KT-454-411

OUTLINE CONTENTS

PART I	**The Constitutional Law of the EU**	**1**
1	The Evolution of the European Union	3
2	The Sources of the Law	33
3	The Nature of Community Law: Supremacy	99
4	The Enforcement of Community Law: 'Dual Vigilance'	109
5	The Direct Effect of Directives	141
6	State Liability	167
7	Article 234: The Preliminary Reference Procedure	187
8	Control of Community Institutions	215
	EPILOGUE TO PART ONE: CONSTITUTIONALISM	275

PART II	**Community Trade Law and Policy**	**287**
9	Law and the Economic Objectives of the Community	289
10	Fiscal Barriers to Trade: Articles 25 and 90	325
11	Physical and Technical Barriers to Trade: Articles 28–30	341
12	Beyond Discrimination: Article 28	381
13	The Free Movement of Workers: Article 39	427
14	Freedom of Establishment and the Free Movement of Services: Articles 43 and 49	445
15	European Citizenship Within an Area of Freedom, Security, and Justice	475
	EPILOGUE TO PART TWO	491

PART III	**Competition Law**	**493**
16	Article 81: Cartels	495
17	Article 82: Dominant Positions	543
18	The Enforcement of the Competition Rules	571
	EPILOGUE TO PART THREE	609

PART IV   **Policy-Making, Governance, and the Constitutional
Debate**   **611**

19 **Harmonization and Common Policy-Making**   613
20 **Subsidiarity, Flexibility, and New Forms of Governance**   653
21 **What Sort of 'Europe'?**   685

EPILOGUE TO PART FOUR: EUROPE'S TRUE SOUL   711

FINAL QUESTIONS   715

SELECTED BIBLIOGRAPHY   716

INDEX   719

DETAILED CONTENTS

Preface	xii
Acknowledgments	xv
Table of Cases	xvii
Table of Legislation	xl
Amsterdam Treaty Table of Equivalence	xlvii
Note on the Citation of Articles of the Treaties in Court Publications	lvii
Abbreviations	lix

PART I	**The Constitutional Law of the EU**	**1**

1	**The Evolution of the European Union**	**3**
SECTION 1:	Introduction	3

2	**The Sources of the Law**	**33**
SECTION 1:	The Treaties	34
SECTION 2:	Legislation	42
	A: Legislation in the European Union	42
	B: The legislative process	45
	C: The principle of attributed competence	59
	D: Reasoning	68
SECTION 3:	General Principles of Community Law	71
	A: Proportionality	71
	B: Fundamental rights	78
	C: Technique	88

3	**The Nature of Community Law: Supremacy**	**99**
SECTION 1:	Supremacy	99
SECTION 2:	Direct Applicability	103
SECTION 3:	Pre-emption	104

4	**The Enforcement of Community Law: 'Dual Vigilance'**	**109**
SECTION 1:	Dual Vigilance	109
SECTION 2:	Control at Community Level	111
	A: The nature of Article 226	111
	B: The effectiveness of Article 226	114
	C: Complaining to the Commission	121
SECTION 3:	Control at National Level	122
	A: The criteria governing direct effect	123
	B: Direct effect as a policy choice	128
	C: Procedure and remedies	131

5	**The Direct Effect of Directives**	**141**
SECTION 1:	Establishing the Principle	141
SECTION 2:	Curtailing the Principle	144
SECTION 3:	The Scope of the Principle: the State	149
SECTION 4:	'Incidental Effect'	152

SECTION 5: The Principle of Indirect Effect, or the Obligation of 'Conform-interpretation'   159

6   State Liability   167

7   Article 234: The Preliminary Reference Procedure   187
SECTION 1: The Purpose of Article 234   187
SECTION 2: The Separation of Functions   188
SECTION 3: The Effect of an Article 234 Ruling   199
SECTION 4: Bodies Competent to Refer   200
SECTION 5: The Obligation to Refer and the Doctrine of *Acte Clair*   203
SECTION 6: The Power to Refer   207
SECTION 7: The Court's Notes for Guidance   209
SECTION 8: Reforming the Court System   211

8   Control of Community Institutions   215
SECTION 1: Introduction   215
SECTION 2: Article 230   216
           A: Article 230, first to third paragraphs   217
           B: Article 230, non-privileged applicants   219
           C: Individual concern   220
           D: Direct concern   224
           E: The example of the anti-dumping cases   226
           F: Grounds for annulment   231
           G: Interim measures   233
SECTION 3: Article 232   234
SECTION 4: Article 241   237
SECTION 5: Article 235 and 288   239
SECTION 6: Article 234   248
           A: The function of Article 234 in judicial review   248
           B: The limitations of Article 234 in judicial review   251
           C: Article 234 and the validity of Community acts   254
           D: The effect of an Article 234 ruling   260
SECTION 7: The Interrelation of the Several Remedies and Pressure for
           Liberalization of the Standing Rules   262
           A: Pressure for liberalization, 1994–2001   262
           B: Pressure for liberalization, 2002 and beyond   268

           EPILOGUE TO PART ONE: CONSTITUTIONALISM   275

PART II   Community Trade Law and Policy   **287**

9   Law and the Economic Objectives of the Community   289
SECTION 1: Introduction   289
SECTION 2: The Common Market   290
SECTION 3: The Internal Market: 1992   294
           A: Background   294
           B: The internal market defined   299
           C: The anticipated benefits of the completion of the internal market   299

SECTION 4: Measuring the Impact of '1992'   303
             A: Measurement in 1996   303
             B: Measurement in 2002   305
             C: The business response   307

SECTION 5: Managing the Internal Market   309

SECTION 6: Economic and Monetary Union   317

10   Fiscal Barriers to Trade: Articles 25 and 90   325

SECTION 1: Article 25   326

SECTION 2: Article 90   330

SECTION 3: Fiscal Harmonization   336

11   Physical and Technical Barriers to Trade: Articles 28–30   341

SECTION 1: The Development of Article 28   341

SECTION 2: The Application of Article 28   346

SECTION 3: Article 30   366
             A: Public morality   367
             B: The protection of health and life of humans, animals, and plants 371

SECTION 4: Eliminating Remaining Barriers to Trade   378

12   Beyond Discrimination: Article 28   381

SECTION 1: Indistinctly Applicable Rules: the *Cassis de Dijon* Formula 381

SECTION 2: Locating the Outer Limit of Article 28   392

SECTION 3: Justifying Indistinctly Applicable Rules   408

SECTION 4: What Sort of Market is Being Made? Some Consequences for
             Consumer Protection   415

13   The Free Movement of Workers: Article 39   427

SECTION 1: Who is a Worker?   428

SECTION 2: To What Advantages is the Worker Entitled?   431

SECTION 3: Exceptions   437

**14   Freedom of Establishment and the Free Movement of
          Services: Articles 43 and 49   445**

SECTION 1: The Rights   445

SECTION 2: Non-discrimination   446

SECTION 3: Beyond Discrimination   449
             A: Challenging and justifying obstructive national measures 450
             B: Cases dealing with company law   460
             C: Cases dealing with particularly sensitive State choices 464

SECTION 4: Harmonization   471

**15   European Citizenship Within an Area of Freedom,
          Security, and Justice   475**

SECTION 1: Introduction   475

SECTION 2: Free Movement of Persons Within an Area of Freedom, Security,
             and Justice   478

SECTION 3: European Citizenship   483

          EPILOGUE TO PART TWO   491

PART III	**Competition Law**	**493**

16	**Article 81: Cartels**	**495**
SECTION 1:	Introduction to Competition Law	495
SECTION 2:	Article 81	496
SECTION 3:	Jurisdiction	500
SECTION 4:	An Agreement	503
SECTION 5:	The Concerted Practice	505
SECTION 6:	Restriction of Competition	510
	A: Preventing or distorting competition	510
	B: Agreements of minor importance	515
	C: Assessing a 'restriction of competition' in its full context	522
	D: State involvement	527
SECTION 7:	Exemption	532
SECTION 8:	Block Exemption	533

17	**Article 82: Dominant Positions**	**543**
SECTION 1:	The Dominant Position: Defining the Market	544
SECTION 2:	Abuse	562

18	**The Enforcement of the Competition Rules**	**571**

	EPILOGUE TO PART THREE	609

PART IV	**Policy-Making, Governance, and the Constitutional Debate**	**611**

19	**Harmonization and Common Policy-Making**	**613**
SECTION 1:	Introduction	613
SECTION 2:	Harmonization Policy	615
	A: Harmonization as an introduction to the wider debate	616
	B: The New Approach to harmonization policy	619
	C: Questioning the New Approach	624
SECTION 3:	Methods of Harmonization	628
	A: Harmonization and the allocation of competence between the EC and the Member States	628
	B: The management of Article 95(4) *et seq*	629
	C: Harmonization, competence, and the scope for minimum rules	633
SECTION 4:	The Example of Consumer Law	638
	A: Minimum harmonization	638
	B: The Product Liability Directive	639
	C: Uniform application of Community consumer law	644
	D: The Product Liability Directive and pre-emption	647

20	**Subsidiarity, Flexibility, and New Forms of Governance**	**653**
SECTION 1:	Subsidiarity	654
SECTION 2:	Variable Integration and Flexibility	665
SECTION 3:	Instruments of Governance	676

21   What Sort of 'Europe'?   685
SECTION 1: The Challenge of National Constitutional Courts   685
SECTION 2: States and Beyond: Multi-level Governance and Constitutionalism   697
SECTION 3: Legitimacy and Democracy   704

EPILOGUE TO PART FOUR: EUROPE'S TRUE SOUL   711

FINAL QUESTIONS   715

SELECTED BIBLIOGRAPHY   716

INDEX   719

PREFACE

It may seem perverse to begin a Preface explaining what a book is *not* about, but in the case of the law of the European Union I think it is justified. The subject has grown at such a pace over recent years that it is no longer possible to aspire to write a book which is truly comprehensive. The best that one can do is to select areas for examination which seem particularly important and then to use those areas as illustrations to draw out the themes and principles on which the law is based. In this way, one can encourage the student to develop a *communautaire* approach which will permit him or her to tackle substantive areas beyond the scope of this book. So, although it is easy to explain away a failure to cover the full extent of the law of the European Union simply by pointing out how much there is of it, I hope that this book has adopted a coherent principle in deciding what to include and what to exclude.

The book is *not* about English law and its reaction to membership of the Union. There is no deep exploration of Parliamentary Sovereignty or the European Communities Act 1972. This is a European law book. Nevertheless, the development of the European Community legal order, and lately a European Union legal order, has not occurred in isolation and is in part dependent on action and reaction at national level. In depicting this process, I have tended to draw on the example of the British experience of the impact of Community membership. However, the *Cohn Bendit* decision (p.147) will provide an example of practice in another Member State and the student should always be prepared to look beyond domestic law. Most of all, the attitudes of German courts cannot be ignored, and I have included the *Brunner* decision relating to ratification of the Maastricht Treaty (p.689) and the *Bananas* decision concerning the protection of fundamental rights (p.693).

I have touched relatively little on matters of external competence. There is, for example, passing reference only to the Common Customs Tariff, the Common Commercial Policy and Treaty-making competence generally. Anti-dumping law is examined more for what it tells us about judicial review than for its substantive importance. The growth of a Common Foreign and Security Policy is located in the context of the three-pillar Union edifice constructed at Maastricht (p.9), but not examined in detail. I have adopted this primarily internal focus with regret, aware that it smacks of an unappealing 'Fortress Europe' attitude. But I think that my choice is in this respect in accordance with most British University degree courses in EU law.

This sixth edition has been written now that the Treaty of Nice has entered into force; it did so on 1 February 2003. I have provided an overview of the progress of recent Union history in the book's first Chapter. Pages 9–14 sweep the reader through a decade of Treaty revision from Maastricht, through Amsterdam to Nice and summarise the relevant changes effected by these instruments. Page 12 explains the most dramatically trivial impact of this process, the re-numbering of the Treaties, which forces the reader to adopt a pre- and a post-Amsterdam sensitivity to numerical change. The table of equivalence between Treaty provisions is set out at p.xlvii and the Community judicature's approach to citation of Treaty articles is found at p.lvii. All the relevant amendments effected at Amsterdam and Nice are, of course, woven into the examination of the law throughout the book.

The Nice Treaty is by no means the end of the line. The future already beckons. Enlargement of the Union will bring ten States from Central, Eastern and Southern Europe into the fold in 2004 (p.14). A further round of Treaty revision is expected, in part to cope with the pressures brought to bear by enlargement but, more ambitiously, to place the institutional and constitutional structure of the Union on a more enduring footing. The role of the Convention on the Future of Europe is examined at pp.30 32 and, as promised, progress will be tracked on this book's Companion Website.

In previous editions, essential updating apart, my approach to amendment has always been to prefer to leave material untouched in cases of doubt rather than fiddle with it. I hope this has ensured the book's familiarity to users. But for this sixth edition I have adopted a different approach. Much familiar material has been retained. But the book's structure has been altered. In part this is in response to some of the trends and challenges that have come to dominate European law scholarship. In part it is designed to freshen up the text. There are now four parts to the book. The first part covers the Constitutional law of the EU. This covers the growth of the system from Community to Union, institutional design, lawmaking and law enforcement and the shaping of a 'constitutionalised' legal order involving attribution of supremacy and direct effect to EC law. The second Part of the book examines Community trade law and policy—the law of the internal market, including assessment of the status of European citizenship. The third part of the book deals with Competition law, covering Articles 81 and 82 EC and their enforcement (but in this new edition excluding with regret the specialist topic of intellectual property). The fourth and final part of the book is entirely new. It is entitled Policy-Making, Governance and the Constitutional Debate. It is designed to expose the reader to some of the most pressing and—I hope—inspiring contemporary challenges in the shaping of an effective, efficient and trustworthy system of governance for Europe—common policymaking, subsidiarity, flexibility, selection of instruments of lawmaking and, more broadly, of governance and, ultimately, the conundrums of legitimacy and democracy beyond the nation State.

As in the previous editions of the book, my concern remains to depict the dynamic process of evolution in the European Union. I have maintained the range of material used in the previous editions., while making some adjustment in the particular sources used. I use lawyers, practising and academic, but also economists, political scientists and journalists. My aim remains to encourage the student to appreciate how the legal order has been developed (and is still in the process of being developed) in response to sometimes conflicting economic, social and political pressures.

I continue to owe countless debts of gratitude. Thank you to everyone who has helped. To those who filled in the Blackstone Press 'Questionnaires', I assure you that these are read and digested—I remain eager to receive consumer views on this book now that Oxford University Press have taken over responsibility for its publication, especially but only in response to the changes I have introduced for this sixth edition. For the past, I thank Blackstone Press, whose enthusiasm and attention to detail is unsurpassed in my experience. For the present and future, I thank Oxford University Press, whose staff have a tough act to follow. But above all I thank Catherine Redgwell, without whom this book would have been written in a much less happy frame of mind.

Stephen Weatherill
July 2003

ACKNOWLEDGEMENTS

The permission of the following authors and publishers, who have kindly agreed to allow the use of material in this book, is gratefully acknowledged:

Extracts from the following article published in the *European Law Review* (Sweet and Maxwell Ltd): J. Usher, 'The Influence of National Concepts on Decisions of the European Court', (1976) 1 EL Rev 359.

Extracts from the following articles published in the *Common Market Law Review* (e Kluwer Academic Publishers):

O. Brouwer, 'Free movement of foodstuffs and quality requirements: has the Commission got it wrong?', (1988) 25 CML Rev 237.

C. Closa, 'The Concept of Citizenship in the Treaty on European Union' (1992) 29 CML Rev 1137.

F. Mancini, 'The Making of a Constitution for Europe', (1989) 26 CML Rev 595.

Extracts from the following article published in the *Journal of Consumer Policy* (Kluwer Academic Publishers): N. Reich, 'Protection of Diffuse Interests in the EEC and the Perspective of Progressively Establishing an Internal Market', (1988) 11 JCP 395.

Extracts from the following articles published in the *Journal of Common Market Studies* (Basil Blackwell, Oxford): J. Pelkmans, 'The New Approach to Technical Harmonization and Standardization', (1986–87) JCMS 249; D. Hodson and I. Maher, 'The Open Method as a new mode of Governance' (2001) 39 JCMS 719.

Extract from the following article published in the *Notre Dame Law Review* (eMatthew Bender Inc., reprinted with permission from the original source, 1983 Fordham Corporate Law Institute, Antitrust and Trade Policies of the EEC): E. Fox, 'Monopolization and Dominance in the US and the EC: Efficiency, Opportunity and Fairness' (1986) 61 Notre Dame Law Rev 981.

Extracts from the following article published in *Legal Issues of European Integration* (Kluwer Academic Publishers): R. Dehousse, '1992 and Beyond: the Institutional Dimension of the Internal Market Programme', [1989/1] LIEI 109.

Extract from the following article published in the *Northern Ireland Legal Quarterly* (SLS Legal Publications): R. Harmsen, 'A European Union of Variable Geometry: Problems and Perspectives' (1994) 45 NILQ 109.

Extract from the following article published in the *Modern Law Review* (Blackwell Publishers, Oxford): F. Snyder, 'The Effectiveness of European Community Law: Institutions, Processes, Tools and Techniques', (1993) 56 MLR 19.

Extract from the following article published in the *Oxford Review of Economic Policy* (Oxford: Oxford University Press): H. Siebert and M.J. Koop, 'Institutional Competition versus Centralization: Quo Vadis Europe?' 9/1 Oxford Rev Ec Pol 15. By permission of Oxford University Press.

Extract from the *Common Market Law Reports* (reproduced with the permission of Sweet and Maxwell Ltd): *Minister of the Interior* v *Cohn Bendit* [1980] 1 CMLR 543.

Extracts from *The European Union: Economics and Policies*, 6th ed. A. M. El-Agraa (2001). Extracts reprinted with the permission of Pearson Education Ltd.

Extracts from *1992: One European Market?*, eds R. Bieber, R. Dehousse, J. Pinder and J. Weiler (1988, Nomos Verlagsgesellschaft, Baden Baden).

Extracts from P. Cecchini, *The European Challenge: 1992, the Benefits of a Single Market* (1988, Wildwood House/Gower Publishing). Permission of the EC Commission is also gratefully acknowledged.

Extracts from *The European Community and the Challenge of the Future*, ed. J. Lodge (1990 and 2nd ed., 1993, Pinter Publishers Ltd, London). All rights reserved.

Extracts from J. Pinder, *European Community: The Building of a Union* (3rd ed., 1998, Oxford University Press). Copyright J. Pinder.

Extracts from R. Merkin, *A Guide to the Consumer Protection Act 1987* (1987, Financial Training Publications Ltd, London).

Extracts from M. Wilke and H. Wallace, *Subsidiarity: Approaches to Power-Sharing in the European Community* (1990, Royal Institute of International Affairs, London). Published as RIIA Discussion Paper 27.

Extract from *The Guardian* of 13 March 1987.

Extract from *The Independent* of 24 November 1989.

For the use of material from the *European Court Reports*, the Court of Justice of the European Communities.

For the use of Community source material, the Commission of the European Communities.

Extract from *The Court of Justice after Maastricht* in D. O'Keeffe and P. Twomey (eds.), *Legal Issues of the Maastricht Treaty* (Chancery, 1994); permission granted by the author, William Robinson.

Extract from *Société Stenuit* v *France* Series A no. 232-A (European Commission on Human Rights), the Council of Europe.

Extract from the following article published in the *Cambridge Law Journal*: R. Caranta, 'Government Liability after Francovich' (1993) 52 CLJ 272, permission kindly granted by both journal and author.

Extracts from the following articles published in *Aussenwirtschaft* (published by Verlag Rüegger AG/ The Swiss Institute for Research into International Economic Relations, Economic Structures and Regional Science at St Gallen): H. Hauser and A. Müller, 'Legitimacy: the Missing Link for Explaining EU-Institution Building' (1995) 50 *Aussenwirtschaft* 17 and D. Curtin, 'The Shaping of a European Constitution and the 1996 IGC' (1995) 50 *Aussenwirtschaft* 237.

Extracts from H.U. Jessurun D'Oliveira, 'Union Citizenship: Pie in the Sky?' in A. Rosas and E. Antola (eds), *A Citizens' Europe* (1995), Sage Publications, London).

Extract from the following article published in the *Yearbook of European Law*: C. Timmermans, 'The constitutionalization of the European Union' (2002) 21 Yearbook of European Law 1.

Extract from Miguel Poiares Maduro, 'Europe and the Constitution: *What if this is As Good As It Gets?*', Constitutionalism Web-Papers (University of Manchester), http://les1.man.ac.uk/conweb/ ConWEB No. 5/2000.

Extracts from A. Menon and S. Weatherill, 'Legitimacy, Accountability and Delegation in the European Union' in A. Arnull and D. Wincott (eds), *Accoutability and Legitimacy in the European Union* (OUP, 2002).

Extracts from T. Kostakopoulou, 'Democracy-talk in the European Union: the Need for a Reflexive Approach', author's original version: edited version to be published subsequently in the Columbia Journal of European Law, 2003.

Extract from V. Heiskaner and K. Kulovesi, *Function and Future of European Law* (Publications of the Faculty of Law, University of Helsinki).

TABLE OF CASES

(Bold face indicates extract material)

Court of Justice of the European Communities (chronological)

Industrie Metallurgische SpA v High Authority of the ECSC (Case 15/57) [1957 and 1958] ECR 133 ... 238

Compagnie des Hauts Fourneaux de Chasse v High Authority of the ECSC (Case 15/57) [1957 and 1958] ECR 211 ... 238

Humblet v Belgium (Case 6/60) [1960] ECR 559 ... 169

Bosch v de Geus (Case 13/61) [1962] ECR 45 ... 187–8

San Michele and Others v Commission (Cases 5–11 and 13–15/62) [1962] ECR 449 ... 588

Germany v Commission (Case 24/62) [1963] ECR 63 ... 69

Plaumann v Commission (Case 25/62) [1963] ECR 95 ... 220–1, 222, 231, 264, 269, 274

Van Gend en Loos v Nederlandse Administratie der Belastingen (Case 26/62) [1963] ECR 1 ... 109–10, 123, 141, 147, 159, 168, 189, 190, 604, 712

Da Costa en Schaake (Cases 28–30/62) [1963] ECR 31 ... 203, 205

Costa v ENEL (Case 6/64) [1964] ECR 585 ... 99–100, 130–1, 168, 189, 190, 604

Établissements Consten SA and Grundig GMbH v Commission (Case 56 & 58/64) [1966] ECR 299, [1966] CMLR 418 ... 497 500, 510, 511, 512, 606

Schwarze v Einfuhr- und Vorratstelle Getreide (Case 16/65) [1965] ECR 877 ... 70

Société Technique Minière v Maschinenbau Ulm (Case 56/65) [1966] ECR 235, [1966] CMLR 357 ... 510

Brasserie de Haecht SA v Wilkin (Case 23/67) [1967] ECR 407, [1968] CMLR 26 ... 518–19, 522, 606

Commission v Italy (Case 7/68) [1968] ECR 423 ... 326–7

Società 'Eridania' Zuccherifici Nazionali v Commission (Cases 10 & 18/68) [1969] ECR 459 ... 236

Commission v Italy (Case 24/68) [1969] ECR 193, [1971] CMLR 611 ... 326, 327–8, 329

Sociaal Fonds voor de Diamantarbeiders v Brachfeld (Cases 2 & 3/69) [1969] ECR 211, [1969] CMLR 335 ... 328

Volk v Verwaecke (Case 5/69) [1969] ECR 295 ... 515

Portelange (Case 10/69) [1969] ECR 309 ... 604

Stauder v Ulm (Case 29/69) [1969] ECR 419, [1970] CMLR 112 ... 81, 188

ACF Chemiefarma v Commission (Quinine) (Cases 41, 44 & 45/69) [1970] ECR 661 416–7, [1986] 1 CMLR 506 ... 136, 503–4

Bilger v Jehle (Case 43/69) [1970] ECR 127 ... 520

ICI v Commission (Dyestuffs) (Case 48/69) [1972] ECR 619, [1972] CMLR 557 ... 500, 505–8

Commission v Belgium (Case 77/69) [1970] ECR 237 ... 112

Chevalley v Commission (Case 15/70) [1970] ECR 975 ... 260

Commission v Council (Case 22/70) [1971] ECR 263 ... 43–4, 104–5, 107, 232

International Fruit Company v Commission (Cases 41–44/70) [1971] ECR 411 ... 43, 44, 219–20, 232, 233

Internationale Handelsgesellschaft [1970] ECR 1125 ... 84

Aktien-Zuckerfabrik Schöppenstedt v Council (Case 5/71) [1971] ECR 975 ... 239–40, 241

Béguelin (Case 22/71) [1971] ECR 949 ... 604

International Fruit Company v Produktschap voor Groenten en Fruit (No. 2) (Cases 51–54/71) [1971] ECR 1107 ... 348–9

Continental Can v Commission (Case 6/72) [1973] ECR 215 ... 559, 561

Vereeniging van Cementhandelaren v Commission (Case 28/72) [1972] ECR 977 ... 523

Commission v Italy (Case 39/72) [1973] ECR 101 ... 113, 605

Brasserie de Haecht II (Case 48/72) [1973] ECR 77 ... 605

Geddo v Ente (Case 2/73) [1973] ECR 865, [1974] 1 CMLR ... 341, 342

Nold v Commission (Case 4/73) [1974] ECR 491 ... 81–2, 84, 86, 587

Balkan-Import-Export v Hauptzollamt Berlin-Packhof (Case 5/73) [1973] ECR 1091 ... 74

Istituto Chemicoterapico Italiano SpA and Commercial Solvents Corporation v Commission (Cases 6 & 7/73) [1974] ECR 223, [1974] 1 CMLR 309 ... 565, 567, 569

Variola v Amministrazione delle Finanze (Case 34/73) [1973] ECR 981 ... 103

Belgische Radio en Televisie v Sabam (Case 127/73) [1974] ECR 313 ... 528, 605

Rheinmühlen-Düsseldorf v Einfuhr- und Vorratsstelle für Getreide und Futtermittel (No. 1) (Case 166/73) [1974] ECR 33 ... 188

Commission v France (Case 167/73) [1974] ECR 359 ... 102

Reyners v Belgian State (Case 2/74) [1974] ECR 631, [1974] 2 CMLR ... 181, 447

Procureur du Roi v Dassonville (Case 8/74) [1974] ECR 837, [1974] 2 CMLR 436 ... 343, **344–5**, 350, 386, 387, 395, 397, 398, 401, 402, 407, 414, 420

Commission v Germany (Case 12/74) [1975] ECR 191 ... 351

Transocean Marine Paint v Commission (Case 17/74) [1974] ECR 1063, [1974] 2 CMLR 459 ... **88–92**, 586

Van Binsbergen v Bedrijfsvereniging Metaalnijverheid (Case 33/74) [1974] ECR 1299 ... 461

Walrave v Association Union Cycliste Internationale (Case 36/74) [1974] ECR 1405 ... 446, 526

Van Duyn v Home Office (Case 41/74) [1974] ECR 1337 ... 123–5, 127, 141, 143–4, 147, 439–40, 442

Cadsky v ICE (Case 63/74) [1975] ECR 281, [1975] 2 CMLR ... 329

Bonsignore (Case 67/74) [1975] ECR 297 ... 442

Rewe-Zentralfinanz Gmbh v Landwirtschaftskammer (Case 4/75) [1975] ECR 843, [1975] 1 CMLR 599 ... 376–8, 633

Cristini v SNCF (Case 32/75) [1975] ECR 1085, [1975] 1 CMLR 573 ... 435–6

Defrenne v SABENA (Case 43/75) [1976] ECR 455 ... 123, **125–8**, 200, 261

REWE (Case 45/75) [1976] ECR 181 ... 334

Procureur du Roi v Royer (Case 48/75) [1976] ECR 497 ... 446

Russo v AIMA (Case 60/75) [1976] ECR 45 ... 169

Tasca (Criminal proceedings against) (Case 65/75) [1976] ECR 291, [1977] 2 CMLR 183 ... 365, 399, 527

Bresciani v Amministrazione Italiana delle Finanze (Case 87/75) [1976] ECR 129, [1976] 2 CMLR 62 ... 328–9

Kramer (Case 3/76) [1976] ECR 1279 ... 105

Donà (Case 13/76) [1976] ECR 1333 ... 526

Schottle v Finanzamt Freudenstadt (Case 20/ 76) [1977] ECR 247, [1977] 2 CMLR ... 330–1

Metro-SB-Grossmärkte GmbH & Co KG v Commission (Case 26/76) [1977] ECR 1875 ... **223–4**, 228, **495**

United Brands v Commission (Case 27/76) [1978] ECR 207, [1978] 1 CMLR 429 ... 544–9, 550, 560, **562–4**

Rewe v Landwirtschaftskammer für das Saarland (Case 33/76) [1976] ECR 1989 ... 158, 169, 172

Comet v Productschap (Case 45/76) [1976] ECR 2043 ... 132–3, 135, 172

Bauhuis v Netherlands (Case 46/76) [1977] ECR 5 ... 329, 350

Nederlandse Ondernemingen (Case 51/76) [1977] 1 ECR 126 ... 142, 147

Thieffry v Conseil de l'Ordre des Avocats à la

Cour de Paris (Case 71/76) [1977] ECR 765, [1977] 2 CMLR 373 ... 446–7, 449, 450, 455

Ianelli & Volpi v Meroni (Case 74/76) [1977] ECR 557 ... 181

Bayerische HNL Vermehrungsbetriebe GmbH & Co. KG v Council (Case 83/76) [1978] ECR 1209 ... 240

HNL and Others v Council and Commission (Cases 83/76, 94/76, 4/77, 40/77, 15/77) [1978] ECR 1209 ... 180, 184

Hoffmann-La Roche v Commission (Case 85/76) [1979] ECR 461 ... 531, 561

Commission v Netherlands (Case 89/76) [1977] ECR 1355 ... 329–30

Hoffman la Roche & Co. AG v Centrafarm Vertriebsgesellschaft Pharmazeutischer Erzeugnisse GmbH (Case 107/76) [1977] ECR 957 ... 191, **203**

Tedeschi v Denkavit (Case 5/77) (1977) ECR 155 ... 378

Sagulo, Brenca and Bakhouche (Case 8/77) [1977] ECR 1495 ... 432

Fink-Frucht GmbH v Hauptzollamt Munchen-Landsbergstrasse (Case 27/77) [1978] ECR 223 ... 334

R v Bouchereau (Case 30/77) [1977] ECR 1999, [1977] 2 CMLR 800 ... 440–1, **442–3**

BP v Commission (Case 77/77) [1978] ECR 1511 ... 566

Openbaar Ministerie v Van Tiggele (Case 82/ 77) [1978] ECR 25, [1978] 2 CMLR 528 ... 365–6, 399

Amministrazione delle Finanze v Simmenthal (Case 106/77) [1978] ECR 629 ... 100–1, 103, 137, 138, 168, 172, 173, 605

NTN Toyo Bearing Co. v Council (Case 113/77) [1979] ECR 1185, [1977] ECR 1721 ... 226–7, 230, **233–4**

UNICME v Council [1978] ECR 845 ... 265

Koninklijke Scholten-Honig NV v Council and Commission (Case 143/77) [1979] ECR 3583 ... 240

Hansen (H.) jun. & O. C. Balle GmbH v Hauptzollamt Flensburg (Case 148/77) [1978] ECR 1787 ... 334

Commission v Belgium (Case 156/77) [1978] ECR 1881 ... 252

Hugin Kassaregister AB v Commission (Case 22/78) [1979] ECR 1869, [1979] 3 CMLR 345 ... **559–60**

BMW v Belgium (Case 32/78) [1979] ECR 2435, [1980] 1 CMLR ... 504

Simmenthal SpA v Commission (Case 92/78) [1979] ECR 777 ... 253

Ministère public v Wesemael and Others (Cases 110–111/78) [1979] ECR 35 ... 451

Knoors (Case 115/78) [1994] ECR I-4795 ... 461

Rewe-Zentrale AG v Bundesmonopolverwaltung für Branntwein (Cassis de Dijon) (Case 120/78) [1979] ECR 649, [1979] 3 CMLR 494 ... 181, 321, 350, 381–3, 385, 386, 387, 388, 392, 393, 397, 399, 400, 403, 406, 408, 411, 414, 415–17, 418, 420, 421, 422, 450, 453, 456, 458, 471, 501, 615, 624

Buitoni v FORMA (Case 122/78) [1979] ECR 677 ... 73

✗ Commission v UK (Case 128/78) [1979] ECR 419 ... 113–14

Denkavit v France (Case 132/78) [1979] ECR 1923 ... 329

France v UK (Case 141/78) [1979] ECR 2923 ... 111

Pubblico Ministero v Ratti (Case 148/78) [1979] ECR 1629, [1980] 1 CMLR 96 ... 141–3, 147, 155, 378

Valsabbia v Commission (Case 154/78) [1980] ECR 907 ... 74–5

Commission v Italy (Case 159/78) [1979] ECR 3247, [1980] 3 CMLR 446 ... 349

Commission v France (Case 168/78) [1980] ECR 347, [1981] 2 CMLR 631 ... 333–4

Commission v UK (Case 170/78) [1983] ECR 2263, [1983] 3 CMLR 512 ... 334–5, 388

Ireks-Arkady v Council and Commission (Case 238/78) [1979] ECR 2955 ... 605

Union Laitière Normande (Case 244/78) [1979] ECR 2663 ... 191

Denkavit (Case 251/78) (1979) ECR 3369 ... 378

Nungesser v Commission (Case 258/78) [1982] ECR 2015, [1983] 1 CMLR 278 ... 510–11, 512, 514

Commission v Council (Case 22/70) [1971] ECR 263 ... 217–18

R v Henn and Darby (Case 34/79) [1979] ECR 3795, [1980] 1 CMLR 246 ... 367–9, 371, 372

Hauer v Rheinland-Pfalz (Case 44/79) [1979] ECR 3727 ... 83–6

Just (Case 68/79) [1980] ECR 501 ... 605

Commission v Italy (Cases 91–92/79) [1980] ECR 1099 ... 52

Foglia v Novello (No. 1) (Case 104/79) [1980] ECR 745, [1981] 1 CMLR 45 ... 191–2, 193

National Panasonic v Commission (Case 136/79) [1090] ECR 2033 ... 586, 592, 593, 595, 596

Roquette Frères v Council (Case 138/79) [1980] ECR 3333 ... 52, 707

Maizena v Council (Case 139/79) [1980] ECR 3393 ... 52

Chemial Farmaceutici v DAF (Case 140/79) [1981] ECR 1 ... 332–3

Commission v Belgium (Case 149/79) [1980] ECR 3881, [1981] 2 CMLR 413 ... 444

AM & S v Commission (Case 155/79) ... 89, 587, 591, 595

R v Pieck (Case 157/79) [1980] ECR 2171, [1980] 3 CMLR 220 ... 432

Commission v Italy (Case 213/79) [1980] ECR 1 ... 333

Philip Morris v Commission (Case 730/79) [1980] ECR 2671 ... 252

Gilli and Andres (Case 788/79) [1980] ECR 2071 ... 350

Calpak SpA Ltd v Commission (Cases 789 & 790/79) [1980] ECR 1949 ... 221–2

Ariete SpA v Amministrazione delle Finanze dello Stato (Case 811/79) [1980] ECR 2545 ... 138

MIRECO SaS v Amministrazione delle Finanze dello Stato (Case 811/79) [1980] ECR 2559 ... 138

Fietje (Case 27/80) [1980] ECR 3839 ... 409–10

L'Oréal v De Nieuwe AMCK (Case 31/80) [1980] ECR 3775 ... 568

Irish Creamery Milk Suppliers v Government of Ireland (Case 36/80) [1981] ECR 735, [1981] 2 CMLR 455 ... 190–1, 207

Cooperatieve Stremsel- en Kleurselfabriek v Commission (Case 61/80) [1981] ECR 851 ... 501, 510

ICC v Amministrazione delle Finanze (Case 66/80) [1981] ECR 1191, [1983] 2 CMLR 593 ... 199, 208, 260, 261

Musique Diffusion Française v Commission (Cases 100–103/80) [1983] ECR 1825 ... 586

Commission v Ireland (Case 113/80) [1981] ECR 1625, [1982] 1 CMLR 706 ... 349–52, 371

Kelderman (Case 130/80) [1981] ECR 351...

Oebel (Case 144/80) [1981] ECR 1993 ... 394

REWE-Handelsgesellschaft Nord GmbH v Hauptzollamt Kiel (Case 158/80) [1981] ECR 1805 ... 70, 169

Commission v Italy (Case 193/80) [1981] ECR 3019 ... 181, 388

Casati (Case 203/80) [1981] ECR 2595 ... 448

Foglia v Novello (No. 2) (Case 244/80) [1981] ECR 3045, [1982] 1 CMLR 585 ... 192–3, 196

Broeckmeulen v Huisarts Registratie Commissie (Case 246/80) [1981] ECR 2311 ... 200–1

Frans-Nederlandse Maatschappij voor Biologische Producten (Case 272/80) [1981] ECR 3277, [1982] 2 CMLR 497 ... 374, 375–6

Webb (Case 279/80) [1981] ECR 3305 ... 235, 450, 451

Diensten Groep v Beele (Case 6/81) [1982] ECR 707 ... 409

Becker v Finanzamt Münster-Innenstadt (Case 8/81) [1982] ECR 53 ... 145, 149, 150, 151, 152, 164

Levin v Staatssecretaris van Justitie (Case 53/81) [1982] ECR 1035, [1982] 2 CMLR 454 ... 428–30

Nordsee v Reederei Mond (Case 102/81) [1982] ECR 1095 ... 201–2

Adoui and Cornuaille v Belgian State (Cases 115 & 116/81) [1982] ECR 1665, [1982] 3 CMLR 631 ... 441–2

Commission v Ireland (Case C-249/81) [1982] ECR 4005, [1983] 2 CMLR 104 ... 357–61, 364

Rau (Walter) v de Smedt (Case 261/81) [1982] ECR 3961 ... 190, 193, 388

Coditel v Ciné-Vog Films (Case 262/81) ... 514

CILFIT (Case 283/81) [1982] ECR 3415, [1983] 1 CMLR 472 ... 204–6

Oosthoek (Case 286/81) [1982] ECR 4575 ... 401

Alusuisse Italia SpA v Council and Commission (Case 307/81) [1982] ECR 3463 ... 227–8, 230

Michelin v Commission (Case 322/81) [1983] ECR 3461 ... 561, 569, 587

Delhaize (Cases 2–4/82) (1982) ECR 2973 ... 378

Morson v Netherlands (Cases 35–36/82) [1982] ECR 3723, [1983] 2 CMLR 720 ... 476

Commission v UK (Case 40/82) [1982] ECR 2793, [1982] 3 CMLR 497 ... 371–3

Commission v France (Case 42/82) [1983] ECR 1013 ... 373

Fromançais SA v FORMA (Case 66/82) [1983] ECR 395 ... 73

Commission v Belgium (Case 132/82) [1983] ECR 1649, [1983] CMLR 600 ... 329

Robards (Case 149/82) [1983] ECR 171 ... 195

Commission v Denmark (Case 158/82) [1983] ECR 3573 ... 329, 335

Officier van Justitie v Sandoz BV (Case 174/82) [1983] ECR 2445, [1984] 3 CMLR 43 ... 373–5, 376, 378, 389, 409

TWD Textilwerke Deggendorf GmbH v Germany (Case C-188/92) [1994] ECR I-833 ... 251–3, 268

EEC Seed Crushers' and Oil Processors' Federation (FEDOIL) v Commission (Case 191/82) [1983] ECR 2913 ... 229

Amministrazione delle Finanze dello Stato v San Giorgio (Case 199/82) [1983] ECR 3595 ... 169, 173, 182

Universität Hamburg v HZA Hamburg-Kehrwieder (Case 216/82) [1983] ECR 2771 ... 248–9, 252, 262

Apple and Pear Development Council v Lewis (Case 222/82) [1983] ECR 4083, [1984] 3 CMLR 733 ... 361, 364

Duphar and Others (Case 238/82) [1984] ECR 523 ... 465

Allied Corporation v Commission (Cases 239 and 275/82) [1984] ECR 1005 ... 230

Timex v Council and Commission (Case 264/82) [1985] ECR 849 ... 228–30, 232

Auer v Ministère Public (Case 271/82) [1983] ECR 2727 ... 472

Luisi and Carbone v Ministero del Tesoro (Cases 286/82 and 26/83) [1984] ECR 377 ... 447

Merck v Hauptzollamt Hamburg-Jonas (Case 292/82) [1983] ECR 3781 ... 635

Commission v Belgium (Case 314/82) [1984] ECR 1543 ... 329, 330

St Nikolaus v Hauptzollamt Krefeld (Case 337/82) [1984] ECR 1051 ... 635

IFG v Freistaat Bayern (Case 1/83) [1984] ECR 349 ... 330

Parliament v Council (Case 13/83) [1985] ECR 1513 ... 234–6

Von Colson and Kamann v Land Nordrhein-Westfalen (Case 14/83) [1984] ECR 1891, [1986] 2 CMLR 430 ... 145, 160–2, 163, 346

Prantl (Criminal proceedings against) (Case C-16/83) [1984] ECR 1299, [1985] 2 CMLR 238 ... 371

Campus Oil v Minister for Industry and Energy (Case 72/83) [1984] ECR 2727 ... 378–9

Harz v Deutsche Tradax (Case 79/83) [1984] ECR 1921 ... 160

Klopp (Case 107/83) [1984] ECR 2971 ... 523

Société de Produits de Màïs v Administration des Douanes (Case 112/83) [1985] ECR 719 ... 200, 261, 262

Adams v Commission (No. 1) (Case 145/83) [1985] ECR 3539 ... 244–8

Kohl v Ringelhan (Case 177/83) [1984] ECR 3651, [1985] 3 CMLR 340 ... 371

Windsurfing v Commission (Case 193/83) [1986] ECR 611 ... 519

Commission v UK (Case 207/83) [1985] ECR 1202, [1985] 2 CMLR 259 ... 352–3, 399

Municipality of Differdange v Commission (Case 222/83) [1984] ECR 2889 ... 224–5

Leclerc and Others v 'Au Blé Vert' and Others (Case 229/83) [1985] ECR 1 ... 461

Parti Écologiste 'Les Verts' v European Parliament (Case 294/83) [1986] ECR 1339 ... 208, 216, 262, 269, 272, 276

Commission v France (Case 21/84) [1985] ECR 1356 ... 354

Remia and Others v Commission (Case 42/84) [1985] ECR 2545 ... 523

Commission v Belgium (Case 52/84) [1986] ECR 89 ... 596

Cinéthèque SA v Fédération Nationale des Cinémas Français (Cases 60 & 61/84) [1985] ECR 2605 ... 394, 399–400

Commission v Italy (Case 103/84) [1986] ECR 1759 ... 122

Humblot v Directeur des Services Fiscaux (Case 112/84) [1985] ECR 1367, [1986] 2 CMLR 338 ... 331–2

Marshall v Southampton AHA (Case 152/84) [1986] ECR 723, [1986] 1 CMLR 688 ... 144–6, 147, 148, 149, 151, 152, 155, 159, 160, 162, 163, 164–5

Pronuptia de Paris GmbH v Pronuptia de Paris Irmgaard Schillgalis (Case 161/84) [1986] ECR 353, [1986] 1 CMLR 414 ... 512–13, 514

Commission v Germany (Case 178/84) ... 177, 181, 387–92, 409

R v Intervention Board, ex parte Man (Sugar) Ltd (Case 181/84) [1985] ECR 2889 ... 72–4, 248

Commission v Germany (Case 205/84) [1986] ECR 3755, [1987] 2 CMLR 69 ... 450–3, 454, 467

Johnston v Chief Constable of the Royal Ulster Constabulary (Case 222/84) [1986] ECR 1651 ... 151, 269, 272, 587

Motte (Case 247/84) [1985] ECR 3887 ... 389–90

Ministère Public v Muller and Others (Case 304/84) [1986] ECR 1511 ... 390

CBEM v CLT and IPB (Case 311/84) [1985] ECR 3261 ... 569

AKZO v Commission (Case 5/85) [1986] ECR 2855 ... 586

Schloh v Auto Controle Technique (Case 50/85) [1986] ECR 1855 ... 346–8

Lawrie-Blum v Land Baden-Württemberg (Case 66/85) [1986] ECR 2121, [1987] 3 CMLR 389 ... 430

Van der Kooy v Commission (Cases 67, 68 and 70/85) [1988] ECR 219 ... 272

Segers (Case 79/85) [1986] ECR 2375 ... 461

Nederlandse Bakkerij v Edah (Cases 80 & 159/85) [1986] ECR 3359, [1988] 2 CMLR 113 ... 392

Ahlström Osakyhtio v Commission (Woodpulp) (Cases 89 et al/85) [1988] ECR 5193, [1988] 4 CMLR 901 ... 502–3, 509

Union Deutsche Lebensmittelwerke v Commission (Case 97/85) [1987] ECR 2265 ... 222–3, 251

Conegate v Customs and Excise Commissioners (Case 121/85) [1986] ECR 1007, [1986] 1 CMLR 739 ... 369–70, 371

Rau (Walter) v BALM (Cases 133–136/85) [1987] ECR 2289 ... 250–1, 252

Maizena (Case 137/85) [1987] ECR 4587 ... 75

Kempf v Staatssecretaris van Justitie (Case 139/85) [1986] ECR 1741, [1987] 1 CMLR 764 ... 430

Commission v Italy (Case 168/85) [1986] ECR 2945 ... 178

Commission v Italy (Case 184/85) [1987] ECR 2013 ... 335

Cooperativa Cofrutta v Amministrazione delle Finanze dello Stato (Case 193/85) [1987] ECR 2085 ... 335

Commission v France (Case 196/85) [1987] ECR 1597, [1988] 2 CMLR 851 ... 333

Barra v Belgium (Case 309/85) [1988] ECR 355 ... 128

Vereniging van Vlaamse Reisbureaus v Sociaale Dienst van de plaatselijke en gewestelijke Overheidsdiensten (Case 311/85) [1987] ECR 3801 ... 528

Foto Frost v HZA Lubeck Ost (Case 314/85) [1987] ECR 4199 ... 207–8, 209, 254, 255, 262, 268, 272, 693

Bond van Adverteerders and Others (Case 352/85) [1988] ECR 2085 ... 465–6

Feldain (Case 433/85) [1987] ECR 3536 ... 332

Commission v Belgium (Case 1/86) [1987] ECR 2797 ... 112–13

Pretore di Salò v X (Case 14/86) [1987] ECR 2545 ... 162

Blaizot v University of Liège (Case 24/86) [1988] ECR 379 ... 128

Lair v Universität Hannover (Case 39/86) [1988] ECR 3161 ... 461

Commission v Council (Case 45/86) [1987] ECR 1493 ... 47, 70–1

Commission v UK (Case 60/86) [1988] ECR 3921 ... 633–4

AKZO v Commission (Case C-62/86) [1991] ECR I-3359 ... 568

Ahmed Saeed Flugreisen v Zentrale zur Bekämpfung unlauteren Wettbewerbs (Case 66/86) [1989] ECR 803, [1990] 4 CMLR 102 ... 528–9

Officier van Justitie v Kolpinghuis Nijmegen (Case 80/86)[1987] ECR 3969 ... 162–3, 167

Unectef v Heylens (Case 222/86) [1987] ECR 4097 ... 456

Commission v Greece (Case 240/86) [1988] ECR 1835 ... 122

Ministère Public v Deserbais (Case 286/86) [1988] ECR 4907 ... 385–6

Enital v Commission and Council (Case C-304/86) [1990] ECR I-2929 ... 230

Neotype Techmashexport v Commission and Council (Case C-305/86) [1990] ECR I-2945 ... 230

Commission v Germany (Case 18/87) [1988] ECR 5427 ... 329–30

Commission v Italy (Case 22/87) [1989] ECR 143 ... 168

Commission v Ireland (Case 45/87) [1988] ECR 4929, [1989] 1 CMLR 225 ... 417–18

Hoechst v Commission (Case 46/87) [1989] ECR 2859, [1991] 4 CMLR 410 ... 82, 83, 587–9, 590, 591, 592, 593, 596

Dow Benelux v Commission (Case 85/87) [1989] ECR 3137 ... 591, 592, 595

Dow Chemical Iberica and Others v Commission (Cases 97–99/87) [1989] ECR 3165 ... 593

Nashua Corporation v Commission (Cases C-133 and C-150/87) [1990] ECR I-719 ... 230

Gestetner Holdings v Council and Commission (Case C-156/87) [1990] ECR I-719 ... 230

Electroimpex v Council [1990] ECR I-3021 ... 230

Cowan v Le Trésor Public (Case 186/87) [1986] ECR 195 ... 447–8

Oberkreisdirektor v Moormann (Case 190/87) [1988] ECR 4689, [1990] 1 CMLR 656 ... 378, 379, 633

Star Fruit Co v Commission (Case 247/87) [1989] ECR 291 ... 114, 121

Bettray v Staatssecretaris van Justitie (Case 344/87) [1989] ECR 1621, [1991] 1 CMLR 459 ... 430

Orkem v Commission (Case 374/87) [1989] ECR 3283 ... 95, 595

Enichem Base and Others v Comune di Cinsello Balsamo (Case 380/87) [1989] ECR 2491 ... 154

Ministère Public v Buet (Case 382/87) [1989] ECR 1235 ... 400–1, 409, 636

Parliament v Council (Case C-70/88) [1991] ECR I-4529 ... 50, 707

Fratelli Costanzo v Comune di Milano (Case 103/88) [1989] ECR 1839 ... 149, 151–2, 164

Commission v Italy (Case C-120/88) [1991] ECR I-621 ... 178

Zuckerfabrik Süderdithmarschen and Zuckerfabrik Soest (Cases C-143/88 and C-92/89) [1991] 1 ECR 415 ... 174, 175, 179, 255–6, 257, 258, 259, 262, 595

Torfaen BC v B & Q plc (Case 145/88) [1989] ECR 765 ... 393–5, 397, 399, 659

Parfumerie Fabrik v Provide (Case C-150/88) [1989] ECR 3891, [1991] 1 CMLR 715 ... 194

Commission v Germany (Case C-217/88) [1990] ECR I-2879 ... 596

ECSC v Acciaierie e Ferriere Busseni (in liquidation) (Case 221/88) ... 151

Messner (Case C-265/88) [1989] ECR 4209, [1991] 2 CMLR 545 ... 433

Dzodzi v Belgian State (Cases C-297/88 and C-197/89) [1990] ECR I-3763 ... 95

Grimaldi v Fonds des Malaises Professionelles (Case C-322/88) [1989] ECR 4407 ... 44

Fedesa and Others (Case C-331/88) [1990] ECR I-4023 ... 595

Procurator Fiscal, Stranraer v Marshall (Case 370/88) [1990] ECR I-420 ... 214

Quietlynn Ltd v Southend on Sea BC (Case C-23/89) [1990] ECR I-3059 ... 397

Procureur de la République v Bouchoucha (Case C-61/89) [1990] ECR I-3560 ... 450, 461

Commission v France (Case C-62/89) [1990] ECR I-925 ... 643

Commission v Netherlands (Case C-68/89) [1991] ECR I-2637 ... 433

Mulder et al v Council and Commission (Cases C-104/89 and C-37/90) [1992] ECR I-3061 ... 241, 270

Marleasing SA v La Comercial Internacional de Alimentacion SA (Case C-106/89) [1990] ECR I-4135 ... 163, 164, 165, 169, 170, 346

Commission v Spain (Case C-119.89) [1991] ECR I-641 ... 178

Commission v Italy (Case C-128/89) [1990] ECR I-3239 ... 373

Commission v France (Case C-154/89) [1991] ECR I-659 ... 454–5

Commission v Italy (Case C-180/89) [1991] ECR I-709 ... 467

Foster v British Gas (Case C-188/89) [1990] ECR I-3313, [1991] 2 CMLR ... 150–1

R v Secretary of State for Transport, ex parte Factortame (Case C-213/89) [1990] ECR I-2433, [1990] 3 WLR 852 ... 136, 137–40, 168, 173, 174, 260, 605

Delimitis (Stergios) v Henninger Brau (Case C-234/89) [1991] ECR I-935, [1992] 5 CMLR 201 ... 514, 519–21, 522, 606

Pall (Case C-238/89) [1990] ECR I-4827 ... 411

Commission v UK (Case C-246/89R) [1989] ECR 3125 ... 117–19, 136

ERT (Case C-260/89) [1991] ECR I-2925 ... 83, 411, 477, 590

Stichting Collectieve Antennevoorziening Gouda v Commissariaat voor de Media (Case C-288/89) [1991] ECR I-4007 ... 456, 459

R v IAT, ex parte Antonissen (Case C-292/89) [1991] ECR I-745, [1991] 2 CMLR 373 ... 430, 431

Gibraltar v Council (Case C-298/89) [1993] ECR I-3605 ... 264

Commission v Council (Case C-300/89) [1991] ECR I-2867 ... 50, 51, 52, 53, 64

Codorniu SA v Council (Case C-309/89) [1994] ECR I-1853 ... 263–4, 265, 267, 268, 272, 273

UDS v Conforama (Case C-312/89) [1991] ECR I-997 ... 396

Marchandise (Case C-332/89) [1991] ECR I-1027 ... 396

Vlassopoulou v Ministerium für Justiz, Bundes- und Europaangelegenheiten Baden-Wurttemberg (Case 340/89) [1991] ECR I-2357 ... 455–6, 472

Sheptonhurst v Newham BC (Case C-350/89) [1991] ECR I-2387 ... 397

Commission v Netherlands (Case C-353/89) [1991] ECR I-4069 ... 411

Extramet v Council (Case C-358/89) [1991] ECR I-2501 ... 230–1, 262–3, 265, 272, 273

Roux v Belgian State (Case C-363/89) [1991] ECR I-273 ... 446

Piageme v BVBA Peeters (Case 369/89) [1991] ECR I-2971 ... 410

Commission v Belgium (Case C-2/90) [1992] ECR I-4431 ... 49, 413, 414

Francovich and Others v Italian State (Cases 6/90 and 9/90) [1991] ECR I-5357, [1993] 2 CMLR ... 121, 154, 167, 168–9, 170, 171, 172,

174, 175, 177, 178, 179, 180, 182, 188, 241, 243, 604, 647

Höfner v Macrotron (Case C-41/90) [1991] ECR I-1979 ... 529

Säger v Dennemeyer & Co Ltd (Case 76/90) [1991] ECR I-4221 ... 456

Society for the Protection of Unborn Children Ireland Ltd (SPUC) v Grogan (Case C-159/90) [1991] ECR I-4685, [1991] 3 CMLR 849 ... 83, 470–1, 590

Emmott v Minister for Social Welfare (Case C-208/90) [1991] 3 CMLR 894 ... 175

Parliament v Council (Case C-295/90) [1992] ECR I-4193 ... 49, 449

Telemarsicabruzzo v Circostel (Cases C-320–322/90) [1993] ECR I-393 ... 196, 197

R v IAT and Singh, ex parte Secretary of State (Case C-370/90) [1992] ECR I-4265, [1992] 3 CMLR 358 ... 476

Meilicke (Wienand) v ADV/ORGA FA Meyer AG (Case C-83/91) [1992] ECR I-4871 ... 195, 196

Dori (Paola Faccini) v Recreb Srl (Case C-91/92) [1994] ECR I-3325 ... 148–9, 153, 156, 160, 163, 165, 170, 171, 488, 636, 644

Ramrath (Case C-106/91) [1992] ECR I-3351 ... 467

ENU v Commission (Case C-107/91) [1993] ECR I-599 ... 260

Veronica Omroep Organisatie v Commissariaat voor de Media (Case C-148/91) [1993] ECR I-487 ... 411, 461

Commission v Council (Case C-155/91) [1993] ECR I-939 ... 48–50, 51, 52, 53, 60

Stoke-on-Trent and Norwich City Councils v B & Q (Case C-169/91), [1992] ECR I-6457, [1993] CMLR 426 ... 396, 659

Commission v Greece (Case C-183/91) [1993] ECR I-3131 ... 252

Kirsammer-Hack v Sidal (Case C-189/91) [1993] ECR I-6185 ... 57

Angelopharm (Case C-212/91) [1994] ECR I-171 ... 56

Radio Téléfis Eireann and Independent Television Publications v Commission (Cases C-241/91P and C-242/91P) [1995] ECR I-801, [1995] 4 CMLR ... 566–7, 569

Keck and Mithouard (Cases C-267–268/91) [1993] ECR I-6097, [1995] 1 CMLR 101 ... 66, 344, 393, 397–8, 398, 399, 400, 401, 402, 403, 404, 405, 406, 407, 408, 418, 457, 458, 501, 659

Marshall v Southampton AHA (Marshall '2') (Case 271/91) [1993] ECR I-4367 ... [1993] 3 CMLR ... 147, 148

General Milk Products v Hauptzollamt Hamburg-Jonas (Case C-8/92) [1993] ECR I-779 ... 461

Kraus v Land Baden-Württemberg (Case C-19/92) [1993] ECR I-1663 ... 462

Commission v Anic (Case C-49/92P) [1999] ECR I-4125 ... 509

Wagner Miret v Fondo de Garantia Salarial (Case C-334/92) [1993] ECR I-6911 ... 163, 164, 165

Banks (H.) & Co. Ltd v British Coal Corporation (Case C-128/92) [1994] ECR I-1209 ... 604

Montecatini v Commission (Case C-235/92) [1999] ECR I-4539 ... 514

DLG (Case C-250/92) [1994] ECR I-5641 ... 514, 524

Customs & Excise Commissioners v Schindler and Schindler (Case C-275/92) [1994] ECR I-1039 ... 457

Schindler (Case C-275/92) [1994] ECR I-1039 ... 411

Hünermund and Others (Case C-292/92) [1993] ECR I-6787 ... 402

ADM Ölmühlen (Case C-339/92) [1993] ECR I-6473 ... 76

Spain v Council (Case C-350/92) [1995] ECR I-1985 ... 62, 66

Peralta (Case C-379/92) [1994] ECR I-3453 ... 531

Commission v UK (Case C-382/92) [1994] ECR I-2435 ... 644

Municipality of Almelo and others v Energiebedrijf IJsselmij NV (Case C-393/92) [1994] ECR I-1477 ... 521–2, 531

Tankstation 't Heukste vof and J. B. E. Boermans (Cases C-401 and C-402/92) [1994] ECR I-2199 ... 398, 400

TV10 v Commissariaat voor de Media (Case C-23/93) [1994] ECR I-4795 ... 461

France v Commission (Case C-41/93) [1994] ECR I-1829 ... 629–30

Brasserie du Pêcheur SA v Germany and R v Secretary of State for Transport: ex parte Factortame and others (Cases C-46/93 and C-48/93) [1996] ECR I-1029, [1996] 1 CMLR 889 ... 177–84, 241, 242, 244

Meyhui NV v Schott Zweisel Glaswerke AG (Case C-51/93) [1994] ECR I-3879 ... 410

van Schaik (Criminal proceedings against) (Case C-55/93) [1994] ECR I-4837 ... 348

Commission v Germany (Case C-131/93) [1994] ECR I-3303 ... 373

Chiquita Banana Co and Others v Council (Case C-276/93) [1993] ECR I-3345 ... 265

Germany v Commission (Case C-280/93) [1993] ECR I-3667, [1994] ECR I-4973 ... 258, 259

BPB Industries and British Gypsum Ltd v Commission (Case C-310/93P) [1995] ECR I-865 ... 566

Vaneetveld v SA Le Foyer (Case C-316/93) [1994] ECR I-763 ... 148, 170

Centre d'insemination de la Crespelle (Case C-323/93) [1994] ECR I-5077 ... 569

Bordessa and Others (Cases C-358/93 and C-416/93) [1995] ECR I-361 ... 468

Roders (F. G.) BV e.a. v Inspecteur der Invoerrechten en Accijnzen (Cases C-367/93–C-377/93) [1995] ECR I-2229 ... 336

Commission v France (Case C-381/93) [1994] ECR I-5145 ... 466

Alpine Investments BV v Minister van Financiën (Case C-384/93) [1995] ECR I-1141 ... 409, 457–9, 460, 476

R v H.M. Treasury, ex parte British Telecommunications (Case C-392/93) [1996] ECR I-1631 ... 184

Oude Lutikhuis and Others (Case C-399/93) ... 514

Leclerc-Siplec (Case C-412/93) [1995] ECR I-179 ... 195

Société d'Importation Edouard Leclerc-Siplec v TF1 Publicité SA and M6 Publicité SA (Case C-412/93) [1995] ECR I-179 ... 401–3, 404

Bosman (Case C-415/93) [1995] ECR I-4921 ... 83, 526, 590

URBSFA v Bosman (Case C-415/93) [1995] ECR I-4921, [1996] All ER (EC) 97 ... 449

Germany v Council (Case C-426/93) [1995] ECR I-3723 ... 75

Saddik (Case C-458/93) [1995] ECR I-511 ... 197

Atlanta Fruchthandelsgesellschaft mbH and others v Bundesamt für Ernährung und Forstwirtschaft (Case C-465/93) [1995] ECR I-3761 ... 256–8, 259, 262

Atlanta Fruchthandelsgesellschaft mbH and others v Bundesamt für Ernährung und Forstwirtschaft (Case C-466/93) [1995] ECR I-3799 ... 258–9

Verein gegen Unwesen in Handel und Gewerbe Köln v Mars GmbH (Case C-470/93) [1995] ECR I-1923 ... 407–8, 411

R v Ministry of Agriculture, Fisheries and Food, ex parte Hedley Lomas (Ireland) Ltd (Case C-5/94) [1996] ECR I-2553 ... 185, 242, 244

P v S and Cornwall County Council (Case C-13/94) [1996] ECR I-2143 ... 93, 94

Gebhard (Reinhard) v Consiglio dell' Ordine degli Avvocati e Procuratori di Milano (Case C-55/94) [1995] ECR I-4165, [1996] 1 CMLR ... 603 ... 321, 322, 385, 450, 456, 462, 472

UK v Council (Case C-84/94) [1996] ECR 1–5755 ... 54–8, 60, 75, 76, 661, 666

CIA Security International SA v Signalson SA and Securitel SPRL (Case C-94/94) [1996] ECR I-2201 ... 153–5, 156, 157, 158, 315

Job Centre Coop. arl (Case C-111/94) [1995] ECR I-3361 ... 202

Hönig (Hans) v Stadt Stockach (Case C-128/94) [1995] ECR I-3389 ... 634–5

DIP SpA v Comune di Bassano del Grappa, (Case C-140/94) [1995] ECR I-3257 ... 530–1

LIDL Italia SrL v Comune di Chioggia (Case C-141/94) [1995] ECR I-3257 ... 530–1

Lingral SrL v Comune di Chioggia (Case C-142/94) [1995] ECR I-3257 ... 530–1

Sanz de Lera (Cases C-163/94, C-165/94 and C-250/94) [1995] ECR I-4821 ... 468

Dillenkofer and Others v Germany (Joined Cases C-178 et al/94) [1996] ECR I-4845 ... 185, 242, 244

El Corte Inglés v Cristina Blasquez Rivero (Case C-192/94) [1996] ECR I-1281 ... 149

Primecrown Ltd v The Medicines Control Agency (Case C-201/94) ... 152, 153

R v The Medicines Control Agency, ex parte Smith & Nephew Pharmaceuticals Ltd (Case C-201/94) ... 152, 153

Brennet v Paletta (Paletta II) (Case C-206/94) [1996] ECR I-2357 ... 461

Germany v Parliament and Council (Case C-223/94) [1997] ECR I-2304 ... 661

Germany v Parliament and Council (Case 233/94) [1997] ECR I-2405 ... 62, 76, 595

Parliament v Council (Case C-271/94) [1996] ECR I-1689 ... 51

Tetra Pak v Commission (Case C-333/94 P) [1996] ECR I-5951 ... 566

Reiseburo Broede v Gerd Sanker (Case C-3/95) [1996] ECR I-6511 ... 457, 523, 524

Deere v Commission (Case C-7/95) [1998] ECR I-3111 ... 243

Konsumentombudsmannen v De Agostini Forlag AB and TV-Shop i Sverige AB (Cases C-34–36/95) [1997] ECR I-3843 ... 404–5, 458

Commission v France (Case C-52/95) [1995] ECR I-4443 ... 356

France v Commission (Case C-57/95) [1997] ECR I-1627 ... 218, 364

Shingara and Radiom (Cases C-65 and C-111/95) [1997] ECR I-3343 ... 442

R v Secretary of State for Social Security, ex parte Sutton (Case C-66/95) [1997] ECR I-2163 ... 185

Sodermare and Others (Case C-70/95) [1997] ECR I-3395 ... 465

Norbrook Laboratories (Case C-127/95) [1998] ECR I-1531 ... 244

Arcaro (Luciano) (Case C-168/95) [1996] ECR I-4705 ... 163, 164

Fantask (Case C-188/95) [1997] ECR I-6783 ... 171

Comateb and Others (Cases C-192–218/95) [1997] ECR I-165 ... 136

GT-Link v DSB (Case C-242/95) [1997] ECR I-4449 ... 568

SAM Schiffahrt (Cases C-248–249/95) [1997] ECR I-4475 ... 86

Palmisani (Case C-261/95) [1997] ECR I-4025 ... 605

Commission v France (Case C-265/95) [1997] ECR I-6959 ... 355–7, 373

Guérin Automobiles v Commission (Case C-282/
95P) [1997] ECR I-1503 ... 605

**Commission v UK (Case C-300/95) [1997] ECR
I-2649 ... 642–4**

**Stichting Greenpeace Council (Greenpeace
International) and others v Commission
(Case C-321/95 P) [1998] ECR I-1651 ...
266–7, 268, 271**

Parfums Christian Dior SA and Parfums
Christian Dior BV v Evora BV (Case C-337/95)
[1997] ECR I-6013 ... 203, 206

Wiener (Case C-338/95) [1997] ECR I-6495 ... 198

**Vereinigte Familiapress Zeitungsverlags- und
vertriebs GmbH v Heinrich Bauer Verlag
(Case C-368/95) [1997] ECR I-3689 ...
411–12, 477**

Belgium v Spain (Case C-388/95) [2000] ECR
I-3123 ... 111

Eurotunnel SA and others v SeaFrance (Case
C-408/95) [1997] ECR I-6315 ... 253

Parliament v Council (Case C-22/96) [1998] ECR
I-3231 ... 51

Deliège (Cases C-51/96 and C-191/97) [2000]
ECR I-2549 ... 466

Job Centre Coop. arl (Case C-55/96) [1997] ECR
I-7119 ... 202

Land Nordrhein-Westfalen v Uecker, Jacquet
(Cases C-64/96 and C-65/96) [1997] ECR
I-3171 ... 488

**Albany International v Stichting
Bedrijfspensioenfonds Textielindustrie
(Case C-67/96) [1999] ECR I-5751 ... 197,
525–6**

Martinez Sala (Marìa) v Freistaat Bayern (Case
C-85/96) [1998] ECR I-2691 ... 431, 488, 489

Verband Deutscher Daihatsu Händler eV v
Daihatsu Deutschland GmbH (Case C-97/96)
[1997] ECR I-6843 ... 149

Mac Quen and Others (Case C-108/96) [2001]
ECR I-837 ... 524

Dorsch Consult (Case C-54/96) [1997] ECR
I-4961 ... 202

Inter-Environment Wallonie ASBL v Région
Wallone (Case C-129/96) [1997] ECR I-7411 ...
143

Portugal v Council (Case C-149/96) [1999] ECR
I-8395 ... 259

National Farmers Union and Others (Case
C-157/96) [1998] ECR I-2211 ... 76

Kohll (Case C-158/96) [1998] ECR I-1931 ... 465,
466

**Commission v Council (Case 170/96) [1998]
ECR I-2763 ... 53–4, 215**

**Jyri Lehtonen, Castors Canada Dry Namur-
Braine ASBL v Fédération Royale Belge des
Sociétés de Basket-ball ASBL (FRBSB) (Case
C-176/96) [2000] ECR I-2681 ... 197**

Commission v France (Foie Gras) (Case C-184/
96) [1998] ECR I-6197 ... 421

Metronome Musik (Case C-200/96) [1998] ECR
I-1953 ... 595

Aprile (Case C-228/96) [1998] ECR I-7141 ... 135

**Grant v South-West Trains Ltd (Case C-249/96)
[1998] ECR I-621 ... 80, 93–5, 96**

Bickel and Franz (C-274/96) [1998] ECR I-7637 ...
489

Didier Tabouillet (Case C-284/96) [1997] ECR
I-7471 ... 332

Javico et al v Yves St Laurent Parfums (Case
C-306/96) [1998] ECR I-1983 ... 522

Levez (Case C-326/96) [1998] ECR I-7835 ... 133,
134

Dilexport (Case C-343/96) ... 135, 136

**Calfa (Donatella) (Case C-348/96) [1999] ECR
I-11 ... 442–3, 446, 448**

Kefalas and Others v Greece (Case C-367/96)
[1998] ECR I-2843 ... 461

Goerres (Hermann Josef) (Case C-385/96) [1998]
ECR I-4431 ... 410

**Bronner (Oscar) GmbH & Co. KG v Mediaprint
(Case C-7/97) [1998] ECR I-7791 ... 568–70**

Colim v Biggs (Case C-33/97) [1999] ECR I-3175
... 410

Autotrasporti Librandi Snc di Librandi F & C
(Case C-38/97) [1998] ECR I-5955 ... 532

**Parliament v Council (Case C-42/97) [1999]
ECR I-869 ... 50–1, 52, 53**

**Büchel & Co Fahrzeugteilefabrik GmbH v
Council and Commission (Cases T-74 and
T-75/97) Judgment 26 September 2000 ... 231**

Atlanta AG and others v Council and
Commission (Case C-104/97P) [1999] ECR
I-6983 ... 259

Brentjens' Handelsonderneming v Stichting
Bedrijfspensioenfonds voor de Handel in
Bouwmaterialen (Cases C-115–117/97) [1999]
ECR I-6025 ... 197

Läärä (Markku Juhani), Cotswold Microsystems
Ltd, Oy Transatlantic Systems (Case C-124/97)
[1999] ECR I-6067 ... 457

**Eco Swiss China Time Ltd v Benetton
International NV (Case C-126/97) [1999]
ECR I-3055 ... 495, 604**

Victoria Films A/S (Case C-134/97) [1998] ECR
I-7023 ... 202

**Centros Ltd v Erhervs- og Selskabsstyrelsen
(Case C-212/97) [1999] ECR I-1459 ... 460–3**

Commission v Germany (Case C-217/97) [1999]
ECR I-5087 ... 164

**Lemmens (Johannes Martinus) (Case C-226/
97) [1998] ECR I-3711 ... 155–6, 158**

Commission v Council (Case 1997/269) [2000]
ECR I-2257 ... 635

Konle (Klaus) v Austria (Case C-302/97) [1999]
ECR I-3099 ... 185

Kortas (Case C-319/97) [1999] ECR I-3143 ... 164, 630

Landesgrundverkehrsreferent der Tiroler Landesregierung v Beck, Bergdorf Wohnbau (Case C-355/97) [1999] ECR I-4977 ... 198

Wijsenbeek (Florius Ariel) (Case C-378/97) [1999] ECR I-6207 ... 433, 478

Haim (Case 1997/424) [2000] ECR I-5123 ... 244

Evangelischer Krankenhausverein Wien (Case C-437/97) [2000] ECR I-1157 ... 128, 196

Preston and Others v Wolverhampton NHS Healthcare Trust and Others (Case C-78/98) [2000] ECR I-3201 ... 133–5

Jägerskiöld (Case C-97/98) [1999] ECR I-7319 ... 476

Gabalfrisa and Others (Cases C-110–147/98) [2000] ECR I-1577 ... 202

Commission v Greece (Case C-214/98) [2000] ECR I-9601 ... 164

D'Hoop (Marie-Nathalie) v Office national de l'emploi (Case C-224/98) Judgment 11 July 2002 ... 490

Océano Grupo Editorial v Salvat Editores (Cases C-240–244/98) [2000] ECR I-4941 ... 165

Angonese (Roman) (Case C-281/98) [2000] ECR I-4139 ... 123, 365, 449, 526

Geffroy (Case C-366/98) [2000] ECR I-6579 ... 410

Germany v Parliament and Council (Case C-376/98) [2000] ECR I-8419 ... 60–5, 66, 67, 636–7, 639, 640, 645, 649, 661, 662

Netherlands v Parliament and Council (Case C-377/98) [2001] ECR I-7079 ... 66

Preussen Elektra (Case C-379/98) [2001] ECR I-2099 ... 414

Konsumentombudsmannen v Gourmet International Products AB (Case C-405/98) [2001] ECR I-1795 ... 405–6

Metallgesellschaft (Case C-410/98) ... 135

Michailidis (Cases 441–442/98) [2000] ECR I-7145 ... 605

Unilever Italia SpA v Central Food SpA (Case C-443/98) Judgment 26 September 2000 ... 156–8

Centrosteel Srl v Adipol GmbH (Case C-456/98) [2000] ECR I-6007 ... 164–5

Industrie des poudres sphériques v Council (Case C-458/98P) [2000] ECR I-8147 ... 231

Commission v Denmark (Case C-467/98) ... 106

Commission v Sweden (Case C-468/98) ... 106

Commission v Finland (Case C-469/98) Judgment of 5 November 2002 ... 106–7

Commission v Belgium (Case C-471/98) ... 106

Commission v Austria (Case C-472/98) ... 106

Commission v Germany (Case C-476/98) ... 106

Laboratoires Pharmaceutiques Bergaderm SA and Jean-Jacques Goupil v Commission

(Case C-3523/98P) [2000] ECR I-5291 ... 241–3, 244, 270

Idéal Tourisme (Case C-36/99) [2000] ECR I-6049 ... 194, 196

Camoroto and Vignone (Cases C-52–53/99) [2001] ECR I-1395 ... 158

Stockholm Lindopark (Case C-150/99) [2001] ECR I-493 ... 185

Geraets-Smits v Stichting Ziekenfonds VGZ, Peerbooms v Stichting CZ Groep Zorgverzekeringen (Case C-157/99) [2001] ECR I-5473 ... 464–9

Saltzmann (Doris) (Case C-178/99) [2001] ECR I-4421 ... 202

Grzelczyk (Rudy) v Centre public d'aide sociale d'Ottignies-Louvain-la-Neuve (Case C-184/99) [2001] ECR I-6193 ... 488–9

Analir and Others (Case C-205/99) [2001] ECR I-1271 ... 468

Neste Markkinoiniti Oy (Case C-214/99) [2000] ECR I-11121 ... 522

Commission v Spain (Case C-232/99) Judgment 16 May 2002 ... 456

Connolly v Commission (Case C-274/99) [2001] ECR I-1611 ... 83, 590

Wouters, J. W. Savelbergh, Price Waterhouse Belastingadviseurs BV v Algemene Raad van de Nederlandse Orde van Advocaten (Case C-309/99) [2002] ECR I-1577 ... 522–5, 526

Baumbast (Case C-413/99) Judgment 17 September 2002 ... 490

Commission v Austria (Case C-424/99) [2001] ECR I-9285 ... 272

Cura Anlagen GmbH v Auto Service Leasing GmbH (Case C-451/99) [2002] ECR I-3193 ... 194–5

Courage Ltd v Bernard Creham (Case C-453/99) [2001] ECR I-6297 ... 604–6

Schmid (Walter) Judgment 30 May 2002 ... 202

Denmark v Commission (Case C-3/00) Judgment 20 March 2003 ... 631

Unión de Pequeños Agricultores v Council (Case C-50/00 P) Judgment 25 July 2002 ... 269, 271–2, 273

Commission v France (Case C-52/00) [2002] ECR I-3827 ... 649, 650

Carpenter (Mary) v Secretary of State for the Home Department (Case C-60/00) Judgment 11 July 2002 ... 475–8, 490

Marks & Spencer plc v Commissioners of Customs & Excise (Case C-62/00) Judgment of 11 July 2002 ... 135–6, 164, 171

Roquette Frères SA v Directeur général de la concurrence, de la consummation et de la répression des frauds (Case C-94/00) 22 October 2002 ... 83, 589–98

Lyckeskog (Kenny Roland) (Case C-99/00) Judgment 4 June 2002 ... 203–4, 206

Laguillaumie [2000] ECR I-4979 ... 196

Bellamy (Christina) (Case C-123/00) [2001] ECR I-2795 ... 198

Danner (Case C-136/00) Judgment 3 October 2002 ... 414

Commission v Greece (Case C-154/00) [2002] ECR I-3879 ... 649, 650

Sapod Audic v Eco-Emballages SA (Case C-159/00) Judgment 6 June 2002 ... 158

González Sánchez (María Victoria) v Medicina Asturiana SA (Case C-183/00) Judgment 25 April 2002 ... 647–9, 650

Überseering BV v Nordic Construction Co Baumanagement GmbH (Case C-208/00) Judgment 5 November 2002 ... 463–4

Käserei Champignon Hofmeister (Case C-210/00) [2002] ECR I-6453 ,,, 76

Commission v Camar and Others (Case C-312/00P) Judgment 10 December 2002 ... 185, 243–4

Bacardi-Martini SAS, Cellier des Dauphins v Newcastle United (Case C-318/00) Judgment 21 January 2003 ... 195–6

Commission v Germany (Case C-325/00) Judgment 5 November 2002 ... 364

AXA Royal Belge (Case C-386/00) [2002] ECR I-2209 ... 165

NFU v Secretariat general du gouvernement (Case C-241/01) Judgment 22 October 2002 ... 254

R v Secretary of State for Health, ex parte British American Tobacco (Investments) Ltd and Imperial Tobacco Ltd (Case C-491/01) Judgment 10 December 2002 ... 66–7, 75–8, 209, 216, 273–4, 637, 639, 661, 663

Court of Justice of the European Communities (alphabetical)

ACF Chemiefarma v Commission (Quinine) (Cases 41, 44 & 45/69) [1970] ECR 661 416–7, [1986] 1 CMLR 506 ... 136, 503–4

Adams v Commission (No. 1) (Case 145/83) [1985] ECR 3539 ... 244–8

ADM Ölmühlen (Case C-339/92) [1993] ECR I-6473 ... 76

Adoui and Cornuaille v Belgian State (Cases 115 & 116/81) [1982] ECR 1665, [1982] 3 CMLR 631 ... 441–2

Ahlström Osakyhtio v Commission (Woodpulp) (Cases 89 et al/85) [1988] ECR 5193, [1988] 4 CMLR 901 ... 502–3, 509

Ahmed Saeed Flugreisen v Zentrale zur Bekämpfung unlauteren Wettbewerbs (Case 66/86) [1989] ECR 803, [1990] 4 CMLR 102 ... 528–9

Aktien-Zuckerfabrik Schöppenstedt v Council (Case 5/71) [1971] ECR 975 ... 239–40, 241

AKZO v Commission (Case 5/85) [1986] ECR 2855 ... 586

AKZO v Commission (Case C-62/86) [1991] ECR I-3359 ... 568

Albany International v Stichting Bedrijfspensioenfonds Textielindustrie (Case C-67/96) [1999] ECR I-5751 ... 197, 525–6

Allied Corporation v Commission (Cases 239 and 275/82) [1984] ECR 1005 ... 230

Alpine Investments BV v Minister van Financiën (Case C-384/93) [1995] ECR I-1141 ... 409, 457–9, 460, 476

Alusuisse Italia SpA v Council and Commission (Case 307/81) [1982] ECR 3463 ... 227–8, 230

AM & S v Commission (Case 155/79) ... 89, 587, 591, 595

Amministrazione delle Finanze dello Stato v San Giorgio (Case 199/82) [1983] ECR 3595 ... 169, 173, 182

Amministrazione delle Finanze v Simmenthal (Case 106/77) [1978] ECR 629 ... 100–1, 103, 137, 138, 168, 172, 173, 605

Analir and Others (Case C-205/99) [2001] ECR I 1271 ... 468

Angelopharm (Case C-212/91) [1994] ECR I 171 ... 56

Angonese (Roman) (Case C-281/98) [2000] ECR I-4139 ... 123, 365, 449, 526

Apple and Pear Development Council v Lewis (Case 222/82) [1983] ECR 4083, [1984] 3 CMLR 733 ... 361, 364

Aprile (Case C-228/96) [1998] ECR I-7141 ... 135

Arcaro (Luciano) (Case C-168/95) [1996] ECR I-4705 ... 163, 164

Ariete SpA v Amministrazione delle Finanze dello Stato (Case 811/79) [1980] ECR 2545 ... 138

Atlanta AG and others v Council and Commission (Case C-104/97P) [1999] ECR I-6983 ... 259

Atlanta Fruchthandelsgesellschaft mbH and others v Bundesamt für Ernährung und Forstwirtschaft (Case C-465/93) [1995] ECR I-3761 ... 256–8, 259, 262

Atlanta Fruchthandelsgesellschaft mbH and others v Bundesamt für Ernährung und Forstwirtschaft (Case C-466/93) [1995] ECR I-3799 ... 258–9

Auer v Ministère Public (Case 271/82) [1983] ECR 2727 ... 472

Autotrasporti Librandi Snc di Librandi F & C (Case C-38/97) [1998] ECR I-5955 ... 532

AXA Royal Belge (Case C-386/00) [2002] ECR I-2209 ... 165

Bacardi-Martini SAS, Cellier des Dauphins v Newcastle United (Case C-318/00) Judgment 21 January 2003 ... 195–6

Balkan-Import-Export v Hauptzollamt Berlin-Packhof (Case 5/73) [1973] ECR 1091 ... 74

Banks (H.) & Co. Ltd v British Coal Corporation (Case C-128/92) [1994] ECR I-1209 ... 604

Barra v Belgium (Case 309/85) [1988] ECR 355 ... 128

Bauhuis v Netherlands (Case 46/76) [1977] ECR 5 ... 329, 350

Baumbast (Case C-413/99) Judgment 17 September 2002 ... 490

Bayerische HNL Vermehrungsbetriebe GmbH & Co. KG v Council (Case 83/76) [1978] ECR 1209 ... 240

Becker v Finanzamt Münster-Innenstadt (Case 8/81) [1982] ECR 53 ... 145, 149, 150, 151, 152, 164

Béguelin (Case 22/71) [1971] ECR 949 ... 604

Belgische Radio en Televisie v Sabam (Case 127/73) [1974] ECR 313 ... 528, 605

Belgium v Spain (Case C-388/95) [2000] ECR I-3123 ... 111

Bellamy (Christina) (Case C-123/00) [2001] ECR I-2795 ... 198

Bettray v Staatssecretaris van Justitie (Case 344/87) [1989] ECR 1621, [1991] 1 CMLR 459 ... 430

Bickel and Franz (C-274/96) [1998] ECR I-7637 ... 489

Bilger v Jehle (Case 43/69) [1970] ECR 127 ... 520

Blaizot v University of Liège (Case 24/86) [1988] ECR 379 ... 128

BMW v Belgium (Case 32/78) [1979] ECR 2435, [1980] 1 CMLR ... 504

Bond van Adverteerders and Others (Case 352/85) [1988] ECR 2085 ... 465–6

Bonsignore (Case 67/74) [1975] ECR 297 ... 442

Bordessa and Others (Cases C-358/93 and C-416/93) [1995] ECR I-361 ... 468

Bosch v de Geus (Case 13/61) [1962] ECR 45 ... 187–8

Bosman (Case C-415/93) [1995] ECR I-4921 ... 83, 526, 590

BP v Commission (Case 77/77) [1978] ECR 1511 ... 566

BPB Industries and British Gypsum Ltd v Commission (Case C-310/93P) [1995] ECR I-865 ... 566

Brasserie de Haecht II (Case 48/72) [1973] ECR 77 ... 605

Brasserie de Haecht SA v Wilkin (Case 23/67) [1967] ECR 407, [1968] CMLR 26 ... 518–19, 522, 606

Brasserie du Pêcheur SA v Germany and R v Secretary of State for Transport, ex parte Factortame and others (Cases C-46/93 and C-48/93) [1996] ECR I-1029, [1996] 1 CMLR 889 ... 177–84, 241, 242, 244

Brennet v Paletta (Paletta II) (Case C-206/94) [1996] ECR I-2357 ... 461

Brentjens' Handelsonderneming v Stichting

Bedrijfspensioenfonds voor de Handel in Bouwmaterialen (Cases C-115–117/97) [1999] ECR I-6025 ... 197

Bresciani v Amministrazione Italiana delle Finanze (Case 87/75) [1976] ECR 129, [1976] 2 CMLR 62 ... 328–9

Broeckmeulen v Huisarts Registratie Commissie (Case 246/80) [1981] ECR 2311 ... 200–1

Bronner (Oscar) GmbH & Co. KG v Mediaprint (Case C-7/97) [1998] ECR I-7791 ... 568–70

Brown (Case 197/86) [1988] ECR 3205 ... 489

Büchel & Co Fahrzeugteilefabrik GmbH v Council and Commission (Cases T-74 and T-75/97) Judgment 26 September 2000 ... 231

Buitoni v FORMA (Case 122/78) [1979] ECR 677 ... 73

Cadsky v ICE (Case 63/74) [1975] ECR 281, [1975] 2 CMLR ... 329

Calfa (Donatella) (Case C-348/96) [1999] ECR I-11 ... 442–3, 446, 448

Calpak SpA Ltd v Commission (Cases 789 & 790/79) [1980] ECR 1949 ... 221–2

Camoroto and Vignone (Cases C-52–53/99) [2001] ECR I-1395 ... 158

Campus Oil v Minister for Industry and Energy (Case 72/83) [1984] ECR 2727 ... 378–9

Carpenter (Mary) v Secretary of State for the Home Department (Case C-60/00) Judgment 11 July 2002 ... 475–8, 490

Casati (Case 203/80) [1981] ECR 2595 ... 448

CBEM v CLT and IPB (Case 311/84) [1985] ECR 3261 ... 569

Centre d'insemination de la Crespelle (Case C-323/93) [1994] ECR I-5077 ... 569

Centros Ltd v Erhervs- og Selskabysstyrelsen (Case C-212/97) [1999] ECR I-1459 ... 460–3

Centrosteel Srl v Adipol GmbH (Case C-456/98) [2000] ECR I-6007 ... 164–5

Chemial Farmaceutici v DAF (Case 140/79) [1981] ECR 1 ... 332–3

Chevalley v Commission (Case 15/70) [1970] ECR 975 ... 260

Chiquita Banana Co and Others v Council (Case C-276/93) [1993] ECR I-3345 ... 265

CIA Security International SA v Signalson SA and Securitel SPRL (Case C-94/94) [1996] ECR I-2201 ... 153–5, 156, 157, 158, 315

CILFIT (Case 283/81) [1982] ECR 3415, [1983] 1 CMLR 472 ... 204–6

Cinéthèque SA v Fédération Nationale des Cinémas Français (Cases 60 & 61/84) [1985] ECR 2605 ... 394, 399–400

Coditel v Ciné-Vog Films (Case 262/81) ... 514

Codorniu SA v Council (Case C-309/89) [1994] ECR I-1853 ... 263–4, 265, 267, 268, 272, 273

Colim v Biggs (Case C-33/97) [1999] ECR I-3175 ... 410

Comateb and Others (Cases C-192–218/95) [1997] ECR I-165 ... 136

Comet v Productschap (Case 45/76) [1976] ECR 2043 ... 132–3, 135, 172

Commission v Anic (Case C-49/92P) [1999] ECR I-4125 ... 509

Commission v Austria (Case C-424/99) [2001] ECR I-9285 ... 272

Commission v Austria (Case C-472/98) ... 106

Commission v Belgium (Case 1/86) [1987] ECR 2797 ... 112–13

Commission v Belgium (Case 52/84) [1986] ECR 89 ... 596

Commission v Belgium (Case 77/69) [1970] ECR 237 ... 112

Commission v Belgium (Case 132/82) [1983] ECR 1649, [1983] CMLR 600 ... 329

Commission v Belgium (Case 149/79) [1980] ECR 3881, [1981] 2 CMLR 413 ... 444

Commission v Belgium (Case 156/77) [1978] ECR 1881 ... 252

Commission v Belgium (Case 314/82) [1984] ECR 1543 ... 329, 330

Commission v Belgium (Case C-2/90) [1992] ECR I-4431 ... 49, 413, 414

Commission v Belgium (Case C-471/98) ... 106

Commission v Camar and Others (Case C-312/00P) Judgment 10 December 2002 ... 185, 243–4

Commission v Council (Case 22/70) [1971] ECR 263 ... 43–4, 104–5, 107, 217–18, 232

Commission v Council (Case 45/86) [1987] ECR 1493 ... 47, 70–1

Commission v Council (Case 170/96) [1998] ECR I-2763 ... 53–4, 215

Commission v Council (Case 1997/269) [2000] ECR I-2257 ... 635

Commission v Council (Case C-155/91) [1993] ECR I-939 ... 48–50, 51, 52, 53, 60

Commission v Council (Case C-300/89) [1991] ECR I-2867 ... 50, 51, 52, 53, 64

Commission v Denmark (Case 158/82) [1983] ECR 3573 ... 329, 335

Commission v Denmark (Case C-467/98) ... 106

Commission v Finland (Case C-469/98) Judgment of 5 November 2002 ... 106–7

Commission v France (Case 21/84) [1985] ECR 1356 ... 354

Commission v France (Case 42/82) [1983] ECR 1013 ... 373

Commission v France (Case 167/73) [1974] ECR 359 ... 102

Commission v France (Case 168/78) [1980] ECR 347, [1981] 2 CMLR 631 ... 333–4

Commission v France (Case 196/85) [1987] ECR 1597, [1988] 2 CMLR 851 ... 333

Commission v France (Case C-52/00) [2002] ECR I-3827 ... 649, 650

Commission v France (Case C-52/95) [1995] ECR I-4443 ... 356

Commission v France (Case C-62/89) [1990] ECR I-925 ... 643

Commission v France (Case C-154/89) [1991] ECR I-659 ... 454–5

Commission v France (Case C-265/95) [1997] ECR I-6959 ... 355–7, 373

Commission v France (Case C-381/93) [1994] ECR I-5145 ... 466

Commission v France (Foie Gras) (Case C-184/96) [1998] ECR I-6197 ... 421

Commission v Germany (Case 12/74) [1975] ECR 191 ... 351

Commission v Germany (Case 18/87) [1988] ECR 5427 ... 329–30

Commission v Germany (Case 178/84) ... 177, 181, 387–92, 409

Commission v Germany (Case 205/84) [1986] ECR 3755, [1987] 2 CMLR 69 ... 450–3, 454, 467

Commission v Germany (Case C-131/93) [1994] ECR I-3303 ... 373

Commission v Germany (Case C-217/88) [1990] ECR I-2879 ... 596

Commission v Germany (Case C-217/97) [1999] ECR I-5087 ... 164

Commission v Germany (Case C-325/00) Judgment 5 November 2002 ... 364

Commission v Germany (Case C-476/98) ... 106

Commission v Greece (Case 240/86) [1988] ECR 1835 ... 122

Commission v Greece (Case C-154/00) [2002] ECR I-3879 ... 649, 650

Commission v Greece (Case C-183/91) [1993] ECR I-3131 ... 252

Commission v Greece (Case C-214/98) [2000] ECR I-9601 ... 164

Commission v Ireland (Case 45/87) [1988] ECR 4929, [1989] 1 CMLR 225 ... 417–18

Commission v Ireland (Case 113/80) [1981] ECR 1625, [1982] 1 CMLR 706 ... 349–52, 371

Commission v Ireland (Case C-249/81) [1982] ECR 4005, [1983] 2 CMLR 104 ... 357–61, 364

Commission v Italy (Case 7/68) [1968] ECR 423 ... 326–7

Commission v Italy (Case 22/87) [1989] ECR 143 ... 168

Commission v Italy (Case 24/68) [1969] ECR 193, [1971] CMLR 611 ... 326, 327–8, 329

Commission v Italy (Case 39/72) [1973] ECR 101 ... 113, 605

Commission v Italy (Case 103/84) [1986] ECR 1759 ... 122

Commission v Italy (Case 159/78) [1979] ECR 3247, [1980] 3 CMLR 446 ... 349

Commission v Italy (Case 168/85) [1986] ECR
2945 ... 178

Commission v Italy (Case 184/85) [1987] ECR
2013 ... 335

Commission v Italy (Case 193/80) [1981] ECR
3019 ... 181, 388

Commission v Italy (Case 213/79) [1980] ECR 1
... 333

Commission v Italy (Case C-120/88) [1991] ECR
I-621 ... 178

Commission v Italy (Case C-128/89) [1990] ECR
I-3239 ... 373

Commission v Italy (Case C-180/89) [1991] ECR
I-709 ... 467

Commission v Italy (Cases 91–92/79) [1980] ECR
1099 ... 52

Commission v Netherlands (Case 89/76) [1977]
ECR 1355 ... 329–30

Commission v Netherlands (Case C-68/89)
[1991] ECR I-2637 ... 433

Commission v Netherlands (Case C-353/89)
[1991] ECR I-4069 ... 411

Commission v Spain (Case C-119.89) [1991] ECR
I-641 ... 178

Commission v Spain (Case C-232/99) Judgment
16 May 2002 ... 456

Commission v Sweden (Case C-468/98) ... 106

**Commission v UK (Case 40/82) [1982] ECR
2793, [1982] 3 CMLR 497 ... 371–3**

**Commission v UK (Case 60/86) [1988] ECR
3921 ... 633–4**

**Commission v UK (Case 128/78) [1979] ECR
419 ... 113–14**

**Commission v UK (Case 170/78) [1983] ECR
2263, [1983] 3 CMLR 512 ... 334–5, 388**

**Commission v UK (Case 207/83) [1985] ECR
1202, [1985] 2 CMLR 259 ... 352–3, 399**

**Commission v UK (Case C-246/89R) [1989]
ECR 3125 ... 117–19, 136**

**Commission v UK (Case C-300/95) [1997] ECR
I-2649 ... 642–4**

Commission v UK (Case C-382/92) [1994] ECR
I-2435 ... 644

Compagnie des Hauts Fourneaux de Chasse v
High Authority of the ECSC (Case 15/57) [1957
and 1958] ECR 211 ... 238

**Conegate v Customs and Excise
Commissioners (Case 121/85) [1986] ECR
1007, [1986] 1 CMLR 739 ... 369–70, 371**

Connolly v Commission (Case C-274/99) [2001]
ECR I-1611 ... 83, 590

Continental Can v Commission (Case 6/72)
[1973] ECR 215 559, 561

**Cooperatieve Stremsel- en Kleurselfabriek v
Commission (Case 61/80) [1981] ECR 851 ...
501, 510**

Cooperativa Cofrutta v Amministrazione delle

Finanze dello Stato (Case 193/85) [1987] ECR
2085 ... 335

**Costa v ENEL (Case 6/64) [1964] ECR 585 ...
99–100, 130–1, 168, 189, 190, 604**

**Courage Ltd v Bernard Creham (Case C-453/
99) [2001] ECR I-6297 ... 604–6**

**Cowan v Le Trésor Public (Case 186/87) [1986]
ECR 195 ... 447–8**

**Cristini v SNCF (Case 32/75) [1975] ECR 1085,
[1975] 1 CMLR 573 ... 435–6**

**Cura Anlagen GmbH v Auto Service Leasing
GmbH (Case C-451/99) [2002] ECR I-3193 ...
194–5**

Customs & Excise Commissioners v Schindler
and Schindler (Case C-275/92) [1994] ECR
I-1039 ... 457

Da Costa en Schaake (Cases 28–30/62) [1963]
ECR 31 ... 203, 205

Danner (Case C-136/00) Judgment 3 October
2002 ... 414

Deere v Commission (Case C-7/95) [1998] ECR
I-3111 ... 243

**Defrenne v SABENA (Case 43/75) [1976] ECR
455 ... 123, 125–8, 200, 261**

Delhaize (Cases 2–4/82) (1982) ECR 2973 ... 378

Deliège (Cases C-51/96 and C-191/97) [2000]
ECR I-2549 ... 466

**Delimitis (Stergios) v Henninger Brau (Case
C-234/89) [1991] ECR I-935, [1992] 5 CMLR
201 ... 514, 519–21, 522, 606**

Denkavit (Case 251/78) (1979) ECR 3369 ... 378

Denkavit v France (Case 132/78) [1979] ECR
1923 ... 329

**Denmark v Commission (Case C-3/00)
Judgment 20 March 2003 ... 631**

D'Hoop (Marie-Nathalie) v Office national de
l'emploi (Case C-224/98) Judgment 11 July
2002 ... 490

Didier Tabouillet (Case C-284/96) [1997] ECR
I-7471 ... 332

Diensten Groep v Beele (Case 6/81) [1982] ECR
707 ... 409

Dilexport (Case C-343/96) ... 135, 136

Dillenkofer and Others v Germany (Joined Cases
C-178 et al/94) [1996] ECR I-4845 ... 185, 242,
244

**DIP SpA v Comune di Bassano del Grappa,
(Case C-140/94) [1995] ECR I-3257 ... 530–1**

DLG (Case C-250/92) [1994] ECR I-5641 ... 514,
524

Donà (Case 13/76) [1976] ECR 1333 ... 526

**Dori (Paola Faccini) v Recreb Srl (Case C-91/
92) [1994] ECR I-3325 ... 148–9, 153, 156,
160, 163, 165, 170, 171, 488, 636, 644**

Dorsch Consult (Case C-54/96) [1997] ECR
I-4961 ... 202

Dow Benelux v Commission (Case 85/87) [1989] ECR 3137 ... 591, 592, 595

Dow Chemical Iberica and Others v Commission (Cases 97–99/87) [1989] ECR 3165 ... 593

Duphar and Others (Case 238/82) [1984] ECR 523 ... 465

Dzodzi v Belgian State (Cases C-297/88 and C-197/89) [1990] ECR I-3763 ... 95

Eco Swiss China Time Ltd v Benetton International NV (Case C-126/97) [1999] ECR I-3055 ... 495, 604

ECSC v Acciaierie e Ferriere Busseni (in liquidation) (Case 221/88) ... 151

EEC Seed Crushers' and Oil Processors' Federation (FEDOIL) v Commission (Case 191/82) [1983] ECR 2913 ... 229

El Corte Inglés v Cristina Blasquez Rivero (Case C-192/94) [1996] ECR I-1281 ... 149

Electroimpex v Council [1990] ECR I-3021 ... 230

Emmott v Minister for Social Welfare (Case C-208/90) [1991] 3 CMLR 894 ... 175

Enichem Base and Others v Comune di Cinsello Balsamo (Case 380/87) [1989] ECR 2491 ... 154

Enital v Commission and Council (Case C-304/86) [1990] ECR I-2929 ... 230

ENU v Commission (Case C-107/91) [1993] ECR I-599 ... 260

ERT (Case C-260/89) [1991] ECR I-2925 ... 83, 411, 477, 590

Établissements Consten SA and Grundig GMBH v Commission (Case 56 & 58/64) [1966] ECR 299, [1966] CMLR 418 ... 497–500, 510, 511, 512, 606

Eurotunnel SA and others v SeaFrance (Case C-408/95) [1997] ECR I-6315 ... 253

Evangelischer Krankenhausverein Wien (Case C-437/97) [2000] ECR I-1157 ... 128, 196

Extramet v Council (Case C-358/89) [1991] ECR I-2501 ... 230–1, 262–3, 265, 272, 273

Fantask (Case C-188/95) [1997] ECR I-6783 ... 171

Fedesa and Others (Case C-331/88) [1990] ECR I-4023 ... 595

Feldain (Case 433/85) [1987] ECR 3536 ... 332

Fietje (Case 27/80) [1980] ECR 3839 ... 409–10

Fink-Frucht GmbH v Hauptzollamt Munchen-Landsbergstrasse (Case 27/77) [1978] ECR 223 ... 334

Foglia v Novello (No. 1) (Case 104/79) [1980] ECR 745, [1981] 1 CMLR 45 ... 191–2, 193

Foglia v Novello (No. 2) (Case 244/80) [1981] ECR 3045, [1982] 1 CMLR 585 ... 192–3, 196

Foster v British Gas (Case C-188/89) [1990] ECR I-3313, [1991] 2 CMLR ... 150–1

Foto Frost v HZA Lubeck Ost (Case 314/85)

[1987] ECR 4199 ... 207–8, 209, 254, 255, 262, 268, 272, 693

France v Commission (Case C-41/93) [1994] ECR I-1829 ... 629–30

France v Commission (Case C-57/95) [1997] ECR I-1627 ... 218, 364

France v UK (Case 141/78) [1979] ECR 2923 ... 111

Francovich and Others v Italian State (Cases 6/90 and 9/90) [1991] ECR I-5357, [1993] 2 CMLR ... 121, 154, 167, 168–9, 170, 171, 172, 174, 175, 177, 178, 179, 180, 182, 188, 241, 243, 604, 647

Frans-Nederlandse Maatschappij voor Biologische Producten (Case 272/80) [1981] ECR 3277, [1982] 2 CMLR 497 ... 374, 375–6

Fratelli Costanzo v Comune di Milano (Case 103/88) [1989] ECR 1839 ... 149, 151–2, 164

Fromançais SA v FORMA (Case 66/82) [1983] ECR 395 ... 73

Gabalfrisa and Others (Cases C-110–147/98) [2000] ECR I-1577 ... 202

Gebhard (Reinhard) v Consiglio dell' Ordine degli Avvocati e Procuratori di Milano (Case C-55/94) [1995] ECR I-4165, [1996] 1 CMLR 603 ... 321, 322, 385, 450, 456, 462, 472

Geddo v Ente (Case 2/73) [1973] ECR 865, [1974] 1 CMLR ... 341, 342

Geffroy (Case C-366/98) [2000] ECR I-6579 ... 410

General Milk Products v Hauptzollamt Hamburg-Jonas (Case C-8/92) [1993] ECR I-779 ... 461

Geraets-Smits v Stichting Ziekenfonds VGZ, Peerbooms v Stichting CZ Groep Zorgverzekeringen (Case C-157/99) [2001] ECR I-5473 ... 464–9

Germany v Commission (Case 24/62) [1963] ECR 63 ... 69

Germany v Commission (Case C-280/93) [1993] ECR I-3667, [1994] ECR I-4973 ... 258, 259

Germany v Council (Case C-426/93) [1995] ECR I-3723 ... 75

Germany v Parliament and Council (Case 233/94) [1997] ECR I-2405 ... 62, 76, 595

Germany v Parliament and Council (Case C-223/94) [1997] ECR I-2304 ... 661

Germany v Parliament and Council (Case C-376/98) [2000] ECR I-8419 ... 60–5, 66, 67, 636–7, 639, 640, 645, 649, 661, 662

Gestetner Holdings v Council and Commission (Case C-156/87) [1990] ECR I-719 ... 230

Gibraltar v Council (Case C-298/89) [1993] ECR I-3605 ... 264

Gilli and Andres (Case 788/79) [1980] ECR 2071 ... 350

Goerres (Hermann Josef) (Case C-385/96) [1998] ECR I-4431 ... 410

González Sánchez (María Victoria) v Medicina Asturiana SA (Case C-183/00) Judgment 25 April 2002 ... 647–9, 650

Grant v South-West Trains Ltd (Case C-249/96) [1998] ECR I-621 ... 80, 93–5, 96

Grimaldi v Fonds des Malaises Professionelles (Case C-322/88) [1989] ECR 4407 ... 44

Grzelczyk (Rudy) v Centre public d'aide sociale d'Ottignies-Louvain-la-Neuve (Case C-184/99) [2001] ECR I-6193 ... 488–9

GT-Link v DSB (Case C-242/95) [1997] ECR I-4449 ... 568

Guérin Automobiles v Commission (Case C-282/95P) [1997] ECR I-1503 ... 605

Haim (Case 1997/424) [2000] ECR I-5123 ... 244

Hansen (H.) jun. & O. C. Balle GmbH v Hauptzollamt Flensburg (Case 148/77) [1978] ECR 1787 ... 334

Harz v Deutsche Tradax (Case 79/83) [1984] ECR 1921 ... 160

Hauer v Rheinland-Pfalz (Case 44/79) [1979] ECR 3727 ... 83–6

HNL and Others v Council and Commission (Cases 83/76, 94/76, 4/77, 40/77, 15/77) [1978] ECR 1209 ... 180, 184

Hoechst v Commission (Case 46/87) [1989] ECR 2859, [1991] 4 CMLR 410 ... 82, 83, 587–9, 590, 591, 592, 593, 596

Hoffman la Roche & Co. AG v Centrafarm Vertriebsgesellschaft Pharmazeutischer Erzeugnisse GmbH (Case 107/76) [1977] ECR 957 ... 191, 203

Hoffmann-La Roche v Commission (Case 85/76) [1979] ECR 461 ... 531, 561

Höfner v Macrotron (Case C-41/90) [1991] ECR I-1979 ... 529

Hönig (Hans) v Stadt Stockach (Case C-128/94) [1995] ECR I-3389 ... 634–5

Hugin Kassaregister AB v Commission (Case 22/78) [1979] ECR 1869, [1979] 3 CMLR 345 ... 559–60

Humblet v Belgium (Case 6/60) [1960] ECR 559 ... 169

Humblot v Directeur des Services Fiscaux (Case 112/84) [1985] ECR 1367, [1986] 2 CMLR 338 ... 331–2

Hünermund and Others (Case C-292/92) [1993] ECR I-6787 ... 402

Ianelli & Volpi v Meroni (Case 74/76) [1977] ECR 557 ... 181

ICC v Amministrazione delle Finanze (Case 66/80) [1981] ECR 1191, [1983] 2 CMLR 593 ... 199, 208, 260, 261

ICI v Commission (Dyestuffs) (Case 48/69) [1972] ECR 619, [1972] CMLR 557 ... 500, 505–8

Idéal Tourisme (Case C-36/99) [2000] ECR I-6049 ... 194, 196

IFG v Freistaat Bayern (Case 1/83) [1984] ECR 349 ... 330

Industrie des poudres sphériques v Council (Case C-458/98P) [2000] ECR I-8147 ... 231

Industrie Metallurgische SpA v High Authority of the ECSC (Case 15/57) [1957 and 1958] ECR 133 ... 238

Inter-Environment Wallonie ASBL v Région Wallone (Case C-129/96) [1997] ECR I-7411 ... 143

International Fruit Company v Commission (Cases 41–44/70) [1971] ECR 411 ... 43, 44, 219–20, 232, 233

International Fruit Company v Produktschap voor Groenten en Fruit (No. 2) (Cases 51–54/71) [1971] ECR 1107 ... 348–9

Internationale Handelsgesellschaft [1970] ECR 1125 ... 84

Ireks-Arkady v Council and Commission (Case 238/78) [1979] ECR 2955 ... 605

Irish Creamery Milk Suppliers v Government of Ireland (Case 36/80) [1981] ECR 735, [1981] 2 CMLR 455 ... 190–1, 207

Istituto Chemicoterapico Italiano SpA and Commercial Solvents Corporation v Commission (Cases 6 & 7/73) [1974] ECR 223, [1974] 1 CMLR 309 ... 565, 567, 569

Jägerskiöld (Case C-97/98) [1999] ECR I-7319 ... 476

Javico et al v Yves St Laurent Parfums (Case C-306/96) [1998] ECR I-1983 ... 522

Job Centre Coop. arl (Case C-55/96) [1997] ECR I-7119 ... 202

Job Centre Coop. arl (Case C-111/94) [1995] ECR I-3361 ... 202

Johnston v Chief Constable of the Royal Ulster Constabulary (Case 222/84) [1986] ECR 1651 ... 151, 269, 272, 587

Just (Case 68/79) [1980] ECR 501 ... 605

Jyri Lehtonen, Castors Canada Dry Namur-Braine ASBL v Fédération Royale Belge des Sociétés de Basket-ball ASBL (FRBSB) (Case C-176/96) [2000] ECR I-2681 ... 197

Käserei Champignon Hofmeister (Case C-210/00) [2002] ECR I-6453 ... 76

Keck and Mithouard (Cases C-267–268/91) [1993] ECR I-6097, [1995] 1 CMLR 101 ... 66, 344, 393, 397–8, 398, 399, 400, 401, 402, 403, 404, 405, 406, 407, 408, 418, 457, 458, 501, 659

Kefalas and Others v Greece (Case C-367/96) [1998] ECR I-2843 ... 461

Kelderman (Case 130/80) [1981] ECR 351 ...

Kempf v Staatssecretaris van Justitie (Case 139/85) [1986] ECR 1741, [1987] 1 CMLR 764 ... 430

Kirsammer-Hack v Sidal (Case C-189/91) [1993] ECR I-6185 ... 57

Klopp (Case 107/83) [1984] ECR 2971 ... 523

Knoors (Case 115/78) [1994] ECR I-4795 ... 461

Kohl v Ringelhan (Case 177/83) [1984] ECR 3651, [1985] 3 CMLR 340 ... 371

Kohll (Case C-158/96) [1998] ECR I-1931 ... 465, 466

Koninklijke Scholten-Honig NV v Council and Commission (Case 143/77) [1979] ECR 3583 ... 240

Konle (Klaus) v Austria (Case C-302/97) [1999] ECR I-3099 ... 185

Konsumentombudsmannen v De Agostini Forlag AB and TV-Shop i Sverige AB (Cases C-34–36/95) [1997] ECR I-3843 ... 404–5, 458

Konsumentombudsmannen v Gourmet International Products AB (Case C-405/98) [2001] ECR I-1795 ... 405–6

Kortas (Case C-319/97) [1999] ECR I-3143 ... 164, 630

Kramer (Case 3/76) [1976] ECR 1279 ... 105

Kraus v Land Baden-Württemberg (Case C-19/92) [1993] ECR I-1663 ... 462

Läärä (Markku Juhani), Cotswold Microsystems Ltd, Oy Transatlantic Systems (Case C 124/97) [1999] ECR I-6067 ... 457

Laboratoires Pharmaceutiques Bergaderm SA and Jean-Jacques Goupil v Commission (Case C-3523/98P) [2000] ECR I-5291 ... 241–3, 244, 270

Laguillaumie [2000] ECR I-4979 ... 196

Lair v Universität Hannover (Case 39/86) [1988] ECR 3161 ... 461

Land Nordrhein Westfalen v Ueeker, Jacquet (Cases C-64/96 and C-65/96) [1997] ECR I-3171 ... 488

Landesgrundverkehrsreferent der Tiroler Landesregierung v Beck, Bergdorf Wohnbau (Case C-355/97) [1999] ECR I-4977 ... 198

Lawrie-Blum v Land Baden-Württemberg (Case 66/85) [1986] ECR 2121, [1987] 3 CMLR 389 ... 430

Leclerc and Others v 'Au Blé Vert' and Others (Case 229/83) [1985] ECR 1 ... 461

Leclerc-Siplec (Case C-412/93) [1995] ECR I-179 ... 195

Lemmens (Johannes Martinus) (Case C-226/97) [1998] ECR I-3711 ... 155–6, 158

Levez (Case C-326/96) [1998] ECR I-7835 ... 133, 134

Levin v Staatssecretaris van Justitie (Case 53/81) [1982] ECR 1035, [1982] 2 CMLR 454 ... 428–30

LIDL Italia SrL v Comune di Chioggia (Case C-141/94) [1995] ECR I-3257 ... 530–1

Lingral SrL v Comune di Chioggia (Case C-142/94) [1995] ECR I-3257 ... 530–1

L'Oréal v De Nieuwe AMCK (Case 31/80) [1980] ECR 3775 ... 568

Luisi and Carbone v Ministero del Tesoro (Cases 286/82 and 26/83) [1984] ECR 377 ... 447

Lyckeskog (Kenny Roland) (Case C-99/00) Judgment 4 June 2002 ... 203–4, 206

Mac Quen and Others (Case C-108/96) [2001] ECR I-837 ... 524

Maizena (Case 137/85) [1987] ECR 4587 ... 75

Maizena v Council (Case 139/79) [1980] ECR 3393 ... 52

Marchandise (Case C-332/89) [1991] ECR I-1027 ... 396

Marks & Spencer plc v Commissioners of Customs & Excise (Case C-62/00) Judgment of 11 July 2002 ... 135–6, 164, 171

Marleasing SA v La Comercial Internacional de Alimentacion SA (Case C-106/89) [1990] ECR I-4135 ... 163, 164, 165, 169, 170, 346

Marshall v Southampton AHA (Case 152/84) [1986] ECR 723, [1986] 1 CMLR 688 ... 144–6, 147, 148, 149, 151, 152, 155, 159, 160, 162, 163, 164–5

Marshall v Southampton AHA (Marshall '2') (Case 271/91) [1993] ECR I-4367 ... [1993] 3 CMLR ... 147, 148

Martinez Sala (Marìa) v Freistaat Bayern (Case C-85/96) [1998] ECR I-2691 ... 431, 488, 489

Meilicke (Wienand) v ADV/ORGA FA Meyer AG (Case C-83/91) [1992] ECR I-4871 ... 195, 196

Merck v Hauptzollamt Hamburg-Jonas (Case 292/82) [1983] ECR 3781 ... 635

Messner (Case C-265/88) [1989] ECR 4209, [1991] 2 CMLR 545 ... 433

Metallgesellschaft (Case C-410/98) ... 135

Metro-SB-Grossmärkte GmbH & Co KG v Commission (Case 26/76) [1977] ECR 1875 ... 223–4, 228, 495

Metronome Musik (Case C-200/96) [1998] ECR I-1953 ... 595

Meyhui NV v Schott Zweisel Glaswerke AG (Case C-51/93) [1994] ECR I-3879 ... 410

Michailidis (Cases 441–442/98) [2000] ECR I-7145 ... 605

Michelin v Commission (Case 322/81) [1983] ECR 3461 ... 561, 569, 587

Ministère Public v Buet (Case 382/87) [1989] ECR 1235 ... 100–1, 409, 636

Ministère Public v Deserbais (Case 286/86) [1988] ECR 4907 ... 385–6

Ministère Public v Muller and Others (Case 304/84) [1986] ECR 1511 ... 390

Ministère public v Wesemael and Others (Cases 110–111/78) [1979] ECR 35 ... 451

MIRECO SaS v Amministrazione delle Finanze dello Stato (Case 811/79) [1980] ECR 2559 ... 138

Montecatini v Commission (Case C-235/92) [1999] ECR I-4539 ... 514

Morson v Netherlands (Cases 35–36/82) [1982] ECR 3723, [1983] 2 CMLR 720 ... 476

Motte (Case 247/84) [1985] ECR 3887 ... 389–90

Mulder et al v Council and Commission (Cases C-104/89 and C-37/90) [1992] ECR I-3061 ... 241, 270

Municipality of Almelo and others v Energiebedrijf IJsselmij NV (Case C-393/92) [1994] ECR I-1477 ... 521–2, 531

Municipality of Differdange v Commission (Case 222/83) [1984] ECR 2889 ... 224–5

Musique Diffusion Française v Commission (Cases 100–103/80) [1983] ECR 1825 ... 586

Nashua Corporation v Commission (Cases C-133 and C-150/87) [1990] ECR I-719 ... 230

National Farmers Union and Others (Case C-157/96) [1998] ECR I-2211 ... 76

National Panasonic v Commission (Case 136/79) [1090] ECR 2033 ... 586, 592, 593, 595, 596

Nederlandse Bakkerij v Edah (Cases 80 & 159/85) [1986] ECR 3359, [1988] 2 CMLR 113 ... 392

Nederlandse Ondernemingen (Case 51/76) [1977] 1 ECR 126 ... 142, 147

Neotype Techmashexport v Commission and Council (Case C-305/86) [1990] ECR I-2945 ... 230

Neste Markkinoiniti Oy (Case C-214/99) [2000] ECR I-11121 ... 522

Netherlands v Parliament and Council (Case C-377/98) [2001] ECR I-7079 ... 66

NFU v Secretariat general du gouvernement (Case C-241/01) Judgment 22 October 2002 ... 254

Nold v Commission (Case 4/73) [1974] ECR 491 ... 81–2, 84, 86, 587

Norbrook Laboratories (Case C-127/95) [1998] ECR I-1531 ... 244

Nordsee v Reederei Mond (Case 102/81) [1982] ECR 1095 ... 201–2

NTN Toyo Bearing Co. v Council (Case 113/77) [1979] ECR 1185, [1977] ECR 1721 ... 226–7, 230, 233–4

Nungesser v Commission (Case 258/78) [1982] ECR 2015, [1983] 1 CMLR 278 ... 510–11, 512, 514

Oberkreisdirektor v Moormann (Case 190/87) [1988] ECR 4689, [1990] 1 CMLR 656 ... 378, 379, 633

Océano Grupo Editorial v Salvat Editores (Cases C-240–244/98) [2000] ECR I-4941 ... 165

Oebel (Case 144/80) [1981] ECR 1993 ... 394

Officier van Justitie v Kolpinghuis Nijmegen (Case 80/86)[1987] ECR 3969 ... 162–3, 167

Officier van Justitie v Sandoz BV (Case 174/82) [1983] ECR 2445, [1984] 3 CMLR 43 ... 373–5, 376, 378, 389, 409

Oosthoek (Case 286/81) [1982] ECR 4575 ... 401

Openbaar Ministerie v Van Tiggele (Case 82/77) [1978] ECR 25, [1978] 2 CMLR 528 ... 365–6, 399

Orkem v Commission (Case 374/87) [1989] ECR 3283 ... 95, 595

Oude Lutikhuis and Others (Case C-399/93) ... 514

P v S and Cornwall County Council (Case C-13/94) [1996] ECR I-2143 ... 93, 94

Pall (Case C-238/89) [1990] ECR I-4827 ... 411

Palmisani (Case C-261/95) [1997] ECR I-4025 ... 605

Parfumerie Fabrik v Provide (Case C-150/88) [1989] ECR 3891, [1991] 1 CMLR 715 ... 194

Parfums Christian Dior SA and Parfums Christian Dior BV v Evora BV (Case C-337/95) [1997] ECR I-6013 ... 203, 206

Parliament v Council (Case 13/83) [1985] ECR 1513 ... 234–6

Parliament v Council (Case C- 42/97) [1999] ECR I-869 ... 50–1, 52, 53

Parliament v Council (Case C-22/96) [1998] ECR I-3231 ... 51

Parliament v Council (Case C-70/88) [1991] ECR I-4529 ... 50, 707

Parliament v Council (Case C-271/94) [1996] ECR I-1689 ... 51

Parliament v Council (Case C-295/90) [1992] ECR I-4193 ... 49, 449

Parti Écologiste 'Les Verts' v European Parliament (Case 294/83) [1986] ECR 1339 ... 208, 216, 262, 269, 272, 276

Peralta (Case C-379/92) [1994] ECR I-3453 ... 531

Philip Morris v Commission (Case 730/79) [1980] ECR 2671 ... 252

Piageme v BVBA Peeters (Case 369/89) [1991] ECR I-2971 ... 410

Plaumann v Commission (Case 25/62) [1963] ECR 95 ... 220–1, 222, 231, 264, 269, 274

Port (T.) GmbH v Bundesanstalt für Landwirtschaft und Ernährung (Case C-68/95) [1996] ECR I-6065, [1997] 1 CMLR 1 ... 259–60, 692

Portelange (Case 10/69) [1969] ECR 309 ... 604

Portugal v Council (Case C-149/96) [1999] ECR I-8395 ... 259

Prantl (Criminal proceedings against) (Case C-16/83) [1984] ECR 1299, [1985] 2 CMLR 238 ... 371

Preston and Others v Wolverhampton NHS Healthcare Trust and Others (Case C-78/98) [2000] ECR I-3201 ... 133–5

Pretore di Salò v X (Case 14/86) [1987] ECR 2545 ... 162

Preussen Elektra (Case C-379/98) [2001] ECR I-2099 ... 414

Primecrown Ltd v The Medicines Control Agency (Case C-201/94) ... 152, 153

Procurator Fiscal, Stranraer v Marshall (Case 370/88) [1990] ECR I-420 ... 214

Procureur de la République v Bouchoucha (Case C-61/89) [1990] ECR I-3560 ... 450, 461

Procureur du Roi v Dassonville (Case 8/74) [1974] ECR 837, [1974] 2 CMLR 436 ... 343, 344–5, 350, 386, 387, 395, 397, 398, 401, 402, 407, 414, 420

Procureur du Roi v Royer (Case 48/75) [1976] ECR 497 ... 446

Pronuptia de Paris GmbH v Pronuptia de Paris Irmgaard Schillgalis (Case 161/84) [1986] ECR 353, [1986] 1 CMLR 414 ... 512–13, 514

Pubblico Ministero v Ratti (Case 148/78) [1979] ECR 1629, [1980] 1 CMLR 96 ... 141–3, 147, 155, 378

Quietlynn Ltd v Southend on Sea BC (Case C-23/89) [1990] ECR I-3059 ... 397

R v Bouchereau (Case 30/77) [1977] ECR 1999, [1977] 2 CMLR 800 ... 440–1, 442–3

R v Henn and Darby (Case 34/79) [1979] ECR 3795, [1980] 1 CMLR 246 ... 367–9, 371, 372

R v H.M. Treasury, ex parte British Telecommunications (Case C-392/93) [1996] ECR I-1631 ... 184

R v IAT, ex parte Antonissen (Case C-292/89) [1991] ECR I-745, [1991] 2 CMLR 373 ... 430, 431

R v IAT and Singh, ex parte Secretary of State (Case C-370/90) [1992] ECR I-4265, [1992] 3 CMLR 358 ... 476

R v Intervention Board, ex parte Man (Sugar) Ltd (Case 181/84) [1985] ECR 2889 ... 72–4, 248

R v Ministry of Agriculture, Fisheries and Food, ex parte Hedley Lomas (Ireland) Ltd (Case C-5/94) [1996] ECR I-2553 ... 185, 242, 244

R v Pieck (Case 157/79) [1980] ECR 2171, [1980] 3 CMLR 220 ... 432

R v Secretary of State for Health, ex parte British American Tobacco (Investments) Ltd and Imperial Tobacco Ltd (Case C-491/01) Judgment 10 December 2002 ... 66–7, 75–8, 209, 216, 273–4, 637, 639, 661, 663

R v Secretary of State for Social Security, ex parte Sutton (Case C-66/95) [1997] ECR I-2163 ... 185

R v Secretary of State for Transport, ex parte Factortame (Case C-213/89) [1990] ECR I-2433, [1990] 3 WLR 852 ... 136, 137–40, 168, 173, 174, 260, 605

R v The Medicines Control Agency, ex parte Smith & Nephew Pharmaceuticals Ltd (Case C-201/94) ... 152, 153

Radio Téléfis Eireann and Independent Television Publications v Commission (Cases C-241/91P and C-242/91P) [1995] ECR I-801, [1995] 4 CMLR ... 566–7, 569

Ramrath (Case C-106/91) [1992] ECR I-3351 ... 467

Rau (Walter) v BALM (Cases 133–136/85) [1987] ECR 2289 ... 250–1, 252

Rau (Walter) v de Smedt (Case 261/81) [1982] ECR 3961 ... 190, 193, 388

Reiseburo Broede v Gerd Sanker (Case C-3/95) [1996] ECR I-6511 ... 457, 523, 524

Remia and Others v Commission (Case 42/84) [1985] ECR 2545 ... 523

REWE (Case 45/75) [1976] ECR 181 ... 334

REWE-Handelsgesellschaft Nord GmbH v Hauptzollamt Kiel (Case 158/80) [1981] ECR 1805 ... 70, 169

Rewe v Landwirtschaftkammer für das Saarland (Case 33/76) [1976] ECR 1989 ... 158, 169, 172

Rewe-Zentrale AG v Bundesmonopolverwaltung für Branntwein (Cassis de Dijon) (Case 120/78) [1979] ECR 649, [1979] 3 CMLR 494 ... 181, 321, 350, 381–3, 385, 386, 387, 388, 392, 393, 397, 399, 400, 403, 406, 408, 411, 414, 415–17, 418, 420, 421, 422, 450, 453, 456, 458, 471, 501, 615, 624

Rewe-Zentralfinanz Gmbh v Landwirtschaftskammer (Case 4/75) [1975] ECR 843, [1975] 1 CMLR 599 ... 376–8, 633

Reyners v Belgian State (Case 2/74) [1974] ECR 631, [1974] 2 CMLR ... 181, 447

Rheinmühlen-Düsseldorf v Einfuhr- und Vorratsstelle für Getreide und Futtermittel (No. 1) (Case 166/73) [1974] ECR 33 ... 188

Robards (Case 149/82) [1983] ECR 171 ... 195

Roders (F. G.) BV e.a. v Inspecteur der Invoerrechten en Accijnzen (Cases C-367/93–C-377/93) [1995] ECR I-2229 ... 336

Roquette Frères SA v Directeur général de la concurrence, de la consummation et de la répression des frauds (Case C-94/00) 22 October 2002 ... 83, 589–98

Roquette Frères v Council (Case 138/79) [1980] ECR 3333 ... 52, 707

Roux v Belgian State (Case C-363/89) [1991] ECR I-273 ... 446

Russo v AIMA (Case 60/75) [1976] ECR 45 ... 169

Saddik (Case C-458/93) [1995] ECR I-511 ... 197

Säger v Dennemeyer & Co Ltd (Case 76/90) [1991] ECR I-4221 ... 456

Sagulo, Brenca and Bakhouche (Case 8/77) [1977] ECR 1495 ... 432

St Nikolaus v Hauptzollamt Krefeld (Case 337/82) [1984] ECR 1051 ... 635

Saltzmann (Doris) (Case C-178/99) [2001] ECR I-4421 ... 202

SAM Schiffahrt (Cases C-248–249/95) [1997] ECR I-4475 ... 86

San Michele and Others v Commission (Cases 5–11 and 13–15/62) [1962] ECR 449 ... 588

Sanz de Lera (Cases C-163/94, C-165/94 and C-250/94) [1995] ECR I-4821 ... 468

Sapod Audic v Eco-Emballages SA (Case C-159/00) Judgment 6 June 2002 ... 158

Schindler (Case C-275/92) [1994] ECR I-1039 ... 411

Schloh v Auto Controle Technique (Case 50/85) [1986] ECR 1855 ... 346–8

Schmid (Walter) Judgment 30 May 2002 ... 202

Schottle v Finanzamt Freudenstadt (Case 20/76) [1977] ECR 247, [1977] 2 CMLR ... 330–1

Schwarze v Einfuhr- und Vorratstelle Getreide (Case 16/65) [1965] ECR 877 ... 70

Segers (Case 79/85) [1986] ECR 2375 ... 461

Sheptonhurst v Newham BC (Case C-350/89) [1991] ECR I-2387 ... 397

Shingara and Radiom (Cases C-65 and C-111/95) [1997] ECR I-3343 ... 442

Simmenthal SpA v Commission (Case 92/78) [1979] ECR 777 ... 253

Sociaal Fonds voor de Diamantarbeiders v Brachfeld (Cases 2 & 3/69) [1969] ECR 211, [1969] CMLR 335 ... 328

Società 'Eridania' Zuccherifici Nazionali v Commission (Cases 10 & 18/68) [1969] ECR 459 ... 236

Société de Produits de Maïs v Administration des Douanes (Case 112/83) [1985] ECR 719 ... 200, 261, 262

Société d'Importation Edouard Leclerc-Siplec v TF1 Publicité SA and M6 Publicité SA (Case C-412/93) [1995] ECR I-179 ... 401–3, 404

Société Technique Minière v Maschinenbau Ulm (Case 56/65) [1966] ECR 235, [1966] CMLR 357 ... 510

Society for the Protection of Unborn Children Ireland Ltd (SPUC) v Grogan (Case C-159/90) [1991] ECR I-4685, [1991] 3 CMLR 849 ... 83, 470–1, 590

Sodermare and Others (Case C-70/95) [1997] ECR I-3395 ... 465

Spain v Council (Case C-350/92) [1995] ECR I-1985 ... 62, 66

Star Fruit Co v Commission (Case 247/87) [1989] ECR 291 ... 114, 121

Stauder v Ulm (Case 29/69) [1969] ECR 419, [1970] CMLR 112 ... 81, 188

Stichting Collectieve Antennevoorziening Gouda v Commissariaat voor de Media (Case C-288/89) [1991] ECR I-4007 ... 456, 459

Stichting Greenpeace Council (Greenpeace International) and others v Commission

(Case C-321/95 P) [1998] ECR I-1651 ... 266–7, 268, 271

Stockholm Lindopark (Case C-150/99) [2001] ECR I-493 ... 185

Stoke-on-Trent and Norwich City Councils v B & Q (Case C-169/91), [1992] ECR I-6457, [1993] CMLR 426 ... 396, 659

Tankstation 't Heukste vof and J. B. E. Boermans (Cases C-401 and C-402/92) [1994] ECR I-2199 ... 398, 400

Tasca (Criminal proceedings against) (Case 65/75) [1976] ECR 291, [1977] 2 CMLR 183 ... 365, 399, 527

Tedeschi v Denkavit (Case 5/77) (1977) ECR 155 ... 378

Telemarsicabruzzo v Circostel (Cases C-320–322/90) [1993] ECR I-393 ... 196, 197

Tetra Pak v Commission (Case C-333/94 P) [1996] ECR I-5951 ... 566

Thieffry v Conseil de l'Ordre des Avocats à la Cour de Paris (Case 71/76) [1977] ECR 765, [1977] 2 CMLR 373 ... 446–7, 449, 450, 455

Timex v Council and Commission (Case 264/82) [1985] ECR 849 ... 228–30, 232

Torfaen BC v B & Q plc (Case 145/88) [1989] ECR 765 ... 393–5, 397, 399, 659

Transocean Marine Paint v Commission (Case 17/74) [1974] ECR 1063, [1974] 2 CMLR 459 ... 88–92, 586

TV10 v Commissariaat voor de Media (Case C-23/93) [1994] ECR I-4795 ... 461

TWD Textilwerke Deggendorf GmbH v Germany (Case C-188/92) [1994] ECR I-833 ... 251–3, 268

Überseering BV v Nordic Construction Co Baumanagement GmbH (Case C-208/00) Judgment 5 November 2002 ... 463–4

UDS v Conforama (Case C-312/89) [1991] ECR I-997 396

UK v Council (Case C-84/94) [1996] ECR 1–5755 ... 54–8, 60, 75, 76, 661, 666

Unectef v Heylens (Case 222/86) [1987] ECR 4097 ... 456

UNICME v Council [1978] ECR 845 ... 265

Unilever Italia SpA v Central Food SpA (Case C-443/98) Judgment 26 September 2000 ... 156–8

Unión de Pequeños Agricultores v Council (Case C-50/00 P) Judgment 25 July 2002 ... 269, 271–2, 273

Union Deutsche Lebensmittelwerke v Commission (Case 97/85) [1987] ECR 2265 ... 222–3, 251

Union Laitière Normande (Case 244/78) [1979] ECR 2663 ... 191

United Brands v Commission (Case 27/76)

[1978] ECR 207, [1978] 1 CMLR 429 ... 544–9, 550, 560, 562–4

Universität Hamburg v HZA Hamburg-Kehrwieder (Case 216/82) [1983] ECR 2771 ... 248–9, 252, 262

URBSFA v Bosman (Case C-415/93) [1995] ECR I-4921, [1996] All ER (EC) 97 ... 449

Valsabbia v Commission (Case 154/78) [1980] ECR 907 ... 74–5

Van Binsbergen v Bedrijfsvereniging Metaalnijverheid (Case 33/74) [1974] ECR 1299 ... 461

Van der Kooy v Commission (Cases 67, 68 and 70/85) [1988] ECR 219 ... 272

Van Duyn v Home Office (Case 41/74) [1974] ECR 1337 ... 123–5, 127, 141, 143–4, 147, 439–40, 442

Van Gend en Loos v Nederlandse Administratie der Belastingen (Case 26/62) [1963] ECR 1 ... 109–10, 123, 141, 147, 159, 168, 189, 190, 604, 712

van Schaik (Criminal proceedings against) (Case C-55/93) [1994] ECR I-4837 ... 348

Vaneetveld v SA Le Foyer (Case C-316/93) [1994] ECR I-763 ... 148, 170

Variola v Amministrazione delle Finanze (Case 34/73) [1973] ECR 981 ... 103

Verband Deutscher Daihatsu Händler eV v Daihatsu Deutschland GmbH (Case C-97/96) [1997] ECR I-6843 ... 149

Vereeniging van Cementhandelaren v Commission (Case 28/72) [1972] ECR 977 ... 523

Verein gegen Unwesen in Handel und Gewerbe Köln v Mars GmbH (Case C-470/93) [1995] ECR I-1923 ... 407–8, 411

Vereinigte Familiapress Zeitungsverlags- und vertriebs GmbH v Heinrich Bauer Verlag (Case C-368/95) [1997] ECR I-3689 ... 411–12, 477

Vereniging van Vlaamse Reisbureaus v Sociaale Dienst van de plaatselijke en gewestelijke Overheidsdiensten (Case 311/85) [1987] ECR 3801 ... 528

Veronica Omroep Organisatie v Commissariaat voor de Media (Case C-148/91) [1993] ECR I-487 ... 411, 461

Victoria Films A/S (Case C-134/97) [1998] ECR I 7023 ... 202

Vlassopoulou v Ministerium für Justiz, Bundes- und Europaangelegenheiten Baden-Wurttemberg (Case 340/89) [1991] ECR I-2357 ... 455–6, 472

Volk v Verwaecke (Case 5/69) [1969] ECR 295 ... 515

Von Colson and Kamann v Land Nordrhein-Westfalen (Case 14/83) [1984] ECR 1891, [1986] 2 CMLR 430 ... 145, 160–2, 163, 346

Wagner Miret v Fondo de Garantia Salarial (Case C-334/92) [1993] ECR I-6911 ... 163, 164, 165

Walrave v Association Union Cycliste Internationale (Case 36/74) [1974] ECR 1405 ... 446, 526

Webb (Case 279/80) [1981] ECR 3305 ... 235, 450, 451

Wiener (Case C-338/95) [1997] ECR I-6495 ... 198

Wijsenbeek (Florius Ariel) (Case C-378/97) [1999] ECR I-6207 ... 433, 478

Windsurfing v Commission (Case 193/83) [1986] ECR 611 ... 519

Wouters, J. W. Savelbergh, Price Waterhouse Belastingadviseurs BV v Algemene Raad van de Nederlandse Orde van Advocaten (Case C-309/99) [2002] ECR I-1577 ... 522–5, 526

Zuckerfabrik Süderdithmarschen and Zuckerfabrik Soest(Cases C-143/88 and C-92/89) [1991] 1 ECR 415 ... 174, 175, 179, 255–6, 257, 258, 259, 262, 595

Opinions

Opinion 1/91 [1991] ECR I-6079 ... 96, 276

Opinion 2/91 [1993] ECR I-1061 ... 55, 106

Opinion 2/92 [1995] ECR I-521 ... 106

Opinion 1/94 [1994] ECR I-5267 ... 105, 106, 107

Opinion 2/94 on Accession to the ECHR [1996] ECR I-1759 ... 80, 95

Court of First Instance

ACAV v Council (Case T-138/98) [2000] ECR II-341 ... 266

Area Cova and Others v Council and Commission (Case T-196/99) [2001] ECR II-3597 ... 270

Atlanta AG and others v Council and Commission (Case T-521/93) [1996] ECR II-1707 ... 259

BPB Industries and British Gypsum Ltd v Commission (Case T-65/89) [1993] ECR II-389 ... 566

Cassa Nazionale di Previdenza ed Assistenza a favore degli Avvocati e Procuratori v Council (Case T-116/94) [1995] ECR II-1 ... 265

Deere (John) v Commission (Case T-35/92) [1994] ECR II-957 ... 509

Dieckmann & Hansen v Commission (Case T-155/99) [2001] ECR II-3143 ... 270

European Night Services v Commission (Case T-374/94) [1998] ECR II-3141 ... 514

Exporteurs in Levende Varkens and Others v Commission (Cases T-481 and 484/93) [1995] ECR II-2941 ... 265

Greenpeace and Others v Commission (Case T-585/93) [1995] ECR II-2205 ... 266

Industrie des poudres sphériques v Council (Case T-2/95) [1998] ECR II-3939 ... 231

Industrie des poudres sphériques v Council (Case T-5/97) [1998] ECR II-3755 ... 231

Jégo-Quéré et Cie SA v Commission (Case T-177/01) Judgment 3 May 2002 ... 269–71, 273

Laboratoires Pharmaceutiques Bergaderm SA and Jean-Jacques Goupil v Commission (Case T-199/96) [1998] ECR II-2805 ... 241

Matra Hachette v Commission (Case T-17/93) [1994] ECR II-595 ... 514

Métropole télévision (M6), Suez-Lyonnais des eaux, France Télécom v Télévision française 1 SA (Case T-112/99) [2001] ECR II-2159 ... 514–15, 522

Montedipe v Commission (Case T-14/89) [1992] ECR II-1155 ... 514

Radio Téléfis Eireann and Independent Television Publications v Commission (Case T-69/89) [1991] ECR II-485 ... 567

Sarrio v Commission (Case T-334/94) [1999] ECR II-1439 ... 509

Terres Rouges v Commission (Case T-47/95) [1997] ECR II-481 ... 264–6, 268

Tiercé Ladbroke v Commission (Case T-504/93) [1997] ECR II-923 ... 568

Tréfilunion v Commission (Case T-148/89) [1995] ECR II-1063 ... 514

TWD Textilwerke Deggendorf GmbH v Commission (Cases T-244/93 and T-486/93) [1995] ECR II-2265 ... 253

Unión de Pequeños Agricultores v Council (Case T-173/98) [1999] ECR II-3357 ... 271

VGB and Others v Commission (Case T-77/94) [1997] ECR II-759 ... 514

European Domestic Cases by Country
French Courts
Minister of the Interior v Cohn Bendit [1980] 1 CMLR 543 ... 147–8, 149, 214

German Courts
Bananas 2 BvL 1/97 ... 690–2, 693
Brunner v European Union Treaty 2 BvR 2134/92, 2 BvR 2159/92 ... 686–9

VAT Directives [1982] 1 CMLR 527 ... 148

Wunsche Handelsgesellschaft [1987] 3 CMLR 225 86–7

Luxembourg Courts
Colot v Mininstre du Trésor (Aff. No 6136) ... 89

Lorse v Ministre des Transport (Aff. No 5811) ... 89

Roth v Ministres de l'Intérieur, de la Santé Publics et les Travaux Publics (Aff. No 5968) ... 89

UK Courts
Arsenal FC v Reed [2002] EWHC 2695 ... 214

Bulmer v Bollinger SA [1974] 3 WLR 202 ... 207

Cooper v Wandsworth Board of Works (1863) 14 CBNS 180 ... 88

Customs & Excise Commissioners v Samex [1983] 1 All ER 1042 ... 207

Duke v GEC Reliance [1988] 2 WLR 359 ... 160

Factortame v Secretary of State for Transport (No 1) [1989] 3 CMLR 1, [1990] 2 AC 85, [1989] 2 All ER 692 ... 137

Malloch v Aberdeen Corporation 1971 SLT 245, [1971] 1 WLR 1578 ... 88

Meat and Livestock Commission v Manchester Wholesale Meat and Poultry Market Ltd [1997] 2 CMLR 361 ... 361

Procurator Fiscal, Stranraer v Marshall [1988] 1 CMLR 657 ... 214

R v Henn and Darby [1978] 1 WLR 1031, [1981] AC 850, [1980] 2 WLR 1031 ... 213

R v Secretary of State, ex parte Bomore [1986] 1 CMLR 228 ... 346

Ridge v Baldwin [1964] AC 40 ... 88

European Commission on Human Rights
B v UK (16106/90) ... 94

Boultif v Switzerland No 54273/00 ECHR 2001-IX ... 477

C and LM v UK (14753/89) ... 94

Camenzind v Switzerland Judgment 16 December 1997, 1997-VIII ... 592

Colas Est and Others v France Judgment 16 April 2002 ... 83, 590, 592

Cossey judgment, 27 September 1990 Series A No 184 ... 94

De Cubber v Belgium Judgment 26 October 1984, Series A No 86 ... 603

Eggs v Switzerland ... 602

Engel and Others v Netherlands Judgment 8 June 1976, Series A No 22 ... 602

Funke v France Judgment 25 February 1992, Series A No 256-A ... 592

Informationsverein Lentia and Others v Austria Series A No 276 ... 412

Kerkhoven and Hinke v Netherlands (15666/89) ... 94

Oztürk v Germany Judgment 21 February 1984, Series A No 73 ... 602

Rees judgment, 17 October 1986 Series A No 106 ... 94

S v UK (11716/85) ... 94

Société Stenuit v France, judgment of 27 February 1992, Series A no. 232-A ... 601–3

Sunday Times v UK Judgment 26 April 1979, Series A No 30 ... 603

X and Y v UK (9369/81) 94

United States Courts

Continental TV v Sylvania 433 US 36 (1977) ... 500

Eastman Kodak Co. v Image Technical Services, Inc. 112 S. Ct. 2072 (1992) ... 561

Commission Decisions

Aerospatiale Alenia/De Havilland [1991] OJ L334/42, [1992] 4 CMLR M2 ... 561

Decision 73/323 Prym-Werke (1973) OJ L296/ 24, [1973] CMLR D250 ... 532–3

Decision 78/258 ... 237

Decision 78/921 WANO Schwarzpulver (1978) OJ L322/26, [1979] 1 CMLR ... 533

Decision 2000/12 1998 Football World Cup [2000] OJ L5/55 ... 559

Decision 2001/571 [2001] OJ L202/46 ... 631–3

Decision 2003/2 Vitamins ... 504

Decision of 21 December 1972 ... 81

TABLE OF LEGISLATION

(Bold face indicates extract material)

European Treaties and Conventions

**Charter of Fundamental Rights of the
European Union** ... 23, 24, 25, 29, 80, 87,
270, 281, 475, 682
art.1–art.2 ... 16
art.3–art.12 ... 17
art.13–art.21 ... 18
art.22 ... 19, 410
art.23–art.31 ... 19
art.32 ... 19–20
art.33–art.36 ... 20
art.37 ... 20, 414
art.38–art.40 ... 20
art.41–art.44 ... 21
art.45 ... 21, **484**
art.46 ... 21
art.47 ... 21, 269, 270
art.48 ... 21–2
art.49–art.50 ... 22
art.51 ... 22
art.51(2) ... 23
art.52–art.54 ... 22
Preamble ... 16

EC Treaty 1957 (Treaty of Rome) ... 7, 11, 34,
36, 37, 40, 80, 96, 99, 129, 130, 141, 177, 277
art.2 ... **290**, 294, 355, 360, 378, 422, 428, 525,
613, 629
art.2(1) ... 95
art.3 ... **293**, 294, 355, 360, 428, 495, 613, 629
art.3(1)(c) ... 62
art.3(1)(g) (former art.3(g)) ... 495, 525, 531,
604
art.3(1)(j) ... 525
art.3(e) ... 105
art.3(f) ... 232, 563
art.4 ... 317
art.5 (former art 3b) ... 62, 659, 660, 662, 663
art.5(1) ... 45, **46**, 53, **59**, 65, 67, **617**, 654, 661,
662, 664
art.5(2) ... **654**, 661, 662, 663, 664
art.5(3) ... 71, **72**, 654, 662
art.6 ... 53
art.10 (former art.5) ... 105, 107, 130, 132, 138,
145, 152, 161, 162, 163, 164, 167, 168, 170,
171, 179, 202, 243, 258, 357, 446, 527, 528,
529, 530, 531, 598
art.10(2) (former art.5(2)) ... 100
art.11 ... 674, 679
art.11(2) ... 674
art.11a ... 674
art.12 (former art.6, earlier art.7) ... 100, 117,
357, 365, 447, 448, 489, 490
art.13 (former art.6a) ... 46, 95, 96
art.13 (repealed) ... 346, 347
art.14 (former art.7a) ... 59, 60, 62, **299**, 316,
325, 336, 349, 355, 366, 371, 373, 379, 423,
478, 479, 630

EC Treaty 1957 (Treaty of Rome) – *continued*
art.15 (repealed) ... 100
art.16 (repealed) ... 132, 326–7, 328, 329
art.17 ... 427, 483
art.17(4) (former art.8(4)) ... 100
art.17(7) (former art.8(7)) ... 234
art.18 (former art.8a) ... 427, 479, **483**, 489
art.18(1) (former art.8a(1)) ... 489
art.19 (former art.8b) ... 427, **484**
art.19(1)–(2) (former art.8b (1)–(2)) ... 686
art.20–art.22 ... 427, 484
art.23 (former art.9) ... 103, **325**, 326, 327,
328, 329
art.25 (former art.12) ... 109, 110, 123, 189,
325, 326, 327, 328, 329, 330, 335, 496, 603,
613
art.26 (former art.13) ... 95, 325, 327, 328, 329
art.28 (former art.30) ... 49, 122, 158, 177,
178, 181, 190, 321, 322, **341**, 343, 344, 345,
346, 347, 348, 349, 350, 352, 353, 354, 355,
357, 358, 360, 361, 362, 363, 364, 365, 366,
367, 369, 371, 373, 374, 376, 377, 381, 382,
383, 385, 386, 387, 389, 391, 392, 393, 394,
395, 396, 397, 398, 399, 400, 401, 402, 403,
404, 405, 406, 407, 409, 410, 412, 413, 414,
415, 417, 418, 419, 421, 427, 450, 457, 458,
496, 501, 510, 526, 527, 531, 603, 613, 615,
616, 633, 640, 659
art.29 ... 341, 414, 457, 633, 640
art.30 (former art.36) ... 327, 330, 341, 346,
347, 348, 349, 350, 359, **366**, 367, 368, 369,
370, 371, 373, 374, 375, 376–7, 378, 379,
390, 393, 394, 404, 409, 413, 414, 419, 420,
457, 585, 615, 632, 633, 640
art.31 (former art.37) ... 381, 382
art.33 (former art.39) ... 86, 232
art.34(3) (former art.40(3)) ... 118, 240
art.36 (former art.42) ... 232
art.37 (former art.43) ... 377, 634–5
art.39 (former art.48) ... 102, 123, 124, 321,
365, **427**, 428, 431, 432, 439, 440, 441, 446,
476, 496, 613, 615
art.39(1) (former art.48(1)) ... 124, 444
art.39(2) (former art.48(2)) ... 102, 124, 444
art.39(3) (former art.48(3)) ... 429, 437, 439,
440, 443, 444, 615
art.39(4) ... 437, 444
art.42 ... 321
art.43 (former art.52) ... 117, 118, 178, 181,
182, **445**, 446, 447, 455, 456, 460, 462, 463,
526, 531
art.43(2) ... 450
art.44(3)(g) (former art.54(3)(g)) ... 461
art.45 ... 446
art.46 (former art.56) ... 147, 148, 441, 442,
446, 460, 462, 467
art.47 (former art.57) ... 447
art.47(2) (former art.57(2)) ... 60–5, 636, 637

EC Treaty 1957 (Treaty of Rome) – *continued*
art.48 (former art.58) ... 118, 460, 462
art.49 (former art.59) ... 195, 234, 235, 321,
  405, 406, 409, 427, 442, **445**, 447, 450, 451,
  453, 454, 456, 457, 458, 459, 465, 466, 468,
  469, 470, 478, 526, 531, 616, 633
art.50 (former art.60) ... 234, 235, 442, 450,
  451, 454, 465, 466, 469, 470
art.50(3) ... 450
art.51 (former art.61) ... 235, 442, 470
art.51(1) (former art.61(1)) ... 235
art.52–art.54 ... 442, 470
art.55 (former art.66) ... 60–5, 442, 446, 470,
  636, 637
art.61 ... 11, 443, **479**
art.62 ... 11, 443, **479–80**
art.63 ... 11, 443, **480**
art.64 ... 11, 443, **480–1**
art.65–art.66 ... 11, 443, **481**
art.67 ... 11, 443, **481**
art.67(2) ... 482
art.68 ... 11, 198, 443, **482**
art.68(2) ... 482
art.69 ... 11, 443, **482**
art.70 (former art.74) ... 105
art.71 (former art.75) ... 44, 105
art.71(1) (former art.75(1)) ... 105
art.71(1)(a)–(b) (former art.75(1)(a)–(b)) ... 235
art.73 (repealed) ... 100
art.81 (former art.85) ... 223, 232, 365, 414,
  495, **496–7**, 498, 501, 502, 503, 505, 509,
  510, 512, 514, 515, 516, 518, 519, 521, 522,
  525, 528, 530, 531, 534, 543, 550, 551, 565,
  571, 604, 605, 606, 609
art.81(1) (former art. 85(1)) ... 90, 223, 497,
  498, 499, 500, 501, 503, 510, 511, 512, 513,
  514, 515, 518, 520, 521, 522, 523, 524, 525,
  526, 527, 528, 529, 551, 571, 589, 603, 605,
  606
art.81(1)(b) (former art. 85(1)(b)) ... 523
art.81(2) (former art.85(2)) ... 495, 525, 571,
  603, 604
art.81(3) (former art.85(3)) ... 90, 223, 496,
  513, 514, 515, 521, 533, 535, 541, 571, 585,
  603, 604
art.81(3)(b) (former art.85(3)(b)) ... 551
art.82 (former art.86) ... 223, 232, 365, 496,
  497, 498, 509, 528, 530, **543**, 545, 546, 550,
  551, 559, 562, 563, 564, 565, 567, 568, 569,
  571, 603, 604, 605, 609
art.83 (former art.87) ... 571
art.86 (former art.90) ... 529, 531
art.86(1)–(2) (former art.90(1)–(2)) ... 528, 529
art.86(3) (former art.90(3)) ... 528
art.87 (former art.92) ... 251, 339, 358, 359,
  362
art.88 (former art.93) ... 251, 358, 359, 362
art.88(2) (former art. 93(2)) ... 100, 252, 253
art.88(3) (former art. 93(3)) ... 100, 359
art.89 (former art.94) ... 251, 362
art.90 (former art.95) ... 112, 191, 321, 322,
  325, 326, 330, 331, 332, 333, 334, 335, 349,
  603, 613, 616
art.90(1)–(2) ... 334

EC Treaty 1957 (Treaty of Rome) – *continued*
art.91 (former art.96) ... 232
art.93 (former art.99) ... 46, 336
art.94 (former art.100) ... 54, 57, 295, 336, 377,
  378, 419, 619, 620, 629, 630, 634, 636, 637,
  638, 639, 640, 648
art.95 (former art.100a) ... 48, 52, 53, 57, **59**,
  60–5, 66, 67, 68, 132, 295, 379, **616–17**, 618,
  622, 628, 629, 630, 632, 634, 636, 637, 639,
  645, 648, 649, 651, 663
art.95(1) (former art.100a(1)) ... 630, 632
art.95(3) ... 67, 76, 618, 622
art.95(4) (former art.100a(4)) ... **629**, 630,
  631, 632, 633, 637, 648
art.95(5) ... **629**
art.95(6) ... 632
art.96–art.97 (former art.101–art.102) ... 132
art.100b (repealed) ... 379
art.133 (former art.113) ... 47, 66, 104, 637
art.134 (former art.114) ... 104
art.136 ... 54, 58
art.137 (former art.118) ... 54, 58, 525
art.138 (former art.118a) ... 54, 55, 56, 57, 58
art.139 (former art.118b) ... 54, 58, 525
art.140 ... 54, 58
art.141 (former art 119) ... 54, 58, 94, 95, 123,
  125–8, 133, 134, 422
art.142–art.145 ... 54, 58
art.148 ... 423
art.151 (former art.128) ... 51, 410
art.151(1) ... 410
art.151(4) ... 410
art.152(1) (former art.129(1)) ... 53, 61, 62
art.152(4) (former art.129(4)) ... 61
art.153 ... 628, 629, 634, 638, 639, 648, 651
art.153(2) ... 53
art.153(3)(a)–(b) ... 628, 648
art.153(5) ... 628
art.157 (former art.130) ... 51
art.174 (former art.130r) ... 49, 52
art.174(2) (former art.130r(2)) ... 413, 414
art.174(4) (former art.130r(4)) ... **654**
art.175 (former art.130s) ... 48, 49, 50, 53, 628
art.175(2) ... 46, 53
art.176 ... 53, 628, 629, 634
art.191 (former art.138a) ... 687
art.220 (former art.164) ... 62, 89, 92, 93, 126,
  178
art.225 ... 213
art.225(1) ... 212
art.225(3) ... 198
art.226 (former art.169) ... 109, 110, **111**, 112,
  114–21, 122, 123, 128, 189, 202, 349, 352,
  357, 450, 641, 643
art.227 (former art.170) ... 109, 110, **111**, 121,
  202
art.228 (former art.171) ... 120, 143, 202, 699
art.228(2) ... 121
art.230 (former art.173) ... 43, 46, 47, 49, 50,
  92, 200, 208, 215, 216, **217**, 218, 219, 220,
  221, 223, 224, 225, 227, 229, 230, 232, 234,
  236, 237, 238, 248, 249, 250, 251, 252, 253,
  254, 255, 257, 260, 261, 262, 263, 264, 266,
  267, 268, 271, 272, 273, 592, 708

EC Treaty 1957 (Treaty of Rome) – *continued*
art.230(4) ... 219, 220, 222, 224, 226, 237, 262, 266, 268, 269, 271, 273
art.231 (former art.174) ... **217**, 261
art.232 (former art.175) ... 114, 215, **234**, 235, 236, 260
art.233 (former art.176) ... 236, 261
art.234 (former art.177) ... 72, 101, 102, 103, 109, 110, 121, 122, 124, 125, 131, 138, 172, 173, 176, **187**, 188–213, 216, 248, 249, 251, 253, 254, 255, 260, 261, 262, 267, 268, 269, 270, 272, 273, 331, 369, 381, 385, 396, 410, 464, 589, 594, 643, 645, 659, 690
art.235 (former art.178) ... 95, 215, **239**, 243, 268, 269, 270, 273
art.240 212
art.241 (former art.184) ... 215, 216, **237**, 238, 249, 252, 253, 262, 268, 272, 273
art.242 (former art.185) ... 174, **233**, 255
art.243 (former art.186) ... 116, 117, 174, **233**, 257
art.249 (former art.189) ... **42**, 43, 44, 46, 100, 103, 104, 113, 124, 131, 141, 142, 145, 146, 147, 149, 152, 161, 162, 163, 164, 167, 169, 170, 178, 211, 218, 220, 222, 227, 339, 644, 653, 659, 676, 677
art.251 (former art.189b) ... 46, 53, 61, 93, 618
art.252 48
art.253 (former art.190) ... 68, **69**, 70
art.254 (former art.191) ... 220, 249
art.257 ... 46
art.263 ... 46
art.281 (former art.210) ... 104
art.287 (former art.214) ... 245, 246
art.288 (former art.215) ... 88, 178, 179, 181, 215, **239**, 240, 242
art.288(2) ... 243, 268, 269, 270, 273
art.294 (former art.221) ... 117, 118
art.296–art.298 (former art.223–art.226) ... 100
art.299 (former art.227) ... 368
art.300 (former art.228) ... 44
art.308 (former art.235) ... 46, **47**, 54, 58, 68, 132, 688, 698
art.310 (former art.238) ... 104
Preamble ... 35
EEA Agreement ... 550, 671
Euratom Treaty ... 7, 34, 277
European Coal and Steel Community Treaty ... 4, 6, 34, 74, 225, 277, 550, 588
art.36 ... 238
art.61 ... 75
European Convention on Human Rights ... 29, 80, 82, 83, 84, 87, 587, 589
art.6 ... 269, 270, 272, 603
art.6(1) ... 602, 603
art.8 ... 83, 94, 477, 589
art.8(1) ... 477, 587
art.8(2) ... 83, 589
art.9 ... 603
art.10 ... 411
art.12 ... 94
art.13 ... 269, 270, 272
First Protocol
art.1 ... 84, 85

Merger Treaty 1965 ... 34

Single European Act 1986 ... 7, 8, 34, 83, 93, 295, 299, 300, 308, 423, 424, 660
Preamble ... 477, 590

Treaty of Amsterdam ... 11, 12, 13, 34, 40, 53, 58, 80, 93, 95, 132, 277, 280, 281, 282, 294, 299, 323, 325, 342, 479, 668
art.12 ... 12
Protocol ... 482, 657–9
Treaty of Nice ... 13–15, 93, 213, 218, 280, 294, 483, 674
Preamble ... 35–6
Treaty on European Union (Maastricht) ... 9–10, 11, 34, 37, 38, 41, 53, 58, 93, 279, 283, 289, 294, 299, 317, 318, 323, 427, 483, 486, 660, 666, 668, 669, 681, 685, 686, 698
art.1... 278
art.1(2) (formerly art.A(2)) ... 686
art.2 ... 283
art.6 ... **78**, 80, 81, 87, 277, 280, 283, 688
art.6(2) (former art.F.2) ... 80, 81, 83, 87, 477, 590
art.7 ... **78–9**, 80, 281
art.11 ... **79**
art.12 ... **44–5**, 677
art.29 ... 45
art.31 ... 281
art.34(2) ... **45**, 128, 677
art.35 ... 11, 198
art.40 ... 674, 679
art.41–art.42 ... 679
art.43 ... **672–3**, 679
art.43(g) ... 674
art.43a–art.43b ... **673**
art.44 ... **673**
art.44a ... **673**
art.45 ... **673**
art.46 (former art.L) ... 46, 53, 54, 80, 87
art.47 (former art.M) ... 53, 54
art.48 ... **15**, 31, 272
art.49 ... 280
art.J3 (pre-Amsterdam) ... 698
art.K3(2) (pre-Amsterdam) ... 53, 54, 698
art.N (pre-Amsterdam) ... 698

Directives

Directive 64/54 ... 374

Directive 64/221 ... 123, 124, 443
art.1 ... **437**
art.1(1) ... 442
art.2 ... **437**
art.3 ... **437–8**, 439, 442
art.3(1) ... 124, 125, 439, 440, 442
art.3(2) ... 440
art.4–art.9 ... **438**
art.10 ... **439**

Directive 65/65 ... 153
art.3 ... 153

Directive 68/151 (Company Law) ... 163

Directive 68/360 ... 431, 446
  art.1 ... 477
  art.1(1)(c) ... 477
  art.2 ... 429
  art.4 ... 428, **431–2**, 477

Directive 69/466 ... 377
  art.3 ... 377
  art.11 ... 377

Directive 70/50 ... 344, 395, 420
  art.1 ... **342**
  art.2 ... **342–3**
  art.2(3)(f) ... 350
  art.2(3)(k) ... 360
  art.3 ... **343**, 386, 394

Directive 70/156 ... 634
  art.13 ... 633–4

Directive 71/188 ... 378

Directive 71/305 ... 152, 417
  art.29(5) ... 152

Directive 73/148 ... 446, 476

Directive 73/173   141

Directive 75/34 ... 446

Directive 75/117 ... 134

Directive 75/442 ... 120, 154

Directive 76/207 (Equal Treatment) ... 144, 145,
    150, 159, 160, 161
  art.1(2) ... 146
  art.2 ... 146
  art.2(1) ... 145, 146
  art.5(1) ... 144, 145, 146
  art.5(2) ... 146
  art.6 ... 160, 161

Directive 76/756 ... 633, 634
  art.5 ... 634

Directive 77/94 ... 374

Directive 77/143 ... 347, 348
  Annex I ... 347

Directive 77/388 (Sixth VAT Directive) ... 135,
    337
  art.35 ... 337

Directive 77/728 ... 142
  art.9 ... 142

Directive 78/319 ... 120

Directive 78/660 ... 462

Directive 79/112 ... 410
  art.14 ... 410

Directive 80/68 ... 112, 113

Directive 80/166 ... 634
  art.1 ... 635
  art.3(1)(a) ... 635

Directive 80/987 ... 168

Directive 81/389 ... 329

Directive 83/189 ... 153, 154, 619
  art.8 ... 154, 155, 156
  art.9 ... 154, 155, 156, 157

Directive 85/337 ... 267

Directive 85/374 (product liability) ... 639, 647,
    649, 650–1, 653, 654
  art.1 ... 639, 640, 642
  art.3 ... 650
  art.3(1)–(2) ... 650
  art.3(3) ... 650, 651
  art.4 ... 642
  art.7 ... 642
  art.7(e) ... 640, 642, 643, 644
  art.12 ... 650
  art.13 ... 647, 648, 649
  art.15(1)(a)–(b) ... 640, 648, 649
  art.15(2) ... 644
  art.16... 648

Directive 85/577 ... 148–9, 636, 637, 638, 645
  art.8 ... 636

Directive 87/601 ... 528

Directive 89/48 ... 321, 472
  art.4(1)(b) ... 472

Directive 89/391 ... 56

Directive 89/428 ... 50, 51, 64

Directive 89/552 ... 63
  art.13 ... 63

Directive 89/622 ... 60, 64, 66
  art.8(1) ... 637

Directive 89/646 ... 472

Directive 89/665 ... 174

Directive 89/666 ... 462

Directive 90/239 ... 66, 67
  art.7(1) ... 64, 637

Directive 90/364 ... 449

Directive 90/365 ... 449

Directive 90/366 ... 449

Directive 90/531
  art.8 ... 184
  art.8(1) ... 184

Directive 91/156 ... 48
  art.1 ... 50
  art.3–art.5 ... 49
  art.7 ... 49, 50
  art.9–art.14 ... 49

Directive 92/12 ... 338

Directive 92/13 ... 174

Directive 92/41 ... 60

Directive 92/51 ... 472

Directive 92/59 ... 621

Directive 92/79 ... 338

Directive 92/80 ... 338

Directive 92/81 ... 338

Directive 92/82 ... 338

Directive 92/83 ... 338

Directive 92/84
  art.1 ... **338**
  art.5 ... **339**

Directive 92/108 ... 338

Directive 93/13 ... 616, 638, 645, 648, 649

Directive 93/37 ... 616

Directive 93/96 ... 449, 489

Directive 93/104 (working time) ... 54, 55, 75
  art.1 ... 56
  art.3–art.4 ... 56
  art.5 ... 55, 56, 58
  art.6 ... 56, 57
  art.6(2) ... 56
  art.7 ... 56, 57
  art.8 ... 56
  art.14 ... 56
  art.15 ... 57
  art.17(1)–(2) ... 56
  art.18 ... 57
  art.18(3) ... 57

Directive 94/46 ... 638

Directive 95/34 ... 241–3

Directive 98/5 ... 472

Directive 98/34 ... 153, 313, 619

Directive 98/43 (tobacco advertising) ... 60–5, 66,
    636, 662
  art.3(1) ... 63
  art.3(2) ... 63, 64, 636
  art.3(3)(a) ... 63
  art.3(4)–(5) ... 63
  art.5 ... 63, 64, 637

Directive 98/48 ... 153, 313

Directive 99/34 ... 641, 649, 650–1

Directive 99/42 ... 472

Directive 2000/13 ... 410
  art.2(1)(a)(iii) ... 364

Directive 2000/38 ... 631, 632
  art.29d(2) ... 632
  art.29d(4) ... 633

Directive 2000/78 ... 96

Directive 2001/19 ... 472

Directive 2001/37 ... 66–7, 75–8, 637
  art.3 ... 76
  art.3(1) ... 76
  art.5 ... 76, 77
  art.5(1) ... 77
  art.7 ... 76, 77, 78
  art.13(1) ... 76, 637

Directive 2001/95 ... 621

Second VAT Directive ... 337

Regulations

Regulation 17/62 ... 550, 551, 571, 586
  art.3(2) ... 223
  art.3(2)(b) ... 223
  art.14 ... 586, 587, 588, 589
  art.14(1) ... 591, 593
  art.14(3) ... 589, 591, 594, 596, 597
  art.14(6) ... 588, 589, 591, 594, 597, 598
  art.20 ... 245

Regulation 99/63 ... 90
  art.2 ... 90, 92
  art.4 ... 90, 92

Regulation 19/65 ... 535

Regulation 1009/67
  art.35 ... 365
  art.37 ... 240
  art.37(1) ... 240

Regulation 234/68
  art.10 ... 132

Regulation 459/68
  art.19(1) ... 226

Regulation 769/68 ... 239, 240

Regulation 805/68
  art.14 ... 237

Regulation 827/68 ... 204

Regulation 1612/68 ... 102, 428, 429, 436, 437,
    488, 489
  art.1–art.3 ... 433
  art.4 ... 433–4
  art.5–art.6 ... 434
  art.7 ... 434
  art.7(2) ... 435, 436, 448
  art.8 ... 434
  art.9 ... 434–5
  art.10 ... 435, 477
  art.11–art.12 ... 435

Regulation 543/69 ... 44, 105
  art.3 ... 105

Regulation 459/70 ... 224, 232
  art.1(2) ... 224
  art.2 ... 224
  art.2(2) ... 43, 219, 224

Regulation 565/70 ... 232
  art.1 ... 219

Regulation 686/70 ... 232

Regulation 816/70 ... 85
  art.17 ... 86

Regulation 983/70 ... 219
  art.1 ... 43, 219

Regulation 1251/70 ... 436, 446
  art.3(1) ... 436
  art.7 ... 436

Regulation 1463/70 ... 113, 114

Regulation 3195/75
  art.3–art.4 ... 249

Regulation 652/76 ... 261

Regulation 1162/76 ... 84, 85, 86

Regulation 1079/77
  art.4 ... 251

Regulation 1778/77 ... 226, 233
  art.1 ... 227
  art.2 ... 227
  art.3 ... 226, 227, 233, 234
  art.3(3) ... 226

Regulation 2900/77 ... 238

Regulation 2901/77 ... 238

Regulation 337/79 ... 85
  art.31 ... 86

Regulation 1697/79
  art.5(2) ... 207

Regulation 3017/79 ... 229
  art.5 ... 229
  art.13(1) ... 229
Regulation 84/82 ... 229
Regulation 1882/82 ... 229
Regulation 170/83 ... 118
  art.5(2) ... 118
Regulation 1880/83 ... 72, 74
  art.12(c) ... 73
  art.13(3) ... 73
Regulation 3309/85 ... 263
Regulation 3975/87 ... 528
Regulation 3976/87 ... 528
Regulation 2045/89 ... 263
Regulation 4064/89 ... 550, 551, 561
  art.2(3) ... 561
Regulation 404/93 ... 256, 257, 258–9, 264, 265,
  266
  art.17 ... 690
  art.18–art.19 ... 265, 690
  art.21(2) ... 690
  art.27 ... 259, 260, 265
Regulation 2309/93
  art.22(1) ... 632
Regulation 3224/94 ... 264, 265, 266
Regulation 820/97 ... 364
Regulation 1103/97 ... 318
Regulation 1310/97 ... 561
Regulation 2679/98 ... 357
  art.2 ... 357
Regulation 2842/98 ... 598, 601
  art.1–art.5 ... 599
  art.6 ... 599–600
  art.7–art.12 ... 600
  art.13 ... 600–1
  art.14–art.16 ... 601
Regulation 1215/99 ... 535
Regulation 2790/99 ... 513, 521, 541
  art.1 ... 537
  art.2 ... 537–8
  art.3 ... 538, 541
  art.4 ... 538–9
  art.5–art.7 ... 539
  art.8 ... 539–40, 541
  art.9 ... 540, 541
  art.10 ... 540
  art.11 ... 540–1
  art.12–art.13 ... 541
  Preamble ... 535–7
Regulation 1760/2000 ... 364
Regulation 2658/2000 ... 542
Regulation 2659/2000 ... 542
Regulation 1/2003 ... 223, 513, 571, 585, 586,
  588, 603, 609, 659
  art.1 ... 572–3
  art.1(2) ... 585
  art.2–art.5 ... 573
  art.6 ... 573, 604
  art.7 223, 574

Regulation 1/2003 – *continued*
  art.8–art.10 ... 574
  art.11 ... 574–5
  art.12–art.13 ... 575
  art.14 ... 575–6
  art.15 ... 576–7
  art.16–art.17 ... 577
  art.18 ... 577–8
  art.19 ... 578
  art.20 ... 578–9, 586, 587, 598
  art.21 ... 579, 586, 598
  art.22 ... 579–80
  art.23 ... 580–1, 601
  art.23(5) ... 603
  art.24 ... 581
  art.25 ... 581–2
  art.26 ... 582
  art.27 ... 582–3
  art.28–art.32 ... 583
  art.33–art.35 ... 584
  art.36–art.42 584
  art.43 ... 584
  art.44–art.45 ... 585
  Preamble ... 572

Court of Justice

EC Statute of the Court of Justice
  art.20 ... 197
  art.51 ... 243

Rules of Procedure ... 211
  art.83(2) ... 233
  art.104(3) ... 199, 211

International Conventions

International Covenant on Civil and Political
  Rights ... 95
  art.28 ... 95
International Labour Organization Convention
  No 100 ... 126
  art.2 ... 126

World Trade Organization Agreement ... 105

Domestic Statutes by country
Australian legislation
Constitution
  s.109 ... 130

Belgian legislation
Royal Decree No 40 of 24 October 1967 ... 126
Royal Decree of 3 March 1927
  art.31–14 ... 112

French legislation
Code du Travail Maritime ... 102
  art.3 ... 102
  art.3(2) ... 102

French legislation – *continued*
Loi Evin ... 195, 196

German legislation
Basic Law *(Grundgesetz)* ... 83, 87, 130, 182
  art.12 ... 84
  art.14 ... 84
  art.14(2) ... 85
  art.23 ... 689
  art.23(1) ... 691
  art.38 ... 687
  art.42(2) ... 85
  art.100(1) ... 690, 691
  art.103 ... 91
Biersteuergesetz ... 387, 389
  art.9 ... 387, 388, 391
  art.9(1)–(2) ... 387, 388
  art.9(7)–(8) ... 388
  art.10 ... 387, 388, 389, 391
Branntweinmonopolgesetz
  art.100 ... 381
Bürgerliches Gesetzbuch
  Para.611a(2) ... 160, 161

Federal Constitutional Court Act
  art.1 ... 690

Zivilprozeßordnung
  art.1040 ... 202

Irish legislation
Companies Act 1963 ... 358, 359
Constitution ... 471
  art.43.2.1 ... 85
  art.43.2.2 ... 85

Merchandise Marks (Restriction on Importation
  of Jewellery) Order 1971 (SI 1971/307) ...
  350, 351
Merchandise Marks (Restriction on Sale of
  Imported Jewellery) Order 1971 (SI 1971/
  306) ... 350, 351

Italian legislation
Constitution ... 91
  art.42(2) ... 85

Law No 313 ... 158
Law No 1089 ... 326

Netherlands legislation
Advocatenwet
  art.28 ... 523

Sickness Fund Law ... 200

Spanish legislation
Civil Code ... 163

Swiss legislation
Penal Code ... 244
  art.273 ... 247

UK legislation
Consumer Protection Act 1987 ... 641
  s.1(1) ... 644
  s.4(1)(e) ... 641, 642, 644
Customs and Excise Act 1952
  s.304 ... 367
Customs Consolidation Act 1876 ... 370
  s.42 ... 367

Equal Pay Act 1970 ... 133, 134

Gas Act 1972 ... 150
Gas Act 1986 ... 151

Health Services Act 1980 ... 145

Merchant Shipping Act 1988 ... 117, 136,
  182
  s.14 ... 117, 118
  s.14(1)(a) ... 119
  s.14(1)(c) ... 119
  s.14(2) ... 119
  s.14(7) ... 119

National Health Service Act 1977 ... 145

Race Relations Act 1976 ... 133

Sale of Goods Act 1979 ... 641
Sex Discrimination Act 1975 ... 94, 133,
  144
  s.6(4) ... 145
Shops Act 1950 ... 395
  art.47 ... 393
  art.59 ... 393
  Sch.5 ... 393

Trade Descriptions (Origin Marking)
  (Miscellaneous Goods) Order 1981 (SI 1981/
  121) ... 352
  art.2 ... 352, 353

United States legislation
Constitution
  art.6 ... 130

Sherman Act ... 513

AMSTERDAM TREATY TABLE OF EQUIVALENCE

The function of this Table of Equivalence, which is annexed to the Amsterdam Treaty, is explained fully at pp. 10–16 below.

Previous numbering	New numbering
Part One	Part One
Article 1	Article 1
Article 2	Article 2
Article 3	Article 3
Article 3a	Article 4
Article 3b	Article 5
Article 3c(*)	Article 6
Article 4	Article 7
Article 4a	Article 8
Article 4b	Article 9
Article 5	Article 10
Article 5a(*)	Article 11
Article 6	Article 12
Article 6a	Article 13
Article 7 (repealed)	–
Article 7a	Article 14
Article 7b (repealed)	–
Article 7c	Article 15
Article 7d(*)	Article 16
Part Two	Part Two
Article 8	Article 17
Article 8a	Article 18
Article 8b	Article 19
Article 8c	Article 20
Article 8d	Article 21
Article 8e	Article 22
Part Three Title I	Part Three Title I
Article 9	Article 23
Article 10	Article 24
Article 11 (repealed)	–
Chapter 1 Section 1 (deleted)	Chapter 1 –
Article 12	Article 25
Article 13 (repealed)	–
Article 14 (repealed)	–
Article 15 (repealed)	–
Article 16 (repealed)	–
Article 17 (repealed)	–
Section 2 (deleted)	–
Article 18 (repealed)	–
Article 19 (repealed)	–

Previous numbering	New numbering
Chapter 1 *continued*	Chapter 1 *continued*
Article 20 (repealed)	–
Article 21 (repealed)	–
Article 22 (repealed)	–
Article 23 (repealed)	–
Article 24 (repealed)	–
Article 25 (repealed)	–
Article 26 (repealed)	–
Article 27 (repealed)	–
Article 28	Article 26
Article 29	Article 27
Chapter 2	Chapter 2
Article 30	Article 28
Article 31 (repealed)	–
Article 32 (repealed)	–
Article 33 (repealed)	–
Article 34	Article 29
Article 35 (repealed)	–
Article 36	Article 30
Article 37	Article 31
Title II	Title II
Article 38	Article 32
Article 39	Article 33
Article 40	Article 34
Article 41	Article 35
Article 42	Article 36
Article 43	Article 37
Article 44 (repealed)	–
Article 45 (repealed)	–
Article 46	Article 38
Article 47 (repealed)	–
Title III	Title III
Chapter 1	Chapter 1
Article 48	Article 39
Article 49	Article 40
Article 50	Article 41
Article 51	Article 42
Chapter 2	Chapter 2
Article 52	Article 43
Article 53	–
Article 54	Article 44
Article 55	Article 45
Article 56	Article 46
Article 57	Article 47
Article 58	Article 48
Chapter 3	Chapter 3
Article 59	Article 49
Article 60	Article 50
Article 61	Article 51

Previous numbering	New numbering
Chapter 3 *continued*	Chapter 3 *continued*
Article 62 (repealed)	–
Article 63	Article 52
Article 64	Article 53
Article 65	Article 54
Article 66	Article 55
Article 67 (repealed)	–
Article 68 (repealed)	–
Article 69 (repealed)	–
Article 70 (repealed)	–
Article 71 (repealed)	–
Article 72 (repealed)	–
Article 73 (repealed)	–
Article 73a (repealed)	–
Article 73b	Article 56
Article 73c	Article 57
Article 73d	Article 58
Article 73e (repealed)	–
Article 73f	Article 59
Article 73g	Article 60
Article 73h (repealed)	–
Title IIIa(**)	Title IV
Article 73i(*)	Article 61
Article 73j(*)	Article 62
Article 73k(*)	Article 63
Article 73l(*)	Article 64
Article 73m(*)	Article 65
Article 73n(*)	Article 66
Article 73o(*)	Article 67
Article 73p(*)	Article 68
Article 73q(*)	Article 69
Title IV	Title V
Article 74	Article 70
Article 75	Article 71
Article 76	Article 72
Article 77	Article 73
Article 78	Article 74
Article 79	Article 75
Article 80	Article 76
Article 81	Article 77
Article 82	Article 78
Article 83	Article 79
Article 84	Article 80
Title V Chapter 1	Title VI Chapter 1
Article 85	Article 81
Article 86	Article 82
Article 87	Article 83
Article 88	Article 84

Previous numbering	New numbering
Chapter 1 *continued*	Chapter 1 *continued*
Article 89	Article 85
Article 90	Article 86
Section 2 (deleted)	–
Article 91 (repealed)	–
Section 3	Section 2
Article 92	Article 87
Article 93	Article 88
Article 94	Article 89
Chapter 2	Chapter 2
Article 95	Article 90
Article 96	Article 91
Article 97 (repealed)	–
Article 98	Article 92
Article 99	Article 93
Chapter 3	Chapter 3
Article 100	Article 94
Article 100a	Article 95
Article 100b (repealed)	–
Article 100c (repealed)	–
Article 100d (repealed)	–
Article 101	Article 96
Article 102	Article 97
Title VI	Title VII
Chapter 1	Chapter 1
Article 102a	Article 98
Article 103	Article 99
Article 103a	Article 100
Article 104	Article 101
Article 104a	Article 102
Article 104b	Article 103
Article 104c	Article 104
Chapter 2	Chapter 2
Article 105	Article 105
Article 105a	Article 106
Article 106	Article 107
Article 107	Article 108
Article 108	Article 109
Article 108a	Article 110
Article 109	Article 111
Chapter 3	Chapter 3
Article 109a	Article 112
Article 109b	Article 113
Article 109c	Article 114
Article 109d	Article 115
Chapter 4	Chapter 4
Article 109e	Article 116
Article 109f	Article 117

Previous numbering	New numbering
Chapter 4 *continued*	Chapter 4 *continued*
Article 109g	Article 118
Article 109h	Article 119
Article 109i	Article 120
Article 109j	Article 121
Article 109k	Article 122
Article 109l	Article 123
Article 109m	Article 124
Title VIa(**)	Title VIII
Article 109n(*)	Article 125
Article 109o(*)	Article 126
Article 109p(*)	Article 127
Article 109q(*)	Article 128
Article 109r(*)	Article 129
Article 109s(*)	Article 130
Title VII	Title IX
Article 110	Article 131
Article 111 (repealed)	–
Article 112	Article 132
Article 113	Article 133
Article 114 (repealed)	–
Article 115	Article 134
Title VIIa(**)	Title X
Article 116(*)	Article 135
Title VIII	Title XI
Chapter 1(***)	Chapter 1
Article 117	Article 136
Article 118	Article 137
Article 118a	Article 138
Article 118b	Article 139
Article 118c	Article 140
Article 119	Article 141
Article 119a	Article 142
Article 120	Article 143
Article 121	Article 144
Article 122	Article 145
Chapter 2	Chapter 2
Article 123	Article 146
Article 124	Article 147
Article 125	Article 148
Chapter 3	Chapter 3
Article 126	Article 149
Article 127	Article 150
Title IX	Title XII
Article 128	Article 151
Title X	Title XIII
Article 129	Article 152

Previous numbering	New numbering
Title XI Article 129a	Title XIV Article 153
Title XII Article 129b Article 129c Article 129d	Title XIV Article 154 Article 155 Article 156
Title XII Article 130	Title XVI Article 157
Title XIV Article 130a Article 130b Article 130c Article 130d Article 130e	Title XVII Article 158 Article 159 Article 160 Article 161 Article 162
Title XV Article 130f Article 130g Article 130h Article 130i Article 130j Article 130k Article 130l Article 130m Article 130n Article 130o Article 130p Article 130q (repealed)	Title XVIII Article 163 Article 164 Article 165 Article 166 Article 167 Article 168 Article 169 Article 170 Article 171 Article 172 Article 173 –
Title XVI Article 130r Article 130s Article 130t	Title XIX Article 174 Article 175 Article 176
Title XVII Article 130u Article 130v Article 130w Article 130x Article 130y	Title XX Article 177 Article 178 Article 179 Article 180 Article 181
Part Four Article 131 Article 132 Article 133 Article 134 Article 135 Article 136 Article 136a	Part Four Article 182 Article 183 Article 184 Article 185 Article 186 Article 187 Article 188

Previous numbering	New numbering
Part Five	Part Five
Title I	Title I
Chapter 1	Chapter 1
Section 1	Section 1
Article 137	Article 189
Article 138	Article 190
Article 138a	Article 191
Article 138b	Article 192
Article 138c	Article 193
Article 138d	Article 194
Article 138e	Article 195
Article 139	Article 196
Article 140	Article 197
Article 141	Article 198
Article 142	Article 199
Article 143	Article 200
Article 144	Article 201
Section 2	Section 2
Article 145	Article 202
Article 146	Article 203
Article 147	Article 204
Article 148	Article 205
Article 149 (repealed)	–
Article 150	Article 206
Article 151	Article 207
Article 152	Article 208
Article 153	Article 209
Article 154	Article 210
Section 3	Section 3
Article 155	Article 211
Article 156	Article 212
Article 157	Article 213
Article 158	Article 214
Article 159	Article 215
Article 160	Article 216
Article 161	Article 217
Article 162	Article 218
Article 163	Article 219
Section 4	Section 4
Article 164	Article 220
Article 165	Article 221
Article 166	Article 222
Article 167	Article 223
Article 168	Article 224
Article 168a	Article 225
Article 169	Article 226
Article 170	Article 227
Article 171	Article 228
Article 172	Article 229
Article 173	Article 230

Previous numbering	New numbering
Section 4 *continued*	Section 4 *continued*
Article 174	Article 231
Article 175	Article 232
Article 176	Article 233
Article 177	Article 234
Article 178	Article 235
Article 179	Article 236
Article 180	Article 237
Article 181	Article 238
Article 182	Article 239
Article 183	Article 240
Article 184	Article 241
Article 185	Article 242
Article 186	Article 243
Article 187	Article 244
Article 188	Article 245
Section 5	Section 5
Article 188a	Article 246
Article 188b	Article 247
Article 188c	Article 248
Chapter 2	Chapter 2
Article 189	Article 249
Article 189a	Article 250
Article 189b	Article 251
Article 189c	Article 252
Article 190	Article 253
Article 191	Article 254
Article 191a(*)	Article 255
Article 192	Article 256
Chapter 3	Chapter 3
Article 193	Article 257
Article 194	Article 258
Article 195	Article 259
Article 196	Article 260
Article 197	Article 261
Article 198	Article 262
Article 198a	Article 263
Article 198b	Article 264
Article 198c	Article 265
Chapter 5	Chapter 5
Article 198d	Article 266
Article 198e	Article 267
Title II	Title II
Article 199	Article 268
Article 200 (repealed)	–
Article 201	Article 269
Article 201a	Article 270
Article 202	Article 271

Previous numbering	New numbering
Title II *continued*	Title II *continued*
Article 203	Article 272
Article 204	Article 273
Article 205	Article 274
Article 205a	Article 275
Article 206	Article 276
Article 206a (repealed)	–
Article 207	Article 277
Article 208	Article 278
Article 209	Article 279
Article 209a	Article 280
Part Six	Part Six
Article 210	Article 281
Article 211	Article 282
Article 212(*)	Article 283
Article 213	Article 284
Article 213a(*)	Article 285
Article 213b(*)	Article 286
Article 214	Article 287
Article 215	Article 288
Article 216	Article 289
Article 217	Article 290
Article 218(*)	Article 291
Article 219	Article 292
Article 220	Article 293
Article 221	Article 294
Article 222	Article 295
Article 223	Article 296
Article 224	Article 297
Article 225	Article 298
Article 226 (repealed)	–
Article 227	Article 299
Article 228	Article 300
Article 228a	Article 301
Article 229	Article 302
Article 230	Article 303
Article 231	Article 304
Article 232	Article 305
Article 233	Article 306
Article 234	Article 307
Article 235	Article 308
Article 236(*)	Article 309
Article 237 (repealed)	–
Article 238	Article 310
Article 239	Article 311
Article 240	Article 312
Article 241 (repealed)	–
Article 242 (repealed)	–
Article 243 (repealed)	–
Article 244 (repealed)	–

Previous numbering	New numbering
Part Six *continued*	Part Six *continued*
Article 245 (repealed)	–
Article 246 (repealed)	–
Final Provisions	Final Provisions
Article 247	Article 313
Article 248	Article 314

(*) New Article introduced by the Treaty of Amsterdam.
(**) New Title introduced by the Treaty of Amsterdam.
(***) Chapter 1 restructured by the Treaty of Amsterdam.

NOTE ON THE CITATION OF ARTICLES OF THE TREATIES IN COURT PUBLICATIONS

Pursuant to the renumbering of the articles of the Treaty on European Union (EU) and of the Treaty establishing the European Community (EC) brought about by the Treaty of Amsterdam, the Court of Justice and the Court of First Instance have introduced, with effect from 1 May 1999, a new method of citation of the articles of the EU, EC, ECSC and Euratom Treaties.

The new method is primarily designed to avoid all risk of confusion between the version of an article as it stood prior to 1 May 1999 and the version applying after that date. The principles on which that method operates are as follows:

— Where reference is made to an article of a Treaty *as it stands after* 1 May 1999, the number of the article is immediately followed by two letters indicating the Treaty concerned:

  — EU for the Treaty on European Union
  — EC for the EC Treaty
  — CS for the ECSC Treaty
  — EA for the Euratom Treaty.

  Thus, 'Article 234 *EC*' denotes the article of that Treaty as it stands *after* 1 May 1999.

— Where, on the other hand, reference is made to an article of a Treaty *as it stood before* 1 May 1999, the number of the article is followed by the words 'of the Treaty on European Union', 'of the EC (or EEC) Treaty', 'of the ECSC Treaty' or 'of the EAEC Treaty', as the case may be.

  Thus, 'Article 85 *of the EC Treaty*' refers to Article 85 of that Treaty *before* 1 May 1999.

— In addition, as regards the EC Treaty and the Treaty on European Union, again where reference is made to an article of a Treaty *as it stood before* 1 May 1999, the initial citation of the article in a text is followed by a reference in brackets to the corresponding provision of the same Treaty as it stands *after* 1 May 1999, as follows:

  — '*Article 85 of the EC Treaty (now Article 81 EC)*' where the article has not been amended by the Treaty of Amsterdam;
  — '*Article 51 of the EC Treaty (now, after amendment, Article 42 EC)*' where the article has been amended by the Treaty of Amsterdam;
  — '*Article 53 of the EC Treaty (repealed by the Treaty of Amsterdam)*', where the article has been repealed by the Treaty of Amsterdam.

— By way of exception to the latter rule, the initial citation of (the former) Articles 117 to 120 of the EC Treaty, which have been replaced *en bloc* by the Treaty of Amsterdam, is followed by the following wording in brackets: '(Articles 117 to 120 of the EC Treaty have been replaced by Articles 136 EC to 143 EC)'.

  For example:

  — '*Article 119 of the EC Treaty (Articles 117 to 120 of the EC Treaty have been replaced by Articles 136 EC to 143 EC)*'.

The same applies to Articles J to J.11 and K to K.9 of the Treaty on European Union. For example:

— *'Article F.2 of the Treaty on European Union (Articles F to F.11 of the Treaty on European Union have been replaced by Articles 11 EU to 28 EU)'*;
— *'Article K.2 of the Treaty on European Union (Articles K to K.9 of the Treaty on European Union have been replaced by Articles 29 EU to 42 EU)'*.

ABBREVIATIONS

AC	Appeal Cases	ICLQ	International and Comparative Law Quarterly
AJCL	American Journal of Comparative Law		
All ER	All England (Law) Reports	ILJ	Industrial Law Journal
CA	Court of Appeal (England)	IRLR	Industrial Relations Law Reports
CDE	Cahiers de Droit Européen		
		JBL	Journal of Business Law
CEE	Charges having equivalent effect (Art. 12)	JCMS	Journal of Common Market Studies
Ch	Chancery Reports	JCP	Journal of Consumer Policy
CLJ	Cambridge Law Journal		
CMLR	Common Market Law Reports	JEL	Journal of Environmental Law
CML Rev	Common Market Law Review	JEPP	Journal of European Public Policy
Cmnd.	Command Paper	JSWFL	Journal of Social Welfare and Family Law
Crim LR	Criminal Law Review		
EC	(ECs) European Community (-ies)	J Law and Econ	Journal of Law and Economics
ECB	European Central Bank	LIEI	Legal Issues of European Integration
ECLJ	European Consumer Law Journal		
		LQR	Law Quarterly Review
ECLR	European Competition Law Review	MEQR	Measures having equivalent effect to a quantitative restriction (Article 28)
ECR	European Court Reports		
ECSC	European Coal and Steel Community		
EEC	European Economic Community	MJ	Maastricht Journal of European & Comparative Law
EEIG	European Economic Interest Grouping	MLR	Modern Law Review
		NILQ	Northern Ireland Legal Quarterly
EIPR	European Intellectual Property Review		
		OJ	Official Journal (of the ECs)
EJIL	European Journal of International Law		
		OJLS	Oxford Journal of Legal Studies
EL Rev	European Law Review		
EU	European Union	QB	Queen's Bench
ERPL	European Review of Private Law	RTDE	Revue Trimistrelle de Droit Européen
EuR	Europarecht	SEA	Single European Act
EURATOM	European Atomic Energy Community	SI	Statutory Instrument
		TEU	Treaty on European Union
GATT	General Agreement on Tariffs and Trade		
		WLR	Weekly Law Reports
HL	House of Lords (UK)	WTO	World Trade Organisation
IBL	International Business Lawyer	YEL	Yearbook of European Law

PART ONE

The Constitutional Law of the EU

1

The Evolution of the European Union

SECTION 1: **INTRODUCTION**

For students in British law schools, European Community (EC) law or, more recently, the wider phenomenon of European Union (EU) law has long held a well-deserved reputation for being extremely difficult to come to grips with. Yet at the end of the course most students tend to look back on it as a subject which they have found more interesting than most of the others which they have studied. There are good reasons for this apparent paradox. European Union law *is* initially difficult, because it represents an adventure into a new legal system. When a student starts the study of a new English or Scots law subject, he or she comes to it with an accumulated fund of knowledge and expectation about the basic principles of the legal order. It is possible immediately to approach the substance of the subject. Not so with European Union law. Indeed, nothing could be worse than to try to leap into the study of this new legal order equipped with domestic preconceptions about what judges do and about how law should be interpreted and applied. EC/EU law is simply different, and it is necessary to learn to walk before one can run. For the law student who had thought that he or she had already picked up a spanking pace in legal education, this return to basic constitutional law can be a dispiriting experience. However, once the essentials of the subject are mastered, EU law is likely to prove a rewarding race to have run. It is a subject which enjoys internal coherence. Its themes and principles are consistent and can be understood and applied relatively easily. There are themes in the substantive law, such as the objective of market integration and the establishment of a common market, and there are principles in the constitutional law, such as the supremacy and direct effect of European Community law. The approach of the judges of the European Court may initially seem odd, but it too displays a certain thematic consistency which can quickly be appreciated. There is even consistency in the difficulties and tensions which beset the development of EU law. The problems of integrating the features of the EU legal order, and in particular its EC dimension, with the traditions of domestic legal systems will be observed on many occasions.

As an academic lawyer with a particular interest in European Union law, I hope that it will one day be possible to abandon these cautionary notes. Most Law Schools are aware of the need to integrate the key elements of the study of EU law into their degree programmes from the earliest possible stage, so that it does not present to the student this initially forbidding prospect. Those who teach substantive European Union law courses remain aware that this task is by no means complete.

Part One of this book deals with the constitutional law of the EU. This covers the sources of Union law in Chapter 2, and then examines in Chapters 3 to 8 the fundamental ground rules of the legal order, with special reference to the European Community. These essential principles are the doctrines of supremacy and of direct effect, and the preliminary reference procedure.

However, given the comments above, is it right to start with Part One? I have already mentioned that the early weeks of study of Community law are difficult, even intimidating. True, in examining a legal system, there is an obvious logic in beginning with its sources. But there is an equally strong argument for starting by acquiring a knowledge of the purpose of the system. This broader perspective can help the subject to come alive more quickly. Chapter 9, in Part Two, therefore deserves the student's examination at an early stage. So too do Chapters 19–21, which comprise Part Four of the book and which help to illustrate what the Union actually does, while also drawing out some bigger questions about its nature and its relationship with the Member States. Equally, once the student has grasped the substantive law of the Community it would be helpful then to refer back once again to the earlier Constitutional law chapters. They will make more sense in the broader context.

It would be ill-advised to approach study of EC law as a purely legal undertaking. Narrowness of focus is damaging in any branch of the law, but perhaps especially so in European law, where economic, political, and social objectives are close to the surface and exert a profound formative influence on the law. From this perspective, then, the student about to read Part One of this book, might be well advised to equip him- or herself in advance with a basic understanding of modern European history and the post-war maelstrom out of which the Community emerged, subsequently to become a Union. Such introductory material may be found in the opening Chapter or Chapters of the major textbooks listed in the Selected Bibliography. Other more general sources of information, which do not offer a specifically legal focus, are also mentioned there and deserve the student's attention.

However, the following extracts provide a short but valuable introductory overview of some of the elements of the Community and Union's past, present, and future, which will be glimpsed, but not studied directly, in the course of this book. The opportunity is also taken to clarify terminology – a Community or a Union?

J. Pinder, The Building of the European Union
(3rd ed, Oxford: OUP, 1998), pp.3–8
[Reproduced by permission of Oxford University Press]

(Footnotes omitted.)

1 CREATING THE COMMUNITY AND THE UNION: NATION-STATE AND FEDERAL IDEA

The European Community, which remains the central element in the European Union, is a remarkable innovation in relations among states. Its institutions are more powerful than those of conventional international organisations, and offer more scope for development. Much of their specific character was determined in a few weeks in the summer of 1950, when representatives of the six founder members, France, the German Federal Republic, Italy, Belgium, the Netherlands, and Luxembourg, agreed on the outline of the Treaty to establish the European Coal and Steel Community. The initiative had been taken by Robert Schuman, the French foreign minister, who explained the gist of his proposal with these words:

. . . the French government proposes to take action immediately on one limited but decisive point . . . to place Franco-German production of coal and steel under a common High Authority, within the framework of an organisation open to the participation of the other countries of Europe . . . The solidarity in production thus established will make it plain that any war between France and Germany becomes not merely unthinkable, but materially impossible . . . this proposal will build the first concrete foundation of a European federation which is indispensable to the preservation of peace . . .

World War II, national sovereignty, the federal idea

World War II was a catastrophe that discredited the previous international order and, for many Europeans, the basic element in that order: the absolutely sovereign nation-state. In the Europe of such states, France and Germany had been at war three times in less than a century, twice at the centre of terrible world wars. Autarky and protection, fragmenting Europe's economy, had caused economic malaise and political antagonism. Fascist glorification of the nation-state had been revealed as a monstrosity; and many felt that insistence on its sovereignty, even without fascist excess, distorted and ossified the political perspective.

This critique pointed towards the limitation of national sovereignty. It was accepted by many people of the anti-fascist resistance, in Germany and Italy as well as the occupied countries. While the idea of limiting sovereignty in a united Europe was widespread, some influential figures were more precise. They envisaged a federal constitution for Europe, giving powers over trade, money, security, and related taxation, to a federal parliament, government, and court, leaving all other powers to be exercised by the institutions of the member states.

Such ideas evoked a ready echo from those Europeans who asked themselves why the war had occurred and what could be done to ensure a better future; and they were encouraged by Winston Churchill who, in a speech in Zurich in September 1946, suggested that France should lead Germany into a United States of Europe. Not everybody noticed that he was reticent about the part that Britain should play in such a union; and many, impressed by the magnanimous vision of the wartime leader with his immense prestige, did not realise how hard it would be to accomplish. For despite the popularity of the federal idea in Continental countries, the structures of the states were gathering strength again and were to prove resistant to radical federal reform.

Some of this resistance stemmed from the principle of national sovereignty as a basic political value. General de Gaulle was to be the most powerful and eloquent exponent of this view; and Mrs Thatcher was a subsequent protagonist. But most of the resisters were more pragmatic. Many bureaucrats, central bankers, and politicians would allow that sovereignty could in principle be shared on the right terms and at the right time: but the right terms were not on offer and the right time would be later.

Two main strategies were devised to overcome the reluctance of governments. One, promoted by the Italian federalist leader, Altiero Spinelli, was to mobilise popular support for a constituent assembly, in which the people's representatives would draw up a European constitution. But this idea bore little fruit until, with the direct elections to the European Parliament in 1979, Spinelli persuaded the people's newly elected representatives to design and approve a Draft Treaty to constitute a European Union. The other strategy, devised by Jean Monnet, was to identify a 'limited but decisive point', as Schuman's declaration put it, on which governments could be persuaded to agree and which, without going the whole way, would mark a significant step towards federation. With this idea, Monnet was to secure an early and spectacular success.

Founding the Community: the ECSC

Monnet's 'limited but decisive point' was the need for a new structure to contain the resurgent heavy industries of the Ruhr, the traditional economic basis for Germany's military might, which had been laid low as a result of the war. It was clear by 1950 that industry in West Germany must develop if Germans were to pay their way in the world and help the West in its rivalry with the Soviet Union, and that this required the revival of German steel production. Of the western Allies then responsible for West Germany, the United States and Britain were increasingly insistent on this. France, through history and geography more sensitive to the potential danger of German power, insisted that the Ruhr's heavy industries should be kept under control. But France lacked the means to restrain the Americans and British; and there were Frenchmen in key positions who realised that the perpetuation of an international Ruhr authority such as had been set up in 1948 to exert control over the Germans, apart from being unacceptable to the two Allies, would be an unstable arrangement, apt to be overturned by Germany at the first opportunity. Hence the idea of a common structure to govern the coal and steel industries, not only of the Ruhr but also of France and other European countries.

This idea was not the invention of Monnet alone. Officials in the French foreign ministry were also working on it. But they would surely have created a conventional international organisation, governed by committees of ministers, whereas Monnet was determined that the new institutions should have a political life independent of the existing governments: that they should be 'the first concrete foundation of a European federation'.

It is the theme of this book that the concept of European institutions which go beyond a conventional system of intergovernmental co-operation, however imperfectly realised so far, has given the Community, and now the Union, its special character: its stability, capacity for achievement, and promise for the future. It is of course possible to argue that the Community is, on the contrary, essentially an intergovernmental organisation to secure free trade and economic co-operation, and that the rest is frills and rhetoric. This book sets out a case for seeing it as more than that.

Monnet, from his vantage point as head of the French *Commissariat du Plan*, persuaded Schuman to adopt the more radical project; and he did it at the moment when the French government was most apt to accept, because a solution to the problem of German steel could no longer be delayed. Monnet's solution had the merit of meeting not only the French national interest in the control of German steel but also a wider interest in the development of European political institutions. The proposal was immediately welcomed by the governments of West Germany, Italy, Belgium, the Netherlands, and Luxembourg; and it was enthusiastically received by the wide sectors of opinion in those countries and in France that could be called broadly federalist, in the sense of supporting steps towards a federal end, even if not all would be precise in defining this. The project also received strong and steady support from the United States.

Support for the federal idea had mushroomed in Britain too in 1939 and the first half of 1940, culminating with the Churchill government's proposal for union with France. But after the fall of France in June 1940, with Nazi domination of the Continent, British interest in European union ebbed. For more than a decade after the war, British governments wanted to confine their relationship with the Continent to no more than a loose association. They were not ready to accept the federal implications of Monnet's proposal. So the six founder members negotiated the Treaty establishing the European Coal and Steel Community (ECSC) without Britain or the other West European countries that took the same view.

As chairman of the intergovernmental conference that drew up the ECSC Treaty, Monnet was well placed to ensure that his basic idea was followed through. The High Authority was to be the executive responsible for policy relating to the coal and steel industries in the member countries, and its decisions were to apply directly to the economic agents in each country, without requiring the approval of its government. The policies envisaged in the Treaty bore the mark of French planning ideas. Investment in the two industries was to be influenced by the High Authority, though not subject to much control. Prices and production could be regulated, but only if there were crises of shortage or over-production. Policies for training, housing, and redeployment were to cater for workers' needs. Competition was at the same time to be stimulated by rules on price transparency, as well as by anti-trust laws on American lines.

Monnet insisted on the principle of the High Authority's independence from the member states' governments because his experience as an international civil servant had convinced him that it would be hamstrung if they controlled it too directly. But that raised the question of the High Authority's accountability. Monnet, in his inaugural speech as the first President of the High Authority in August 1952, was to explain the Treaty's answer like this. The High Authority was responsible to an Assembly (now called the European Parliament), which would eventually be directly elected, and which had the power to dismiss it. There was recourse to the European Court of Justice in cases that concerned the High Authority's acts. In short, the powers defined by the Treaty would be exercised by institutions with federal characteristics, sovereign within the limits of their competences. The policy of the High Authority and those of the member states would be 'harmonised' by a Council of ministers, voting by majority 'save in exceptional cases'. Monnet ensured that the federal elements in the Community would be clearly explained by employing Spinelli's help in drafting the speech.

Monnet's idea was that the European federation would be built over the years on this 'first concrete foundation' as new sectors of activity were brought within the scope of the pre-federal institutions; and the establishment of the European Economic Community and Euratom in 1958 lent remarkable support to this view. But he does not appear to have foreseen how much the Council would come to dominate the politics of the Community, as the political structures of member states came to assert themselves against the realisation of the federal idea. This reaction led to a long-drawn-out conflict within the Community, which began with a major assault by General de Gaulle as President of France and continued up to the 1990s, with Britain succeeding de Gaulle as champion of national sovereignty . . .

NOTE
The Treaties of Rome, signed in 1957 and creating the EEC and EURATOM in 1958, led to a deepening of the process. The EEC envisaged the creation of a common market and was not limited to particular sectors of the economy. Its institutions followed the pattern of the ECSC. The EEC had a Commission, where the ECSC has a High Authority. (Since 1967 the two have functioned as one under the title 'Commission'.) The EEC also had three other institutions – Council, Parliament, and Court. The system is rooted in International Treaties agreed between States, but it represents a much more institutionally sophisticated and intricate model of co-operation than can be found in the orthodox type of 'intergovernmental co-operation' to which international Treaty-making is dedicated. Admittedly the roots remain deep and each time the Treaty is revised the process of ratification by States offers a reminder of their foundational role. But there is much more to it than mere intergovernmental co-operation. The dynamic process of institutional interplay *within* the system endows it with a momentum that is not capable of crude control by Member State political élites. It operates as a layer of governance for Europe that is driven by motives that are distinct from, though certainly influenced by, those dear to individual Member States. To this extent the system is *not only* intergovernmental *but also* quasi-federal.

Questions about political accountability and institutional development demand the attention of any student with an interest in the European Union. If the institutions of the Union are to develop autonomous policy-making competence, it is necessary to provide the appropriate democratic safeguards. The evolution of the Union is increasingly characterized by controversial debates about how best to subject the institutions to political and legal control. It is impossible for this book to explore these issues in detail. The next extract covers some specific points which will not yet be familiar, but the themes which it introduces are already valuable. It depicts the Community in the wake of subjection to its first major process of formal Treaty revision. This was effected by the *Single European Act*, which entered into force in 1987, and which took as a major objective the renovation of the institutional and constitutional system in order to improve its capacity to deliver the political objective of completing the internal market by the end of 1992.

R. Dehousse, '1992 and Beyond: the Institutional Dimension of the
Internal Market Programme'
[1989/1] LIEI 109, 133–36

(Footnotes omitted.)

The evolution of the Community in the last few years teaches us a series of lessons on what might be called the politics of institutional reform. The first conclusion to be drawn from this experience is that institutional reform is easier to arrive at when it is not pursued for its own sake, but emerges as a logical implication of other political choices. Once the general idea of completing the internal market by 1992 had been accepted, it proved possible to convince even the most reluctant Member States that a shift towards more majority voting was necessary. Had the objective itself not met with consensus, the change would not have been possible. The same logic is apparent in the Single Act's provisions on economic and social cohesion, on research and technological development or on the environment. In all these sectors, unanimous agreement is needed in order to define the objectives to be pursued at Community level; it is only at a second stage that resort to majority voting can be envisaged. The rationale of all these provisions is the same: when a decision of principle is to be taken, Member States must be able to preserve what they regard as their essential interests but, precisely because they have been given this guarantee, no vital interest to be harmed at the implementation stage; the 'Community interest' – and in particular the necessity of an efficient decision-making system – can therefore be given precedence.

Thus, most of the developments which have taken place in these years find their origin in the Commission's capacity to capitalise on the political pressures exerted by the Parliament and to define a 'new frontier' which would be acceptable to all Member States. But the way in which the institutional reform was accomplished also deserves attention. The main feature of the process was certainly its piecemeal character, which is often the case with compromises achieved in decentralised systems. As is known, the Single European Act was not the result of an inspired exercise in constitution-making, but the product of strenuous international negotiation. This cumbersome process had a direct incidence on the final result, which reflects the various aspirations and fears of more or less all Member States. In a typical *quid pro quo* exercise, France and Germany secured the adoption of provisions on political cooperation, and the backward countries a general commitment in favour of the reinforcement of economic and social cohesion within the Community, while several countries managed to limit the Community's capacity to act autonomously as far as the environment is concerned. Several of the institutional problems mentioned above are linked to the complexity of the structure which eventually emerged. The lengthy discussions on the subject of legal basis offer good examples of difficulties connected with the ambiguity of the compromises made at the time of drafting the Single Act.

With the White Paper on the internal market, questions which were previously considered as essentially technical gained the status of major political objectives. This change was paralleled by an evolution in the decision-making process: the creation of an internal market Council, with its induced effects at national level, has made it easier to coordinate national and Community action in this sphere. The introduction of majority voting has had a similar effect. Even if it is not systematically used, the possibility of a vote reinforces the weight of political decision-makers over that of specialised departments, which are to a large extent deprived of the veto right they had in the past.

These changes account for the relatively positive results reached so far. The Commission has now presented most of the proposals envisaged in the White Paper; approximately one third of them have been adopted so far, which certainly represents no meagre achievement. However, these figures should not generate an excessive optimism, for the most delicate matters – tax harmonisation, the free movement of persons, and the social dimension of the internal market – remain to be dealt with. It is therefore not unreasonable to think that the pace of implementation of the White Paper programme will slow down in coming months. Much will certainly depend on the Commission's capacity to forge the coalitions which are needed for the adoption of its proposals, and to transpose into operational terms the choices made in the White Paper. It is one thing to make a conceptual distinction between what is essential and what is not, and quite another to draw a clear line between the two in different sectors.

In spite of all the difficulties which can be foreseen, it is clear that the Community has now embarked on an era of dynamism which few expected a couple of years ago. Part of this dynamism finds its origin in external factors like the economic growth experienced in recent years; but it is equally clear that the momentum generated by the White Paper would not have been possible without its healthy institutional pragmatism. Not only did this approach make possible advances generally regarded as beyond reach not so long ago; but it might lead to even further-reaching results. For whether it is achieved by 1992 or only later, completion of the internal market could well generate its own dynamic. It has, for instance, often been argued that the liberalisation of capital movements in a Community with stable exchange rates will make it more difficult for Member States to pursue autonomous macro-economic policies. If at some stage two thirds of the economic and social legislation will have to be adopted at the Community level, as President Delors recently hinted, Community citizens and interest groups might press for a stronger voice in the decision-making process. At the same time, Member States might also realise that more systematic resort to voting, or a stronger involvement of Parliament in the legislative process, do not necessarily mean unbearable threats to their national interests . . .

NOTE

Even before the deadline for the completion of the internal market, the end of 1992, both the dynamism and the taste for ambiguous compromises noted by Dehousse in this extract were redeployed. In December 1991 agreement was reached at Maastricht on the next step forward – the Treaty on European Union. The Treaty was signed at Maastricht on 7 February 1992. However, only on 1 November 1993 did the Treaty finally come into force following hard-fought campaigns surrounding the ratification process in several Member States. The Danish people voted narrowly against ratification in a referendum in 1992 before voting in favour by a slightly larger margin in a second referendum in 1993. The British government chose not to hold a referendum, but John Major's government secured Parliamentary approval only by a slim majority amid turbulent Parliamentary scenes in summer 1993. Germany was the last of the 12 Member States to ratify and could do so only after its Constitutional Court had ruled in October 1993 that ratification was not incompatible with the German Constitution ([1994] 1 CMLR 57: see further Chapter 20, p.686 below).

The basic structure instituted by the Maastricht Treaty on European Union is best presented in diagrammatic form.

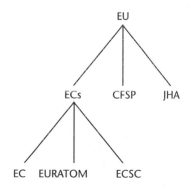

The Treaty on European Union declared that 'The Union shall be founded on the European Communities'. Be that as it may, the Union structure fashioned at Maastricht is built on three pillars and the European Communities are only one of those three pillars. Two of the pillars, those relating to a Common Foreign and Security Policy (the 'second pillar') and Cooperation in the Fields of Justice and Home Affairs (the 'third pillar'), exist outside the traditional, developed EC structure and are much more overtly intergovernmental in nature. Meanwhile, the three European Communities remained in existence as components of what is commonly termed the European Community pillar, or the 'first pillar'. So there is an EC – but it is not co-terminous with the EU. It is a part of the EU. In fact, the most important of the three Communities, the EEC, was formally renamed the EC by the Maastricht Treaty. It was also amended in a number of more substantial respects, such as the inclusion of new Titles enhancing the Community's competences, the creation of the status of Citizenship of the Union, and adjustments to the legislative procedure which enhance the position of the Parliament. Perhaps the centrepiece of the Treaty is the insertion into the EC Treaty of detailed provisions designed to lead to Economic and Monetary Union. These provisions carry immense constitutional significance. The Treaty timetable was adhered to and the third stage of economic and monetary union was launched on 1 January 1999, when 11 Member States (all save Denmark, Greece, Sweden, and the UK) adopted the euro as their common currency. Euro banknotes and coins have circulated validly since 1 January 2002. EMU is further discussed, albeit briefly, at p.317 below.

There is a disjointed facade to the European Union. The nature of each of the three pillars is different. The Council seems to be the only institution which is in any significant sense an institution of the whole Union. In November 1993, it accordingly chose to rename itself the Council of the European Union. The Commission, Parliament, and Court remain institutions whose principal role is within the European Community pillar. The impression of a disjointed structure is heightened when one appreciates that even within the EC there are emerging tendencies towards fragmentation. Denmark and the United Kingdom, most prominently, were permitted certain 'opt-outs' from EC policies (see p.668 below on Social Policy). A flavour of the debate at the time can be acquired from Deirdre Curtin's famous expressions of concern about the growth of a 'Europe of Bits and Pieces' (Curtin, D., 'The Constitutional Structure of the Union: a Europe of Bits and Pieces' (1993) 30 CML Rev 17). The picture was complicated yet further by the coming into existence of the European Economic Area at the start of 1994, which extended a mass of EC rules relevant to free trade into the wider area of the majority of the European Free Trade Association States, Austria, Finland, Iceland, Norway, and Sweden (but not Switzerland or Liechtenstein). The EEA structure established further institutions: the EEA Council, Joint Committee, Joint Parliamentary Committee, and Consultative Committee. The accession of Austria, Finland, and Sweden to the Union at the start of 1995 greatly reduced the practical importance of the EEA, while swelling the EU to a membership of 15.

It has been astutely commented that 'the success of the internal market programme lay in its apparent lack of ambition' (Dehousse, Joerges, Majone, Snyder (eds), 'Europe after 1992: New Regulatory Strategies', EUI Working Paper Law 92/31, Florence). In sharp contrast, as the European Union project unfolds, what is increasingly apparent is the breadth of the ambition. How this will affect the prospects for success dominates the European agenda.

■ QUESTION

'Since EU matters will be dealt with by the same people, sitting in the same rooms . . . as EC matters, it is hard to imagine a sufficient justification for creating the charade of constitutional obscurity which is EU . . . It would have been perfectly possible to devise exceptional but constitutionally coherent Title V [second pillar] and Title VI [third pillar] systems within the EC system itself.' (P. Allott, Written Evidence to the House of Lords Scrutiny of the Intergovernmental Pillars of the European Union (1992–93) HL 124.)

Discuss.

NOTE
The process of Treaty revision continues. An intergovernmental conference opened in Turin in March 1996 and was concluded at Amsterdam in June 1997, where the Treaty of Amsterdam was agreed. It was formally signed in October 1997. The Treaty of Amsterdam secured ratification according to domestic constitutional procedures in the 15 Member States while attracting noticeably less opposition than the Maastricht Treaty and it duly entered into force on 1 May 1999. The Amsterdam changes to the Treaties were incremental. They did not disturb the basic existence of the three-pillar structure of the Union.

Already post-Maastricht, the legal structure of the Union, understood in formal terms, was not one-dimensional. There is EC law, which is part of EU law. There is also 'non-EC EU law', emerging from the other two pillars of the Union. What emerges from the traditional architecture of the EC – from the EC Treaty itself, and from the activity of the Council, Commission, and Parliament, all of which is supervised by the Courts – is called EC law in this book. It is submitted that completely to replace the label 'EC law' with 'EU law' is to misrepresent the divided and peculiar reality of the three-pillar EU. However, such scrupulousness may eventually have to be set aside. As the practice of the EU evolved post-Maastricht it was increasingly possible to make a case in favour of fusion based on legal analysis and on observation of practice. The Amsterdam Treaty added velocity to this trend (see A. Von Bogdandy, 'The legal case for unity: the EU as a single organisation with a single legal system' (1999) 36 CML Rev 887; B. De Witte, 'The Pillar Structure and the Nature of the European Union: Greek Temple or French Gothic Cathedral?' in T. Heukels, N. Blokker, and M. Brus, *The European Union after Amsterdam* (Dordrecht: Kluwer Law International, 1998)).

In principle, the EU after Amsterdam maintains the three-pillar structure of the Union presented in diagrammatic form at p.9 above. However, the Amsterdam Treaty moved material between the pillars. Of greatest significance is the transfer of material relevant to the free movement of people within the Union from the third pillar to the first pillar, the EC. A new Title is inserted into the EC Treaty on 'Visas, asylum, immigration and other policies related to free movement of persons' which is dedicated to the progressive establishment of 'an area of freedom, security and justice'. This is Title IV and comprises Articles 61–69 EC. The Title is built around a five-year timetable for dismantling internal borders, although special provision is made in Protocols to the Treaty for Denmark, the United Kingdom, and Ireland; see further p.479 below. This Title in the EC Treaty is home to modified versions of material that had been allocated to the 'third pillar' by the Maastricht Treaty on European Union. So the first pillar, the EC, gained ground at the expense of the third, formerly dealing with Justice and Home Affairs but now re-worked and re-styled *Provisions on Police and Judicial Co-operation in Criminal Matters*. This suggests that Amsterdam saw a triumph of EC institutional and constitutional method over the species of intergovernmentalism found in the non-EC EU. However, that perspective should be tempered by awareness that the new Title, although part of the EC Treaty, is marked by some aspects which are alien to the EC system. As part of the package deal according to which these apparent additions to the scope of *communautaire* method were made, aspects of 'non-EC EU' method are now absorbed into the EC pillar, most notably with regard to the role of the Court (p.482 below) while, conversely, the third pillar is itself endowed with characteristics of a type more familiar to the EC pillar (for example, Article 35 EU confers an enhanced role for the European Court, largely shut out of the third pillar by the Maastricht Treaty).

So there are clear signs of a move towards a unified 'EU legal order' involving a rapprochement between the EC and the non-EC EU, which for Advocate-General Fennelly, writing in his personal capacity, represents 'the most positive general aspect of the Amsterdam Treaty' ('Preserving the Legal Coherence within the new Treaty' (1998) 5 MJ 185). But this process of rapprochement is not yet complete. And, in fact, there are counter trends towards fragmentation, because, as will be seen in this book, legal sub-systems of an increasingly distinct nature govern matters such as the law of persons (p.478), economic and monetary union (p.317), and, broader still, the Amsterdam innovation of 'closer cooperation' involving enhanced activity in common agreed by most but not all Member States (p.672).

As is true of every process of Treaty revision, the Amsterdam changes mean that there is EU law 'pre-Amsterdam' and there is EU law 'post-Amsterdam', and this must be taken into account when reading older legislative materials and judicial pronouncements. But the pre-Amsterdam legal world is also numerically distinct from the post-Amsterdam. The Amsterdam Treaty's most immediately visible feature was the re-numbering from start to finish of the whole EC Treaty and of the EU Treaty (pursuant to Article 12 of the Treaty of Amsterdam). Both Treaties now run from Article 1 upwards (to Article 314 in the case of the EC Treaty; Article 53 in the EU Treaty). This cleans out the unwieldy insertions made by the Single European Act and the Maastricht Treaty that littered the EC Treaty with Articles denoted as numbers-plus-letters (e.g., Articles 3b, 100a); and it eliminates entirely the lettering system used in the TEU (which in turn makes it now vital to be clear whether one is referring to the EC Treaty or to the TEU since both use numbers). The obvious disadvantage of this spring-clean lies in the need to become accustomed to the replacement of familiar numbers for Articles of the Treaty with new numbers. Article 30 EC became Article 28 EC; Article 177 EC, Article 234 EC, and so on. This change will always have to be borne in mind when reading pre-Amsterdam texts, including legislation and Court judgments, and in fact the EU lawyer will need to become adept at this form of 'currency conversion'. Page xlvii of this book contains the table of equivalence between the previous and the new numbering which is annexed to the Amsterdam Treaty, and the reader will find frequent resort to that table invaluable while he or she is making the necessary mental adjustments. Moreover (see Preface, p.xii above), references to the numerical changes are made in introducing key Treaty provisions throughout the book. The Court's own approach to the citation of Treaty articles is set out at p.lvii above, and this will be adhered to in this book.

FURTHER READING ON THE AMSTERDAM TREATY

Special Issue, 'The European Union and the Treaty of Amsterdam', (1999) 22 *Fordham International Law Journal*.

Favret, B., 'Le Traité d'Amsterdam: une revision à minima de la Charte constitutionnelle de l'Union européenne' (1997) 33 CDE 555.

Heukels, T., Blokker, N., and Brus, M., *The European Union after Amsterdam* (Dordrecht: Kluwer Law International, 1998).

Moravscik, A., and Nicolaides, K., 'Explaining the Treaty of Amsterdam' (1999) 37 JCMS 59.

O'Keeffe, D. and Twomey, P., 'Legal Issues of the Amsterdam Treaty' (Oxford: Hart Publishing, 1999 – a collection of 23 essays).

Pernice, I., 'Multilevel Constitutionalism and the Treaty of Amsterdam: European Constitution-Making Revisited?' (1999) 36 CML Rev 703.

Piris, J.-C., 'Does the European Union have a Constitution? Does It Need One?' (1999) 24 EL Rev 557.

Michel Petite, The Treaty of Amsterdam
(1998), published as a Harvard Jean Monnet Chair Working Paper, 2/98
available at http://www.law.harvard.edu/Programs/JeanMonnet

The Amsterdam Treaty is by no means the last word on European integration. Like its predecessors it marks a further stage in the process. However one views it, it probably represents the most that the Member States were prepared to agree among themselves at a given moment.
  . . . Two simple remarks suggest cause for both humility and perseverance:

— firstly, all of the delegations asserted their commitment to maintaining the institutional balance (yet this balance is constantly shifting, as exemplified by the increased role of the European Parliament); this commitment means that everyone wants to build on the foundations of the achievements of forty years of European integration – and will continue to do so for the foreseeable future. There will be no *tabula rasa* on which radically new institutional formulas will be rebuilt;
— secondly, there is no magic formula that can confound the mathematics: the organisation will inevitably be more difficult for a group of 21, 26 or 30 than one of 6 or even 15. Enlargement has certain inherent consequences.

What this amounts to is that the reforms to be undertaken in response to the demands of enlargement cannot be achieved by new constitutional formulas so much as by a less headline-grabbing series of changes to the way our institutions operate. Most of these reforms are a question of fine-tuning, and many rightfully belong in the internal rules of procedure rather than in the Treaty itself.

NOTE
For good or ill (*cf* p.10 above), the Amsterdam Treaty seems bereft of any 'big idea'. For J. Weiler, finding 'no shared agenda and no mobilising force behind the exercise', this was 'an Intergovernmental Conference which should never have started'; and in the light of the complexity of the unresolved issues, 'it was, too, an Intergovernmental Conference which should never have ended'. The product was 'an inconclusive Treaty leaving all hard issues for tomorrow' ((1997) 3 ELJ, Editorial, 309, 310).

Tomorrow always comes, and unfinished business needed to be addressed. Some institutional and constitutional questions, relating most of all to Council voting and the composition of the Commission, were left unresolved by the Amsterdam Treaty. These had to be settled in order to re-shape the Union's institutional architecture in anticipation of the pressures imposed by enlargement into central and eastern Europe, which presents itself as the next great challenge for the European Union. A new intergovernmental conference opened in February 2000. It concluded in December 2000 at Nice, where a new amending Treaty was agreed. The broad purpose of the Nice Treaty is to perform surgery designed to improve the efficiency of the EU's institutions without delaying enlargement.

The Nice Treaty, like the Amsterdam Treaty before it, maintains the three-pillar structure of the Union, while making detailed adjustments to each of the pillars. The Nice Treaty too is essentially incremental in its impact. It was agreed in December 2000, but – like the Maastricht Treaty, but unlike the Amsterdam Treaty – it gathered a considerable amount of opposition when put to the test of domestic ratification. The people of Denmark had been the 'problem' in the Maastricht process; now it was the people of Ireland who asserted their right to choose in a referendum held in 2001. The Nice Treaty was rejected in a popular referendum. It was frankly difficult to identify any particular provision of the Nice Treaty to which the Irish objected. The Nice Treaty is largely concerned to make technical adjustments to the Union in order to make fit for enlargement into Central and Eastern Europe. It alters arcane matters such as voting rules in Council and the number of seats allocated to each State in the European Parliament. But the Nice Treaty's absence of defining features was perhaps precisely the point; the people of Ireland had little understanding of what they being asked to vote on, and a reading of the dismally dull and dry text of the Treaty would leave most citizens only vaguely aware that something important was afoot, but that they could not grasp exactly what. A patient campaign of information by the Irish government prepared the ground for a second referendum and in Autumn 2002 the Irish once again followed the example of the Danish approach to Maastricht and, second time round, voted 'yes'. Duly ratified by all 15 Member States, the Nice Treaty entered into force on 1 February 2003. The accession of the new Member States in Central and Eastern Europe is planned to proceed according to a timetable agreed at the December 2002 European Council in Copenhagen. Provided negotiations are satisfactorily concluded and treaties of accession duly agreed and ratified, ten more countries will join the Union from 1 May 2004: Cyprus, the Czech Republic, Estonia, Hungary, Latvia, Lithuania, Malta, Poland, Slovakia, and Slovenia. Progress will be tracked on this book's Companion Website.

FURTHER READING ON THE TREATY OF NICE

Bradley, K. StC., 'Institutional design in the Treaty of Nice' (2001) 38 CML Rev 1095.

Dashwood, A., 'The Constitution of the European Union After Nice: Law-making Procedures' (2001) 26 EL Rev 215.

Moberg, A., 'The Nice Treaty and Voting Rules in the Council' (2002) 40 JCMS 259.

Shaw, J., 'The Treaty of Nice: Legal and Constitutional Implications' (2001) 7 *European Public Law* 195.

Wouters, J., 'Institutional and Constitutional Challenges for the European Union – Some Reflections in the Light of the Treaty of Nice' (2001) 26 EL Rev 342.

Yatganas, X., 'The Treaty of Nice: The Sharing of Power and the Institutional Balance in the European Union – a Continental Perspective' (2001) 7 ELJ 242.

There is much discussion about the nature of the entity into which the European Union is evolving. Although not itself a State, the Community (and, to a lesser extent, the Union) possesses an institutional and constitutional sophistication which marks it out from normal intergovernmental associations. Moreover, the creature has developed not only through the formal process of periodic Treaty revision, but also (as will be traced in this book) through wide-ranging legislative action and through the remarkable activism of its Court. So the Community/Union may not be a State, but it displays some State-like features and it affects the nature of the States that are members of it. The concluding Chapter of this book will devote further attention to these broader questions, once the reader has acquired a fuller understanding of constitutional and substantive law. This Chapter is concerned only to trace the trajectory of the process. But Nice is likely to prove to be the last Treaty that respects the pattern for the European Union cautiously mapped at Maastricht. It is increasingly probable that the next stage of reform will eliminate the three pillars as constitutionally and institutionally distinct methods of law- and policy-making, and replace them with a single trunk. Most of all, the aspiration is to move away form the tortuous and largely hidden process of intergovernmental conferences as the breeding grounds of Treaty revision, and to establish a supplementary mechanism that will be more transparent and capable of encouraging deeper and wider participation by the peoples of Europe in the planning of their destinies. There is a strong political impetus to dispel the alienation of citizens from the project of European integration. It is to be made more comprehensible, in the (far from uncontroversial) expectation that this will make it more appealing. The European Union is to be made more *legitimate*.

From a formal perspective the legitimacy of the process of European integration is guaranteed by the requirement that Treaty revision be conducted with respect for the domestic constitutional arrangements of each Member State and with the support of all of them. The procedure is mapped out in Article 48 EU.

ARTICLE 48 EU

The government of any Member State or the Commission may submit to the Council proposals for the amendment of the Treaties on which the Union is founded.

If the Council, after consulting the European Parliament and, where appropriate, the Commission, delivers an opinion in favour of calling a conference of representatives of the governments of the Member States, the conference shall be convened by the President of the Council for the purpose of determining by common accord the amendments to be made to those Treaties. The European Central Bank shall also be consulted in the case of institutional changes in the monetary area.

The amendments shall enter into force after being ratified by all the Member States in accordance with their respective constitutional requirements.

NOTE
Some Member States are obliged to hold or choose to hold a referendum before proceeding to ratification. This caused awkwardness in the process of ratification of both the Maastricht Treaty (to which the Danes voted first 'no', and only subsequently 'yes') and the Nice Treaty (which generated a similar 'first no, then yes' pattern in Ireland). Other Member States prefer to confine discussion of ratification to Parliamentary processes. This is true of the UK, which has never held a referendum on ratification (although it did hold a referendum on the question of continued membership in 1975). But the key point is that from a formal perspective the Treaty can be revised, and the EU's powers extended, only provided each Member State agrees. The nature of the legal order as a creature of international law is most vividly demonstrated when intergovernmental conferences leading to Treaty revision take place pursuant to Article 48 EU.

But legitimacy has dimensions that stretch beyond the formal. Do the peoples of Europe treat the European Union as a legitimate source of authority? This is a matter of social observation, not a matter of formal legal authority The inter-governmental conference is on the one hand the means of conferring formal State approval on the shaping of the Union, but it is on the other hand a powerful statement to citizens that the Union is remote from their concerns, the plaything of political élites – that it is, in short, none of their business.

Efforts have been devoted to investing the Union with a greater degree of social legitimacy. It is to be brought closer to the citizen. Relevant devices include the creation of the status of Citizenship of the Union (Chapter 15) and the irresistible rise of the principle of subsidiarity (Chapter 20). And central to this quest is the EU Charter of Fundamental Rights. The European Council of December 2000 held in Nice did not simply agree the text of the Nice Treaty. At that meeting a Charter of Fundamental Rights of the European Union was signed and solemnly proclaimed by the Presidents of the European Parliament, the Council, and the Commission at the European Council meeting in Nice on 7 December 2000 [2000] OJ C364.

CHARTER OF FUNDAMENTAL RIGHTS OF THE EUROPEAN UNION

PREAMBLE

The peoples of Europe, in creating an ever closer union among them, are resolved to share a peaceful future based on common values.

Conscious of its spiritual and moral heritage, the Union is founded on the indivisible, universal values of human dignity, freedom, equality and solidarity; it is based on the principles of democracy and the rule of law. It places the individual at the heart of its activities, by establishing the citizenship of the Union and by creating an area of freedom, security and justice.

The Union contributes to the preservation and to the development of these common values while respecting the diversity of the cultures and traditions of the peoples of Europe as well as the national identities of the Member States and the organisation of their public authorities at national, regional and local levels; it seeks to promote balanced and sustainable development and ensures free movement of persons, goods, services and capital, and the freedom of establishment.

To this end, it is necessary to strengthen the protection of fundamental rights in the light of changes in society, social progress and scientific and technological developments by making those rights more visible in a Charter.

This Charter reaffirms, with due regard for the powers and tasks of the Community and the Union and the principle of subsidiarity, the rights as they result, in particular, from the cons-titutional traditions and international obligations common to the Member States, the Treaty on European Union, the Community Treaties, the European Convention for the Protection of Human Rights and Fundamental Freedoms, the Social Charters adopted by the Community and by the Council of Europe and the case law of the Court of Justice of the European Communities and of the European Court of Human Rights.

Enjoyment of these rights entails responsibilities and duties with regard to other persons, to the human community and to future generations.

The Union therefore recognises the rights, freedoms and principles set out hereafter.

CHAPTER I – DIGNITY

Article 1: Human dignity

Human dignity is inviolable. It must be respected and protected.

Article 2: Right to life

1. Everyone has the right to life.
   2. No one shall be condemned to the death penalty, or executed.

Article 3: Right to the integrity of the person

1. Everyone has the right to respect for his or her physical and mental integrity.
    2. In the fields of medicine and biology, the following must be respected in particular:
        - the free and informed consent of the person concerned, according to the procedures laid down by law,
        - the prohibition of eugenic practices, in particular those aiming at the selection of persons,
        - the prohibition on making the human body and its parts as such a source of financial gain,
        - the prohibition of the reproductive cloning of human beings.

Article 4: Prohibition of torture and inhuman or degrading treatment or punishment

No one shall be subjected to torture or to inhuman or degrading treatment or punishment.

Article 5: Prohibition of slavery and forced labour

1. No one shall be held in slavery or servitude.
    2. No one shall be required to perform forced or compulsory labour.
    3. Trafficking in human beings is prohibited.

CHAPTER II – FREEDOMS

Article 6: Right to liberty and security

Everyone has the right to liberty and security of person.

Article 7: Respect for private and family life

Everyone has the right to respect for his or her private and family life, home and communications.

Article 8: Protection of personal data

1. Everyone has the right to the protection of personal data concerning him or her.
    2. Such data must be processed fairly for specified purposes and on the basis of the consent of the person concerned or some other legitimate basis laid down by law. Everyone has the right of access to data which has been collected concerning him or her, and the right to have it rectified.
    3. Compliance with these rules shall be subject to control by an independent authority.

Article 9: Right to marry and right to found a family

The right to marry and the right to found a family shall be guaranteed in accordance with the national laws governing the exercise of these rights.

Article 10: Freedom of thought, conscience and religion

1. Everyone has the right to freedom of thought, conscience and religion. This right includes freedom to change religion or belief and freedom, either alone or in community with others and in public or in private, to manifest religion or belief, in worship, teaching, practice and observance.
    2. The right to conscientious objection is recognised, in accordance with the national laws governing the exercise of this right.

Article 11: Freedom of expression and information

1. Everyone has the right to freedom of expression. This right shall include freedom to hold opinions and to receive and impart information and ideas without interference by public authority and regardless of frontiers.
    2. The freedom and pluralism of the media shall be respected.

Article 12: Freedom of assembly and of association

1. Everyone has the right to freedom of peaceful assembly and to freedom of association at all levels, in particular in political, trade union and civic matters, which implies the right of everyone to form and to join trade unions for the protection of his or her interests.
    2. Political parties at Union level contribute to expressing the political will of the citizens of the Union.

Article 13: Freedom of the arts and sciences

The arts and scientific research shall be free of constraint. Academic freedom shall be respected.

Article 14: Right to education

1. Everyone has the right to education and to have access to vocational and continuing training.

2. This right includes the possibility to receive free compulsory education.

3. The freedom to found educational establishments with due respect for democratic principles and the right of parents to ensure the education and teaching of their children in conformity with their religious, philosophical and pedagogical convictions shall be respected, in accordance with the national laws governing the exercise of such freedom and right.

Article 15: Freedom to choose an occupation and right to engage in work

1. Everyone has the right to engage in work and to pursue a freely chosen or accepted occupation.

2. Every citizen of the Union has the freedom to seek employment, to work, to exercise the right of establishment and to provide services in any Member State.

3. Nationals of third countries who are authorised to work in the territories of the Member States are entitled to working conditions equivalent to those of citizens of the Union.

Article 16: Freedom to conduct a business

The freedom to conduct a business in accordance with Community law and national laws and practices is recognised.

Article 17: Right to property

1. Everyone has the right to own, use, dispose of and bequeath his or her lawfully acquired possessions. No one may be deprived of his or her possessions, except in the public interest and in the cases and under the conditions provided for by law, subject to fair compensation being paid in good time for their loss. The use of property may be regulated by law insofar as is necessary for the general interest.

2. Intellectual property shall be protected.

Article 18: Right to asylum

The right to asylum shall be guaranteed with due respect for the rules of the Geneva Convention of 28 July 1951 and the Protocol of 31 January 1967 relating to the status of refugees and in accordance with the Treaty establishing the European Community.

Article 19: Protection in the event of removal, expulsion or extradition

1. Collective expulsions are prohibited.

2. No one may be removed, expelled or extradited to a State where there is a serious risk that he or she would be subjected to the death penalty, torture or other inhuman or degrading treatment or punishment.

CHAPTER III – EQUALITY

Article 20: Equality before the law

Everyone is equal before the law.

Article 21: Non-discrimination

1. Any discrimination based on any ground such as sex, race, colour, ethnic or social origin, genetic features, language, religion or belief, political or any other opinion, membership of a national minority, property, birth, disability, age or sexual orientation shall be prohibited.

2. Within the scope of application of the Treaty establishing the European Community and of the Treaty on European Union, and without prejudice to the special provisions of those Treaties, any discrimination on grounds of nationality shall be prohibited.

Article 22: Cultural, religious and linguistic diversity

The Union shall respect cultural, religious and linguistic diversity.

Article 23: Equality between men and women

Equality between men and women must be ensured in all areas, including employment, work and pay. The principle of equality shall not prevent the maintenance or adoption of measures providing for specific advantages in favour of the under-represented sex.

Article 24: The rights of the child

1. Children shall have the right to such protection and care as is necessary for their well-being. They may express their views freely. Such views shall be taken into consideration on matters which concern them in accordance with their age and maturity.

   2. In all actions relating to children, whether taken by public authorities or private institutions, the child's best interests must be a primary consideration.

   3. Every child shall have the right to maintain on a regular basis a personal relationship and direct contact with both his or her parents, unless that is contrary to his or her interests.

Article 25: The rights of the elderly

The Union recognises and respects the rights of the elderly to lead a life of dignity and independence and to participate in social and cultural life.

Article 26: Integration of persons with disabilities

The Union recognises and respects the right of persons with disabilities to benefit from measures designed to ensure their independence, social and occupational integration and participation in the life of the community.

CHAPTER IV – SOLIDARITY

Article 27: Workers' right to information and consultation within the undertaking

Workers or their representatives must, at the appropriate levels, be guaranteed information and consultation in good time in the cases and under the conditions provided for by Community law and national laws and practices.

Article 28: Right of collective bargaining and action

Workers and employers, or their respective organisations, have, in accordance with Community law and national laws and practices, the right to negotiate and conclude collective agreements at the appropriate levels and, in cases of conflicts of interest, to take collective action to defend their interests, including strike action.

Article 29: Right of access to placement services

Everyone has the right of access to a free placement service.

Article 30: Protection in the event of unjustified dismissal

Every worker has the right to protection against unjustified dismissal, in accordance with Community law and national laws and practices.

Article 31: Fair and just working conditions

1. Every worker has the right to working conditions which respect his or her health, safety and dignity.

   2. Every worker has the right to limitation of maximum working hours, to daily and weekly rest periods and to an annual period of paid leave.

Article 32: Prohibition of child labour and protection of young people at work

The employment of children is prohibited. The minimum age of admission to employment may not be lower than the minimum school-leaving age, without prejudice to such rules as may be more favourable to young people and except for limited derogations. Young people admitted to work must have working conditions appropriate to their age and be protected against economic exploitation and any work likely to harm their safety, health or physical, mental, moral or social development or to interfere with their education.

Article 33: Family and professional life

1. The family shall enjoy legal, economic and social protection.

2. To reconcile family and professional life, everyone shall have the right to protection from dismissal for a reason connected with maternity and the right to paid maternity leave and to parental leave following the birth or adoption of a child.

Article 34: Social security and social assistance

1. The Union recognises and respects the entitlement to social security benefits and social services providing protection in cases such as maternity, illness, industrial accidents, dependency or old age, and in the case of loss of employment, in accordance with the procedures laid down by Community law and national laws and practices.

2. Everyone residing and moving legally within the European Union is entitled to social security benefits and social advantages in accordance with Community law and national laws and practices.

3. In order to combat social exclusion and poverty, the Union recognises and respects the right to social and housing assistance so as to ensure a decent existence for all those who lack sufficient resources, in accordance with the procedures laid down by Community law and national laws and practices.

Article 35: Health care

Everyone has the right of access to preventive health care and the right to benefit from medical treatment under the conditions established by national laws and practices. A high level of human health protection shall be ensured in the definition and implementation of all Union policies and activities.

Article 36: Access to services of general economic interest

The Union recognises and respects access to services of general economic interest as provided for in national laws and practices, in accordance with the Treaty establishing the European Community, in order to promote the social and territorial cohesion of the Union.

Article 37: Environmental protection

A high level of environmental protection and the improvement of the quality of the environment must be integrated into the policies of the Union and ensured in accordance with the principle of sustainable development.

Article 38: Consumer Protection

Union policies shall ensure a high level of consumer protection.

CHAPTER V – CITIZEN'S RIGHTS

Article 39: Right to vote and to stand as a candidate at elections to the European Parliament

1. Every citizen of the Union has the right to vote and to stand as a candidate at elections to the European Parliament in the Member State in which he or she resides, under the same conditions as nationals of that State.

2. Members of the European Parliament shall be elected by direct universal suffrage in a free and secret ballot.

Article 40: Right to vote and to stand as a candidate at municipal elections

Every citizen of the Union has the right to vote and to stand as a candidate at municipal elections in the Member State in which he or she resides under the same conditions as nationals of that State.

Article 41: Right to good administration

1. Every person has the right to have his or her affairs handled impartially, fairly and within a reasonable time by the institutions and bodies of the Union.

   2. This right includes:
   - the right of every person to be heard, before any individual measure which would affect him or her adversely is taken;
   - the right of every person to have access to his or her file, while respecting the legitimate interests of confidentiality and of professional and business secrecy;
   - the obligation of the administration to give reasons for its decisions.

   3. Every person has the right to have the Community make good any damage caused by its institutions or by its servants in the performance of their duties, in accordance with the general principles common to the laws of the Member States.

   4. Every person may write to the institutions of the Union in one of the languages of the Treaties and must have an answer in the same language.

Article 42: Right of access to documents

Any citizen of the Union, and any natural or legal person residing or having its registered office in a Member State, has a right of access to European Parliament, Council and Commission documents.

Article 43: Ombudsman

Any citizen of the Union and any natural or legal person residing or having its registered office in a Member State has the right to refer to the Ombudsman of the Union cases of maladministration in the activities of the Community institutions or bodies, with the exception of the Court of Justice and the Court of First Instance acting in their judicial role.

Article 44: Right to petition

Any citizen of the Union and any natural or legal person residing or having its registered office in a Member State has the right to petition the European Parliament.

Article 45: Freedom of movement and of residence

1. Every citizen of the Union has the right to move and reside freely within the territory of the Member States.

   2. Freedom of movement and residence may be granted, in accordance with the Treaty establishing the European Community, to nationals of third countries legally resident in the territory of a Member State.

Article 46: Diplomatic and consular protection

Every citizen of the Union shall, in the territory of a third country in which the Member State of which he or she is a national is not represented, be entitled to protection by the diplomatic or consular authorities of any Member State, on the same conditions as the nationals of that Member State.

CHAPTER VI – JUSTICE

Article 47: Right to an effective remedy and to a fair trial

Everyone whose rights and freedoms guaranteed by the law of the Union are violated has the right to an effective remedy before a tribunal in compliance with the conditions laid down in this Article. Everyone is entitled to a fair and public hearing within a reasonable time by an independent and impartial tribunal previously established by law. Everyone shall have the possibility of being advised, defended and represented.

Legal aid shall be made available to those who lack sufficient resources insofar as such aid is necessary to ensure effective access to justice.

Article 48: Presumption of innocence and right of defence

1. Everyone who has been charged shall be presumed innocent until proved guilty according to law.

2. Respect for the rights of the defence of anyone who has been charged shall be guaranteed.

Article 49: Principles of legality and proportionality of criminal offences and penalties

1. No one shall be held guilty of any criminal offence on account of any act or omission which did not constitute a criminal offence under national law or international law at the time when it was committed. Nor shall a heavier penalty be imposed than that which was applicable at the time the criminal offence was committed. If, subsequent to the commission of a criminal offence, the law provides for a lighter penalty, that penalty shall be applicable.

2. This Article shall not prejudice the trial and punishment of any person for any act or omission which, at the time when it was committed, was criminal according to the general principles recognised by the community of nations.

3. The severity of penalties must not be disproportionate to the criminal offence.

Article 50: Right not to be tried or punished twice in criminal proceedings for the same criminal offence

No one shall be liable to be tried or punished again in criminal proceedings for an offence for which he or she has already been finally acquitted or convicted within the Union in accordance with the law.

CHAPTER VII – GENERAL PROVISIONS

Article 51: Scope

1. The provisions of this Charter are addressed to the institutions and bodies of the Union with due regard for the principle of subsidiarity and to the Member States only when they are implementing Union law. They shall therefore respect the rights, observe the principles and promote the application thereof in accordance with their respective powers.

2. This Charter does not establish any new power or task for the Community or the Union, or modify powers and tasks defined by the Treaties.

Article 52: Scope of guaranteed rights

1. Any limitation on the exercise of the rights and freedoms recognised by this Charter must be provided for by law and respect the essence of those rights and freedoms. Subject to the principle of proportionality, limitations may be made only if they are necessary and genuinely meet objectives of general interest recognised by the Union or the need to protect the rights and freedoms of others.

2. Rights recognised by this Charter which are based on the Community Treaties or the Treaty on European Union shall be exercised under the conditions and within the limits defined by those Treaties.

3. Insofar as this Charter contains rights which correspond to rights guaranteed by the Convention for the Protection of Human Rights and Fundamental Freedoms, the meaning and scope of those rights shall be the same as those laid down by the said Convention. This provision shall not prevent Union law providing more extensive protection.

Article 53: Level of protection

Nothing in this Charter shall be interpreted as restricting or adversely affecting human rights and fundamental freedoms as recognised, in their respective fields of application, by Union law and international law and by international agreements to which the Union, the Community or all the Member States are party, including the European Convention for the Protection of Human Rights and Fundamental Freedoms, and by the Member States' constitutions.

Article 54: Prohibition of abuse of rights

Nothing in this Charter shall be interpreted as implying any right to engage in any activity or to perform any act aimed at the destruction of any of the rights and freedoms recognised in this Charter or at their limitation to a greater extent than is provided for herein.

NOTE

The Charter sounds clear echoes of *inter alia* the fundamental rights and freedoms recognised by the European Convention on Human Rights, the constitutional traditions of the Member States, the Council of Europe's Social Charter, and the Community Charter of Fundamental Social Rights of Workers. But it is a distinctive EU document. It suggests itself as a benchmark against which to judge the validity of the exercise of public power. It is also capable of being taken as a statement of the EU's concern to infuse a system largely focused on economic integration with concern to show respect for wider social and political values. The protection of fundamental rights in the EU does not begin with the Charter – see Chapter 2, p.78 below – but the Charter offers a more comprehensive statement of the nature and scope of fundamental rights than has been previously available. Accordingly the Charter will be the subject of regular cross-reference in this book, in particular in order to question whether it may be used to challenge orthodox *communautaire* assumptions.

At present the influence of the Charter is best summarized as currently weak yet potentially strong. It is weak in the sense that it is not legally binding. It is a solemn proclamation. It is intended that it will permeate the Union's institutional political culture but not that it should of itself provide a basis for judicial review. And the general provisions in Chapter VII, especially Article 51(2), demonstrate the absence of ambition to extend the formal reach of the law. But the Charter is (potentially) strong for what it may become. It is currently non-binding, but it carries with it a claim to a central role in any more ambitious constitutional re-shaping of the Union. After all it is not politically easy to resist the claims of a 'Charter of Fundamental Rights'.

■ QUESTION

'Good constitutions are short and enigmatic' (C. Engel, 'The European Charter of Fundamental Rights' (2001) 7 ELJ 151). Measured on this scale, how does the Charter of Fundamental Rights rate as a potential constitutional document? Is this anyway an appropriate scale?

The Charter represents a significant development in the evolution of the European Union not only because of its content and its likely future impact. The manner of its drafting is of itself remarkable – and groundbreaking.

The Cologne European Council of June 1999 resolved to establish a Charter of Fundamental Rights. The European Council meeting in Tampere (Finland) in October 1999 entrusted the drafting task to an *ad hoc* body called a 'Convention'. This was made up of representatives of the heads of State and government of the 15 Member States, a representative of the President of the European Commission, 16 members of the European Parliament and 30 members of Parliaments in the Member States. Representatives of the European Court and of the Council of Europe were invited to attend as observers, and input was sought from the applicant States. More generally, maximum transparency was sought in the drafting process, in order to allow input from a wide range of sources in society. This was a much more open process than the orthodox, and typically secretive, intergovernmental conference. The 'Convention' lacked formal legitimacy in the sense that it could not create binding rules. But its relatively open procedure was intended to confer on it a much greater degree of popular legitimacy.

The Convention met for the first time in December 1999 and succeeded in reaching a consensus on a draft Charter by early October 2000. The Presidents of the European Parliament, the Council, and the Commission signed and proclaimed the Charter on behalf of their institutions on 7 December 2000 in Nice. The text is set out above.

FURTHER READING ON THE CHARTER OF FUNDAMENTAL RIGHTS

Alonso Garcia R., 'The General Provisions of the Charter of Fundamental Rights of the European Union' (2002) 8 ELJ 492.

De Búrca, G., 'The Drafting of the European Union Charter of Fundamental Rights' (2001) 26 EL Rev 126.

De Witte, B., 'The Legal Status of the Charter: Vital Question or Non-Issue?' (2001) 8 ELJ 81.

Eeckhout, P., 'The EU Charter of Fundamental Rights and The Federal Question' (2002) 39 CML Rev 945.

Heringa, A.W. and Verhey, L., 'The EU Charter: Text and Structure' (2001) 8 MJ 11.

Jacobs, F., 'The EU Charter of Fundamental Rights', Ch. 16 in A. Arnull and D. Wincott, *Accountability and Legitimacy in the European Union* (Oxford: OUP, 2002).

Sadurski, W., 'Charter and Enlargement' (2002) 8 ELJ 340.

The process of European integration does not stand still. This is work-in-progress. The European Council meeting in Nice in December 2000 adopted a Declaration on the Future of the Union (Declaration 23) calling *inter alia* for further consideration of the status of the Charter of Fundamental Rights. But the agenda was broader.

DECLARATION ON THE FUTURE OF THE UNION
(adopted by the Conference at Nice)

1. Important reforms have been decided in Nice. The Conference welcomes the successful conclusion of the Conference of Representatives of the Governments of the Member States and commits the Member States to pursue the early ratification of the Treaty of Nice.

2. It agrees that the conclusion of the Conference of Representatives of the Governments of the Member States opens the way for enlargement of the European Union and underlines that, with ratification of the Treaty of Nice, the European Union will have completed the institutional changes necessary for the accession of new Member States.

3. Having thus opened the way to enlargement, the Conference calls for a deeper and wider debate about the future of the European Union. In 2001, the Swedish and Belgian Presidencies, in cooperation with the Commission and involving the European Parliament, will encourage wide-ranging discussions with all interested parties: representatives of national parliaments and all those reflecting public opinion, namely political, economic and university circles, representatives of civil society, etc. The candidate States will be associated with this process in ways to be defined.

4. Following a report to be drawn up for the European Council in Goteborg [Gothenburg] in June 2001, the European Council, at its meeting in Laeken/Brussels in December 2001, will agree on a declaration containing appropriate initiatives for the continuation of this process.

5. The process should address, inter alia, the following questions:
   — how to establish and monitor a more precise delimitation of powers between the European Union and the Member States, reflecting the principle of subsidiarity;

— the status of the Charter of Fundamental Rights of the European Union, proclaimed in Nice, in accordance with the conclusions of the European Council in Cologne;

— a simplification of the Treaties with a view to making them clearer and better understood without changing their meaning;

— the role of national parliaments in the European architecture.

6. Addressing the abovementioned issues, the Conference recognises the need to improve and to monitor the democratic legitimacy and transparency of the Union and its institutions, in order to bring them closer to the citizens of the Member States.

7. After these preparatory steps, the Conference agrees that a new Conference of the Representatives of the Governments of the Member States will be convened in 2004, to address the abovementioned items with a view to making corresponding changes to the Treaties.

8. The Conference of Member States shall not constitute any form of obstacle or pre-condition to the enlargement process. Moreover, those candidate States which have concluded accession negotiations with the Union will be invited to participate in the Conference. Those candidate States which have not concluded their accession negotiations will be invited as observers.

NOTE

As envisaged in paragraph 4 of this Declaration the European Council met in Laeken (Belgium) in December 2001 and agreed to convene a Convention on the 'Future of Europe'. This is designed to pave the way for the next Intergovernmental Conference, to be convened in 2004 (according to para 7 of this Declaration). The Laeken Declaration picks up the four matters to which specific attention is drawn in para 5 of this Declaration, but it goes much further. It attempts to set in motion a process of deliberation that will do justice to the grand aspirations contained in para 6. And the model of a 'Convention', distinct from intergovernmental ortho-doxy, was considered sufficiently to have proved its worth in the drafting of the Charter of Fundamental Rights to deserve redeployment in the search for a blueprint for the 'Future of Europe'.

THE LAEKEN DECLARATION

I. EUROPE AT A CROSSROADS

For centuries, peoples and states have taken up arms and waged war to win control of the European continent. The debilitating effects of two bloody wars and the weakening of Europe's position in the world brought a growing realisation that only peace and concerted action could make the dream of a strong, unified Europe come true. In order to banish once and for all the demons of the past, a start was made with a coal and steel community. Other economic activities, such as agriculture, were subsequently added in. A genuine single market was eventu-ally established for goods, persons, services and capital, and a single currency was added in 1999. On 1 January 2002 the euro is to become a day-to-day reality for 300 million European citizens.

The European Union has thus gradually come into being. In the beginning, it was more of an economic and technical collaboration. Twenty years ago, with the first direct elections to the European Parliament, the Community's democratic legitimacy, which until then had lain with the Council alone, was considerably strengthened. Over the last ten years, construction of a political union has begun and cooperation been established on social policy, employment, asylum, immi-gration, police, justice, foreign policy and a common security and defence policy.

The European Union is a success story. For over half a century now, Europe has been at peace. Along with North America and Japan, the Union forms one of the three most prosperous parts of the world. As a result of mutual solidarity and fair distribution of the benefits of economic development, moreover, the standard of living in the Union's weaker regions has increased enormously and they have made good much of the disadvantage they were at.

Fifty years on, however, the Union stands at a crossroads, a defining moment in its existence.

The unification of Europe is near. The Union is about to expand to bring in more than ten new Member States, predominantly Central and Eastern European, thereby finally closing one of the darkest chapters in European history: the Second World War and the ensuing artificial division of Europe. At long last, Europe is on its way to becoming one big family, without bloodshed, a real transformation clearly calling for a different approach from fifty years ago, when six countries first took the lead.

The democratic challenge facing Europe

At the same time, the Union faces twin challenges, one within and the other beyond its borders.

Within the Union, the European institutions must be brought closer to its citizens. Citizens undoubtedly support the Union's broad aims, but they do not always see a connection between those goals and the Union's everyday action. They want the European institutions to be less unwieldy and rigid and, above all, more efficient and open. Many also feel that the Union should involve itself more with their particular concerns, instead of intervening, in every detail, in matters by their nature better left to Member States' and regions' elected representatives. This is even perceived by some as a threat to their identity. More importantly, however, they feel that deals are all too often cut out of their sight and they want better democratic scrutiny.

Europe's new role in a globalised world

Beyond its borders, in turn, the European Union is confronted with a fast-changing, globalised world. Following the fall of the Berlin Wall, it looked briefly as though we would for a long while be living in a stable world order, free from conflict, founded upon human rights. Just a few years later, however, there is no such certainty. The eleventh of September has brought a rude awakening. The opposing forces have not gone away: religious fanaticism, ethnic nationalism, racism and terrorism are on the increase, and regional conflicts, poverty and underdevelopment still provide a constant seedbed for them.

What is Europe's role in this changed world? Does Europe not, now that is finally unified, have a leading role to play in a new world order, that of a power able both to play a stabilising role worldwide and to point the way ahead for many countries and peoples? Europe as the continent of humane values, the Magna Carta, the Bill of Rights, the French Revolution and the fall of the Berlin Wall; the continent of liberty, solidarity and above all diversity, meaning respect for others' languages, cultures and traditions. The European Union's one boundary is democracy and human rights. The Union is open only to countries which uphold basic values such as free elections, respect for minorities and respect for the rule of law.

Now that the Cold War is over and we are living in a globalised, yet also highly fragmented world, Europe needs to shoulder its responsibilities in the governance of globalisation. The role it has to play is that of a power resolutely doing battle against all violence, all terror and all fanaticism, but which also does not turn a blind eye to the world's heartrending injustices. In short, a power wanting to change the course of world affairs in such a way as to benefit not just the rich countries but also the poorest. A power seeking to set globalisation within a moral framework, in other words to anchor it in solidarity and sustainable development.

The expectations of Europe's citizens

The image of a democratic and globally engaged Europe admirably matches citizens' wishes. There have been frequent public calls for a greater EU role in justice and security, action against cross-border crime, control of migration flows and reception of asylum seekers and refugees from far-flung war zones. Citizens also want results in the fields of employment and combating poverty and social exclusion, as well as in the field of economic and social cohesion. They want a common approach on environmental pollution, climate change and food safety, in short, all transnational issues which they instinctively sense can only be tackled by working together. Just as they also want to see Europe more involved in foreign affairs, security and defence, in other words, greater and better coordinated action to deal with trouble spots in and around Europe and in the rest of the world.

At the same time, citizens also feel that the Union is behaving too bureaucratically in numerous other areas. In coordinating the economic, financial and fiscal environment, the basic issue should continue to be proper operation of the internal market and the single currency, without this jeopardising Member States' individuality. National and regional differences frequently stem from history or tradition. They can be enriching. In other words, what citizens understand by 'good governance' is opening up fresh opportunities, not imposing further red tape. What they expect is more results, better responses to practical issues and not a European superstate or European institutions inveigling their way into every nook and cranny of life.

In short, citizens are calling for a clear, open, effective, democratically controlled Community approach, developing a Europe which points the way ahead for the world. An approach that provides concrete results in terms of more jobs, better quality of life, less crime, decent education and better health care. There can be no doubt that this will require Europe to undergo renewal and reform.

II. CHALLENGES AND REFORMS IN A RENEWED UNION

The Union needs to become more democratic, more transparent and more efficient. It also has to resolve three basic challenges: how to bring citizens, and primarily the young, closer to the European design and the European institutions, how to organise politics and the European political area in an enlarged Union and how to develop the Union into a stabilising factor and a model in the new, multipolar world. In order to address them a number of specific questions need to be put.

A better division and definition of competence in the European Union

Citizens often hold expectations of the European Union that are not always fulfilled. And vice versa – they sometimes have the impression that the Union takes on too much in areas where its involvement is not always essential. Thus the important thing is to clarify, simplify and adjust the division of competence between the Union and the Member States in the light of the new challenges facing the Union. This can lead both to restoring tasks to the Member States and to assigning new missions to the Union, or to the extension of existing powers, while constantly bearing in mind the equality of the Member States and their mutual solidarity.

A first series of questions that needs to be put concerns how the division of competence can be made more transparent. Can we thus make a clearer distinction between three types of competence: the exclusive competence of the Union, the competence of the Member States and the shared competence of the Union and the Member States? At what level is competence exercised in the most efficient way? How is the principle of subsidiarity to be applied here? And should we not make it clear that any powers not assigned by the Treaties to the Union fall within the exclusive sphere of competence of the Member States? And what would be the consequences of this?

The next series of questions should aim, within this new framework and while respecting the 'acquis communautaire', to determine whether there needs to be any reorganisation of competence. How can citizens' expectations be taken as a guide here? What missions would this produce for the Union? And, vice versa, what tasks could better be left to the Member States? What amendments should be made to the Treaty on the various policies? How, for example, should a more coherent common foreign policy and defence policy be developed? Should the Petersberg tasks be updated? Do we want to adopt a more integrated approach to police and criminal law cooperation? How can economic-policy coordination be stepped up? How can we intensify cooperation in the field of social inclusion, the environment, health and food safety? But then, should not the day-to-day administration and implementation of the Union's policy be left more emphatically to the Member States and, where their constitutions so provide, to the regions? Should they not be provided with guarantees that their spheres of competence will not be affected?

Lastly, there is the question of how to ensure that a redefined division of competence does not lead to a creeping expansion of the competence of the Union or to encroachment upon the exclusive areas of competence of the Member States and, where there is provision for this, regions. How are we to ensure at the same time that the European dynamic does not come to a halt? In the future as well the Union must continue to be able to react to fresh challenges and developments and must be able to explore new policy areas. Should Articles 95 and 308 of the Treaty be reviewed for this purpose in the light of the 'acquis jurisprudentiel'?

Simplification of the Union's instruments

Who does what is not the only important question; the nature of the Union's action and what instruments it should use are equally important. Successive amendments to the Treaty have on each occasion resulted in a proliferation of instruments, and directives have gradually evolved towards more and more detailed legislation. The key question is therefore whether the Union's various instruments should not be better defined and whether their number should not be reduced.

In other words, should a distinction be introduced between legislative and executive measures? Should the number of legislative instruments be reduced: directly applicable rules, framework legislation and non-enforceable instruments (opinions, recommendations, open coordination)? Is it or is it not desirable to have more frequent recourse to framework legislation, which affords the Member States more room for manoeuvre in achieving policy objectives? For which areas of competence are open coordination and mutual recognition the most appropriate instruments? Is the principle of proportionality to remain the point of departure?

More democracy, transparency and efficiency in the European Union

The European Union derives its legitimacy from the democratic values it projects, the aims it pursues and the powers and instruments it possesses. However, the European project also derives its legitimacy from democratic, transparent and efficient institutions. The national parliaments also contribute towards the legitimacy of the European project. The declaration on the future of the Union, annexed to the Treaty of Nice, stressed the need to examine their role in European integration. More generally, the question arises as to what initiatives we can take to develop a European public area.

The first question is thus how we can increase the democratic legitimacy and transparency of the present institutions, a question which is valid for the three institutions.

How can the authority and efficiency of the European Commission be enhanced? How should the President of the Commission be appointed: by the European Council, by the European Parliament or should he be directly elected by the citizens? Should the role of the European Parliament be strengthened? Should we extend the right of co-decision or not? Should the way in which we elect the members of the European Parliament be reviewed? Should a European electoral constituency be created, or should constituencies continue to be determined nationally? Can the two systems be combined? Should the role of the Council be strengthened? Should the Council act in the same manner in its legislative and its executive capacities? With a view to greater transparency, should the meetings of the Council, at least in its legislative capacity, be public? Should citizens have more access to Council documents? How, finally, should the balance and reciprocal control between the institutions be ensured?

A second question, which also relates to democratic legitimacy, involves the role of national parliaments. Should they be represented in a new institution, alongside the Council and the European Parliament? Should they have a role in areas of European action in which the European Parliament has no competence? Should they focus on the division of competence between Union and Member States, for example through preliminary checking of compliance with the principle of subsidiarity?

The third question concerns how we can improve the efficiency of decision-making and the workings of the institutions in a Union of some thirty Member States. How could the Union set its objectives and priorities more effectively and ensure better implementation? Is there a need for more decisions by a qualified majority? How is the co-decision procedure between the Council and the European Parliament to be simplified and speeded up? What of the six-monthly rotation of the Presidency of the Union? What is the future role of the European Parliament? What of the future role and structure of the various Council formations? How should the coherence of European foreign policy be enhanced? How is synergy between the High Representative and the competent Commissioner to be reinforced? Should the external representation of the Union in international fora be extended further?

Towards a Constitution for European citizens

The European Union currently has four Treaties. The objectives, powers and policy instruments of the Union are currently spread across those Treaties. If we are to have greater transparency, simplification is essential.

Four sets of questions arise in this connection. The first concerns simplifying the existing Treaties without changing their content. Should the distinction between the Union and the Communities be reviewed? What of the division into three pillars?

Questions then arise as to the possible reorganisation of the Treaties. Should a distinction be made between a basic treaty and the other treaty provisions? Should this distinction involve separating the texts? Could this lead to a distinction between the amendment and ratification procedures for the basic treaty and for the other treaty provisions?

Thought would also have to be given to whether the Charter of Fundamental Rights should be included in the basic treaty and to whether the European Community should accede to the European Convention on Human Rights.

The question ultimately arises as to whether this simplification and reorganisation might not lead in the long run to the adoption of a constitutional text in the Union. What might the basic features of such a constitution be? The values which the Union cherishes, the fundamental rights and obligations of its citizens, the relationship between Member States in the Union?

III. CONVENING OF A CONVENTION ON THE FUTURE OF EUROPE

In order to pave the way for the next Intergovernmental Conference as broadly and openly as possible, the European Council has decided to convene a Convention composed of the main parties involved in the debate on the future of the Union. In the light of the foregoing, it will be the task of that Convention to consider the key issues arising for the Union's future development and try to identify the various possible responses.

The European Council has appointed Mr V. Giscard d'Estaing as Chairman of the Convention and Mr G. Amato and Mr J.L. Dehaene as Vice-Chairmen.

Composition

In addition to its Chairman and Vice-Chairmen, the Convention will be composed of 15 representatives of the Heads of State or government of the Member States (one from each Member State), 30 members of national parliaments (two from each Member State), 16 members of the European Parliament and two Commission representatives. The accession candidate countries will be fully involved in the Convention's proceedings. They will be represented in the same way as the current Member States (one government representative and two national parliament members) and will be able to take part in the proceedings without, however, being able to prevent any consensus which may emerge among the Member States.

The members of the Convention may only be replaced by alternate members if they are not present. The alternate members will be designated in the same way as full members.

The Praesidium of the Convention will be composed of the Convention Chairman and Vice-Chairmen and nine members drawn from the Convention (the representatives of all the governments holding the Council Presidency during the Convention, two national parliament representatives, two European Parliament representatives and two Commission representatives).

Three representatives of the Economic and Social Committee with three representatives of the European social partners; from the Committee of the Regions: six representatives (to be appointed by the Committee of the Regions from the regions, cities and regions with legislative powers), and the European Ombudsman will be invited to attend as observers. The Presidents of the Court of Justice and of the Court of Auditors may be invited by the Praesidium to address the Convention.

Length of proceedings

The Convention will hold its inaugural meeting on 1 March 2002, when it will appoint its Praesidium and adopt its rules of procedure. Proceedings will be completed after a year, that is to say in time for the Chairman of the Convention to present its outcome to the European Council.

Working methods

The Chairman will pave the way for the opening of the Convention's proceedings by drawing conclusions from the public debate. The Praesidium will serve to lend impetus and will provide the Convention with an initial working basis.

The Praesidium may consult Commission officials and experts of its choice on any technical aspect which it sees fit to look into. It may set up ad hoc working parties.

The Council will be kept informed of the progress of the Convention's proceedings. The Convention Chairman will give an oral progress report at each European Council meeting, thus enabling Heads of State or government to give their views at the same time.

The Convention will meet in Brussels. The Convention's discussions and all official documents will be in the public domain. The Convention will work in the Union's eleven working languages.

Final document

The Convention will consider the various issues. It will draw up a final document which may comprise either different options, indicating the degree of support which they received, or recommendations if consensus is achieved.

Together with the outcome of national debates on the future of the Union, the final document will provide a starting point for discussions in the Intergovernmental Conference, which will take the ultimate decisions.

Forum

In order for the debate to be broadly based and involve all citizens, a Forum will be opened for organisations representing civil society (the social partners, the business world, non-governmental organisations, academia, etc.). It will take the form of a structured network of organisations receiving regular information on the Convention's proceedings. Their contributions will serve as input into the debate. Such organisations may be heard or consulted on specific topics in accordance with arrangements to be established by the Praesidium.

Secretariat

The Praesidium will be assisted by a Convention Secretariat, to be provided by the General Secretariat of the Council, which may incorporate Commission and European Parliament experts.

NOTE

And the Convention was duly established. It held its inaugural session under the Chairmanship of Valery Giscard d'Estaing in February 2002. Its website is located at http://european-convention.eu.int/bienvenue.asp?lang=EN&Content=. The model of broader participation employed in the drafting of the Charter was maintained. Representatives of heads of State and government were joined by representatives of the Parliament and the Commisisson and of national Parliaments. Representatives from candidate accession countries were also included.

Eleven working groups were established to delve into the range of relevant material, and by early 2003 each had submitted a Final Report. These are available on the Convention's website. The 11 areas covered by the explorations of the working groups were I Subsidiarity; II Charter/European Convention on Human Rights; III Legal Personality; IV National Parliaments; V Complementary Competencies; VI Economic Governance; VII External Action; VIII Defence; IX Simplification; X Freedom, Security and Justice; XI Social Europe.

A *preliminary draft Constitutional Treaty* (CONV 369/02) was published as a focus for debate in October 2002. It was no more than a skeleton. Even the name was open for discussion: European Community *or* European Union *or* United States of Europe *or* United Europe. (A wager on the third of these alternatives is not recommended.) By the Spring of 2003 firmer proposals for draft Treaty Articles were being advanced, tranche by tranche. The intention was to present a complete draft by

June 2003. As a matter of law it is then for the orthodox process envisaged by Article 48 EU to set in motion the process of Treaty revision. An intergovernmental conference will be convened. As a matter of politics, it is envisaged – by some observers, at least – that if the Convention produces a text that is backed by most shades of opinion, it will be difficult for the heads of State and government of the Member States to resist the legitimacy of the agreed text. To this extent what emerges will be a text that is orthodox in its legal character – it will be a Treaty requiring ratification before it may enter into force – but which is intended to carry particularly profound constitutional implications in the shaping of a legitimate political order for Europe.

It is a full-time and only sporadically rewarding job to keep abreast of all the documentation that has cascaded across the Convention's website. *Que sera, que sera* – and the Companion Website to this book will provide up-dated summaries of which ideas for the future have been accepted into the mainstream and which have been discarded. In the meantime consult the Convention's own website at http://european-convention.eu.int/bienvenue.asp?lang=EN&Content=.

The last word which this book is able to offer before it goes to press is that the expectation of presentation in June 2003 of a complete text agreed at the Convention was fulfilled, but that the aspiration to produce a tightly-drawn harmonious whole that would be a strong candidate for acceptance without amendment appears to have been over optimistic. Instead the text submitted to the June 2003 European Council in Thessalonika by Giscard d'Estaing contains many imaginative and valuable contributions to meeting the aims set out in the Laeken Declaration, but is hardly likely to supply the last word in a process that will now move to the forum of an intergovernmental conference ('IGC') scheduled to open in the Autumn of 2003 and likely to agree a text some time in 2004. That agreed text – a Treaty which might also be labelled a constitution – will in turn require ratification by all Member States, including the new entrants in Central and Eastern Europe whose date of entry is set for 1 May 2004 (p. 14 above).

The June 2003 draft constitutional text is based on four Parts. The second Part contains the text of the Charter of Fundamental Rights (p.16 above); the third Part contains detailed treatment of substantive competences, policies, and the functioning of the Union (see p.491 below); and the fourth Part contains general and final provisions. The attention throughout the Convention has been focused on Part One. The June 2003 draft offers a division of Part One into Nine Titles. These comprise Definition and Objectives of the Union; Fundamental Rights and Citizenship; Competences and Actions; Institutions; Exercise of Competence; the Democratic Life of the Union; Finances; the Union and its Immediate Environment; and Membership. This, then, is designed to provide treatment of the core workings of the Union's system – and it is the *Union* that is at stake: the 'three pillar' structure will be abandoned. It is, of course, anything but surprising that a perfectly elegant text backed by untroubled unanimity has not emerged. The variety of interest groups involved could hardly be expected to reach accommodation without the toughest of (at times inelegant) bargaining. It seems probable that institutional questions will continue to provoke the most awkward wrangles and, despite the ambitions to take the process of Treaty revision out of the unedifying grip of late-night haggling by exhausted leaders at the close of intergovernmental conferences, it will be no surprise if the resolution of institutional questions and associated anxieties to secure adequate accountability is delayed until (in political terms) five minutes to midnight. The institutional structure of the EU, sketched below at pp.36–42, is designed to produce a system that all participants accept as, ultimately, generating more benefits from membership than costs. How to ensure that perception of 'better in than out' endures? Bigger States have tended to regard the Council and European Council as the habitat in which their preferences can be most effectively advanced; smaller States cherish the mediating role played by the Commission. And all the while periodic Treaty revision has increased the power of the Parliament. The aim is to improve the performance of all these institutions without causing damaging disturbance to the balance that has proved so successful since the 1950s. The reader is encouraged to track the debate, and this book's Companion Website will serve to depict the trajectory of a debate that, on current estimates, will generate the entry into force of a new Treaty in late 2004 or some time in 2005.

Be aware that much of the debate on such fast-moving issues is today conducted electronically, rather than in academic journals. Sites that deserve your attention for their topicality, although their intellectual interest is not confined to the Convention and its aftermath, include:

Robert Schumann Centre for Advanced Studies in the European University Institute, Florence: http://www.iue.it/RSCAS/Research/Institutions/.

Jurist EU Legal Education Network (Universidade Nova de Lisboa, Faculdade de Direito): http://www.fd.unl.pt/je/index.htm.

The Federal Trust: http://www.fedtrust.co.uk/projects.htm.

The Federal Union: http://www.federalunion.org.uk/.

One Europe or Several? The Dynamics of Change across Europe (programme supported by the Economic and Social Research Committee): http://www.one-europe.ac.uk/.

ConWEB: Constitutionalism Web-Papers (Manchester School of Law): http://www.les1.man.ac.uk/conweb/.

Jean Monnet Working Papers (Jean Monnet Center, NYU School of Law): http://www.jeanmonnetprogram.org/papers/index.html.

And do not neglect more conventional forms of publication:

Lenaerts, K. and Desomer, M., 'New Models of Constitution-making in Europe: the Quest for Legitimacy' (2002) 39 CML Rev 1217.

NOTE

For additional material and resources see the Companion Website at: www.oup.co.uk/best.textbooks/law/weatherill6e

2

The Sources of the Law

The three major sources of the law of the European Union are examined in this Chapter. Section 1 discusses the founding Treaties; Section 2 explains the nature and method of adoption of legislation; Section 3 examines the general legal principles which have been shaped by the Court of Justice of the European Communities. Another basis for making this three-fold classification is to view Section 1, the Treaties, as the product of the Member States, Section 2, legislation, as the product of the system's autonomous political institutions acting as a legislature, and Section 3, general principles, as the contribution of the judicial institution.

It is the law of the European Community – the first pillar – that is the principal focus of this Chapter. This is the most institutionally and constitutionally sophisticated species of law created within the European Union. It is moreover that which exerts the broadest functional influence. However, reference will be made, where appropriate, to law-making under pillars two and three of the Union (Common Foreign and Security Policy and Police and Judicial Cooperation in Criminal Matters respectively). The grip of 'intergovernmentalism' – the Member States, acting in Council and the European Council – is much firmer in pillars two and three of the Union than in the first pillar; the role of the Commission, Parliament, and of the Community judicature is correspondingly much less prominent. But none of these institutions is wholly excluded from the non-EC EU pillars. And the non-EC EU is capable of generating binding rules, albeit not according to the *communautaire* orthodoxy found in the first (EC) pillar. So it must not be neglected.

It is, however, that *communautaire* orthodoxy nurtured under the first pillar on which this Chapter concentrates. In *A Guide to European Community Law* Professor Mathijsen declares that 'the Community legal order grew and developed mainly at the hands of the Community judges' (p. 54). The Court's creativity will be introduced in Section 3 of this Chapter, but it also exerts an important influence over the sources in Sections 1 and 2 by virtue of its interpretative function. The activism of the judges will be observed throughout this book in many aspects of the Community's constitutional and institutional law. Two questions in particular will be addressed. First, to what extent is such judicial activism appropriate? This raises the general jurisprudential issue of the respective roles of courts and legislators. The second, more modern, more specifically European, question is the extent to which such judicial initiative is still forthcoming. Some observers have identified a more cautious, 'minimalist' approach by the European Court; see T. Koopmans (then a judge of the Court) (1986) 35 ICLQ 925 and *Further Reading* at the end of this Chapter.

SECTION 1: **THE TREATIES**

The Community has three founding Treaties. The Treaty of Paris came into force in 1952 and established the European Coal and Steel Community (ECSC). The two Treaties of Rome came into force in 1958 and established EURATOM, The European Atomic Energy Community, and the EEC, the European Economic Community. The six original parties were France, Germany, Luxembourg, Belgium, The Netherlands, and Italy. Since the Merger Treaty 1965, the three Communities have been administered on a day-to-day basis as one – hence the common label 'European Community'.

The first major formal Treaty revision which the original Treaties underwent was the Single European Act 1986 (SEA). This adjusted several aspects of the Community structure and brought about a modest extension in its competence. The SEA was chiefly motivated by the plan to complete the internal market of the Community by the end of 1992.

The Treaties share common principles. The two Treaties of Rome are closely analogous in their specific provisions. The Treaty of Paris contained certain distinct features, but the European Coal and Steel Community, unlike EURATOM and the EEC, was limited to a span of only 50 years and so in July 2002 it reached the end of its natural life and control of the coal and steel sectors was brought under the umbrella of the EC. The primary focus of this book is on the most important of the Communities – what was the EEC, becoming the EC, the 'European Community' proper, on the entry into force of the Maastricht Treaty on 1 November 2003.

The alteration in name – EEC to EC – represented just a small piece of the Maastricht Treaty reforms. Effective from 1 November 1993 that Treaty created a 'European Union'. The original Treaties from the 1950s remained in force under the European Union umbrella. The EC Treaty was amended significantly, most notably through the insertion of detailed provisions for the establishment of Economic and Monetary Union.

The Amsterdam Treaty, which entered into force on 1 May 1999 (p.11 above), retains the overall three-pillar structure of the Union, though it moves some matters from the Third Pillar into the First Pillar, the EC (see Chapter 15)). It also amends a substantial number of provisions of the EC Treaty. And most recently the Nice Treaty, which entered into force on 1 February 2003 (p.13 above), also respects the three-pillar structure of the Union, while amending a number of detailed provisions.

The creation of an integrated economy which transcends national frontiers is the most prominent of the tasks undertaken by this Treaty-based system. The substantive legal provisions in the EC Treaty which are examined in this book are primarily concerned to eliminate barriers to trade between Member States and to establish a common market. The constitutional principles too are shaped in accordance with this central objective. However, it is important to appreciate that, first, the European Community and now, more widely, the European Union are about more than economics. This is plain even from a superficial understanding of the tensions in post-war Europe from which the Communities emerged. It is wise to begin by reading the Preambles to the Treaties in order to appreciate that the Communities are based on a vision rather less tangible, but, to many, more inspiring, than Gross Domestic Product.

TREATY OF ROME ESTABLISHING THE EUROPEAN ECONOMIC COMMUNITY 1957, PREAMBLE

His Majesty The King of the Belgians, the President of the Federal Republic of Germany, the President of the French Republic, the President of the Italian Republic, Her Royal Highness the Grand Duchess of Luxembourg, Her Majesty The Queen of the Netherlands,

Determined to lay the foundations of an ever closer union among the peoples of Europe,

Resolved to ensure the economic and social progress of their countries by common action to eliminate the barriers which divide Europe,

Affirming as the essential objective of their efforts the constant improvement of the living and working conditions of their peoples,

Recognising that the removal of existing obstacles calls for concerted action in order to guarantee steady expansion, balanced trade and fair competition,

Anxious to strengthen the unity of their economies and to ensure their harmonious development by reducing the differences existing between the various regions and the backwardness of the less favoured regions,

Desiring to contribute, by means of a common commercial policy, to the progressive abolition of restrictions on international trade,

Intending to confirm the solidarity which binds Europe and the overseas countries and desiring to ensure the development of their prosperity, in accordance with the principles of the Charter of the United Nations,

Resolved by thus pooling their resources to preserve and strengthen peace and liberty, and calling upon the other peoples of Europe who share their ideal to join in their efforts,

Have decided to create a European Economic Community . . .

TREATY ON EUROPEAN UNION (POST-NICE) CONSOLIDATED VERSION [2002] OJ C325, PREAMBLE

[His Majesty the King of the Belgians, Her Majesty the Queen of Denmark, The President of the Federal Republic of Germany, the President of the Hellenic Republic, His Majesty the King of Spain, the President of the French Republic, the President of Ireland, the President of the Italian Republic, His Royal Highness the Grand Duke of Luxembourg, Her Majesty the Queen of the Netherlands, the Federal President of the Republic of Austria, the President of the Portuguese Republic, the President of the Republic of Finland, His Majesty the King of Sweden, Her Majesty the Queen of the United Kingdom of Great Britain and Northern Ireland]

Resolved to mark a new stage in the process of European integration undertaken with the establishment of the European Communities,

Recalling the historic importance of the ending of the division of the European continent and the need to create firm bases for the construction of the future Europe,

Confirming their attachment to the principles of liberty, democracy and respect for human rights and fundamental freedoms and of the rule of law,

Confirming their attachment to fundamental social rights as defined in the European Social Charter signed at Turin on 18 October 1961 and in the 1989 Community Charter of the Fundamental Social Rights of Workers,

Desiring to deepen the solidarity between their peoples while respecting their history, their culture and their traditions,

Desiring to enhance further the democratic and efficient functioning of the institutions so as to enable them better to carry out, within a single institutional framework, the tasks entrusted to them,

Resolved to achieve the strengthening and the convergence of their economies and to establish an economic and monetary union including, in accordance with the provisions of this Treaty, a single and stable currency,

Determined to promote economic and social progress for their peoples, taking into account the principle of sustainable development and within the context of the accomplishment of the internal market and of reinforced cohesion and environmental protection, and to implement policies ensuring that advances in economic integration are accompanied by parallel progress in other fields,

Resolved to establish a citizenship common to nationals of their countries,

Resolved to implement a common foreign and security policy including the progressive framing of a common defence policy, which might lead to a common defence in accordance with the provisions of Article 17, thereby reinforcing the European identity and its independence in order to promote peace, security and progress in Europe and in the world,

Resolved to facilitate the free movement of persons, while ensuring the safety and security of their peoples, by establishing an area of freedom, security and justice, in accordance with the provisions of this Treaty,

Resolved to continue the process of creating an ever closer union among the peoples of Europe, in which decisions are taken as closely as possible to the citizen in accordance with the principle of subsidiarity,

In view of further steps to be taken in order to advance European integration,

Have decided to establish a European Union . . .

NOTE
These sentiments must be taken to influence the more specific provisions of the Treaty which are examined in the course of this book.

The institutions are established by the Treaties, and in practice a great deal of the energy of the Union is contributed by the interplay of the institutions. The next extract provides an outline summary of the Community's institutional structure, focusing on the three main political institutions, the Council of the European Union, the European Commission, and the European Parliament.

Key Players in EU Legislation, available via http://www.europa.eu.int/eur-lex/en/about/pap/index.html

Key players in the EU legislative process

THE COUNCIL OF THE EUROPEAN UNION

Function and responsibilities

The Council – also referred to as the Council of Ministers – is the European Union's main decision-making institution and final legislative authority. The Council of the European Union, as an EU institution, should not be confused with the European Council – which brings together the Heads of State or Government of the Member States of the European Union and the President of the European Commission – or with the Council of Europe which is an international organisation.

Under the Treaty establishing the European Community, the main responsibilities of the Council are the following:

the Council is the Community's legislative body; for a wide range of Community issues, it exercises that legislative power in co-decision with the European Parliament;
the Council coordinates the general economic policies of the Member States;
the Council concludes, on behalf of the European Communities, international agreements (which

are negotiated by the Commission and require, in some cases, Parliament's consultation or assent) between the Communities and a State, a group of States or international organisations; the Council and the Parliament constitute the budgetary authority adopting the Community's budget.

Under the Treaty on European Union, the Council also:

takes the decisions necessary for defining and implementing the common foreign and security policy on the basis of general guidelines established by the European Council;
coordinates the activities of the Member States and adopts measures in the field of police and judicial cooperation in criminal matters.

The Council is a body with the characteristics of both a supranational and an intergovernmental organisation. This is reflected by the composition and Presidency of the Council, as well as the working procedures associated with the Council's activities.

The role of the Council in the decision-making and legislative process

The role of the Council as the main decision-making institution in Community activities is defined in terms of the three pillars set out in the Treaty on European Union (the Treaty of Maastricht).

The first pillar – covering a wide range of Community policies such as agriculture, transport, environment, energy, research and development – is designed and implemented according to a well-proven decision-making process which starts with a Commission proposal. Following detailed examination by experts and at the political level, the Council may either adopt the Commission proposal, amend it or ignore it. The Treaty of Maastricht strengthened the role of the European Parliament in this context by creating a co-decision procedure. As a consequence, a wide range of legislation (such as that pertaining to the single market, consumer affairs, trans-European networks, education and health) is adopted by both the Parliament and the Council. The 'social partners' and other interest groups are consulted via the Economic and Social Committee and local and regional authorities represented in the Committee of the Regions in a number of fields.

The Treaties lay down that, depending on the subject, the Council acts by a simple majority of its members, by a qualified majority or by unanimous decision. Where the Council acts by a qualified majority, the votes of each of its members are weighted. In the Community sphere, a large proportion of legislative decisions are taken by qualified majority. The policy areas in the first pillar which remain subject to unanimity include taxation, industry, culture, regional and social funds and the framework programme for research and technology development. For the other two pillars created by the Treaty on European Union, the Council is the decision-maker as well as the promoter of initiatives. On common foreign and security policy the Council takes the decisions necessary for defining and implementing this policy, on the basis of general guidelines specified by the European Council. It recommends common strategies to the European Council and implements them, particularly by deciding on joint actions and common positions. On police and judicial cooperation in criminal matters, the Council, at the initiative of a Member State or of the Commission, decides on common positions, framework decisions and decisions, and draws up conventions. Unanimity is the rule in both pillars, except for the implementation of a joint action, which can be decided by qualified majority.

Legislation

In the framework of the Treaty establishing the European Community, Community law, adopted by the Council – or by the Parliament and the Council in the framework of the co-decision procedure – may take the following forms:

Regulations
Directives
Decisions
Recommendations and opinions.

. . . The Council may also adopt conclusions of a political nature or other types of acts such as *Declarations* or *Resolutions*. Furthermore, the Council establishes requirements for exercising the implementing powers conferred on the Commission or reserved to the Council itself.

Community legislation as well as the Council's common positions forwarded to the European Parliament are published in the *Official Journal of the European Communities* in all the official EC languages.

THE EUROPEAN COMMISSION

Function and responsibilities

The European Commission, a political body, has various responsibilities and plays a major role in the European Union's policy-making process as EU laws are mainly enforced by Commission action. The Single European Act of 1986 as well as the Treaty on European Union and the Amsterdam Treaty confirmed and expanded the scope of the Union and the Commission's responsibility in additional areas. These include the environment, education, health, consumer affairs, the trans-European networks, R&D policy, culture, and economic and monetary union (EMU). In 1995 the composition of the Commission was adapted to account for the accession of Finland, Sweden and Austria. Commission proposals, actions and decisions are in various ways scrutinised, checked and judged by the other institutions (except the European Investment Bank). The Commission does not, however, take any decisions on EU policies and priorities, as this is the prerogative of the Council and, in some cases, also of the European Parliament.

The European Commission has three distinct functions:

initiator of proposals for legislation;
guardian of the Treaties;
manager and executor of EU policies and of international trade relations.

Legislative initiative

The Commission has a monopoly on the initiative in Community decision-making and drafts proposals for a decision by the two decision-making institutions: the Parliament and the Council. Thus, the legislative process begins with Commission proposals (for regulations or directives) which need to be in line with the Treaties and help to implement them. Normally, the Commission takes guidelines of national authorities into account. Commission proposals must encompass three core objectives:

identifying the European interest;
organising consultation as widely as necessary;
respecting the principle of subsidiarity.

Once the Commission has formally sent a proposal for legislation to the Council and the Parliament, the Union's law-making process is dependent on effective cooperation between three institutions – the Council, the Commission and the European Parliament. In agreement with the Commission, the Council can amend a proposal by a qualified majority (if the Commission does not agree, the change requires unanimity). The European Parliament shares the power of co-decision with the Council in most areas and has to be consulted in others. When revising its proposals, the Commission is required to take amendments of the Parliament into consideration. The Commission's initiative is limited with regard to recommendations or opinions. The Commission has also the budgetary initiative, drawing up the preliminary draft budget, which is put to the Council.

The Commission does not have an exclusive right of initiative in the two areas of intergovernmental cooperation covered by the Treaty on European Union: common foreign and security policy and cooperation on justice and home affairs. But it may submit a proposal and participates in discussions at all levels.

Guardian of the Treaties

A major responsibility of the Commission is to ensure that EU law is applied properly by the Member States. If it is considered that a Member State does not fulfil its obligations under the Treaty, the Commission, mainly through the 'failure to act' procedure, can initiate proceedings by requiring the State concerned to submit its observations. If these do not satisfy the Commission, a reasoned opinion is delivered, requiring the matter to be sorted out by a specific date. After that Commission action in this respect may also include legal proceedings before the Court of Justice. Under certain circumstances, the Commission can fine individuals, firms and organisations for infringing Treaty law.

Manager and negotiator

The Commission manages the Union's annual budget with responsibility for public expenditure and for administering the four major Community funds. Of these the European Agricultural Guidance and Guarantee Fund and the Structural Funds account for a considerable proportion of the budget and are designed to even out the economic disparities between the richer and the poorer areas.

The role of the European Commission is also characterised by its major executive responsibilities:

It delegates powers to make rules covering the details of Council legislation.
It can introduce preventive measures for a limited period to protect the Community market from dumping by third countries.
It enforces the Treaty's competition rules and regulates mergers and acquisitions above a certain size.

The EU's competitiveness in the world is enhanced by the Commission's role as negotiator of international trade and cooperation agreements with third countries, or groups of countries, which are then put to the Council for conclusion. In this context, the Commission has important responsibilities for aid and development programmes in third countries.

The role of the European Commission in the legislative process

Given its central position in the structure of the European Union, the Commission has special links with each of the other institutions. It works most intensively with the Council of Ministers and the European Parliament in drafting EU legislation and attends Council and Parliament meetings. In addition, the President of the Commission participates alongside the Heads of State and/or Government of the Member States at the twice-yearly meetings of the European Council. The President also participates as a representative of the Union as a whole at the annual economic summits of the Group of Seven (G-7) leading industrialised nations.

The Commission is answerable to the European Parliament, which has the power to dismiss it by a vote of censure or no confidence. The Commission attends all sessions of the European Parliament and must explain and justify its policies if so requested by members of the house. It must reply to written or oral questions put by MEPs.

The Commission's functions regularly involve the European Court of Justice, which is the final arbiter of European law. The Commission refers cases to the Court where directives or regulations are not being respected by governments or companies. The Court can also be consulted by the Member States and enterprises when, for instance, they want to appeal against fines imposed by the Commission.

The Commission's management of the EU budget is scrutinised by the Court of Auditors which is responsible for examining the legality and regularity of revenue and expenditure and for ensuring the sound financial management of the EU budget. The common goal of both institutions is to eliminate fraud and wastage. On the basis of the Court of Auditors' reports, it is the European Parliament which gives the Commission final discharge for the execution of the annual budget.

Finally, the Commission works closely with the Union's two consultative bodies, the Economic and

Social Committee and the Committee of the Regions, and consults them on most items of draft legislation.

THE EUROPEAN PARLIAMENT

Function and responsibilities

The European Parliament (EP) as an institution represents the 370 million citizens of the European Union. It is the largest multinational parliament in the world and forms the democratic basis of the Community. Since 1979 direct elections to the European Parliament are held every five years in all the EU Member States. The composition of the EP represents all the EU's major political currents. Today, the most important mandates of the EP are the following:

Legislative power: the EP considers the Commission's proposals and is associated with the Council in the legislative process by means of various procedures.

Budgetary powers: the EP shares budgetary powers with the Council in voting on the annual budget and overseeing its implementation.

Supervision of the executive: the EP has the power of control over the Union's activities through its confirmation of the appointment of the Commission, the right to censure the Commission and through the written and oral questions which can be put to the Commission and the Council.

These roles are reflected by the EP's working procedures.

The role of the European Parliament in the legislative process

Legislative power

Originally, the Treaty of Rome (1957) gave the European Parliament (EP) a consultative role only, whereas the Commission was entitled to propose and the Council of Ministers to decide legislation. Subsequent Treaties have extended the EP's influence from a purely advisory role to full involvement in the Community's legislative process. The EP is now empowered to amend and even adopt legislation. Thus, in a large number of areas the power of decision is shared by the Council and the EP. Depending on the individual legal basis, the EP takes part, to varying degrees, in the drafting of Community legislation. The different legal bases and associated procedures defined in the Treaties are as follows.

Co-decision procedure

According to the Amsterdam Treaty, the simplified co-decision procedure shares decision-making power equally between the EP and the Council. A legal act is adopted if Council and EP agree at first reading. If these institutions disagree, a 'conciliation committee' – made up of equal numbers of Members of Parliament and of the Council, with the Commission present – convenes, seeking a compromise on a text that the Council and Parliament can both subsequently endorse. If this conciliation does not result in an agreement, the Parliament can reject the proposal outright by an absolute majority. The co-decision procedure, which strengthens the role of the EP as co-legislator, applies to a wide range of issues (39 legal bases in the EC Treaty), such as the free movement of workers, consumer protection, education, culture, health and trans-European networks.

Consultation procedure

The consultation procedure requires an opinion from the EP before the Council can adopt a legislative proposal from the Commission. Neither the Commission nor the Council is obliged to accept the amendments listed in the opinion of the EP. Once the EP has given its opinion, the Council can adopt the proposal without amendments or adopt it in an amended form. However, the EP can refuse to give an opinion. The consultation procedure applies to agriculture (price review), taxation, competition, harmonisation of legislation not related to the single market, industrial policy, aspects of social and environmental policy (subject to unanimity), most aspects pertaining to the creation of an area of freedom, security and justice, and adoption of general rules and principles for comitology. For the purpose of the approximation of laws and regulations, this procedure also applies to a new framework-decision instrument created by the Amsterdam Treaty under the third pillar.

Cooperation procedure

The cooperation procedure allows the EP to improve proposed legislation by amendment. This requires an opinion and involves two readings by the EP, giving its members ample opportunity to review and amend the Commission's proposal as well as the Council's preliminary position. The Commission indicates which amendments it accepts before forwarding its proposal to the Council. This results in a 'common position' of the Council. At second reading the Council is obliged to take into account those amendments of the EP that were adopted by an absolute majority in so far as they have been taken on board by the Commission. The Treaty of Amsterdam has simplified the various legislative procedures by significantly extending the co-decision procedure, which is in practice almost replacing the cooperation procedure. As a consequence, the cooperation procedure applies to very few cases (two EMU provisions).

Assent procedure

The assent procedure applies to those legislative areas in which the Council acts by unanimous decision, limited, since the Amsterdam Treaty, to the organisation and objectives of the Structural and Cohesion Funds. The EP's assent is also required for important international agreements concluded between the Union and a non-member country or group of countries, such as the accession of new Member States and association agreements with third countries (absolute majority of the EP's total membership required).

The right of initiative

Since the Maastricht Treaty, the EP has a limited right of legislative initiative in that it has the possibility of asking the Commission to put forward a proposal.

Budgetary powers

As one of the two arms of the budgetary authority, the EP is involved in the budgetary procedure from the preparation stage, notably in laying down the general guidelines and the type of spending.

Supervision of the executive

Executive power in the EU is shared between the Commission and the Council of Ministers; their representatives appearing regularly before Parliament. The EP exercises overall political supervisory functions of the way policies are conducted by exercising democratic control over the executive.

Appeals to the Court of Justice

In cases of alleged violation of the Treaty by another institution, the EP has the right to institute proceedings before the Court of Justice. This may take the following forms:

the right to intervene, i.e., to support one of the parties to the proceedings, in cases before the Court;
in an action for 'failure to act' the Parliament may institute proceedings against an institution before the Court for violation of the Treaty;
for the purpose of protecting its prerogatives, the EP may bring an action to annul an act of another institution. The EP may be the defending party in an action against an act adopted under the co-decision procedure or when one of its acts is intended to produce legal effects *vis-à-vis* third parties.

The European Parliament and the EU citizens

Petitions

The EP defines itself as the guardian of European interests and the defender of citizens' rights. In this context, EU citizens have a right of petition – individually or as a group – to the EP.

The European Ombudsman

The EP also appoints an Ombudsman whose main responsibilities as defined in the EU Treaty are:

  to improve the protection of citizens in cases of maladministration;
  to strengthen the democratic accountability of the Community's institutions.

For this purpose, the Ombudsman is empowered to receive and investigate complaints raised by EU citizens regarding alleged maladministration in the activities of the institutions or bodies of the European Union. Natural or legal persons residing or having their registered office in a Member State may also consult the Ombudsman.

SECTION 2: **LEGISLATION**

A: **Legislation in the European Union**

The Treaties are *traite cadre*: frameworks which set out an overall design, but which require more specific amplification. That task belongs to the political and judicial institutions of the Union. The creative role of the Court of Justice of the European Communities (the Court) is considered below, but it is the other three principal institutions, the Council, the Commission, and the Parliament, which are responsible for the adoption of legislation. The roles of each institution varies according to the applicable legislative procedure. This was sketched above. Most fundamental of all, the procedures and instruments are quite different depending which of the three pillars of the Union is relevant to the subject-matter at hand.

   For the first pillar, the European Community, the available measures are set out in Article 249 EC:

ARTICLE 249 EC

In order to carry out their task and in accordance with the provisions of this Treaty, the European Parliament acting jointly with the Council, the Council and the Commission shall make regulations and issue directives, take decisions, make recommendations or deliver opinions.

   A regulation shall have general application. It shall be binding in its entirety and directly applicable in all Member States.

   A directive shall be binding, as to the result to be achieved, upon each Member State to which it is addressed, but shall leave to the national authorities the choice of form and methods.

   A decision shall be binding in its entirety upon those to whom it is addressed.

   Recommendations and opinions shall have no binding force.

NOTE
Article 249 EC was Article 189 pre-Amsterdam (p.12 above), but the text remains unaltered.

The Court has insisted that the different acts available under Article 249 are distinguishable on the basis of their nature, not their form. A label is not conclusive. In *International Fruit Company* v *Commission* (Cases 41–44/70) [1971] ECR 411, a measure was labelled a Regulation. The applicant company argued that in reality it was a set of Decisions. The Court's examination of the substance of the measure led it to agree with the applicant:

International Fruit Company v *Commission* (Cases 41–44/70)
[1971] ECR 411, Court of Justice of the European Communities

[21] Consequently, Article 1 of Regulation No 983/70 is not a provision of general application within the meaning of the second paragraph of Article 189 of the Treaty, but must be regarded as a conglomeration of individual decisions taken by the Commission under the guise of a regulation pursuant to Article 2(2) of Regulation No 459/70, each of which decisions affects the legal position of each author of an application for a licence.

NOTE
The primary significance which flows from classifying a measure under one Article 249 pigeonhole rather than another relates to the individual's opportunity to challenge its validity. Showing a measure to be a Decision, rather than a Regulation, greatly increases the likelihood that an applicant can persuade the Court to hold the legislation invalid. Judicial review of Community legislation will be examined in more depth in Chapter 8.

To return to the task of identifying the types of Community legislation which exist, the Court held in the next case that the list of measures in Article 249 is not exhaustive. Community institutions are capable of adopting other acts of legal significance.

Commission v *Council* (Case 22/70)
[1971] ECR 263, Court of Justice of the European Communities

The Member States acting together in Council had adopted a Resolution on 20 March 1970, in which they agreed to coordinate their approaches in negotiations for the conclusion of a European Road Transport Agreement (ERTA/AETR). The question of the Resolution's legal status arose when the Commission brought proceedings under Article 173 of the EC Treaty (now, after amendment, Article 230 EC), which provides for judicial review of Community acts. Was the Resolution an act? The Council observed that it did not fit into any of the categories in Article 189 of the EC Treaty (now Article 249 EC). The Court, however, was more concerned to identify whether the Resolution had legal effects. That possibility could not be excluded simply because the resolution was not within the Article 189 list.

[44] In the course of the meeting on 20 March 1970, the Council, after an exchange of views between its members and the representative of the Commission, reached a number of 'conclusions' on the attitude to be taken by the Governments of the Member States in the decisive negotiations on the AETR.

[45] These proceedings were concerned partly with the objective of the negotiations and partly with negotiating procedure.

[46] As regards the objective to be pursued, the Council settled on a negotiating position aimed at having the AETR adapted to the provisions of the Community system, apart from the concession of certain derogations from that system which would have to be accepted by the Community.

[47] Having regard to the objective thus established, the Council invited the Commission to put forward, at the appropriate time and in accordance with the provisions of Article 75 of the Treaty, the necessary proposals with a view to amending Regulation No 543/69.

[48] As regards negotiating, the Council decided, in accordance with the course of action decided upon at its previous meetings, that the negotiations should be carried on and concluded by the six Member States, which would become contracting parties to the AETR.

[49] Throughout the negotiations and at the conclusion of the agreement, the States would act in common and would constantly coordinate their positions according to the usual procedure in close association with the Community institutions, the delegation of the Member State currently occupying the Presidency of the Council acting as spokesman.

[50] It does not appear from the minutes that the Commission raised any objections to the definition by the Council of the objective of the negotiations.

[51] On the other hand, it did lodge an express reservation regarding the negotiating procedure, declaring that it considered that the position adopted by the Council was not in accordance with the Treaty, and more particularly with Article 228.

[52] It follows from the foregoing that the Council's proceedings dealt with a matter falling within the power of the Community, and that the Member States could not therefore act outside the framework of the common institutions.

[53] It thus seems that in so far as they concerned the objective of the negotiations as defined by the Council, the proceedings of 20 March 1970 could not have been simply the expression or the recognition of a voluntary coordination, but were designed to lay down a course of action binding on both the institutions and the Member States, and destined ultimately to be reflected in the tenor of the regulation.

[54] In the part of its conclusions relating to the negotiating procedure, the Council adopted provisions which were capable of derogating in certain circumstances from the procedure laid down by the Treaty regarding negotiations with third countries and the conclusion of agreements.

[55] Hence, the proceedings of 20 March 1970 had definite legal effects both on relations between the Community and the Member States and on the relationship between institutions.

NOTES
1. The significance of finding that the Council's act, although not mentioned in Article 189 of the EC Treaty (now Article 249 EC), nevertheless had legal effects, was that its validity could be challenged by the Commission before the Court. As in the *International Fruit Company* case, above, the task of identifying a legal act occurred in the context of a challenge to it. *Commission* v *Council* (Case 22/70) will be considered again in Chapter 8 which examines challenges to Community acts.
2. Community law is becoming increasingly multi-dimensional. An increasingly wide range of acts may carry direct or indirect legal implications. Read Case C-322/88 *Grimaldi* v *Fonds des Malaises Professionelles* [1989] ECR 4407 and J. Klabbers, 'Informal Instruments before the European Court of Justice' (1994) 31 CML Rev 997.
3. Outwith the first pillar – and outwith the principal focus of this book – there are different procedures and instruments, which may nevertheless generate binding legal rules, albeit that they will not be *Community* rules.
    In the 'second pillar', the Provisions on the definition and implementation of a Common Foreign and Security Policy found in Title V of the Treaty on European Union, as amended most recently by the Treaty of Nice, it is provided in Article 12 that:

ARTICLE 12 EU

The Union shall pursue the objectives set out in Article 11 by:

— defining the principles of and general guidelines for the common foreign and security policy,

— deciding on common strategies,

— adopting joint actions,

— adopting common positions,

— strengthening systematic cooperation between Member States in the conduct of policy.

In the 'third pillar', the provisions on police and judicial co-operation in criminal matters located in Title VI of the Treaty on European Union, Article 29 EU sets out an objective 'to provide citizens with a high level of safety within an area of freedom, security and justice by developing common action among the Member States in the fields of police and judicial cooperation in criminal matters and by preventing and combating racism'.

ARTICLE 34(2) EU

The Council shall take measures and promote cooperation, using the appropriate form and procedures as set out in this title, contributing to the pursuit of the objectives of the Union. To that end, acting unanimously on the initiative of any Member State or of the Commission, the Council may:

(a) adopt common positions defining the approach of the Union to a particular matter;

(b) adopt framework decisions for the purpose of approximation of the laws and regulations of the Member States. Framework decisions shall be binding upon the Member States as to the result to be achieved but shall leave to the national authorities the choice of form and methods. They shall not entail direct effect;

(c) adopt decisions for any other purpose consistent with the objectives of this title, excluding any approximation of the laws and regulations of the Member States. These decisions shall be binding and shall not entail direct effect; the Council, acting by a qualified majority, shall adopt measures necessary to implement those decisions at the level of the Union;

(d) establish conventions which it shall recommend to the Member States for adoption in accordance with their respective constitutional requirements. Member States shall begin the procedures applicable within a time limit to be set by the Council. Unless they provide otherwise, conventions shall, once adopted by at least half of the Member States, enter into force for those Member States. Measures implementing conventions shall be adopted within the Council by a majority of two thirds of the Contracting Parties.

B: The legislative process

The Union has neither a general legislative competence nor a single uniform legislative procedure. The same is true of the Community. The competence is that conferred by the Treaty. And the manner in which that competence is exercised is detailed in the Treaty. In this vein Article 5(1) EC is constitutionally fundamental.

ARTICLE 5(1) EC

The Community shall act within the limits of the powers conferred upon it by this Treaty and of the objectives assigned to it therein.

As a general observation the Community system involves the allocation of an almost, but not quite, exclusive power of legislative initiative to the Commission (the exceptions lie in Title IV of the EC Treaty: see Chapter 15). But the Commission is almost entirely denied legislative power of its own under the Treaty. The adoption of legislation prepared and proposed by the Commission is the preserve of the Parliament and the Council. In many cases this power is exercised according to the 'co-decision' procedure established by Article 251 EC, which has steadily gained ground on periodic Treaty revision as the dominant method of lawmaking in the Community. 'Co-decision' requires *inter alia* only a qualified majority in Council for the adoption of legislation, in combination with Parliamentary support. However there are residual areas to which other procedures apply, according to which Parliamentary involvement is weaker and/or a rule of unanimity in Council is retained (for example see Articles 13, 93, 175(2), 308 of the EC Treaty).

In short, the EC legislative procedure represents a relatively sophisticated network of institutional interdependence involving the Council, the Parliament, and the Commission (plus other less powerful actors such as the Economic and Social Committee established under Article 257 EC and the Committee of the Regions created by Article 263 EC). By contrast the two non-EC EU pillars are characterised by a much more powerful assertion of Member State control. In institutional terms this means the lawmaking process is dominated by the Council and/or the European Council, with both the Parliament and the Commission confined to a subordinate role. Moreover unanimity in Council is the normal voting rule, though exceptions are made. The 'second pillar' is more heavily marked than the third by preservation of State prerogatives and anxiety to confine the involvement of exclusion of the Parliament and the Commission but the detailed provisions are embedded in Titles V and VI of the EU Treaty and the weary reader is compassionately advised that in order to master the detail there is no substitute for poring over them Article by Article.

It is plainly possible to challenge legislation on the basis that it has not been made in accordance with the required procedures. This is reflected in Article 249 EC (p.42 above), which insists that legislation be made 'in accordance with the provisions of this Treaty'. Legal challenge to Community legislation is accordingly possible, and this is explicitly provided for in Article 230 EC (Chapter 8). Legal challenge to measures adopted in the non-EC EU is also possible – but the jurisdiction of the European Court is severely circumscribed: see Article 46 EU. Therefore it is judicial control of the exercise of EC – first pillar – competence that is of greatest practical significance.

Specific provisions (or 'bases') granting particular legislative powers are scattered throughout the text of the EC Treaty. Different procedures govern the making of legislation in different (but often not unconnected) areas. The result is that it may matter a great deal to the institutions and/or to the Member States which legal base in the Treaty is chosen to assert Community competence. The case law provoked by the need to choose is complex and appears rather technical, but its inspection is recommended for it reveals much about the tensions felt by the Member States and by the European institutions as the shape of the Community develops.

In case of dispute, the European Court is forced to decide which is the correct Treaty base for legislative action. It has consistently insisted that the correct base is as a matter of law identifiable, not a matter of unfettered discretion enjoyed by the political institutions.

Commission v *Council* (Case 45/86)

[1987] ECR 1493, Court of Justice of the European Communities

A Council Regulation dealing with external trade policy contained no explicit statement of its legal base. The Council, challenged by the Commission under Article 173 of the EC Treaty (now, after amendment, Article 230 EC), informed the European Court that the base was Articles 113 and 235 of the EC Treaty (now, after amendment, Articles 133 and 308 EC). The Court observed:

[11] It must be observed that in the context of the organization of the powers of the Community the choice of the legal basis for a measure may not depend simply on an institution's conviction as to the objective pursued but must be based on objective factors which are amenable to judicial review.

Different rules governed Articles 113 and 235 – the former allowed qualified majority voting in Council, whereas the latter insisted on unanimity. (The same is true of the current versions, Articles 133 and 308.) Article 235, which is now Article 308 and has not been textually altered, provides the broadest statement of Community legislative competence to be found in the Treaty:

ARTICLE 308 EC

If action by the Community should prove necessary to attain, in the course of the operation of the common market, one of the objectives of the Community and this Treaty has not provided the necessary powers, the Council shall, acting unanimously on a proposal from the Commission and after consulting the European Parliament, take the appropriate measures.

The Court continued:

Commission v *Council* (Case 45/86)

[1987] ECR 1493, Court of Justice of the European Communities

[13] It follows from the very wording of Article 235 [now 308] that its use as the legal basis for a measure is justified only where no other provision of the Treaty gives the Community institutions the necessary power to adopt the measure in question.

[14] It must therefore be considered whether in this case the Council had the power to adopt the contested regulations pursuant to Article 113 [now, in amended form, 133] of the Treaty alone, as the Commission maintains.

The Court held that the measures were adoptable under Article 113; that accordingly adoption under Article 235 was unjustified; and held them void.

NOTE

This judgment asserts that a *specific* legal base for legislation, if available in the Treaty, must be preferred over the *more general* base now found in Article 308 EC. The Court has never deviated from this view. Nor has it deviated from its insistence that the legal basis for a measure must be based on objective factors which are amenable to judicial review. But in subsequent case law the Court has been challenged to deal not with the 'general vs specific' issue, but instead to choose between two competing specific legal bases. Finding relevant 'objective factors' has proved more awkward.

Most prominent among the early cases were those involving disputes about whether measures establishing common standards of environmental protection for the territory of the Union should be adopted as measures aimed at making the internal market (Article 95 (ex 100a) EC) or as measures of environmental protection (Article 175 (ex 130s) EC). One might be forgiven for supposing that such legislation fits into both categories. And one would be forgiven for regarding the matter as profoundly uninteresting, were internal market rules and rules of environmental protection made according to the same legislative procedure. But they are not. And this affects the interests and influence of the political institutions engaged in the lawmaking process. The differences between the applicable legislative procedures have duly stimulated litigation. Periodic Treaty revision has altered the precise nature of relevant variation between the Treaty provisions concerned, and the detailed incentives generating litigation in the next case, which concerned the pre-Maastricht pattern of the EC Treaty, have now been adjusted (and much reduced). But the Court's need to umpire such disputes persists, and this case helps to reveal its approach.

Commission v *Council* (Case C-155/91)
[1993] ECR I-939, Court of Justice of the European Communities

The Commission, supported by the Parliament, brought an action for the annulment of Council Directive 91/156/EEC on waste disposal. The Commission proposal had opted for Article 100a (now, in amended form, 95) EC as the legal basis, and the Parliament agreed, but the Council had instead preferred Article 130s (now, in amended form, 175) EC. Why not use both? Case law reveals that where an institution's power is based on two provisions of the Treaty, it is bound to adopt the relevant measures on the basis of the two relevant provisions (e.g., Case 165/87 *Commission* v *Council* [1988] ECR 5545). Failure to do so will result in the annulment of the act, unless the error constitutes a purely formal defect giving rise to no irregularity in the procedure for adoption (e.g., Case C-491/01 *R* v *Secretary of State, ex parte BAT and Imperial Tobacco* judgment of 10 December 2002). However, that approach was fundamentally unsuitable in the present case. The combined use of both Article 100a and Article 130s would be unacceptable because of the detrimental impact on the role of the Parliament. Under the then applicable Treaty rules Article 100a required recourse to the 'cooperation procedure' (which today is found in Article 252 EC but survives only in relation to acts adopted under Title VII of the EC Treaty governing Economic and Monetary Policy), whereas Article 130s required the Council to act unanimously after merely consulting the European Parliament. The cooperation procedure envisages Council action by qualified majority where it intends accepting the amendments to its common position proposed by the Parliament and included by the Commission in its re-examined proposal, whereas it must secure unanimity if it intends taking a decision after its common position has been rejected by the Parliament or if it intends modifying the Commission's re-examined proposal. But the leverage thereby conferred on the

Parliament would be eliminated were the Council required in any event to act unanimously pursuant to Article 130s. Use of both provisions as a joint legal basis would rob the cooperation procedure of its purpose. So the Commission, supported by the Parliament, objected to the Council's use of Article 130s and brought an action under Article 173 (now, in amended form, 230) EC for the annulment of the Directive. But how to choose? The Court stepped back and examined the objects of the measure in order to determine which provision or provisions of the Treaty could provide a valid legal base.

[7] According to what is now settled case law, in the context of the organization of the powers of the Community, the choice of a legal basis for a measure must be based on objective factors which are amenable to judicial review. Those factors include, in particular, the aim and content of the measure (see, most recently, the judgment in Case C-295/90 *Parliament* v *Council* [1992] ECR I-4193, paragraph 13).

[8] As for the aim pursued by Directive 91/156, the fourth, sixth, seventh and ninth recitals in its preamble state that, in order to achieve a high level of environmental protection, the Member States must take measures to restrict the production of waste and to encourage the recycling of waste and its re-use as raw materials, and they must become self-sufficient in waste disposal and reduce movements of waste.

[9] As for the content of the directive, it requires the Member States, in particular, to encourage the prevention or reduction of waste production and waste recovery and disposal without endangering human health and without harming the environment and to prohibit the abandonment, dumping and uncontrolled disposal of waste (Articles 3 and 4). Accordingly, the directive requires the Member States to establish an integrated and adequate network of disposal installations which will enable the Community as a whole and the Member States individually to become self-sufficient in waste disposal, with the waste being disposed of in one of the nearest installations (Article 5). In order to attain those objectives, the Member States are to draw up waste management plans and may prevent movements of waste which are not in accordance with those plans (Article 7). Lastly, the directive requires the Member States to subject disposal undertakings and establishments to rules providing for permits, registration and inspections (Articles 9 to 14) and confirms, in the field of waste disposal, the 'polluter pays' principle enshrined in Article 130r(2) of the Treaty (Article 15).

[10] It appears from the above particulars that, according to its aim and content, the directive at issue has the object of ensuring the management of waste, whether it is of industrial or domestic origin, in accordance with the requirements of environmental protection.

[11] However, the Commission adds that the directive implements the principle of the free movement of waste intended for recovery and subjects the free movement of waste intended for disposal to conditions consistent with the internal market.

[12] Admittedly, waste, whether recyclable or not, is to be regarded as goods the movement of which, in accordance with Article 30 [now 28] of the Treaty, must in principle not be prevented (judgment in Case C-2/90 *Commission* v *Belgium* [1992] ECR I-4431, paragraph 28).

[13] However, the Court has held that imperative requirements relating to the protection of the environment justify exceptions to the free movement of waste. In that context, the Court has acknowledged that the principle that environmental damage should as a matter of priority be remedied at source, laid down by Article 130r(2) of the Treaty as a basis for action by the Community relating to the environment, entails that it is for each region, municipality or other local authority to take appropriate steps to ensure that its own waste is collected, treated and disposed of; it must accordingly be disposed of as close as possible to the place where it is produced, in order to limit as far as possible the transport of waste (judgment in *Commission* v *Belgium*, cited above, paragraph 34).

[14] The aim of the directive is to implement those principles. It lays down, in particular in Article 5, the principle that the place at which waste is disposed of should be near the place where it was

produced in order to ensure, as far as possible, that each Member State is self-sufficient in waste disposal. Moreover, Article 7 of the directive authorises Member States to prevent movements of waste for recovery or disposal which are not in accordance with their waste management plans.

[15] In those circumstances, the directive cannot be regarded as intended to implement the free movement of waste within the Community, as, moreover, the Commission admitted at the hearing.

[16] The Commission further argues that the directive leads to the approximation of legislation inasmuch as Article 1 introduces a single, common definition of waste and related activities. In that connection, it refers in particular to the fifth recital in the preamble to the directive, according to which any disparity between Member States' laws on waste disposal and recovery can affect the quality of the environment and interfere with the functioning of the internal market.

[17] Lastly, the Commission refers to the fact that the directive also contributes to harmonisation of the conditions of competition, at the level of both industrial production and waste disposal. In that connection, it argues that to some extent the directive brings to an end the advantages enjoyed by industries in certain Member States in terms of production costs owing to the fact that their legisla-tion on the treatment of waste is less strict than that of other Member States. Accordingly, it argues that the wording of Article 4, which provides for the recovery and disposal of waste 'without risk to water, air, soil and plants and animals', is sufficiently precise to ensure that the burdens on economic operators will henceforth be largely equivalent in all the Member States, provided that it is faithfully transposed into national law.

[18] Admittedly, it must be acknowledged that some provisions of the directive, in particular the definitions set out in Article 1, affect the functioning of the internal market.

[19] However, contrary to the Commission's contention, the mere fact that the establishment or functioning of the internal market is affected is not sufficient for Article 100a of the Treaty to apply. It appears from the Court's case law that recourse to Article 100a is not justified where the measure to be adopted has only the incidental effect of harmonising market conditions within the Community (judgment in Case C-70/88 *Parliament v Council* [1991] ECR I-4529, paragraph 17).

[20] That is the case here. The harmonisation provided for in Article 1 of the directive has as its main object to ensure, with a view to protecting the environment, the effective management of waste in the Community, regardless of its origin, and has only ancillary effects on the conditions of competition and trade. As a result, it differs from Council Directive 89/428/EEC of 21 June 1989 on procedures for harmonising the programmes for the reduction and eventual elimination of pollution caused by waste from the titanium dioxide industry (OJ 1989 L 201, p. 56), which was the subject of the judgment in the titanium dioxide case, [Case C-300/89 *Commission v Council* [1991] ECR I-2867] . . ., and is intended to approximate national rules concerning production conditions in a given industrial sector with the aim of eliminating distortions of competition in that sector.

[21] Accordingly, the contested directive must be deemed to have been validly adopted on the sole basis of Article 130s of the Treaty. The plea alleging that the wrong legal basis was chosen for the directive must therefore be rejected.

NOTE
A 'main object' test (paragraph 20) took the Court to its conclusion. The same is true in the next case, which concerns two different competing legal bases according to the pattern of the Treaty post-Maastricht and pre-Amsterdam. Here the applicant argues for a dual legal base, but fails to persuade the Court.

European Parliament v Council of the European Union (Case C-42/97)
[1999] ECR I-869, Court of Justice of the European Communities

The Parliament brought an action under Article 173 (now, in amended form, 230) EC Treaty for the annulment of Council Decision 96/664/EC on the adoption of a multiannual programme to promote the linguistic diversity of the Community in the information society. It argued that the legal basis of that decision should have been not only Article 130 EC on industry (now, in amended form, Article 157), the sole base chosen by the Council, but also Article 128 EC on culture (now, in amended form, Article 151). The Parliament's incentive to worry about such matters is today greatly diminished as a result of Treaty revision that has brought the two bases into closer alignment. But at the time the Parliament fared much better under the Treaty Article on culture than that on industry.

[36] According to settled case law, in the context of the organisation of the powers of the Community the choice of the legal basis for a measure must be based on objective factors which are amenable to judicial review. Those factors include in particular the aim and the content of the measure (see, in particular, Case C-271/94 *Parliament* v *Council* [1996] ECR I-1689, paragraph 14, and Case C-22/96 *Parliament* v *Council* [1998] ECR I-3231, paragraph 23).

[37] It must be pointed out that the wording of the title of a measure cannot by itself determine its legal basis and, in this case, that the words 'to promote . . . linguistic diversity' appearing in the title of the contested decision cannot be isolated from the measure as a whole and interpreted independently.

[38] In order to determine whether the dual legal basis contended for by the Parliament was necessary, it is appropriate to consider whether, according to its aim and content, as they appear from its actual wording, the contested decision is concerned, indissociably, both with industry and with culture (see, to that effect, Case C-300/89 *Commission* v *Council* [1991] ECR I-2867, paragraph 13).

[39] In that connection, it is not sufficient for the contested decision to pursue a twofold purpose or for an analysis of its content to disclose the existence of a twofold component.

[40] If it were apparent from an examination of the decision that its 'industrial' component is identifiable as the main or predominant component, whereas the 'cultural' component is merely incidental, it would follow that the only appropriate legal basis for it was Article 130 of the Treaty.

[41] That interpretation conforms with the actual text of Article 128(4) of the Treaty, according to which the Community is to take cultural aspects into account in its action under other provisions of the Treaty.

[42] It is clear from that provision that not every description of the cultural aspects of Community action necessarily implies that recourse must be had to Article 128 as the legal basis, where culture does not constitute an essential and indissociable component of the other component on which the action in question is based but is merely incidental or secondary to it.

NOTE
The Court, examining the measure in the light of this approach, concluded that culture was not an essential component of the contested decision, in the same way as industry. The main aim of the proposed action was to ensure that undertakings were not eliminated from the market or suffer damage to their competitiveness as a result of communications costs caused by linguistic diversity. Linguistic diversity was addressed as an essentially economic matter and only incidentally under a cultural perspective. The Parliament's application for annulment therefore failed.

The Judgments in both Case C-155/91 *Commission* v *Council* (para 20) and C-42/97 *Parliament* v *Council* (para 38) refer to one of the earliest rulings of the Court in these realms – Case C-300/89 *Commission* v *Council* [1991] ECR I-2867, in which Directive 89/428 approximating national programmes for reducing and eventually eliminating pollution caused by waste in the production of titanium dioxide was challenged. Case C-300/89, 'Titanium Dioxide', like Case C-155/91 on the Waste Directive, concerned the 'internal market *vs* environmental protection' issue: what was then Article 100a *vs* Article 130s, and is now Article 95 *vs* Article 175. That landmark 'Titanium Dioxide' ruling is regrettably not easy to interpret. However, it seems best explained as a case in which both legal bases were equally plausible – in contrast to Case C-155/91 and Case C-42/97, extracted above, which were successfully resolved with reference to a 'main object' test. But in 'Titanium Dioxide' the two bases were nevertheless mutually incompatible (for the reasons relating to the detrimental impact on the Parliament set out above at p.48 in introducing Case C-155/91). The Court, forced to choose, grasped a differentiating factor rooted in broad appreciation of accountable governance:

Commission v *Council* (Case C-300/89)
[1991] ECR I-2867, Court of Justice of the European Communities

[20] The very purpose of the cooperation procedure, which is to increase the involvement of the European Parliament in the legislative process of the Community, would . . . be jeopardized [were both legal bases to be applied]. As the Court stated in its judgments in Case 138/79 *Roquette Frères* v *Council* [1980] ECR 3333 and Case 139/79 *Maizena* v *Council* [1980] ECR 3393, paragraph 34, that participation reflects a fundamental democratic principle that the peoples should take part in the exercise of power through the intermediary of a representative assembly.

[21] It follows that in the present case recourse to the dual legal basis of Articles 100a and 130s is excluded and that it is necessary to determine which of those two provisions is the appropriate legal basis.

[22] It must be observed in the first place that, pursuant to the second sentence of Article 130r(2) of the Treaty, 'environmental protection requirements shall be a component of the Community's other policies'. That principle implies that a Community measure cannot be covered by Article 130s merely because it also pursues objectives of environmental protection.

[23] Secondly, as the Court held in its judgments in Cases 91/79 and 92/79 *Commission* v *Italy* [1980] ECR 1099 (paragraph 8) and 1115 (paragraph 8), provisions which are made necessary by considerations relating to the environment and health may be a burden upon the undertakings to which they apply and, if there is no harmonisation of national provisions on the matter, competition may be appreciably distorted. It follows that action intended to approximate national rules concerning production conditions in a given industrial sector with the aim of eliminating distortions of competition in that sector is conducive to the attainment of the internal market and thus falls within the scope of Article 100a, a provision which is particularly appropriate to the attainment of the internal market.

[24] Finally, it must be observed that Article 100a(3) requires the Commission, in its proposals for measures for the approximation of the laws of the Member States which have as their object the establishment and functioning of the internal market, to take as a base a high level of protection in matters of environmental protection. That provision thus expressly indicates that the objectives of environmental protection referred to in Article 130r may be effectively pursued by means of harmonising measures adopted on the basis of Article 100a.

[25] In view of all the foregoing considerations, the contested measure should have been based on Article 100a of the EEC Treaty and must therefore be annulled.

NOTE

The invocation of 'democratic principle' as a basis for choosing the legal base that maximizes the involvement of the European Parliament is striking (para 20 of the judgment), but Case C-155/91 (p. 48 above) makes plain that this factor is *not* relevant if one base prevails over the other when the 'main object' test is applied.

■ QUESTION

How realistic is the Court's 'main object' test, given that public regulation of the market is inevitably multi-functional? And how can the 'main object' test be reconciled with the assertion of linkage between different policy areas made by horizontal clauses in the Treaty such as Articles 6, 152(1) and 153(2) EC?

These awkward and constitutionally sensitive cases have proliferated before the Court in recent years as the number of legal bases for legislation in the Treaty has been steadily increased by periodic Treaty revision. The precise context in which the decision on which base to choose is taken depends on the Treaty as then in force. Both Case C-300/89, the 'Titanium Dioxide' case, and Case C-155/91, on the 'Waste Framework' Directive, discussed above, were decided against the background of the Treaty as it stood before the entry into force of the Maastricht Treaty. The amendments to the Treaty effected by the Maastricht Treaty both increased the variety of available legislative procedures and also added new competences which are not easy to demarcate from existing competences. Case C-42/97 on linguistic diversity arose under the post-Maastricht pre-Amsterdam arrangements. Gratifyingly more recent Treaty revision has reduced the likelihood of mutual incompatibility between legal bases. The Amsterdam Treaty, in particular, greatly reduced the incentives to litigate about choice of legal base, most prominently by helpfully asserting a strong preference for the 'co-decision' procedure under Article 251 EC as the dominant form of Community lawmaking. But discrepancies still lurk in the Treaty: for example, even today Article 95 and Article 175, the internal market and environmental protection provisions that generated such notable case law in the years after the entry into force of the Single European Act, do not run in perfect parallel – consider Article 175(2) and Article 176 EC.

Moreover, the creation of the European Union constructed on three pillars under the Maastricht Treaty added an extra dimension to the issue of choosing the correct procedure. Article 5(1) EC (p.46) states that the Community shall act within the limits of the powers conferred on it by its Treaty. The same is in principle true of the two non-EC EU pillars. But, as mentioned at p.11, the Court's jurisdiction to police the exercise of Union competence outwith the EC pillar is severely limited according to Article 46 EU. In the next case the Court asserts its jurisdiction in an 'inter-pillar' dispute.

Commission v *Council* (Case-170/96)
[1998] ECR I-2763, Court of Justice of the European Communities

The Council had adopted a measure on airport transit arrangements as a 'third pillar' measure (96/197/JAI [1996] OJ L63/8) pursuant to (what was then) Article K3(2) EU. The measure was designed to harmonise Member States' policies as regards the requirement of an airport transit visa. This was in turn designed to improve control of perceived use of air routes to take up residence illegally within the territory of the Member States. The Commission, supported by the Parliament, would have enjoyed much greater involvement in the process of adoption of the act had it been instead treated as a 'first pillar' EC measure. They therefore sought its annulment under Article 173 (now, after amendment, 230) EC. But could the Court review a measure purportedly adopted outwith the EC Treaty pursuant to the procedure for judicial review created by the EC Treaty? It could.

[14] Article M of the Treaty on European Union [*see now Art 47 EU*] makes it clear that a provision such as Article K.3(2), which provides for the adoption of joint action by the Council in the areas

referred to in Article K.1 of the Treaty on European Union, does not affect the provisions of the EC Treaty.

[15] In accordance with Article L of the Treaty on European Union [*see now Art 46 EU*], the provisions of the EC Treaty concerning the powers of the Court of Justice and the exercise of those powers apply to Article M of the Treaty on European Union.

[16] It is therefore the task of the Court to ensure that acts which, according to the Council, fall within the scope of Article K.3(2) of the Treaty on European Union do not encroach upon the powers conferred by the EC Treaty on the Community.

After examining the substance of the matter the Court dismissed the application.

NOTE
This judgment was delivered in the pre-Amsterdam era and the detailed relationship between the first and third pillars have been changed (p.11 above). However it remains important in understanding the scope of judicial supervision in the EU. But it is atypical. Most cases involve 'intra-EC' disputes. The Parliament might have incentives to argue about legal base, most commonly because its influence is not the same between two candidate legal bases. The Commission too engages in this inter-institutional horseplay. That is the character of the cases considered above. Member States too might have incentives to argue about choice of legal base, most commonly because the applicable voting rule in Council is not the same between two candidate legal bases. This forms the background to the next case.

United Kingdom v *Council* (Case C-84/94)
[1996] ECR I-5755, Court of Justice of the European Communities

The UK's attempt in the post-Maastricht, pre-Amsterdam era to preserve a veto in Council prompted it to seek to persuade the Court that Directive 93/104 concerning the organization of working time had been wrongly treated by the Council as capable of adoption under (what was then) Article 118a of the EC Treaty, authorising legislation to improve the health and safety of workers especially in the working environment. The UK argued that Article 100 or Article 235 should have provided the legal base. Its point was one of practical politics. Article 118a required only a qualified majority vote in Council. Articles 100 and 235 demanded unanimity. So the UK would be able to prevent the adoption in Council of social policy legislation to which it was politically opposed only provided it could persuade the Court that the organization of working time, governed by the Directive, was not covered by Article 118a's focus on health and safety at work. The detailed implications of this ruling, like those of the cases considered above, has been altered by subsequent Treaty revision that has extended the scope of EC competence in the field of social policy and altered the Council voting rules in most circumstances to qualified majority (see Articles 136–145 EC). But the basic point that the Court is entrusted with the task of determining the proper reach of the Treaty is of enduring importance. In this case its fulfilment of that task led it to rule against the UK.

[15] There is nothing in the wording of Article 118a to indicate that the concepts of 'working environment', 'safety' and 'health' as used in that provision should, in the absence of other indications, be interpreted restrictively, and not as embracing all factors, physical or otherwise, capable of affecting the health and safety of the worker in his working environment, including in particular certain aspects of the organization of working time. On the contrary, the words 'especially in the working environment' militate in favour of a broad interpretation of the powers which Article 118a confers upon the Council for the protection of the health and safety of workers. Moreover, such an interpretation of the words 'safety' and 'health' derives support in particular from the preamble to

the Constitution of the World Health Organization to which all the Member States belong. Health is there defined as a state of complete physical, mental and social well-being that does not consist only in the absence of illness or infirmity.

The Court, having explained the nature and purpose of Article 118a, repeated its view that the choice of legal basis must be based on objective factors amenable to judicial review. This is a familiar statement – see p.48 above. It then proceeded to examine Directive 93/104 on Working Time.

[26] As regards the aim of the directive, the applicant argues that it represents a continuation of the Community's earlier thinking and of a series of earlier initiatives at Community level concerned with the organization of working time in the interests of job creation and reduced unemployment. It is in reality a measure concerned with the overall improvement of the living and working conditions of employees and with their general protection, and is so broad in its scope and coverage as to be capable of classification as a social policy measure, for the adoption of which other legal bases exist.

[27] It is to be noted in that respect that, according to the sixth recital in its preamble, the directive constitutes a practical contribution towards creating the social dimension of the internal market. However, it does not follow from the fact that the directive falls within the scope of Community social policy that it cannot properly be based on Article 118a, so long as it contributes to encouraging improvements as regards the health and safety of workers. Indeed, Article 118a forms part of Chapter 1, headed 'Social Provisions', of Title VIII of the Treaty, which deals in particular with 'Social Policy'. This led the Court to conclude that that provision conferred on the Community internal legislative competence in the area of social policy (Opinion 2/91, cited above, [[1993] ECR I-1061] paragraph 17).

[28] Furthermore, as the Advocate-General has demonstrated in points 85 to 90 of his Opinion, the organization of working time is not necessarily conceived as an instrument of employment policy. In this case, the fifth recital in the preamble to the directive states that the improvement of workers' safety, hygiene and health at work is an objective which should not be subordinated to 'purely economic considerations'. Were the organization of working time to be viewed as a means of combating unemployment, a number of economic factors would have to be taken into account, such as, for example, its impact on the productivity of undertakings and on workers' salaries.

[29] The approach taken by the directive, viewing the organization of working time essentially in terms of the favourable impact it may have on the health and safety of workers, is apparent from several recitals in its preamble. Thus, for example, the eighth recital states that, in order to ensure the safety and health of Community workers, they must be granted minimum rest periods and adequate breaks and that it is also necessary in that context to place a maximum limit on weekly working hours. In addition, the eleventh recital states that 'research has shown that . . . long periods of night work can be detrimental to the health of workers and can endanger safety at the workplace', while the fifteenth recital states that specific working conditions may have detrimental effects on the safety and health of workers and that the organization of work according to a certain pattern must take account of the general principle of adapting work to the worker.

[30] While, in the light of those considerations, it cannot be excluded that the directive may affect employment, that is clearly not its essential objective.

[31] As regards the content of the directive, the applicant argues that the connection between the measures it lays down, on the one hand, and health and safety, on the other, is too tenuous for the directive to be based on Article 118a of the Treaty.

[32] In that respect, it argues that no adequate scientific evidence exists to justify the imposition of a general requirement to provide for breaks where the working day is longer than six hours (Article 4), a general requirement to provide for a minimum uninterrupted weekly rest period of twenty-four hours in addition to the usual eleven hours' daily rest (Article 5, first sentence), a requirement that the minimum rest period must, in principle, include Sunday (Article 5, second sentence), a general requirement to ensure that the average working time for each seven-day period, including overtime,

does not exceed forty-eight hours (Article 6(2)), and a general requirement that every worker is to have a minimum of four weeks' paid annual leave (Article 7).

[33] The applicant points out in that connection that Directive 89/391 provides for employers to carry out assessments to evaluate specific risks to the health and safety of workers, taking into account the nature of the activities of the undertaking. The risk assessment procedure laid down by Directive 89/391 could not apply to the restrictions on working time contained in Section II of the contested directive (and is applicable only to a very limited extent in Section III), the provisions in question being quite simply mandatory and leaving no scope for such an assessment in order to determine whether they are to apply.

[34] The applicant maintains, moreover, that unlike other provisions based on Article 118a of the Treaty, the contested measures were not referred to the Advisory Committee on Safety, Hygiene and Health Protection at Work for an opinion (on the role of such committees, it cites Case C-212/91 *Angelopharm* [1994] ECR I-171, paragraphs 31 and 32). Although consultation of that committee is not expressly provided for in cases such as this, the fact that the Council did not call on the Commission to undertake such consultation casts further doubt on the link between the directive and the health and safety of workers.

[35] Finally, in the applicant's view, contrary to the requirements of Article 118a(2), the provisions of the directive do not constitute 'minimum requirements for gradual implementation, having regard to the conditions and technical rules obtaining in each of the Member States and do not take account of their effects on the creation and development of small and medium-sized undertakings'.

[36] In order to deal with those arguments, a distinction must be drawn between the second sentence of Article 5 of the directive and its other provisions.

[37] As to the second sentence of Article 5, whilst the question whether to include Sunday in the weekly rest period is ultimately left to the assessment of Member States, having regard, in particular, to the diversity of cultural ethnic and religious factors in those States (second sentence of Article 5, read in conjunction with the tenth recital), the fact remains that the Council has failed to explain why Sunday, as a weekly rest day, is more closely connected with the health and safety of workers than any other day of the week. In those circumstances, the applicant's alternative claim must be upheld and the second sentence of Article 5, which is severable from the other provisions of the directive, must be annulled.

[38] The other measures laid down by the directive, which refer to minimum rest periods, length of work, night work, shift work and the pattern of work, relate to the 'working environment' and reflect concern for the protection of 'the health and safety of workers'. The scope of those terms has been explained in paragraph 15 of this judgment. Moreover, as the Belgian Government has pointed out, the evolution of social legislation at both national and international level confirms the existence of a link between measures relating to working time and the health and safety of workers.

[39] Legislative action by the Community, particularly in the field of social policy, cannot be limited exclusively to circumstances where the justification for such action is scientifically demonstrated (see points 165 to 167 of the Advocate-General's Opinion).

[40] Similarly, the applicant's argument that the directive precludes any assessment of the risks involved for certain workers or for those working in a particular sector cannot be regarded as well founded. The Community legislature did take certain special situations into account, as is demonstrated by Article 1 of the directive, which excludes certain sectors or activities from its scope; by Article 14, which excludes occupations and occupational activities where more specific Community provisions apply; and by Article 17(1) and (2) which allow derogations from Articles 3, 4, 5, 6 and 8 in respect of certain groups of workers or certain sectors of activity (see points 114 to 117 of the Advocate-General's Opinion).

[41] It is true that the Council did not consult the Advisory Committee on Safety, Hygiene and Health Protection at Work established by Council Decision 74/325/EEC of 27 June 1974 (OJ 1974 L 185, p. 15) with regard to the measures envisaged by the directive. However, under Article 2(1) of that decision,

such consultation is intended only '[to assist] the Commission in the preparation and implementation of activities in the fields of safety, hygiene and health protection at work', and does not therefore constitute a condition precedent for action by the Council. In those circumstances, failure to consult that committee cannot be relied on to cast doubt on the link between the measures laid down by the directive and the protection of the health and safety of workers.

[42] Furthermore, the provisions of the directive are 'minimum requirements' within the meaning of Article 118a of the Treaty. Whilst ensuring a certain level of protection for workers, the directive authorises Member States in Article 15 to apply, or facilitate the application of, measures which are more favourable to the protection of the health and safety of workers, thereby guaranteeing them a more stringent level of protection, in accordance with Article 118a(3). Similarly, Article 18(3) of the directive states that, whilst Member States may provide for different measures in the field of working time, subject to compliance with the requirements it lays down, implementation of the directive does not constitute valid grounds for reducing the general level of protection afforded to workers.

[43] The measures laid down by the directive are also, in accordance with Article 118a, 'for gradual implementation, having regard to the conditions and technical rules obtaining in each of the Member States'. In the first place, it is not in dispute that legislation in all the Member States includes measures on the organization of working time. Furthermore, Article 18 of the directive authorises Member States, subject to certain conditions, not to apply, after the expiry of the time-limit for implementing the directive (23 November 1996), the provisions of Article 6 on weekly working time or, for a three-year transitional period, the provisions of Article 7 on paid annual leave, which may during that period be limited to three weeks.

[44] Finally, the directive has taken account of the effects which the organization of working time for which it provides may have on small and medium-sized undertakings. Thus, the second recital in the preamble to the directive refers to the overriding requirement not to hold back the development of such undertakings. Moreover, as the Court held in its judgment in Case C-189/91 *Kirsammer-Hack* v *Sidal* [1993] ECR I-6185, paragraph 34, by providing that directives adopted in the field of health and safety of workers are to avoid imposing administrative, financial and legal constraints such as to hold back the creation and development of small and medium-sized undertakings, the second sentence of Article 118a(2) indicates that such undertakings may be the subject of special economic measures. Contrary to the view taken by the applicant, however, that provision does not prevent those undertakings from being subject to binding measures.

[45] Since it is clear from the above considerations that, in terms of its aim and content, the directive has as its principal objective the protection of the health and safety of workers by the imposition of minimum requirements for gradual implementation, neither Article 100 nor Article 100a could have constituted the appropriate legal basis for its adoption.

[46] The applicant further maintains that the Community legislature neither fully considered nor adequately demonstrated whether there were transnational aspects which could not be satisfactorily regulated by national measures, whether such measures would conflict with the requirements of the EC Treaty or significantly damage the interests of Member States or, finally, whether action at Community level would provide clear benefits compared with action at national level. In its submission, Article 118a should be interpreted in the light of the principle of subsidiarity, which does not allow adoption of a directive in such wide and prescriptive terms as the contested directive, given that the extent and the nature of legislative regulation of working time vary very widely between Member States. The applicant explains in this context, however, that it does not rely upon infringement of the principle of subsidiarity as a separate plea.

[47] In that respect, it should be noted that it is the responsibility of the Council, under Article 118a, to adopt minimum requirements so as to contribute, through harmonisation, to achieving the objective of raising the level of health and safety protection of workers which, in terms of Article 118a(1), is primarily the responsibility of the Member States. Once the Council has found that it is necessary to improve the existing level of protection as regards the health and safety of workers and to harmonise the conditions in this area while maintaining the improvements made,

achievement of that objective through the imposition of requirements necessarily presupposes Community-wide action, which otherwise, as in this case, leaves the enactment of the detailed implementing provisions required largely to the Member States. The argument that the Council could not properly adopt measures as general and mandatory as those forming the subject-matter of the directive will be examined below in the context of the plea alleging infringement of the principle of proportionality.

[48] Finally, as regards Article 235 of the Treaty, it is sufficient to point to the Court's case law, which holds that that article may be used as the legal basis for a measure only where no other Treaty provision confers on the Community institutions the necessary power to adopt it (see, in particular, *Parliament* v *Council*, cited above, paragraph 13).

[49] It must therefore be held that the directive was properly adopted on the basis of Article 118a, save for the second sentence of Article 5, which must accordingly be annulled . . .

The Court, having allowed the UK only an insignificant shred of success (paras 37, 49), then concluded its judgment by rejecting pleas of breach of the proportionality principle (p.75 below) and of infringement of essential procedural requirements.

NOTE

The background to this litigation lies in the hostility of the UK Government at the time to an enhanced EC competence in the social field. This generated the so-called UK opt-out from the extra commitments undertaken in the field by all the other Member States in the Maastricht Treaty, although that mechanism was not directly at issue in this case. The election of a Labour Government in the UK in 1997 cleared the way for the deletion by the Amsterdam Treaty of these special arrangements for the UK, and the EC Treaty's coverage of social policy is now found in renovated form, applying to all 15 Member States, in Articles 136–145 EC, which replace Articles 117–120. The Court's ruling in Case C-84/94 on 'Working Time' retains significance in principle in fixing the post-Amsterdam demarcation between Articles 95 and 308, on the one hand, and the renovated Articles 136–145 EC on social policy on the other, but the Court's firm embrace of the wide interpretation of health and safety preferred by the majority of Member States, combined with the electoral elimination of the UK grit in the EU oyster, reduces the incentives to pursue litigation on this particular point. But the case constitutes compelling evidence of the possibility that a State unsuccessful in winning an argument in Council about the desirable intensity of EC regulation may take the matter to the Court in the guise of an argument that the political preferences of the majority in Council have generated legislation that goes beyond the mandate provided by the Treaty. The UK lost before the Court. In the next case the dissentient minority State succeeds.

FURTHER READING ON THE ISSUE OF CHOICE OF LEGAL BASE – BUT NOTE THAT THESE CONTRIBUTIONS, THOUGH ILLUMINATING, PRE-DATE THE EXTREMELY IMPORTANT 'TOBACCO ADVERTISING' JUDGMENT (CASE C-376/98), EXAMINED AT P.60 BELOW:

Cullen, H. and Charlesworth, A., 'Diplomacy by Other Means: the Use of Legal Basis Litigation as a Political Strategy by the European Parliament and Member States' (1999) 36 CML Rev 1243.

Dashwood, A., 'Community Decision-making after Amsterdam' (1998) 1 *Cambridge Yearbook of European Legal Studies* 25.

Mischo, J., 'The Contribution of the Court of Justice to the Protection of the "Federal Balance" in the EC', Ch. 5 in O'Keeffe, D. (ed), *Judicial Review in European Union Law: Liber Amicorum Gordon Slynn* (The Hague: Kluwer Law International, 2000).

C: **The principle of attributed competence**

In the absence of a single legislative procedure, it may matter acutely to the relative influence of the Parliament, the Commission, and States in the Council which Treaty provision is relied on for the adoption of a particular measure. The correct Treaty base for proposed legislation must be identified, because different Treaty provisions dealing with different subject matter demand different procedures. This has provided the background to the litigation considered above. But these have been wrangles about *how* the Community should act. There is, however, a more fundamental question – whether the Community is competent to act *at all*. Article 5(1) EC was set out above (p.46) but as a constitutionally fundamental statement it bears repetition.

ARTICLE 5(1) EC

The Community shall act within the limits of the powers conferred upon it by this Treaty and of the objectives assigned to it therein.

NOTE

This is the principle of attributed competence. The EC is not omnicompetent. If the Community is not competent to act at all, then the matter rests with the Member States, and in principle the attitude of the Member States in Council is irrelevant. It is not in the gift of the Community legislature to override the limits of powers conferred upon the Community. Only Treaty revision, and due confirmation through national constitutional processes leading to Treaty ratification, can change the settlement. The point comes clearly into view when litigation is directed at showing that the chosen legal base is invalid *and no other candidate is available under the Treaty*.

Article 100a EC was amended and re-numbered as Article 95 by the Treaty of Amsterdam. It provides the most vivid testing ground.

ARTICLES 95(1)–(3) EC

1. By way of derogation from Article 94 and save where otherwise provided in this Treaty, the following provisions shall apply for the achievement of the objectives set out in Article 14. The Council shall, acting in accordance with the procedure referred to in Article 251 and after consulting the Economic and Social Committee, adopt the measures for the approximation of the provisions laid down by law, regulation or administrative action in Member States which have as their object the establishment and functioning of the internal market.

2. Paragraph 1 shall not apply to fiscal provisions, to those relating to the free movement of persons nor to those relating to the rights and interests of employed persons.

3. The Commission, in its proposals envisaged in paragraph 1 concerning health, safety, environmental protection and consumer protection, will take as a base a high level of protection, taking account in particular of any new development based on scientific facts. Within their respective powers, the European Parliament and the Council will also seek to achieve this objective.

NOTE

This provides a competence to 'approximate' or to harmonize national laws. But such approximation or harmonization must have as its object the establishment and functioning of the internal market. The internal market, according to Article 14 EC, 'shall comprise an area without internal frontiers in which the free movement of goods, persons, services, and capital is ensured in accordance with the provisions of this Treaty'. Case C-155/91 *Commission* v *Council* (p.48 above) establishes that recourse to Article 95 (ex 100a) is not justified where the measure has only the incidental effect of harmonizing market conditions within the Community. Case C-84/94 *UK* v *Council* concluded that the legal base authorizing harmonization could not have constituted the appropriate legal basis for the adoption of the 'Working Time' Directive since its 'principal objective' (para 45) was the protection of the health and safety of workers. In each case other Treaty provisions took the strain – Article 130s (now, after amendment, Article 175) in Case C-155/91, and Article 118a (now, after amendment, Article 137) in Case C-84/94. In the next case it is harmonization or nothing. And the Court, in the famous 'Tobacco Advertising' judgment of October 2000, finds that constitutionally the answer is nothing – the Community lacks competence to adopt the contested measure.

Germany v *European Parliament and Council of the European Union* (Case C-376/98)
[2000] ECR I-8419, Court of Justice of the European Communities

Directives based on Article 100a prohibit the sale of oral snuff and high tar cigarettes (Directives 89/622 [1989] OJ L359/1, and 92/41 [1992] OJ L158/30). In 1998 a third measure of harmonization was added to the package of Directives governing tobacco products. This was Directive 98/43 [1998] OJ L213/9 imposing severe restrictions on the advertising of tobacco products. It too was based on Article 100a, now, after amendment, Article 95 (and also Articles 57(2) & 66, now Articles 47(2) and 55, governing the services sector). These provisions require only a qualified majority in Council pursuant to the Article 251 EC co-decision procedure and the Directive had been adopted despite German opposition. Germany brought an action under Article 173 (now, after amendment, Article 230) EC to challenge the validity of the Directive. The German objections covered a number of matters, but the core of the application, which succeeded before the Court, attacked the 'Tobacco Advertising' Directive as being inadequately closely connected to the process of market-making to which the Treaty provisions on harmonization are dedicated. Germany was, in short, alleging that the Community – in the shape of a qualified majority of States in Council allied with the Parliament – had trespassed into an area lying beyond the authorized scope of Community powers.

Advocate-General Fennelly's Opinion charted a route to which the Court subsequently adhered. In his Opinion he stated:

[83] . . . the internal market is not a value-free synonym for general economic governance . . . the conferral of competence to pursue its establishment and functioning, under both Article 100A and more specific provisions such as Article 57(2), cannot, in my view, be equated with creation of a general Community regulatory power. These competences are conferred either to facilitate the exercise of the four freedoms or to equalise the conditions of competition.

[89] . . . the pursuit of equal conditions of competition does not give *carte blanche* to the Community legislator to harmonize any national rules that meet the eye, be it in a liberalizing or restrictive fashion . . . I would say that it would risk transferring general Member State regulatory competence to the Community if recourse to Article 100A to adopt harmonising measures in the interests of undistorted competition were not subject to some test of the reality of the link between such measures and internal market objectives. The silence of Articles 7A and 100A of the Treaty regarding equal conditions of competition furnishes an additional reason to avoid turning Article 100A into an instrument of general economic governance on this ground.

This is the detailed manifestation of a much broader constitutional anxiety about the need to police legislative excesses perpetrated by the Community legislature at the expense of other interests and actors in the political process. Mr Fennelly had introduced his inquiry in the following terms:

[4] The legal basis invoked by the Advertising Directive relates to the internal market. The Community's internal market competence is not limited, a priori, by any reserved domain of Member State power. It is a horizontal competence, whose exercise displaces national regulatory competence in the field addressed. Judicial review of the exercise of such a competence is a delicate and complex matter. On the one hand, unduly restrained judicial review might permit the Community institutions to enjoy, in effect, general or unlimited legislative power, contrary to the principle that the Community only enjoys those limited competences, however extensive, which have been conferred on it by the Treaty with a view to the attainment of specified objectives. This could permit the Community to encroach impermissibly on the powers of the Member States. On the other hand, the Court cannot, in principle, restrict the legitimate performance by the Community legislator of its task of removing barriers and distortions to trade in goods and services. It is the task of the Court, as the repository of the trust and confidence of the Community institutions, the Member States and the citizens of the Union, to perform this difficult function of upholding the constitutional division of powers between the Community and the Member States on the basis of objective criteria.

The Court was playing for high constitutional stakes, not least because of the risk that if it was perceived to apply a soft standard of review when invited to police the margins of EC competence, it might risk triggering rebellion among national judiciaries anxious to protect the reserved domain of State power. This judicial interplay is examined further at p.686 below. In 'Tobacco Advertising' the Court devoted close analysis to the scope of the Treaty-conferred competence to harmonize national laws.

[76] The Directive is concerned with the approximation of laws, regulations and administrative provisions of the Member States relating to the advertising and sponsorship of tobacco products. The national measures affected are to a large extent inspired by public health policy objectives.

[77] The first indent of Article 129(4) of the Treaty excludes any harmonization of laws and regulations of the Member States designed to protect and improve human health.

[78] But that provision does not mean that harmonising measures adopted on the basis of other provisions of the Treaty cannot have any impact on the protection of human health. Indeed, the third paragraph of Article 129(1) provides that health requirements are to form a constituent part of the Community's other policies.

[79] Other articles of the Treaty may not, however, be used as a legal basis in order to circumvent the express exclusion of harmonization laid down in Article 129(4) of the Treaty.

This explains the observation made above that this case, unlike earlier 'legal base' cases, involved harmonization or nothing. If the Directive, which severely restricted tobacco advertising, albeit on a common EC-wide basis, was treated as a public health measure, then it fell beyond the scope of the EC's legislative competence. Public health is a competence conferred on the EC, but Article 129(4) (now 152(4)) EC explicitly excludes harmonization of laws under that Title. So the Directive would be ruled invalid unless it properly took the Treaty provisions governing harmonization as its bases.

[81] Article 100a(1) of the Treaty empowers the Council, acting in accordance with the procedure referred to in Article 189b (now, after amendment, Article 251 EC) and after consulting the Economic and Social Committee, to adopt measures for the approximation of the provisions laid down by law, regulation or administrative action in Member States which have as their object the establishment and functioning of the internal market.

[82] Under Article 3(c) of the EC Treaty (now, after amendment, Article 3(1)(c) EC), the internal market is characterized by the abolition, as between Member States, of all obstacles to the free movement of goods, persons, services and capital. Article 7a of the EC Treaty (now, after amendment, Article 14 EC), which provides for the measures to be taken with a view to establishing the internal market, states in paragraph 2 that that market is to comprise an area without internal frontiers in which the free movement of goods, persons, services and capital is ensured in accordance with the provisions of the Treaty.

[83] Those provisions, read together, make it clear that the measures referred to in Article 100a(1) of the Treaty are intended to improve the conditions for the establishment and functioning of the internal market. To construe that article as meaning that it vests in the Community legislature a general power to regulate the internal market would not only be contrary to the express wording of the provisions cited above but would also be incompatible with the principle embodied in Article 3b of the EC Treaty (now Article 5 EC) that the powers of the Community are limited to those specifically conferred on it.

[84] Moreover, a measure adopted on the basis of Article 100a of the Treaty must genuinely have as its object the improvement of the conditions for the establishment and functioning of the internal market. If a mere finding of disparities between national rules and of the abstract risk of obstacles to the exercise of fundamental freedoms or of distortions of competition liable to result therefrom were sufficient to justify the choice of Article 100a as a legal basis, judicial review of compliance with the the proper legal basis might be rendered nugatory. The Court would then be prevented from discharging the function entrusted to it by Article 164 of the EC Treaty (now Article 220 EC) of ensuring that the law is observed in the interpretation and application of the Treaty.

[85] So, in considering whether Article 100a was the proper legal basis, the Court must verify whether the measure whose validity is at issue in fact pursues the objectives stated by the Community legislature (see, in particular, *Spain v Council*, cited above [Case C-350/92], paragraphs 25 to 41, and Case C-233/94 *Germany v Parliament and Council* [1997] ECR I-2405, paragraphs 10 to 21).

[86] It is true, as the Court observed in paragraph 35 of its judgment in *Spain v Council*, cited above, that recourse to Article 100a as a legal basis is possible if the aim is to prevent the emergence of future obstacles to trade resulting from multifarious development of national laws. However, the emergence of such obstacles must be likely and the measure in question must be designed to prevent them.

[87] The foregoing considerations apply to interpretation of Article 57(2) of the Treaty, read in conjunction with Article 66 thereof, which expressly refers to measures intended to make it easier for persons to take up and pursue activities by way of services. Those provisions are also intended to confer on the Community legislature specific power to adopt measures intended to improve the functioning of the internal market.

[88] Furthermore, provided that the conditions for recourse to Articles 100a, 57(2) and 66 as a legal basis are fulfilled, the Community legislature cannot be prevented from relying on that legal basis on the ground that public health protection is a decisive factor in the choices to be made. On the contrary, the third paragraph of Article129(1) provides that health requirements are to form a constituent part of the Community's other policies and Article 100a(3) expressly requires that, in the process of harmonization, a high level of human health protection is to be ensured.

[89] It is therefore necessary to verify whether, in the light of the foregoing, it was permissible for the Directive to be adopted on the basis of Articles 100a, 57(2) and 66 of the Treaty.

The Directive

[90] In the first recital in the preamble to the Directive, the Community legislature notes that differences exist between national laws on the advertising and sponsorship of tobacco products and observes that, as a result of such advertising and sponsorship transcending the borders of the Member States, the differences in question are likely to give rise to barriers to the movement of the products which serve as the media for such activities and the exercise of freedom to provide services

in that area, as well as to distortions of competition, thereby impeding the functioning of the internal market.

[91] According to the second recital, it is necessary to eliminate such barriers, and, to that end, approximate the rules relating to the advertising and sponsorship of tobacco products, whilst leaving Member States the possibility of introducing, under certain conditions, such requirements as they consider necessary in order to guarantee protection of the health of individuals.

[92] Article 3(1) of the Directive prohibits all forms of advertising and sponsorship of tobacco products and Article 3(4) prohibits any free distribution having the purpose or the effect of promoting such products. However, its scope does not extend to communications between professionals in the tobacco trade, advertising in sales outlets or in publications published and printed in third countries which are not principally intended for the Community market (Article 3(5)).

[93] The Directive also prohibits the use of the same names both for tobacco products and for other products and services as from 30 July 1998, except for products and services marketed before that date under a name also used for a tobacco product, whose use is authorized under certain conditions (Article 3(2)). With effect from 30 July 2001, tobacco products must not bear the brand name, trade-mark, emblem or other distinctive feature of any other product or service, unless the tobacco product has already been traded under that brand name, trade-mark, emblem or other distinctive feature before that date (Article 3(3)(a)).

[94] Pursuant to Article 5, the Directive is not to preclude Member States from laying down, in accordance with the Treaty, such stricter requirements concerning the advertising or sponsorship of tobacco products as they deem necessary to guarantee the health protection of individuals.

[95] It is therefore necessary to verify whether the Directive actually contributes to eliminating obstacles to the free movement of goods and to the freedom to provide services, and to removing distortions of competition.

Elimination of obstacles to the free movement of goods and the freedom to provide services

[96] It is clear that, as a result of disparities between national laws on the advertising of tobacco products, obstacles to the free movement of goods or the freedom to provide services exist or may well arise.

[97] In the case, for example, of periodicals, magazines and newspapers which contain advertising for tobacco products, it is true, as the applicant has demonstrated, that no obstacle exists at present to their importation into Member States which prohibit such advertising. However, in view of the trend in national legislation towards ever greater restrictions on advertising of tobacco products, reflecting the belief that such advertising gives rise to an appreciable increase in tobacco consumption, it is probable that obstacles to the free movement of press products will arise in the future.

[98] In principle, therefore, a Directive prohibiting the advertising of tobacco products in periodicals, magazines and newspapers could be adopted on the basis of Article 100a of the Treaty with a view to ensuring the free movement of press products, on the lines of Directive 89/552, Article 13 of which prohibits television advertising of tobacco products in order to promote the free broadcasting of television programmes.

[99] However, for numerous types of advertising of tobacco products, the prohibition under Article 3(1) of the Directive cannot be justified by the need to eliminate obstacles to the free movement of advertising media or the freedom to provide services in the field of advertising. That applies, in particular, to the prohibition of advertising on posters, parasols, ashtrays and other articles used in hotels, restaurants and cafés, and the prohibition of advertising spots in cinemas, prohibitions which in no way help to facilitate trade in the products concerned.

[100] Admittedly, a measure adopted on the basis of Articles 100a, 57(2) and 66 of the Treaty may incorporate provisions which do not contribute to the elimination of obstacles to exercise of the fundamental freedoms provided that they are necessary to ensure that certain prohibitions imposed

in pursuit of that purpose are not circumvented. It is, however, quite clear that the prohibitions mentioned in the previous paragraph do not fall into that category.

[101] Moreover, the Directive does not ensure free movement of products which are in conformity with its provisions.

[102] Contrary to the contentions of the Parliament and Council, Article 3(2) of the Directive, relating to diversification products, cannot be construed as meaning that, where the conditions laid down in the Directive are fulfilled, products of that kind in which trade is allowed in one Member State may move freely in the other Member States, including those where such products are prohibited.

[103] Under Article 5 of the Directive, Member States retain the right to lay down, in accordance with the Treaty, such stricter requirements concerning the advertising or sponsorship of tobacco products as they deem necessary to guarantee the health protection of individuals.

[104] Furthermore, the Directive contains no provision ensuring the free movement of products which conform to its provisions, in contrast to other directives allowing Member States to adopt stricter measures for the protection of a general interest (see, in particular, Article 7(1) of Council Directive 90/239/EEC of 17 May 1990 on the approximation of the laws, regulations and administrative provisions of the Member States concerning the maximum tar yield of cigarettes (OJ 1990 L 137, p. 36) and Article 8(1) of Council Directive 89/622/EEC of 13 November 1989 on the approximation of the laws, regulations and administrative provisions of the Member States concerning the labelling of tobacco products (OJ 1989 L 359, p. 1)).

[105] In those circumstances, it must be held that the Community legislature cannot rely on the need to eliminate obstacles to the free movement of advertising media and the freedom to provide services in order to adopt the Directive on the basis of Articles 100a, 57(2) and 66 of Treaty.

Elimination of distortion of competition

[106] In examining the lawfulness of a directive adopted on the basis of Article 100a of the Treaty, the Court is required to verify whether the distortion of competition which the measure purports to eliminate is appreciable (*Titanium Dioxide*, cited above [Case C-300/89], paragraph 23).

[107] In the absence of such a requirement, the powers of the Community legislature would be practically unlimited. National laws often differ regarding the conditions under which the activities they regulate may be carried on, and this impacts directly or indirectly on the conditions of competition for the undertakings concerned. It follows that to interpret Articles 100a, 57(2) and 66 of the Treaty as meaning that the Community legislature may rely on those articles with a view to eliminating the smallest distortions of competition would be incompatible with the principle, already referred to in paragraph 83 of this judgment, that the powers of the Community are those specifically conferred on it.

[108] It is therefore necessary to verify whether the Directive actually contributes to eliminating appreciable distortions of competition.

[109] First, as regards advertising agencies and producers of advertising media, undertakings established in Member States which impose fewer restrictions on tobacco advertising are unquestionably at an advantage in terms of economies of scale and increase in profits. The effects of such advantages on competition are, however, remote and indirect and do not constitute distortions which could be described as appreciable. They are not comparable to the distortions of competition caused by differences in production costs, such as those which, in particular, prompted the Community legislature to adopt Council Directive 89/428/EEC of 21 June 1989 on procedures for harmonising the programmes for the reduction and eventual elimination of pollution caused by waste from the titanium dioxide industry (OJ 1989 L 201, p. 56).

[110] It is true that the differences between certain regulations on tobacco advertising may give rise to appreciable distortions of competition. As the Commission and the Finnish and United Kingdom

Governments have submitted, the fact that sponsorship is prohibited in some Member States and authorized in others gives rise, in particular, to certain sports events being relocated, with considerable repercussions on the conditions of competition for undertakings associated with such events.

[111] However, such distortions, which could be a basis for recourse to Article 100a of the Treaty in order to prohibit certain forms of sponsorship, are not such as to justify the use of that legal basis for an outright prohibition of advertising of the kind imposed by the Directive.

[112] Second, as regards distortions of competition in the market for tobacco products, irrespective of the applicant's contention that such distortions are not covered by the Directive, it is clear that, in that sector, the Directive is likewise not apt to eliminate appreciable distortions of competition.

[113] Admittedly, as the Commission has stated, producers and sellers of tobacco products are obliged to resort to price competition to influence their market share in Member States which have restrictive legislation. However, that does not constitute a distortion of competition but rather a restriction of forms of competition which applies to all economic operators in those Member States. By imposing a wide-ranging prohibition on the advertising of tobacco products, the Directive would in the future generalise that restriction of forms of competition by limiting, in all the Member States, the means available for economic operators to enter or remain in the market.

[114] In those circumstances, it must be held that the Community legislature cannot rely on the need to eliminate distortions of competition, either in the advertising sector or in the tobacco products sector, in order to adopt the Directive on the basis of Articles 100a, 57(2) and 66 of the Treaty.

[115] In view of all the foregoing considerations, a measure such as the directive cannot be adopted on the basis of Articles 100a, 57(2) and 66 of the Treaty.

NOTE

The Court had no need to consider other pleas advanced by Germany, which included breach of the principles of subsidiarity, proportionality, and freedom of expression (although these issues are addressed in the Opinion of Advocate-General Fennelly). It annulled the Directive.

The Court makes it quite clear that it is *not* denying that public health concerns may play a part in the shaping of harmonization legislation (paras 78, 88). Nor is it holding it impermissible to ban particular practices in pursuit of the internal market (paras 98, 110–11). But it is insistent that harmonization must be tied to market-making. Were harmonization a competence *per se* the EC would in practice enjoy open-ended competence (paras 83–84, 107). That is not what Article 5(1) EC stipulates.

So, according to paragraph 95 of the 'Tobacco Advertising' judgment, a Directive must actually contribute to eliminating obstacles to the free movement of goods and to the freedom to provide services, and to removing distortions of competition. The challenged Directive did not.

Expect further litigation designed to refine understanding of the limits of Article 95. As 'Tobacco Advertising' (Case C-376/98) reveals, the rise of qualified majority voting in Council increases the likelihood of dissentient States outvoted in Council but willing to pursue the matter before the Court. But challenges to the validity of EC acts may also be advanced before national courts, who have available the Article 234 preliminary reference procedure as a means for bringing the matter before the Court in Luxembourg (see pp.207, 248 below). This is how the next case reached the Court and it supplied an opportunity to revisit the kernel of 'Tobacco Advertising'.

R v *Secretary of State for Health, ex parte British American Tobacco (Investments) Ltd and Imperial Tobacco Ltd* (Case C-491/01)

Judgment of 10 December 2002, Court of Justice of the European Communities

Health Warning: Don't mix up your Tobacco Directives! Directive 98/43 was annulled in Case C-376/98, extracted above. It concerned advertising. This case concerns Directive 2001/37. It amended and extended common rules governing tar yields and warnings on tobacco product packaging. It was based on Article 95 EC and, in view of its impact on external trade, Article 133 EC.

[60] First of all, it is clear from paragraphs 83, 84 and 95 of the tobacco advertising judgment that the measures referred to in that provision are intended to improve the conditions for the establishment and functioning of the internal market and must genuinely have that object, actually contributing to the elimination of obstacles to the free movement of goods or to the freedom to provide services, or to the removal of distortions of competition.

[61] Also, it follows from that case law that while recourse to Article 95 EC as a legal basis is possible if the aim is to prevent the emergence of future obstacles to trade resulting from multifarious development of national laws, the emergence of such obstacles must be likely and the measure in question must be designed to prevent them (see, to that effect, Case C-350/92 *Spain* v *Council* [1995] ECR I-1985, paragraph 35; the tobacco advertising judgment, paragraph 86, and Case C-377/98 *Netherlands* v *Parliament and Council* [2001] ECR I-7079, paragraph 15).

[62] Finally, provided that the conditions for recourse to Article 95 EC as a legal basis are fulfilled, the Community legislature cannot be prevented from relying on that legal basis on the ground that public health protection is a decisive factor in the choices to be made (see, to that effect, the tobacco advertising judgment, paragraph 88). Moreover, the first subparagraph of Article 152(1) EC provides that a high level of human health protection is to be ensured in the definition and implementation of all Community policies and activities, and Article 95(3) EC explicitly requires that, in achieving harmonization, a high level of protection of human health should be guaranteed.

NOTE

It is worth making a small but significant textual point here. In paragraph 60 of Case C-491/01 the Court refers to measures that are 'intended to improve the conditions for the establishment and functioning of the internal market and must genuinely have that object, actually contributing to the elimination of obstacles to the free movement of goods or to the freedom to provide services, or to the removal of distortions of competition'. In paragraph 95 of 'Tobacco Advertising' it referred instead to actually contributing 'to eliminating obstacles to the free movement of goods *and* to the freedom to provide services, *and* to removing distortions of competition'. It is submitted that the replacements of two *and*s by two *or*s in the later ruling, Case C-491/01, represents an improvement in precision. Moreover, the tenor of both judgments is that it is *appreciable* distortions of competition that must be removed (see paras 106–108 of 'Tobacco Advertising' above).

Directive 2001/37 was put to this (amended) test. Unlike Directive 98/43 which was at stake in 'Tobacco Advertising' (Case C-376/98), it survived.

[64] . . . national rules laying down the requirements to be met by products, in particular those relating to their designation, composition or packaging, are in themselves liable, in the absence of harmonization at Community level, to constitute obstacles to the free movement of goods (see, to that effect, Joined Cases C-267/91 and C-268/91 *Keck and Mithouard* [1993] ECR I-6097, paragraph 15).

[65] Notwithstanding the Community harmonization measures already adopted, namely, Directive 89/622 concerning the labelling of tobacco products and Directive 90/239 concerning the maximum tar yield of cigarettes, differences between the Member States' laws, regulations and

administrative provisions on the manufacture, presentation and sale of tobacco products, which create obstacles to trade, had already emerged, or were likely to emerge, by the time the Directive was adopted.

The vital 'market-making' connection was therefore established.

[75] It follows that the Directive genuinely has as its object the improvement of the conditions for the functioning of the internal market and that it was, therefore, possible for it to be adopted on the basis of Article 95 EC, and it is no bar that the protection of public health was a decisive factor in the choices involved in the harmonising measures which it defines.

[76] That conclusion is not called into question by the argument that, since the Community legislature had established a fully harmonised regime applicable to the tar yields of cigarettes, it could not legislate afresh on the basis of Article 95 EC in order to settle that matter or, in any event, could do so only on the basis of new scientific facts.

[77] The fact is that since the Community legislature made exhaustive provision in Directive 90/239 over the question of fixing the maximum tar yield of cigarettes, the Member States no longer had the power to enact individual rules in that area. As the Advocate-General has observed in paragraph 124 of his Opinion, the Community legislature can properly carry out its task of safeguarding the general interests recognised by the Treaty, such as public health, only if it has the freedom to amend the relevant Community legislation so as to take account of any change in perceptions or circumstances.

[78] It follows that, even where a provision of Community law guarantees the removal of all obstacles to trade in the area it harmonises, that fact cannot make it impossible for the Community legislature to adapt that provision in step with other considerations.

[79] With regard in particular to the protection of public health, it follows from Article 95(3) EC that the Community legislature, in harmonising the legislation, must guarantee a high level of protection, taking particular account of any new development based on scientific facts.

[80] Progress in scientific knowledge is not, however, the only ground on which the Community legislature can decide to adapt Community legislation since it must, in exercising the discretion it possesses in that area, also take into account other considerations, such as the increased importance given to the social and political aspects of the anti-smoking campaign.

NOTES
1. The Court plainly allows a margin of discretion to the legislature in choosing the level of intensity at which to pitch its harmonized measures of market regulation – *provided* the threshold that the measures be 'intended to improve the conditions for the establishment and functioning of the internal market and must genuinely have that object, actually contributing to the elimination of obstacles to the free movement of goods or to the freedom to provide services, or to the removal of distortions of competition' is crossed. In Case C-491/01 it was. In Case C-376/8 it was not.
2. The broad question of how to exercise 'control' over perceived legislative expansionism in the EC has been increasingly prominent on the political and legal agendas in recent years. 'Subsidiarity' has been an all-embracing label covering a range of concerns associated with the perceived need to protect Member States from excessive encroachment by Community intervention. But subsidiarity was not dealt with at all by the Court in the 'Tobacco Advertising' case. In fact the Court's decision in that case demonstrates logical precision. It analysed the matter from the perspective of Article 5(1) EC – did the Community have competence? It did not, and therefore subsidiarity, which is located in Article 5(2), simply did not come into play. However, subsidiarity is clearly relevant to decisions about whether and, if so, how to exercise a Community competence once it is shown to exist in principle. It will be explored in its full legal and political context in Chapter 20 as part of a broader investigation of strategies for regulation and governance in the functionally and geographically expanded European Union.

3. The Laeken Declaration of December 2001 contributed to setting the agenda for the Convention (p.25 above). It includes the observation that many citizens 'feel that the Union should involve itself more with their particular concerns, instead of intervening, in every detail, in matters by their nature better left to Member States' and regions' elected representatives. This is even perceived by some as a threat to their identity'. It continues: 'In coordinating the economic, financial and fiscal environment, the basic issue should continue to be proper operation of the internal market and the single currency, without this jeopardising Member States' individuality'. So what is to be done? The Laeken Declaration continues: '. . . the important thing is to clarify, simplify and adjust the division of competence between the Union and the Member States . . . there is the question of how to ensure that a redefined division of competence does not lead to a creeping expansion of the competence of the Union or to encroachment upon the exclusive areas of competence of the Member States and, where there is provision for this, regions. How are we to ensure at the same time that the European dynamic does not come to a halt? In the future as well the Union must continue to be able to react to fresh challenges and developments and must be able to explore new policy areas. Should Articles 95 and 308 of the Treaty be reviewed for this purpose in the light of the *acquis jurisprudentiel*?'.

■ QUESTION

Why are Articles 95 and 308 (alone of all the provisions of the EC Treaty) picked out in the Laeken Declaration as ripe for review? To what extent has the Court's case law already met the anxieties expressed about the role of Article 95?

FURTHER READING

Hervey, T., 'Community and National Competence in Health after Tobacco Advertising' (2001) 38 CML Rev 1421.

Khanna, D., 'The Defeat of the European Tobacco Advertising Directive: a Blow for Health' (2001) 20 YEL 113.

Slot, P-J., 'A Contribution to the Constitutional Debate in the EU in the Light of the Tobacco Judgment: What can be Learned from the USA?' [2002] Euro Bus Law Rev 3.

Tridimas, P. and Tridimas, G., 'The European Court of Justice and the Annulment of the Tobacco Advertisement Directive' (2002) 14 Euro Jnl Law & Economics 171.

Usher, J., 'Annotation' (2001) 38 CML Rev 1519.

■ QUESTION

What reforms would you advocate for the Community's legislative procedure in order to improve:
    (i) the efficacy of judicial control; and
    (ii) democratic accountability?

D: **Reasoning**

Article 253 declares that Community administrative and legislative acts must be reasoned.

ARTICLE 253 EC

Regulations, directives and decisions adopted jointly by the European Parliament and the Council, and such acts adopted by the Council or the Commission shall state the reasons on which they are based and shall refer to any proposals or opinions which were required to be obtained pursuant to this Treaty.

NOTES
1. Article 253 was Article 190 pre-Amsterdam, though the text is unaltered.
2. In an early decision, the Court explained the objective and scope of the requirement to give reasons in the following terms:

Germany v *Commission* (Case 24/62)
[1963] ECR 63, Court of Justice of the European Communities

In imposing upon the Commission the obligation to state reasons for its decisions, Article 190 is not taking mere formal considerations into account but seeks to give an opportunity to the parties of defending their rights, to the Court of exercising its supervisory functions and to Member States and to all interested nationals of ascertaining the circumstances in which the Commission has applied the Treaty. To attain these objectives, it is sufficient for the Decision to set out, in a concise but clear and relevant manner, the principal issues of law and of fact upon which it is based and which are necessary in order that the reasoning which has led the Commission to its Decision may be understood. . . .

Applying this test, the Court proceeded to consider whether the Commission had supplied sufficient information to support a Decision which granted Germany a wine tariff quota far below that for which it had submitted a request:

. . .[T]he Commission has been content to rely upon 'the information collected', without specifying any of it, in order to reach a conclusion 'that the production of the wines in question is amply sufficient'.

This elliptical reasoning is all the more objectionable because the Commission gave no indication, as it did belatedly before the Court, of the evolution and size of the surpluses, but only repeated, without expanding the reasons for it, the same statement 'that there was no indication that the existing market situation within the Community did not allow these branches of the Industry in the German Federal Republic a supply which is adequate in quantity and in quality'. On the other hand, although it maintained that the production of the Community was sufficient, the Commission restricted itself to 'deducing from this' that 'the grant of a tariff quota of the volume requested might therefore lead to serious disturbances of the market in the products in question', but these disturbances were not specified. Thus it neither described the risk involved in this case, nor did it disclose what it considered to be the necessary and sufficient connexion in the present case between the two concepts which it links one with the other by a simple deduction. However, by granting a restricted quota notwithstanding its description of production as 'amply sufficient', and thereby admitting that Article 25(3) applied, the Commission thus conceded that this factor was not enough to make it possible 'to deduce from it' the risk of serious disturbance.

Thus the statement of reasons expressed appears on this point to be contradictory, since in spite of its statement with regard to an adequate supply and of the automatic conclusion to be drawn therefrom the Commission grants a quota and thereby implies that it would not cause any serious disturbance. Moreover, several of the recitals in the German text, which is authentic, lack the necessary clarity.

It follows from these factors that the inadequacy, the vagueness and the inconsistency of the statement of reasons for the Decision, both in respect of the refusal of the quota requested and of the concession of the quota, granted, do not satisfy the requirements of Article 190.

Those parts of the Decision which have been submitted to the Court must therefore be annulled.

NOTE

The extent of the detail which must be provided in support of a measure will vary according to the circumstances.

Schwarze v *Einfuhr- und Vorratsstelle Getreide* (Case 16/65)
[1965] ECR 877, Court of Justice of the European Communities

The challenged Decision fixed prices for cereals. It referred back to an earlier Decision without explicitly setting out the reasons contained therein. The Court accepted that given the manner in which one measure built on the other in the administration of the policy, it was permissible for the Commission simply to refer back in this way. But were the reasons in the original Decision, thus incorporated, themselves sufficient?

The degree of precision of the statement of reasons for such a decision must be weighed against practical realities and the time and technical facilities available for making such a decision. A specific statement of reasons for each individual decision fixing a free-at-frontier price as envisaged by the Finanzgericht would mean the publication and technical evaluation of all the facts submitted by the exporting Member State or gathered by the Commission's staff for several hundreds of prices requiring to be fixed. In view, first, of the time available for the issue of the decisions and, secondly, of the number of prices to be fixed, the requirement of such a specific statement of reasons would be incompatible with the proper functioning of the machinery provided for in Regulation No 19 of the Council and Regulation No 89 of the Commission. The preparation and drafting of this kind of statement of reasons would take up so much time that the determination of prices would run the risk of being, to some extent, out of date by the time it was issued.

Moreover a comparison of the free-at-frontier prices as fixed with the general criteria published is sufficient to inform persons with a legitimate interest of the character of the data on the basis of which the decision was taken and of the conclusions to be drawn therefrom. The need to protect the parties to whom the decision is addressed and nationals of Member States affected by the decision, as also the need for proper judicial review, is sufficiently met as long as the Commission, as here, puts at the disposal of the parties the technical data used by it in fixing the free-at-frontier prices whenever the decision is challenged before a court having the appropriate jurisdiction.

For these reasons it must be concluded that the Commission was entitled to confine itself to setting out in a general form the essential factors to and the procedure which formed the background to its evaluation of the facts without its being necessary to specify the facts themselves.

NOTES

1. The Court is concerned with the balance between protecting the rights of the individual and imposing unreasonable burdens on administrative authorities in complicated, rapidly moving areas of market regulation.
2. *Commission* v *Council* (Case 45/86) was examined above (p.47). The Court held that the measures were adopted on the wrong legal basis. It also found them flawed for inadequate reasoning on this point:

Commission v *Council* (Case 45/86)
[1987] ECR 1493, Court of Justice of the European Communities

[5] Article 190 of the Treaty provides that: 'Regulations, directives and decisions of the Council and of the Commission shall state the reasons on which they are based'. According to the case law of the Court (in particular the judgment of 7 July 1981 in Case 158/80 *REWE-Handelsgesellschaft Nord GmbH* v *Hauptzollamt Kiel* [1981] ECR 1805), in order to satisfy that requirement to state reasons, Community measures must include a statement of the facts and law which led the institution in question to adopt them, so as to make possible review by the Court and so that the Member States and the nationals concerned may have knowledge of the conditions under which the Community institutions have applied the Treaty.

[6] It is therefore necessary to consider whether the contested regulations satisfy those requirements.

[7] In that connection the Council contends that, although the indication of the legal basis is not precise, the recitals in the preambles to the regulations, taken as a whole, provide sufficient alternative information as to the aims pursued by the Council, that is to say both commercial aims and aims of development-aid policy.

[8] However, those indications are not sufficient to identify the legal basis by virtue of which the Council acted. Although the recitals in the preambles to the regulations do refer to improving access for developing countries to the markets of the preference-giving countries, they merely state that adaptations to the Community system of generalized preferences have proved to be necessary in the light of experience in the first 15 years. Moreover, according to information given the Court by the Council itself, the wording 'Having regard to the Treaty' was adopted as a result of differences of opinion about the choice of the appropriate legal basis. Consequently, the wording chosen was designed precisely to leave the legal basis of the regulations in question vague.

[9] Admittedly, failure to refer to a precise provision of the Treaty need not necessarily constitute an infringement of essential procedural requirements when the legal basis for the measure may be determined from other parts of the measure. However, such explicit reference is indispensable where, in its absence, the parties concerned and the Court are left uncertain as to the precise legal basis.

SECTION 3: **GENERAL PRINCIPLES OF COMMUNITY LAW**

The substance of Community law concerns market integration, market regulation, and the establishment of a common market. These provisions are examined in Part Two of this book. Because these rules of law, which permit regulation of the economy, directly affect individuals, the procedures must respect the position of the individual. Community law accordingly contains important principles protecting the individual. The legislative and administrative tasks performed by the Community institutions are subject to review on the basis of these principles.

The Treaty contains some explicit principles which protect the individual. Article 12, for example, imposes a requirement that there shall be no discrimination on grounds of nationality within the scope of application of the Treaty. However, the Court has proved vigorous in developing a substantial body of principles independently of explicit Treaty support. These principles are important in themselves. More generally, the Court's influence in this area reveals its concern to develop a broadly based Community legal system. Some of these principles are considered below. For an extended analysis see J. Schwarze, *European Administrative Law* (London: Sweet & Maxwell, 1992); T. Tridimas, *The General Principles of EC Law* (Oxford: OUP, 1999).

A: **Proportionality**

The principle of proportionality is not spelled out in those terms in the EC Treaty. But Article 5(3) captures the concept.

ARTICLE 5(3) EC

Any action by the Community shall not go beyond what is necessary to achieve the objectives of this Treaty.

This statement is amplified by the Protocol attached to the EC Treaty on the application of the principles of subsidiarity and proportionality, which, admittedly, is more concerned to elucidate the former principle than the latter. (See p.654 below on subsidiarity.)

NOTE
Article 5(3) is a relative newcomer to the EC Treaty. It was inserted by the Maastricht Treaty and therefore entered into force only in 1993 (p.9 above). The Court had long before already developed proportionality as a basis for checking the exercise of power in the Community. So Article 5(3) clearly establishes the shape of the principle, but it is the Court's case law that amplifies what is at stake in applying the principle of proportionality.

The following case arose before English courts. It reached the European Court via the Article 234 preliminary reference procedure which allows national courts to cooperate with the Community Court and is discussed in Chapter 7. It allows the European Court to answer questions about Community law referred to it by a national court. The European Court took the opportunity in this case to insist that Community legislation must conform to the principle of proportionality.

R v *Intervention Board, ex parte Man (Sugar) Ltd* (Case 181/84)
[1985] ECR 2889, Court of Justice of the European Communities

The case involved the sugar market, which is regulated by Community legislation administered at national level. Man, a British sugar trader, submitted to the Intervention Board, the regulatory agency, tenders for the export of sugar to States outside the Community. It lodged securities with a bank. Under relevant Community legislation, Man ought to have applied for export licences by noon on 2 August 1983. It was nearly four hours late, because of its own internal staff difficulties. The Board, acting pursuant to Community Regulation 1880/83, declared the security forfeit. This amounted to £1,670,370 lost by Man. Man claimed that this penalty was disproportionate; a small error resulted in a severe sanction. It accordingly instituted judicial review proceedings before the English courts in respect of the Board's action and argued that the authorising Community legislation was invalid because of its disproportionate effect. The matter was referred to the European Court under the preliminary reference procedure. Man's submission was explained by the Court as follows:

[16] . . . Man Sugar maintains that, even if it is accepted that the obligation to apply for an export licence is justifiable, the forfeiture of the entire security for failure to comply with that obligation infringes the principle of proportionality, in particular for the following reasons: the contested regulation unlawfully imposes the same penalty for failure to comply with a secondary obligation – namely, the obligation to apply for an export licence – as for failure to comply with the primary obligation to export the sugar. The obligation to apply for an export licence could be enforced by other, less drastic means than the forfeiture of the entire security and therefore the burden imposed is not necessary for the achievement of the aims of the legislation. The severity of the penalty bears no relation to the nature of the default, which may, as in the present case, be only minimal and purely technical.

The Court held:

[20] It should be noted that, as the Court held in its judgments of 20 February 1979 (Case 122/78, *Buitoni* v *FORMA*, [1979] ECR 677) and of 23 February 1983 (Case 66/82, *Fromançais SA* v *FORMA*, [1983] ECR 395), in order to establish whether a provision of Community law is in conformity with the principle of proportionality it is necessary to ascertain whether the means which it employs are appropriate and necessary to attain the objective sought. Where Community legislation makes a distinction between a primary obligation, compliance with which is necessary in order to attain the objective sought, and a secondary obligation, essentially of an administrative nature, it cannot, without breaching the principle of proportionality, penalize failure to comply with the secondary obligation as severely as failure to comply with the primary obligation.

[21] It is clear from the wording of the abovementioned Council and Commission regulations concerning standing invitations to tender for exports of white sugar, from an analysis of the preambles thereto and from the statements made by the Commission in the proceedings before the Court that the system of securities is intended above all to ensure that the undertaking, voluntarily entered into by the trader, to export the quantities of sugar in respect of which tenders have been accepted is fulfilled. The trader's obligation to export is therefore undoubtedly a primary obligation, compliance with which is ensured by the initial lodging of a security of 9 ECU per 100 kilograms of sugar.

[22] The Commission considers, however, that the obligation to apply for an export licence within a short period, and to comply with that time-limit strictly, is also a primary obligation and as such is comparable to the obligation to export; indeed, it is that obligation alone which guarantees the proper management of the sugar market. In consequence, according to the Commission, failure to comply with that obligation, and in particular failure to comply with the time-limit, even where that failure is minimal and unintentional, justifies the forfeiture of the entire security, just as much as the total failure to comply with the primary obligation to export justifies such a penalty.

[23] In that respect the Commission contended, both during the written procedure and in the oral argument presented before the Court, that export licences fulfil four separate and important functions:

   (i)   They make it possible to control the release onto the market of sugar.
   (ii) They serve to prevent speculation.
   (iii) They provide information for the relevant Commission departments.
   (iv) They establish the system of monetary compensatory amounts chosen by the exporter.

[24] As regards the use of export licences to control the release onto the world market of exported sugar, it must be noted that the traders concerned have a period of five months within which to export the sugar and no Community provision requires them to export it at regular, staggered intervals. They may therefore release all their sugar onto the market over a very short period. In those circumstances export licences cannot be said to have the controlling effect postulated by the Commission. That effect is guaranteed, though only in part, simply by staggering the invitations to tender.

[25] The Commission considers, secondly, that the forfeiture of the entire security for failure to comply with the time-limit for applying for an export licence makes it possible to prevent traders from engaging in speculation with regard to fluctuations in the price of sugar and in exchange rates and accordingly delaying the submission of their applications for export licences.

[26] Even if it is assumed that there is a real risk of such speculation, it must be noted that Article 12(c) of Regulation No 1880/83 requires the successful tenderer to pay the additional security provided for in Article 13(3) of the same regulation. The Commission itself recognised at the hearing that that additional security removes any risk of speculation by traders. It is true that at the hearing the Commission expressed doubts about the applicability of Article 13(3) before export licences have been issued. However, even if those doubts are well founded, the fact remains that a simple amendment of the rules regarding the payment of an additional security, requiring for example that, in an appropriate case, the additional security should be paid during the tendering procedure, in other words, even before the export licence has been issued, would make it possible to attain the

objective sought by means which would be much less drastic for the traders concerned. The argument that the fight against speculation justifies the contested provision of Regulation No 1880/83 cannot therefore be accepted.

[27] With regard to the last two functions attributed by the Commission to export licences, it is true that those licences make it possible for the Commission to monitor accurately exports of Community sugar to non-member countries, although they do not provide it with important new information not contained in the tenders and do not, in themselves, guarantee that the export will actually take place. It is also true that the export licence makes it possible for the exporter to state whether he wishes the monetary compensatory amounts to be fixed in advance.

[28] However, although it is clear from the foregoing that the obligation to obtain export licences performs a useful administrative function from the Commission's point of view, it cannot be accepted that that obligation is as important as the obligation to export, which remains the essential aim of the Community legislation in question.

[29] It follows that the automatic forfeiture of the entire security, in the event of an infringement significantly less serious than the failure to fulfil the primary obligation, which the security itself is intended to guarantee, must be considered too drastic a penalty in relation to the export licence's function of ensuring the sound management of the market in question.

[30] Although the Commission was entitled, in the interests of sound administration, to impose a time-limit for the submission of applications for export licences, the penalty imposed for failure to comply with that time-limit should have been significantly less severe for the traders concerned than forfeiture of the entire security and it should have been more consonant with the practical effects of such a failure.

[31] The reply to the question submitted must therefore be that Article 6(3) of Regulation No 1880/83 is invalid inasmuch as it prescribes forfeiture of the entire security as the penalty for failure to comply with the time-limit imposed for the submission of applications for export licences.

NOTE
A key element in the practical expression of the principle of proportionality is the need to show a link between the nature and scope of the measures taken and the object in view. The next extract is taken from a case in which a firm sought to show that a measure affected it disproportionately and that it was accordingly invalid. The issue arose in the coal and steel sector, and therefore the provisions in question were found in the ECSC Treaty, which has now expired (p.34 above). However, the Court explained the nature of the principle of proportionality in terms of general application.

Valsabbia v *Commission* (Case 154/78)
[1980] ECR 907, Court of Justice of the European Communities

[117] It is now necessary to examine whether in view of the omissions established the obligations imposed upon the undertakings cast disproportionate burdens upon the applicants which would constitute an infringement of the principle of proportionality. In reply to the applicants' allegations on this matter, the Commission states that the validity of a general decision cannot depend on the existence or absence of other formally independent decisions.

[118] That argument is not relevant in this case and the Court must inquire whether the defects established imposed disproportionate burdens upon the applicants, having regard to the objectives laid down by Decision No 962/77. But the Court has already recognised in its judgment of 24 October 1973 in Case 5/73, *Balkan-Import-Export* v *Hauptzollamt Berlin-Packhof* [1973] ECR 1091, that 'In exercising their powers, the Institutions must ensure that the amounts which commercial operators are charged are no greater than is required to achieve the aim which the authorities are to accomplish; however, it does not necessarily follow that that obligation must be measured in relation to the individual situation of any one particular group of operators'.

[119] It appears that, on the whole, the system established by Decision No 962/77 worked despite

the omissions disclosed and in the end attained the objectives pursued by that decision. Although it is true that the burden of the sacrifices required of the applicants may have been aggravated by the omissions in the system, that does not alter the fact that that decision did not constitute a disproportionate and intolerable measure with regard to the aim pursued.

[120] In those circumstances, and taking into consideration the fact that the objective laid down by Decision No 962/77 is in accordance with the Commission's duty to act in the common interest, and that a necessary consequence of the very nature of Article 61 of the ECSC Treaty is that certain undertakings must, by virtue of European solidarity, accept greater sacrifices than others, the Commission cannot be accused of having imposed disproportionate burdens upon the applicants.

NOTE
The nature of the Court's scrutiny is influenced by the type of act subject to challenge. (See, for example, Bermann, G., 'Proportionality and Subsidiarity' Ch. 3 in Barnard, C. and Scott, J., *The Law of the Single European Market* (Oxford: Hart Publishing, 2002).) It was mentioned above (p.58) that the UK's submission that Directive 93/104 on Working Time violated the principle of proportionality was rejected. The Court explained its role in the following terms.

United Kingdom v *Council* (Case C-84/94)
[1996] ECR I-5755, Court of Justice of the European Communities

[57] As regards the principle of proportionality, the Court has held that, in order to establish whether a provision of Community law complies with that principle, it must be ascertained whether the means which it employs are suitable for the purpose of achieving the desired objective and whether they do not go beyond what is necessary to achieve it (see, in particular, Case C-426/93 *Germany* v *Council* [1995] ECR I-3723, paragraph 42).

[58] As to judicial review of those conditions, however, the Council must be allowed a wide discretion in an area which, as here, involves the legislature in making social policy choices and requires it to carry out complex assessments. Judicial review of the exercise of that discretion must therefore be limited to examining whether it has been vitiated by manifest error or misuse of powers, or whether the institution concerned has manifestly exceeded the limits of its discretion.

There were no such flaws and consequently the plea failed. Notice that in Case 181/84 (p.72 above) Man Sugar was not complaining about a broad legislative choice. The matter was more specific to its circumstances. In Case C-84/94 the Court's concession that the legislature be allowed a 'wide discretion' in areas of policy choice means that the principle of proportionality, though flexible and therefore a tempting addition to any challenge to the validity of a Community act, is only infrequently held to have been violated where broad legislative choices are impugned. This is well illustrated by revisiting a ruling already considered above.

R v *Secretary of State for Health, ex parte British American Tobacco (Investments) Ltd and Imperial Tobacco Ltd* (Case C-491/01)
Judgment of 10 December 2002, Court of Justice of the European Communities

The validity of Directive 2001/37, which amended and extended common rules governing tar yields and warnings on tobacco product packaging, was challenged in this case. As explained above (p.66), the Court was not persuaded that an incorrect legal base had been chosen. The applicant fared no better by alleging the measure violated the principle of proportionality.

[122] As a preliminary point, it ought to be borne in mind that the principle of proportionality, which is one of the general principles of Community law, requires that measures implemented through Community provisions should be appropriate for attaining the objective pursued and must not go beyond what is necessary to achieve it (see, *inter alia*, Case 137/85 *Maizena* [1987] ECR 4587,

paragraph 15; Case C-339/92 *ADM Ölmühlen* [1993] ECR I-6473, paragraph 15, and Case C-210/00 *Käserei Champignon Hofmeister* [2002] ECR I-6453, paragraph 59).

[123] With regard to judicial review of the conditions referred to in the previous paragraph, the Community legislature must be allowed a broad discretion in an area such as that involved in the present case, which entails political, economic and social choices on its part, and in which it is called upon to undertake complex assessments. Consequently, the legality of a measure adopted in that sphere can be affected only if the measure is manifestly inappropriate having regard to the objective which the competent institution is seeking to pursue (see, to that effect, Case C-84/94 *United Kingdom* v *Council* [1996] ECR I-5755, paragraph 58; Case C-233/94 *Germany* v *Parliament and Council* [1997] ECR I-2405, paragraphs 55 and 56, and Case C-157/96 *National Farmers' Union and Others* [1998] ECR I-2211, paragraph 61).

[124] With regard to the Directive, the first, second and third recitals in the preamble thereto make it clear that its objective is, by approximating the rules applicable in this area, to eliminate the barriers raised by differences which, notwithstanding the harmonization measures already adopted, still exist between the Member States' laws, regulations and administrative provisions on the manufacture, presentation and sale of tobacco products and impede the functioning of the internal market. In addition, it is apparent from the fourth recital that, in the attaining of that objective, the Directive takes as a basis a high level of health protection, in accordance with Article 95(3) of the Treaty.

[125] During the procedure various arguments have been put forward in order to challenge the compatibility of the Directive with the principle of proportionality, particularly so far as Articles 3, 5 and 7 are concerned.

[126] It must first be stated that the prohibition laid down in Article 3 of the Directive on releasing for free circulation or marketing within the Community cigarettes that do not comply with the maximum levels of tar, nicotine and carbon monoxide, together with the obligation imposed on the Member States to authorise the import, sale and consumption of cigarettes which do comply with those levels, in accordance with Article 13(1) of the Directive, is a measure appropriate for the purpose of attaining the objective pursued by the Directive and one which, having regard to the duty of the Community legislature to ensure a high level of health protection, does not go beyond what is necessary to attain that objective.

[127] Secondly, as pointed out in paragraph 85 above, the purpose of the prohibition, also laid down in Article 3 of the Directive, on manufacturing cigarettes which do not comply with the maximum levels fixed by that provision is to avoid the undermining of the internal market provisions in the tobacco products sector which might be caused by illicit reimports into the Community or by deflections of trade within the Community affecting products which do not comply with the requirements of Article 3(1).

[128] The proportionality of that ban on manufacture has been called into question on the ground that it is not a measure for the purpose of attaining its objective and that it goes beyond what is necessary to attain it since, in particular, an alternative measure, such as reinforcing inspections of imports from non-member countries, would have been sufficient.

[129] It must here be stated that, while the prohibition at issue does not of itself make it possible to prevent the development of the illegal trade in cigarettes in the Community, having particular regard to the fact that cigarettes which do not comply with the requirements of Article 3(1) of the Directive may also be placed illegally on the Community market after being manufactured in non-member countries, the Community legislature did not overstep the bounds of its discretion when it considered that such a prohibition nevertheless constitutes a measure likely to make an effective contribution to limiting the risk of growth in the illegal trafficking of cigarettes and to preventing the consequent undermining of the internal market.

[130] Nor has it been established that reinforcing controls would in the circumstances be enough to attain the objective pursued by the contested provision. It must be observed that the prohibition on manufacture at issue is especially appropriate for preventing at source deflections in trade

affecting cigarettes manufactured in the Community for export to non-member countries, deflections which amount to a form of fraud which, *ex hypothesi*, it is not possible to combat as efficiently by means of an alternative measure such as reinforcing controls on the Community's frontiers.

[131] As regards Article 5 of the Directive, the obligation to show information on cigarette packets as to the tar, nicotine and carbon monoxide levels and to print on the unit packets of tobacco products warnings concerning the risks to health posed by those products are appropriate measures for attaining a high level of health protection when the barriers raised by national laws on labelling are removed. Those obligations in fact constitute a recognised means of encouraging consumers to reduce their consumption of tobacco products or of guiding them towards such of those products as pose less risk to health.

[132] Accordingly, by requiring in Article 5 of the Directive an increase in the percentage of the surface area on certain sides of the unit packet of tobacco products to be given over to those indications and warnings, in a proportion which leaves sufficient space for the manufacturers of those products to be able to affix other material, in particular concerning their trade marks, the Community legislature has not overstepped the bounds of the discretion which it enjoys in this area.

[133] Article 7 of the Directive calls for the following observations.

[134] The purpose of that provision is explained in the 27th recital in the preamble to the Directive, which makes it clear that the reason for the ban on the use on tobacco product packaging of certain texts, such as 'low-tar', 'light', 'ultra-light', 'mild', names, pictures and figurative or other signs is the fear that consumers may be misled into the belief that such products are less harmful, giving rise to changes in consumption. That recital states in this connection that the level of inhaled substances is determined not only by the quantities of certain substances contained in the product before consumption, but also by smoking behaviour and addiction, which fact is not reflected in the use of such terms and so may undermine the labelling requirements set out in the Directive.

[135] Read in the light of the 27th recital in the preamble, Article 7 of the Directive has the purpose therefore of ensuring that consumers are given objective information concerning the toxicity of tobacco products.

[136] Such a requirement to supply information is appropriate for attaining a high level of health protection on the harmonization of the provisions applicable to the description of tobacco products.

[137] It was possible for the Community legislature to take the view, without overstepping the bounds of its discretion, that stating those tar, nicotine and carbon monoxide levels in accordance with Article 5(1) of the Directive ensured that consumers would be given objective information concerning the toxicity of tobacco products connected to those substances, whereas the use of descriptors such as those referred to in Article 7 of the Directive did not ensure that consumers would be given objective information.

[138] As the Advocate-General has pointed out in paragraphs 241 to 248 of his Opinion, those descriptors are liable to mislead consumers. In the first place, they might, like the word 'mild', for example, indicate a sensation of taste, without any connection with the product's level of noxious substances. In the second place, terms such as 'low-tar', 'light', 'ultra-light', do not, in the absence of rules governing the use of those terms, refer to specific quantitative limits. In the third place, even if the product in question is lower in tar, nicotine and carbon monoxide than other products, the fact remains that the amount of those substances actually inhaled by consumers depends on their manner of smoking and that that product may contain other harmful substances. In the fourth place, the use of descriptions which suggest that consumption of a certain tobacco product is beneficial to health, compared with other tobacco products, is liable to encourage smoking.

[139] Furthermore, it was possible for the Community legislature to take the view, without going beyond the bounds of the discretion which it enjoys in this area, that the prohibition laid down in Article 7 of the Directive was necessary in order to ensure that consumers be given objective

information concerning the toxicity of tobacco products and that, specifically, there was no alternative measure which could have attained that objective as efficiently while being less restrictive of the rights of the manufacturers of tobacco products.

[140] It is not clear that merely regulating the use of the descriptions referred to in Article 7, as proposed by the claimants in the main proceedings and by the German, Greek and Luxembourg Governments, or saying on the tobacco products' packaging, as proposed by Japan Tobacco, that the amounts of noxious substances inhaled depend also on the user's smoking behaviour would have ensured that consumers received objective information, having regard to the fact that those descriptions are in any event likely, by their very nature, to encourage smoking.

[141] It follows from the preceding considerations concerning Question 1(c) that the Directive is not invalid by reason of infringement of the principle of proportionality.

NOTE
The principle of proportionality applies not only to Community legislation, but also arises in the application of substantive Treaty provisions. It will be examined further in several of the Chapters in Part Two of this book.

....

B: **Fundamental rights**

The EU Treaty vigorously asserts the central role played by the protection of fundamental rights in the lifestyle of the Union.

ARTICLE 6 EU

1. The Union is founded on the principles of liberty, democracy, respect for human rights and fundamental freedoms, and the rule of law, principles which are common to the Member States.

2. The Union shall respect fundamental rights, as guaranteed by the European Convention for the Protection of Human Rights and Fundamental Freedoms signed in Rome on 4 November 1950 and as they result from the constitutional traditions common to the Member States, as general principles of Community law.

3. The Union shall respect the national identities of its Member States.

4. The Union shall provide itself with the means necessary to attain its objectives and carry through its policies.

NOTE
Article 7 EU adds a procedure for taking action against defaulting States.

ARTICLE 7 EU

1. On a reasoned proposal by one third of the Member States, by the European Parliament or by the Commission, the Council, acting by a majority of four fifths of its members after obtaining the assent of the European Parliament, may determine that there is a clear risk of a serious breach by a Member State of principles mentioned in Article 6(1), and address appropriate recommendations to that State. Before making such a determination, the Council shall hear the Member State in question and, acting in accordance with the same procedure, may call on independent persons to submit within a reasonable time limit a report on the situation in the Member State in question.

The Council shall regularly verify that the grounds on which such a determination was made continue to apply.

2. The Council, meeting in the composition of the Heads of State or Government and acting by unanimity on a proposal by one third of the Member States or by the Commission and after obtaining the assent of the European Parliament, may determine the existence of a serious and persistent breach by a Member State of principles mentioned in Article 6(1), after inviting the Government of the Member State in question to submit its observations.

3. Where a determination under paragraph 2 has been made, the Council, acting by a qualified majority, may decide to suspend certain of the rights deriving from the application of this Treaty to the Member State in question, including the voting rights of the representative of the Government of that Member State in the Council. In doing so, the Council shall take into account the possible consequences of such a suspension on the rights and obligations of natural and legal persons.

The obligations of the Member State in question under this Treaty shall in any case continue to be binding on that State.

4. The Council, acting by a qualified majority, may decide subsequently to vary or revoke measures taken under paragraph 3 in response to changes in the situation which led to their being imposed.

5. For the purposes of this Article, the Council shall act without taking into account the vote of the representative of the Government of the Member State in question. Abstentions by members present in person or represented shall not prevent the adoption of decisions referred to in paragraph 2. A qualified majority shall be defined as the same proportion of the weighted votes of the members of the Council concerned as laid down in Article 205(2) of the Treaty establishing the European Community.

This paragraph shall also apply in the event of voting rights being suspended pursuant to paragraph 3.

6. For the purposes of paragraphs 1 and 2, the European Parliament shall act by a two-thirds majority of the votes cast, representing a majority of its Members.

NOTE
This procedure has not (yet) been used against a Member State. The action controversially taken against Austria in 2000 was *not* taken pursuant to Article 7 EU: see Merlingen, M., Mudde, C., and Sedelemeier, U., 'The Right and the Righteous: European Norms, Domestic Politics and the Sanctions against Austria' (2001) 39 JCMS 59.

The EU Treaty provisions on a common foreign and security policy (the 'second pillar', p.9 above) make explicit reference to the importance of promoting protection of human rights.

ARTICLE 11 EU

1. The Union shall define and implement a common foreign and security policy covering all areas of foreign and security policy, the objectives of which shall be:
  — to safeguard the common values, fundamental interests, independence and integrity of the Union in conformity with the principles of the United Nations Charter,
  — to strengthen the security of the Union in all ways,
  — to preserve peace and strengthen international security, in accordance with the principles of the United Nations Charter, as well as the principles of the Helsinki Final Act and the objectives of the Paris Charter, including those on external borders,
  — to promote international cooperation,
  — to develop and consolidate democracy and the rule of law, and respect for human rights and fundamental freedoms.

NOTE
Within the EC Treaty both Article 177 EC (development co-operation) and Article 181a (economic, financial, and technical cooperation measures with third countries) 'shall contribute to the general objective of developing and consolidating democracy and the rule of law, and to the objective of respecting human rights and fundamental freedoms'. Consequently EC legislative

acts may take account of the promotion of such virtues (although the scope of this competence must be read in the light of the Court's cautious Opinion 2/94 on Accession to the ECHR [1996] ECR I-1759; see *Further Reading* p.87 below, and also para 45 of Case C-249/96 *Grant* p.93 below).

Furthermore the Charter of Fundamental Rights, solemnly proclaimed at Nice in December 2001 (p.16 above), constitutes a powerful assertion of the importance of weaving the protection of fundamental rights deep into the very fabric of the Union's wide sweep of activities. The European Union, on the face of it, is marked by an embedded commitment to subordinate majoritarian practices in democratic polities to respect for the rights and freedoms of individuals. In this, it seems to share with its States the deep concern to craft legal/constitutional protection for individual rights that has been one of the most important hallmarks of the reconstruction of European political systems and societies since (in Western Europe) the end of the Second World War in 1945 and (in Eastern Europe) the collapse of the hegemony of the Soviet Union beginning in 1989.

But all is not what it seems. Or, at least, with regard to judicial enforcement all is not what it seems. All the Member States are party to the European Convention for the Protection of Human Rights and Fundamental Freedoms signed in Rome on 4 November 1950 mentioned in Article 6 EU. But this, commonly referred to as the European Convention on Human Rights, is an instrument of the Council of Europe, not the European Union. The EU is not party to the European Convention on Human Rights. In fact the European Court has ruled that under the current Treaty arrangements it is not open to the EC to accede to the Convention (Opinion 2/94 on Accession to the ECHR [1996] ECR I-1759). Treaty revision would be required to allow for such a possibility, but there has been no such revision subsequently. So the EU cannot be directly called to account before the European Court of Human Rights, based in Strasbourg. In principle the EU can be controlled by its own Court, the European Court based in Luxembourg. But most of the provisions set out above are located in the non-EC sphere of the EU and they are not justiciable before the European Court. Pursuant to Article 46 EU the Court enjoys jurisdiction over the provisions set out above only with respect to Article 6(2) EU with regard to action of the institutions in so far as the Court has jurisdiction under the EC and EU Treaties and, in Article 7 EU, the purely procedural stipulations, with the Court acting at the request of the Member State concerned within one month from the date of the determination by the Council provided for in that Article.

Moreover, the Charter of Fundamental Rights is not legally binding. So the commitment made by the Union in Article 6 EU to respect fundamental rights is, on closer inspection, deficient in enforcement back-up. This raises two questions, one pertaining to the current position and one to the future. For the time being what exactly is the scope of judicially-enforced protection of fundamental rights? And will it be extended?

Future revision is considered at p.87 below, but the next cases reveal the scope of protection allowed by the limited jurisdiction conferred on the Court by Article 46 EU. What is now Article 7 was introduced only by the Amsterdam Treaty, while what has now become Article 6 EU was introduced for the first time by the Maastricht Treaty with effect from 1993. Before that time the Treaty was bare of explicit commitment to the protection of fundamental rights. The absence of explicit protection in the Treaty of Rome was in part due to the impossibility of predicting in 1957 how deeply the Community legal order would intrude into the social sphere and the field of individual rights. However, once that development had occurred it would have been unacceptable for the Community to fail to show respect for the protection of fundamental rights. The Court began to plug the gap more than two decades before the Maastricht Treaty. In understanding the scope of the Court's competence to review acts of the institutions against the standards of fundamental rights, recognised by Article 6 EU, it is necessary to inspect the older case law. This will also reveal the source of the wording now found in Article 6(2) EU.

The Court made a hesitant start; a terse start. The preliminary reference to the European Court by a German court in *Stauder* v *Ulm* (Case 29/69) arose out of concern that a provision of Community legislation infringed fundamental rights.

Stauder v *Ulm* (Case 29/69)
[1969] ECR 419, Court of Justice of the European Communities

[7] . . . the provision at issue contains nothing capable of prejudicing the fundamental human rights enshrined in the general principles of Community law and protected by the Court.

NOTE
The next case constituted a much more serious judicial commitment to the protection of fundamental rights as part of the Community legal order.

Nold v *Commission* (Case 4/73)
[1974] ECR 491, Court of Justice of the European Communities

Nold, a wholesale coal and construction materials dealer, sought annulment of a Commission Decision. The Decision had authorised Nold's supplier, Ruhrkohle AG, to sell coal only subject to onerous conditions which Nold could not fulfil. Nold therefore suffered damage to its business due to the Decision, because it could no longer buy direct from its supplier. The Court first considered Nold's submissions relating to discrimination and inadequate reasoning:

[9] In the reasoning given in its Decision the Commission emphasized that it was aware that the introduction of the new terms of business would mean that a number of dealers would lose their entitlement to buy direct from the producer, due to their inability to undertake the obligations specified above.

It justifies this measure by the need for Ruhrkohle AG, in view of the major decline in coal sales, to rationalize its marketing system in such a way as to limit direct business association to dealers operating on a sufficient scale.

The requirement that dealers contract for an annual minimum quantity is in fact intended to ensure that the collieries can market their products on a regular basis and in quantities suited to their production capacity.

[10] It emerges from the explanations given by the Commission and the interveners that the imposition of the criteria indicated above can be justified on the grounds not only of the technical conditions appertaining to coal mining but also of the particular economic difficulties created by the recession in coal production.

It therefore appears that these criteria, established by an administrative act of general application, cannot be considered discriminatory and, for the purposes of law, were sufficiently well-reasoned in the Decision of 21 December 1972.

As regards the application of these criteria, it is not alleged that the applicant is treated differently from other undertakings which, having failed to meet the requirements laid down under the new rules, have likewise lost the advantage of their entitlement to purchase direct from the producer.

[11] These submissions must therefore be dismissed.

The Court then examined the status of fundamental rights:

[12] The applicant asserts finally that certain of its fundamental rights have been violated, in that the restrictions introduced by the new trading rules authorized by the Commission have the effect, by depriving it of direct supplies, of jeopardizing both the profitability of the undertaking and the free development of its business activity, to the point of endangering its very existence.

In this way, the Decision is said to violate, in respect of the applicant, a right akin to a proprietary right, as well as its right to the free pursuit of business activity, as protected by the Grundgesetz of the Federal Republic of Germany and by the Constitutions of other Member States and various international treaties, including in particular the Convention for the Protection of Human Rights and Fundamental Freedoms of 4 November 1950 and the Protocol to that Convention of 20 March 1952.

[13] As the Court has already stated, fundamental rights form an integral part of the general principles of law, the observance of which it ensures.

In safeguarding these rights, the Court is bound to draw inspiration from constitutional traditions common to the Member States, and it cannot therefore uphold measures which are incompatible with fundamental rights recognized and protected by the Constitutions of those States.

Similarly, international treaties for the protection of human rights on which the Member States have collaborated or of which they are signatories, can supply guidelines which should be followed within the framework of Community law.

The submissions of the applicant must be examined in the light of these principles.

[14] If rights of ownership are protected by the constitutional laws of all the Member States and if similar guarantees are given in respect of their right freely to choose and practice their trade or profession, the rights thereby guaranteed, far from constituting unfettered prerogatives, must be viewed in the light of the social function of the property and activities protected thereunder.

For this reason, rights of this nature are protected by law subject always to limitations laid down in accordance with the public interest.

Within the Community legal order it likewise seems legitimate that these rights should, if necessary, be subject to certain limits justified by the overall objectives pursued by the Community, on condition that the substance of these rights is left untouched.

As regards the guarantees accorded to a particular undertaking, they can in no respect be extended to protect mere commercial interests or opportunities, the uncertainties of which are part of the very essence of economic activity.

[15] The disadvantages claimed by the applicant are in fact the result of economic change and not of the contested Decision.

It was for the applicant, confronted by the economic changes brought about by the recession in coal production, to acknowledge the situation and itself carry out the necessary adaptations.

[16] This submission must be dismissed for all the reasons outlined above.

NOTES
1. This is a 'give and take' judgment. Nold fails on the facts; its rights must yield. However, of more importance in the long-term development of the law, the Court explicitly acknowledges the importance of fundamental rights within the Community legal order.
2. In *Hoechst* v *Commission* (Case 46/87) [1989] ECR 2859, [1991] 4 CMLR 410, the Court insisted that the exercise of the Commission's powers of investigation under the Treaty competition law regime must respect fundamental rights. This case is considered in its substantive context at p.587, but in its constitutional aspects it belongs here as a demonstration of the link between constitutional principles and the substantive law of Community market integration and regulation. In the next case, also concerning the application of the Treaty competition rules, the Court seizes the opportunity to provide a statement of the contemporary extent of the direct and indirect influence of fundamental rights in the EC legal order.

Roquette Frères SA v *Directeur général de la concurrence, de la consommation et de la répression des frauds* (Case C-94/00)

22 October 2002, Court of Justice of the European Communities

[23] According to settled case law, fundamental rights form an integral part of the general principles of law observance of which the Court ensures. For that purpose, the Court draws inspiration from the constitutional traditions common to the Member States and from the guidelines supplied by international treaties for the protection of human rights on which the Member States have collaborated or to which they are signatories. The ECHR has special significance in that respect (see, in particular, *Hoechst*, paragraph 13 [Case 46/87], and Case C-274/99 P *Connolly* v *Commission* [2001] ECR I-1611, paragraph 37).

[24] As the Court has also stated, the principles established by that case law have been reaffirmed in the preamble to the Single European Act and in Article F.2 of the Treaty on European Union (Case C-415/93 *Bosman* [1995] ECR I-4921, paragraph 79). They are now set out in Article 6(2) EU (*Connolly* v *Commission*, cited above, paragraph 38).

[25] In a different connection, the Court has likewise consistently held that, where national rules fall within the scope of Community law and reference is made to it for a preliminary ruling, it must provide all the criteria of interpretation needed by the national court to determine whether those rules are compatible with the fundamental rights the observance of which the Court ensures and which derive in particular from the ECHR (see, in particular, Case C-260/89 *ERT* [1991] ECR I-2925, paragraph 42, and Case C-159/90 *Society for the Protection of Unborn Children Ireland* [1991] ECR I-4685, paragraph 31).

This preliminary reference concerned the scope of legal protection of business premises subject to search. The Court proceeded to emphasize that the absence of an organic link between the EC legal order and that of the ECHR does not preclude it, sitting in Luxembourg, from explicit recognition of decisions taken by the European Court of Human Rights in Strasbourg.

[29] For the purposes of determining the scope of that principle in relation to the protection of business premises, regard must be had to the case law of the European Court of Human Rights subsequent to the judgment in *Hoechst*. According to that case-law, first, the protection of the home provided for in Article 8 of the ECHR may in certain circumstances be extended to cover such premises (see, in particular, the judgment of 16 April 2002 in *Colas Est and Others v. France*, not yet published in the *Reports of Judgments and Decisions*, § 41) and, second, the right of interference established by Article 8(2) of the ECHR 'might well be more far-reaching where professional or business activities or premises were involved than would otherwise be the case' (*Niemietz v. Germany*, cited above, § 31).

NOTE
The Court knows that it will earn (and deserve) the confidence of national constitutional courts only if it demonstrates that the Community observes fundamental rights. Without such a guarantee one could expect that national courts would deny the legitimacy and autonomy of Community law by testing it against national fundamental constitutional principles. This prospect seems to motivate the Court's observations in the next case.

Hauer v *Rheinland-Pfalz* (Case 44/79)

[1979] ECR 3727, Court of Justice of the European Communities

The case was a preliminary reference from a German court and concerned the validity of a Regulation. The first paragraph set out below details the anxiety of the national court. The *Grundgesetz* is the Federal Republic's Basic Law, established immediately after the war, and understandably much cherished. The Court responds by delicately but firmly re-writing the question.

[13] In its order making the reference, the Verwaltungsgericht states that if Regulation No 1162/76 must be interpreted as meaning that it lays down a prohibition of general application, so as to include even land appropriate for wine growing, that provision might have to be considered inapplicable in the Federal Republic of Germany owing to doubts existing with regard to its compatibility with the fundamental rights guaranteed by Articles 14 and 12 of the Grundgesetz concerning, respectively, the right to property and the right freely to pursue trade and professional activities.

[14] As the Court declared in its judgment of 17 December 1970, *Internationale Handelsgesellschaft* [1970] ECR 1125, the question of a possible infringement of fundamental rights by a measure of the Community institutions can only be judged in the light of Community law itself. The introduction of special criteria for assessment stemming from the legislation or constitutional law of a particular Member State would, by damaging the substantive unity and efficacy of Community law, lead inevitably to the destruction of the unity of the Common Market and the jeopardizing of the cohesion of the Community.

[15] The Court also emphasized in the judgment cited, and later in the judgment of 14 May 1974, *Nold* [1974] ECR 491, that fundamental rights form an integral part of the general principles of the law, the observance of which it ensures; that in safeguarding those rights, the Court is bound to draw inspiration from constitutional traditions common to the Member States, so that measures which are incompatible with the fundamental rights recognised by the constitutions of those States are unacceptable in the Community; and that, similarly, international treaties for the protection of human rights on which the Member States have collaborated or of which they are signatories, can supply guidelines which should be followed within the framework of Community law. That conception was later recognised by the joint declaration of the European Parliament, the Council and the Commission of 5 April 1977, which, after recalling the case law of the Court, refers on the one hand to the rights guaranteed by the constitutions of the Member States and on the other hand to the European Convention for the Protection of Human Rights and Fundamental Freedoms of 4 November 1950 (Official Journal C 103, 1977, p. 1).

[16] In these circumstances, the doubts evinced by the Verwaltungsgericht as to the compatibility of the provisions of Regulation No 1162/76 with the rules concerning the protection of fundamental rights must be understood as questioning the validity of the regulation in the light of Community law. In this regard, it is necessary to distinguish between, on the one hand, a possible infringement of the right to property and, on the other hand, a possible limitation upon the freedom to pursue a trade or profession.

The Court then proceeded to examine the nature of the right to property:

[17] The right to property is guaranteed in the Community legal order in accordance with the ideas common to the constitutions of the Member States, which are also reflected in the first Protocol to the European Convention for the Protection of Human Rights.

[18] Article 1 of the Protocol provides as follows:

'Every natural or legal person is entitled to the peaceful enjoyment of his possessions. No one shall be deprived of his possessions except in the public interest and subject to the conditions provided for by law and by the general principles of international law.

The preceding provisions shall not, however, in any way impair the right of a State to enforce such laws as it deems necessary to control the use of property in accordance with the general interest or to secure the payment of taxes or other contributions or penalties.'

[19] Having declared that persons are entitled to the peaceful enjoyment of their property, that provision envisages two ways in which the rights of a property owner may be impaired, according as the impairment is intended to deprive the owner of his right or to restrict the exercise thereof. In this case it is incontestable that the prohibition on new planting cannot be considered to be an act depriving the owner of his property, since he remains free to dispose of it or to put it to other uses which are not prohibited. On the other hand, there is no doubt that that prohibition restricts the use

of the property. In this regard, the second paragraph of Article 1 of the Protocol provides an important indication in so far as it recognises the right of a State 'to enforce such laws as it deems necessary to control the use of property in accordance with the general interest'. Thus the Protocol accepts in principle the legality of restrictions upon the use of property, whilst at the same time limiting those restrictions to the extent to which they are deemed 'necessary' by a State for the protection of the 'general interest'. However, that provision does not enable a sufficiently precise answer to be given to the question submitted by the Verwaltungsgericht.

[20] Therefore, in order to be able to answer that question, it is necessary to consider also the indications provided by the constitutional rules and practices of the nine Member States. One of the first points to emerge in this regard is that those rules and practices permit the legislature to control the use of private property in accordance with the general interest. Thus some constitutions refer to the obligations arising out of the ownership of property (German Grundgesetz, Article 14(2), first sentence), to its social function (Italian constitution, Article 42(2)), to the subordination of its use to the requirements of the common good (German Grundgesetz, Article 14(2), second sentence, and the Irish constitution, Article 43.2.2), or of social justice (Irish constitution, Article 43.2.1). In all the Member States, numerous legislative measures have given concrete expression to that social function of the right to property. Thus in all the Member States there is legislation on agriculture and forestry, the water supply, the protection of the environment and town and country planning, which imposes restrictions, sometimes appreciable, on the use of real property.

[21] More particularly, all the wine-producing countries of the Community have restrictive legislation, albeit of differing severity, concerning the planting of vines, the selection of varieties and the methods of cultivation. In none of the countries concerned are those provisions considered to be incompatible in principle with the regard due to the right to property.

[22] Thus it may be stated, taking into account the constitutional precepts common to the Member States and consistent legislative practices, in widely varying spheres, that the fact that Regulation No 1162/76 imposed restrictions on the new planting of vines cannot be challenged in principle. It is a type of restriction which is known and accepted as lawful, in identical or similar forms, in the constitutional structure of all the Member States.

[23] However, that finding does not deal completely with the problem raised by the Verwaltungsgericht. Even if it is not possible to dispute in principle the Community's ability to restrict the exercise of the right to property in the context of a common organization of the market and for the purposes of a structural policy, it is still necessary to examine whether the restrictions introduced by the provisions in dispute in fact correspond to objectives of general interest pursued by the Community or whether, with regard to the aim pursued, they constitute a disproportionate and intolerable interference with the rights of the owner, impinging upon the very substance of the right to property. Such in fact is the plea submitted by the plaintiff in the main action, who considers that only the pursuit of a qualitative policy would permit the legislature to restrict the use of wine-growing property, with the result that she possesses an unassailable right from the moment that it is recognized that her land is suitable for wine growing. It is therefore necessary to identify the aim pursued by the disputed regulation and to determine whether there exists a reasonable relationship between the measures provided for by the regulation and the aim pursued by the Community in this case.

[24] The provisions of Regulation No 1162/76 must be considered in the context of the common organization of the market in wine which is closely linked to the structural policy envisaged by the Community in the area in question. The aims of that policy are stated in Regulation (EEC) No 816/70 of 28 April 1970 laying down additional provisions for the common organization of the market in wine (Official Journal, English Special Edition 1970 (1), p. 234), which provides the basis for the disputed regulation, and in Regulation No 337/79 of 5 February 1979 on the common organization of the market in wine (Official Journal L 54, p. 1), which codifies all the provisions governing the common organization of the market. Title III of that regulation, laying down 'rules concerning production and for controlling planting', now forms the legal framework in that sphere. Another factor which makes it possible to perceive the Community policy pursued in that field is the Council Resolution of

21 April 1975 concerning new guidelines to balance the market in table wines (Official Journal C 90, p. 1).

[25] Taken as a whole, those measures show that the policy initiated and partially implemented by the Community consists of a common organization of the market in conjunction with a structural improvement in the wine-producing sector. Within the framework of the guidelines laid down by Article 39 of the EEC Treaty that action seeks to achieve a double objective, namely, on the one hand, to establish a lasting balance on the wine market at a price level which is profitable for producers and fair to consumers and, secondly, to obtain an improvement in the quality of wines marketed. In order to attain that double objective of quantitative balance and qualitative improvement, the Community rules relating to the market in wine provide for an extensive range of measures which apply both at the production stage and at the marketing stage for wine.

[26] In this regard, it is necessary to refer in particular to the provisions of Article 17 of Regulation No 816/70, re-enacted in an extended form by Article 31 of Regulation No 337/79, which provide for the establishment by the Member States of forecasts of planting and production, co-ordinated within the framework of a compulsory Community plan. For the purpose of implementing that plan measures may be adopted concerning the planting, re-planting, grubbing-up or cessation of cultivation of vineyards.

[27] It is in this context that Regulation No 1162/76 was adopted. It is apparent from the preamble to that regulation and from the economic circumstances in which it was adopted, a feature of which was the formation as from the 1974 harvest of permanent production surpluses, that that regulation fulfils a double function: on the one hand, it must enable an immediate brake to be put on the continued increase in the surpluses; on the other hand, it must win for the Community institutions the time necessary for the implementation of a structural policy designed to encourage high-quality production, whilst respecting the individual characteristics and needs of the different wine-producing regions of the Community, through the selection of land for grape growing and the selection of grape varieties, and through the regulation of production methods.

[28] It was in order to fulfil that twofold purpose that the Council introduced by Regulation No 1162/76 a general prohibition on new plantings, without making any distinction, apart from certain narrowly defined exceptions, according to the quality of the land. It should be noted that, as regards its sweeping scope, the measure introduced by the Council is of a temporary nature. It is designed to deal immediately with a conjunctural situation characterised by surpluses, whilst at the same time preparing permanent structural measures.

[29] Seen in this light, the measure criticized does not entail any undue limitation upon the exercise of the right to property. Indeed, the cultivation of new vineyards in a situation of continuous over-production would not have any effect, from the economic point of view, apart from increasing the volume of the surpluses; further, such an extension at that stage would entail the risk of making more difficult the implementation of a structural policy at the Community level in the event of such a policy resting on the application of criteria more stringent than the current provisions of national legislation concerning the selection of land accepted for wine-growing.

[30] Therefore it is necessary to conclude that the restriction imposed upon the use of property by the prohibition on the new planting of vines introduced for a limited period by Regulation No 1162/76 is justified by the objectives of general interest pursued by the Community and does not infringe the substance of the right to property in the form in which it is recognised and protected in the Community legal order.

NOTE
Citing *Nold* (Case 4/73), the Court also concluded that there was no breach of the freedom to pursue a trade or profession. For a more recent decision, comparable in both its reasoning and result, see Cases C-248/95 and C-249/95 *SAM Schiffahrt* [1997] ECR I-4475.

In *Wunsche Handelsgesellschaft* [1987] 3 CMLR 225, the German Federal Constitutional Court, the *Bundesverfassungsgericht*, declared it would not test

Community legislation against the requirements of the German Constitution, because it was satisfied that the Community legal order offered adequate protection against violation of fundamental rights. The Community legal order has thus been shaped in the context of litigation at national level and in response to national constitutional concerns. This matter will be examined further in Chapter 3, for it impinges on the doctrine of the supremacy of Community law. A distinct but connected concern surrounds the question of whether a national court can invalidate a Community act as lying beyond the competence conferred by the Treaty. The European Court's view is perfectly clear – only it possesses this jurisdiction. National courts do not all agree. This too has generated a form of indirect judicial dialogue between national (especially German) and European courts: see Chapter 21.

The Court's case law has plainly inspired the text of Article 6 EU, even if the jurisdiction of the Court to secure the protection of 'fundamental rights, as guaranteed by the European Convention for the Protection of Human Rights and Fundamental Freedoms signed in Rome on 4 November 1950 and as they result from the constitutional traditions common to the Member States, as general principles of Community law' pursuant to Article 6(2) EU is defined in limited fashion by Article 46 EU. The Helsinki European Council in December 1999 took the opportunity to issue a 'millennium declaration' which asserted that the European Union is based on democracy and the rule of law and that its citizens are joined by common values such as freedom, tolerance, equality, solidarity, and cultural diversity. Then, in December 2000, the Charter of Fundamental Rights was solemnly proclaimed after a process of drafting that was consciously adopted as a model for the Convention that began in March 2002 (p.25 above). The Charter is not binding. Nonetheless it has been cited increasingly commonly by Advocates General and by the Court. And the consensus in the Convention is evidently that the Charter should be embedded within a new Treaty as a centrally important and legally binding component of a new Treaty. (See this book's Companion Website for up-dates on the progress of this debate.)

■ QUESTION

The European Court is the only Community institution not susceptible to legal challenge. Would it be desirable to establish a control over the European Court by putting it in turn under the supervision of the European Court of Human Rights?

FURTHER READING

Alston, P., (ed), *The EU and Human Rights* (Oxford: OUP, 1999 – a collection of 28 essays).

Curtin, D., 'The EU Human Rights Charter and the Union Legal Order: the Banns before the Marriage', Ch.20 in O'Keeffe, D., (ed), *Judicial Review in European Union Law: Liber Amicorum Gordon Slynn* (The Hague: Kluwer Law International, 2000).

Duvigneau, J.L., 'From Advisory Opinion 2/94 to the Amsterdam Treaty: Human Rights Protection in the EU' [1998/2] LIEI 61.

Fierro, E., 'Legal Basis and Scope of the Human Rights Clauses in EC Bilateral Agreements: Any Room for Positive Interpretation?' (2001) 7 ELJ 41.

Lenaerts, K., 'Fundamental Rights in the European Union' (2000) 25 EL Rev 575.

McGoldrick, D., 'The European Union after Amsterdam: An Organisation with general Human Rights Competence?', in D. O'Keeffe and P. Twomey, *Legal Issues of the Amsterdam Treaty* (Oxford: Hart Publishing, 1999), Ch. 15.

Von Bogdandy, A., 'The EU as a Human Rights Organisation? Human Rights and the Core of the EU' (2000) 37 CML Rev 1307.

....

C: **Technique**

The Court's technique in realizing the elaboration of the principles of Community law is of more general interest beyond the content of those principles. Article 288 of the EC Treaty, examined in Chapter 8, requires the Court to construct a principle of non-contractual liability, 'in accordance with the general principles common to the laws of the Member States'. It has become increasingly apparent that Article 288 is a statement of a broader principle of Community legal technique. The Court develops Community law by building from the foundations of national law. As the fundamental rights case law shows, this is an incremental process. The comparative tradition in the Court is often most visible in the Opinions of its Advocates-General.

Transocean Marine Paint v *Commission* **(Case 17/74)**
[1974] ECR 1063, Court of Justice of the European Communities

Advocate-General Warner was concerned to establish the nature of the principle of a fair hearing to which a party under investigation by the Commission is entitled. It is the method of his inquiry, rather than the substance, which is particularly interesting in this context. After explaining the problem of identifying the scope of the Commission's obligation to offer a hearing, he continued:

ADVOCATE-GENERAL WARNER: There is a rule embedded in the law of some of our countries that an administrative authority, before wielding a statutory power to the detriment of a particular person, must in general hear what that person has to say about the matter, even if the statute does not expressly require it. '*Audi alteram partem*' or, as it is sometimes expressed, '*audiatur et altera pars*'. I say that the rule applies 'in general' because it is subject to exceptions, as are most legal principles.

In the law of England the rule is centuries old, firmly established and of daily application. It is considered to be a 'rule of natural justice', a somewhat flamboyant and sometimes criticized phrase embodying a concept akin to what is, in French-speaking countries, more soberly and, I think, more accurately, referred to as 'les principes généraux du droit'. The late Professor de Smith, in his book 'Judicial Review of Administrative Action' (3rd Ed. at p. 134 *et seq*), traced its origins and development. I will not take up your Lordships' time with an account of them. The most often cited expression of the rule is in the judgment of Byles J. in *Cooper* v *Wandsworth Board of Works* (1863) 14 CBNS 180, where he said that 'although there are no positive words in a statute requiring that the party shall be heard, yet the justice of the common law will supply the omission of the legislature'. In England today there is no scope for controversy about the existence of the rule, but only about the circumstances in which it may be held inapplicable and about the manner in which it is to be applied in particular instances – consider the judgments in the House of Lords in *Ridge* v *Baldwin* [1964] AC 40. I know, my Lords, of no exception to the rule, acknowledged in English law, which could have deprived the Applicants in the circumstances of the present case of the right to be heard before being subjected to an obligation such as that contained in Article 3(1)(d) of the Commission's Decision.

There can be no doubt that the rule forms part also of the law of Scotland (consider *Malloch* v *Aberdeen Corporation* 1971 SLT 245; [1971] 1 WLR 1578) and of the laws of Denmark (see Andersen, 'Dansk Forvaltningsret', at p. 337 *et seq*), of Germany (see Forsthoff, 'Lehrbuch des Verwaltungsrechts', 10th Ed., at p. 235 *et seq*) and of Ireland (see Kelly, 'Fundamental Rights in the Irish Law and Constitutions', at pp. 313–314).

It has been said by Professor Vedel that the rule *'audi alteram partem'* does not exist in French administrative law (see, for instance, his 'Cours de Droit Administratif', p. 536). Professor Waline, on the other hand, in an article on the rule ('Livre Jubilaire' du Conseil d'État du Grand-Duché de Luxembourg, 1957, pp. 495–506) suggests on the contrary that it does. In my opinion, it matters little whether the applicable rule is subsumed under the title *'audi alteram partem'* or, as Professor Vedel would prefer, under the concept of the 'droits de la défense'. What is undoubted is that French administrative law does acknowledge the existence of those 'principes généraux du droit' which I have mentioned and which are applicable even in the absence of any specific legislative provision. The relevant decisions of the Conseil d'État are collected by Professor Waline in his article, and I need not rehearse them. It appears that the principle here in question is of fairly recent origin in French law, and that its scope is not yet settled. The decisions of the Conseil d'État evince three different approaches: the narrowest being to apply it only when the decision of the administrative authority concerned is in the nature of a sanction; a slightly wider approach which would apply it in any case where the decision of that authority is based on the character or on the behaviour of the person to be affected; and a third approach which is virtually as wide as that of the English common law. I should perhaps add that Professor Vedel refers to French law as being in this respect 'plutôt retardataire' and 'en voie d'évolution' (see 'Cours de Droit Administratif', p. 534, and 'Droit Administratif' 5th Ed., p. 279), and this is echoed by Professor Waline who refers to the principle *'audi alteram partem'* as 'un principe en voie de développement' (p. 496).

The position in Belgium and in Luxembourg is similar, though the Conseils d'État of those countries seem to have been less hesitant in developing the principle than that of France (see as to Belgium an article by Professor L. P. Suetens in Tijdschrift voor Bestuurswetensschappen en Publiek Recht, 1970, et p. 388, and as to Luxembourg the decisions of the Conseil d'État of 13 April 1961 in *Lorse* v *Ministre des Transports* (Aff. No 5811), of 5th August 1966 in *Roth* v *Ministres de l'Intérieur, de la Santé Publique et des Travaux Publics* (Aff. No 5968) and of 9th July 1971 in *Colot* v *Ministre du Trésor* (Aff. No 6136)).

In Italy the Consiglio di Stato has held that there is no general principle of law requiring an administrative authority to inform those concerned of its proposals so as to enable them to comment (Sez. IV, 15 May 1970, n. 345, Rass. Cons. di Stato 1970, I, p. 828, at p. 834). And it seems that the law of the Netherlands is similar, in this respect, to that of Italy.

My Lords, that review, which I have sought to keep short, of the laws of the Member States, must, I think, on balance, lead to the conclusion that the right to be heard forms part of those rights which 'the law' referred to in Article 164 of the Treaty upholds, and of which, accordingly, it is the duty of this Court to ensure the observance.

I would therefore reject the contention of the Commission that it was under no duty to inform the Applicants of what it had in mind before imposing on them the obligation contained in Article 3(1)(d) of its Decision.

NOTE

Chapter 18 examines in greater depth the procedures involved in Community competition law. *AM & S v Commission* (Case 155/79) provides a similar example of legal technique, in connection with legal professional privilege; see p.586.

The next extract comments on the approach taken in the *Transocean Marine Paint* case. As footnote 84 indicates, it is rather well-informed!

J. Usher, 'The Influence of National Concepts on Decisions of the European Court'
(1976) 1 EL Rev 359

A case-study: the Transocean case[78]

A study may now be made of the techniques involved in applying national concepts in a case before the Court.

---

78 Case 17/74, *Transocean Marine Paint Association* v *Commission* [1974] ECR 1063, [1974] 2 CMLR 459.

In 1967 the Commission had granted an exemption under Article 85(3) EEC [now 81(3) EC] with regard to the agreement between the undertakings forming the Transocean Marine Paint Association, subject to a condition obliging the Association to keep the Commission informed, *inter alia*, of any change in the composition of its membership.[79] In December 1973[80] this exemption was renewed subject to certain new conditions, including Article 3(1)(*d*) which required members of the Association to inform the Commission without delay of 'any links by way of common directors or managers between a member of the Association and any other company or firm in the paints sector or any financial participation by a member of the Association in such outside companies or vice versa including all changes in such links or participations already in existence.'

The applicants brought an action to annul this provision of the decision, on the basis that, since it had neither been mentioned in the Commission's 'Notice of Objections' nor raised at the hearing before the Commission, the Commission had infringed the rules of procedure laid down in Regulation 99/63,[81] in particular Articles 2 and 4 thereof.

The Commission had in fact indicated that it was willing to renew the exemption for five years, subject to certain fresh conditions and obligations. One of these was that the Association should, according to the literal English translation, 'notify any change in the participatory relationships of the members,' which could be interpreted, amongst other things, as requiring merely that the information which had already had to be supplied under the 1967 decision be supplemented by the notification of any links which might exist between the undertakings which were members of the association.

On the question of Regulation 99/63, Advocate-General Warner suggested in his Opinion,[82] and the Court in fact decided,[83] that Articles 2 and 4 of Regulation 99/63 concern the objections which would either bring an agreement within Article 85(1) or prevent it being granted an exemption under Article 85(3) and do not deal with conditions which may be imposed upon a grant of an exemption.

However, the Court is not dependent solely upon the arguments which the parties choose to put before it. Its purpose is to ensure as far as possible the uniform application of Community law and to a certain degree it has its own staff which it can use to enable it to do this. There exists a 'Library and Research Division,'[84] the members of which when requested by members of the Court provide research notes on points of law. In this particular case, as Advocate-General Warner was of the opinion that, at any rate in English law, this would be a situation where *audi alteram partem* could be invoked, he requested a comparative study of the laws of the other Member States to see whether this was a principle generally accepted in other Member States.

It should hardly be necessary in this *Review* to cite the well-known English cases on the question,[85] although in fact the *dictum* which is perhaps most appropriate to the facts of that particular case was pronounced in an extra-judicial capacity by Lord Morris of Borth-y-Gest when he said that 'if someone has a right to be heard he must be entitled to know what he needs to be heard about. He must know what is the case against him. He must know what he has to meet.'[86]

Turning then to the various national legal systems, and looking first at French law, it is interesting to note that an English text book on French administrative law[87] states that the French concept, *droit de la défense*, is much wider than the English concept of *audi alteram partem*; on the other hand, a

---

79 Decision of June 27, 1967, JO 1967, 163/10, [1967] CMLR D9.

80 Decision of December 21, 1973, OJ 1974, L19/18, [1974] CMLR D11.

81 Commission Reg. 99/63 of July 25, 1963, JO 1963, 2268.

82 [1974] ECR 1063, 1087.

83 *Ibid.* p. 1079.

84 Of which the present writer was a member at the time.

85 e.g., *Cooper v Wandsworth Board of Works* (1863) 14 CB (NS) 180; *Ridge v Baldwin* [1964] AC 40.

86 *Current Legal Problems*, 1973, p. 11.

87 Brown and Garner, *French Administrative Law* 2nd ed, p. 124–125, citing *Trompier-Gravier* (Counseil d'État, May 5, 1944, *Sirey* 1945, 3, 14) and *SA Co-opérative d'HBM de Vichy-Cusset-Bellerive* (Counseil d'État, April 24, 1964, *Recueil*, p. 244).

French writer, Professor Vedel,[88] is of the opinion that the rule *audi alteram partem* is much wider than the principle of *droit de la défense* in French law, largely because he is of the opinion that the doctrine of *droit de la défense* only applies where the administrative measure in question has been taken by reason of the character or personal conduct of the person concerned. However, other writers take a somewhat wider view, notably Professor Waline, in a contribution to a publication celebrating the centenary of the Luxembourg Conseil d'État,[89] where he deduces from the many specific statutory instances, as well as the case law, that the principle is in the course of development.

In the case of the Federal Republic, it is interesting to note that Article 103 of the Basic Law provides only that the right to be heard applies before the ordinary civil law courts. There is no specific provision for it in administrative law. However, commentators seem to agree that the principle applies despite the absence of any legislative necessity for it. In fact one text book[90] manages to quote 14 pre-Federal Republic decisions supporting the general idea that the right to a hearing (*das rechtliche Gehör*) is an essential element of correct procedure not by virtue of principles of written law but by principles of unwritten law, i.e., as a general principle of law.[91] This principle has been taken up by the Federal German courts and a clear illustration is a decision of the Verwaltungsgerichtshof of Kassel in 1956[92] concerned with an administrative decision to change what might be termed a 'milk-catchment area' (*Milcheinzugsgebiet*) It was stated there that even without any express provision of a statute the administration must, as a requirement of the rule of law, hear the persons affected before taking a decision imposing any burden on them.

Similar formulations can be found, for example, in the case law of the Luxembourg Conseil d'État, which has held that in the case of administrative decisions which might affect proprietary interests, the administration must hear those affected, even if the actual legislation in question is silent upon the point.[93]

The same would appear to be true in Ireland,[94] Scotland[95] and Denmark.[96] As far as Belgian law is concerned, there do not appear to be any decisions directly in point though academic opinion is in favour of giving a person affected by an administrative decision the right to be heard.[97] It appears, however, that there is no general right to be heard in Dutch administrative law, and the problem is complicated by the fact that there is no general right of appeal against administrative decisions, in the absence of a special statutory provision. However, a law of June 20, 1963, provides for appeals against the administrative acts of the central government authorities.[98]

Finally, in Italy, it has been held that the right to be heard is not protected by the Constitution in administrative proceedings[99] and that there is no general principle of administrative law requiring the Administration to communicate preparatory acts to those liable to be affected to enable them to put their view.[100]

Mr Warner reviewed the position under the various national legal systems in his Opinion and concluded that the right to be heard forms part of those rights which 'the law' referred to in

---

88 *Droit Administratif*, p. 281; *Cours de Droit Administratif*, p. 536.

89 *Livre Jubilaire*, 1957, pp. 495–506; see also his *Droit Administratif*, 9th ed, at pp. 460, 552, 586 and 606 for specific examples.

90 Forsthoff, *Lehrbuch des Verwaltungsrechts*, 10th ed, p. 235 *et seq.*

91 See e.g., Decision of administrative court of Saxony (Sächs OVG), October 24, 1908, *Jahrbuch* 13 p. 97.

92 May 18, 1956, *Neue juristische Wochenschrift*, 1956, p. 1940.

93 August 5, 1966, Aff. No 5968, *Roth v Ministres de l'Intérieur, de la Santé Publique et des Travaux Publics* – the number of Ministers involved was the result of the subject-matter of the action, a refusal of an authorisation to work a quarry so as to protect underground water supplies.

94 Kelly, *Fundamental Rights in the Irish Law and Constitution*, pp. 313–314.

95 *Malloch v Aberdeen Corporation* [1971] 1 WLR 1578.

96 Anderson, *Dansk Forvaltningsret*, at pp. 337 and 339.

97 See e.g., Dembour, *Droit Administratif*, p. 266.

98 See Van Wijk, Netherlands Report, 8 *International Congress of Comparative Law* 1970, pp. 303 *et seq.*

99 Cons. di Stato, Sez. IV, 9 nov. 1971, n. 959, Rass. Cons. di Stato 1971, I, p. 2076.

100 Cons. di Stato, Sez. IV, 15 mai 1970, n. 345, Rass. Cons. di Stato 1970, I, p. 828 (834).

Article 164 EEC [now 220 EC] upholds and of which accordingly it is the duty of the Court to ensure the observance.[101]

The way the Court introduced this general principle into its judgment was to state that notwithstanding the cases specifically dealt with in Articles 2 and 4 of Regulation 99/63, the Regulation is an application of 'the general rule that a person whose interests are perceptibly affected by a decision taken by a public authority, must be given the opportunity to make his point of view known.'[102] Under the Court's formulation it was stated that the rule requires that an undertaking be clearly informed in good time of the essence of conditions to which the Commission intends to subject an exemption and it must have the opportunity to submit its observations to the Commission. 'This is especially so in the case of conditions which, as in this case, impose considerable obligations having far-reaching effects.'

The Court deduced from this that breach of the rule would be regarded as a breach of an essential procedural requirement under Article 173 of the Treaty, and that this was the case with regard to Article 3(1)(*d*) of the Decision. Since this condition was severable, it alone was annulled, and the rest of the decision was allowed to stand whilst the Commission was given the opportunity to reach a fresh decision on the point after hearing the observations or suggestions of the members of the association.[103]

Conclusion

It is hoped that this article will have shown the importance of concepts derived from national sources in the case law of the European Court, subject always to the proviso that once adopted by the Court, they are applicable as principles of Community law, not as rules of national law.

From the point of view of English readers, it will be evident from the account of the *Transocean* case that English concepts are beginning to make their presence felt. However, it will also have been noticed that certain of the most important principles applied by the Court can be regarded as derived from German sources or at least as having become principles of Community law in a formulation closely resembling that current in the Federal Republic, a point which may not be totally unconnected with the fact that of the 353 cases referred to the Court by national courts up to the end of 1975, no fewer than 167 were referred by courts in the Federal Republic. In the nature of things, judges tend to regard as common principles those which they hear cited before them day-in, day-out; perhaps there is something of a moral here for English (and Scottish) courts and lawyers.

NOTES
1. National law spills over into Community law and *vice versa*. The Community legal order is broadened and replenished by the comparative approach. In 'European Public Law: Reality and Prospects' [1991] *Public Law* 53, at p.58, T. Koopmans, a former judge of the Court, refers to general principles 'defined and developed at the Community level . . . [which] tend to extend their influence to the application of purely national law. They are discovered, by the Court of Justice, on the basis of the existing national legal systems, but they then "travel back" to these same systems with a kind of added force'. Our examination of fundamental rights shows that sources such as the European Convention on Human Rights are also heavily influential, even though organically independent of the Union structure. Aspects of Community law can be understood as an exercise in applied comparative law: K. Lenaerts, 'Le droit comparé dans le travail du juge communautaire' (2001) 37 RTDE 487.
2. It is notable that these principles are developed both in Article 230 judicial review actions and in Article 234 preliminary reference procedures. There is more than one context in which the European Court is offered the opportunity to develop the Community's legal order.

    In *The Community Legal Order*, J.-V. Louis points out that the Court, in shaping the principles of Community law, must 'determine the solution that appears most appropriate having regard to the requirements of the Community legal order'. However, he warns that 'it may not . . . usurp the role of the Community legislator if the deficiency could be filled by

101 [1974] ECR 1063, 1089.
102 [1974] ECR 1063, 1080.
103 The new Decision was in fact taken on October 23, 1975, OJ 1975 L286/24.

legislation . . . In applying the general principles common to the laws of the Member States it must exercise self-restraint' (pp.98–99). Has it? The most notable proponent of the view that the Court lacks such due inhibition is H. Rasmussen. In *On Law and Policy in the ECJ*, he comments (at p.508) that 'The Court of Justice's lawmaking activities, defiant of much European tradition in that respect, were regularly preceded by deep involvements in making choices between competing public policies' for which the available sources of law did not offer the Court judicially applicable guidelines'.

Rasmussen's more recent views may be explored in *European Court of Justice* (Copenhagen: Gadjura, 1998), although this is explicitly *not* designed as a 2nd edition of *On Law and Policy in the ECJ* (p. 36).

3. 'Judicial activism' is a phrase commonly, though troublingly imprecisely, used to describe the approach of the Court. There will be much more discussion of this issue later in the book, but do not expect the European Court to follow the methods of an English court. As Advocate-General Warner observed in the extract at p.89 above, Article 164 of the EC Treaty (now Article 220 EC) declares that, 'The Court of Justice shall ensure that in the interpretation and application of this Treaty the law is observed'. Yet many of the Treaty obligations are loosely worded, which has given the Court great latitude in developing the shape of the law. It is expected to be creative in pursuit of broad general objectives in an overt manner unfamiliar to the English judiciary. Clearly, however, the relationship between the three sources of law considered in this Chapter is not static. This book contains many examples of remarkably ambitious 'activist' decisions issued by the European Court. Many, though by no means all, pre-date the entry into force of the Single European Act in 1987. That was the first major formal revision of the founding Treaties, the subject of examination in Section 1 of this Chapter, but since then there have been three further significant revisions (Maastricht, Amsterdam and Nice). Moreover, the nature and method of adoption of legislation, covered in Section 2 of this Chapter, has been altered by those Treaties, *inter alia* by expanding the fields in which the EC is competent to legislate and, eventually, by establishing the 'co-decision' procedure under Article 251 EC as the dominant legislative procedure. So the environment within which the Court develops general principles – Section 3 of this Chapter – has changed, both because of the correspondingly broader application of those principles and the realization that today the Court takes its place as a lawmaker alongside a process of Treaty revision and legislation which is much more dynamic than it was in the first 30 years of the system's lifecycle. Awareness of this changed institutional context is plain in the next case. It is chosen less for its substantive importance than for its value in putting the reader on notice that an enduring question, to be kept in mind in traversing the material contained in this book, is how far the Court *should* go in renovating the legal order. This is a question about the nature and legitimacy of legal reasoning and it is obviously not unique to the EC's constitutional order.

Lisa Jacqueline Grant v *South-West Trains Ltd* (Case C-249/96)
[1998] ECR I-621, Court of Justice of the European Communities

The applicant, Ms Grant, had been denied travel benefits for her female partner by her employer, South-West Trains (SWT). SWT granted such benefits to an unmarried partner only if of the opposite sex to the employee. Discrimination based on sex was addressed explicitly by EC law, but discrimination based on sexual orientation, of which Ms Grant had fallen victim, was not. The Court, in receipt of a preliminary reference made by an Industrial Tribunal in Southampton, was pressed to interpret the existing EC rules to accommodate a prohibition against discrimination based on sexual orientation. Two years earlier, in Case C-13/94 *P* v *S and Cornwall County Council* [1996] ECR I-2143, it had agreed that the principle of equality, which it treated as one of the fundamental principles of Community law, favoured a broad interpretation of the scope of the provisions combatting discrimination and it held them applicable to a case of discrimination based on the worker's gender reassignment. Ms Grant was not so fortunate before the Court.

[29] . . . the Court must consider whether, with respect to the application of a condition such as that in issue in the main proceedings, persons who have a stable relationship with a partner of the same sex are in the same situation as those who are married or have a stable relationship outside marriage with a partner of the opposite sex.

[30] Ms Grant submits in particular that the laws of the Member States, as well as those of the Community and other international organisations, increasingly treat the two situations as equivalent.

[31] While the European Parliament, as Ms Grant observes, has indeed declared that it deplores all forms of discrimination based on an individual's sexual orientation, it is nevertheless the case that the Community has not as yet adopted rules providing for such equivalence.

[32] As for the laws of the Member States, while in some of them cohabitation by two persons of the same sex is treated as equivalent to marriage, although not completely, in most of them it is treated as equivalent to a stable heterosexual relationship outside marriage only with respect to a limited number of rights, or else is not recognised in any particular way.

[33] The European Commission of Human Rights for its part considers that despite the modern evolution of attitudes towards homosexuality, stable homosexual relationships do not fall within the scope of the right to respect for family life under Article 8 of the Convention (see in particular the decisions in application No 9369/81, *X. and Y.* v *the United Kingdom*, 3 May 1983, *Decisions and Reports* 32, p. 220; application No 11716/85, *S.* v *the United Kingdom*, 14 May 1986, D.R. 47, p. 274, paragraph 2; and application No 15666/89, *Kerkhoven and Hinke* v *the Netherlands*, 19 May 1992, unpublished, paragraph 1), and that national provisions which, for the purpose of protecting the family, accord more favourable treatment to married persons and persons of opposite sex living together as man and wife than to persons of the same sex in a stable relationship are not contrary to Article 14 of the Convention, which prohibits *inter alia* discrimination on the ground of sex (see the decisions in *S.* v *the United Kingdom*, paragraph 7; application No 14753/89, *C. and L.M.* v *the United Kingdom*, 9 October 1989, unpublished, paragraph 2; and application No 16106/90, *B.* v *the United Kingdom*, 10 February 1990, D.R. 64, p. 278, paragraph 2).

[34] In another context, the European Court of Human Rights has interpreted Article 12 of the Convention as applying only to the traditional marriage between two persons of opposite biological sex (see the *Rees* judgment of 17 October 1986, Series A no.106, p. 19, § 49, and the *Cossey* judgment of 27 September 1990, Series A no.184, p. 17, § 43).

[35] It follows that, in the present state of the law within the Community, stable relationships between two persons of the same sex are not regarded as equivalent to marriages or stable relationships outside marriage between persons of opposite sex. Consequently, an employer is not required by Community law to treat the situation of a person who has a stable relationship with a partner of the same sex as equivalent to that of a person who is married to or has a stable relationship outside marriage with a partner of the opposite sex.

[36] In those circumstances, it is for the legislature alone to adopt, if appropriate, measures which may affect that position.

[37] Finally, Ms Grant submits that it follows from *P* v *S* that differences of treatment based on sexual orientation are included in the 'discrimination based on sex' prohibited by Article 119 of the Treaty.

[38] In *P* v *S* the Court was asked whether a dismissal based on the change of sex of the worker concerned was to be regarded as 'discrimination on grounds of sex' within the meaning of Directive 76/207.

[39] The national court was uncertain whether the scope of that directive was wider than that of the Sex Discrimination Act 1975, which it had to apply and which in its view applied only to discrimination based on the worker's belonging to one or other of the sexes.

[40] In their observations to the Court the United Kingdom Government and the Commission submitted that the directive prohibited only discrimination based on the fact that the worker concerned belonged to one sex or the other, not discrimination based on the worker's gender reassignment.

[41] In reply to that argument, the Court stated that the provisions of the directive prohibiting discrimination between men and women were simply the expression, in their limited field of application, of the principle of equality, which is one of the fundamental principles of Community law. It considered that that circumstance argued against a restrictive interpretation of the scope of those provisions and in favour of applying them to discrimination based on the worker's gender reassignment.

[42] The Court considered that such discrimination was in fact based, essentially if not exclusively, on the sex of the person concerned. That reasoning, which leads to the conclusion that such discrimination is to be prohibited just as is discrimination based on the fact that a person belongs to a particular sex, is limited to the case of a worker's gender reassignment and does not therefore apply to differences of treatment based on a person's sexual orientation.

[43] Ms Grant submits, however, that, like certain provisions of national law or of international conventions, the Community provisions on equal treatment of men and women should be interpreted as covering discrimination based on sexual orientation. She refers in particular to the International Covenant on Civil and Political Rights of 19 December 1966 (*United Nations Treaty Series*, Vol. 999, p. 171), in which, in the view of the Human Rights Committee established under Article 28 of the Covenant, the term 'sex' is to be taken as including sexual orientation (communication No 488/1992, *Toonen* v *Australia*, views adopted on 31 March 1994, 50th session, point 8.7).

[44] The Covenant is one of the international instruments relating to the protection of human rights of which the Court takes account in applying the fundamental principles of Community law (see, for example, Case 374/87 *Orkem* v *Commission* [1989] ECR 3283, paragraph 31, and Joined Cases C-297/88 and C-197/89 *Dzodzi* v *Belgian State* [1990] ECR I-3763, paragraph 68).

[45] However, although respect for the fundamental rights which form an integral part of those general principles of law is a condition of the legality of Community acts, those rights cannot in themselves have the effect of extending the scope of the Treaty provisions beyond the competences of the Community (see, *inter alia*, on the scope of Article 235 of the EC Treaty as regards respect for human rights, Opinion 2/94 [1996] ECR I-1759, paragraphs 34 and 35).

[46] Furthermore, in the communication referred to by Ms Grant, the Human Rights Committee, which is not a judicial institution and whose findings have no binding force in law, confined itself, as it stated itself without giving specific reasons, to 'noting . . . that in its view the reference to "sex" in Articles 2, paragraph 1, and 26 is to be taken as including sexual orientation'.

[47] Such an observation, which does not in any event appear to reflect the interpretation so far generally accepted of the concept of discrimination based on sex which appears in various international instruments concerning the protection of fundamental rights, cannot in any case constitute a basis for the Court to extend the scope of Article 119 of the Treaty. That being so, the scope of that article, as of any provision of Community law, is to be determined only by having regard to its wording and purpose, its place in the scheme of the Treaty and its legal context. It follows from the considerations set out above that Community law as it stands at present does not cover discrimination based on sexual orientation, such as that in issue in the main proceedings.

[48] It should be observed, however, that the Treaty of Amsterdam amending the Treaty on European Union, the Treaties establishing the European Communities and certain related acts, signed on 2 October 1997, provides for the insertion in the EC Treaty of an Article 6a which, once the Treaty of Amsterdam has entered into force, will allow the Council under certain conditions (a unanimous vote on a proposal from the Commission after consulting the European Parliament) to take appropriate action to eliminate various forms of discrimination, including discrimination based on sexual orientation.

NOTE

Notice that the Court refers to a number of sources of law that lie outwith the formal bounds of the EC legal order. This resembles the approach taken in the fundamental rights cases, considered above. But in *Grant* the Court places limits on the porous nature of the EC legal order. 'The principle of equality, which is one of the fundamental principles of Community law' (para 41) cannot help the applicant, for the Court is unprepared to interpret the existing law in a manner that brings the discriminatory conduct within the ambit of EC law's protection. It is striking that the Treaty provision authorizing legislation to which the Court in refers in the concluding paragraph of the above extract was at the time of the judgment not even in force. It is now – it was Article 6a and it is now Article 13 EC. Legislation designed to provide a basis for attacking *inter alia* discrimination based on sexual orientation in employment has now been adopted: see Directive 2000/78 [2000] OJ L303/16.

■ QUESTIONS

1. It is striking that both proportionality and fundamental rights were first developed as legal principles by the Court, and only later embraced within the body of the Treaty. To what extent does the rise of regular Treaty revision dampen the likelihood of future judicial willingness to elaborate principles of law that exert control over the exercise of legislative and administrative discretion? Is the Charter of Fundamental Rights properly seen as an inhibition on future improvements rather than as a new stage in the process of rights protection?

2. In the light of your knowledge of techniques of judicial reasoning in the EC and more generally, do you think the Court's deferral to other forms of lawmaking (paras 36, 48 of the *Grant* judgment) is justified? How does one measure 'justification'?

NOTE

The European Court contends that the 'Treaty, albeit concluded in the form of an international agreement, nonetheless constitutes the constitutional charter of a Community based on the rule of law' (Opinion 1/91 [1991] ECR I-6079). Beyond Treaty sources and secondary legislation, there are general principles which permeate the fabric of the law. The Community offers both a Constitution for economic integration and a Constitution for the protection of the individual. This twin purpose of Community law will be observed in many manifestations throughout this book. And in fact tracing this process of 'constitutionalization' of what began as, and in formal terms still is, a legal order founded on an international Treaty holds the key to understanding the remarkable evolution of the EU legal order. Moreover, it raises fascinating yet deeply sensitive questions about how sustainable the Court's vision of the nature of the legal order over which it presides truly is. The Court's 'constitutionalization' of the EC Treaty has attracted increasing attention as one part of a broader inquiry into the nature of the Union and its impact on the constitutional structures of the Member States. These are matters to which to return. We shall do so both at the end of Part One of this book, in assessing the scope of the process of 'constitutionalization' of EC law (p.275), and then, more broadly, in Chapter 21, when attention will be focused on what it may mean to advance the case for a formal 'Constitution' for the European Union.

FURTHER READING

Bengoetxea, J., MacCormick, N., and Moral Soriano, I., 'Integration and Integrity in the Legal Reasoning of the European Court of Justice', Ch. 3 in de Búrca, G. and Weiler, J.H.H., *The European Court of Justice* (Oxford: OUP, 2001).

De Búrca, G., 'Proportionality and *Wednesbury* Unreasonableness: The Influence of European Legal Concepts on UK Law' (1997) 3 *Euro Public Law* 561.

Dehousse, R., *The European Court of Justice* (Basingstoke: Macmillan Press, 1998).

Ellis, E. (ed), *The Principle of Proportionality in the Laws of Europe* (Oxford: Hart Publishing, 1999).

Lenaerts, K., 'Le droit comparé dans le travail du juge communautaire' (2001) 37 RTDE 487.

Mestmäcker, E.-J., 'On the Legitimacy of European Law' (1994) 58 *Rabels Z* 615.

Shapiro, M., 'The European Court of Justice' in Craig, P. and de Búrca, G., *The Evolution of EU Law* (Oxford: OUP, 1999).

Van Gerven, W., 'Comparative Law in a texture of Communitarization of National Laws and Europeanization of Community Law', Ch. 28 in O'Keeffe, D., (ed), *Judicial Review in European Union Law: Liber Amicorum Gordon Slynn* (The Hague: Kluwer Law International, 2000).

Weiler, J., 'The Transformation of Europe' (1991) 100 Yale LJ 2403.

Wilhelmsson, T., 'Jack-in-the-box theory of European Community Law', in Krämer, L., *et al* (eds), *Law and Diffuse Interests in the European Legal Order* (Baden-Baden: Nomos, 1997), p. 177.

NOTE

For additional material and resources see the Companion Website at: www.oup.co.uk/best.textbooks/law/weatherill6e

3

The Nature of Community Law: Supremacy

The Court's development of the key notions of *supremacy* and of *direct effect* represents a classic exercise of the teleological interpretative function favoured by the Court. Nowhere in the EC Treaty is it possible to find an explicit commitment to the idea that Community law shall be supreme, nor to the notion that it shall be directly effective. Yet the Court has deduced the existence of both these fundamental principles from the *object* of the Treaty. It would be impossible to create the structure envisaged by the Treaties *unless* the law is supreme and directly effective. So, reasoned the Court, the Treaty impliedly contains the principles of supremacy and direct effect. This Chapter examines supremacy and its consequences; the next Chapter studies direct effect. And the focus here is on the EC, the 'first pillar' of the EU (p.9). The law of the second and third pillars does not bear the stamp of supremacy and direct effect, which constitutes one of the principal reasons for treating 'EU law' as a potentially misleading label. The law found in the three pillars is not of a uniform constitutional character. It is EC law that is the most sophisticated and it is EC law that is supreme and capable of direct effect.

SECTION 1: **SUPREMACY**

The case of *Costa* v *ENEL* (Case 6/64) provided the Court with one of its earliest opportunities to explain the nature of the Community legal order. (Naturally, the references to Treaty Articles use the 'old', i.e., pre-Amsterdam, numbering – see p.12 above.)

Costa v *ENEL* (Case 6/64)
[1964] ECR 585, Court of Justice of the European Communities

By contrast with ordinary international treaties, the EEC Treaty has created its own legal system which, on the entry into force of the Treaty, became an integral part of the legal systems of the Member States and which their courts are bound to apply.

By creating a Community of unlimited duration, having its own institutions, its own personality, its own legal capacity and capacity of representation on the international plane and, more particularly, real powers stemming from a limitation of sovereignty or a transfer of powers from the States to the Community, the Member States have limited their sovereign rights, albeit within limited fields, and have thus created a body of law which binds both their nationals and themselves.

The integration into the laws of each Member State of provisions which derive from the Community, and more generally the terms and the spirit of the Treaty, make it impossible for the States, as a corollary, to accord precedence to a unilateral and subsequent measure over a legal system accepted by them on a basis of reciprocity. Such a measure cannot therefore be inconsistent with that legal system. The executive force of Community law cannot vary from one State to another in deference to subsequent domestic laws, without jeopardizing the attainment of the objectives of the Treaty set out in Article 5(2) and giving rise to the discrimination prohibited by Article 7.

The obligations undertaken under the Treaty establishing the Community would not be unconditional, but merely contingent, if they could be called in question by subsequent legislative acts of the signatories. Wherever the Treaty grants the States the right to act unilaterally, it does this by clear and precise provisions (for example, Articles 15, 93(3), 223, 224 and 225). Applications, by Member States for authority to derogate from the Treaty are subject to a special authorization procedure (for example, Articles 8(4), 17(4), 25, 26, 73, the third subparagraph of Article 93(2), and 226) which would lose their purpose if the Member States could renounce their obligations by means of an ordinary law.

The precedence of Community law is confirmed by Article 189, whereby a regulation 'shall be binding' and 'directly applicable in all Member States'. This provision, which is subject to no reservation, would be quite meaningless if a State could unilaterally nullify its effects by means of a legislative measure which could prevail over Community law.

It follows from all these observations that the law stemming from the Treaty, an independent source of law, could not, because of its special and original nature, be overridden by domestic legal provisions, however framed, without being deprived of its character as Community law and without the legal basis of the Community itself being called into question.

The transfer by the States from their domestic legal system to the Community legal system of the rights and obligations arising under the Treaty carries with it a permanent limitation of their sovereign rights, against which a subsequent unilateral act incompatible with the concept of the Community cannot prevail . . .

NOTE
In the next case the Court made plain its view of the implications of Community law before national courts asked to rule on a conflict between Community law and domestic law.

Amministrazione delle Finanze v *Simmenthal* (Case 106/77)
[1978] ECR 629, Court of Justice of the European Communities

[14] . . . [R]ules of Community law must be fully and uniformly applied in all the Member States from the date of their entry into force and for so long as they continue in force.

[15] These provisions are therefore a direct source of rights and duties for all those affected thereby, whether Member States or individuals, who are parties to legal relationships under Community law.

[16] This consequence also concerns any national court whose task it is as an organ of a Member State to protect, in a case within its jurisdiction, the rights conferred upon individuals by Community law.

[17] Furthermore, in accordance with the principle of the precedence of Community law, the relationship between provisions of the Treaty and directly applicable measures of the institutions on the one hand and the national law of the Member States on the other is such that those provisions and measures not only by their entry into force render automatically inapplicable any conflicting provision of current national law but – in so far as they are an integral part of, and take precedence in, the legal order applicable in the territory of each of the Member States – also preclude the valid adoption of new national legislative measures to the extent to which they would be incompatible with Community provisions.

[18] Indeed any recognition that national legislative measures which encroach upon the field within which the Community exercises its legislative power or which are otherwise incompatible with the provisions of Community law had any legal effect would amount to a corresponding denial of the effectiveness of obligations undertaken unconditionally and irrevocably by Member States pursuant to the Treaty and would thus imperil the very foundations of the Community.

[19] The same conclusion emerges from the structure of Article 177 of the Treaty which provides that any court or tribunal of a Member State is entitled to make a reference to the Court whenever it considers that a preliminary ruling on a question of interpretation or validity relating to Community law is necessary to enable it to give judgment.

[20] The effectiveness of that provision would be impaired if the national court were prevented from forthwith applying Community law in accordance with the decision or the case law of the Court.

[21] It follows from the foregoing that every national court must, in a case within its jurisdiction, apply Community law in its entirety and protect rights which the latter confers on individuals and must accordingly set aside any provision of national law which may conflict with it, whether prior or subsequent to the Community rule.

[22] Accordingly any provision of a national legal system and any legislative, administrative or judicial practice which might impair the effectiveness of Community law by withholding from the national court having jurisdiction to apply such law the power to do everything necessary at the moment of its application to set aside national legislative provisions which might prevent Community rules from having full force and effect are incompatible with those requirements which are the very essence of Community law.

[23] This would be the case in the event of a conflict between a provision of Community law and a subsequent national law if the solution of the conflict were to be reserved for an authority with a discretion of its own, other than the court called upon to apply Community law, even if such an impediment to the full effectiveness of Community law were only temporary.

[24] The first question should therefore be answered to the effect that a national court which is called upon, within the limits of its jurisdiction, to apply provisions of Community law is under a duty to give full effect to those provisions, if necessary refusing of its own motion to apply any conflicting provision of national legislation, even if adopted subsequently, and it is not necessary for the court to request or await the prior setting aside of such provision by legislative or other constitutional means.

[25] The essential point of the *second question* is whether – assuming it to be accepted that the protection of rights conferred by provisions of Community law can be suspended until any national provisions which might conflict with them have been in fact set aside by the competent national authorities – such setting aside must in every case have unrestricted retroactive effect so as to prevent the rights in question from being in any way adversely affected.

[26] It follows from the answer to the first question that national courts must protect rights conferred by provisions of the Community legal order and that it is not necessary for such courts to request or await the actual setting aside by the national authorities empowered so to act of any national measures which might impede the direct and immediate application of Community rules.

[27] The second question therefore appears to have no purpose.

The Court's ruling in response to the questions referred was:

A national court which is called upon, within the limits of its jurisdiction, to apply provisions of Community law is under a duty to give full effect to those provisions, if necessary refusing of its own motion to apply any conflicting provision of national legislation, even if adopted subsequently, and it is not necessary for the court to request or await the prior setting aside of such provisions by legislative or other constitutional means.

NOTE
The cases dealing with fundamental rights in Chapter 2 should be recalled. It was precisely Community law's aspiration to supremacy that led to concern at national level about respect for fundamental rights. That in turn motivated the Court to develop the content of Community law to meet such concerns. So was built the Community legal order. It remains a developing project.

The next case examines the scope of the obligation on Member States to ensure that the influence of Community law, which is supreme, is not obstructed. (Once again, it should be borne in mind that the vintage of the case means that pre-Amsterdam Treaty numbering is used.)

Commission v France (Case 167/73)
[1974] ECR 359, Court of Justice of the European Communities

The French *Code du Travail Maritime* required the crew of merchant ships to comprise at least three French for every non-French sailor. This is in principle unlawful discrimination on grounds of nationality, forbidden by Community law. However, the French authorities were prepared in practice to allow nationals of other Member States to count as French for these purposes. It was argued that because it was proper to focus on the application of the law in practice, not its terms in the abstract, France had not violated Community law.

[41] . . . [A]lthough the objective legal position is clear, namely, that Article 48 and Regulation No 1612/68 are directly applicable in the territory of the French Republic, nevertheless the maintenance in these circumstances of the wording of the Code du Travail Maritime gives rise to an ambiguous State of affairs by maintaining, as regards those subject to the law who are concerned, a State of uncertainty as to the possibilities available to them of relying on Community law.

[42] This uncertainty can only be reinforced by the internal and verbal character of the purely administrative directions to waive the application of the national law.

[43] The free movement of persons, and in particular workers, constitutes, as appears both from Article 3(c) of the Treaty and from the place of Articles 48 to 51 in Part Two of the Treaty, one of the foundations of the Community.

[44] According to Article 48(2) it entails the abolition of any discrimination based on nationality, whatever be its nature or extent, between workers of the Member States as regards employment, remuneration and other conditions of work and employment.

[45] The absolute nature of this prohibition, moreover, has the effect of not only allowing in each State equal access to employment to the nationals of other Member States, but also, in accordance with the aim of Article 177 of the Treaty, of guaranteeing to the State's own nationals that they shall not suffer the unfavourable consequences which could result from the offer or acceptance by nationals of other Member States of conditions of employment or remuneration less advantageous than those obtaining under national law, since such acceptance is prohibited.

[46] It thus follows from the general character of the prohibition on discrimination in Article 48 and the objective pursued by the abolition of discrimination that discrimination is prohibited even if it constitutes only an obstacle of secondary importance as regards the equality of access to employment and other conditions of work and employment.

[47] The uncertainty created by the maintenance unamended of the wording of Article 3 of the Code du Travail Maritime constitutes such an obstacle.

[48] It follows that in maintaining unamended, in these circumstances, the provisions of Article 3(2) of the Code du Travail Maritime as regards the nationals of other Member States, the French Republic has failed to fulfil its obligations under Article 48 of the Treaty and Article 4 of Regulation No 1612/68 of the Council of 15 October 1968.

SECTION 2: **DIRECT APPLICABILITY**

The attribute of *direct applicability*, referred to in *Simmenthal* (Case 106/77) at p.100 above, is linked to the doctrine of supremacy. Article 249 EC declares Regulations to be directly applicable in the national legal order. This means that they are automatically law in all the Member States when made under the Community legislative procedure. In principle it is not open to Member States to interfere with the direct application of the Regulation in the national legal order. Only exceptionally will a Regulation require implementation at national level.

Variola v *Amministrazione delle Finanze* (Case 34/73)
[1973] ECR 981, Court of Justice of the European Communities

[9] In the fourth and fifth questions, the Court is, in effect, asked to determine whether the disputed provisions of the Regulations can be introduced into the legal order of Member States by internal measures reproducing the contents of Community provisions in such a way that the subject-matter is brought under national law, and the jurisdiction of the Court is thereby affected.

[10] The direct application of a Regulation means that its entry unto force and its application in favour of or against those subject to it are independent of any measure of reception into national law.

By virtue of the obligations arising from the Treaty and assumed on ratification, Member States are under a duty not to obstruct the direct applicability inherent in Regulations and other rules of Community law.

Strict compliance with this obligation is an indispensable condition of simultaneous and uniform application of Community Regulations throughout the Community.

[11] More particularly, Member States are under an obligation not to introduce any measure which might affect the jurisdiction of the Court to pronounce on any question involving the interpretation of Community law or the validity of an act of the institutions of the Community, which means that no procedure is permissible whereby the Community nature of a legal rule is concealed from those subject to it.

Under Article 177 of the Treaty in particular, the jurisdiction of the Court is unaffected by any provisions of national legislation which purport to convert a rule of Community law into national law.

. . .

[15] A legislative provision of internal law could not be set up against the direct effect, in the legal order of Member States, of Regulations of the Community and other provisions of Community law, including the prohibition, under Articles 9 *et seq.* of the Treaty, of charges having equivalent effect to customs duties, without compromising the essential character of Community rules as such and the fundamental principle that the Community legal system is supreme.

This is particularly true as regards the date from which the Community rule becomes operative and creates rights in favour of private parties.

The freedom of each Member State to vary, in relation to itself and without express authority, the date on which a Community rule comes into force is excluded by reason of the need to ensure uniform and simultaneous application of Community law throughout the Community.

SECTION 3: **PRE-EMPTION**

A further aspect of the nature of the Community legal order is that in some fields the competence of the Community is exclusive. In order to maintain integrity and uniformity in the application of the Community's legal order, Member States are held to have lost the power to act independently in particular areas.

Commission v *Council* (Case 22/70) was examined in Chapter 2 as an instance of an act, a Council Resolution, falling outside the list in Article 189 of the EC Treaty (now Article 249 EC), which was held nevertheless to have legal effects. Of interest here is exactly what that act related to – its substance.

***Commission* v *Council* (Case 22/70)**

[1971] ECR 263, Court of Justice of the European Communities

The Resolution adopted by the States relating to negotiation of the European Road Transport Agreement (the common acronym 'AETR' reflects the French version of this name) was based on the assumption that it was for the Member States to participate independently in the conclusion of the Agreement. The ostensible purpose of the Commission's challenge was to show that it was for the Community to participate, and that it had replaced the Member States as the competent actor in the field. The Court embarked on a close examination of the Treaty in order to determine the correct allocation of competence.

[12] In the absence of specific provisions of the Treaty relating to the negotiation and conclusion of international agreements in the sphere of transport policy – a category into which, essentially, the AETR falls – one must turn to the general system of Community law in the sphere of relations with third countries.

[13] Article 210 provides that 'The Community shall have legal personality'.

[14] This provision, placed at the head of Part Six of the Treaty, devoted to 'General and Final Provisions', means that in its external relations the Community enjoys the capacity to establish contractual links with third countries over the whole field of objectives defined in Part One of the Treaty, which Part Six supplements.

[15] To determine in a particular case the Community's authority to enter into international agreements, regard must be had to the whole scheme of the Treaty no less than to its substantive provisions.

[16] Such authority arises not only from an express conferment by the Treaty – as is the case with Articles 113 and 114 for tariff and trade agreements and with Article 238 for association agreements – but may equally flow from other provisions of the Treaty and from measures adopted, within the framework of those provisions, by the Community institutions.

[17] In particular, each time the Community, with a view to implementing a common policy envisaged by the Treaty, adopts provisions laying down common rules, whatever form these may take, the Member States no longer have the right, acting individually or even collectively, to undertake obligations with third countries which affect those rules.

[18] As and when such common rules come into being, the Community alone is in a position to assume and carry out contractual obligations towards third countries affecting the whole sphere of application of the Community legal system.

[19] With regard to the implementation of the provisions of the Treaty the system of internal Community measures may not therefore be separated from that of external relations.

[20] Under Article 3(e), the adoption of a common policy in the sphere of transport is specially mentioned amongst the objectives of the Community.

[21] Under Article 5, the Member States are required on the one hand to take all appropriate measures to ensure fulfilment of the obligations arising out of the Treaty or resulting from action taken by the institutions and, on the other hand, to abstain from any measure which might jeopardize the attainment of the objectives of the Treaty.

[22] If these two provisions are read in conjunction, it follows that to the extent to which Community rules are promulgated for the attainment of the objectives of the Treaty, the Member States cannot, outside the framework of the Community institutions, assume obligations which might affect those rules or alter their scope.

[23] According to Article 74, the objectives of the Treaty in matters of transport are to be pursued within the framework of a common policy.

[24] With this in view, Article 75(1) directs the Council to lay down common rules and, in addition, 'any other appropriate provisions'.

[25] By the terms of subparagraph (a) of the same provision, those common rules are applicable 'to international transport to or from the territory of a Member State or passing across the territory of one or more Member States'.

[26] This provision is equally concerned with transport from or to third countries, as regards that part of the journey which takes place on Community territory.

[27] It thus assumes that the powers of the Community extend to relationships arising from inter-national law, and hence involve the need in the sphere in question for agreements with the third countries concerned.

[28] Although it is true that Articles 74 and 75 do not expressly confer on the Community authority to enter into international agreements, nevertheless the bringing into force, on 25 March 1969, of Regulation No 543/69 of the Council on the harmonization of certain social legislation relating to road transport (OJ L **77**, p.49) necessarily vested in the Community power to enter into any agreements with third countries relating to the subject-matter governed by that regulation.

[29] This grant of power is moreover expressly recognized by Article 3 of the said regulation which prescribes that: 'The Community shall enter into any negotiations with third countries which may prove necessary for the purpose of implementing this regulation'.

[30] Since the subject-matter of the AETR falls within the scope of Regulation No 543/69, the Community has been empowered to negotiate and conclude the agreement in question since the entry into force of the said regulation.

[31] These Community powers exclude the possibility of concurrent powers on the part of Member States, since any steps taken outside the framework of the Community institutions would be incompatible with the unity of the Common Market and the uniform application of Community law.

NOTES

1. It is clearly apparent from the final paragraph of this extract that the ruling is based on the nature of the Community legal order. However, despite this ruling in principle in favour of the Community at the expense of the Member States acting independently, the Com mission's application was rejected on the facts. Given the long history of negotiations on the Agreement, the Community had not yet fully assumed competence in this particular matter. The resolution was not invalid.

2. See also *Kramer* (Case 3/76) [1976] ECR 1279, in which the Court was still firmer in its insistence on pre-emption. Some of these issues have already been explored in part in Chapter 2. A more recent significant ruling on the allocation of competences between Community and Member States in external relations is Opinion 1/94 [1994] ECR I-5267. The Court found that some aspects of the World Trade Organization Agreement fell within the EC's exclusive competence, while others fell outside the scope of exclusive competence.

The case law was duly re-visited in the context of external competence in the air transport sector in a group of cases decided by the Court on 5 November 2002: Case C-467/98 *Commission* v *Denmark,* Case C-468/98 *Commission* v *Sweden,* Case C-471/98 *Commission* v *Belgium,* Case C-472/98 *Commission* v *Luxembourg,* Case C-475/98 *Commission* v *Austria,* Case C-476/98 *Commission* v *Germany,* and the following ruling involving Finland.

Commission v *Finland* (Case 469/98)
Judgment of 5 November 2002, Court of Justice of the European Communities

[75]. . . whilst Article 84(2) of the Treaty does not establish an external Community competence in the field of air transport, it does make provision for a Community power of action in that area, albeit one that is dependent on there being a prior decision by the Council.

[76] It was, moreover, by taking that provision as a legal basis that the Council adopted the 'third package' of legislation in the field of air transport.

[77] The Court has already held, in paragraphs 16 to 18 and 22 of the *AETR* judgment, that the Community's competence to conclude international agreements arises not only from an express conferment by the Treaty but may equally flow from other provisions of the Treaty and from measures adopted, within the framework of those provisions, by the Community institutions; that, in particular, each time the Community, with a view to implementing a common policy envisaged by the Treaty, adopts provisions laying down common rules, whatever form these may take, the Member States no longer have the right, acting individually or even collectively, to undertake obligations towards non-member countries which affect those rules or distort their scope; and that, as and when such common rules come into being, the Community alone is in a position to assume and carry out contractual obligations towards non-member countries affecting the whole sphere of application of the Community legal system.

[78] Since those findings imply recognition of an exclusive external competence for the Community in consequence of the adoption of internal measures, it is appropriate to ask whether they also apply in the context of a provision such as Article 84(2) of the Treaty, which confers upon the Council the power to decide 'whether, to what extent and by what procedure appropriate provisions may be laid down' for air transport, including, therefore, for its external aspect.

[79] If the Member States were free to enter into international commitments affecting the common rules adopted on the basis of Article 84(2) of the Treaty, that would jeopardise the attainment of the objective pursued by those rules and would thus prevent the Community from fulfilling its task in the defence of the common interest.

[80] It follows that the findings of the Court in the *AETR* judgment also apply where, as in this case, the Council has adopted common rules on the basis of Article 84(2) of the Treaty.

[81] It must next be determined under what circumstances the scope of the common rules may be affected or distorted by the international commitments at issue and, therefore, under what circumstances the Community acquires an external competence by reason of the exercise of its internal competence.

[82] According to the Court's case law, that is the case where the international commitments fall within the scope of the common rules (*AETR* judgment, paragraph 30), or in any event within an area which is already largely covered by such rules (Opinion 2/91, [1993] ECR I-1061), paragraph 25). In the latter case, the Court has held that Member States may not enter into international commitments outside the framework of the Community institutions, even if there is no contradiction between those commitments and the common rules (Opinion 2/91, paragraphs 25 and 26).

[83] Thus it is that, whenever the Community has included in its internal legislative acts provisions relating to the treatment of nationals of non-member countries or expressly conferred on its institutions powers to negotiate with non-member countries, it acquires an exclusive external competence in the spheres covered by those acts (Opinion 1/94, paragraph 95; Opinion 2/92, [1995] ECR I-521, paragraph 33).

[84] The same applies, even in the absence of any express provision authorising its institutions to negotiate with non-member countries, where the Community has achieved complete harmonisation in a given area, because the common rules thus adopted could be affected within the meaning of the *AETR* judgment if the Member States retained freedom to negotiate with non-member countries (Opinion 1/94, paragraph 96; Opinion 2/92, paragraph 33).

[85] On the other hand, it follows from the reasoning in paragraphs 78 and 79 of Opinion 1/94 that any distortions in the flow of services in the internal market which might arise from bilateral 'open skies' agreements concluded by Member States with non-member countries do not in themselves affect the common rules adopted in that area and are thus not capable of establishing an external competence of the Community.

[86] There is nothing in the Treaty to prevent the institutions arranging, in the common rules laid down by them, concerted action in relation to non-member countries or to prevent them prescribing the approach to be taken by the Member States in their external dealings (Opinion 1/94, paragraph 79).

[87] It is in the light of those considerations that it falls to be determined whether the common rules relied on by the Commission in the present action are capable of being affected by the international commitments entered into by the Republic of Finland.

Examining the matter, the Court concluded that the common rules were capable of being affected by the international commitments concerning air fares and rates entered into by Finland. This constituted an unlawful intrusion into the Community's exclusive external competence contrary to Article 10 EC.

NOTE

Comparable issues of competence-allocation arise in the Community's internal legal order. So where the Community legislates, for example, in the area of health inspections for animals, Member States may be precluded from adopting different legislation in that area. Here too anxiety to protect 'the unity of the Common Market and the uniform application of Community law' mentioned in para 31 of Case 22/70 (above) is prominent. This is examined in Chapter 12 in relation to the free movement of goods in the Community under Articles 28–30. Broader questions relating to the respective competences of the Community and the Member States are addressed in Chapter 19.

 For additional material and resources see the Companion Website at: www.oup.co.uk/best.textbooks/law/weatherill6e

4

The Enforcement of Community Law: 'Dual Vigilance'

SECTION 1: **DUAL VIGILANCE**

A Member State in breach of the EC Treaty may be brought before the European Court by the Commission in the context of the Article 226 procedure (Article 169 pre-Amsterdam), or, less common, by another Member State in reliance on Article 227 (Article 170 pre-Amsterdam). However, the State may also be challenged at national level by litigants relying on the direct effect of Community law. It is then for national courts to grant appropriate remedies against the State in breach, if necessary after seeking the assistance of the European Court in matters of interpretation of Community law via an Article 234 reference (Article 177 pre-Amsterdam: see Chapter 7).

According to this model of enforcement there are two routes for protecting rights arising under Community law; that means, two routes for tackling State action that is contrary to Community law. The first, the 'European-level' infringement procedure under Articles 226 and 227 (ex 169 and 170) EC, was clearly marked out in the Treaty from the day of its entry into force in 1958. The second, the 'national-level' control, was not set out in the Treaty. It is the child of creative jurisprudence. 'Direct effect' is one of the Court's most remarkable achievements and it addressed the matter at an early stage in the development of the Community.

No decision in Community law is more important than the following:

Van Gend en Loos v *Nederlandse Administratie der Belastingen* (Case 26/62)
[1963] ECR 1, Court of Justice of the European Communities

Van Gend en Loos had imported ureaformaldehyde from Germany into The Netherlands. It had been charged a customs duty. This violated the principle of the free movement of goods between Member States – specifically Article 12 of the Treaty of Rome (which is now Article 25 post-Amsterdam, Chapter 10). Van Gend en Loos claimed reimbursement of the sum before the Dutch courts. The Dutch court made a preliminary reference to the European Court under Article 177 (which is now Article 234 post-Amsterdam) in order to discover whether Article 12 of the Treaty could assist a private litigant before a national court.

The first question of the Tariefcommissie is whether Article 12 of the Treaty has direct application in national law in the sense that nationals of Member States may on the basis of this Article lay claim to rights which the national court must protect.

To ascertain whether the provisions of an international treaty extend so far in their effects it is necessary to consider the spirit, the general scheme and the wording of those provisions.

The objective of the EEC Treaty, which is to establish a Common Market, the functioning of which is of direct concern to interested parties in the Community, implies that this Treaty is more than an agreement which merely creates mutual obligations between the contracting states. This view is confirmed by the preamble to the Treaty which refers not only to governments but to peoples. It is also confirmed more specifically by the establishment of institutions endowed with sovereign rights, the exercise of which affects Member States and also their citizens. Furthermore, it must be noted that the nationals of the states brought together in the Community are called upon to cooperate in the functioning of this Community through the intermediary of the European Parliament and the Economic and Social Committee.

In addition the task assigned to the Court of Justice under Article 177, the object of which is to secure uniform interpretation of the Treaty by national courts and tribunals, confirms that the states have acknowledged that Community law has an authority which can be invoked by their nationals before those courts and tribunals.

The conclusion to be drawn from this is that the Community constitutes a new legal order of international law for the benefit of which the states have limited their sovereign rights, albeit within limited fields, and the subjects of which comprise not only Member States but also their nationals. Independently of the legislation of Member States, Community law therefore not only imposes obligations on individuals but is also intended to confer upon them rights which become part of their legal heritage. These rights arise not only where they are expressly granted by the Treaty, but also by reason of obligations which the Treaty imposes in a clearly defined way upon individuals as well as upon the Member States and upon the institutions of the Community.

The Court then addressed the objection that Articles 169 and 170 (now 226 and 227) of the Treaty had already created a system for exercising supervision of alleged violations of EC law by Member States, and that enforcement before national courts should therefore be excluded.

In addition the argument based on Articles 169 and 170 of the Treaty put forward by the three Governments which have submitted observations to the Court in their statements of case is misconceived. The fact that these Articles of the Treaty enable the Commission and the Member States to bring before the Court a State which has not fulfilled its obligations does not mean that individuals cannot plead these obligations, should the occasion arise, before a national court, any more than the fact that the Treaty places at the disposal of the Commission ways of ensuring that obligations imposed upon those subject to the Treaty are observed, precludes the possibility, in actions between individuals before a national court, of pleading infringements of these obligations.

A restriction of the guarantees against an infringement of Article 12 by Member States to the procedures under Article 169 and 170 would remove all direct legal protection of the individual rights of their nationals. There is the risk that recourse to the procedure under these Articles would be ineffective if it were to occur after the implementation of a national decision taken contrary to the provisions of the Treaty.

The vigilance of individuals concerned to protect their rights amounts to an effective supervision in addition to the supervision entrusted by Articles 169 and 170 to the diligence of the Commission and of the Member States.

NOTE

The final sentence of this extract provides the source of the title of this Chapter – the 'vigilance of individuals' supplements that of the Commission and (albeit rarely) Member States in securing the enforcement of Community law. This is a system of 'dual vigilance'. The Court shows itself in this judgment determined carefully to justify its discovery of the key principle of direct effect from the point of view of the purpose of Community law. The inclusion of individuals as those capable of benefiting from and being subject to Community law immeasurably deepens the impact of Community law. It also makes it more likely to be observed. Breach of Community law may be challenged at Community level and also at national level. The two routes are now examined in turn.

SECTION 2: **CONTROL AT COMMUNITY LEVEL**

ARTICLES 226 AND 227 EC

Article 226

If the Commission considers that a Member State has failed to fulfil an obligation under this Treaty, it shall deliver a reasoned opinion on the matter after giving the State concerned the opportunity to submit its observations.

If the State concerned does not comply with the opinion within the period laid down by the Commission the latter may bring the matter before the Court of Justice.

Article 227

A Member State which considers that another Member State has failed to fulfil an obligation under this Treaty may bring the matter before the Court of Justice.

Before a Member State brings an action against another Member State for an alleged infringement of an obligation under this Treaty, it shall bring the matter before the Commission.

The Commission shall deliver a reasoned opinion after each of the States concerned has been given the opportunity to submit its own case and its observations on the other party's case both orally and in writing.

If the Commission has not delivered an opinion within three months of the date on which the matter was brought before it, the absence of such opinion shall not prevent the matter from being brought before the Court of Justice.

NOTE

Article 227 is plainly politically sensitive and has been little used (but see *France* v *UK* (Case 141/78) [1979] ECR 2923; and *Belgium* v *Spain* (Case C-388/95) [2000] ECR I-3123).

Articles 226 and 227 EC were Articles 169 and 170 EC pre-Amsterdam, though the text of both was unaffected by the Amsterdam Treaty, and it is also left untouched by the Treaty of Nice.

. . . .

A: **The nature of Article 226**

> **R. White and A. Dashwood**, 'Enforcement Actions under Articles 169 and 170 EEC'
> [now 226 and 227 EC]
> (1989) 14 EL Rev 388, 388–89

(Footnotes omitted; numbering altered to reflect the post-Amsterdam Treaty.)

The nature of Articles 226 and 227 EC

. . . Under both Article [226] and Article [227] the procedure falls into two distinct phases. In a first 'administrative' phase, the Commission receives observations on the allegation of non-compliance from the Member State (or in proceedings under Article [227], the Member States) concerned and defines its own position in a reasoned opinion. An attempt is made to reach a satisfactory settlement without resorting to litigation, and in the great majority of cases this has proved possible. Where it is not, an action is brought by the Commission or by the complaining Member State in the European Court. The aim of the action is to obtain a declaration by the European Court that the defendant Member State has failed in a specified manner to fulfil its obligation under specified provisions of Community law. The Member State will be bound under Article [228] to take the necessary measures to comply with the judgment.

The procedure under Article [226] represents a considerable advance on the rules that normally apply in public international law where a State fails to fulfil its obligations under a treaty. In the first place, a right to prosecute infringements is given to the Commission, an institution specifically charged with protecting and promoting the interests of the Community as a whole. This makes it much more likely that effective action will be taken than if the Decision depended exclusively on Member State's estimation as to what would best serve their particular interests. Secondly, by virtue of their adherence to the EEC Treaty, Member States accept the compulsory jurisdiction of the European Court. No express declaration of acceptance is required; and no reservations or time limit may be imposed. These special features of the procedure are explained by the vital role the Member States are called upon to play in the concrete implementation of Community policies and rules.

NOTE
A State may be liable even for violations committed by bodies which are constitutionally independent.

Commission v Belgium (Case 77/69)
[1970] ECR 237, Court of Justice of the European Communities

The action arose out of a discriminatory tax on wood imposed by Belgium. This was a violation of Article 95 of the EC Treaty (now Article 90 EC) (see Chapter 10).

[11] The defendant does not dispute the existence of discrimination resulting from the provisions which form the subject-matter of the proceedings.

[12] Following a series of steps taken by the Commission the first of which dates back to 1963, the Belgian government has shown its willingness to take the necessary measures with a view to eliminating the discrimination complained of.

[13] A draft law intended to make possible a revision of the disputed scheme was put before Parliament in 1967 and provisions were later adopted in order to revive this draft law which had lapsed owing to the dissolution of the Belgian Parliament in the meanwhile.

[14] In these circumstances the Belgian government considers that the delay in enacting the law amounts as far as it is concerned to a 'case of *force majeure*'.

[15] The obligations arising from Article 95 of the Treaty devolve upon States as such and the liability of a Member State under Article 169 arises whatever the agency of the State whose action or inaction is the cause of the failure to fulfil its obligations, even in the case of a constitutionally independent institution.

[16] The objection raised by the defendant cannot therefore be sustained.

[17] In these circumstances, by applying a duty at the same rate, as laid down by Article 31–14 of the Royal Decree of 3 March 1927 as amended, to home-grown wood transferred standing or felled and to imported wood calculated on its value at the time of the declaration of entry for home use, the Kingdom of Belgium has failed to fulfil its obligations under Article 95 of the Treaty.

Commission v Belgium (Case 1/86)
[1987] ECR 2797, Court of Justice of the European Communities

Belgium had failed to implement in time Directive 80/68, a measure designed to combat water pollution.

[8] The Belgian government has explained that the delay in transposing the Directive in respect of the entire country is due to the fact that, as a result of the institutional reforms of 8 August 1980, the national government's powers in regard to the environment have been transferred to the regions, which involved the creation and organization of new institutions, such as the Brussels region, established in 1985. Furthermore, it has pointed out that a draft decree has been approved by the Walloon Executive for the purpose of implementing the Directive in the Walloon region and is shortly to be submitted to the Conseil d'État (State Council) before being submitted to the Conseil régional wallon (Walloon Regional Council), and that for the Brussels region a draft royal decree is in preparation.

[9] It must be stated that the fact that the procedure for the adoption of implementing measures has been initiated in respect of the Walloon region and the Brussels region does not put an end to the failure to fulfil obligations. Furthermore, according to settled case law, a Member State may not plead provisions, practices or circumstances existing in its internal legal system in order to justify a failure to comply with obligations resulting from Community Directives.

[10] Accordingly, it must be held that, by failing to adopt within the prescribed period all the measures necessary to comply with Council Directive 80/68 of 17 December 1979, the Kingdom of Belgium has failed to fulfil its obligations under the EEC Treaty.

NOTE
Practical difficulties are no excuse for infringement of Treaty obligations.

Commission v *UK* (Case 128/78)
[1979] ECR 419, Court of Justice of the European Communities

The UK failed to introduce legislation requiring the use of recording equipment in road transport – tachographs.

[6] It is not denied that provision for the installation and use of the recording equipment has been made by the British legislation only on an optional and voluntary basis as regards both vehicles engaged in intra-Community transport and those engaged in national transport. On the other hand, the British legislation has maintained in force the obligations relating to the keeping of an individual control book which were abolished by the said Regulation.

[7] The defendant claims that this arrangement is sufficient to meet the objectives of promoting road safety, of social progress for workers and of the harmonization of conditions of competition. It maintains that the implementation of Regulation No 1463/70 on its territory is best achieved by the installation and use of the recording equipment on a voluntary basis, though this may be made compulsory at an appropriate time. It adds that implementation of the Regulation involving compulsory measures would meet with active resistance from the sectors concerned, in particular the trade unions, which would result in strikes in the transport sector and would therefore seriously damage the whole economy of the country.

[8] It contends that since, in the case of the United Kingdom, the objectives of the Community policy in this field can be achieved just as satisfactorily by the maintenance of the system of the individual control book as by the compulsory introduction of recording equipment, the alleged failure to fulfil an obligation is of a purely technical nature and, in view of the difficulties referred to, should not be taken into account. Moreover the installation and use of recording equipment is in practice already guaranteed in respect of intra-Community transport by the fact that the other Member States have made it compulsory.

[9] Article 189 of the Treaty provides that a Regulation shall be binding 'in its entirety' in the Member States. As the Court has already stated in its judgment of 7 February 1973 (Case 39/72 *Commission* v *Italian Republic* [1973] ECR 101) it cannot therefore be accepted that a Member State should apply in an incomplete or selective manner provisions of a Community Regulation so as to render abortive certain aspects of Community legislation which it has opposed or which it considers contrary to its national interests. In particular, as regards the putting into effect of a general rule intended to eliminate certain abuses to which workers are subject and which in addition involve a threat to road safety, a Member State which omits to take, within the requisite period and simultaneously with the other Member States, the measures which it ought to take, undermines Community solidarity by imposing, in particular as regards intra-Community transport, on the other Member States the necessity of remedying the effects of its own omissions, while at the same time taking an undue advantage to the detriment of its partners.

[10] As the Court said in the same judgment, practical difficulties which appear at the stage when a Community measure is put into effect cannot permit a Member State unilaterally to opt out of fulfilling its obligations. The Community institutional system provides the Member State concerned

with the necessary means to ensure that its difficulties be given due consideration, subject to compliance with the principles of the common market and the legitimate interests of the other Member States.

[11] In these circumstances, the possible difficulties of implementation alleged by the defendant cannot be accepted as a justification.

[12] Further, as the Court said in the case mentioned above, in permitting Member States to profit from the advantages of the Community, the Treaty imposes on them also the obligation to respect its rules. For a State unilaterally to break, according to its own conception of national interest, the equilibrium between the advantages and obligations flowing from its adherence to the Community brings into question the equality of Member States before Community law and creates discrimination at the expense of their nationals. This failure in the duty of solidarity accepted by Member States by the fact of their adherence to the Community strikes at the very root of the Community legal order.

[13] It appears therefore that, in deliberately refusing to give effect on its territory to the provisions of Regulation No 1463/70, the United Kingdom has markedly failed to fulfil the obligation which it has assumed by virtue of its membership of the European Economic Community.

....

B: **The effectiveness of Article 226**

The procedure under Article 226 occupies two phases – the administrative and the judicial. As the extract from White and Dashwood observes (p.111 above), most cases are resolved to mutual satisfaction as a result of dialogue within (or even before) the first phase. Some, a minority, are brought before the Court. The Commission enjoys a discretion in choosing how to deal with a suspected infringement of Community law, and its hand cannot be forced.

Star Fruit Co. v *Commission* (Case 247/87)
[1989] ECR 291, Court of Justice of the European Communities

Star Fruit, a Belgian banana trader, felt itself prejudiced by French banana market regulation which it believed to be contrary to the Treaty. It considered that the Commission's failure to institute infringement proceedings under Article 169 of the EC Treaty (now Article 226 EC) against France constituted a failure to act, which it was entitled to challenge under Article 175 of the EC Treaty (now, after amendment, Article 232 EC: see Chapter 8, p.234 below).

[10] In so far as it is based on the third paragraph of Article 175 of the Treaty, the purpose of the application is to obtain a declaration that in not commencing against the French Republic proceedings to establish its breach of obligations the Commission infringed the Treaty by failing to take a decision.

[11] However, it is clear from the scheme of Article 169 of the Treaty that the Commission is not bound to commence the proceedings provided for in that provision but in this regard has a discretion which excludes the right for individuals to require that institution to adopt a specific position.

[12] It is only if it considers that the Member State in question has failed to fulfil one of its obligations that the Commission delivers a reasoned opinion. Furthermore, in the event that the State does not comply with the opinion within the period allowed, the institution has in any event the right, but not the duty, to apply to the Court of Justice for a declaration that the alleged breach of obligations has occurred.

The next extract provides a statistical flavour of Commission practice. A preference for informal resolution of disputes is motivated by a strong desire on the part of the Commission for cost-effective, non-litigious rule enforcement.

The Commission's Nineteenth Annual Report on monitoring the application of Community law, 2001
COM(2002) 324, pp.6, 7–9

http://europa.eu.int/comm/secretariat_general/sgb/droit_com/index_en.htm

1. INTRODUCTION

Whereas . . . prime responsibility for applying Community law lies with national administrations and Courts, it falls to the Commission to monitor the transposal of Community law where necessary, the compatibility with Community law of the national provisions transposing that law and the proper application of Community law by various bodies in the Member States. The White Paper on European Governance points out that the impact of Community law 'depends on the willingness and capacity of Member State authorities to ensure that they are transposed and enforced effectively, fully and on time'. The Commission's activity in monitoring the application of Community law covers Community law in its entirety. As such, it is not unusual for the Commission to take action against a Member State for adopting or maintaining legislation or rules which are contrary to the fundamental principles of Community law as enshrined in the Treaties.

Within this framework, cooperation between administrative bodies in the Member States and the Commission forms a vital component of the Commission's remit, as vested in it by the Treaties, to act as the guardian of Community law. In this spirit the Commission seeks to promote, at all stages of infringement proceedings, contacts between its departments and the national administrations. The primary objective of infringement proceedings (Article 226 EC and Article 141 Euratom), particularly in the pre-litigation stage, is to encourage the Member State involved to comply voluntarily with Community law as quickly as possible. Optimal exploitation of the pre-litigation stage is thus the best way of achieving the objectives vested in the Commission by the Treaties. This duty of cooperation is formally enshrined in Article 10 of the EC Treaty . . .

1.1. Statistics for 2001

The statistics for 2001 reflect, once again, a degree of stability in the number of complaints registered by the Commission: up slightly on 2000 but still below the number recorded in 1999. Complaints still form the bulk of infringement proceedings initiated by the Commission against the Member States, and a corresponding decline is observed in the number of cases opened by the Commission on the basis of its own investigations.

The statistics for 2001 can be summed up as follows:

— The **total** number of infringement cases initiated by the Commission is **down 11.65%**, the lowest figure since 1999.
— The number of **complaints** registered by the Commission increased in 2001 (6.12% up on 2000) but remains slightly below the 1999 record. In 2001 complaints accounted for six infringement cases out of ten initiated by the Commission in that year. Inversely, the Commission opened a smaller number of cases based on its own investigations than in previous years. In 2001 there were 273 such cases, excluding infringement proceedings for failure to communicate national transposal measures. The number of proceedings for failure to notify is down to the lowest level since 1996.
— **1 050 letters of formal notice** were issued in 2001, 25.43% down on 2000, when 1 317 notifications were registered. However, it should be emphasised that because the backlog in operations for the issue of formal notice had been cleared by the beginning of 2000, the particularly high number of letters of formal notice based on failure to communicate national transposal measures had inflated the year's figures. The 2001 figure should therefore be compared with the 1999 figure (1075), suggesting a degree of

stability. It should be noted that the time necessary for operations for the issue of formal notice based on failure to notify had been considerably reduced in 2000 and that this trend continued in 2001 thanks to the continued development of the Asmodée II 'directives' database.

— The number of **reasoned opinions** rose in 2001 from 460 to 569, an increase of 23.7%. However, reasoned opinions as a proportion of outstanding files remains stable (27.80% in 2001 against 23.76% in 2000). The sudden upturn in 2001 therefore seems to be largely due to the considerable increase in the speed of notification to Member States (reduced from 29 calendar days to approximately 24 hours on average): thus, for the first time, the reasoned opinions issued in December 2001 were notified during that same year. Accordingly, the figures for 2001 represent the total number of reasoned opinions issued in December 2000 and those issued in December 2001. Only by examining the 2002 figures can the trend be determined.

— The number of **cases referred to the Court of Justice** fell by 5.82%, from 172 in 2000 to 162 in 2001. But this slight decrease must be seen against the higher number of reasoned opinions in 2001 and the reduction in processing times for reasoned opinion decisions and referral decisions. The rate of referrals is fairly stable (up from 9.77% to 10.33%).

— **Processing times have increased** slightly for letters of notice, 73% of them relating to infringement proceedings commenced in 2001. But they are down for reasoned opinions, with only 23% of reasoned opinions served concerning proceedings commenced in that year, against 14% in 2000. However, the slight increase in processing times for letters of notice must be relativised in view of the significant number of letters of formal notice based on failure to notify issued in 2000; the opening of those files is linked to notification of the letter of formal notice; the only element of complaint, i.e., failure to notify, is established purely on the basis that the deadline for transposal has passed. But overall, processing times have not increased. Whereas 49% of cases opened in 2000 were still pending at 31 December 2000, as at 31 December 2001 the corresponding figure for files opened in 2001 was 45.77%.

— At the same time, the efficiency of the pre-litigation procedure was confirmed by the number of **termination** decisions, which stabilised at 1 915 in 2001 (1 899 in 2000);

— Lastly, the Commission's policy of transparency intensified in 2000, chiefly through greater use of the internet as a means of disseminating information (see below). Since 17 January 2001, the Commission has announced all recent decisions to issue letters of formal notice and reasoned opinions, to refer cases to the Court of Justice and to terminate cases on the Secretariat-General's Europa website at: http://europa.eu.int/comm/secretariat_general/sgb/droit_com/index_en.htm – infractions

All this information is now freely accessible, whereas it used to be available only to the Member State concerned. The Commission also issued 93 press releases in 2001.

NOTE
The White Paper on European Governance, mentioned in the first paragraph of this extract, is discussed further in Chapter 20, p.681 below.

Although the Commission brings alleged infringements before the Court in only a minority of cases, there are two important elements in furthering the effectiveness of Article 226 which depend on recourse to the Court. The first is the Court's ability to make interim orders against defaulting States; the second is the power to impose fines. The power to make interim orders is conferred by Article 243, which states: 'The Court of Justice may in any cases before it prescribe any necessary interim measures'.

This is a flexible provision, but the Court has imposed relatively strict conditions on its own capacity to make interim orders. This runs parallel to its attitude to the grant of interim relief against acts of the Community institutions discussed subsequently in Chapter 8, at p.233 below.

Commission v UK (Case C-246/89R)
[1989] ECR 3125, Court of Justice of the European Communities

The Commission's action related to the UK's Merchant Shipping Act 1988. The Commission took the view that the Act violated Community rules forbidding discrimination on grounds of nationality. Under the arrangements governing the accession of Spain to the Community, the volume of catches which Spanish fishing vessels could make in Community waters was regulated. Many Spanish fishing vessels were re-registered by their owners as British and fished under the British flag, thereby taking advantage of enhanced access to Community waters, but continued to land catches in Spain and to earn profits for Spanish nationals. At the start of January 1986, the UK introduced new licensing requirements for British fishing vessels. These were supplemented by the Merchant Shipping Act 1988. The thrust of the requirements was the demand that a genuine economic link with the UK be shown beyond the mere fact of registration. British ownership and management was required. In challenging the 1988 Act, the Commission argued that its provisions contravened the Treaty rules prohibiting discrimination on grounds of nationality contained in Articles 7, 52, and 221 of the EC Treaty (now, after amendment, Articles 12, 43, and 294 EC). It initiated an action under Article 169 of the EC Treaty (now Article 226 EC), but it also asked the Court to make an interim order against the UK under Article 186 of the EEC Treaty (now Article 243 EC).

[20] Under Article 186 of the EEC Treaty the Court may in any cases before it prescribe any necessary interim measures.

[21] Under Article 83(2) of the Rules of Procedure, interim measures such as those requested may not be ordered unless there are circumstances giving rise to urgency and factual and legal grounds establishing a prima-facie case for the measures applied for.

[22] It must be considered whether these conditions are satisfied in this case.

[23] As regards first of all the condition of existence of a prima-facie case, the Commission points out that it is contesting solely the nationality requirements laid down by section 14 of the Merchant Shipping Act 1988. These requirements prohibit nationals of the other Member States from acquiring, through a company, a British fishing vessel and from managing a company operating such a vessel under the same conditions as British nationals. This constitutes direct discrimination, in flagrant breach of the prohibition of discrimination on grounds of nationality, which cannot be justified either by the Community rules on fishing quotas or by the United Kingdom's obligations under international law.

[24] For its part, the United Kingdom considers that the national provisions contested by the Commission do not infringe Community law. Any Member State is at liberty to lay down the conditions for registration of ships and for flying its flag. International law requires the United Kingdom to lay down these conditions in such a way that the ship has a genuine link with the United Kingdom, enabling that country to exercise effectively its jurisdiction and control over the ship. The conditions contained in the Merchant Shipping Act 1988 correspond to those imposed by other Member States for flying their flag.

[25] The United Kingdom further considers that the nationality requirements introduced by the 1988 Act are justified by the present Community legislation on fisheries; that legislation, although it establishes a common system, is based on a principle of nationality for the purposes of the

distribution of fishing quotas. Under Article 5(2) of Council Regulation 170/83 it is for the Member States to determine the detailed rules for the utilization of the quotas allocated to them and thus to lay down the conditions which the vessels authorized to fish from these quotas must satisfy.

[26] It must be observed that the system of national quotas established by Council Regulation 170/83 constitutes, as the United Kingdom contends, a derogation from the principle of equal access for Community fishermen to fishing grounds and to the exploitation thereof in waters coming within the jurisdiction of the Member States, which is itself a specific expression of the principle of non-discrimination laid down in Article 40(3) of the EEC Treaty.

[27] That derogation is justified, according to the recitals in the preamble to Regulation No 170/83, by the need, in a situation where there is a dearth of fishery resources, to ensure a relative stability in regard to fishing activities in order to safeguard the particular needs of regions where local populations are especially dependent on fisheries and related industries.

[28] The possibility cannot therefore be excluded that in their legislation concerning in particular the registration of fishing vessels and access to fishing activities the Member States may be led to introduce requirements whose compatibility with Community law can be justified only by the necessity to attain the objectives of the Community system of fishing quotas. As the Commission itself has admitted in these proceedings, such requirements may be necessary in order to ensure that there is a genuine link with the fishing industry of the Member State against whose quota the vessel may fish.

[29] However there is nothing which would prima facie warrant the conclusion that such requirements may derogate from the prohibition of discrimination on grounds of nationality contained in Articles 52 and 221 of the EEC Treaty regarding, respectively, the right of establishment and the right to participate in the capital of companies or firms within the meaning of Article 58.

[30] The rights deriving from the abovementioned provisions of the Treaty include not only the rights of establishment and of participation in the capital of companies or firms but also the right to pursue an economic activity, as the case may be through a company, under the conditions laid down by the legislation of the country of establishment for its own nationals.

[31] These rights prima facie also include the right to incorporate and manage a company whose object is to operate a fishing vessel registered in the State of establishment under the same conditions as a company controlled by nationals of that State.

[32] As regards the United Kingdom's first submission based on its obligations under international law, it is sufficient to note, at this stage, that in this respect nothing has been put forward which at first sight could necessitate any derogation from the abovementioned rights under Community law in order to ensure the effective exercise of British jurisdiction and control over the vessels in question.

[33] It must therefore be held that, at the stage of these proceedings for the grant of interim relief, the application in the main proceedings does not appear to be without foundation and that the requirement of a prima-facie case is thus satisfied.

[34] As regards, next, the condition relating to urgency, it should be borne in mind that the urgency of an application for interim measures must be assessed in relation to the necessity for an order granting interim relief in order to prevent serious and irreparable damage.

[35] The Commission makes the observation that the establishment of the new register of British fishing vessels has had the effect of forcing the entire 'Anglo-Spanish' fleet to remain idle. According to its information the registration in that register of a number of those vessels is precluded solely by reason of the nationality requirements at issue, since the vessels in question could satisfy the other requirements under section 14 of the Merchant Shipping Act 1988, in particular that relating to management and control from the United Kingdom. The owners of the vessels in question are suffering heavy losses as a result of the vessels' remaining idle and will in the short term be forced to sell them under very adverse conditions. Under British civil law these losses cannot later be recovered by means of actions brought against the British authorities.

[36] The United Kingdom contends that the interim measures applied for would in practice be ineffectual. Leaving aside the nationality requirements, the United Kingdom denies that the vessels forced to remain idle would be able to satisfy the requirements for registration, in particular those relating to residence in the United Kingdom and the management of the vessel from the United Kingdom. The suspension of the application of the nationality requirements, requested by the Commission, could not, therefore, prevent the damage alleged and there is accordingly no urgency. The United Kingdom stresses moreover that the interest which the Commission may have in obtaining these interim measures must be weighed against the United Kingdom's interest in achieving a lasting settlement of the problems caused by the 'Anglo-Spanish' vessels for the British fishing industry. The measures adopted to that end by the British authorities in 1983 and 1986 remained ineffective and only the introduction of requirements that are clear and easy to administer makes it possible to resolve these problems.

[37] It must be held in the first place that for fishing vessels which until 31 March 1989 were flying the British flag and fishing under a British fishing licence the loss of the flag and the cessation of their activities entail serious damage. There is no ground for believing that, pending delivery of the judgment in the main proceedings, these vessels can be operated in the pursuit of alternative fishing activities. The aforesaid damage must also, should the application in the main proceedings be granted, be regarded as irreparable.

[38] It is true that, for there to be urgency, it is necessary that the interim measures requested should be of a nature to prevent the alleged damage. At the present stage of the proceedings the possibility cannot however be excluded that a number of the vessels in question may, as the Commission maintains, satisfy the registration requirements if the application of the nationality requirement is suspended.

[39] Finally, as regards the balance of interests, it is not established that the interim measures applied for may jeopardize the objective pursued by the British legislation at issue, namely to ensure the existence of a genuine link between the vessels fishing against the British quotas and the British fishing industry.

[40] It appears prima facie that the registration requirements laid down by the new legislation, other than those relating to nationality, and the measures adopted by the United Kingdom authorities in 1983 and 1986 would be sufficient to ensure the existence of such a link. The United Kingdom itself considers that the 'Anglo-Spanish' vessels, which do not have that link with the United Kingdom, will not be able to satisfy the aforesaid requirements.

[41] It is true that the nationality requirements would be easier to administer than the requirements relating to the actual operation of a vessel. A Member State may not however plead administrative difficulties in order not to comply with the obligations laid on it by Community law.

[42] It follows that the condition relating to urgency is also satisfied. The interim measures applied for must therefore be ordered.

On those grounds, THE PRESIDENT hereby orders:

(1) Pending delivery of the judgment in the main proceedings, the United Kingdom shall suspend the application of the nationality requirements laid down in section 14(1)(a) and (c) of the Merchant Shipping Act 1988, read in conjunction with paragraphs (2) and (7) of that section, as regards the nationals of other Member States and in respect of fishing vessels which, until 31 March 1989, were pursuing a fishing activity under the British flag and under a British fishing licence.

   (2) The costs, including those relating to the intervention, are reserved.

NOTE
Read generally, C. Gray, 'Interim Measures of Protection in the European Court' (1979) 4 EL Rev 80. In October 1991, the full Court ruled that the UK was indeed in breach of its Treaty obligations ([1991] ECR I-4585). The substance of this case will be readdressed below, for challenge to the Act was also initiated before the English courts.

A power to impose financial sanctions is obviously helpful in inducing improved State compliance with EC law. The Maastricht Treaty added such a procedure, which is now found in Article 228 EC.

ARTICLE 228 EC

1. If the Court of Justice finds that a Member State has failed to fulfil an obligation under this Treaty, the State shall be required to take the necessary measures to comply with the judgment of the Court of Justice.

2. If the Commission considers that the Member State concerned has not taken such measures it shall, after giving that State the opportunity to submit its observations, issue a reasoned opinion specifying the points on which the Member State concerned has not complied with the judgment of the Court of Justice.

If the Member State concerned fails to take the necessary measures to comply with the Court's judgment within the time-limit laid down by the Commission, the latter may bring the case before the Court of Justice. In so doing it shall specify the amount of the lump sum or penalty payment to be paid by the Member State concerned which it considers appropriate in the circumstances.

If the Court of Justice finds that the Member State concerned has not complied with its judgment it may impose a lump sum or penalty payment on it.

This procedure shall be without prejudice to Article 227.

NOTE

The Commission has publicized the criteria on which it will base its assessment of the amount to be paid by a defaulting Member State pursuant to Article 228(2); [1996] OJ C242/6, [1997] OJ C63/2. Lump sum fines or penalty payments have been threatened infrequently and imposed just once, but Article 228 has not proved to be a dead letter.

The Commission's Nineteenth Annual Report on monitoring the application of Community law, 2001
COM(2002) 324, pp.6, 7–9
http://europa.eu.int/comm/secretariat_general/sgb/droit_com/index_en.htm

1.7. Application by the Commission of Article 228 of the EC Treaty (developments in 2001)

... The Commission also adopted three second referral decisions with demands for penalty payments from Spain, France and Luxembourg. The fields covered by these decisions were very diverse: one concerned the environment (Spain), one fisheries (France) and one transport (Luxembourg). The diversity of areas concerned shows that the second referral procedure with penalty payments is no longer, as it once was, mainly limited to the environmental and social fields and therefore covers the whole range of infringements. It should also be noted that the second referral decision against France is the first in the fisheries field. Several files were also wound up in 2001 after the Member States concerned had taken steps to comply with the Court judgment. One such example was the file on the Kouroupitos rubbish tip, the only case to date in which the Court has required a Member State to make penalty payments. Given that measures to implement the first Court judgment were adopted by the Greek authorities on 26 February 2001, the latter paid a total of 5 400 000 in penalty payments for the period from July 2000 to March 2001. This case concerned Greece's failure to take the necessary measures to ensure the elimination of toxic and dangerous waste in the Chania region of Crete (more specifically, closure of the illegal rubbish tip located at the mouth of the river Kouroupitos), in violation of the obligations imposed by Council Directive 75/442/EEC of 15 July 1975 on waste and Council Directive 78/319/EEC of 20 March 1978 on toxic and dangerous waste. In 2001 the Commission also closed previous cases for which a solution designed to ensure compliance with the Court judgment was provided by the Member State concerned. No file in which a second referral decision was taken in 2000 or previously is still pending.

NOTE

In assessing the likely impact of Article 228(2) on the incidence of default by Member States, you should also take account of the Court's ruling in *Francovich* (Cases C-6/90 and C-9/90, p.168 below) that Member States may be liable to individuals in damages before national courts, elaborated in the package of rulings of March 1996 including '*Factortame III*' (Case C-48/93), p.177 below. Remember 'dual vigilance' at p.110 above.

C: **Complaining to the Commission**

R. White and A. Dashwood, 'Enforcement Actions under Articles 169 and 170 EEC'
[now 226 and 227 EC]
(1989) 14 EL Rev 388, 388–89

. . . However, the procedure does not go so far as to allow an action to be brought in the European Court by individuals or firms whose interests have been harmed by a Member State's failure to fulfil an obligation under the EEC Treaty. Two courses are open to a private party in such circumstances. One would be to lodge a complaint with the Commission, which might lead to the initiation of proceedings under Article [226]. The other would be to bring proceedings in the courts of the Member State concerned, assuming the Community provision in question is a directly effective one, and an appropriate national remedy is available. To help establish the infringement, it may be necessary to ask the national court to make a reference to the European Court under Article [234] for a preliminary ruling on the interpretation of the Community provision.

The Court's ruling in *Star Fruit Co. v Commission* (Case 247/87, p.114 above) confirms the inability of the complainant to *require* the Commission to initiate proceedings under Article 226. However, complaints frequently provide the Commission with valuable information on malpractice. So the Commission is sometimes prepared to act on complaints and open an investigation. In 2001 six out of ten cases initiated by the Commission were on the basis of complaints (19th Annual Report, p.120 above) and the Commission makes available a standard form for complaints ([2002] OJ C244/1, also available via http://europa.eu.int/comm/ secretariat_general/sgb/lexcomm/index_en.htm).

Effective and fair complaint handling is also the subject of a Commission communication to the European Parliament and the European Ombudsman on relations with the complainant in respect of infringements of community law, [2002] OJ C244/5. The notice was the result of the European Ombudsman's own-initiative enquiry and the Commission's subsequent undertaking to comply with certain administrative formalities, and in particular to inform the complainant in advance of any decision to close a case. The Commission takes care in this Communication to insist on its 'discretionary power in deciding whether or not to commence infringement proceedings and to refer a case to the Court', recognized by the Court. For discussion of the several interests at stake in the management of complaints by the Commission, see R. Rawlings, 'Engaged Elites: Citizen Action and Institutional Attitudes in Commission Enforcement' (2000) 6 ELJ 4, which locates the matter in the broader context of enforcement in the public interest.

NOTE

The fact that a State puts an end to its violation before the Court has the opportunity to rule on the matter does not automatically lead to the proceedings being dropped by the Commission. In the next case the Court refers to the value such an action may have from the perspective of parties affected by the (discontinued) infringement of Community law, which may include complainants.

Commission v *Greece* (Case 240/86)

[1988] ECR 1835, Court of Justice of the European Communities

The Commission's action related to obstacles to cereal imports which it considered incompatible with *inter alia* Article 30 of the EC Treaty (now, after amendment, Article 28 EC). When the matter reached the stage of a hearing before the Court, the Greek government contested the case's admissibility.

[12] The Greek government considers that since the barriers to cereal imports were lifted before the action was commenced it is devoid of purpose.

[13] At the hearing the Commission acknowledged that the failure to fulfil obligations had been remedied but nevertheless asserted that it had an interest in obtaining a ruling in respect of measures adopted by the Hellenic Republic in the past.

[14] As the Court has consistently held (see most recently the judgment of 5 June 1986 in Case 103/ 84 *Commission* v *Italian Republic* [1986] ECR 1759), the subject-matter of an action brought under Article 169 [now 226] is established by the Commission's reasoned opinion and even where the default has been remedied after the period laid down pursuant to the second paragraph of that article has elapsed, an interest still subsists in pursuing the action. That interest may consist in establishing the basis for a liability which a Member State may incur, by reason of its failure to fulfil its obligations, towards those to whom rights accrue as a result of that failure.

[15] Since the Hellenic Republic did not comply with the reasoned opinon of 25 November 1985 within the period stipulated by the Commission the action is admissible in so far as it concerns the subject-matter of the dispute as defined by that opinion.

SECTION 3: **CONTROL AT NATIONAL LEVEL**

The Court's ruling in *Commission* v *Greece* (Case 240/86 above) leads logically into the next stage of the discussion; control at national level. The Court mentions the possibility of liability arising out of the State's violation of Community law obligations (para 14). A State in violation of Community law may be challenged before its own national courts. The principles of direct effect, supremacy and the Article 234 preliminary reference procedure all come into play. A complainant unable to persuade the Commission to investigate the matter may be able to resort to this second limb of 'dual vigilance', national-level control. Even a complainant able to provoke a Commission investigation under Article 226 may in addition choose to bring proceedings at national level in so far as that may offer legal protection unavailable at EC level: this will be the case in particular if the applicant seeks compensation for loss suffered as a result of State violation of EC law (Chapter 6 below).

The structure also permits private parties to challenge at national level acts of other private parties in violation of Community law. This is illustrated by many of the cases connected with the competition rules, the enforcement of which is examined separately in Chapter 18. It also applies to other provisions of the Treaty that are capable of application directly against private parties such as the rule requiring equal pay for equal work between the sexes, now found in Article 141 EC (e.g., *Defrenne* v *SABENA* (Case 43/75) [1976] ECR 455) and the Treaty provisions concerning freedom of movement of persons (*Roman Angonese* (Case C-281/98) [2000] ECR I-4139; see Chapter 13). However the first limb of 'dual vigilance' is deficient here: Article 226 proceedings may not be brought against private parties.

....

A: **The criteria governing direct effect**

Van Gend en Loos (Case 26/62) was encountered above (p.109). It is the seminal case concerning direct effect, which the Court identifies as flowing from the objectives of the EC Treaty, if not from its explicit terms. Once the Court had established the point of principle that provisions of the Treaty are capable of direct effect, the Court then considered Article 12 of the Treaty itself (now, remember, Article 25 EC post-Amsterdam). Community law *can* be directly effective before a national court; but is Article 12?

Van Gend en Loos v *Nederlandse Administratie der Belastingen* (Case 26/62)
[1963] ECR 1, Court of Justice of the European Communities

The wording of Article 12 contains a clear and unconditional prohibition which is not a positive but a negative obligation. This obligation, moreover, is not qualified by any reservation on the part of states which would make its implementation conditional upon a positive legislative measure enacted under national law. The very nature of this prohibition makes it ideally adapted to produce direct effects in the legal relationship between Member States and their subjects.

The Implementation of Article 12 does not require any legislative intervention on the part of the states. The fact that under this Article it is the Member States who are made the subject of the negative obligation does not imply that their nationals cannot benefit from this obligation . . .

It follows from the foregoing considerations that, according to the spirit, the general scheme and the wording of the Treaty, Article 12 must be interpreted as producing direct effects and creating individual rights which national courts must protect.

NOTE
In the next two cases the Court repeats its views of the nature and purpose of the direct effect doctrine. It also explains further the conditions which must be satisfied before a provision will be held directly effective. The test is one which will more readily be fulfilled than might initially have been expected. Direct effect, it seems, is the rule rather than the exception.

Van Duyn v *Home Office* (Case 41/74)
[1974] ECR 1337, Court of Justice of the European Communities

Van Duyn, a Dutch woman, had been refused leave to enter the UK, where she wished to take up employment with the Church of Scientology. Her action against the Home Office was based on Community law guaranteeing the free movement of workers. This is contained in Article 48 of the EC Treaty (now, after amendment, Article 39 EC) and amplified in other measures, including Directive 64/221. Chapter 13 of this book examines these provisions. There is a basic right to travel from Member State A to Member State B to take up work, subject to exceptions based on, *inter alia*, public policy. The UK sought to exclude Van Duyn on the basis of the exceptions, claiming the Church of Scientology to be socially undesirable. The High Court made a preliminary reference to the European Court to seek clarification of the issues involved. The first two questions concerned the enforceability of Community law provisions before national courts – direct effect.

[4] By the first question, the Court is asked to say whether Article 48 of the EEC Treaty is directly applicable so as to confer on individuals rights enforceable by them in the courts of a Member State.

[5] It is provided, in Article 48(1) and (2), that freedom of movement for workers shall be secured by the end of the transitional period and that such freedom shall entail 'the abolition of any discrimination based on nationality between workers of Member States as regards employment, remuneration and other conditions of work and employment'.

[6] These provisions impose on Member States a precise obligation which does not require the adoption of any further measure on the part either of the Community institutions or of the Member States and which leaves them, in relation to its implementation, no discretionary power.

[7] Paragraph 3, which defines the rights implied by the principle of freedom of movement for workers, subjects them to limitations justified on grounds of public policy, public security or public health. The application of these limitations is, however, subject to judicial control, so that a Member State's right to invoke the limitations does not prevent the provisions of Article 48, which enshrine the principle of freedom of movement for workers, from conferring on individuals rights which are enforceable by them and which the national courts must protect.

[8] The reply to the first question must therefore be in the affirmative.

Second question

[9] The second question asks the Court to say whether Council Directive No 64/221 of 25 February 1964 on the co-ordination of special measures concerning the movement and residence of foreign nationals which are justified on grounds of public policy, public security or public health is directly applicable so as to confer on individuals rights enforceable by them in the courts of a Member State.

[10] It emerges from the order making the reference that the only provision of the Directive which is relevant is that contained in Article 3(1) which provides that 'measures taken on grounds of public policy or public security shall be based exclusively on the personal conduct of the individual concerned'.

[11] The United Kingdom observes that, since Article 189 of the Treaty distinguishes between the effects ascribed to regulations, directives and decisions, it must therefore be presumed that the Council, in issuing a directive rather than making a regulation, must have intended that the directive should have an effect other than that of a regulation and accordingly that the former should not be directly applicable.

[12] If, however, by virtue of the provisions of Article 189 regulations are directly applicable and, consequently, may by their very nature have direct effects, it does not follow from this that other categories of acts mentioned in that Article can never have similar effects. It would be incompatible with the binding effect attributed to a directive by Article 189 to exclude, in principle, the possibility that the obligation which it imposes may be invoked by those concerned. In particular, where the Community authorities have, by directive, imposed on Member States the obligation to pursue a particular course of conduct, the useful effect of such an act would be weakened if individuals were prevented from relying on it before their national courts and if the latter were prevented from taking it into consideration as an element of Community law. Article 177, which empowers national courts to refer to the Court questions concerning the validity and interpretation of all acts of the Community

institutions, without distinction, implies furthermore that these acts may be invoked by individuals in the national courts. It is necessary to examine, in every case, whether the nature, general scheme and wording of the provision in question are capable of having direct effects on the relations between Member States and individuals.

[13] By providing that measures taken on grounds of public policy shall be based exclusively on the personal conduct of the individual concerned, Article 3(1) of Directive No 64/221 is intended to limit the discretionary power which national laws generally confer on the authorities responsible for the entry and expulsion of foreign nationals. First, the provision lays down an obligation which is not subject to any exception or condition and which, by its very nature, does not require the intervention of any act on the part either of the institutions of the Community or of Member States. Secondly, because Member States are thereby obliged, in implementing a clause which derogates from one of the fundamental principles of the Treaty in favour of individuals, not to take account of factors extraneous to personal conduct, legal certainty for the persons concerned requires that they should be able to rely on this obligation even though it has been laid down in a legislative act which has no automatic direct effect in its entirety.

[14] If the meaning and exact scope of the provision raise questions of interpretation, these questions can be resolved by the courts, taking into account also the procedure under Article 177 of the Treaty.

[15] Accordingly, in reply to the second question, Article 3(1) of Council Directive No 64/221 of 25 February 1964 confers on individuals rights which are enforceable by them in the courts of a Member State and which the national courts must protect.

Defrenne v *SABENA* (Case 43/75)
[1976] ECR 455, Court of Justice of the European Communities

This was a preliminary reference from a Brussels court. It concerned Article 119, which contained the principle of equal pay for equal work. The post-Amsterdam version is found in Article 141 EC, though, as explained in Chapter 20, the Amsterdam Treaty made significant alterations to the Treaty provisions on social policy. It is the Treaty's major provision in the field of sex discrimination. Defrenne, an air hostess, was seeking compensation from SABENA, her employer, for low pay she had received in comparison with male workers. But could she rely on the Treaty provision before a national court?

[16] Under the terms of the first paragraph of Article 119, the Member States are bound to ensure and maintain 'the application of the principle that men and women should receive equal pay for equal work'.

[17] The second and third paragraphs of the same article add a certain number of details concerning the concepts of pay and work referred to in the first paragraph.

[18] For the purposes of the implementation of these provisions a distinction must be drawn within the whole area of application of Article 119 between, first, direct and overt discrimination which may be identified solely with the aid of the criteria based on equal work and equal pay referred to by the article in question and, secondly, indirect and disguised discrimination which can only be identified by reference to more explicit implementing provisions of a Community or national character.

[19] It is impossible not to recognise that the complete implementation of the aim pursued by Article 119, by means of the elimination of all discrimination, direct or indirect, between men and women workers, not only as regards individual undertakings but also entire branches of industry and even of the economic system as a whole, may in certain cases involve the elaboration of criteria whose implementation necessitates the taking of appropriate measures at Community and national level.

[20] This view is all the more essential in the light of the fact that the Community measures on this question, to which reference will be made in answer to the second question, implement Article 119 from the point of view of extending the narrow criterion of 'equal work', in accordance in particular with the provisions of Convention No 100 on equal pay concluded by the International Labour Organization in 1951, Article 2 of which establishes the principle of equal pay for work 'of equal value'.

[21] Among the forms of direct discrimination which may be identified solely by reference to the criteria laid down by Article 119 must be included in particular those which have their origin in legislative provisions or in collective labour agreements and which may be detected on the basis of a purely legal analysis of the situation.

[22] This applies even more in cases where men and women receive unequal pay for equal work carried out in the same establishment or service, whether public or private.

[23] As is shown by the very findings of the judgment making the reference, in such a situation the court is in a position to establish all the facts which enable it to decide whether a woman worker is receiving lower pay than a male worker performing the same tasks.

[24] In such situation, at least, Article 119 is directly applicable and may thus give rise to individual rights which the courts must protect.

[25] Furthermore, as regards equal work, as a general rule, the national legislative provisions adopted for the implementation of the principle of equal pay as a rule merely reproduce the substance of the terms of Article 119 as regards the direct forms of discrimination.

[26] Belgian legislation provides a particularly apposite illustration of this point, since Article 14 of Royal Decree No 40 of 24 October 1967 on the employment of women merely sets out the right of any female worker to institute proceedings before the relevant court for the application of the principle of equal pay set out in Article 119 and simply refers to that article.

[27] The terms of Article 119 cannot be relied on to invalidate this conclusion.

[28] First of all, it is impossible to put forward an argument against its direct effect based on the use in this article of the word 'principle', since, in the language of the Treaty, this term is specifically used in order to indicate the fundamental nature of certain provisions, as is shown, for example, by the heading of the first part of the Treaty which is devoted to 'Principles' and by Article 113, according to which the commercial policy of the Community is to be based on 'uniform principles'.

[29] If this concept were to be attenuated to the point of reducing it to the level of a vague declaration, the very foundations of the Community and the coherence of its external relations would be indirectly affected.

[30] It is also impossible to put forward arguments based on the fact that Article 119 only refers expressly to 'Member States'.

[31] Indeed, as the Court has already found in other contexts, the fact that certain provisions of the Treaty are formally addressed to the Member States does not prevent rights from being conferred at the same time on any individual who has an interest in the performance of the duties thus laid down.

[32] The very wording of Article 119 shows that it imposes on States a duty to bring about a specific result to be mandatorily achieved within a fixed period.

[33] The effectiveness of this provision cannot be affected by the fact that the duty imposed by the Treaty has not been discharged by certain Member States and that the joint institutions have not reacted sufficiently energetically against this failure to act.

[34] To accept the contrary view would be to risk raising the violation of the right to the status of a principle of interpretation, a position the adoption of which would not be consistent with the task assigned to the Court by Article 164 of the Treaty.

[35] Finally, in its reference to 'Member States', Article 119 is alluding to those States in the exercise of all those of their functions which may usefully contribute to the implementation of the principle of equal pay.

[36] Thus, contrary to the statements made in the course of the proceedings this provision is far from merely referring the matter to the powers of the national legislative authorities.

[37] Therefore, the reference to 'Member States' in Article 119 cannot be interpreted as excluding the intervention of the courts in direct application of the Treaty.

[38] Furthermore it is not possible to sustain any objection that the application by national courts of the principle of equal pay would amount to modifying independent agreements concluded privately or in the sphere of industrial relations such as individual contracts and collective labour agreements.

[39] In fact, since Article 119 is mandatory in nature, the prohibition on discrimination between men and women applies not only to the action of public authorities, but also extends to all agreements which are intended to regulate paid labour collectively, as well as to contracts between individuals.

[40] The reply to the first question must therefore be that the principle of equal pay contained in Article 119 may be relied upon before the national courts and that these courts have a duty to ensure the protection of the rights which this provision vests in individuals, in particular as regards those types of discrimination arising directly from legislative provisions or collective labour agreements, as well as in cases in which men and women receive unequal pay for equal work which is carried out in the same establishment or service, whether private or public.

NOTES
1. In *Van Duyn* v *Home Office* (Case 41/74), the Court found the provisions directly effective despite the existence of derogations available to Member States; in *Defrenne* v *SABENA* (Case 43/75), direct effect was upheld despite the very broad, underdeveloped terms of the provision in question.
2. Two particular aspects of *Defrenne* v *SABENA* (Case 43/75) should not be overlooked. First, the Treaty provision was held directly effective against a private party, the employer (para 39 above). Treaty provisions, then, are capable of binding not only the State, as in *Van Gend en Loos* and *Van Duyn* (so-called vertical direct effect), but also private parties (horizontal direct effect). This was mentioned at p.123 above. The second aspect worthy of attention is that the Court decided to restrict the implications of its ruling:

Defrenne v *SABENA* (Case 43/75)
[1976] ECR 455, Court of Justice of the European Communities

[69] The Governments of Ireland and the United Kingdom have drawn the Court's attention to the possible economic consequences of attributing direct effect to the provisions of Article 119, on the ground that such a decision might, in many branches of economic life, result in the introduction of claims dating back to the time at which such effect came into existence.

[70] In view of the large number of people concerned such claims, which undertakings could not have foreseen, might seriously affect the financial situation of such undertakings and even drive some of them to bankruptcy.

[71] Although the practical consequences of any judicial decision must be carefully taken into account, it would be impossible to go so far as to diminish the objectivity of the law and compromise its future application on the ground of the possible repercussions which might result, as regards the past, from such a judicial decision.

[72] However, in the light of the conduct of several of the Member States and the views adopted by the Commission and repeatedly brought to the notice of the circles concerned, it is appropriate to take exceptionally into account the fact that, over a prolonged period, the parties concerned have been led to continue with practices which were contrary to Article 119, although not yet prohibited under their national law.

[73] The fact that, in spite of the warnings given, the Commission did not initiate proceedings under Article 169 against the Member States concerned on grounds of failure to fulfil an obligation was likely to consolidate the incorrect impression as to the effects of Article 119.

[74] In these circumstances, it is appropriate to determine that, as the general level at which pay would have been fixed cannot be known, important considerations of legal certainty affecting all the interests involved, both public and private, make it impossible in principle to reopen the question as regards the past.

[75] Therefore, the direct effect of Article 119 cannot be relied on in order to support claims concerning pay periods prior to the date of this judgment, except as regards those workers who have already brought legal proceedings or made an equivalent claim.

NOTE

The Court has subsequently insisted that it alone can declare that a directly effective provision may not be relied on retrospectively. This power does not belong to a national court; see *Blaizot* v *University of Liège* (Case 24/86) [1988] ECR 379; *Barra* v *Belgium* (Case 309/85) [1988] ECR 355; and *Evangelischer Krankenhausverein Wien* (Case C-437/97) [2000] ECR I-1157.

B: **Direct effect as a policy choice**

The Court has made a conscious policy choice in asserting the central significance of direct effect in the Community legal order. Most of the key substantive provisions of Community law studied in Parts Two and Three of this book are directly effective and therefore susceptible to enforcement by private individuals before national courts.

Read particularly P. Pescatore, 'The Doctrine of Direct Effect: an infant disease of Community law' (1983) 8 EL Rev 155. At p.157 he observes that, 'the reasoning of the Court shows that the judges had "une certaine ideé de l'Europe" of their own and that it is this idea which has been decisive and not arguments based on the legal technicalities of the matter'.

Read also R. Lecourt, *L'Europe des Juges* (Brussels: Bruylant, 1976). At p.248 he explains that:

En effet, ou bien la Communauté est, pour les particuliers, une séduisante mais lointaine abstraction intéressant seulement les gouvernements qui leur en appliquent discrétionnairement les règles; ou bien elle est pour eux une réalité effective et par conséquence créatrice de droits.

The vigour of directly effective law is a key constitutional feature of the EC legal order. It is missing from the non-EC pillars of the EU, a distinction that is one of the more fundamental in explaining how and why 'EU Law' is not a unified category (p.11 above). In Article 34(2) EU, a 'third pillar' provision set out at p.45 above, the Treaty goes so far as explicitly to provide that 'framework decisions' and other decisions taken for purposes consistent with the objectives of this title shall be binding but 'shall not entail direct effect'. So, in discussing direct effect, it is EC law alone – the first pillar – that we are discussing.

The following extract provides an elegantly written overview of the course pursued by the Court in shaping the constitutional principles of the Community legal order. The author is not impartial. He was a judge of the Court from 1988 until his death in 1999.

F. Mancini, 'The Making of a Constitution for Europe'
(1989) 26 CML Rev 595
[Reproduced by permission of Kluwer Academic Publishers]

(Some footnotes omitted.)

1. For educated observers of European affairs, whether friends or foes of a strong Community, the magnitude of the contribution made by the Court of Justice to the integration of Europe has almost become a by-word. It is unnecessary to quote the friends, which in any event, since they tend to be enthusiastic, would be somewhat embarrassing for a member of the Court. Far more interesting are the enemies or the less than lukewarm supporters of a united Europe. In England politicians who openly criticise judges are frowned upon; Mrs Thatcher, a barrister, is aware of this rule and cannot therefore be quoted, though her private reactions to judgments encroaching on British sovereign rights and interests are easy to visualise. But that old, unredeemed Gaullist, the former Prime Minister Michel Debré, is eminently quotable: 'J'accuse la Cour de Justice' – he said as late as 1979 – 'de mégalomanie maladive', by which, of course, he meant insufficient deference to the sovereign rights and interests of France.

If one were asked to synthesise the direction in which the case law produced in Luxembourg has moved since 1957, one would have to say that it coincides with the making of a constitution for Europe. Unlike the United States, the EC was born as a peculiar form of international organisation. Its peculiarity resided in the unique institutional structure and the unprecedented law-making and judicial powers it was given. But these features – admittedly reminiscent of a federal State – should not overshadow two essential facts. First: while the American Declaration of Independence spoke of '*one people*' dissolving the bonds which connected them with '*another people*', the preamble of the Rome Treaty recites that the contracting parties are 'determined to lay the foundations of an ever closer union among the *peoples* of Europe'. Second and more important: the instrument giving rise to the Community was a traditional multilateral *treaty*.

Treaties are basically different from constitutions. In many countries (and 'many' includes even some of the founding States of the EC) they do not enjoy the status of higher law. The interpretation of treaties is subject to canons unlike all others (such as, for example, the presumption that States do not lose their sovereignty). As a rule, treaties devise systems of checks and balances whose main function is to keep under control the powers of the organisation which they set up. In the case of the Rome Treaty these differences are emphasised by two highly significant characteristics. The Treaty does not safeguard the fundamental rights of the individuals affected by its application, nor does it recognise, even in an embryonic form, a constitutional right to European citizenship. Europe cannot confer citizenship; this remains the prerogative of the Member States. By the same token, individual citizens of a Member State are entitled to move from their State to another Member State exclusively by virtue of their being workers, self-employed persons or providers of services, that is *qua* units of a production factor.

The main endeavour of the Court of Justice has precisely been to remove or reduce the differences just mentioned. In other words, the Court has sought to 'constitutionalise' the Treaty, that is to fashion a constitutional framework for a federal-type structure in Europe. Whether this effort was always inspired by a clear and consistent philosophy is arguable, but that is not really important. What really matters are its achievements – and they are patent to all.

To be sure, the Court has been helped by favourable circumstances. The combination of being, as it were, out of sight and out of mind by virtue of its location in the fairy-tale Grand Duchy of Luxembourg and the benign neglect of the media has certainly contributed to its ability to create a sense of belonging on the part of its independent-minded members and, where necessary, to convert them into confirmed Europeans. Furthermore, the judges and advocates general have usually been middle-aged and at least half of them have been academics. As a group, therefore, they have never met the three conditions of Lord Diplock's famous verdict: 'by training, temperament and age judges are too averse to change to be entrusted with the development of rules of conduct for a brave new world'.

Nevertheless, these circumstances do not explain the whole story. The Court would have been far less successful had it not been assisted by two mighty allies: the national courts and the

Commission. The institutional position of the former will be clarified below. It is sufficient to mention here that by referring to Luxembourg sensitive questions of interpretation of Community law they have been indirectly responsible for the boldest judgments the Court has made. Moreover, by adhering to these judgments in deciding the cases before them, and therefore by lending them the credibility which national judges usually enjoy in their own countries, they have rendered the case law of the Court both effective and respected throughout the Community.

As to the Commission, the founding fathers and especially Jean Monnet conceived it as a sort of 'Platonic embodiment of Communitarian spirit, with Gallic élan, self-confidence and expertise'. As the executive-political branch of the Community, the Commission may not have always lived up to those expectations, but as 'watchdog of the Treaty', that is both as the prosecutor of Member State infractions and as an *amicus curiae* in cases referred by the national courts, it has undoubtedly played a positive rôle. In other words, the Commission has led the Court – particularly by assuaging the concern some of the judges may have felt regarding the acceptability of their rulings – on the path toward further integration and increased Community power.

On the other hand, the Parliament and the Council are not natural allies of the Court. The Parliament evinced great sympathy for the Court in the 1960s and the 1970s, but then its function was simply that of a debating forum. More recently, however, the Parliament has been involved in a permanent trial of strength with the Council: the stake is a new allocation of power in the budgetary and legislative areas. The Court is a victim of this (in itself entirely legitimate) turbulence. The reason is obvious. Luxembourg is more and more encumbered by increasingly political and emotion-loaded intra-Community controversies: hence a visibility and an exposure to scrutiny by the media that are in sharp contrast with the conditions under which progress was made in the past.

The Council, the Community legislative body, is bound not to be an ally of the Court. Although formally an institution with supranational characteristics like the others, it was drawn by its very composition – a gathering of national Ministers – into resembling an intergovernmental round table often characterised by all the warmth of a love match in a snake-pit. In other words, its members regularly speak, and no doubt think, in terms of negotiating with their partners much as they would do in any other international context. The observation that 'decisionally, the Community is closer to the United Nations than it is to the United States' is therefore particularly telling.

This situation is heightened by the weight acquired in the area of law-making by COREPER (the Committee of Permanent Representatives of the Member States) and its many subcommittees. The permanent representatives are ambassadors and the subcommittees are composed of national officials. While a minister may occasionally be expected to deal with a given problem in a supra-national spirit, it would be naïve to expect an ambassador or a national bureaucrat, whatever his leanings, to assist willfully in the process of the wasting away of Member State power, thereby blighting his own career.

2. It was noted above that, unlike federal constitutions, the treaties creating international organisations do not usually enjoy higher-law status with regard to the laws of the contracting powers. Article VI of the American Constitution reads: 'the laws of the United States . . . shall be the supreme law of the land; and the judges in every state shall be bound thereby; any thing in the constitution or laws of any state to the contrary notwithstanding'. In the same vein section 109 of the Australian Constitution provides that 'When a law of a State is inconsistent with the law of the Commonwealth the latter shall prevail and the former shall be . . . invalid', and the German Fundamental Law stipulates just as clearly that *Bundesrecht bricht Landesrecht*. On the contrary, the Rome Treaty, while including some hortatory provisions to the same effect (Article 5 [now 10]), fails to state squarely whether Community law is pre-eminent *vis-à-vis* prior and subsequent Member State law.

The now undisputed existence of a supremacy clause in the Community framework is therefore a product of judicial creativeness. In *Costa* v *Enel*, a case which arose in the early 1960s before a *giudice conciliatore* (local magistrate) in Milan, a shareholder of a nationalised power company challenged as being contrary to the Treaty the Italian law nationalising the electric industry. The Italian Government claimed before the Court of Justice that the Court had no business to deal with the matter: the magistrate, it said, should apply the nationalisation law as the most current indication of parliamentary intention and could not avail of the reference procedure provided for by the Treaty.

But the Court ruled that 'by creating a Community of unlimited duration, having its own institutions, its own personality . . . and, more particularly, real powers stemming from a limitation of sovereignty or a transfer of powers from the States to the Community, the Member States have limited their sovereign rights . . . and have thus created a body of law which binds both their nationals and themselves'.

Is this line of reasoning entirely cogent? Some legal writers doubt it and a few have regarded *Costa v Enel* as an example of judicial activism 'running wild'.[10] Yet, the Court's supremacy doctrine was accepted by the judiciaries and the administrations of both the original and the new Member States, with the exception of some grumblings by the French *Conseil d'Etat*, the Italian *Corte costituzionale* and a couple of English law lords. Lord Denning, a majestic but irritable elderly gentleman, was caught intimating that 'once a bill is passed by Parliament, that will dispose of all this discussion about the Treaty'.[11] A few years later, however, Lord Diplock admitted that even subsequent acts of Parliament must be interpreted in line with Community law, no matter how far-fetched the interpretation.[12] Lord Diplock, and many other national judges before him, obviously realised that the alternative to the supremacy clause would have been a rapid erosion of the Community; and this was a possibility that nobody really envisaged, not even the most intransigent custodians of national sovereignty. Actually, the 'or else' argument, though not fully spelled out, was used by the Court, and it was this argument, much more than the one I have quoted, that led to a ready reception of the doctrine in *Costa v Enel*.

But the recognition of Community pre-eminence was not only an indispensable development, it was also a logical development. It is self-evident that in a federal or quasi-federal context the issue of supremacy will arise only if federal norms are to apply directly, that is to bear upon the federation's citizens without any need of intervention by the Member States. Article 189 of the Rome Treaty identifies a category of Community norms that do not require national implementing measures but are binding on the States and their citizens as soon as they enter into force: the founding fathers called them 'regulations' and provided them principally for those areas where the Treaty itself merely defines the thrust of Community policy and leaves its elaboration to later decisions of the Council and the Commission. One year before *Costa v Enel*, however, the Court had enormously extended the Community power to deal directly with the public by ruling in *Van Gend en Loos* that even Treaty provisions may be relied upon by private individuals if they expressly grant them rights and impose on the Member States an obligation so precise and unconditional that it can be fulfilled without the necessity of further measures.

■ QUESTION

How persuasive is the *or else* argument, set out in the final sentence of the penultimate paragraph of this extract?

....

C: Procedure and remedies

Community law establishes substantive rights. It also establishes the constitutional principles which allow a private individual to rely on those rights at national level to defeat conflicting national law – direct effect, plus supremacy, plus the preliminary reference under Article 234. However, Community law also exerts an impact on the national law of procedure and remedies. National autonomy is in principle respected, but subjected to overriding requirements imposed by

---

10 Rasmussen, *On Law and Policy in the European Court of Justice: A Comparative Study in Judicial Policy-making* (Dordrecht-Boston-Lancaster: Martinus Nijhoff, 1986). [*Cf* p.93 above.]

11 *Felixstowe Dock and Ry Co.* v *British Transport Docks Board* [1976] 2 CMLR 655.

12 *Garland* v *British Rail Engineering* [1982] 2 All ER 402.

Community law. The Court's first clear explanation of the division of function between Community law and national law was supplied in the next case.

Comet v *Produktschap* (Case 45/76)
[1976] ECR 2043, Court of Justice of the European Communities

Comet argued before Dutch courts that it had paid sums to Produktschap on the export of plants and bulbs which were incompatible with (what was then) Article 16 (Chapter 10; Article 16 was a transitional provision deleted by the Treaty of Amsterdam). It sought reimbursement. The defendant argued that the claim could not succeed because it had been lodged after the expiry of the limitation period for such actions under Dutch law. A Community right; but national procedures. The issue was referred to the European Court. In the following extract, the Court first explains the nature of Comet's argument designed to defeat Dutch procedural law, and then disposes of the case.

[9] The applicant in the main action contends, on the other hand, that the primacy of Community law means that it overrules any decision which constitutes an infringement of it and that, before the national courts, which are bound to protect the rights conferred on it by Article 16, it possesses, in consequence, an independent right of action which is unaffected by limitations provided for under national law which are liable to weaken the impact of the direct effect of that article in the legal order of the Member States.

[10] Thus, the question referred seeks to establish whether the procedural rules for proceedings designed to ensure the protection of the rights which individuals acquire as a result of the direct effect of a Community provision, in the present case Article 16 of the Treaty and Article 10 of Regulation No 234/68, especially the rules concerning the period within which an action must be brought are governed by the national law of the Member State where the action is brought or whether, on the other hand, they are independent and fall to be determined only by Community law itself.

[11] The prohibition laid down in Article 16 of the Treaty and that contained in Article 10 of Regulation No 234/68 have direct effect and confer on individuals rights which the national courts must protect.

[12] Thus, in application of the principle of cooperation laid down in Article 5 [now 10] of the Treaty, the national courts are entrusted with ensuring the legal protection conferred on individuals by the direct effect of the provisions of Community law.

[13] Consequently, in the absence of any relevant Community rules, it is for the national legal order of each Member State to designate the competent courts and to lay down the procedural rules for proceedings designed to ensure the protection of the rights which individuals acquire through the direct effect of Community law, provided that such rules are not less favourable than those governing the same right of action on an internal matter.

[14] Articles 100 to 102 [now 95 to 97] and 235 [now 308] of the Treaty enable the appropriate steps to be taken as necessary, to eliminate differences between the provisions laid down in such matters by law, regulation or administrative action in Member States if these differences are found to be such as to cause distortion or to affect the functioning of the common market.

[15] In default of such harmonization measures, the rights conferred by Community law must be exercised before the national courts in accordance with the rules of procedure laid down by national law.

[16] The position would be different only if those rules and time-limits made it impossible in practice to exercise rights which the national courts have a duty to protect.

[17] This does not apply to the fixing of a reasonable period of limitation within which an action must be brought.

[18] The fixing, as regards fiscal proceedings, of such a period is in fact an application of a fundamental principle of legal certainty which protects both the authority concerned and the party from whom payment is claimed.

[19] The answer must therefore be that, in the case of a litigant who is challenging before the national courts a decision of a national body for incompatibility with Community law, that law, in its present state, does not prevent the expiry of the period within which proceedings must be brought under national law from being raised against him, provided that the procedural rules applicable to his case are not less favourable than those governing the same right of action on an internal matter.

NOTE

At first glance, then, the applicant able to show a violation of Community law is dependent on existing national procedures, which may thwart the claim. Procedural law varies from State to State, with the result that in practice the means of enforcement of Community law are not uniform State by State. (See J. Bridge, 'Procedural Aspects of the Enforcement of EC Law through the Legal Systems of the Member States' (1984) 9 EL Rev 28.) Paragraph 14 of *Comet* (Case 45/76) hints at the way to resolve such disunity, but little progress has been made (except in the special case of public procurement).

However, the judgment in *Comet* (Case 45/76) does not confer absolute autonomy on the national system. In the concluding words of para 13, and in para 16, it offers two Community law qualifications to the approach which a national court may adopt in providing remedies for a litigant which has suffered loss as a result of violation of Community law. These have become commonly known as the 'the principle of equivalence' and the 'principle of effectiveness' respectively.

The 'principle of equivalence' was discussed by the Court in the next case.

Shirley Preston and Others v *Wolverhampton NHS Healthcare Trust and Others* (Case C-78/98)

[2000] ECR I-3201, Court of Justice of the European Communities

This was a sex equality claim based on the Equal Pay Act 1970 which in turn constituted the UK's implementation of Article 119 of the EC Treaty (Articles 117 to 120 of the EC Treaty have now been replaced by Articles 136 EC to 143 EC). The applicant claimed to be subject to procedures that were less favourable than those applying to similar domestic claims under the Sex Discrimination Act 1975 and the Race Relations Act 1976. The Court began with a statement of principle:

[31] First, it should be borne in mind that, according to settled case law, in the absence of relevant Community rules, it is for the national legal order of each Member State to designate the competent courts and to lay down the procedural rules for proceedings designed to ensure the protection of the rights which individuals acquire through the direct effect of Community law, provided that such rules are not less favourable than those governing similar domestic actions (principle of equivalence) and are not framed in such a way as to render impossible in practice the exercise of rights conferred by Community law (principle of effectiveness).

It proceeded to conduct a more specific examination:

[49] In order to verify whether the principle of equivalence has been complied with in the present case, it is for the national court, which alone has direct knowledge of the procedural rules governing actions in the field of domestic law, to verify whether the procedural rules intended to ensure that the rights derived by individuals from Community law are safeguarded under domestic law comply with that principle and to consider both the purpose and the essential characteristics of allegedly similar domestic actions (see Case C-326/96 *Levez* [1998] ECR I-7835, paragraphs 39 and 43).

[50] However, with a view to the appraisal to be carried out by the national court, the Court may provide guidance for the interpretation of Community law.

[51] It must be borne in mind that the Court held, in paragraph 46 of *Levez*, a judgment delivered after the House of Lords sought a ruling in this case, that the EPA was the domestic legislation which gave effect to the Community principle of non-discrimination on grounds of sex in relation to pay, pursuant to Article 119 of the Treaty and Council Directive 75/117/EEC of 10 February 1975 on the approximation of the laws of the Member States relating to the application of the principle of equal pay for men and women (OJ 1975 L 45, p.19). In paragraph 47 of the same judgment, the Court stated that the fact that the same procedural rules applied to two comparable claims, one relying on a right conferred by Community law, the other on a right acquired under domestic law, was not enough to ensure compliance with the principle of equivalence, since one and the same form of action was involved.

[52] Since, following the accession of the United Kingdom to the Communities, the EPA constituted the legislation by means of which the United Kingdom discharged its obligations under Article 119 of the Treaty and, subsequently, under Directive 75/117, the Court concluded that the EPA could not provide an appropriate ground of comparison against which to measure compliance with the principle of equivalence (*Levez* paragraph 48).

[53] The answer to the first part of the second question must therefore be that an action alleging infringement of a statute such as the EPA does not constitute a domestic action similar to an action alleging infringement of Article 119 of the Treaty.

[54] By the second part of its second question the House of Lords seeks to ascertain the Community-law criteria for identifying a similar action in domestic law.

[55] The principle of equivalence requires that the rule at issue be applied without distinction, whether the infringement alleged is of Community law or national law, where the purpose and cause of action are similar (*Levez*, paragraph 41).

[56] In order to determine whether the principle of equivalence has been complied with in the present case, the national court – which alone has direct knowledge of the procedural rules governing actions in the field of employment law – must consider both the purpose and the essential characteristics of allegedly similar domestic actions (*Levez*, paragraph 43).

[57] In view of the foregoing, the answer to the second part of the second question must be that, in order to determine whether a right of action available under domestic law is a domestic action similar to proceedings to give effect to rights conferred by Article 119 of the Treaty, the national court must consider whether the actions concerned are similar as regards their purpose, cause of action and essential characteristics.

[58] By the third part of its second question, the House of Lords seeks to ascertain what are the relevant criteria for determining whether the procedural rules governing any claim which it may have identified as being similar are more favourable than the procedural rules which govern the enforcement of rights conferred by Article 119 of the Treaty.

[59] For the purposes of the appraisal to be undertaken by the national court, regard must be had to the relevant guidance as to the interpretation of Community law given in *Levez*.

[60] Thus, in paragraph 51, the Court stated that the principle of equivalence would be infringed if a person relying on a right conferred by Community law were forced to incur additional costs and delay by comparison with a claimant whose action was based solely on domestic law.

[61] More generally, it observed that whenever it fell to be determined whether a procedural provision of national law was less favourable than those governing similar domestic actions, the national court must take into account the role played by that provision in the procedure as a whole, as well as the operation and any special features of that procedure before the different national courts (*Levez*, paragraph 44).

[62] It follows that the various aspects of the procedural rules cannot be examined in isolation but must be placed in their general context. Moreover, such an examination may not be carried out subjectively by reference to circumstances of fact but must involve an objective comparison, in the abstract, of the procedural rules at issue.

[63] In view of the foregoing, the answer to the third part of the second question must be that, in order to decide whether procedural rules are equivalent, the national court must verify objectively, in the abstract, whether the rules at issue are similar taking into account the role played by those rules in the procedure as a whole, as well as the operation of that procedure and any special features of those rules.

NOTE

Recognition that the national court alone has direct knowledge of the relevant procedural rules (para 56) justifies caution on the part of the European Court when invited to intrude on national procedural autonomy. However, turning from the 'principle of equivalence' to the 'principle of effectiveness' (a modern rewriting of para 16 of the judgment in *Comet* (Case 45/76)) the European Court has been increasingly prepared to make specific the nature of the obligation cast on national judges by Community law. In defence of legal certainty all legal systems impose time limits. Such limits have proved a particular favourite target of litigants basing their action on Community law. *Comet* (Case 45/76, p.132 above) was a case of this nature. In the next case a time limit complied with the 'principle of equivalence' but fell foul of the 'principle of effectiveness'.

Marks and Spencer plc v *Commissioners of Customs and Excise* (Case C-62/00)
Judgment of 11 July 2002, Court of Justice of the European Communities

The UK was in breach of the Sixth VAT Directive, Directive 77/388. The relevant provisions had direct effect, so Marks and Spencer could rely on them before the English courts to seek recovery of money wrongly paid to the tax authorities. But the company was faced by rules that retroactively curtailed the period within which repayment of sums could be sought.

[34] It should be recalled at the outset that in the absence of Community rules on the repayment of national charges wrongly levied it is for the domestic legal system of each Member State to designate the courts and tribunals having jurisdiction and to lay down the detailed procedural rules governing actions for safeguarding rights which individuals derive from Community law, provided, first, that such rules are not less favourable than those governing similar domestic actions (the principle of equivalence) and, second, that they do not render virtually impossible or excessively difficult the exercise of rights conferred by Community law (the principle of effectiveness) (see, *inter alia*, Case C-228/96 *Aprile* [1998] ECR I-7141, paragraph 18, and the judgments cited above in *Dilexport*, [Case C-343/96] paragraph 25, and *Metallgesellschaft*, [Case C-410/98], paragraph 85).

[35] As regards the latter principle, the Court has held that in the interests of legal certainty, which protects both the taxpayer and the administration, it is compatible with Community law to lay down reasonable time-limits for bringing proceedings (*Aprile*, paragraph 19, and the case law cited therein). Such time-limits are not liable to render virtually impossible or excessively difficult the exercise of the rights conferred by Community law. In that context, a national limitation period of three years which runs from the date of the contested payment appears to be reasonable (see, in particular, *Aprile*, paragraph 19, and *Dilexport*, paragraph 26).

[36] Moreover, it is clear from the judgments in *Aprile* (paragraph 28) and *Dilexport* (paragraphs 41 and 42) that national legislation curtailing the period within which recovery may be sought of sums charged in breach of Community law is, subject to certain conditions, compatible with Community law. First, it must not be intended specifically to limit the consequences of a judgment of the Court to the effect that national legislation concerning a specific tax is incompatible with Community law. Secondly, the time set for its application must be sufficient to ensure that the right to repayment is effective. In that connection, the Court has held that legislation which is not in fact retrospective in scope complies with that condition.

[37] It is plain, however, that that condition is not satisfied by national legislation such as that at issue in the main proceedings which reduces from six to three years the period within which repayment may be sought of VAT wrongly paid, by providing that the new time-limit is to apply immediately to

all claims made after the date of enactment of that legislation and to claims made between that date and an earlier date, being that of the entry into force of the legislation, as well as to claims for repayment made before the date of entry into force which are still pending on that date.

[38] Whilst national legislation reducing the period within which repayment of sums collected in breach of Community law may be sought is not incompatible with the principle of effectiveness, it is subject to the condition not only that the new limitation period is reasonable but also that the new legislation includes transitional arrangements allowing an adequate period after the enactment of the legislation for lodging the claims for repayment which persons were entitled to submit under the original legislation. Such transitional arrangements are necessary where the immediate application to those claims of a limitation period shorter than that which was previously in force would have the effect of retroactively depriving some individuals of their right to repayment, or of allowing them too short a period for asserting that right.

[39] In that connection it should be noted that Member States are required as a matter of principle to repay taxes collected in breach of Community law (Joined Cases C-192/95 to C-218/95 *Comateb and Others* [1997] ECR I-165, paragraph 20, and *Dilexport*, paragraph 23), and whilst the Court has acknowledged that, by way of exception to that principle, fixing a reasonable period for claiming repayment is compatible with Community law, that is in the interests of legal certainty, as was noted in paragraph 35 hereof. However, in order to serve their purpose of ensuring legal certainty limitation periods must be fixed in advance (Case 41/69 *ACF Chemiefarma* v *Commission* [1970] ECR 661, paragraph 19).

[40] Accordingly, legislation such as that at issue in the main proceedings, the retroactive effect of which deprives individuals of any possibility of exercising a right which they previously enjoyed with regard to repayment of VAT collected in breach of provisions of the Sixth Directive with direct effect must be held to be incompatible with the principle of effectiveness.

[41] That applies notwithstanding the argument of the United Kingdom Government to the effect that the enactment of the legislation at issue in the main proceedings was motivated by the legitimate purpose of striking a due balance between the individual and the collective interest and of enabling the State to plan income and expenditure without the disruption caused by major unforeseen liabilities.

[42] Whilst such a purpose may serve to justify fixing reasonable limitation periods for bringing claims, as was noted in paragraph 35, it cannot permit them to be so applied that rights conferred on individuals by Community law are no longer safeguarded.

NOTE

It is plain that the 'principle of effectiveness' has potency before national courts. There is now a significant Community input into national law governing procedure and remedies.

Consider *Commission* v *UK* (Case C-246/89R), at p.117 above. Re-read the summary of the facts. While the Commission was pursuing the UK at Community level, private parties were acting before English courts to protect their interests. Factortame was one of several Spanish fishing undertakings holding a British registration which alleged that it had been discriminated against on grounds of nationality contrary to Community law. It saw the imminent prospect of severe curtailment of its fishing operations. Factortame wished to challenge the UK's Merchant Shipping Act 1988, which it did by an application for judicial review of the decision of the Secretary of State for Transport which brought particular provisions of the Act into force. This raises fundamental issues of constitutional law in the UK relating to Parliamentary Sovereignty. The *Factortame* litigation provides an extremely important indication of modern British judicial thinking about the constitutional implications of membership of the Community. However, in the present context the tale deserves attention for the European Court's view of the impact of Community law on national remedies and procedures.

R v *Secretary of State for Transport, ex parte Factortame* (Case C-213/89)
[1990] ECR I-2433, [1990] 3 WLR 852, Court of Justice of the European Communities

Factortame's claim that the Act violated Community rules prohibiting discrimination was initially treated in straightforward fashion; a reference was made by the High Court to the European Court requesting assistance in the interpretation of relevant points of Community law ([1989] 2 CMLR 353, Case C-221/89 – eventually, in July 1991, the Court ruled in terms favourable to Factortame – [1991] ECR I-3905.) But what should happen pending that ruling? Should the Act apply, or should it be suspended? The House of Lords ruled that as a matter of English law it had no power to make the award of interim relief against the application of the statute which Factortame had sought (*Factortame v Secretary of State for Transport (No 1)* [1989] 3 CMLR 1, [1990] 2 AC 85, [1989] 2 All ER 692). However the House of Lords referred to the European Court the following questions relating to the impact of Community law on available remedies:

1. Where:

    (i) a party before the national court claims to be entitled to rights under Community law having direct effect in national law ('the rights claimed'),
    (ii) a national measure in clear terms will, if applied, automatically deprive that party of the rights claimed,
    (iii) there are serious arguments both for and against the existence of the rights claimed and the national court has sought a preliminary ruling under Article 177 [now 234] as to whether or not the rights claimed exist,
    (iv) the national law presumes the national measure in question to be compatible with Community law unless and until it is declared incompatible,
    (v) the national court has no power to give interim protection to the rights claimed by suspending the application of the national measure pending the preliminary ruling,
    (vi) if the preliminary ruling is in the event in favour of the rights claimed, the party entitled to those rights is likely to have suffered irremediable damage unless given such interim protection,

    does Community law either

    (a) oblige the national court to grant such interim protection of the rights claimed; or
    (b) give the Court power to grant such interim protection of the rights claimed?

2.   If Question 1(a) is answered in the negative and Question 1(b) in the affirmative, what are the criteria to be applied in deciding whether or not to grant such interim protection of the rights claimed?

The European Court ruled within 13 months in June 1990.

[17] It is clear from the information before the Court, and in particular from the judgment making the reference and, as described above, the course taken by the proceedings in the national courts before which the case came at first and second instance, that the preliminary question raised by the House of Lords seeks essentially to ascertain whether a national court which, in a case before it concerning Community law, considers that the sole obstacle which precludes it from granting interim relief is a rule of national law, must disapply that rule.

[18] For the purpose of replying to that question, it is necessary to point out that in its judgment of 9 March 1978 in Case 106/77 (*Amministrazione delle Finanze dello Stato v Simmenthal SpA* [1978] ECR 629) the Court held that directly applicable rules of Community law 'must be fully and uniformly applied in all the Member States from the date of their entry into force and for so long as they continue in force' (paragraph 14) and that 'in accordance with the principle of the precedence of Community law, the relationship between provisions of the Treaty and directly applicable measures of the institutions on the one hand and the national law of the Member States on the other is such

that those provisions and measures... by their entry into force render automatically inapplicable any conflicting provision of . . . national law' (paragraph 17).

[19] In accordance with the case-law of the Court, it is for the national courts, in application of the principle of co-operation laid down in Article 5 of the EEC Treaty [now Article 10 EC], to ensure the legal protection which persons derive from the direct effect of provisions of Community law (see, most recently, the judgments of 10 July 1980 in Case 811/79 *Ariete SpA* v *Amministrazione delle Finanze dello Stato* [1980] ECR 2545 and *MIRECO SaS* v *Amministrazione delle Finanze dello Stato* [1980] ECR 2559).

[20] The Court has also held that any provision of a national legal system and any legislative, administrative or judicial practice which might impair the effectiveness of Community law by with-holding from the national court having jurisdiction to apply such law the power to do everything necessary at the moment of its application to set aside national legislative provisions which might prevent, even temporarily, Community rules from having full force and effect are incompatible with those requirements, which are the very essence of Community law (judgment of 9 March 1978 in *Simmenthal*, cited above, at paragraphs 22 and 23).

[21] It must be added that the full effectiveness of Community law would be just as much impaired if a rule of national law could prevent a court seised of a dispute governed by Community law from granting interim relief in order to ensure the full effectiveness of the judgment to be given on the existence of the rights claimed under Community law. It follows that a court which in those circum-stances would grant interim relief, if it were not for a rule of national law, is obliged to set aside that rule.

[22] That interpretation is reinforced by the system established by Article 177 of the EEC Treaty whose effectiveness would be impaired if a national court, having stayed proceedings pending the reply by the Court of Justice to the question referred to it for a preliminary ruling, were not able to grant interim relief until it delivered its judgment following the reply given by the Court of Justice.

[23] Consequently, the reply to the question raised should be that Community law must be inter-preted as meaning that a national court which, in a case before it concerning Community law, considers that the sole obstacle which precludes it from granting interim relief is a rule of national law must set aside that rule.

NOTE
The Court's brisk reformulation of the question causes it to be rather dismissive of the view advanced by the UK that *Simmenthal* (Case 106/77, p.100 above) was not directly in point because the rights under Community law in that case had been firmly established and were not, as in *Factortame*, merely claimed. Advocate-General Tesauro was rather fuller in his treatment of the role of interim protection in a system of effective remedies.

R v *Secretary of State for Transport, ex parte Factortame* (Case C-213/89)
[1990] ECR I-2433, [1990] 3 WLR 852, Court of Justice of the European Communities

ADVOCATE-GENERAL TESAURO: . . . Sometimes the right's existence is established too late for the right claimed to be fully and usefully exercised, which is the more likely to be the case the more structured and complex, and the more probably rich in safeguards, is the procedure culminating in the definitive establishment of the right. The result is that in such a case the utility as well as the effectiveness of judicial protection may be lost and there could be a betrayal of the principle, long established in jurisprudence, according to which the need to have recourse to legal proceedings to enforce a right should not occasion damage to the party in the right.

Interim protection has precisely that objective purpose, namely to ensure that the time needed to establish the existence of the right does not in the end have the effect of irremediably depriving the right of substance, by eliminating any possibility of exercising it; in brief, the purpose of interim protection is to achieve that fundamental objective of every legal system, the effectiveness of judicial protection. Interim protection is intended to prevent so far as possible the damage occasioned by the fact that the establishment and the existence of the right are not fully contemporaneous from prejudicing the effectiveness and the very purpose of establishing the right, which was also specifically affirmed by the Court when it linked interim protection to a requirement that, when delivered, the judgment will be fully effective; or to the need to 'preserve the existing position pending a decision on the substance of the case'.

Now that the function of interim protection has been brought into focus, such protection can be seen to be a fundamental and indispensable instrument of any judicial system, which seeks to achieve, in the particular case and always in an effective manner, the objective of determining the existence of a right and more generally of giving effect to the relevant legal provision, whenever the duration of the proceedings is likely to prejudice the attainment of this objective and therefore to nullify the effectiveness of the judgment.

The requirement for interim protection, moreover, as has already been noted, arises in the same terms, both where the establishment of the right's existence involves the facts and, consequently, the determination of the correct provision to be applied, that is to say where the uncertainty as to the outcome of the application involves – although the expression is not perhaps a happy one – 'the facts', and where it is a question of choosing between two or more provisions which may be applicable (for example, a classification problem), irrespective of whether both are presumed to be valid or whether one is presumed to be incompatible with the other, which is of a higher order or in any event has precedence.

In particular, where, as in the case now before the Court, the determination as to the existence of the right not only involves a choice between two or more provisions which may be applicable but also involves a prior review of the validity or compatibility of one provision vis à vis another of a higher order or in any event having precedence, the difference is merely one of appearance, particularly when that review is entrusted to a court on which special jurisdiction has been conferred for the purpose. This situation, too, is fully covered by the typical function of judicial proceedings, which seek to establish the existence of and hence to give effect to the right, so that the requirement that the individual's position be protected on a provisional basis remains the same, inasmuch as it is a question of determining, interpreting and applying to the case in question the relevant (and valid) legal rules.

It follows that what is commonly called the presumption of validity, which attaches to laws or administrative acts no less than it does to Community acts, until such time as it is established by judicial determination that the measure in question is incompatible with a rule of law of a higher order or in any event having precedence, *to the extent that such a procedure is provided for*, does not constitute a formal obstacle to the interim protection of enforceable legal rights. In fact, precisely because what is concerned is a presumption, which as such may be rebutted by the final determination, it remains necessary to provide a remedy to compensate for the fact that the final ruling establishing the existence of the right may come too late and therefore be of no use to the successful party.

In fact, it is certain and undeniable that a provision, whether it is contained in an Act of Parliament or a Community act, or in an administrative act, must be presumed to be valid. But that cannot and must not mean that the courts are precluded from temporarily paralysing its effects with regard to the concrete case before them where, pending a final determination on its validity *vis-à-vis* or compatibility with a provision of a higher order or having precedence, one or other of the legal rights in question is likely to be irremediably impaired and there is a suspicion (the degree of which must be established) that the final determination may entail a finding that the statute or administrative act in question is invalid.

In brief, the presumption that a law or an administrative act is valid may not and must not mean that the very possibility of interim protection is precluded *where the measure in question may form the subject of a final judicial review of its validity*.

Far from running counter to the principle of the validity of laws or administrative acts, which finds expression in a presumption that may always be rebutted by a final determination, interim protection in fact removes the risk that that presumption may lead to the perverse result, certainly not desired by any legal system, negating the function of judicial review and, in particular, of the review of the validity of laws. To take a different view would amount to radically denying the possibility of interim protection, not only in relation to laws, but absolutely, given that any act of a public authority, whether it is a rule-making instrument properly so-called or an individual decision, is presumed to be valid until the outcome of the judicial review of its validity.

NOTE

It was then for the House of Lords, equipped with the ruling that it possessed the power to grant interim relief, to decide whether to exercise that power on the facts of the case before it. Their Lordships considered the case appropriate for the grant of relief in favour of Factortame, pending the final ruling ([1991] 1 All ER 70, [1990] 3 CMLR 375). Lord Bridge was moved by some well-publicized denunciations of the European Court's alleged intrusion on the sovereignty of the UK (see especially Hansard, HC Debs, vol. 174, 20 June 1990) to remark that

there is nothing in any way novel in according supremacy to rules of Community law in those areas to which they apply and to insist that, in the protection of rights under Community law, national courts must not be inhibited by rules of national law from granting interim relief in appropriate cases is no more than a logical recognition of that supremacy.

FURTHER READING

Craufurd Smith, R., 'Remedies for Breach of EU Law in National Courts' Ch. 8 in P. Craig and G. de Búrca, *The Evolution of EU Law* (Oxford: OUP, 1999).

Girerd, P., 'Les principes d'équivalence et d'effectivité: encadrement ou désencadrement de l'autonomie procédurale des Etats members?'(2002) 38 RTDE 75.

Van Gerven, W., 'Of Rights, Remedies and Procedures' (2000) 37 CML Rev 501.

NOTE

For additional material and resources see the Companion Website at: www.oup.co.uk/best.textbooks/law/weatherill6e

5

The Direct Effect of Directives

SECTION 1: **ESTABLISHING THE PRINCIPLE**

The most difficult area relating to 'direct effect' arises in the application of the notion to EC *Directives*. Although the rest of this Chapter concentrates on this area, it is important not to develop an inflated notion of the importance of the problem of the direct effect of Directives. Directives are after all only one source of Community law. However, the issue deserves examination in some depth, not least because Directives play a major role in elaborating the detailed scope of Community policy-making in respect of which the Treaty provides a mere framework. Moreover, Directives are a rather peculiar type of act – Community law but implemented at national level through national legal procedures. An examination of this area, then, should reveal much about the general problem of the interrelation of national law with the Community legal order.

The starting point is Article 249 EC, formerly Article 189, set out at p.42. This suggests that a Directive, in contrast to a Regulation, would *not* be directly effective. Regulations are directly applicable, and if they meet the *Van Gend en Loos* (Case 26/62) test for direct effect they are directly effective too. They are law in the Member States (direct applicability) and they may confer legally enforceable rights on individuals (direct effect). Directives, in marked contrast, are clearly dependent on implementation by each State, according to Article 249. When made by the Community, they are not designed to be law in that form at national level. Nor are they designed directly to affect the individual. Yet in *Van Duyn* (Case 41/74), at p.123 above, the Court held that a Directive might be relied on by an individual before a national court. In the next case, *Pubblico Ministero* v *Ratti* (Case 148/78), the European Court explains how, when and why Directives can produce direct effects (or, at least, effects analogous thereto) at national level.

Pubblico Ministero v *Ratti* (Case 148/78)

[1979] ECR 1629, [1980] 1 CMLR 96, Court of Justice of the European Communities

Directive 73/173 required Member States to introduce into their domestic legal orders rules governing the packaging and labelling of solvents. This had to be done by December 1974. Italy had failed to implement the Directive and maintained in force a different national regime. Ratti produced his solvents in accordance with the Directive, not the Italian law. In 1978 he found himself the subject of criminal proceedings in Milan for non-compliance with Italian law. Could he rely on the Directive which Italy had left unimplemented?

[18] This question raises the general problem of the legal nature of the provisions of a directive adopted under Article 189 of the Treaty.

[19] In this regard the settled case law of the Court, last reaffirmed by the judgment of 1 February 1977 in Case 51/76 *Nederlandse Ondernemingen* [1977] 1 ECR 126, lays down that, whilst under Article 189 regulations are directly applicable and, consequently, by their nature capable of producing direct effects, that does not mean that other categories of acts covered by that article can never produce similar effects.

[20] It would be incompatible with the binding effect which Article 189 ascribes to directives to exclude on principle the possibility of the obligations imposed by them being relied on by persons concerned.

[21] Particularly in cases in which the Community authorities have, by means of directive, placed Member States under a duty to adopt a certain course of action, the effectiveness of such an act would be weakened if persons were prevented from relying on it in legal proceedings and national courts prevented from taking it into consideration as an element of Community law.

[22] Consequently a Member State which has not adopted the implementing measures required by the directive in the prescribed periods may not rely, as against individuals, on its own failure to perform the obligations which the directive entails.

[23] It follows that a national court requested by a person who has complied with the provisions of a directive not to apply a national provision incompatible with the directive not incorporated into the internal legal order of a defaulting Member State, must uphold that request if the obligation in question is unconditional and sufficiently precise.

[24] Therefore the answer to the first question must be that after the expiration of the period fixed for the implementation of a directive a Member State may not apply its internal law – even if it is provided with penal sanctions – which has not yet been adapted in compliance with the directive, to a person who has complied with the requirements of the directive.

NOTE
Directive 77/728 applied a similar regime to varnishes. But here Ratti had jumped the gun. The deadline for implementation was November 1979. Yet in 1978 his varnishes were already being made according to the Directive, not Italian law. In the criminal prosecution for breach of Italian law he sought to rely on this Directive too. He argued that he had a legitimate expectation that compliance with the Directive prior to its deadline for implementation would be permissible:

Pubblico Ministero v *Ratti* (Case 148/78)
[1979] ECR 1629, [1980] 1 CMLR 96, Court of Justice of the European Communities

[43] It follows that, for the reasons expounded in the grounds of the answer to the national court's first question, it is only at the end of the prescribed period and in the event of the Member State's default that the directive – and in particular Article 9 thereof – will be able to have the effects described in the answer to the first question.

[44] Until that date is reached the Member States remain free in that field.

[45] If one Member State has incorporated the provisions of a directive into its internal legal order before the end of the period prescribed therein, that fact cannot produce any effect with regard to other Member States.

[46] In conclusion, since a directive by its nature imposes obligations only on Member States, it is not possible for an individual to plead the principle of 'legitimate expectation' before the expiry of the period prescribed for its implementation.

[47] Therefore the answer to the fifth question must be that Directive No 77/728 of the Council of the European Communities of 7 November 1977, in particular Article 9 thereof, cannot bring about with respect to any individual who has complied with the provisions of the said directive before the

expiration of the adaptation period prescribed for the Member State any effect capable of being taken into consideration by national courts.

NOTE

A small indentation into the Court's insistence that the expiry of the period prescribed for a Directive's implementation is the vital trigger for its relevance in law before national courts was made in Case C-129/96 *Inter-Environnement Wallonie ASBL* v *Région Wallone* [1997] ECR I-7411. In advance of the deadline, Member States are obliged 'to refrain . . . from adopting measures liable seriously to compromise the result prescribed' by the Directive. In normal circumstances, however, it is the expiry of the prescribed deadline which converts an unimplemented (and sufficiently unconditional) Directive into a provision on which an individual may rely before a national court.

■ QUESTION

Why did the European Court decide to uphold Ratti's ability to rely on the unimplemented 1973 solvents Directive in the face of the apparently conflicting wording of the Treaty (Article 189, now 249)? One may return to Judge Mancini for one explanation:

F. Mancini, 'The Making of a Constitution for Europe'
(1989) 26 CML Rev 595

(Footnotes omitted.)

3. *Costa* v *Enel* may be therefore regarded as a sequel of *Van Gend en Loos*. It is not the only sequel, however. Eleven years after *Van Gend en Loos*, the Court took in *Van Duyn* v *Home Office* a further step forward by attributing direct effect to provisions of Directives not transposed into the laws of the Member States within the prescribed time limit, so long as they met the conditions laid down in *Van Gend en Loos*. In order to appreciate fully the scope of this development it should be borne in mind that while the principal subjects governed by Regulations are agriculture, transport, customs and the social security of migrant workers, Community authorities resort to Directives when they intend to harmonise national laws on such matters as taxes, banking, equality of the sexes, protection of the environment, employment contracts and organisation of companies. Plain cooking and haute cuisine, in other words. The hope of seeing Europe grow institutionally, in matters of social relationships and in terms of quality of life rests to a large extent on the adoption and the implementation of Directives.

Making Directives immediately enforceable poses, however, a formidable problem. Unlike Regulations and the Treaty provisions dealt with by *Van Gend en Loos*, Directives resemble international treaties, in so far as they are binding *only* on the States and *only* as to the result to be achieved. It is understandable therefore that, whereas the *Van Gend en Loos* doctrine established itself within a relatively short time, its extension to Directives met with bitter opposition in many quarters. For example, the French *Conseil d'État* and the German *Bundesfinanzhof* bluntly refused to abide by it and Professor Rasmussen, in a most un-Danish fit of temper, went so far as to condemn it as a case of 'revolting judicial behaviour'.

Understandable criticism is not necessarily justifiable. It is mistaken to believe that in attributing direct effect to Directives not yet complied with by the Member States, the Court was only guided by political considerations, such as the intention of by-passing the States in a strategic area of law-making. Non-compliance with Directives is the most typical and most frequent form of Member State infraction; moreover, the Community authorities often turn a blind eye to it and, even when the Commission institutes proceedings against the defaulting State under Article 169 of the Treaty, the Court cannot impose any penalty on that State. [See now Article 228 EC, a Maastricht innovation, p.120 above.] This gives the Directives a dangerously elastic quality: Italy, Greece or Belgium may agree to accept the enactment of a Directive with which it is uncomfortable knowing that the price to pay for possible failure to transpose it is non-existent or minimal.

Given these circumstances, it is sometimes submitted that the *Van Duyn* doctrine was essentially concerned with assuring respect for the rule of law. The Court's main purpose, in other words, was 'to ensure that neither level of government can rely upon its malfeasance – the Member State's failure to comply, the Community's failure or even inability to enforce compliance', with a view to frustrating the legitimate expectation of the Community citizens on whom the Directive confers rights. Indeed, 'if a Court is forced to condone wholesale violation of a norm, that norm can no longer be termed law'; nobody will deny that 'Directives are intended to have the force of law under the Treaty'.

Doubtless, in arriving at its judgment in *Van Duyn*, the Court may also have considered that by reducing the advantages Member States derived from non-compliance, its judgment would have strengthened the 'federal' reach of the Community power to legislate and it may even have welcomed such a consequence. But does that warrant the revolt staged by the *Conseil d'État* or the *Bundesfinanzhof*? The present author doubts it; and so did the German Constitutional Court, which sharply scolded the *Bundesfinanzhof* for its rejection of the *Van Duyn* doctrine. This went a long way towards restoring whatever legitimacy the Court of Justice had lost in the eyes of some observers following *Van Duyn*. The wound, one might say, is healed and the scars it has left are scarcely visible.

■ **QUESTION**

Do you agree with Mancini that the Court's work in this area is 'essentially concerned with assuring respect for the rule of law'? See also N. Green, 'Directives, Equity and the Protection of Individual Rights' (1984) 9 EL Rev 295.

NOTE
Difficult constitutional questions arise at Community level and at national level in relation to the direct effect of Directives. You will quickly notice that many of the issues have arisen in the context of cases about sex discrimination. This has happened because equality between the sexes constitutes an area of Community competence which is given shape by a string of important Directives, often inadequately implemented at national level.

SECTION 2: **CURTAILING THE PRINCIPLE**

The next case allowed the Court to refine its approach to the direct effect of Directives.

Marshall v *Southampton Area Health Authority* (Case 152/84)
[1986] ECR 723, [1986] 1 CMLR 688, Court of Justice of the European Communities

Ms Marshall was dismissed by her employers, the Health Authority, when she reached the age of 62. A man would not have been dismissed at that age. This was discrimination on grounds of sex. But was there a remedy in law? Apparently not under the UK's Sex Discrimination Act 1975, because of a provision excluding discrimination arising out of treatment in relation to retirement. Directive 76/207, requiring equal treatment between the sexes, *did* appear to envisage a legal remedy for such discrimination, but that Directive had not been implemented in the UK, even though the deadline was past. So could Ms Marshall base a claim on the unimplemented Community Directive before an English court? The European Court was asked this question in a preliminary reference by the Court of Appeal.

The European Court first held that Ms Marshall's situation was an instance of discrimination on grounds of sex contrary to the Directive. It continued:

[39] Since the first question has been answered in the affirmative, it is necessary to consider whether Article 5(1) of Directive No 76/207 may be relied upon by an individual before national courts and tribunals.

[40] The appellant and the Commission consider that that question must be answered in the affirmative. They contend in particular, with regard to Articles 2(1) and 5(1) of Directive No 76/207, that those provisions are sufficiently clear to enable national courts to apply them without legislative intervention by the Member States, at least so far as overt discrimination is concerned.

[41] In support of that view, the appellant points out that directives are capable of conferring rights on individuals which may be relied upon directly before the courts of the Member States; national courts are obliged by virtue of the binding nature of a directive, in conjunction with Article 5 of the EEC Treaty, to give effect to the provisions of directives where possible, in particular when construing or applying relevant provisions of national law (judgment of 10 April 1984 in Case 14/83 *von Colson and Kamann* v *Land Nordrhein-Westfalen* [1984] ECR 1891). Where there is any inconsistency between national law and Community law which cannot be removed by means of such a construction, the appellant submits that a national court is obliged to declare that the provision of national law which is inconsistent with the directive is inapplicable.

[42] The Commission is of the opinion that the provisions of Article 5(1) of Directive No 76/207 are sufficiently clear and unconditional to be relied upon before a national court. They may therefore be set up against section 6(4) of the Sex Discrimination Act, which, according to the decisions of the Court of Appeal, has been extended to the question of compulsory retirement and has therefore become ineffective to prevent dismissals based upon the difference in retirement ages for men and for women.

[43] The respondent and the United Kingdom propose, conversely, that the second question should be answered in the negative. They admit that a directive may, in certain specific circumstances, have direct effect as against a Member State in so far as the latter may not rely on its failure to perform its obligations under the directive. However, they maintain that a directive can never impose obligations directly on individuals and that it can only have direct effect against a Member State *qua* public authority and not against a Member State *qua* employer. As an employer a State is no different from a private employer. It would not therefore be proper to put persons employed by the State in a better position than those who are employed by a private employer.

[44] With regard to the legal position of the respondent's employees the United Kingdom states that they are in the same position as the employees of a private employer. Although according to United Kingdom constitutional law the health authorities, created by the National Health Service Act 1977, as amended by the Health Services Act 1980 and other legislation, are Crown bodies and their employees are Crown servants, nevertheless the administration of the National Health Service by the health authorities is regarded as being separate from the government's central administration and its employees are not regarded as civil servants.

[45] Finally, both the respondent and the United Kingdom take the view that the provisions of Directive No 76/207 are neither unconditional nor sufficiently clear and precise to give rise to direct effect. The directive provides for a number of possible exceptions, the details of which are to be laid down by the Member States. Furthermore, the wording of Article 5 is quite imprecise and requires the adoption of measures for its implementation.

[46] It is necessary to recall that, according to a long line of decisions of the Court (in particular its judgment of 19 January 1982 in Case 8/81 *Becker* v *Finanzamt Münster-Innenstadt* [1982] ECR 53), wherever the provisions of a directive appear, as far as their subject-matter is concerned, to be unconditional and sufficiently precise, those provisions may be relied upon by an individual against the State where that State fails to implement the directive in national law by the end of the period prescribed or where it fails to implement the directive correctly.

[47] That view is based on the consideration that it would be incompatible with the binding nature which Article 189 confers on the directive to hold as a matter of principle that the obligation imposed thereby cannot be relied on by those concerned. From that the Court deduced that a Member State which has not adopted the implementing measures required by the directive within the prescribed period may not plead, as against individuals, its own failure to perform the obligations which the directive entails.

[48] With regard to the argument that a directive may not be relied upon against an individual, it must be emphasised that according to Article 189 of the EEC Treaty the binding nature of a directive, which constitutes the basis for the possibility of relying on the directive before a national court, exists only in relation to 'each Member State to which it is addressed'. It follows that a directive may not of itself impose obligations on an individual and that a provision of a directive may not be relied upon as such against such a person. It must therefore be examined whether, in this case, the respondent must be regarded as having acted as an individual.

[49] In that respect it must be pointed out that where a person involved in legal proceedings is able to rely on a directive as against the State he may do so regardless of the capacity in which the latter is acting, whether employer or public authority. In either case it is necessary to prevent the State from taking advantage of its own failure to comply with Community law.

[50] It is for the national court to apply those considerations to the circumstances of each case; the Court of Appeal has, however, stated in the order for reference that the respondent, Southampton and South West Hampshire Area Health Authority (Teaching), is a public authority.

[51] The argument submitted by the United Kingdom that the possibility of relying on provisions of the directive against the respondent *qua* organ of the State would give rise to an arbitrary and unfair distinction between the rights of State employees and those of private employees does not justify any other conclusion. Such a distinction may easily be avoided if the Member State concerned has correctly implemented the directive in national law.

[52] Finally, with regard to the question whether the provision contained in Article 5(1) of Directive No 76/207, which implements the principle of equality of treatment set out in Article 2(1) of the directive, may be considered, as far as its contents are concerned, to be unconditional and sufficiently precise to be relied upon by an individual as against the State, it must be stated that the provision, taken by itself, prohibits any discrimination on grounds of sex with regard to working conditions, including the conditions governing dismissal, in a general manner and in unequivocal terms. The provision is therefore sufficiently precise to be relied on by an individual and to be applied by the national courts.

[53] It is necessary to consider next whether the prohibition of discrimination laid down by the directive may be regarded as unconditional, in the light of the exceptions contained therein and of the fact that according to Article 5(2) thereof the Member States are to take the measures necessary to ensure the application of the principle of equality of treatment in the context of national law.

[54] With regard, in the first place, to the reservation contained in Article 1(2) of Directive No 76/207 concerning the application of the principle of equality of treatment in matters of social security, it must be observed that, although the reservation limits the scope of the directive *ratione materiae*, it does not lay down any condition on the application of that principle in its field of operation and in particular in relation to Article 5 of the directive. Similarly, the exceptions to Directive No 76/207 provided for in Article 2 thereof are not relevant to this case.

[55] It follows that Article 5 of the Directive No 76/207 does not confer on the Member States the right to limit the application of the principle of equality of treatment in its field of operation or to subject it to conditions and that that provision is sufficiently precise and unconditional to be capable of being relied upon by an individual before a national court in order to avoid the application of any national provision which does not conform to Article 5(1).

[56] Consequently, the answer to the second question must be that Article 5(1) of Council Directive No 76/207 of 9 February 1976, which prohibits any discrimination on grounds of sex with regard to working conditions, including the conditions governing dismissal, may be relied upon as against a State authority acting in its capacity as employer, in order to avoid the application of any national provision which does not conform to Article 5(1).

NOTES
1. Ms Marshall was able to rely on the Directive because she was employed by the State. Her subsequent quest for compensation took her back to the European Court, where it was made

clear that national limits on compensatory awards should not be applied in so far as they impede an effective remedy (Case C-271/91 [1993] ECR I-4367). However, had she been employed by a private firm she would have been unable to rely on the direct effect of the Directive. So, as far as direct effect is concerned, there are requirements which always apply – those explained above in *Van Gend en Loos* (Case 26/62) (p.123). But for Directives there are extra requirements: first, that the implementation date has passed; and, second, that the State is the party against which enforcement is claimed. Directives may be vertically directly effective, but not horizontally directly effective.

2. In rejecting the horizontal direct effect of Directives, the Court in fact made a choice between competing rationales for the direct effect of Directives. In its early decisions the Court laid emphasis on the need to extend direct effect in this area in order to secure the 'useful effect' of measures left unimplemented by defaulting States. Consider para 12 of *Van Duyn* (Case 41/74) (p.123 above); and, for example, in *Nederlandse Ondernemingen* (Case 51/76) [1977] ECR 113, the Court observed (at para 23) that:

    > where the Community authorities have, by Directive, imposed on Member States the obli-
    > gation to pursue a particular course of conduct, the useful effect of such an act would be
    > weakened if individuals were prevented from relying on it before their national courts and
    > if the latter were prevented from taking it into consideration as an element of Community
    > law.

    This dictum came in the context of a case against the State, but this logic would lead a bold court to hold an unimplemented Directive enforceable against a private party too, in order to improve its useful effect. However, in *Ratti* (Case 148/78) (p.141 above) and in *Marshall* (Case 152/84) (p.144 above), the Court appears to switch its stance away from the idea of 'useful effect' to a type of 'estoppel' as the legal rationale for holding Directives capable of direct effect. See para 49 of the judgment in *Marshall* (Case 152/84).

3. The Court's curtailment of the impact of Directives before national courts may also be seen as a manifestation of judicial minimalism, mentioned at p.33 above. The realist would examine the awareness of the Court that in this area it risks assaulting national sensitivities if it insists on deepening the impact of Community law in the national legal order. The next case was mentioned in passing by Judge Mancini (p.143 above), but the decision deserves further attention.

Minister of the Interior v Cohn Bendit
[1980] 1 CMLR 543, Conseil d'État

The matter concerned the exclusion from France of Cohn Bendit, a noted political radical (who subsequently became a Member of the European Parliament!). He relied on Community rules governing free movement to challenge the exclusion. The Conseil d'État, the highest court in France dealing with administrative law, addressed itself to the utility of a Directive in Cohn Bendit's action before the French courts.

According to Article 56 of the Treaty instituting the European Economic Community of 25 March 1957, no requirement of which empowers an organ of the European Communities to issue, in matters of *ordre public*, regulations which are directly applicable in the member-States, the co-ordination of statute and of subordinate legislation (*dispositions législatives et réglementaires*) 'providing for special treatment for foreign nationals on grounds of public policy (*ordre public*), public security or public health' shall be the subject of Council directives, enacted on a proposal from the Commission and after consultation with the European Assembly. It follows clearly from Article 189 of the Treaty of 25 March 1957 that while these directives bind the member-States 'as to the result to be achieved' and while, to attain the aims set out in them, the national authorities are required to adapt the statute law and subordinate legislation and administrative practice of the member-States to the directives which are addressed to them, those authorities alone retain the power to decide on the form to be given to the implementation of the directives and to fix themselves, under the control of the national courts, the means appropriate to cause them to produce effect in national law. Thus, whatever the detail that they contain for the eyes of the member-States, directives may not be invoked by the nationals of such States in support of an action brought against an individual administrative act. It follows that M. Cohn-Bendit could not effectively maintain, in requesting the Tribunal Administratif of Paris to annul the decision of the Minister of the Interior of 2 February 1976, that that decision infringed the provisions of the directive enacted on 25 February 1964 by the Council of the European Communities with a view to coordinating, in the circumstances laid down in Article 56 of the EEC Treaty, special measures concerning the movement and residence of foreign nationals which are justified on grounds of public policy, public security or public health. Therefore, in the absence of any dispute on the legality of the administrative measures taken by the French Government to comply with the directives enacted by the Council of the European Communities, the solution to be given to the action brought by M. Cohn-Bendit may not in any case be made subject to the interpretation of the directive of 25 February 1964. Consequently, without it being necessary to examine the grounds of the appeal, the Minister of the Interior substantiates his argument that the Tribunal Administratif of Paris was wrong when in its judgment under appeal of 21 December 1977 it referred to the Court of Justice of the European Communities questions relating to the interpretation of that directive and stayed proceedings until the decision of the European Court.

In the circumstances the case should be referred back to the Tribunal Administratif of Paris to decide as may be the action of M. Cohn-Bendit.

NOTE

See, similarly, the *Bundesfinanzhof* (German federal tax court) in *VAT Directives* [1982] 1 CMLR 527.

As D. Anderson observed in the wake of the Court's rejection in *Marshall* (Case 152/84) of the enforceability of unimplemented Directives against private parties, '[t]he present concern of the Court is to consolidate the advances of the 1970s rather than face the legal complexities and political risks of attempting to extend the doctrine [of direct effect] further' (*Boston College International & Comparative Law Review* (1988) XI 91, 100). This implies that the Court might be expected to return to the matter. This proved correct. In 1993 and 1994 three Advocates-General pressed the Court to reconsider its rejection of the horizontal direct effect of Directives: Van Gerven in '*Marshall 2*' (Case C-271/91) [1993] ECR I-4367; Jacobs in *Vaneetveld* v *SA Le Foyer* (Case C-316/93) [1994] ECR I-763 and Lenz in *Paola Faccini Dori* v *Recreb Srl* (Case C-91/92) [1994] ECR I-3325. Advocate-General Lenz insisted that the Citizen of the Union was entitled to expect equality before the law throughout the territory of the Union and observed that, in the absence of horizontal direct effect, such equality was compromised by State failure to implement Directives. Advocate-General Jacobs thought that the effectiveness principle militated against drawing distinctions based on the status of a defendant. All three believed that the pursuit of coherence in the Community legal order dictated acceptance of the horizontal direct effect of Directives. Only in the third of these cases, *Faccini Dori* v *Recreb*, was the European Court unable to avoid addressing the issue directly.

Paola Faccini Dori v *Recreb Srl* (Case C-91/92)
[1994] ECR I-3325, Court of Justice of the European Communities

Ms Dori had concluded a contract at Milan Railway Station to buy an English language correspondence course. By virtue of Directive 85/577, which harmonizes laws governing the protection of consumers in respect of contracts negotiated away from business premises, the so-called 'Doorstep Selling Directive', she ought to have been entitled to a 'cooling-off' period of at least seven days within which she could exercise a right to withdraw from the contract. However, she found herself unable to exercise that right under Italian law because Italy had not implemented the Directive. She therefore sought to rely on the Directive to defeat the claim brought against her by the private party with which she had contracted. The ruling in *Marshall* (Case 152/84) appeared to preclude reliance on the Directive and the Court, despite the promptings of Advocate-General Lenz, *refused* to over-rule *Marshall*. It maintained that Directives are incapable of horizontal direct effect.

[23] It would be unacceptable if a State, when required by the Community legislature to adopt certain rules intended to govern the State's relations – or those of State entities – with individuals and to confer certain rights on individuals, were able to rely on its own failure to discharge its obligations so as to deprive individuals of the benefits of those rights. Thus the Court has recognised that certain provisions of directives on conclusion of public works contracts and of directives on harmonisation of turnover taxes may be relied on against the State (or State entities) (see the judgment in Case 103/88 *Fratelli Costanzo* v *Comune di Milano* [1989] ECR 1839 and the judgment in Case 8/81 *Decker* v *Finanzamt Münster-Innenstadt* [1982] ECR 53)

[24] The effect of extending that case law to the sphere of relations between individuals would be to recognise a power in the Community to enact obligations for individuals with immediate effect, whereas it has competence to do so only where it is empowered to adopt regulations.

[25] It follows that, in the absence of measures transposing the directive within the prescribed time-limit, consumers cannot derive from the directive itself a right of cancellation as against traders with whom they have concluded a contract or enforce such a right in a national court.

NOTE
Paragraph 48 of the ruling in *Marshall* expresses comparable sentiments to those expressed in para 24 of the *Dori* ruling, but the emphasis in the latter on the limits of Community competence (specifically under Article 189 – now 249 – EC) is noticeably firmer. Although the Court did not consider that Ms Dori was wholly barred from relying on the Directive (see p.163 below on 'indirect' effect and p.170 on a claim against the defaulting State), it nevertheless refused to allow a Directive to exert direct effect in relations between private individuals. In rulings subsequent to *Dori*, the Court has repeated its rejection of the horizontal direct effect of Directives: e.g., Case C-192/94 *El Corte Inglés* v *Cristina Blasquez Rivero* [1996] ECR I-1281; Case C-97/96 *Verband Deutscher Daihatsu Händler eV* v *Daihatsu Deutschland GmbH* [1997] ECR I-6843. The reader is invited to consider whether, just as the Conseil d'État's ruling in *Cohn Bendit* (p.147 above) may have prompted the European Court's caution in *Marshall*, so too national judicial anxieties, expressed with particular force by the the *Bundesverfassungsgericht*, about Treaty amendment in the guise of judicial interpretation may have prompted the European Court in *Dori* to emblazon its fidelity to the text of the EC Treaty by declining to extend Community legislative competence to include the enactment of obligations for individuals with immediate effect. Chapter 21 will examine this material in depth.

SECTION 3: **THE SCOPE OF THE PRINCIPLE: THE STATE**

Whatever one's view of the Court's motivations in ruling against the horizontal direct effect of Directives in *Marshall* (Case 152/84), confirmed in *Dori* (Case C-91/92) and subsequently, the decision left many questions unanswered. First, what is the 'State'? The more widely this is interpreted, the more impact the unimplemented Directive will have.

Foster v *British Gas* (Case C-188/89)
[1990] ECR I-3133, Court of Justice of the European Communities

The applicant wished to rely on the Equal Treatment Directive 76/207 against her employer before English courts. She and other applicants had been compulsorily retired at an age earlier than male employees. This raised the familiar issue of the enforceability of Directives before national courts where national law is inadequate. The Court examined the nature of the defendant (the British Gas Corporation: BGC).

[3] By virtue of the Gas Act 1972, which governed the BGC at the material time, the BGC was a statutory corporation responsible for developing and maintaining a system of gas supply in Great Britain, and had a monopoly of the supply of gas.

[4] The members of the BGC were appointed by the competent Secretary of State. He also had the power to give the BGC directions of a general character in relation to matters affecting the national interest and instructions concerning its management.

[5] The BGC was obliged to submit to the Secretary of State periodic reports on the exercise of its functions, its management and its programmes. Those reports were then laid before both Houses of Parliament. Under the Gas Act 1972 the BGC also had the right, with the consent of the Secretary of State, to submit proposed legislation to Parliament.

[6] The BGC was required to run a balanced budget over two successive financial years. The Secretary of State could order it to pay certain funds over to him or to allocate funds to specified purposes.

It then proceeded to explain the legal approach to defining the 'State' for these purposes:

[13] Before considering the question referred by the House of Lords, it must first be observed as a preliminary point that the United Kingdom has submitted that it is not a matter for the Court of Justice but for the national courts to determine, in the context of the national legal system, whether the provisions of a directive may be relied upon against a body such as the BGC.

[14] The question what effects measures adopted by Community institutions have and in particular whether those measures may be relied on against certain categories of persons necessarily involves interpretation of the articles of the Treaty concerning measures adopted by the institutions and the Community measure in issue.

[15] It follows that the Court of Justice has jurisdiction in proceedings for a preliminary ruling to determine the categories of persons against whom the provisions of a directive may be relied on. It is for the national courts, on the other hand, to decide whether a party to proceedings before them falls within one of the categories so defined.

The Court then disposed of the question referred:

[16] As the Court has consistently held (see the judgment of 19 January 1982 in Case 8/81, *Becker* v *Hauptzollamt Münster-Innenstadt*, [1982] ECR 53 at paragraphs 23 to 25), where the Community authorities have, by means of a directive, placed Member States under a duty to adopt a certain course of action, the effectiveness of such a measure would be diminished if persons were prevented from relying upon it in proceedings before a court and national courts were prevented from taking it into consideration as an element of Community law. Consequently, a Member State which has not adopted the implementing measures required by the directive within the prescribed period may not plead, as against individuals, its own failure to perform the obligations which the directive entails. Thus, wherever the provisions of a directive appear, as far as their subject-matter is concerned, to be unconditional and sufficiently precise, those provisions may, in the absence of implementing measures adopted within the prescribed period, be relied upon as against any national

provision which is incompatible with the directive or in so far as the provisions define rights which individuals are able to assert against the State.

[17] The Court further held in its judgment of 26 February 1986 in Case 152/84 (*Marshall*, at paragraph 49) that where a person is able to rely on a directive as against the State he may do so regardless of the capacity in which the latter is acting, whether as employer or as public authority. In either case it is necessary to prevent the State from taking advantage of its own failure to comply with Community law.

[18] On the basis of those considerations, the Court has held in a series of cases that unconditional and sufficiently precise provisions of a directive could be relied on against organizations or bodies which were subject to the authority or control of the State or had special powers beyond those which result from the normal rules applicable to relations between individuals.

[19] The Court has accordingly held that provisions of a directive could be relied on against tax authorities (the judgments of 19 January 1982 in Case 8/81, *Becker*, cited above, and of 22 February 1990 in Case C-22188, *ECSC* v *Acciaierie e Ferriere Busseni* (*in liquidation*)), local or regional authorities (judgment of 22 June 1989 in Case 103/88, *Fratelli Costanzo* v *Comune di Milano*), constitutionally independent authorities responsible for the maintenance of public order and safety (judgment of 15 May 1986 in Case 222/84, *Johnston* v *Chief Constable of the Royal Ulster Constabulary*, [1986] ECR 1651), and public authorities providing public health services (judgment of 26 February 1986 in Case 152/84, *Marshall*, cited above).

[20] It follows from the foregoing that a body, whatever its legal form, which has been made responsible, pursuant to a measure adopted by the State, for providing a public service under the control of the State and has for that purpose special powers beyond those which result from the normal rules applicable in relations between individuals is included in any event among the bodies against which the provisions of a directive capable of having direct effect may be relied upon.

[21] With regard to Article 5(1) of Directive 76/207 it should be observed that in the judgment of 26 February 1986 in Case 152/84 (*Marshall*, cited above, at paragraph 52), the Court held that that provision was unconditional and sufficiently precise to be relied on by an individual and to be applied by the national courts.

[22] The answer to the question referred by the House of Lords must therefore be that Article 5(1) of Council Directive 76/207/EEC of 9 February 1976 may be relied upon in a claim for damages against a body, whatever its legal form, which has been made responsible, pursuant to a measure adopted by the State, for providing a public service under the control of the State and has for that purpose special powers beyond those which result from the normal rules applicable in relations between individuals.

NOTE
The case has been widely commented upon; see, e.g., N. Grief, (1991) 16 EL Rev 136; E. Szyszczak, (1990) 27 CML Rev 859. For a full examination of the policy issues, see D. Curtin, 'The Province of Government', (1990) 15 EL Rev 195.

■ QUESTION

The case arose before British Gas was 'privatized' under the Gas Act 1986 (sold to the private sector). What difference would this sale make to the application of the Court's test?

NOTE
The notion of the 'State' embraces local authorities.

Fratelli Costanzo v *Milano* (Case 103/88)
[1989] ECR 1839, Court of Justice of the European Communities

The case arose out of the alleged failure of the municipal authorities in Milan to respect *inter alia* a Community Directive in awarding contracts for the construction of a football stadium for the 1990 World Cup. Could a disappointed contractor rely on the unimplemented Directive before Italian courts against the municipal authorities? The matter reached the European Court by way of a preliminary reference.

[28] In the fourth question the national court asks whether administrative authorities, including municipal authorities, are under the same obligation as a national court to apply the provisions of Article 29(5) of Council Directive 71/305 and to refrain from applying provisions of national law which conflict with them.

[29] In its judgments of 19 January 1982 in Case 8/81 *Becker* v *Finanzamt Münster-Innenstadt* [1982] ECR 53, at p.71 and 26 February 1986 in Case 152/84 *Marshall* v *Southampton and South-West Hampshire Area Health Authority* [1986] ECR 723, at p.748, the Court held that wherever the provisions of a directive appear, as far as their subject-matter is concerned, to be unconditional and sufficiently precise, those provisions may be relied upon by an individual against the State where that State has failed to implement the directive in national law by the end of the period prescribed or where it has failed to implement the Directive correctly.

[30] It is important to note that the reason for which an individual may, in the circumstances described above, rely on the provisions of a directive in proceedings before the national courts is that the obligations arising under those provisions are binding upon all the authorities of the Member States.

[31] It would, moreover, be contradictory to rule that an individual may rely upon the provisions of a directive which fulfil the conditions defined above in proceedings before the national courts seeking an order against the administrative authorities, and yet to hold that those authorities are under no obligation to apply the provisions of the directive and refrain from applying provisions of national law which conflict with them. It follows that when the conditions under which the Court has held that individuals may rely on the provisions of a directive before the national courts are met, all organs of the administration, including decentralized authorities such as municipalities, are obliged to apply those provisions.

[32] With specific regard to Article 29(5) of Directive 71/305, it is apparent from the discussion of the first question that it is unconditional and sufficiently precise to be relied upon by an individual against the State. An individual may therefore plead that provision before the national courts and, as is clear from the foregoing, all organs of the administration, including decentralized authorities such as municipalities, are obliged to apply it.

SECTION 4: **'INCIDENTAL EFFECT'**

It has been shown that Directives are incapable of application against private individuals before national courts. It is only when the State has fulfilled its Treaty obligation of implementation pursuant to Articles 10 and 249 EC that the Directive, duly transformed, becomes 'live' for the purposes of imposing obligations on private parties.

But this is not to say that an unimplemented Directive will never exert an effect before a national court that is prejudicial to a private party. Without abandoning its stance against horizontal direct effect the Court has nevertheless chosen to recognise circumstances in which the State's default may incidentally affect the position of a private individual.

Case C-201/94 *R* v *The Medicines Control Agency, ex parte Smith & Nephew Pharmaceuticals Ltd* and *Primecrown Ltd* v *The Medicine Control Agency* [1996] ECR I-5819 concerned Article 3 of Directive 65/65. This provided that no proprietary medicinal product could be placed on the market in a Member State unless a prior authorisation had been issued by the competent authority of that Member State – the Medicines Control Agency (MCA) in the UK. The UK's Medicines Control Agency (MCA) had issued to Primecrown a licence to import a proprietary medicinal product of Belgian origin bearing the same name, and manufactured under an agreement with the same (American) licensor, as a product for which Smith & Nephew already held a marketing authorisation in the United Kingdom. But the MCA decided it was in error and it withdrew the authorisation. Both Primecrown and Smith & Nephew initiated proceedings before the English courts and, in a preliminary reference, the European Court was asked to provide an interpretation of the Directive's rules governing authorisation. But it was also asked whether Smith & Nephew, as the holder of the original authorisation issued under the normal procedure referred to in Directive 65/65, could rely on the Directive in proceedings before a national court in which it contested the validity of a marketing authorisation granted by a competent public authority to one of its competitors. The Court decided that it could. The consequence is that Primecrown's position could be detrimentally affected by a competitor's reliance on a Directive in proceedings against the public authorities. True, Smith & Nephew did not rely on the Directive in an action against Primecrown. This is *not* horizontal direct effect of the type painstakingly excluded by the Court in *Dori* (Case C-91/92, p.148 above). But it is a case in which the application of a Directive by a national court *incidentally* affected the legal position of a private party.

The Court has developed this case law further. Without any direct challenge to its dogged resistance to the horizontal direct effect of Directives, it has nevertheless extended the *incidental* effect of Directives on private parties in national proceedings.

Council Directive 83/189/EEC provided for Member States to give advance notice to the Commission and other Member States of plans to introduce new product specifications. The amendments were consolidated in Directive 98/34 [1998] OJ L204/37, itself amended by Directive 98/48 [1998] OJ L217/18. The purpose of this notification system is to avoid the introduction of new measures having equivalent effect to quantitative restrictions on trade (and to supply the Commission with a possible basis for developing its harmonisation programme). It is an 'early warning system' (see Chapter 9 more generally on 'market management').

In the next case the Court decided that non-notification of a draft technical regulation (as defined by the Directive) affected the enforceability of that measure before the courts of the defaulting Member State.

CIA Security International SA v *Signalson SA and Securitel Sprl* (Case C-194/94)
[1996] ECR I-2201, Court of Justice of the European Communities

Signalson and Securitel sought a court order from a Belgian court requiring that their competitor CIA Security cease marketing a burglar alarm. The alarm was not compatible with Belgian technical standards. But the Belgian technical standards had not been notified to the Commission, as was required by Directive 83/189. Did this State default have any effect in the national proceedings involving two private parties? The Directive did not address the matter. This did not deter the Court.

[42] It is settled law that, wherever provisions of a directive appear to be, from the point of view of their content, unconditional and sufficiently precise, they may be relied on against any national provision which is not in accordance with the directive (see the judgment in Case 8/81 *Becker* [1982] ECR 53 and the judgment in Joined Cases C-6/90 and C-9/90 *Francovich and Others* [1991] ECR I-5357).

[43] The United Kingdom considers that the provisions of Directive 83/189 do not satisfy those criteria on the ground, in particular, that the notification procedure contains a number of elements that are imprecise.

[44] That view cannot be adopted. Articles 8 and 9 of Directive 83/189 lay down a precise obligation on Member States to notify draft technical regulations to the Commission before they are adopted. Being, accordingly, unconditional and sufficiently precise in terms of their content, those articles may be relied on by individuals before national courts.

[45] It remains to examine the legal consequences to be drawn from a breach by Member States of their obligation to notify and, more precisely, whether Directive 83/189 is to be interpreted as meaning that a breach of the obligation to notify, constituting a procedural defect in the adoption of the technical regulations concerned, renders such technical regulations inapplicable so that they may not be enforced against individuals.

[46] The German and Netherlands Governments and the United Kingdom consider that Directive 83/189 is solely concerned with relations between the Member States and the Commission, that it merely creates procedural obligations which the Member States must observe when adopting technical regulations, their competence to adopt the regulations in question after expiry of the suspension period being, however, unaffected, and, finally, that it contains no express provision relating to any effects attaching to non-compliance with those procedural obligations.

[47] The Court observes first of all in this context that none of those factors prevents non-compliance with Directive 83/189 from rendering the technical regulations in question inapplicable.

[48] For such a consequence to arise from a breach of the obligations laid down by Directive 83/189, an express provision to this effect is not required. As pointed out above, it is undisputed that the aim of the directive is to protect freedom of movement for goods by means of preventive control and that the obligation to notify is essential for achieving such Community control. The effectiveness of Community control will be that much greater if the directive is interpreted as meaning that breach of the obligation to notify constitutes a substantial procedural defect such as to render the technical regulations in question inapplicable to individuals.

[49] That interpretation of the directive is in accordance with the judgment given in Case 380/87 *Enichem Base and Others* v *Comune di Cinisello Balsamo* [1989] ECR 2491, paragraphs 19 to 24. In that judgment, in which the Court ruled on the obligation for Member States to communicate to the Commission national draft rules falling within the scope of an article of Council Directive 75/442/EEC of 15 July 1975 on waste (OJ 1975 L 194, p.39), the Court held that neither the wording nor the purpose of the provision in question provided any support for the view that failure by the Member States to observe their obligation to give notice in itself rendered unlawful the rules thus adopted. In this regard, the Court expressly considered that the provision in question was confined to imposing an obligation to give prior notice which did not make entry into force of the envisaged rules subject to the Commission's agreement or lack of opposition and which did not lay down the procedure for Community control of the drafts in question. The Court therefore concluded that the provision under examination concerned relations between the Member States and the Commission but that it did not afford individuals any right capable of being infringed in the event of breach by a Member State of its obligation to give prior notice of its draft regulations to the Commission.

[50] In the present case, however, the aim of the directive is not simply to inform the Commission. As already found in paragraph 41 of this judgment, the directive has, precisely, a more general aim of eliminating or restricting obstacles to trade, to inform other States of technical regulations envisaged by a State, to give the Commission and the other Member States time to react and to propose amendments for lessening restrictions to the free movement of goods arising from the envisaged

measure and to afford the Commission time to propose a harmonising directive. Moreover, the wording of Articles 8 and 9 of Directive 83/189 is clear in that those articles provide for a procedure for Community control of draft national regulations and the date of their entry into force is made subject to the Commission's agreement or lack of opposition

NOTE

The *effectiveness* rationale contained in para 48 is remarkably far-reaching. It was also encountered in *Ratti* (Case 148/78 para 21, p.141 above)). But the reasoning in *Ratti* was treated more circumspectly by the Court subsequently in *Marshall* (Case 152/84, p.144), and the approach taken in *CIA Security* has also been curtailed in the light of the salutary experience provided by litigation.

Johannes Martinus Lemmens (Case C-226/97)
[1998] ECR I-3711, Court of Justice of the European Communities

Lemmens was charged with driving while under the influence of alcohol. He argued that the breathalyser was made according to a technical standard that had not been notified to the Commission and that accordingly, following *CIA Security*, it was incompatible with Community law to rely on such evidence before national (criminal) courts.

Para 12 of the judgment records Mr Lemmens' disingenuous but ingenious idea:

It is apparent from the order for reference that, in the course of the criminal proceedings instituted against him, Mr Lemmens said 'I understand from the press that there are difficulties regarding the breath-analysis apparatus. I maintain that this apparatus has not been notified to Brussels and wonder what the consequences of this could be for my case'.

The Court concluded that the Dutch Regulation governing breathalyser kits constituted a technical regulation which should, prior to its adoption, have been notified to the Commission in accordance with Article 8 of the Directive. But with what consequence?

[32] . . . it should be noted that, in paragraph 40 of its judgment in *CIA Security International*, cited above, the Court emphasised that the Directive is designed to protect, by means of preventive control, freedom of movement for goods, which is one of the foundations of the Community. This control serves a useful purpose in that technical regulations covered by the Directive may constitute obstacles to trade in goods between Member States, such obstacles being permissible only if they are necessary to satisfy compelling requirements relating to the public interest.

[33] In paragraphs 48 and 54 of that judgment, the Court pointed out that the obligation to notify is essential for achieving such Community control and went on to State that the effectiveness of such control will be that much greater if the Directive is interpreted as meaning that breach of the obligation to notify constitutes a substantial procedural defect such as to render the technical regulations in question inapplicable, and thus unenforceable against individuals.

[34] In criminal proceedings such as those in the main action, the regulations applied to the accused are those which, on the one hand, prohibit and penalise driving while under the influence of alcohol and, on the other, require a driver to exhale his breath into an apparatus designed to measure the alcohol content, the result of that test constituting evidence in criminal proceedings. Such regulations differ from those which, not having been notified to the Commission in accordance with the Directive, are unenforceable against individuals.

[35] While failure to notify technical regulations, which constitutes a procedural defect in their adoption, renders such regulations inapplicable inasmuch as they hinder the use or marketing of a product which is not in conformity therewith, it does not have the effect of rendering unlawful any use of a product which is in conformity with regulations which have not been notified.

[36] The use of the product by the public authorities, in a case such as this, is not liable to create an obstacle to trade which could have been avoided if the notification procedure had been followed.

[37] The answer to the first question must therefore be that the Directive is to be interpreted as meaning that breach of the obligation imposed by Article 8 thereof to notify a technical regulation on breath-analysis apparatus does not have the effect of making it impossible for evidence obtained by means of such apparatus, authorised in accordance with regulations which have not been notified, to be relied upon against an individual charged with driving while under the influence of alcohol.

Paragraph 35 of *Lemmens* provides a re-focusing of the test applied in *CIA Security*. Paragraph 36 constitutes a narrower reading of the *effectiveness* rationale. In the next case the Court explicitly adopts the reasoning advanced in *Lemmens* but accepts the application of the notification Directive in litigation between two contracting parties in which, at first glance, the State had no involvement.

Unilever Italia SpA v *Central Food SpA* (Case C-443/98)
[2000] ECR I-7535, Court of Justice of the European Communities

Unilever had supplied Central Food with a quantity of virgin olive oil. Central Food rejected the goods on the basis that they were not labelled in accordance with a relevant Italian law. This law had been notified to the Commission but Italy had not observed the Directive's 'standstill' obligation, which required it to wait a defined period before bringing the law into force. The Court treated breach of the 'standstill' obligation as indistinguishable for these purposes from outright failure to notify (which was the nature of the default in both *CIA Security* and *Lemmens*). Unilever submitted that the law should not be applied and sued Central Food under the contract for the price of the goods.

[46] . . . in civil proceedings of that nature, application of technical regulations adopted in breach of Article 9 of Directive 83/189 may have the effect of hindering the use or marketing of a product which does not conform to those regulations.

[47] That is the case in the main proceedings, since application of the Italian rules is liable to hinder Unilever in marketing the extra virgin olive oil which it offers for sale.

[48] Next, it must be borne in mind that, in *CIA Security*, the finding of inapplicability as a legal consequence of breach of the obligation of notification was made in response to a request for a preliminary ruling arising from proceedings between competing undertakings based on national provisions prohibiting unfair trading.

[49] Thus, it follows from the case law of the Court that the inapplicability of a technical regulation which has not been notified in accordance with Article 8 of Directive 83/189 can be invoked in proceedings between individuals for the reasons set out in paragraphs 40 to 43 of this judgment. The same applies to non-compliance with the obligations laid down by Article 9 of the same directive, and there is no reason, in that connection, to treat disputes between individuals relating to unfair competition, as in the *CIA Security* case, differently from disputes between individuals concerning contractual rights and obligations, as in the main proceedings.

[50] Whilst it is true, as observed by the Italian and Danish Governments, that a directive cannot of itself impose obligations on an individual and cannot therefore be relied on as such against an individual (see Case C-91/92 *Faccini Dori* [1994] ECR I-3325, paragraph 20), that case-law does not apply where non-compliance with Article 8 or Article 9 of Directive 83/189, which constitutes a substantial procedural defect, renders a technical regulation adopted in breach of either of those articles inapplicable.

[51] In such circumstances, and unlike the case of non-transposition of directives with which the case-law cited by those two Governments is concerned, Directive 83/189 does not in any way define

the substantive scope of the legal rule on the basis of which the national court must decide the case before it. It creates neither rights nor obligations for individuals.

[52] In view of all the foregoing considerations, the answer to the question submitted must be that a national court is required, in civil proceedings between individuals concerning contractual rights and obligations, to refuse to apply a national technical regulation which was adopted during a period of postponement of adoption prescribed in Article 9 of Directive 83/189.

NOTE

This is *not* horizontal direct effect. The Directive did not impose an obligation on Central Food. The contract with Unilever imposed the obligation. This seems to be the Court's point in para 51. But the invocation of the Directive completely changed the legal position that had appeared to prevail between the two parties under the contract. It transplanted the commercial risk.

Advocate-General Jacobs had argued vigorously in his Opinion in *Unilever* that legal certainty would be damaged by a finding that the notification Directive be relevant to the status of the contractual claim between private parties.

ADVOCATE-GENERAL JACOBS:

[99] . . . The fact that a Member State did not comply with the procedural requirements of the directive as such should not, in my view, entail detrimental effects for individuals.

[100] That is, first, because such effects would be difficult to justify in the light of the principle of legal certainty. For the day-to-day conduct of trade, technical regulations which apply to the sale of goods must be clearly and readily identifiable as enforceable or as unenforceable. Although the present dispute concerns a relatively small quantity of bottled olive oil of a value which may not affect the finances of either Unilever or Central Food to any drastic extent, it is easy to imagine an exactly comparable case involving highly perishable goods and sums of money which represent the difference between prosperity and ruin for one or other of the parties concerned. In order to avoid difficulties in his contractual relations, an individual trader would have to be aware of the existence of Directive 83/189, to know the judgment in *CIA Security*, to identify a technical regulation as such, and to establish with certainty whether or not the Member State in question had complied with all the procedural requirements of the directive. The last element in particular might prove to be extremely difficult because of the lack of publicity of the procedure under the directive. There is no obligation on the Commission to publish the fact that a Member State has notified or failed to notify a given draft technical regulation. In respect of the standstill periods under Article 9 of the directive, there is no way for individuals to know that other Member States have triggered the six-month standstill period by delivering detailed opinions to the Commission. Similarly, the Commission is also not required to publish the fact that it has informed a Member State of intended or pending Community legislation.

[101] The second problem is possible injustice. If failure to notify were to render a technical regulation unenforceable in private proceedings an individual would lose a case in which such a regulation was in issue, not because of his own failure to comply with an obligation deriving from Community law, but because of a Member State's behaviour. The economic survival of a firm might be threatened merely for the sake of the effectiveness of a mechanism designed to control Member States' regulatory activities. That would be so independently of whether the technical regulation in question constituted an obstacle to trade, a measure with neutral effects on trade, or even a rule furthering trade. The only redress for a trader in such a situation would be to bring *ex post* a hazardous and costly action for damages against a Member State. Nor is there any reason for the other party to the proceedings to profit, entirely fortuitously, from a Member State's failure to comply with the directive.

[102] It follows, in my view, that the correct solution in proceedings between individuals is a substantive solution. The applicability of a technical regulation in proceedings between individuals

should depend only on its compatibility with Article 30 [now 28: Chapter 11 of this book] of the Treaty. If in the present case Italian Law No 313 complies with Article 30, I can see no reason why Central Food, which understandably relied on the rules laid down in the Italian statute book, should lose the case before the national court. If, however, Italian Law No 313 infringes Article 30 then the national court should be obliged to set the Law aside on that ground.

[103] I accordingly conclude that as against an individual another individual should not be able to rely on a Member State's failure to comply with the requirements of Directive 83/189 in order to set aside a technical regulation.

NOTE
Plainly these anxieties did not move the Court in *Unilever*. It did not follow the Advocate-General and it did not limit the matter to resolution under Article 28 (ex 30) EC, concerning the free movement of goods. It accepted the incidental effect of the notification Directive on the contractual claim. This thrusts EC law of market integration deep into national contract law in so far as private compliance with technical standards is at stake. In the next case the Court nonetheless adopts an additional line of reasoning which may be capable of providing a basis for softening some of the harsh commercial uncertainty likely to flow from the principle that technical standards may be treated as unenforceable by national courts if the requirements of the notification Directive are not observed by the State.

Sapod Audic v *Eco-Emballages SA* (Case C-159/00)
Judgment of 6 June 2002, Court of Justice of the European Communities

[49] . . . it should be observed, first, that according to settled case law Directive 83/189 must be interpreted as meaning that a failure to observe the obligation to notify laid down in Article 8 of that directive constitutes a substantial procedural defect such as to render the technical regulations in question inapplicable and thus unenforceable against individuals (see, in particular, *CIA Security International*, paragraphs 48 and 54, and *Lemmens*, paragraph 33).

[50] Second, it should be borne in mind that according to the case law of the Court the inapplicability of a technical regulation which has not been notified to the Commission in accordance with Article 8 of Directive 83/189 may be invoked in legal proceedings between individuals concerning, *inter alia*, contractual rights and duties (see *Unilever*, paragraph 49).

[51] Accordingly, if the national court were to interpret the second paragraph of Article 4 of Decree No 92–377 as establishing an obligation to apply a mark or label and, hence, as constituting a technical regulation within the meaning of Directive 83/189, it would be incumbent on that court to refuse to apply that provision in the main proceedings.

[52] It should, however, be observed that the question of the conclusions to be drawn in the main proceedings from the inapplicability of the second paragraph of Article 4 of Decree No 92–377 as regards the severity of the sanction under the applicable national law, such as nullity or unenforceability of the contract between Sapod and Eco-Emballages, is a question governed by national law, in particular as regards the rules and principles of contract law which limit or adjust that sanction in order to render its severity proportionate to the particular defect found. However, those rules and principles may not be less favourable than those governing similar domestic actions (principle of equivalence) and may not be framed in such a way as to render impossible in practice the exercise of rights conferred by Community law (principle of effectiveness) (see, *inter alia*, Case 33/76 *Rewe* v *Landwirtschaftskammer für das Saarland* [1976] ECR 1989, paragraph 5, and Joined Cases C-52/99 and C-53/99 *Camorotto and Vignone* [2001] ECR I-1395, paragraph 21).

NOTE
The principles of equivalence and effectiveness, mentioned in para 52, were examined above in Chapter 4, p.133 above. With reference to relevant national rules on remedies with which you are familiar, consider what they may mean in the context sketched by the Court in para 52 of *Sapod Audic*.

In conclusion, none of these decisions on 'incidental' effect overturns the Court's long-standing exclusion of the horizontal direct effect of Directives. After all in none of these cases did a Directive impose an obligation directly on a private party. However these decisions do demonstrate that the legal position of private parties may be prejudicially affected by the lurking presence of an unimplemented Directive of which they may be perfectly unaware.

■ QUESTION

The Court's case law places a sharp distinction between the horizontal direct effect of Directives (which is not allowed) and the 'incidental' effect of Directives of private parties (which is allowed). Is this distinction fair?

FURTHER READING

On the 'incidental effect' case law and its implications

Dougan, M., 'Annotation of *Supod Audle*' (2003) 40 CML Rev 193.

Figuero Reguiero, P., 'Invocability of Substitution and Invocability of Exclusion: Bringing Legal Realism to the Current Developments of the Case Law of "Horizontal" Direct Effect of Directives', Jean Monnet Working Paper 7/02 via http://www.jeanmonnetprogram.org/papers/papers02.html.

Weatherill, S., 'Breach of Directives and Breach of Contract' (2001) 26 EL Rev 177.

More generally

Jans, J., 'National Legislative Autonomy? The Procedural Constraints of European Law' [1998/1] LIEI 25.

Weatherill, S., 'A Case Study in Judicial Activism in the 1990s: the Status before national courts of measures wrongfully un-notified to the Commission', Ch. 31 in D. O'Keeffe (ed), *Judicial Review in European Union Law: Liber Amicorum Gordon Slynn* (The Hague: Kluwer Law International, 2000).

SECTION 5: **THE PRINCIPLE OF INDIRECT EFFECT, OR THE OBLIGATION OF 'CONFORM-INTERPRETATION'**

The previous section questioned the extent to which the rejected notion that Directives may exert horizontal direct effect can be rationally sealed off from the phenomenon of incidental effect. But however one chooses to categorize the horizontal direct effect/incidental effect case law, and however one defines the 'State' for the purposes of fixing the outer limits of 'vertical' direct effect (Case 152/84 *Marshall*, p.144 above), an unavoidable anomaly taints the law governing the scope of the direct effect of Directives. Consider the sex discrimination Directives. If a State has failed to implement a Directive properly, then, provided that the standard *Van Gend en Loos* (Case 26/62) 'test' for direct effect is met by the provision in question, a State employee can rely on the direct effect of the Directive (vertical direct effect). A private employee cannot (horizontal direct effect). So, in the UK, where Directive 76/207 on Equal Treatment of the Sexes was not properly implemented in time, Ms Marshall (above), a State employee, succeeded in relying on Community law, whereas Ms Duke (*Duke* v *GEC Reliance* [1988] 2 WLR 359, [1988] 1 All ER 626), who was making the same complaint, failed, for she happened to be a private sector employee.

The UK had made this point in *Marshall* (Case 152/84) as a reason for *withholding* direct effect, but its objections were swept aside by the Court in para 51 of the judgment (p.146 above). Yet the anomaly is real, even if the Court's refusal to permit a recalcitrant State to benefit from pointing it out is understandable. Submissions in *Dori* (Case C-91/92, p.148 above) urged the Court to eliminate the anomaly by *extending* direct effect, but these were not successful.

The European Court's contribution to the resolution of this anomaly first began to take shape in *Von Colson and Kamann* v *Land Nordrhein-Westfalen* (Case 14/83) and *Harz* v *Deutsche Tradax* (Case 79/83). Mention is made of Case 14/83 in para 41 of the judgment in *Marshall* at p.145 above, but the Court's approach in the case deserves careful separate attention.

Von Colson and Kamann v Land Nordrhein-Westfalen (Case 14/83)
[1984] ECR 1891, [1986] 2 CMLR 430, Court of Justice of the European Communities

The case was a preliminary reference from Germany, and concerned that fertile source of litigation, the Equal Treatment Directive 76/207. The issue was described by the Court as follows:

[2] Those questions were raised in the course of proceedings between two qualified social workers, Sabine von Colson and Elisabeth Kamann, and the Land Nordrhein-Westfalen. It appears from the grounds of the order for reference that Werl prison, which caters exclusively for male prisoners and which is administered by the Land Nordrhein-Westfalen, refused to engage the plaintiffs in the main proceedings for reasons relating to their sex. The officials responsible for recruitment justified their refusal to engage the plaintiffs by citing the problems and risks connected with the appointment of female candidates and for those reasons appointed instead male candidates who were however less well-qualified.

[3] The Arbeitsgericht Hamm held that there had been discrimination and took the view that under German law the only sanction for discrimination in recruitment is compensation for 'Vertrauensschaden', namely the loss incurred by candidates who are victims of discrimination as a result of their belief that there would be no discrimination in the establishment of the employment relationship. Such compensation is provided for under Paragraph 611a(2) of the Bürgerliches Gesetzbuch.

[4] Under that provision, in the event of discrimination regarding access to employment, the employer is liable for 'damages in respect of the loss incurred by the worker as a result of his reliance on the expectation that the establishment of the employment relationship would not be precluded by such a breach [of the principle of equal treatment]'. That provision purports to implement Council Directive No 76/207.

[5] Consequently the Arbeitsgericht found that, under German law, it could order the reimbursement only of the travel expenses incurred by the plaintiff von Colson in pursuing her application for the post (DM 7.20) and that it could not allow the plaintiffs' other claims.

Von Colson's objection centred on Article 6 of the Directive:

[18] Article 6 requires Member States to introduce into their national legal systems such measures as are necessary to enable all persons who consider themselves wronged by discrimination 'to pursue their claims by judicial process'. It follows from the provision that Member States are required to adopt measures which are sufficiently effective to achieve the objective of the directive and to ensure that those measures may in fact be relied on before the national courts by the persons

concerned. Such measures may include, for example, provisions requiring the employer to offer a post to the candidate discriminated against or giving the candidate adequate financial compensation, backed up where necessary by a system of fines. However the directive does not prescribe a specific sanction; it leaves Member States free to choose between the different solutions suitable for achieving its objective.

Was this adhered to in the German legal order? The Court's approach was markedly different from standard 'direct effect' analysis:

[22] It is impossible to establish real equality of opportunity without an appropriate system of sanctions. That follows not only from the actual purpose of the directive but more specifically from Article 6 thereof which, by granting applicants for a post who have been discriminated against recourse to the courts, acknowledges that those candidates have rights of which they may avail themselves before the courts.

[23] Although, as has been stated in the reply to Question 1, full implementation of the directive does not require any specific form of sanction for unlawful discrimination, it does entail that that sanction be such as to guarantee real and effective judicial protection. Moreover it must also have a real deterrent effect on the employer. It follows that where a Member State chooses to penalize the breach of the prohibition of discrimination by the award of compensation, that compensation must in any event be adequate in relation to the damage sustained.

[24] In consequence it appears that national provisions limiting the right to compensation of persons who have been discriminated against as regards access to employment to a purely nominal amount, such as, for example, the reimbursement of expenses incurred by them in submitting their application, would not satisfy the requirements of an effective transposition of the directive.

[25] The nature of the sanctions provided for in the Federal Republic of Germany in respect of discrimination regarding access to employment and in particular the question whether the rule in Paragraph 611a (2) of the Bürgerliches Gesetzbuch excludes the possibility of compensation on the basis of the general rules of law were the subject of lengthy discussion before the Court. The German Government maintained in the oral procedure that that provision did not necessarily exclude the application of the general rules of law regarding compensation. It is for the national court alone to rule on that question concerning the interpretation of its national law.

[26] However, the Member States' obligation arising from a directive to achieve the result envisaged by the directive and their duty under Article 5 of the Treaty to take all appropriate measures, whether general or particular, to ensure the fulfilment of that obligation, is binding on all the authorities of Member States including, for matters within their jurisdiction, the courts. It follows that, in applying the national law and in particular the provisions of a national law specifically introduced in order to implement Directive No 76/207, national courts are required to interpret their national law in the light of the wording and the purpose of the directive in order to achieve the result referred to in the third paragraph of Article 189.

[27] On the other hand, as the above considerations show, the directive does not include any unconditional and sufficiently precise obligation as regards sanctions for discrimination which, in the absence of implementing measures adopted in good time may be relied on by individuals in order to obtain specific compensation under the directive, where that is not provided for or permitted under national law.

[28] It should, however, be pointed out to the national court that although Directive No 75/207/EEC, for the purpose of imposing a sanction for the breach of the prohibition of discrimination, leaves the Member States free to choose between the different solutions suitable for achieving its objective, it nevertheless requires that if a Member State chooses to penalize breaches of that prohibition by the award of compensation, then in order to ensure that it is effective and that it has a deterrent effect, that compensation must in any event be adequate in relation to the damage sustained and must therefore amount to more than purely nominal compensation such as, for example, the reimbursement only of the expenses incurred in connection with the application. It is for the national

court to interpret and apply the legislation adopted for the implementation of the directive in conformity with the requirements of Community law, in so far as it is given discretion to do so under national law.

NOTE

J. Steiner, (1985) 101 LQR 491, observed that the decision marks 'a subtle but significant change of direction' in the European Court's approach to the enforceability of EEC Directives before national courts'. P. Morris, (1989) JBL 233, at p.241, suggested that 'if national judiciaries respond positively to this exhortation [in *Von Colson*] something approaching horizontal direct effect may be achieved by a circuitous route'. B. Fitzpatrick, (1989) 9 OJLS 336, at p.346, refers to *Von Colson* having established a principle of 'indirect effect' and suggests that 'it may effectively bridge the gap between vertical and horizontal direct effect'.

■ QUESTION

To what extent do you think the *Von Colson* approach offers a route for resolving the anomalies of the horizontal/vertical direct effect distinction which emerges from the Court's ruling in *Marshall* (Case 152/84)?

NOTE

In the *Von Colson* (Case 14/83) judgment itself, one can pick out important contradictions in respect of the national court's task of 'conform-interpretation' (para 28). Compare the second sentence of para 26 with the more qualified statement in the concluding sentence of the Court's ruling in answer to the questions referred to above. The next two cases are both worthy of examination from the perspective of clarifying the ambit of *Von Colson* (Case 14/83).

Officier van Justitie v *Kolpinghuis Nijmegen* (Case 80/86)
[1987] ECR 3969, Court of Justice of the European Communities

A criminal prosecution was brought against a café owner for stocking mineral water which was in fact simply fizzy tap water. The Dutch authorities sought to supplement the basis of the prosecution by relying on definitions of mineral water detrimental to the defendant which were contained in a Directive which had not been implemented in The Netherlands. A preliminary reference was made to the European Court.

The Court ruled that 'a national authority may not rely, as against an individual, upon a provision of a Directive whose necessary implementation in national law has not yet taken place'. It then turned to the third question referred to it:

[11] The third question is designed to ascertain how far the national court may or must take account of a directive as an aid to the interpretation of a rule of national law.

[12] As the Court stated in its judgment of 10 April 1984 in Case 14/83 *Von Colson and Kamann* v *Land Nordrhein-Westfalen* [1984] ECR 1891, the Member States' obligation arising from a directive to achieve the result envisaged by the directive and their duty under Article 5 of the Treaty to take all appropriate measures, whether general or particular, to ensure the fulfilment of that obligation, is binding on all the authorities of Member States including, for matters within their jurisdiction, the courts. It follows that, in applying the national law and in particular the provisions of a national law specifically introduced in order to implement the directive, national courts are required to interpret their national law in the light of the wording and the purpose of the directive in order to achieve the result referred to in the third paragraph of Article 189 of the Treaty.

[13] However, that obligation on the national court to refer to the content of the directive when interpreting the relevant rules of its national law is limited by the general principles of law which form part of Community law and in particular the principles of legal certainty and non-retroactivity. Thus the Court ruled in its judgment of 11 June 1987 in Case 14/86 *Pretore di Salò* v *X* [1987] ECR 2545 that a directive cannot, of itself and independently of a national law adopted by a Member State for

its implementation, have the effect of determining or aggravating the liability in criminal law of persons who act in contravention of the provisions of that directive.

[14] The answer to the third question should therefore be that in applying its national legislation a court of a Member State is required to interpret that legislation in the light of the wording and the purpose of the directive in order to achieve the result referred to in the third paragraph of Article 189 of the Treaty, but a directive cannot, of itself and independently of a law adopted for its implementation, have the effect of determining or aggravating the liability in criminal law of persons who act in contravention of the provisions of that directive.

NOTE

The Court is anxious to emphasise the importance of preserving legal certainty and protecting reasonable expectations. See also Case C-168/95 *Luciano Arcaro* [1996] ECR I-4705.

Marleasing SA v La Comercial Internacional de Alimentación SA (Case C-106/89)
[1990] ECR I-4135, Court of Justice of the European Communities

The case arose out of a conflict between the Spanish Civil Code and Community Company Law Directive (68/151) which was unimplemented in Spain. The litigation was between private parties, which, following *Marshall* (Case 152/84), ruled out the direct effect of the Directive. The European Court explained the national court's duty of interpretation in the following terms:

[8] . . . [T]he Member States' obligation arising from a directive to achieve the result envisaged by the directive and their duty under Article 5 of the Treaty to take all appropriate measures, whether general or particular, to ensure the fulfilment of that obligation, is binding on all the authorities of Member States including, for matters within their jurisdiction, the courts. It follows that, in applying national law, whether the provisions in question were adopted before or after the directive, the national court called upon to interpret it is required to do so, as far as possible, in the light of the wording and the purpose of the directive in order to achieve the result pursued by the latter and thereby comply with the third paragraph of Article 189 of the Treaty.

NOTE

The obligation imposed on national courts in *Marleasing* (Case C-108/89) has a firmer feel than that in *Von Colson* (Case 14/83, p.160 above). See J. Stuyck and P. Wytinck, (1991) 28 CML Rev 205.

The Court also confirmed the obligation of sympathetic interpretation that is cast on national courts by virtue of what was Article 5 and is now Article 10 EC post-Amsterdam in its ruling in *Paola Faccini Dori* (Case C-91/92). Even though Ms Dori was not able to rely directly on the unimplemented Directive in proceedings involving another private party (p.148 above), she was entitled to expect that the national court would not simply ignore the Directive in applying national law.

Paola Faccini Dori v Recreb Srl (Case C-91/92)
[1994] ECR I-3325, Court of Justice of the European Communities

[26] It must also be borne in mind that, as the Court has consistently held since its judgment in Case 14/83 *Von Colson and Kamann* v *Land Nordrhein-Westfalen* [1984] ECR 1891, paragraph 26, the Member States' obligation arising from a directive to achieve the result envisaged by the directive and their duty under Article 5 of the Treaty to take all appropriate measures, whether general or particular, is binding on all the authorities of Member States, including, for matters within their jurisdiction, the courts. The judgments of the Court in Case C-106/89 *Marleasing* v *La Comercial Internacional de Alimentación* [1990] ECR I-4135, paragraph 8, and Case C-334/92 *Wagner Miret* v *Fondo de Garantia Salarial* [1993] ECR I-6911, paragraph 20, make it clear that, when applying national law, whether adopted before or after the directive, the national court that has to interpret that law must do so, as far as possible, in the light of the wording and the purpose of the directive so as to achieve the result it has in view and thereby comply with the third paragraph of Article 189 of the Treaty.

NOTE

The logic of this reasoning leads to the conclusion that the Community law obligations pertaining to the absorption of a Directive into the national legal order are enduring, and do not come to an end on the Directive's transposition 'on paper' into national law. This is made clear in the next case.

Marks and Spencer plc v Commissioners of Customs and Excise (C-62/00)

Judgment of 11 July 2002, Court of Justice of the European Communities

[24] . . . it should be remembered, first, that the Member States' obligation under a directive to achieve the result envisaged by the directive and their duty under Article 5 of the EC Treaty (now Article 10 EC) to take all appropriate measures, whether general or particular, to ensure fulfilment of that obligation are binding on all the authorities of the Member States, including, for matters within their jurisdiction, the courts (see, *inter alia*, Case C-168/95 *Arcaro* [1996] ECR I-4705, paragraph 41). It follows that in applying domestic law the national court called upon to interpret that law is required to do so, as far as possible, in the light of the wording and purpose of the directive, in order to achieve the purpose of the directive and thereby comply with the third paragraph of Article 189 of the EC Treaty (now the third paragraph of Article 249 EC) (see, in particular, Case C-106/89 *Marleasing* [1990] ECR I-4135, paragraph 8, and Case C-334/92 *Wagner Miret* [1993] ECR I-6911, paragraph 20).

[25] Second, as the Court has consistently held, whenever the provisions of a directive appear, so far as their subject-matter is concerned, to be unconditional and sufficiently precise, they may be relied upon before the national courts by individuals against the State where the latter has failed to implement the directive in domestic law by the end of the period prescribed or where it has failed to implement the directive correctly (see, *inter alia*, Case 8/81 *Becker* [1982] ECR 53, paragraph 25; Case 103/88 *Fratelli Costanzo* [1989] ECR 1839, paragraph 29; and Case C-319/97 *Kortas* [1999] ECR I-3143, paragraph 21).

[26] Third, it has been consistently held that implementation of a directive must be such as to ensure its application in full (see to that effect, in particular, Case C-217/97 *Commission* v *Germany* [1999] ECR I-5087, paragraph 31, and Case C-214/98 *Commission* v *Greece* [2000] ECR I-9601, paragraph 49).

[27] Consequently, the adoption of national measures correctly implementing a directive does not exhaust the effects of the directive. Member States remain bound actually to ensure full application of the directive even after the adoption of those measures. Individuals are therefore entitled to rely before national courts, against the State, on the provisions of a directive which appear, so far as their subject-matter is concerned, to be unconditional and sufficiently precise whenever the full application of the directive is not in fact secured, that is to say, not only where the directive has not been implemented or has been implemented incorrectly, but also where the national measures correctly implementing the directive are not being applied in such a way as to achieve the result sought by it.

[28] As the Advocate General noted in point 40 of his Opinion, it would be inconsistent with the Community legal order for individuals to be able to rely on a directive where it has been implemented incorrectly but not to be able to do so where the national authorities apply the national measures implementing the directive in a manner incompatible with it.

NOTE

The scope of the obligation to interpret national law in conformity with a Directive was taken a step further in the next case. However, the Court did not help to stabilize and clarify the State of the law by introducing textual anomalies into its ruling.

Centrosteel Srl v Adipol GmbH (Case C-456/98)

[2000] ECR I-6007, Court of Justice of the European Communities

[15] It is true that, according to settled case law of the Court, in the absence of proper transposition into national law, a directive cannot of itself impose obligations on individuals (Case 152/84 *Marshall*

v *Southampton and South-West Hampshire Health Authority* [1986] ECR 723, paragraph 48, and Case C-91/92 *Faccini Dori* v *Recreb* [1994] ECR I-3325, paragraph 20).

[16] However, it is also apparent from the case law of the Court (Case C-106/89 *Marleasing* v *La Comercial Internacional de Alimentación* [1990] ECR I-4135, paragraph 8; Case C-334/92 *Wagner Miret* v *Fondo de Garantía Salarial* [1993] ECR I-6911, paragraph 20; *Faccini Dori*, paragraph 26; and Joined Cases C-240/98 to C-244/98 *Océano Grupo Editorial* v *Salvat Editores* [2000] ECR I-4941, paragraph 30) that, when applying national law, whether adopted before or after the directive, the national court that has to interpret that law must do so, as far as possible, in the light of the wording and the purpose of the directive so as to achieve the result it has in view and thereby comply with the third paragraph of Article 189 of the EC Treaty (now the third paragraph of Article 249 EC).

[17] Where it is seised of a dispute falling within the scope of the Directive and arising from facts postdating the expiry of the period for transposing the Directive, the national court, in applying provisions of domestic law or settled domestic case law, as seems to be the case in the main proceedings, must therefore interpret that law in such a way that it is applied in conformity with the aims of the Directive . . .

The reference in para 17 to the application of 'settled domestic case law' in conformity with the aims of the Directive is striking. However, this phrase is missing from the formal ruling.

Council Directive 86/653/EEC of 18 December 1986 on the coordination of the laws of the Member States relating to self-employed commercial agents precludes national legislation which makes the validity of an agency contract conditional upon the commercial agent being entered in the appropriate register. The national court is bound, when applying provisions of domestic law predating or postdating the said Directive, to interpret those provisions, so far as possible, in the light of the wording and purpose of the Directive, so that those provisions are applied in a manner consistent with the result pursued by the Directive.

NOTE

In its subsequent ruling in *AXA Royal Belge* (Case C-386/00 [2002] ECR I-2209) the Court referred explicitly to its own ruling in *Centrosteel* (Case C-456/98), but cited only paragraphs 15 and 16, not 17!

■ QUESTIONS

1. *Marleasing* seems clearly to require interpretation of pre-existing national legislation in the light of a subsequent Directive and this is confirmed in *Dori* and *Centrosteel*. This is by no means uncontroversial. Lord Slynn, who served as both Advocate-General and judge in Luxembourg before assuming the role of a Law Lord, has observed extra-judicially that:

   I find it difficult to say that a statute of 1870 must be interpreted in the light of a 1991 directive. If the former is in conflict with the latter, it is not for judges to strain language but for Governments to introduce new legislation. (*Introducing a European Legal Order*, Stevens/Sweet and Maxwell, 1992, p.124; see also 'Looking at European Community Texts' (1993) 14/1 Statute L Rev 12)

   What are the limits of 'interpretation'? Do you think the European Court is improperly asking national courts to perform tasks which belong with national legislatures?

2. How might the Community legal order rid itself of the complexities engendered by the extension of the notion of direct effect to Directives?

FURTHER READING (COVERING MOST OR ALL ASPECTS OF THIS CHAPTER)

Boch, C., 'The Iroquois at the Kirchberg: or Some Naive Remarks on the Status and Relevance of Direct Effect' in J. Usher (ed), *The State of the European Union* (Harlow: Longman, 2000).

De Witte, B., 'Direct Effect, Supremacy and the Nature of the Legal Order', in Craig, P., and de Búrca, G. (eds), *The Evolution of EU Law* (Oxford: OUP, 1999), Ch. 5.

Hilson, C. and Downes, T., 'Making Sense of Rights: Community Rights in EC Law' (1999) 24 EL Rev 121.

Maher, I., 'National Courts as European Community Courts' (1994) 14 *Legal Studies* 226.

Mastroianni, R., 'On the Distinction Between Vertical and Horizontal Direct Effect of Directives: What Role for the Principle of Equality?' (1999) 5 *Euro Public Law* 417.

Prechal, S., 'Does Direct Effect Matter?' (2000) 37 CML Rev 1047.

Timmermans, C., 'Community Directives Revisited' (1997) 17 YEL 1.

Van Gerven, W., 'The Horizontal Effect of Directive Provisions Revisited: the Reality of Catchwords' in Curtin, D. and Heukels, T. (eds), *Institutional Dynamics of European Integration* (Dordrecht: Martinus Nijhoff, 1994).

NOTE

For additional material and resources see the Companion Website at: www.oup.co.uk/best.textbooks/law/weatherill6e

6

State Liability

Chapter 5 explained that Directives are capable of direct effect – but only against the State. The unimplemented Directive is barred from application against private parties, although it may exert an incidental effect on private parties. Chapter 5 concluded with examination of the obligation imposed on national courts to interpret national rules in order to conform with relevant Directives. This represents an ingenious strategy for embedding EC Directives within national legal orders even where the State authorities have failed to effect the legal transplant between EC and national level envisaged by Article 249 EC. However, there are difficulties in defining the proper scope of the obligation of judicial interpretation. And those difficulties are in effect multiplied by 15 (and soon even more), since courts in all the Member States are forced to grapple with the issue. One may doubt whether the notion of 'indirect effect' or 'conform interpretation' underpinned by Article 10 EC is a fully satisfactory method of securing the application at national level of unimplemented Community Directives.

In any event even if the national court is willing and able to carry out the interpretative function, there remains a persisting concern about its consequences. Where national courts actively interpret national law in the light of unimplemented Community Directives, interference with the legitimate expectations of private parties may result. Private parties may find themselves bound by obligations drawn by interpretation from Directives of which they are quite unaware. That concern seems to motivate the Court's reluctance to sanction 'indirect effect' in *Kolpinghuis Nijmegen* (Case 80/86, p.162 above) where the State would be the beneficiary. In cases involving private parties alone, it might be possible to contend that this interpretative approach is justified as a means of protecting the expectations of the intended beneficiary of rights under an unimplemented Directive. In that sense, the issue is a choice between two deserving private parties, one of which must ultimately be prejudiced. Moreover, in the 'incidental effect' cases the Court seems to have been carefree in imposing unexpected burdens on private parties *via* the medium of unimplemented Directives. Yet at bottom the problem is that this route fails to impose a burden on the party responsible for the gap in legal protection – the *Member State* which has failed to implement the Directive. There is a strong case for holding that the primary target for the individual who has suffered loss through non-implementation of a Directive should be the public authorities. This was a point astutely made by commentators (N. Green, (1984) 9 EL Rev 295, 321–4; J. Usher, (1989) 10 Statute Law Rev 95, 102; D. Curtin, (1990) 27 CML Rev 709, 729). The Court took the chance to develop its jurisprudence in the direction of State liability in Cases C-6/90 and C-9/90 *Francovich and Others* v *Italian State*

[1991] ECR I-5357. In shaping our understanding of the application of EC law by national courts and tribunals *Francovich* is a landmark case of a stature comparable to *Van Gend en Loos* (Case 26/62, p.109).

Directive 80/987 required Member States to set up guarantee funds to compensate workers in the event of employer insolvency. Italy failed to implement the Directive. That Treaty violation had already been recorded in a Court ruling – Case 22/87, *Commission* v *Italy* [1989] ECR 143. Italian workers, among them Andrea Francovich, believed themselves denied the protection envisaged by the Directive but not transposed into Italian law. Proceedings before the Italian courts yielded a preliminary reference to the European Court.

The Court determined that the workers could claim no directly effective rights, for the relevant provisions of the Directive lacked sufficient unconditionality. The provider of the guarantee could not be identified. The Court then turned to the question of the liability of the State to make good loss suffered by individuals as a result of the failure to implement. The Court considered that this was an issue which fell to be considered in the light of the general system of the Treaty and its fundamental principles:

Francovich and Others v *Italian State* (Cases C-6/90 and C-9/90)
[1991] ECR I-5357, Court of Justice of the European Communities

(a) The existence of State liability as a matter of principle

[31] It should be borne in mind at the outset that the EEC Treaty has created its own legal system, which is integrated into the legal systems of the Member States and which their courts are bound to apply. The subjects of that legal system are not only the Member States but also their nationals. Just as it imposes burdens on individuals, Community law is also intended to give rise to rights which become part of their legal patrimony. Those rights arise not only where they are expressly granted by the Treaty but also by virtue of obligations which the Treaty imposes in a clearly defined manner both on individuals and on the Member States and the Community institutions (see the judgments in Case 26/62 *Van Gend en Loos* [1963] ECR 1 and Case 6/64 *Costa* v *ENEL* [1964] ECR 585).

[32] Furthermore, it has been consistently held that the national courts whose task it is to apply the provisions of Community law in areas within their jurisdiction must ensure that those rules take full effect and must protect the rights which they confer on individuals (see in particular the judgments in Case 106/77 *Amministrazione delle Finanze dello Stato* v *Simmenthal* [1978] ECR 629, paragraph 16, and Case C-213/89 *Factortame* [1990] ECR I-2433, paragraph 19).

[33] The full effectiveness of Community rules would be impaired and the protection of the rights which they grant would be weakened if individuals were unable to obtain redress when their rights are infringed by a breach of Community law for which a Member State can be held responsible.

[34] The possibility of obtaining redress from the Member State is particularly indispensable where, as in this case, the full effectiveness of Community rules is subject to prior action on the part of the State and where, consequently, in the absence of such action, individuals cannot enforce before the national courts the rights conferred upon them by Community law.

[35] It follows that the principle whereby a State must be liable for loss and damage caused to individuals as a result of breaches of Community law for which the State can be held responsible is inherent in the system of the Treaty.

[36] A further basis for the obligation of Member States to make good such loss and damage is to be found in Article 5 of the Treaty, under which the Member States are required to take all appropriate measures, whether general or particular, to ensure fulfilment of their obligations under Community law. Among these is the obligation to nullify the unlawful consequences of a breach of Community

law (see, in relation to the analogous provision of Article 86 of the ECSC Treaty, the judgment in Case 6/60 *Humblet* v *Belgium* [1960] ECR 559).

[37] It follows from all the foregoing that it is a principle of Community law that the Member States are obliged to make good loss and damage caused to individuals by breaches of Community law for which they can be held responsible.

(b) The conditions for State liability

[38] Although State liability is thus required by Community law, the conditions under which that liability gives rise to a right to reparation depend on the nature of the breach of Community law giving rise to the loss and damage.

[39] Where, as in this case, a Member State fails to fulfil its obligation under the third paragraph of Article 189 of the Treaty to take all the measures necessary to achieve the result prescribed by a directive, the full effectiveness of that rule of Community law requires that there should be a right to reparation provided that three conditions are fulfilled.

[40] The first of those conditions is that the result prescribed by the directive should entail the grant of rights to individuals. The second condition is that it should be possible to identify the content of those rights on the basis of the provisions of the directive. Finally, the third condition is the existence of a causal link between the breach of the State's obligation and the loss and damage suffered by the injured parties.

[41] Those conditions are sufficient to give rise to a right on the part of individuals to obtain reparation, a right founded directly on Community law.

[42] Subject to that reservation, it is on the basis of the rules of national law on liability that the State must make reparation for the consequences of the loss and damage caused. In the absence of Community legislation, it is for the internal legal order of each Member State to designate the competent courts and lay down the detailed procedural rules for legal proceedings intended fully to safeguard the rights which individuals derive from Community law (see the judgments in Case 60/75 *Russo* v *AIMA* [1976] ECR 45, Case 33/76 *Rewe* v *Landwirtschaftskammer Saarland* [1976] ECR 1989 and Case 158/80 *Rewe* v *Hauptzollamt Kiel* [1981] ECR 1805).

[43] Further, the substantive and procedural conditions for reparation of loss and damage laid down by the national law of the Member States must not be less favourable than those relating to similar domestic claims and must not be so framed as to make it virtually impossible or excessively difficult to obtain reparation (see, in relation to the analogous issue of the repayment of taxes levied in breach of Community law, *inter alia* the judgment in Case 199/82 *Amministrazione delle Finanze dello Stato* v *San Giorgio* [1983] ECR 3595).

[44] In this case, the breach of Community law by a Member State by virtue of its failure to transpose Directive 80/987 within the prescribed period has been confirmed by a judgment of the Court. The result required by that directive entails the grant to employees of a right to a guarantee of payment of their unpaid wage claims. As is clear from the examination of the first part of the first question, the content of that right can be identified on the basis of the provisions of the directive.

[45] Consequently, the national court must, in accordance with the national rules on liability, uphold the right of employees to obtain reparation of loss and damage caused to them as a result of failure to transpose the directive.

[46] The answer to be given to the national court must therefore be that a Member State is required to make good loss and damage caused to individuals by failure to transpose Directive 80/987.

NOTE
It should be appreciated that this ruling, like that in *Marleasing* (Case C-106/89), makes an important contribution to the vigour of Community law at national level *even in circumstances where direct effect is lacking.*

The Court repeated its formulation in *Dori* (Case C-91/92). Having denied Ms Dori the possibility of relying on the Directive as such to defeat the claim against her by a private supplier (p.149 above), the Court proceeded to rule that the Italian court was subject to the obligation of interpretation drawn from Article 5, now Article 10 EC post-Amsterdam ('indirect effect' or 'conform-interpretation', p.163 above). It then directed Dori to a different target – the defaulting State.

Paola Faccini Dori v Recreb Srl (Case C-91/92)

[1994] ECR I-3325, Court of Justice of the European Communities

[27] If the result prescribed by the directive cannot be achieved by way of interpretation, it should also be borne in mind that, in terms of the judgment in Joined Cases C-6/90 and C-9/90 *Francovich and Others v Italy* [1991] ECR I-5357, paragraph 39, Community law requires the Member States to make good damage caused to individuals through failure to transpose a directive, provided that three conditions are fulfilled. First, the purpose of the directive must be to grant rights to individuals. Second, it must be possible to identify the content of those rights on the basis of the provisions of the directive. Finally, there must be a causal link between the breach of the State's obligation and the damage suffered.

[28] The directive on contracts negotiated away from business premises is undeniably intended to confer rights on individuals and it is equally certain that the minimum content of those rights can be identified by reference to the provisions of the directive alone (see paragraph 17 above).

[29] Where damage has been suffered and that damage is due to a breach by the State of its obligation, it is for the national court to uphold the right of aggrieved consumers to obtain reparation in accordance with national law on liability.

■ QUESTION

To what extent do the techniques of, first, 'indirect effect'/'conform interpretation' and, second, State liability under *Francovich* provide an adequate protection for the individual deprived of rights against a private party that are envisaged under an unimplemented Directive? (See, in particular, the Opinion of Advocate-General Jacobs in *Vaneetveld v SA Le Foyer* (Case C-316/93) [1994] ECR I-763.) Has the Court repaired the damage done to individual protection by its refusal in *Marshall* and *Dori* to accept that Directives are capable of horizontal direct effect?

NOTE
Article 10 EC, which was Article 5 EC pre-Amsterdam, requires national authorities, including the judiciary, actively to support EC law and if necessary to adjust their 'normal' approach under domestic law. 'The principle of effectiveness' was examined in Chapter 4 in its application to national courts charged with the mission to apply EC law (p.133 above). It also underlies the obligations which the European Court has imposed on national courts to give effect to unimplemented Directives. *Francovich*, like *Factortame*, examined in Chapter 4 (p.137 above), demands that national courts adjust their domestic law of remedies where this is required in order to provide effective protection to EC law rights. *Francovich*, like *Factortame*, envisages a minimum level of protection which must be available to the Community law litigant in the national system. *Francovich* demonstrates the operation of the principle of effectiveness beyond the limits of direct effect.

The *Francovich* focus on State liability appears to be acquiring an increasing priority within the Community system governing effective judicial protection at national level, at the expense of other devices for addressing the consequences of State failures to implement Directives in accordance with Articles 10 and 249 EC.

Chapter 4 included discussion of the impact of Community law on time limits in national proceedings brought to secure repayment of charges levied, or payment of sums not made, in breach of a Directive that has not been properly implemented. The 'principle of effectiveness' may be invoked to challenge such restrictions (p.135 above), but the European Court has accepted that restrictions on backdating claims may be imposed under national law; and that reasonable time limits may be applied in the interests of legal certainty. So these procedural rules may be permissible even though they may serve to shelter the State from the full consequences of its unlawful failure to implement unless, exceptionally, the Member State has made the exercise of rights excessively difficult (*cf* Case C-62/00 *Marks and Spencer*, p.135 above).

Advocate-General Jacobs in *Fantask* (Case C-188/95 [1997] ECR I-6783) argued strongly in favour of the contribution to legal security made by the application of time limits even in cases involving unimplemented Directives and suggested that a *Francovich* claim was the appropriate method of protecting an individual suffering loss in such circumstances. This approach to the protection of the individual would place great emphasis on the significance of the defaulting State's culpability as an element in the criteria governing *Francovich* liability (pp.177 and 185 below).

More broadly still, H. Schermers has argued that in the wake of rulings such as *Francovich* and *Faccini Dori* 'we do not need direct effect for directives any more. When Member States do not fulfil their obligations under a directive, the affected individuals will be able to claim damages' ('No Direct Effect for Directives' (1997) 3 *Euro Public Law* 527, 539). He observes that the abandonment of the capacity of Directives to exert direct effect in favour of emphasis on *Francovich* claims against the defaulting State would expel from the Community legal order the current imbalance, which lends direct effect to Directives only in *some* circumstances (individual versus State). Does this provocative suggestion appeal to you?

It is, however, important to appreciate that the increasing tendency of *Francovich* to take centre stage in the pattern of individual protection developed by the European Court has not been universally welcomed. C. Harlow ('Francovich and the Problem of the Disobedient State' (1996) 2 ELJ 199), for example, finds the theoretical underpinnings for State liability in the EC to be weak, and fears that the intermingling of Community law with national liability systems may corrupt both. One may certainly question the *practical* feasibility of pursuing a *Francovich* claim other than in instances involving very wealthy applicants; yet Community law is supposed to confer rights on a wider range of interest groups than large commercial concerns.

The judgment in *Francovich* counts as one of the European Court's most remarkable. It has created a remedy defined by criteria under Community law which must be absorbed into the national legal order. *Francovich* represents a statement of the European Court's readiness to employ Article 5, now Article 10 EC post-Amsterdam, as a basis for establishing a system of judicial remedies that will further the cause of effective protection of Community law rights. But, at a more general level, the Court is presiding over the development of a Community 'common law'. The next extract traces the Court's development of the notion of effective judicial protection (at national level), already introduced in Chapter 4 (p.136 above), before concluding with observations in this wider context.

R. Caranta, 'Government Liability after Francovich'
(1993) 52 Cambridge Law Journal 272, 279–82

. . . The ground upon which the *Francovich* case was decided is the principle of effective protection of individuals.

The case law concerning this principle has evolved remarkably during the past ten years, the court having moved from an initial position which amounted to almost complete indifference to the remedial aspect of the rights conferred on individuals by Community law, to an ever greater involvement in questions concerning the conditions under which the protection of such rights is ensured by the judiciary of the Member States.

The initial position was the result of a widespread belief that Community law in general was only interested in substantive aspects of law, the procedural aspects having been left to the competence of the Member States. In the *Rewe*[42] and *Comet*[43] cases, for example, the court ruled that it was for each national legal system to determine the procedural aspects of actions claiming the protection of individual rights provided by Community law. There were two qualifications, namely that the domestic remedies had to be no less favourable than those established for comparable national rights, and that in any case the remedies conferred had to be effective, but the actual incidence of Community law on procedure was virtually non-existent.

The *Francovich* decision does maintain the traditional rule whereby procedures to ensure the execution of Community law are left to national legal systems, but with a small, and not so innocent, change; the competence of Member States ceases to be the governing principle, and becomes the rule only in the absence of relevant Community provisions.[44]

These qualifications of the principle of the competence of Member States in procedural matters acquired relevance long before *Francovich*. In the *Simmenthal* case, notably, the principle of the effectiveness of judicial protection ceased to be a mere obiter dictum and began to bite. In that case another Italian judge of first instance, the *Pretore* of Susa, had asked the Court of Justice whether it was consistent with Community law for a national system of judicial review of legislation to make it the duty of every judge, before excluding the operation of a national legal provision in conflict with Community law, to request a preliminary ruling by the country's Constitutional Court. The European Court, as is well known, held that:[45]

> any provision of a national legal system and any legislative, administrative or judicial practice which might impair the effectiveness of Community law by withholding from the national court having jurisdiction to apply such law the power to do everything necessary at the moment of its application to set aside national legal provisions which might prevent Community rules from having full force and effect are incompatible with those requirements which are the very essence of Community law.

On this ground the Court held that a system of centralised judicial review such as the one existing in Italy which delayed the final decision by requiring the matter to be referred to the Constitutional Court was not compatible with the principle of the effective protection of individual rights which was based upon Community law, and for this reason had to be set aside by every judge in the Member State.

Even in *Simmenthal*, however, it could be thought that the real issue was not just the effective protection of individuals; what was actually at stake in that case was which court was to have the last word when national law conflicted with Community law. If every national judge had to make a reference to the Constitutional Court, it would be that Court which determined the consistency of the national law with Community law, without even consulting the Court of Justice, because the Italian Constitutional Court in practice never made a reference under article 177 of the EEC Treaty. On the other hand, if every judge was left free to decide the conflict between national and Community

---

42 Case 33/76, [1976], ECR 1997, cons. 5.

43 Case 45/76, [1976] ECR 2053, cons. 12–17.

44 But for a traditional reading of the rule *see* G. de Búrca, 'Giving Effect to European Community Directives' (1992) 55 MLR 215, at p.238.

45 Case 106/77, [1978] ECR 629, para 22.

law on his own, he would probably resort to the European Court to have Community law interpreted and the question of compatibity assessed. It was a contest for power, the Court of Justice against the Italian Constitutional Court, and the latter finally bowed to the supremacy of Community law and of its court.[46]

More relevant to the protection of individuals were the decisions concerning the repayment of wrongly paid taxes. On references by some Italian courts, the Court of Justice in the *San Giorgio* case[47] held it to be inconsistent with Community law for a national provision to subject the right to restitution of sums paid pursuant to a national tax law contrary to Community law to proof that the charge had not been transferred to the final consumer of the goods; the court thought it contrary to the principle of effective judicial protection to impose on citizens invoking their Community law rights an onus of proof which it was almost impossible to discharge.

There can be no doubt that *Factortame*[48] is the most important decision so far concerning the consequences of the principle of the effectiveness of judicial protection of individuals; its impact upon the respective roles of the Community and Member States in the creation of remedies for infringements of Community law rights seriously undermines the position according to which procedure is a matter to be left to Member States.

The facts which constitute the background to, and the legal questions involved in, the *Factortame* decision are widely known on the Continent as well as in Britain.[49] It is sufficient to recall that some Spanish owners of fishing vessels had challenged the conformity with Community law of a British statute and regulations designed to ensure that ships flying the Union Jack were owned and operated by British citizens or corporations.

Fearing that irrecoverable damage could accrue pending the judgment, the plaintiffs had asked for an interim injunction, but this was refused by the Court of Appeal[50] which held that courts had no authority under the law to suspend the application of a legal provision which had not yet been judicially determined to be in conflict with Community law. The House of Lords,[51] having come to the same conclusion on the point of English law as the Court of Appeal, thought it necessary to ask the Court of Justice for a preliminary ruling under article 177 whether, in relation to the grant of interim protection in the circumstances of the case, Community law overrode English law.[52] The Court of Justice, following the learned conclusions of Advocate General Tesauro, held that:[53]

> Community law must be interpreted as meaning that a national court which, in a case before it concerning Community law, considers that the sole obstacle which precludes it from granting interim relief is a rule of national law must set aside that rule.

Decisive to the outcome of the *Factortame* case was, according to the Court of Justice which laid great emphasis on its previous decision in the *Simmenthal* case,[54] the consideration that:[55]

---

46 Corte cost, 8 giugno 1984 n. 170, in *Giurisprudenza constituzionale* 1984, I, 1098: for a commentary see J-V. Louis, 'Droit communautaire et loi postérieure: un revirement de la Cour constitutionelle italienne', in *Cah. dr. europ*, 1986, 194.

47 Case 199/82, [1983] ECR 3595.

48 *R* v *Secretary of State for Transport, ex parte Factortame Ltd No 2*. [1991] 1 AC 603; see the commentaries by D. Oliver, 'Fishing on the Incoming Tide' (1991) 54 MLR 442, and A.G. Toth (1990) 27 CML Rev 574; see also H.W.R. Wade, 'What has Happened to the Sovereignty of Parliament?' (1991) 107 LQR 1; *Id.*, 'Injunctive Relief against the Crown and Ministers' *ibidem*, 4; N.P. Gravells, 'Disapplying an Act of Parliament Pending Ruling: Constitutional Enormity or Community Law Right?' [1989] PL 568; A. Barav, 'Enforcement of Community Rights in the National Courts: The Case for Jurisdiction to Grant an Interim Relief' (1989) 26 CML Rev 369 ff.

49 See R.R. Churchill, ' "Quota hopping": The Common Fisheries Policy Wrongfooted?' (1990) 27 CML Rev 209, and the commentary by the same author in (1992) 29 CML Rev 415.

51 [1989] 2 CMLR 353.

51 [1990] 2 AC 85.

52 [1990] 2 AC 85 at 152, *per* Lord Bridge of Harwich, with whom all the other Law Lords concurred.

53 [1991] 1 AC 603, 644.

54 [1991] 1 AC 603, 643–4.

55 [1991] 1 AC 603, 644.

the full effectiveness of Community law would be . . . much impaired if a rule of national law could prevent a court seised of a dispute governed by Community law from granting interim relief in order to ensure the full effectiveness of the judgment to be given on the existence of the rights claimed under Community law.

Just as in *Factortame* it was from the principle of the effectiveness of Community law that the Court of Justice deduced the necessity for interim protection, so in *Francovich* it distilled the necessity for an entitlement to damages when Community law is infringed.

These decisions, it is submitted, mark the definitive departure by the Court of Justice from the model, recalled above, according to which Community law was confined to the substantive aspects of law, to the definition of rights and duties, while the rules governing the actual enforcement of such rights and duties depended entirely on the possibly different legal rules in force in the various Member States.

The new approach is not limited to the case law. It is sufficient to mention two EEC directives, namely directive 89/665[56] and the more recent 92/13,[57] both designed to promote uniformity of national remedies for violation of Community rules applicable to public works and procurement contracts.[58]

From a comparative point of view it is clear that, under the mounting pressure exerted by the case law of the Court of Justice and also by the legislator, Community law has increasingly begun to 'fasten upon remedies', in this way introducing at a continental level a style of legal thinking which was characteristic of common law rather than civil law systems.

The author concludes his examination in the following terms (pp.296–7):

. . . The *Francovich* decision has a relevance which goes beyond the field of governmental liability. It marks the birth of a 'jus commune', of a law common to all the Member States and to the Community itself, in the field of the judicial protection of individuals against public powers.[107]

In *Factortame* and to a larger degree in *Zuckerfabrik Süderdithmarschen*[108] the Court of Justice laid down the rules to be applied by domestic courts when granting interim relief in Community law cases. The rules were the same as those applied by the European Court itself in proceedings under articles 185 and 186 of the EEC Treaty, the first of which was explicitly referred to by the court.[109]

In *Francovich* the the Court of Justice applied to actions of the Member States inconsistent with Community law the same rules which had been elaborated by the court itself in relation to non-contractual liability for invalid acts of Community organs – but with a qualification: it forgot that in Community law the breach has to be 'sufficiently serious'. But qualifications are inconsistent with a 'jus commune'; they destroy its inherent condition, namely, to be common. . . .

The next extract locates these rulings in the context of a process of the judicial harmonization of national remedies and invites consideration of the wider role played by the Court in the Community system.

---

56 OJEC 1989, No L. 395/34.

57 OJEC 1992, No L. 76/14.

58 See M. Bronckers, 'Private Enforcement of 1992: Do Trade and Industry Stand a Chance against Member States?' (1989) 26 CML Rev 528.

107 See more generally J. Schwarze, 'Tendencies towards a Common Administrative Law in Europe' (1991) 16 EL Rev 3; J. Rivero, 'Vers un droit commun européen: nouvelles perspectives en droit administratif', in *Pages de doctrine* (Paris 1980), p.489 *et. seq.*; M.P. Chiti, 'I signori del diritto comunitario: la Corte di giustizia e lo sviluppo del diritto amministrativo europeo', in *Rivista trimestrale di diritto pubblico* 1991, 796.

108 Joint Cases C-143/88 and C-92/89, [1991] 1 ECR 415; the decision was considered by Lord Goff of Chieveley in *Kirklees Metropolitan Borough Council* v *Wickes Building Supplies Ltd* [1992] 3 WLR 170, 187.

109 See cons. 27.

F. Snyder, 'The Effectiveness of European Community Law: Institutions,
Processes, Tools and Techniques'
(1993) 56 MLR 19, 45–7

In *Francovich*, the Court of Justice recalled that, in the absence of Community provisions, it was for national legal systems to lay down the procedural steps for legal action to ensure the full protection of Community rights.[156] These 'conditions of substance and form' were not to be less favourable than those governing national remedies, and they were not to make the enforcement of Community rights impossible.[157] While thus recognising that Community rights are to be enforced primarily in national courts,[158] the Court's jurisprudence has nonetheless impinged increasingly on national legal remedies. At the same time as national administrative law is being influenced considerably by general principles of Community law, such as proportionality,[159] the Court of Justice is beginning to contribute to the restructuring of national procedural systems.[160]

In the celebrated *Factortame*[161] case, the Court of Justice set aside the rule of English constitutional law that an injunction cannot be granted against the Crown, at least where the rule prevents the enforcement of a right conferred by Community law. In *Emmott* it declared that, where an individual wishes to rely as against a Member State on rights contained in a directly effective directive, time does not begin to run, and therefore the individual cannot be time-barred even under the normal domestic rules on limitations on actions, until such time as the directive has been properly transposed into national law.[162] More recently, in *Zuckerfabrik*,[163] the Court held that interim measures should be available when the legality of Community law was being questioned before a national court, and a national court has a duty to consider granting such relief if requested by a party to do so.[164] These steps towards the gradual reshaping of national remedies can be viewed as a fourth element in the Community judicial liability system.

The four elements in this system need to be appreciated as a whole from two different perspectives. Seen from the bottom up, they help to provide judicial protection for the individual. Seen from the top down, they perform an essentially political function of social control.[165] These two perspectives are complementary, one representing the view of individual actors or organisations, and the other representing a conception of the Community legal system as a whole. Both perspectives are essential in order to understand the contribution and the limits of the judicial liability system in ensuring the effectiveness of Community law.

---

156 [Joined cases C-6/90 and C-9/90 *Francovich and Bonifaci v Italy*, para 42 of the judgment].

157 See Case 45/76, *Comet v Produktschap voor Siergewassen* [1976] ECR 2043.

158 See Green and Barav, 'Damages in the National Courts for Breach of Community Law' (1986) 6 YEL 55; Oliver, 'Enforcing Community Rights in English Courts' (1987) 50 MLR 881, Steiner, 'How to Make the Action Suit the Case: Domestic Remedies for Breach of EEC Law' (1987) 12 EL Rev 102; Ward, 'Government Liability in the United Kingdom for Breach of Individual Rights in European Community Law' (1990) 19 *Anglo-American Law Review* 1.

159 See Schwarze, *European Administrative Law* (London: Sweet and Maxwell, 1992).

160 See Duffy, [(1992) 17 EL Rev 133], pp.137–138.

161 Case C221/89, *R v Secretary of State for Transport, ex p Factortame Ltd and Others* [1990] ECR I-2433.

162 Including where the directive has been implemented but in terms which vary from the directive such that the implementing measure does not fully represent the rights contained in the directive: Case C208/90, *Emmott v Minister for Social Welfare* [1991] 3 CMLR 894, 916 (para 23).

163 Joined Cases C-143/88 and C-92/89, *Zuckerfabrik Süderdithmarschen et Zuckerfabrik Soest v Hauptzollamt Itzehoe* [1991] *Recueil* I-415, nyr in English, noted Schermers (1992) 29 CML Rev 133.

164 In addition, the conditions for suspending community acts could not vary from one Member State to another. See further Oliver, 'Interim Measures: Some Recent Developments' (1992) 27 CML Rev 7, 24–25; Barav, 'Enforcement of Community Rights in the National Courts: The Case for Jurisdiction to Grant Interim Relief' (1989) 26 CML Rev 369.

165 This point is argued forcefully with regard to appeal courts in general: Shapiro, 'Appeal' (1980) 14 *Law and Society Review* 629. Note that a similar dual role in the Community legal order is played by the concept of institutional balance: see the Opinion by Advocate-General Van Gerven in Case 70/88, *European Parliament v Council* [1990] ECR I-2041. Whether such a duality of function is characteristic of other basic concepts of Community constitutional and administrative law remains to be seen.

Seen from the second perspective, the judicial liability system embodies a type of structural reform, not by administrative negotiation but by adjudication. In the United States, constitutional lawyers have focused on the Supreme Court. In the late 1970s, they identified a new kind of public law litigation, 'institutional litigation', which typically requires the courts to scrutinize the operation of large public institutions. The suits are generally brought by persons subject to the control of the institutions who seek as relief some relatively elaborate rearrangement of the institution's mode of operation.[166]

Views have differed as to the novelty of institutional litigation.[167] All agree, however, that in institutional litigation, '[l]itigation inevitably becomes an explicitly political forum and the court a visible arm of the political process'.[168]

It is tempting to apply these observations to the Court of Justice. After all, in the Community, as in the United States, the institutional vacuum resulting from executive and legislative inaction led to an increased role for the judiciary. In both systems, the appropriateness of such a judicial response has been the subject of intense controversy.[169]

It is suggested, however, that the precise analogy is misplaced. First, the Court of Justice is activated by individuals and organisations who, in contrast to plaintiffs in American institutional litigation, are not inmates of institutions in any specific sense. Second, the judicial liability system in the Community has been developed by the Court of Justice mainly through the Article 177 [now 234] procedure: the reach of the Court into the operation of national public institutions, including administrations, is restricted by the fact that its jurisdiction is limited in principle to interpreting (or ruling on the validity of) Community law. Third, and consequently, Community litigation does not involve the negotiation by the Court of Justice with defendant institutional parties of detailed rules regarding the internal organisation of national institutions.

In the United States, it has been argued that:

> The demands of structural reform have magnified the explicitly political dimensions of litigation. Parties have used litigation less as a method for authoritative resolution of conflict than as a means of reallocation of power. Rather than an isolated, self-contained transaction, the lawsuit becomes a component of the continuous political bargaining process that determines the shape and content of public policy. This transformation in the character of litigation necessarily transforms the judge's role as well.[170]

In the Community, it is suggested, the role of 'political powerbroker'[171] in this strong sense has been resisted thus far by the Court of Justice. Nonetheless, there are common features and this brief comparison with the United States Supreme Court is instructive. It enables us to begin to situate Community law litigation in the political process, at both the Community and the national levels, and it illuminates the political dimension of the Community judicial liability system. By elaborating the elements of this system, rather than by institutional litigation in the American sense, the Court of Justice has played a central role in organising and reshaping relations among Community institutions and between the Community and the Member States.

---

166 Eisenberg and Yeazell, 'The Ordinary and the Extraordinary in Institutional Litigation' (1980) 93 *Harvard Law Review* 465, 467–468. See also, e.g., Chayes, 'The Role of the Judge in Public Law Litigation' (1976) 89 *Harvard Law Review* 1281; Cox, 'The New Dimensions of Constitutional Litigation' (1976) 51 *Washington Law Review* 791; Diver, 'The Judge as Political Powerbroker: Superintending Structural Change in Public Institutions' (1979) 65 *Virginia Law Review* 43.

167 Chayes and Cox argue that its procedures and remedies depart significantly from the model of traditional litigation: see Chayes, *op cit* n 166; Cox, *op cit* n 166. In contrast, Eisenberg and Yeazell, *op cit* n 166, suggest that the only new features are its substance, especially new rights, and its power.

168 Chayes, *op cit* n 166, p.1304; Diver, [(1979) 65 *Virginia Law Review* 43], p.65.

169 With regard to the Community, see Pescatore, 'La carence du législateur et le devoir du juge' in *Rechtsvergleichung, Europarecht und Staateninegration, Gedachtnisschrift für L.-J. Constantinesco* (Saarbrucken: Europa Institute, 1983) and Rasmussen, *On Law and Policy in the European Court of Justice* (Dordrecht: Martinus Nijhoff, 1986).

170 Diver, [(1979) 65 *Virginia Law Review* 43], p.45.

171 *ibid.*

NOTE

It is apparent that the issue of effective protection extends far beyond the question of the application of Directives alone and beyond questions of a remedy in damages alone. *Francovich* is part of a wider phenomenon. The European Court is building a notion of effective protection as a general principle of the Community legal order. This was already plain from the *Factortame* saga, mentioned by Caranta and Snyder and examined at p.137 above.

The one sure consequence of *Francovich* was that the Court would be invited to clarify the scope of liability. The Court's rulings in March 1996, including a further episode in the *Factortame* saga, '*Factortame III*' (Case C-48/93), are now crucial. These are relevant beyond the specific issue of unimplemented Directives.

Brasserie du Pêcheur SA v *Germany* and *R* v *Secretary of State for Transport, ex parte Factortame Ltd and Others*

(Joined Cases C-46/93 and C-48/93), [1996] ECR I-1029, [1996] 1 CMLR 889,
Court of Justice of the European Communities

Factortame was not content with its success in establishing the availability of interim protection against a domestic statute (p.137 above), or with the final ruling that the UK had acted in violation of its Treaty obligations (p.137 above.) Factortame sought compensation for loss suffered as a result of action in 1989 by the UK authorities that had been shown to be unlawful under EC law. This raised questions about the application of *Francovich* liability to violations of primary Treaty provisions, rather than in the specific instance of failure to implement a Directive. Questions of the culpability required to ground liability, which (as R. Caranta observes in the extract at p.172 above) had not been addressed in *Francovich*, were also raised. A preliminary reference was made by the High Court in the UK. This was joined to a reference made by the *Bundesgerichtshof*, the German Federal Court of Justice, which arose out of a complaint by a French company based in Alsace which claimed that it had suffered loss as a result of German restrictions on trade in beer which had been shown to be incompatible with Article 30 of the EC Treaty (now, after amendment, Article 28 EC): see the 'Beer Purity' case, *Commission* v *Germany* (Case 178/84, p.387 below). Here too the national court was in search of elaboration of the scope of State liability in damages for loss caused by violation of Community law.

The Court first traced the nature and scope of the principle of State liability for acts and omissions of the national legislature contrary to Community law:

[16] By their first questions, each of the two national courts essentially seeks to establish whether the principle that Member States are obliged to make good damage caused to individuals by breaches of Community law attributable to the State is applicable where the national legislature was responsible for the infringement in question.

[17] In joined Cases C-6/90 and C-9/90 *Francovich and Others* [1991] ECR I-5357, paragraph 37, the Court held that it is a principle of Community law that Member States are obliged to make good loss and damage caused to individuals by breaches of Community law for which they can be held responsible.

[18] The German, Irish and Netherlands Governments contend that Member States are required to make good loss or damage caused to individuals only where the provisions breached are not directly effective: in *Francovich and Others* the Court simply sought to fill a lacuna in the system for safeguarding rights of individuals. In so far as national law affords individuals a right of action enabling them to assert their rights under directly effective provisions of Community law, it is

unnecessary, where such provisions are breached, also to grant them a right to reparation founded directly on Community law.

[19] That argument cannot be accepted.

[20] The Court has consistently held that the right of individuals to rely on the directly effective provisions of the Treaty before national courts is only a minimum guarantee and is not sufficient in itself to ensure the full and complete implementation of the Treaty (see, in particular, Case 168/85 *Commission* v *Italy* [1986] ECR 2945, paragraph 11, Case C-120/88 *Commission* v *Italy* [1991] ECR I-621, paragraph 10, and C-119/89 *Commission* v *Spain* [1991] ECR I-641, paragraph 9). The purpose of that right is to ensure that provisions of Community law prevail over national provisions. It cannot, in every case, secure for individuals the benefit of the rights conferred on them by Community law and, in particular, avoid their sustaining damage as a result of a breach of Community law attributable to a Member State. As appears from paragraph 33 of the judgment in *Francovich and Others*, the full effectiveness of Community law would be impaired if individuals were unable to obtain redress when their rights were infringed by a breach of Community law.

[21] This will be so where an individual who is a victim of the non-transposition of a directive and is precluded from relying on certain of its provisions directly before the national court because they are insufficiently precise and unconditional, brings an action for damages against the defaulting Member State for breach of the third paragraph of Article 189 [now 249] of the Treaty. In such circumstances, which obtained in the case of *Francovich and Others*, the purpose of reparation is to redress the injurious consequences of a Member State's failure to transpose a directive as far as beneficiaries of that directive are concerned.

[22] It is all the more so in the event of infringement of a right directly conferred by a Community provision upon which individuals are entitled to rely before the national courts. In that event, the right to reparation is the necessary corollary of the direct effect of the Community provision whose breach caused the damage sustained.

[23] In this case, it is undisputed that the Community provisions at issue, namely Article 30 [now 28] of the Treaty in Case C-46/93 and Article 52 [now 43] in Case C-48/93, have direct effect in the sense that they confer on individuals a right upon which they are entitled to rely directly before the national courts. Breach of such provisions may give rise to reparation.

[24] The German Government further submits that a general right to reparation for individuals could be created only by legislation and that for such a right to be recognised by judicial decision would be incompatible with the allocation of powers as between the Community institutions and the Member States and with the institutional balance established by the Treaty.

[25] It must, however, be stressed that the existence and extent of State liability for damage ensuing as a result of a breach of obligations incumbent on the State by virtue of Community law are questions of Treaty interpretation which fall within the jurisdiction of the Court.

[26] In this case, as in *Francovich and Others*, those questions of interpretation have been referred to the Court by national courts pursuant to Article 177 [now 234] of the Treaty.

[27] Since the Treaty contains no provision expressly and specifically governing the consequences of breaches of Community law by Member States, it is for the Court, in pursuance of the task conferred on it by Article 164 [now 220] of the Treaty of ensuring that in the interpretation and application of the Treaty the law is observed, to rule on such a question in accordance with generally accepted methods of interpretation, in particular by reference to the fundamental principles of the Community legal system and, where necessary, general principles common to the legal systems of the Member States.

[28] Indeed, it is to the general principles common to the laws of the Member States that the second paragraph of Article 215 [now 288] of the Treaty refers as the basis of the non-contractual liability of the Community for damage caused by its institutions or by its servants in the performance of their duties.

[29] The principle of the non-contractual liability of the Community expressly laid down in Article 215 [now 288] of the Treaty is simply an expression of the general principle familiar to the legal systems of the Member States that an unlawful act or omission gives rise to an obligation to make good the damage caused. That provision also reflects the obligation on public authorities to make good damage caused in the performance of their duties.

[30] In any event, in many national legal systems the essentials of the legal rules governing State liability have been developed by the courts.

[31] In view of the foregoing considerations, the Court held in *Francovich and Others*, at paragraph 35, that the principle of State liability for loss and damage caused to individuals as a result of breaches of Community law for which it can be held responsible is inherent in the system of the Treaty.

[32] It follows that that principle holds good for any case in which a Member State breaches Community law, whatever be the organ of the State whose act or omission was responsible for the breach.

[33] In addition, in view of the fundamental requirement of the Community legal order that Community law be uniformly applied (see, in particular, Joined Cases C-143/88 and C-92/89 *Zuckerfabrik Süderdithmarschen and Zuckerfabrik Soest* [1991] ECR I-415, paragraph 26), the obligation to make good damage caused to individuals by breaches of Community law cannot depend on domestic rules as to the division of powers between constitutional authorities.

[34] As the Advocate General points out in paragraph 38 of his Opinion, in international law a State whose liability for breach of an international commitment is in issue will be viewed as a single entity, irrespective of whether the breach which gave rise to the damage is attributable to the legislature, the judiciary or the executive. This must apply *a fortiori* in the Community legal order since all State authorities, including the legislature, are bound in performing their tasks to comply with the rules laid down by Community law directly governing the situation of individuals.

[35] The fact that, according to national rules, the breach complained of is attributable to the legislature cannot affect the requirements inherent in the protection of the rights of individuals who rely on Community law and, in this instance, the right to obtain redress in the national courts for damage caused by that breach.

[36] Consequently, the reply to the national courts must be that the principle that Member States are obliged to make good damage caused to individuals by breaches of Community law attributable to the State is applicable where the national legislature was responsible for the breach in question.

The Court then turned to the conditions under which the State may incur liability:

[37] By these questions, the national courts ask the Court to specify the conditions under which a right to reparation of loss or damage caused to individuals by breaches of Community law attributable to a Member State is, in the particular circumstances, guaranteed by Community law.

[38] Although Community law imposes State liability, the conditions under which that liability gives rise to a right to reparation depend on the nature of the breach of Community law giving rise to the loss and damage (*Francovich and Others*, paragraph 38).

[39] In order to determine those conditions, account should first be taken of the principles inherent in the Community legal order which form the basis for State liability, namely, first, the full effectiveness of Community rules and the effective protection of the rights which they confer and, second, the obligation to cooperate imposed on Member States by Article 5 [now 10] of the Treaty (*Francovich and Others*, paragraphs 31 to 36).

[40] In addition, as the Commission and the several governments which submitted observations have emphasised, it is pertinent to refer to the Court's case-law on non-contractual liability on the part of the Community.

[41] First, the second paragraph of Article 215 [now 288] of the Treaty refers, as regards the non-contractual liability of the Community, to the general principles common to the laws of the Member States, from which, in the absence of written rules, the Court also draws inspiration in other areas of Community law.

[42] Second, the conditions under which the State may incur liability for damage caused to individuals by a breach of Community law cannot, in the absence of particular justification, differ from those governing the liability of the Community in like circumstances. The protection of the rights which individuals derive from Community law cannot vary depending on whether a national authority or a Community authority is responsible for the damage.

[43] The system of rules which the Court has worked out with regard to Article 215 [now 288] of the Treaty, particularly in relation to liability for legislative measures, takes into account, *inter alia*, the complexity of the situations to be regulated, difficulties in the application or interpretation of the texts and, more particularly, the margin of discretion available to the author of the act in question.

[44] Thus, in developing its case law on the non-contractual liability of the Community, in particular as regards legislative measures involving choices of economic policy, the Court has had regard to the wide discretion available to the institutions in implementing Community policies.

[45] The strict approach taken towards the liability of the Community in the exercise of its legislative activities is due to two considerations. First, even where the legality of measures is subject to judicial review, exercise of the legislative function must not be hindered by the prospect of actions for damages whenever the general interest of the Community requires legislative measures to be adopted which may adversely affect individual interests. Second, in a legislative context characterised by the exercise of a wide discretion, which is essential for implementing a Community policy, the Community cannot incur liability unless the institution concerned has manifestly and gravely disregarded the limits on the exercise of its powers (Joined Cases 83/76, 94/76, 4/77 and 40/77, 15/77 *HNL and Others* v *Council and Commission* [1978] ECR 1209, paragraphs 5 and 6).

[46] That said, the national legislature – like the Community institutions – does not systematically have a wide discretion when it acts in a field governed by Community law. Community law may impose upon it obligations to achieve a particular result or obligations to act or refrain from acting which reduce its margin of discretion, sometimes to a considerable degree. This is so, for instance, where, as in the circumstances to which the judgment in *Francovich and Others* relates, Article 189 [now 249] of the Treaty places the Member State under an obligation to take, within a given period, all the measures needed in order to achieve the result required by a directive. In such a case, the fact that it is for the national legislature to take the necessary measures has no bearing on the Member State's liability for failing to transpose the directive.

[47] In contrast, where a Member State acts in a field where it has a wide discretion, comparable to that of the Community institutions in implementing Community policies, the conditions under which it may incur liability must, in principle, be the same as those under which the Community institutions incur liability in a comparable situation.

[48] In the case which gave rise to the reference in Case C-46/93, the German legislature had legislated in the field of foodstuffs, specifically beer. In the absence of Community harmonisation, the national legislature had a wide discretion in that sphere in laying down rules on the quality of beer put on the market.

[49] As regards the facts of Case C-48/93, the United Kingdom legislature also had a wide discretion. The legislation at issue was concerned, first, with the registration of vessels, a field which, in view of the State of development of Community law, falls within the jurisdiction of the Member States and, secondly, with regulating fishing, a sector in which implementation of the common fisheries policy leaves a margin of discretion to the Member States.

[50] Consequently, in each case the German and United Kingdom legislatures were faced with situations involving choices comparable to those made by the Community institutions when they adopt legislative measures pursuant to a Community policy.

[51] In such circumstances, Community law confers a right to reparation where three conditions are met: the rule of law infringed must be intended to confer rights on individuals; the breach must be sufficiently serious; and there must be a direct causal link between the breach of the obligation resting on the State and the damage sustained by the injured parties.

[52] Firstly, those conditions satisfy the requirements of the full effectiveness of the rules of Community law and of the effective protection of the rights which those rules confer.

[53] Secondly, those conditions correspond in substance to those defined by the Court in relation to Article 215 [now 288] in its case-law on liability of the Community for damage caused to individuals by unlawful legislative measures adopted by its institutions.

[54] The first condition is manifestly satisfied in the case of Article 30 [now 28] of the Treaty, the relevant provision in Case C-46/93, and in the case of Article 52 [now 43], the relevant provision in Case C-48/93. Whilst Article 30 imposes a prohibition on Member States, it nevertheless gives rise to rights for individuals which the national courts must protect (Case 74/76 *Iannelli & Volpi* v *Meroni* [1977] ECR 557, paragraph 13). Likewise, the essence of Article 52 is to confer rights on individuals (Case 2/74 *Reyners* [1974] ECR 631, paragraph 25).

[55] As to the second condition, as regards both Community liability under Article 215 [now 288] and Member State liability for breaches of Community law, the decisive test for finding that a breach of Community law is sufficiently serious is whether the Member State or the Community institution concerned manifestly and gravely disregarded the limits on its discretion.

[56] The factors which the competent court may take into consideration include the clarity and precision of the rule breached, the measure of discretion left by that rule to the national or Community authorities, whether the infringement and the damage caused was intentional or involuntary, whether any error of law was excusable or inexcusable, the fact that the position taken by a Community institution may have contributed towards the omission, and the adoption or retention of national measures or practices contrary to Community law.

[57] On any view, a breach of Community law will clearly be sufficiently serious if it has persisted despite a judgment finding the infringement in question to be established, or a preliminary ruling or settled case-law of the Court on the matter from which it is clear that the conduct in question constituted an infringement.

[58] While, in the present cases, the Court cannot substitute its assessment for that of the national courts, which have sole jurisdiction to find the facts in the main proceedings and decide how to characterise the breaches of Community law at issue, it will be helpful to indicate a number of circumstances which the national courts might take into account.

[59] In Case C-46/93 a distinction should be drawn between the question of the German legislature's having maintained in force provisions of the Biersteuergesetz concerning the purity of beer prohibiting the marketing under the designation 'Bier' of beers imported from other Member States which were lawfully produced in conformity with different rules, and the question of the retention of the provisions of that same law prohibiting the import of beers containing additives. As regards the provisions of the German legislation relating to the designation of the product marketed, it would be difficult to regard the breach of Article 30 by that legislation as an excusable error, since the incompatibility of such rules with Article 30 was manifest in the light of earlier decisions of the Court, in particular Case 120/78 *Rewe-Zentral* [1979] ECR 649 ('Cassis de Dijon') and Case 193/80 *Commission* v *Italy* [1981] ECR 3019 ('vinegar'). In contrast, having regard to the relevant case law, the criteria available to the national legislature to determine whether the prohibition of the use of additives was contrary to Community law were significantly less conclusive until the Court's judgment of 12 March 1987 in *Commission* v *Germany*, cited above, in which the Court held that prohibition to be incompatible with Article 30.

[60] A number of observations may likewise be made about the national legislation at issue in Case C-48/93.

[61] The decision of the United Kingdom legislature to introduce in the Merchant Shipping Act 1988 provisions relating to the conditions for the registration of fishing vessels has to be assessed differently in the case of the provisions making registration subject to a nationality condition, which constitute direct discrimination manifestly contrary to Community law, and in the case of the provisions laying down residence and domicile conditions for vessel owners and operators.

[62] The latter conditions are prima facie incompatible with Article 52 of the Treaty in particular, but the United Kingdom sought to justify them in terms of the objectives of the common fisheries policy. In the judgment in *Factortame II*, cited above, the Court rejected that justification.

[63] In order to determine whether the breach of Article 52 thus committed by the United Kingdom was sufficiently serious, the national court might take into account, *inter alia*, the legal disputes relating to particular features of the common fisheries policy, the attitude of the Commission, which made its position known to the United Kingdom in good time, and the assessments as to the state of certainty of Community law made by the national courts in the interim proceedings brought by individuals affected by the Merchant Shipping Act.

[64] Lastly, consideration should be given to the assertion made by Rawlings (Trawling) Ltd, the 37th claimant in Case C-48/93, that the United Kingdom failed to adopt immediately the measures needed to comply with the Order of the President of the Court of 10 October 1989 in *Commission* v *United Kingdom*, cited above, and that this needlessly increased the loss it sustained. If this allegation – which was certainly contested by the United Kingdom at the hearing – should prove correct, it should be regarded by the national court as constituting in itself a manifest and, therefore, sufficiently serious breach of Community law.

[65] As for the third condition, it is for the national courts to determine whether there is a direct causal link between the breach of the obligation borne by the State and the damage sustained by the injured parties.

[66] The aforementioned three conditions are necessary and sufficient to found a right in individuals to obtain redress, although this does not mean that the State cannot incur liability under less strict conditions on the basis of national law.

[67] As appears from paragraphs 41, 42 and 43 of *Francovich and Others*, cited above, subject to the right to reparation which flows directly from Community law where the conditions referred to in the preceding paragraph are satisfied, the State must make reparation for the consequences of the loss and damage caused in accordance with the domestic rules on liability, provided that the conditions for reparation of loss and damage laid down by national law must not be less favourable than those relating to similar domestic claims and must not be such as in practice to make it impossible or excessively difficult to obtain reparation (see also Case 199/82 *Amministrazione delle Finanze dello Stato* v *San Giorgio* [1983] ECR 3595).

[68] In that regard, restrictions that exist in domestic legal systems as to the non-contractual liability of the State in the exercise of its legislative function may be such as to make it impossible in practice or excessively difficult for individuals to exercise their right to reparation, as guaranteed by Community law, of loss or damage resulting from the breach of Community law.

[69] In Case C-46/93 the national court asks in particular whether national law may subject any right to compensation to the same restrictions as apply where a law is in breach of higher-ranking national provisions, for instance, where an ordinary Federal law infringes the Grundgesetz of the Federal Republic of Germany.

[70] While the imposition of such restrictions may be consistent with the requirement that the conditions laid down should not be less favourable than those relating to similar domestic claims, it is still to be considered whether such restrictions are not such as in practice to make it impossible or excessively difficult to obtain reparation.

[71] The condition imposed by German law where a law is in breach of higher-ranking national provisions, which makes reparation dependent upon the legislature's act or omission being referable to an individual situation, would in practice make it impossible or extremely difficult to obtain

effective reparation for loss or damage resulting from a breach of Community law, since the tasks falling to the national legislature relate, in principle, to the public at large and not to identifiable persons or classes of person.

[72] Since such a condition stands in the way of the obligation on national courts to ensure the full effectiveness of Community law by guaranteeing effective protection for the rights of individuals, it must be set aside where an infringement of Community law is attributable to the national legislature.

[73] Likewise, any condition that may be imposed by English law on State liability requiring proof of misfeasance in public office, such an abuse of power being inconceivable in the case of the legislature, is also such as in practice to make it impossible or extremely difficult to obtain effective reparation for loss or damage resulting from a breach of Community law where the breach is attributable to the national legislature.

[74] Accordingly, the reply to the questions from the national courts must be that, where a breach of Community law by a Member State is attributable to the national legislature acting in a field in which it has a wide discretion to make legislative choices, individuals suffering loss or injury thereby are entitled to reparation where the rule of Community law breached is intended to confer rights upon them, the breach is sufficiently serious and there is a direct causal link between the breach and the damage sustained by the individuals. Subject to that reservation, the State must make good the consequences of the loss or damage caused by the breach of Community law attributable to it, in accordance with its national law on liability. However, the conditions laid down by the applicable national laws must not be less favourable than those relating to similar domestic claims or framed in such a way as in practice to make it impossible or excessively difficult to obtain reparation.

The Court proceeded to deal with three further, related questions, and provided the following answers to the questions referred to:

1. The principle that Member States are obliged to make good damage caused to individuals by breaches of Community law attributable to the State is applicable where the national legislature was responsible for the breach in question.

2. Where a breach of Community law by a Member State is attributable to the national legislature acting in a field in which it has a wide discretion to make legislative choices, individuals suffering loss or injury thereby are entitled to reparation where the rule of Community law breached is intended to confer rights upon them, the breach is sufficiently serious and there is a direct causal link between the breach and the damage sustained by the individuals. Subject to that reservation, the State must make good the consequences of the loss or damage caused by the breach of Community law attributable to it, in accordance with its national law on liability. However, the conditions laid down by the applicable national laws must not be less favourable than those relating to similar domestic claims or framed in such a way as in practice to make it impossible or excessively difficult to obtain reparation.

3. Pursuant to the national legislation which it applies, reparation of loss or damage cannot be made conditional upon fault (intentional or negligent) on the part of the organ of the State responsible for the breach, going beyond that of a sufficiently serious breach of Community law.

4. Reparation by Member States of loss or damage which they have caused to individuals as a result of breaches of Community law must be commensurate with the loss or damage sustained. In the absence of relevant Community provisions, it is for the domestic legal system of each Member State to set the criteria for determining the extent of reparation. However, those criteria must not be less favourable than those applying to similar claims or actions based on domestic law and must not be such as in practice to make it impossible or excessively difficult to obtain reparation. National legislation which generally limits the damage for which reparation may be granted to damage done to certain, specifically protected individual interests not including loss of profit by individuals is not compatible with Community law. Moreover, it must be possible to award specific damages, such as the exemplary damages provided for by English law, pursuant to claims or actions founded on Community law, if such damages may be awarded pursuant to similar claims or actions founded on domestic law.

5. The obligation for Member States to make good loss or damage caused to individuals by breaches of Community law attributable to the State cannot be limited to damage sustained after the delivery of a judgment of the Court finding the infringement in question.

NOTE

The Court has clearly taken the scope of *Francovich* liability beyond the specific issue of non-implementation of Directives and it has established an approach which places emphasis on the context of particular infractions. As para 46 of the ruling indicates, the issue of non-implementation of Directives itself could lead to liability in circumstances as clear-cut as those prevailing in *Francovich* itself, but not in others. This was made plain in a ruling delivered just three weeks later.

R v H.M. Treasury, ex parte British Telecommunications (Case C-392/93)
[1996] ECR I-1631, Court of Justice of the European Communities

The litigation arose out of the UK's implementation of Article 8(1) of Directive 90/531, in the field of public procurement. The Court ruled that the UK had not implemented the Directive correctly. It was asked to consider the scope of State liability in a case of incorrect implementation.

[40] . . . A restrictive approach to State liability is justified in such a situation, for the reasons already given by the Court to justify the strict approach to non-contractual liability of Community institutions or Member States when exercising legislative functions in areas covered by Community law where the institution or State has a wide discretion – in particular, the concern to ensure that the exercise of legislative functions is not hindered by the prospect of actions for damages whenever the general interest requires the institutions or Member States to adopt measures which may adversely affect individual interests (see, in particular, the judgments in Joined Cases 83/76, 94/76, 4/77, 15/77 and 40/77 *HNL and Others* v *Council and Commission* [1978] ECR 1209, paragraphs 5 and 6, and in *Brasserie du Pêcheur and Factortame*, paragraph 45).

[41] Whilst it is in principle for the national courts to verify whether or not the conditions governing State liability for a breach of Community law are fulfilled, in the present case the Court has all the necessary information to assess whether the facts amount to a sufficiently serious breach of Community law.

[42] According to the case-law of the Court, a breach is sufficiently serious where, in the exercise of its legislative powers, an institution or a Member State has manifestly and gravely disregarded the limits on the exercise of its powers (judgments in *HNL and Others* v *Council and Commission*, cited above, paragraph 6, and in *Brasserie du Pêcheur and Factortame*, paragraph 55). Factors which the competent court may take into consideration include the clarity and precision of the rule breached (judgment in *Brasserie du Pêcheur and Factortame*, paragraph 56).

[43] In the present case, Article 8(1) is imprecisely worded and was reasonably capable of bearing, as well as the construction applied to it by the Court in this judgment, the interpretation given to it by the United Kingdom in good faith and on the basis of arguments which are not entirely devoid of substance (see paragraphs 20 to 22 above). That interpretation, which was also shared by other Member States, was not manifestly contrary to the wording of the directive or to the objective pursued by it.

[44] Moreover, no guidance was available to the United Kingdom from case law of the Court as to the interpretation of the provision at issue, nor did the Commission raise the matter when the 1992 Regulations were adopted.

[45] In those circumstances, the fact that a Member State, when transposing the directive into national law, thought it necessary itself to determine which services were to be excluded from its scope in implementation of Article 8, albeit in breach of that provision, cannot be regarded as a sufficiently serious breach of Community law of the kind intended by the Court in its judgment in *Brasserie du Pêcheur and Factortame*.

NOTES

1. In relation to all breaches of Community law, not simply those arising out of the process of implementation of Directives, it appears that an assessment of the gravity of the breach is required in determining the availability of compensation. This is a condition the fulfilment of which seems hard to predict in advance. For further examples involving exploration of the seriousness of the breach for these purposes, see *R v Ministry of Agriculture, Fisheries and Food, ex parte Hedley Lomas (Ireland) Ltd* (Case C-5/94) [1996] ECR I-2553; *Dillenkofer v Germany* (Joined Cases C-178 *et al*/94) [1996] ECR I-4845; *R v Secretary of State for Social Security, ex parte Sutton* (Case C-66/95) [1997] ECR I-2163; *Klaus Konle v Austria* (Case C-302/97), [1999] ECR I-3099; Case C-150/99 *Stockholm Lindopark* [2001] ECR I-493.

2. The Court has brought the rules on State liability for breach of Community law into alignment with the rules governing the liability of Community institutions for unlawful conduct. The latter system is envisaged by the Treaty. It is set out in Articles 235 and 288(2), which are examined in Chapter 8, p.239 below. The former is by contrast the product of the Court's ingenuity. This correspondence means that the case law arising in recent years in one branch is helpful in understanding the case law in the other. See for example *Commission v Camar and Others* (Case C-312/00P), p.243 below.

3. The Commission tracks application at national level of the rulings in *Francovich* and *Brasserie du Pêcheur/Factortame* and refers to them routinely in its Annual Reports on monitoring the application of Community law (currently available via http://europa.eu.int/comm/secretariat_general/sgb/droit_com/index_en.htm). This reflects the significance of these legal principles in improving the policing of State compliance with Community law.

FURTHER READING

Barav, A., 'State Liability in Damages for Breach of Community Law in the National Courts' (1996) 16 YEL 87.

Craig, P., 'Once More unto the Breach: the Community, the State and Damages Liability' (1997) 113 LQR 67.

Craufurd Smith, R., 'Remedies for Breaches of EC Law in National Courts: Legal Variation and Selection', in P. Craig and G. de Búrca, *The Evolution of EU Law* (Oxford: OUP, 1999).

Steiner, J., 'The Limits of State Liability for Breach of EC Law' (1998) 4 *Euro Public Law* 69.

Swaine, E., 'Subsidiarity and Self-Interest: Federalism at the European Court of Justice' (2000) 41 Harvard Intl Law Jnl 1.

Tesauro, G., 'The Effectiveness of Judicial Protection and Co-operation between the Court of Justice and the National Courts' (1993) 13 YEL 1.

Tridimas, T., 'Liability for Breach of Community Law: Growing Up and Mellowing Down' (2001) 38 CML Rev 301.

Van Gerven, W., 'Bridging the Unbridgeable: Community and National Tort Laws after Francovich and Brasserie' (1996) 45 ICLQ 507.

■ QUESTIONS

1. To what extent are public authorities entitled to expect protection under the law where an honest but mistaken attempt to meet legal obligations may result in liability to an indeterminate class for an indeterminate time and in an indeterminate amount? To what extent has the European Court responded to such concerns?

2. To what extent do the Court's recent judgments in this area display a willingness to perform a task of harmonization of Community and national rules relating to interim protection and liability in damages which ought to be the preserve of the legislature, not the courts?

3. (Imaginary) Directive 1/2000 provides that from January 2003, all workers shall be entitled to bring a claim that they have been unfairly dismissed before a national tribunal, provided they have been employed for at least one year prior to dismissal. A UK Statutory Instrument made in 1988 provides that the relevant qualifying period for an unfair dismissal claim in the UK is two years. The UK has not implemented the Directive. It ought to have done so by 1 July 2001, but the government has been unable to introduce implementing measures because of protests by the opposition parties and some of its own backbench MPs. At the start of 2002, Alice took up a post with British Stodge plc, a firm which supplies catering services to National Health Service hospitals. It is June 2003 and she has just been dismissed. Advise Alice of any assistance she may derive from EC law.

NOTE

For additional material and resources see the Companion Website at: www.oup.co.uk/best.textbooks/law/weatherill6e

7

Article 234: The Preliminary Reference Procedure

ARTICLE 234 EC

The Court of Justice shall have jurisdiction to give preliminary rulings concerning:

(a) the interpretation of this Treaty;
(b) the validity and interpretation of acts of the institutions of the Community and of the ECB;
(c) the interpretation of the statutes of bodies established by an act of the Council, where those statutes so provide.

Where such a question is raised before any court or tribunal of a Member State, that court or tribunal may, if it considers that a decision on the question is necessary to enable it to give judgment, request the Court of Justice to give a ruling thereon.

Where any such question is raised in a case pending before a court or tribunal of a Member State, against whose decisions there is no judicial remedy under national law, that court or tribunal shall bring the matter before the Court of Justice.

NOTE

The text was untouched by the Treaty of Nice. Nor did the Treaty of Amsterdam make any changes to this Article, except for its numbering (see p.12 above): Article 234 was formerly Article 177. Clearly this numerical adjustment must be borne in mind when reading pre-Amsterdam documents, including judgments of the Court.

SECTION 1: THE PURPOSE OF ARTICLE 234

The purpose of Article 234 can be traced directly to the need to secure uniformity in the Community legal order throughout the Member States. The introduction delivered by Advocate-General Lagrange 40 years ago in his Opinion in *Bosch* v *de Geus* (Case 13/61), can hardly be bettered:

Bosch v *de Geus* (Case 13/61)

[1962] ECR 45, Court of Justice of the European Communities

ADVOCATE-GENERAL LAGRANGE: *Mr President, Members of the Court,*

This case – the first submitted to you under the provisions of Article 177 of the Treaty establishing the European Economic Community – is of importance under that head alone, since it involves the working of a procedure for the submission of preliminary questions which is apparently designed to play a central part in the application of the Treaty. The progressive integration of the Treaty into the legal, social and economic life of the Member States must involve more and more frequently the application and, when the occasion arises, the interpretation of the Treaty in municipal litigation, whether public or private, and not only the provisions of the Treaty itself but also those of the Regulations adopted for its implementation will give rise to questions of interpretation and indeed of legality. Applied judiciously – one is tempted to say loyally – the provisions of Article 177 must lead to a real and fruitful collaboration between the municipal courts and the Court of Justice of the Communities with mutual regard for their respective jurisdictions. It is in this spirit that each side must solve the sometimes delicate problems which may arise in all systems of preliminary procedure, and which are necessarily made more difficult in this case by the differences in the legal systems of the Member States as regards this type of procedure.

Rheinmühlen-Düsseldorf v *Einfuhr- und Vorratsstelle für Getreide und Futtermittel (No 1)* **(Case 166/73)**
[1974] ECR 33, Court of Justice of the European Communities

Article 177 is essential for the preservation of the Community character of the law established by the Treaty and has the object of ensuring that in all circumstances the law is the same in all States of the Community.

NOTE

Stauder v *Ulm* (Case 29/69) was examined at p.81 above in connection with the protection of fundamental rights. The case was also illuminating for its use of the preliminary reference procedure to secure uniform interpretation of Community texts:

Stauder v *Ulm* **(Case 29/69)**
[1969] ECR 419, Court of Justice of the European Communities

[2] . . . Article 4 of Decision No 69/71 stipulates in two of its versions, one being the German version, that the States must take all necessary measures to ensure that beneficiaries can only purchase the product in question on presentation of a 'coupon indicating their names', whilst in the other versions, however, it is only stated that a 'coupon referring to the person concerned' must be shown, thus making it possible to employ other methods of checking in addition to naming the beneficiary. It is therefore necessary in the first place to ascertain exactly what methods the provision at issue prescribes.

[3] When a single decision is addressed to all the Member States the necessity for uniform application and accordingly for uniform interpretation makes it impossible to consider one version of the text in isolation but requires that it be interpreted on the basis of both the real intention of its author and the aim he seeks to achieve, in the light in particular of the versions in all four languages.

NOTES
1. It will be recalled from p.81 above, that the Court's interpretation led it to reject the contention that the rules infringed fundamental rights.
2. The preliminary reference procedure's role in securing authoritative interpretation of Community law places it alongside the principles of supremacy and direct effect and the notion of effective judicial protection (which, as illustrated in *Francovich* (Cases C-6 and C-9/90, p.168 above), extends beyond direct effect) as one of the pillars of the Community legal order. Its deepening significance may be appreciated when one realizes that the four official languages to which the Court refers in *Stauder* have now increased to 11, and enlargement will increase the number still further.

SECTION 2: **THE SEPARATION OF FUNCTIONS**

The preliminary reference procedure under Article 234 EC – which was Article 177 pre-Amsterdam – is based on a separation of function. It does not elevate the European Court to an appellate status. The Court may not rule on the validity of national law. This was made clear in *Van Gend en Loos* (Case 26/62), which was examined at p.109 above for its explanation of the nature of direct effect. It will be recalled that the substance of the case concerned the compatibility of a Dutch levy with the Treaty.

Van Gend en Loos v *Nederlandse Administratie der Belastingen* (Case 26/62)
[1963] ECR 1, Court of Justice of the European Communities

According to the observations of the Belgian and Netherlands Governments, the wording of this question appears to require, before it can be answered, an examination by the Court of the tariff classification of ureaformaldehyde imported into the Netherlands, a classification on which Van Gend & Loos and the Inspector of Customs and Excise at Zaandam hold different opinions with regard to the 'Tariefbesluit' of 1947. The question clearly does not call for an interpretation of the Treaty but concerns the application of Netherlands customs legislation to the classification of aminoplasts, which is outside the jurisdiction conferred upon the Court of Justice of the European Communities by subparagraph (a) of the first paragraph of Article 177.

The Court has therefore no jurisdiction to consider the reference made by the Tariefcommissie

However, the real meaning of the question put by the Tariefcommissie is whether, in law, an effective increase in customs duties charged on a given product as a result not of an increase in the rate but of a new classification of the product arising from a change of its tariff description contravenes the prohibition in Article 12 of the Treaty.

Viewed in this way the question put is concerned with an interpretation of this provision of the Treaty and more particularly of the meaning which should be given to the concept of duties applied before the Treaty entered into force.

Therefore the Court has jurisdiction to give a ruling on this question.

As to whether the facts of the case disclosed a violation of Article 12, which is Article 25 post-Amsterdam, the Court concluded:

The Court has no jurisdiction to check the validity of the conflicting views on this subject which have been submitted to it during the proceedings but must leave them to be determined by the national courts

NOTE
The same approach may be observed in *Costa* v *ENEL* (Case 6/64), examined above at p.99 in relation to the doctrine of the supremacy of Community law.

Costa v *ENEL* (Case 6/64)
[1964] ECR 585, Court of Justice of the European Communities

The complaint is made that the intention behind the question posed was to obtain, by means of Article 177, a ruling on the compatibility of a national law with the Treaty.

By the terms of this Article, however, national courts against whose decisions, as in the present case, there is no judicial remedy, must refer the matter to the Court of Justice so that a preliminary ruling may be given upon the 'interpretation of the Treaty' whenever a question of interpretation is raised before them. This provision gives the Court no jurisdiction either to apply the Treaty to a specific case or to decide upon the validity of a provision of domestic law in relation to the Treaty, as it would be possible for it to do under Article 169.

Nevertheless, the Court has power to extract from a question imperfectly formulated by the national court those questions which alone pertain to the interpretation of the Treaty. Consequently a decision should be given by the Court not upon the validity of an Italian law in relation to the Treaty, but only upon the interpretation of the abovementioned Articles in the context of the points of law stated by the Giudice Conciliatore.

NOTE

However, the Court's inability to rule on the validity of national law may not be as absolute as it first seems. In *Walter Rau* v *de Smedt* (Case 261/81), the Court was asked to interpret Article 30 of the EC Treaty (now, after amendment, Article 28; see Chapter 11). The case concerned a challenge to Belgian rules requiring the packaging of margarine in cubes. The Court's response was rather more full and direct than mere interpretation of Community law.

Walter Rau v *de Smedt* (Case 261/81)
[1982] ECR 3961, Court of Justice of the European Communities

The application in one Member State to margarine imported from another Member State and lawfully produced and marketed in that State of legislation prohibiting the marketing of margarine or edible fats where each block or its external packaging does not have a particular shape, for example the shape of a cube, in circumstances in which the consumer may be protected and informed by means which hinder the free movement of goods to a lesser degree constitutes a measure having an effect equivalent to a quantitative restriction within the meaning of Article 30 of the Treaty.

NOTES

1. Look out for other examples of the Court adopting an approach beyond mere interpretation in its answers to questions referred.
2. In fact, it would be rather unrealistic to expect the Court to adhere to the abstract in its answers. It also typically expands its answers when it is eager to ensure that an important principle is fully understood; *Van Gend en Loos* (Case 26/62) (p.109 above) stands as a classic example of this.
3. Since the European Court's formal role under the Article 234 procedure relates to Community law only, it should not question the national court's decision in the case before it to make a reference. Whether it is necessary to obtain a decision on a question is a matter for the national court. This stems from the separation of functions between national courts and the European Court.

Van Gend en Loos v *Nederlandse Administratie der Belastingen* (Case 26/62)
[1963] ECR 1, Court of Justice of the European Communities

The Belgian Government further argues that the Court has no jurisdiction on the ground that no answer which the Court could give to the first question of the Tariefcommissie would have any bearing on the result of the proceedings brought in that court.

However, in order to confer jurisdiction on the Court in the present case it is necessary only that the question raised should clearly be concerned with the interpretation of the Treaty. The considerations which may have led a national court or tribunal to its choice of questions as well as the relevance which it attributes to such questions in the context of a case before it are excluded from review by the Court of Justice.

It appears from the wording of the questions referred that they relate to the interpretation of the Treaty. The Court therefore has the jurisdiction to answer them.

Costa v *ENEL* (Case 6/64)
[1964] ECR 585, Court of Justice of the European Communities

The complaint is made that the Milan court has requested an interpretation of the Treaty which was not necessary for the solution of the dispute before it.

Since, however, Article 177 is based upon a clear separation of functions between national courts and the Court of Justice, it cannot empower the latter either to investigate the facts of the case or to criticize the grounds and purpose of the request for interpretation.

Irish Creamery Milk Suppliers v *Government of Ireland* (Case 36/80)
[1981] ECR 735, Court of Justice of the European Communities

[4] The first question raised by the High Court of Ireland is worded as follows:

'Was the decision by the High Court, at this stage of the hearing, to refer to the European Court under Article 177 of the Treaty the question set out in paragraph 2 below a correct exercise on the part of the High Court of its discretion pursuant to the said article?'.

[5] Before an answer is given to that question it should be recalled that Article 177 of the Treaty establishes a framework for close co-operation between the national courts and the Court of Justice based on the assignment to each of different functions. The second paragraph of that article makes it clear that it is for the national court to decide at what stage in the proceedings it is appropriate for that court to refer a question to the Court of Justice for a preliminary ruling.

[6] The need to provide an interpretation of Community law which will be of use to the national court makes it essential, as the Court has already stated in its judgment of 12 July 1979 (*Union Laitière Normande*, Case 244/78 [1979] ECR 2663) to define the legal context in which the interpretation requested should be placed. From that aspect it might be convenient, if circumstances permit, for the facts in the case to be established and for questions of purely national law to be settled at the time the reference is made to the Court of Justice so as to enable the latter to take cognizance of all the features of fact and of law which may be relevant to the interpretation of Community law which it is called upon to give.

[7] However, those considerations do not in any way restrict the discretion of the national court, which alone has a direct knowledge of the facts of the case and of the arguments of the parties, which will have to take responsibility for giving judgment in the case and which is therefore in the best position to appreciate at what stage in the proceedings it requires a preliminary ruling from the Court of Justice.

[8] Hence it is clear that the national court's decision when to make a reference under Article 177 must be dictated by considerations of procedural organization and efficiency to be weighed by that court.

[9] The reply to the first question which has been raised should therefore be that under Article 177 the decision at what stage in proceedings before it a national court should refer a question to the Court of Justice for a preliminary ruling is a matter for the discretion of the national court.

NOTES

1. It is perfectly permissible to refer in interim proceedings, although this will not be normal; *Hoffman la Roche* v *Centrafarm* (Case 107/76) [1977] ECR 957.
2. An outstanding exception to the receptiveness of the Court to references made by national courts is found in the two *Foglia* v *Novello* cases (Cases 104/79 and 244/80).

Foglia v *Novello (No 1)* (Case 104/79)
[1980] ECR 745, Court of Justice of the European Communities

Foglia, an Italian wine dealer, dispatched goods to Novello in France. The contract stipulated that Novello would not be liable for any charges levied by the French or Italian authorities which were incompatible with Community law. A tax then levied by the French authorities formed the basis of the litigation. Novello refused to bear the cost. Foglia sued Novello before the Italian courts; Novello's defence was based on the incompatibility of the charge with Community law (Article 95 of the EC Treaty (now Article 90 EC)). A reference was made by the Italian judge, the *Pretura di Bra*.

[8] The parties to the main action submitted a certain number of documents to the Pretura which enabled it to investigate the French legislation concerning the taxation of liqueur wines and other comparable products. The court concluded from its investigation that such legislation created a 'serious discrimination' against Italian liqueur wines and natural wines having a high degree of alcoholic strength by means of special arrangements made for French liqueur wines termed 'natural sweet wines' and preferential tax treatment accorded certain French natural wines with a high

degree of alcoholic strength and bearing a designation of origin. On the basis of that conclusion the court formulated the questions which it has submitted to the Court of Justice.

[9] In their written observations submitted to the Court of Justice the two parties to the main action have provided an essentially identical description of the tax discrimination which is a feature of the French legislation concerning the taxation of liqueur wines; the two parties consider that that legislation is incompatible with Community law. In the course of the oral procedure before the Court Foglia stated that he was participating in the procedure before the Court in view of the interest of his undertaking as such and as an undertaking belonging to a certain category of Italian traders in the outcome of the legal issues involved in the dispute.

[10] It thus appears that the parties to the main action are concerned to obtain a ruling that the French tax system is invalid for liqueur wines by the expedient of proceedings before an Italian court between two private individuals who are in agreement as to the result to be attained and who have inserted a clause in their contract in order to induce the Italian court to give a ruling on the point. The artificial nature of this expedient is underlined by the fact that Danzas [the carrier] did not exercise its rights under French law to institute proceedings over the consumption tax although it undoubtedly had an interest in doing so in view of the clause in the contract by which it was also bound and moreover of the fact that Foglia paid without protest that undertaking's bill which included a sum paid in respect of that tax.

[11] The duty of the Court of Justice under Article 177 of the EEC Treaty is to supply all courts in the Community with the information on the interpretation of Community law which is necessary to enable them to settle genuine disputes which are brought before them. A situation in which the Court was obliged by the expedient of arrangements like those described above to give rulings would jeopardize the whole system of legal remedies available to private individuals to enable them to protect themselves against tax provisions which are contrary to the Treaty.

[12] This means that the questions asked by the national court, having regard to the circumstances of this case, do not fall within the framework of the duties of the Court of Justice under Article 177 of the Treaty.

[13] The Court of Justice accordingly has no jurisdiction to give a ruling on the questions asked by the national court.

NOTE
The judge was evidently perplexed that the Court seemed to have abandoned its policy of non-interference with the decision of the referring judge, and referred further questions in the second *Foglia* v *Novello* case.

Foglia v *Novello (No 2)* (Case 244/80)
[1981] ECR 3045, Court of Justice of the European Communities

[17] In order that the Court of Justice may perform its task in accordance with the Treaty it is essential for national courts to explain, when the reasons do not emerge beyond any doubt from the file, why they consider that a reply to their questions is necessary to enable them to give judgment.

[18] It must in fact be emphasised that the duty assigned to the Court by Article 177 is not that of delivering advisory opinions on general or hypothetical questions but of assisting in the administration of justice in the Member States. It accordingly does not have jurisdiction to reply to questions of interpretation which are submitted to it within the framework of procedural devices arranged by the parties in order to induce the Court to give its views on certain problems of Community law which do not correspond to an objective requirement inherent in the resolution of a dispute. A declaration by the Court that it has no jurisdiction in such circumstances does not in any way trespass upon the prerogatives of the national court but makes it possible to prevent the application of the procedure under Article 177 for purposes other than those appropriate for it.

[19] Furthermore, it should be pointed out that, whilst the Court of Justice must be able to place as much reliance as possible upon the assessment by the national court of the extent to which

the questions submitted are essential, it must be in a position to make any assessment inherent in the performance of its own duties in particular in order to check, as all courts must, whether it has jurisdiction. Thus the Court, taking into account the repercussions of its decisions in this matter, must have regard, in exercising the jurisdiction conferred upon it by Article 177, not only to the interests of the parties to the proceedings but also to those of the Community and of the Member States. Accordingly it cannot, without disregarding the duties assigned to it, remain indifferent to the assessments made by the courts of the Member States in the exceptional cases in which such assessments may affect the proper working of the procedure laid down by Article 177.

[20] Whilst the spirit of co-operation which must govern the performance of the duties assigned by Article 177 to the national courts on the one hand and the Court of Justice on the other requires the latter to have regard to the national court's proper responsibilities, it implies at the same time that the national court, in the use which it makes of the facilities provided by Article 177, should have regard to the proper function of the Court of Justice in this field.

[21] The reply to the first question must accordingly be that whilst, according to the intended role of Article 177, an assessment of the need to obtain an answer to the questions of interpretation raised, regard being had to the circumstances of fact and of law involved in the main action, is a matter for the national court it is nevertheless for the Court of Justice, in order to confirm its own jurisdiction, to examine, where necessary, the conditions in which the case has been referred to it by the national court.

The Court then observed:

[25] The reply to the fourth question must accordingly be that in the case of preliminary questions intended to permit the national court to determine whether provisions laid down by law or regulation in another Member State are in accordance with Community law the degree of legal protection may not differ according to whether such questions are raised in proceedings between individuals or in an action to which the State whose legislation is called in question is a party, but that in the first case the Court of Justice must take special care to ensure that the procedure under Article 177 is not employed for purposes which were not intended by the Treaty.

NOTES

1. In the result, the Court did not significantly modify the stance which it had taken in the first *Foglia* v *Novello* case (Case 104/79). There are sound arguments both for and against the Court's stance. See, e.g., discussion by A. Barav (1980) 5 EL Rev 443; D. Wyatt (1982) 7 EL Rev 186; and G. Behr (1982) 19 CML Rev 421.

2. However, contrary to the impression left by these two judgments, subsequent case law confirms that the Court had *not* chosen to embark on a new policy of inquiry into the national court's decision to refer. It is striking that in the main the Court has routinely declined subsequent invitations to repeat the *Foglia* v *Novello* approach. In *Walter Rau* (Case 261/81), mentioned above at p.190, the Court was curt when presented with objections to its jurisdiction:

Walter Rau v *de Smedt* (Case 261/81)
[1982] ECR 3961, Court of Justice of the European Communities

[8] The Belgian Government points out that the importation of margarine into Belgium by the defendant in the main action is already the subject of criminal proceedings in Belgium and that the Court should therefore inquire whether the dispute which gave rise to the request for a preliminary ruling is a genuine dispute. In this regard the Belgian Government recalls the judgment of the Court of 16 December 1981 in Case 244/80 *Foglia* [1981] ECR 3045.

[9] In this instance there is nothing in the file on the case which provides grounds for doubting that the dispute is genuine. Therefore there is no reason for concluding that the Court has no jurisdiction.

NOTE

In *Parfumerie-Fabrik* v *Provide* (Case C-150/88), the Court confirmed that it will not lightly infer an absence of a genuine dispute.

Parfumerie-Fabrik v *Provide* (Case C-150/88)
[1989] ECR 3891, Court of Justice of the European Communities

[11] The Italian Government notes that the preliminary questions arose in the context of a dispute between individuals, the genuineness of which is open to doubt, and that they are intended to permit a court in one Member State to determine whether the rules of another Member State are compatible with Community law. Referring to the Court's judgment of 16 December 1981 in Case 244/80 *Foglia* v *Novello* [1981] ECR 3045, the Italian Government therefore expresses its doubts as to the propriety of the request for a preliminary ruling. It further maintains that the Court has no jurisdiction under Article 177 to rule on the compatibility of national legislation with Community law.

[12] Those objections must be dismissed. First, the documents before the Court do not allow any doubt as to the genuineness of the dispute in the main proceedings or, therefore, the propriety of the request for a preliminary ruling. Secondly, the Court has consistently held (see, in particular, its judgment of 9 October 1984 in Joined Cases 91 and 127/83 *Heineken Brouwerijen BV* v *Inspecteurs der Vennootschapsbelasting, Amsterdam and Utrecht* [1984] ECR 3435) that, when ruling on questions intended to permit the national court to determine whether national provisions are in accordance with Community law, the Court may provide the criteria for the interpretation of Community law which will enable the national court to solve the legal problem with which it is faced. The same is true when it is to be determined whether the provisions of a Member State other than that of the court requesting the ruling are compatible with Community law.

NOTE

It is pertinent to recall that the fact that the parties to litigation may be in agreement about the desired result does not necessarily eliminate the existence of a real dispute calling for a ruling by the European Court. The Court made this point in *Société d'Importation Édouard Leclerc-Siplec* v *TFI Publicité SA & M6 Publicité SA* (Case C-412/93) [1995] ECR I-179 and expanded on it in the next case.

Cura Anlagen GmbH v *Auto Service Leasing GmbH* (Case C-451/99)
[2002] ECR I-3193, Court of Justice of the European Communities

Cura Anlagen, an Austrian company, rented a German-registered car from Auto Service Leasing, a company based in Germany. But Cura Anlagen could not use the car because Austrian rules prevented the driving of a vehicle with foreign plates in Austria for more than three days. In an action on the contract brought before a court in Vienna the question of the compatibility of the Austrian rules with the EC Treaty's free movement provisions was raised and duly referred to Luxembourg under the Article 234 procedure. But was it admissible?

[16] According to settled case law, it is solely for the national court before which the dispute has been brought, and which must assume responsibility for the subsequent judicial decision, to determine in the light of the particular circumstances of the case both the need for a preliminary ruling in order to enable it to deliver judgment and the relevance of the questions which it submits to the Court. Nevertheless, the Court has held that it cannot give a preliminary ruling on a question submitted by a national court where it is quite obvious that the ruling sought by that court on the interpretation or validity of Community law bears no relation to the actual facts of the main action or its purpose, where the problem is hypothetical, or where the Court does not have before it the factual or legal material necessary to give a useful answer to the questions submitted to it (see, in particular, Case C-36/99 *Idéal Tourisme* [2000] ECR I-6049, paragraph 20, and the case law cited therein). . . .

[21] The Austrian Government. . . argues that the dispute in the main proceedings concerns the interpretation and performance of a private law contract which bears no relation to the question referred.

[23] It should be noted in that respect that, pursuant to Article 234 EC, where a question on the interpretation of the Treaty or of subordinate acts of the institutions of the Community is raised before any court or tribunal of a Member State, that court or tribunal may, if it considers that a decision on the question is necessary to enable it to give judgment, request the Court of Justice to give a ruling thereon (see, in particular, Case C-412/93 *Leclerc-Siplec* [1995] ECR I-179, paragraph 9).

[23] In the context of that procedure for making a reference, the national court, which alone has direct knowledge of the facts of the case, is in the best position to assess, with full knowledge of the matter before it, the need for a preliminary ruling to enable it to give judgment (see, in particular, *Leclerc-Siplec*, paragraph 10).

[24] Moreover, as the Advocate General has pointed out in paragraph 23 of his Opinion, it is important for a court which is asked to order the enforcement or annulment of a contract to know whether the national provisions which appear to hinder its performance are compatible with Community law or not. The question therefore appears to be relevant.

[25] Finally, the Austrian Government challenges the genuineness of the dispute in the main proceedings, which it claims is to a large extent contrived.

[26] In that respect, the Court of Justice has held that, in order to determine whether it has jurisdiction, it must examine the conditions in which the case has been referred to it by the national court. The spirit of cooperation which must prevail in the preliminary ruling procedure requires the national court to have regard to the function entrusted to the Court of Justice, which is to assist in the administration of justice in the Member States and not to deliver advisory opinions on general or hypothetical questions (Case 149/82 *Robards* [1983] ECR 171, paragraph 19; Case C-83/91 *Meilicke* [1992] ECR I-4871, paragraph 25).

[27] In this case, even if some of the information on the file might give rise to a suspicion that the situation underlying the main proceedings was contrived with a view to obtaining a decision from the Court of Justice on a question of Community law of general interest, it cannot be denied that there is a genuine contract the performance or annulment of which undeniably depends on a question of Community law.

NOTE

The question was therefore treated as admissible. This judgment strengthens the impression that *Foglia* v *Novello* continues to be treated as an exception to a general rule of receptivity to preliminary references. But, though an exception, it is not dead, as the next case demonstrates.

Bacardi-Martini SAS, Cellier des Dauphins v *Newcastle United* (Case C-318/00)
Judgment of 21 January 2003, Court of Justice of the European Communities

Newcastle United permitted the broadcasting of football matches from their home ground, at which advertisements for alcoholic drinks were displayed. This was compatible with English law but in conflict with the highly restrictive French *Loi Évin* governing advertising of alcohol. After a match against Metz was transmitted on French television, litigation was commenced between the companies whose products had been advertised and the club. The possible application of EC rules governing the free movement of services (Article 49 EC: Chapter 14) was raised and the High Court in London referred questions to Luxembourg under Article 234. But they were held inadmissible.

[42] . . . The spirit of cooperation which must prevail in preliminary ruling proceedings requires the national court for its part to have regard to the function entrusted to the Court of Justice, which is to

contribute to the administration of justice in the Member States and not to give opinions on general or hypothetical questions . . .

[43] Thus the Court has held that it has no jurisdiction to give a preliminary ruling on a question submitted by a national court where it is quite obvious that the interpretation or the assessment of the validity of a provision of Community law sought by that court bears no relation to the actual facts of the main action or its purpose, or where the problem is hypothetical, or where the Court does not have before it the factual or legal material necessary to give a useful answer to the questions submitted to it (see *Bosman*, paragraph 61; Case C-437/97 *EKW and Wein & Co* [2000] ECR I-1157, paragraph 52; and Case C-36/99 *Idéal Tourisme* [2000] ECR I-6049, paragraph 20).

[44] In order that the Court may perform its task in accordance with the Treaty, it is essential for national courts to explain, when the reasons do not emerge beyond any doubt from the file, why they consider that a reply to their questions is necessary to enable them to give judgment (Case 244/80 *Foglia* [1981] ECR 3045, paragraph 17). Thus the Court has held that it is essential that the national court should give at the very least some explanation of the reasons for the choice of the Community provisions which it requires to be interpreted and of the link it establishes between those provisions and the national legislation applicable to the dispute (order in Case C-116/00 *Laguillaumie* [2000] ECR I-4979, paragraph 16).

[45] Moreover, the Court must display special vigilance when, in the course of proceedings between individuals, a question is referred to it with a view to permitting the national court to decide whether the legislation of another Member State is in accordance with Community law (*Foglia*, paragraph 30).

[46] In the present case, as the questions referred are intended to enable the national court to assess the compatibility with Community law of the legislation of another Member State, the Court must be informed in some detail of that court's reasons for considering that an answer to the questions is necessary to enable it to give judgment.

[47] It appears from the High Court's account of the legal context that it has to apply English law in the main proceedings. It nevertheless considers that 'the issue of the legality of the Loi Évin provisions is central to resolution of the proceedings before [it]'. It does not, however, state positively that an answer to that question is necessary to enable it to give judgment.

[48] On being requested by the Court to explain more fully the basis on which Newcastle could rely on the Loi Évin, the High Court has essentially confined itself to repeating the defendant's argument that it could reasonably anticipate that a failure to give instructions to remove the advertisements in the stadium would result in a breach of French law.

[49] On the other hand, the High Court has not said whether it itself considered that Newcastle could reasonably suppose that it was obliged to comply with the French legislation, and there is nothing else to that effect before the Court.

These deficiencies led the Court to conclude that it did not have the material before it to show that it was 'necessary to rule on the compatibility with the Treaty of legislation of a Member State other than that of the court making the reference'. The questions were therefore inadmissible.

NOTE

In *Wienand Meilicke v ADV/ORGA FA Meyer AG* (Case C-83/91) [1992] ECR I-4871, mentioned in paragraph 26 of *Cura Anlagen* (Case C-451/99, p.195 above), the Court declined to answer questions referred to it by a German court because it considered it was being asked to rule on a purely hypothetical general problem. It had not had made available to it information necessary to enable it to provide a useful reply. In *Telemarsicabruzzo v Circostel* (Cases C-320–322/90) [1993] ECR I-393, the Court refused to give a ruling where it had been supplied with inadequate background information. The rulings, in conjunction with *Newcastle United* (Case C-318/00) may be taken in part as an encouragement to a referring court to take more care in the preparation of relevant documentation (see *Further Reading* at the end of this Chapter). In this vein the Court in the next case was ready to pick and choose the questions in respect of which it had jurisdiction, while offering fuller explanation of why it does not leave the door unconditionally open:

Jyri Lehtonen, Castors Canada Dry Namur-Braine ASBL v *Fédération Royale Belge des Sociétés de Basket-ball ASBL (FRBSB)* (Case C-176/96)

[2000] ECR I-2681, Court of Justice of the European Communities

[22] According to settled case-law, the need to provide an interpretation of Community law which will be of use to the national court makes it necessary that the national court define the factual and legal context of the questions it is asking or, at the very least, explain the factual circumstances on which those questions are based. Those requirements are of particular importance in certain areas, such as that of competition, where the factual and legal situations are often complex (see, in particular, Joined Cases C-320/90 to C-322/90 *Telemarsicabruzzo and Others* [1993] ECR I-393, paragraphs 6 and 7, Case C-67/96 *Albany International* v *Stichting Bedrijfspensioenfonds Textielindustrie* [1999] ECR I-5751, paragraph 39, and Joined Cases C-115/97 to C-117/97 *Brentjens' Handelsonderneming* v *Stichting Bedrijfspensioenfonds voor de Handel in Bouwmaterialen* [1999] ECR I-6025, paragraph 38).

[23] The information provided in decisions making references must not only enable the Court to reply usefully but also give the governments of the Member States and other interested parties the opportunity to submit observations pursuant to Article 20 of the EC Statute of the Court of Justice. It is the Court's duty to ensure that that opportunity is safeguarded, bearing in mind that, by virtue of the abovementioned provision, only the decisions making references are notified to the interested parties (see *inter alia* the order in Case C-458/93 *Saddik* [1995] ECR I-511, paragraph 13, and the judgments in *Albany International*, paragraph 40, and *Brentjens' Handelsonderneming*, paragraph 39).

[24] In the main proceedings, it appears, first, from the observations submitted by the parties, the Governments of the Member States and the Commission pursuant to Article 20 of the EC Statute of the Court of Justice that the information in the order for reference enabled them properly to state their position on the question put to the Court, in so far as it concerns the Treaty rules on freedom of movement for workers.

However, this was only part of the reference submitted by the Belgian court. The Court continued:

[28] In so far as the question put concerns the competition rules applicable to undertakings, on the other hand, the Court considers that it does not have enough information to give guidance as to the definition of the market or markets at issue in the main proceedings. Nor does the order for reference show clearly the character and number of undertakings operating on that market or markets. In addition, the information provided by the national court does not enable the Court to make meaningful findings as to the existence and volume of trade between Member States or as to the possibility of that trade being affected by the rules on transfers of players.

[29] The order for reference therefore does not contain sufficient information to satisfy the requirements described in paragraphs 22 and 23 above, as far as the competition rules are concerned.

[30] Accordingly, the Court should answer the question referred in so far as it relates to the interpretation of the Treaty rules on the principle of the prohibition of discrimination on grounds of nationality and on freedom of movement for workers. The question is inadmissible, however, in so far as it relates to the interpretation of the competition rules applicable to undertakings.

NOTE

For a further example of a case in which the Court inspected the documentation provided by the referring court but felt itself unable to provide a 'useful answer', see *Christina Bellamy* (Case C-123/00) [2001] ECR I-2795. Nonetheless this outcome remains unusual. In the absence of exceptional circumstances, the European Court's readiness to answer questions of interpretation of Community law which a national court chooses to refer seems likely to continue. In *Landesgrundverkehrsreferent der Tiroler Landesregierung* v *Beck, Bergdorf Wohnbau* (Case C-355/97), [1999] ECR I-4977, for example, questions posed by an Austrian court were answered despite submissions by the Austrian Government and the Commission that answers could be of no value whatsoever in resolving the dispute. The 'presumption of relevance' attaching to questions referred was not rebutted on the facts. In *Wiener* (Case C-338/95) [1997] ECR I-6495, the Court coolly ignored Advocate-General Jacobs' plea for more self-restraint by both national courts and the European Court. That does not rule out the possibility that national courts may refer fewer cases to Luxembourg as they gain confidence in their ability to handle Community law materials. However, in recent years the number of referrals has remained fairly constant. The figures are 264 in 1998, 255 in 1999, 224 in 2000 and 237 in 2001. In 1998 Spain led the way (55 referrals), but since then the top three positions have been held by Austria, Germany, and Italy, albeit not always in that order. Austrian courts made the highest number of referrals in 1999 (56), followed by Germany (49) and Italy (43). In 2000, Italy was the most prolific (50), followed by Germany (47) and Austria (31), while in 2001 the ranking placed Austria first (57), Germany second (53) and Italy third (40). Courts in the UK made 22 references to Luxembourg in 1999, 26 in 2000 and 21 in 2000 (this information is available *via* the Court's website, http://curia.eu.int). It is plausible that the weight of preliminary references transmitted to the Court will increase, under pressures caused by *inter alia* enlargement of the Union and the enhanced albeit unorthodox jurisdiction conferred on the Court by the Amsterdam Treaty (in Article 68 EC, discussed in Chapter 15, and even outside the EC pillar of the Union, in a modified version of the preliminary reference procedure found in Article 35 EU). The heavier the Court's workload, the more intense will become the pressure for reform of the system. The Treaty of Nice made a relatively modest contribution by providing for the possibility of equipping the Court of First Instance with jurisdiction to deliver preliminary rulings in specific areas. This is now found in Article 225(3):

Article 225(3) EC: The Court of First Instance shall have jurisdiction to hear and determine questions referred for a preliminary ruling under Article 234, in specific areas laid down by the Statute. Where the Court of First Instance considers that the case requires a decision of principle likely to affect the unity or consistency of Community law, it may refer the case to the Court of Justice for a ruling. Decisions given by the Court of First Instance on questions referred for a preliminary ruling may exceptionally be subject to review by the Court of Justice, under the conditions and within the limits laid down by the Statute, where there is a serious risk of the unity or consistency of Community law being affected.

No such 'specific areas' have yet been laid down.

■ QUESTION

F. Mancini has compared the structure of the preliminary reference procedure with 'a fully fledged dual system of federal courts as can be found in the US', and found it 'legally frailer, but politically more faithful to the federal ethos' ((1989) 26 CML Rev 595, at p.605; see also D. Edward (also a judge at the Court) (1995) 20 EL Rev 539, 546–7). Discuss. What alterations to the Article 234 division of function might improve the procedure?

SECTION 3: **THE EFFECT OF AN ARTICLE 234 RULING**

ICC v *Amministrazione delle Finanze* (Case 66/80)

[1981] ECR 1191, Court of Justice of the European Communities

[9] Article 177 of the Treaty provides that the Court shall have jurisdiction to give preliminary rulings on the interpretation of the Treaty and on the validity and interpretation of acts of the institutions of the Community, including regulations of both the Council and the Commission. The second and third paragraphs of that provision go on to state that national courts may or must, as the case may be, bring such matters before the Court where they need a decision on that issue in order to give their judgment.

[10] The scope of judgments given under this head should be viewed in the light of the aims of Article 177 and the place it occupies in the entire system of judicial protection established by the Treaties.

[11] The main purpose of the powers accorded to the Court by Article 177 is to ensure that Community law is applied uniformly by national courts. Uniform application of Community law is imperative not only when a national court is faced with a rule of Community law the meaning and scope of which need to be defined; it is just as imperative when the Court is confronted by a dispute as to the validity of an act of the institutions.

[12] When the Court is moved under Article 177 to declare an act of one of the institutions to be void there are particularly imperative requirements concerning legal certainty in addition to those concerning the uniform application of Community law. It follows from the very nature of such a declaration that a national court may not apply the act declared to be void without once more creating serious uncertainty as to the Community law applicable.

[13] It follows therefrom that although a judgment of the Court given under Article 177 of the Treaty declaring an act of an institution, in particular a Council or Commission regulation, to be void is directly addressed only to the national court which brought the matter before the Court, it is sufficient reason for any other national court to regard that act as void for the purposes of a judgment which it has to give.

[14] That assertion does not however mean that national courts are deprived of the power given to them by Article 177 of the Treaty and it rests with those courts to decide whether there is a need to raise once again a question which has already been settled by the Court where the Court has previously declared an act of a Community institution to be void. There may be such a need in particular if questions arise as to the grounds, the scope and possibly the consequences of the invalidity established earlier.

[15] If that is not the case national courts are entirely justified in determining the effect on the cases brought before them of a judgment declaring an act void given by the Court in an action between other parties.

NOTES

1. Case 66/80 concerned a reference relating to the validity of Community legislation. A comparable approach should be taken in relation to the effect of preliminary rulings on the interpretation of Community law. Read A. Toth, 'The Authority of Judgments of the European Court of Justice: Binding Force and Legal Effects' (1984) 4 YEL 1.
2. The point that a preliminary ruling exerts an impact beyond the case in which it is delivered may affect the way in which the Court handles a request for a reference. In the current (2001) version of the Court's *Rules of Procedure* (available at http://curia.eu.int) Article 104(3) states that where the question referred is identical to one on which the Court has already ruled, where the answer may be clearly deduced from existing case law or where the answer admits of no reasonable doubt the Court may simply issue a reasoned order rather than proceeding to judgment.

3. The Court has the competence to restrict the temporal effects of its rulings; see, e.g., in relation to a ruling on interpretation (*Defrenne* (Case 43/75)) and the other cases mentioned at p.127 above; and read W. Alexander (1988) 8 YEL 11. These issues will be re-addressed in the next Chapter. The Court is determined to construct a comprehensive Community system of remedies which is coherent. It accordingly draws inspiration in interpreting Article 234 from other Treaty provisions, notably Article 230 (e.g., *Société de Produits de Màis* v *Administration des Douanes* (Case 112/83), at p.261 below).

SECTION 4: **BODIES COMPETENT TO REFER**

Broeckmeulen v *Huisarts Registratie Commissie* (Case 246/80)

[1981] ECR 2311, Court of Justice of the European Communities

Broeckmeulen was refused registration as (the equivalent of) a General Practitioner in the Netherlands by the defendant *Commissie*. He held a Belgian medical qualification and sought to rely on Community rules relating to the free movement of professionals between Member States. The first issue for the European Court to consider was whether the Appeals Committee was competent to refer questions relating to Community law under Article 177 – now, remember, Article 234 post-Amsterdam – which refers only to a 'court or tribunal of a Member State'.

[10] According to the internal rules of the Society, the Appeals Committee, appointed for a period of five years, is composed of three members appointed by the Netherlands medical faculties, three members appointed by the Board of the Society and three members, including the chairman (preferably a high-ranking judge), who are appointed by the ministers responsible for higher education and health respectively. It may therefore be seen that the composition of the Appeals Committee entails a significant degree of involvement on the part of the Netherlands public authorities.

[11] Pursuant to those rules, the Appeals Committee determines disputes on the adversarial principle, that is to say having heard the Registration Committee and the doctor concerned, as well as his adviser or lawyer, if necessary.

[12] The Netherlands Government stated that, in its opinion, the Appeals Committee cannot be considered a court or tribunal under Netherlands law. However, it pointed out that that fact is not decisive for the interpretation of Article 177 of the Treaty and suggested that the question whether a body such as the Appeals Committee is entitled to refer a case to the Court under that provision should be determined in the light of the function performed by that body within the system of remedies available to those who consider that their rights under Community law have been infringed.

[13] In this regard, the order for reference mentions a Royal Decree of 1966, the decree concerning benefits ('Verstreckingenbesluit'), adopted under the Sickness Fund Law; for the purposes of that decree the term 'general practitioner' refers exclusively to a doctor enrolled on the register of general practitioners maintained by the Society. The practice of a doctor who is not enrolled on the register would thus not be recognized by the sickness insurance schemes. Under those circumstances a doctor who is not enrolled on the register is unable to treat, as a general practitioner, patients covered by the social security system. In fact, private practice is likewise made impossible by the fact that private insurers also define the term 'general practitioner' in their policies in the same way as the provisions of the decree concerning benefits.

[14] A study of the Netherlands legislation and of the statutes and internal rules of the Society shows that a doctor who intends to establish himself in the Netherlands may not in fact practise either as a specialist, or as an expert in social medicine, or as a general practitioner, without being recognized and registered by the organs of the Society. In the same way it may be seen that the system thus established is the result of close cooperation between doctors who are members of the Society, the medical faculties and the departments of State responsible for higher education and health.

[15] It is thus clear that both in the sector covered by the social security system and in the field of private medicine the Netherlands system of public health operates on the basis of the status accorded to doctors by the Society and that registration as a general practitioner is essential to every doctor wishing to establish himself in the Netherlands as a general practitioner.

[16] Therefore a general practitioner who avails himself of the right of establishment and the freedom to provide services conferred upon him by Community law is faced with the necessity of applying to the Registration Committee established by the Society, and, in the event of his application's being refused, must appeal to the Appeals Committee. The Netherlands Government expressed the opinion that a doctor who is not a member of the Society would have the right to appeal against such a refusal to the ordinary courts, but stated that the point had never been decided by the Netherlands courts. Indeed all doctors, whether members of the Society or not, whose application to be registered as a general practitioner is refused, appeal to the Appeals Committee, whose decisions to the knowledge of the Netherlands Government, have never been challenged in the ordinary courts.

[17] In order to deal with the question of the applicability in the present case of Article 177 of the Treaty, it should be noted that it is incumbent upon Member States to take the necessary steps to ensure that within their own territory the provisions adopted by the Community institutions are implemented in their entirety. If, under the legal system of a Member State, the task of implementing such provisions is assigned to a professional body acting under a degree of governmental super-vision, and if that body, in conjunction with the public authorities concerned, creates appeal pro-cedures which may affect the exercise of rights granted by Community law, it is imperative, in order to ensure the proper functioning of Community law, that the Court should have an opportunity of ruling on issues of interpretation and validity arising out of such proceedings.

[18] As a result of all the foregoing considerations and in the absence, in practice, of any right of appeal to the ordinary courts, the Appeals Committee, which operates with the consent of the public authorities and with their cooperation, and which, after an adversarial procedure, delivers decisions which are in fact recognized as final, must, in a matter involving the application of Community law, be considered as a court or tribunal of a Member State within the meaning of Article 177 of the Treaty. Therefore, the Court has jurisdiction to reply to the question asked.

NOTE
The Court thus felt itself able to proceed to examine the substance of the case.

Nordsee v *Reederei Mond* (Case 102/81)
[1982] ECR 1095, Court of Justice of the European Communities

This was a reference by an arbitrator in a dispute between three German firms.

[7] Since the arbitration tribunal which referred the matter to the Court for a preliminary ruling was established pursuant to a contract between private individuals the question arises whether it may be considered as a court or tribunal of one of the Member States within the meaning of Article 177 of the Treaty.

[8] The first question put by the arbitrator concerns that problem. It is worded as follows:

'Is a German arbitration court, which must decide not according to equity but according to law, and whose decision has the same effects as regards the parties as a definitive

judgment of a court of law (Article 1040 of the Zivilprozeßordnung [rules of civil pro-
cedure]) authorized to make a reference to the Court of Justice of the European
Communities for a preliminary ruling pursuant to the second paragraph of Article 177 of
the EEC Treaty?'

[9] It must be noted that, as the question indicates, the jurisdiction of the Court to rule on questions
referred to it depends on the nature of the arbitration in question.

[10] It is true, as the arbitrator noted in his question, that there are certain similarities between
the activities of the arbitration tribunal in question and those of an ordinary court or tribunal
inasmuch as the arbitration is provided for within the framework of the law, the arbitrator must
decide according to law and his award has, as between the parties, the force of *res judicata*, and
may be enforceable if leave to issue execution is obtained. However, those characteristics are not
sufficient to give the arbitrator the status of a 'court or tribunal of a Member State' within the
meaning of Article 177 of the Treaty.

[11] The first important point to note is that when the contract was entered into in 1973 the parties
were free to leave their disputes to be resolved by the ordinary courts or to opt for arbitration by
inserting a clause to that effect in the contract. From the facts of the case it appears that the parties
were under no obligation, whether in law or in fact, to refer their disputes to arbitration.

[12] The second point to be noted is that the German public authorities are not involved in the
decision to opt for arbitration nor are they called upon to intervene automatically in the proceedings
before the arbitrator. The Federal Republic of Germany, as a Member State of the Community
responsible for the performance of obligations arising from Community law within its territory
pursuant to Article 5 and Articles 169 to 171 of the Treaty, has not entrusted or left to private
individuals the duty of ensuring that such obligations are complied with in the sphere in question in
this case.

[13] It follows from these considerations that the link between the arbitration procedure in this
instance and the organization of legal remedies through the courts in the Member State in question
is not sufficiently close for the arbitrator to be considered as a 'court or tribunal of a Member State'
within the meaning of Article 177.

Doris Saltzmann (Case C-178/99)
[2001] ECR I-4421, Court of Justice of the European Communities

[13] In order to determine whether a referring body is a court or tribunal within the meaning of
Article 177 of the Treaty, which is a question governed by Community law alone, the Court takes
account of a number of factors, such as whether the body is established by law, whether it is
permanent, whether its jurisdiction is compulsory, whether its procedure is *inter partes*, whether it
applies rules of law and whether it is independent (see, in particular, Case C-54/96 *Dorsch Consult*
[1997] ECR I-4961, paragraph 23, and the case law cited therein, and in Joined Cases C-110/98 to
C-147/98 *Gabalfrisa and Others* [2000] ECR I-1577, paragraph 33).

NOTE
For further illustrations of the Court's approach to the determination of whether a referring
body is a court or tribunal for these purposes, see Case C-111/94 *Job Centre Coop. arl* [1995] ECR
I-3361 (referral by administrative body performing a non-judicial function inadmissible, though
an appeal to a court against the decision of the administrative body prompted an admissible
reference in Case C-55/96 *Job Centre Coop. arl* [1997] ECR I-7119; Case C-134/97 *Victoria
Film A/S* [1998] ECR I-7023 (referral by body within Swedish tax administration inadmissible);
Case C-516/99 *Walter Schmid* judgment of 30 May 2002 (body's absence of independence from
the tax administration fatal – referral inadmissible).

SECTION 5: **THE OBLIGATION TO REFER AND THE DOCTRINE OF**
ACTE CLAIR

Article 234 makes a distinction in paragraphs 2 and 3 between courts which can refer and those which must. The obligation to refer latter category covers highest courts. Its function was explained by the Court as follows:

Hoffman la Roche v *Centrafarm* (Case 107/76)
[1977] ECR 957, Court of Justice of the European Communities

[5] In the context of Article 177, whose purpose is to ensure that Community law is interpreted and applied in a uniform manner in all the Member States, the particular objective of the third paragraph is to prevent a body of national case law not in accord with the rules of Community law from coming into existence in any Member State . . .

NOTE

A question arises as to which courts are subject to this obligation to refer. The highest courts within Member States are obviously covered by the obligation. But what of a court whose decisions will be examined by a superior court only if that superior court declares an appeal to be admissible?

Kenny Roland Lyckeskog (Case C-99/00)
Judgment of 4 June 2002, Court of Justice of the European Communities

[14] The obligation on national courts against whose decisions there is no judicial remedy to refer a question to the Court for a preliminary ruling has its basis in the cooperation established, in order to ensure the proper application and uniform interpretation of Community law in all the Member States, between national courts, as courts responsible for applying Community law, and the Court. That obligation is in particular designed to prevent a body of national case law that is not in accordance with the rules of Community law from coming into existence in any Member State (see, *inter alia*, *Hoffmann-La Roche*, cited above, paragraph 5, and Case C-337/95 *Parfums Christian Dior* [1997] ECR I-6013, paragraph 25)

[15] That objective is secured when, subject to the limits accepted by the Court of Justice (*CILFIT*), supreme courts are bound by this obligation to refer (*Parfums Christian Dior*, cited above) as is any other national court or tribunal against whose decisions there is no judicial remedy under national law (Joined Cases 28/62, 29/62 and 30/62 *Da Costa en Schaake* [1963] ECR 31).

[16] Decisions of a national appellate court which can be challenged by the parties before a supreme court are not decisions of a 'court or tribunal of a Member State against whose decisions there is no judicial remedy under national law' within the meaning of Article 234 EC. The fact that examination of the merits of such appeals is subject to a prior declaration of admissibility by the supreme court does not have the effect of depriving the parties of a judicial remedy.

[17] That is so under the Swedish system. The parties always have the right to appeal to the Högsta domstol against the judgment of a hovrätt, which cannot therefore be classified as a court delivering a decision against which there is no judicial remedy. Under Paragraph 10 of Chapter 54 of the Rättegångsbalk, the Högsta domstol may issue a declaration of admissibility if it is important for guidance as to the application of the law that the appeal be examined by that court. Thus, uncertainty as to the interpretation of the law applicable, including Community law, may give rise to review, at last instance, by the supreme court.

[18] If a question arises as to the interpretation or validity of a rule of Community law, the supreme court will be under an obligation, pursuant to the third paragraph of Article 234 EC, to refer a question to the Court of Justice for a preliminary ruling either at the stage of the examination of admissibility or at a later stage.

[19] The answer to the first question must therefore be that, where the decisions of a national court or tribunal can be appealed to the supreme court under conditions such as those that apply to decisions of the referring court in the present case, that court or tribunal is not under the obligation referred to in the third paragraph of Article 234 EC.

NOTE

But even highest courts, so defined, need not refer if the doctrine of *acte clair* applies. The European Court carefully explained the nature of this doctrine in the following case.

CILFIT (Case 283/81)
[1982] ECR 3415, Court of Justice of the European Communities

[1] By order of 27 March 1981, which was received at the Court on 31 October 1981, the Corte Suprema di Cassazione [Supreme Court of Cassation] referred to the Court of Justice for a preliminary ruling under Article 177 of the EEC Treaty a question on the interpretation of the third paragraph of Article 177 of the EEC Treaty.

[2] That question was raised in connection with a dispute between wool importers and the Italian Ministry of Health concerning the payment of a fixed health inspection levy in respect of wool imported from outside the Community. The firms concerned relied on Regulation (EEC) No 827/68 of 28 June 1968 on the common organization of the market in certain products listed in Annex II to the Treaty (Official Journal, English Special Edition 1968 (I) p.209). Article 2(2) of that regulation prohibits Member States from levying any charge having an effect equivalent to a customs duty on imported 'animal products', not specified or included elsewhere, classified under heading 05.15 of the Common Customs Tariff. Against that argument the Ministry for Health contended that wool is not included in Annex II to the Treaty and is therefore not subject to a common organization of agricultural markets.

[3] The Ministry of Health infers from those circumstances that the answer to the question concerning the interpretation of the measure adopted by the Community institutions is so obvious as to rule out the possibility of there being any interpretative doubt and thus obviates the need to refer the matter to the Court of Justice for a preliminary ruling. However, the companies concerned maintain that since a question concerning the interpretation of a regulation has been raised before the Corte Suprema di Cassazione, against whose decisions there is no judicial remedy under national law, that court cannot, according to the terms of the third paragraph of Article 177, escape the obligation to bring the matter before the Court of Justice.

[4] Faced with those conflicting arguments, the Corte Suprema di Cassazione referred to the Court the following question for a preliminary ruling:

'Does the third paragraph of Article 177 of the EEC Treaty, which provides that where any question of the same kind as those listed in the first paragraph of that article is raised in a case pending before a national court or tribunal against whose decisions there is no judicial remedy under national law that court or tribunal must bring the matter before the Court of Justice, lay down an obligation so to submit the case which precludes the national court from determining whether the question raised is justified or does it, and if so within what limits, make that obligation conditional on the prior finding of a reasonable interpretative doubt?'

[5] In order to answer that question it is necessary to take account of the system established by Article 177, which confers jurisdiction on the Court of Justice to give preliminary rulings on, *inter alia*, the interpretation of the Treaty and the measures adopted by the institutions of the Community.

[6] The second paragraph of that article provides that any court or tribunal of a Member State *may*, if it considers that a decision on a question of interpretation is necessary to enable it to give judgment, request the Court of Justice to give a ruling thereon. The third paragraph of that article provides that, where a question of interpretation is raised in a case pending before a court or tribunal of a Member State against whose decisions there is no judicial remedy under national law, that court or tribunal *shall* bring the matter before the Court of Justice.

[7] That obligation to refer a matter to the Court of Justice is based on cooperation, established with a view to ensuring the proper application and uniform interpretation of Community law in all the Member States, between national courts, in their capacity as courts responsible for the application of Community law, and the Court of Justice. More particularly, the third paragraph of Article 177 seeks to prevent the occurrence within the Community of divergences in judicial decisions on questions of Community law. The scope of that obligation must therefore be assessed, in view of those objectives, by reference to the powers of the national courts, on the one hand, and those of the Court of Justice, on the other, where such a question of interpretation is raised within the meaning of Article 177.

[8] In this connection, it is necessary to define the meaning for the purposes of Community law of the expression 'where any such question is raised' in order to determine the circumstances in which a national court or tribunal against whose decisions there is no judicial remedy under national law is obliged to bring a matter before the Court of Justice.

[9] In this regard, it must in the first place be pointed out that Article 177 does not constitute a means of redress available to the parties to a case pending before a national court or tribunal. Therefore the mere fact that a party contends that the dispute gives rise to a question concerning the inter-pretation of Community law does not mean that the court or tribunal concerned is compelled to consider that a question has been raised within the meaning of Article 177. On the other hand, a national court or tribunal may, in an appropriate case, refer a matter to the Court of Justice of its own motion.

[10] Secondly, it follows from the relationship between the second and third paragraphs of Article 177 that the courts or tribunals referred to in the third paragraph have the same discretion as any other national court or tribunal to ascertain whether a decision on a question of Community law is necessary to enable them to give judgment. Accordingly, those courts or tribunals are not obliged to refer to the Court of Justice a question concerning the interpretation of Community law raised before them if that question is not relevant, that is to say, if the answer to that question, regardless of what it may be, can in no way affect the outcome of the case.

[11] If, however, those courts or tribunals consider that recourse to Community law is necessary to enable them to decide a case, Article 177 imposes an obligation on them to refer to the Court of Justice any question of interpretation which may arise.

[12] The question submitted by the Corte di Cassazione seeks to ascertain whether, in certain circumstances, the obligation laid down by the third paragraph of Article 177 might none the less be subject to certain restrictions.

[13] It must be remembered in this connection that in its judgment of 27 March 1963 in Joined Cases 28 to 30/62 (*Da Costa* v *Nederlandse Belastingadministratie* [1963] ECR 31) the Court ruled that: 'Although the third paragraph of Article 177 unreservedly requires courts or tribunals of a Member State against whose decisions there is no judicial remedy under national law . . . to refer to the Court every question of interpretation raised before them, the authority of an interpretation under Article 177 already given by the Court may deprive the obligation of its purpose and thus empty it of its substance. Such is the case especially when the question raised is materially identical with a question which has already been the subject of a preliminary ruling in a similar case.'

[14] The same effect, as regards the limits set to the obligation laid down by the third paragraph of Article 177, may be produced where previous decisions of the Court have already dealt with the point of law in question, irrespective of the nature of the proceedings which led to those decisions, even though the questions at issue are not strictly identical.

[15] However, it must not be forgotten that in all such circumstances national courts and tribunals, including those referred to in the third paragraph of Article 177, remain entirely at liberty to bring a matter before the Court of Justice if they consider it appropriate to do so.

[16] Finally, the correct application of Community law may be so obvious as to leave no scope for any reasonable doubt as to the manner in which the question raised is to be resolved. Before it comes to

the conclusion that such is the case, the national court or tribunal must be convinced that the matter is equally obvious to the courts of the other Member States and to the Court of Justice. Only if those conditions are satisfied, may the national court or tribunal refrain from submitting the question to the Court of Justice and take upon itself the responsibility for resolving it.

[17] However, the existence of such a possibility must be assessed on the basis of the characteristic features of Community law and the particular difficulties to which its interpretation gives rise.

[18] To begin with, it must be borne in mind that Community legislation is drafted in several languages and that the different language versions are all equally authentic. An interpretation of a provision of Community law thus involves a comparison of the different language versions.

[19] It must also be borne in mind, even where the different language versions are entirely in accord with one another, that Community law uses terminology which is peculiar to it. Furthermore, it must be emphasised that legal concepts do not necessarily have the same meaning in Community law and in the law of the various Member States.

[20] Finally, every provision of Community law must be placed in its context and interpreted in the light of the provisions of Community law as a whole, regard being had to the objectives thereof and to its State of evolution at the date on which the provision in question is to be applied.

[21] In the light of all those considerations, the answer to the question submitted by the Corte Suprema di Cassazione must be that the third paragraph of Article 177 of the EEC Treaty is to be interpreted as meaning that a court or tribunal against whose decisions there is no judicial remedy under national law is required, where a question of Community law is raised before it, to comply with its obligation to bring the matter before the Court of Justice, unless it has established that the question raised is irrelevant or that the Community provision in question has already been interpreted by the Court or that the correct application of Community law is so obvious as to leave no scope for any reasonable doubt. The existence of such a possibility must be assessed in the light of the specific characteristics of Community law, the particular difficulties to which its interpretation gives rise and the risk of divergences in judicial decisions within the Community.

■ QUESTION

'The real strategy of *CILFIT* is not to incorporate an *acte clair* concept into Community law. It is to call the national judiciaries to circumspection when they are faced with problems of interpretation and application of Community law' (H. Rasmussen (1984) 9 EL Rev 242). Discuss.

NOTE
The Court explored these realms in the unusual context of the Benelux Court in Case C-337/95 *Parfums Christian Dior SA and Parfums Christian Dior BV v Evora BV* [1997] ECR I-6013, a reference made by the Dutch Hoge Raad (Supreme Court) and cited in the above extract from the judgment in *Lyckeskog* (Case C-99/00). The Benelux Court was established by a 1965 Treaty between Belgium, Luxembourg, and The Netherlands. Given that the Benelux Court interprets Community rules in the performance of its functions, it was treated by the European Court in *Dior* as capable of making preliminary references in order to ensure the uniform interpretation of Community law. The Court, citing *CILFIT*, then added that in so far as no appeal lies against its decisions, the Benelux Court may be *obliged* to make a reference. However, the authority of an interpretation provided by the Court under the procedure may deprive that obligation of its purpose and thus empty it of its substance. In the Benelux context, this may arise where, prior to making a reference to the Benelux Court, a national court has already made use of its power to submit the question raised to Luxembourg. The obligation imposed by the third paragraph of Article 234 loses its purpose when the question raised is 'substantially the same' as a question already the subject of a preliminary ruling in the same national proceedings.

SECTION 6: **THE POWER TO REFER**

When should a lower court exercise its Article 234(2) discretion to make a reference?

NOTES

1. The European Court's approach is distinctly flexible. In acknowledging 'considerations of procedural organization and efficiency to be weighed by [the national] court', the ruling in *Irish Creamery Milk Suppliers* (Case 36/80, at p.190 above) shows an openness on the part of the European Court and a concern not to raise technical obstacles to referral. Remember also how in *CILFIT* (Case 283/81) the Court pointed out the perils of non-referral (p.204 above).

2. In the English courts, the notoriously mechanistic attitude expounded by Lord Denning MR in *Bulmer* v *Bollinger SA* [1974] 3 WLR 202 has been superseded by a more flexible, *communautaire* approach. In *Customs and Excise Commissioners* v *Samex* [1983] 1 All ER 1042, Bingham J (as he then was) made a reference to Luxembourg after conceding

   > the advantages enjoyed by the Court of Justice. It has a panoramic view of the Community and its institutions, a detailed knowledge of the treaties and of much subordinate legislation made under them, and an intimate familiarity with the functioning of the Community market which no national judge denied the collective experience of the Court of Justice could hope to achieve.

   For discussion see D. Chalmers, 'The Application of Community Law in the United Kingdom, 1994–1998' (2000) 37 CML Rev 83; L. Gormley, 'References for a Preliminary Ruling: Article 234 EC from the United Kingdom Viewpoint' (2002) 66 *Rabels Z* 459.

3. In one respect, however, the European Court has decided to abandon its flexible approach to the power to refer. This is where the *validity* of Community acts is at stake. In the next case it takes to itself an important jurisdiction, thus insisting on referral.

Firma Foto Frost v *HZA Lubeck Ost* (Case 314/85)
[1987] ECR 4199, Court of Justice of the European Communities

Foto Frost instituted proceedings before the German courts in order to secure the annulment of a demand by the customs authorities for payment of duties on imported binoculars. The basis for the customs authorities' demand was a Commission Decision addressed to Germany. The basis of Foto Frost's application was that the Commission Decision was invalid. The referring court (*Finanzgericht*) addresses in its first question the important jurisdictional point.

[11] In its first question the Finanzgericht asks whether it itself is competent to declare invalid a Commission decision such as the decision of 6 May 1983. It casts doubt on the validity of that decision on the ground that all the requirements laid down by Article 5(2) of Regulation No 1697/79 for taking no action for the post-clearance recovery of duty seem to be fulfilled in this case. However, it considers that in view of the division of jurisdiction between the Court of Justice and the national courts set out in Article 177 of the EEC Treaty only the Court of Justice is competent to declare invalid acts of the Community institutions.

[12] Article 177 confers on the Court jurisdiction to give preliminary rulings on the interpretation of the Treaty and of acts of the Community institutions and on the validity of such acts. The second paragraph of that article provides that national courts may refer such questions to the Court and the third paragraph of that article puts them under an obligation to do so where there is no judicial remedy under national law against their decisions.

[13] In enabling national courts, against those decisions where there is a judicial remedy under national law, to refer to the Court for a preliminary ruling questions on interpretation or validity,

Article 177 did not settle the question whether those courts themselves may declare that acts of Community institutions are invalid.

[14] Those courts may consider the validity of a Community act and, if they consider that the grounds put forward before them by the parties in support of invalidity are unfounded, they may reject them, concluding that the measure is completely valid. By taking that action they are not calling into question the existence of the Community measure.

[15] On the other hand, those courts do not have the power to declare acts of the Community institutions invalid. As the Court emphasised in the judgment of 13 May 1981 in Case 66/80 *International Chemical Corporation* v *Amministrazione delle Finanze* [1981] ECR 1191, the main purpose of the powers accorded to the Court by Article 177 is to ensure that Community law is applied uniformly by national courts. That requirement of uniformity is particularly imperative when the validity of a Community act is in question. Divergences between courts in the Member States as to the validity of Community acts would be liable to place in jeopardy the very unity of the Community legal order and detract from the fundamental requirement of legal certainty.

[16] The same conclusion is dictated by consideration of the necessary coherence of the system of judicial protection established by the Treaty. In that regard it must be observed that requests for preliminary rulings, like actions for annulment, constitute means for reviewing the legality of acts of the Community institutions. As the Court pointed out in its judgment of 23 April 1986 in Case 294/83 *Partiécologiste 'les Verts'* v *European Parliament* [1986] ECR 1339), 'in Articles 173 and 184, on the one hand, and in Article 177, on the other, the Treaty established a complete system of legal remedies and procedures designed to permit the Court of Justice to review the legality of measures adopted by the institutions'.

[17] Since Article 173 [now 230: see Chapter 8] gives the Court exclusive jurisdiction to declare void an act of a Community institution, the coherence of the system requires that where the validity of a Community act is challenged before a national court the power to declare the act invalid must also be reserved to the Court of Justice.

[18] It must also be emphasised that the Court of Justice is in the best position to decide on the validity of Community acts. Under Article 20 of the Protocol on the Statute of the Court of Justice of the EEC, Community institutions whose acts are challenged are entitled to participate in the proceedings in order to defend the validity of the acts in question. Furthermore, under the second paragraph of Article 21 of that Protocol the Court may require the Member States and institutions which are not participating in the proceedings to supply all information which it considers necessary for the purposes of the case before it.

[19] It should be added that the rule that national courts may not themselves declare Community acts invalid may have to be qualified in certain circumstances in the case of proceedings relating to an application for interim measures; however, that case is not referred to in the national court's question.

[20] The answer to the first question must therefore be that the national courts have no jurisdiction themselves to declare that acts of Community institutions are invalid.

The Court proceeded to hold the contested Commission Decision invalid.

■ QUESTION

Why did the Court deny national courts competence to declare Community acts invalid? Read G. Bebr (1988) 25 CML Rev 667.

NOTES
1. *Foto-Frost* (Case 314/85) involved a challenge to the validity of a Community provision before a national court, which duly sparked a preliminary reference. The next Chapter examines in more depth the ways in which Article 234 can be used as a device to support such an indirect challenge to the legality of Community legislation. The matter of interim protection, referred

to in paragraph 19 of *Foto-Frost*, has now been elucidated in subsequent case law (p.255 below). The matter is also touched on in the next subsection of this Chapter.

2. The case law considered at p.196 above concerning the inadmissibility of irrelevant or hypothetical questions is in principle equally applicable to references concerning the validity of Community acts. But it is in any circumstances exceptional for the Court to reject a reference and in *R v Secretary of State, ex parte BAT and Imperial Tobacco* (Case C-491/01) judgment of 10 December 2002 the Court, faced with objections, nonetheless found that a reference concerning validity was admissible.

3. There are intriguing general questions about the nature of the relationship between national courts and the European Court under this procedure. The logic of the Court's reasoning in *Foto-Frost* (Case 314/85) appears to be that it would assert its own exclusive jurisdiction in all cases where the validity of Community acts are challenged, including those involving alleged interference with areas of exclusive national competence. Such litigation would be a great deal more constitutionally sensitive than the relatively technical matters at stake in *Foto-Frost* itself. The Court's approach in *Foto-Frost* offers a perfectly clear statement of EC law, but the willingness of national courts to accept with due deference the Court's claim to exclusive competence in the matter of the validity of Community acts is a question to which to return later, once the challenges to the Court's approach that have lately emerged among the national judiciaries who are expected to absorb and apply these rulings have been explored. Of particular interest will be the stance of the German *Bundesverfassungsgericht* p.686 below.

SECTION 7: **THE COURT'S NOTES FOR GUIDANCE**

In 1996 the Court issued guidelines on the use of what was then Article 177 EC, now Article 234 EC post-Amsterdam (p.12 above). These serve as a useful distillation of the principles of law and the practice explained in the course of this Chapter.

Note for guidance on references by national courts for preliminary rulings issued by the European Court of Justice

The development of the Community legal order is largely the result of cooperation between the Court of Justice of the European Communities and national courts and tribunals through the preliminary ruling procedure under Article 177 of the EC Treaty and the corresponding provisions of the ECSC and Euratom Treaties.[1]

In order to make this cooperation more effective, and so enable the Court of Justice better to meet the requirements of national courts by providing helpful answers to preliminary questions, this Note for Guidance is addressed to all interested parties, in particular to all national courts and tribunals.

It must be emphasised that the Note is for guidance only and has no binding or interpretative effect in relation to the provisions governing the preliminary ruling procedure. It merely contains practical information which, in the light of experience in applying the preliminary ruling procedure, may help to prevent the kind of difficulties which the Court has sometimes encountered.

---

1 A preliminary ruling procedure is also provided for by protocols to several conventions concluded by the Member States, in particular the Brussels Convention on Jurisdiction and the Enforcement of Judgments in Civil and Commercial Matters.

1. Any court or tribunal of a Member State may ask the Court of Justice to interpret a rule of Community law, whether contained in the Treaties or in acts of secondary law, if it considers that this is necessary for it to give judgment in a case pending before it.

Courts or tribunals against whose decisions there is no judicial remedy under national law must refer questions of interpretation arising before them to the Court of Justice, unless the Court has already ruled on the point or unless the correct application of the rule of Community law is obvious.[2]

2. The Court of Justice has jurisdiction to rule on the validity of acts of the Community institutions. National courts or tribunals may reject a plea challenging the validity of such an act. But where a national court (even one whose decision is still subject to appeal) intends to question the validity of a Community act, it must refer that question to the Court of Justice.[3]

Where, however, a national court or tribunal has serious doubts about the validity of a Community act on which a national measure is based, it may, in exceptional cases, temporarily suspend application of the latter measure or grant other interim relief with respect to it. It must then refer the question of validity to the Court of Justice, stating the reasons for which it considers that the Community act is not valid.[4]

3. Questions referred for a preliminary ruling must be limited to the interpretation or validity of a provision of Community law, since the Court of Justice does not have jurisdiction to interpret national law or assess its validity. It is for the referring court or tribunal to apply the relevant rule of Community law in the specific case pending before it.

4. The order of the national court or tribunal referring a question to the Court of Justice for a preliminary ruling may be in any form allowed by national procedural law. Reference of a question or questions to the Court of Justice generally involves stay of the national proceedings until the Court has given its ruling, but the decision to stay proceedings is one which it is for the national court alone to take in accordance with its own national law.

5. The order for reference containing the question or questions referred to the Court will have to be translated by the Court's translators into the other official languages of the Community. Questions concerning the interpretation or validity of Community law are frequently of general interest and the Member States and Community institutions are entitled to submit observations. It is therefore desirable that the reference should be drafted as clearly and precisely as possible.

6. The order for reference should contain a statement of reasons which is succinct but sufficiently complete to give the Court, and those to whom it must be notified (the Member States, the Commission and in certain cases the Council and the European Parliament), a clear understanding of the factual and legal context of the main proceedings.[5]

In particular, it should include:

— a statement of the facts which are essential to a full understanding of the legal significance of the main proceedings;
— an exposition of the national law which may be applicable;
— a statement of the reasons which have prompted the national court to refer the question or questions to the Court of Justice; and
— where appropriate, a summary of the arguments of the parties.

The aim should be to put the Court of Justice in a position to give the national court an answer which will be of assistance to it.

The order for reference should also be accompanied by copies of any documents needed for a proper understanding of the case, especially the text of the applicable national provisions. However, as the case-file or documents annexed to the order for reference are not always

---

2 Judgment in Case 283/81 *CILFIT* v *Ministry of Health* [1982] ECR 3415.

3 Judgment in Case 314/85 *Foto-Frost* v *Hauptzollamt Lübeck-Ost* [1987] ECR 4199.

4 Judgments in Joined Cases C-143/88 and C-92/89 *Zuckerfabrik Süderdithmarschen and Zuckerfabrik Soest* [1991] ECR I-415 and in Case C-465/93 *Atlanta Fruchthandelsgesselschaft* [1995] ECR I-3761.

5 E.g., intellectual property (trade marks, patents and industrial designs, etc.).

translated in full into the other official languages of the Community, the national court should ensure that the order for reference itself includes all the relevant information.

7. A national court or tribunal may refer a question to the Court of Justice as soon as it finds that a ruling on the point or points of interpretation or validity is necessary to enable it to give judgment. It must be stressed, however, that it is not for the Court of Justice to decide issues of fact or to resolve disputes as to the interpretation or application of rules of national law. It is therefore desirable that a decision to refer should not be taken until the national proceedings have reached a stage where the national court is able to define, if only as a working hypothesis, the factual and legal context of the question; on any view, the administration of justice is likely to be best served if the reference is not made until both sides have been heard.[6]

8. The order for reference and the relevant documents should be sent by the national court directly to the Court of Justice, by registered post, addressed to:

> The Registry
> Court of Justice of the European Communities
> L-2925 Luxembourg
> Telephone (352) 43031

The Court Registry will remain in contact with the national court until judgment is given, and will send copies of the various documents (written observations, Report for the Hearing, Opinion of the Advocate-General). The Court will also send its judgment to the national court. The Court would appreciate being informed about the application of its judgment in the national proceedings and being sent a copy of the national court's final decision.

9. Proceedings for a preliminary ruling before the Court of Justice are free of charge. The Court does not rule on costs.

NOTE

The Court is also able to use its *Rules of Procedure* to shape and clarify the management of the preliminary reference procedure. Familiarity with the *Rules* is therefore also helpful in understanding the practice. As mentioned above at p.199, in the current 2001 version (available at http://curia.eu.int) it is provided in Article 104(3) of the *Rules* that where the question asked is identical to one on which the Court has already ruled, where the answer may be clearly deduced from existing case law or where the answer admits of no reasonable doubt the Court may deal with the reference by an expedited procedure. It will in such circumstances issue a reasoned order rather than proceeding to judgment.

SECTION 8: **REFORMING THE COURT SYSTEM**

Institutional reform was the *leitmotif* of the intergovernmental conference that commenced in 2000 and ultimately generated the Treaty of Nice. The structure of the Court was on the agenda. The preliminary reference procedure was one of the main points for consideration in the Report of the Working Party on the Future of the European Communities' Court System established by the Commission under the Chairmanship of Ole Due, former President of the European Court, which was published in January 2000. On this report was based the Commission's contribution to the intergovernmental conference on reform of the Community courts. The success of the preliminary reference procedure was trumpeted, but adjustment proposed.

---

6 As provided by, for instance, Article 68(3) of the Treaty.

Reform of the Community Courts (additional Commission contribution to the Intergovernmental Conference on institutional reform), COM (2000) 109, 1 March 2000

a. Preliminary rulings

(i) Jurisdiction of the Court of Justice

The preliminary ruling procedure is undoubtedly the keystone of the Community's legal order. Forty years' experience have shown that it is the most effective means of securing the uniform application of Community law throughout the Union and that it is an exceptional factor for integration owing to the simple, direct dialogue which it establishes with national courts. The Commission considers that this regulating function, which is essential to the Community legal order, must therefore in principle be the exclusive responsibility of the Court of Justice.

The Working Party shares this opinion. But it proposes that the last sentence of Article 225(1) of the EC Treaty be deleted to give the CFI exceptional jurisdiction to give preliminary rulings in very specialised areas of Community law.[5] The Working Party considers that special categories of case, including preliminary questions in such areas, should be entrusted as a whole to the CFI and that the Court of Justice, as the supreme court of the Union, should become involved where appropriate only in appeals on points of law lodged by the Commission.[6]

This proposal will have to be examined in connection with any specific changes to jurisdiction that will have to be provided for in certain categories of special case, such as intellectual property proceedings.

(ii) Clarification of the roles of the Court of Justice and the national courts

To preserve the effectiveness of the preliminary ruling procedure, it is essential that the Court of Justice should be able to concentrate on genuinely new questions and give its judgments considerably sooner. To this end, the Commission believes it is necessary to amend Article 234 (ex Article 177) of the Treaty in order to clarify the distribution of jurisdiction between the Court of Justice and national courts.

1. The first amendment proposed seeks to give national courts greater responsibility as courts of ordinary law in Community matters. At present, this function is not expressly laid down in the Treaty. It can only be inferred from reading Articles 234 and 240 together. It is therefore essential to correct this omission by spelling out the introductory provision in Article 234, clearly stating that it is for the national courts in the first place to apply Community law to the cases before them and that they may consult the Court of Justice when faced with a specific problem of interpretation.

2. In similar vein, it could be worthwhile amending the second paragraph of Article 234, so as to invite national courts other than those of final instance to specify why they have doubts as to the meaning of the rule of Community law applicable in the case before them and why they feel the need to put a question to the Court of Justice. This provision could be accompanied by the requisite corollary changes to the Rules of Procedure.

3. As part of this clarification exercise, it is necessary, lastly, to insert in Article 234 the rule established in case-law whereby, **in cases of doubt as to the validity of a Community act**, all national courts must consult the Court of Justice since the latter has the monopoly of the review of Community legality.

The Commission does not feel it would be right to give flexibility to the obligation on courts of final instance to refer preliminary questions, currently laid down in the third paragraph of Article 234, requiring them to consult the Court of Justice only if the question were sufficiently important for Community law and if, after examination by the lower courts, there were still reasonable doubts as to the reply. The Commission considers that the advantages of such

---

5 E.g., intellectual property (trade marks, patents and industrial designs, etc.).

6 As provided by, for instance, Article 68(3) of the Treaty.

flexibility as far as the Court's workload is concerned are very slight and that there are real dangers for the uniform application of Community law, especially with enlargement on the horizon. It therefore thinks it is essential to stick with the current wording of the third paragraph of Article 234. Naturally, the flexibility introduced by case-law would continue to apply.

The Commission further wonders whether it might be worth harmonising the procedure for preliminary rulings in matters of free movement of persons (Title IV) with the ordinary procedure . . .

Proposed new wording

ARTICLE 234

1. **Subject to the provisions of this Article, the courts and tribunals of the Member States shall rule on the questions of Community law which they encounter in exercise of their national jurisdiction.**

   2. The Court of Justice shall have jurisdiction to give preliminary rulings concerning:

   (a) the interpretation of this Treaty,
   (b) the validity and interpretation of acts of the institutions of the Community and of the ECB;
   (c) the interpretation of the statutes of bodies established by an act of the Council, where those statutes so provide.

   3. Where such a question is raised before any national court or tribunal, that court or tribunal may, if it considers that a decision on the question is necessary to enable it to give a judgement, request the Court of Justice to give a ruling thereon. **In that event, it shall specify why the validity or interpretation of the rule of Community law raises difficulties in the case before it.**

   4. Where any such question is raised in a case pending before a national court or tribunal against whose decisions there is no judicial remedy under national law, that court or tribunal shall bring the matter before the Court of Justice.

   5. **A national court or tribunal must consult the Court of Justice where it proposes not to apply an act of Community law on the grounds that the latter is invalid.**

■ QUESTIONS

1. It is mentioned above (p.198) that the Treaty of Nice made relatively technical adjustments to Article 225 in order to provide for the possible involvement of the Court of First Instance in dealing with preliminary references. But at Nice the text of Article 234 itself was left untouched. Consider the strengths and weaknesses of this (rejected) proposed new wording. Was the Nice Treaty too conservative?

2. 'Preliminary rulings should be replaced by *post hoc* and selective review by the Court of Justice of national court decisions' (P. Allott, 'Preliminary Rulings – Another Infant Disease' (2000) 25 EL Rev 538). Discuss.

3. Read the following decisions. Comment critically on their application of Article 234 of the EC Treaty. What do the decisions tell you about the strengths and weaknesses of the preliminary reference procedure? Would the proposals extracted above, if adopted at some time in the future, make any difference to the way in which such cases would be dealt with by national courts?

   R v Henn and Darby; contrast the Court of Appeal [1978] 1 WLR 1031 with the House of Lords [1981] AC 850, [1980] 2 WLR 597;

Minister of the Interior v *Cohn Bendit* [1980] 1 CMLR 543 (p.147 above);

Procurator Fiscal, Stranraer v *Marshall* [1988] 1 CMLR 657 (this case eventually reached the Court as Case 370/88 via the High Court in Edinburgh, and the Court's decision is reported at [1990] ECR I-4071);

R v *International Stock Exchange, ex parte Else Ltd* [1993] 1 All ER 420;

Arsenal Football Club v *Reed* ([2002] EWHC 2695, available via http://www.courtservice.gov.uk/judgmentsfiles/j1493/arsenal_v_reed.htm); currently on appeal.

4. 'Two somewhat contradictory principles – the effectiveness of Community law and the procedural autonomy of the State – must be reconciled. The result is that the direct effect of Community law is to some extent restricted while national autonomy must sometimes yield to the requirements of Community law'. (R. Kovar, *Thirty Years of Community Law* (Luxembourg: Office for Official Publications of the ECs, 1983), p.146). Discuss.

FURTHER READING

Arnull, A., 'The Evolution of the Court's Jurisdiction under Article 177 EEC' (1993) 18 EL Rev 129.

Barnard, C. and Sharpston, E., 'The Changing Face of Article 177 References' (1997) 34 CML Rev 1113.

De La Mare, T., 'Article 177 in Social and Political Context', in Craig, P. and de Búrca, G., *The Evolution of EU Law* (Oxford: OUP, 1999), Ch. 6.

Dyrberg, P., 'What Should the Court of Justice be Doing?' (2001) 26 EL Rev 291.

Edward, D., 'Reform of Article 234 Procedure: the Limits of the Possible', in O'Keeffe, D. (ed), *Judicial Review in European Union Law: Liber Amicorum Gordon Slynn* (The Hague: Kluwer, 2000), Ch. 9.

Johnston, A., 'Judicial Reform and the Treaty of Nice' (2001) 38 CML Rev 499.

Mancini, F., and Keeling, D., 'From *CILFIT* to *ERT*: the Constitutional Challenge Facing the European Court' (1991) 11 YEL 1.

O'Keeffe, D., 'Is the Spirit of Article 177 Under Attack?' (1998) 23 EL Rev 509.

Rasmussen, H., 'Remedying the Crumbling EC Judicial System' (2000) 37 CML Rev 1071.

Tridimas, T., 'Knocking on Heaven's Door: Fragmentation, Efficiency and Defiance in the Preliminary Reference Procedure' (2003) 40 CML Rev 9.

Voss, R., 'The National Perception of the Court of First Instance and the European Court of Justice' (1993) 30 CML Rev 1119.

NOTE

For additional material and resources see the Companion Website at: www.oup.co.uk/best.textbooks/law/weatherill6e

8

Control of Community Institutions

SECTION 1: **INTRODUCTION**

All legal systems contain administrative law and a law of remedies in some form. The substance of the Community's system therefore deserves attention, but it should neither be considered unique nor be viewed in isolation. Its study can be enriched by drawing comparisons with other national and international systems. However, what is of especial interest is the pattern of development of the Community legal order. This has occurred in a fashion which *is* peculiar to the Community. The original structure owed a great deal to French administrative law traditions. The Community legal order still retains many of these features but has increasingly developed a life of its own, drawing on diverse national traditions. Under the influence of the Court, it has evolved along distinctive lines in response to the needs of the institutional and constitutional structures of the maturing Community.

And it is, almost exclusively, the Community, rather than the non-EC elements of the Union, that is the subject of examination in this Chapter. As explained in Chapter 2, the Court is able to police the line of demarcation between the EC pillar and other forms of co-operation pursued under the EU mantle (Case C-170/96 *Commission* v *Council* [1998] ECR I-2763, p.53), but the Treaty confers on the Court only a severely limited jurisdiction outside the EC 'pillar' (p.10).

The acts of the Community institutions may be supervised at Community level through proceedings before the Court of Justice of the European Communities or, since 1989, the Court of First Instance, which enjoys only limited jurisdiction. Article 230 (Article 173 pre-Amsterdam) provides an action to annul Community acts. Article 232 (Article 175 pre-Amsterdam) provides a complementary action aimed at controlling failure to act. Article 241 (Article 184 pre-Amsterdam) allows a measure to be challenged indirectly in an action brought against another measure. Articles 235 and 288 (Articles 178 and 215 respectively pre-Amsterdam) allow claims to be brought against the Community institutions for compensation for loss suffered as a result of unlawful action. In some circumstances, however, it will be possible to challenge the validity of Community acts without the need to institute a direct challenge before the Court in Luxembourg. Provided a national cause of action can be established, it may be possible to claim before a national tribunal that a relevant Community act is unlawful. Typically this will arise where national authorities are responsible for the implementation of Community legislation. A challenge at national level to the national authorities' acts will involve a plea that the legal basis for the act, Community legislation, is invalid. Where enforcement before a national court is in issue, the bridge between the action at national level and proceedings at Community level is the Article 234 procedure (Article 177 pre-Amsterdam). It will be recalled from the previous Chapter that Article 234 ensures that points of Community law raised at national level are interpreted authoritatively at Community level. This is essential in order to preserve the uniformity and integrity of the Community legal order.

The inter-relationship between remedies may seem complicated, but the central point is that the Court has consistently endeavoured to treat the several strands as contributions to a coherent whole. There is a complete system of remedies.

Parti Ecologiste 'Les Verts' v Parliament (Case 294/83)
[1986] ECR 1339, Court of Justice of the European Communities

[23] It must first be emphasised in this regard that the European Economic Community is a Community based on the rule of law, inasmuch as neither its Member States nor its institutions can avoid a review of the question whether the measures adopted by them are in conformity with the basic constitutional charter, the Treaty. In particular, in Articles 173 [now 230] and 184 [now 241], on the one hand, and in Article 177 [now 234], on the other, the Treaty established a complete system of legal remedies and procedures designed to permit the Court of Justice to review the legality of measures adopted by the institutions. Natural and legal persons are thus protected against the application to them of general measures which they cannot contest directly before the Court by reason of the special conditions of admissibility laid down in the second paragraph of Article 173 [now the fourth paragraph of Article 230] of the Treaty. Where the Community institutions are responsible for the administrative implementation of such measures, natural or legal persons may bring a direct action before the Court against implementing measures which are addressed to them or which are of direct and individual concern to them and, in support of such an action, plead the illegality of the general measure on which they are based. Where implementation is a matter for the national authorities, such persons may plead the invalidity of general measures before the national courts and cause the latter to request the Court of Justice for a preliminary ruling.

R v Secretary of State, ex parte BAT and Imperial Tobacco (Case C-491/01)
Judgment of 10 December 2002, Court of Justice of the European Communities

[39] . . . in the complete system of legal remedies and procedures established by the EC Treaty with a view to ensuring judicial review of the legality of acts of the institutions, where natural or legal persons cannot, by reason of the conditions for admissibility laid down in the fourth paragraph of that article [Article 230], directly challenge Community measures of general application, they are able, depending on the case, either indirectly to plead the invalidity of such acts before the Community judicature under Article 241 EC or to do so before the national courts and ask them, since they have no jurisdiction themselves to declare those measures invalid, to make a reference to the Court of Justice for a preliminary ruling on validity . . .

NOTE
This quest for a 'complete system' of remedies within a Community based on the rule of law governs the Court's approach to the interpretation of each relevant Treaty provision. Fixing the scope of one source of judicial protection may be influenced by the possibilities and limitations under another.

SECTION 2: **ARTICLE 230**

Article 230 provides a procedure whereby Community acts may be annulled by the European Court.

ARTICLE 230 EC

The Court of Justice shall review the legality of acts adopted jointly by the European Parliament and the Council, of acts of the Council, of the Commission and of the ECB, other than recommendations and opinions, and of acts of the European Parliament intended to produce legal effects vis-à -vis third parties.

It shall for this purpose have jurisdiction in actions brought by a Member State, the European Parliament, the Council or the Commission on grounds of lack of competence, infringement of an essential procedural requirement, infringement of this Treaty or of any rule of law relating to its application, or misuse of powers.

The Court of Justice shall have jurisdiction under the same conditions in actions brought by the Court of Auditors and by the ECB for the purpose of protecting their prerogatives.

Any natural or legal person may, under the same conditions, institute proceedings against a decision addressed to that person or against a decision which, although in the form of a regulation or a decision addressed to another person, is of direct and individual concern to the former.

The proceedings provided for in this article shall be instituted within two months of the publication of the measure, or of its notification to the plaintiff, or, in the absence thereof, of the day on which it came to the knowledge of the latter, as the case may be.

Article 231 specifies the consequences and offers the Court some flexibility in its rulings.

ARTICLE 231 EC

If the action is well founded, the Court of Justice shall declare the act concerned to be void.

In the case of a regulation, however, the Court of Justice shall, if it considers this necessary, state which of the effects of the regulation which it has declared void shall be considered as definitive.

NOTE

The case law which has arisen under Article 230 is vast, and this selection is designed merely to draw out the main principles. However, perhaps the most useful starting point is the general observation that most applications for the annulment of acts of the Community institutions fail. This is especially striking in relation to the fourth paragraph of Article 230, which contains restrictive standing rules which must be satisfied before the merits of an application for annulment will be heard.

....

A: Article 230, first to third paragraphs

It is useful first to return to a case already considered in Chapter 2, in order to appreciate the nature of acts susceptible to review by the Court under this procedure.

Commission v *Council* (Case 22/70)
[1971] ECR 263, Court of Justice of the European Communities

The Member States had participated in the conclusion of the AETR/ERTA (European Road Transport Agreement). They had expressed agreement to coordinate their approach to the ERTA in a resolution adopted at an EEC Council meeting on 20 March 1970. The Commission formed the view that the matter fell within the competence of the Community, not the individual Member States. In order to test its view of the correct allocation of competence in this field, it brought proceedings to annul the Council resolution. However, the resolution was not a Regulation, a Directive, or a Decision, acts mentioned in Article 189 of the EC Treaty (now Article 249 EC) which are clearly reviewable by the Court under Article 173 of the EC Treaty (now, after amendment, Article 230 EC). Was the resolution susceptible to review?

[34] The Council considers that the proceedings of 20 March 1970 do not constitute an act, within the meaning of the first sentence of the first paragraph of Article 173, the legality of which is open to review.

[35] Neither by their form nor by their subject-matter or content, it is argued, were these proceedings a regulation, a decision or a directive within the meaning of Article 189.

[36] They were really nothing more than a coordination of policies amongst Member States within the framework of the Council, and as such created no rights, imposed no obligations and did not modify any legal position.

[37] This is said to be the case more particularly because in the event of a dispute between the institutions admissibility has to be appraised with particular rigour.

[38] Under Article 173, the Court has a duty to review the legality 'of acts of the Council . . . other than recommendations or opinions'.

[39] Since the only matters excluded from the scope of the action for annulment open to the Member States and the institutions are 'recommendations or opinions' – which by the final paragraph of Article 189 are declared to have no binding force – Article 173 treats as acts open to review by the Court all measures adopted by the institutions which are intended to have legal force.

[40] The objective of this review is to ensure, as required by Article 164, observance of the law in the interpretation and application of the Treaty.

[41] It would be inconsistent with this objective to interpret the conditions under which the action is admissible so restrictively as to limit the availability of this procedure merely to the categories of measures referred to by Article 189.

[42] An action for annulment must therefore be available in the case of all measures adopted by the institutions, whatever their nature or form, which are intended to have legal effects.

NOTE
The Court then proceeded to determine that the resolution was of this character (see the extract at p.43 above). Remember also the Court's willingness to review (and annul) a Commission 'communication' in Case C-57/95 *France v Commission* [1997] ECR I-1627, p.364 below.

We here now appreciate the full significance of designating the resolution a legal 'act'; it was therefore susceptible to review. Several of the constitutional cases discussed in Part One of this book will be seen in this Part in the broader context of judicial review.

The second paragraph of Article 230 makes it clear that the Parliament is a 'privileged applicant' occupying the same status as the Council, Commission, or a Member State. It may bring an action without a need to show any particular interest in the matter. It has not always been so well-equipped. This is an improvement brought about by the Nice Treaty. Prior to Nice the Parliament was lodged alongside the Court of Auditors and the ECB in the third paragraph of Article 230. Prior to Maastricht the Parliament was completely absent from the list of privileged applicants and had to take its chances in the same way as other non-privileged applicants.

B: **Article 230, non-privileged applicants**

Whereas the first three paragraphs of Article 230 confer a special status on privileged applicants, most applicants for annulment must use the non-privileged route. The efficacy of this route is heavily qualified by the standing rules. The relevant paragraph of Article 230 is the fourth (p.217 above). Between 1993 and 1999 this was the fourth paragraph of Article 173. However, prior to the Maastricht amendments that paragraph was the second. Therefore references in the following cases and discussion of Article 173(2) EEC or to the second paragraph of Article 173 EEC should be read with an awareness that this became Article 173(4) EC in 1993; and that in turn this became Article 230(4) EC on the entry into force of the Amsterdam Treaty on 1 May 1999.

It should also be added at this point that in 1993 the Court of First Instance had transferred to it jurisdiction to hear applications brought by natural or legal persons except those concerned with anti-dumping matters (Dec 93/350 [1993] OJ L144/21). In 1994 jurisdiction over anti-dumping matters too was transferred to the CFI (Dec 94/149 [1994] OJ L66/29).

Not every act can be challenged. The act under attack must be defined carefully.

International Fruit Company v *Commission* (Cases 41–44/70)
[1971] ECR 411, Court of Justice of the European Communities

According to the Commission, the acts in question were of general application to the importation of dessert apples into the Community. They were Regulations. The applicant argued that it was picked out specially by the terms of the measures. When adopted, they referred back to importers who had already applied for import licences. The 'class' was closed and the applicant was within it. These were Decisions. The terms of what was the second paragraph of Article 173 EEC and is now the fourth paragraph of Article 230 EC (p.217 above) make it plain that it was essential to classify the act correctly in order to establish whether the applicant had standing to bring its challenge.

[16] It is indisputable that Regulation No 983/70 was adopted [on 28 May 1970] with a view on the one hand to the state of the market and on the other to the quantities of dessert apples for which applications for import licences had been made in the week ending on 22 May 1970.

[17] It follows that when the said regulation was adopted, the number of applications which could be affected by it was fixed.

[18] No new application could be added.

[19] To what extent, in percentage terms, the applications could be granted, depended on the total quantity in respect of which applications had been submitted.

[20] Accordingly, by providing that the system introduced by Article 1 of Regulation No 565/70 should be maintained for the relevant period, the Commission decided, even though it took account only of the quantities requested, on the subsequent fate of each application which had been lodged.

[21] Consequently, Article 1 of Regulation No 983/70 is not a provision of general application within the meaning of the second paragraph of Article 189 of the Treaty, but must be regarded as a conglomeration of individual decisions taken by the Commission under the guise of a regulation pursuant to Article 2(2) of Regulation No 459/70, each of which decisions affects the legal position of each author of an application for a licence.

[22] Thus, the decisions are of individual concern to the applicants.

NOTE

Here, again, one returns to the different types of Community legislation examined in Chapter 2, and realizes the true significance of the distinctions.

In addition to the fact that not every act can be challenged, the non-privileged route under Article 230 makes it clear that not every applicant is capable of making a challenge. Unless the addressee of a Decision, the applicant needs to establish 'direct and individual concern'. Unless this standing requirement is satisfied, the Court will not even examine the merits of the action for annulment.

....

C: **Individual concern**

The phrase is already familiar from the extract from *International Fruit Company* (Cases 41–44/70) above. The problem of defining 'individual concern' has been addressed in a string of cases arising out of *general* market regulation by the Community which adversely affects *individual* firms.

Plaumann v *Commission* (Case 25/62)

[1963] ECR 95, Court of Justice of the European Communities

Plaumann was a German importer of clementines. In importing clementines from third countries outside the Community, it had to pay a customs duty of 13%. This sum was due under the Community's Common Customs Tariff, part of the uniform trade policy which the Community presents to the wider world. The German government asked the Commission to authorise it to levy only 10% duty. The Commission refused. That refusal became the act challenged by Plaumann. No doubt Plaumann was prejudiced by it. But could it challenge it before the European Court given the limitations contained in what was then Article 173(2) EEC, now Article 230(4) EC?

Admissibility

Under the second paragraph of Article 173 of the EEC Treaty 'any natural or legal person may . . . institute proceedings against a decision . . . which, although in the form of . . . a decision addressed to another person, is of direct and individual concern to the former'. The defendant contends that the words 'other person' in this paragraph do not refer to Member States in their capacity as sovereign authorities and that individuals may not therefore bring an action for annulment against the decisions of the Commission or of the Council addressed to Member States.

However the second paragraph of Article 173 does allow an individual to bring an action against decisions addressed to 'another person' which are of direct and individual concern to the former, but this Article neither defines nor limits the scope of these words. The words and the natural meaning of this provision justify the broadest interpretation. Moreover provisions of the Treaty regarding the right of interested parties to bring an action must not be interpreted restrictively. Therefore, the Treaty being silent on the point, a limitation in this respect may not be presumed.

It follows that the defendant's argument cannot be regarded as well founded.

The defendant further contends that the contested decision is by its very nature a regulation in the form of an individual decision and therefore action against it is no more available to individuals than in the case of legislative measures of general application.

It follows however from Articles 189 and 191 of the EEC Treaty that decisions are characterized by the limited number of persons to whom they are addressed. In order to determine whether or not a measure constitutes a decision one must enquire whether that measure concerns specific persons.

The contested Decision was addressed to the government of the Federal Republic of Germany and refuses to grant it authorisation for the partial suspension of customs duties on certain products imported from third countries. Therefore the contested measure must be regarded as a decision referring to a particular person and binding that person alone.

Under the second paragraph of Article 173 of the Treaty private individuals may institute proceedings for annulment against decisions which, although addressed to another person, are of direct and individual concern to them, but in the present case the defendant denies that the contested decision is of direct and individual concern to the applicant.

It is appropriate in the first place to examine whether the second requirement of admissibility is fulfilled because, if the applicant is not individually concerned by the decision, it becomes unnecessary to enquire whether he is directly concerned.

Persons other than those to whom a decision is addressed may only claim to be individually concerned if that decision affects them by reason of certain attributes which are peculiar to them or by reason of circumstances in which they are differentiated from all other persons and by virtue of these factors distinguishes them individually just as in the case of the person addressed. In the present case the applicant is affected by the disputed Decision as an importer of clementines, that is to say, by reason of a commercial activity which may at any time be practised by any person and is not therefore such as to distinguish the applicant in relation to the contested Decision as in the case of the addressee.

For these reasons the present action for annulment must be declared inadmissible.

NOTE

A string of cases have been decided in similar fashion, to the detriment of the applicant.

Calpak SpA v *Commission* (Cases 789 and 790/79)
[1980] ECR 1949, Court of Justice of the European Communities

The applicant, an Italian firm, sought annulment under Article 173 of the EC Treaty (now, after amendment, Article 230 EC) of Regulations governing the grant of production aid for Williams pears preserved in syrup. It observed that an identifiable class of producers, including the applicant itself, was affected by the measure. It added that, even within that group it was especially prejudiced, because the Commission's aid was fixed according to production in 1978/79 when Italian production was unusually low. *Plaumann* was a Decision addressed to another; here is a prima facie Regulation. The issue, however, is the same; does the applicant have individual concern in the matter? The Court first explains the Commission's view and then disposes of the application.

[6] The Commission's main contention is that as the disputed provisions were adopted in the form of regulations their annulment may only be sought if their content shows them to be, in fact, decisions. But in the Commission's view the provisions in question, which lay down rules of general application, are truly in the nature of regulations within the meaning of Article 189 of the Treaty. By selecting the 1978/79 marketing year as the reference period the Commission's intention was to limit and stabilize production at a level as low as that of that year. It is said to be possible, but certainly not indefensible that such a restriction has a greater incidence upon marginal producers such as the applicants than, for example, upon co-operatives, but that does not mean that the applicants are individually concerned within the meaning of the second paragraph of Article 173, which hypothesis the Commission denies in any case.

[7] The second paragraph of Article 173 empowers individuals to contest, *inter alia*, any decision which, although in the form of a regulation, is of direct and individual concern to them. The objective of that provision is in particular to prevent the Community institutions from being in a position, merely by choosing the form of a regulation, to exclude an application by an individual against a decision which concerns him directly and individually; it therefore stipulates that the choice of form cannot change the nature of the measure.

[8] By virtue of the second paragraph of Article 189 of the Treaty the criterion for distinguishing between a regulation and a decision is whether the measure at issue is of general application or not.

As the amendment to Regulation No 1530/78 made by Article 1(3) of Regulation No 1732/79 concerning the information to be submitted in support of the application for aid is merely the natural consequence of the limitation imposed by Article 1 of Regulation No 1731/79, consideration need only be given to the nature of the latter provision.

[9] A provision which limits the granting of production aid for all producers in respect of a particular product to a uniform percentage of the quantity produced by them during a uniform preceding period is by nature a measure of general application within the meaning of Article 189 of the Treaty. In fact the measure applies to objectively determined situations and produces legal effects with regard to categories of persons described in a generalized and abstract manner. The nature of the measure as a regulation is not called in question by the mere fact that it is possible to determine the number or even the identity of the producers to be granted the aid which is limited thereby.

[10] Nor is the fact that the choice of reference period is particularly important for the applicants, whose production is subject to considerable variation from one marketing year to another as a result of their own programme of production, sufficient to entitle them to an individual remedy. Moreover, the applicants have not established the existence of circumstances such as to justify describing that choice – the conformity of which with the Council's regulations, and especially with the basic regulation, is only relevant to the substantive issues of the case – as a decision adopted specifically in relation to them and, as such, entitling them to institute proceedings under the second paragraph of Article 173.

[11] It follows that the objection raised by the Commission must be accepted as regards the applications for the annulment of the provisions in the two regulations in question.

The action was dismissed as inadmissible.

Union Deutsche Lebensmittelwerke v *Commission* (Case 97/85)
[1987] ECR 2265, Court of Justice of the European Communities

By a Decision addressed to Germany, the Commission authorized a scheme for selling cheap butter for a short period on the West Berlin market. The object was market research into consumer demand for butter. However, promoting butter hurt sales of margarine. The applicant was a German margarine producer active on the Berlin market. It sought annulment of the Decision addressed to Germany under the second paragraph of Article 173 EEC (now the fourth paragraph of Article 230 EC).

[9] It should be noted that, according to the second paragraph of Article 173 of the EEC Treaty, proceedings instituted by a natural or legal person against a decision addressed to another person are admissible only if that decision is of direct and individual concern to the applicant.

[10] The Court has consistently held, since its judgment of 15 July 1963 in Case 25/62 *Plaumann* [1963] ECR 95, that a decision addressed to a Member State is of direct and individual concern to natural or legal persons only if that decision affects them by reason of certain attributes which are peculiar to them, or by reason of circumstances in which they are differentiated from all other persons, and by virtue of these factors distinguishes them individually just as in the case of the person addressed.

[11] In this case it must be stated that the contested decision does not apply to a closed circle of persons who were known at the time of its adoption and whose rights the Commission intended to regulate. Although the contested decision affects the applicants, that is only because of the effects it produces on their position on the market. In that regard, the decision is of concern to

the applicants just as it was to any other person supplying margarine on the West Berlin market while the contested operation was in progress, and it is not therefore of individual concern to them for the purposes of the second paragraph of Article 173 of the EEC Treaty.

[12] The applicants' argument to the effect that this application should be declared admissible so as to enable them to enjoy full legal protection must be rejected. It must be pointed out that, in support of an action challenging a national measure implementing a Community decision, the applicant may plead the illegality of that decision and thereby require the national court to adjudicate on all the allegations formulated in that respect, if necessary after making a reference to the Court of Justice for a ruling on the validity of the decision in question. The fact that the national court is empowered to determine which questions it intends to submit to the Court is an inherent feature of the system of means of redress established by the Treaty and is not therefore an argument which is capable of justifying a broad interpretation of the conditions of admissibility laid down in the second paragraph of Article 173 of the EEC Treaty.

NOTE

Paragraph 12 of the judgment indicates that this was not the only avenue of redress open to the applicant. The telling of the tale of the Berlin butter will be resumed later in this Chapter. It provides a fine illustration of the pattern of interrelation of the remedies in the Community system, mentioned in the introduction to this Chapter.

Note that the Court never even reaches the merits of the challenge to the contested act in these cases.

These decisions indicate that the issue of individual concern and the issue whether the meas ure is a true Regulation or in reality a Decision (*International Fruit Company* (Cases 41–44/70) at p.219 above) are conceptually similar. A genuinely normative measure is not susceptible to challenge.

The next case arose from the enforcement of the competition rules. They will be examined in Chapters 16–18. It clearly involves a Decision addressed to another person, and the Court focuses on the problem of individual concern.

Metro-SB-Grossmärkte GmbH & Co. KG v *Commission* (Case 26/76)

[1977] ECR 1875, Court of Justice of the European Communities

Metro complained to the Commission under Article 3(2) of Regulation 17/62 about SABA's distributorship network. (This has been replaced by Regulation 1/2003 with effect from 1 May 2004 but the system of complaint is retained by Article 7 Reg 1/2003, p.572 below): Metro had been excluded from it, and suggested that SABA was acting in violation of the Treaty competition rules. Contrary to Metro's hopes, the Commission ruled that some terms of SABA's system did not violate Article 85(1) of the EC Treaty (now Article 81(1) EC); others were exemptable under Article 85(3) (now Article 81(3) of the EC Treaty, see Chapter 18)). That ruling became the contested act. Metro wished to challenge under Article 173 of the EC Treaty (now, after amendment, Article 230 EC) the Decision addressed to SABA giving it a clean bill of health.

... [T]he contested decision was adopted in particular as the result of a complaint submitted by Metro and that it relates to the provisions of SABA's distribution system, on which SABA relied and continues to rely as against Metro in order to justify its refusal to sell to the latter or to appoint it as a wholesaler, and which the applicant had for this reason impugned in its complaint.

It is in the interests of a satisfactory administration of justice and of the proper application of Articles 85 and 86 that natural or legal persons who are entitled, pursuant to Article 3(2)(b) of Regulation No 17, to request the Commission to find an infringement of Articles 85 and 86 should be able, if their request is not complied with either wholly or in part, to institute proceedings in order to protect their legitimate interests.

In those circumstances the applicant must be considered to be directly and individually concerned, within the meaning of the second paragraph of Article 173, by the contested decision and the application is accordingly admissible.

....

D: **Direct concern**

This additional element of the Article 230, fourth paragraph standing rules requires the existence of a direct causal link between the challenged Community act and the impact on the applicant.

International Fruit Company v *Commission* (Cases 41–44/70)
[1971] ECR 411, Court of Justice of the European Communities

The case has already been examined above, at p.219. Individual concern was there established. In the following extract the Court looks for the applicant's direct concern in the matter.

[23] Moreover, it is clear from the system introduced by Regulation No 459/70, and particularly from Article 2(2) thereof, that the Decision on the grant of import licences is a matter for the Commission.

[24] According to this provision, the Commission alone is competent to assess the economic situation in the light of which the grant of import licences must be justified.

[25] Article 1(2) of Regulation No 459/70, by providing that 'the Member States shall in accordance with the conditions laid down in Article 2, issue the licence to any interested party applying for it', makes it clear that the national authorities do not enjoy any discretion in the matter of the issue of licences and the conditions on which applications by the parties concerned should be granted.

[26] The duty of such authorities is merely to collect the data necessary in order that the Commission may take its Decision in accordance with Article 2(2) of that Regulation, and subsequently adopt the national measures needed to give effect to that Decision.

[27] In these circumstances as far as the interested parties are concerned, the issue of or refusal to issue the import licences must be bound up with this Decision.

[28] The measure whereby the Commission decides on the issues of the import licences thus directly affects the legal position of the parties concerned.

[29] The applications thus fulfil the requirements of the second paragraph of Article 173 of the Treaty, and are therefore admissible.

NOTE
Typically, the insertion of a discretionary power vested by Community legislation in national authorities will preclude a direct challenge to the Community act establishing the general system.

Municipality of Differdange v *Commission* (Case 222/83)
[1984] ECR 2889, Court of Justice of the European Communities

The contested act was addressed by the Commission to Luxembourg. It authorized Luxembourg to grant aids to steel firms, provided they undertook reductions in capacity. The applicant municipality argued it was directly and individually concerned by the Commission's Decision on the following grounds:

[5] . . . Although the contested decision is addressed to the Grand Duchy of Luxembourg it is, from two points of view, of direct and individual concern to the applicants within the meaning of the

second paragraph of Article 173 of the EEC Treaty. In the first place the reduction of production capacity and the closure of factories located in their municipal territory results, they claim, in a reduction of the yield from local taxes. In the second place, they contend that according to a principle of administrative law known to several Member States, which also applies in Community law, the interests of the inhabitants of a municipality and the interests of the undertakings established in the municipal territory must be regarded as the municipalities' own interests.

The Court found the applicant had no standing under the ECSC Treaty and turned to the EEC rules:

[9] With regard, secondly, to the admissibility of the action under the EEC Treaty it must be recalled that the second paragraph of Article 173 of the Treaty makes the admissibility of an action brought by a natural or legal person other than the person to whom a Council or Commission Decision is addressed, for a declaration that the measure in question is void, subject to the requirement that the contested Decision is of direct and individual concern to him. The purpose of that provision is to ensure that legal protection is also available to a person who, whilst not the person to whom the contested measure is addressed, is in fact affected by it in the same way as is the addressee.

[10] In this case the contested measure, which is addressed to the Grand Duchy of Luxembourg, authorises it to grant certain aids to the undertakings named therein provided that they reduce their production capacity by a specified amount. However, it neither identifies the establishments in which the production must be reduced or terminated nor the factories which must be closed as a result of the termination of production. In addition, the Decision states that the Commission was to be notified of the closure dates only by 31 January 1984 so that the undertakings affected were free until that date to fix, where necessary with the agreement of the Luxembourg Government, the detailed rules for the restructuring necessary to comply with the conditions laid down in the Decision.

[11] That conclusion is, moreover, confirmed by Article 2 of the Decision according to which the capacity reductions may also be carried out by other undertakings.

[12] It follows that the contested Decision left to the national authorities and undertakings concerned such a margin of discretion with regard to the manner of its implementation and in particular with regard to the choice of the factories to be closed, that the Decision cannot be regarded as being of direct and individual concern to the municipalities with which the undertakings affected, by virtue of the location of their factories, are connected.

[13] Since the action is therefore inadmissible also to the extent to which it is based on the provisions of the EEC Treaty, it must be dismissed.

NOTE

Notice that where the intervention of the national authorities prevents an Article 230 action against the Community act, it may instead be possible to challenge the acts of the national authorities at national level, p.248 below. Indirectly this may permit a challenge to the Community act. Here, then, is a further example of the construction of a complete system of remedies through the interrelation of the several Treaty provisions. This structure will become clearer once the material in this Chapter is fully understood.

FURTHER READING

Craig, P., 'Legality, Standing and Substantive Review in Community Law' (1994) 14 Ox JLS 507.

Harlow, C., 'Access to Justice as a Human Right: the European Convention and the European Union' in P. Alston (ed), *The EU and Human Rights* (Oxford: OUP, 1999).

Rasmussen, H., 'Why is Article 173 Interpreted against Private Plaintiffs?' (1980) 5 EL Rev 112.

....

E: **The example of the anti-dumping cases**

Anti-dumping procedures are taken where the Commission determines that goods are being dumped on the Community market by traders in third States at unfairly low prices. In order to prevent distortion of the Community market, action is taken in the form of anti-dumping duties imposed by Regulation. These are levies imposed on the products being dumped, thereby raising their price. There is, then, a *general* policy; but it affects *particular* traders. Those traders are naturally eager to protect their interests by challenging the Community measure imposing the duty. But do they have standing? They must show that the act is challengeable *and* that they have standing; two procedural hurdles which are to some extent interdependent. Several important cases have been fought on the issue. All four cases extracted in this sub-section are from the pre-Maastricht era. Consequently they refer to Article 173(2) EEC. Post-Amsterdam, this is Article 230(4) EC (p.217 above).

NTN Toyo Bearing Co. v *Council* (Case 113/77)
[1979] ECR 1185, Court of Justice of the European Communities

A Regulation imposed an anti-dumping duty on ball-bearings originating in Japan. NTN, a Japanese ball-bearing producer, and its subsidiary companies sought annulment of the measure in so far as it affected them.

The admissibility of the application

[7] The Council has raised an objection of inadmissibility claiming that the contested Article forms part of a Regulation and that the applicants are therefore not entitled to request annulment of it under the second paragraph of Article 173 of the Treaty. It claims that in the present case this is not a Decision adopted in the guise of a Regulation since Regulation No 1778/77 in fact constitutes a general rule which affects all the products in question originating in Japan and which must, according to Article 19(1) of Regulation No 459/68 of the Council of 5 April 1968 on protection against dumping or the granting of bounties or subsidies by countries which are not members of the European Economic Community (Official Journal, English Special Edition 1968 (I), p.80), be adopted in the form of a Regulation.

[8] The applicants reply that the contested Article, although drafted in abstract terms, in fact affects only the first applicant and three other Japanese undertakings which produce the products in question (hereinafter referred to as 'the major producers'), as well as their subsidiaries in the Community. The preliminary investigation carried out before the adoption of Regulation No 1778/77 was limited to inquiries made first at the premises of the European subsidiaries and then at the premises of the major producers in Japan. The specific nature of the measure is confirmed by Article 3 of Regulation No 1778/77 which provides for the collection of the amounts secured by way of provisional duty only as regards the products manufactured and exported by the major producers. The contested Article therefore constitutes a Decision which affects only the major producers and their subsidiaries and must therefore be considered to be a Decision concerning them adopted in the guise of a Regulation.

[9] Before commencing the examination of the admissibility of the application, it should be stated that NTN and its subsidiaries are sufficiently closely associated for the Commission to have considered, during its examination of the matter, that it was necessary to apply to them the special provisions concerning export prices laid down in Article 3(3) of the basic Regulation, Regulation No 459/68. In these circumstances there is no need, as regards the question whether the contested measure is of direct and individual concern to the applicants, to make a distinction in relation to them between producers on the one hand and importers on the other.

[10] Regulation No 1778/77 contains essentially three provisions:

(i) Article 1 imposes a definitive anti-dumping duty of 15% on the products in question originating in Japan and suspends the application of that duty without prejudice to Article 2;

(ii) Article 2 regulates the monitoring of the undertakings given by the major Japanese producers and empowers the Commission to terminate the suspension of the application of the duty if it finds that these undertakings are being evaded, not being observed or have been withdrawn;

(iii) Article 3 provides, in respect of the products manufactured by the major producers, for the collection of the amounts secured by way of provisional duty in application of the imposition by previous Regulations of a provisional duty.

[11] Article 3 constitutes accordingly a collective Decision relating to named addressees. Although the collection of the amounts secured by way of provisional anti-dumping duty is *per se* of direct concern to any importer who has imported the products in question subject to such duty, the special feature of Article 3 which sets it apart is that it does not concern all importers but only those who have imported the products manufactured by the four major Japanese producers named in that Article. The allegation of the Council and the intervener that only implementing measures adopted by the national authorities are of direct concern to the importers and that these importers should therefore, where appropriate, bring the matter before the national courts having jurisdiction disregards the fact that such implementation is purely automatic and, moreover, in pursuance not of intermediate national rules but of Community rules alone.

[12] Article 3 of Regulation No 1778/77 is therefore of direct and individual concern to those importers and consequently the applications lodged by the susidiaries, as importers of NTN products, are admissible. As a result the application lodged by NTN against that Article is also admissible.

NOTE
The applicants in the next case were less successful. You will obtain valuable insight into the Court's approach by carefully contrasting this decision with *NTN Toyo Bearing*, above.

Alusuisse Italia SpA v *Council and Commission* (Case 307/81)
[1982] ECR 3463, Court of Justice of the European Communities

The Regulation imposed an anti-dumping duty on orthoxylene originating in Puerto Rico and the USA. The applicant, a company based in Milan, needed orthoxylene as a raw material in its production processes. It imported orthoxylene independently – it was not linked to a manufacturer or an exporting firm. Did it have standing to challenge the measure imposing the duty, which had affected it by raising the prices it had to pay?

[7] The second paragraph of Article 173 of the Treaty makes the admissibility of proceedings instituted by an individual for a declaration that a measure is void dependent on fulfilment of the condition that the contested measure, although in the form of a Regulation, in fact constitutes a Decision which is of direct and individual concern to him. The objective of that provision is in particular to prevent the Community institutions, merely by choosing the form of a Regulation, from being able to exclude an application by an individual against a Decision of direct and individual concern to him and thus to make clear that the choice of form may not alter the nature of a measure.

[8] Nevertheless an action brought by an individual is not admissible in so far as it is directed against a Regulation having general application within the meaning of the second paragraph of Article 189 [now 249] of the Treaty, the test for distinguishing between a Regulation and a Decision, according to the settled case law of the Court, being whether or not the measure in question has general application. It is therefore necessary to appraise the nature of the contested measures and in particular the legal effects which they are intended to produce or in fact produce.

[9] In that connection it should be borne in mind that the Regulations at issue have as their object the imposition of an anti-dumping duty on all imports of orthoxylene originating in the United States of

America and Puerto Rico, subject to certain exemptions laid down for products exported by undertakings expressly named. Consequently, such measures constitute, as regards independent importers who, in contrast to exporters, are not expressly named in the Regulations, measures having general application within the meaning of the second paragraph of Article 189 of the Treaty, because they apply to objectively determined situations and entail legal effects for categories of persons regarded generally and in the abstract.

[10] The applicant claims in that connection that, although the contested measures were adopted in the form of Regulations, they in fact constitute Decisions concerning it since importers of orthoxylene who are also users of that substance form a closed category of traders of a limited number whose identity was known at the date when the Regulations were adopted.

[11] That argument must be rejected. As the Court has already stated, a measure does not cease to be a regulation because it is possible to determine the number or even the identity of the persons to whom it applies at any given time as long as it is established that such application takes effect by virtue of an objective legal or factual situation defined by the measure in relation to its purpose. That applies to independent importers of orthoxylene. Under the Regulations the anti-dumping duty is imposed on persons importing the product from the countries in question solely by reference to the objective criterion that they are importers of that product. Consequently, the Regulations at issue constitute, as regard such importers, measures having general application within the meaning of the second paragraph of Article 189 of the Treaty and not Decisions of direct and individual concern to them.

[12] In favour of the admissibility of its application the applicant also argues that the particular features of the procedure leading to the adoption of the anti-dumping Regulations, in particular the participation of the various interested parties in the successive stages of that procedure, lead to the conclusion that the measures in question constitute individual administrative measures which may be contested by individuals under the second paragraph of Article 173 of the Treaty.

[13] That argument must also be rejected since the distinction between a Regulation and a Decision may be based only on the nature of the measure itself and the legal effects which it produces and not on the procedures for its adoption. That solution is furthermore in conformity with the system of remedies provided for by Community law since importers may contest before the national courts individual measures taken by the national authorities in application of the Community Regulations.

[14] For all those reasons, it must be concluded that the contested measures are Regulations and not Decisions within the meaning of the second paragraph of Article 173 of the Treaty, so that the application must be dismissed as inadmissible.

NOTE

The next case confirms, as in *Metro* v *Commission* (Case 26/76), at p.223 above, that complainants enjoy a special status. However, unlike in *Metro*, the challenged act seems to be a Regulation, not a Decision. The Court here appears ready to hold a measure a Regulation, but a Decision as far as the applicant is concerned – a hybrid measure.

Timex v *Council and Commission* **(Case 264/82)**
[1985] ECR 849, Court of Justice of the European Communities

A Regulation imposed an anti-dumping duty on wrist watches from the Soviet Union. Timex sought annulment for reasons quite distinct from those motivating the applicants in the previous two cases. As a producer of watches based in the Community, it wanted the duties annulled because they were too *low* to protect it from unfair Soviet competition. But did it have standing?

[9] In support of their objection of inadmissibility the defendants argue that the contested Regulation is not addressed to Timex, that Timex is not mentioned by name in its Articles and that Timex is not directly and individually concerned by the Regulation, which in their view affects all manufacturers of mechanical wrist-watches in the Community alike. That view is not altered by the fact that Timex may

be entitled to request the opening of an anti-dumping proceeding, since, according to the Decisions of the Court, the distinction between a Regulation and a Decision depends solely on the nature of the measure itself and its consequences in law.

[10] On the other hand, Timex and the parties intervening in its support contend that the action is admissible because the contested Regulation constitutes in reality a Decision which is of direct and individual concern to Timex within the meaning of the second paragraph of Article 173 of the EEC Treaty. They submit that the Regulation was adopted as a result of a complaint lodged on behalf of Timex, amongst others, and that it therefore constitutes the culmination of an administrative proceeding initiated at Timex's request. Its interest in bringing proceedings is all the more evident in so far as it is the only remaining manufacturer of mechanical wrist-watches in the United Kingdom and the anti-dumping duty in question was fixed exclusively by reference to its economic situation.

[11] The questions of admissibility raised by the Council and the Commission must be resolved in the light of the system established by Regulation No 3017/79 and, more particularly, of the nature of the anti-dumping measures provided for by that Regulation, regard being had to the provisions of the second paragraph of Article 173 of the EEC Treaty.

[12] Article 13(1) of Regulation No 3017/79 provides that 'Anti-dumping or countervailing duties, whether provisional or definitive, shall be imposed by Regulation'. In the light of the criteria set out in the second paragraph of Article 173, the measures in question are, in fact, legislative in nature and scope, inasmuch as they apply to traders in general; nevertheless, their provisions may be of direct and individual concern to some of those traders. In this regard, it is necessary to consider in particular the part played by the applicant in the anti-dumping proceedings and its position on the market to which the contested legislation applies.

[13] It should be pointed out first of all that the complaint under Article 5 of Regulation No 3017/79 which led to the adoption of Regulation No 1882/82 was lodged by the British Clock and Watch Manufacturers' Association Limited on behalf of manufacturers of mechanical watches in France and the United Kingdom, including Timex. According to the documents before the Court, that association took action because a complaint which Timex had itself lodged in April 1979 had been rejected by the Commission on the ground that it came from only one Community manufacturer.

[14] The complaint which led to the opening of the investigation procedure therefore owes its origin to the complaints originally made by Timex. Moreover, it is clear from the preamble to Commission Regulation No 84/82 and the preamble to Council Regulation No 1882/82 that Timex's views were heard during that procedure.

[15] It must also be remembered that Timex is the leading manufacturer of mechanical watches and watch movements in the Community and the only remaining manufacturer of those products in the United Kingdom. Furthermore, as is also clear from the preambles to Regulations Nos 84/82 and 1882/82, the conduct of the investigation procedure was largely determined by Timex's observations and the anti-dumping duty was fixed in the light of the effect of the dumping on Timex. More specifically, the preamble to Regulation No 1882/82 makes it clear that the definitive anti-dumping duty was made equal to the dumping margin which was found to exist 'taking into account the extent of the injury caused to Timex by the dumped imports'. The contested Regulation is therefore based on the applicant's own situation.

[16] It follows that the contested Regulation constitutes a Decision which is of direct and individual concern to Timex within the meaning of the second paragraph of Article 173 of the EEC Treaty. As the Court held in its judgment of 4 October 1983 in Case 191/82 *EEC Seed Crushers' and Oil Processors' Federation (FEDIOL) v Commission* ([1983] ECR 2913), the applicant is therefore entitled to put before the Court any matters which would facilitate a review as to whether the Commission has observed the procedural guarantees granted to complainants by Regulation No 3017/79 and whether or not it has committed manifest errors in its assessment of the facts, has omitted to take any essential matters into consideration or has based the reasons for its Decision on considerations amounting to a misuse of powers. In that respect, the Court is required to exercise its normal powers of review over a discretion granted to a public authority, even though it has no

jurisdiction to intervene in the exercise of the discretion reserved to the Community authorities by the aforementioned Regulation.

[17] Since the action is therefore admissible, the objection of inadmissibility raised by the Council and the Commission must be dismissed.

NOTE

R. Greaves, writing in 1986, surveyed *NTN Toyo Bearing* (Case 113/77) and *Alusuisse* (Case 307/ 81) and other cases in the area ('Locus Standi under Article 173 EEC when seeking Annulment of a Regulation' (1986) 11 EL Rev 119). She concluded:

What of the future? The Decisions of the Court seem to suggest that cases concerning particular areas of EEC Law such as the competition rules and dumping rules may well encourage a more flexible approach from the Court where admissibility under Article 173, second paragraph, is in dispute. This will be so particularly where the applicant not only has to show direct and individual concern but also that the Regulation is really a Decision within the measure of that Article. How far it will be possible to transpose the Court's rulings in these specific areas to the general body of Community law one can only guess. It would not be surprising if the Court, encouraged by its Advocate Generals and by commentators, took a much more liberal approach in the future and gave Article 173, second paragraph, a more vital role in assisting individuals to subject more of the Community acts to judicial review.

NOTE

This area of the law continues to provide the Court with a fertile field of litigation. As Greaves indicates, the Court's policy is in a state of flux and is only partly predictable. It is a policy which is susceptible to adjustment. The next case, a 1991 decision, follows neatly from Greaves's concluding sentence, and suggests the Court decided to take a more liberal approach to the standing rules.

Extramet v *Council* (Case C-358/89)
[1991] ECR I-2501, Court of Justice of the European Communities

Extramet, a French firm, sought the annulment of a Regulation imposing an anti-dumping duty on imports of calcium metal from China and the Soviet Union. The Council disputed the admissibility of the application on the basis that Extramet was an independent importer lacking individual concern. The Council referred to the Court's line of authority which, it submitted, showed Extramet had no standing.

[14]. . .[M]easures imposing anti-dumping duties may, without losing their character as regulations, be of individual concern in certain circumstances to certain traders who therefore have standing to bring an action for their annulment.

[15] The Court has acknowledged that this was the case, in general, with regard to producers and exporters who are able to establish that they were identified in the measures adopted by the Commission or the Council or were concerned by the preliminary measures (see the judgments in Joined Cases 239/82 and 275/82 *Allied Corporation* v *Commission* [1984] ECR 1005, and in Joined Cases C-133/87 and C-150/87 *Nashua Corporation* v *Commission and Council* [1990] ECR I–719, and in Case C-156/87 *Gestetner Holdings* v *Council and Commission* [1990] ECR I–781), and with regard to importers whose retail prices for the goods in question have been used as a basis for establishing the export prices (see, most recently, the judgments in Case C-304/86 *Enital* v *Commission and Council* [1990] ECR I-2939, Case C-305/86 *Neotype Techmashexport* v *Commission and Council* [1990] ECR I-2945, and Case C-157/87 *Electroimpex* v *Council* [1990] ECR I-3021).

[16] Such recognition of the right of certain categories of traders to bring an action for the annulment of an anti-dumping regulation cannot, however, prevent other traders from also claiming to be individually concerned by such a regulation by reason of certain attributes which are peculiar to

them and which differentiate them from all other persons (see the judgment in Case 25/62 *Plaumann* v *Commission* [1963] ECR 95).

[17] The applicant has established the existence of a set of factors constituting such a situation which is peculiar to the applicant and which differentiates it, as regards the measure in question, from all other traders. The applicant is the largest importer of the product forming the subject-matter of the anti-dumping measure and, at the same time, the end-user of the product. In addition, its business activities depend to a very large extent on those imports and are seriously affected by the contested regulation in view of the limited number of manufacturers of the product concerned and of the difficulties which it encounters in obtaining supplies from the sole Community producer, which, moreover, is its main competitor for the processed product.

[18] It follows that the objection of inadmissibility raised by the Council must be dismissed.

NOTE

The novel feature of the decision is that the Court held admissible an action by an independent importer unconnected with any producer or exporter subject to the anti-dumping duty. Subsequently the measure was declared void ([1992] ECR I-3813), although the dispute continued (Case T-2/95 *Industrie des poudres sphériques* v *Council* [1998] ECR II-3939; Case C-458/98P *Industrie des poudres sphériques* v *Council* [2000] ECR I-8147; Case T-5/97 *Industrie des poudres sphériques* v *Council* [2000] ECR II-3755).

■ QUESTIONS

1. What factors peculiar to the case induced the Court to hear Extramet's application? Can you distinguish this case from *Alusuisse* (Case 307/81) at p.227 above?

2. Was the measure in *Extramet* a Regulation or a Decision? Does it matter?

NOTE

But the Court of First Instance has taken seriously the comments made in para 17 of *Extramet*. The rules of standing in anti-dumping cases may have been adjusted, but they remain obstructive of private litigation in most circumstances.

Büchel & Co. Fahrzeugteilefabrik GmbH v Council of the European Union and the European Commission (Joined Cases T–74/97 and T–75/97)

Judgment of 26 September 2000, Court of Justice of the European Communities

An importer of bicycle parts from China sought to challenge the imposition of an anti-dumping duty. It failed.

[63] Finally, the applicant also has failed to establish the existence of a series of factors constituting a particular situation differentiating it from any other person. In particular, it has not shown that it is in a situation comparable to that of the applicant in Case C-358/89 *Extramet Industrie* v *Council* [1991] I-2501. With a market share of less than 2.5% of all imports of bicycle parts from the People's Republic of China, it is obviously not the largest Community importer of the products concerned. Similarly, by merely stating that the sale of parts from China represented 20% of its turnover between 1992 and 1996, it has not adduced sufficient evidence to support the conclusion that its activities depend to a large extent upon imports affected by the extension regulation.

F: Grounds for annulment

Having established sufficient standing, the applicant must show the measure is flawed in order to win annulment. The grounds for review are made clear in the Article itself:

. . . lack of competence, infringement of an essential procedural requirement, infringement of this Treaty or of any rule of law relating to its application, or misuse of powers.

These grounds seem broad. Of particular interest is 'any rule of law relating to [the Treaty's] application'. It is here that the significance of the Court's development of the general principles of Community law referred to in Chapter 2 becomes apparent. The validity of Community acts can be tested against these principles. Indeed, many of the principles have been developed by the Court in the context of Article 173 of the EC Treaty (now, after amendment, Article 230 EC) applications.

International Fruit Company v *Commission* (Cases 41–44/70)
[1971] ECR 411, Court of Justice of the European Communities

(The facts are set out at p.219 above.) The Court, having held the application admissible, proceeded to examine the merits. It held the application unfounded. The next extract explains the Court's rejection of one of the grounds of complaint.

[66] . . . [T]he applicants claim that Regulations Nos 565/70 and 686/70 are void or at least are not applicable to them, inasmuch as they establish a system of import licences which is in conflict with Articles 3(f), 85 and 96 of the Treaty.

[67] Moreover, these regulations are said to be insufficiently supported by reasons, inasmuch as the grounds on which the system was necessary or at least permissible under the said articles and under Article 39 of the Treaty are not stated.

[68] Article 3 of the Treaty lists several general objectives, towards the attainment and harmonization of which the Commission has to direct its activities.

[69] Amongst these objectives Article 3 specifies not only 'the institution of a system ensuring that competition in the common market is not distorted', but also (subparagraph (d)) 'the adoption of a common policy in the sphere of agriculture'.

[70] The Treaty attaches very great importance to the attainment of this latter objective in the sphere of agriculture, devoting Article 39 to it and providing, in the first paragraph of Article 42, that the provisions relating to competition shall apply to agricultural products only to the extent determined by the Council, account being taken of the objectives set out in Article 39.

[71] It follows from this that the application of protective measures in the form of a restriction of imports from third countries might in the present case prove to be necessary with a view to preventing, in the market in the products in question, serious disturbances capable of endangering the objectives of Article 39.

[72] In these circumstances an explicit statement of the reasons for the measures in question, in relation to Articles 85 and 86 of the Treaty, was not indispensable.

[73] It may well be that the grant of import licences according to the criterion of a reference quantity led in the present case to a crystallization of the previously existing trade relations with third countries. Yet, on the other hand, the laying down of objective criteria for calculating the quantities of which import was permitted made it possible to avoid discrimination among those who received licences on the basis of previously existing trade relations with third countries.

[74] This system was the one best adapted to distort competition to the smallest possible extent.

[75] For these reasons, the submissions directed against Regulations Nos 459/70, 565/70 and 686/70 must be rejected.

NOTE
In *Timex* v *Council* (Case 264/82) (p.228 above) the measure was annulled, for Timex had been inadequately involved in the inquiry in breach of relevant Community legislation; an infringement of an essential procedural requirement. In *Commission* v *Council* (Case 22/70) (p.217

above), however, the application for annulment was rejected. In *UK* v *Council* (Case C–84/94) (p.54 above) the Court rejected the UK's application for annulment of the 'Working Time' Directive almost in its entirety, but it should be noted that in para 58 (p.75 above) the Court observed that its review of compliance with the principle of proportionality would be confined to examining whether the legislature's 'wide discretion' had been vitiated by manifest error or misuse of powers, or whether the limits of that discretion had been manifestly exceeded. A similar approach may be traced in *R* v *Secretary of State for Health, ex parte British American Tobacco (Investments) Ltd and Imperial Tobacco Ltd* (Case C-491/01) (p.66 above).

G: **Interim measures**

ARTICLES 242 AND 243 EC

Article 242

Actions brought before the Court of Justice shall not have suspensory effect. The Court of Justice may, however, if it considers that circumstances so require, order that application of the contested act be suspended.

Article 243

The Court of Justice may in any cases before it prescribe any necessary interim measures.

These provisions, which were Articles 185 and 186 EC respectively pre-Amsterdam, confer a wide discretion on the Court. It has generally been slow to grant interim relief from Community acts. Here, however, is a successful interim application made in respect of anti-dumping duties imposed on Japanese ball bearings under Regulation 1778/77.

NTN Toyo Bearing Co. v *Council* (Case 113/77R)

[1977] ECR 1721, Court of Justice of the European Communities

[4] . . . The Council has not contested that the competent British, French and German customs authorities are insisting that the payments required under Article 3 of Regulation No 1778/77 shall be made forthwith. Nor has it contested that the NTN Group will incur the additional charges referred to by NTN in the event of the dismissal of the latter's application for the adoption of interim measures.

[5] It has not been possible to establish conclusively within the context of the present proceedings whether, in the event of NTN's being successful in the main action, this expenditure would be wholly recouped.

[6] Having regard to the probable duration of the procedure in the main action, charges at the rate quoted by the applicant cannot be regarded as negligible.

[7] On the other hand the Council has not been able to demonstrate that the adoption of the interim measures applied for would cause appreciable detriment to the European Economic Community if the NTN Group were to maintain the existing bank guarantees in the sums to be paid in accordance with Article 3 of Regulation No 1778/77 and if NTN were to be unsuccessful in the main action.

[8] NTN has thus substantiated the circumstances giving rise to urgency and the factual and legal grounds establishing a prima facie case for the suspension of the application, as far as the NTN Group is concerned, of the abovementioned Article 3 (Article 83(2) of the Rules of Procedure of the Court of Justice).

[9] To that extent therefore the application of the said Article must be suspended until the final judgment in the case of *NTN* v *Council* (Case 113/77) on condition that and for so long as the NTN

Group continues to provide security for the performance of its obligation in the amounts which it is required to pay in pursuance of Article 3 of Regulation No 1778/77.

NOTE
Case 113/77 subsequently reached full trial (see p.226 above).

■ **Question**

Compare and contrast the Community's rules on judicial review, especially those relating to standing, with those of any other administrative law system with which you are familiar.

SECTION 3: **ARTICLE 232**

ARTICLE 232 EC

Should the European Parliament, the Council or the Commission, in infringement of this Treaty, fail to act, the Member States and the other institutions of the Community may bring an action before the Court of Justice to have the infringement established.

The action shall be admissible only if the institution concerned has first been called upon to act. If, within two months of being so called upon, the institution concerned has not defined its position, the action may be brought within a further period of two months.

Any natural or legal person may, under the conditions laid down in the preceding paragraphs, complain to the Court of Justice that an institution of the Community has failed to address to that person any act other than a recommendation or an opinion.

The Court of Justice shall have jurisdiction, under the same conditions, in actions or proceedings brought by the ECB in the areas falling within the latter's field of competence and in actions or proceedings brought against the latter.

Whereas Article 230 concerns challenges to acts, Article 232 concerns challenges to omissions. It complements Article 230. While Article 230 was numbered Article 173 pre-Amsterdam, Article 175 has become Article 232. In the next case the Parliament obtained a ruling that the Council had unlawfully remained inactive.

Parliament v *Council* (Case 13/83)
[1985] ECR 1513, Court of Justice of the European Communities

The matter concerned the Council's alleged failure to ensure freedom to provide services in the sphere of international transport, and to lay down the conditions under which non-resident carriers may operate transport services in a Member State.

[59] The Commission and the Netherlands Government point out that the Court has held the provisions of Articles 59 and 60 to be directly applicable since the expiry of the transitional period. They both contend that the fact that Article 61 requires the provision of services in relation to transport to be liberalized within the framework of a common transport policy does not in itself constitute a sufficient ground for suspending indefinitely the effect of the provisions relating to services when the Council has for years failed to introduce a common policy.

[60] The Netherlands Government states that according to Article 8(7) of the Treaty the expiry of the transitional period is to constitute the latest date by which all the measures required for establishing the common market must be implemented; there is no ground for making the transport market an exception thereto. It also points out that the absence of express implementing

provisions in the Treaty has never prevented the application of the general rules of the Treaty or its basic principles. From this it concludes that since the end of the transitional period freedom to provide services must apply even in the transport sector. Since the direct application of the provisions of Articles 59 and 60 is sufficient to achieve the aims of a common transport policy without any further intervention by the Council, that institution cannot be said to have failed to act.

[61] The Commission, on the other hand, considers that Articles 59 and 60 are not directly applicable in the transport sector. Pursuant to Article 61 freedom to provide services in relation to transport must be achieved within the framework of the rules provided for by Article 75(1)(a) and (b). The aim of that provision is to allow the Council an appropriate period, extending if necessary beyond the expiry of the transitional period, within which to achieve freedom to provide services in relation to transport within the framework of a common policy. That appropriate period cannot, however, extend indefinitely, and now that more than 15 years have elapsed since the end of the transitional period it must almost have reached its end; if it were otherwise freedom to provide services, although guaranteed by the Treaty, would apply in all but one sector of activity, a situation which in the long term would be likely to cause distortion of competition. In those circumstances the Court should indicate by way of a warning in the present judgment what is a reasonable period for the purposes of Article 61.

[62] It should first be borne in mind that Article 61(1) provides that freedom to provide services in the field of transport is to be governed by the provisions of the Title relating to transport. Application of the principles governing freedom to provide services, as established in particular by Articles 59 and 60 of the Treaty, must therefore be achieved, according to the Treaty, by introducing a common transport policy and, more particularly, by laying down common rules applicable to international transport and the conditions under which non-resident carriers may operate transport services, the rules and conditions of which are referred to in Article 75(1)(a) and (b) and necessarily affect freedom to provide services.

[63] Accordingly, the argument of the Netherlands Government to the effect that on the expiry of the transitional period the provisions of Articles 59 and 60 are of direct application even in the transport sector cannot be accepted.

[64] However, the Parliament, the Commission and the Netherlands Government have rightly contended that the obligations imposed on the Council by Article 75(1)(a) and (b) include the introduction of freedom to provide services in relation to transport, and that the scope of that obligation is clearly defined by the Treaty. Pursuant to Articles 59 and 60 the requirements of freedom to provide services include, as the Court held in its judgment of 17 December 1981 (Case 279/80 *Webb* [1981] ECR 3305), the removal of any discrimination against the person providing services based on his nationality or the fact that he is established in a Member State other than that where the services are to be provided.

[65] It follows that in that respect the Council does not have the discretion on which it may rely in other areas of the common transport policy. Since the result to be achieved is determined by the combined effect of Articles 59, 60, 61 and 75(1)(a) and (b), the exercise of a certain measure of discretion is allowed only as regards the means employed to obtain that result, bearing in mind, as required by Article 75, those features which are special to transport.

[66] In so far as the obligations laid down in Article 75(1)(a) and (b) relate to freedom to provide services, therefore, they are sufficiently well-defined for disregard of them to be the subject of a finding of failure to act pursuant to Article 175.

[67] The Council was required to extend freedom to provide services to the transport sector before the expiry of the transitional period, pursuant to Article 75(1)(a) and (2), in so far as the extension related to international transport to or from the territory of a Member State or across the territory of one or more Member States and, within the framework of freedom to provide services in the transport sector, to lay down, pursuant to Article 75(1)(b) and (2), the conditions under which non-resident carriers may operate transport services within a Member State. It is common ground that the necessary measures for that purpose have not yet been adopted.

[68] On that point the Court must therefore hold that the Council has failed to act since it has failed to adopt measures which ought to have been adopted before the expiry of the transitional period and whose subject-matter and nature may be determined with a sufficient degree of precision.

[69] The Parliament, the Commission and the Netherlands Government also refer to the legal situation which would arise if, after judgment against it, the Council still failed to act. That problem is, however, hypothetical. Article 176 requires the Council to take the measures necessary to comply with this judgment; since that provision does not prescribe a time-limit for such compliance it must be inferred that the Council has a reasonable period for that purpose. It is not necessary in the present judgment to consider what would be the consequences if the Council still fails to act.

[70] Accordingly, the Court must find that in breach of the Treaty the Council has failed to ensure freedom to provide services in the sphere of international transport and to lay down the conditions under which non-resident carriers may operate transport services in a Member State.

[71] The Council is at liberty to adopt, in addition to the requisite measures of liberalization, such accompanying measures as it considers necessary and to do so in the order it holds to be appropriate.

NOTE

The case is a good illustration of the nature and purpose of Article 232. It might also be noted as an example of inter-institutional wrangling in the quest to develop Community policymaking in an important sector.

The next case demonstrates that although Article 232 complements Article 230, it does not offer a method of outflanking the limitations to Article 230. An applicant may find one available, but not both.

Societá 'Eridania' Zuccherifici Nazionali v Commission (Cases 10 and 18/68)
[1969] ECR 459, Court of Justice of the European Communities

The application for annulment of Commission Decisions had failed to clear the standing hurdles in Article 173 of the EC Treaty (now, after amendment, Article 230 EC). It was then argued that the Commission's failure to revoke the Decisions despite the applicant's requests was challengeable under Article 175 of the EC Treaty (now, after amendment, Article 232 EC) as a failure to act. On admissibility, the Court held as follows:

[16] The action provided for in Article 175 is intended to establish an illegal omission as appears from that article, which refers to a failure to act 'in infringement of this Treaty' and from Article 176 which refers to a failure to act declared to be 'contrary to this Treaty'.

Without stating under which provision of Community law the Commission was required to annul or to revoke the said decisions, the applicants have confined themselves to alleging that those decisions were adopted in infringement of the Treaty and that this fact alone would thus suffice to make the Commission's failure to act subject to the provisions of Article 175.

[17] The Treaty provides, however, particularly in Article 173, other methods of recourse by which an allegedly illegal Community measure may be disputed and if necessary annulled on the application of a duly qualified party.

To admit, as the applicants wish to do, that the parties concerned could ask the institution from which the measure came to revoke it and, in the event of the Commission's failing to act, refer such failure to the Court as an illegal omission to deal with the matter would amount to providing them with a method of recourse parallel to that of Article 173, which would not be subject to the conditions laid down by the Treaty.

[18] This application does not therefore satisfy the requirements of Article 175 of the Treaty and must thus be held to be inadmissible.

SECTION 4: **ARTICLE 241**

ARTICLE 241 EC

Notwithstanding the expiry of the period laid down in the fifth paragraph of Article 230, any party may, in proceedings in which a regulation adopted jointly by the European Parliament and the Council, or a regulation of the Council, of the Commission, or of the ECB is at issue, plead the grounds specified in the second paragraph of Article 230 in order to invoke before the Court of Justice the inapplicability of that regulation.

Article 241 was re-numbered from Article 184 on the entry into force of the Treaty of Amsterdam. The nature and purpose of Article 241 would be immediately apparent to a lawyer familiar with French administrative law, which contains the similar *exception d'illégalité*. Article 241 is, however, initially peculiar to British eyes. It is commonly referred to as the 'plea of illegality', which hardly invites instant recognition of its function. The following extract from '*Les Verts*' v *Parliament* (Case 294/83) (mentioned at p.216 above) provides an explanation of the place of Article 241 in the system of judicial remedies instituted by the Treaty.

Parti Ecologiste 'Les Verts' v *Parliament* (Case 294/83)
[1986] ECR 1339, Court of Justice of the European Communities

[23] . . . Natural and legal persons are.. . protected against the application to them of general measures which they cannot contest directly before the Court by reason of the special conditions of admissibility laid down in the second paragraph of Article 173 [now the fourth paragraph of Article 230] of the Treaty. Where the Community institutions are responsible for the administrative implementation of such measures, natural or legal persons may bring a direct action before the Court against implementing measures which are addressed to them or which are of direct and individual concern to them and, in support of such an action, plead the illegality of the general measure on which they are based. . . .

NOTE
This, then, is the plea of illegality – Article 241. It is a form of indirect challenge to a measure which the applicant is unable to challenge directly.
    Article 241's operation may be explained with reference to the next case.

Simmenthal SpA v *Commission* (Case 92/78)
[1979] ECR 777, Court of Justice of the European Communities

The applicant sought annulment of a February 1978 Decision. The basis of the challenge was the alleged invalidity of several Regulations and Notices from which that Decision of February 1978 derived. The limitations in Article 173 of the EC Treaty (now, after amendment, Article 230 EC), relating to standing and time limits, impeded direct challenge to those 'parent' measures. This application challenged those measures indirectly via a direct challenge to the February 1978 measure which stemmed from them. The Court explained the nature of Article 184 of the EC Treaty (now Article 241 EC) in these circumstances.

[34] While the applicant formally challenges Commission Decision No 78/258 it has at the same time criticized, in reliance on Article 184 of the EEC Treaty, certain aspects of the 'linking' system in the form in which it has been implemented pursuant to the new Article 14 of Regulation No 805/68, by

Regulation No 2900/77 and No 2901/77 and also by the notices of invitations to tender of 13 January 1978.

[35] Article 184 reads: 'Notwithstanding the expiry of the period laid down in the third paragraph of Article 173, any party may, in proceedings in which a Regulation of the Council or the Commission is in issue, plead the grounds specified in the first paragraph of Article 173, in order to invoke before the Court of Justice the inapplicability of that Regulation'.

[36] There is no doubt that this provision enables the applicant to challenge indirectly during the proceedings, with a view to obtaining the annulment of the contested Decision, the validity of the measures laid down by Regulation which form the legal basis of the latter.

[37] On the other hand there are grounds for questioning whether Article 184 applies to the notices of invitations to tender of 13 January 1978 when according to its wording it only provides for the calling in question of 'Regulations'.

[38] These notices are general acts which determine in advance and objectively the rights and obligations of the traders who wish to participate in the invitations to tender which these notices make public.

[39] As the Court in its judgment of 12 June 1958 in Case 15/57, *Compagnie des Hauts Fourneaux de Chasse* v *High Authority of the European Coal and Steel Community* [1957 and 1958] ECR 211, and in its judgment of 13 June 1956 in Case 9/56, *Meroni & Co., Industrie Metallurgische SpA* v *High Authority of the European Coal and Steel Community* [1957 and 1958] ECR 133, has already held in connexion with Article 36 of the ECSC Treaty, Article 184 of the EEC Treaty gives expression to a general principle conferring upon any party to proceedings the right to challenge, for the purpose of obtaining the annulment of a Decision of direct and individual concern to that party, the validity of previous acts of the institutions which form the legal basis of the Decision which is being attacked, if that party was not entitled under Article 173 of the Treaty to bring a direct action challenging those acts by which it was thus affected without having been in a position to ask that they be declared void.

[40] The field of application of the said Article must therefore include acts of the institutions which, although they are not in the form of a Regulation, nevertheless produce similar effects and on those grounds may not be challenged under Article 173 by natural or legal persons other than Community institutions and Member States.

[41] This wide interpretation of Article 184 derives from the need to provide those persons who are precluded by the second paragraph of Article 173 from instituting proceedings directly in respect of general acts with the benefit of a judicial review of them at the time when they are affected by implementing Decisions which are of direct and individual concern to them.

[42] The notices of invitations to tender of 13 January 1978 in respect of which the applicant was unable to initiate proceedings are a case in point, seeing that only the Decision taken in consequence of the tender which it had submitted in answer to a specific invitation to tender could be of direct and individual concern to it.

[43] There are therefore good grounds for declaring that the applicant's challenge during the proceedings under Article 184, which relates not only to the above-mentioned Regulations but also to the notices of invitations to tender of 13 January 1978, is admissible, although the latter are not in the strict sense measures laid down by Regulation.

NOTE

On the merits the application succeeded. The grounds for review under Article 241 are the same as those applicable to Article 230 (see p.231 above).

SECTION 5: **ARTICLES 235 AND 288**

ARTICLES 235 AND 288 EC

Article 235

The Court of Justice shall have jurisdiction in disputes relating to the compensation for damage provided for in the second paragraph of Article 288.

Article 288

The contractual liability of the Community shall be governed by the law applicable to the contract in question.

In the case of non-contractual liability, the Community shall, in accordance with the general principles common to the laws of the Member States, make good any damage caused by its institutions or by its servants in the performance of their duties.

The preceding paragraph shall apply under the same conditions to damage caused by the ECB or by its servants in the performance of their duties.

The personal liability of its servants towards the Community shall be governed by the provisions laid down in their Staff Regulations or in the Conditions of Employment applicable to them.

Articles 235 and 288 EC were Articles 178 and 215 EC respectively prior to the entry into force of the Treaty of Amsterdam, p.12 above.

The early development of the case law was marked by a very restrictive approach to the imposition of non-contractual liability on the institutions of the Community.

Aktien-Zuckerfabrik Schöppenstedt v *Council* (Case 5/71)

[1971] ECR 975, Court of Justice of the European Communities

[1] By application filed at the Registry on 13 February 1971 the undertaking Aktien-Zuckerfabrik Schöppenstedt asks the Court under the second paragraph of Article 215 of the EEC Treaty to order the Council to make good the damage which it caused the applicant by adopting Regulation No 769/68 of 18 June 1968 (OJ 1968, L 143) laying down the measures needed to offset the difference between national sugar prices and prices valid from 1 July 1968. Its principal claim is for the payment by the Council of 38 852.78 u.a., that is DM 155 411.13, representing the loss of income which it suffered in relation to the former German price of raw sugar. In the alternative it seeks moreover to be compensated otherwise for the damage which it has suffered.

ADMISSIBILITY

[2] The Council contests the admissibility of the application contending in the first place that it is aimed in fact not at compensation for damage due to its wrongful act or omission but to the removal of the legal effects arising from the contested measure. To recognize the admissibility of the application would frustrate the contentious system provided for by the Treaty in particular in the second paragraph of Article 173, under which individuals are not entitled to bring applications for annulment of regulations.

[3] The action for damages provided for by Articles 178 and 215, paragraph 2, of the Treaty was introduced as an autonomous form of action, with a particular purpose to fulfil within the system of actions and subject to conditions on its use dictated by its specific nature. It differs from an application for annulment in that its end is not the abolition of a particular measure, but compensation for damage caused by an institution in the performance of its duties.

[4] The Council further contends that the principal conclusions are inadmissible in that they involve the substitution of new rules, in accordance with the criteria described by the applicant, for the rules in question, a substitution which the Court has not the power to order.

[5] The principal conclusions seek only an award of damages and, therefore, a benefit intended solely to produce effects in the case of the applicant. Therefore this submission must be dismissed.

NOTE

This remains good law, and represents an authoritative statement of the function of the action for damages as 'an autonomous form of action' (para 3 above). The Court then proceeded to examine the nature of the violation required to generate a liability to compensate.

[11] In the present case the non-contractual liability of the Community pre-supposes at the very least the unlawful nature of the act alleged to be the cause of the damage. Where legislative action involving measures of economic policy is concerned, the Community does not incur noncontractual liability for damage suffered by individuals as a consequence of that action, by virtue of the provisions contained in Article 215, second paragraph, of the Treaty, unless a sufficiently flagrant violation of a superior rule of law for the protection of the individual has occurred. For that reason the Court, in the present case, must first consider whether such a violation has occurred.

[12] Regulation No 769/68 was adopted pursuant to Article 37(1) of Regulation No 1009/67 which requires the Council to adopt provisions concerning the measures needed to offset the difference between national sugar prices and prices valid from 1 July 1968, and it authorises the Member State in which the price of white sugar is higher than the target price to grant compensation for such quantities of white sugar and raw sugar which are in free circulation in its territory at 0.00 hours on 1 July 1968. The applicant points out that as regards Member States with a low price this regulation provides for the payment of dues on sugar stocks only if the previous prices were less than the intervention price valid from 1 July 1968 and concludes from this that by adopting different criteria for the right to compensation of sugar producers in a Member State with high prices, the regulation infringes the provision of the last subparagraph of Article 40(3) of the Treaty according to which any common price policy shall be based on common criteria and uniform methods of calculation.

[13] The difference referred to does not constitute discrimination because it is the result of a new system of common organization of the market in sugar which does not recognize a single fixed price but has a maximum and minimum price and lays down a framework of prices within which the level of actual prices depends on the development of the market. Thus it is not possible to challenge the justification of transitional rules which proceeded on the basis that where the previous prices were already within the framework set up they must be governed by market forces and which therefore required the payment of dues only in cases where the previous prices were still too low to come within the new framework of prices and authorised compensation only in cases where the previous prices were too high to come within the said framework.

[14] In addition, having regard to the special features of the system established with effect from 1 July 1968, the Council by adopting Regulation No 769/68 satisfied the requirements of Article 37 of Regulation No 1009/67.

[15] It is also necessary to dismiss the applicant's claim that Regulation No 769/68 infringed the provisions of Article 40 of the Treaty because the method of calculating the compensation and dues for the raw sugar stocks was derived from that adopted for white sugar, which could, according to the applicant, result in the unequal treatment of the producers of raw sugar. Although, relying on hypothetical cases, the applicant stated that the calculation methods selected did not necessarily lead to uniform results with regard to producers of raw sugar, it was not proved that this could have been the case on 1 July 1968.

[16] The applicant's action founded upon the Council's liability does not therefore satisfy the first condition mentioned above and must be dismissed.

NOTE

The Court's test in para 11 of the judgment appeared extremely difficult to satisfy. This was borne out by subsequent case law in which claims for compensation were regularly rejected. See also, e.g., *Bayerische HNL Vermehrungsbetriebe GmbH & Co. KG v Council* (Case 83/76) [1978] ECR 1209; *Koninklijke Scholten-Honig NV v Council and Commission* (Case 143/77) [1979] ECR 3583.

There were only occasional successes; see, e.g., *Mulder et al* v *Council & Commission* (Cases C-104/89 and C-37/90) [1992] ECR I-3061 and, on assessing compensation, [2000] ECR I-203.

Article 288's second paragraph requires the Court to develop Community law in this area in accordance with the general principles common to the law of the Member States. It is worth considering with reference to systems of administrative liability with which you are familiar whether the Court's test in *Schöppenstedt* (Case 5/71) was appropriate. However the case law has lately taken a new turn. Principles of liability under Article 288 applicable to *Community* institutions cannot rationally be developed in isolation from those developed under Community law applicable to *national* institutions. Chapter 6 explored the Court's reliance on Article 10 (ex 5) EC to craft a system of liability applicable to national institutions accused of infringing Community law rights. The landmark case was *Francovich* (Cases C–6 and C–9/90, p.168 above). The principle was elucidated and its scope of application expanded in *Brasserie du Pêcheur and Factortame* (Joined Cases C-46/93 and C-48/93, p.177). The pressure to bring the principles of liability into alignment irrespective of the national or Community origin of the challenged institution has convinced the Court to depart from the *Schöppenstedt* formula.

Laboratoires Pharmaceutiques Bergaderm SA and Jean-Jacques Goupil v *Commission* (Case C-352/98P)
[2000] ECR I-5291, Court of Justice of the European Communities

This was an appeal against the Court of First Instance's decision in Case T-199/96 *Laboratoires Pharmaceutiques Bergaderm and Goupil v Commission* [1998] ECR II-2805. Bergaderm had applied for compensation for damage which they claimed to have suffered as a result of the adoption of Directive 95/34/EC, adapting the regime governing cosmetic products. This measure had the effect of preventing the sale of one of Bergaderm's sun oil products by introducing restrictions on permissible ingredients on scientific grounds associated with perceived risks to health. The Court of First Instance dismissed the application. On appeal, the Court began by setting out the basis for the Court of First Instance's decision which was now being challenged before it.

[13] In the contested judgment, the Court of First Instance recalled that, as regards liability arising from legislative measures, the conduct with which the Community is charged must constitute a breach of a higher-ranking rule of law for the protection of individuals (paragraph 48). It held that the Adaptation Directive was a measure of general application (paragraph 50) and concluded that it was necessary therefore to determine whether the Commission had disregarded a higher-ranking rule of law for the protection of individuals (paragraph 51).

[14] Without deeming it necessary to determine whether the provisions governing the procedure for the adoption of the Adaptation Directive contained higher-ranking rules of law for the protection of individuals, the Court of First Instance concluded that the Commission had not infringed those provisions (paragraph 56). It stated that they did not provide for the protection of certain rights of the defence (paragraph 59) and that, in any event, the appellants had had the opportunity to express their views before the adoption of the Adaptation Directive (paragraph 60).

[15] As regards the plea alleging manifest error of assessment and breach of the principle of proportionality, the Court of First Instance held that, in the light of the evidence before the Court, the Commission's conduct and the measure adopted by it could not be regarded as vitiated by a manifest error of assessment or as disproportionate (paragraph 67).

[16] Finally, as regards the plea alleging misuse of powers, the Court of First Instance held that the

appellants had failed to provide evidence such as to show that the Adaptation Directive had been adopted with the exclusive or main purpose of achieving an end other than that stated (paragraphs 69 and 70).

The appeal was based on three grounds: (i) that the Court of First Instance erred in law in declaring that the Adaptation Directive was a legislative measure, (ii) that the Court of First Instance committed a manifest error in assessing the Commission's exercise of its powers, and (iii) in the alternative, that there was a breach of higher-ranking rules of law. The Court took the first two grounds of appeal together.

[38] By their first two grounds of appeal, the appellants essentially claim that, in the light of the nature of the measure adopted by the Commission, the Court of First Instance erred in law in concluding, in paragraph 67 of the contested judgment, that the Commission's conduct and the measure adopted by it to restrict to 1 mg/kg the maximum level of psoralens in sun protection products cannot be regarded as vitiated by a manifest error of assessment or as disproportionate.

[39] The second paragraph of Article 215 of the Treaty provides that, in the case of non-contractual liability, the Community is, in accordance with the general principles common to the laws of the Member States, to make good any damage caused by its institutions or by its servants in the performance of their duties.

[40] The system of rules which the Court has worked out with regard to that provision takes into account, *inter alia*, the complexity of the situations to be regulated, difficulties in the application or interpretation of the texts and, more particularly, the margin of discretion available to the author of the act in question (Joined Cases C-46/93 and C-48/93 *Brasserie du Pêcheur and Factortame* [1996] ECR I-1029, paragraph 43).

[41] The Court has stated that the conditions under which the State may incur liability for damage caused to individuals by a breach of Community law cannot, in the absence of particular justification, differ from those governing the liability of the Community in like circumstances. The protection of the rights which individuals derive from Community law cannot vary depending on whether a national authority or a Community authority is responsible for the damage (*Brasserie du Pêcheur and Factortame*, paragraph 42).

[42] As regards Member State liability for damage caused to individuals, the Court has held that Community law confers a right to reparation where three conditions are met: the rule of law infringed must be intended to confer rights on individuals; the breach must be sufficiently serious; and there must be a direct causal link between the breach of the obligation resting on the State and the damage sustained by the injured parties (*Brasserie du Pêcheur and Factortame*, paragraph 51).

[43] As to the second condition, as regards both Community liability under Article 215 of the Treaty and Member State liability for breaches of Community law, the decisive test for finding that a breach of Community law is sufficiently serious is whether the Member State or the Community institution concerned manifestly and gravely disregarded the limits on its discretion (*Brasserie du Pêcheur and Factortame*, paragraph 55; and Joined Cases C-178/94, C-179/94, C-188/94, C-189/94, C-190/94 *Dillenkofer and Others* v *Germany* [1996] ECR I-4845, paragraph 25).

[44] Where the Member State or the institution in question has only considerably reduced, or even no, discretion, the mere infringement of Community law may be sufficient to establish the existence of a sufficiently serious breach (see, to that effect, Case C-5/94 *Hedley Lomas* [1996] ECR I-2553, paragraph 28).

[45] It is therefore necessary to examine whether, in the present case, as the appellants assert, the Court of First Instance erred in law in its examination of the way in which the Commission exercised its discretion when it adopted the Adaptation Directive.

[46] In that regard, the Court finds that the general or individual nature of a measure taken by an institution is not a decisive criterion for identifying the limits of the discretion enjoyed by the institution in question.

[47] It follows that the first ground of appeal, which is based exclusively on the categorisation of the Adaptation Directive as an individual measure, has in any event no bearing on the issue and must be rejected.

[48] By the first limb of the second ground of appeal, the appellants challenge the finding, by the Court of First Instance, that there existed disputed scientific studies and data as regards the risk for human health caused by the use of furocoumarines present in natural essences, even when associated with sun filters.

[49] Article 168a of the Treaty and Article 51 of the EC Statute of the Court of Justice state that an appeal is to be limited to points of law and, therefore, the Court of First Instance has exclusive jurisdiction, first, to establish the facts except where the substantive inaccuracy of its findings is apparent from the documents submitted to it and, second, to assess those facts (Case C–7/95 P *Deere* v *Commission* [1998] ECR I-3111, paragraphs 18 and 21).

[50] Before the Court, the appellants have not shown either by their arguments or by the documents they have submitted that the Court of First Instance distorted the nature of the evidence submitted to it by holding, in paragraph 63 of the contested judgment, that 'there is nothing in the documents before the Court to support the conclusion that the Commission misunderstood the scientific arguments'.

[51] Therefore, since the first limb of the second ground of appeal contests a finding of fact, without showing that the facts were distorted, it must be declared inadmissible.

[52] By the second limb of that ground of appeal, the appellants dispute the reference to the precautionary principle in paragraph 66 of the contested judgment.

[53] However, paragraph 66 of the contested judgment, which begins with the word 'furthermore', is a statement of reasons added for completeness, since the Court of First Instance had already concluded its reasoning in paragraph 65 by stating that the Commission could not be criticised for placing the matter before the Scientific Committee or for complying with that body's opinion, which was drawn up on the basis of a large number of meetings, visits and specialist reports.

[54] It follows that the second limb of the second ground of appeal is irrelevant and must be rejected.

The third ground of appeal based on breach of higher-ranking rules of law was re-interpreted by the Court:

[62] Having regard to the conditions, set out in paragraphs 41 and 42 above, that must be met for Community liability to be incurred, the third ground of appeal must be interpreted as alleging that the Court of First Instance misinterpreted the legislation in considering that the Commission did not infringe a rule of law intended to confer rights on individuals.

But this too failed to persuade, and the appeal was dismissed.

Having made the key statement of principle in para 41 of the judgment in *Bergaderm* (above), the Court is now adept at weaving together the case law concerning the liability of Community institutions pursuant to Articles 235 and 288(2) EC and the liability of national authorities pursuant to the *Francovich* and *Brasserie du Pêcheur/Factortame* case law developed on the basis of Article 10 EC. This is a single stream of legal principle.

Commission v *Camar and Others* (Case C-312/00P)
Judgment of 10 December 2002, Court of Justice of the European Communities

[52] . . . the system of rules which the Court has worked out in relation to the non-contractual liability of the Community takes into account, *inter alia*, the complexity of the situations to be regulated, difficulties in the application or interpretation of the texts and, more particularly, the margin of discretion available to the author of the act in question (see Joined Cases C-46/93 and C-48/93

Brasserie du pêcheur and Factortame [1996] ECR I-1029, paragraph 43, and *Bergaderm and Goupil* v *Commission*, cited above, paragraph 40).

[53] It is appropriate to point out also that, Community law confers a right to reparation where three conditions are met: the rule of law infringed must be intended to confer rights on individuals; the breach must be sufficiently serious; and there must be a direct causal link between the breach of the obligation resting on the author of the act and the damage sustained by the injured parties (see the judgments cited above *Brasserie du pêcheur and Factortame*, paragraph 51, and *Bergaderm and Goupil* v *Commission*, paragraphs 41 and 42).

[54] As to the second condition, the decisive test for finding that a breach of Community law is sufficiently serious is whether the Community institution concerned manifestly and gravely disregarded the limits on its discretion (see the judgments cited above *Brasserie du pêcheur and Factortame*, paragraph 55, and *Bergaderm and Goupil* v *Commission*, paragraph 43). Where that institution has only considerably reduced, or even no, discretion, the mere infringement of Community law may be sufficient to establish the existence of a sufficiently serious breach (Case C-5/94 *Hedley Lomas* [1996] ECR I-2553, paragraph 28; Joined Cases C-178/94, C-179/94 and C-188/94 to C-190/94 *Dillenkofer and Others* [1996] ECR I-4845, paragraph 25; Case C-127/95 *Norbrook Laboratories* [1998] ECR I-1531, paragraph 109; Case C-424/97 *Haim* [2000] ECR I-5123, paragraph 38, and *Bergaderm and Goupil* v *Commission*, cited above, paragraph 44).

[55] It follows from the foregoing that the decisive test for determining whether there has been such an infringement is not the individual nature of the act in question, but the discretion available to the institution when it was adopted.

NOTE

Outside the field of economic policymaking which was at issue in these cases, the Court seems a little more receptive to claims for compensation. 'Administrative illegality' is subject to rules that are more favourable to an applicant than 'legislative illegality'. The next case, which involves 'administrative illegality', tells a tragic tale. It is thankfully outside the mainstream of Community practice, but deserves attention as an example of how the Court can adopt a flexible approach to these rules.

Adams v *Commission (No 1)* (Case 145/83)

[1985] ECR 3539, Court of Justice of the European Communities

Stanley Adams sought compensation for damage he claimed to have suffered as a result of wrongful acts on the part of the Commission. Adams, an employee of the Swiss firm Hoffman-La Roche, had 'leaked' to the Commission documents which showed that Roche had been acting contrary to the Treaty competition rules. He requested the Commission to keep his identity secret. In the course of the inquiry, which culminated in the imposition of a fine on Roche, the Commission had let the firm see documents which indicated its participation in unlawful practices. Roche was able to deduce from the documents that the Commission's informant was Adams. Adams was charged with economic espionage under the Swiss Penal Code. He had left Roche and moved to Italy, but in 1974 he was arrested as he crossed the Swiss/Italian border. He was held in solitary confinement. He was not allowed to communicate with his family. His wife committed suicide. He received a one-year suspended prison sentence.

In the following extract from the judgment the Court examines breaches of the duty of confidentiality and the duty to warn Adams as the basis for the Commission's liability to him.

[28] The applicant claims that the relationship between the Commission and himself was in fact confidential in nature, as is clear both from his first letter to the Commission, dated 25 February

1973, and the discussion which he had with the Commission officials at the meeting on 9 April 1973. The existence of a duty of confidentiality follows, moreover, from the general principles common to the laws of the Member States and from the obligations imposed on the Commission by Article 214 of the EEC Treaty and by Article 20 of Regulation No 17 of the Council of 6 February 1962 (Official Journal, English Special Edition 1959–1962, p.87).

[29] In particular the applicant points out that the fact that he indicated in his letter of 25 February 1973 that he would be prepared to give evidence on oath before the Court as to the accuracy of his statements showed that his identity was to be disclosed by himself alone after the Commission investigation had been completed and the proceedings before the Court initiated. The applicant maintains that he never gave the Commission to understand that after he had left Roche he would no longer insist on that duty of confidentiality in regard to him. Finally, in the applicant's view, the Commission's conduct proved that it considered itself bound by such a duty. Thus on several occasions, both before and after the applicant had left Roche, the Commission deliberately refused to name its informant – until the beginning of 1975 when Mr Schlieder disclosed his name.

[30] Although the Commission was therefore bound by a duty of confidentiality towards the applicant, in his view it acted in breach of that obligation on three occasions in particular. In the first place, the disclosure of the copies of the documents to the Roche employees in October 1974 enabled Roche to infer therefrom that the applicant was the most likely informant. Secondly, the Commission failed to warn the applicant of the risk that he would inevitably run if he returned to Switzerland. In the applicant's view, it was the Commission's duty to warn him of that risk, either after the documents had been handed over to the Roche employees or, and in any event, after Dr Alder's first visit to the Commission in November 1974, when the Commission was made fully aware of the gravity of that risk. In that respect, the applicant points out that Dr Alder had told the Commission officials that Roche was considering the possibility of criminal proceedings against the informant and that the lawyer had even explained the contents of the relevant provision of the Swiss Penal Code. Thirdly, and finally, in February 1975 Mr Schlieder named the applicant as the Commission's informant.

[31] The Commission denies that it was bound by a duty of confidentiality towards the applicant after he had left his employment with Roche. It bases its contention in particular on the applicant's express statement in his letter of 25 February 1973 that, after he had left Roche, he would be willing to appear before any court, in other words not only before the Court of Justice, to confirm on oath the statements he had made. Moreover, the applicant's conduct after he had left Roche gave the Commission good reason to believe that it was a matter of indifference to him whether he was identified as the informant, since he had not even informed the Commission of his new address. According to the Commission the fact that it repeatedly declined to identify its informant in no way establishes that it considered itself bound by a duty of confidentiality. Its conduct was dictated entirely by its general practice of not divulging the identity of its informants.

[32] In any event the Commission contends that even if it were under a duty of confidentiality regarding the applicant's identity, it did not act in breach of that duty. The fact that it handed over photocopies to the Roche employees did not amount to such a breach, since it could not possibly have been foreseen that Roche would be able to identify the source of the documents by examining the copies. The applicant never requested the Commission not to disclose those documents to Roche. On the other hand, he agreed that the Commission could use the documents in connection with an investigation of that firm. The Commission had considered that it was necessary to disclose them to Roche but it nevertheless took care to remove anything which looked as though it might indicate their specific source. Moreover, the documents in question had no evident connection with the applicant, who could have been identified only by someone with a highly detailed knowledge of the organization and the operation of Roche. The applicant had never warned the Commission of such a risk.

[33] As regards the possible existence of a duty on the part of the Commission to warn the applicant, the Commission contends that such a duty cannot be inferred from any duty of confidentiality which may have existed. In so far as the applicant is putting forward a separate submission in this

respect, the Commission adds that it is impossible to establish in law that, following Dr Alder's visit, it was under a duty to warn the applicant of the risks that he would run if he returned to Switzerland. In addition, the Commission had no reason to believe that Roche would be able to identify the applicant as the informant. Finally, during his telephone conversation with Dr Alder at the beginning of February 1975, Mr Schlieder revealed nothing that Roche and the Swiss authorities did not already know, since by then the applicant had already admitted that he was the Commission's informant.

[34] As regards the existence of a duty of confidentiality it must be pointed out that Article 214 of the EEC Treaty lays down an obligation, in particular for the members and the servants of the institutions of the Community 'not to disclose information of the kind covered by the obligation of professional secrecy, in particular information about undertakings, their business relations or their cost components'. Although that provision primarily refers to information gathered from undertakings, the expression 'in particular' shows that the principle in question is a general one which applies also to information supplied by natural persons, if that information is 'of the kind' that is confidential. That is particularly so in the case of information supplied on a purely voluntary basis but accompanied by a request for confidentiality in order to protect the informant's anonymity. An institution which accepts such information is bound to comply with such a condition.

[35] As regards the case before the Court, it is quite clear from the applicant's letter of 25 February 1973 that he requested the Commission not to reveal his identity. It cannot therefore be denied that the Commission was bound by a duty of confidentiality towards the applicant in that respect. In fact the parties disagree not so much as to the existence of such a duty but as to whether the Commission was bound by a duty of confidentiality after the applicant had left his employment with Roche.

[36] In that respect it must be pointed out that the applicant did not qualify his request by indicating a period upon the expiry of which the Commission would be released from its duty of confidentiality regarding the identity of its informant. No such indication can be inferred from the fact that the applicant was prepared to appear before any court after he had left Roche. The giving of evidence before a court implies that the witness has been duly summoned, that he is under a duty to answer the questions put to him, and is, in return, entitled to all the guarantees provided by a judicial procedure. The applicant's offer to confirm the accuracy of his information under such conditions cannot therefore be interpreted as a general statement releasing the Commission from its duty of confidentiality. Nor can any such intention be inferred from the applicant's subsequent conduct.

[37] It must therefore be stated that the Commission was under a duty to keep the applicant's identity secret even after he had left his employer.

[38] Of the events mentioned by the applicant, the only occasion on which the Commission directly revealed the identity of its informant was the telephone conversation between Mr Schlieder and Dr Alder at the beginning of February 1975. However, that conversation took place after the applicant had caused an anonymous letter to be sent to the Commission informing it of his detention and seeking its help. It is difficult to see how the Commission could have acted on that request without confirming, at least by implication, that the applicant was indeed its informant. Moreover, it transpired subsequently that at that time the applicant had already admitted to the Swiss police that he had given information, at least orally, to the Commission and it is clear from the decisions of the Swiss courts that the confirmation of that fact by Mr Schlieder did not have a decisive bearing on the applicant's conviction. The disclosure of the applicant's identity at that time and in those circumstances cannot be regarded as constituting a breach of the duty of confidentiality which could give rise to the Commission's liability *vis-à-vis* the applicant.

[39] On the other hand, it is clear that the handing over of the edited photocopies to members of the staff of the Roche subsidiaries enabled Roche to identify the applicant as the main suspect in the complaint which it lodged with the Swiss Public Prosecutor's Office. It was therefore that handing over of the documents which led to the applicant's arrest and which in addition supplied the police and the Swiss courts with substantial evidence against him.

[40] It appears from the documents before the Court that the Commission was fully aware of the risk that the handing over to Roche of the photocopies supplied by the applicant might reveal the informant's identity to the company. For that reason the Commission officials first attempted to obtain other copies of the documents in question from the Roche subsidiaries in Paris and Brussels. When that attempt failed, the Commission prepared new copies of the documents which it considered were the least likely to lead to the discovery of the applicant's identity and it took care to remove from those copies any indication which it considered might reveal the source of the documents. However, since it was not familiar with Roche's practices regarding the distribution of the documents in question within the company, the Commission could not be sure that those precautions were sufficient to eliminate all risk of the applicant's being identified by means of the copies handed over to Roche. The Commission was therefore, in any event, imprudent in handing over those copies to Roche without having consulted the applicant.

[41] It is not however necessary to decide whether, in view of the situation at the time and in particular of the information in the Commission's possession, the handing over of the documents is sufficient to give rise to the Commission's liability regarding the consequences of the applicant's being identified as the informant. Although the Commission was not necessarily aware, when those documents were handed over, of the gravity of the risk to which it was exposing the applicant, Dr Alder's visit on 8 November 1974, on the other hand, provided it with all the necessary information in that respect. Following that visit the Commission knew that Roche was determined to discover how the Commission had come into possession of the documents in question and that it was preparing to lay a complaint against the informant under Article 273 of the Swiss Penal Code, the contents of which Dr Alder even took care to explain. The Commission also knew that there was a possibility of obtaining from Roche, in return for the disclosure of the informant's identity, an undertaking not to take action against him. It could not however pursue that possibility without the applicant's consent.

[42] In those circumstances it was not at all sufficient for the Commission merely to take the view that it was unlikely that the applicant would be identified, that he was probably never going to return to Switzerland and that, in any event, the Swiss authorities did not intend to institute criminal proceedings against him. On the contrary, the Commission was under a duty to take every possible step to warn the applicant, thereby enabling him to make his own arrangements in the light of the information given by Dr Alder, and to consult him as to the approach to be adopted in relation to Dr Alder's proposals.

[43] Although the applicant had not left any precise address making it possible for the Commission to contact him easily, in his letter of 25 February 1973 he had already indicated his intention of setting up his own meat business in Italy, near Rome. Even in the absence of other indications, that information would have enabled the Commission to make inquiries with a view to discovering where the applicant was staying. It is common ground that the Commission did not even attempt to find the applicant although it allowed almost one month to elapse before communicating to Dr Alder its final refusal to discuss the origin of the documents in its possession, a refusal which was followed by the lodging of Roche's complaint at the Swiss Public Prosecutor's Office.

[44] It must therefore be concluded that, by failing to make all reasonable efforts to pass on to the applicant the information which was available to it following Dr Alder's visit of 8 November 1974, even though the communication of that information might have prevented, or at least limited, the damage which was likely to result from the discovery of the applicant's identity by means of the documents which it had handed over to Roche, the Commission has incurred liability towards the applicant in respect of that damage.

The Court then rejected the Commission's submission that the action was time-barred. In what may seem a cruel concluding twist, it awarded Adams compensation, but halved the sum payable on the following basis:

[53] It must therefore be concluded that in principle the Community is bound to make good the damage resulting from the discovery of the applicant's identity by means of the documents

handed over to Roche by the Commission. It must however be recognized that the extent of the Commission's liability is diminished by reason of the applicant's own negligence. The applicant failed to inform the Commission that it was possible to infer his identity as the informant from the documents themselves, although he was in the best position to appreciate and to avert that risk. Nor did he ask the Commission to keep him informed of the progress of the investigation of Roche, and in particular of any use that might be made of the documents for that purpose. Lastly, he went back to Switzerland without attempting to make any inquiries in that respect, although he must have been aware of the risks to which his conduct towards his former employer had exposed him with regard to Swiss legislation.

[54] Consequently, the applicant himself contributed significantly to the damage which he suffered. In assessing the conduct of the Commission on the one hand and that of the applicant on the other, the Court considers it equitable to apportion responsibility for that damage equally between the two parties.

NOTE

On this case read J. Meade (1986) 37 NILQ 370; N. March Hunnings (1987) 24 CML Rev 65.

SECTION 6: **ARTICLE 234**

A: **The function of Article 234 in judicial review**

The restrictive standing rules under the fourth paragraph of Article 230 and the time limit in its fifth paragraph conspire to diminish the efficacy of direct challenge to Community legislation before the European Court. However, the existence of the Article 234 preliminary reference procedure allows indirect challenge to be brought before national courts. In practice, this is of immense value to the private litigant.

R v *Intervention Board, ex parte Man (Sugar) Ltd* (Case 181/84) was examined in Chapter 2 and deserves re-reading (p.72 above). It is an example of an action instituted at national level in which the validity of Community legislation is called into question. The Article 234 reference allows the Court to rule on the Community measure's validity. So, once Community legislation finds expression in national implementing legislation, a challenge to the validity of the Community legislation may be achieved via a challenge at national level to the national implementing acts.

Universität Hamburg v *HZA Hamburg-Kehrwieder* (Case 216/82)
[1983] ECR 2771, Court of Justice of the European Communities

The dispute between the University and the German customs authorities related to the levy due on a Spectrometer imported from the USA for use in laboratory experiments on animals. A Commission Decision addressed to all Member States indicated an outcome unfavourable to the University, and the German authorities confirmed this. The University then brought proceedings at national level against the German authorities. The Finance Court in Hamburg made a preliminary reference questioning the lawfulness of the Commission Decision, but first it asked whether Article 177 of the EC Treaty (now Article 234 EC) could be used in this fashion. After all, the University had failed to use Article 173 of the EC Treaty (now, after amendment, Article 230 EC) directly to challenge the Commission's Decision before the European Court.

The first two questions

[5] By these questions the national court in substance seeks to ascertain whether, by not having brought proceedings under the second paragraph of Article 173 against a Decision of the Commission of the type in question within the periods stipulated in the third paragraph of that Article, the person or persons concerned by that Decision are, according to Community law, precluded from relying upon the invalidity of that Decision in proceedings before a national court. For the purpose of resolving that issue the procedure established by the aforesaid Regulations should be considered.

[6] Article 3 of Regulation No 3195/75 requires an application for duty-free admission to be submitted to the competent authority of the Member State in which the scientific establishment in question is situated. Article 4 requires that national authority to give a direct Decision on applications in all cases where the information at its disposal enables it to decide whether or not there exist apparatus of equivalent scientific value which are currently manufactured in the Community. Only if the national authority considers that it is unable to decide that question for itself is it therefore bound to refer it to the Commission and Community law does not require the applicant to be informed of that reference.

[7] The Decision adopted by the Commission is addressed to all the Member States. By virtue of Article 191 of the Treaty it must therefore be notified to the Member States and it takes effect upon such notification. However, it does not have to be notified to the person applying for exemption from customs duty and it is not one of the measures which the Treaty requires to be published. Even if in practice the Decision is in fact published in the *Official Journal of the European Communities*, its wording does not necessarily enable the applicant to ascertain whether it was adopted in relation to the procedure which he initiated.

[8] Since the Decision is binding on the Member States, the national authority must reject the application for duty-free admission in the event of a negative Decision on the part of the Commission; however, Community law does not require it to refer to the Commission's Decision in its own Decision rejecting the application. Furthermore, as this case demonstrates, the national authority's Decision may be adopted some time after the notification of the Commission's Decision.

[9] Finally, as the Finanzgericht rightly points out, for the purpose of bringing an action under the second paragraph of Article 173 of the Treaty against the Commission's Decision, the scientific establishment in question must demonstrate that the Decision is of direct and individual concern to it.

[10] In those circumstances the rejection by the national authority of the scientific establishment's application is the only measure which is directly addressed to it, of which it has necessarily been informed in good time and which the establishment may challenge in the courts without encountering any difficulty in demonstrating its interest in bringing proceedings. According to a general principle of law which finds its expression in Article 184 of the EEC Treaty, in proceedings brought under national law against the rejection of his application the applicant must be able to plead the illegality of the Commission's Decision on which the national Decision adopted in his regard is based.

[11] That statement is sufficient to provide an answer capable of dispelling the doubts expressed by the national court without there being any need to consider the wider issue of the general relationship between Articles 173 and 177 of the Treaty or to give a separate answer to the first question.

[12] The answer to the first two questions of the Finanzgericht should therefore be that the person or persons concerned by a Decision adopted by the Commission pursuant to Article 4 of Regulation No 3195/75 may plead the illegality of the Decision before the national court in proceedings against the fixing of customs duty and that the question of the validity of the Decision may therefore be referred to the Court in proceedings for a preliminary ruling.

On the merits, however, the Court found no reason to impugn the validity of the Decision.

Walter Rau v *BALM* (Case 133/85)
[1987] ECR 2289, Court of Justice of the European Communities

The Community instituted a scheme whereby cheap butter was sold on the West Berlin market in order to test consumer reaction. German margarine producers challenged the scheme before German courts arguing that the German implementing measures were unlawful because their source, the Community scheme, was unlawful. The national court was immediately concerned whether this line of argument could properly be advanced before it, given the existence of the direct action to challenge Community acts before the European Court under Article 173 of the EC Treaty (now, after amendment, Article 230 EC).

[11] It must be emphasized that there is nothing in Community law to prevent an action from being brought before a national court against a measure implementing a Decision adopted by a Community institution where the conditions laid down by national law are satisfied. When such an action is brought, if the outcome of the dispute depends on the validity of that Decision the national court may submit questions to the Court of Justice by way of a reference for a preliminary ruling, without there being any need to ascertain whether or not the plaintiff in the main proceedings has the possibility of challenging the Decision directly before the Court.

[12] The answer to the first question must therefore be that the possibility of bringing a direct action under the second paragraph of Article 173 of the EEC Treaty against a Decision adopted by a Community institution does not preclude the possibility of bringing an action in a national court against a measure adopted by a national authority for the implementation of that Decision on the ground that the latter Decision is unlawful.

However, the Court held that none of several submissions provided a basis for holding the Community scheme invalid. On the issue of proportionality, for example, the Court held:

[33] In its eighth question the national court asks whether the Decision of 25 February 1985 is compatible with the principle of proportionality in so far as the expansion of the markets or the search for new outlets may be achieved by action which has less impact on the workings of the market.

[34] By way of explanation, the national court states that rules which interfere with the fundamental right to exercise a trade or profession are justified only if they are dictated by objectives in the general interest which are of such overriding importance that they deserve to take precedence over that fundamental right. The national court considers that that is not the case in this instance. If, on the one hand, the purpose of the operation was to reduce public stocks by 900 tonnes of butter, it could have been achieved by measures which had a less serious effect on the position of competitors protected by fundamental rights. Thus the 900 tonnes of butter could have been distributed over a longer period or over a wider area. If, on the other hand, the purpose of the operation was the search for new outlets, the national court doubts whether the operation is capable of yielding useful results. A measure which is such as to interfere with fundamental rights but not such as to help achieve the aim pursued can never be justified by overriding considerations pertaining to the general interest.

[35] It follows from those considerations that the question raised by the national court was, more precisely, whether the principle of proportionality had been contravened on the ground that the aim of reducing public stocks by 900 tonnes of butter was attainable by methods which had a serious effect on the position of competitors and that it was doubtful whether a test market such as West Berlin was capable of yielding useful results.

[36] It must be remembered in the first place that, as the Court stated in reply to the third question, the operation did not have as its purpose to reduce intervention stocks by 900 tonnes of butter and

did not conflict with the principle of freedom to pursue a trade or profession, the principle of general freedom to pursue any lawful activity and the principle of freedom of competition.

[37] Next, it must be emphasized that the operation constituted, as it was intended to, the basis of a scientific survey from which the Commission was able to derive useful information. Furthermore, the Commission chose the West Berlin market because of its isolated geographical location and the possibility of carrying out there, in view of its limited size, an operation at relatively low cost. In so doing, the Commission would not appear to have exceeded the discretion conferred upon it by the Council in Article 4 of Regulation No 1079/77.

[38] Accordingly, the answer to the eighth question must be that consideration of the decision of 25 February 1985 has not disclosed any evidence of a breach of the principle of proportionality.

NOTE

The value of the preliminary reference procedure to the applicant is clear when it is appreciated that the applicant's direct action was doomed to fail as inadmissible without any examination of the merits of the claim; it was *Union Deutsche Lebensmittelwerke* (Case 97/85) (p.222 above), and this is the promised next episode in the saga of the Berlin butter.

B· The limitations of Article 234 in judicial review

Resort to the Article 234 'indirect' route for challenging Community acts has real attractions for the individual confronted by the high hurdles of Article 230. Moreover, the process emphasizes the role of national courts acting for these purposes as ordinary courts of Community law. It has a flavour of subsidiarity (p.654 below). The availability of Article 234 in addition to Article 230 gives the individual flexibility in acting to secure protection of interests affected by EC acts, although the value of Article 234 is limited *inter alia* by the individual's inability to *require* that a referral be made. Nevertheless, the next ruling amounts to a sharp rejection of any notion that an individual is entitled to choose to surrender an opportunity to sue under Article 230 and subsequently await reliance on Article 234.

TWD Textilwerke Deggendorf GmbH v *Germany* (Case C-188/92)
[1994] ECR I-833, Court of Justice of the European Communities

A Commission Decision addressed to Germany declared that aid paid to TWD Textilwerke Deggendorf GmbH, a Bavarian producer of polyamide and polyester yarn, was incompatible with the rules on State aid, Articles 92–94 of the EC Treaty (now, after amendment, Articles 87–89 EC). Germany was required to recover the aid. No direct action was initiated by either Germany or the firm, TWD, even though TWD had received a copy of the Commission Decision from the relevant German Ministry, which had also informed TWD that it could employ Article 173 of the EC Treaty (now, after amendment, Article 230 EC) to challenge the Decision (circumstances emphasized by the referring court). Subsequently in national proceedings to recover the aid, TWD raised challenges to the validity of the Commission Decision on which the national action was based. This led to a preliminary reference relating to the validity of the Commission Decision. But the European Court focused on TWD's tactics in selecting remedies.

[14] The undertaking in receipt of individual aid which is the subject-matter of a Commission decision adopted on the basis of Article 93 of the Treaty has the right to bring an action for annulment under the second paragraph of Article 173 of the Treaty even if the decision is addressed to a Member

State (judgment in Case 730/79 *Philip Morris* v *Commission* [1980] ECR 2671). By virtue of the third paragraph of that article, the expiry of the time-limit laid down in that provision has the same time-barring effect vis-à-vis such an undertaking as it does vis-à-vis the Member State which is the addressee of the decision.

[15] It is settled law that a Member State may no longer call in question the validity of a decision addressed to it on the basis of Article 93(2) of the Treaty once the time-limit laid down in the third paragraph of Article 173 of the Treaty has expired (see the judgments in Case 156/77 *Commission* v *Belgium* [1978] ECR 1881 and Case C-183/91 *Commission* v *Greece* [1993] ECR I-3131).

[16] That case law, according to which it is impossible for a Member State which is the addressee of a decision taken under the first paragraph of Article 93(2) of the Treaty to call in question the validity of the decision in the proceedings for non-compliance provided for in the second paragraph of that provision, is based in particular on the consideration that the periods within which applications must be lodged are intended to safeguard legal certainty by preventing Community measures which involve legal effects from being called in question indefinitely.

[17] It follows from the same requirements of legal certainty that it is not possible for a recipient of aid, forming the subject-matter of a Commission decision adopted on the basis of Article 93 of the Treaty, who could have challenged that decision and who allowed the mandatory time-limit laid down in this regard by the third paragraph of Article 173 of the Treaty to expire, to call in question the lawfulness of that decision before the national courts in an action brought against the measures taken by the national authorities for implementing that decision.

[18] To accept that in such circumstances the person concerned could challenge the implementation of the decision in proceedings before the national court on the ground that the decision was unlawful would in effect enable the person concerned to overcome the definitive nature which the decision assumes as against that person once the time-limit for bringing an action has expired.

[19] It is true that in its judgment in Joined Cases 133 to 136/85 *Rau* v *BALM* [1987] ECR 2289, on which the French Government relies in its observations, the Court held that the possibility of bringing a direct action under the second paragraph of Article 173 of the EEC Treaty against a decision adopted by a Community institution did not preclude the possibility of bringing an action in a national court against a measure adopted by a national authority for the implementation of that decision, on the ground that the latter decision was unlawful.

[20] However, as is clear from the Report for the Hearing in those cases, each of the plaintiffs in the main proceedings had brought an action before the Court of Justice for the annulment of the decision in question. The Court did not therefore rule, and did not have to rule, in that judgment on the time-barring effects of the expiry of time-limits. It is precisely that issue with which the question referred by the national court in this case is concerned.

[21] This case is also distinguishable from Case 216/82 *Universität Hamburg* v *Hauptzollamt Hamburg-Kehrwieder* [1983] ECR 2771.

[22] In the judgment in that case the Court held that a plaintiff whose application for duty-free admission had been rejected by a decision of a national authority taken on the basis of a decision of the Commission addressed to all the Member States had to be able to plead, in proceedings brought under national law against the rejection of his application, the illegality of the Commission's decision on which the national decision adopted in his regard was based.

[23] In that judgment the Court took into account the fact that the rejection of the application by the national authority was the only measure directly addressed to the person concerned of which it had necessarily been informed in good time and which it could challenge in the courts without encountering any difficulty in demonstrating its interest in bringing proceedings. It held that in those circumstances the possibility of pleading the unlawfulness of the Commission's decision derived from a general principle of law which found its expression in Article 184 of the EEC Treaty, namely the principle which confers upon any party to proceedings the right to challenge, for the purpose of obtaining the annulment of a decision of direct and individual concern to that party, the validity of

previous acts of the institutions which form the legal basis of the decision which is being attacked, if that party was not entitled under Article 173 of the Treaty to bring a direct action challenging those acts by which it was thus affected without having been in a position to ask that they be declared void (see the judgment in Case 92/78 *Simmenthal* v *Commission* [1979] ECR 777).

[24] In the present case, it is common ground that the applicant in the main proceedings was fully aware of the Commission's decision and of the fact that it could without any doubt have challenged it under Article 173 of the Treaty.

[25] It follows from the foregoing that, in factual and legal circumstances such as those of the main proceedings in this case, the definitive nature of the decision taken by the Commission pursuant to Article 93 of the Treaty vis-à-vis the undertaking in receipt of the aid binds the national court by virtue of the principle of legal certainty.

[26] The reply to be given to the first question must therefore be that the national court is bound by a Commission decision adopted under Article 93(2) of the Treaty where, in view of the implementation of that decision by the national authorities, the recipient of the aid to which the implementation measures are addressed brings before it an action in which it pleads the unlawfulness of the Commission's decision and where that recipient of aid, although informed in writing by the Member State of the Commission's decision, did not bring an action against that decision under the second paragraph of Article 173 of the Treaty, or did not do so within the period prescribed.

NOTE.

See also the analogy drawn in *TWD Textilwerke Deggendorf GmbH* v *Commission* (Cases T-244/93 and T-486/93) [1995] ECR II-2265, where the Court of First Instance limited access to Article 184 of the EC Treaty (now Article 241 EC) (p.237) where an available action under Article 173 of the EC Treaty (now, after amendment, Article 230 EC) had not been initiated. In the above ruling the Court is careful to make plain that it does not intend to overturn its pre-existing receptivity to the use of Article 177 of the EC Treaty (now Article 234 EC) as a means of indirect challenge to Community acts. Rather, it considers that it is dealing with a special situation in which a firm declining to pursue the available routes of the direct action should not subsequently be able to rely on the preliminary reference procedure. By contrast, in *Eurotunnel SA and Others* v *SeaFrance* (Case C-408/95) [1997] ECR I-6315, challenge to the validity of Directives 91/680 and 92/12 establishing transitional arrangements for 'duty free' shops failed on the merits, but was treated as permissibly advanced via proceedings at national level involving a preliminary reference under Article 177 of the EC Treaty (now Article 234 EC) even though the applicant had not attempted to employ Article 173 of the EC Treaty (now, after amendment, Article 230 EC), for it was not obvious that the applicant would have had individual concern for the purposes of a direct action and clearly would not have had direct concern. The message is that a firm immediately affected by a Community act must decide its litigation strategy with an eye to the two-month time-limit contained in the final paragraph of Article 230. Read M. Ross (1994) 19 EL Rev 641, A. Arnull (1995) 32 CML Rev 7, J. Usher in A. Campbell and M. Voyatzi (eds), *Legal Reasoning and Judicial Interpretation in European Law* (London: Trenton Publishing, 1996).

■ QUESTIONS

1. *In principle* do you accept the Court's concern in Case C-188/92 that legal certainty would be compromised were a party in the applicant's position permitted to avail itself of national proceedings supplemented by Article 234 in order to contest Community acts?

2. *In practice*, in the light of your examination in this Chapter of the twists and turns of the Court's approach to standing under Article 230, do you consider that the Court's reference to the ability *without any doubt* (para 24 of the ruling in Case C-188/92) of the applicant to make use of Article 230 represents a workable

criterion for lawyers who in future must advise clients as to when they should invest time and money in pursuing an Article 230 challenge, in order to preclude the subsequent unpleasant discovery that the Article 234 route is barred? Consider in this vein also Case C-241/01 *NFU v Secretariat general du gouvernement* judgment of 22 October 2002 (a recipient who 'could undoubtedly have challenged that decision' under Article 230 may not call its lawfulness into question before a national court, para 35 of the judgment).

C: **Article 234 and the validity of Community acts**

The next case was an important milestone in the Court's development of the preliminary reference procedure as a tool of judicial review of Community legislation. It has already been discussed at p.207 above, but the core of the judgment bears repetition here.

Foto Frost v *HZA Lubeck Ost* (Case 314/85)
[1987] ECR 4199, Court of Justice of the European Communities

[15] . . . [T]he main purpose of the powers accorded to the Court by Article 177 [now 234] is to ensure that Community law is applied uniformly by national courts. That requirement of uniformity is particularly imperative when the validity of a Community act is in question. Divergences between courts in the Member States as to the validity of Community acts would be liable to place in jeopardy the very unity of the Community legal order and detract from the fundamental requirement of legal certainty.

. . .

[17] Since Article 173 [now 230] gives the Court exclusive jurisdiction to declare void an act of a Community institution, the coherence of the system requires that where the validity of a Community act is challenged before a national court the power to declare the act invalid must also be reserved to the Court of Justice.

. . .

[19] It should be added that the rule that national courts may not themselves declare Community acts invalid may have to be qualified in certain circumstances in the case of proceedings relating to an application for interim measures; however, that case is not referred to in the national court's question.

[20] The answer to the first question must therefore be that the national courts have no jurisdiction themselves to declare that acts of Community institutions are invalid.

The Commission Decision was held invalid.

NOTE
Once this case is placed in the general context of the Community's judicial review procedures, it is perhaps easier to appreciate why the Court was eager to deny the competence of national courts to hold Community legislation unlawful (*cf* p.207 above). The proposition that the European Court is indeed properly treated as 'the ultimate umpire of the system' is carefully defended by J. Weiler and U. Haltern in 'The Autonomy of the Community Legal Order – Through the Looking Glass' (1996) 37 Harvard Intl L Jnl 411. The stance of national courts on judicial competence to fix the outer limits of Community competence has the potential to cause tension in the light of the European Court's perception that its own exclusive jurisdiction is essential to the very unity of the Community legal order. This is considered more fully in Chapter 21.

Zuckerfabrik Süderdithmarschen v *HZA Itzehoe* (Case C-143/88); *Zuckerfabrik Soest* v *HZA Paderborn* (Case C-92/89)

[1991] ECR I-415, Court of Justice of the European Communities

These cases involved two separate disputes between firms and German customs offices concerning demands for the payment of levies. The firms challenged the national administrative measures before German courts; the basis of the challenge was the validity of the Community legislation setting up the structure. The questions referred to the European Court concerned, first, the circumstances in which the national court could grant interim relief against the contested measures, it being clear from *Foto Frost* that the final decision on validity of Community legislation belongs with the European Court; and, secondly, questions about the validity of the challenged Regulation itself.

The Court insisted that in order to ensure that the preliminary reference procedure under Article 177 of the EC Treaty (now Article 234 EC) works effectively, it must be possible for a national court to grant interim relief suspending the operation of a national measure based on impugned Community legislation, pending the Court's final ruling on validity. It pointed out that it had already ruled that interim relief must be available before a national court asked to rule on the compatibility of national law with Community law (*Factortame*, p.137 below), and added that no different solution should apply where the dispute was about the compatibility of secondary Community law with Community law. The Court then went on to explain the circumstances in which such interim relief should be granted by a national court.

[23] It must first of all be noted that interim measures suspending enforcement of a contested measure may be adopted only if the factual and legal circumstances relied on by the applicants are such as to persuade the national court that serious doubts exist as to the validity of the Community regulation on which the contested administrative measure is based. Only the possibility of a finding of invalidity, a matter which is reserved to the court, can justify the granting of suspensory measures.

[24] It should next be pointed out that suspension of enforcement must retain the character of an interim measure. The national court to which the application for interim relief is made may therefore grant a suspension only until such time as the Court has delivered its ruling on the question of validity. Consequently, it is for the national court, should the question not yet have been referred to the Court of Justice, to refer that question itself, setting out the reasons for which it believes that the regulation must be held to be invalid.

[25] As regards the other conditions concerning the suspension of enforcement of administrative measures, it must be observed that the rules of procedure of the courts are determined by national law and that those conditions differ according to the national law governing them, which may jeopardize the uniform application of Community law.

[26] Such uniform application is a fundamental requirement of the Community legal order. It therefore follows that the suspension of enforcement of administrative measures based on a Community regulation, whilst it is governed by national procedural law, in particular as regards the making and examination of the application, must in all the Member States be subject, at the very least, to conditions which are uniform so far as the granting of such relief is concerned.

[27] Since the power of national courts to grant such a suspension corresponds to the jurisdiction reserved to the Court of Justice by Article 185 in the context of actions brought under Article 173, those courts may grant such relief only on the conditions which must be satisfied for the Court of Justice to allow an application to it for interim measures.

[28] In this regard, the Court has consistently held that measures suspending the operation of a contested act may be granted only in the event of urgency, in other words, if it is necessary for them to be adopted and to take effect before the decision on the substance of a case, in order to avoid serious and irreparable damage to the party seeking them.

[29] With regard to the question of urgency, it should be pointed out that damage invoked by the applicant must be liable to materialize before the Court of Justice has been able to rule on the validity of the contested Community measure. With regard to the nature of the damage, purely financial damage cannot, as the Court has held on numerous occasions, be regarded in principle as irreparable. However, it is for the national court hearing the application for interim relief to examine the circumstances particular to the case before it. It must in this connection consider whether immediate enforcement of the measure which is the subject of the application for interim relief would be likely to result in irreversible damage to the applicant which could not be made good if the Community act were to be declared invalid.

[30] It should also be added that a national court called upon to apply, within the limits of its jurisdiction, the provisions of Community law is under an obligation to ensure that full effect is given to Community law and, consequently, where there is doubt as to the validity of Community regulations, to take account of the interest of the Community, namely that such regulations should not be set aside without proper guarantees.

[31] In order to comply with that obligation, a national court seised of an application for suspension must first examine whether the Community measure in question would be deprived of all effectiveness if not immediately implemented.

[32] If suspension of enforcement is liable to involve a financial risk for the Community, the national court must also be in a position to require the applicant to provide adequate guarantees, such as the deposit of money or other security.

[33] It follows from the foregoing that the reply to the second part of the first question put to the Court by the Finanzgericht Hamburg must be that suspension of enforcement of a national measure adopted in implementation of a Community regulation may be granted by a national court only:

(i) if that court entertains serious doubts as to the validity of the Community measure and, should the question of the validity of the contested measure not already have been brought before the Court, itself refers that question to the Court;

(ii) if there is urgency and a threat of serious and irreparable damage to the applicant;

(iii) and if the national court takes due account of the Community's interests.

NOTE

There is a sure indication that the Court was aware in the *Zuckerfabrik* cases that it was establishing an important principle. The decision is against the applicants; the legislation is held valid. Yet the Court had not dealt with the matter in brief, as it could have done. It took time to explain the applicable principles of law.

In the next case the Court added a further, fourth criterion. There seems little doubt that the addition reflects the Court's concern to sustain uniformity in the application of Community law. The decision is a preliminary ruling on questions referred from a German court, the *Verwaltungsgericht* of Frankfurt-am-Main.

Atlanta Fruchthandelsgesellschaft mbH and Others v *Bundesamt für Ernährung und Forstwirtschaft* (Case C-465/93)

[1995] ECR I-3761, Court of Justice of the European Communities

The challenged act was Council Regulation 404/93 on the common organization of the market in bananas, establishing a common import regime. The applicants, traditional importers of bananas, found themselves with import quotas which they viewed as insufficient. Among other strategies to challenge the system, they brought proceedings before the German courts to attack measures associated with the implementation of the EC regime. The European Court was asked questions on the national court's power to order interim measures disapplying an EC Regulation pending a preliminary ruling by the Court on its validity. The Court stated that the case afforded it 'an opportunity to clarify' the conditions established in *Zuckerfabrik* (Cases C-143/88, C-92/89), p.255 above.

[35] In *Zuckerfabrik* (paragraph 23) the Court held that interim measures may be adopted only if the factual and legal circumstances relied on by the applicants are such as to persuade the national court that serious doubts exist as to the validity of the Community regulation on which the contested administrative measure is based. Only the possibility of a finding of invalidity, a matter which is reserved to the Court, can justify the grant of interim relief.

[36] That requirement means that the national court cannot restrict itself to referring the question of the validity of the regulation to the Court for a preliminary ruling, but must set out, when making the interim order, the reasons for which it considers that the Court should find the regulation to be invalid.

[37] The national court must take into account here the extent of the discretion which, having regard to the Court's case-law, the Community institutions must be allowed in the sectors concerned.

[38] The Court further held in *Zuckerfabrik* (paragraph 24) that the grant of relief must retain the character of an interim measure. The national court to which the application for interim relief is made may therefore order interim measures and maintain them only for so long as the Court has not ruled that consideration of the questions referred for a preliminary ruling has disclosed no factor of such a kind as to affect the validity of the regulation in question.

[39] Since the power of national courts to order interim relief corresponds to the jurisdiction reserved to the Court of Justice by Article 186 in the context of actions brought under Article 173 of the Treaty, those national courts may grant such relief only on the same conditions as apply when the Court of Justice is dealing with an application for interim measures (*Zuckerfabrik*, paragraph 27).

[40] In that respect the Court held in *Zuckerfabrik* (paragraph 28), on the basis of settled case law, that interim measures may be ordered only where they are urgent, that is to say, where it is necessary for them to be adopted and take effect before the decision on the substance of the case, in order to avoid serious and irreparable damage to the party seeking them.

[41] As to urgency, the damage relied on by the applicant must be such as to materialise before the Court of Justice has been able to rule on the validity of the contested Community act. As to the nature of the damage, purely financial damage cannot, as the Court has held on numerous occasions, be regarded in principle as irreparable. However, it is for the national court hearing the application for interim relief to examine the circumstances particular to the case before it. It must in this connection consider whether immediate enforcement of the measure with respect to which the application for interim relief is made would be likely to result in irreversible damage to the applicant which could not be made good if the Community act were to be declared invalid (*Zuckerfabrik*, paragraph 29).

[42] Furthermore, a national court called upon to apply, within the limits of its jurisdiction, the provisions of Community law is under an obligation to ensure that full effect is given to Community law and, consequently, where there is doubt as to the validity of Community regulations, to take account of the interest of the Community, namely that such regulations should not be set aside without proper guarantees (*Zuckerfabrik*, paragraph 30).

[43] In order to comply with that obligation, the national court to which an application for interim relief has been made must first examine whether the Community act in question would be deprived of all effectiveness if not immediately implemented (*Zuckerfabrik*, paragraph 31).

[44] In that respect the national court must take account of the damage which the interim measure may cause the legal regime established by that regulation for the Community as a whole. It must consider, on the one hand, the cumulative effect which would arise if a large number of courts were also to adopt interim measures for similar reasons and, on the other, those special features of the applicant's situation which distinguish him from the other operators concerned.

[45] If the grant of interim relief represents a financial risk for the Community, the national court must also be in a position to require the applicant to provide adequate guarantees, such as the deposit of money or other security (*Zuckerfabrik*, paragraph 32).

[46] When assessing the conditions for the grant of interim relief, the national court is obliged under Article 5 [now 10] of the Treaty to respect what the Community court has decided on the questions at issue before it. Thus if the Court of Justice has dismissed on the merits an action for annulment of the regulation in question or has held, in the context of a reference for a preliminary ruling on validity, that the reference disclosed nothing to affect the validity of that regulation, the national court can no longer order interim measures or must revoke existing measures, unless the grounds of illegality put forward before it differ from the pleas in law or grounds of illegality rejected by the Court in its judgment. The same applies if the Court of First Instance, in a judgment which has become final and binding, has dismissed on the merits an action for annulment of the regulation or a plea of illegality.

[47] In the present case the Court, adjudicating on the same factual situation as that which gave rise to the proceedings before the national court, has held that the Member States which bring an action for annulment of the regulation, being responsible for the interests, in particular those of an economic and social nature, which are regarded as general interests at national level, are entitled to take judicial proceedings to defend such interests. They may therefore invoke damage affecting a whole sector of their economy, in particular when the contested Community measure may entail unfavourable repercussions on the level of employment and the cost of living (order in *Germany* v *Council*, cited above [Case C-280/93 R) [1993] ECR I-3667], paragraph 27).

[48] The national court, when called upon to protect the rights of individuals, may indeed assess the extent to which refusal to order an interim measure may be liable to have a serious and irreparable effect on important individual interests.

[49] However, if an applicant is unable to show a specific situation which distinguishes him from other operators in the relevant sector, the national court must accept any findings already made by the Court of Justice concerning the serious and irreparable nature of the damage.

[50] The national court's obligation to respect a decision of the Court of Justice applies in particular to the Court's assessment of the Community interest and the balance between that interest and that of the economic sector concerned.

[51] Accordingly, the answer to the second question put to the Court by the Verwaltungsgericht Frankfurt am Main must be that interim relief, with respect to a national administrative measure adopted in implementation of a Community regulation, can be granted by a national court only if:

(1) that court entertains serious doubts as to the validity of the Community act and, if the validity of the contested act is not already in issue before the Court of Justice, itself refers the question to the Court of Justice;

(2) there is urgency, in that the interim relief is necessary to avoid serious and irreparable damage being caused to the party seeking the relief;

(3) the court takes due account of the Community interest; and

(4) in its assessment of all those conditions, it respects any decisions of the Court of Justice or the Court of First Instance ruling on the lawfulness of the regulation or on an application for interim measures seeking similar interim relief at Community level.

NOTE
On the very same day the Court answered questions relating to the validity of the same Regulation, 404/93, referred to it by the same court in litigation between the same parties: *Atlanta Fruchthandelsgesellschaft mbH and others* v *Bundesamt für Ernährung und Forstwirtschaft* (Case

C-466/93) [1995] ECR I-3799. The Court observed that an action for annulment of the Regulation brought by Germany under Article 173 of the EC Treaty (now, after amendment, Article 230 EC), based on comparable pleas to those covered by the questions referred, had already been dismissed as unfounded (*Germany* v *Council* (Case C-280/93) [1994] ECR I-4973). The European Court had there found no violation of Community law principles including that of undistorted competition, nor of fundamental rights including the right to property; neither had the Court in Case C-280/93 been prepared to test the Regulation against the standards of the GATT which it viewed as too 'flexible' to be apt for application in the context of a direct action for annulment (the Court has subsequently transplanted this reluctance to the incorporation of the Standards of the WTO, which has replaced the GATT: Case C-149/96 *Portugal* v *Council* [1999] ECR I-8395). Nothing new had been advanced in the preliminary reference to alter the Court's findings in Case C-280/93, excepting only a submission based on lack of reasons within the meaning of Article 190 of the EC Treaty (now Article 235 EC) (p.68 above) which the Court did not accept. The Court therefore found no basis to impugn the validity of the Regulation. Subsequently, a claim for damages was unsuccessful; Case T-521/93 *Atlanta AG and Others* v *Council and Commission* [1996] ECR II-1707, from which an appeal failed in substance in Case C-104/97P *Atlanta AG and Others* v *Council and Commission* [1999] ECR I-6983. (On some of the background tensions in the 'banana cases', see N. Reich (1996) 7 EJIL 103; S. Peers (1999) 4 *Euro Foreign Affairs Rev* 195; and the *Bundesverfassungsgericht* ruling in *Bananas* is set out in Chapter 21, p.690 below.)

Whereas *Atlanta* (Case C-465/93) explores the criteria according to which the application of national measures adopted pursuant to a Community act may exceptionally be suspended in national proceedings in which the validity of the Community act is impugned, the next case in this saga, also involving the Community's disputed bananas regime founded on Regulation 404/93, saw the Court unwilling further to extend the powers of national courts.

T. Port GmbH v *Bundesanstalt für Landwirtschaft und Ernährung* (Case C-68/95)
[1996] ECR I-6065, [1997] 1 CMLR 1, Court of Justice of the European Communities

The applicant company's aim was to secure an increased quota of bananas. Proceedings were initiated before a German court, which made a preliminary reference asking for guidance on the powers of a national court to grant interim relief to traders pending a Commission determination on a request for an increased quota; specifically, could the national court make an interim order granting an increase? This goes beyond that which the Court accepted was within the competence of a national court in *Zuckerfabrik* and *Atlanta*, and in *T. Port* the Court, having referred to those cases, was not prepared to make that extension. Traders must seek judicial protection before the Community judicature in such circumstances.

[52] However, the situation now raised by the national court is different from the situation at issue in those cases. The present case is not about granting interim measures in the context of the implementation of a Community regulation whose validity is being contested, in order to ensure interim protection of rights which individuals derive from the Community legal system, but about granting traders interim judicial protection in a situation where, by virtue of a Community regulation, the existence and scope of traders' rights must be established by a Commission measure which the Commission has not yet adopted.

[53] The Treaty makes no provision for a reference for a preliminary ruling by which a national court asks the Court of Justice to rule that an institution has failed to act. Consequently, national courts have no jurisdiction to order interim measures pending action on the part of the institution. Judicial review of alleged failure to act can be exercised only by the Community judicature.

[54] In a situation such as that in the present case, only the Court of Justice or the Court of First Instance, as the case may be, can ensure judicial protection for the persons concerned.

[55] It is to be remembered that, under the procedure provided for in Article 27 of the Regulation,

the Commission is to adopt transitional measures following an opinion of the Management Committee before which the matter is brought by a representative of the Commission or of a Member State.

[56] In circumstances such as those in the main proceedings, it is for the relevant Member State, urged if necessary by the trader concerned, to request initiation of the Management Committee procedure, should this be necessary.

[57] Having regard to the hardship which the applicant in the main proceedings claims to be suffering, the applicant may also approach the Commission directly and request it to adopt, in accordance with the Article 27 procedure, the specific measures which its situation requires.

[58] Where the Community institution fails to act, the Member State may bring an action for failure to act before the Court of Justice. Likewise, the trader concerned, who would be the addressee of the measure which the Commission is alleged to have failed to adopt, or at least directly and individually concerned by it, could bring such an action before the Court of First Instance (see Case C-107/91 *ENU* v *Commission* [1993] ECR I-599).

[59] It is true that the third paragraph of Article 175 of the Treaty entitles legal and natural persons to bring an action for failure to act when an institution has failed to address to them any act other than a recommendation or an opinion. The Court has, however, held that Articles 173 and 175 merely prescribe one and the same method of recourse (Case 15/70 *Chevalley* v *Commission* [1970] ECR 975, paragraph 6). It follows that, just as the fourth paragraph of Article 173 allows individuals to bring an action for annulment against a measure of an institution not addressed to them provided that the measure is of direct and individual concern to them, the third paragraph of Article 175 must be interpreted as also entitling them to bring an action for failure to act against an institution which they claim has failed to adopt a measure which would have concerned them in the same way. The possibility for individuals to assert their rights should not depend upon whether the institution concerned has acted or failed to act.

NOTE

Notice in these cases the Court's concern to build through analogies between Community level and national level. The Treaty provisions governing remedies are singularly incomplete, and the Court here shows itself bent on developing the system. What is particularly interesting in this area is the extent to which the European Court is presiding over the development of a coherent legal order governing remedies. These cases concern interim relief at national level from Community acts. *Factortame* (Case C-213/89) concerns interim relief at national level from Member State practices allegedly incompatible with Community law; p.137 above. Interim relief at Community level is examined at p.233 in relation to Community acts, at p.116 in relation to Member State practices. It is interesting and important to assess the extent to which the Court is bringing all these procedures into line. The process is far from complete, and naturally lacks the comprehensive coverage of legislation, but the Court appears gradually to be building the Community legal order through jurisprudence in linked but not identical areas.

....

D: **The effect of an Article 234 ruling**

ICC v *Amministrazione delle Finanze* **(Case 66/80)**

[1981] ECR 1191, [1983] 2 CMLR 593, Court of Justice of the European Communities

The facts are set out at p.199 above. The Court held:

. . . [A]lthough a judgment of the Court given under Article 177 [now 234] of the Treaty declaring an act of an institution, in particular a Council or Commission Regulation, to be void is directly addressed only to the national court which brought the matter before the Court, it is sufficient reason for any other national court to regard that act as void for the purposes of a judgment which it has to give.

NOTE
Accordingly, a finding in Article 234 proceedings that Community legislation is invalid should be respected by other national courts. In practice, the effects of an Article 234 ruling of invalidity may not be significantly different from the impact of an Article 230 ruling, which according to Article 231 renders the act 'void'.

The Court has also claimed the power under Article 234 to rule on the validity of Community legislation in a nuanced manner. Validity need not be all or nothing.

Société de Produits de Màïs v *Administration des Douanes* (Case 112/83)
[1985] ECR 719, Court of Justice of the European Communities

This was a reference under Article 177 of the EC Treaty (now Article 234 EC) from a French court relating to the validity of Commission Regulation 652/76.

[16] It should in the first place be recalled that the Court has already held in its judgment of 13 May 1981 (Case 66/80 *International Chemical Corporation* [1981] ECR 1191) that although a judgment of the Court given under Article 177 of the Treaty declaring an act of an institution, in particular a Council or Commission Regulation, to be void is directly addressed only to the national court which brought the matter before the Court, it is sufficient reason for any other national court to regard that act as void for the purposes of a judgment which it has to give.

[17] Secondly, it must be emphasized that the Court's power to impose temporal limits on the effects of a declaration that a legislative act is invalid, in the context of preliminary rulings under indent (b) of the first paragraph of Article 177, is justified by the interpretation of Article 174 [now 231] of the Treaty having regard to the necessary consistency between the preliminary ruling procedure and the action for annulment provided for in Articles 173, 174 and 176 of the Treaty, which are two mechanisms provided by the Treaty for reviewing the legality of acts of the Community institutions. The possibility of imposing temporal limits on the effects of the invalidity of a Community Regulation, whether under Article 173 or Article 177, is a power conferred on the Court by the Treaty in the interest of the uniform application of Community law throughout the Community. In the particular case of the judgment of 15 October 1980, referred to by the Tribunal [Case 145/79], the use of the possibility provided for in the second paragraph of Article 174 was based on reasons of legal certainty more fully explained in paragraph 52 of that judgment.

[18] It must be pointed out that where it is justified by overriding considerations the second paragraph of Article 174 [now 231] gives the Court discretion to decide, in each particular case, which specific effects of a Regulation which has been declared void must be maintained. It is therefore for the Court, where it makes use of the possibility of limiting the effect on past events of a declaration in proceedings under Article 177 [now 234] that a measure is void, to decide whether an exception to that temporal limitation of the effect of its judgment may be made in favour of the party which brought the action before the national court or of any other trader which took similar steps before the declaration of invalidity or whether, conversely, a declaration of invalidity applicable only to the future constitutes an adequate remedy even for traders who took action at the appropriate time with a view to protecting their rights.

NOTE
Cf the second paragraph of Article 231, at p.217 above. Notice once again the Court's interest in bringing about coherence between the different routes for challenging Community acts.

The Court's approach in this case to the validity of Community legislation also finds a parallel in its approach to the interpretation of Community law. In *Defrenne* v *SABENA* (Case 43/75), at p.127 above, it insisted that it alone has the competence to limit the implications of its ruling at national level.

SECTION 7: **THE INTERRELATION OF THE SEVERAL REMEDIES AND PRESSURE FOR LIBERALIZATION OF THE STANDING RULES**

It should now be plain that although Article 230 constitutes the major direct means of challenging Community acts before the Court, other avenues of redress may be open to applicants. These include other avenues before the Court, as well as procedures at national level involving the use of the Article 234 preliminary reference procedure.

An extract from para 23 of '*Les Verts*' (Case 294/83) was set out at p.237 above to demonstrate how at Community level Article 241 may allow the applicant to circumvent the hurdles of the Article 230 direct action. Here now is the full text of para 23, which confirms how in addition Article 234 may serve that purpose via the action at national level.

Parti Ecologiste 'Les Verts' v *Parliament* (Case 294/83)
[1986] ECR 1339, Court of Justice of the European Communities

[23] It must first be emphasised in this regard that the European Economic Community is a Community based on the rule of law, inasmuch as neither its Member States nor its institutions can avoid a review of the question whether the measures adopted by them are in conformity with the basic constitutional charter, the Treaty. In particular, in Articles 173 [now 230] and 184 [now 241], on the one hand, and in Article 177 [now 234], on the other, the Treaty established a complete system of legal remedies and procedures designed to permit the Court of Justice to review the legality of measures adopted by the institutions. Natural and legal persons are thus protected against the application to them of general measures which they cannot contest directly before the Court by reason of the special conditions of admissibility laid down in the second paragraph of Article 173 [now the fourth paragraph of Article 230] of the Treaty. Where the Community institutions are responsible for the administrative implementation of such measures, natural or legal persons may bring a direct action before the Court against implementing measures which are addressed to them or which are of direct and individual concern to them and, in support of such an action, plead the illegality of the general measure on which they are based. Where implementation is a matter for the national authorities, such persons may plead the invalidity of general measures before the national courts and cause the latter to request the Court of Justice for a preliminary ruling.

NOTE
In this Chapter there have been many other examples of the Court's concern to draw analogies between different levels of enforcement and remedies in order to ensure the structure displays an internal coherence. See the *Zuckerfabrik* cases at p.255 above; and read para 10 of the judgment in *Universität Hamburg* (Case 216/82), at p.249 above; para 17, *Foto Frost* (Case 314/85), at p.254 above; para 39, *Atlanta* (Case 465/93), at p.256 above; para 17, *Société de Produits de Maïs* (Case 112/83), at p.261 above. This is part of the Court's process of 'constitutionalising' the Treaty (p.275 below).

A: **Pressure for liberalization, 1994–2001**

However, there is a degree of pressure to loosen the standing rules that apply to applications made under Article 230(4) EC. This is an unstable area of law at present. In the anti-dumping cases the relatively liberal attitude in *Extramet*

(Case C-358/89, p.230 above) could be attributed to the unusually heavy impact of the EC measure on the applicant's trade in the case and, more generally, to the special circumstances prevailing in the sphere of anti-dumping. However, in the next case the Court hints at a possible transplant of the liberal approach accepted in specific sectors such as anti-dumping into the broad area of challenges to general market regulation. The applicant employs *Extramet* as a lever.

Codorniu SA v *Council* (Case C-309/89)
[1994] ECR I-1853, Court of Justice of the European Communities

Codorniu, a Spanish producer of sparkling wines, sought to annul a provision in Council Regulation 2045/89, amending Regulation 3309/85, laying down general rules for the description and presentation of sparkling wines. The measure reserved the term *crémant* for certain quality sparkling wines manufactured in France and Luxembourg. It was explained in the recitals to the Regulation that this protected traditional descriptions used in those two countries. Codorniu had held and, since 1924, had used the Spanish trade mark *Gran Crémant de Codorniu* to designate one of its wines. It wished to challenge the Regulation. The Council objected to the admissibility of the application.

[14] In support of its objection of inadmissibility the Council states that it did not adopt the contested provision on the basis of the circumstances peculiar to certain producers but on the basis of a choice of wine-marketing policy in relation to a particular product. The contested provision reserves the use of the term 'crémant' to quality sparkling wines psr manufactured under specific conditions in certain Member States. It thus constitutes a measure applicable to an objectively determined situation which has legal effects in respect of categories of persons considered in a general and abstract manner.

[15] According to the Council, Codorniu is concerned by the contested provision only in its capacity as a producer of quality sparkling wine psr using the term 'crémant', like any other producer in an identical situation. Even if when that provision was adopted the number or identity of producers of sparkling wines using the term 'crémant' could theoretically be determined, the measure in question remains essentially a regulation inasmuch as it applies on the basis of an objective situation of law or fact defined by the measure in relation to its objective.

[16] Codorniu alleges that the contested provision is in reality a decision adopted in the guise of a regulation. It has no general scope but affects a well-determined class of producers which cannot be altered. Such producers are those who on 1 September 1989 traditionally designated their sparkling wines with the term 'crémant'. For that class the contested provision has no general scope. Furthermore, the direct result of the contested provision will be to prevent Codorniu from using the term 'Gran Cremant' which will involve a loss of 38% of its turnover. The effect of that damage is to distinguish it, within the meaning of the second paragraph of Article 173 of the Treaty, from any other trader. Codorniu alleges that the Court has already recognized the admissibility of an action for annulment brought by a natural or legal person against a regulation in such circumstances (see the judgment in Case C-358/89 *Extramet Industrie* v *Council* [1991] ECR I-2501).

[17] Under the second paragraph of Article 173 of the Treaty the institution of proceedings by a natural or legal person for a declaration that a regulation is void is subject to the condition that the provisions of the regulation at issue in the proceedings constitute in reality a decision of direct and individual concern to that person.

[18] As the Court has already held, the general applicability, and thus the legislative nature, of a measure is not called in question by the fact that it is possible to determine more or less exactly the number or even the identity of the persons to whom it applies at any given time, as long as it is established that it applies to them by virtue of an objective legal or factual situation defined by the

measure in question in relation to its purpose (see most recently the judgment in Case C-298/89 *Gibraltar* v *Council* [1993] ECR I-3605, paragraph 17).

[19] Although it is true that according to the criteria in the second paragraph of Article 173 of the Treaty the contested provision is, by nature and by virtue of its sphere of application, of a legislative nature in that it applies to the traders concerned in general, that does not prevent it from being of individual concern to some of them.

[20] Natural or legal persons may claim that a contested provision is of individual concern to them only if it affects them by reason of certain attributes which are peculiar to them or by reason of circumstances in which they are differentiated from all other persons (see the judgment in Case 25/62 *Plaumann* v *Commission* [1963] ECR 95).

[21] Codorniu registered the graphic trade mark 'Gran Cremant de Codorniu' in Spain in 1924 and traditionally used that mark both before and after registration. By reserving the right to use the term 'crémant' to French and Luxembourg producers, the contested provision prevents Codorniu from using its graphic trade mark.

[22] It follows that Codorniu has established the existence of a situation which from the point of view of the contested provision differentiates it from all other traders.

[23] It follows that the objection of inadmissibility put forward by the Council must be dismissed.

NOTE
The Court proceeded to determine that the measure's discrimination between producers from different countries lacked objective justification. The contested provision was accordingly declared void. The ruling is more generous to the admissibility of an application by an individual firm affected by a measure of market regulation than past European Court practice might have led one to expect. The acceptance that a measure of a general legislative nature could be of individual concern to traders who are particularly heavily affected by it offers a route to wider access to justice for non-privileged applicants.

After *Codorniu* the development of the law rested initially with the Court of First Instance (p.219 above). *Codorniu* is plainly a significant ruling, but there were special factors affecting the applicant's position, most notably its property right in the trade mark, which were capable of being used as a basis for limiting the decision's contribution to the general liberalization of the rules affecting non-privileged applicants. And initially the *Codorniu*-inspired optimism of proponents of more generous standing rules proved 'largely misplaced' (A. Arnull, 'Private Applicants and the action for annulment since *Codorniu*' (2001) 38 CML Rev 7). The important statement at para 19 of the ruling in *Codorniu* (above), that a measure may be 'of a legislative nature in that it applies to the traders concerned in general' yet simultaneously of 'individual concern to some of them', is rehearsed in CFI rulings, yet applicants have consistently found it very difficult to persuade the CFI that their situation falls within this hybrid pattern.

Terres Rouges v *Commission* (Case T-47/95)
[1997] ECR II-481, Court of First Instance of the European Communities

Challenge was directed at Regulation 3224/94, which amended Regulation 404/93 and in doing so significantly reduced the tariff quota entitlement for non-traditional ACP (African, Caribbean and Pacific) bananas from Côtè d'Ivoire (Ivory Coast). The applicants submitted that they, as importers into the EU of 70% of the banana production of Côte d'Ivoire, would be prejudiced by the downwards adjustment of the figure and that they were therefore directly and individually concerned.

[41] In this case the contested regulation does not have any features which would enable it to be classed as a decision taken in the form of a regulation. It is drafted in general and abstract terms and is applicable in all the Member States, without any regard being had to the situation of individual producers. It is designed to amend the arrangements for the import of bananas laid down by Regulation No 404/93 in order to adapt them to the changes introduced by the Framework Agreement entered into with the Latin American countries concerned.

[42] It follows that the contested regulation applies to situations which have been determined objectively and has legal effects with respect to a category of persons viewed in a general and abstract manner.

[43] As regards the question whether the applicants are individually concerned by the contested regulation, it is settled law that, in certain circumstances, even a legislative measure applying to the traders concerned in general may concern some of them individually (judgments in Case C-358/89 *Extramet Industrie* v *Council* [1991] ECR I-2501, paragraph 13, and Case C-309/89 *Codorniu* v *Council* [1994] ECR I-1853, paragraph 19, and order of 11 January 1995 in Case T-116/94 *Cassa Nazionale di Previdenza ed Assistenza a favore degli Avvocati e Procuratori* v *Council* [1995] ECR II-1, paragraph 26). In such circumstances, a Community measure could be of a legislative nature and, at the same time, in the nature of a decision *vis-à-vis* some of the traders concerned (Joined Cases T-481/93 and T-484/93 *Exporteurs in Levende Varkens and Others* v *Commission* [1995] ECR II-2941, paragraph 50).

[44] However, the possibility of determining more or less precisely the number or even the identity of the persons to whom a measure applies by no means implies that it must be regarded as being of individual concern to them (Case 123/77 *UNICME* v *Council* [1978] ECR 845, paragraph 16).

[45] In that regard, the legislative provisions relevant to this dispute should be borne in mind. Article 19 of Regulation No 404/93 provides that the tariff quota is to be opened as to 66.5% for the category of operators who marketed third-country and/or non-traditional ACP bananas (category A); as to 30% for the category of operators who marketed Community and/or traditional ACP bananas (category B); and as to 3.5% for the category of operators established in the Community who started marketing bananas other than Community and/or traditional ACP bananas from 1992 (category C). Supplementary criteria to be met by operators are to be laid down in accordance with the procedure provided for in Article 27 of the regulation. Operators who satisfy those conditions and who are granted import licences by the competent authorities of the relevant Member State may import third-country or non-traditional ACP bananas within the tariff quota, whatever category of importer they fall within.

[46] In addition, the Court of Justice has held that the purpose of Articles 18 and 19 of Regulation No 404/93 is to establish arrangements for trade in bananas with third countries and a mechanism for the allocation of the tariff quota between categories of traders defined according to objective criteria. Those provisions accordingly apply to situations which have been determined objectively and have legal effects as regards categories of persons viewed in a general and abstract manner. It follows that the contested measure is of concern to the applicants only in their objective capacity as traders engaged in the marketing of bananas from third countries in the same way as any other trader in an identical position (order of 21 June 1993 in Case C-276/93 *Chiquita Banana Company and Others* v *Council* [1993] ECR I-3345, paragraphs 10, 11 and 12).

[47] Regulation No 3224/94 admittedly restricted the quantity of non-traditional ACP bananas that Côte d'Ivoire could export within the tariff quota. However, under Regulation No 404/93 (see paragraph 45 of this judgment), all importers in categories A, B and C are entitled to import bananas from Côte d'Ivoire. Regulation No 3224/94 thus affects every importer wishing to import bananas from Côte d'Ivoire and the fact that the applicants currently import a large proportion of Côte d'Ivoire's bananas does not amount to circumstances differentiating them from other importers.

[48] The applicants' argument that Regulation No 3224/94 fundamentally altered the rights conferred by Regulation No 404/93 must be rejected.

[49] It is based on the premiss that, before Regulation No 3224/94 was adopted, Côte d'Ivoire could

have placed approximately 50,000 tonnes of non-traditional ACP bananas on the Community market in addition to the 155,000 tonnes of traditional ACP bananas allocated to it by Regulation No 404/93 (see paragraphs 34 to 38 of this judgment).

[50] First, Regulation No 3224/94 does not in any way preclude the applicants from importing into the Community traditional ACP bananas from Côte d'Ivoire. They can still import 70%, or even more, of the 155,000 tonnes of traditional ACP bananas allocated to that country.

[51] Secondly, as the Commission stated at the hearing and the applicants did not dispute, the total amount of traditional ACP and non-traditional ACP bananas exported from Côte d'Ivoire in 1993 and 1994 after the new arrangements had been established by Regulation No 404/93 did not exceed 160,000 tonnes per year. Those exports did not therefore exceed the quantity of 162,500 tonnes constituted by the reserve of 155,000 tonnes of traditional ACP bananas and the share of 7,500 tonnes of non-traditional ACP bananas reserved for Côte d'Ivoire by Regulation No 3224/94. The truth is that the figure of 50,000 tonnes quoted by the applicants is only an estimate of the potential production of Côte d'Ivoire's plantations and does not refer to current exports. Contrary to the applicants' submissions, therefore, their position has not in actual fact been affected by the adoption of Regulation No 3224/94.

The Court of First Instance concluded that Regulation 3224/94 concerned the applicants only in their objective capacity as importers of third-country bananas, and that their legal position was not affected by circumstances in which they were differentiated from the other traders in the same position. It was therefore not of individual concern to them. The CFI added that under Regulation 404/93 importers of third-country bananas must obtain an import licence from the authorities of a Member State, and that only decisions on whether or not to grant a licence affect the applicants directly. The quota allocated by Regulation 3224/94 was therefore not capable of affecting the applicants' legal position directly, as was required under Article 173(4) of the EC Treaty (now, after amendment, Article 230(4) EC), p.224 above. The Court dismissed the application as inadmissible after commenting:

[59] Nor have the applicants established that in appropriate circumstances it would be impossible for them to challenge the validity of Regulation No 3224/94 before a national court, for example in an action brought against a refusal by the competent national authorities to issue them with import licences for non-traditional ACP bananas from Côte d'Ivoire, and to request the national court to seek a preliminary ruling in that regard from the Court of Justice pursuant to Article 177 [now 234] of the Treaty.

NOTE
See similarly Case T-138/98 *ACAV* v *Council* [2000] ECR II-341. The next case also offered no joy to the private applicants.

Stichting Greenpeace Council (Greenpeace International) and Others v Commission (Case C-321/95 P)
[1998] ECR I-1651, Court of Justice of the European Communities

In Case T-585/93 *Greenpeace and Others* v *Commission* [1995] ECR II-2205, the CFI held inadmissible an action for the annulment of a Commission decision to allocate funds to Spain within the framework of the European Regional Development Fund for the construction of two power stations in the Canary Islands. It was alleged that EC rules on environmental protection had been neglected, but the CFI adhered to existing case law and treated the applicants, who included associations concerned with the protection of the environment, as lacking any distinct interest in the matter of the type necessary to establish 'individual concern' within the meaning of Article 173 of the EC Treaty (now, after amendment, Article 230 EC). On appeal to the Court of Justice, the applicants observed *inter alia* that the CFI's approach 'creates a legal vacuum in ensuring compliance with Community environmental legislation, since in this area the interests are, by their very nature, common and shared, and the rights relating to those interests are liable to be held by a potentially large number of individuals so that there could never be a closed class of applicants satisfying the criteria adopted by the Court of First Instance'. The Court of Justice was then pressed to take the lead in relaxing the strict approach. The Court's 'Findings' occupy no more than nine short paragraphs.

Findings of the Court

27. The interpretation of the fourth paragraph of Article 173 of the Treaty that the Court of First Instance applied in concluding that the appellants did not have *locus standi* is consonant with the settled case law of the Court of Justice.

28. As far as natural persons are concerned, it follows from the case-law, cited at both paragraph 48 of the contested order and at paragraph 7 of this judgment, that where, as in the present case, the specific situation of the applicant was not taken into consideration in the adoption of the act, which concerns him in a general and abstract fashion and, in fact, like any other person in the same situation, the applicant is not individually concerned by the act.

29. The same applies to associations which claim to have *locus standi* on the basis of the fact that the persons whom they represent are individually concerned by the contested decision. For the reasons given in the preceding paragraph, that is not the case.

30. In appraising the appellants' arguments purporting to demonstrate that the case-law of the Court of Justice, as applied by the Court of First Instance, takes no account of the nature and specific characteristics of the environmental interests underpinning their action, it should be emphasised that it is the decision to build the two power stations in question which is liable to affect the environmental rights arising under Directive 85/337 that the appellants seek to invoke.

31. In those circumstances, the contested decision, which concerns the Community financing of those power stations, can affect those rights only indirectly.

32. As regards the appellants' argument that application of the Court's case-law would mean that, in the present case, the rights which they derive from Directive 85/337 would have no effective judicial protection at all, it must be noted that, as is clear from the file, Greenpeace brought proceedings before the national courts challenging the administrative authorisations issued to Unelco concerning the construction of those power stations. TEA and CIC also lodged appeals against CUMAC's declaration of environmental impact relating to the two construction projects (see paragraphs 6 and 7 of the contested order, reproduced at paragraph 2 of this judgment).

33. Although the subject-matter of those proceedings and of the action brought before the Court of First Instance is different, both actions are based on the same rights afforded to individuals by Directive 85/337, so that in the circumstances of the present case those rights are fully protected by the national courts which may, if need be, refer a question to this Court for a preliminary ruling under Article 177 of the Treaty.

34. The Court of First Instance did not therefore err in law in determining the question of the appellants' *locus standi* in the light of the criteria developed by the Court of Justice in the case law set out at paragraph 7 of this judgment.

35. In those circumstances the appeal must be dismissed.

NOTE

Although the applicants in *Greenpeace* referred to *Codorniu* in urging that a restrictive interpretation of Article 173 of the EC Treaty (now, after amendment, Article 230 EC) be eschewed, it will be noted that the Court made no direct mention of it, or any other decision, in these 'Findings'. Moreover, although environmental cases may in principle be decided according to generally applicable rules of law, the dispersed impact of acts affecting the environment creates special problems in determining standing (especially where, as in *Greenpeace*, both national and EC acts are involved). Consequently, the outcome of such cases may not be indicative of trends in the wider arena of challenge to forms of economic regulation. However, even with those *caveats*, *Greenpeace*, in its style and brevity, offered no encouragement to those seeking a hint that the Court of Justice might be inclined to issue any corrective to the CFI's doggedly restrictive reading of *Codorniu*.

■ QUESTION

Could decisions by EC institutions affecting the environment *ever* be of individual concern to individuals or groups concerned to secure protection of the environment?

B: **Pressure for liberalization, 2002 and beyond**

The model developed by the Court envisages two principal routes for the judicial protection of parties whose interests are prejudiced by the adoption of Community acts which they wish to challenge as unlawful. The first takes an applicant to Luxembourg, and it is the application for annulment created by Article 230 EC (supplemented, in appropriate cases, by Article 241 and, in combination, Articles 235/288(2)). The second is located in the ordinary courts of the Member States, where a challenge may be brought to a national act within which the question of the validity of a parent Community act may be raised. A national court may not rule the Community act invalid, but rather must follow the route to Luxembourg created by the Article 234 preliminary reference procedure, in the manner envisaged by the Court in *Foto Frost* and subsequent cases (pp.254–260 above). The two routes to judicial protection are independent of each other, subject only to the limited exception created in *TWD Deggendorf* (Case T-188/92 p.251 above) and refined subsequently, according to which the undoubted but neglected availability of an Article 230 action may preclude reliance on an Article 234.

Accordingly one may interpret this model as a recognition by the Court that although the standing rules under Article 230 impose severe restrictions on the access of private parties to the courts in Luxembourg, the availability of an action at national level supplemented by the Article 234 preliminary reference procedure offers compensation. The latter secures judicial protection in circumstances where it is denied under the former. In this vein, it is notable that in *Terres Rouges* (Case T-47/95, p.264 above) and in *Greenpeace* (Case C-321/95P, p.266 above) a finding of inadmissibility under Article 230(4) was accompanied by comment on the availability of judicial protection before national courts able to make preliminary references.

But can the law be so neat? The year 2002 has seen vigorous judicial debate. In the next case the Court of First Instance, unpersuaded by the adequacy of protection secured *via* national courts, launched a spirited attack on the long-established and restrictive interpretative approach to the standing rules under Article 230.

Jégo-Quéré et Cie SA v *Commission of the European Communities* (Case T-177/01)
Judgment of 3 May 2002, Court of First Instance

The applicants, a French fishing company, challenged a Regulation designed to reduce catches of young hake. The Commission claimed that the Regulation was a measure of general application, and that the applicants lacked individual concern within the meaning of Article 230(4). The Court of First Instance agreed, citing *inter alia* Case 25/62 *Plaumann* v *Commission* [1963] ECR 95 (p.220 above). So far, so orthodox. But the matter was taken further.

[39] However, the applicant asserts that, were its action to be dismissed as inadmissible, it would be denied any legal remedy enabling it to challenge the legality of the contested provisions. Since the regulation does not provide for the adoption of any implementing measures by the Member States, the applicant maintains that, in the present case, it would have no right of action before the national courts.

[40] The Commission, on the other hand, takes the view that the applicant is not denied access to the courts, since it can bring an action for non-contractual liability pursuant to Article 235 EC and the second paragraph of Article 288 EC.

[41] In that regard, it should be borne in mind that the Court of Justice itself has confirmed that access to the courts is one of the essential elements of a community based on the rule of law and is guaranteed in the legal order based on the EC Treaty, inasmuch as the Treaty established a complete system of legal remedies and procedures designed to permit the Court of Justice to review the legality of acts of the institutions (Case 294/83 *Les Verts* v *European Parliament* [1986] ECR 1339, paragraph 23). The Court of Justice bases the right to an effective remedy before a court of competent jurisdiction on the constitutional traditions common to the Member States and on Articles 6 and 13 of the ECHR (Case 222/84 *Johnston* [1986] ECR 1651, paragraph 18).

[42] In addition, the right to an effective remedy for everyone whose rights and freedoms guaranteed by the law of the Union are violated has been reaffirmed by Article 47 of the Charter of Fundamental Rights of the European Union proclaimed at Nice on 7 December 2000 (OJ 2000 C 364, p.1).

[43] It is therefore necessary to consider whether, in a case such as this, where an individual applicant is contesting the lawfulness of provisions of general application directly affecting its legal situation, the inadmissibility of the action for annulment would deprive the applicant of the right to an effective remedy.

[44] In that regard, it should be recalled that, apart from an action for annulment, there exist two other procedural routes by which an individual may be able to bring a case before the Community judicature – which alone have jurisdiction for this purpose – in order to obtain a ruling that a Community measure is unlawful, namely proceedings before a national court giving rise to a reference to the Court of Justice for a preliminary ruling under Article 234 EC and an action based on the non-contractual liability of the Community, as provided for in Article 235 EC and the second paragraph of Article 288 EC.

[45] However, as regards proceedings before a national court giving rise to a reference to the Court of Justice for a preliminary ruling under Article 234 EC, it should be noted that, in a case such as the present, there are no acts of implementation capable of forming the basis of an action before national courts. The fact that an individual affected by a Community measure may be able to bring its validity before the national courts by violating the rules it lays down and then asserting their illegality in subsequent judicial proceedings brought against him does not constitute an adequate means of judicial protection. Individuals cannot be required to breach the law in order to gain access to justice (see point 43 of the Opinion of Advocate General Jacobs delivered on 21 March 2002 in Case C-50/00 P *Unión de Pequeños Agricultores* v *Council* [2002] 3 CMLR 1 not yet published in the European Court Reports).

[46] The procedural route of an action for damages based on the non-contractual liability of the Community does not, in a case such as the present, provide a solution that satisfactorily protects

the interests of the individual affected. Such an action cannot result in the removal from the Community legal order of a measure which is nevertheless necessarily held to be illegal. Given that it presupposes that damage has been directly occasioned by the application of the measure in issue, such an action is subject to criteria of admissibility and substance which are different from those governing actions for annulment, and does not therefore place the Community judicature in a position whereby it can carry out the comprehensive judicial review which it is its task to perform. In particular, where a measure of general application, such as the provisions contested in the present case, is challenged in the context of such an action, the review carried out by the Community judicature does not cover all the factors which may affect the legality of that measure, being limited instead to the censuring of sufficiently serious infringements of rules of law intended to confer rights on individuals (see Case C-352/98 P *Bergaderm and Goupil* v *Commission* [2000] ECR I-5291, paragraphs 41 to 43; Case T-155/99 *Dieckmann & Hansen* v *Commission* [2001] ECR II-3143, paragraphs 42 and 43; see also, as regards an insufficiently serious infringement, Joined Cases C-104/89 and C-37/90 *Mulder and Others* v *Council and Commission* [1992] ECR I-3061, paragraphs 18 and 19, and, for a case in which the rule invoked was not intended to confer rights on individuals, paragraph 43 of the judgment of 6 December 2001 in Case T-196/99 *Area Cova and Others* v *Council and Commission* [2001] ECR II-3597).

[47] On the basis of the foregoing, the inevitable conclusion must be that the procedures provided for in, on the one hand, Article 234 EC and, on the other hand, Article 235 EC and the second paragraph of Article 288 EC can no longer be regarded, in the light of Articles 6 and 13 of the ECHR and of Article 47 of the Charter of Fundamental Rights, as guaranteeing persons the right to an effective remedy enabling them to contest the legality of Community measures of general application which directly affect their legal situation.

NOTE

So the Court of First Instance found that the right to an effective remedy, drawn *inter alia* from the Charter of Fundamental Rights, was inadequately protected by the model of judicial protection developed over decades since *Plaumann*. But was it open to it to put things right?

[48] It is true that such a circumstance cannot constitute authority for changing the system of remedies and procedures established by the Treaty, which is designed to give the Community judicature the power to review the legality of acts of the institutions. In no case can such a circumstance allow an action for annulment brought by a natural or legal person which does not satisfy the conditions laid down by the fourth paragraph of Article 230 EC to be declared admissible . . .

[49] However, as Advocate General Jacobs stated in point 59 of his Opinion in *Unión de Pequeños Agricultores* v *Council* (cited in paragraph 45 above), there is no compelling reason to read into the notion of individual concern, within the meaning of the fourth paragraph of Article 230 EC, a requirement that an individual applicant seeking to challenge a general measure must be differentiated from all others affected by it in the same way as an addressee.

[50] In those circumstances, and having regard to the fact that the EC Treaty established a complete system of legal remedies and procedures designed to permit the Community judicature to review the legality of measures adopted by the institutions (paragraph 23 of the judgment in *Les Verts* v *Parliament*, cited in paragraph 41 above), the strict interpretation, applied until now, of the notion of a person individually concerned according to the fourth paragraph of Article 230 EC, must be reconsidered.

[51] In the light of the foregoing, and in order to ensure effective judicial protection for individuals, a natural or legal person is to be regarded as individually concerned by a Community measure of general application that concerns him directly if the measure in question affects his legal position, in a manner which is both definite and immediate, by restricting his rights or by imposing obligations on him. The number and position of other persons who are likewise affected by the measure, or who may be so, are of no relevance in that regard.

[52] In the present case, obligations are indeed imposed on Jégo-Quéré by the contested provisions.

The applicant, whose vessels are covered by the scope of the regulation, carries on fishing operations in one of the areas in which, by virtue of the contested provisions, such operations are subjected to detailed obligations governing the mesh size of the nets to be used.

[53] It follows that the contested provisions are of individual concern to the applicant.

[54] Since those provisions are also of direct concern to the applicant (see paragraph 26 above), the objection of inadmissibility raised by the Commission must be dismissed and an order made for the action to proceed.

NOTE

This is plainly a remarkably ambitious judgment – an audacious judgment, no less. But can such a history of 'strict interpretation' (para 50 above) be upset in this manner? The Court of First Instance refers in paragraphs 45 and 49 to the Opinion of Advocate-General Jacobs in *Unión de Pequeños Agricultores* v *Council*. The ruling of the European Court in that case was delivered shortly after that of the Court of First Instance in *Jégo-Quéré*. In the senior forum a more conservative mood prevailed.

Unión de Pequeños Agricultores v *Council of the European Union* (Case C-50/00P)
Judgment of 25 July 2002, Court of Justice of the European Communities

The applicants, UPA, a trade association representing small Spanish agricultural businesses, sought annulment of a Regulation amending the scheme for the common organization of the olive oil market in the EC. In the Court of First Instance they failed (Case T-173/98 *Unión de Pequeños Agricultores* v *Council* [1999] ECR II-3357), on the basis that their action was inadmissible under Article 230(4) EC. The contested regulation was treated as concerning the applicant's members on the same basis as all operators trading in the relevant markets. This conclusion was not challenged on appeal. UPA's appeal was targeted squarely on the issue of grant of effective judicial protection under the Community legal order.

The applicant submitted that the disputed provisions required no national implementing legislation nor did they occasion the taking of any administrative measures. Furthermore, the applicant submitted it was not even possible to infringe the provisions so as to be in a position to challenge the validity of any duly imposed sanction. An action before the Spanish courts was impossible and a reference for a preliminary ruling to assess their validity therefore precluded. (The Commission disputed this analysis, but the Court's ruling is at the level of general principle, and it chose not to resolve this disagreement.) The applicant sought to have the Court of First Instance's decision set aside on the ground that, in the alleged absence of any legal remedy before the national courts, the right to effective judicial protection required that standing be conceded under Article 230 before the courts in Luxembourg. The applicant drew on paragraphs 32 and 33 of the judgment in Case C-321/95P *Greenpeace Council and Others* v *Commission* [1998] ECR I-1651 (p.266 above), which, in its submission, confirms that where there is no legal remedy under national law an application for annulment under the fourth paragraph of Article 230 of the Treaty must be held admissible. The Court did not accept this argument.

[38] The European Community is . . . a community based on the rule of law in which its institutions are subject to judicial review of the compatibility of their acts with the Treaty and with the general principles of law which include fundamental rights.

[39] Individuals are therefore entitled to effective judicial protection of the rights they derive from the Community legal order, and the right to such protection is one of the general principles of law

stemming from the constitutional traditions common to the Member States. That right has also been enshrined in Articles 6 and 13 of the European Convention for the Protection of Human Rights and Fundamental Freedoms (see, in particular, Case 222/84 *Johnston* [1986] ECR 1651, paragraph 18, and Case C-424/99 *Commission v Austria* [2001] ECR I-9285, paragraph 45).

[40] By Article 173 [now 230] and Article 184 . . . [now 241], on the one hand, and by Article 177 [now 234], on the other, the Treaty has established a complete system of legal remedies and procedures designed to ensure judicial review of the legality of acts of the institutions, and has entrusted such review to the Community Courts (see, to that effect, *Les Verts v Parliament*, paragraph 23). Under that system, where natural or legal persons cannot, by reason of the conditions for admissibility laid down in the fourth paragraph of Article 173 [now 230] of the Treaty, directly challenge Community measures of general application, they are able, depending on the case, either indirectly to plead the invalidity of such acts before the Community Courts under Article 184 [now 241] of the Treaty or to do so before the national courts and ask them, since they have no jurisdiction themselves to declare those measures invalid (see Case 314/85 *Foto-Frost* [1987] ECR 4199, paragraph 20), to make a reference to the Court of Justice for a preliminary ruling on validity.

[41] Thus it is for the Member States to establish a system of legal remedies and procedures which ensure respect for the right to effective judicial protection.

[42] In that context, in accordance with the principle of sincere cooperation laid down in Article 5 [now 10] of the Treaty, national courts are required, so far as possible, to interpret and apply national procedural rules governing the exercise of rights of action in a way that enables natural and legal persons to challenge before the courts the legality of any decision or other national measure relative to the application to them of a Community act of general application, by pleading the invalidity of such an act.

[43] As the Advocate General has pointed out in paragraphs 50 to 53 of his Opinion, it is not acceptable to adopt an interpretation of the system of remedies, such as that favoured by the appellant, to the effect that a direct action for annulment before the Community Court will be available where it can be shown, following an examination by that Court of the particular national procedural rules, that those rules do not allow the individual to bring proceedings to contest the validity of the Community measure at issue. Such an interpretation would require the Community Court, in each individual case, to examine and interpret national procedural law. That would go beyond its jurisdiction when reviewing the legality of Community measures.

[44] Finally, it should be added that, according to the system for judicial review of legality established by the Treaty, a natural or legal person can bring an action challenging a regulation only if it is concerned both directly and individually. Although this last condition must be interpreted in the light of the principle of effective judicial protection by taking account of the various circumstances that may distinguish an applicant individually (see, for example, Joined Cases 67/85, 68/85 and 70/85 *Van der Kooy v Commission* [1988] ECR 219, paragraph 14; *Extramet Industrie v Council*, paragraph 13, and *Codorniu v Council*, paragraph 19), such an interpretation cannot have the effect of setting aside the condition in question, expressly laid down in the Treaty, without going beyond the jurisdiction conferred by the Treaty on the Community Courts.

[45] While it is, admittedly, possible to envisage a system of judicial review of the legality of Community measures of general application different from that established by the founding Treaty and never amended as to its principles, it is for the Member States, if necessary, in accordance with Article 48 EU, to reform the system currently in force.

[46] In the light of the foregoing, the Court finds that the Court of First Instance did not err in law when it declared the appellant's application inadmissible without examining whether, in the particular case, there was a remedy before a national court enabling the validity of the contested regulation to be examined.

[47] The appeal must therefore be dismissed.

NOTE

The Court does not choose explicitly to overrule the Court of First Instance. But the approach in *UPA* is quite different. It is more limited in its readiness to entertain applications for review by private parties. The Court of First Instance in *Jégo-Quéré* does not believe the current model of judicial protection, based on Article 230 buttressed by Articles 241 and 235/288(2) supplemented by the availability of Article 234 preliminary references made by national courts, will always offer an effective remedy to an individual. The European Court in *UPA* does not disagree. But whereas the Court of First Instance, prompted *inter alia* by the Charter on Fundamental Rights, felt it had room to interpret Article 230(4) more generously than has been past practice in order to upgrade judicial protection, the European Court, ignoring the Charter, felt it had no such room for manoeuvre. Improvements in the scope of protection afforded by Article 230(4) would have to be delivered by the process of Treaty revision (see para 45 of the judgment in Case C-50/00P). And inadequacies in protection available through national procedures would have to be remedied at national level, albeit in the light of the Community law obligation of sincere co-operation found in Article 10 EC.

Further litigation might yet elucidate just what can be done about the standing rules in Article 230(4). *Jégo-Quéré* goes unmentioned in *UPA*, which leaves its status ambiguous. Paragraph 44 of *UPA* insists that the notion of individual concern 'must be interpreted in the light of the principle of effective judicial protection by taking account of the various circumstances that may distinguish an applicant individually'. Probably this is to be taken simply as a reference to existing niche concessions to private parties already recognized in the case law – after all explicit reference is made to *Extramet* (p.230 above) and to *Codorniu* (p.263 above). But it is at least arguable that this phrase may yet be used by the European Court to launch a renewed extension of individuality for the purposes of Article 230(4), in the direction, if not to the full extent, of that promoted by the Court of First Instance in *Jégo-Quéré*. In the meantime one may also expect the Court to remain vigilant to keep as open as possible the protection of individuals *via* national courts.

R v *Secretary of State, ex parte BAT and Imperial Tobacco* (Case C-491/01)
Judgment of 10 December 2002, Court of Justice of the European Communities

The Court cannot give a preliminary ruling on a question submitted by a national court where *inter alia* it is quite obvious that the ruling sought by that court on the interpretation or validity of Community law bears no relation to the actual facts of the main action or its purpose or where the problem is hypothetical (p.196 above). Here the validity of a Directive was challenged before the English courts before the expiry of the deadline for implementation. A preliminary reference was made. But was this too early?

[39] As for the argument that to accept the admissibility of the order for reference seeking a decision on validity in a situation such as that in the main proceedings could be tantamount to circumventing the requirements of Article 230 EC, it must be stated that, in the complete system of legal remedies and procedures established by the EC Treaty with a view to ensuring judicial review of the legality of acts of the institutions, where natural or legal persons cannot, by reason of the conditions for admissibility laid down in the fourth paragraph of that article, directly challenge Community measures of general application, they are able, depending on the case, either indirectly to plead the invalidity of such acts before the Community judicature under Article 241 EC or to do so before the national courts and ask them, since they have no jurisdiction themselves to declare those measures invalid, to make a reference to the Court of Justice for a preliminary ruling on validity (Case C-50/00 P *Unión de Pequeños Agricultores* v *Council* [2002] ECR I-6677, paragraph 40).

[40] The opportunity open to individuals to plead the invalidity of a Community act of general application before national courts is not conditional upon that act's actually having been the subject of implementing measures adopted pursuant to national law. In that respect, it is sufficient if the national court is called upon to hear a genuine dispute in which the question of the validity of such an act is raised indirectly. That condition is amply fulfilled in the circumstances of the case in the main proceedings . . .

■ QUESTION

What do these cases reveal to you about the nature of legal interpretation practised by the Community judicature? In so far as there are deficiencies in the rules governing standing whose job is it to repair them?

NOTE

This fascinating pair of cases has naturally attracted eager academic comment: see, e.g., M.-P. Granger (2003) 66 MLR 124; F. Ragolle (2003) 28 EL Rev 90. Consult this book's Companion Website for further references.

■ QUESTIONS RELATING TO THE MATERIAL COVERED IN THIS CHAPTER

1. In *Plaumann* v *Commission* (Case 25/62) (p.220 above) the Court commented that 'provisions of the Treaty regarding the right of interested parties to bring an action must not be interpreted restrictively'. Has the Court adhered to this view in its treatment of applications for annulment of the acts of the Community institutions? Should it?

2. 'It is ill-advised to consider whether natural and legal persons should enjoy more generous rules on standing in order to enhance their capacity to control acts of Community institutions in isolation from questions about the adequacy of the systems of accountability to citizens to which EC institutions are subject and the propensity of those systems for securing representative and responsive governance in the Union'. Discuss.

NOTE

For additional material and resources see the Companion Website at: www.oup.co.uk/best.textbooks/law/weatherill6e

Epilogue To Part One: Constitutionalism

'The Court has sought to "constitutionalise" the Treaty, that is to fashion a constitutional framework for a federal-type structure in Europe'. These words were written in 1989 by Mancini and are set out in the extract at p.129 above. The shaping of inter-State relations according to EC law has at least as much, and perhaps more, in common with the modes of internal distribution of power within a federal State than it does with the structuring of an international organization established by a Treaty. The principles of supremacy and direct effect are central to this claim that the EC legal regime operates in many respects *as if* it were organizing the internal governance of a (federal) State. This reveals that 'constitutionalism' has equipped the EC with a working method that allows it to avoid choices about whether it is 'really' international law or 'really' State law. It is both; it is neither; it doesn't matter (in practice).

'Constitutionalization' provides an insight into the deeper mission of European integration. Joerges and Sand describe constitutionalism 'as a metaphor for the challenges that the emerging transnational governance presents to the notion of democratic legitimacy' (*Constitutionalism and transnational governance*, unpublished paper). It is vital to escape imprisonment in thinking that assumes the rise of transfrontier markets generates a need for geographical bigger States. Economic structures migrate in ways that do not have to be followed and frequently cannot be followed by political institutions. The EU is part of the necessary leap of imagination in the direction of an understanding of governance that transcends the State, either acting alone or in constructing inter-State bargains. The 'constitutionalized' legal order serves to bind together national and transnational actors within a system that does not require choices to be made about where to locate ultimate political and legal authority, nor to require the wholesale transfer of authority from a State to a 'Euro-State'. A more subtle network of governance is envisaged. The debate about the EU's legitimacy will be rejoined in Chapter 20 but it suffices for present purposes to observe that from this perspective, criticism of the EU as lacking the democratic credentials that are characteristic of a State is not to take as given that which is contested. It is to take as given that which is denied. The EU is not a State nor is it to become one.

Once one assembles the several pieces of the jigsaw – supremacy, direct effect, effective judicial protection, preliminary rulings, judicial review – Community law has functional resemblances to a Constitution for a federal-type State. In particular, supremacy appears to dictate a hierarchical relationship between the two levels of law-making, placing the (quasi-) federal rules on top. There is much more to the claim to constitutionalization. Beyond Treaty sources and secondary legislation, there are general principles which permeate the fabric of the law, in some instances without explicit textual support in the Treaty; and the Treaty establishes institutionally relatively sophisticated forms of lawmaking which reflect forms of representative democracy at both national and European level, in the shape of the Council and the Parliament respectively. So it functions as a constitution in the 'thin' sense that it is constitutive of the system that is the EC legal order. But the Court is rhetorically bolder. In *Parti Ecologiste 'Les Vert'* v *Parliament* (Case 294/83, p.216 above) the Court described the Community as 'a Community based on the rule of law, inasmuch as neither its Member States nor its institutions can avoid a review of the question whether the measures adopted by them are in conformity with the basic constitutional charter, the Treaty . . .' (see similarly Opinion 1/91 on the draft EEA Agreement [1991] ECR I–6079). What seems to be at stake here is a constitution that is characterized by an assumption of the subjection of the exercise of public power to judicial control even in circumstances where this is not explicitly foreseen in the governing texts. The legal control of the institutions of the Community itself, which is what was in dispute in *Parti Ecologiste 'Les Verts'*, was deepened by the Court's readiness to extend its powers of review beyond those explicitly conferred by the Treaty. This tends towards a stronger and thicker kind of constitution, of a type that might not be readily associated with an organization existing beyond the State. The Community offers both a Constitution for economic integration and a Constitution for the protection of the individual. This twin purpose of Community law has been and will be observed in many manifestations throughout this book. And in fact tracing this process of 'constitutionalization' of what began as, and in formal terms still is, a legal order founded on an international Treaty holds the key to understanding the remarkable evolution of the EU legal order. Moreover, it raises fascinating yet deeply sensitive questions about how sustainable the Court's vision of the nature of the legal order over which it presides truly is – and how sustainable it should be.

The next paper pulls together the themes that connect much of the material in Part One of this book, while also offering tantalizing glimpses forward to matters that remain to be investigated.

C. Timmermans, 'The constitutionalization of the European Union'
(2002) 21 Yearbook of European Law*

Introduction

1. Europe and its Constitution (or a constitution for Europe) is almost a popular theme, nowadays. It is in the air. Philip Allott wrote a couple of years ago in a remarkable article in the Common Market Law Review: 'A sort of self-induced constitutional depression has settled over the people and the peoples of Europe'.[1] Without being able to announce complete recovery, I think the least we can say is that recently, a lot of fresh air has been blown into the constitutional debate on Europe.

However, what shall be discussed in this contribution are neither the issue of a European Constitution, nor the agenda setting for the 2004 Intergovernmental Conference or the post Laeken process . . . [cf pp.24–32 above]

---

* The following text is the edited version of a speech delivered on 1 November 2001 at King's College, London before the United Kingdom Association for European Law.

1 Philip Allott, The crisis of European constitutionalism. Reflections on the revolution in Europe. CML Rev 1997, 439 (at 469).

A process of constitutionalization, what does it mean?

2. What I find certainly as interesting, particularly since the reform of the EU-Treaty brought about by the Treaty of Amsterdam, is the ongoing, almost creeping process of constitutionalization of the European Union. These solemn words require some explanation.

3. What do we mean by saying that the European Union is in a process of being constitutionalized? In a way the founding instruments, and speaking in this context, the founding Treaty or Treaties of an international organization could always be referred to as the 'Constitution' of the organisation (as has been done, for instance, in the founding Treaty of the International Labour Organization). That is not what we have in mind, of course, when referring to constitutionalization.[2] This process is one by which the legal system of the organisation acquires some fundamental characteristics and is going to respect a number of basic values, and in doing so, is making that system at the same time more independent from the contracting parties who brought it into being. That process is the more important for those international organizations which dispose of real decision-making powers the exercise of which can be binding upon its members, or even upon individuals.

4. We need not discuss this in the abstract because the development of the legal order of the European Communities gives a striking example of such a process of constitutionalization and the need for such a process. It has taken a fairly long time before national politics, the civil society, the public at large have become aware of the reality of the transfer of powers to the EC and the restrictions of Member States' sovereign rights deriving therefrom, to quote the euphemism of Van Gend en Loos;[3] the reality of shared sovereignty to use a more current expression. People have become well aware of the reality of a Community legislator and executive, whatever its institutional structuring might be. Most people are unable to distinguish between the Council and the European Commission or at any rate to give some indication of their respective roles. However, any reference to Brussels is fairly well understood. That explains why the debate on the legitimacy, the accountability and the quality of the Community legal system has become so intense. And this also is one of the motives for the call for a European Constitution.

Indeed, when we refer to 'a constitution', we mean more than a technical instrument embodying the organizational chart for a state spelling out who should do what and in doing so be controlled by whom. The term constitution, at least to me, implies values of a more fundamental nature; values that should underpin and penetrate the institutional structuring of the state system and its functioning. That is why it is possible to have a Constitution without a written text and why we can use the term constitutionalization. These values which are the guarantees for a proper organisation and exercise of State power, and also constitute to some extent the basic objectives to be pursued by State action, are more particularly expressed in terms of protection of fundamental rights, democracy and the rule of law.

5. How real the process of constitutionalization of the EC has been, is perhaps most conspicuously expressed by the fact that no clear reference to these constitutional values can be found in the founding treaties, the ECSC Treaty of 1952 and the EEC/Euratom Treaties of 1957. At present you will find ample reference to most of these values, first of all in the preambles of the Treaties, and more particularly in Article 6 of the EU-Treaty.

6. As you know, the Court of Justice qualified the EC Treaty already in 1984 as a Constitutional Charter of a Community based on the rule of law.[4] Indeed, the fact that the Treaty instruments, as far as the Communities are concerned, can already now (that is in the absence of a European Constitution), be qualified as of a constitutional nature is mainly due to the Court of Justice. Not, of

---

2 See on this concept, Pierre Pescatore, Die gemeinschaftsverträge als Verfassungsrecht – ein Kapitel Verfassungsgeschichte in der Perspektive des europäischen Gerichtshofs, systematisch geordnet, in Europäische Gerichtsbarkeit und nationale verfassungsgerichtsbarkeit, Festschrift zum 70. Geburtstag von Hans Kutscher, Wilhelm Grewe, Hans Rupp und Hans Schneider (Hrsg.), Baden-Baden 1981, p.319, and Ingolf Pernice, Multilevel Constitutionalism and the Treaty of Amsterdam: European Constitution-Making Revisited? CML Rev 1999, p.703.

3 Case 26/62, [1963] ECR 23.

4 Case 294/83, *Les Verts* [1986] ECR 1339, para 23.

course, because the Court has said so, but because, what one may call, the constitutional stepping stones or building blocks of a European Constitution have been patiently carved out by the Court over the years in its case law. It will be sufficient to refer to four of these blocks:

— First of all, and most importantly, the qualification of the EC as an autonomous legal system, a legal order in its own right, integrated into the national legal systems but preserving its special characteristics.[5]

— Secondly, the concepts of direct effect and supremacy of EC law, directly derived from that notion of an autonomous Community legal order. Community law is law of the land.[6]

— Thirdly, the respect of general principles of law, and amongst these, of fundamental rights, not only as safeguards to be respected by the Communities in their legislative and executive action, but also by the Member States to the extent that they act within the scope of EC law.[7]

— Fourthly, and finally, as a basic element in this process of constitutionalization of the EC, one should refer to the case-law by which national systems of legal protection are being mobilized in order to allow the enforcement of Community law rights by national courts, and this subject to the tests of non-discrimination (or equivalence) and effectiveness.[8] This latter test of effectiveness might occasionally imply that a Member State will have to reinforce its system of legal protection or even introduce new forms of relief, which as such are not available under the national system.[9] In this context a reference should be added to the principle of state liability for violation of Community law rules as developed in Francovich, Factortame and subsequent case-law.[10] And after the recent judgment in Courage we may add now also the principle of liability of private parties for damages caused by violations of the competition rules of the Treaty.[11]

One might say that the EC legal system, by this process of constitutionalization has evolved into a real *legal order*, that is a system of law-making and law-abidance, ensuring respect of the rule of law and the principles of what German constitutionalists would call 'Rechtsstaatlichkeit'.

How to fit in the EU?

7. Now, the question I would like to address more particularly is where to situate the European Union in this process of constitutionalization? That question can and should be raised because, albeit that the European Communities are part of the European Union, the Union does not automatically partake in the characteristics of the legal order of the EC. Indeed, Member States, in crafting the present structure, have been keen on keeping the Union separate from the EC. They have not wanted one single structure. The Union, in the wording of Article 1 of the EU Treaty, is founded on the European Communities which continue to exist as separate international organizations with their own legal personality, and their own, I venture to say, constitution.

The structure of the Union, more particularly as to the relationship between the Union and the European Communities is complex and opaque (perhaps best illustrated by the fact that we still have a Council of the European Union, but a Commission and a Court of the European Communities; how to explain that to the citizens of the European Union who, a further example, to discover their rights

---

5 See *Van Gend en Loos, supra* note 3 and Case 6/64, *Costa vs ENEL*, [1964], ECR 1203.

6 See too *Van Gend en Loos* and *Costa vs ENEL supra* note 5.

7 See e.g., Opinion 2/94 (accession of the EC to the European Human Rights Convention), [1996] ECR I-1759, Case C-274/99P, *Connolly* [2001] ECR I-1589, Case 5/88, *Wachauf* [1989] ECR 2609.

8 Case 158/80, *Rewe* [1981] ECR 1805, Case C-19/92, *Kraus* [1993] ECR I-1663, Case C-430/93, *Van Schijndel* [1995] ECR I-4705.

9 Case C-213/89, *Factortame* [1990] ECR I-2433, Case 97/91, *Borelli* [1992] ECR I-6313, Case C-269/99, *Kühne*, Judgment of 6 December 2001 (not yet published).

10 Case C-6/90 and 9/90, *Francovich* [1991] ECR I-5357, Cases C-46/93 and C-48/93, *Brasserie du Pêcheur and Factortame* [1996] ECR I-1029.

11 Case C-453/99, *Courage* [2001] ECR 6297.

as citizens of the Union, have to look into the EC, not the EU Treaty?). The Union's structure, to put it mildly, has no inherent institutional logic of its own. Its logic is a historical one, it can only be understood and explained as a product of political compromise and negotiation during the relevant intergovernmental conferences.[12]

8. Just a few comments to refresh your memories. The inception of the European Union as the overarching structure of the European Communities and the separate pillars for CFSP and Justice and Home Affairs, as it then was, stems from the Treaty of Maastricht. It might be useful to recall that the Intergovernmental Conference leading up to that Treaty had as its main point on the agenda Economic and Monetary Union; it was only at a late stage of preparation for this Conference that the construction of a political union was added to the agenda, an initiative of Chancellor Kohl intended to anchor a reunified Germany still more firmly into an integrated Europe. You might recall the abortive attempt of the Dutch presidency to achieve one single Union structure, by which the Communities would be absorbed. The flat refusal of all other delegations, apart from Belgium, even to discuss that proposal, is still freshly remembered, at least in The Hague, as the black Monday of Dutch diplomacy. Indeed, the logic of the Dutch presidency's draft might have been impeccable, but it took too little account of national sensitivities. The fear of most Member States being that a single structure would inevitably pollute the institutional functioning of the Union as such with ingredients of the Community method, also through the case law of the Court.

So the result of the Maastricht Treaty was to encapsulate the Communities into the rather loose structure of a Union with its own fields of activity but of a rather amorphous content. Moreover, this Union structure was only intended to be a provisional one, a more definitive structure to be discussed during the forthcoming intergovernmental conference, already scheduled by the Maastricht Treaty for 1996. Academic writing on European law, was apparently not very much impressed by this new structure. New editions of Textbooks and Manuals, incorporating the results of the Maastricht Treaty, continued to refer to European *Community* law. The European Union and its second and third pillar activities were very much treated as European Political Cooperation (EPC) had been before, that is mostly with benign neglect.

9. Nowadays, some eight years after the entering into force of the Maastricht Treaty, it is striking to see how this institutional weakling, I mean the Union, has developed. From a loose, provisional, over-arching non-entity, the Union has acquired a firm political and institutional presence. It has become a global reality. To mention some examples:

— The Union has decided to set up a military intervention force (Rapid Reaction Force) which should be operational as from 2003.[13] In the meantime there have been created a Political and Security Committee and a Military Committee of the European Union. The European Union has now also its own Military staff headed by a Chief of Staff.[14]

— Missions in Brussels from third countries and international organisations are accredited with the European Union, not any more with the European Communities.

— Three weeks after the events of 11 September 2001 the Belgian Prime Minister Guy Verhofstadt and Romano Prodi visited the President of the United States as representatives of the European Union in order to inform him about and discuss the

---

12 *Cf* E.P. Wellenstein, Community, Union – What's in a name, CML Rev 1992, p.205; U. Everling, Reflections on the Structure of the European Union, CML Rev 1992, p.1053; N.M. Blokker and T. Heukels, The European Union. Historical Origins and Institutional Challenges, in T. Heukels/N. Blokker/M. Brus (eds), The European Union after Amsterdam, 1998, p.9. See also the contribution to this book by Bruno de Witte, The pillar Structure and the nature of the European Union: Greek Temple or French Gothic Cathedral, p.51; also Deirdre Curtin and Ige Dekker, The EU as a 'layered' Institutional Organization: Institutional Unity in Disguise, in Craig and De Búrca (eds), The Evolution of EU law (1999), p.83.

13 The implementation of this decision which was taken by the European Council of Nice (2000) and Göteborg (2001) appears however to be particularly cumbersome. *Cf* also the Declaration adopted by the European Council of Laeken (2001), Presidency conclusions, Annex II.

14 See the relevant decisions published in OJ 2001, L27.

Union's action plan to fight terrorism including the introduction of a European arrest warrant.
— The European Union is setting up missions in third countries, so for example the European Union monitoring mission for the Western Balkans.[15] Some months ago there was published in the Official Journal the text of an international agreement concluded by the Council of the Union with the Federal Republic of Yugoslavia as to the status of this mission.[16] This agreement states explicitly that it is concluded on behalf of the EU. This could be an important precedent, as a step into the direction of seeing the EU acquire international legal personality, and that despite the unwillingness of the Member States when drafting the Treaty of Maastricht and again when negotiating the Treaty of Amsterdam, to grant such legal personality explicitly to the Union.[17]

10. The EU appears capable of functioning as an organization. It is 'funktionsfähig'. As has often been the case in the history of European integration, 'c'est le provisoire qui dure'. But there is more to it than this. My impression is that we can detect elements of a process of constitutionalization of the EU itself. The European Union is developing into an international organization of its own right with its own legal order.

11. Of course, the Amsterdam Treaty has greatly contributed to this evolution by reinforcing substantially the structure of the Union. The Common Foreign and Security Policy (CFSP) as well as cooperation in the field of police and criminal justice have become policies of the Union itself; so are the decision-making powers granted to that effect. It cannot be argued any more, as was still possible under the Treaty of Maastricht, that the Union is no more than a framework for cooperation between Member States, CFSP being a policy of the Member States, not of the Union itself. It is becoming increasingly clear that treaty-making power has been granted to the EU as such for CFSP and also the third pillar; the treaty concluded with the Federal Republic of Yugoslavia, just mentioned, appears to confirm this. As to the institutional framework of the Union, a remarkable feature of the Amsterdam Treaty is the strengthening of the position of the European Council which acquires for the first time formal decision-making powers.[18] In the third pillar some elements of the Community method were injected by reinforcing (modestly) the respective roles of the European Parliament and the Commission, and also by granting some, limited jurisdiction to the Court of Justice.[19] Another example of reinforcement of the Union's structure is the general regime as to enhanced cooperation which is embodied in the Union Treaty. This general regime defines obligations which Member States and the institutions have to respect when applying this regime not only within the third pillar, but also the EC.[20] The Treaty of Nice still further strengthens this EU regime for enhanced cooperation.

Finally, I should mention, of course, as a more particular token of the constitutionalization of the EU by the Amsterdam treaty the new Article 6 of the EU Treaty, subjecting the EU itself explicitly to respect the principles of liberty, democracy, respect of fundamental rights and the rule of law. Not only the Union, also the Member States are bound to respect these principles, first of all as an explicit condition to be admitted as a Member of the Union (Article 49 of the EU Treaty) but furthermore as a permanent condition for membership. It is interesting to note that the sanction mechanism provided

---

15 Council Joint Action of 22 December 2000 on the European Union Monitoring Mission, OJ 2000, L328.

16 Council Decision 2001/682/CFSP, OJ 2001, L241.

17 *Cf* on the question of the legal personality of the Union, the articles referred to in fn. 12; see also Manfred Zuleeg, Die Organisationsstruktur der Europäischen Union – Eine Analyse der Klammerbestimmungen des Vertrags von Amsterdam – Europarecht 1998, p.151 and Antonio Tizzano, La personnalité internationale de l'Union européenne, Revue du Marché Unique Européen 4/1998, 11.

18 E.g., decisions on common strategies to be implemented by Council decisions to be adopted with qualified majority, Articles 13 and 23, para 2 of the EC Treaty; decisions on 'appeal' in cases where a Member State, by invoking 'important and stated reasons of national policy', blocks the decision-making in the Council, Articles 23, para 2 and 40 para 2 of the EU treaty.

19 Article 35 of the EU Treaty.

20 Title VII of the EU Treaty.

for by Article 7 of the EU Treaty in case of a serious and persistent breach of the principles just mentioned has not been limited to the scope ratione materiae of the treaties, but is of general application. The Union has thus acquired its own responsibility for ensuring the respect by Member States for these principles. The Treaty of Nice will add a mechanism of ex ante surveillance in order to improve, after the experience with the sanctions against Austria, the exercise of these responsibilities.

By the way, legal practice has now become aware of these new procedures. It appears that the European Commission has received a series of complaints with regard to the length of judicial procedures in Italy. It cannot be excluded that the Commission, also under the impetus of the European Parliament and the European Ombudsman, may take initiatives in this field.

Of course, one should mention in this context also the EU Charter of fundamental rights. First of all, to underline that it is an EU not an EC Charter. Secondly, to say that the Charter, whatever one thinks about its legal status, cannot be disregarded when applying these Union procedures with regard to respect for fundamental rights, as an authoritative and up to date statement of the content of these rights. The European Parliament has recently announced its intention to proceed along those lines by submitting the situation in the Member States to an annual review, the results of which are to be published in an annual report.[21]

12. These changes in the position and the structure of the Union brought about by the Amsterdam treaty, have not escaped European law specialists. The focus has definitely changed now from EC law to EU law. The nature and status of the Union, its relationship to the EC, are the subject of intensive research. Some even advocate considering the European Union and the European Community as one, integrated legal order.[22]

Relationship EU-EC

13. The least one can say, is that the Treaty of Amsterdam has made the relationship between EU and EC more complex. If one could, after the Treaty of Maastricht, still largely regard the EC as a separate compartment within the Union, safely protected from interference by the Union, this is less so now. Of course, the European Communities continue to exist as separate organizations, each with its own legal personality. They still form a legal order of their own but the walls between EC and EU have become less impenetrable than before. The cases in which the EC is explicitly made subject to decision-making by the Union have become more frequent.

More generally, it can be said that the interdependence of EU and EC has become more intense. It is true that in a way this interdependence has existed from the start for the relationship between CFSP and the external policies of the EC, particularly the common commercial policy. Practice has largely succeeded in carrying out these policies in a coherent way, respecting the fairly different legal regimes of CFSP and EC (see the example of dual-use goods before the relevant regime became exclusively Community law based).[23] But, the Amsterdam Treaty has clearly increased this interdependence. So, the development of an area of freedom, security and justice, which is an overall objective of the *Union* will have to be achieved by joint action under the third pillar and title IV of the EC Treaty. Article 62 of the EC Treaty even subjects the abolition of all internal bordercontrols on persons to measures of harmonization of criminal law under Article 31 of the EU Treaty, as a

---

21 Resolution of the European Parliament on the situation as regards fundamental rights in the European Union (2000) of 5 July 2001 (2000/2231 (INI)).

22 *Cf* with further references the article of Deirdre Curtin and Ige Dekker referred to in fn. 12, Armin von Bogdandy, The Legal Case for Unity: The European Union as a Single Organization with a Single Legal System, CML Rev 1999, p.887; Ramses A. Wessel, The inside looking out: consistency and delimitation in EU external relations, CML Rev 2000, p.1135; by the same author, Revisiting the international legal status of the EU, European Foreign Affairs Review, Vol. 5 (2000), 4, p.507; Ulrich Everling, Von der Europäischen Gemeinschaften zur Europäischen Union Durch Konvergenz zu Kohärenz, in 'In einem vereinten Europa dem Frieden der Welt zu dienen . . .', Liber Amicorum Thomas Oppermann, Herausgegeben von Claus Dieter Classen, etc., Berlin 2001, p.163.

23 Council Regulation 3381/94 and Decision 94/942/CFSP, OJ 1994, L367. The latter Decision has been repealed by Decision 2000/402/CFSP, OJ 2000, L218 subsequent to the judgments of the ECJ in cases C-70/94, *Werner* [1995] ECR I-3189, C-83/94, *Leifer* [1995] ECR I-3231 and Case C-124/95, *Centro-Com* [1997] ECR I-81.

preliminary condition. More examples could be given, to mention only one: the transparency regime, that is the regulation on access to documents, recently adopted, applies indiscriminately to the EC and Union activities.[24]

14. This increasing interdependence between EC and EU is not without risk for the maintenance of the autonomy of the EC. Some colonising of the EC by the EU cannot be excluded. Because of the more intergovernmental decision-making of the Union, this is not without danger for the Community method and the position of the more supranational institutions as the European Parliament and the Commission. It is, for instance, remarkable that the executive function within the framework of CFSP is almost exclusively reserved to the Council;[25] for that purpose the Council is building up its own executive machinery. To put it more generally: a process of constitutionalization of the European Union might go hand in hand with some constitutional erosion of the EC.[26] I immediately add that the prerogatives of the EC, particularly as to the delimitation of its powers and those under the other Union pillars, can be protected by the Court.[27]

15. The strengthening of the Union as such by the Amsterdam Treaty on the one hand and the growing interwovenness between EC and EU on the other, raises a number of interesting questions with regard to the qualities of the legal system of the EU itself, more particularly in comparison with the EC:

— the principle of supremacy, the concept of direct effect, the principles of state liability under the rule in Francovich, the general principles of law, as developed in the Court's case-law, do they apply to EU law? Does there exist a general principle of loyalty to the Union, as inscribed in Article 10 EC with regard to the EC? And quid with regard to the principles governing the division of internal and external powers between EC and Member States (preemption, ERTA doctrine), do they apply also for the Union?

In other words, can the constitutional principles characterizing the legal order of the Communities be transposed to the EU?

16. These questions cannot be brushed aside as being of mere theoretical interest and without practical relevance. Not only might they arise in national courts, also the Court of Justice will quite probably be confronted with them, since it has now obtained jurisdiction, albeit limited, with regard to the Union, more particularly in the third pillar. It is true that direct effect has been excluded for decisions taken within the framework of the third pillar. However, that exclusion does not apply to all legal instruments available under the third pillar. Moreover, what exactly does it mean to say that decisions have no direct effect? In view of the possible preliminary jurisdiction of the Court as to those decisions, they can apparently at least be invoked within national courts for the purposes of consistent interpretation or to contest their validity.

17. Let me centre, more particularly, on the question of supremacy.[28] When applying the criteria of Van Gend en Loos and Costa ENEL, it is fairly clear that the legal system of the Union does not satisfy all of the conditions or it does so only to a more limited extent. More particularly, the impact of Union law on individuals, both in terms of imposing obligations or granting them rights, will be less direct than for Community law. For CFSP this will be so because of the very nature of foreign policy, for the third pillar this is largely the consequence of the exclusion of direct effect.

Is that sufficient to exclude supremacy? I do not think so. Even if the Union is not capable of legislating directly with regard to citizens' rights and obligations, there remain sufficient arguments

---

24 Regulation 1049/2001, OJ 2001, L145.

25 See the interesting comments of the Court of Auditors in its Special Report 13/2001 on CFSP, OJ 2001, C338.

26 I have borrowed that term from the farewell lecture by Richard H. Lauwaars when leaving his chair at the University of Amsterdam, Constitutionele erosie van de Europese Gemeenschappen, Groningen 1994.

27 See Case C-170/96, *Airport Transit Visas* [1998] ECR I-2763.

28 *Cf* on this question Ulrich Everling op.cit. fn. 22 at p.184 and Jan Wouters, National Constitutions and the European Union, Legal Issues of Economic Integration Vol. 27, p.25 (at 85).

to qualify the Union Treaty as being more than an agreement which merely creates mutual obligations between the contracting states, to quote once again Van Gend en Loos.[29] In view of the general objectives, as spelled out in the preamble ('an ever closer Union among the peoples of Europe'), the function of the Union as guardian of the respect for fundamental rights, also in and by the Member States, and finally, as far as the third pillar is concerned, the granting of real powers to the Union in order to establish an area of freedom, security and justice, it would be difficult to deny that the Union has a direct and immediate impact on the citizens of the Member States and their interests. Another argument in favour of accepting supremacy of Union law would be that the Union being so emphatically based on respect for the rule of law according to Article 6 of the EU Treaty, it would be unacceptable for Member States to free themselves unilaterally, by acts of national law, from their obligations imposed by Union law.

18. Moreover, it would be difficult to exclude that the quality and characteristics of the Community legal order will have some radiation effect on the Union's legal system. The case-law of the Court gives an illustration of this phenomenon. The principle of supremacy and respect for fundamental rights have, without much argument, been transposed to the Brussels I Convention on the recognition and enforcement of judgments in civil and commercial matters (Judgments in cases Duijnstee and Krombach).[30] This Convention (now a regulation)[31] remained a classic instrument of international cooperation, but because of its close link with the Community legal order, it has been able to benefit from some of the characteristics of Community law itself.

The existence of a single institutional structure for the Union and the EC, the interdependence of the Communities and the Union, of Community law and Union law, as already mentioned, will make it difficult and artificial to exclude such a radiation effect or 'Reflex Wirkung' as Germans would call it. But would it not precisely be artificial to try to attribute to the Union, the qualities of the Community legal order, like a Von Münchhausen drawing himself by his own hair out of the swamp? I do not think so. In a way, ironically enough, it is precisely the structure of the Union, even if it is not a single one, which fosters such an effect. Indeed, the Union is not separate from the Communities, it has to act through the Communities to achieve its own objectives. We should not forget that the objectives of the Communities, as set out in Article 2 of the Union Treaty, are at the same time the objectives of the Union.

19. I see only one major objection to this transplant of the principles of the Community legal order to the Union as such. Is the Union system in view of its institutional structuring and its incomplete system of dispute settlement and law enforcement at all apt to be qualified as a separate *legal order* as the Communities can? Is it sufficiently legitimized both in terms of democratic legitimation and respect for the principles of the Rechtsstaat, to be able to claim supremacy over national law? I have as yet no final answer to this dilemma. Much will depend on how institutional practice will evolve, and what role the Court of Justice will be able and allowed to play.

Conclusion

20. As a conclusion, we end up with a paradox. Through a process of what I have called the constitutionalization of the European Union, institutional reality might go largely beyond what the drafters of the European Union Treaty had in mind. What was so keenly meant to remain separate, is growing into an organic whole. It might be that by natural evolution the EU will very much develop into a single system, just as the ECSC, EC and Euratom have grown into one single legal order. Technically, it may not be too difficult to respect at the same time the legal and institutional varieties between the EC and the two other pillars. There remains however the problem of opacity, the lack of transparency for the non-initiated which seriously undermines the legitimacy of the Union in the eyes of the citizen.

Now if practice continues indeed to develop in the direction of an osmosis between EC and EU, there is much to be said in favour of drawing the logical consequences during the forthcoming

29 Case 26/62, [1963] ECR 23.

30 Case 288/82, *Duijnstee* [1983] ECR 3663 and Case C-7/98, *Krombach* [2000] ECR I-1956.

31 Regulation 44/2001 on jurisdiction and the recognition and enforcement of judgments in civil and commercial matters, OJ 2001, L12.

intergovernmental conference and devising one single Union structure, absorbing EC and Euratom which would then cease to exist. For institutional practice that need not have to constitute a fundamental change, legal basis and decision-making procedures remaining what they are. On the contrary, transparency and, in the end, legitimacy of the Union would substantially gain.

However, we know that the evolution of the process of European integration is not just a matter of logic, particularly not when the institutional setting is concerned.

'But of the crooked timber of humanity nothing entirely straight was ever made'.[32]

This favourite quotation of Isaiah Berlin (adapted from Kant) certainly also applies to the structure of the European Union.

FURTHER READING ON 'CONSTITUTIONALIZATION' IN PARTICULAR AND THE ROLE OF THE COURT IN GENERAL

Alter, K., *Establishing the Supremacy of European Law* (Oxford: OUP, 2001)

Dehousse, R., *The European Court of Justice* (Basingstoke: Macmillan Press, 1998).

Mestmäcker, E.-J., 'On the Legitimacy of European Law' (1994) 58 *Rabels Z* 615.

Joerges, C., 'Taking the Law Seriously: On Political Science and the Role of Law in the Process of European Integration' (1996) 2 ELJ 195.

Lenaerts, K., 'Constitutionalism and the Many Faces of Federalism' (1990) 38 AJCL 205.

Petersmann, E.-U., 'Proposals for a New Constitution for the European Union: Building Blocks for a Constitutional Theory and Constitutional Law of the EU' (1995) 32 CML Rev 1123.

Shapiro, M., 'The European Court of Justice' in Craig, P. and de Búrca, G., *The Evolution of EU Law* (Oxford: OUP, 1999).

Snyder, F., 'Governing Economic Globalisation: Global Legal Pluralism and European Law' (1999) 5 ELJ 334.

Weiler, J., 'The Transformation of Europe' (1991) 100 Yale LJ 2403.

Wilhelmsson, T., 'Jack-in-the-box Theory of European Community Law', in Krämer, L., *et al* (eds), *Law and Diffuse Interests in the European Legal Order* (Baden-Baden: Nomos, 1997), p.177.

■ QUESTION

To what extent is it appropriate today to examine under the label 'constitutionali-zation' not only the depening and widening of the EC legal order but also the process of reliably policing its outer limits? What is the vision of a constitutional-ized legal order that emerges from the Laeken Declaration? (p.25 above). And what does the outcome of the Convention on the 'Future of Europe' reveal about the limits of the EU's 'constitutionalized' incursion into national competence?

The existence of a 'constitutionalized' legal order does not presuppose the existence of a Constitution of the type familiar in most modern European States.

P. Craig, 'Constitutions, Constitutionalism and the European Union'
(2001) 7 ELJ 125, 150

It has been argued that the EC has indeed been transformed from an international to a constitutional legal order, and that the arguments to the contrary are not convincing. This does not however mean that it has or should have a constitution which draws together in a separate document the constitutional norms presently enshrined in the Treaties, together with constitutional doctrine emanating from the European Court of Justice, and national courts.

---

32 See Noel Annan, The Dons, 2000, p.222.

The impetus to make the Union more transparent has been examined in Chapter 1 and it will be re-assessed in Chapters 20 and 21. But the lure of transparency is perilous in so far as it is provokes a desire to fit the European Union into institutional and constitutional structures of the type familiar among States. That is to impoverish the Union's novelty.

PART TWO

Community Trade Law and Policy

9

Law and the Economic Objectives of the Community

SECTION 1: **INTRODUCTION**

This Part of the book examines the major provisions of European Community substantive law. These are the provisions which are designed to eliminate barriers to trade between Member States and to suppress distortions in the competitive structure of the market. These provisions are the instruments for transforming the territory of the European Union into a common market. This heartland of trade law is almost exclusively the preserve of the first pillar and orthodox *communautaire* method, so the label 'EC law' or 'Community law' will be routinely employed. Only in relation to parts of the law governing the free movement of persons is a brand of unorthodox lawmaking to be found; this discussion is reserved to Chapter 15.

Chapter 9 provides an introduction to the subject. It explains basic economic theory. It shows why a common market is economically advantageous and discusses the shortcomings of the Community hitherto. It also examines the project which in the late 1980s and early 1990s catapulted the Community into the forefront of national and international affairs – the completion of the single (or internal) market by the end of 1992. It shows how this is a dynamic process, reverberating long after the 1992 deadline has passed. Chapter 9 concludes with an introduction to the pursuit of the objective of Economic and Monetary Union which was elaborated in the (Maastricht) Treaty on European Union.

Thereafter Chapters 10–15 examine the legal provisions which permit the opening up of the market. This is achieved by prohibiting States from imposing barriers to the free movement of the factors of production (goods, persons, services, capital) between Member States. Chapters 10 to 12 examine the legal instruments for securing the free movement of goods; Chapters 13 and 14 examine the free movement of persons and services. These provisions are 'negative' in the sense that they involve prohibitions on State action. Chapter 15 looks at the broadening of the project of integration in the shape of the creation of European Citizenship and the quest to establish an 'area of freedom, security and justice'. These notions operate at a grander and more constitutionally demanding level than the pursuit of market integration and have injected some serious controversy into the nature and scope of European-level policy-making.

SECTION 2: **THE COMMON MARKET**

ARTICLE 2 EC

The Community shall have as its task, by establishing a common market and an economic and monetary union and by implementing common policies or activities referred to in Articles 3 and 4, to promote throughout the Community a harmonious, balanced and sustainable development of economic activities, a high level of employment and of social protection, equality between men and women, sustainable and non-inflationary growth, a high degree of competitiveness and convergence of economic performance, a high level of protection and improvement of the quality of the environment, the raising of the standard of living and quality of life, and economic and social cohesion and solidarity among Member States.

NOTE
It may first be observed that the Community has chosen to place emphasis on the establishment of a *common market*. What distinguishes the common market from other types of economic integration?

A. M. El-Agraa (ed), The European Union: Economics and Policies
(6th ed, Harlow: Prentice Hall, 2001), pp.1–3

International economic integration (hereafter, simply economic integration) is one aspect of 'international economics' which has been growing in importance for almost five decades. The term itself has a rather short history; indeed, Machlup [*A History of Thought on Economic Integration* (Macmillan, 1977)] was unable to find a single instance of its use prior to 1942. Since then the term has been used at various times to refer to practically any area of international economic relations. By 1950, however, the term had been given a specific definition by economists specializing in international trade to denote a state of affairs or a process which involves the amalgamation of separate economies into larger free trading regions. It is in this more limited sense that the term is used today. However, one should hasten to add that economists not familiar with this branch of international economics have for quite a while been using the term to mean simply increasing economic interdependence between nations.

More specifically, economic integration is concerned with the discriminatory removal of all trade impediments between at least two participating nations and with the establishment of certain elements of cooperation and coordination between them. The latter depends entirely on the actual form that integration takes. Different forms of economic integration can be envisaged and many have actually been implemented (see Table 1.1 for schematic presentation):

1. *Free trade areas*, where the member nations remove all trade impediments among themselves but retain their freedom with regard to the determination of their own policies *vis-à-vis* the outside world (the non-participant – for example, the European Free Trade Association (EFTA) and the defunct Latin American Free Trade Area (LAFTA) and the North American Free Trade Agreement (NAFTA) but which also covers investment).

2. *Customs unions*, which are very similar to free trade areas except that member nations must conduct and pursue common external commercial relations – for instance, they must adopt common external tariffs (CETs) on imports from the non-participants as is the case in, *inter alia*, the European Union (EU, which is in this particular sense a customs union, but, as we shall presently see, it is more than that), the Central American Common Market (CACM) and the Caribbean Community and Common Market (CARICOM).

3. *Common markets*, which are custom unions that allow also for free factor mobility across national member frontiers, i.e., capital, labour, technology and enterprises should move unhindered between the participating countries – for example, the EU (but again it is more complex).

Table 1.1 Schematic presentation of economic integration schemes

Scheme	Free intrascheme trade	Common commercial policy	Free factor mobility	Common monetary and fiscal policy	One Government
Free trade area	Yes	No	No	No	No
Customs union	Yes	Yes	No	No	No
Common market	Yes	Yes	Yes	No	No
Economic union	Yes	Yes	Yes	Yes	No
Political union	Yes	Yes	Yes	Yes	Yes

4. *Complete economic unions*, which are common markets that ask for complete unification of monetary and fiscal policies, i.e., the participants must introduce a central authority to exercise control over these matters so that member nations effectively become regions of the same nation – the EU is heading in this direction.
5. *Complete political unions*, where the participating countries become literally one nation, i.e., the central authority needed in complete economic unions should be paralleled by a common parliament and other necessary institutions needed to guarantee the sovereignty of one state – an example of this is the unification of the two Germanies in 1990.

However, one should hasten to add that political integration need not be, and in the majority of cases will never be, part of this list. Nevertheless, it can of course be introduced as a form of unity and for no economic reason whatsoever, as was the case with the two Germanies and as is the case with the pursuit of the unification of the Korean Peninsula, although one should naturally be interested in its economic consequences (see below). More generally, one should indeed stress that each of these forms of economic integration can be introduced in its own right; hence they should not be confused with *stages* in a *process* which eventually leads to either complete economic or political union.

It should also be noted that there may be *sectoral* integration, as distinct from general across-the-board integration, in particular areas of the economy as was the case with the European Coal and Steel Community (ECSC), created in 1950, but sectoral integration is a form of cooperation not only because it is inconsistent with the accepted definition of economic integration but also because it may contravene the rules of the General Agreement on Tariffs and Trade (GATT), now called the World Trade Organization (WTO) – see below. Sectoral integration may also occur within any of the mentioned schemes, as is the case with the EU's Common Agricultural Policy (CAP), but then it is nothing more than a 'policy'.

One should further point out that it has been claimed that economic integration can be *negative* or *positive*. The term negative integration was coined by Tinbergen (*International Economic Integration* (Elsevier, 1954)) to refer to the removal of impediments on trade between the participating nations or to the elimination of any restrictions on the process of trade liberalization. The term positive integration relates to the modification of existing instruments and institutions and, more importantly, to the creation of new ones so as to enable the market of the integrated area to function properly and effectively and also to promote other broader policy aims of the scheme. Hence, at the risk of oversimplification, according to this classification, it can be stated that sectoral integration and free trade areas are forms of economic integration which require only negative integration, while the remaining types require positive integration, since, as a minimum, they need the positive act of adopting common relations. However, in reality this distinction is oversimplistic not only because practically all existing types of economic integration have found it essential to introduce some elements of positive integration, but also because theoretical considerations clearly indicate that no scheme of economic integration is viable without certain elements of positive integration.

■ QUESTION

What are the economic advantages of integration in general and a common market in particular?

A. M. El-Agraa (ed), The European Union: Economics and Policies
(6th ed, Harlow: Prentice Hall, 2001), pp.17–18

At the customs union (CU) and free trade area (FTA) levels, the possible sources of economic gain from economic integration can be attributed to:

1. enhanced efficiency in production made possible by increased specialization in accordance with the law of comparative advantage, due to the liberalized market of the participating nations;

2. increased production levels due to better exploitation of economies of scale made possible by the increased size of the market;

3. an improved international bargaining position, made possible by the larger size, leading to better terms of trade (cheaper imports from the outside world and higher prices for exports to them);

4. enforced changes in efficiency brought about by intensified competition between firms;

5. changes affecting both the amount and quality of the factors of production due to technological advances, themselves encouraged by (4).

If the level of economic integration is to go beyond the free trade area and customs union levels, then further sources of economic gain also become possible:

6. factor mobility across the borders of the member nations will materialize only if there is a net economic incentive for them, thus leading to higher national incomes;

7. the coordination of monetary and fiscal policies may result in cost reductions since the pooling of efforts may enable the achievement of economies of scale;

8. the unification of efforts to achieve better employment levels, lower inflation rates, balanced trade, higher rates of economic growth and better income distribution may make it cheaper to attain these targets.

It should be apparent that some of these possible gains relate to static resource reallocation effects while the rest relate to long-term or dynamic effects. It should also be emphasized that these are *possible* economic gains, i.e., there is no guarantee that they can ever be achieved; everything would depend on the nature of the particular scheme and the type of competitive behaviour prevailing prior to integration. Indeed, it is quite feasible that in the absence of 'appropriate' competitive behaviour, economic integration may worsen the situation. Thus the possible attainment of these benefits must be considered with great caution.

Membership of an economic grouping cannot of itself guarantee to a member state or the group a satisfactory economic performance, or even a better performance than in the past. The static gains from integration, although significant, can be – and often are – swamped by the influence of factors of domestic or international origin that have nothing to do with integration. The more fundamental factors influencing a country's economic performance (the dynamic factors) are unlikely to be affected by integration except in the long run. It is clearly not a necessary condition for economic success that a country should be a member of an economic community as the experience of several small countries confirms, although such countries might have done better as members of a suitable group. Equally, a large integrated market is in itself no guarantee of performance, as the experience of India suggests. However, although integration is dearly no panacea for all economic ills, nor indispensable to success, there are many convincing reasons for supposing that significant economic benefits may be derived from properly conceived arrangements for economic integration. (Robson, *The Economics of International Integration* Allen & Unwin, 1985).

However, in the case of the EU, one should always keep in mind that the 'founding fathers' had the formation of a United States of Western (hopefully all) Europe as the ultimate goal and that economic integration became the immediate objective so as to facilitate the attainment of political unity via the back door . . . Those who fail to appreciate this will always undermine the EU's serious attempts at the achievement of economic and monetary union via the Maastricht Treaty . . .

NOTE

The Community is a response to the post-war devastation of the continent of Europe, and grew in part because of the perceived failure of the nation State as an international actor. The final paragraph of the preceding extract makes the particularly important point that the Community encompasses aspirations beyond economics. This should already have become clear from your reading of the material in Chapter 1 of this book.

What, then, is the role of law in achieving these goals?

ARTICLE 3 EC

1. For the purposes set out in Article 2, the activities of the Community shall include, as provided in this Treaty and in accordance with the timetable set out therein:

   (a) the prohibition, as between Member States, of customs duties and quantitative restrictions on the import and export of goods, and of all other measures having equivalent effect;

   (b) a common commercial policy;

   (c) an internal market characterized by the abolition, as between Member States, of obstacles to the free movement of goods, persons, services and capital;

   (d) measures concerning the entry and movement of persons as provided for in Title IV;

   (e) a common policy in the sphere of agriculture and fisheries;

   (f) a common policy in the sphere of transport;

   (g) a system ensuring that competition in the internal market is not distorted;

   (h) the approximation of the laws of Member States to the extent required for the functioning of the common market;

   (i) the promotion of coordination between employment policies of the Member States with a view to enhancing their effectiveness by developing a coordinated strategy for employment;

   (j) a policy in the social sphere comprising a European Social Fund;

   (k) the strengthening of economic and social cohesion;

   (l) a policy in the sphere of the environment;

   (m) the strengthening of the competitiveness of Community industry;

   (n) the promotion of research and technological development;

   (o) encouragement for the establishment and development of trans-European networks;

   (p) a contribution to the attainment of a high level of health protection;

   (q) a contribution to education and training of quality and to the flowering of the cultures of the Member States;

   (r) a policy in the sphere of development cooperation;

   (s) the association of the overseas countries and territories in order to increase trade and promote jointly economic and social development;

   (t) a contribution to the strengthening of consumer protection;

   (u) measures in the spheres of energy, civil protection and tourism.

2. In all the activities referred to in this Article, the Community shall aim to eliminate inequalities, and to promote equality, between men and women.

NOTES

1. Article 3 sets out the 'four fundamental freedoms' in Community trade law: the free movement of goods, persons, services, and capital. In addition, it refers to the need for common policy-making in several areas. The Maastricht Treaty on European Union and the Amsterdam Treaty both added significantly to the list of such areas (one consequence of which is the increased profile of cases involving choice of 'legal base' for EC legislation, p.53 above). The Nice Treaty, a more modest document (p.13), made no change to the list.

2. There are, then, both negative and positive aspects to Community law. The law is negative in the sense that it is designed to eliminate national laws which act as obstacles to trade within the wider Community market. It is positive in the sense that it implies regulation of that wider market through Community legislation. Sometimes positive Community policy-making may be seen as a means of breaking down remaining barriers to trade which are lawful under Community law. This will be observed in the Chapters that follow (in particular, Chapter 10, p.336, Chapter 11, p.378, and Chapter 14, p.471). It is also examined more broadly in Chapter 19. On other occasions Community policies may be designed more to cope with the consequences of free movement rather than simply to bring it about. Some of the material in Chapters 13 and 15 may be usefully addressed from this perspective, but the discussion in Chapters 20 and 21 takes the inquiry onto a broader plane.

3. The substantive provisions of Community law which are studied in the Chapters that follow are essentially the provisions alluded to in Article 3 EC, which are designed to achieve the common market broadly conceived.

■ QUESTION

To what extent are the *substantive* rules alluded to in Article 3 EC achievable only through the development of the *constitutional* principles examined in Chapters 2–7? Could a common market be achieved without a legal system which is supreme and directly effective; or without a procedure under which authoritative uniform interpretation of the law can be supplied?

SECTION 3: **THE INTERNAL MARKET: 1992**

....

A: **The background**

Why does the common market referred to in Article 2 EC not exist? Economic barriers to trade proved enduring in the early years. Moreover the institutional and legislative apparatus of the Community also proved inadequate to secure the advancement of the Community. There was a marked weakening in political will. Difficult decisions were stifled by the effect of the requirement in practice of unanimity in voting in Council. Violation of Community law became more common. The Community was in a state of stagnation by the early-1980s. Loss of confidence in its prospects reduced cross-border investment.

Leon Brittan, EC Commissioner, Annual General Meeting of JUSTICE
London, 7 July 1989

... [W]hy [was] the 1992 process ... necessary in the first place. Really, in a way, it was necessary because of the recognition that the prescriptions of the Treaty of Rome had not been fully fulfilled. The idea of a single European market in which there would be freedom of goods and services had manifestly not been created by the early 1980s, and although there was freedom of physical goods, the unseen barriers to trade were so substantial that you could not say that we had created a single Common Market. That perception was allied with the further perception that in order to achieve that progress towards a genuine single market, it was necessary for there to be constitutional change in the Community, because as long as all decisions had to be taken by unanimity, in practice, if not in strict theory, it was impossible to remove the non-tariff barriers, whether in public procurement, whether through the abuse of standards, whatever their nature, towards the creation of a genuine single market. And so, alongside the programmes of 1992, went the Single European Act and the constitutional changes, giving greater power to the European Parliament, and the ability for decisions to be taken in many, if not all, areas by qualified majority vote. It was that that provided the impetus to 1992.

NOTE

For a collection of essays, see D. Swann (ed), *The Single European Market and Beyond* (Routledge, 1992).

Thus, the 1992 project is properly seen as an attempt to secure the reinvigoration of the Community. It is the New Impetus, without which the Community would at best have remained marginalized and at worst have collapsed.

The blueprint for the 1992 programme was provided by COM (85) 310 – the Commission White Paper on Completing the Internal Market. This declared that 'A well developed free trade area offers significant advantages . . . but it would fail and fail dismally to release the energies of the people of Europe; it would fail to deploy Europe's immense economic resources to the maximum advantage; and it would fail to satisfy the aspirations of the people of Europe' (para 220). The White Paper provided a policy agenda of some 300 measures which needed to be adopted by the end of 1992 in order to make the internal market a reality. The legal propulsion to give the plan the might to succeed was provided by the Single European Act, which came into force on 1 July 1987. That Treaty amended the Treaty of Rome in certain important respects; most notably for present purposes it shifted voting procedures in relation to 1992 measures towards qualified majority voting, instead of unanimous voting (contrast Article 100a, introduced by the SEA, with the original Treaty's Article 100 – becoming Articles 95 and 94 respectively post-Amsterdam). More generally, the Member States had committed themselves to a new wave of European integration through an explicit political act.

H. Schmitt von Sydow, 'Basic Strategies of the Commission's White Paper',
in R. Bieber, R. Dehousse, J. Pinder, J. Weiler (eds), 1992: One European Market?
(Baden-Baden: Nomos Verlagsgesellschaft, 1988), pp.79, 86–92

(Footnotes omitted.)

The idea

A successful politician does not always need to have brilliant ideas, but he must be aware of existing problems and possible solutions and, most of all, he needs a sense of good timing, knowing when an ambitious idea is ripe to be pushed with vigour.

When the Delors Commission took office in January 1985, the Commissioners – 14 out of 17 were newcomers – looked for a motto, for a major goal to be achieved during the next four or eight years, the lifetime of one or two Commissions.

There were about five topics to choose from. Two concerned the reform of the agricultural policy and of the budget. These were significant tasks and, no doubt, they had to be fulfilled. But were they sufficient to give a positive trade mark to the Commission? Repairing the errors of the past was important, but a quantum leap forward was even more so.

Institutional reform and progress towards political union were overdue, but would they be sufficient to reach the citizens of Europe? The man on the street would not be convinced of the usefulness of Community institutions as long as, crossing the borders between Member States, he met the same old customs officials and had to take along the same whole set of different currencies in order to pay the local taxi driver. Commissioners were influenced by the disappointing results of the 1984 election to the European Parliament where the campaigns had focused on national policies and where voters had snubbed the polling stations not only because the Parliament was lacking powers, but also because the whole Community did not seem able to solve citizens' problems.

These problems concern employment and economic prosperity, and they need a regenerative impetus of which the European countries are intrinsically capable if they overcome the fragmentation of their economies and their markets. The instruments for this kind of integration are Economic and Monetary Union and the Internal Market.

Economic and Monetary Union was certainly an attractive goal, especially to the five Commissioners who previously had been Ministers of Finance in their national governments; and there was no doubt that it should be pursued vigourously. But Member States' fears regarding its political and financial impact made it difficult to draft a realistic timetable.

So the choice became the Internal Market. Indeed this file was ripe for a decisive breakthrough.

First of all, since 1983, a new momentum in the right direction had been taking shape, which just needed a determined push and a precise perspective. Never before had there been such a promising basis for removing all visible and most of the invisible barriers to free movement inside the Community.

Second, there was a clear political will. Since the early 1980s, Heads of State and Government, as well as Parliament and Commission, had repeatedly committed themselves to achieve the goals – already enshrined in the Treaty – of the internal market. Even down in the Council's expert groups, there was no fundamental opposition, neither from economic, regional nor sectoral interests, to the completion of the internal market. Delays were mainly due to procedural difficulties such as quarrels about legal base, reluctance to delegate powers of implementation, conflicting priorities, and lack of flexibility fostered by the practice of unanimity. These difficulties within the institutions were supposed to vanish once the global vision of the immense economic advantages of an integrated market became consolidated by a binding overall programme.

Third, the completion of the internal market required no additional spending from national or Community budgets. On the contrary, it would set free gains several times superior to the Community budget. The European Parliament had just given widespread publicity to the calculations of Messrs. Albert and Ball demonstrating that money lost by the fragmentation of public markets and by the delays encountered by barriers at intra-Community borders was equal to two years' Community budgets. And these were only two items on the costs of Non-Europe bill; if one added the expenses for the infrastructure of intra-Community borders and the potential prosperity resulting, directly and indirectly, from the increased competitivenes of industry in a home market of continental dimensions, then it became increasingly surprising that Heads of State and Government had personally, for years and years, wasted time and energy on trying to adjust percentages of national contributions to the Community budget, neglecting the internal market with its much greater, intrinsic benefits. As was stated in the House of Lords, the cost of just one single barrier to trade, namely the discriminatory element of tax levied from 1978 to 1981 on Scotch Whisky, was four times as much as the British annual net contribution to the Community budget.

The formulation

The Commission lost no time. Only one week after he took office, President Delors went to the Parliament and announced the new Commission's intention to ask the European Council to pledge itself to completion of a fully unified internal market by 1992, to be achieved with the help of a programme comprising a realistic and binding timetable. This intention was repeated in the overall 'Programme of the Commission for 1985'.

The members of the Parliament and the Heads of State and Government could not help but approve the target and the procedure. In its meeting of 29 and 30 March, the European Council identified as its first priority 'action to achieve a single large market by 1992 thereby creating a more favourable environment for stimulating enterprise, competition and trade'; it called upon the Commission to draw up a detailed programme with a specific timetable before its next meeting.

The Commission's White Paper in response to this invitation was rapid, bold and radical. The document was written in seven weeks. It covered a vast series of topics and left no stone unturned. Seldom before had a single paper required such detailed inter-service discussions with so many Commission departments necessitating the redefinition of so many policies. It took seventeen drafts before Lord Cockfield, the Vice-President responsible for internal market, could present the Paper to the public on Saturday, 15 June 1985. He was aware that the strategy proposed in the White Paper implied a profound change in the habits and traditional ways of thinking; but he also knew the pledge of the Heads of State and Government to the target of 1992. 'They asked for it', he calmly said, 'they have got it'.

The contents

The White Paper does not propose the target of 1992, nor does it rehearse the arguments in favour of that target. Instead the Commission, given the European Council's clear commitment to the target, just spells out the logical consequences of the commitment, together with an action programme for achieving the objective.

Consequently, the fields of action proposed by the White Paper have not been chosen because of their feasibility, but because of their necessity. The question to be answered was not: 'What can be realistically done by 1992?', but: 'What must be done in order to achieve the internal market and how could one squeeze it into the 1992 timetable?' Paradoxically, this 'unrealistic' approach has largely contributed to the Paper's credibility, since the global vision of what has to be done – with no jack-in-the-box-barriers hidden – helps to make the overall efforts measurable and to scale the 'unfeasible' actions down to their real political and economic proportions. During the drafting of the White Paper, all Commission departments had been warned that afterwards they would not be allowed to raise additional problems, and they responded to the challenge as if they – and not national administrations – were personally responsible for the emergence of new barriers to the free movement.

Identifying all problems without exception, the White Paper did not hesitate to tackle sensitive areas where no realistic immediate solution was at hand, e.g., commercial policy vis-à-vis third countries, nor to deal with policies for which no clear Community competence could be established, e.g. the right of asylum or the fight against terrorism. Whatever the underlying reason giving rise to a physical or technical barrier is, the White Paper spells it out and examines how justified interests can be taken care of without disturbing free movement inside the Community.

On the other hand, there are numerous other policies, such as regional, social, environmental, consumer, transport, research, competition, economic and monetary policies, which are closely linked to the internal market and the integration of economies; but they are touched by the White Paper only where they have a direct bearing on the abolition of physical and technical barriers. While progress on these policies becomes even more important because of the completion of the internal market, and indeed has been positively enhanced by the verve of the White Paper and the perspective of the great 'rendez-vous' of 1992, they must not constitute a precondition to completing the internal market. The White Paper mentions them only for the record refraining from offering any recipe.

Similarly, institutional reforms are not explicitly called for in the White Paper. Its main merit is not to have presented detailed solutions, but to have identified the problems. Of course, where problems had been tackled for a long time and where formal Commission proposals were already on the table, the White Paper refers, in many cases, to those proposals. But in cases where the problems had not been tackled at Community level before or where rapid but realistic solutions were difficult to define, such as asylum or commercial policy, the White Paper just sketches the responsibilities and possible ways of solution, maintaining nevertheless the pressure stemming from the time schedule.

Comprehensive as the White Paper's strategy is, its fields of action form a single entity. One cannot extract individual files which seem to have a higher priority or to be easier, and postpone the decision on other files, without jeopardising the objective of complete abolition of all border controls.

This objective has been confirmed by the Single European Act which defines the internal market as 'an area without internal frontiers in which the free movement of goods, persons, services and capital is ensured'. A Europe without internal frontiers – not a Europe with fewer or simpler controls, but one with no such divisive frontier controls at all.

The structure

In line with this comprehensive character, the chapters of the White Paper do not follow the legal categories of the Treaty (goods, persons, services, capital) but the types of barriers which are met in practice; hence the division of the Paper in three parts dealing with physical, technical and fiscal barriers.

The physical barriers at the customs posts are the most obvious and glaring manifestation of the continued fragmentation of the Community; they must be removed for both economic and political reasons. It should be noted that the White Paper understands the notion of 'border' not in a geographical, but in a practical sense. Physical barriers are to be abolished not only where they are carried out at the very frontier of Member States, but also where they are carried out, thanks for example to the Community Transit Procedure, inside the Member States' territory at the premises of consignors and consignees of goods. In this sense, physical barriers are those barriers which are triggered by the fact of crossing a border; which are discriminatory insofar as they are opposed only to goods, persons, services and capital coming from abroad and are not identical to, and an integrated part of, internal controls.

The technical barriers result from national legislation which, in practice, hampers free movement even if, from a legal point of view, it does not refer to border crossings, and which is indistinctly applied to foreign and indigenous goods, persons, services and capital. Again, the White Paper's definition goes beyond the traditional notion of technical barriers: It is not limited to goods but intentionally includes services, capital movements, public procurement, industrial property and other national policies insofar as they risk to obstruct free movement and to annihilate the benefits of the removal of physical barriers.

The fiscal barriers appear in both forms, as physical and as technical barriers. The White Paper devotes a special chapter to them because they are the most important single group of impediments; their abolition had fallen a long way behind the advances made in other fields of integration, and they required a particularly radical change of strategy.

The Annex to the White Paper contains a detailed timetable for approximately 300 Commission proposals and Council decisions in order to implement the Commission's proposed programme . . .

R. Bieber, R. Dehousse, J. Pinder, J. Weiler, 'Back to the Future: Policy, Strategy and
Tactics of the White Paper on the Creation of a Single European Market',
in R. Bieber *et al* (eds), 1992: One European Market (Baden-Baden:
Nomos Verlagsgesellschaft, 1988), pp.13–16

(Footnotes omitted.)

The Aim and Method

If you want to attract support for a big political project, you do well to explain in half a dozen words what it is all about. The Cockfield White Paper selected the words 'action to achieve a single market by 1992'. At a time when the EC member governments disagreed about most major issues, it was possible to focus their minds and secure their agreement on making a priority of this apparently simple aim . . .

Yet the apparent simplicity of the aim and the definition conceal the enormous complexity of the undertaking . . . it involves the most intricate adjustment of regulations, taxes and laws. Completing a single market among advanced industrial economies is an exercise not of laissez-faire but of *Ordnungspolitik*; and *Ordnungspolitik* has become immensely more complicated since the idea of the social market economy was developed nearly half a century ago. In the terms of integration theory, negative integration, or the removal of barriers to transactions across the frontiers of different states, implies also the more exacting effort to achieve positive integration, or common policies with aims going beyond the straightforward removal of discrimination, when the barriers are not just tariffs and quotas, but differing regulations, taxes or laws. The White Paper gives rise, indeed, to some large and complex political, social and even ideological problems . . .

Virtues and Limits of an Inductive Method

What we have learnt in the intervening thirty years is a healthy disrespect of programmes which are not linked to specific executory commitments and to adequate institutional arrangements.

The White Paper presents a striking difference from other ambitious attempts to reform the Community in depth. Unlike the Draft Treaty Establishing the European Union adopted by the European Parliament which invited theological debates about the nature of Community governance, the White Paper is essentially inductive. It spells out in detail over 300 specific measures which will have to be adopted to complete the internal market; it even sets a proximate goal which, while it may fall short of a fully-formed single market, is at least unambiguous: to do away with frontier controls in their entirety by the end of 1992.

B: The internal market defined

What exactly *was* the 1992 project? What constitutes the completion of the internal market?

Article 8a was inserted into the original Treaty of Rome by the Single European Act; it was renumbered as Article 7a by the Treaty on European Union. But since the entry into force of the Treaty of Amsterdam the relevant Article is numbered Article 14 and it has read as follows:

Article 14

1. The Community shall adopt measures with the aim of progressively establishing the internal market over a period expiring on 31 December 1992, in accordance with the provisions of this Article and of Articles 15, 26, 47(2), 49, 80, 93 and 95 and without prejudice to the other provisions of this Treaty.

2. The internal market shall comprise an area without internal frontiers in which the free movement of goods, persons, services and capital is ensured in accordance with the provisions of this Treaty.

3. The Council, acting by a qualified majority on a proposal from the Commission, shall determine the guidelines and conditions necessary to ensure balanced progress in all the sectors concerned.

NOTE

Lord Cockfield was the Commissioner responsible from 1985–1989 for the development of the 1992 strategy. Speaking in London on 22 February 1988, he confirmed the uncompromising nature of the objective: '[it is] *not* an area where frontier controls have merely been simplified or are retained for this reason or that: but an area *without* internal frontiers' (Lord Cockfield reflects on the project in *The European Union* (Chichester: Wiley Chancery Law, 1994)).

■ QUESTION

To what extent does the pursuit of the internal market remain less ambitious than a common market?

C: The anticipated benefits of the completion of the internal market

Much of the comment above about the economic advantages of a *common* market applies to the aspiration to create an *internal* market. The Commission supported its campaign to set the Community the medium-term objective of completing the internal market by funding an extensive survey of the 'The Costs of Non-Europe' – the Cecchini Report.

An immensely optimistic picture is painted by the following summary of the survey's conclusions:

> **P. Cecchini,** The European Challenge: 1992, the Benefits of a Single Market
> (Aldershot: Wildwood House/Gower Publishing, 1988), pp.xvii–xxi

(Endnotes omitted.)

The research

The outlook emerges from an unprecedented research programme, launched in 1986 by EC Commission vice-president Lord Cockfield. Its purpose was to provide a solid body of scientifically-assembled evidence as a means of judging the extent of the market fragmentation confronting European business and Community policy-makers alike. In the process, the research has thrown up a vivid illustration and rigorous analysis of the costs imposed on Europeans by the mosaic of non-tariff barriers which – 30 years after the Community's birth – continue to mock the term 'common market'. The findings of this research into the 'costs of non-Europe', are outlined in their essential detail in the pages of this book.

The research is unprecedented for various reasons – first for the sheer size of its scope, but also because of the novelty of the subject-matter and the methodological difficulties that were encountered in making the analysis and calculations based on it. A further problem was the unevenness of the empirical data on European market fragmentation. Yet despite these fragilities, the results that emerge tell an unmistakable story.

They estimate the size of the costs and thus a potential for gains exceeding Ecu 200 billions. This basic benefit, which could be magnified by modestly positive economic policies, is the reward for removing the barriers targeted by the 1992 legislative programme set out in the EC's 1985 White Paper *Completing the Internal Market*. Thus when EC political decisions are taken and the business community has fully adjusted to the new competitive environment, gains of this order of magnitude would be acquired once and for all, meaning that the European economy would be lifted onto a higher plane of overall performance.

The barriers – like border controls and customs red-tape, divergent standards and technical regulations, conflicting business laws and protectionist procurement practice – are well enough known by name. But not until now has their impact, and that of their removal, been charted and costed. These results, the product of the extensive field-work and subsequent analysis, are outlined in Part I, together with illustrations of the workings of non-Europe in a broad range of industries and services.

Likewise, the White Paper's legislative programme for removing market barriers, reinforced since mid-1987 by the Single European Act, is also well known. But what has not been estimated until now is the value of the ultimate prize which Community governments could, by enacting it in full, deliver to Europe's citizens, its companies – and to themselves. Detailed estimates of these overall gains, and the mechanisms by which they are to be realized, are made by two separate but complementary approaches – respectively a micro-economic and a macro-economic analysis – and are presented in simplified form in Part II.

The shock and the prospect

For all the complexities, the essential mechanism is simple. The starting point of the whole process of economic gain is the removal of non-tariff barriers.

The release of these constraints will trigger a supply-side shock to the Community economy as a whole. The name of the shock is European market integration. Costs will come down. Prices will follow as business, under the pressure of new rivals on previously protected markets, is forced to develop fresh responses to a novel and permanently changing situation. Ever-present competition will ensure the completion of a self-sustaining virtuous circle. The downward pressure on prices will in turn stimulate demand, giving companies the opportunity to increase output, to exploit resources better and to scale them up for European, and global, competition.

However, the effect of the shock is to be gauged not just in terms of the market, and of the companies and consumers who buy and sell there. Its waves will ripple out into the economy at large. By its very size, the shock will have reverberations on general economic management. Over time, creation of a European home market will unbind the macro-economic constraints which have chronically fettered the prospects of sustained growth in Europe for the best part of twenty years.

Public deficits will be eased, under the dual impact of open public procurement and the economy's regeneration. Inflation, traditionally growth's ugly sister, will be cooled down by the drop in prices provoked by open markets. The jolt so imparted to Europe's competitivity should ensure that growth is achieved without damage to the Community's external trade position.

But, perhaps most important of all, is the medium-term impact of market integration on employment. With its injection of inflation-free growth, coupled with a loosening of the constraints on public exchequers in the Community's member states, the European home market of the 1990s raises the prospect, for the first time since the early 1970s, of very substantial job creation. The added financial elbow-room given to governments should, in addition, enable any unevenness in the rewards distributed by market integration to be compensated.

This medium-term prospect of substantial growth is not just a boon for Europe. The world economy of the late 1980s and early 1990s, overshadowed by American deficits, a fickle dollar and the spectre of a US recession, needs to take confidence where it can. The expectation may be that a dynamic European market, trading with the world on a footing of revamped competitivity, will provide a much-needed shot in the arm for other markets and economies in less buoyant shape.

In return, EC governments will have the right to expect appropriate responses from the Community's economic partners abroad, notably the US and Japan. If the fruits of the European home market are to be shared internationally, there must also be a fair share-out of the burdens of global economic responsibility, with market opening measures extended internationally on a firm basis of clear reciprocity.

The actors and the opportunity

The European home market will not materialize at the wave of a wand. 1992 will not come by whispering words of mysterious Eurospeak into a receding future, or the future will return the compliment by staying conveniently out of reach. For business and government, the two main actors, the road to market integration will be paved with tough adjustments and the need for new strategies.

For business, removing protective barriers creates a permanent opportunity, but signals a definitive end to national soft options. Cost reductions will be good news, but market opening means also the permanent threat, actual or potential, of competition. This is also good news for the company which is gearing up to capitalize on the enlarged market's enhanced opportunities for innovation and economies of scale. But profits which derive from cashing in on monopoly or protected positions will tend to be squeezed. The situation will be one of constant competitive renewal.

Managing change will mean changing management – or rather the focus of its business strategy. There is already widespread evidence that this is happening, as companies – ahead of 1992 and often way ahead of the politicians – are adjusting both their management goals and business structures in readiness for new patterns of competition. But opportunities must continue to be seized – merely to neglect them will create a threat. One thing is certain. Firms from outside the EC, who are already positioning themselves in Community markets in anticipation of the White Paper programme's success, will not miss opportunities overlooked by their indigenous rivals.

Governments, already being watched closely by business, will be expected to give clear signs of their commitment to the 1992 goal. The credibility of the European market as an operational environment for business depends in the first instance on the legislator persuading companies of the seriousness of its intentions. There is only one way of doing this. EC governments must enact the White Paper programme fully and on schedule. In so doing, they will release the costs, outlined in this book, which presently inhibit Europe's market and economic expansion.

This means a further role for companies. Business cannot afford to sit passively by, idly expecting governments to keep to long-term legislative commitments, unaided. There is a need of more active political involvement, in the sense of constructive input to policy, orchestrated at Community level but targetted above all at the seats of national political power.

But governments must do more than achieve the European home market. They must maintain it – and, once again, give companies tangible proof that they are committed to doing so.

No great insight is needed to see that maintaining market integration will in turn pose the Community with some ineluctable choices. The business managers of the European market of the 1990s cannot be indefinitely divorced from the political managers of the Community economy.

Attempting to sustain this unserviceable dichotomy would be to invite disaster. Market integration, for example, particularly in its early stages, is likely to accentuate pressures on exchange rates and thus the need for firm currency management and for a stronger European monetary system. Without an institutional framework to deal effectively with these and other problems inherent in the success of the 1992 programme, the European home market will soon be put in jeopardy. The tensions that will be created will not be susceptible of management in an institutional vacuum. In short, for Europe to meet its market challenge, it must also, sooner rather than later, review the overall structure of its economic organisation.

NOTE

The following extract is rather more restrained.

A. M. El-Agraa (ed), The European Union: Economics and Policies
(6th ed, Harlow: Prentice Hall, 2001), pp.182–83

. . . There are two reservations to consider. The first is advanced by Pelkmans and Robson (1987). It is that the categorisation by the EC of these three types of barrier is somewhat arbitrary. Physical barriers are concerned with frontier controls on the movement of goods and persons. Fiscal barriers consist of all impediments and substantial distortions among member states that emanate from differences in the commodity base as well as in the rates of VAT and the duties on excises. . . . All remaining impediments fall into the category of technical barriers. Therefore, this category comprises not only barriers arising from absence of technical harmonisation and public procurement procedures, but also institutional impediments on the free movement of people, capital and financial services, including transport and data transmission. It also comprises a miscellaneous collection of obstacles to the business environment which take the form of an inadequately harmonised company law, the lack of an EC patent and of an EC trademark, together with issues of corporate taxation and several diverse problems concerned with the national application of EC law. However, even though this categorisation may make analysis more cumbersome, the approach adopted in this book shows that this is not a serious reservation.

The second reservation is more serious. It is that the estimates given in the Cecchini Report should not be taken at face value. First, in spite of the endorsement of the SEA by all the member nations, there does not seem to be a philosophy common to all of them to underpin the internal market. Second, these estimates do not take into consideration the costs to be incurred by firms, regions and governments in achieving them. Third, the internal market aims at the elimination of internal barriers to promote the efficient restructuring of supply, but it remains silent on the question of demand; thus the internal market seems to be directed mainly at the production side. Fourth, putting too much emphasis on economies of scale, when their very existence has to be proved, will encourage concentration rather than competition, and there is no evidence to support the proposition that there is a positive correlation between increased firm size and competitive success. Finally, the estimates are for the EC as a whole; thus it is likely that each member nation will strive to get the maximum gain for itself with detrimental consequences for all, i.e., this is like the classical oligopoly problem where the best solution for profit-maximisation purposes is for oligopolists to behave as joint monopolists, but if each oligopolist firm tries to maximise its own share of the joint profit, the outcome may be losses all round.

NOTES

1. The study referred to is J. Pelkmans and P. Robson, 'The Aspirations of the White Paper', (1987) 25 JCMS 181.

2. It should be apparent from this analysis that these issues have not suddenly dropped from view after the end of 1992. Market integration is a continuing process. Building and maintaining an internal market demands a long-term agenda.

SECTION 4: **MEASURING THE IMPACT OF '1992'**

....

A: **Measurement in 1996**

Roughly a decade after providing the impetus needed to pilot the Community on a course to complete the internal market by the end of 1992, the Commission sponsored a research programme designed to discover what economic benefits had actually accrued. The fruits were published in a set of 38 sector-specific volumes, divided into six sub-sets: impact on manufacturing; impact on services; dismantling of barriers; impact on trade and investment; impact on competition and scale effects; and aggregate and regional impact. These volumes were co-published in 1997 by the Commission and Kogan Page. Naturally, the inquiry is not straightforward, for, sector by sector, it is difficult to demarcate advantages accruing from the '1992' initiative and those that would have occurred in any event or which are attributable to other factors such as global trade liberalization. Moreover, the essence of the internal market programme is that benefits will be felt not only in the short term, but also in the long term, and accordingly measurement cannot yet be decisive. However, the Commission, presenting a Communication to the Parliament and Council on 30 October 1996, summarized the results of its research in the following broadly positive terms.

Summary – The Impact and Effectiveness of the Single Market
(available via http://europa.eu.int/comm/dg15/en/update/impact/smsumen.htm)

1. Jobs and sustainable growth are at the top of the Union's agenda. The Commission's Confidence Pact, 'Action for Employment in Europe', identified the Single Market as the launching pad for attaining higher levels of job creation and sustainable growth. The Commission now has solid evidence of the positive effects of the Single Market, based on a first exhaustive survey of its economic impact and effectiveness conducted over the past two years.

2. In terms of economic impact the news is encouraging. It is still too early for many Single Market measures to have taken full effect but there are clear signs of significant change in the European economy. We now have evidence of the following positive, albeit preliminary effects of the Single Market in triggering the expected reinforcement of integration, competition, economic performance and benefits for consumers:

— growing competition between companies in both manufacturing and services;
— an accelerated pace of industrial restructuring, with the resultant benefits in terms of greater competitiveness;
— a wider range of products and services available to public sector, industrial and domestic consumers at lower prices, particularly in newly liberalised service sectors such as transport, financial services, telecommunications and broadcasting;
— faster and cheaper cross-frontier deliveries resulting from the absence of border controls on goods;

— greater mobility between Member States for both workers and those not economically active (including students and retired people).

3. Calculations of the overall economic effects of these changes suggest that the SMP has resulted in:

— between 300,000 and 900,000 more jobs than would have existed in the absence of the Single Market;
— an extra increase in EU income of 1.1–1.5% over the period 1987–93;
— inflation rates which are 1.0–1.5% lower than they would be in the absence of the SMP;
— economic convergence and cohesion between different EU regions.

4. These benefits have been gained without any reduction in safety standards for consumers or workers. In many areas standards of protection for the citizen have in fact increased. Citizens of the Union also enjoy more personal freedom and have more choice than ever before. The Commission's survey confirms that Community legislation in the Single Market area has, taken as a whole, created the basic conditions for free movement and economic efficiency. The situation in today's Single Market is in sharp contrast to that of the mid–1980s when:

— all goods were stopped and subject to checks at frontiers;
— most products had to comply with different laws in each Member State;
— services such as transport, telecommunications, banking and broadcasting were not subject to competition; and
— citizens who were not employed could be subject to restrictions on residence and risk losing social security rights in another Member State.

5. It is up to economic operators to make the most of the Single Market. The role of public authorities at national and Community level is confined to creating appropriate economic and institutional conditions. In the context of a more favourable economic climate, operators will be better placed to exploit to the full the opportunities that are now available. This report shows that where these opportunities are taken the benefits are significant.

6. The Commission's analysis suggests that these opportunities would have been even greater if Member States had been more diligent in putting in place the Single Market measures already agreed and applying the principles of the Community law on which they are based. Delays in applying and enforcing Single Market rules at national level continue to limit the Single Market's positive contribution to growth, competitiveness and more employment.

7. The Community must build on its successes and iron out the remaining political and practical difficulties which inhibit the Single Market's full potential from being achieved. The Commission is putting forward clear policy recommendations for action at two levels:

— first and foremost, *at the national level*, where the main responsibility for applying Single Market rules lies. The Commission is urging that enforcement of Single Market legislation and Treaty rules be stepped up. In addition, the Commission calls for vigorous action to be taken to reduce excessive regulation at national level which inhibits both competition and competitiveness;
— at the *Community level*, where further efforts must be made to complete the 1985 agenda in a few key areas (such as abolition of border controls on persons, taxation and company law), where further means have to be devoted to the control of implementation and to updating the legislation and where Community policies in related areas such as competition, consumer policy, information and the environment may need to be developed further in order to ensure the most effective use and development of the Single Market.

The introduction of a single currency in 1999 will also make the Single Market more effective, by eliminating the constraints which now result from exchange risks and by generally increasing transparency and competition.

8. In its conclusions to this report, the Commission calls for action to deliver a properly working Single Market. It spells out what is required in terms of a renewed commitment to the Single

Market, not only at the highest political level – the European Council in Dublin – but also from all those who must contribute to making the Single Market a success – national authorities, the European Institutions and, above all, economic operators themselves.

....

B: **Measurement in 2002**

The tenth anniversary of 'deadline 2002' prompted the Commission to return to the quest to measure the gains achieved through the programme. Once again it was confronted by the unavoidable absence of reliable data on what would have occurred had the internal market *not* been pursued in the chosen manner, but it made the following assessment.

The macroeconomic Effects of the Single market Programme after Ten Years
http://europa.eu.int/comm/internal_market/10years/background_en.htm

At the end of 1992, the single market programme (SMP) came into force in Europe. It was aimed at eliminating the remaining barriers to trade among member countries. The expected consequences were increases in competition, industrial restructuring and reallocation of economic activities. In turn, these consequences were intended to induce three categories of gain. Allocative efficiency gain: when producers have market power, prices deviate substantially and persistently from marginal costs. Thus the structure of consumption is distorted and total output is kept below its socially optimal level. Productive efficiency gain: while firms produce at lowest cost under conditions of competition, they begin to operate inefficiently (through overstaffing, higher wages, lack of response to new opportunities, poor management) in situations of poor competition. Dynamic efficiency gain: fostering product and process innovations and, hence, speeding up the move to the modern technology frontier, which is a major source of growth. Recent empirical studies have tried to assess the allocative and productive efficiency gains from trade liberalization focusing on industries. Although similar gains are expected in services, no study provides a quantitative assessment.

A recent study by Salgado (2002) investigates the impact of trade, domestic product market and domestic labor market reforms on productivity performance. The analysis is based on panel data for 20 OECD countries over the period 1965–1998. The results suggest that trade and domestic product market reforms explain the trend in productivity growth. Their impact on total factor productivity growth is weak in the short run but substantial in the long run (i.e. between 0.2 and 0.3 percentage points a year). This is, however, an average estimate over OECD countries. Given the difference in the coverage and speed of reforms across these countries, the estimate may not be a reliable measure of the impact of the SMP. Notaro (2002) focused on the impact of the SMP on industrial productivity in a panel of 6 European countries and 30 industries. Using Buigues et al. (1990) methodology, these industries are classified as non-sensitive, moderately sensitive and highly sensitive to the SMP. The econometric evidence provided strong support to the positive impact of the SMP on industrial productivity in the last category of industries. In 1992 and 1993 the productivity in the high and medium sensitive sector increased by around 2%.

Allen et al. (1998) studied the impact of the SMP distinguishing among its effect on patterns of production and trade and its effects on price-cost margins and industrial restructuring. They also classified the industries according to their sensitivity to the SMP. The results showed that the SMP was mainly trade creating: the domestic production share of demand has fallen by 5.4 percentage point on average while the shares of both intra-European trade and extra-European trade have increased by 2.95 and 2.45 percentage point respectively. With respect to price, the result suggested that price competition has increased: on the average, price-cost margins have fallen by

3.6 percentage points in the high and medium sensitive industries. Bottasso and Sembenelli (2001) examined the impact of the SMP on market power of a large sample of Italian firms using a similar industry split. They found that in the most sensitive industries, firms' market power decreased by around 10 percentage points during the implementation of the SMP.

The results of these studies point to a consistent positive (negative) impact of the SMP on productivity (mark-up) in the high and medium sensitive industries. However, no clear pattern emerged in the other industries. The high and medium sensitive industries represent around 25% of the EU GDP. To get an estimate of the impact of the SMP on mark-up and productivity at the EU economy as a whole, we take the estimates by Notaro (2002) and Allen et al. (1998) and weight them by the share of the high and medium sensitive industries in the EU GDP. This implies an average decrease of mark-up by around 0.9 percentage points and an increase of productivity by around 0.5%. The evidence on services is not clear yet and there exists no study which provides a quantitative assessment of the Internal Market effect on services. There are, however some results from network industries (telecom, electricity and transportation) which have been used for our macro assessment. Nevertheless, our results should be considered as a 'lower bound' to the overall impact of the SMP on the EU economy.

Ranges of these estimates are also computed using the standard deviation provided in the respective papers. These ranges give a lower bound of 0.45 and an upper bound of 1.35 percentage points for mark-up decrease. The bounds for productivity increase are respectively 0.25% and 0.75%.

The Commission's QUEST II model is used to assess the macroeconomic effect of these two shocks. The following question is asked in this exercise: What would have been the level of GDP and employment in 2002, 2012 and 2022 if the single market programme would not have been implemented? Various simulations are performed depending on whether average, upper or lower bounds of the SMP impact on productivity and mark-up are considered. Moreover, three scenarios are envisaged concerning the time it takes for the full realization of the TFP increase and the mark-up reduction: 3, 5 and 7 years. The results emanating from the manufacturing sector and the network industries separately have been calculated separately. A table at the end of the note gives the total results.

Macroeconomic Effects of Liberalizing Manufacturing

The simulation results suggest that real GDP would have been 1.4% lower (with a lower and upper of .76 and 2.05) in 2002 without the internal market programme. Small additional gains are to be expected in this and the next decade, with an additional GDP effect of .4% until 2012 and .5 in 2022. Similarly the level of employment would have been .86% lower (with a lower bound of .43 and an upper bound of 1.3%) compared to its actual current level in 2002 without the single market programme. However, according to the simulation results no further employment gains should be expected. Both the increase in efficiency of production and increased competition contribute about equally to the GDP gain, while about 80% of the increase in employment is due to the removal of restrictions impeding competition.

Macroeconomic Effects of Liberalizing Network Industries

Not much empirical work has so far been undertaken in assessing the effects of liberalization in network industries. Some preliminary evidence for the electricity sector (Roeger and Warzynski, 2002) suggest a decline in the price cost margin from 25% to 19%. Given that the price decline in the telecom sector (relative to the consumer price deflator) has been more significant, namely about 23% relative to 9% in the electricity sector since 1996, profit margins have most likely been reduced more strongly in that sector. This would also be consistent with the more advanced state of liberalization in telecommunication. Taking into account the relative GDP weights and making the cautious assumption that mark-ups in the telecom sector have only decreased by 50% more compared to electricity would yield an aggregate mark-up decline of about .5%.

In the forthcoming European Economy Review 2002, the GDP and employment effects from the more recent liberalization of network industries, in particular electricity and telecom markets, are estimated to be .4% and .6% respectively after 4 years already and GDP will increase by .6% after 10 years. These effects are somewhat stronger than the internal market effects because in these simulations it is assumed that deregulation also has an effect on rent sharing between workers and firms. Thus the decline in price cost mark-ups is associated with a decline in the mark-up of wages over the reservation wage.

The following table provides absolute GDP and employment figures from the SMP and the liberalization of network industries.

Table 1 – Simulation Results of the Total Effect

Scenario	Additional GDP (Bio of Euros) in			Additional Employment (1000 of persons) in		
	2002	2012	2022	2002	2012	2022
Average	164.5	203.1	214.0	2450.6	2463.8	2463.8
Lower Bound	105.6	127.5	158.4	1733.9	1741.5	1741.5
Upper Bound	223.2	264.2	273.3	3189.2	3202.3	3202.3

References

Allen, C., Gasiorek, M. and Smith, A. (1998), 'European Single Market: How the programme has fostered competition', Economic Policy, 441–486.

Buigues, P., Ilzkovitz, F. and Lebrun, J.F. (1990), 'The impact of the internal market by industrial sector: The challenge for the Member States', European Economy, special edition.

Bottasso, A. and Sembenelli, A. (2001), 'Market power, productivity and the EU Single Market Programme: Evidence from a panel of Italian firms', European Economic Review, vol. 45, 167–186.

Notaro, G. (2002), 'European Integration and Productivity: Exploring the Gains of the Single Market', London Economics, Working Paper.

Roeger, W and F. Warzynski (2002), 'A Joint Estimation of Price-Cost Margins and the Importance of Fixed Costs in the European Electricity sector using Firm Level data', work in progress.

Salgado, R. (2002), 'Impact of structural reforms on productivity growth in industrial countries', IMF Working Paper, January.

NOTE
Regular reports are made available at http://europa.eu.int/comm/internal_market/en/index.htm.

....

C: **The business response**

The assumption must be that the opportunities presented by the completion of the internal market will be seized by business. As the Commission insists in the above extract, it is essentially private commercial interests, not governments, that will make 1992 a visible reality. Business, then, must plan ahead. More: it must *keep* planning!

R. Dudley, 1992: Strategies for the Single Market (1990), pp.74–75
[reproduced by permission of Kogan Page]

The effects of competition on industry structures
The intensification of business activity triggered by the creation of the Single Market will have a number of effects on the shaping of industry structures across the community. The main elements will be:

— the exit of a number of firms due to competitive intensity;
— the relocation of production by companies needing to produce more competitive products in recognised centres of excellence or needing to find lower-cost production centres;

— the acquisition by predatory companies of firms located within Community markets to provide or strengthen their marketing and manufacturing dispositions in target markets or to acquire essential technology;

— acquisition of smaller companies which may in themselves be at a competitive disadvantage but are attractive enough for them to successfully offer themselves to larger firms;

— acquisitions by external Community firms as a means of creating an indigenous presence;

— acquisition and mergers for vertical integration reasons to control upstream and downstream elements of their industry's value system; and

— mergers and joint ventures to reinforce the strength and position of companies in the face of the need to scale up activities, collaborate on distribution, meet R & D needs etc.

It is these potential changes to industry structures which will affect the competitive conditions under which both suppliers and customers will have to operate. It is vital, therefore, that managers look more closely at the risks of change and the impact they will bring to their individual firms.

NOTE
The effect of the completion of the single market varies according to the sector of the economy under review, but no sector escapes unaffected. A firm planning its internal market strategy must consider a range of factors touching, for example, its production, marketing and distribution strategies, opportunities for structural growth through takeovers and research and development policy.

In addition to decisions about responding to the nature of the market, business must become accustomed to dealing with the Community regulatory authorities.

R. Dudley, 1992: Strategies for the Single Market
(London: Kogan Page, 1990), pp.60–61

(Footnote omitted.)

With such an amount of change being brought about by the SEA [Single European Act] a new feature of company strategy development will be the need to become adept at the political level. The European Community recognises the need for companies to become involved in the development of a number of legal areas. It encourages their participation in the processes of eliminating discriminatory anti-competitive activity. It provides forums for the views of industry to be heard. It provides the machinery for firms to involve themselves with product standards and so on . . .

Companies need, therefore, to put a political strategy somewhere towards the top of their agenda. They will need to understand the political motivations of the different member states within the Community and the workings of the Community's executive and legislative. Competition is no longer a mere market phenomenon, it is exercised at the political level. Companies, therefore, not having their views and interests represented will have to accept what is handed out to them whether or not it is in their interests.

■ QUESTIONS

1. This extract insists on the need for a 'political strategy'. To what extent is the increasing *power* of the Community authorities matched by increased *responsibility* (e.g., to electors)? How, if at all, would you like to see the institutional framework of the Community adjusted in order to improve democratic accountability for the decisions which are presently being taken?

2. The Community is firmly on the national political agenda in a way which would have seemed scarcely credible 25 years ago. As an advertising campaign slogan, '1992' proved a remarkable success.

'As a mobilising theme, as an impulse for innovation and restructuring, as a justification and sometimes as an alibi for unpopular decisions, the myth of 1992 has had a deep influence which we have every reason to be satisfied with and must congratulate those who conceived it.' (Mertens de Wilmars [1989/1] LIEI 1 (Editorial))

Who do you think make up the 'we' who have every reason to be satisfied?

SECTION 5: **MANAGING THE INTERNAL MARKET**

The end of 1992 plainly had major significance for the Commission, but it signified a shift in its internal market strategy rather than a termination of it. It was true that most of the major measures had been prepared by the Commission and agreed by the Member States by the end of 1992 (although some matters remained outstanding, not least those concerning persons), but there then arose questions of monitoring compliance. The summary at p.303 above highlights the central role of proper application of the rules of the internal market in ensuring full realization of its economic advantages. The Commission produces an annual report on the monitoring of the application of Community law, which provides information on *inter alia* the progress of implementation of Directives. These reports have typically told of an accelerating pace of implementation by the Member States, but there remain many gaps between Community law on paper and Community law in practice. Enlargement into Central and Eastern Europe offers a new challenge.

The reports contain 'league tables' which reveal in percentage terms the success of each Member State in complying with its obligation to notify its transposition measures to the Commission. In order to sharpen this statistical spur to the Member States to respond to the obligations agreed in Directives, the Commission established a 'Single Market Scoreboard' in 1997. This is available, and is regularly updated, on the website of the Directorate-General which deals with internal market matters. Enter via http://europa.eu.int (it is currently at http://europa.eu.int/comm/internal_market/en/index.htm); the site also carries a great deal of up-to-date information on broader policy direction. The first published scoreboard revealed that on 1 November 1997, over 25% of internal market Directives were not implemented in all Member States. Particular problem areas were the transport and public procurement sectors, where over 50% of Directives were unimplemented in one or more States. The data available in the Eleventh Scoreboard, published in November 2002, set out below, suggests steady improvement when judged against the early years of the internal market project, but it draws attention to a more recent interruption to the record of increasingly faithful compliance. Pockets of non-compliance remain stubbornly hard to shift.

Internal Market Scoreboard No 11, 11 November 2002

MAIN FINDINGS: Implementing the Internal Market's Legal Framework

- The transposition deficit has dropped considerably from 21.4% in 1992 to 2.1% today. However, the latest score is up from 1.8% only 6 months ago.

- Only 5 Member States (Sweden, Finland, Denmark, Netherlands, UK) now meet the European Council's target for spring 2003 of having a transposition deficit of 1.5% or less. The transposition deficit of 3 Member States (France, Greece, Portugal) is more than double the European Council's target.
- Finland is the only Member State which has already met the European Council's other target of transposing all directives whose transposition deadline is overdue by 2 years or more. 4 Member States (France, Germany, Luxembourg, Greece) will need to transpose 10 or more 'old' directives in the next 6 months to meet it.
- The total number of Internal Market infringement proceedings remains stubbornly high at more than 1500 open cases. France and Italy continue to have the highest number, together accounting for nearly 30% of all cases.
- Only Denmark has managed to reduce the number of infringement proceedings relating to misapplication of legislation by 10% or more, as called for in the Commission's 2002 Internal Market Strategy Review. Most others have seen their numbers actually go up. More than half of all cases take more than 2 years to be resolved – reinforcing the argument that cases should, where possible, be resolved by other means.
- Compared to 10 years ago standardisation today mainly takes place on the European level and is to a very large extent (over 80%) initiated by industry. Problems with long development times remain in several areas of standardisation.

Only 5 Member States (Sweden, Finland, Denmark, the Netherlands and the UK) and 2 EFTA countries have met the European Council's standard of achieving – or maintaining – their deficits at 1.5% or below (see figure 2). This is worse than 6 months ago when Belgium and Spain were also part of this leading group. As only 7 Member States had achieved the European Council's standard by March 2002, the Barcelona European Council decided to extend the deadline until next spring.

Figure 2: Two thirds of Member States fail to meet the 1.5% target

no. of directives	56	48	46	42	40	38	38	34	30	23	21	19	10	9	6
percentage	3.8	3.3	3.1	2.9	2.7	2.6	2.6	2.3	2.0	1.6	1.4	0.7	0.6	0.4	1.3
State	F	EL	P	A	D	I	IRL	L	B	E	UK	NL	DK	FIN	S

NOTE
These statistics relate only to legislative measures concerned with the internal market. More general information on the pattern of transposition is provided in the Annual Report on Monitoring the Application of Community Law, currently available via http://europa.eu.int/comm/secretariat_general/sgb/droit_com/index_en.htm. The 19th such Annual Report was published in 2001 (COM (2002) 324).

In its Internal Market Scoreboard No 11, above, the Commission confesses that 'The Internal Market will never be "completed". The effort to maximise its performance is a process, not an event'. The dynamic nature of the process of market-building and market-management, which makes enduring demands of the Commission's capacities, is captured in the next extract, taken from a major survey of the evolving political, institutional, and legal implications of a 'post-1992' Community.

K. Armstrong and S. Bulmer, The Governance of the Single European Market
(Manchester: Manchester University Press, 1998), pp.307–308

In procedural terms there are serious concerns about the 'holy trinity' of transposition, enforcement and redress. Although the Commission report states that the transposition rate for the White Paper measures was on average 90% for the EU-15, it notes that 'fifty-six per cent . . . have been transposed in *every* Member State' ([COM (96) 520]). That yields a rather different picture and one which is arguably more pertinent to those firms conducting business across the SEM. The comparability of enabling legislation also remains a concern. Enforcement is more complex still because the relevant agencies may be national, regional or local, thus making it extremely difficult to monitor the impact of the SEM 'on the ground' to ensure equivalence across the EU. The Commission's resources simply do not permit sufficient oversight of this dimension . . . Finally, the ability of private parties to secure redress through the courts is complex and variable because of differences in national legal systems.

A final issue worthy of mention here concerns over-zealous regulation: where national transposition introduces costs over and above those necessitated by the relevant EC Directive. This phenomenon, known in the UK as 'gold-plating', lies behind the recent emphasis in SEM policy on reducing the regulatory burden . . .

Despite the legislation to open up public procurement in the utilities . . ., the results in this area of activity have been much more limited. Although a major area of economic activity – 11.5 per cent of EU GDP in 1994 – the achievements have been limited, with only 10 per cent import penetration of import markets. A major explanation for this situation is 'the substantial delay in incorporating the 11 procurement Directives into national legislation and enforcing them effectively' ([COM (96) 520]). The 1996 Florence European Council underlined the importance of accelerating national transposition in this area. Finally, it is worth mentioning that the general impact of the single market upon small and medium-sized enterprises has been rather limited.

The Commission is aware that it requires a more sophisticated strategy than mere publication of figures and establishment of timetables. In order to foster a 'compliance culture' among the Member States, it has placed an increasing post-1992 emphasis on administrative cooperation as a basis for managing the internal market. The Commission, energized by Mario Monti, the Commissioner who held responsibility for the internal market until 1999, prepared an *Action Plan for the Single Market*, which was published in June 1997. It was submitted to the European Council in Amsterdam in that month, where it was firmly endorsed as a basis for renewed effort to eliminate remaining obstacles to realization of the full benefits of the single market programme. The *Action Plan* picked out four priority areas ripe for action designed to improve the functioning of the internal market.

Action Plan for the Single Market, Communication of the Commission to the European Council, CSE(97)1, final, 4 June 1997

Four Strategic Targets

The Action Plan follows the Commission's report on the Impact and Effectiveness of the Single Market. It sets priorities to give a clear and strategic vision of what is now needed. Four *Strategic Targets* have been set. They are of equal importance and must be pursued in parallel:

1. **Making the rules more effective:** The Single Market is based on confidence. Proper enforcement of common rules is the only way to achieve this goal. Simplification of rules at Community and national level is also essential to reduce the burden on business and create more jobs.

2. **Dealing with key market distortions:** There is general agreement that tax barriers and anti-competitive behaviour constitute distortions that need to be tackled.

3. **Removing sectoral obstacles to market integration:** The Single Market will only deliver its full potential if barriers that remain – and, of course, any new ones that emerge – are removed. This may require legislative action to fill gaps in the Single Market framework, but it also calls for a significant change in national administrations' attitudes towards the Single Market.

4. **Delivering a Single Market for the benefit of all citizens:** The Single Market generates employment, increases personal freedom and benefits consumers, while ensuring high levels of both health and safety and environmental protection. But further steps are needed, including steps to enhance the social dimension of the Single Market. And to enjoy their Single Market rights to the full, citizens must be aware of them and be able to obtain speedy redress.

Within the first Strategic Target, 'Making the Rules More Effective', the Commission offers the following observations on the need to establish a framework for enforcement and problem-solving:

The primary responsibility for enforcing Single Market rules rests with the Member States. The Single Market will not operate effectively unless they ensure that the rules are fully respected by all concerned. Those who breach the rules should be subject to penalties under national law that are effective and proportionate and that act as a deterrent. Problems also need to be sorted out quickly in today's Single Market to avoid undermining the confidence of business and consumers. The informal arrangements for cooperation on enforcement and problem solving between Member States, and between them and the Commission, have proved only partly successful and now need to be upgraded. The Commission will therefore press each Member State to designate a coordination centre within its administration responsible for ensuring that problems raised by other Member States or the Commission are solved by the national or regional authorities directly concerned within strict deadlines. Easily identifiable contact points must also be designated in national administrations to which citizens and businesses can address any Single Market problems. These coordination centres and contact points will be key components in a simple but effective framework for enforcement cooperation and problem solving. It will provide for more transparency about enforcement structures and peer review or mutual audit of national enforcement. Telematic links between enforcement authorities will be further developed under the second IDA programme. If necessary, the Commission will submit serious cases of non-application to the Internal Market Council to allow strong commitment and involvement in problem solving to be demonstrated at political level. The Commission will accelerate the investigation of complaints from business and individuals and the treatment of infringement proceedings. For their part, Member States must respect strictly the procedures laid down for infringement proceedings and ensure, expeditiously, operational results. In cases of serious breach of Community law which gravely affect the functioning of the Single Market, the Commission should be able to take urgent action against Member States which fail in these obligations, using sanctions where necessary. Strengthening of the Commission's enforcement powers would contribute to this end and to the reduction of delays in problem solving.

NOTE

Lists of the 'contact points' referred to in the final paragraph of this extract as methods for facilitating problem-solving may now be accessed via the website of the Directorate-General for the internal market (enter via http://europa.eu.int). Contact Points are available for both citizens and business. 'SOLVIT' – Problem Solving in the Internal Market – is the Commission's latest punchy idea for raising the profile of effective market management: http://europa.eu.int/comm/internal_market/solvit/index_en.htm.

In November 1999 the Commission published its *Strategy for Europe's Internal Market*, designed to cover the next five years. The scope of the programme is mapped in the next extract:

European Commission, Strategy for Europe's Internal Market (1999), pp.2–3

THE STRATEGY

This strategy for the Internal Market provides a coherent framework for policy development for the years 2000–2004. It sets out a longer-term strategic vision which should direct the identification of more immediate priorities for action. The overarching aim is constantly to improve the performance of the Internal Market in the years ahead for the benefit of citizens and business alike. The Commission recognises that the credibility of the Internal Market will depend on its delivering and being seen to deliver these benefits. The strategy has been conceived to reflect the characteristics of a more mature Internal Market:

— the need to enhance the competitiveness of the European economy as well as to improve the quality of life of European citizens. Where the interests of business and the consumer diverge, they must be equitably reconciled. Community policies on the environment, economic and social cohesion, health and safety and consumer rights need not only to be co-ordinated with Internal Market policies but integrated into them, as required by the Treaty.

— the need to involve all stakeholders in the continuing development of the Internal Market, be they citizens or business and whatever their location and circumstances. The continuing development of the Internal Market should be at the heart of bringing the EU closer to its citizens through its impact on their daily lives, as employees, employers, consumers, pensioners, students, borrowers, savers, investors and taxpayers.

— the need to remove all unjustified barriers to the free movement of goods, services, persons and capital. The new legal framework, created by integrating national markets must function optimally, in order to maximise the benefits to consumers, citizens and business. A proper balance will be sought between legislative and non-legislative activity and between harmonisation and mutual recognition. Wherever appropriate, the Commission will support self-regulation and ensure that it achieves results in an open and transparent way.

— the need to promote comprehensive structural reform and modernisation through the microeconomic strand of the process of multilateral economic surveillance, as established by the Cardiff European Council.

— the need to monitor and review the effects of existing Internal Market measures by using and developing instruments such as the Scoreboard and the Cardiff report.[4] The Dialogue with Citizens and Business should make full use of the opportunities created by information technology to enhance inclusive and interactive policy-shaping.

— the need to provide an adequate framework to unleash the great potential for the development of the Internal Market for information and communication technologies, including e-commerce.

— the need to prepare for the next enlargement of the Union. The accession of ten or more countries represents a major challenge to both current and future Member States. The operation of the existing rules needs to be improved and the candidate countries associated as soon as possible in their practical application.

— the need to look beyond the borders of the Union. The internet and e-commerce offer even the smallest of companies the opportunity to trade globally. The Union's experience in creating its Internal Market provides extensive experience on which discussions with its main trading partners can be based.

NOTE

In December 2002 the Commission released a Communication aimed at better 'monitoring' of the application of the law.

Commission Communication, Better Monitoring of the Application of Community Law, COM (2002) 725, 11 December 2002

To ensure that Community policies are effectively implemented and have the desired effect, thereby gaining the public's confidence, the institutions must now try not just to improve the quality of legislation but also to ensure further downstream that its application is efficiently

---

4 The Single Market Scoreboard has proved to be a valuable monitor of legal and administrative progress. The Cardiff report provides an annual assessment of the functioning of product and capital markets.

monitored. In this regard, the discussion on the *White Paper on European Governance*, focuses on the quality of Community legislation and the improvement of monitoring. The two issues are clearly linked.

The White Paper on European Governance is explored in Chapter 20. In it the Commission comments that 'Late transposition, bad transposition and weak enforcement all contribute to the public impression of a Union which is not delivering' (COM (01) 428 p.25). In its December 2002 Communication, the Commission proceeds to develop the notion of administrative co-operation as a basis for generating the required public confidence in the viability of the internal market.

2.1. Improving cooperation between the Commission and the Member States in the field of prevention

Preventive action to enforce Community law begins with selecting the best instrument. But once a selection has been made, it continues with cooperation on the implementation of the legislation. A variety of practical cooperation instruments have already been tried out with a view to preventing infringements. These include:

(1) Interpretative communications on a specific matter of Community law (both the Treaty and secondary legislation).[6]

(2) The obligation to notify the Commission of draft technical regulations arising from Directives 98/34/EC (goods) and 98/48/EC (information society services)[7] in the non-harmonised sector of the internal market.

(3) The regular publication of statistics by the Commission in the internal market score-board; the annual report on monitoring the application of Community law which aims to promote peer pressure between the Member States by creating a form of mutual monitoring of efforts to apply European legislation. Commission reports on the application of directives provided for by certain of them play a similar role.[8]

(4) Anticipation of major events, linked, for example, to infrastructure projects: experience shows that when investments have to be made on a national scale the national authorities involved are occasionally inclined to take insufficient account of Community regulations.[9] This approach has been followed in the field of public procurement, in the case of both the Treaty and secondary legislation, and could usefully be extended to the prevention of infringements in the area of the environment[10] and, if appropriate to other sectors.

---

6 For example, interpretative communications on the major freedoms in the internal market and public procurement or on the removal of tax barriers to the cross-border provision of occupational pensions (OJ C165, 8.6.2001, p.4).

7 The application of these directives makes it possible, through prior notification of draft national technical rules, to identify possible barriers to trade before they enter into force and thus to avoid the need to initiate many infringement procedures. This procedure also enables a particular emphasis to be placed on the principle of mutual recognition (by the introduction of mutual recognition clauses). The Court of Justice has also ruled that failure to notify a technical regulation can be invoked in a dispute between individuals; it is then for the national judge to refuse to apply this provision and to establish the consequences for the contract brought before him in the light of national law.

8 Example: report on the application of Council Directive 98/49/EC of 29.6.1998 on safeguarding the supplementary pension rights of employed and self-employed persons moving within the Community.

9 In its *Green Paper on public procurement*, the Commission was thus able to state that the anticipation of certain events was an effective preventive element, limiting considerably the risk of incorrect application (e.g., dialogue with the Greek authorities about the major works for the 2004 Olympic Games and with the Italian authorities for the Winter Olympics).

10 In particular, to fulfilment of obligations deriving from the environmental impact Directive 85/337/EC on the assessment of the effects of certain public and private projects.

(5) Training, information and transparency campaigns intended for national administrations and judges, along the lines of the Grotius II civil and criminal programmes,[11] or, in connection with enlargement, twinning arrangements between national administrations.[12]

(6) For the purposes of the exchange of information and good practice, regarding both the Treaty and secondary legislation, the use of expert committees and networks to assist the Commission, or the setting up of *ad hoc* groups of experts in particular fields.[13]

NOTE

The second of these points, the obligation to notify draft technical regulations, has already been encountered in its constitutional context. The Court's rulings in Case C-194/94 *CIA Security International SA* v *Signalson SA and Securitel SPRL* [1996] ECR I-2201 *et al.* were examined in Chapter 5, pp.152–59, and they concerned this 'early warning' procedure. In *CIA Security* the Court was vigorous in interpreting the consequences before national courts of breach of the Directive in the light of the demands of effective market-management. Here one can observe a community of interest between the Court and the Commission in strengthening the incentives for States to adhere to the system of notification. The Commission was pleased. In 1986, in Communication 86/C 245/05 [1986] OJ C245/4 it had argued for the outcome reached in *CIA Security*; and indeed the Court cited this Communication in para 36 of *CIA Security*. The Commission in turn routinely cites this judgment with pride when it publishes notified technical rules in the Official Journal – see for example [2001] OJ C152/4

■ QUESTION

Is concern for effective market management a sufficient justification for the Court's willingness to tweak the principle of direct effect to exert an 'incidental' effect prejudicial to private parties in cases where the State has failed to comply with this Directive? How does *Unilever* (Case C-443/98, p.156) help?

FURTHER READING ON 'MARKET MANAGEMENT'

Armstrong, K., 'Governance and the Single European Market' in P. Craig and G. De Búrca, *The Evolution of EU Law* (Oxford: OUP, 1999).

Mortelmans, K., 'The Common Market, the Internal Market and the Single Market, What's in a Market?' (1998) 35 CML Rev 101.

Weatherill, S., 'New Strategies for Managing the EC's Internal Market', in M. Freeman (ed), *Current Legal Problems* (Oxford: OUP, vol. 53, 2000).

11 Council Regulation (EC) No 743/2002 of 25 April 2002 establishing a general Community framework of activities to facilitate the implementation of judicial cooperation in civil matters and Council Decision of 28 June 2001 establishing a second phase of the programme of incentives and exchanges, training and cooperation for legal practitioners (Grotius II Criminal).

12 *European Governance – A white paper*, COM (2001) 428, p.49. The possibility of extending such twinning arrangements to all Member States' administrations had already been mentioned in the Governance White Paper.

13 The Commission has set up such groups of government experts in the field of the directives on the posting of workers (96/71/EC) and the 'anti-discrimination' directives (2000/43/EC and 2000/78/EC). These groups met before the transposal date and provided a forum for discussion and the exchange of best practice. In the same way, Regulation (EC) 1408/71 set up the Advisory Committee on Social Security for Migrant Workers, made up of government experts, which is playing a very active role before the Commission presents its proposals for updating this Regulation. Another example is the network of contact points on professional qualifications.

NOTE

For commerce too, as well as for the institutions of the Community, it should be apparent from much of the material in this Chapter that the significance of the 'legal deadline' of 31 December 1992 in Article 14 EC should not be accorded undue weight. Important though the end of 1992 was, the development of the internal market is commercially an evolving process. The Cecchini Report (p.299 above) is based on the perception that the benefits of integration persist over time – they are not obtained once and for all. Equally, the debate about how extensive the benefits of the internal market will really prove to be, presented through the foregoing extracts, continues as integration evolves. For commerce, the process involves questions about how best to restructure operations which will persist for many years yet.

Integration also poses questions about the patterns of supporting legal regulation. This issue was visible in 1988 as the internal market programme began to take shape.

R. Bieber, R. Dehousse, J. Pinder, J. Weiler, 1992: One European Market?
(Baden-Baden: Nomos Verlagsgesellschaft, 1988), pp.30–31

Despite the beguiling simplicity of the ideas of completing the single market and abolishing the frontier controls, it is not hard to see that the project outlined by the White Paper is a complex one: a vast exercise in harmonising laws, regulations and practices, presenting a tough challenge to the Community's political and institutional capacity. That is hardly contestable. More open to judgment, but nevertheless plausible, are the propositions that the process of completion carries with it pressures for related policies in fields such as the environment, competition, industry, cohesion, monetary integration and macro economic management. These in turn would not only require the creation of new common policy instruments, but also imply the strengthening of Community institutions, in matters such as majority voting in the Council, codecision with the Parliament, and enhancing the Community's juridical capacity and the Commission's role. All this would not only develop the Community internally, but would also strengthen its international position and bargaining power, not only in trade policy but also in the fields of money and of technological development.

In so far as this is accepted, the White Paper should be viewed not in the minimalist perspective of a Community which emphasises free trade at the expense of other values, but as a bold initiative to impel the Community forward where agreement among all the member governments was possible, which, if it succeeds, will imply also a major effort of policy integration in related fields and development of the Community institutions.

This perception has much in common with the fruits of a more recent investigation into the way in which the process of market-building and market-management has made deep demands of the institutional capacity of the Community.

M. Egan, Constructing a European Market
(Oxford: OUP, 2001), p.260

(Footnotes omitted.)

The governance of the market has inspired considerable debate. Part of that discussion has focused on the relationship between states and markets, and their effectiveness as alternative mechanisms for coordinating economic activity, setting parameters, and simplifying and stabilizing conditions of choice. While the pendulum appears to have shifted towards markets, many neoliberal reforms, often touted as a means of 'rolling back the state', contain elements that actually strengthen the state in some ways. In fact, the divorce of markets from states is untenable, and markets are absolutely dependent on public authority. The market-oriented reforms enacted by the European Union are particularly striking in this regard since the effort to create 'freer markets' has resulted in 'more rules' and strengthened the authority of the European Union in exercising market governance.

The analysis of market integration in this book has sought to explain this puzzle by demonstrating that the regulatory agenda of the EU has come to dominate the regulatory agenda of the member states, as the supply of and demand for European regulations has produced thousands of regulations in a host of policy areas. As the EU increasingly recognised the need to tackle the growing number of national regulations and standards, since these could threaten market integration, the central task facing the EU seemed to be finding the most efficient way to achieve its public policy goals and objectives. In trying to find an effective mechanism to bridge the gap between different regulatory traditions, European governments grapple with a double challenge They have to reduce obstacles to trade to promote competition and find more efficient ways to regulate, while also protecting important welfare policy goals. In the end, however, there is more at stake in the discussion of regulation than the question of an efficient choice of instruments.

'Free markets' ... 'more rules'. This is a crisp catchphrase for the conundrum of European integration.

SECTION 6: **ECONOMIC AND MONETARY UNION**

The questions raised in the penultimate extract of the preceding subsection remain high on the agenda. They may be assessed in the light of the impact of the Maastricht Treaty on European Union. The most specific next step of policy integration envisaged by that Treaty was the process of Economic and Monetary Union. Cecchini (p.299 above) identified the single currency as a potential major element in the integrative process.

Article 4 EC provides an outline for the plan.

ARTICLE 4 EC

Article 4

1. For the purposes set out in Article 2, the activities of the Member States and the Community shall include, as provided in this Treaty and in accordance with the timetable set out therein, the adoption of an economic policy which is based on the close coordination of Member States' economic policies, on the internal market and on the definition of common objectives, and conducted in accordance with the principle of an open market economy with free competition.

2. Concurrently with the foregoing, and as provided in this Treaty and in accordance with the timetable and the procedures set out therein, these activities shall include the irrevocable fixing of exchange rates leading to the introduction of a single currency, the ecu, and the definition and conduct of a single monetary policy and exchange-rate policy the primary objective of both of which shall be to maintain price stability and, without prejudice to this objective, to support the general economic policies in the Community, in accordance with the principle of an open market economy with free competition.

3. These activities of the Member States and the Community shall entail compliance with the following guiding principles: stable prices, sound public finances and monetary conditions and a sustainable balance of payments.

NOTE
Title VII of the EC Treaty, 'Economic and Monetary Policy', which occupies Articles 112–124 EC, provides elaboration of the plan. The economic convergence criteria on which the entry into being of the single currency is predicated are found in Article 121:

— the achievement of a high degree of price stability; this will be apparent from a rate of inflation which is close to that of, at most, the three best performing Member States in terms of price stability;

— the sustainability of the government financial position; this will be apparent from having achieved a government budgetary position without a deficit that is excessive as determined in accordance with Article 104(6);

— the observance of the normal fluctuation margins provided for by the exchange-rate mechanism of the European Monetary System, for at least two years, without devaluing against the currency of any other Member State;

— the durability of convergence achieved by the Member State and of its participation in the exchange-rate mechanism of the European Monetary System being reflected in the long-term interest-rate levels.

After conformity with these criteria was (in some instances, controversially) confirmed in accordance with Article 121 EC (see Decision 98/317, [1998] OJ L139/30), the third stage of economic and monetary union began on 1 January 1999, with 11 participants: Belgium, Germany, Spain, France, Ireland, Italy, Luxembourg, the Netherlands, Austria, Portugal, and Finland. The exchange rates between these States' currencies were fixed. In effect, the national currencies became simply representations of the euro. Greece joined in 2001. The UK has an opt-out from the third stage, secured at the time of the Maastricht negotiations, and its currency remains outside 'euroland' and therefore continues to fluctuate against the euro. Coins and banknotes of the euro – which according to Regulation 1103/97 is the term that should be used in preference to the Treaty term 'ecu' – have been physically available from 1 January 2002, and, after a brief period of overlap, national currencies of the 12 participants were withdrawn. The next extract offers a broader perspective on the prospects for Economic and Monetary Union.

H. Siebert and M. Koop, Institutional Competition versus Centralization:
Quo Vadis Europe?
(1993) 9 Oxford Review of Economic Policy 15, 25–27

VII. HARMONIZING MONEY

The Maastricht Treaty has put macroeconomics back on the EC's agenda and it has done so by applying the *ex-ante* harmonisation approach. The most exposed single issue is the creation of the European Monetary Union (EMU), the design of a single currency for twelve different nations with twelve heterogeneous sets of preferences regarding price level stability, twelve distinct histories of monetary policies, twelve track records on inflation, and twelve systems of administering monetary policy.

The risk of creating a weak European currency partly derives from the possibility of merging countries with different attitudes towards monetary stability and different levels of economic development. Therefore, participation in EMU was made dependent on the fulfilment of various convergence criteria: total government debt must be less than 60 per cent of GDP and annual budget deficits must be smaller than 3 per cent of GDP. The inflation rate may only be 1.5 percentage points above the average inflation rate of the three lowest inflation rates in the EC. Finally, the exchange rate may not have been devalued two years before entering EMU and long-term interest rates must broadly be in line with comparable rates in the low inflation countries.

By setting quantitative criteria in advance, the Maastricht Treaty seeks to mitigate the risk of a weak Euro-currency. However, two objections must be raised. First, the quality of some indicators is uncertain. For obvious reasons, the requirement of a low budget deficit in the year before entering EMU should have been extended for a number of consecutive years and it should include stealth budgets. The criterion on indebtedness conveys limited information. It reflects a long history of running up debts and it does not take into account whether the funds were used for consumption or investment. Therefore, the number 60 seems to be chosen arbitrarily. On the other hand, the interest rate and inflation criteria are useful measures because they comprise an element of competition. If, for example, a low-inflation country reduces its inflation rate it simultaneously forces high-inflation countries to follow suit – a competition for stable money. To enhance this competition, the European Council and the Commission will be constantly assessing the stabilization efforts (and success) of the member countries. In the second half of the decade they will even be allowed to enforce this goal by withholding EC benefits – another safeguard clause for achieving economic stability.

Second, a serious question will be to what extent the criteria will be interpreted in a politically soft way in order to bring countries into EMU that would normally not qualify for membership. For instance, the wish of the EC-founding countries, Belgium and Italy, also to co-found EMU may generate pressures to soften the interpretation of the convergence criteria. In that case monetary stability would be at risk because a European monetary policy that aims for stable money needs accommodation by sound national fiscal policies.

The main problem for the EMU will be to transfer credibility from the national central banks to their European successor. One important aspect is that the national central banks are independent before a European currency would start. A period of independence of at least two years in which national central banks could build up a reputation of pursuing an independent monetary policy would be helpful. The political decision of some countries to make the central bank independent just the second before the starting signal of monetary union, calls into question the independence of the European Central Bank (ECB) and undermines its credibility even before it is founded.

Even if the ECB is legally independent, it may not be in practice. National ECB governors who seek reappointment after serving a relatively short term may choose to please their national governments by voting for a less stringent monetary policy. The most decisive issue, however, is whether a European monetary policy can be insulated from the moral-hazard problem of political pressure. A European monetary policy affects each region of Europe in a uniform way – the same interest rate will be effective from Aberdeen to Heraklion; but the policy-making process remains at the national level. This represents a systematic source of conflict, and it is hard to say to what extent a European monetary policy can withstand this conflict. A European Central Bank needs extremely strong safeguards in such a context and it is open to question whether institutional arrangements with respect to fiscal policy can provide sufficiently strong ones.

Leaving aside such intricate issues as the ECB's independence, the level of transfers needed in a currency union without exchange rates, and the willingness of countries to pay the price of transfers in favour of European integration, the central question is whether the EC is an optimum currency area. As Eichengreen (1991) shows, the EC does not fulfil the requirements for an optimum currency area too well, i.e., high factor mobility and no region-specific shocks and disturbances. Possibly, the Internal Market leads to more specialization of regions, owing to the fact that firms are increasingly able to exploit economies of scale. This would make European economies even more diverse – not less. As German unification has proved, asymmetric shocks cannot be ruled out. Then, flexible nominal exchange rates are more important than before to adjust to real shocks. The foreign exchange turmoil of mid-September 1992 has lent additional support to this view. Two devaluations and suspension of two currencies from the European Exchange Rate Mechanism (ERM) have shown that the degree of economic convergence is lower than expected.

Although the ERM has, by and large, functioned properly, its recent shake-up made it obvious that the system is in need of repair. A solution may consist in allowing competition between the national central banks and the institutional rules defining their behaviour such as operating procedures, monetary policy instruments, money targets, and the space to manoeuvre in open-market operations. Those banks and currencies that have similar institutional arrangements (reflecting similar preferences on stable money) and low inflation rates, and that represent economies that have converged close enough to make exchange rates unnecessary for internal adjustments, could merge of their own free will. This leaves open how many currencies join and when they do. The 'new' central bank could start with the credibility it inherits from its national predecessors that must be truly independent beforehand. Imagine the Netherlands, Germany, and Austria forming a currency union, institutionalizing the policies they have pursued for years. The other countries would be left with an adjustment mechanism to absorb real shocks that hit their economies, and the central banks would face an incentive to build up their own credibility. This solution, however, calls for a more flexible approach to EC membership than the current 'all or none'.

NOTES
1. The reference to Eichengreen is to 'Is Europe an Optimum Currency Area?', NBER Working Paper, 3579, Cambridge MA, National Bureau of Economic Research. For further reading from a legal perspective, try P. Beaumont and N. Walker, *The Legal Framework of the Single European Currency* (Oxford: Hart Publishing, 1999).
2. Economic, political, and legal perspectives converge in acknowledging that the significance of Economic and Monetary Union is profound. One rather central question asks: will it prove a success?

D. Dinan, Ever Closer Union: an Introduction to European Integration
(London: Macmillan Press, 1999), p.477

WILL EMU WORK?

The short answer to the question 'Will EMU work?' is yes, it *will* work because a majority of Europeans have decided that it *must* work. During the transition stages, member states displayed a determination to make it happen; new and existing administrative bodies demonstrated the necessary expertise to bring it about; and public opinion showed surprising compliance with it. Having concluded during the transition stages not only that EMU was feasible but also that the political and economic costs of failure were greater than the costs of success, politicians, technocrats, and ordinary Europeans alike were bound to conclude after the launch of Stage III that the costs of maintaining the single currency are considerably less than the costs of its collapse.

NOTE
The phenomenon of EMU deserves no more than a brief introduction, or else a profound exploration of its economic, institutional, and constitutional consequences. This book is compelled to take the first option. But the interested reader is encouraged to read more widely. This is a project on a dauntingly ambitious scale.

Analysis now turns over the following chapters contained in Part Two of this book to the substantive legal rules which serve to eliminate national rules which act as impediments to trade between Member States. The concern, then, is initially with the negative aspect of the creation of the internal/common market. Chapters 10 to 12 and Chapters 13 to 15 examine 'Opening up the Market', first in relation to the free movement of goods, then in relation to the free movement of persons and services.

As the maintenance of border controls declines, in part as a result of legal prohibition but also because of the irrelevance of border controls to supervision of technologically advanced economic activity, so the question for negative Community law becomes more one of coping with regulatory diversity between the Member States rather than physical frontiers or discriminatory practices. In many fields it is the simple fact of differences between non-discriminatory regulatory standards State-by-State that impedes traders from constructing an integrated strategy for the territory of the whole Community. Where States tax products at different rates, the trader in a low-taxing state will face a demand for extra payment when he or she tries to sell the product in the high-taxing state. Where States make different demands with regard to the composition of, say, foodstuffs, the trader in a State which allows use of ingredient *alpha* will be unable to gain access to the market of a State which forbids use of *alpha*. And where States apply different standards of professional qualification, a lawyer trained in State X may be refused the opportunity of working, establishing him- or herself or providing services in State Y simply because State Y has a different training regime.

Were these cases based on overt discrimination against out-of-State providers, then they would be rather easy to resolve in favour of free trade. But there is no discrimination in such cases; all products are highly taxed irrespective of origin in the first example, all products are denied use of ingredient *alpha* in the second example, and all lawyers must meet the host State's requirements in the third. The rules are different, but this tends to lead to protection of home State producers who naturally comply with their own State's rules. The rules restrict cross-border trade. The validity of such rules comes into sharper focus as the integrative process evolves and such less-than-obvious technical barriers to trade are revealed. In the EC, the three examples given above would be considered under different Treaty provisions – Article 90 (tax, Chapter 10), Article 28 (goods, Chapters 11 and 12), and Articles 39, 42, and 49 (persons, Chapter 13, services, Chapter 14) respectively. They would not be dealt with in precisely the same way; but they raise the same policy issue – the compatibility with EC trade law of regulatory diversity between the States in so far as that diversity acts as an impediment to integration.

The European Court has developed principles for judging the acceptable limits of regulatory diversity where trade restriction is caused. The roots of this case law pre-date '1992' by over a decade (*Cassis de Dijon*, p.381), which emphasizes once again that 1992 was a dynamic process, constructed on already well-established principles that are of continuing significance; but the management of regulatory diversity is a quintessentially post-1992, post-border control issue.

Reinhard Gebhard v *Consiglio dell'Ordine degli Avvocati e Procuratori di Milano* (Case C-55/94)

[1995] ECR I-4165, [1996] 1 CMLR 603, Court of Justice of the European Communities

Gebhard, a German national and a member of the Bar of Stuttgart, was resident in Italy. He had worked as a lawyer in Milan, but found himself the subject of disciplinary proceedings by the Milan Bar Council on the ground that he had infringed Italian law by pursuing a professional activity in Italy on a permanent basis using the title *avvocato*. The Court rejected the view of the Milan Bar Council that Gebhard could not be regarded for the purposes of the Treaty as 'established' in Italy unless he belonged to the professional body, or at least pursued his activity in collaboration or in association with persons belonging to that body. The Court conceded that the pursuit of certain self-employed activities may be conditional on complying with certain provisions justified by 'the general good', such as rules relating to organization, qualification, professional ethics, supervision, and liability. It added that where the pursuit of a specific activity is subject to such conditions in the host State, a national of another Member State intending to pursue that activity must in principle comply with them. This concedes regulatory diversity, and the Court referred to the role of secondary Community legislation governing recognition of professional qualifications (especially Directive 89/48, p.472 below). It then stated:

[37] It follows, however, from the Court's case-law that national measures liable to hinder or make less attractive the exercise of fundamental freedoms guaranteed by the Treaty must fulfil four conditions: they must be applied in a non-discriminatory manner; they must be justified by imperative requirements in the general interest; they must be suitable for securing the attainment of the objective which they pursue; and they must not go beyond what is necessary in order to attain it . . .

NOTE

The *Gebhard* case concerned the free movement of persons, but the principle stated is capable of application in the context of Article 28, which deals with the free movement of goods (though not, it would seem, to Article 90 where the Court's control of non-discriminatory regulatory diversity is less assertive, Chapter 10 below). This is part of an emerging, though (as will be seen) not entirely consistent, pattern of EC trade law applicable to all national rules that impede the exercise of economic freedoms. The principles expressed by the Court in this ruling will be traced through the Chapters on negative trade law that follow.

It is plain that the Court envisages that States may justify rules against standards recognised under Community law (e.g, environmental and consumer protection) even where there is a restrictive effect on cross-border trade. How, then, can integration be achieved? As already suggested above in connection with *Gebhard*, the classic Community answer is to move beyond negative law to positive law – to harmonize the diverse national laws so that a common Community rule is put in place. The Community measure governs the interests that underpinned national intervention but achieves protection of those interests at Community level. Traders may then plan integrated strategies according to this common rule which applies throughout the common market territory.

Areas in which a positive contribution from Community law is required may be observed on several occasions, and accordingly the themes set out in this Chapter will be seen to underlie the substantive rules. This becomes more explicit in the remaining Chapters of this book. Part Three, Chapters 16 to 18, concerns the competition rules. Part Four of the book takes the discussion on to a broader plane. Chapter 19 considers harmonization and common policy-making, where several of the themes introduced in the present Chapter are reassessed in the light of the substantive law examined in Chapters 10–15. Chapter 20 looks more broadly still at questions of subsidiarity, flexibility, and new forms of governance. It will be seen that the beguiling notion of common rules for a common market is under strain. In part this is attributable to the geographic and functional expansion of the EC which renders agreement increasingly hard to achieve. The range of interests at stake in the EC cannot readily be reduced to a single agreed norm. More fundamentally, there is an increasingly voiced case against harmonization. Better, it is said by some sources, to allow traders access to the markets of all Member States subject only to compliance with the rules of their home State. The host State could retain a regulatory regime different from other States, but could not use those regulatory differences as a basis for denying access to an out-of-State trader. This would be a system of mutual recognition of national rules. Firms could then choose where to locate in order to supply the whole market, and their choice would be informed by prevailing regulatory strategies. Firms – the market – would select which regulatory regime suited them best. It can readily be appreciated that this approach not only downplays the need for harmonization and a level playing field, it also portrays harmonization as an undesirable suppression of a market in which regulators compete for customers. The debate is not only directed at the internal aspects of EC policy; it is also argued that externally the EC will lose its competitive position if it locks itself into a single standard.

This is an inevitably superficial summary of a key philosophical debate about the Community's future. This preference for 'competition between regulators' over the 'level playing field' is most closely associated with the now ousted Thatcher/

Major administrations in the UK, although it is a debate with global resonances. The debate is being conducted in many sectors, although Social Policy was the most high-profile example at Maastricht. The United Kingdom fought against provisions permitting a deepening of regulation; unable to win that argument, it then successfully argued that it should be insulated from the regulations that other Member States wished to introduce. The United Kingdom thus competed in social policy standards against the other 11, then 14, in the area covered by the Protocol-plus-Agreement. This is touched on in Chapter 20 (p.666) although, via the Amsterdam Treaty, the UK's exclusion was brought to an end by the Labour Government which took office in May 1997. At a more general level, the reader should consider whether the EC is adjusting to new patterns of growth to which all members need not necessarily subscribe, or whether these patterns of fragmentation are fatal to its survival. Chapter 20 contains relevant material. This is variable geometry – and it challenges many of the assumptions about the role of positive law beyond negative law. It is nothing new. Variable geometry has already been touched on in this Chapter (and see the final sentence of the extract from Siebert and Koop above (p.319)), but, as the EC pursues its path of geographic and functional expansion marked by periodic intergovernmental conferences, the debate about how far to move beyond deregulation and market liberalization towards patterns of substantive and institutional re-regulation (in common or not) is becoming increasingly acute. The Treaty provisions on 'closer cooperation' envisaged by the Treaty of Amsterdam constitute an intriguing manifestation. They are examined in Chapter 20 (p.672 below). Chapter 20 also investigates new forms of governance which assume a less rigid form than orthodox patterns of EC rule-making and rule-application (p.676). Chapter 21 concludes the book by placing this debate in the context of that which will shape the 'Future of Europe'. But it is time now to usher the reader towards closer study of the relevant patterns of substantive EC law.

NOTE

 For additional material and resources see the Companion Website at: www.oup.co.uk/ best.textbooks/law/weatherill6e

10

Fiscal Barriers to Trade: Articles 25 and 90

NOTE

Article 23 of the Treaty commits the Community to the creation of a customs union.

ARTICLE 23 EC

The Community shall be based upon a customs union which shall cover all trade in goods and which shall involve the prohibition between Member States of customs duties on imports and exports and of all charges having equivalent effect, and the adoption of a common customs tariff in their relations with third countries.

NOTE

Article 26 EC empowers the Council acting by qualified majority on a proposal from the Commission to fix common customs tariff duties. It is the internal aspects of the customs union which form the focus of this Chapter.

ARTICLE 25 EC

Customs duties on imports and exports and charges having equivalent effect shall be prohibited between Member States. This prohibition shall also apply to customs duties of a fiscal nature.

NOTE

The elimination of customs duties on trade between Member States is essential as part of the process of market integration, but it is not enough on its own to secure origin neutrality in fiscal law. Consequently the provisions which prohibit customs duties are supplemented by provisions directed at the internal taxation systems of the Member States. Article 90 forbids discrimination against imported goods in the State's internal system of taxation.

ARTICLE 90 EC

No Member State shall impose, directly or indirectly, on the products of other Member States any internal taxation of any kind in excess of that imposed directly or indirectly on similar domestic products.

Furthermore, no Member State shall impose on the products of other Member States any internal taxation of such a nature as to afford indirect protection to other products.

NOTES

1. These are fundamentally important provisions. Both plainly connect with Article 14, examined in the previous Chapter. The wording, though not the substance, of both provisions was adjusted by the Amsterdam Treaty. That Treaty also adjusted the numbering

(p.12 above). Article 25 was formerly Article 12; Article 90 was Article 95. This must be kept in mind when reading pre-Amsterdam case law.

2. It has become axiomatic in Community law that Article 25 and Article 90 are *complementary but mutually exclusive*. Both are directed at the abolition of fiscal barriers to trade; but a charge is controlled by one or the other, not both. There is no overlap. (See *Commission* v *Italy* (Case 24/68), p.327 below.)

3. The nature of the control exercised over domestic competence to levy tax is distinct. Article 25 forbids customs duties and charges having equivalent effect. Article 90 does not forbid internal taxation; it merely forbids discrimination according to nationality. States remain otherwise free to levy taxation as they see fit.

SECTION 1: **ARTICLE 25**

The Court has used the prohibition on customs duties and charges having equivalent effect to challenge a range of levies imposed on goods which cross a frontier. The Court is concerned with the restrictive *effect* on trade, not the purpose of the charge. The following cases, both infringement proceedings against Italy (see Chapter 4), illustrate the Court's application of the Article 25 prohibition (which, at the time the cases were decided, was contained in Article 12).

Commission v *Italy* (Case 7/68)
[1968] ECR 423, Court of Justice of the European Communities

The case concerned an Italian tax on the export of artistic, historical, and archaeological articles.

1. *The scope of the disputed tax*

By basing its action on Article 16 of the Treaty, the Commission considers that articles of an artistic, historic, archaeological or ethnographic nature, which are the subject of the Italian Law of 1 June 1939, No 1089, fall under the provisions relating to the customs union. This point of view is disputed by the defendant, which considers that the articles in question cannot be assimilated to 'consumer goods or articles of general use' and are not therefore subject to the provisions of the Treaty which apply to 'ordinary merchandise'; for that reason they are excluded from the application of Article 16 of the Treaty.

Under Article 9 of the Treaty the Community is based on a customs union 'which shall cover all trade in goods'. By goods, within the meaning of that provision, there must be understood products which can be valued in money and which are capable, as such, of forming the subject of commercial transactions.

The articles covered by the Italian Law, whatever may be the characteristics which distinguish them from other types of merchandise, nevertheless resemble the latter, inasmuch as they can be valued in money and so be the subject of commercial transactions. That view corresponds with the scheme of the Italian Law itself, which fixes the tax in question in proportion to the value of the articles concerned.

It follows from the above that the rules of the Common Market apply to these goods subject only to the exceptions expressly provided by the Treaty.

2. *The classification of the disputed tax having regard to Article 16 of the Treaty*

In the opinion of the Commission the tax in dispute constitutes a tax having an effect equivalent to a customs duty on exports and therefore the tax should have been abolished, under Article 16 of the Treaty, no later than the end of the first stage of the common market, that is to say, from 1 January

1962. The defendant argues that the disputed tax does not come within the category, as it has its own particular purpose which is to ensure the protection and safety of the artistic, historic and archaeological heritage which exists in the national territory. Consequently, the tax does not in any respect have a fiscal nature, and its contribution to the budget is insignificant.

Article 16 of the Treaty prohibits the collection in dealings between Member States of any customs duty on exports and of any charge having an equivalent effect, that is to say, any charge which, by altering the price of an article exported, has the same restrictive effect on the free circulation of that article as a customs duty. This provision makes no distinction based on the purpose of the duties and charges the abolition of which it requires.

It is not necessary to analyse the concept of the nature of fiscal systems on which the defendant bases its argument upon this point, for the provisions of the section of the Treaty concerning the elimination of customs duties between the Member States exclude the retention of customs duties and charges having equivalent effect without distinguishing in that respect between those which are and those which are not of a fiscal nature.

The disputed tax falls within Article 16 by reason of the fact that export trade in the goods in question is hindered by the pecuniary burden which it imposes on the price of the exported articles.

NOTE

The Court went on to reject Italian arguments of justification based on Article 30 (formerly 36). Article 30 is available only in respect of physical and technical barriers to trade caught by Article 28, and is unavailable in the field of fiscal barriers to trade. Chapter 11 examines Articles 28–30.

Commission v *Italy* (Case 24/68)

[1969] ECR 193, [1971] CMLR 611, Court of Justice of the European Communities

Italy collected a levy on goods exported to other Member States in order to fund the compilation of statistical data relating to trade patterns. The Court began by examining the nature of the Article 25 (then Article 12) prohibition before proceeding to find the charge incompatible with the Treaty.

[6] . . . the purpose of the abolition of customs barriers is not merely to eliminate their protective nature, as the Treaty sought on the contrary to give general scope and effect to the rule on the elimination of customs duties and charges having equivalent effect, in order to ensure the free movement of goods.

[7] It follows from the system as a whole and from the general and absolute nature of the prohibition of any customs duty applicable to goods moving between Member States that customs duties are prohibited independently of any consideration of the purpose for which they were introduced and the destination of the revenue obtained therefrom.

The justification for this prohibition is based on the fact that any pecuniary charge, however small, imposed on goods by reason of the fact that they cross a frontier constitutes an obstacle to the movement of such goods.

[8] The extension of the prohibition of customs duties to charges having equivalent effect is intended to supplement the prohibition against obstacles to trade created by such duties by increasing its efficiency.

The use of these two complementary concepts thus tends, in trade between Member States, to avoid the imposition of any pecuniary charge on goods circulating within the Community by virtue of the fact that they cross a national frontier.

[9] Thus, in order to ascribe to a charge an effect equivalent to a customs duty, it is important to consider this effect in the light of the objectives of the Treaty, in the Parts, Titles and Chapters in which Articles 9, 12, 13 and 16 are to be found, particularly in relation to the free movement of goods.

Consequently, any pecuniary charge, however small and whatever its designation and mode of application, which is imposed unilaterally on domestic or foreign goods by reason of the fact that they cross a frontier, and which is not a customs duty in the strict sense, constitutes a charge having equivalent effect within the meaning of Articles 9, 12, 13 and 16 of the Treaty, even if it is not imposed for the benefit of the State, is not discriminatory or protective in effect and if the product on which the charge is imposed is not in competition with any domestic product.

[10] It follows from all the provisions referred to and from their relationship with the other provisions of the Treaty that the prohibition of new customs duties or charges having equivalent effect, linked to the principle of the free movement of goods, constitutes a fundamental rule which, without prejudice to the other provisions of the Treaty, does not permit of any exceptions.

. . .

[15] The Italian Government further maintains that the disputed charge constitutes the consideration for a service rendered and as such cannot be designated as a charge having equivalent effect.

According to the Italian Government the object of the statistics in question is to determine precisely the actual movements of goods and, consequently, changes the state of the market. It claims that the exactness of the information thus supplied affords importers a better competitive position in the Italian market whilst exporters enjoy a similar advantage abroad and that the special advantages which dealers obtain from the survey justifies their paying for this public service and moreover demonstrates that the disputed charge is in the nature of a *quid pro quo*.

[16] The statistical information in question is beneficial to the economy as a whole and *inter alia* to the relevant administrative authorities.

Even if the competitive position of importers and exporters were to be particularly improved as a result, the statistics still constitute an advantage so general, and so difficult to assess, that the disputed charge cannot be regarded as the consideration for a specific benefit actually conferred.

[17] It appears from the abovementioned considerations that in so far as the disputed charge is levied on exports it is contrary to Article 16 of the Treaty.

NOTES
1. Paragraph 9 of the judgment constitutes the Court's definition of the scope of the prohibition; a formula which has proved enduring through subsequent case law.
2. See also, on the Court's approach, e.g., *Sociaal Fonds voor de Diamantarbeiders* v *Brachfeld* (Cases 2 and 3/69) [1969] ECR 211, [1969] CMLR 335.
3. The Court accepts that a State is permitted to levy a fee for services provided to an importer. Such a charge is demanded as part of a commercial transaction, not because of the passage of the goods across a frontier. The charge is accordingly not caught by Article 25. However, the risk that States may use this approach as a device for imposing charges on importers for unwanted services which impede free trade has led the Court to scrutinize with great care arguments of this nature. In paras 15 and 16 of its judgment in *Commission* v *Italy* (Case 24/68) above, the Court rejected submissions along these lines by the Italian Government. It took a similar approach in *Bresciani* v *Amministrazione Italiana delle Finanze* (Case 87/75).

Bresciani v *Amministrazione Italiana delle Finanze* (Case 87/75)
[1976] ECR 129, [1976] 2 CMLR 62, Court of Justice of the European Communities

The case involved the imposition of a charge for compulsory veterinary and public health inspections carried out on the importation of raw cowhides. The Court was asked by a court in Genoa to consider whether such a levy constitutes a charge having equivalent effect to a customs duty on imports.

[9] . . . [A]ny pecuniary charge, whatever its designation and mode of application, which is unilaterally imposed on goods imported from another Member State by reason of the fact that they cross a frontier, constitutes a charge having an effect equivalent to a customs duty. In appraising a duty of the type at issue it is . . . of no importance that it is proportionate to the quantity of the imported goods and not to their value.

[10] Nor, in determining the effects of the duty on the free movement of goods, is it of any importance that a duty of the type at issue is proportionate to the costs of a compulsory public

health inspection carried out on entry of the goods. The activity of the administration of the State intended to maintain a public health inspection system imposed in the general interest cannot be regarded as a service rendered to the importer such as to justify the imposition of a pecuniary charge. If, accordingly, public health inspections are still justified at the end of the transitional period, the costs which they occasion must be met by the general public which, as a whole, benefits from the free movement of Community goods.

[11] The fact that the domestic production is, through other charges, subjected to a similar burden matters little unless those charges and the duty in question are applied according to the same criteria and at the same stage of production, thus making it possible for them to be regarded as falling within a general system of internal taxation applying systematically and in the same way to domestic and Imported products.

NOTE

Arguments of fee-for-service also failed in, e.g., *Cadsky* v *ICE* (Case 63/74) [1975] ECR 281, [1975] 2 CMLR 246. See *Commission* v *Belgium* (Case 132/82) [1983] ECR 1649, [1983] 3 CMLR 600 for discussion of circumstances in which a fee might legitimately be demanded; the case was nonetheless still decided against the charging State.

However, where the inspection is carried out under mandatory provisions of Community law, then a charge may be lawful.

Commission v Germany (Case 18/87)

[1988] ECR 5427, Court of Justice of the European Communities

German *Länder* (regions) charged fees on the importation of live animals to cover costs of inspections undertaken under Directive 81/389. The Court adopted a step-by-step approach in ruling on the compatibility of the system with Community law.

[5] It should be observed in the first place that, as the Court has held on a number of occasions, the justification for the prohibition of customs duties and any charges having an equivalent effect lies in the fact that any pecuniary charge, however small, imposed on goods by reason of the fact that they cross a frontier, constitutes an obstacle to the movement of goods which is aggravated by the resulting administrative formalities. It follows that any pecuniary charge, whatever its designation and mode of application, which is imposed unilaterally on goods by reason of the fact that they cross a frontier and Is not a customs duty in the strict sense constitutes a charge having an equivalent effect to a customs duty within the meaning of Articles 9, 12, 13 and 16 of the Treaty.

[6] However, the Court has held that such a charge escapes that classification if it relates to a general system of internal dues applied systematically and in accordance with the same criteria to domestic products and imported products alike (judgment of 31 May 1979 in Case 132/78 *Denkavit* v *France* [1979] ECR 1923), if it constitutes payment for a service in fact rendered to the economic operator of a sum in proportion to the service (judgment of 9 November 1983 in Case 158/82 *Commission* v *Denmark* [1983] ECR 3573), or again, subject to certain conditions, if it attaches to inspections carried out to fulfil obligations imposed by Community law (judgment of 25 January 1977 in Case 46/76 *Bauhuis* v *Netherlands* [1977] ECR 5).

[7] The contested fee, which is payable on importation and transit, cannot be regarded as relating to a general system of internal dues. Nor does it constitute payment for a service rendered to the operator, because this condition is satisfied only if the operator in question obtains a definite specific benefit (see judgment of 1 July 1969 in Case 24/68 *Commission* v *Italy* [1969] ECR 193), which is not the case if the inspection serves to guarantee, in the public interest, the health and life of animals in international transport (see judgment of 20 March 1984 in Case 314/82 *Commission* v *Belgium* [1984] ECR 1543).

[8] Since the contested fee was charged in connection with inspections carried out pursuant to a Community provision, it should be noted that according to the case-law of the Court (judgment of 25 January 1977 in *Bauhuis*, cited above; judgment of 12 July 1977 *Commission* v *Netherlands*

[1977] ECR 1355; judgment of 31 January 1984 in Case 1/83 *IFG* v *Freistaat Bayern* [1984] ECR 349) such fees may not be classified as charges having an effect equivalent to a customs duty if the following conditions are satisfied:

(a) they do not exceed the actual costs of the inspections in connection with which they are charged;

(b) the inspections in question are obligatory and uniform for all the products concerned in the Community;

(c) they are prescribed by Community law in the general interest of the Community;

(d) they promote the free movement of goods, in particular by neutralizing obstacles which could arise from unilateral measures of inspection adopted in accordance with Article 36 of the Treaty.

[9] In this instance these conditions are satisfied by the contested fee . . .

NOTE

The Court appears prepared to accept in such a case that the Community as a whole obtains a benefit from the facilitation of free trade secured through a harmonized system of health inspections, and that accordingly the State is permitted to pass on the costs to individual traders. It has adopted the same view in respect of inspections mandatory under international conventions to which all Member States are party; *Commission* v *Netherlands* (Case 89/76) [1977] ECR 1355.

It should however be noted that where Community law does no more than permit the inspection, any fee levied to cover costs is incompatible with Article 25; *Commission* v *Belgium* (Case 314/82) [1984] ECR 1543.

SECTION 2: **ARTICLE 90**

A charge may fall to be considered in the light of Article 90 (text at p.325 above) where it is imposed not on an importer as such, but instead on all traders irrespective of origin. If the State can show that the charge 'relates to a general system of internal dues applied systematically and in accordance with the same criteria to domestic products and imported products alike' (para 6 of *Commission* v *Germany* (Case 18/87 at p.329 above)), then the charge is lawful, provided only that the non-discrimination requirements of Article 90 are complied with.

The next case shows the application of Article 90 to an internal system of taxation which was held to favour the domestic trader over the importer. Remember that pre-Amsterdam Article 90 was numbered Article 95.

Schottle v *Finanzamt Freudenstadt* (Case 20/76)
[1977] ECR 247, [1977] 2 CMLR 98, Court of Justice of the European Communities

The case arose out of German taxation of carriage of goods by road. Long-distance road transport was taxed as part of a policy to encourage use of rail and waterways instead, but no tax was imposed on short-distance road transport. The definition of 'short distance' included special arrangements for importers. The net result was that a short journey might be exempt if purely internal to Germany, but subject to tax if it crossed a border.

[20] The first paragraph of Article 95 is infringed where the taxation on the imported product and that on the similar domestic product are calculated in a different manner on the basis of different

criteria which lead, if only in certain cases, to higher taxation being imposed on the imported product.

[21] Higher taxation of the imported product exists when the conditions under which the carrier is subject to tax are different with regard to International transport and purely domestic transport so that in comparable situations the product moving within the Member State is not subject to the tax to which an imported product is subject. Indeed in order to compare the tax on goods moving within the national territory with that on the imported product for the purposes of the application of Article 95, account must be taken of both the basis of assessment of the tax and the advantages or exemptions which each tax carries with it. For the taxation of the imported product to be higher it is sufficient that in certain circumstances the national product may be transported without being subject to tax for the same distance within the Member State while the imported product is subject to the tax solely because the border was crossed. In this respect it is for the national judge to compare in specific cases the situations which may arise.

[22] The information supplied by the national court shows that a real obstacle to free movement of goods may sometimes result from the application of different conditions for the imposition of taxation with regard to both international transport and domestic transport. The minor and inci-dental nature of the obstacle created by a national tax and the fact that it could only have been avoided in practice by abolishing the tax are not sufficient to prevent Article 95 from being applic-able. Title IV of Part Two of the Treaty concerning the common transport policy enables Member States to resolve problems of competition between means of transport without however adversely affecting the free movement of goods. However the lack of such a policy is no justification for a derogation from Article 95 of the Treaty.

NOTE

The tax system lacked origin neutrality. However, States are commonly more devious. It is pos-sible to avoid direct discrimination on grounds of nationality (the problem in *Schottle*), but to achieve a similar result by instead basing a taxation system on criteria which indirectly prejudice the imported product. In the following case the Court decided that such indirect discrimination on grounds of nationality is also capable of falling foul of Article 90.

Humblot v Directeur des Services Fiscaux (Case 112/84)

[1985] ECR 1367, [1986] 2 CMLR 338. Court of Justice of the European Communities

France imposed two different types of annual car tax. The key threshold between the two was 16 CV, a power rating. Below that level the tax increased gradually in proportion to the car's power, up to a maximum of 1,100 francs. Above 16 CV a flat rate of 5,000 francs was imposed. No French car was rated above 16 CV, so only imported vehicles were burdened by the high flat rate. M. Humblot, charged 5,000 francs tax on his 36 CV imported car, claimed the tax violated what was then Article 95, now Article 90, and sought a refund. The French court in Belfort referred questions under Article 177 (Article 234 post-Amsterdam).

[12] It is appropriate in the first place to stress that as Community law stands at present the Member States are at liberty to subject products such as cars to a system of road tax which increases progressively in amount depending on an objective criterion, such as the power rating for tax purposes, which may be determined in various ways.

[13] Such a system of domestic taxation is, however, compatible with Article 95 only in so far as it is free from any discriminatory or protective effect.

[14] That is not true of a system like the one at issue in the main proceedings. Under that system there are two distinct taxes: a differential tax which increases progressively and is charged on cars not exceeding a given power rating for tax purposes and a fixed tax on cars exceeding that rating which is almost five times as high as the highest rate of the differential tax. Although the system embodies no formal distinction based on the origin of products it manifestly exhibits discriminatory

or protective features contrary to Article 95, since the power rating determining liability to the special tax has been fixed at a level such that only imported cars, in particular from other Member States, are subject to the special tax whereas all cars of domestic manufacture are liable to the distinctly more advantageous differential tax.

[15] In the absence of considerations relating to the amount of the special tax, consumers seeking comparable cars as regards such matters as size, comfort, actual power, maintenance costs, durability, fuel consumption and price would naturally choose from among cars above and below the critical power rating laid down by French law. However, liability to the special tax entails a much larger increase in taxation than passing from one category of car to another in a system of progressive taxation embodying balanced differentials like the system on which the differential tax is based. The resultant additional taxation is liable to cancel out the advantages which certain cars imported from other Member States might have in consumers' eyes over comparable cars of domestic manufacture, particularly since the special tax continues to be payable for several years. In that respect the special tax reduces the amount of competition to which cars of domestic manufacture are subject and hence is contrary to the principle of neutrality with which domestic taxation must comply.

[16] In the light of the foregoing considerations the question raised by the national court for a preliminary ruling should be answered as follows: Article 95 of the EEC Treaty prohibits the charging on cars exceeding a given power rating for tax purposes of a special fixed tax the amount of which is several times the highest amount of the progressive tax payable on cars of less than the said power rating for tax purposes, where the only cars subject to the special tax are imported, in particular from other Member States.

NOTES
1. An amended French car tax system was also found incompatible with Article 95 (now Article 90) in *Feldain* (Case 433/85) [1987] ECR 3536. In Case C-284/96 *Didier Tabouillot* [1997] ECR I-7471, the Court was able to avoid answering questions about the French system since the vehicle had been imported directly into France from the USA, a situation falling outside the scope of this Article of the Treaty.
2. However, the establishment of a taxation system based on a criterion which indirectly affects imported goods more severely than domestic products is not automatically unlawful. It is open to the State to show that there is an objective justification for the use of that criterion which is not connected with nationality. The tax may then be accepted as compatible with Article 90.

Chemial Farmaceutici v *DAF* (Case 140/79)
[1981] ECR 1, Court of Justice of the European Communities

Italian taxation of denatured synthetic ethyl alcohol was higher than taxation of denatured ethyl alcohol obtained by fermentation, although the products were interchangeable in use. Italy produced little of the more heavily taxed synthetic version of the product. The Court explained that the facts and the result were distinguishable from *Humblot* (Case 112/84).

[13] . . . the different taxation of synthetic alcohol and of alcohol produced by fermentation in Italy is the result of an economic policy decision to favour the manufacture of alcohol from agricultural products and, correspondingly, to restrain the processing into alcohol of ethylene, a derivative of petroleum, in order to reserve that raw material for other more important economic uses. It accordingly constitutes a legitimate choice of economic policy to which effect is given by fiscal means. The implementation of that policy does not lead to any discrimination since although it results in discouraging imports of synthetic alcohol into Italy, it also has the consequence of hampering the development in Italy itself of production of alcohol from ethylene, that production being technically perfectly possible.

[14] As the Court has stated on many occasions, particularly in the judgments cited by the Italian

Government, in its present stage of development Community law does not restrict the freedom of each Member State to lay down tax arrangements which differentiate between certain products on the basis of objective criteria, such as the nature of the raw materials used or the production processes employed. Such differentiation is compatible with Community law if it pursues economic policy objectives which are themselves compatible with the requirements of the Treaty and its secondary law and if the detailed rules are such as to avoid any form of discrimination, direct or indirect, in regard to imports from other Member States or any form of protection of competing domestic products.

[15] Differential taxation such as that which exists in Italy for denatured synthetic alcohol on the one hand and denatured alcohol obtained by fermentation on the other satisfies these requirements. It appears in fact that that system of taxation pursues an objective of legitimate industrial policy in that it is such as to promote the distillation of agricultural products as against the manufacture of alcohol from petroleum derivatives. That choice does not conflict with the rules of Community law or the requirements of a policy decided within the framework of the Community.

[16] The detailed provisions of the legislation at issue before the national court cannot be considered as discriminatory since, on the one hand, it is not disputed that imports from other Member States of alcohol obtained by fermentation qualify for the same tax treatment as Italian alcohol produced by fermentation and, on the other hand, although the rate of tax prescribed for synthetic alcohol results in restraining the importation of synthetic alcohol originating in other Member States, it has an equivalent economic effect in the national territory in that it also hampers the establishment of profitable production of the same product by Italian industry.

Note
Notice that it is only indirect discrimination on grounds of nationality which may be justified in this way; never direct discrimination. Concessions must be made available to all products meeting the criteria, even if in practice few imports conform. See, e.g., *Commission v Italy* (Case 213/79) [1980] ECR 1.

■ QUESTION

Advise a State which has several regions which suffer from abnormally high rainfall and which wishes to introduce a tax which favours production of goods typical of high-rainfall areas in order to confer economic support on the farmers of such areas.

See *Commission v France* (Case 196/85) [1987] ECR 1597, [1988] 2 CMLR 851.

NOTES
1. The second paragraph of Article 90 (p.325 above) broadens the scope of the provisions beyond tax equality for similar products to equality for competing products. This involves an economic assessment of the relationship of products in order to reveal whether the State is engaged in conferring protection on its domestic producers by imposing undue burdens on competing imports.
2. The Court explained the nature of the control exercised by the first and second paragraphs of what was then Article 95, now Article 90, in the 'Spirits' cases, a series of cases concerned to challenge taxation laws relating to alcohol alleged to favour domestic products.

Commission v France (Case 168/78)
[1980] ECR 347, [1981] 2 CMLR 631, Court of Justice of the European Communities

[4] [Article 95 supplements] within the system of the Treaty, the provisions on the abolition of customs duties and charges having equivalent effect. Their aim is to ensure free movement of goods between the Member States in normal conditions of competition by the elimination of all forms of protection which result from the application of internal taxation which discriminates against products from other Member States. As the Commission has correctly stated, Article 95 must guarantee the complete neutrality of internal taxation as regards competition between domestic products and imported products.

[5] The first paragraph of Article 95, which is based on a comparison of the tax burdens imposed on domestic products and on imported products which may be classified as 'similar', is the basic rule in this respect. This provision, as the Court has had occasion to emphasize in its judgment of 10 October 1978 in Case 148/77, *H. Hansen jun. & O.C. Balle GmbH & Co.* v *Hauptzollamt Flensburg* [1978] ECR 1787, must be interpreted widely so as to cover all taxation procedures which conflict with the principle of the equality of treatment of domestic products and imported products; it is therefore necessary to interpret the concept of 'similar products' with sufficient flexibility. The Court specified in the judgment of 17 February 1976 in the *REWE* case (Case 45/75 [1976] ECR 181) that it is necessary to consider as similar products which 'have similar characteristics and meet the same needs from the point of view of consumers'. It is therefore necessary to determine the scope of the first paragraph of Article 95 on the basis not of the criterion of the strictly identical nature of the products but on that of their similar and comparable use.

[6] The function of the second paragraph of Article 95 is to cover, in addition, all forms of indirect tax protection in the case of products which, without being similar within the meaning of the first paragraph, are nevertheless in competition, even partial, indirect or potential, with certain products of the importing country. The Court has already emphasized certain aspects of that provision in its judgment of 4 April 1978 in Case 27/77, *Firma Fink-Frucht GmbH* v *Hauptzollamt Munchen-Landsbergerstrasse* [1978] ECR 223, in which it stated that for the purposes of the application of the first paragraph of Article 95 it is sufficient for the imported product to be in competition with the protected domestic production by reason of one or several economic uses to which it may be put, even though the condition of similarity for the purposes of the first paragraph of Article 95 is not fulfilled.

[7] Whilst the criterion indicated in the first paragraph of Article 95 consists in the comparison of tax burdens, whether in terms of the rate, the mode of assessment or other detailed rules for the application thereof, in view of the difficulty of making sufficiently precise comparisons between the products in question, the second paragraph of that article is based upon a more general criterion, in other words the protective nature of the system of internal taxation.

NOTE

Most of the 'Spirits' cases, including *Commission* v *France* (Case 168/78), were decided on the basis that the Treaty prohibition was plainly infringed, and without detailed examination of the two paragraphs separately. This was not possible in the most difficult of the cases, *Commission* v *UK* (Case 170/78), which involved tax differentials between wine and beer. These products are not similar within Article 90(1), and therefore argument centred on the possible application of Article 90(2) (then, of course, Article 95(2)). So complex were the economic calculations that the Court declined to give final judgment at the same time as it upheld the Commission's complaints in the other 'Spirits' cases ([1980] ECR 417). Eventually, however, after deeper investigation had been presented to the Court, the UK was held in breach of the Treaty.

Commission v *UK* (Case 170/78)

[1983] ECR 2263, [1983] 3 CMLR 512, Court of Justice of the European Communities

The Court first explored the nature of the competitive relationship between wine and beer, and built on its initial findings three years earlier.

[8] As regards the question of competition between wine and beer, the Court considered that, to a certain extent at least, the two beverages in question were capable of meeting identical needs, so that it had to be acknowledged that there was a degree of substitution for one another. It pointed out that, for the purpose of measuring the possible degree of substitution, attention should not be confined to consumer habits in a Member State or in a given region. Those habits, which were essentially variable in time and space, could not be considered to be immutable; the tax policy of a Member State must not therefore crystallize given consumer habits so as to consolidate an advantage acquired by national industries concerned to respond to them.

[9] The Court nonetheless recognized that, in view of the substantial differences between wine and beer, it was difficult to compare the manufacturing processes and the natural properties of those beverages, as the Government of the United Kingdom had rightly observed. For that reason, the Court requested the parties to provide additional information with a view to dispelling the doubts which existed concerning the nature of the competitive relationship between the two products.

. . .

[11] The Italian Government contended in that connection that it was inappropriate to compare beer with wines of average alcoholic strength or, *a fortiori*, with wines of greater alcoholic strength. In its opinion, it was the lightest wines with an alcoholic strength in the region of 9, that is to say the most popular and cheapest wines, which were genuinely in competition with beer. It therefore took the view that those wines should be chosen for purposes of comparison where it was a question of measuring the incidence of taxation on the basis of either alcoholic strength or the price of the products.

[12] The Court considers that observation by the Italian Government to be pertinent. In view of the substantial differences in the quality and, therefore, in the price of wines, the decisive competitive relationship between beer, a popular and widely consumed beverage, and wine must be established by reference to those wines which are the most accessible to the public at large, that is to say, generally speaking, the lightest and cheapest varieties. Accordingly, that is the appropriate basis for making fiscal comparisons by reference to the alcoholic strength or to the price of the two beverages in question.

Having established a competitive relationship between the products, the Court then examined the effect of the taxation system:

[26] After considering the information provided by the parties, the Court has come to the conclusion that, if a comparison is made on the basis of those wines which are cheaper than the types of wine selected by the United Kingdom and of which several varieties are sold in significant quantities on the United Kingdom market, it becomes apparent that precisely those wines which, in view of their price, are most directly in competition with domestic beer production are subject to a considerably higher tax burden.

[27] It is clear, therefore, following the detailed inquiry conducted by the Court – whatever criterion for comparison is used, there being no need to express a preference for one or the other – that the United Kingdom's tax system has the effect of subjecting wine imported from other Member States to an additional tax burden so as to afford protection to domestic beer production, inasmuch as beer production constitutes the most relevant reference criterion from the point of view of competition. Since such protection is most marked in the case of the most popular wines, the effect of the United Kingdom tax system is to stamp wine with the hallmarks of a luxury product which, in view of the tax burden which it bears, can scarcely constitute in the eyes of the consumer a genuine alternative to the typical domestically produced beverage.

NOTES
1. For analysis of the Court's approach see A. J. Easson (1984) 6 EL Rev 57.
2. A product which is available entirely or mainly only as an import can be subject to taxation, provided the tax on that product falls within the general scheme of internal taxation. A State which wishes to tax, for example, an exotic fruit or a raw material of which it has no supplies of its own, will have to demonstrate that the tax is simply an aspect of its broader tax regime for fruit or raw materials of that general type. If it cannot do so – if the tax is a special charge introduced for that import alone – then the charge is covered by Article 25. Even if the charge is part of the internal system, it must nevertheless be shown to be compatible with Article 90 – it must be neither discriminatory nor protective.

   See *Commission* v *Denmark* (Case 158/82) [1983] ECR 3573, [1984] 2 CMLR 658 for an example of violation of Article 25; *Cooperativa Cofrutta* v *Amministrazione delle Finanze dello Stato* (Case 193/85) [1987] ECR 2085, *Commission* v *Italy* (Case 184/85) [1987] ECR 2013,

Cases C-367/93-C-377/93 *F.G. Roders BV et al* v *Inspecteur der Invoerrechten en Accijnzen* [1995] ECR I-2229 on the application of Article 90.

FURTHER READING

Danusso, M., and Denton, R., 'Does the European Court of Justice look for a Protectionist Motive under Article 95?' [1990/1] LIEI 67.

Hedemann-Robinson, M., 'Indirect Discrimination: Article 95 EC Back to Front and Inside Out?' (1995) 1 *European Public Law* 439.

SECTION 3: **FISCAL HARMONIZATION**

The prohibition on discriminatory internal taxation is insufficient to achieve unrestricted free movement of goods in accordance with Article 14 EC, p.299 above, as the following extract from COM (85) 310, the '1992 blueprint', the White Paper on the Completion of the Internal Market, explains.

COM (85) 310, 'COMPLETING THE INTERNAL MARKET', WHITE PAPER FROM THE COMMISSION TO THE EUROPEAN COUNCIL, 14 JUNE 1985

160. Fiscal checks feature prominently among the functions carried out at the Community's internal frontiers. Consequently, the removal of frontier controls is bound to have inescapable implications for the Member States as far as indirect taxes are concerned. The adjustments that will be needed to solve these practical problems are also very much in line with the terms of the commitment undertaken by those who signed the Treaties and with historical developments since then.

161. When the Customs Union was achieved in 1968, it was already apparent that the mere removal of tariffs would not enable a true common internal market to be created; and that differences in turnover taxes in particular were the source of serious distortion and hence a serious obstacle to the completion of the Internal Market. That such a situation might arise was foreseen in the Treaty itself. Article 99 specifically provided that the Commission should make proposals for the approximation of indirect taxation when this was needed for the completion of the internal market; and Article 100 provided the legal means for so doing.

162. Accordingly, in 1967, the Member States decided that the existing turnover taxes must be replaced by a Value Added Tax levied on a common basis. It was recognized from the outset that the imposition of such a tax on a common basis would raise many difficulties for Member States and would have to be phased in over a period of years. But it is clear from both the First and the Second VAT Directives which gave effect to this decision that a common basis was not only intended but was regarded as essential.

163. The adoption of a harmonized VAT was given further impetus by the Council Decision in 1970 that the Community should be financed through 'own resources'. A significant element in this new 'own resources' regime was the allocation to the Community of the yield of part (not to exceed a rate of 1 per cent) of the harmonized VAT. It is clear from the Directives that what was in mind was not a notional calculation but the allocation of a specific share of an actual harmonized tax. The following year (1971) saw the adoption of a Council Resolution confirming its intention to create an area within which goods, services and capital could circulate freely and without distortions of competition. Not only was a common tax base regarded as essential to achieve this end,

but common tax rates as well were contemplated. In the words of the Resolution: 'Before the end of the first stage, the Council will deliberate on the studies undertaken, and on the proposals made, by the Commission concerning the approximation of rates of value added tax and of excise duties.'

164. The broad principles of the harmonized common tax base for VAT were laid down in outline in the Second VAT Directive dated 11 April 1967. This was followed after a period of intensive consideration and discussion, by the Sixth VAT Directive, adopted in 1977 which set out in great detail the provisions of the common base. Because of the problems involved in reaching agreement on a number of difficult and contentious issues, the Sixth Directive contains a number of lacunae as well as special schemes, derogations and transitional provisions. At the same time, Article 35 of the Directive specifically provided that these derogations and special arrangements should ultimately be brought to an end. Nowhere is the general philosophy set out more succinctly than in the preamble to the Directive. This declares:

'Whereas account should be taken of the objective of abolishing the imposition of tax on the importation and the remission of tax on exportation in trade between Member States; whereas it should be ensured that the common system of turnover taxes is non-discriminatory as regards the origin of goods and services, so that a common market permitting fair competition and resembling a real internal market may ultimately be achieved.'

Since 1977 a number of supplementary Directives have been adopted and a number await the Council's decision.

165. Soon after the first steps were taken to harmonize turnover taxes, the Community turned its attention to excise duties. As a first step the Commission identified tobacco, alcoholic drinks and hydrocarbon oils as the products on which excises should be levied – a choice which coincides with the coverage adopted by most Member States.

166. In the case of tobacco, a limited degree of harmonization has already been achieved. The basic directive adopted in 1972 defined the structures of excise duty on cigarettes; provided for harmonization in successive stages; and defined a range of relationships between the specific duty and the total duty. In the case of alcoholic drinks and hydrocarbon oils, little progress has been made despite the presentation by the Commission of a whole range of directives. At the same time, however, a limited degree of progress has been made as a result of judgments by the European Court which have compelled Member States to abandon tax arrangements which benefited domestic producers to the detriment of producers in other Member States.

167. It is clear from what has been said above that the harmonization of indirect taxation has always been regarded as an essential and integral part of achieving a true common market. Momentum has been lost in recent years but this was due essentially to the impact of the recession on the economic policies of Member States and preoccupation with other problems. But progress is being resumed and now we must proceed vigorously if we are to achieve the target date of 1992 for the completion of the Internal Market.

168. If goods and services and people are to move freely from one member State to another in just the same way as they can move within a member State, it is essential that frontier controls be abolished. Since these are primarily designed to ensure that each member State can collect the revenue in the form of indirect taxation to which it feels entitled, there are clear implications for the indirect taxation policies of individual Member States. Let us be quite clear that we are talking here not in terms of frontier facilitation, i.e., simplifying frontier procedures in the way that the Directive on the Harmonization of Frontier Procedures and the Single Administrative Document aim to do, but in terms of removing the frontiers altogether as only in this way is it possible to achieve the stated objective of free movement of goods and of people.

As this extract suggests, harmonization of taxation is extremely complex. A major obstacle is the political symbolism of the power to levy tax. Yet progress is being made, although this is an area which continues to demand delicate negotiation far beyond the end of 1992, the deadline for the completion of the internal market.

As is well known, the pattern chosen for the internal market after the end of 1992 is based on a sharp distinction between private consumers and commercial traders. Private consumers are free to shop in a State other than their own and to take goods back home without having to pay sums representing the difference between the taxes levied in the State of purchase and their home State. The popularity of day-trips from England to France to buy alcohol is, to the dismay of British brewers, a direct result of this EC initiative; in the area of private consumption there is a 'competition between regulators' in fixing VAT and excise duties (p.322 above). A high-taxing State unwilling to accept the shortfall in tax revenues may choose to raise rates, but this risks provoking even higher levels of cross-border shopping. The alternative is a reduction in rates to competitive levels in order to remove the incentive to shop elsewhere. See M. McKelvey, 'Cheap Beer or Economic Harmony' (1995) XVIII *Boston College International and Comp Law Rev* 457. However, in commercial trade the tax differentials which persist between the Member States have led to the introduction of a scheme which requires collection of taxes, although not at physical borders. The scheme is found in Directives 92/12 [1992] OJ L76/1 and 92/108 [1992] OJ L390/124.

The technical nature of the subject of tax harmonization precludes exhaustive treatment in this book. However, issues of tax harmonization remain high profile, even though legislative progress has been relatively slow. The method chosen has typically been 'minimum harmonization'. States may not set rates lower than the Community minimum, though they may set higher rates. This reflects the political complexity of the subject – States are not prepared to allow their competence to set tax rates to be totally preempted by the Community and, illuminatingly, unanimous voting in Council remains the rule in the area of taxation. Minimum harmonization yields both a degree of harmonization and, above the minimum rate, a competition between regulators. This is to be observed in relation to value added tax and excise duties. On the latter, some progress was made in a package of Directives adopted in October 1992. Directives 92/79 and 92/80 [1992] OJ L316/8, 10 set minimum rates for cigarettes and other tobacco products respectively; Directives 92/81 and 92/82 [1992] OJ L316/12, 19 set minimum rates for petroleum products; Directives 92/83 and 92/84 [1992] OJ L316/21, 29 cover the harmonization of the structure and of the rates respectively of excise duties on alcoholic beverages. Minimum rates are set for beer, wine, and other defined categories of alcoholic beverage. The text below reveals the rather remarkable choice made of the minimum figure for excise rates levied on still and sparkling wine.

COUNCIL DIRECTIVE 92/84/EEC ON THE APPROXIMATION OF THE RATES OF EXCISE DUTY ON ALCOHOL AND ALCOHOLIC BEVERAGES
[1992] OJ L316/29

Article 1

Not later than 1 January 1993, Member States shall apply minimum rates of excise duty in accordance with the rules laid down in this Directive.

. . .

Article 5

As from 1 January 1993, the minimum rate of excise duty on wine shall be fixed:

 — for still wine at ECU 0, and
 — for sparkling wine at ECU 0

per hectolitre of product.

■ QUESTION

Is minimum harmonization of this type worthwhile? What alternatives are available to the EC in developing a tax policy for the internal market?

NOTE

At a much broader level, in December 1997 the Finance Ministers of the Member States in Council agreed to a package of measures designed to counter 'Harmful Tax Competition'. This was the result of a vigorous Commission initiative (COM (96) 546, COM (97) 564). Binding legislation within the meaning of Article 249 EC is not involved. A code of conduct on company taxation has been agreed, which includes a review process, and a commitment is made to consider new legislation on a minimum tax on savings income. Naturally, the title chosen for this initiative begs the delicate question of what is truly *harmful* competition and what are merely different choices about tax rates and policies. This is closely related to the intriguing issue of reconciling a 'competition between regulators' with the pursuit of a level playing field, introduced at p.322 above and further examined in Chapters 19 and 20. Furthermore, in order to site this new package in its wider legal context, it should be appreciated that tax concessions may in some circumstances fall foul of Article 87 EC governing State aids (p.527 below). The most recent overview of tax policy by the Commission may be found in COM (2001) 260, Commission Communication of 23 May 2001, *Tax Policy in the European Union – Priorities for the Years Ahead*. This and other relevant documentation may be tracked *via* http://europa.eu.int/comm/taxation_customs/taxation/genindex_en.htm

FURTHER READING

Bratton W., and McCahery, J., 'Tax Co-ordination and Tax Competition in the EU: Evaluating the Code of Conduct on Business Taxation' (2001) 38 CML Rev 677.

Farmer, P. and Lyal, R., *EC Tax Law* (Oxford: Clarendon Press, 1994).

Terra, B., and Wattel, P., *European Tax Law* (The Hague: Kluwer, 2002).

Vanistendael, F., 'The limits to the new Community tax order' (1994) 31 CML Rev 293.

See also for some consideration of the association of economic and monetary union with fiscal harmonization, D. McKay, 'Policy Legitimacy and Institutional Design' (2000) 38 JCMS 25.

NOTE

For additional material and resources see the Companion Website at: www.oup.co.uk/best.textbooks/law/weatherill6e

11

Physical and Technical Barriers to Trade: Articles 28–30

SECTION 1: **THE DEVELOPMENT OF ARTICLE 28**

The brevity of Article 28 is out of all proportion to its immense significance as an instrument for the creation of a market in which the free circulation of goods is ensured.

ARTICLE 28 EC

Quantitative restrictions on imports and all measures having equivalent effect shall be prohibited between Member States.

Article 29 applies a similarly worded prohibition to restrictions on exports.

Article 30 permits Member States to advance justifications for obstacles to trade contrary to Articles 28 and 29. Such purported justifications will be closely scrutinized, for they imply lawful trade barriers which handicap the pursuit of a common market.

Here, more than in most areas, it is vital to remember that pre-Amsterdam material contains pre-Amsterdam Treaty numbering (p.12 above). Articles 28 and 29 were Articles 30 and 34 respectively, while, in the most unfortunate of all the Amsterdam re-numberings, what is now Article 30 was previously Article 36. Remember this when reading the texts in this Chapter and the next.

Articles 28 and 29 on the one hand and Article 30 on the other, are provisions which seek to strike a balance between the impetus towards free trade and the acceptance that Member States retain a strictly defined competence lawfully to restrict free trade in order to protect certain important domestic interests. The interpretation and location of this balance by the judges is itself an interesting exercise in judicial assessment of competing interests. The Chapters which follow will frequently refer to the Court's role as an arbiter in this field. Eventually, however, restrictive national rules which remain justifiable may be replaced by Community rules which set common standards for the Community. This is the process of harmonization. It is designed to secure protection of important interests (as is Article 30), but (unlike Article 30) that protection is achieved within the framework of a Community, not a national, structure, which will permit and stimulate free cross-border trade.

The Court defined the 'quantitative restriction' in *Geddo* v *Ente* (Case 2/73) [1973] ECR 865, [1974] 1 CMLR 13, as 'measures which amount to a total or partial restraint of, according to the circumstances, imports, exports or goods in transit'.

But what of the measure 'having equivalent effect' to the quantitative restriction which, according to Article 28, also falls within the scope of the prohibition?

In *Geddo* v *Ente* (Case 2/73), the Court followed its definition of the quantitative restriction given above by stating briefly that 'measures having equivalent effect not only take the form of restraint described: whatever the description or technique employed, they can also consist of encumbrances having the same effect'.

Further elucidation of the notion may be found in Directive 70/50. Directive 70/50 was formally only of application to the transitional period of the Community's development, which has long since expired, and the relevant Treaty provisions in this area were repealed by the Treaty of Amsterdam. Yet its influence as an indication of the Commission's view of the scope of this Article of the EC Treaty has persisted and the Court continues to refer to it on occasion. The Directive is, then, a useful source of guidance on the nature of the practices which fall foul of the prohibition on 'MEQRs' (measures having equivalent effect to a quantitative restriction).

DIRECTIVE 70/50 EEC ON THE ABOLITION OF MEASURES WHICH HAVE AN EFFECT EQUIVALENT TO THE QUANTITATIVE RESTRICTIONS ON IMPORTS AND ARE NOT COVERED BY OTHER PROVISIONS ADOPTED IN PURSUANCE OF THE EEC TREATY
[1970] OJ (Special Edition) (I), p.17

Article 1
The purpose of this Directive is to abolish the measures referred to in Articles 2 and 3, which were operative at the date of entry into force of the EEC Treaty.

Article 2
1. This Directive covers measures, other than those applicable equally to domestic or imported products, which hinder imports which could otherwise take place, including measures which make importation more difficult or costly than the disposal of domestic production.

2. In particular, it covers measures which make imports or the disposal at any marketing stage, of imported products subject to a condition – other than a formality – which is required in respect of imported products only, or a condition differing from that required for domestic products and more difficult to satisfy. Equally, it covers, in particular, measures which favour domestic products or grant them a preference, other than an aid, to which conditions may or may not be attached.

3. The measures referred to must be taken to include those measures which:

   (a) lay down, for imported products only, minimum or maximum prices below or above which imports are prohibited, reduced or made subject to conditions liable to hinder importation;
   (b) lay down less favourable prices for imported products than for domestic products;
   (c) fix profit margins or any other price components for imported products only or fix these differently for domestic products and for imported products, to the detriment of the latter;
   (d) preclude any increase in the price of the imported product corresponding to the supplementary costs and charges inherent in importation;
   (e) fix the prices of products solely on the basis of the cost price or the quality of domestic products at such a level as to create a hindrance to importation;
   (f) lower the value of an imported product, in particular by causing a reduction in its intrinsic value, or increase its costs;
   (g) make access of imported products to the domestic market conditional upon having an agent or representative in the territory of the importing Member State;

(h) lay down conditions of payment in respect of imported products only, or subject imported products to conditions which are different from those laid down for domestic products and more difficult to satisfy;

(i) require, for imports only, the giving of guarantees or making of payments on account;

(j) subject imported products only to conditions, in respect, in particular of shape, size, weight, composition, presentation, identification or putting up, or subject imported products to conditions which are different from those for domestic products and more difficult to satisfy;

(k) hinder the purchase by private individuals of imported products only, or encourage, require or give preference to the purchase of domestic products only;

(l) totally or partially preclude the use of national facilities or equipment in respect of imported products only, or totally or partially confine the use of such facilities or equipment to domestic products only;

(m) prohibit or limit publicity in respect of imported products only, or totally or partially confine publicity to domestic products only;

(n) prohibit, limit or require stocking in respect of imported products only; totally or partially confine the use of stocking facilities to domestic products only, or make the stocking of imported products subject to conditions which are different from those required for domestic products and more difficult to satisfy;

(o) make importation subject to the granting of reciprocity by one or more Member States;

(p) prescribe that imported products are to conform, totally or partially, to rules other than those of the importing country;

(q) specify time limits for imported products which are insufficient or excessive in relation to the normal course of the various transactions to which these time limits apply;

(r) subject imported products to controls, other than those inherent in the customs clearance procedure, to which domestic products are not subject or which are stricter in respect of imported products than they are in respect of domestic products, without this being necessary in order to ensure equivalent protection;

(s) confine names which are not indicative of origin or source to domestic products only.

Article 3

This Directive also covers measures governing the marketing of products which deal, in particular, with shape, size, weight, composition, presentation, identification or putting up and which are equally applicable to domestic and imported products, where the restrictive effect of such measures on the free movement of goods exceeds the effects intrinsic to trade rules.

This is the case, in particular, where:

— the restrictive effects on the free movement of goods are out of proportion to their purpose;

— the same objective can be attained by other means which are less of a hindrance to trade.

NOTES

1. The Directive, then, discloses two types of 'MEQR' (measure having equivalent effect to a quantitative restriction), divided according to their application. Article 2 covers national rules which discriminate against imports, which are taken to infringe Article 28; Article 3 covers national rules which apply equally to all goods, which are taken normally to conform to the demands of Article 28.

2. The vigorous work of the Court has transformed Article 28 into a fundamentally important means of dismantling national barriers to the free movement of goods. The Court was naturally little confined by the explicit terms of the Treaty Article in building its approach, for the provision is of such brevity as to yield almost any interpretation. In its celebrated decision in *Dassonville* (Case 8/74) (p.344 below), the Court selected an interpretation of Article 28 which is firmly orientated towards market integration through the abolition of obstructive national rules.

The Court declared that Article 28 (then 30) prohibits as MEQRs 'all trading rules enacted by Member States which are capable of hindering, directly or indirectly, actually or potentially, intra-Community trade'. Article 28 has, according to Lord Cockfield, the Commissioner responsible for internal market policy in the 1980s, a 'magnificent sweep'.

On its literal terms, the *Dassonville* formula could even be taken to catch any national measure which circumscribes commercial freedom, even if neither discriminatory against imports nor protective of home production. The Court chose in *Keck and Mithouard* (Joined Cases C-267 and C-268/91) [1993] ECR I-6097, [1995] 1 CMLR 101, to refine the *Dassonville* formula in order to make it clear that Article 28 cannot be invoked where the rule in question impedes trade in imported goods no more than it impedes trade in domestic goods. The Court stated that 'the application to products from other Member States of national provisions restricting or prohibiting certain selling arrangements is not such as to hinder, directly or indirectly, actually or potentially, trade between Member States, provided that the provisions apply to all affected traders operating within the national territory and provided that they affect in the same manner, in law and in fact, the marketing of domestic products and those from other Member States'. The implications of the cautious *Keck* ruling, and its requirement of legal or factual inequality as a threshold to the application of Article 28, are examined more fully at p.397 below.

At the heart of the Court's declaration in *Dassonville* is the perception that the application of the Article 28 prohibition is dependent on the *effects* of the measure. Article 28 bites where a national rule is shown to have an effect prejudicial to the integration of the markets of the Member States.

3. The Court's emphasis differs from that in Directive 70/50. Discrimination is *not* the key. Unequal treatment of domestic and imported goods is likely to violate Article 28 because of the consequential restrictive effect on cross-border trade, but such discrimination is plainly not a pre-condition for the application of Article 28. The essential element is *the restrictive effect on inter-State trade*.

Procureur du Roi v *Dassonville* (Case 8/74)
[1974] ECR 837, [1974] 2 CMLR 436, Court of Justice of the European Communities

The Court indicated that a Belgian requirement that importers of Scotch whisky possess a British certificate of authentication was incompatible with Article 30 of the EC Treaty (now, after amendment, Article 28 EC). The rule favoured direct importers over traders importing Scotch whisky into Belgium from other Member States in which the goods were already in free circulation. The rule 'channelled' trade and distorted the market.

[1] By Judgment of 11 January 1974, received at the Registry of the Court on 8 February 1974, the Tribunal de Première Instance of Brussels referred, under Article 177 of the EEC Treaty, two questions on the interpretation of Articles 30, 31, 32, 33, 36 and 85 of the EEC Treaty, relating to the require-ment of an official document issued by the government of the exporting country for products bearing a designation of origin.

[2] By the first question it is asked whether a national provision prohibiting the import of goods bearing a designation of origin where such goods are not accompanied by an official docu-ment issued by the government of the exporting country certifying their right to such designation constitutes a measure having an effect equivalent to a quantitative restriction within the meaning of Article 30 of the Treaty.

[3] This question was raised within the context of criminal proceedings instituted in Belgium against traders who duly acquired a consignment of Scotch whisky in free circulation in France and imported it into Belgium without being in possession of a certificate of origin from the British customs authorities, thereby infringing Belgian rules.

[4] It emerges from the file and from the oral proceedings that a trader, wishing to import into

Belgium Scotch whisky which is already in free circulation in France, can obtain such a certificate only with great difficulty, unlike the importer who imports directly from the producer country.

[5] All trading rules enacted by Member States which are capable of hindering, directly or indirectly, actually or potentially, intra-Community trade are to be considered as measures having an effect equivalent to quantitative restrictions.

[6] In the absence of a Community system guaranteeing for consumers the authenticity of a product's designation of origin, if a Member State takes measures to prevent unfair practices in this connexion, it is however subject to the condition that these measures should be reasonable and that the means of proof required should not act as a hindrance to trade between Member States and should, in consequence, be accessible to all Community nationals.

[7] Even without having to examine whether or not such measures are covered by Article 36, they must not, in any case, by virtue of the principle expressed in the second sentence of that Article, constitute a means of arbitrary discrimination or a disguised restriction on trade between Member States.

[8] That may be the case with formalities, required by a Member State for the purpose of proving the origin of a product, which only direct importers are really in a position to satisfy without facing serious difficulties.

[9] Consequently, the requirement by a Member State of a certificate of authenticity which is less easily obtainable by importers of an authentic product which has been put into free circulation in a regular manner in another Member State than by importers of the same product coming directly from the country of origin constitutes a measure having an effect equivalent to a quantitative restriction as prohibited by the Treaty.

■ QUESTION

What is meant by the Court's suggestion in para 6 that 'reasonable' measures would not infringe Article 28 (then Article 30)? Could the Belgian authorities have devised an authentication system compatible with Article 28? (The issue of locating the limit to the scope of Article 28 as a means of challenging trade restrictions will be readdressed in the next Chapter.)

NOTES

1. The fundamental aim of Article 28 is to preclude the isolation of national markets and thereby to induce efficient competition irrespective of the existence of national frontiers. Competition yields consumer choice, lower prices, and higher quality. In this way the benefits of a common market are realised. The economic advantages were discussed more generally in Chapter 9.
2. It is not misleading to view the Court's activism in this area as judicial lawmaking. This integrationist jurisprudence finds little explicit basis in the Treaty or in secondary legislation. Yet implied support exists. The Court has moulded its conception of Article 28 in accordance with the objects of the Treaty. The objective of market integration and, eventually, the establishment of a common market, provide the inspiration for the development of appropriate substantive rules of law. Just as Part One of this book showed how the Court was not constrained by the absence of explicit instruction in the Treaty from eliciting the constitutional doctrines of supremacy and direct effect as the pillars of the Community's legal order in order to achieve the objectives of the Treaty, so too in the area of substantive law the Court is prepared to construct a body of interpretation which is loosely derived from Article 28, but which, more significantly, is justified as a method of bringing to fruition the Treaty objective of market integration.
3. This approach is certainly distinct from that of the English judges. The traditional English technique is to follow rules laid down with more precision than is the style of the Treaty of Rome. Judicial development of codified law is less readily acknowledged as either familiar or appropriate in the UK.

R v *Secretary of State, ex parte Bomore*

[1986] 1 CMLR 228, Court of Appeal

MAY LJ: [The European] Court adopts an approach substantially different from that familiar to lawyers in this country . . . the Court of Justice in its decisions on Article 30 has sought both to flesh it out and at the same time to limit its apparent generality so as to produce, by a process of judge-made legislation, a developing code of law, founded upon Article 30.

■ QUESTIONS

1. Should English judges adopt a more purposive or, perhaps, creative approach (i) in interpreting Community law, (ii) in interpreting domestic law? (Remember the discussion of the implications of *Von Colson* (Case 14/83) and *Marleasing* (Case C-106/89) in Chapter 5.)

   You might read Chapter 8 on 'Judicial Creativity' in J. Griffith's *The Politics of the Judiciary* (London: Fontana, 1997), and consider how the debate there presented might be applied to the development of Community law.

2. Can you think of any examples from any area of Community law where the European Court has adopted an unduly activist, creative stance which has failed to command respect? Are there cases which demonstrate caution about the perils of judicial overeagerness? Read generally H. Rasmussen, *On Law and Policy in the ECJ* (Dordrecht: Martinus Nijhoff, 1986) and K. Alter, *Establishing the Supremacy of European Law* (Oxford: OUP, 2001), and reconsider some of the material in Part One of this book.

SECTION 2: **THE APPLICATION OF ARTICLE 28**

Examples of the application of Article 28 follow. The consistent theme is the breadth of Article 28 as a prohibition on national measures which have an effect which is restrictive of trade between Member States. In reading these cases, remember that prior to the re-numbering effected by the Amsterdam Treaty, what is now Article 28 EC was, with minor amendment, Article 30; and what is now Article 30 EC was Article 36.

Schloh v *Auto Controle Technique* (Case 50/85)

[1986] ECR 1855, Court of Justice of the European Communities

Mr Schloh bought a Ford Granada estate car in Germany. He obtained from a Ford dealer in Belgium a certificate of conformity with vehicle types approved in Belgium. In Belgium he was required to submit his car to two roadworthiness tests, for which fees were charged. He challenged the tests on the basis of Article 30 (now 28), the fees on the basis of Article 13 (now deleted). (See Chapter 10 on fiscal charges.) The matter reached the European Court by way of a preliminary reference from a Belgian court (see Chapter 7). The Court summed up the questions referred as follows:

[9] It is apparent from the terms of those questions that the Court is being asked in substance:

(a) first, whether it is in accordance with Article 30 of the Treaty for a car imported from another Member State and carrying a certificate of conformity to the vehicle types approved in the importing Member State to be subject to a roadworthiness test for the purposes of registration in the latter State;

(b) secondly, whether it is in accordance with Article 30 of the Treaty for the same car to be subject to a second roadworthiness test carried out a few days after the first test;

(c) thirdly, whether it is in accordance with Article 13 of the Treaty for a fee to be levied at the time of each roadworthiness test.

The first roadworthiness test

[10] The Danish Government and the Commission take the view that national measures whereby a new imported vehicle carrying a certificate of conformity to the safety standards of the importing Member State is subject to a roadworthiness test constitute measures having an effect equivalent to quantitative restrictions contrary to Article 30 of the Treaty; moreover, they are not justified by any of the imperative requirements referred to in the judgments of the Court or any of the reasons enumerated in Article 36 of the Treaty. However, the Danish Government states that where the vehicle is imported in a used condition a roadworthiness test may be justified by the need to check at least its state of repair.

[11] It should be noted first of all that, although Council Directive 77/143/EEC of 29 December 1976 (Official Journal 1977, L 47, p.47) laid down a number of measures for the harmonization of roadworthiness tests for motor vehicles, the terms of Annex I to the directive make it inapplicable to vehicles in the category to which the plaintiff's vehicle belongs. At this stage in the development of Community law it is therefore for the Member States – provided that they comply with the provisions of the Treaty – to lay down rules for the roadworthiness testing of vehicles in that category in order to ensure road safety.

[12] Under the terms of Article 30 of the Treaty, quantitative restrictions on imports and all measures having equivalent effect are prohibited between Member States. Roadworthiness testing is a formality which makes the registration of imported vehicles more difficult and more onerous and consequently is in the nature of a measure having an effect equivalent to a quantitative restriction.

[13] Nevertheless, Article 36 may justify such a formality on grounds of the protection of human health and life, provided that it is established, first, that the test at issue is necessary for the attainment of that objective and, secondly, that it does not constitute a means of arbitrary discrimination or a disguised restriction on trade between Member States.

[14] As far as the first condition is concerned, it must be acknowledged that roadworthiness testing required prior to the registration of an imported vehicle may, even though the vehicle carries a certificate of conformity to the vehicle types approved in the importing Member State, be regarded as necessary for the protection of human health and life where the vehicle in question has already been put on the road. In such cases roadworthiness testing performs a useful function inasmuch as it makes it possible to check that the vehicle has not been damaged and is in a good state of repair. However, such testing cannot be justified on those grounds where it relates to an imported vehicle carrying a certificate of conformity which has not been placed on the road before being registered in the importing Member State.

[15] As far as the second condition is concerned, it must be stated that the roadworthiness testing of imported vehicles cannot, however, be justified under the second sentence of Article 36 of the Treaty if it is established that such testing is not required in the case of vehicles of national origin presented for registration in the same circumstances. If that were the case it would become apparent that the measure in question was not in fact inspired by a concern for the protection of human health and life but in reality constituted a means of arbitrary discrimination in trade between Member States. It is for the national court to verify that such non-discriminatory treatment is in fact ensured.

[16] It must therefore be stated in reply to the juge de paix of Schaerbeek that Article 30 of the Treaty must be interpreted as meaning that a national measure which requires a roadworthiness test for the purpose of registering an imported vehicle carrying a certificate of its conformity to the vehicle types approved in the importing Member State constitutes a measure having an effect equivalent to

a quantitative restriction on imports. Nevertheless, such a measure is justified under Article 36 of the Treaty in so far as it relates to vehicles put on the road before such registration and applies without distinction to vehicles of national origin and imported vehicles.

The second roadworthiness test

[17] The Commission, which was alone in presenting observations on this point, takes the view that the second test, being imposed for the purpose of exempting the vehicle from regular annual testing for the first four years, constitutes a measure having equivalent effect contrary to Article 30 of the Treaty and not justified by Article 36. In that connection the Commission notes that an exemption from regular annual tests could have been obtained simply by means of a declaration concerning the use of the vehicle made on the occasion of the first roadworthiness test.

[18] It should be pointed out that, as the Court has consistently held, national rules cannot benefit from an exception provided for by Article 36 of the Treaty if the objective pursued by that exception can be as effectively realised by measures which do not restrict intra-Community trade so much.

[19] It must consequently be accepted that Article 36 does not provide justification for road-worthiness testing whose purpose is to obtain from the owner of the imported vehicle a written declaration certifying that the use of the vehicle qualifies it for exemption from annual testing. That purpose may be achieved simply by requiring the owner to supply that written declaration, without its being necessary for the vehicle to be presented to an approved vehicle testing agency.

[20] It must therefore be stated in reply to the question put by the juge de paix of Schaerbeek that Articles 30 and 36 of the Treaty must be interpreted as meaning that, where the roadworthiness testing of an imported vehicle has the purpose of obtaining a written declaration from the owner of the vehicle, it constitutes a measure having an effect equivalent to a quantitative restriction on imports contrary to the Treaty.

The Court held the fees unlawful where the test itself violated Article 30 (now 28), but capable of accommodation within a general system of taxation compatible with Article 95 (now 90) where the inspection itself was lawful under Article 36 (now 30).

NOTES
1. Notice how (para 11) the Court observes that the matter is untouched by the Community's harmonization programme and that therefore the Treaty alone supplies the basis for judging the permissibility of Member State action. The legal assessment would be different if (as is increasingly common in many sectors) the field had been entered by Community secondary legislation; p.378 below.
2. See also Case C-55/93 *Criminal Proceedings against Johannis Gerrit Cornelis van Schaik* [1994] ECR I-4837, in which the Court held that neither primary Treaty provisions including Article 28 nor Directive 77/143 preclude legislation of a Member State which does not permit test certificates in respect of cars registered in that State to be issued by garages established in another Member State.

International Fruit Company v *Produktschap voor Groenten en Fruit (No 2)* (Cases 51–54/71)
[1971] ECR 1107, Court of Justice of the European Communities

The Court was asked to consider whether Article 30 of the EC Treaty (now, after amendment, Article 28 EC) applies to 'national legislative provisions prohibiting imports and exports without a licence but which in fact are not applied because exemptions are granted from the prohibition and, where this is not so, because the licence is always issued on request'.

[6] The question put refers both to the system of quantitative restrictions on intra-Community trade and the system of such restrictions on trade with third countries.

[7] It is however clear from the scheme of the Treaty that those two systems must be distinguished.

[8] Under Articles 30 and 34(1) of the Treaty quantitative restrictions and measures having equivalent effect are prohibited between Member States both with regard to imports and exports.

[9] Consequently, apart from the exceptions for which provision is made by Community law itself those provisions preclude the application to intra-Community trade of a national provision which requires, even purely as a formality, import or export licences or any other similar procedure.

NOTE
The Court concluded its judgment by taking a more permissive view of the lawfulness of controls over trade with third countries outside the Community.

In *Commission* v *Italy* (Case 159/78) the Court accepted the opportunity to declare its view of the application of Article 30 of the EC Treaty (now, after amendment, Article 28 EC) to customs formalities at frontiers which impede intra-Community trade.

Commission v *Italy* (Case 159/78)
[1979] ECR 3247, [1980] 3 CMLR 446, Court of Justice of the European Communities

[7] As regards intra-Community trade, since all customs duties on imports and exports and all charges having equivalent effect and all quantitative restrictions on imports and exports and measures having equivalent effect had to be abolished, pursuant to Title I of the Treaty, by the end of the transitional period at the latest, it should be emphasised that customs controls properly so-called have lost their *raison d'être* as regards such trade. Frontier controls remain justified only in so far as they are necessary either for the implementation of the exceptions to free movement referred to in Article 36 of the Treaty; or for the levying of internal taxation within the meaning of Article 95 of the Treaty when the crossing of the frontier may legitimately be assimilated to the situation which, in the case of domestic goods, gives rise to the levying of the tax; or for transit controls; or finally when they are essential in order to obtain reasonably complete and accurate information on movement of goods within the Community. These residuary controls must nevertheless be reduced as far as possible so that trade between Member States can take place in conditions as close as possible to those prevalent on a domestic market.

NOTE
The final sentence is to some extent a statement of the Community's overall objective.

The completion of, initially, an internal market and, subsequently, a common market (Chapter 9) requires the creation of common Community rules to deal with problems of this nature without the need to impose impediments to cross-frontier trade. The realisation of Article 14's 'area without internal frontiers' demands a deeper intrusion into national competence than is envisaged in the above extract. Community legislation of this nature will be discussed further below.

Most of the cases considered so far involve controls imposed at frontiers. Such barriers are by definition applicable only to imports and therefore discriminatory. However, there is a further large category of discriminatory measures also caught by Article 28. These are measures which involve discrimination against imports once they have reached the market of the State of destination. The discrimination may apply at a different stage in the marketing chain, but the restrictive effect on inter-State trade is equally apparent.

Commission v *Ireland* (Case 113/80)
[1981] ECR 1625, [1982] 1 CMLR 706, Court of Justice of the European Communities

[1] By an application lodged at the Court Registry on 28 April 1980, the Commission instituted proceedings under Article 169 of the EEC Treaty, for a declaration that Ireland had failed to fulfil its

obligations under Article 30 of the EEC Treaty by requiring that the imported goods falling within the scope of the Merchandise Marks (Restriction on Sale of Imported Jewellery) Order 1971 (SI No 306, Iris Oifigiúil of 21 November 1971) and the Merchandise Marks (Restriction on Importation of Jewellery) Order 1971 (SI No 307, Iris Oifigiúil of 21 November 1971) bear an indication of origin or the word 'foreign'.

[2] According to the explanatory notes thereto, Statutory Instrument No 306 (hereinafter referred to as 'the Sale Order') prohibits the sale or exposure for sale of imported articles of jewellery depicting motifs or possessing characteristics which suggest that they are souvenirs of Ireland, for example an Irish character, event or scene, wolfhound, round tower, shamrock etc. and Statutory Instrument No 307 (hereinafter referred to as 'the Importation Order') prohibits the importation of such articles unless, in either case, they bear an indication of their country of origin or the word 'foreign'.

[3] The articles concerned are listed in a schedule to each order. However, in order to come within the scope of the orders the article must be made of precious metal or rolled precious metal or of base metal, including polished or plated articles suitable for setting.

[4] In the Commission's opinion, the restrictions on the free movement of the goods covered by the two orders constitute measures having an effect equivalent to quantitative restrictions on imports, contrary to the provisions of Article 30 of the EEC Treaty; it also observes that according to Article 2(3)(f) of Directive 70/50/EEC of 22 December 1969, based on the provisions of Article 33(7) of the Treaty, on the abolition of measures which have an effect equivalent to quantitative restrictions on imports and are not covered by other provisions adopted in pursuance of the EEC Treaty (Official Journal, English Special Edition 1970 (I), p.17) 'measures which lower the value of an imported product, in particular by causing a reduction in its intrinsic value, or increase its costs' must be regarded as measures having an effect equivalent to quantitative restrictions, contrary to Article 30 of the EEC Treaty.

[5] The Irish Government does not dispute the restrictive effects of these orders on the free movement of goods. However, it contends that the disputed measures are justified in the interests of consumer protection and of fairness in commercial transactions between producers. In this regard, it relies upon Article 36 of the Treaty which provides that Articles 30 to 34 shall not preclude prohibitions or restrictions on imports justified on grounds of public policy or the protection of industrial and commercial property.

[6] The defendant is, however, mistaken in placing reliance on Article 36 of the Treaty as the legal basis for its contention.

[7] In fact, since the Court stated in its judgment of 25 January 1977 in Case 46/76 *Bauhuis* [1977] ECR 5 that Article 36 of the Treaty 'constitutes a derogation from the basic rule that all obstacles to the free movement of goods between Member States shall be eliminated and must be interpreted strictly', the exceptions listed therein cannot be extended to cases other than those specifically laid down.

[8] In view of the fact that neither the protection of consumers nor the fairness of commercial transactions is included amongst the exceptions set out in Article 36, those grounds cannot be relied upon as such in connexion with that article.

[9] However, since the Irish Government describes its recourse to these concepts as 'the central issue in the case', it is necessary to study this argument in connexion with Article 30 and to consider whether it is possible, in reliance on those concepts, to say that the Irish orders are not measures having an effect equivalent to quantitative restrictions on imports within the meaning of that article, bearing in mind that, according to the established case-law of the Court, such measures include 'all trading rules enacted by Member States which are capable of hindering, directly or indirectly, actually or potentially, intra-Community trade' (judgment of 11 July 1974 in Case 8/74 *Dassonville* [1974] ECR 837).

[10] In this respect, the Court has repeatedly affirmed (in the judgments of 20 February 1979 in Case 120/78 *REWE* [1979] ECR 649, 26 June 1980 in Case 788/79 *Gilli and Andres* [1980] ECR 2071,

19 February 1981 in Case 130/80 *Kelderman* [1981] ECR) that 'in the absence of common rules relating to the production and marketing of the product in question it is for Member States to regulate all matters relating to its production, distribution and consumption on their own territory subject, however, to the condition that those rules do not present an obstacle . . . to intra-Community trade' and that 'it is only where national rules, which apply without discrimination to both domestic and imported products, may be justified as being necessary in order to satisfy imperative requirements relating in particular to . . . the fairness of commercial transactions and the defence of the consumer that they may constitute an exception to the requirements arising under Article 30'.

[11] The orders concerned in the present case are not measures which are applicable to domestic products and to imported products without distinction but rather a set of rules which apply only to imported products and are therefore discriminatory in nature, with the result that the measures in issue are not covered by the decisions cited above which relate exclusively to provisions that regulate in a uniform manner the marketing of domestic products and imported products.

[12] The Irish Government recognises that the contested measures apply solely to imported articles and render their importation and sale more difficult than the sale of domestic products. However, it maintains that this difference in the treatment awarded to home-produced articles and to imported articles does not constitute discrimination on the ground that the articles referred to in the contested orders consist mainly of souvenirs; the appeal of such articles lies essentially in the fact of their being manufactured in the place where they are purchased and they bear in themselves an implied indication of their Irish origin, with the result that the purchaser would be misled if the souvenir bought in Ireland was manufactured elsewhere. Consequently, the requirement that all imported 'souvenirs' covered by the two orders must bear an indication of origin is justified and in no way constitutes discrimination because the articles concerned are different on account of the differences between their essential characteristics.

[13] The Commission rejects this reasoning. In reliance on the judgment of 20 February 1975 in Case 12/74 *Commission* v *Federal Republic of Germany* [1975] ECR 191, it submits that it is unnecessary for a purchaser to know whether or not a product is of a particular origin, unless such origin implies a certain quality, basic materials or process of manufacture or a particular place in the folklore or tradition of the region in question; since none of the articles referred to in the orders display these features, the measures in question cannot be justified and are therefore 'overtly discriminatory'.

[14] It is therefore necessary to consider whether the contested measures are indeed discriminatory or whether they constitute discrimination in appearance only.

[15] The souvenirs referred to in the Sale Order and in the Importation Order are generally articles of ornamentation of little commercial value representing or incorporating a motif or emblem which is reminiscent of an Irish place, object, character or historical event or suggestive of an Irish symbol and their value stems from the fact that the purchaser, more often than not a tourist, buys them on the spot. The essential characteristic of the souvenirs in question is that they constitute a pictorial reminder of the place visited which does not by itself mean that a souvenir, as defined in the orders, must necessarily be manufactured in the country of origin.

[16] Furthermore, leaving aside the point argued by the Commission – with regard to the articles covered by the contested orders – that it would not be enough to require a statement of origin to be affixed to domestic products also, it is important to note that the interests of consumers and fair trading would be adequately safeguarded if it were left to domestic manufacturers to take appropriate steps such as affixing, if they so wished, their mark of origin to their own products or packaging.

[17] Thus by granting souvenirs imported from other Member States access to the domestic market solely on condition that they bear a statement of origin, whilst no such statement is required in the case of domestic products, the provisions contained in the Sale Order and the Importation Order indisputably constitute a discriminatory measure.

[18] The conclusion to be drawn therefore is that by requiring all souvenirs and articles of jewellery imported from other Member States which are covered by the Sale Order and the Importation Order

to bear an indication of origin or the word 'foreign', the Irish rules constitute a measure having equivalent effect within the meaning of Article 30 of the EEC Treaty. Ireland has consequently failed to fulfil its obligations under the article.

Commission v *UK* (Case 207/83)

[1985] ECR 1202, [1985] 2 CMLR 259, Court of Justice of the European Communities

[1] By an application lodged at the Court Registry on 15 September 1983 the Commission of the European Communities brought an action before the Court under Article 169 of the EEC Treaty for a declaration that, by prohibiting the retail sale of certain goods imported from other Member States unless they are marked with or accompanied by an indication of origin, the United Kingdom has failed to fulfil an obligation incumbent on it under Article 30 of the EEC Treaty.

[2] The national legislation challenged by the Commission is the Trade Descriptions (Origin Marking) (Miscellaneous Goods) Order 1981 (Statutory Instrument 1981 No 121) which entered into force on 1 January 1982.

[3] Article 2 of that Order provides that no person may supply or offer to supply by retail the goods listed in the Schedule to the Order, other than second-hand goods and goods supplied in certain special circumstances, unless the goods are marked with or accompanied by an indication of origin. In a case in which the goods are exposed for supply and the indication of origin would not be conveyed until after delivery, such an indication must also be displayed near the goods. The indication of origin must be clear and legible; it must not in any way be hidden or obscured or reduced in conspicuousness by any other matter, whether pictorial or not.

[4] According to Article 1 of the Order, the 'origin' of goods means 'the country in which the goods were manufactured or produced'.

[5] The Schedule to the Order lists the goods to which the Order applies. Those goods are divided into four categories: clothing and textile goods, domestic electrical appliances, footwear and cutlery.

. . .

[13] The United Kingdom's defence is in substance limited to developing the two arguments which it has already put forward during the procedure prior to the application to the Court. First, it contends that the Order is a national measure which applies to imported and national products alike and the effect of which on trade between Member States is uncertain, if not non-existent. Secondly, it maintains that, in the case of the goods to which the Order applies, the requirements relating to indications of origin meet the requirements of consumer protection since consumers regard the origin of the goods which they buy as an indicator of their quality or true value.

[14] Those two arguments must be examined in turn.

[15] As regards the possible effect of the contested Order on trade, the United Kingdom points out that the requirements laid down in Article 2 of the Order concern the retail sale of all the goods covered by the Order, whether imported or not. Some of those goods, for example woollen knitwear and cutlery, are produced in the United Kingdom in substantial quantities.

[16] It should first be observed, with regard to that argument, that in order to escape the obligations imposed on him by the legislation in question the retailer will tend, as the Commission has rightly pointed out, to ask his wholesalers to supply him with goods which are already origin-marked. That tendency has been confirmed by complaints received by the Commission. Thus, it emerges from the documents before the Court that the Groupement des industries françaises des appareils déquipe-ment ménager [French Domestic Appliance Manufacturers' Association] informed the Commission that French manufacturers of domestic appliances who wish to sell their products on the United Kingdom market have had to mark such products systematically in response to pressure brought to bear on them by their distributors. The effects of the contested provisions are therefore liable to spread to the wholesale trade and even to manufacturers.

[17] Secondly, it has to be recognised that the purpose of indications of origin or origin-marking is to

enable consumers to distinguish between domestic and imported products and that this enables them to assert any prejudices which they may have against foreign products. As the Court has had occasion to emphasise in various contexts, the Treaty, by establishing a common market and progressively approximating the economic policies of the Member States seeks to unite national markets in a single market having the characteristics of a domestic market. Within such a market, the origin-marking requirement not only makes the marketing in a Member State of goods produced in other Member States in the sectors in question more difficult; it also has the effect of slowing down economic interpenetration in the Community by handicapping the sale of goods produced as the result of a division of labour between Member States.

[18] It follows from those considerations that the United Kingdom provisions in question are liable to have the effect of increasing the production costs of imported goods and making it more difficult to sell them on the United Kingdom market.

[19] The second argument advanced by the United Kingdom is in effect that the contested legislation, applicable without distinction to domestic and imported products, is necessary in order to satisfy imperative requirements relating to consumer protection. It states that a survey carried out amongst United Kingdom consumers has shown that they associate the quality of certain goods with the countries in which they are made. They like to know, for example, whether leather shoes have been made in Italy, woollen knitwear in the United Kingdom, fashion-wear in France and domestic electrical appliances in Germany.

[20] That argument must be rejected. The requirements relating to the indication of origin of goods are applicable without distinction to domestic and imported products only in form because, by their very nature, they are intended to enable the consumer to distinguish between those two categories of products, which may thus prompt him to give his preference to national products.

[21] It must also be observed that the fact that United Kingdom consumers associate a product's quality with its national origin does not appear to have been a consideration which prompted the United Kingdom Government when it suggested to the Commission that, as far as the Member States of the Community were concerned, it was prepared to accept the indication 'Made in the European Community'. Besides, if the national origin of goods brings certain qualities to the minds of consumers, it is in manufacturers' interests to indicate it themselves on the goods or on their packaging and it is not necessary to compel them to do so. In that case, the protection of consumers is sufficiently guaranteed by rules which enable the use of false indications of origin to be prohibited. Such rules are not called in question by the EEC Treaty.

[22] Those considerations lead to the conclusion that Article 2 of the Order constitutes a measure which makes the marketing of goods imported from other Member States more difficult than the marketing of domestically-produced goods and for which Community law does not recognise any ground of justification. That provision therefore falls within the prohibition laid down in Article 30 of the EEC Treaty.

[23] It must therefore be declared that, by prohibiting the retail sale of certain goods imported from other Member States unless they are marked with or accompanied by an indication of origin, the United Kingdom has failed to fulfil an obligation incumbent on it under Article 30 of the EEC Treaty.

NOTE

Notice that para 17 of the judgment in this case envisages a rather extended notion of discrimination.

In *Commission* v *UK* (Case 207/83), the UK had at an earlier stage in its negotiations with the Commission suggested that it would be prepared to amend its law in order to allow a choice between indicating national origin or marking the item 'Made in the European Community'. The Commission was not dissuaded by this suggestion from bringing the matter before the Court. Paragraph 21 of the Court's judgment shows that this concession ultimately weakened the UK's case.

■ QUESTION

Could a Member State require all products marketed in its territory to carry a 'Made in the EC' label?

Commission v *France* (Case 21/84)
[1985] ECR 1356, Court of Justice of the European Communities

The Commission alleged that France had violated Article 30 of the EC Treaty (now, after amendment, Article 28 EC) by refusing to approve postal franking machines from other Member States. The action arose out of a complaint to the Commission by a British manufacturer which, despite repeated applications, had failed to secure the approval of the French authorities, even after France had eliminated an earlier law which explicitly envisaged a preference for domestic machines.

[11] The fact that a law or regulation such as that requiring prior approval for the marketing of postal franking machines conforms in formal terms to Article 30 of the EEC Treaty is not sufficient to discharge a Member State of its obligations under that provision. Under the cloak of a general provision permitting the approval of machines imported from other Member States, the administration might very well adopt a systematically unfavourable attitude towards imported machines, either by allowing considerable delay in replying to applications for approval or in carrying out the examination procedure, or by refusing approval on the grounds of various alleged technical faults for which no detailed explanations are given or which prove to be inaccurate.

[12] The prohibition on measures having an effect equivalent to quantitative restrictions would lose much of its useful effect if it did not cover protectionist or discriminatory practices of that type.

[13] It must however be noted that for an administrative practice to constitute a measure prohibited under Article 30 that practice must show a certain degree of consistency and generality. That generality must be assessed differently according to whether the market concerned is one on which there are numerous traders or whether it is a market, such as that in postal franking machines, on which only a few undertakings are active. In the latter case, a national administration's treatment of a single undertaking may constitute a measure incompatible with Article 30.

[14] In the light of those principles it is clear from the facts of the case that the conduct of the French postal administration constitutes an impediment to imports contrary to Article 30 of the EEC Treaty.

[15] It must therefore be concluded that by refusing without proper justification to approve postal franking machines from another Member State, the French Republic has failed to fulfil its obligations under Article 30 of the EEC Treaty.

NOTE
Read a casenote by L. Gormley (1985) 10 EL Rev 449.

■ QUESTIONS

1. What is a measure, what is a mere isolated act, for the purposes of the application of Article 28? Why did the Court consider the structure of the market relevant in the case of the refusal to authorize postal franking machines (para 13)?

2. Consider whether the following are capable of falling within Article 28:

    (a) The determined policy adopted by an official at Dover as a result of personal prejudice to obstruct wherever possible the importation of goods originating in Greece. Would it make any difference if the officer's superiors turned a blind eye to these practices?

(b) A party political broadcast on behalf of the Government declaring an intent 'to protect British interests by stopping importers of foodstuffs thinking they can enjoy a free-for-all on the UK marketplace'.

NOTE

In the next case, the Court is astute to maintain a broad approach in defining the 'measure' susceptible to control under Article 28. The dispute related to the alleged passive approach of the French authorities in the face of actions such as the interception of lorries transporting imported fruit and vegetables in France and the destruction of their loads, violence against lorry drivers, and threats against French supermarkets selling imported agricultural products.

Commission v *France* (Case C-265/95)

[1997] ECR I-6959, Court of Justice of the European Communities

[24] In order to determine whether the Commission's action is well founded, it should be stressed from the outset that the free movement of goods is one of the fundamental principles of the Treaty.

[25] Article 3(c) of the EC Treaty provides that, for the purposes set out in Article 2, the activities of the Community are to include an internal market characterized by the abolition, as between Member States, of, *inter alia*, obstacles to the free movement of goods

[26] Pursuant to the second paragraph of Article 7a of the EC Treaty, the internal market is to comprise an area without internal frontiers in which the free movement of goods is ensured in accordance with the provisions of the Treaty.

[27] That fundamental principle is implemented by Article 30 et seq. of the Treaty.

[28] In particular, Article 30 provides that quantitative restrictions on imports and all measures having equivalent effect are prohibited between Member States.

[29] That provision, taken in its context, must be understood as being intended to eliminate all barriers, whether direct or indirect, actual or potential, to flows of imports in intra-Community trade.

[30] As an indispensable instrument for the realisation of a market without internal frontiers, Article 30 therefore does not prohibit solely measures emanating from the State which, in themselves, create restrictions on trade between Member States. It also applies where a Member State abstains from adopting the measures required in order to deal with obstacles to the free movement of goods which are not caused by the State.

[31] The fact that a Member State abstains from taking action or, as the case may be, fails to adopt adequate measures to prevent obstacles to the free movement of goods that are created, in particular, by actions by private individuals on its territory aimed at products originating in other Member States is just as likely to obstruct intra-Community trade as is a positive act.

[32] Article 30 therefore requires the Member States not merely themselves to abstain from adopting measures or engaging in conduct liable to constitute an obstacle to trade but also, when read with Article 5 of the Treaty, to take all necessary and appropriate measures to ensure that that fundamental freedom is respected on their territory.

[33] In the latter context, the Member States, which retain exclusive competence as regards the maintenance of public order and the safeguarding of internal security, unquestionably enjoy a margin of discretion in determining what measures are most appropriate to eliminate barriers to the importation of products in a given situation.

[34] It is therefore not for the Community institutions to act in place of the Member States and to prescribe for them the measures which they must adopt and effectively apply in order to safeguard the free movement of goods on their territories.

[35] However, it falls to the Court, taking due account of the discretion referred to above, to verify, in cases brought before it, whether the Member State concerned has adopted appropriate measures for ensuring the free movement of goods.

The Court proceeded from this statement of legal principle to determine that the violent acts had created obstacles to intra-Community trade; and that France had failed to meet its legal obligations to respond. In reaching this conclusion, the Court referred to:

— the duration of the incidents (which had been occurring regularly for more than 10 years);

— failure of the French police to attend, despite the fact that in certain cases the competent authorities had been warned of the imminence of demonstrations by farmers, or, even if present, to intervene, even where they far outnumbered the perpetrators;

— the fact that although a number of acts of attacks by identifiable individuals were filmed by television cameras, a very small number of persons had been identified and prosecuted.

[52] In the light of all the foregoing factors, the Court, while not discounting the difficulties faced by the competent authorities in dealing with situations of the type in question in this case, cannot but find that, having regard to the frequency and seriousness of the incidents cited by the Commission, the measures adopted by the French Government were manifestly inadequate to ensure freedom of intra-Community trade in agricultural products on its territory by preventing and effectively dissuading the perpetrators of the offences in question from committing and repeating them.

[53] That finding is all the more compelling since the damage and threats to which the Commission refers not only affect the importation into or transit in France of the products directly affected by the violent acts, but are also such as to create a climate of insecurity which has a deterrent effect on trade flows as a whole.

[54] The above finding is in no way affected by the French Government's argument that the situation of French farmers was so difficult that there were reasonable grounds for fearing that more determined action by the competent authorities might provoke violent reactions by those concerned, which would lead to still more serious breaches of public order or even to social conflict.

[55] Apprehension of internal difficulties cannot justify a failure by a Member State to apply Community law correctly (see, to that effect, Case C-52/95 *Commission* v *France* [1995] ECR I-4443, paragraph 38).

[56] It is for the Member State concerned, unless it can show that action on its part would have consequences for public order with which it could not cope by using the means at its disposal, to adopt all appropriate measures to guarantee the full scope and effect of Community law so as to ensure its proper implementation in the interests of all economic operators.

[57] In the present case the French Government has adduced no concrete evidence proving the existence of a danger to public order with which it could not cope.

[58] Moreover, although it is not impossible that the threat of serious disruption to public order may, in appropriate cases, justify non-intervention by the police, that argument can, on any view, be put forward only with respect to a specific incident and not, as in this case, in a general way covering all the incidents cited by the Commission.

The Court concluded by declaring that 'by failing to adopt all necessary and proportionate measures in order to prevent the free movement of fruit and vegetables from being obstructed by actions by private individuals, the French Republic has failed to fulfil its obligations under Article 30 of the EC Treaty, in conjunction with Article 5 of that Treaty, and under the common organizations of the markets in agricultural products'.

NOTE

1. The Court's ruling in this case provided a stimulus to the adoption of Regulation 2679/98 [1998] OJ L337/8 on the functioning of the internal market in relation to the free movement of goods. The Commission is equipped with special powers to act in cases of serious obstacles to free movement, and the Regulation expressly includes inaction by public authorities, not simply action, within its scope for these purposes.

2. Article 2 of Regulation 2679/98 on the functioning of the internal market in relation to the free movement of goods provides that 'This Regulation may not be interpreted as affecting in any way the exercise of fundamental rights as recognised in Member States, including the right or freedom to strike. These rights may also include the right or freedom to take other actions covered by the specific industrial relations systems in Member States'. So where a Member States does not take action to break a lawful strike that is causing an impediment to cross-border trade, it will not fall foul of the Regulation. But would it fall foul of Article 28 (ex 30)? How far does the Court's reasoning in Case C-295/95 reach in placing obligations on Member States to suppress private practices such as industrial action or broader forms of public protest that might have an effect hostile to trade integration? The issue is a potential collision between what the Court describes as a 'fundamental freedom' to trade (para 32 above) and other fundamental freedoms, such as the right to strike or, more generally, the right of assembly or freedom of expression. You should consult the EU Charter of Fundamental Rights at p.16 above, in particular Articles 12 and 28, and consider its possible influence, notwithstanding its non-binding character. The Commission's Report to the Council and Parliament on the application of Regulation 2679/98 (COM (2001) 160 makes an explicit reference to Art 28 of the Charter in footnote 27. See further C. Barnard and I. Hare, 'Police Discretion and the Rule of Law: Economic Community Rights versus Civil Rights' (2000) 63 MLR 581; G. Orlandini, 'The Free Movement of Goods as a Possible Community Limitation on Industrial Conflict' (2000) 6 ELJ 341.

3. The next case also raises the question of what constitutes a measure for the purposes of defining the MEQR caught by Article 28. The decision confirms that even a State's course of conduct which is merely designed to induce discriminatory practices among private individuals can be held in violation of Article 28. Neither the absence of binding character nor the absence of sanctions for refusal to comply with the State's policy necessarily deprive the act of the required quality. The Court avoids a formalistic assessment of the legal status of the act and concentrates instead on its purpose and effect. However, in addition to its interpretation of the concept of a measure, the 'Buy Irish' case has much to commend it as a broader illustration of the scope of Article 30 of the EC Treaty (now, after amendment, Article 28 EC).

Commission v Ireland (Case 249/81)

[1982] ECR 4005, [1983] 2 CMLR 104, Court of Justice of the European Communities

[1] By an application lodged at the Court Registry on 15 September 1981 the Commission of the European Communities brought an action before the Court under Article 169 of the EEC Treaty for a declaration that by organizing a campaign to promote the sale and purchase of Irish products in its territory Ireland has failed to fulfil its obligations under the Treaty.

I – The subject-matter of the application

[2] In a reasoned opinion addressed to Ireland on 25 February 1981 concerning the 'Buy Irish' campaign, the Commission noted that in January 1978 the Irish Government had introduced a three-year programme to help to promote Irish products. The campaign was launched on 18 January 1978 in a speech delivered by the Irish Minister for Industry, Commerce and Energy. The Minister declared on that occasion that the aim of the campaign was to achieve 'a switch from imports to Irish products equivalent to 3% of total consumer spending' and that the campaign was 'a carefully

thought out set of initiatives that add up to an integrated programme for promoting Irish goods, with specific proposals to involve the producer, distributor and consumer'.

[3] The Irish Government, it was said, had taken and was continuing to take a series of measures designed to promote Irish products in accordance with the terms of that speech. The reasoned opinion cited the following measures:

(a) The organization of a free information service for consumers wishing to know which products in a particular category of goods are made in Ireland and where they may be obtained (the Shoplink Service);

(b) The provision of exhibition facilities, exclusively for exhibiting Irish products, in a large exhibition centre in Dublin run by the Irish Goods Council, which is, it is claimed, a public authority;

(c) The encouragement of the use of the 'Guaranteed Irish' symbol for products made in Ireland together with the organization by the Irish Goods Council of a special system for investigating complaints about products bearing that symbol;

(d) The organization of a big publicity campaign by the Irish Goods Council in favour of Irish products, involving in particular the publication and distribution by that institution of literature encouraging consumers to buy only domestic products.

[4] The Commission notes in the application that the activities connected with the Shoplink Service and the exhibition facilities in Dublin have now been abandoned by the Irish Government. However, the other two activities have continued, even after the expiry of the three-year period for which the campaign was to last. Moreover, the publicity campaign has been gradually extended, in particular by means of widespread advertising in favour of Irish products in the press and on television.

[5] The Irish Government admits that there was a three-year programme in favour of buying Irish products in Ireland. It says that since the Shoplink Service and the exhibition facilities in Dublin were abandoned at the request of the Commission the programme consists merely of an advertising campaign, by means of the press and television, the publication of posters and pamphlets and the use of the 'Guaranteed Irish' symbol, designed to make Irish consumers better acquainted with products made in Ireland and to stimulate awareness in the Irish public of the link between the marketing of such products in Ireland and the unemployment problem in that country.

[6] As far as the advertising campaign is concerned, the Irish Government confirms that it forms part of the activities of the Irish Goods Council. However, that institution cannot be regarded as a public authority; it is merely an arrangement whereby the various industries in Ireland may cooperate for their common good. The activities of the Irish Goods Council are not based on any official enactment and the involvement of the Government consists exclusively of financial aid and moral support.

[7] The Commission maintains that the actions of the Irish Goods Council are unquestionably attributable to the Irish Government. It points out, in particular, that the members of the Management Committee of the Council are appointed, under the Articles of Association of that body, by the Minister for Industry, Commerce and Energy.

[8] The Commission is of the opinion that the campaign to promote the sale and purchase of Irish products in Ireland must be regarded as a measure having an effect equivalent to a quantitative restriction on imports. Ireland contends, first, that the Irish Government has never adopted 'measures' within the meaning of Article 30 of the Treaty and, secondly, that the financial aid given to the Irish Goods Council must be judged in the light of Articles 92 and 93 of the Treaty, and not Article 30.

[9] Before asssessing the merits of those arguments the position of the Irish Goods Council must be considered.

II – The Irish Goods Council

[10] The Irish Goods Council was created on 25 August 1978, a few months after the disputed campaign was launched, in the form of a company limited by guarantee and not having a share capital; it was registered in accordance with Irish company law (Companies Act 1963). The Council

is in fact the result of the amalgamation of two bodies, the National Development Council, a company limited by guarantee and registered under the Companies Act, and the Working Group on the Promotion and Sale of Irish Goods.

[11] The Irish Government maintains that the Irish Goods Council was created under the sponsorship of the government in order to encourage Irish industry to overcome its own difficulties. The Council was established for the purpose of creating a framework within which the various industries could come together in order to cooperate for their common good.

[12] The Management Committee of the Irish Goods Council consists, according to the Articles of Association of that institution, of 10 persons appointed in their individual capacities by the Minister for Industry, Commerce and Energy; the same Minister appoints the chairman from among the members of the Management Committee. The members and the chairman are appointed for a period of three years, and their appointments may be renewed. In practice, the members of the Management Committee are selected by the Minister in such a manner as to represent the appropriate sectors of the Irish economy.

[13] It appears from the information supplied by the Irish Government at the request of the Court that the activities of the Irish Goods Council are financed by subsidies paid by the Irish Government and by private industry. The subsidies from the State and from the private sector amounted, respectively to IRL 1 005 000 and IRL 175 000 for the period between August 1978 and December 1979; IRL 940 000 and IRL 194 000 for 1980; and IRL 922 000 and IRL 238 000 for 1981.

[14] The Irish Government has not denied that the activities of the Irish Goods Council consist in particular, after the abandonment of the Shoplink Service and the exhibition facilities offered to Irish manufacturers in Dublin, in the organization of an advertising campaign in favour of the sale and purchase of Irish products, and in promoting the use of the 'Guaranteed Irish' symbol.

[15] It is thus apparent that the Irish Government appoints the members of the Management Committee of the Irish Goods Council, grants it public subsidies which cover the greater part of its expenses and, finally, defines the aims and the broad outline of the campaign conducted by that institution to promote the sale and purchase of Irish products. In the circumstances the Irish Government cannot rely on the fact that the campaign was conducted by a private company in order to escape any liability it may have under the provisions of the Treaty.

III – The applicability of Articles 92 and 93 of the Treaty

[16] The Irish Government maintains that, even if the purpose or the effect of the campaign was to discourage imports from other Member States, it must be judged on the basis of Articles 92 and 93 of the Treaty, which deal with State aids. The applicability of those provisions excludes the applicability of Article 30 of the Treaty, upon which the Commission has based its case.

[17] The Irish Government states that the campaign has in fact been conducted by the Irish Goods Council and that the role of the government has been restricted to moral support and financial assistance. If, as the Commission maintains, the campaign was liable to hinder the free movement of goods within the Community by promoting domestic products at the expense of imported ones that circumstance is attributable solely to a single government decision, namely the decision to subsidize the Irish Goods Council.

[18] It must be observed, however, that the fact that a substantial part of the campaign is financed by the Irish Government, and that Articles 92 and 93 of the Treaty may be applicable to financing of that kind, does not mean that the campaign itself may escape the prohibitions laid down in Article 30.

[19] In any case, if the Irish Government considered that such financing amounted to aid within the meaning of Articles 92 and 93 it ought to have notified the aid to the Commission in accordance with Article 93 (3).

IV – The application of Article 30 of the Treaty

[20] The Commission maintains that the 'Buy Irish' campaign and the measures taken to prosecute the campaign must be regarded, as a whole, as measures encouraging the purchase of domestic

products only. Such measures are said to be contrary to the obligations imposed on the Member States by Article 30. The Commission refers to Article 2(3)(k) of Commission Directive No 70/50/EEC of 22 December 1969, based on the provisions of Article 33(7), on the abolition of measures which have an effect equivalent to quantitative restrictions on imports and are not covered by other provisions adopted in pursuance of the EEC Treaty (Official Journal, English Special Edition 1970 (I), p.17). According to Article 2(3)(k), measures which encourage the purchase of domestic products only must be regarded as contrary to the prohibitions contained in the Treaty.

[21] The Irish Government maintains that the prohibition against measures having an effect equivalent to quantitative restrictions in Article 30 is concerned only with 'measures', that is to say, binding provisions emanating from a public authority. However, no such provision has been adopted by the Irish Government, which has confined itself to giving moral support and financial aid to the activities pursued by the Irish industries.

[22] The Irish Government goes on to emphasise that the campaign has had no restrictive effect on imports since the proportion of Irish goods to all goods sold on the Irish market fell from 49.2% in 1977 to 43.4% in 1980.

[23] The first observation to be made is that the campaign cannot be likened to advertising by private or public undertakings, or by a group of undertakings, to encourage people to buy goods produced by those undertakings. Regardless of the means used to implement it, the campaign is a reflection of the Irish Government's considered intention to substitute domestic products for imported products on the Irish market and thereby to check the flow of imports from other Member States.

[24] It must be remembered here that a representative of the Irish Government stated when the campaign was launched that it was a carefully thought-out set of initiatives constituting an integrated programme for promoting domestic products; that the Irish Goods Council was set up at the initiative of the Irish Government a few months later; and that the task of implementing the integrated programme as it was envisaged by the government was entrusted, or left, to that Council.

[25] Whilst it may be true that the two elements of the programme which have continued in effect, namely the advertising campaign and the use of the 'Guaranteed Irish' symbol, have not had any significant success in winning over the Irish market to domestic products, it is not possible to overlook the fact that, regardless of their efficacy, those two activities form part of a government programme which is designed to achieve the substitution of domestic products for imported products and is liable to affect the volume of trade between Member States.

[26] The advertising campaign to encourage the sale and purchase of Irish products cannot be divorced from its origin as part of the government programme, or from its connection with the introduction of the 'Guaranteed Irish' symbol and with the organization of a special system for investigating complaints about products bearing that symbol. The establishment of the system for investigating complaints about Irish products provides adequate confirmation of the degree of organization surrounding the 'Buy Irish' campaign and of the discriminatory nature of the campaign.

[27] In the circumstances the two activities in question amount to the establishment of a national practice, introduced by the Irish Government and prosecuted with its assistance, the potential effect of which on imports from other Member States is comparable to that resulting from government measures of a binding nature.

[28] Such a practice cannot escape the prohibition laid down by Article 30 of the Treaty solely because it is not based on decisions which are binding upon undertakings. Even measures adopted by the government of a Member State which do not have binding effect may be capable of influencing the conduct of traders and consumers in that State and thus of frustrating the aims of the Community as set out in Article 2 and enlarged upon in Article 3 of the Treaty.

[29] That is the case where, as in this instance, such a restrictive practice represents the implementation of a programme defined by the government which affects the national economy as a whole and

which is intended to check the flow of trade between Member States by encouraging the purchase of domestic products, by means of an advertising campaign on a national scale and the organization of special procedures applicable solely to domestic products, and where those activities are attributable as a whole to the government and are pursued in an organized fashion throughout the national territory.

[30] Ireland has therefore failed to fulfil its obligations under the Treaty by organizing a campaign to promote the sale and purchase of Irish goods within its territory.

NOTE

A delicate but important distinction from the 'Buy Irish' case was made in *Apple and Pear Development Council* v *Lewis* (Case 222/82). The case involved the submission that the fruit promotions undertaken by the Council, a body set up in the UK under statutory instrument, infringed *inter alia* Article 30 of the EC Treaty (now, after amendment, Article 28 EC) in so far as they concerned the promotion of varieties typical of English and Welsh production.

Apple and Pear Development Council v *Lewis* (Case 222/82)

[1983] ECR 4083, [1984] 3 CMLR 733, Court of Justice of the European Communities

[17] As the Court held in its judgment of 24 November 1982 in Case 249/81 (*Commission* v *Ireland* [1982] ECR 4005), a publicity campaign to promote the sale and purchase of domestic products may, in certain circumstances, fall within the prohibition contained in Article 30 of the Treaty, if the campaign is supported by the public authorities. In fact, a body such as the Development Council, which is set up by the government of a Member State and is financed by a charge imposed on growers, cannot under Community law enjoy the same freedom as regards the methods of advertising used as that enjoyed by producers themselves or producers' associations of a voluntary character.

[18] In particular, such a body is under a duty not to engage in any advertising intended to discourage the purchase of products of other Member States or to disparage those products in the eyes of consumers. Nor must it advise consumers to purchase domestic products solely by reason of their national origin.

[19] On the other hand, Article 30 does not prevent such a body from drawing attention, in its publicity, to the specific qualities of fruit grown in the Member State in question or from organizing campaigns to promote the sale of certain varieties, mentioning their particular properties, even if those varieties are typical of national production.

[20] In the observations which it submitted to the Court, the Commission stated that campaigns to promote certain varieties might result in the exclusion of other varieties from the market and make it necessary, either in the Member State in question or in other Member States which export the latter varieties, to apply the intervention measures provided for in the common organization of the market in relation to those varieties.

[21] Although it is true that such a distortion of the conditions of competition, which would be incompatible with the proper functioning of the common organization of the markets, might occur in a market where the publicity measures related exclusively or essentially to certain varieties to the exclusion of the others, that consideration cannot justify the prohibition of all publicity campaigns whereby an organization such as the Development Council draws attention to the properties of certain varieties and indicates the uses for which those varieties are specifically suitable.

NOTES

1. For subsequent litigation in this area before English courts, see *Meat and Livestock Commission* v *Manchester Wholesale Meat and Poultry Market Ltd* [1997] 2 CMLR 361.
2. The Commission attempted to extract some general principles from these judgments in order to foster predictable application of the law to such practices in the future. In 1986 it issued guidelines on *Member States' Involvement in the Promotion of Agricultural and Fisheries Products*. These were replaced in 2001 by the following text.

COMMUNITY GUIDELINES FOR STATE AID FOR ADVERTISING OF PRODUCTS LISTED IN ANNEX I TO THE EC TREATY AND OF CERTAIN NON-ANNEX I PRODUCTS,
[2001] OJ C252/5

The principal target of the guidelines is aid provided by public authorities in the Member States to finance the promotion and advertising of products. Aid is subject to supervision pursuant to Articles 87–89 EC. The guidelines also consider the compatibility with Article 28 of the promotion schemes themselves, and the relevant extracts are set out below.

3.1.1. Aid for campaigns contrary to Article 28 of the Treaty

18. National aid for an advertising campaign which infringes Article 28 of the Treaty prohibiting quantitative restrictions on imports and all measures having equivalent effect between Member States cannot in any circumstances be considered compatible with the common market within the meaning of Article 87(3)(c) of the Treaty. The Commission will therefore seek assurances from the Member State concerned that the principles as described in point 19 and as derived from the jurisprudence of the Court of Justice of the European Communities will be respected. In case of doubt, the Commission will request samples or mock-ups of the advertising material concerned before approving the aid scheme. Furthermore, the Commission will require the Member State concerned to submit an annual report containing information about the activities undertaken during the previous year (see point 6.2).

19. The following are forms of advertising which are clearly not open to objection under Article 28 of the Treaty:

(a) advertising campaigns organized directly or indirectly by one Member State on the market of another Member State;
(b) advertising campaigns organized on the home market of a Member State which advertise the product in a purely generic manner making no reference whatsoever to its national origin;
(c) campaigns on the home market promoting specific qualities or varieties of products even though they are typical of national production; these are campaigns which make no specific references to the national origin of the product other than which may be evident from the references made to the qualities or varieties concerned or to the normal designation of the product.

20. The following are forms of advertising which clearly infringe Article 28 of the Treaty:

(a) advertising which advises consumers to buy national products solely because of their national origin;
(b) campaigns intended to discourage the purchase of products from other Member States or which disparage those products in the eyes of consumers (negative advertising); positive statements about a Member State's home product should not be phrased in such a way as to imply that other Member State's products are necessarily inferior.

21. Some advertising on a Member State's home market may, because of the references made to the national origin of the products, and unless certain restraints are observed, be open to objection under Article 28 of the Treaty.

22. Advertising drawing attention to the varieties or qualities of products produced within a Member State frequently draws attention to the national origin of the products, even though those products and their qualities are similar to those of products produced elsewhere. If undue emphasis is placed on the national origin of the product in such advertising there is a danger of breach of Article 28 of the Treaty. The Commission therefore requests Member States to ensure particularly that point 23 is strictly respected.

23. Identification of the producing country by word or by symbol may be made providing that a reasonable balance is struck between references to, on the one hand, qualities and varieties of the product and, on the other hand, its national origin. The references to national origin should be subsidiary to the main message put over to consumers by the campaign and should not constitute the principal reason why consumers are being advised to buy the product.

24. Certain advertising mentioning the national origin of agricultural and other products may, even though they respect the criteria referred to in points 22 and 23, nevertheless infringe Article 28 of the Treaty if they reflect a considered intention of a Member State to substitute domestic products for products imported from other Member States(8).

. . .

4.1. Advertising of products of a particular Member State or region where origin is (part of) the message

Advertising where origin is the primary message

35. Article 28 of the Treaty states that quantitative restrictions on imports and all measures having equivalent effect shall be prohibited between Member States. Advertising of home-grown products by a Member State which is aimed at domestic consumption is considered as such an equivalent measure as the measure may lead, or is intended to lead, to favour the consumption of home-grown products in place of the consumption of imported products.

36. However, advertising campaigns that are undertaken with a view to introducing consumers to the agricultural and other products of a particular Member State or region do not necessarily have to have such an effect. Sometimes such campaigns concern a single category of products, such as wine, cheese or beer. Sometimes they may concern a wide range of agricultural and other products produced in the Member State or region concerned, for example through the organization of 'food weeks' in which consumers in one Member State are encouraged to try products from another Member State. In addition to advertising, such campaigns may include other measures, for example the organization of free tasting sessions for consumers or professionals working in the food and catering sectors.

37. The Commission considers that one of the major benefits of the realisation of the internal market in the agricultural and foodstuffs sector has been to provide consumers with access to the very wide range of products produced in the Member States in accordance with different practices and traditions. Advertising campaigns which encourage consumers to try these different products benefit the internal market and contribute to the development of the agricultural sector. Therefore, despite the fact that the primary focus of such campaigns is inevitably on the national or regional origin of the products concerned, the Commission takes a favourable view of them provided that certain conditions are met.

38. The objective of such campaigns should be to introduce consumers to products with which they are not familiar. Therefore, as a general rule, the campaign should be undertaken outside the Member State or region in which the agricultural and other products are produced. Unless appropriate explanations can be provided to suggest the contrary, publicly subsidised campaigns focused on the origin of the products and aimed at consumers residing in the Member State or region of production, who may be presumed to be familiar with the products concerned, would appear to be intended to reinforce possible existing preferences to buy local products, and would therefore be contrary to the common interest. This would not, however, be the case for advertising campaigns which are aimed at visitors to the Member State or region, and which encourage them to try local products, and possibly encourage them to visit local production facilities.

39. It is acceptable for such campaigns to include information about the objective characteristics of the products concerned, such as the ingredients used, the taste and texture of the product, or the method of production, e.g., animal welfare standards or biological production. However, they should not, subject to the guidance given in point 4.2, include subjective claims about the quality of the products. In essence, the focus of such a campaign should be limited to encouraging consumers or the trade to try the product, and leaving it to them to form a judgment as to its quality.

Advertising where origin is the secondary message

40. In line with point 3.1.1, advertising which mentions the (regional) origin of the product as a subsidiary message would not infringe Article 28 of the Treaty.

41. To assess whether the origin is indeed a subsidiary message, the Commission will take into account the overall importance of text and/or symbol, including pictures and general presentation, referring to origin and the importance of text and/or symbol referring to the unique selling point of the advertisement, i.e., the part of the advertising message which does not focus on origin.

Advertising concerning traceability systems

42. Regulation (EC) No 1760/2000 of the European Parliament and of the Council of 17 July 2000 establishing a system for the identification and registration of bovine animals and regarding the labelling of beef and beef products and repealing Council Regulation (EC) No 820/97(13) has improved the transparency of the conditions for the production and marketing of beef and beef products. Through that regulation Community legislation has made traceability of origin obligatory for some products. Member States may want to finance advertising campaigns explaining the mechanisms of such a system to the general public.

43. A general advertising campaign explaining the fact that traceability has become obligatory and/or explaining how such a system is managed would not emphasise a particular origin. Therefore, such a campaign (if it is State aid at all) would comply with Article 28 of the Treaty.

44. However, claims that products of a certain origin are special because of the existence of a traceability system, when in fact they simply meet the relevant legislative requirements applicable to the marketing of all similar products concerned, may mislead the consumer, because they suggest that the product possesses special characteristics when in fact all similar products possess the same characteristics (see Article 2(1)(a)(iii) of Directive 2000/13/EC). In this case, the payment of aid for such campaigns cannot be considered to be in the common interest. However, information stemming from a traceability system may be integrated into a campaign in line with the principles on advertising where origin is the secondary message referred to in point 23.

NOTE

Wherever possible, the Commission wisely has an eye to developing broadly-based interpretation of the law by building on the accidents of litigation. By expanding understanding of the reach of Community law, it hopes to improve observance through education. However, in Case C-57/95 *France* v *Commission* [1997] ECR I-1627, the Court was alert to the risk that the Commission might seek in this way improperly to impose new obligations on Member States and annulled a communication on pension funds as a binding act in respect of which the Commission lacked the necessary competence. Accordingly, communications and guidelines must be limited to clarification. Moreover the Commission has developed a practice of organizing bilateral meetings with national authorities at which non-contentious solutions to instances of infringement are sought (see the Annual Reports on monitoring the application of Community law, http://europa.eu.int/comm/secretariat_general/sgb/droit_com/index_en.htm). Reactive, *ad hoc* litigation can be only one component of supervision. Pursuit of administrative cooperation as a basis for management of the internal market is a prominent feature of the Commission's strategies sketched in Chapter 9 (p.309 above).

■ QUESTIONS

1. Could a campaign which involved the use of a national flag as a campaign logo fall on the lawful side of the line?

2. In both the 'Buy Irish' and the *Apple and Pear Council* cases (Cases 249/81 and 222/82), the Court dismissed arguments that the acts complained of were those of a private body insufficiently closely aligned to the State to fall within the scope of Article 30 of the EC Treaty (now, after amendment, Article 28 EC). What factors persuaded the Court that the State was sufficiently involved in the practices of the Irish Goods Council and the Apple and Pear Development Council? See also Case C-325/00 *Commission* v *Germany* judgment of 5 November 2002.

3. Would discrimination by a private body on grounds of nationality fall foul of Community law? Consider, for example, a policy decision by a UK supermarket chain to stock only British-made goods; or only French-made goods. You should make reference to the scope of Article 12; and Articles 81 and 82. For Article 39, see Case C-281/98 *Roman Angonese* [2000] ECR I-4139 (Chapter 13). Consider also the issue of obligatory compliance with national standards. The Commission expressed its view in Written Question 835/82 [1983] OJ C93/1; Written Question 862/83 [1983] OJ C315/15.

4. What other areas of Community law demand close attention to the extent of State involvement (see p.144 on the direct effect of Directives)? Are the tests used identical? If not, why not? Read D. Curtin, 'The Province of Government', (1990) 15 EL Rev 195.

NOTE

Interventionist governments are fond of price-fixing schemes. As a matter of Community law, such schemes must give the importer an opportunity to benefit from any competitive advantage the imported goods may possess (by setting a lower price than the competing domestic product), or to take account of any disadvantage they may possess (by setting a higher price). Schemes which exclude the importer's ability to achieve such flexibility are capable of violating Article 28. These are simply instances of the application of Article 28 to discriminatory practices, but here the discrimination lies in treating imported goods in the *same* way as domestic goods where such equal treatment is not objectively justified, rather than in treating goods differently when in objective terms they should be treated in the same way.

Criminal proceedings against Riccardo Tasca (Case 65/75)

[1976] ECR 291, [1977] 2 CMLR 183, Court of Justice of the European Communities

[12] The second question asks whether Article 30 of the EEC Treaty and Article 35 of Regulation No 1009/67, especially the prohibition against the application in intra-Community trade of measures having an effect equivalent to quantitative restrictions, prohibit the fixing of maximum prices valid only for the territory of a single Member State.

[13] Article 30 of the Treaty prohibits in trade between Member States all measures having an effect equivalent to quantitative restrictions and this prohibition is repeated in Article 35 of Regulation No 1009/67 as regards the market in sugar. For the purposes of this prohibition it is sufficient that the measures in question are likely to constitute an obstacle, directly or indirectly, actually or potentially, to imports between Member States. Although a maximum price applicable without distinction to domestic and imported products does not in itself constitute a measure having an effect equivalent to a quantitative restriction, it may have such an effect, however, when it is fixed at a level such that the sale of imported products becomes, if not impossible, more difficult than that of domestic products. A maximum price, in any event in so far as it applies to imported products, constitutes therefore a measure having an effect equivalent to a quantitative restriction, especially when it is fixed at such a low level that, having regard to the general situation of imported products compared to that of domestic products, dealers wishing to import the product in question into the Member State concerned can do so only at a loss.

[14] It is for the national court to decide whether this is so in the present case.

Openbaar Ministerie v *Van Tiggele* (Case 82/77)

[1978] ECR 25, [1978] 2 CMLR 528, Court of Justice of the European Communities

[16] First a national provision which prohibits without distinction the retail sale of domestic products and imported products at prices below the purchase price paid by the retailer cannot produce effects detrimental to the marketing of imported products alone and consequently cannot constitute a measure having an effect equivalent to a quantitative restriction on imports.

[17] Furthermore the fixing of the minimum profit margin at a specific amount, and not as a percentage of the cost price, applicable without distinction to domestic products and imported products is likewise incapable of producing an adverse effect on imported products which may be cheaper, as in the present case where the amount of the profit margin constitutes a relatively insignificant part of the final retail price.

[18] On the other hand this is not so in the case of a minimum price fixed at a specific amount which, although applicable without distinction to domestic products and imported products, is capable of having an adverse effect on the marketing of the latter in so far as it prevents their lower cost price from being reflected in the retail selling price.

[19] This is the conclusion which must be drawn even though the competent authority is empowered to grant exemptions from the fixed minimum price and though this power is freely applied to imported products, since the requirement that importers and traders must comply with the administrative formalities inherent in such a system may in itself constitute a measure having an effect equivalent to a quantitative restriction.

[20] The temporary nature of the application of the fixed minimum prices is not a factor capable of justifying such a measure since it is incompatible on other grounds with Article 30 of the Treaty.

[21] The answer to the first question must therefore be that Article 30 of the EEC Treaty must be interpreted to mean that the establishment by a national authority of a minimum retail price fixed at a specific amount and applicable without distinction to domestic products and imported products constitutes, in conditions such as those laid down in the regulation made by the Produktschap voor Gedistilleerde Dranken on 17 December 1975, a measure having an effect equivalent to a quantitative restriction on imports which is prohibited under the said Article 30.

SECTION 3: **ARTICLE 30**

ARTICLE 30 EC

The provisions of Articles 28 and 29 shall not preclude prohibitions or restrictions on imports, exports or goods in transit justified on grounds of public morality, public policy or public security; the protection of health and life of humans, animals or plants; the protection of national treasures possessing artistic, historic or archaeological value; or the protection of industrial and commercial property. Such prohibitions or restrictions shall not, however, constitute a means of arbitrary discrimination or a disguised restriction on trade between Member States.

It is an unfortunate coincidence that the Amsterdam re-numbering of the EC Treaty (p.341 above) converted what was Article 36 into what is now Article 30. It will be recalled that what was Article 30 is now Article 28.

As a general principle of Community trade law, any derogation from freedom of movement is to be construed strictly, because it is hostile to the aim of achieving a common market. This principle can be seen in concrete form in Article 30. In its first sentence, an exhaustive list of possible grounds of derogation is set out. In its second sentence, a caution is issued that reliance on any derogation must be objectively justifiable, not a ruse to protect domestic industry. Moreover, the invocation of Article 30 should be read in the light of Article 14's commitment to an area without internal frontiers (p.299 above).

The Court, in assessing purported justification under Article 30, consistently requires Member States to show not simply a protectable interest, but also that the means chosen are proportionate to the end in view and the least restrictive of trade available which are necessary to meet that objective.

....

A: **Public morality**

R v Henn and Darby **(Case 34/79)**

[1979] ECR 3795, [1980] 1 CMLR 246, Court of Justice of the European Communities

The defendants were convicted of being 'knowingly concerned in the fraudulent evasion of the prohibition of the importation of indecent or obscene articles' contrary to the Customs Consolidation Act 1876, s.42, and the Customs and Excise Act 1952, s.304. They had shipped pornography into Felixstowe from Rotterdam. Their appeal against conviction was based on the submission that the legal control of pornography restricted the free circulation of goods in the Community contrary to Article 30 of the EC Treaty (now, after amendment, Article 28 EC). The matter reached the House of Lords which referred questions of interpretation under Article 177 (now Article 234, Chapter 7) to the European Court. The Court first accepts the applicability of Article 30 (now 28) before proceeding to discuss Article 36 (now 30).

[11] The first question asks whether a law of a Member State which prohibits the import into that State of pornographic articles is a measure having equivalent effect to a quantitative restriction on imports within the meaning of Article 30 of the Treaty.

[12] That Article provides that 'quantitative restrictions on imports and all measures having equivalent effect' shall be prohibited between Member States. It is clear that this provision includes a prohibition on imports inasmuch as this is the most extreme form of restriction. The expression used in Article 30 must therefore be understood as being the equivalent of the expression 'prohibitions or restrictions on imports' occurring in Article 36.

[13] The answer to the first question is therefore that a law such as that referred to in this case constitutes a quantitative restriction on imports within the meaning of Article 30 of the Treaty.

Second and third questions

[14] The second and third questions are framed in the following terms:

'2. If the answer to Question 1 is in the affirmative, does the first sentence of Article 36 upon its true construction mean that a Member State may lawfully impose prohibitions on the importation of goods from another Member State which are of an indecent or obscene character as understood by the laws of that Member State?

3. In particular:

(i) is the member State entitled to maintain such prohibitions in order to prevent, to guard against or to reduce the likelihood of breaches of the domestic law of all constituent parts of the customs territory of the State?

(ii) is the Member State entitled to maintain such prohibitions having regard to the national standards and characteristics of that State as demonstrated by the domestic laws of the constituent parts of the customs territory of that State including the law imposing the prohibition, notwithstanding variations between the laws of the constituent parts?'

It is convenient to consider these questions together.

[15] Under the terms of Article 36 of the Treaty the provisions relating to the free movement of goods within the Community are not to preclude prohibitions on imports which are justified *inter alia* 'on grounds of public morality'. In principle, it is for each Member State to determine in accordance with its own scale of values and in the form selected by it the requirements of public morality in its territory. In any event, it cannot be disputed that the statutory provisions applied by the United

Kingdom in regard to the importation of articles having an indecent or obscene character come within the powers reserved to the Member States by the first sentence of Article 36.

[16] Each Member State is entitled to impose prohibitions on imports justified on grounds of public morality for the whole of its territory, as defined in Article 227 of the Treaty, whatever the structure of its constitution may be and however the powers of legislating in regard to the subject in question may be distributed. The fact that certain differences exist between the laws enforced in the different constituent parts of a Member State does not thereby prevent that State from applying a unitary concept in regard to prohibitions on imports imposed, on grounds of public morality, on trade with other Member States.

[17] The answer to the second and third questions must therefore be that the first sentence of Article 36 upon its true construction means that a Member State may, in principle, lawfully impose prohibitions on the importation from any other Member State of articles which are of an indecent or obscene character as understood by its domestic laws and that such prohibitions may lawfully be applied to the whole of its national territory even if, in regard to the field in question, variations exist between the laws in force in the different constituent parts of the Member State concerned.

Fourth, fifth and sixth questions

[18] The fourth, fifth and sixth questions are framed in the following terms:

'4. If a prohibition on the importation of goods is justifiable on grounds of public morality or public policy, and imposed with that purpose, can that prohibition nevertheless amount to a means of arbitrary discrimination or a disguised restriction on trade contrary to Article 36?

5. If the answer to Question 4 is in the affirmative, does the fact that the prohibition imposed on the importation of such goods is different in scope from that imposed by the criminal law upon the possession and publication of such goods within the Member State or any part of it necessarily constitute a means of arbitrary discrimination or a disguised restriction on trade between Member States so as to conflict with the requirements of the second sentence of Article 36?

6. If it be the fact that the prohibition imposed upon importation is, and a prohibition such as is imposed upon possession and publication is not, capable as a matter of administration of being applied by customs officials responsible for examining goods at the point of importation, would that fact have any bearing upon the answer to Question 5?'

[19] In these questions the House of Lords takes account of the appellants' submissions based upon certain differences between, on the one hand, the prohibition on importing the goods in question, which is absolute, and, on the other, the laws in force in the various constituent parts of the United Kingdom, which appear to be less strict in the sense that the mere possession of obscene articles for non-commercial purposes does not constitute a criminal offence anywhere in the United Kingdom and that, even if it is generally forbidden, trade in such articles is subject to certain exceptions, notably those in favour of articles having scientific, literary, artistic or educational interest. Having regard to those differences the question has been raised whether the prohibition on imports might not come within the second sentence of Article 36.

[20] According to the second sentence of Article 36 the restrictions on imports referred to in the first sentence may not 'constitute a means of arbitrary discrimination or a disguised restriction on trade between Member States'.

[21] In order to answer the questions which have been referred to the Court it is appropriate to have regard to the function of this provision, which is designed to prevent restrictions on trade based on the grounds mentioned in the first sentence of Article 36 from being diverted from their proper purpose and used in such a way as either to create discrimination in respect of goods originating in other Member States or indirectly to protect certain national products. That is not the purport of a prohibition, such as that in force in the United Kingdom, on the importation of articles which are of an indecent or obscene character. Whatever may be the differences between the laws on this subject in force in the different constituent parts of the United Kingdom, and notwithstanding the

fact that they contain certain exceptions of limited scope, these laws, taken as a whole, have as their purpose the prohibition, or at least, the restraining, of the manufacture and marketing of publications or articles of an indecent or obscene character. In these circumstances it is permissible to conclude, on a comprehensive view, that there is no lawful trade in such goods in the United Kingdom. A prohibition on imports which may in certain respects be more strict than some of the laws applied within the United Kingdom cannot therefore be regarded as amounting to a measure designed to give indirect protection to some national product or aimed at creating arbitrary discrimination between goods of this type depending on whether they are produced within the national territory or another Member State.

[22] The answer to the fourth question must therefore be that if a prohibition on the importation of goods is justifiable on grounds of public morality and if it is imposed with that purpose the enforcement of that prohibition cannot, in the absence within the Member State concerned of a lawful trade in the same goods, constitute a means of arbitrary discrimination or a disguised restriction on trade contrary to Article 36.

[23] In these circumstances it is not necessary to answer the fifth and sixth questions.

NOTE
Both Articles 30 and 36 of the EC Treaty (now, after amendment, Articles 28 and 30 EC) applied. The convictions were accordingly upheld.

The course of the litigation prior to the Court's decision deserves attention. The decision of the Court of Appeal is an instructive misapplication of Article 30 (now 28): [1978] 1 WLR 1031. The House of Lords' approach to Article 177 (now 234, Chapter 7) is an instructive explanation of the function of that provision: [1980] 2 WLR 597.

Conegate v *Customs and Excise Commissioners* (Case 121/85)
[1986] ECR 1007, [1986] 1 CMLR 739, Court of Justice of the European Communities

This case also involved the seizure of pornography. Similar arguments were advanced in relation to the lawfulness of the seizure under EC law. There was, however, a different background under the (non-existent, but for these purposes deemed) 'law of the UK'.

[13] The Court would observe that the first question raises, in the first place, the general problem of whether a prohibition on the importation of certain goods may be justified on grounds of public morality where the legislation of the Member State concerned contains no prohibition on the manufacture or marketing of the same products within the national territory.

[14] So far as that problem is concerned, it must be borne in mind that according to Article 36 of the EEC Treaty the provisions relating to the free movement of goods within the Community do not preclude prohibitions on imports justified 'on grounds of public morality'. As the Court held in its judgment of 14 December 1979, cited above [*Henn*] in principle it is for each Member State to determine in accordance with its own scale of values and in the form selected by it the requirements of public morality in its territory.

[15] However, although Community law leaves the Member States free to make their own assessments of the indecent or obscene character of certain articles, it must be pointed out that the fact that goods cause offence cannot be regarded as sufficiently serious to justify restrictions on the free movement of goods where the Member State concerned does not adopt, with respect to the same goods manufactured or marketed within its territory, penal measures or other serious and effective measures intended to prevent the distribution of such goods in its territory.

[16] It follows that a Member State may not rely on grounds of public morality in order to prohibit the importation of goods from other Member States when its legislation contains no prohibition on the manufacture or marketing of the same goods on its territory.

[17] It is not for the Court, within the framework of the powers conferred upon it by Article 177 of the EEC Treaty, to consider whether, and to what extent, the United Kingdom legislation contains such a

prohibition. However, the question whether or not such a prohibition exists in a State comprised of different constituent parts which have their own internal legislation, can be resolved only by taking into consideration all the relevant legislation. Although it is not necessary, for the purposes of the application of the above-mentioned rule, that the manufacture and marketing of the products whose importation has been prohibited should be prohibited in the territory of all the constituent parts, it must at least be possible to conclude from the applicable rules, taken as a whole, that their purpose is, in substance, to prohibit the manufacture and marketing of those products.

[18] In this instance, in the actual wording of its first question the High Court took care to define the substance of the national legislation the compatibility of which with Community law is a question which it proposes to determine. Thus it refers to rules in the importing Member State under which the goods in question may be manufactured freely and marketed subject only to certain restrictions, which it sets out explicitly, namely an absolute prohibition on the transmission of such goods by post, a restriction on their public display and, in certain areas of the Member State concerned, a system of licensing of premises for the sale of those goods to customers aged 18 years and over. Such restrictions cannot however be regarded as equivalent in substance to a prohibition on manufacture and marketing.

[19] At the hearing, the United Kingdom again stressed the fact that at present no articles comparable to those imported by Conegate are manufactured on United Kingdom territory, but that fact, which does not exclude the possibility of manufacturing such articles and which, moreover, was not referred to by the High Court, is not such as to lead to a different assessment of the situation.

[20] In reply to the first question it must therefore be stated that a Member State may not rely on grounds of public morality within the meaning of Article 36 of the Treaty in order to prohibit the importation of certain goods on the grounds that they are indecent or obscene, where the same goods may be manufactured freely on its territory and marketed on its territory subject only to an absolute prohibition on their transmission by post, a restriction on their public display and, in certain regions, a system of licensing of premises for the sale of those goods to customers aged 18 and over.

[21] That conclusion does not preclude the authorities of the Member State concerned from applying to those goods, once imported, the same restrictions on marketing which are applied to similar products manufactured and marketed within the country.

■ QUESTIONS

1. What is presented as the key distinction between these two cases? Explain how the concept of the prohibition on 'arbitrary discrimination' found in the second sentence of Article 30 is reflected in the decisions.

2. T. Van Rijn (1988) 25 CML Rev 593, at pp.608–9 argues as follows:

> the test in *Conegate* depends on whether the purpose of the internal legislation was, in substance, to prohibit the manufacture and marketing of those products. One may wonder, however, whether that criterion is satisfactory in so far as it refers to prohibitions on marketing. The operation of importation takes place on the same level as the operation of manufacture. Imported products are marketed in the Member State after their importation and are then subject to the same rules as products manufactured in that Member State, as the Court rightly underlined. Control of the marketing of imported indecent products should therefore not take place on the basis of legislation on imports (such as the Customs Consolidation Act), but on the basis of the legislation governing the marketing of nationally manufactured products.

Do you agree?

Might it be open to the UK to argue that importation and manufacture are objectively distinct and may therefore be treated differently? The special position of the UK as an island may more readily yield justification for controls at the border, on the basis that control there is the most efficient location. Land borders may lose their economic relevance as market integration accelerates; the same may not be true of division by sea. Can such an argument survive the establishment of an internal market in accordance with Article 14?

3. Chapter 14 examines EC trade law's application to the services sector, but the reader should ponder here how Article 30's recognition of permissible variation in standards of morality can be translated into laws capable of effective enforcement in a world of cable and satellite broadcasting and the 'Internet'.

4. Could the UK Government have argued that since the morality laws in question were enforced by criminal sanctions, the area fell within the scope of public policy, which is also a protectable interest under Article 30? See *Criminal proceedings against Karl Prantl* (Case 16/83) [1984] ECR 1299, [1985] 2 CMLR 238.

   Consider also the Court's refusal to interpret Article 30's reference to public policy in such a way as to include the protection of the economic interests of the consumer in *Commission v Ireland* (Case 113/80) [1981] ECR 1625, [1982] 1 CMLR 706, p.349 above and *Kohl v Ringelhan* (Case 177/83) [1984] ECR 3651, [1985] 3 CMLR 340.

5. One of the issues in both *Henn and Darby* (Case 34/79) and *Conegate* (Case 121/85) was the absence of uniformity in the law of the constituent elements of the UK. How did the Court resolve the problem of applying Article 28 in such circumstances? Is its approach satisfactory? If the sale of an object is banned or severely restricted in Scotland but not in England, what measures could be taken to restrict its importation? Would it matter if importation was into Aberdeen or into Hull? Would it matter if the law was in practice rarely enforced anyway?

....

B: The protection of health and life of humans, animals, and plants

Commission v *UK* **(Case 40/82)**

[1982] ECR 2793, [1982] 3 CMLR 497, Court of Justice of the European Communities

The UK adopted what amounted in practice to an import ban on poultrymeat and eggs from all other Member States except Denmark and Ireland. The stated purpose of the system was to prevent the spread of Newcastle disease, a contagious disease affecting poultry. The Commission considered that the measures adopted went beyond the scope of action permissible under the Treaty, whereas the UK defended them as necessary to protect public health. The Court first explained the factual background:

[22] First, there is agreement among the parties that imports of poultrymeat and poultry products into the United Kingdom from other Member States showed a remarkable rise in the years preceding the introduction of the 1981 measures. This increase concerned in particular imports of slaughtered whole turkeys; in 1980 imports of whole turkeys from France showed a steep rise as compared with those in 1979.

[23] It is also agreed that by mid-1981 the United Kingdom Government and British producers were gravely concerned by the continuing increase in the importation of turkeys from France, and that

British poultry producers made it known that they were troubled about government subsidies which, they asserted, had been made available to French producers. In these circumstances, a certain pressure was put on the United Kingdom Government, by articles in the press and in other ways, to take action in order to reduce imports of poultry products from France.

[24] Secondly, the United Kingdom does not deny that the date chosen for the introduction of the 1981 measures was such as to prevent imports of Christmas turkeys from France into Great Britain for the 1981 season, and that these imports had constituted a very substantial part of the total imports of turkeys in the preceding years.

[25] It is also an established fact that France tried to retain its poultry outlets on the British market by introducing, in September 1981, a policy on Newcastle disease which was broadly similar to the one recently adopted by the United Kingdom. As from 16 September 1981, it prohibited the use of vaccine and instituted a policy of compulsory slaughter in the event of an outbreak of disease. The British authorities refused, however, to admit French poultry products to their territory on the ground that France had not restricted poultry imports from non-member countries, notably from Spain and from some East European countries, where vaccine was still in use. The French Government maintains that it had previously been able to come to arrangements with Switzerland when outbreaks of the disease occurred in France but not in Switzerland, in such a way that French imports into that country could continue, although health controls at the frontier were substantially reinforced.

It then proceeded to examine whether the UK was entitled to act in this manner:

[36] As the Court has already observed in its judgment of 14 December 1979 in Case 34/79 *Henn and Darby* [1979] ECR 3795, the second sentence of Article 36 is designed to prevent restrictions on trade mentioned in the first sentence of that article from being diverted from their proper purpose and used in such a way as either to create discrimination in respect of goods originating in other Member States or indirectly to protect certain national products.

[37] Certain established facts suggest that the real aim of the 1981 measures was to block, for commercial and economic reasons, imports of poultry products from other Member States, in particular from France. The United Kingdom Government had been subject to pressure from British poultry producers to block these imports. It hurriedly introduced its new policy with the result that French Christmas turkeys were excluded from the British market for the 1981 season. It did not inform the Commission and the Member States concerned in good time, as the letter in which the Commission was informed of the new measures – which took effect on 1 September 1981 – was dated 27 August 1981. It did not find it necessary to discuss the effects of the new measures on imports with the Community institutions, with the Standing Veterinary Committee or with the Member States concerned.

[38] It should be noted, in this context, that when the United Kingdom abandoned, in 1964, the policy of non-vaccination and compulsory slaughter conducted till then in Great Britain, in order to adopt a policy of control of Newcastle disease by vaccination, this change of policy was thoroughly prepared by an elaborate report of a committee of experts, by various studies and by prolonged discussions among veterinary experts. The evidence available in the present case does not suggest that any comparable effort was made before the Government decided, in 1981, to reintroduce the policy which it had applied before 1964. The deduction must be made that the 1981 measures did not form part of a seriously considered health policy.

[39] This conclusion is reinforced by the way in which the United Kingdom dealt with French demands that French poultry products should be readmitted to Great Britain after the French Republic had fulfilled the three conditions laid down by the United Kingdom Government, namely that the exporting country should be totally free from outbreaks of Newcastle disease, should prohibit vaccination and should apply a policy of compulsory slaughter in the event of any future outbreak of the disease. By refusing French imports on the ground that France had not closed its frontiers to poultry imports from non-member countries where vaccine was still in use, the United Kingdom added in fact a fourth condition to the three which it had previously stated in its letter to

the Commission of 27 August 1981, and which it still states in its defence in the present case as the only applicable conditions.

[40] Taken together, these facts are sufficient to establish that the 1981 measures constitute a disguised restriction on imports of poultry products from other Member States, in particular from France, unless it can be shown that, for reasons of animal health, the only possibility open to the United Kingdom was to apply the strict measures which are at issue in this case and that, therefore, the methods prescribed by the 1981 measures for obtaining the high standards of animal health which the United Kingdom Government had in mind when it changed its policy with regard to Newcastle disease, were not more restrictive than was necessary for the protection of the health of poultry flocks in Great Britain.

[41] It follows from the information given to the Court during the proceedings that there are less stringent measures for attaining the same result. Thus, the manner in which the Danish authorities deal with imports of poultry products from other Member States – even from those where recent outbreaks of Newcastle disease have been recorded – suggests that it is possible to preserve the highest standard of freedom from Newcastle disease without completely blocking imports from countries where vaccine is still in use.

The UK was accordingly found in breach of Article 30 of the EC Treaty (now, after amendment, Article 28 EC).

NOTE
The case reflects the Court's determination to scrutinize closely purported reliance on Article 30. The Court must be satisfied, first, that a genuine threat to one of the interests specified in Article 30 has been established. Then, the Member State must show that the measures taken are apt to achieve protection from the perceived threat and that they are proportionate to the end in view. As an aspect of this rigorous approach to derogation, the State will fail if the Court considers that it was open to the State to achieve protection of a recognised interest through means which are less restrictive of trade.

At the heart of this approach is the key idea expressed in the second sentence of Article 30 that national measures shall not constitute 'arbitrary discrimination'.

See also, e.g., *Commission v France* (Case 42/82) [1983] ECR 1013, [1984] 1 CMLR 160; *Commission v Italy* (Case C-128/89) [1990] ECR I-3239; *Commission v Germany* (Case C-131/93) [1994] ECR I-3303. *Cf* the extract from Case C-265/95 *Commission v France*, p.355 above.

■ QUESTION

If the UK had instituted a fully considered genuine control of the spread of Newcastle disease, including effective domestic regulation, what type of controls over imports could have been introduced in conformity with Article 30 (and Article 14)?

NOTE
The health risks of many artificial substances are the subject of debate. A Member State may be able to impose controls on products even in the absence of *conclusive* proof of their harmful properties, provided that there is some *objective* reason for doubting the safety of the product. As ever, the State must avoid *arbitrary* discrimination.

Officier van Justitie v *Sandoz BV* (Case 174/82)
[1983] ECR 2445, [1984] 3 CMLR 43, Court of Justice of the European Communities

Sandoz wished to sell in the Netherlands muesli bars to which vitamins had been added. These bars were freely marketable in Belgium and Germany. Authorization to sell was refused by the Dutch authorities on the basis that the vitamins were dangerous to public health. Questions relating to the applicability of Articles 30 and 36 of the EC Treaty (now, after amendment, Articles 28 and 30 EC) were referred to Luxembourg. The Court had no doubt that a breach of Article 30 (now 28) was established. It proceeded to examine the relevance of Article 36 (now 30).

[11] It appears from the file that vitamins are not in themselves harmful substances but on the contrary are recognised by modern science as necessary for the human organizm. Nevertheless excessive consumption of them over a prolonged period may have harmful effects, the extent of which varies according to the type of vitamin: there is generally a greater risk with vitamins soluble in fat than with those soluble in water. According to the observations submitted to the Court, however, scientific research does not appear to be sufficiently advanced to be able to determine with certainty the critical quantities and the precise effects.

[12] It is not disputed by the parties who have submitted observations that the concentration of vitamins contained in the foodstuffs of the kind in issue is far from attaining the critical threshold of harmfulness so that even excessive consumption thereof cannot in itself involve a risk to public health. Nevertheless such a risk cannot be excluded in so far as the consumer absorbs with other foods further quantities of vitamins which it is impossible to monitor or foresee.

[13] The addition of vitamins is thus subject to the general policy in relation to food additives, which are already to a limited extent the subject of Community harmonization. Thus in particular the Council Directive of 23 October 1962 on the approximation of the rules of the Member States concerning the colouring matters authorized for use in foodstuffs intended for human consumption (Official Journal, English Special Edition 1959–62, p.279) and Council Directive No 64/54/EEC of 5 November 1963 on the approximation of the laws of the Member States concerning the preservatives authorized for use in foodstuffs intended for human consumption (Official Journal, English Special Edition 1963–64, p.99), as amended, require the Member States to authorize only the colouring matters and preservatives set out in the list annexed but leave the Member States free to restrict, in certain circumstances, the use even of the substances listed.

[14] As regards foodstuffs intended for particular nutritional uses there has been some degree of harmonization in Council Directive No 77/94/EEC of 21 December 1976 on the approximation of the laws of the Member States relating to foodstuffs for particular nutritional uses (Official Journal 1977, L 26, p.55). Article 7 thereof requires the Member States to adopt all the measures necessary to ensure that trade in the said products cannot be impeded by the application of non-harmonized national provisions governing the composition, manufacturing specifications, packaging or labelling of foodstuffs, subject nevertheless to provisions justified on grounds, *inter alia*, of protection of public health.

[15] The abovementioned Community measures clearly show that the Community legislature accepts the principle that it is necessary to restrict the use of food additives to the substances specified, whilst leaving the Member States a certain discretion to adopt stricter rules. The measures thus testify to great prudence regarding the potential harmfulness of additives, the extent of which is still uncertain in respect of each of the various substances, and leave a wide discretion to the Member States in relation to such additives.

[16] As the Court found in its judgment of 17 December 1981 in Case 272/80 (*Frans-Nederlandse Maatschappij voor Biologische Producten* [1981] ECR 3277), in so far as there are uncertainties at the present state of scientific research it is for the Member States, in the absence of harmonization, to decide what degree of protection of the health and life of humans they intend to assure, having regard however for the requirements of the free movement of goods within the Community.

[17] Those principles also apply to substances such as vitamins which are not as a general rule harmful in themselves but may have special harmful effects solely if taken to excess as part of the general nutrition, the composition of which is unforeseeable and cannot be monitored. In view of the uncertainties inherent in the scientific assessment, national rules prohibiting, without prior authorization, the marketing of foodstuffs to which vitamins have been added are justified on principle within the meaning of Article 36 of the Treaty on grounds of the protection of human health.

[18] Nevertheless the principle of proportionality which underlies the last sentence of Article 36 of the Treaty requires that the power of the Member States to prohibit imports of the products in question from other Member States should be restricted to what is necessary to attain the legitimate aim of protecting health. Accordingly, national rules providing for such a prohibition are justified only if authorizations to market are granted when they are compatible with the need to protect health.

[19] Such an assessment is, however, difficult to make in relation to additives such as vitamins the abovementioned characteristics of which exclude the possibility of foreseeing or monitoring the quantities consumed as part of the general nutrition and the degree of harmfulness of which cannot be determined with sufficient certainty. Nevertheless, although in view of the present stage of harmonization of national laws at the Community level a wide discretion must be left to the Member States, they must, in order to observe the principle of proportionality, authorize marketing when the addition of vitamins to foodstuffs meets a real need, especially a technical or nutritional one.

[20] The first question must therefore be answered to the effect that Community law permits national rules prohibiting without prior authorization the marketing of foodstuffs lawfully marketed in another Member State to which vitamins have been added, provided that the marketing is authorized when the addition of vitamins meets a real need, especially a technical or nutritional one.

Second question

[21] In the second question the national court asks in essence whether Community law precludes national rules such as those referred to by the national court where the authorization to market is subject to proof by the importer that the product in question is not harmful to health.

[22] Inasmuch as the question arises as to where the onus of proof lies when there is a request for authorization, in view of the answer to the first question, it must be remembered that Article 36 of the Treaty creates an exception, which must be strictly interpreted, to the rule of free movement of goods within the Community which is one of the fundamental principles of the common market. It is therefore for the national authorities who rely on that provision in order to adopt a measure restricting intra-Community trade to check in each instance that the measure contemplated satisfies the criteria of that provision.

[23] Accordingly, although the national authorities may, in so far as they do not have it themselves, ask the importer to produce the information in his possession relating to the composition of the product and the technical or nutritional reasons for adding vitamins, they must themselves assess, in the light of all the relevant information, whether authorization must be granted pursuant to Community law.

[24] The second question must therefore be answered to the effect that Community law does not permit national rules which subject authorization to market to proof by the importer that the product in question is not harmful to health, without prejudice to the right of the national authorities to ask the importer to submit all the information in his possession needed to assess the facts.

NOTE

The circumstances in which a State may impose a health check on products which have already been subjected to a check in the State of origin are closely circumscribed. The key, once again, is the elimination of trade restriction which constitutes 'arbitrary discrimination'.

Frans-Nederlandse Maatschappij voor Biologische Producten (Case 272/80)

[1981] ECR 3277, [1982] 2 CMLR 497, Court of Justice of the European Communities

The case concerned Dutch checks on plant protection products imported from France where the products had been approved and lawfully marketed.

[13] . . . [I]t is not disputed that the national rules in question are intended to protect public health and that they therefore come within the exception provided for by Article 36. The measures of control applied by the Netherlands authorities, in particular as regards the approval of the product,

may not therefore be challenged in principle. However, that leaves open the question whether the detailed procedures governing approvals, as indicated by the national court, may possibly constitute a disguised restriction, within the meaning of the last sentence of Article 36, on trade between Member States, in view, on the one hand, of the dangerous nature of the product and, on the other hand, of the fact that it has been the subject of a procedure for approval in the Member State where it has been lawfully marketed.

[14] Whilst a Member State is free to require a product of the type in question, which has already received approval in another Member State, to undergo a fresh procedure of examination and approval, the authorities of the Member States are nevertheless required to assist in bringing about a relaxation of the controls existing in intra-Community trade. It follows that they are not entitled unnecessarily to require technical or chemical analyses or laboratory tests where those analyses and tests have already been carried out in another Member State and their results are available to those authorities, or may at their request be placed at their disposal.

[15] For the same reasons, a Member State operating an approvals procedure must ensure that no unnecessary control expenses are incurred if the practical effects of the control carried out in the Member State of origin satisfy the requirements of the protection of public health in the importing Member State. On the other hand, the mere fact that those expenses weigh more heavily on a trader marketing small quantities of an approved product than on his competitor who markets much greater quantities, does not justify the conclusion that such expenses constitute arbitrary discrimination or a disguised restriction within the meaning of Article 36.

[16] The reply to be given to the question submitted to the Court must therefore be that it follows from Article 30 in conjunction with Article 36 of the Treaty that a Member State is not prohibited from requiring plant protection products to be subject to prior approval, even if those products have already been approved in another Member State. The authorities of the importing State are however not entitled unnecessarily to require technical or chemical analyses or laboratory tests when the same analyses and tests have already been carried out in another Member State and their results are available to those authorities or may at their request be placed at their disposal.

[17] It is for the national court to examine, in the light of the foregoing considerations, whether, and if so to what extent, the procedures governing approvals laid down by the national legislation are justified under Article 36.

NOTE

The judgment in *Sandoz* (Case 174/82) (p.373 above) indicates that unilateral Member State action in derogation from the basic principle of free movement may be robbed of its legal justification by the introduction of Community legislation which secures the protection of the particular interest in issue. Community legislation was not yet sufficiently comprehensive in that case (para 19). This is the 'dual function' of harmonization legislation: a common Community rule which *facilitates* free trade but on terms which *protect* the interests which might previously have justified national rules. The Community's work has been particularly intense in the field of health controls. It has sought to establish a system of controls and checks which will allow the dismantling of the existing obstructions of differing rules in each State, because, as recognised in *Biologische Producten* (Case 272/80), it remains lawful to impose 'double checks' in exceptional circumstances where the legitimate concerns of the State of importation are not met by the exporting State.

This has given rise to some difficulty in law in ascertaining the scope of permissible Member State action in areas subject to Community legislative intervention.

Rewe-Zentralfinanz Gmbh v *Landwirtschaftskammer* (Case 4/75)
[1975] ECR 843, [1975] 1 CMLR 599, Court of Justice of the European Communities

The case concerned checks of imported apples by the German authorities. This constituted a clear breach of Article 30 of the EC Treaty (now, after amendment, Article 28 EC). Were the checks justifiable? Reliance on Article 36 of the EC Treaty (now, after amendment, Article 30 EC) was complicated by the existence of Community legislation governing the type of controls at issue.

[5] . . . [P]hytosanitary inspections at the frontier which plant products, such as apples, coming from another Member State are required to undergo, constitute measures having an effect equivalent to quantitative restrictions within the meaning of Article 30 of the Treaty, and are prohibited under that provision subject to the exceptions laid down by Community law.

[6] Under the first sentence of Article 36 of the Treaty, the provisions of Articles 30 to 34 are not to preclude restrictions on imports and, therefore, measures having equivalent effect, which are justified for reasons of protection of the health of plants.

Council Directive No 69/466/EEC of 8 December 1969 (OJ 1969, L 323, p.5) on the control of San José Scale, lays down a series of provisions which are common to all the Member States of the Community.

The purpose of this Directive is to introduce certain minimum measures common to all the Member States by which certain harmful organizms may be controlled 'simultaneously and methodically' throughout the Community and prevented from spreading.

At the same time the Directive, which was adopted under Articles 43 and 100 of the Treaty, forms part of the measures intended to remove obstacles to the free movement of agricultural products within the Common Market.

[7] Its fourth recital shows, however, that the measures laid down are intended to supplement and not to replace the protective measures taken against the introduction of harmful organizms into each Member State.

By authorizing those States to adopt such additional or stricter provisions as may be required to control San José Scale or to prevent it from spreading, Article 11 reserves to them the power to maintain such measures in force to the extent necessary.

In the light of the current Community rules in this matter, a phytosanitary inspection carried out by a Member State on the importation of plant products constitutes, in principle, one of the restrictions on imports which are justified under the first sentence of Article 36 of the Treaty.

[8] However, the restrictions on imports referred to in the first sentence of Article 36 cannot be accepted under the second sentence of that article if they constitute a means of arbitrary discrimination.

The fact that plant products imported from another Member State are subject to a phytosanitary inspection although domestic products are not subject to an equivalent examination when they are despatched within the Member State might constitute arbitrary discrimination within the meaning of the abovementioned provision.

Therefore, the phytosanitary inspection of imported products which are shown to originate in areas other than those referred to in Article 3 of Council Directive No 69/466/EEC may constitute an additional or stricter measure which is not justified by Article 11 of that directive and should be regarded as a means of arbitrary discrimination within the meaning of the second sentence of Article 36 of the Treaty.

The different treatment of imported and domestic products, based on the need to prevent the spread of the harmful organizm could not, however, be regarded as arbitrary discrimination if effective measures are taken in order to prevent the distribution of contaminated domestic products and if there is reason to believe, in particular on the basis of previous experience, that there is a risk of the harmful organizm's spreading if no inspection is held on importation.

[9] The reply to the questions put must therefore be that a requirement to submit imports of plant products, such as apples, from another Member State to a phytosanitary inspection at the frontier in order to establish whether such products are carriers of certain organizms harmful to plants constitutes a measure having an effect equivalent to quantitative restrictions within the meaning of Article 30 of the Treaty and is prohibited under that provision, subject to the exceptions laid down in Article 36 of the Treaty.

The additional or stricter provisions which may be required under Article 11 of Council Directive No 69/466/EEC of 8 December 1969 in order to control San José Scale and prevent it from spreading entitle the Member States to make phytosanitary inspections of imported products if effective measures are taken in order to prevent the distribution of contaminated domestic products and if there is reason to believe, in particular on the basis of previous experience, that there is a risk of the harmful organizm's spreading if no inspection is held on importation.

Oberkreisdirektor v *Moormann* (Case 190/87)
[1988] ECR 4689, [1990] 1 CMLR 656, Court of Justice of the European Communities

[10] The Court has consistently held that where, in application of Article 100 of the Treaty, Community directives provide for the harmonization of the measures necessary to ensure *inter alia* the protection of animal and human health and establish Community procedures to check that they are observed, recourse to Article 36 is no longer justified and the appropriate checks must be carried out and protective measures adopted within the framework outlined by the harmonizing directive (judgments of 5 October 1977 in 5/77, *Tedeschi* v *Denkavit* ((1977)) ECR 155; 5 April 1979 in Case 148/78, *Ratti* ((1979)) ECR 1629; and 8 November 1979 in Case 251/78, *Denkavit* ((1979)) ECR 3369).

[11] As the Court has already held in its judgment of 6 October 1983 in Joined Cases 2 to 4/82 (*Delhaize* ((1982)) ECR 2973), Council Directive 71/188/EEC of 15 February 1971 on health problems affecting trade in fresh poultrymeat (Official Journal, English Special Edition 1971 (I), p.106) introduced a harmonized system of health inspections. This system of health inspections, harmonized at Community level and based on full inspection of the goods in the exporting State, replaces inspection in the State of destination and is intended to allow the free movement of the goods concerned under the same conditions as those of an internal market.

[12] Consequently, with regard to trade in fresh poultrymeat, health inspection carried out systematically on goods when they cross the frontier can no longer be justified on grounds of the protection of health under Article 36 of the Treaty.

[13] Only occasional health inspections carried out by the State of destination are permissible, provided that they are not increased to such an extent as to constitute a disguised restriction on trade between the Member States (see judgment of 6 October 1983, *Delhaize*, cited above).

NOTE

Establishing a balance between the responsibility of the Community authorities and those at the national level is perhaps the paramount problem confronting the shapers of the internal market. It is not a problem which miraculously vanished on the last day of 1992! It is deceptively simple to declare that in principle the passage of Community harmonization legislation precludes an individual State's reliance on Article 30; and that the interest can be protected in a Community measure which also facilitates free trade. The reality is that in a heterogenous Community of 15 Member States a single Community rule cannot encompass all the diffuse interests at work in the structure. So in practice national derogations and differing standards may be judged necessary. Both the two cases just considered illustrate this. The Community has a responsibility to develop a framework in which the objective of free trade will be pursued in accompaniment with the protection of and respect for national diversity and social traditions – see Article 2 EC, p.290 above. This implies a careful mix between responsibility at Community level and responsibility at national level. In addition, the administration of the law must be allocated to the appropriate level in the structure.

Further discussion of these issues is found below at p.420 and in Chapters 19 and 20.

SECTION 4: **ELIMINATING REMAINING BARRIERS TO TRADE**

It has been observed that *Sandoz* (Case 174/82) (at p.373 above) is a decision which allows national rules to restrict trade pending Community harmonization in the pursuit of the protection of public health; *Campus Oil Ltd* v *Minister for Industry and*

Energy (Case 72/83) [1984] ECR 2727 provides a parallel example of trade restrictions to protect domestic energy production, permissible in the interest of public security given the inadequacy of existing Community rules guaranteeing energy supplies; *Moormann* (Case 190/87) (at p.378 above) demonstrates the interaction of Community rules and national competence, again in the area of health protection.

Are all the heads of justification under Article 30 susceptible to harmonization, or do they perform different functions calling for different solutions? How could a Community approach to public morality or protection of national treasures be achieved which yields free trade? How will the Community develop? To what extent is a balance between the exclusive competence of the Community and the legitimate concerns of the diverse Member States feasible? This is the very essence of the Community's task.

It falls to be considered how these questions have been addressed in the context of the completion of the internal market in accordance with Article 14. As already suggested (in Chapter 9 and subsequently), the problems persist beyond the target date of the end of 1992. However, Articles 100a and 100b were inserted into the Treaty by the Single European Act with a view to resolving some of these issues. In practice, much internal market legislation has been based on Article 100a. The Amsterdam Treaty repealed Article 100b, which proved superfluous, but it amended and re-numbered Article 100a. It is now Article 95 and it is set out at p.616 in Chapter 19, where harmonization policy is discussed in its wider context.

■ QUESTIONS

Discuss the impact of Community law in the following cases:

1. The French authorities uncover a scandal involving the use of anti-freeze by wine producers. The adulterated wine has already caused several deaths in France.

   The UK immediately introduces a system whereby all French wine must be inspected and granted a licence before it may be imported. The procedure at the ports can result in the detention of goods for up to one month.

   A flat rate fee of £1 per case is imposed on all French wine subject to this procedure.

   How would your answer differ if the French authorities, in an effort to minimize the detrimental effect of the scandal on their wine export trade, had already introduced a similar system of checks on all wine exported from France?

2. Franco exports dairy products from France to Germany. He has always sold his milk in Germany in cartons bearing the French flag. He believes that this is a valuable marketing technique. However, he learns that a new German law prohibits the use of national flags in product promotion. This law is part of a programme introduced by the German Government to make its population more aware of European integration and less likely to exercise national prejudice.

NOTE

For additional material and resources see the Companion Website at: www.oup.co.uk/ best.textbooks/law/weatherill6e

12

Beyond Discrimination: Article 28

SECTION 1 **INDISTINCTLY APPLICABLE RULES: THE *CASSIS DE DIJON* FORMULA**

The previous Chapter examined a range of rules which discriminated against imports. However, even in the absence of discrimination against imported goods, national trading rules are capable of impeding the free circulation of goods in the Community. Article 28 may apply even to national legislation which makes no distinction between domestic and imported goods. The scope and application of Community law in this area is primarily the consequence of the Court's activism, and therefore it is appropriate to allow the leading case to provide the introductory means of explanation. Remember that Article 30, referred to in the judgment, was re-numbered by the Treaty of Amsterdam and is now, with minor amendment, Article 28.

Rewe-Zentrale AG v *Bundesmonopolverwaltung für Branntwein* (Case 120/78)
[1979] ECR 649, [1979] 3 CMLR 494, Court of Justice of the European Communities

[1] By order of 28 April 1978, which was received at the Court on 22 May, the Hessisches Finanzgericht referred two questions to the Court under Article 177 of the EEC Treaty for a preliminary ruling on the interpretation of Articles 30 and 37 of the EEC Treaty, for the purpose of assessing the compatibility with Community law of a provision of the German rules relating to the marketing of alcoholic beverages fixing a minimum alcoholic strength for various categories of alcoholic products.

[2] It appears from the order making the reference that the plaintiff in the main action intends to import a consignment of 'Cassis de Dijon' originating in France for the purpose of marketing it in the Federal Republic of Germany.

The plaintiff applied to the Bundesmonopolverwaltung (Federal Monopoly Administration for Spirits) for authorization to import the product in question and the monopoly administration informed it that because of its insufficient alcoholic strength the said product does not have the characteristics required in order to be marketed within the Federal Republic of Germany.

[3] The monopoly administration's attitude is based on Article 100 of the Branntweinmonopolgesetz and on the rules drawn up by the monopoly administration pursuant to that provision, the effect of which is to fix the minimum alcohol content of specified categories of liqueurs and the potable spirits (Verordnung über den Mindestweingeistgehalt von Trinkbranntweinen of 28 February 1958, Bundesanzeiger No 48 of 11 March 1958).

Those provisions lay down that the marketing of fruit liqueurs, such as 'Cassis de Dijon', is conditional upon a minimum alcohol content of 25%, whereas the alcohol content of the product in question, which is freely marketed as such in France, is between 15 and 20%.

[4] The plaintiff takes the view that the fixing by the German rules of a minimum alcohol content leads

to the result that well-known spirits products from other Member States of the Community cannot be sold in the Federal Republic of Germany and that the said provision therefore constitutes a restriction on the free movement of goods between Member States which exceeds the bounds of the trade rules reserved to the latter.

In its view it is a measure having an effect equivalent to a quantitative restriction on imports contrary to Article 30 of the EEC Treaty.

Since, furthermore, it is a measure adopted within the context of the management of the spirits monopoly, the plaintiff considers that there is also an infringement of Article 37, according to which the Member States shall progressively adjust any State monopolies of a commercial character so as to ensure that when the transitional period has ended no discrimination regarding the conditions under which goods are procured or marketed exists between nationals of Member States.

[5] In order to reach a decision on this dispute the Hessisches Finanzgericht has referred two questions to the Court, worded as follows:

> 1. Must the concept of measures having an effect equivalent to quantitative restrictions on imports contained in Article 30 of the EEC Treaty be understood as meaning that the fixing of a minimum wine-spirit content for potable spirits laid down in the German Branntweinmonopolgesetz, the result of which is that traditional products of other Member States whose wine-spirit content is below the fixed limit cannot be put into circulation in the Federal Republic of Germany, also comes within this concept?
> 2. May the fixing of such a minimum wine-spirit content come within the concept of 'discrimination regarding the conditions under which goods are procured and marketed . . . between nationals of Member States' contained in Article 37 of the EEC Treaty?

[6] The national court is thereby asking for assistance in the matter of interpretation in order to enable it to assess whether the requirement of a minimum alcohol content may be covered either by the prohibition on all measures having an effect equivalent to quantitative restrictions in trade between Member States contained in Article 30 of the Treaty or by the prohibition on all discrimination regarding the conditions under which goods are procured and marketed between nationals of Member States within the meaning of Article 37.

[7] It should be noted in this connexion that Article 37 relates specifically to State monopolies of a commercial character.

That provision is therefore irrelevant with regard to national provisions which do not concern the exercise by a public monopoly of its specific function – namely, its exclusive right – but apply in a general manner to the production and marketing of alcoholic beverages, whether or not the latter are covered by the monopoly in question.

That being the case, the effect on intra-Community trade of the measure referred to by the national court must be examined solely in relation to the requirements under Article 30, as referred to by the first question.

[8] In the absence of common rules relating to the production and marketing of alcohol – a proposal for a regulation submitted to the Council by the Commission on 7 December 1976 (Official Journal C 309, p.2) not yet having received the Council's approval – it is for the Member States to regulate all matters relating to the production and marketing of alcohol and alcoholic beverages on their own territory.

Obstacles to movement within the Community resulting from disparities between the national laws relating to the marketing of the products in question must be accepted in so far as those provisions may be recognised as being necessary in order to satisfy mandatory requirements relating in particular to the effectiveness of fiscal supervision, the protection of public health, the fairness of commercial transactions and the defence of the consumer.

[9] The Government of the Federal Republic of Germany, intervening in the proceedings, put forward various arguments which, in its view, justify the application of provisions relating to the minimum alcohol content of alcoholic beverages, adducing considerations relating on the one hand to the protection of public health and on the other to the protection of the consumer against unfair commercial practices.

[10] As regards the protection of public health the German Government states that the purpose of the fixing of minimum alcohol contents by national legislation is to avoid the proliferation of alcoholic beverages on the national market, in particular alcoholic beverages with a low alcohol content, since, in its view, such products may more easily induce a tolerance towards alcohol than more highly alcoholic beverages.

[11] Such considerations are not decisive since the consumer can obtain on the market an extremely wide range of weakly or moderately alcoholic products and furthermore a large proportion of alcoholic beverages with a high alcohol content freely sold on the German market is generally consumed in a diluted form.

[12] The German Government also claims that the fixing of a lower limit for the alcohol content of certain liqueurs is designed to protect the consumer against unfair practices on the part of producers and distributors of alcoholic beverages.

This argument is based on the consideration that the lowering of the alcohol content secures a competitive advantage in relation to beverages with a higher alcohol content, since alcohol constitutes by far the most expensive constituent of beverages by reason of the high rate of tax to which it is subject.

Furthermore, according to the German Government, to allow alcoholic products into free circulation wherever, as regards their alcohol content, they comply with the rules laid down in the country of production would have the effect of imposing as a common standard within the Community the lowest alcohol content permitted in any of the Member States, and even of rendering any requirements in this field inoperative since a lower limit of this nature is foreign to the rules of several Member States.

[13] As the Commission rightly observed, the fixing of limits in relation to the alcohol content of beverages may lead to the standardization of products placed on the market and of their designations, in the interests of a greater transparency of commercial transactions and offers for sale to the public.

However, this line of argument cannot be taken so far as to regard the mandatory fixing of minimum alcohol contents as being an essential guarantee of the fairness of commercial transactions, since it is a simple matter to ensure that suitable information is conveyed to the purchaser by requiring the display of an indication of origin and of the alcohol content on the packaging of products.

[14] It is clear from the foregoing that the requirements relating to the minimum alcohol content of alcoholic beverages do not serve a purpose which is in the general interest and such as to take precedence over the requirements of the free movement of goods, which constitutes one of the fundamental rules of the Community.

In practice, the principal effect of requirements of this nature is to promote alcoholic beverages having a high alcohol content by excluding from the national market products of other Member States which do not answer that description.

It therefore appears that the unilateral requirement imposed by the rules of a Member State of a minimum alcohol content for the purposes of the sale of alcoholic beverages constitutes an obstacle to trade which is incompatible with the provisions of Article 30 of the Treaty.

There is therefore no valid reason why, provided that they have been lawfully produced and marketed in one of the Member States, alcoholic beverages should not be introduced into any other Member State; the sale of such products may not be subject to a legal prohibition on the marketing of beverages with an alcohol content lower than the limit set by the national rules.

[15] Consequently, the first question should be answered to the effect that the concept of 'measures having an effect equivalent to quantitative restrictions on imports' contained in Article 30 of the Treaty is to be understood to mean that the fixing of a minimum alcohol content for alcoholic beverages intended for human consumption by the legislation of a Member State also falls within the prohibition laid down in that provision where the importation of alcoholic beverages lawfully produced and marketed in another Member State is concerned.

NOTE

Notice that such trade restrictions arise simply because national laws are different within the Community. Typical French products were excluded from the German market by a rule which on its face made no reference whatsoever to national origin. The result was the isolation of the German market and the protection of the German producer from competition. Such market partitioning subverts the concept of a common market.

P. Cecchini, The European Challenge: 1992, the Benefits of a Single Market
(Aldershot: Wildwood House, 1988), pp.24–27

Divergences in technical regulations and standards – costs difficult to quantify but impossible to ignore

Rated by companies themselves as one of the most acute problems they face in their European operations . . ., disparities between national technical regulations and standards are a complex and, to the outside observer, an arcane subject. Yet their adverse impact on industry seeking to exploit the full dimension of the EC market, a priority matter for the Community policy-maker as for the businessman, is now widely accepted.

It is not difficult to see why. In an increasing number of sectors, firms will be obliged to survive by selling in quantities much larger than are likely to be absorbed by their share of a single, narrow national market. To compete, they need to produce on a larger scale. To amortize this investment in new plant, and also their spiralling expenditure on research and innovation, they need the larger, European market.

National product regulations and standards, however, impose an entirely contrary logic. They tend, by their differences, to force companies to do what their business strategy tells them is wrong: produce for the national market, innovate for the national market. Manufacturers are thus often constrained either to limit themselves to a sub-optimal market, or to attack new markets via a range of sub-optimal plants and narrowly relevant technology. Either option implies extensive costs – the costs of non-Europe.

Adverse effects are thus not limited to restrictions on cross-border trade. They impact on the core functions of business – production and technology. And the costs they incur are often compounded by their use in combination with other obstacles to market entry, notably restrictive public procurement, e.g., telecommunications equipment . . . Among the worst affected by these and related barriers are high tech sectors which are precisely those where market fragmentation has a proven track record in putting Europe at a competitive disadvantage with the US and Japan.

Barriers in this field result from differences between EC countries for three types of arrangement: technical regulations, standards, testing and certification procedures.

Technical regulations lay down legal requirements, enacted by the national legislator mainly in the interests of health, safety and the environment; often these requirements refer to standards.

Standards are not legally binding in themselves, since they are written by private national standard-isation bodies like DIN (in Germany), BSI (in Britain) and AFNOR (in France). However, although standards are only voluntary codifications for products and product processes, they often assume a quasi-legal status because of their use as a reference in technical regulations and, for example, in insurance and product liability claims, as well as in calls for tender for public procurement.

Testing and certification procedures are used to check that a product or process complies either with voluntary standards or with statutory regulations. If successfully passed, they result in the issuance of certificates of conformity. However, a typical problem is non-recognition by one EC country of another's certification process, meaning at best additional testing and at worst an absolute market entry barrier.

Costs: multi-sector impact

The costs . . . imposed by these barriers hit manufacturing industries right across the board. But they do so in a manner which is so sector-specific and which, even then, is often inextricably combined with the impact of other barriers, as to make a quantified extrapolation at the general level impossible to undertake. But on an individual industry basis, the story is clear. It is illustrated by the investigations carried out by the research into certain selected industries . . . Their results are in turn corroborated and amplified by company executives themselves in the general survey of manufacturing business conducted for the research.

Telecom equipment, automobiles, foodstuffs, pharmaceuticals and the building products sector are . . . five major EC industries where standards and technical regulations, alone or in combination with other obstacles, inject heavy doses of inefficiency into business operations.

This is most spectacularly the case in the telecom sector. Here the industry's regulators – usually the national PTTs – have traditionally sustained their restrictive procurement practices by demanding observance of narrowly relevant standards reinforced by discriminating certification procedures. The overall cost of these mutually supportive barriers is estimated as high as Ecu 4.8 billion. The experience of telecom equipment, moreover, is to an extent indicative of the massive losses imposed by divergent standards on other high technology sectors, where burgeoning R&D expenditure can only be recouped by manufacturing products to widely marketable standards.

At the other end of industry's product range, foodstuffs and building products have their own experiences to tell. Thus of the total estimated costs of up to Ecu 1 billion attributable to market barriers in the foodstuffs sector, content and ingredient regulations on just four items (chocolates, beer, ice-cream and pasta) contribute over 80% . . . In the building products sector, research shows unequivocally that divergent standards and lengthy certification (whose procedures can last years rather than months) are the primary causes of non-Europe costs estimated in total at around Ecu 2.5 billion. Pharmaceutical companies, meanwhile, face serious problems and significant costs in getting new products authorized and admitted to the market.

Motor manufacturing enjoys a paradoxical but costly situation. It is both the sector where the removal of technical barriers is judged as most necessary by business itself . . . and yet the one where the Community has had most apparent success in harmonising technical regulations. As many as 41 EC harmonisation directives, dealing with specifications for various parts of the automobile, have been adopted over the years. But the key problem is that there remain three further directives which need to be adopted before full EC type approval can be achieved. In the absence of Community type approval (which is being held up on political rather than technical grounds), and thus of a European certification procedure, EC wide manufacturers are generally being forced into costly duplications.

NOTE

The ruling in 'Cassis de Dijon' (Case 120/78) is one of the main pillars of EC trade law. As already discussed in Chapter 9 (p.321 above), the Court has constructed a strategy for judging the permissibility of regulatory diversity between the States in an integrating market. The principles set out by the Court in its ruling in *Gebhard* (Case C-55/94, p.321 above), have their roots in the fertile soil of the '*Cassis de Dijon*' ruling.

A further simple example of market partitioning caused by national laws which in effect enshrine a preference for typical national produce is provided by the following case.

Ministère Public v *Deserbais* (Case 286/86)

[1988] ECR 4907, Court of Justice of the European Communities

French legislation restricted the use of the name 'Edam' to cheese with a minimum fat content of 40%. M. Deserbais imported cheese from Germany where it was lawfully produced with a fat content of only 34.3%. When he marketed the cheese in France as 'Edam', he was prosecuted for unlawful use of a trade name. M. Deserbais argued that Article 30 of the EC Treaty (now, after amendment, Article 28 EC) provided him with a complete defence to the charge. The matter was referred to the Court under the Article 177 preliminary reference procedure, found in Article 234 post-Amsterdam (Chapter 7).

[10] [T]he national court starts from the premise that the cheese in question, containing 34% fat, has

been lawfully and traditionally produced in the Federal Republic of Germany under the name 'Edam' in accordance with the laws and regulations applicable to it there, and that consumers' attention is adequately drawn to that fact by the labelling.

[11] It must also be stated that at the present stage of development of Community law there are no common rules governing the names of the various types of cheeses in the Community. Accordingly, it cannot be stated in principle that a Member State may not lay down rules making the use by national producers of a name for a cheese subject to the observance of a traditional minimum fat content.

[12] However, it would be incompatible with Article 30 of the Treaty and the objectives of a common market to apply such rules to imported cheeses of the same type where those cheeses have been lawfully produced and marketed in another Member State under the same generic name but with a different minimum fat content. The Member State into which they are imported cannot prevent the importation and marketing of such cheeses where adequate information for the consumer is ensured.

[13] The question may arise whether the same rule must be applied where a product presented under a particular name is so different, as regards its composition or production, from the products generally known by that name in the Community that it cannot be regarded as falling within the same category. However, no situation of that kind arises in the circumstances described by the national court in this case.

The Court's reply to the question referred was accordingly:

Article 30 *et seq.* of the Treaty must be interpreted as precluding a Member State from applying national legislation making the right to use the trade name of a type of cheese subject to the observance of a minimum fat content to products of the same type imported from another Member State when those products have been lawfully manufactured and marketed under that name in that Member State and consumers are provided with proper information.

NOTE

There is every reason to insist that Article 28 is capable of applying to such national rules because of the clear restrictive *effect* on intra-Community trade. The *'Cassis de Dijon'* (Case 120/78) approach has this emphasis on effect in common with the *Dassonville* (Case 8/74) formula (p.344 above). This interpretation of Article 28 is crucial to the attack on national protectionism and market division. According to P. Verloren van Themaat (1982) 18 CDE 123, at p.135:

La crise économique actuelle augmente sans doute la tentation pour les Etats membres de prendre des mesures qui sont susceptibles d'entraver directement ou indirectement, actuellement ou potentiellement, le commerce intracommunautaire . . .

The Court's application of Article 28 constitutes an important corrective to that persisting temptation.

■ QUESTION

To what extent has the Court adopted a more vigorous pro-free trade stance than that envisaged by Article 3 of Directive 70/50 (p.342 above)?

NOTES

1. The result of the Court's approach is that goods produced to a standard which entitles access to the market of the Member State of production should normally be recognised as a sufficient standard to deserve access to the market of any other Member State. It is assumed that all Member States have a broadly equivalent approach to basic standards of health and safety, and that they should recognise this in dealing with imports from other Member States. The approach

taken in *'Cassis de Dijon'* (Case 120/78) is an important impetus towards market integration. A State can no longer present an importer with a rule book full of technical standards and demand that the importer's goods conform to those standards of manufacture or designation.

2. Only in exceptional circumstances can a State stand on its technical rules to prevent the import of a product from another Member State – when it can show that the rules are necessary to satisfy a mandatory requirement. There is, then, a strong presumption in favour of free trade inherent in the Court's approach.

Commission v Germany (Case 178/84)
[1987] ECR 1227, [1988] 1 CMLR 780, Court of Justice of the European Communities

This was an infringement procedure against Germany (see Chapter 4) alleging breach of Article 30 of the EC Treaty (now, after amendment, Article 28 EC). Germany prohibited the marketing on its territory of beer lawfully produced and marketed in other Member States if the beer failed to comply with the provisions of the *Biersteuergesetz* of 1952. The law applied equally to all beer produced in Germany itself, so there was no question of discrimination against imports. There were two limbs to the *Biersteuergesetz* which the Commission was concerned to challenge. In the first place, the name 'Bier' could be used only for products brewed using malted barley, hops, yeast, and water alone. The use of other ingredients such as maize did not preclude the marketing of the finished product, but it could not be sold as 'Bier'.

[25] [T]he Commission concedes that as long as harmonisation has not been achieved at Community level the Member States have the power in principle to lay down rules governing the manufacture, the composition and the marketing of beverages. It stresses, however, that rules which, like Article 10 of the Biersteuergesetz, prohibit the use of a generic designation for the marketing of products manufactured partly from raw materials, such as rice and maize, other than those whose use is prescribed in the national territory are contrary to Community law. In any event, such rules go beyond what is necessary in order to protect the German consumer, since that could be done simply by means of labelling or notices. Those rules therefore constitute an impediment to trade contrary to Article 30 of the EEC Treaty.

[26] The German Government has first sought to justify its rules on public-health grounds. It maintains that the use of raw materials other than those permitted by Article 9 of the Biersteuergesetz would inevitably entail the use of additives. However, at the hearing the German Government conceded that Article 10 of the Biersteuergesetz, which is merely a rule on designation, was exclusively intended to protect consumers. In its view, consumers associate the designation 'Bier' with a beverage manufactured from only the raw materials listed in Article 9 of the Biersteuergesetz. Consequently, it is necessary to prevent them from being misled as to the nature of the product by being led to believe that a beverage called 'Bier' complies with the Reinheitsgebot when that is not the case. The German Government maintains that its rules are not protectionist in aim. It stresses in that regard that the raw materials whose use is specified in Article 9(1) and (2) of the Biersteuergesetz are not necessarily of national origin. Any trader marketing products satisfying the prescribed rules is free to use the designation 'Bier' and those rules can readily be complied with outside the Federal Republic of Germany.

[27] According to a consistent line of decisions of the Court (above all, the judgment of 11 July 1974 in Case 8/74 *Procureur du Roi v Dassonville* [1974] ECR 837) the prohibition of measures having an effect equivalent to quantitative restrictions under Article 30 of the EEC Treaty covers 'all trading rules enacted by Member States which are capable of hindering, directly or indirectly, actually or potentially, intra-Community trade'.

[28] The Court has also consistently held (in particular in the judgment of 20 February 1979 in Case 120/78 *REWE-Zentrale AG* v *Bundesmonopolverwaltung* [1979] ECR 649, and the judgment of 10 November 1982 in Case 261/81 *Walter Rau Lebensmittelwerke* v *De Smedt* [1982] ECR 3961) that 'in the absence of common rules relating to the marketing of the products concerned, obstacles to free movement within the Community resulting from disparities between the national laws must be accepted in so far as such rules, applicable to domestic and to imported products without distinction, may be recognised as being necessary in order to satisfy mandatory requirements relating *inter alia* to consumer protection. It is also necessary for such rules to be proportionate to the aim in view. If a Member State has a choice between various measures to attain the same objective it should choose the means which least restricts the free movement of goods'.

[29] It is not contested that the application of Article 10 of the Biersteuergesetz to beers from other Member States in whose manufacture raw materials other than malted barley have been lawfully used, in particular rice and maize, is liable to constitute an obstacle to their importation into the Federal Republic of Germany.

[30] Accordingly, it must be established whether the application of that provision may be justified by imperative requirements relating to consumer protection.

[31] The German Government's argument that Article 10 of the Biersteuergesetz is essential in order to protect German consumers because, in their minds, the designation 'Bier' is inseparably linked to the beverage manufactured solely from the ingredients laid down in Article 9 of the Biersteuergesetz must be rejected.

[32] Firstly, consumers' conceptions which vary from one Member State to the other are also likely to evolve in the course of time within a Member State. The establishment of the common market is, it should be added, one of the factors that may play a major contributory role in that development. Whereas rules protecting consumers against misleading practices enable such a development to be taken into account, legislation of the kind contained in Article 10 of the Biersteuergesetz prevents it from taking place. As the Court has already held in another context (judgment of 27 February 1980 in Case 170/78 *Commission* v *United Kingdom* [1980] ECR 417), the legislation of a Member State must not 'crystallize given consumer habits so as to consolidate an advantage acquired by national industries concerned to comply with them'.

[33] Secondly, in the other Member States of the Community the designations corresponding to the German designation 'Bier' are generic designations for a fermented beverage manufactured from malted barley, whether malted barley on its own or with the addition of rice or maize. The same approach is taken in Community law as can be seen from heading No 22.03 of the Common Customs Tariff. The German legislature itself utilizes the designation 'Bier' in that way in Article 9(7) and (8) of the Biersteuergesetz in order to refer to beverages not complying with the manufacturing rules laid down in Article 9(1) and (2).

[34] The German designation 'Bier' and its equivalents in the languages of the other Member States of the Community may therefore not be restricted to beers manufactured in accordance with the rules in force in the Federal Republic of Germany.

[35] It is admittedly legitimate to seek to enable consumers who attribute specific qualities to beers manufactured from particular raw materials to make their choice in the light of that consideration. However, as the Court has already emphasized (judgment of 9 December 1981 in Case 193/80 *Commission* v *Italy* [1981] ECR 3019), that possibility may be ensured by means which do not prevent the importation of products which have been lawfully manufactured and marketed in other Member States and, in particular, 'by the compulsory affixing of suitable labels giving the nature of the product sold'. By indicating the raw materials utilized in the manufacture of beer 'such a course would enable the consumer to make his choice in full knowledge of the facts and would guarantee transparency in trading and in offers to the public'. It must be added that such a system of mandatory consumer information must not entail negative assessments for beers not complying with the requirements of Article 9 of the Biersteuergesetz.

[36] Contrary to the German Government's view, such a system of consumer information may

operate perfectly well even in the case of a product which, like beer, is not necessarily supplied to consumers in bottles or in cans capable of bearing the appropriate details. That is borne out, once again, by the German legislation itself.

Article 26(1) and (2) of the aforementioned regulation implementing the Biersteuergesetz provides for a system of consumer information in respect of certain beers, even where those beers are sold on draught, when the requisite information must appear on the casks or the beer taps.

[37] It follows from the foregoing that by applying the rules on designation in Article 10 of the Biersteuergesetz to beers imported from other Member States which were manufactured and marketed lawfully in those States the Federal Republic of Germany has failed to fulfil its obligations under Article 30 of the EEC Treaty.

NOTE

The second limb of the rules involved an absolute ban on the marketing of beers containing additives. This rule also applied to all beers wherever produced; it was not origin specific. Arguments relating to the protection of public health which were rather more powerful than those advanced in relation to the first limb of the *Biersteuergesetz* were advanced.

Commission v Germany (Case 178/84)

[1987] ECR 1227, [1988] 1 CMLR 780, Court of Justice of the European Communities

[38] In the Commission's opinion the absolute ban on the marketing of beers containing additives cannot be justified on public-health grounds. It maintains that the other Member States control very strictly the utilization of additives in foodstuffs and do not authorize the use of any given additive until thorough tests have established that it is harmless. In the Commission's view, there should be a presumption that beers manufactured in other Member States which contain additives authorized there represent no danger to public health. The Commission argues that if the Federal Republic of Germany wishes to oppose the importation of such beers then it bears the onus of proving that such beers are a danger to public health. The Commission considers that in this case that burden of proof has not been discharged. In any event, the rules on additives applying to beer in the Federal Republic of Germany are disproportionate in so far as they completely preclude the use of additives whereas the rules for other beverages, such as soft drinks, are much more flexible.

[39] For its part, the German Government considers that in view of the dangers resulting from the utilization of additives whose long-term effects are not yet known and in particular of the risks resulting from the accumulation of additives in the organism and their interaction with other substances, such as alcohol, it is necessary to minimize the quantity of additives ingested. Since beer is a foodstuff of which large quantities are consumed in Germany, the German Government considers that it is particularly desirable to prohibit the use of any additive in its manufacture, especially in so far as the use of additives is not technologically necessary and can be avoided if only the ingredients laid down in the Biersteuergesetz are used. In those circumstances, the German rules on additives in beer are fully justified by the need to safeguard public health and do not infringe the principle of proportionality.

[40] It is not contested that the prohibition on the marketing of beers containing additives constitutes a barrier to the importation from other Member States of beers containing additives authorized in those States, and is to that extent covered by Article 30 of the EEC Treaty. However, it must be ascertained whether it is possible to justify that prohibition under Article 36 of the Treaty on grounds of the protection of human health.

[41] The Court has consistently held (in particular in the judgment of 14 July 1983 in Case 174/82 *Sandoz BV* [1983] ECR 2445) that 'in so far as there are uncertainties at the present state of scientific research it is for the Member States, in the absence of harmonisation, to decide what degree of protection of the health and life of humans they intend to assure, having regard however to the requirements of the free movement of goods within the Community'.

[42] As may also be seen from the decisions of the Court (and especially the judgment of 14 July 1983 in the *Sandoz* case, cited above, the judgment of 10 December 1985 in Case 247/84 *Motte*

[1985] ECR 3887, and the judgment of 6 May 1986 in Case 304/84 *Ministère public* v *Muller and Others* [1986] ECR 1511), in such circumstances Community law does not preclude the adoption by the Member States of legislation whereby the use of additives is subjected to prior authorization granted by a measure of general application for specific additives, in respect of all products, for certain products only or for certain uses. Such legislation meets a genuine need of health policy, namely that of restricting the uncontrolled consumption of food additives.

[43] However, the application to imported products of prohibitions on marketing products containing additives which are authorized in the Member State of production but prohibited in the Member State of importation is permissible only in so far as it complies with the requirements of Article 36 of the Treaty as it has been interpreted by the Court.

[44] It must be borne in mind, in the first place, that in its judgments in the *Sandoz, Motte* and *Muller* cases, cited above, the Court inferred from the principle of proportionality underlying the last sentence of Article 36 of the Treaty that prohibitions on the marketing of products containing additives authorized in the Member State of production but prohibited in the Member State of importation must be restricted to what is actually necessary to secure the protection of public health. The Court also concluded that the use of a specific additive which is authorized in another Member State must be authorized in the case of a product imported from that Member State where, in view, on the one hand, of the findings of international scientific research, and in particular of the work of the Community's Scientific Committee for Food, the Codex Alimentarius Committee of the Food and Agriculture Organization of the United Nations (FAO) and the World Health Organization, and, on the other hand, of the eating habits prevailing in the importing Member State, the additive in question does not present a risk to public health and meets a real need, especially a technical one.

[45] Secondly, it should be remembered that, as the Court held in its judgment of 6 May 1986 in the *Muller* case, cited above, by virtue of the principle of proportionality, traders must also be able to apply, under a procedure which is easily accessible to them and can be concluded within a reasonable time, for the use of specific additives to be authorized by a measure of general application.

[46] It should be pointed out that it must be open to traders to challenge before the courts an unjustified failure to grant authorization. Without prejudice to the right of the competent national authorities of the importing Member State to ask traders to produce the information in their possession which may be useful for the purpose of assessing the facts, it is for those authorities to demonstrate, as the Court held in its judgment of 6 May 1986 in the *Muller* case, cited above, that the prohibition is justified on grounds relating to the protection of the health of its population.

[47] It must be observed that the German rules on additives applicable to beer result in the exclusion of all the additives authorized in the other Member States and not the exclusion of just some of them for which there is concrete justification by reason of the risks which they involve in view of the eating habits of the German population; moreover those rules do not lay down any procedure whereby traders can obtain authorization for the use of a specific additive in the manufacture of beer by means of a measure of general application.

[48] As regards more specifically the harmfulness of additives, the German Government, citing experts' reports, has referred to the risks inherent in the ingestion of additives in general. It maintains that it is important, for reasons of general preventive health protection, to minimize the quantity of additives ingested, and that it is particularly advisable to prohibit altogether their use in the manufacture of beer, a foodstuff consumed in considerable quantities by the German population.

[49] However, it appears from the tables of additives authorized for use in various foodstuffs submitted by the German Government itself that some of the additives authorized in other Member States for use in the manufacture of beer are also authorized under the German rules, in particular the Regulation on Additives, for use in the manufacture of all, or virtually all, beverages. Mere reference to the potential risks of the ingestion of additives in general and to the fact that beer is a foodstuff consumed in large quantities does not suffice to justify the imposition of stricter rules in the case of beer.

[50] As regards the need, and in particular the technological need, for additives, the German Government argues that there is no need for additives if beer is manufactured in accordance with the requirements of Article 9 of the Biersteuergesetz.

[51] It must be emphasized that mere reference to the fact that beer can be manufactured without additives if it is made from only the raw materials prescribed in the Federal Republic of Germany does not suffice to preclude the possibility that some additives may meet a technological need. Such an interpretation of the concept of technological need, which results in favouring national production methods, constitutes a disguised means of restricting trade between Member States.

[52] The concept of technological need must be assessed in the light of the raw materials utilized and bearing in mind the assessment made by the authorities of the Member State where the product was lawfully manufactured and marketed. Account must also be taken of the findings of international scientific research and in particular the work of the Community's Scientific Committee for Food, the Codex Alimentarius Committee of the FAO and the World Health Organization.

[53] Consequently, in so far as the German rules on additives in beer entail a general ban on additives, their application to beers imported from other Member States is contrary to the requirements of Community law as laid down in the case law of the Court, since that prohibition is contrary to the principle of proportionality and is therefore not covered by the exception provided for in Article 36 of the EEC Treaty.

[54] In view of the foregoing considerations it must be held that by prohibiting the marketing of beers lawfully manufactured and marketed in another Member State if they do not comply with Articles 9 and 10 of the Biersteuergesetz, the Federal Republic of Germany has failed to fulfil its obligations under Article 30 of the EEC Treaty.

■ QUESTIONS

1. Is the beer market so important? Why did the Commission deploy scarce resources pursuing an infringement action in this sector? (The fact that the cutting reproduced below appeared on the front page of the newspaper may assist you in finding an answer.)

2. How is the German brewer likely to react to this judgment (consider p.290 above on the nature and purpose of a common market)? What factors might the German brewer choose to emphasize in launching a campaign in order to maintain customer loyalty now that the protectionist isolation of the domestic beer market has been broken?

3. How is the German consumer likely to react to this judgment?

The following item appeared on p.1 of *The Guardian* of 13 March 1987, shortly after the judgment.

'Parts British beers will still not reach', by Anna Tomforde
The Guardian, 13 March 1987

To a chorus of 'Deutschesbier Allein' (German beer only) regulars at Bonn's Haehnchen pub (The Cock) raised their glasses yesterday and vowed to remain true to domestic brews. This is despite a European Court ruling in favour of the import of foreign beers, regarded as impure under Germany's ancient rules.

'The verdict is the best possible advertisement for German beer', said Detlef Haberland, a 40-year-old doctor enjoying a few pints on his afternoon off. 'It will enhance solidarity among German beer drinkers and stir the German national conscience'.

More than 99 per cent of the 94 million hectolitres of beer drunk each year by Europe's thirstiest country, originates in the country's 1,200 breweries. This, according to the top clientele, will not change.

Judging by comments in the pub, the British Brewers' Society's view that there will now be a 'Willkommen' for the British pint amongst the discerning German beer drinkers, is premature and unduly optimistic.

'I drink an English ale once in a while but I miss the froth. I find it tasteless and without charm,' said Mr Hans Pfotenhauer, a vegetable market worker. 'The German beer drinker wants quality'.

This quality, pub-goers believe, is best guaranteed by a 16th century purity law, the 'Reinheitsgebot', which states that German beer must consist only of water, hops, malt and yeast. 'After the Austrian wine scandal and general anxiety over chemicals in our food, at least we know our beer is pure', Dr Haberland said. His friends agreed, ordering another round.

The Luxembourg ruling, given by the court president, Lord Mackenzie Stuart, means that West Germany can no longer exclude foreign beers which do not meet the 471-year-old German beer law, and which contain different ingredients and additives.

'The laws of a member country must not serve to foster consumer habits in the interests of the national industry', the ruling says in a key sentence that marked the end of a five-year legal battle. The case was brought by a French exporter.

The West German Brewers' Association, which stressed yesterday that it would make sure that additives and ingredients of foreign beers are clearly marked on the labels, said it would mount a £415,000 advertising campaign in all West German newspapers this weekend to reassure consumers that Germany's 4,000 domestic brews will continue to be produced according to the purity rules, promulgated by Duke Wilhelm of Bavaria in 1516.

A publicity campaign is also being planned by French and Dutch brewers, as well as the British, in an attempt to penetrate the German market. Behind the outwardly defiant German reaction there is great anxiety that poor Germans will be tempted by cheaper imported beer on supermarket shelves.

'I can well imagine that broad sections of the public will buy the cheaper beer, and that small, family-run pubs and restaurants will be forced to sell it', said the barman at The Cock.

■ QUESTION

How is the German Government likely to react to the judgment? Could it introduce labelling requirements relating to ingredients for beers marketed in Germany (see para 35 of the judgment)?

Is the German government obliged to abolish the mandatory purity laws for domestic producers too?

Nederlandse Bakkerij v *Edah* (Cases 80 and 159/85)

[1986] ECR 3359, [1988] 2 CMLR 113, Court of Justice of the European Communities

[18] It is also impossible to accept Edah BV's argument that such provisions are contrary to Article 30 of the EEC Treaty because they enable imported bread to be sold below the minimum selling price applicable to domestically produced bread when the purchase price is sufficiently low. The purpose of that article is to eliminate obstacles to the importation of goods and not to ensure equal treatment in all cases for goods of national origin and imported goods. Unequal treatment which does not have the effect of hindering imports or making the sale of imported goods more difficult but instead favours them does not fall within the prohibition laid down by that article.

SECTION 2: **LOCATING THE OUTER LIMIT OF ARTICLE 28**

The key to '*Cassis de Dijon*' (Case 120/78) rules is that although they impose burdens on all products irrespective of origin, imported goods feel an extra burden because they have *already* been subject to the technical rules or traditions of the

State of origin. In this manner, the *'Cassis de Dijon'* rules protect the domestic economy by subjecting imported goods to *different* technical standards from those to which they have already been exposed in their State of origin. Such rules may be applied to imported goods only provided they are justified. In the cases extracted above the national measures were not shown to be justified: the question of the scope of justification is addressed further below. But the Court has also been obliged to consider rules which *restrict* trade but which do not *protect* the home market. Are these too to be put to the test of justification?

For almost a decade the Court was prepared to allow the invocation of Article 30 of the EC Treaty (now, after amendment, Article 28 EC) even where both the application of the rules *and* the consequential burden was felt equally by all goods. However, in its November 1993 ruling in *Keck and Mithouard* (Cases C-267 and 268/91) it changed its mind and set an outer limit to the application of this Article of the Treaty. In order to appreciate the background to the *Keck* ruling, it is appropriate to look first at the notorious 'Sunday trading' litigation.

Torfaen BC v *B & Q plc* (Case 145/88)
[1989] ECR 765, Court of Justice of the European Communities

[1] By order of 25 April 1988, which was received at the Court on 24 May 1988, Cwmbran Magistrates' Court, United Kingdom, referred to the Court for a preliminary ruling under Article 177 of the EEC Treaty three questions on the interpretation of Articles 30 and 36 of the EEC Treaty in order to assess the compatibility with those provisions of national rules prohibiting trading on Sunday.

[2] The questions were raised in proceedings between Torfaen Borough Council (hereinafter referred to as 'the Council') and B&Q PLC, formerly B&Q (Retail) Limited (hereinafter referred to as 'B&Q'), which operates do-it-yourself centres and garden centres.

[3] The Council alleges that B&Q contravened sections 47 and 59 of the United Kingdom Shops Act 1950 by causing its retail shop premises to be open for the serving of customers on Sunday other than for the transactions mentioned in the Fifth Schedule to that Act. B&Q is therefore liable to a maximum fine of £1,000.

[4] The Fifth Schedule to the Shops Act lists the items which, by way of exception, may be sold in shops on Sundays. Those items include intoxicating liquors, certain foodstuffs, tobacco, newspapers and other products of everyday consumption.

[5] Before the national court B&Q submitted that section 47 of the Shops Act was a measure having an effect equivalent to a quantitative restriction on imports within the meaning of Article 30 of the EEC Treaty and that it was not justified under Article 36 of the EEC Treaty or by virtue of any 'mandatory requirement'.

[6] The Council denied that the ban on Sunday trading constituted a measure having an effect equivalent to a quantitative restriction on the ground that it applied to domestic and imported products alike and did not put imported products at any disadvantage.

[7] The national court found that in the instant case the ban on Sunday trading had the effect of reducing B&Q's total sales, that approximately 10% of the goods sold by B&Q came from other Member States and that a corresponding reduction of imports from other Member States would therefore ensue.

[8] Having reached those findings the national court took the view that the case raised questions concerning the interpretation of Community law. It therefore requested the Court to give a preliminary ruling on the following questions:

'1. Where a Member State prohibits retail premises from being open on Sunday for the sale of goods to customers, save in respect of certain specified items, sales of which are permitted, and where the effect of the prohibition is to reduce in absolute terms the sales of goods in those premises, including goods manufactured in other Member States, and correspondingly to reduce the volume of imports of goods from other Member States, is such a prohibition a measure having equivalent effect to a quantitative restriction on imports within the meaning of Article 30 of the Treaty?

2. If the answer to Question 1 is in the affirmative, does such a measure benefit from any of the exceptions to Article 30 contained in Article 36, or from any other exception recognised by Community law?

3. Is the answer to Question 1 or Question 2 above affected by any factor so as to render the measure in question a means of arbitrary discrimination or a disguised restriction on trade between Member States or a measure lacking in proportionality or otherwise unjustified?'

[9] Reference is made to the Report for the Hearing for a fuller account of the legal background to, and the facts of, the main proceedings, the course of the procedure and the written observations submitted to the Court, which are mentioned or discussed hereinafter only in so far as is necessary for the reasoning of the Court.

The first question

[10] By its first question the national court seeks to establish whether the concept of measures having an effect equivalent to quantitative restrictions within the meaning of Article 30 of the Treaty also covers provisions prohibiting retailers from opening their premises on Sunday if the effect of the prohibition is to reduce in absolute terms the sales of goods in those premises, including goods imported from other Member States.

[11] The first point which must be made is that national rules prohibiting retailers from opening their premises on Sunday apply to imported and domestic products alike. In principle, the marketing of products imported from other Member States is not therefore made more difficult than the marketing of domestic products.

[12] Next, it must be recalled that in its judgment of 11 July 1985 in Joined Cases 60 and 61/84 (*Cinéthèque SA and Others* v *Fédération Nationale des Cinémas Françaises* ([1985]) ECR 2618) the Court held, with regard to a prohibition of the hiring of video-cassettes applicable to domestic and imported products alike, that such a prohibition was not compatible with the principle of the free movement of goods provided for in the Treaty unless any obstacle to Community trade thereby created did not exceed what was necessary in order to ensure the attainment of the objective in view and unless that objective was justified with regard to Community law.

[13] In those circumstances it is therefore necessary in a case such as this to consider first of all whether rules such as those at issue pursue an aim which is justified with regard to Community law. As far as that question is concerned, the Court has already stated in its judgment of 14 July 1981 in Case 155/80 (*Oebel* [1981] ECR 1993) that national rules governing the hours of work, delivery and sale in the bread and confectionery industry constitute a legitimate part of economic and social policy, consistent with the objectives of public interest pursued by the Treaty.

[14] The same consideration must apply as regards national rules governing the opening hours of retail premises. Such rules reflect certain political and economic choices in so far as their purpose is to ensure that working and non-working hours are so arranged as to accord with national or regional socio-cultural characteristics, and that, in the present state of Community law, is a matter for the Member States. Furthermore, such rules are not designed to govern the patterns of trade between Member States.

[15] Secondly, it is necessary to ascertain whether the effects of such national rules exceed what is necessary to achieve the aim in view. As is indicated in Article 3 of Commission Directive 70/50/EEC of 22 December 1969 (Official Journal, English Special Edition 1970 (I), p.17), the prohibition laid down in Article 30 covers national measures governing the marketing of products where the

restrictive effect of such measures on the free movement of goods exceeds the effects intrinsic to trade rules.

[16] The question whether the effects of specific national rules do in fact remain within that limit is a question of fact to be determined by the national court.

[17] The reply to the first question must therefore be that Article 30 of the Treaty must be interpreted as meaning that the prohibition which it lays down does not apply to national rules prohibiting retailers from opening their premises on Sunday where the restrictive effects on Community trade which may result therefrom do not exceed the effects intrinsic to rules of that kind.

■ QUESTIONS

1. Why does the Court choose to refer to Directive 70/50 but not to *Dassonville* (Case 8/74)?

2. Did the Council or the company 'win' the case in Luxembourg?

'Rivals claim victory after EC ruling on Sunday trade', by Patricia Wynn Davies
The Independent, 24 November 1989

A European Court of Justice ruling on whether Britain's Sunday trading ban breaks EC rules was hailed as a victory yesterday by supporters and opponents of the law.

The DIY chain B&Q had claimed that the 1950 Shops Act was an unlawful restraint on cross border trade within the European Community, breaching article 30 of the Treaty of Rome.

The Luxembourg court said the article would not apply to the Act if its restrictive effects did not exceed the socio-cultural aims of the Sunday trading ban. The magistrates' court which referred the case had to decide whether the Act fell within that limit.

Sunday traders still face prosecution, but this could change once the Luxembourg decision is tested here. A higher court ruling will probably be needed to resolve the uncertainty.

The confusing upshot of the court challenge brought enthusiastic responses from pro-Sunday groups and reform campaigners.

B&Q said the ruling was a victory for consumers, two-thirds of whom support liberalising Sunday shopping laws. It means the 1950 Act would breach article 30 if the effects on intra-community trade were found by UK courts to be excessively restrictive.

But Lord Brentford, chairman of the Keep Sunday Special Campaign, a pressure group of retailers and trade associations, said: 'Sunday is a key part of the shared European cultural tradition and we are very grateful that the court has upheld this vital part of our heritage'.

Bill Connor, deputy general secretary of the Union of Shop, Distributive and Allied Workers, which opposes Sunday opening, said: 'We now want to see every retailer who breaks the law taken to court and fined'.

Roger Boaden, director of the Shopping Hours Reform Council, said: 'The judgment contains a clear message for the UK Government. It is quite simply to sort out the mess of your own making'. He said about 60,000 shops in Britain were now trading on a Sunday, of which only 600 were DIY stores.

B&Q was taken to court by Torfaen Borough Council, South Wales, for opening its branch in Cwmbran, Gwent, on a Sunday. Cwmbran magistrates referred the case to Luxembourg when B&Q invoked EC law in its defence.

Bill Whiting, the company's marketing director, said there was now a possibility of having different interpretations of the law in different parts of the country.

Research by the Sunday Shopping Hours Reform Council shows the law is strictly enforced in Norwich, Coventry, the London Borough of Bromley, and Wellingborough, Northamptonshire. Swansea, Blackpool, Birmingham, Bradford, and Cambridge also take a strong enforcement line. But many councils tend to prosecute only as a result of a direct complaint, mainly because of the cost.

The Consumers' Association said Parliament must 'grit its teeth' and take action on the 'appalling muddle'.

The law, passed in 1936, bans most goods from being sold on a Sunday but contains a curious amalgam of past lobbying. Meals may be sold, unless they happen to be fish and chips.

Newly-cooked provisions and cooked or partly-cooked tripe are allowed. Milk and cream, including clotted cream, may be sold, but dried or tinned milk is banned. Tinned fruit and vegetables are off-limits, but fodder for horses, mules, ponies and donkeys may be purchased at any farm, stables, hotel or inn. Buying DIY goods is prohibited, but if you need to repair a jumbo jet the necessary supplies can be obtained, along with motor and cycle accessories. You can buy a bible, but only at a railway station or airport – where you can also buy pornography.

■ QUESTION

What does the Court's judgment and this divided response tell you about the division of function between national and Community court under the Article 234 preliminary reference procedure? (See Chapter 7.)

NOTE
This ruling created confusion at national level, where different English and Welsh courts adopted different views of the compatibility of the Sunday trading laws with the Treaty. (See A. Arnull (1991) 16 EL Rev 112.)

In May 1991, a further preliminary reference was made by the House of Lords. This was motivated in part by the European Court rulings of February 1991 in *Marchandise* (Case C-332/89) [1991] ECR I-1027 and *UDS* v *Conforama* (Case C-312/89) [1991] ECR I-997. These cases, though factually comparable to *Torfaen*, had revealed the European Court much readier explicitly to rule national measures compatible with Article 30 of the EC Treaty (now, after amendment, Article 28 EC). The second reference yielded a much clearer response from the European Court in December 1992:

Stoke-on-Trent and Norwich City Councils v *B & Q* (Case C-169/91)
[1992] ECR I-6457, [1993] 1 CMLR 426, Court of Justice of the European Communities

[15] Appraising the proportionality of national rules which pursue a legitimate aim under Community law involves weighing the national interest in attaining that aim against the Community interest in ensuring the free movement of goods. In that regard, in order to verify that the restrictive effects on intra-Community trade of the rules at issue do not exceed what is necessary to achieve the aim in view, it must be considered whether those effects are direct, indirect or purely speculative and whether those effects do not impede the marketing of imported products more than the marketing of national products.

[16] It was on the basis of those considerations that in its judgments in the *Conforama* and *Marchandise* cases the court ruled that the restrictive effects on trade of national rules prohibiting the employment of workers on Sundays in certain retailing activities were not excessive in relation to the aim pursued. For the same reasons, the court must make the same finding with regard to national rules prohibiting shops from opening on Sundays.

[17] It must therefore be stated in reply to the first question that Article 30 of the Treaty is to be interpreted as meaning that the prohibition which it lays down does not apply to national legislation prohibiting retailers from opening their premises on Sundays.

NOTE
For comment, see R. Rawlings (1993) 20 *Journal of Law and Society* 309; A. Arnull (1993) 18 EL Rev 314. Eventually, the law in England and Wales was amended, and made more coherent, by the Sunday Trading Act 1994.

■ QUESTION

What does *this* ruling tell you about the division of function between national and Community court under Article 234?

NOTE

Lurking beneath this litigation was the point made in para 6 of the ruling in Case 145/88 (p.393 above). The Sunday trading rules did not put imported goods at a disadvantage in comparison with domestic goods. All goods were equally affected. Had EC free movement law been pushed beyond its proper scope by the ingenuity of the Sunday traders' lawyers? Many commentators took this view and tried to develop a test which would allow a reorientation towards rules which partitioned national markets rather than general trading rules unconnected with the process of market integration. Such thoughtful efforts include:

Chalmers, D., 'Free Movement of Goods within the European Community: an Unhealthy Addiction to Scotch Whisky?' (1993) 42 ICLQ 269.

Mortelmans, K., 'Article 30 of the EEC Treaty and Legislation Relating to Market Circumstances: Time to Consider a New Definition?' (1991) 28 CML Rev 115.

Wils, W., 'The Search for the Rule in Article 30 EEC: Much Ado about Nothing?' (1993) 18 EL Rev 475.

In the period between the two Sunday trading rulings there had already been indications that the European Court was ready to rethink its approach in this area. In *Quietlynn Ltd* v *Southend on Sea BC* (Case C-23/89) [1990] ECR I-3059 and in *Sheptonhurst* v *Newham BC* (Case C-350/89) [1991] ECR I-2387, the Court found no effect on inter-State trade adequate to permit the invocation of Article 30 of the EC Treaty (now, after amendment, Article 28 EC). Accordingly, questions of justification of national rules simply did not arise, in contrast to the Sunday trading cases. The Court had the chance to provide a bolder formula in *Keck and Mithouard*.

Bernard Keck and Daniel Mithouard (Cases C-267 and C-268/91)

[1993] ECR I-6097, [1995] 1 CMLR 101, Court of Justice of the European Communities

MM. Keck and Mithouard had resold goods at a loss. This violated a French law forbidding such practices. Keck and Mithouard submitted that the law restricted the volume of sales of imported goods by depriving them of a method of sales promotion and that it was therefore incompatible with Article 30 of the EC Treaty (now, after amendment, Article 28 EC). Any restrictive effect on trade plainly affected *all* goods, not just imports.

[14] In view of the increasing tendency of traders to invoke Article 30 of the Treaty as a means of challenging any rules whose effect is to limit their commercial freedom even where such rules are not aimed at products from other Member States, the Court considers it necessary to re-examine and clarify its case-law on this matter.

[15] In 'Cassis de Dijon' (Case 120/78 *Rewe-Zentral* v *Bundesmonopolverwaltung für Branntwein* [1979] ECR 649) it was held that, in the absence of harmonisation of legislation, measures of equivalent effect prohibited by Article 30 include obstacles to the free movement of goods where they are the consequence of applying rules that lay down requirements to be met by such goods (such as requirements as to designation, form, size, weight, composition, presentation, labelling, packaging) to goods from other Member States where they are lawfully manufactured and marketed, even if those rules apply without distinction to all products unless their application can be justified by a public-interest objective taking precedence over the free movement of goods.

[16] However, contrary to what has previously been decided, the application to products from other Member States of national provisions restricting or prohibiting certain selling arrangements is not such as to hinder directly or indirectly, actually or potentially, trade between Member States within the meaning of the *Dassonville* judgment (Case 8/74 [1974] ECR 837), provided that those provisions apply to all affected traders operating within the national territory and provided that they affect in

the same manner, in law and in fact, the marketing of domestic products and of those from other Member States.

[17] Where those conditions are fulfilled, the application of such rules to the sale of products from another Member State meeting the requirements laid down by that State is not by nature such as to prevent their access to the market or to impede access any more than it impedes the access of domestic products. Such rules therefore fall outside the scope of Article 30 of the Treaty.

[18] Accordingly, the reply to be given to the national court is that Article 30 of the EEC Treaty is to be interpreted as not applying to legislation of a Member State imposing a general prohibition on resale at a loss.

■ QUESTION

In 1989, E. White proposed that Article 30 should be interpreted as catching 'the application by a Member State to products legally produced and marketed in another Member State of its national rules relating to the characteristics required of such products on its territory (which therefore prevents this product from benefitting in the importing Member State from the advantages arising out of its production in the different legal and economic environment prevailing in the other Member State' ('In Search of the Limits to Article 30 of the EEC Treaty' (1989) 26 CML Rev 235). Does this proposal conform to the Court's policy in *Keck*?

NOTE

The Commission declared that in *Keck* 'the Court has completed its case law' ([1993] OJ C353/6). It is doubtless the case that in future traders will find it more difficult to employ the Treaty provisions governing free movement of goods to require Member States to justify rules which inhibit commercial freedom. This is well illustrated by the next case, decided by the Court less than seven months after *Keck*, in which a challenge to Dutch rules relating to the compulsory closing of shops at stipulated times was curtly rejected.

Tankstation 't Heukste vof and J.B.E. Boermans (Cases C-401 and C-402/92)
[1994] ECR I-2199, Court of Justice of the European Communities

[12] . . . the application to products from other Member States of national provisions restricting or prohibiting certain selling arrangements is not such as to hinder, directly or indirectly, actually or potentially, trade between Member States within the meaning of the *Dassonville* judgment . . . provided that those provisions apply to all relevant traders operating within the national territory and provided that they affect in the same manner, in law and in fact, the marketing of domestic products and of those from other Member States. Where those conditions are fulfilled, the application of such rules to the sale of products from another Member State meeting the requirements laid down by that State is not by nature such as to prevent their access to the market or to impede access any more than it impedes the access of domestic products. Such rules therefore fall outside the scope of Article 30 of the Treaty (see the judgment in Joined Cases C-267/91 and C-268/91 *Keck and Mithouard* [1993] ECR I-6097, paragraphs 16 and 17).

[13] The conditions laid down in the judgment last cited are fulfilled in the case of rules such as those at issue in the main proceedings.

[14] The rules in question relate to the times and places at which the goods in question may be sold to consumers. However, they apply to all relevant traders without distinguishing between the origin of the products in question and do not affect the marketing of products from other Member States in a manner different from that in which they affect domestic products.

[15] Consequently, the reply to be given to the Gerechtshof is that Article 30 of the Treaty is to be interpreted as not applying to national rules concerning the closing of shops which apply to all traders operating within the national territory and which affect in the same manner, in law and in fact, the marketing of domestic products and of products from other Member States.

NOTE

It was suggested above (at p.385) that the *'Cassis de Dijon'* case law represents the Court's strategy for judging the permissibility of regulatory diversity between the States in an integrating market; *Keck* reflects the Court's concern to establish where regulatory diversity does not affect the integrative process for the purposes of application of Article 28 and where, accordingly, States remain free to make their own regulatory choices unhindered by the demands of EC trade law. The key jurisdictional point is that where a national measure is excluded from the reach of Article 28 (ex 30) by virtue of the reasoning found in *Keck* then (in contrast to the 'Sunday Trading' cases) the national regulator does not even fall under an obligation to justify the measure according to standards recognised by the Court. But although *Keck* is, as a general proposition, designed to curtail the reach of Article 28 (ex 30) and thereby to immunize certain areas of local market regulation from the threat of challenge based on Article 28 (ex 30), the detailed impact of the ruling is not yet settled – not least because ingenious litigants have continued to fight battles over just how much power EC law confers on traders to challenge obstructive national rules of market regulation.

It is instructive to consider cases decided prior to *Keck* in order to determine whether it would now be considered that a sufficient adverse effect on imported products had been shown such as to permit the invocation of Article 28. Consider from this perspective the extracts in *Commission v UK* (Case 207/83) at p.352 above; *Tasca* (Case 65/75) and *Van Tiggele* (Case 82/77) at p.365 above.

The decision in *Cinéthèque* (Cases 60 and 61/84) was mentioned at para 12 in the *Torfaen* ruling (Case 145/88, p.393 above) as a basis for the need to embark on consideration of justification of the Sunday trading rules. In the ruling in *Cinéthèque* there was a divergence of approach between the Court and its Advocate-General, although both agreed in the result that the French rules were compatible with the Treaty.

Cinéthèque SA v *Fédération Nationale des Cinémas Français* (Cases 60 and 61/84)
[1985] ECR 2605, [1986] 1 CMLR 365, Court of Justice of the European Communities

French legislation prohibited the selling or hiring of video cassettes of films within the first year of the film receiving its performance certificate. The objective was to encourage attendance at cinemas. Yet the legislation eliminated the market for videos during that year's grace allowed to the cinema. Imported videos could not be sold in France. But neither could French-made videos. A distributor of videos used Article 30 of the EC Treaty (now, after amendment, Article 28 EC) before French courts to challenge the law as a trade barrier.

[21] . . . [I]t must be observed that such a system, if it applies without distinction to both video-cassettes manufactured in the national territory and to imported video-cassettes, does not have the purpose of regulating trade patterns; its effect is not to favour national production as against the production of other Member States, but to encourage cinematographic production as such.

[22] Nevertheless, the application of such a system may create barriers to intra-Community trade in video-cassettes because of the disparities between the systems operated in the different Member States and between the conditions for the release of cinematographic works in the cinemas of those States. In those circumstances a prohibition of exploitation laid down by such a system is not compatible with the principle of the free movement of goods provided for in the Treaty unless any obstacle to intra-Community trade thereby created does not exceed that which is necessary in order to ensure the attainment of the objective in view and unless that objective is justified with regard to Community law.

[23] It must be conceded that a national system which, in order to encourage the creation of cinematographic works irrespective of their origin, gives priority, for a limited initial period, to the distribution of such works through the cinema, is so justified.

[24] The reply to the questions referred to the Court is therefore that Article 30 of the EEC Treaty must be interpreted as meaning that it does not apply to national legislation which regulates the distribution of cinematographic works by imposing an interval between one mode of distributing such works and another by prohibiting their simultaneous exploitation in cinemas and in video-cassette form for a limited period, provided that the prohibition applies to domestically produced and imported cassettes alike and any barriers to intra-Community trade to which its implementation may give rise do not exceed what is necessary for ensuring that the exploitation in cinemas of cinematographic works of all origins retains priority over other means of distribution.

Cinéthèque SA v *Fédération Nationale des Cinémas Français* (Cases 60 and 61/84)

[1985] ECR 2605, [1986] 1 CMLR 365, Court of Justice of the European Communities

ADVOCATE-GENERAL SLYNN: It seems to me in summary that a measure is in breach of Article 30 (a) if it forbids imports or restricts imports quantitatively; (b) if it discriminates against imports by e.g., imposing more stringent standards on importers than on domestic producers so that in practice importation may be made more difficult and thereby imports may be restricted; (c) if, although not directed to importation as such but covering both national goods and imports, it requires a producer or distributor to take steps additional to those which he would normally and lawfully take in the marketing of his goods, which thereby render importation more difficult, so that imports may be restricted and national producers be given protection in practice. The last category, (c) will not be in breach of Article 30 if it can be shown that the measure is justified by mandatory requirements of the kind contemplated in *Cassis de Dijon*.

On the other hand, in an area in which there are no common Community standards or rules, where a national measure is not specifically directed at imports, does not discriminate against imports, does not make it any more difficult for an importer to sell his products than it is for a domestic producer, and gives no protection to domestic producers, then in my view, *prima facie*, the measure does not fall within Article 30 even if it does in fact lead to a restriction or reduction of imports.

In the present case the law does not discriminate against imports. The importer can in fact import. He is then on exactly the same footing as the domestic trader. The latter gets no extra benefit over the importer, the former suffers no extra detriment over the French trader as a result of the ban on the exploitation of video-cassettes. The factor which would lead a trader in France not to buy from a French video distributor (inability to sell or hire) is the same as that which would lead him not to buy from a distributor in another Member State. In this respect both distributors are subject to the same conditions of trade. They are effectively operating in the same market. Article 30 cannot have been intended in this respect to give the distributor in another Member State better conditions than the domestic distributor. It may be that if it was patently unreasonable to put imports on the same footing as domestic products that the measure could be bad for that reason. That however is not the position here and in my view this law does not fall within Article 30.

■ QUESTION

In *Tankstation 't Heukste vof and J.B.E. Boermans* (Cases C-401/92 and C-402/92, p.398 above), Advocate-General Van Gerven commented that the legislation challenged in *Cinéthèque* 'would in any event fulfil the second condition introduced by "provided that" in the judgment in *Keck and Mithouard*'. Do you agree with his view that the law would escape the scope of application of Article 28? Would this be a desirable outcome?

Ministère Public v *Buet* (Case 382/87)

[1989] ECR 1235, Court of Justice of the European Communities

A trader was convicted under French law forbidding canvassing at private dwellings for the purpose of selling educational material. It was submitted that the law was incompatible with Article 30 of the EC Treaty (now, after amendment, Article 28 EC). The Court found an obstacle to the free movement of goods:

[7] As the Court held in its judgment of 15 December 1982 in Case 286/81 *Oosthoek* [1982] ECR 4575, the possibility cannot be ruled out that to compel a trader either to adopt advertising or sales promotion schemes which differ from one Member State to another or to discontinue a scheme which he considers to be particularly effective may constitute an obstacle to imports even if the legislation in question applies to domestic and imported products without distinction.

[8] That finding applies *a fortiori* when the rules in question deprive the trader concerned of the possibility of using not a means of advertising but a method of marketing whereby he realizes almost all his sales.

[9] Application of a prohibition on canvassing in order to sell foreign-language teaching material from another Member State must therefore be regarded as constituting an obstacle to imports.

The Court then concluded that the French rule was compatible with the Treaty, notwithstanding the obstacle to trade, in view of its contribution to the protection of the consumer.

■ QUESTION

Would the ruling in *Keck* make any difference in such circumstances?

NOTE

It seems likely that cases involving restrictions on marketing methods will provide the sternest challenges to the Court's attempt in *Keck* to realign its case law in order to introduce a coherent basis for locating the outer limit of Article 28. The next case features distinct approaches taken by the Court and its Advocate-General when confronted by this issue.

Société d'Importation Edouard Leclerc-Siplec v *TF1 Publicité SA and M6 Publicité SA* (Case C-412/93)

[1995] ECR I-179, Court of Justice of the European Communities

TF1 and M6 refused to broadcast an advertisement concerning distribution of fuel in Leclerc supermarkets. The refusal was based on French rules excluding the distribution sector from televised advertising. It was submitted that the rules impeded sales opportunities for imported fuel and that they were therefore susceptible to challenge under Article 30 of the EC Treaty (now, after amendment, Article 28 EC). The *Tribunal de Commerce de Paris* made a preliminary reference to the Court in search of an authoritative interpretation.

[18] It has been consistently held that all rules enacted by Member States which are capable of hindering, directly or indirectly, actually or potentially, intra-Community trade are to be considered as measures having an effect equivalent to quantitative restrictions (judgment in Case 8/74 *Procureur du Roi* v *Dassonville* [1974] ECR 837, paragraph 5).

[19] A law or regulation such as that at issue in the main proceedings, which prohibits televised advertising in the distribution sector, is not designed to regulate trade in goods between Member States. Moreover, such a prohibition does not prevent distributors from using other forms of advertising.

[20] Such a prohibition may, admittedly, restrict the volume of sales, and hence the volume of sales of products from other Member States, in so far as it deprives distributors of a particular form of advertising their goods. But the question remains whether such a possibility is sufficient to characterise the prohibition in question as a measure having equivalent effect to a quantitative restriction on imports within the meaning of Article 30 of the Treaty.

[21] The application to products from other Member States of national provisions restricting or prohibiting certain selling arrangements it not such as to hinder directly or indirectly, actually or potentially, trade between Member States within the meaning of the *Dassonville* judgment, cited above, so long as those provisions apply to all relevant traders operating within the national territory and so long as they affect in the same manner, in law and in fact, the marketing of domestic products and of those from other Member States. Provided that those conditions are fulfilled, the application of such rules to the sale of products from another Member State meeting the requirements laid down by that State is not by nature such as to prevent their access to the market or to impede access any more than it impedes the access of domestic products. Such rules therefore fall outside the scope of Article 30 of the Treaty (see the judgment in Joined Cases C-267/91 and 268/91 *Keck and Mithouard* [1993] ECR I-6097, paragraphs 16 and 17, and Case C-292/92 *Hünermund and Others* [1993] ECR I-6787, paragraph 21).

[22] A provision such as that at issue in the main proceedings concerns selling arrangements since it prohibits a particular form of promotion (televised advertising) of a particular method of marketing products (distribution).

[23] Furthermore, those provisions, which apply regardless of the type of product to all traders in the distribution sector, even if they are both producers and distributors, affect the marketing of products from other Member States and that of domestic products in the same manner.

[24] The reply should accordingly be that on a proper construction Article 30 of the Treaty does not apply where a Member State, by statute or by regulation, prohibits the broadcasting of televised advertisements for the distribution sector.

In his Opinion in the case Advocate-General Jacobs embarked on a careful examination of *Keck*. Although his views were not reflected in the Court's ruling, they deserve attention for the light they shed on some of the complexities generated by the Court's refinement of the law in *Keck*. Advocate-General Jacobs stated that he found the Court's reasoning in *Keck* unsatisfactory, although he agreed with the result. He continued (remember that Article 30, to which he refers, was re-numbered Article 28 by the Amsterdam Treaty):

[41] The question then is what test should be applied in order to determine whether a measure falls within the scope of Article 30. There is one guiding principle which seems to provide an appropriate test: that principle is that all undertakings which engage in a legitimate economic activity in a Member State should have unfettered access to the whole of the Community market, unless there is a valid reason for denying them full access to a part of that market. In spite of occasional inconsistencies in the reasoning of certain judgments, that seems to be the underlying principle which has inspired the Court's approach from *Dassonville* through 'Cassis de Dijon' to *Keck*. Virtually all of the cases are, in their result, consistent with the principle, even though some of them appear to be based on different reasoning.

[42] If the principle is that all undertakings should have unfettered access to the whole of the Community market, then the appropriate test in my view is whether there is a substantial restriction on that access. That would of course amount to introducing a *de minimis* test into Article 30. Once it is recognised that there is a need to limit the scope of Article 30 in order to prevent excessive interference in the regulatory powers of the Member States, a test based on the extent to which a measure hinders trade between Member States by restricting market access seems the most obvious solution. Indeed it is perhaps surprising that, in view of the avowed aim of preventing excessive recourse to Article 30, the Court did not opt for such a solution in *Keck*. The reason may be that the Court was concerned lest a *de minimis* test, if applied to all measures affecting trade in goods, might induce national courts, who have primary responsibility for applying Article 30, to exclude too many measures from the scope of the prohibition laid down by that provision. Caution must therefore be exercised and if a *de minimis* test is to be introduced it will be necessary to define carefully the circumstances in which it should apply.

[43] Clearly it would not be appropriate to apply a *de minimis* test to measures which overtly discriminate against goods from other Member States. Such measures are prohibited by Article 30 (unless justified under Article 36) even if their effect on inter-State trade is slight: there is a *per se* prohibition of overtly discriminatory measures.

[44] Only in relation to measures which are applicable without distinction to domestic goods and goods from other Member States would it be necessary to introduce a requirement that the restriction, actual or potential, on access to the market must be substantial. The impact on access to the market of measures applicable without distinction may vary greatly, depending on the nature of the measure in issue. Where such a measure prohibits the sale of goods lawfully placed on the market in another Member State (as in 'Cassis de Dijon'), it may be presumed to have a substantial impact on access to the market, since the goods are either denied access altogether or can gain access only after being modified in some way; the need to modify goods is itself a substantial barrier to market access.

[45] Where, on the other hand, a measure applicable without distinction simply restricts certain selling arrangements, by stipulating when, where, how, by whom or at what price goods may be sold, its impact will depend on a number of factors, such as whether it applies to certain goods (as in *Blesgen*, *Buet* or *Quietlynn*), or to most goods (as in *Torfaen*), or to all goods (as in *Keck*), on the extent to which other selling arrangements remain available, and on whether the effect of the measure is direct or indirect, immediate or remote, or purely speculative[36] and uncertain.[37] Accordingly, the magnitude of the barrier to market access may vary enormously: it may range from the insignificant to a quasi-prohibition. Clearly, this is where a *de minimis* test could perform a useful function. The distinction recognised in *Keck* between a prohibition of the kind in issue in 'Cassis de Dijon' and a mere restriction on certain selling arrangements is therefore valuable: the former inevitably creates a substantial barrier to trade between Member States, whereas the latter may create such a barrier. But it cannot be maintained that the latter type of measure is not capable of hindering trade contrary to Article 30 in the absence of discrimination. It should therefore be recognised that such measures, unless overtly discriminatory, are not automatically caught by Article 30, as are measures of the type at issue in 'Cassis de Dijon', but may be caught if the restriction which they cause on access to the market is substantial.

Advocate-General Jacobs concluded that 'Article 30 should be regarded as applying to non-discriminatory measures which are liable substantially to restrict access to the market'. Applying this test to the French measures, he continued:

[55] . . . The restriction affects only one form of advertising, although the most effective as far as mass consumer goods are concerned; and advertisement of the goods themselves is not affected other than indirectly. As in the case of legislation restricting the opening hours of shops . . . the measure may result in a slight reduction in the total volume of sales of goods, including imports. But it cannot be said to have a substantial impact on access to the market. It therefore falls in my view outside the scope of Article 30.

■ QUESTIONS

1. Is the approach advocated by Advocate-General Jacobs likely to breed consistency in the application of (what is now) Article 28 by national courts? Is it more or less likely to achieve this objective than the Court's own test laid down in *Keck* and repeated in *Société d'Importation Edouard Leclerc-Siplec* v *TF1 Publicité SA and M6 Publicité SA* (Case C-412/93)?

---

36 As in paragraph 15 of the judgment in *Stoke-on-Trent Council* v *B&Q* . . . [p. 396 above].
37 As in Case C-69/88 *Krantz* [1990] ECR I-583, paragraph 11 of the judgment.

2. M. Ross identifies 'patchwork pragmatism' and an avoidance of long-term commitment to principle in the Court's recent approach in this area ((1995) 20 EL Rev 507, 512). He finds this 'disappointing, since the central question to be addressed is simple enough to formulate: what does the notion of a single market require and permit?'. Discuss.

NOTE

The Court continues to be fed a steady diet of cases involving challenge to national rules which limit commercial freedom. *Keck* notwithstanding, there remains scope for argument about the nature of the impediment to market access that must be shown for Article 28 to come into play where national rules deprive traders of the use of particular practices or require them to adopt practices which they do not favour.

Konsummentombudsmannen v *De Agostini Forlag AB and TV-Shop i Sverige AB* (Joined Cases C-34/95, C-35/95, and C-36/95)
[1997] ECR I-3843, Court of Justice of the European Communities

The background to this case is provided by satellite broadcasting of television programmes, an activity particularly apt for cross-border commerce. The questions referred were prompted by action taken by the Swedish consumer *ombud* to restrain forms of television advertising *inter alia* on the ground that contrary to Swedish law they were targeted at children less than 12 years of age. The Court ruled that Directive 89/552 harmonising laws governing television broadcasting did not preclude a Member State from taking action to protect consumers in respect of advertisements broadcast from another Member State, provided that this did not prevent retransmission as such. As regards Article 30 of the EC Treaty (now, after amendment, Article 28 EC):

[39] In paragraph 22 of its judgment in *Leclerc-Siplec*, cited above [Case C-412/93], the Court held that legislation which prohibits television advertising in a particular sector concerns selling arrangements for products belonging to that sector in that it prohibits a particular form of promotion of a particular method of marketing products.

[40] In Joined Cases C-267/91 and C-268/91 *Keck and Mithouard* [1993] ECR I-6097, at paragraph 16, the Court held that national measures restricting or prohibiting certain selling arrangements are not covered by Article 30 of the Treaty, so long as they apply to all traders operating within the national territory and so long as they affect in the same manner, in law and in fact, the marketing of domestic products and of those from other Member States.

[41] The first condition is clearly fulfilled in the cases before the national court.

[42] As regards the second condition, it cannot be excluded that an outright ban, applying in one Member State, of a type of promotion for a product which is lawfully sold there might have a greater impact on products from other Member States.

[43] Although the efficacy of the various types of promotion is a question of fact to be determined in principle by the referring court, it is to be noted that in its observations De Agostini stated that television advertising was the only effective form of promotion enabling it to penetrate the Swedish market since it had no other advertising methods for reaching children and their parents.

[44] Consequently, an outright ban on advertising aimed at children less than 12 years of age and of misleading advertising, as provided for by the Swedish legislation, is not covered by Article 30 of the Treaty, unless it is shown that the ban does not affect in the same way, in fact and in law, the marketing of national products and of products from other Member States.

[45] In the latter case, it is for the national court to determine whether the ban is necessary to satisfy overriding requirements of general public importance or one of the aims listed in Article 36 of the EC

Treaty if it is proportionate to that purpose and if those aims or requirements could not have been attained or fulfilled by measures less restrictive of intra-Community trade.

NOTE

The Court proceeded to take a rather different line in response to questions about the impact of Article 59 of the EC Treaty (now, after amendment, Article 49 EC), which concerns the free movement of services (see p.458 below).

■ QUESTION

Would a law forbidding retail outlets for widgets from being opened within 10 kilometres of each other be susceptible to challenge under Community law? What about a law forbidding advertising of widgets other than in retail outlets? Or a law forbidding advertising of widgets entirely?

NOTE

The subjection of rules affecting advertising strategies to Article 28 continues to pose the sternest tests for the law re-shaped by the Court in *Keck*. In the next case the Court shows itself receptive to the argument that the dynamic role of advertising in generating the re-structuring of markets should be taken into account in fixing the scope of Article 28.

Konsumentombudsmannen (KO) v *Gourmet International Products AB (GIP)* (Case C-405/98)

[2001] ECR I-1795, Court of Justice of the European Communities

Pursuant to Swedish public health policy, Gourmet International Products AB (hereinafter 'GIP') was restrained from placing advertisements for alcoholic beverages in magazines. It was accepted that the prohibition affected sales of alcoholic beverages there, including those imported from other Member States, since the specific purpose of the Swedish legislation was to reduce the consumption of alcohol.

But advertising was prohibited irrespective of the source of the products. Did this not bring the matter within the '*Keck* formula' – and outwith Article 28? In his Opinion Advocate-General Jacobs drew attention to the flaw in this analysis:

A consumer who is unaware of alternatives to the products he or she is in the habit of purchasing is unlikely to go to any great lengths to discover whether such alternatives exist and is thus likely to continue to purchase the same products. The role of advertising is primordial in launching a new product or in penetrating a new market.

In its judgment the Court did not neglect the crucial point that an advertising ban tends to work to the benefit of the traders currently active in the market.

[18] It should be pointed out that, according to paragraph 17 of its judgment in *Keck and Mithouard*, if national provisions restricting or prohibiting certain selling arrangements are to avoid being caught by Article 30 of the Treaty, they must not be of such a kind as to prevent access to the market by products from another Member State or to impede access any more than they impede the access of domestic products.

[19] The Court has also held, in paragraph 42 of its judgment in Joined Cases C-34/95 to C-36/95 *De Agostini and TV-Shop* [1997] ECR I-3843, that it cannot be excluded that an outright prohibition, applying in one Member State, of a type of promotion for a product which is lawfully sold there might have a greater impact on products from other Member States.

[20] It is apparent that a prohibition on advertising such as that at issue in the main proceedings not only prohibits a form of marketing a product but in reality prohibits producers and importers from directing any advertising messages at consumers, with a few insignificant exceptions.

[21] Even without its being necessary to carry out a precise analysis of the facts characteristic of the Swedish situation, which it is for the national court to do, the Court is able to conclude that, in the case of products like alcoholic beverages, the consumption of which is linked to traditional social practices and to local habits and customs, a prohibition of all advertising directed at consumers in the form of advertisements in the press, on the radio and on television, the direct mailing of unsolicited material or the placing of posters on the public highway is liable to impede access to the market by products from other Member States more than it impedes access by domestic products, with which consumers are instantly more familiar.

This left only the question of justification. The rules would be permitted 'unless it is apparent that, in the circumstances of law and of fact which characterise the situation in the Member State concerned, the protection of public health against the harmful effects of alcohol can be ensured by measures having less effect on intra-Community trade'.

The Court also considered the matter from the standpoint of the law governing the free movement of services. It concluded that

[39] A measure such as the prohibition on advertising at issue in the proceedings before that court, even if it is non-discriminatory, has a particular effect on the cross-border supply of advertising space, given the international nature of the advertising market in the category of products to which the prohibition relates, and thereby constitutes a restriction on the freedom to provide services within the meaning of Article 59 of the Treaty (see, in that regard, *Alpine Investments*, cited above, paragraph 35).

Here too the case accordingly turned on the availability of justification.

FURTHER READING ON THE IMPLICATIONS OF THE *KECK* RULING

Chalmers, D., 'Repackaging the Internal Market – the Ramifications of the *Keck* Judgment' (1994) 19 EL Rev 385.

Friedbacher, T., 'Motive Unmasked: The European Court of Justice, the Free Movement of Goods and the Search for Legitimacy' (1996) 2 ELJ 226.

Greaves, R., 'Advertising Restrictions and the Free Movement of Goods and Services' (1998) 23 EL Rev 305.

NicShuibhne, N., 'The Free Movement of Goods and Article 28 EC: an Evolving Framework' (2002) 27 EL Rev 408.

Oliver, P., 'Some Further Reflections on the Scope of Articles 28–30 (ex 30–36) EC' (1999) 36 CML Rev 783.

Poiares Maduro, M., 'Reforming the Market or the State? Article 30 and the European Constitution: Economic Freedom and Political Rights' (1997) 3 ELJ 55.

Reich, N., 'The November Revolution of the European Court of Justice: *Keck, Meng* and *Audi* Revisited' (1994) 31 CML Rev 459.

Weatherill, S., 'After *Keck*: Some Thoughts on how to Clarify the Clarification' (1996) 33 CML Rev 885.

NOTE
However the *Keck* ruling may be shaped in future as a method for sheltering national regulatory choices from challenge based on Article 28, it is appropriate to conclude by emphasizing that the Court has not lost its determination to use the *'Cassis de Dijon'* principle to root out measures that segregate national markets and deny consumers choice between goods of different origins.

Verein gegen Unwesen in Handel und Gewerbe Köln v ***Mars GmbH* (Case C-470/93)**
[1995] ECR I-1923, Court of Justice of the European Communities

Mars ice-creams were presented in wrappers marked '10%'. This was part of a Europe-wide publicity campaign during which the quantity of the product was increased by 10%. Proceedings were initiated before a German court to restrain this practice as incompatible with German rules forbidding unfair competition. The question of the impact of Article 30 of the EC Treaty (now, after amendment, Article 28 EC) on such intervention in the market was referred to the European Court under the preliminary reference procedure. The European Court observed:

[11] The first question to be examined is whether a prohibition of the marketing of goods bearing on their packaging a publicity marking such as that in question in the main proceedings constitutes a measure having an effect equivalent to a quantitative restriction within the meaning of Article 30 of the Treaty.

[12] According to the case-law of the Court, Article 30 is designed to prohibit any trading rules of Member States which are capable of hindering, directly or indirectly, actually or potentially, intra-Community trade (see the judgment in Case 8/74 *Procureur du Roi* v *Dassonville* [1974] ECR 837, paragraph 5). The Court has held that, in the absence of harmonisation of legislation, obstacles to the free movement of goods that are the consequence of applying, to goods coming from other Member States where they are lawfully manufactured and marketed, rules that lay down requirements to be met by such goods, such as those relating, for example, to their presentation, labelling and packaging, are prohibited by Article 30, even if those rules apply without distinction to national products and to imported products (judgment in Joined Cases C-267/91 and C-268/91 *Keck and Mithouard* [1993] ECR I-6097, paragraph 15).

[13] Although it applies to all products without distinction, a prohibition such as that in question in the main proceedings, which relates to the marketing in a Member State of products bearing the same publicity markings as those lawfully used in other Member States, is by nature such to hinder intra-Community trade. It may compel the importer to adjust the presentation of his products according to the place where they are to be marketed and consequently to incur additional packaging and advertising costs.

[14] Such a prohibition therefore falls within the scope of Article 30 of the Treaty.

Critical to the *Keck* formula is the point that once a law is shown to apply equally in law and in fact, the State is *not* required to justify its law against standards recognised by Community law. By contrast, in this case, the threshold for invocation of Article 28 was crossed and therefore the State *was* required to show justification for its rules. It was unable to do this to the Court's satisfaction:

The consumer's expectation that the price previously charged is being maintained

[17] It is argued that the '10%' marking may lead the consumer to think that the 'new' product is being offered at a price identical to that at which the 'old' product was sold.

[18] As the Advocate-General points out in Paragraphs 39 to 42 of his Opinion, on the assumption that the consumer expects the price to remain the same, the referring court considers that the consumer could be the victim of deception within the meaning of Paragraph 3 of the UWG and that if the price did not increase the offer would meet the consumer's expectation but then a question would arise concerning the application of Paragraph 15 of the GWB, which prohibits manufacturers from imposing prices on retailers.

[19] As regards the first possibility, it must be observed first of all that Mars has not actually profited from the promotional campaign in order to increase its sale prices and that there is no evidence that retailers have themselves increased their prices. In any case, the mere possibility that importers and

retailers might increase the price of the goods and that consequently consumers may be deceived is not sufficient to justify a general prohibition which may hinder intra-Community trade. That fact does not prevent the Member States from taking action, by appropriate measures, against duly proved actions which have the effect of misleading consumers.

[20] As regards the second possibility, the principle of freedom of retail trade in the matter of the fixing of prices, provided for by a system of national law, and intended in particular to guarantee the consumer genuine price competition, may not justify an obstacle to intra-Community trade such as that in question in the main proceedings. The constraint imposed on the retailer not to increase his prices is in fact favourable to the consumer. It does not arise from any contractual stipulation and has the effect of protecting the consumer from being misled in any way. It does not prevent retailers from continuing to charge different prices and applies only during the short duration of the publicity campaign in question.

The visual presentation of the '10%' marking and its alleged misleading effect

[21] It is accepted by all the parties that the '10%' marking is accurate in itself.

[22] However, it is contended that the measure in question is justified because a not insignificant number of consumers will be induced into believing, by the band bearing the '10%' marking, which occupies more than 10% of the total surface area of the wrapping, that the increase is larger than that represented.

[23] Such a justification cannot be accepted.

[24] Reasonably circumspect consumers are supposed to know that there is not necessarily a link between the size of publicity markings relating to an increase in a product's quantity and the size of that increase.

[25] The reply to the preliminary question must therefore be that Article 30 of the Treaty is to be interpreted as precluding a national measure from prohibiting the importation and marketing of a product lawfully marketed in another Member State, the quantity of which was increased during a short publicity campaign and the wrapping of which bears the marking '10%',

- (a) on the ground that the presentation may induce the consumer into thinking that the price of the goods offered is the same as that at which the goods had previously been sold in their old presentation,
- (b) on the ground that the new presentation gives the impression to the consumer that the volume and weight of the product have been considerably increased.

SECTION 3: **JUSTIFYING INDISTINCTLY APPLICABLE RULES**

The ruling in *Mars* provides a helpful bridge back to the mainstream of '*Cassis de Dijon*' case law. Whether or not a national measure constitutes a trade barrier that requires justification depends on an application of the formula crafted by the Court in *Keck*, which does not disturb the pure stream of *Cassis de Dijon* but rather siphons off the contaminations added by rulings such as the *Sunday Trading* pair (p.393 above), in which the Court mistakenly called on the regulating State to justify rules which subjected imports to no greater interference than domestic production. Once it is established that a trade barrier requiring justification is at stake, the *Cassis* formula – the 'mandatory requirements' – applies undisturbed by *Keck*. In '*Cassis de Dijon*' (Case 120/78), the Court indicated that measures 'necessary to satisfy mandatory requirements' are capable of being held compatible with Article 28 despite their restrictive effect on trade. This allows justification in circumstances extending beyond those allowed by Article 30 (ex 36) EC, albeit only where there is no discrimination against imported goods. But most cases have been decided against the regulating State – that is, no adequate justification has been shown.

In *Cassis* itself the Court was clearly not satisfied that the German rules on alcohol strength were necessary to satisfy mandatory requirements. In *Commission v Germany* (Case 178/84) arguments of justification were similarly dismissed. In both cases no compelling reasons for impeding trade were shown to exist. And *Mars* found the Court in robust mood: 'Reasonably circumspect consumers are supposed to know that there is not necessarily a link between the size of publicity markings relating to an increase in a product's quantity and the size of that increase' (para 24). So Germany was 'over-regulating' its market, according to the standards recognised by the European Court. Presumably the interests of German consumers who are *not* reasonably circumspect and who might be confused by the markings on the chocolate bars are judged less important in aggregate than the interests of consumers more generally in participating an integrated, more competitive European market.

The assumption, then, is that consumers benefit from increased cross border trade in goods. Competition is stimulated; quality should rise while prices fall. This is basic economics – see Chapter 9. The Court's application of Article 28 in this manner generates deregulation within the territory of the Member State in question. However, the Court does not insist on a 'lowest common denominator' of regulatory protection within the EC (see S. Weatherill, *EC Consumer Law and Policy* (Harlow: Longman, 1997), Ch. 2). As is plain in cases concerning scientific uncertainty about the safety of products (Case 174/82, p.373 above), the application of Article 28 is not inevitably destructive of national choices. Laws curtailing practices perceived to be 'unfair' were found compatible with Article 30 in *Diensten Groep* v *Beele* (Case 6/81) [1982] ECR 707 and *Buet* (Case 382/87, p.400 above); and see also, in connection with similar issues arising in the services sector under Article 49 EC, *Alpine Investments* (Case C-384/93, p.457 below).

But the law of free movement increasingly impinges on matters of wider impact than market economics. The deceptively bland notion that trade restrictions may be 'justified' is capable of becoming very sensitive indeed as its scope becomes more visible.

Fietje (Case 27/80)
[1980] ECR 3839, Court of Justice of the European Communities

[10] Although the extension to imported products of an obligation to use a certain name on the label does not wholly preclude the importation into the Member State concerned of products originating in other Member States or in free circulation in those States it may none the less make their marketing more difficult, especially in the case of parallel imports. As the Netherlands Government itself admits in its observations, such an extension of that obligation is thus capable of impeding, at least indirectly, trade between Member States. It is therefore necessary to consider whether it may be justified on the ground of the public interest in consumer protection, which, according to the observations of the Netherlands Government and according to the 'Warenwet', underlies the rules in question.

[11] If national rules relating to a given product include the obligation to use a description that is sufficiently precise to inform the purchaser of the nature of the product and to enable it to be distinguished from products with which it might be confused, it may well be necessary, in order to give consumers effective protection, to extend this obligation to imported products also, even in such a way as to make necessary the alteration of the original labels of some of these products. At the level of Community legislation, this possibility is recognised in several directives on the approximation of the laws of the Member States relating to certain foodstuffs as well as by Council Directive 79/112/EEC of 18 December 1978 on the approximation of the laws of the Member States relating to the labelling, presentation and advertising of foodstuffs for sale to the ultimate consumer (Official Journal 1979, L 33, p.1 [now replaced by Directive 2000/13 OJ 2000 L109/29]).

[12] However, there is no longer any need for such protection if the details given on the original label of the imported product have as their content information on the nature of the product and that content includes at least the same information, and is just as capable of being understood by consumers in the importing State, as the description prescribed by the rules of that State. In the context of Article 177 of the EEC Treaty, the making of the findings of fact necessary in order to establish whether there is such equivalence is a matter for the national court.

NOTE
In *Piageme* v *BVBA Peeters* (Case C-369/89) [1991] ECR I-2971, the Court ruled that 'Article 30 of the EEC Treaty and Article 14 of Directive 79/112 preclude a national law from requiring the exclusive use of a specific language for the labelling of foodstuffs, without allowing for the possibility of using another language easily understood by purchasers or of ensuring that the purchaser is informed by other measures'. (See also Case C-85/94 between the same parties, [1995] ECR I-2955; and Case C-385/96 *Hermann Josef Goerres* [1998] ECR I-4431; Case C-33/97 *Colim* v *Biggs* [1999] ECR I-3175; Case C-366/98 *Geffroy* [2000] ECR I-6579.) In November 1993, the Commission published a communication concerning the use of languages in the marketing of foodstuffs in the light of Case C-369/89 – COM (93) 532. This is a further example of the Commission's penchant for issuing interpretation of specific Court rulings (*cf* p.364 above). The communication observes that 'The grounds of consumer protection which may justify the imposition of the official language(s) of a Member State no longer apply when foreign terms and expressions appearing on product labelling are easily understood and therefore fulfil their informative function'. (On review of *Community* rules specifying use of particular languages against the requirements of the Treaty rules governing free movement of goods, see *Meyhui NV* v *Schott Zwiesel Glaswerke AG* (Case C-51/93) [1994] ECR I-3879.) See J. Usher, 'Disclosure Rules (Information) as a Primary Tool in the Doctrine on Measures having Equivalent Effect', in S. Grundmann, W. Kerber and S. Weatherill (eds), *Party Autonomy in the Internal Market* (Berlin: De Gruyter, 2001).

■ QUESTIONS

1. To what extent is the linguistic competence of consumers relevant to the compatibility of labelling requirements with Community law?

2. Instead of basing justification on the risk of consumer confusion, could one 're-package' and thereby strengthen the defence of a mandatory language rule as a contribution to protecting and promoting local culture? How strong is the argument that language protection is a cultural matter that should not be threatened by Article 28? *Cf* Article 151 EC, especially Articles 151(1), (4) EC; also Article 22 of the EU Charter of Fundamental Rights, p.16 above. Read C. Boch, 'Language Protection and Free Trade: the Triumph of the Homo McDonaldus' (1998) 4 *Euro Public Law* 379.

An unusual example of the range of issues involved in the Court's process of adjudication is provided by the next case.

Vereinigte Familiapress Zeitungsverlags- und vertriebs GmbH v *Heinrich Bauer Verlag* (Case C-368/95)

[1997] ECR I-3689, Court of Justice of the European Communities

A German publisher fell foul of Austrian law when it tried to market a magazine containing a prize crossword. Such an inducement was lawful in Germany but prohibited in Austria as a means to protect small publishers from damaging competition from bigger rivals with deeper pockets. The rule obstructed cross-border trade but Austria sought to justify it as a means to sustain diversity in media ownership. The Court's ruling exposes the collison of values at stake.

[18] Maintenance of press diversity may constitute an overriding requirement justifying a restriction on free movement of goods. Such diversity helps to safeguard freedom of expression, as protected by Article 10 of the European Convention on Human Rights and Fundamental Freedoms, which is one of the fundamental rights guaranteed by the Community legal order (see Case C-353/89 *Commission* v *Netherlands* [1991] ECR I-4069, paragraph 30, and Case C-148/91 *Vereiniging Veronica Omroep Organisatie* v *Commissariaat voor de Media* [1993] ECR I-487, paragraph 10).

[19] However, the Court has also consistently held (*Cassis de Dijon*, cited above; Case C-230/89 *Rau* [1990] ECR I-4827, paragraph 12, and Case C-470/93 *Mars* [1995] ECR I-1923, paragraph 15) that the provisions of national law in question must be proportionate to the objective pursued and that objective must not be capable of being achieved by measures which are less restrictive of intra-Community trade.

[20] Admittedly, in Case C-275/92 *Schindler* [1994] ECR I-1039, paragraph 61, concerning freedom to provide services, the Court held that the special features of lotteries justify allowing national authorities a sufficient degree of latitude to determine what is required to protect the players and, more generally, in the light of the specific social and cultural features of each Member State, to maintain order in society, as regards the manner in which lotteries are operated, the size of the stakes and the allocation of the profits they yield. The Court therefore considered that it was for the national authorities to assess not only whether it is necessary to restrict the activities of lotteries but also whether they should be prohibited, provided that those restrictions are not discriminatory.

[21] Games such as those at issue in the main proceedings are not, however, comparable to the lotteries the features of which were considered in *Schindler*.

[22] The facts on which that judgment was based were concerned exclusively, as the Court expressly pointed out, with large-scale lotteries in respect of which the discretion enjoyed by national authorities was justified because of the high risk of crime or fraud, given the amounts which could be staked and the winnings which could be held out to players (paragraphs 50, 51 and 60).

[23] By contrast, such concerns for the maintenance of order in society are not present in this case. The draws in question are organized on a small scale and less is at stake; they do not constitute an economic activity in their own right but are merely one aspect of the editorial content of a magazine; and under Austrian legislation, draws are prohibited only in the press.

[24] Furthermore, it is to be noted that where a Member State relies on overriding requirements to justify rules which are likely to obstruct the exercise of free movement of goods, such justification must also be interpreted in the light of the general principles of law and in particular of fundamental rights (see Case C-260/89 *ERT* [1991] ECR I-2925, paragraph 43).

[25] Those fundamental rights include freedom of expression, as enshrined in Article 10 of the European Convention for the Protection of Human Rights and Fundamental Freedoms (*ERT*, paragraph 44).

[26] A prohibition on selling publications which offer the chance to take part in prize games competitions may detract from freedom of expression. Article 10 of the European Convention for the Protection of Human Rights and Fundamental Freedoms does, however, permit derogations from that freedom for the purposes of maintaining press diversity, in so far as they are prescribed by law

and are necessary in a democratic society (see the judgment of the European Court of Human Rights of 24 November 1993 in *Informationsverein Lentia and Others* v *Austria* Series A No 276).

[27] In the light of the considerations set out in paragraphs 19 to 26 of this judgment, it must therefore be determined whether a national prohibition such as that in issue in the main proceedings is proportionate to the aim of maintaining press diversity and whether that objective might not be attained by measures less restrictive of both intra-Community trade and freedom of expression.

[28] To that end, it should be determined, first, whether newspapers which offer the chance of winning a prize in games, puzzles or competitions are in competition with those small press publishers who are deemed to be unable to offer comparable prizes and whom the contested legislation is intended to protect and, second, whether such a prospect of winning constitutes an incentive to purchase capable of bringing about a shift in demand.

[29] It is for the national court to determine whether those conditions are satisfied on the basis of a study of the Austrian press market.

[30] In carrying out that study, it will have to define the market for the product in question and to have regard to the market shares of individual publishers or press groups and the trend thereof.

[31] Moreover, the national court will also have to assess the extent to which, from the consumer's standpoint, the product concerned can be replaced by papers which do not offer prizes, taking into account all the circumstances which may influence the decision to purchase, such as the presence of advertising on the title page referring to the chance of winning a prize, the likelihood of winning, the value of the prize or the extent to which winning depends on a test calling for a measure of ingenuity, skill or knowledge.

[32] The Belgian and Netherlands Governments consider that the Austrian legislature could have adopted measures less restrictive of free movement of goods than an outright prohibition on the distribution of newspapers which afford the chance of winning a prize, such as blacking out or removing the page on which the prize competition appears in copies intended for Austria or a statement that readers in Austria do not qualify for the chance to win a prize.

[33] The documents before the Court suggest that the prohibition in question would not constitute a barrier to the marketing of newspapers where one of the above measures had been taken. If the national court were nevertheless to find that this was the case, the prohibition would be disproportionate.

[34] In the light of the foregoing considerations, the answer to be given to the national court's question must be that Article 30 of the EC Treaty is to be interpreted as not precluding application of legislation of a Member State the effect of which is to prohibit the distribution on its territory by an undertaking established in another Member State of a periodical produced in that latter State containing prize puzzles or competitions which are lawfully organized in that State, provided that that prohibition is proportionate to maintenance of press diversity and that that objective cannot be achieved by less restrictive means. This assumes, *inter alia*, that the newspapers offering the chance of winning a prize in games, puzzles or competitions are in competition with small newspaper publishers who are deemed to be unable to offer comparable prizes and the prospect of winning is liable to bring about a shift in demand. Furthermore, the national prohibition must not constitute an obstacle to the marketing of newspapers which, albeit containing prize games, puzzles or competitions, do not give readers residing in the Member State concerned the opportunity to win a prize. It is for the national court to determine whether those conditions are satisfied on the basis of a study of the national press market concerned.

The deployment of the language of fundamental rights in the law of free movement is highly significant in showing the permeation of trade law by wider values. But notice that *both* parties in this case are able to play the fundamental rights card. How would you, as a national judge, decide the case in the light of the Court's ruling?

For recent surveys of case law, see S. Weatherill, 'Recent Case Law Concerning the Free Movement of Goods: Mapping the Frontiers of Market Deregulation' (1999) 36 CML Rev 51; M. Poiares Maduro, 'The Saga of Article 30 EC Treaty: To Be Continued' (1998) 5 MJ 298.

It is notable that arguments based on the protection of interests that go unrecognized in Article 30 (ex 36) were considered available in principle, if rejected on the merits of most of these cases. It will be remembered from the preceding Chapter that this had induced both the Irish and the British Governments to defend their origin marking rules as measures of consumer protection (pp.349 and 352 above). In both instances the Court held the argument misplaced because both States had established a *discriminatory* system. The element of discrimination against imported goods precluded reliance on the 'mandatory requirements' encompassing, for example, the protection of the economic interests of the consumer. The insistence on the elimination of discrimination is also plain in *Gebhard* (Case C-55/94, pp.321 and 386 above).

Even though the Court ruled against the invocation of the mandatory requirements on the facts of the cases considered above ('Cassis', beer purity, etc.), the availability of 'defences' not found in Article 30 indicates a greater willingness to respect national competence to regulate in a manner incompatible with free trade, provided discrimination does not contaminate the system.

Cases concerning environmental protection have provided the sternest challenge to the Court's refusal to permit the 'mandatory requirements' to save discriminatory State measures. In *Commission* v *Belgium* (Case C-2/90) [1992] ECR I-4431, [1993] 1 CMLR 365 Wallonia (a region of Belgium) prohibited the storage, tipping, or dumping of waste from other Member States or from elsewhere in Belgium. The measure was aimed at protecting Wallonia from becoming the target for waste from areas with tighter regulatory regimes. The Commission challenged the rule as a violation of Article 30 of the EC Treaty (now, after amendment, Article 28 EC), but the application was rejected by the Court. This was a restriction on the importation of goods of commercial value, but the Court found it justified as a measure of environmental protection. The Court observed that '[t]he accumulation of waste . . . constitutes a threat to the environment because of the limited capacity of each region or locality for receiving it'. The oddity in the ruling is that the regime appeared to be discriminatory – Walloon waste was treated in Wallonia, waste from outside could not be. It is explained above that discriminatory measures are not justifiable with reference to 'the mandatory requirements' which include environmental protection. The Court expressly confirmed this principle in Case C-2/90, but evaded the problem by finding the Walloon measures to be indistinctly applicable and therefore capable of justification as measures of environmental protection. It drew on the principle expressed in Article 130r(2) of the EC Treaty (now, after amendment, Article 174(2) EC) that 'environmental damage should as a priority be rectified at source', which dictates a need to minimize transport of waste. Accordingly the Court commented that it 'follows that, having regard to the differences between waste produced in one place and that in another and its connection with the place where it is produced, the contested measures cannot be considered to be discriminatory'.

The ruling attracted divergent comment on its implications (Hancher and Sevenster (1993) 30 CML Rev 351; Von Wilmowsky, *ibid.*, 541; Geradin (1993)

18 EL Rev 144). The Court's reasoning that the measure was *not* discriminatory is not wholly convincing and is contradicted by Advocate-General Jacobs's Opinion in the case. However, the Court's reasoning enabled it to achieve a result in conformity with general Treaty principles on environmental protection. It may be as well not to overestimate the ruling's importance, given that this area is increasingly occupied by legislative initiatives which replace the need to test national initiatives against Articles 28–30. Indeed, in Case C-2/90 the Court had also examined Belgian compliance with relevant Directives. At the very least, the decision further demonstrates the sensitivity of Article 28 litigation which raises the potential collision between national environmental protection and market integration. (See further L. Kramer, 'Environmental Protection and Article 30 EEC Treaty' (1993) 30 CML Rev 111; D. Geradin, 'Trade and Environmental Protection: Community Harmonization and National Environmental Standards' (1993) 13 YEL 151.)

Some commentators take these cases as evidence of the Court tacitly changing its mind about its refusal to extend the 'mandatory requirements' to permit justification of discriminatory practices; others would regard environmental cases as quite distinct, in particular because of the impact of the principle that environmental damage be rectified at source (Article 174(2) EC) which may be taken to mean that transported waste is simply not the same as local waste and can therefore be treated differently without this being treated as 'discrimination'. And consider too how Article 6 EC should interact with Article 28 EC; and so too Article 37 of the EU Charter of Fundamental Rights – how 'permeable' is the law of free movement? As a minimum – note how the notion of 'discrimination' carries a heavy weight – perhaps too heavy a weight – in structuring the law on the scope of available justifications. What is the proper basis of comparison? (See, e.g., the contributions of De Búrca and of Scott to Barnard and Scott (eds), *The Law of the Single European Market* (Oxford: Hart Publishing, 2001).)

In Case C-379/98 *Preussen Elektra* [2001] ECR I-2099 Advocate-General Jacobs called on the Court to improve legal certainty by adopting a unified test that would apply the full spectrum of justifications to all barriers to trade. The presence of discrimination would be relegated to the assessment of whether the national rules should be accepted as proportionate. But the Court did not address the point, and maintained its orthodox approach (as it did in a subsequent case dealing with the free movement of services, Case C-136/00 *Danner*, judgment of 3 October 2002).

Notice finally how in '*Cassis de Dijon*' (Case 120/78) and in subsequent cases a key precondition to the application of Article 28 is the absence of common Community rules in the area. Article 28 operates pending Community intervention in the field. How might environmental laws be framed in this area in order to remove the barriers to trade caused by divergent national legislation? At what level should the rules be administered and enforced – Community, national, or a combination of both? (See, more generally, Chapters 19 and 20.)

■ QUESTIONS

1. Consider the necessity to satisfy mandatory requirements in '*Cassis de Dijon*' (Case 120/78) and the rule of reason in *Dassonville* (Case 8/74) (p.344 above). Do these concepts serve the same *function*; and are they identical in substance? Consider also Article 81 (p.513).

2. Joe imports alcoholic drink from the Republic of Ireland into England. However, he has recently become increasingly frustrated due to a variety of British regulations which impede his business. He seeks your advice about the impact of Community law on the following problems he has encountered with his latest consignment:

(a) British legislation forbids the marketing of whisky above a specified maximum alcohol strength. Joe is therefore unable to sell his 'Super de Luxe Special Irish Whiskey' because it is too strong.

(b) Joe is unable to sell his beers which are marketed in blue glass bottles, because British legislation reserves the use of blue bottles for medicines.

SECTION 4: WHAT SORT OF MARKET IS BEING MADE? SOME CONSEQUENCES FOR CONSUMER PROTECTION

THE COMMISSION'S INTERPRETATION OF THE JUDGMENT IN *CASSIS DE DIJON*

The Court's decision in *'Cassis de Dijon'* (Case 120/78) was seized on with enthusiasm by the Commission as a means of advancing the attack on national rules which partition the market.

COMMISSION COMMUNICATION
[1980] OJ C256/2, 3 OCTOBER 1980

The following is the text of a letter which has been sent to the member States; the European Parliament and the Council have also been notified of it.

In the Commission's Communication of 6 November 1978 on 'Safeguarding free trade within the Community', it was emphasised that the free movement of goods is being affected by a growing number of restrictive measures.

The judgment delivered by the Court of Justice on 20 February 1979 in Case 120/78 (the *'Cassis de Dijon'* case), and recently reaffirmed in the judgment of 26 June 1980 in Case 788/79, has given the Commission some interpretative guidance enabling it to monitor more strictly the application of the Treaty rules on the free movement of goods, particularly Articles 30 to 36 of the EEC Treaty.

The Court gives a very general definition of the barriers to free trade which are prohibited by the provisions of Article 30 *et seq.* of the EEC Treaty. These are taken to include 'any national measure capable of hindering, directly or indirectly, actually or potentially, intra-Community trade'.

In its judgment of 20 February 1979 the Court indicates the scope of this definition as it applies to technical and commercial rules.

Any product lawfully produced and marketed in one member-State must, in principle, be admitted to the market of any other member-State.

Technical and commercial rules, even those equally applicable to national and imported products, may create barriers to trade only where those rules are necessary to satisfy mandatory requirements and to serve a purpose which is in the general interest and for which they are an essential guarantee. This purpose must be such as to take precedence over the requirements of the free movement of goods, which constitutes one of the fundamental rules of the Community.

The conclusions in terms of policy which the Commission draws from this new guidance are set out below.

— Whereas member-States may, with respect to domestic products and in the absence of relevant Community provisions, regulate the terms on which such products are marketed, the case is different for products imported from other member-States.

Any product imported from another member-State must in principle be admitted to the territory of the importing member-State if it has been lawfully produced, that is, conforms to rules and processes of manufacture that are customarily and traditionally accepted in the exporting country, and is marketed in the territory of the latter.

This principle implies that member-States, when drawing up commercial or technical rules liable to affect the free movement of goods, may not take an exclusively national viewpoint and take account only of requirements confined to domestic products. The proper functioning of the common market demands that each member-State also give consideration to the legitimate requirements of the other member-States.

Only under very strict conditions does the Court accept exceptions to this principle; barriers to trade resulting from differences between commercial and technical rules are only admissible:

— if the rules are necessary, that is appropriate and not excessive, in order to satisfy mandatory requirements (public health, protection of consumers or the environment, the fairness of commercial transactions, etc.);

— if the rules serve a purpose in the general interest which is compelling enough to justify an exception to a fundamental rule of the Treaty such as the free movement of goods;

— if the rules are essential for such a purpose to be attained, *i.e.* are the means which are the most appropriate and at the same time least hinder trade.

The Court's interpretation has induced the Commission to set out a number of guidelines

— The principles deduced by the Court imply that a member-State may not in principle prohibit the sale in its territory of a product lawfully produced and marketed in another member-State even if the product is produced according to technical or quality requirements which differ from those imposed on its domestic products. Where a product 'suitably and satisfactorily' fulfils the legitimate objective of a member-State's own rules (public safety, protection of the consumer or the environment, etc.), the importing country cannot justify prohibiting its sale in its territory by claiming that the way it fulfils the objective is different from that imposed on domestic products.

In such a case, an absolute prohibition of sale could not be considered 'necessary' to satisfy a 'mandatory requirement' because it would not be an 'essential guarantee' in the sense defined in the Court's judgment.

The Commission will therefore have to tackle a whole body of commercial rules which lay down that products manufactured and marketed in one member-State must fulfil technical or qualitative conditions in order to be admitted to the market of another and specifically in all cases where the trade barriers occasioned by such rules are inadmissible according to the very strict criteria set out by the Court.

The Commission is referring in particular to rules covering the composition, designation, presentation and packaging of products as well as rules requiring compliance with certain technical standards.

— The Commission's work of harmonisation will henceforth have to be directed mainly at national laws having an impact on the functioning of the common market where barriers to trade to be removed arise from national provisions which are admissible under the criteria set by the Court.

The Commission will be concentrating on sectors deserving priority because of their economic relevance to the creation of a single internal market.

To forestall later difficulties, the Commission will be informing member-States of potential objections, under the terms of Community law, to provisions they may be considering introducing which come to the attention of the Commission.

It will be producing suggestions soon on the procedures to be followed in such cases.

The Commission is confident that this approach will secure greater freedom of trade for the Community's manufacturers, so strengthening the industrial base of the Community, while meeting the expectations of consumers.

NOTE

The Commission thus believes that the extension of Article 30 of the EC Treaty (now, after amendment, Article 28 EC) to cover '*Cassis de Dijon*' (Case 120/78) type rules has reduced the need for harmonisation.

■ QUESTION

What would have been the consequence for national diversity and tradition if harmonization at Community level had been required to remove the trade distortive effect of rules governing the content of fruit liqueurs, the fat levels of Edam cheese, and the designation of beers?

NOTE

The Commission's view that States 'drawing up commercial or technical rules liable to affect the free movement of goods, may not take an exclusively national viewpoint' is reflected in the next case.

Commission v Ireland (Case 45/87)

[1988] ECR 4929, [1989] 1 CMLR 225, Court of Justice of the European Communities

The contract specification for the Dundalk Water Supply Augmentation Scheme provided that the asbestos cement pressure pipes to be used should be certified as complying with Irish Standard 188:1975 in accordance with the Irish Standard Mark Licensing Scheme of the Institute for Industrial Research and Standards (IIRS). The Commission brought infringement proceedings alleging a violation of Article 28 (ex 30) EC.

[19] In that connection, it must first be pointed out that the inclusion of such a clause in an invitation to tender may cause economic operators who produce or utilize pipes equivalent to pipes certified as complying with Irish standards to refrain from tendering

[20] It further appears from the documents in the case that only one undertaking has been certified by the IIRS to IS 188:1975 to apply the Irish Standard Mark to pipes of the type required for the purposes of the public works contract at issue. That undertaking is located in Ireland. Consequently, the inclusion of Clause 4.29 had the effect of restricting the supply of the pipes needed for the Dundalk scheme to Irish manufacturers alone.

[21] The Irish Government maintains that it is necessary to specify the standards to which materials must be manufactured, particularly in a case such as this where the pipes utilized must suit the existing network. Compliance with another standard, even an international standard such as ISO 160:1980, would not suffice to eliminate certain technical difficulties.

[22] That technical argument cannot be accepted. The Commission's complaint does not relate to compliance with technical requirements but to the refusal of the Irish authorities to verify whether those requirements are satisfied where the manufacturer of the materials has not been certified by the IIRS to IS 188. By incorporating in the notice in question the words 'or equivalent' after the reference to the Irish standard, as provided for by Directive 71/305 where it is applicable, the Irish authorities could have verified compliance with the technical conditions without from the outset restricting the contract only to tenderers proposing to utilize Irish materials.

[23] The Irish Government further objects that in any event the pipes manufactured by the Spanish undertaking in question whose use was provided for in the rejected tender did not meet the technical requirements, but that argument, too, is irrelevant as regards the compatibility with the Treaty of the inclusion of a clause like Clause 4.29 in an invitation to tender.

[24] The Irish Government further maintains that protection of public health justifies the requirement of compliance with the Irish standard in so far as that standard guarantees that there is no contact between the water and the asbestos fibres in the cement pipes, which would adversely affect the quality of the drinking water.

[25] That argument must be rejected. As the Commission has rightly pointed out, the coating of the pipes, both internally and externally, was the subject of a separate requirement in the invitation to tender. The Irish Government has not shown why compliance with that requirement would not be such as to ensure that there is no contact between the water and the asbestos fibres, which it considers to be essential for reasons of public health.

[26] The Irish Government has not put forward any other argument to refute the conclusions of the Commission and the Spanish Government and those conclusions must consequently be upheld.

[27] It must therefore be held that by allowing the inclusion in the contract specification for tender for a public works contract of a clause stipulating that the asbestos cement pressure pipes must be certified as complying with Irish Standard 188:1975 in accordance with the Irish Standard Mark Licensing Scheme of the Institute for Industrial Research and Standards, Ireland has failed to fulfil its obligations under Article 30 of the EEC Treaty.

NOTES
1. The application of Article 28 stimulates competition. Competition yields consumer choice, lower prices, and higher quality. In this way the benefits of a common market are realized.
2. In the 1985 White Paper (p.295 above), the Commission located the *'Cassis de Dijon'* (Case 120/78) interpretation of the law governing free movement of goods firmly within the framework of the rules designed to complete the internal market by the end of 1992. The fact that market integration did not stop at the end of 1992, but, as is made plain in Chapter 9, continues to evolve, means that this analysis remains true for the future, subject to the refinements brought about by the ruling in *Keck* (Cases C-267 & C-268/91, p.397 above).

COM (85) 310, COMPLETING THE INTERNAL MARKET
White Paper from the Commission to the European Council, 14 June 1985

PART TWO: THE REMOVAL OF TECHNICAL BARRIERS

57. The elimination of border controls, important as it is, does not of itself create a genuine common market. Goods and people moving within the Community should not find obstacles inside the different Member States as opposed to meeting them at the border.

58. This does not mean that there should be the same rules everywhere, but that goods as well as citizens and companies should be able to move freely within the Community. Subject to certain important constraints (see paragraph 65 below), the general principle should be approved that, if a product is lawfully manufactured and marketed in one Member State, there is no reason why it should not be sold freely throughout the Community. Indeed, the objectives of national legislation, such as the protection of human health and life and of the environment, are more often than not identical. It follows that the rules and controls developed to achieve those objectives, although they may take different forms, essentially come down to the same thing, and so should normally be accorded recognition in all Member States, not forgetting the possibilities of cooperation between national authorities. What is true for goods, is also true for services and for people. If a Community citizen or a company meets the requirements for its activity in one member State, there should be no valid reason why those citizens or companies should not exercise their economic activities also in other parts of the Community.

59. The Commission is fully aware that this strategy implies a change in habits and in traditional ways of thinking. What is needed is a radical change of attitude which would lead to new and innovative solutions for problems – real or apparent – which may appear when border controls no longer exist.

I. Free movement of goods

60. Whilst the physical barriers dealt with in Part One impede trade flows and add unacceptable administrative costs (ultimately paid by the consumer), barriers created by different national product regulations and standards have a double-edged effect: they not only add extra costs, but they also distort production patterns; increase unit costs; increase stock holding costs; discourage business cooperation, and fundamentally frustrate the creation of a common market for industrial products. Until such barriers are removed, Community manufacturers are forced to focus on national rather than continental markets and are unable to benefit from the economies of scale which a truly unified internal market offers. Failure to achieve a genuine industrial common market becomes increasingly serious since the research, development and commercialisation costs of the new technologies, in order to have a realistic prospect of being internationally competitive, require the background of a home market of continental proportions.

The need for a new strategy

61. The harmonization approach has been the cornerstone of Community action in the first 25 years and has produced unprecedented progress in the creation of common rules on a Community-wide basis. However, over the years, a number of shortcomings have been identified . .

63. In principle, therefore, given the Council's recognition (Conclusions on Standardization, 16 July 1984) of the essential equivalence of the objectives of national legislation, mutual recognition could be an effective strategy for bringing about a common market in a trading sense. This strategy is supported in particular by Articles 30 to 36 of the EEC Treaty, which prohibit national measures which would have excessively and unjustifiably restrictive effects on free movement.

64. But while a strategy based purely on mutual recognition would remove barriers to trade and lead to the creation of a genuine common trading market, it might well prove inadequate for the purposes of the building up of an expanding market based on the competitiveness which a continental-scale uniform market can generate. On the other hand experience has shown that the alternative of relying on a strategy based totally on harmonization would be over-regulatory, would take a long time to implement, would be inflexible and could stifle innovation. What is needed is a strategy that combines the best of both approaches but, above all, allows for progress to be made more quickly than in the past.

The chosen strategy

65. The Commission takes into account the underlying reasons for the existence of barriers to trade, and recognizes the essential equivalence of Member States' legislative objectives in the protection of health and safety, and of the environment. Its harmonization approach is based on the following principles:

- a clear distinction needs to be drawn in future internal market initiatives between what it is essential to harmonize, and what may be left to mutual recognition of national regulations and standards; this implies that, on the occasion of each harmonization initiative, the Commission will determine whether national regulations are excessive in relation to the mandatory requirements pursued and, thus, constitute unjustified barriers to trade according to Article 30 to 36 of the EEC Treaty;
- legislative harmonization (Council Directives based on Article 100) will in future be restricted to laying down essential health and safety requirements which will be obligatory in all Member States. Conformity with this will entitle a product to free movement;
- harmonization of industrial standards by the elaboration of European standards will be promoted to the maximum extent, but the absence of European Standards should not be allowed to be used as a barrier to free movement. During the waiting period while European Standards are being developed, the mutual acceptance of national standards, with agreed procedures, should be the guiding principle.

NOTES

1. *Cf* p.342 above on the present standing of Directive 70/50.
2. The reaction to the Commission's strategy has been mixed.

R. Dehousse, 'Completing the Internal Market: Institutional Constraints and Challenges'
in R. Bieber *et al* (eds) 1992: One European Market?
(Baden-Baden: Nomos Verlagsgesellschaft, 1988), pp.311, 324–29

(Footnotes omitted.)

The success of a programme as ambitious as the White Paper depends not only on changes in rules governing decision-making alone but also on the proposed programme itself and the way in which it takes account of the institutional context. The connection between the decision-making procedure and the decisions which eventually emerge is not purely a one-way system. Just as the way in which a decision is taken can largely determine its content, so the way that the decision-making procedure operates can be modified by altering the final product that is expected to emerge. To some extent the means used for a given end condition the feasibility of the undertaking. To give a specific example: basically it would appear simpler to persuade the Twelve to refrain from introducing new provisions that might harm intra-Community trade, rather than to get them to agree on a definition of the technical specifications which a given product must satisfy. Equally it is possible – without tampering with the existing decision-making structures at all – to reduce the degree of consensus needed by cutting down the number of participants involved: all that has to be done is to circumscribe the problem in such a way that only a few Member States are directly concerned. Another possibility is to reduce the bargaining costs by proposing no more than a general agreement which leaves each Member State some room for manoeuvre, either by allowing relative freedom of implementation or by means of exemptions or safeguard clauses. These are some simple ways of getting round the joint-decision trap referred to earlier. Viewed from this angle, a number of recent developments catch the eye.

The broad interpretation given to the notion of 'measures having equivalent effect to quantitative restrictions' in the *Dassonville* and *Cassis de Dijon* cases unquestionably opened up new avenues for the Commission. The Court has stated that a Member State may not in principle prohibit the sale in its territory of a product lawfully produced and marketed in another Member State even if this product is produced according to technical or quality requirements which differ from those imposed on its domestic products. In the absence of Community provisions, only measures covered by article 36 or 'necessary in order to satisfy mandatory requirements' like the effectiveness of fiscal supervision, the protection of public health and of the environment, the fairness of commercial transactions and the defence of the consumer, can take precedence over the requirements of the free movements of goods. By extending the scope of article 30, the Court has rendered possible an emphasis on the removal of technical barriers to trade in areas where it was generally thought that only harmonization of national measures was possible.

The new strategy outlined in the White Paper rests on the implicit premise of this case law, namely the essential equivalence of national legislative objectives concerning the protection of human health and safety, and of the environment. In its conclusions on standardization of July 1984, the Council has explicitly recognised that

> 'the objectives being pursued by the Member States to protect the safety and health of their people as well as the consumer are equally valid in principle, even if different techniques are used to achieve them.'

The White Paper takes this new situation to a logical conclusion and proposes a theoretical distinction between matters where harmonization is essential and those where it is sufficient for there to be mutual recognition of the equivalence of the various basic requirements laid down under national law. The concept of mutual recognition also appears in several other places in the White Paper: it is referred to in connection with health controls, frontier checks, University degrees and vocational training, and even in such a sensitive matter as financial services.

This approach has many advantages in view of the cumbersome nature of the decision-making process. Unlike harmonization, mutual recognition does not involve the transfer of powers to the Community but, at the very worst, somewhat restricts the freedom of action of the Member States. Furthermore, this emphasis on mutual recognition avoids all the difficulties linked to the necessity of drafting directives so as to suit the substantive concerns of twelve different actors or the specific requirements of their legal system. Thus the lengthy bargaining which tends to accompany harmonization can be reduced to a minimum, with greater reliance being placed on the (politically more neutral) supervision of the Court to ensure that the continued existence of national rules does not constitute a barrier to trade. Both from a political and from a legalistic viewpoint, this new direction should be easier to follow.

. . .

The reliance on mutual recognition is nothing more than the rediscovery of a principle which is fairly common in structures of a federal type – and to which the draft Treaty on European Union gave a prominent place: the principle of subsidiarity. The essence of this principle is very simple: the higher level of government should only intervene when it can provide public goods that lower levels cannot supply. In the Community context, this would imply that Community action should be limited to fields where it is absolutely necessary for market integration, or where it can reach better results than the Member States. As is so often the case, the espousal of this principle seems dictated by a combination of theoretical considerations as to the level at which certain powers would be most fruitfully exercised and more practical considerations of how best to simplify the decision-making process. In this particular case, it is perfectly in line with the Treaty inclination towards negative integration.

NOTE
Some of these issues have already been touched on in Chapter 9. Some, especially those connected with harmonization policy and subsidiarity, will be readdressed in Chapters 19 and 20. It bears repetition that these are general issues for the evolution of the Community market. They were not suddenly solved at the end of 1992.

An interesting and under-researched question is whether 'mutual recognition' really works in practice. In the Commission's Second Biennial Report on the Application of the Principle of Mutual Recognition in the Single Market, COM (2002) 419 (available via http://europa.eu.int/comm/internal_market/en/goods/ mutrec.htm) it is stated in para 5.1 that 'The Commission has always found it very difficult to obtain . . . a clear and reliable picture of how the principle of mutual recognition is actually applied in practice'. This is quite a confession! But the principle plays an enduring role on paper. For a recent example of the Court's insistence on the guiding role of mutual recognition, see Case C-184/96 *Commission* v *France* ('Foie Gras') [1998] ECR I-6197. The Court agreed with the Commission that it is in breach of Article 28 EC to adopt a national rule 'without including in it a mutual recognition clause for products coming from a Member State and complying with the rules laid down by that State'. This provides assistance to the Commission in its quest for transparent *market management* (Chapter 9, p.309 above).

Many commentators have expressed enthusiasm for the '*Cassis de Dijon*' (Case 120/78) decision as a means of improving the consumer's position. Spurious national rules of consumer protection which were in truth rules of producer protection are exposed as unlawful trade barriers. This opens up the market to competition, which, as far as the consumer is concerned, ought to mean increased choice, lower prices, and higher quality.

Bureau Européen des Unions de Consommateurs,
Discussion Document 237/84 on Protectionism and Consumer Protection (1985), p.3

. . . [T]he case law of the European Court of Justice . . . serves as a model of how to expose false consumer protection arguments and identify consumers' real interests.

N. Reich, 'European Consumer Law', in Bourgoignie (ed),
Community Consumer Law (Brussels: Story-Scienta, 1982), p.223

The Court does not denounce consumer policy in general but criticizes *false consumer policy*. In studying consumer law in the EC Member States on a comparative basis, I have come to the conviction that many regulations which carry the label of consumer protection do not really serve the consumer but instead hinder unwanted competition.

■ QUESTION

Which cases might be cited in support of (or in opposition to) these views?

NOTE

Nevertheless, concern has been expressed about the consequences of the '*Cassis de Dijon*' (Case 120/78) judgment, and particularly the legislative and administrative policy which has developed in its wake. The fears lie essentially in the perception that the judgment is heavily biased towards establishing free trade. Member States wishing to uphold national protection bear a heavy burden of proof that the rules are necessary to satisfy mandatory requirements. The Commission's expressed relief at the reduction in the need for Community regulation implies a *negative* rather than a *positive* approach to regulating the Community market. This is capable of depriving the trader of certainty about the terms of inter-State trade, and the consumer of confidence about the safety of products originating in other Member States.

N. Reich, 'Protection of Diffuse Interests in the EEC and the Perspective of
Progressively Establishing an Internal Market'
(1988) 11 JCP 395

(References omitted.)

'Negative Integration'

The concept of 'integration' defines the central political object of the Community since its coming into existence. Integration looks at Member States' regulations which have an effect on the free circulation of goods, services, persons, and capital transfers as restrictions, whatever their political and legal justifications. The thrust of primary and secondary Community law is directed *against* member-State regulations. The Community integrates by eliminating member-State law which is in opposition to its functioning. The term 'negative integration' . . . helps to explain this activity of the Community. Pelkmans . . . therefore defines the Community as a free trade zone which has been enlarged by a customs union. Theories of free trade ideas harmonise well with classical liberal and neo-liberal economic thought, which has always been popular in Germany, because it recognises the de-regulatory spirit of Community law. Oppermann . . . has therefore defined as the basic rule of Community law 'European market freedom.'

Importance of Diffuse Interests

The second point of this complex triangular relation can be defined by employing the theory of *diffuse interests* . . . It aims at an explanation of the economic and social paradoxes of aggregating and integrating diffuse interests into consumer, environmental, and equal rights protection. From its very beginning the Community did not intend to protect diffuse interests in the quality of life, even though article 2 of the EEC Treaty might be read and has been read in this sense. The Community had primarily allocated right to business, viz., a far-reaching right of market access in the entire common market, in order to achieve economic integration as previously defined. It has only recently tried to develop rights protecting diffuse interests, beginning with article 119 of the EEC Treaty concerning equal treatment of men and women in working conditions [see now Article 148 EC]. The social reform movement which had also reached the Community through the Paris declaration of 1972 of the Heads of States and Governments has added separate Community policies in environmental . . ., consumer . . ., health . . ., and workplace protection without formally amending the Treaty. Secondary EEC law, based on broad powers of discretion for the EEC institutions, has been responsive in developing social policies of the EEC to protect diffuse interests. This might be called 'positive integration' . . . The Community is trying to develop its own standards common to all member states and therefore applying to all citizens, and allowing a certain common level in the protection of diffuse interests.

. . . One could conclude from these remarks that the process of positive integration will neither harmonise protective standards nor promote integration. The EEC citizen who has suffered damage from defective products will have to look for his basic right to safety and health where he has left it, more precisely, where it has been violated. An enterprise wanting to compete in a single market via harmonised conditions of liability at uniform insurance rates is subjected to subtle fragmentations, which make impossible a uniform marketing strategy and an EEC-wide product monitoring. Private international law rules, though being viewed somewhat suspiciously by the EEC institutions, still continue to be applied. Does this mean that positive integration will not work?

A solution is only possible if one neither overstrains laws or protective policies nor looks at integration in a somewhat reduced fashion. Harmonisation does not mean uniformity. The EEC is not really an autonomous political entity but must be brought to life, be accepted, and legitimised for action by the member states. Community law should therefore be regarded as running *parallel* to member state law . . . and not, in the words of the Court, as '*limit(ing) their sovereign rights.*' Therefore, the doctrine of supremacy and preemption of Community law should be regarded with a certain scepticism. This doctrine, to take a recent example, will in the eyes of the Court prevent Denmark from selling more protective standards in the trade of hazardous chemicals by obliging importers to notify certain risks to the Danish authorities. The notion of total harmonisation on the basis of which the Court disapproved of the Danish regulation is used as a petrified legal argument to create the illusion that Community law may really regulate all the possible hazards arising in intra-community trade. The principle of market access without restrictions (except those allowed by Community law) does not go along with the previously mentioned balancing test. It also makes it impossible for Denmark and other countries to fulfil obligations which they have under their constitution and under international law in the protection of their own and foreign citizens.

. . . There is an inherent conflict between market integration, protection of diffuse interests, and the rule of law within the Community. Some trends have turned into a genuine 'acquis communautaire'. Others have been taken up by the Single Act but may not have led to the clear solutions which lawyers are always looking for. The role of law itself becomes a main concern within the Community. It is interesting to note that the autonomy and function of law has been reduced and not increased by the Single Act, quite in contrast to 'post-modern legal theory' which insists on the need for autonomy and reformalisation ('autopoiesis') . . . of law.

The main dilemma of EEC law in the future will be whether the objectives of integration, protection, and rule-of-law can really be balanced and harmonised to an equal extent. Mainstream political and legal thinking in the EEC still has as its starting point a basic right to market access for which law is a mere instrument. Protection enters only through a sort of hidden door, or it is regarded as a restriction to free trade. It is quite revealing to read article 8A in this light [see now Article 14 EC]: It comes as no surprise that the free circulation of *goods* is mentioned *before* the free circulation of *persons*! . . .

R. Dehousse, 'Completing the Internal Market: Institutional Constraints and Challenges'
in R. Bieber *et al* (eds), 1992: One European Market?
(Baden-Baden: Nomos Verlagsgesellschaft, 1988), pp.334–36

(Footnotes omitted.)

As much as one may approve the White Paper's emphasis on negative integration and the removal of borders, it is clear that market unity will not be possible without a measure of positive integration,

even if only in a limited way, for example for the setting up of minimal health and safety requirements or the organization of the cooperation among national customs administrations, which is
necessary in order to achieve a real elimination of physical borders. It is likely that the difficulties that
traditionally beset Community decision-making will surface again at that level. The Single Act has
tried to ease somewhat the taking of decision with a mixture of majority voting and differentiation.
The two are closely linked; in a Community of twelve, renewed progress would not be possible
without a simplification of decision-making procedures but, at the same time, the latter would
have been unthinkable without a measure of flexibility. In substantive terms, additional flexibility is
also rendered necessary by the sometimes wide differences which exist between Member States'
economies and societal choices. To a certain extent, the impact of these new mechanisms will
probably depend on the Commission's ability to maintain a certain degree of momentum in its White
Paper programme. At least it will benefit in its quest for an enhanced room for manoeuvre for, as
we have seen, the combination of majority voting and derogatory provisions should reinforce the
strategic importance of its proposals.

At some point, however, a major challenge will have to be faced, for the objective of market
integration itself remains unacceptable, politically speaking, for some Member States if it is not
accompanied by a specific effort to improve the social and economic cohesion within the
Community. It is worth recalling in this respect that economically weaker countries have been
reluctant to accept majority voting, precisely because they are those who might suffer most in the
short term from the creation of a single market. Of the many problems linked to the completion of
the internal market, this one is perhaps the most difficult: unlike the concerns for a high level of
protection for health, consumer safety or the environment, this kind of fear cannot be allayed by
derogatory measures alone. A parallel in the Community's allocative and redistributive policies has
been strongly advocated by recent studies, both from a theoretical and from a practical viewpoint.
The Single Act pledges the Community to reinforce its action in favour of backward areas; it even
explicitly states that the completion of the internal market should be pursued taking into account the
existence of different levels of development within the Community [see now Article 158]. However,
it fails to give the Community additional means to reach that end. The crucial point is that, at a given
stage, progress towards the single European market might be conditioned by the capacity to tackle
the problem of structural imbalances: if the Community does not find a way to offer some compensation to those countries which feel they have more to lose, market integration could be severely
hampered. More than institutional pragmatism will be needed in order to cut this Gordian knot.

NOTE
The issues discussed are illustrative of some of the most fundamental which confront the
Community. How are the differing demands of national interest groups to be accommodated
in a broader structure committed to free trade? The Community's harmonisation programme
must satisfy many often competing interests. No one doubts that the Community must regulate
certain matters in order to achieve genuine integration. Much doubt remains about the nature
and scope of that regulation. The rival notions of the 'level playing field' and 'competition
between regulators' were introduced at p.322 above. The future shape of the Community
will be governed by the nature of choices about the allocation of responsibility for different
functions to different levels of government in the Community – European, national, regional,
local. Lately this complex issue has come to be denoted by catchphrases such as *subsidiarity* and
flexibility. These matters are re-visited in Chapters 19 and 20.

N. Reich, Internal Market and Diffuse Interests
(Brussels: Story-Scienta, 1990), pp.18–19

On the one hand, the Internal Market may lead to standards which abide to the lowest common
denominator. This would be true if there are highly divergent standards, for instance relating to
product safety, to environmental quality, or to the contents of contracts in the service areas, and
if the EC will simply open up the borders by allowing for a free movement of goods or services
without control by the receiving state. Therefore, tendencies in new EC legislation, namely to impose
a standard-of-origin principle as a Community-wide rule for marketing, must be viewed with
scepticism . . .

On the other hand, where high Community standards already exist and where they are implemented responsibly by the Member States, one cannot simply forecast a 'dumping' of consumer and environmental standards. One must have regard to a certain 'acquis communautaire'. This is true, e.g., for medicinal products. Protective consumer legislation at the EC level and in the Member States has practically offset the principle of the free circulation of goods, with the exception of so-called arbitrage as parallel imports, and has tightly segregated markets. This shows that a wide variety of options in the area of standard-setting for trade practices must be taken into account. Any simplistic solution will therefore not help political and legal analysis.

. . . As the integration process within the EC develops and as the Internal Market is completed, more powers will be transferred to Community institutions, thus making *federal solutions* in Community law-making and law application more realistic, as far as the protection of diffuse interests is concerned. This means that the future will be characterized by different options, ranging, on the one hand, from a complete deregulation to, on the other hand, a remaining of market segregation by different standards. The first model is true in areas where price/quality relations are concerned, legitimately allowing for consumers' free choice, the second in areas where either health and safety aspects are concerned, or where 'highly sensitive areas' of consumer policy like insurance or job placement services are to be considered . . . If we take the imperatives of the federal model seriously, Community law will develop a set of rules allowing for a coordination of different areas of law-making and law-implementation. This will explain the paradox, why independent Member State policies protecting diffuse interests will become ever more important if the process of Community integration continues. We therefore reject, as we have mentioned above, any hierarchical model of Community law and will suggest federal solutions for existing or coming conflicts.

NOTES
1. For a collection of essays grouped around the notion of *diffuse interests*, see L. Krämer, *et al* (eds), 'Law and diffuse interests in the European Legal Order: Liber Amicorum Norbert Reich' (1997). See also the collection of articles grouped around the theme 'Governance in the Internal Market' in (1997) 4 JEPP, Issue 4 (Special Issue).
2. These are inevitably matters of intense political debate. Yet they are vital for the lawyer too, because the legal rules and institutional structures which emerge and which form the lawyer's working materials will be the product of that political debate.

J. Pelkmans, 'A Grand Design by the Piece? An Appraisal of the Internal Market Strategy'
in R Bieber *et al* (eds), 1992: One European Market? (Baden-Baden:
Nomos Verlagsgesellschaft, 1988), p.371

Finally whether one likes it or not, an Internal Market cutting so deep into the regulatory environment of consumers, traders and producers and limiting even more severely the Member States in their policy instruments *can no longer pretend to be a-political*. In completing the Internal Market by the piece, it becomes more and more artificial to expect conservatives, liberals, progressives, radicals, christian-democrats and socialists to agree, for the mere sake of 'Europe'. The verbal emphasis in the White Paper is, rightly, on fully free and unhindered mutual market access. But it is not very helpful to postulate that the *'positive integration' needed for that, will come forward and be solved, for the good purpose*. As more and more positive integration reduces the national policy autonomy needed to accentuate different positions in domestic politics, the greater the sensitivity to the Community's implicit or explicit political bias. As one begins to touch upon the most deeply entrenched forms of protection and the most cherished state instruments the process of positive integration will become more politicized.

NOTE
Such problems have been deepened by the 'ambiguous compromises' (p.9 above) of the Maastricht, Amsterdam, and Nice Treaties. The process continues.

 For additional material and resources see the Companion Website at: www.oup.co.uk/ best.textbooks/law/weatherill6e

13

The Free Movement of Workers: Article 39

ARTICLE 39 EC

1. Freedom of movement for workers shall be secured within the Community.

2. Such freedom of movement shall entail the abolition of any discrimination based on nationality between workers of the Member States as regards employment, remuneration and other conditions of work and employment.

3. It shall entail the right, subject to limitations justified on grounds of public policy, public security or public health:

    (a) to accept offers of employment actually made;

    (b) to move freely within the territory of Member States for this purpose;

    (c) to stay in a Member State for the purpose of employment in accordance with the provisions governing the employment of nationals of that State laid down by law, regulation or administrative action;

    (d) to remain in the territory of a Member State after having been employed in that State, subject to conditions which shall be embodied in implementing regulations to be drawn up by the Commission.

4. The provisions of this Article shall not apply to employment in the public service.

NOTE

The Treaty of Amsterdam merely deleted the words 'by the end of the transitional period at the latest' from the first paragraph, and altered to Article 39 the number of this Article, which was previously 48. The Nice Treaty left Article 39 untouched.

At one level, the Treaty secures the free movement of workers simply as an adjunct to the other freedoms, such as the free movement of goods (Article 28), and services (Article 49). These freedoms all contribute to the realization of mobility within a common market. But the free movement of persons has implications beyond the economics of market integration. It concerns human beings. It identifies people as the beneficiaries of the Treaty rules in a more direct sense than any other area of Community law. The treatment of people in the EU immediately encourages contemplation of the status of Citizenship of the European Union, created at Maastricht and legally articulated in Articles 17–22 EC. But that temptation will be resisted. Citizenship is examined in Chapter 15. In this Chapter and the next the predominantly market-focused evolution of the rules on persons and services is examined in the belief that this will allow a clearer appreciation of the possibilities and limitations facing the law of the European Union as it gropes beyond the 'market citizen' towards a system that builds fundamental rights and Citizenship.

Article 39 concerns both labour mobility and the rights of the individual. Both the Court and the legislature have developed the scope of the rights conferred upon the migrant worker. These developments mean that, independently of the

Maastricht-created notion of Citizenship, an individual has an extensive range of rights, first, to move freely between Member States to take up employment and, second, to enjoy non-discriminatory access to social protection once installed in the host Member State. This Chapter explores the scope of the worker's right to free movement.

SECTION 1: WHO IS A WORKER?

Levin v *Staatssecretaris van Justitie* (Case 53/81)

[1982] ECR 1035, [1982] 2 CMLR 454, Court of Justice of the European Communities

Mrs Levin was a British national married to a South African national. She was refused a residence permit by the Dutch authorities because she was not in gainful employment. She challenged the refusal before the Dutch courts. Questions were referred to the European Court. The Court was asked to explain the notion of a 'worker' for Community law purposes. The Dutch court was particularly concerned to elucidate the scope of Article 48 of the EC Treaty (now, after amendment, Article 39 EC) where an individual earns an income less than the minimum required for subsistence as defined under national law. The Court observed that no authoritative definition of 'worker' is to be found in the Treaty or secondary legislation. It then claimed for itself the job of carrying out that interpretative task.

[11] . . . [T]he terms 'worker' and 'activity as an employed person' may not be defined by reference to the national laws of the Member States but have a Community meaning. If that were not the case, the Community rules on freedom of movement for workers would be frustrated, as the meaning of those terms could be fixed and modified unilaterally, without any control by the Community institutions, by national laws which would thus be able to exclude at will certain categories of persons from the benefit of the Treaty.

[12] Such would, in particular, be the case if the enjoyment of the rights conferred by the principle of freedom of movement for workers could be made subject to the criterion of what the legislation of the host State declares to be a minimum wage, so that the field of application *ratione personae* of the Community rules on this subject might vary from one Member State to another. The meaning and the scope of the terms 'worker' and 'activity as an employed person' should thus be clarified in the light of the principles of the legal order of the Community.

[13] In this respect it must be stressed that these concepts define the field of application of one of the fundamental freedoms guaranteed by the Treaty and, as such, may not be interpreted restrictively.

[14] In conformity with this view the recitals in the preamble to Regulation (EEC) No 1612/68 contain a general affirmation of the right of all workers in the Member States to pursue the activity of their choice within the Community, irrespective of whether they are permanent, seasonal or frontier workers or workers who pursue their activities for the purpose of providing services. Furthermore, although Article 4 of Directive 68/360/EEC grants the right of residence to workers upon the mere production of the document on the basis of which they entered the territory and of a confirmation of engagement from the employer or a certificate of employment, it does not subject this right to any condition relating to the kind of employment or to the amount of income derived from it.

[15] An interpretation which reflects the full scope of these concepts is also in conformity with the objectives of the Treaty which include, according to Articles 2 and 3, the abolition, as between Member States, of obstacles to freedom of movement for persons, with the purpose *inter alia* of

promoting throughout the Community a harmonious development of economic activities and a raising of the standard of living. Since part-time employment, although it may provide an income lower than what is considered to be the minimum required for subsistence, constitutes for a large number of persons an effective means of improving their living conditions, the effectiveness of Community law would be impaired and the achievement of the objectives of the Treaty would be jeopardized if the enjoyment of rights conferred by the principle of freedom of movement for workers were reserved solely to persons engaged in full-time employment and earning, as a result, a wage at least equivalent to the guaranteed minimum wage in the sector under consideration.

[16] It follows that the concepts of 'worker' and 'activity as an employed person' must be interpreted as meaning that the rules relating to freedom of movement for workers also concern persons who pursue or wish to pursue an activity as an employed person on a part-time basis only and who, by virtue of that fact obtain or would obtain only remuneration lower than the minimum guaranteed remuneration in the sector under consideration. In this regard no distinction may be made between those who wish to make do with their income from such an activity and those who supplement that income with other income, whether the latter is derived from property or from the employment of a member of their family who accompanies them.

[17] It should however be stated that whilst part-time employment is not excluded from the field of application of the rules on freedom of movement for workers, those rules cover only the pursuit of effective and genuine activities, to the exclusion of activities on such a small scale as to be regarded as purely marginal and ancillary. It follows both from the statement of the principle of freedom of movement for workers and from the place occupied by the rules relating to that principle in the system of the Treaty as a whole that those rules guarantee only the free movement of persons who pursue or are desirous of pursuing an economic activity.

[18] The answer to be given to the first and second questions must therefore be that the provisions of Community law relating to freedom of movement for workers also cover a national of a Member State who pursues, within the territory of another Member State, an activity as an employed person which yields an income lower than that which, in the latter State, is considered as the minimum required for subsistence, whether that person supplements the income from his activity as an employed person with other income so as to arrive at that minimum or is satisfied with means of support lower than the said minimum, provided that he pursues an activity as an employed person which is effective and genuine.

[19] The third question essentially seeks to ascertain whether the right to enter and reside in the territory of a Member State may be denied to a worker whose main objectives, pursued by means of his entry and residence, are different from that of the pursuit of an activity as an employed person as defined in the answer to the first and second questions.

[20] Under Article 48(3) of the Treaty the right to move freely within the territory of the Member States is conferred upon workers for the 'purpose' of accepting offers of employment actually made. By virtue of the same provision workers enjoy the right to stay in one of the Member States 'for the purpose' of employment there. Moreover, it is stated in the preamble to Regulation (EEC) No 1612/68 that freedom of movement for workers entails the right of workers to move freely within the Community 'in order to' pursue activities as employed persons, whilst Article 2 of Directive 68/360/EEC requires the Member States to grant workers the right to leave their territory 'in order to' take up activities as employed persons or to pursue them in the territory of another Member State.

[21] However, these formulations merely give expression to the requirement, which is inherent in the very principle of freedom of movement for workers, that the advantages which Community law confers in the name of that freedom may be relied upon only by persons who actually pursue or seriously wish to pursue activities as employed persons. They do not, however, mean that the enjoyment of this freedom may be made to depend upon the aims pursued by a national of a Member State in applying for entry upon and residence in the territory of another Member State, provided that he there pursues or wishes to pursue an activity which meets the criteria specified above, that is to say, an effective and genuine activity as an employed person.

[22] Once this condition is satisfied, the motives which may have prompted the worker to seek employment in the Member State concerned are of no account and must not be taken into consideration.

[23] The answer to be given to the third question put to the Court by the Raad van State must therefore be that the motives which may have prompted a worker of a Member State to seek employment in another Member State are of no account as regards his right to enter and reside in the territory of the latter State provided that he there pursues or wishes to pursue an effective and genuine activity.

Kempf v *Staatssecretaris van Justitie* (Case 139/85)

[1986] ECR 1741, [1987] 1 CMLR 764, Court of Justice of the European Communities

The Court took the opportunity in this case to refine further its definition.

[11] As regards, first, the criterion of effective and genuine work as opposed to marginal and ancillary activities not covered by the relevant Community rules, the Netherlands Government expressed doubts at the hearing as to whether the work of a teacher who gives 12 lessons a week may be regarded as constituting in itself effective and genuine work within the terms of the judgment in *Levin*.

[12] There is, however, no need to consider that question since the Raad van State, in the grounds of the judgment making the reference, expressly found that Mr Kempf's work was not on such a small scale as to be purely a marginal and ancillary activity. According to the division of jurisdiction between national courts and the Court of Justice in connection with references for a preliminary ruling, it is for national courts to establish and to evaluate the facts of the case. The question submitted for a preliminary ruling must therefore be examined in the light of the assessment made by the Raad van State.

[13] The Court has consistently held that freedom of movement for workers forms one of the foundations of the Community. The provisions laying down that fundamental freedom and, more particularly, the terms 'worker' and 'activity as an employed person' defining the sphere of application of those freedoms must be given a broad interpretation in that regard, whereas exceptions to and derogations from the principle of freedom of movement for workers must be interpreted strictly.

[14] It follows that the rules on this topic must be interpreted as meaning that a person in effective and genuine part-time employment cannot be excluded from their sphere of application merely because the remuneration he derives from it is below the level of the minimum means of subsistence and he seeks to supplement it by other lawful means of subsistence. In that regard it is irrelevant whether those supplementary means of subsistence are derived from property or from the employment of a member of his family, as was the case in *Levin*, or whether, as in this instance, they are obtained from financial assistance drawn from the public funds of the Member State in which he resides, provided that the effective and genuine nature of his work is established.

NOTE

The Court is plainly concerned in these decisions to establish a broad definition of the worker entitled to Community law rights (see also *Lawrie-Blum* v *Land Baden-Württemberg* (Case 66/85) [1986] ECR 2121, [1987] 3 CMLR 389; but note some caution in *Bettray* v *Staatssecretaris van Justitie* (Case 344/87) [1989] ECR 1621). Notice that the notion of worker is held to be a concept of Community, not national, law in order to preclude the destruction of the integrity of Community law through differing national approaches.

It had long been a matter of doubt whether this provision of the Treaty protects an individual who migrates in order to seek work, rather than to take up a job already offered. The Court decided in *R* v *IAT, ex parte Antonissen* (Case C-292/89) that a jobseeker may be a worker, but not indefinitely.

R v IAT, ex parte Antonissen (Case C-292/89)

[1991] ECR I-745, [1991] 2 CMLR 373, Court of Justice of the European Communities

Antonissen, a Belgian, sought to rely on Article 48 of the EC Treaty (now, after amendment, Article 39 EC) to defeat a UK deportation order against him. He had been seeking employment in the UK for more than six months and the Tribunal's view was that he had no Community law rights. *Held* by the European Court:

It is not contrary to the provisions of Community law governing the free movement of workers for the legislation of a Member State to provide that a national of another Member State who entered the first State in order to seek employment may be required to leave the territory of that State (subject to appeal) if he has not found employment there after six months, unless the person concerned provides evidence that he is continuing to seek employment and that he has genuine chances of being engaged.

The equation of genuine jobseeker and 'worker' under Article 39 was confirmed by the Court in *Maria Martinez Sala* v *Freistaat Bayern* (Case C-85/96) [1998] ECR I-2691.

SECTION 2: TO WHAT ADVANTAGES IS THE WORKER ENTITLED?

Directive 68/360 on the Abolition of Restrictions on Movement and Residence within the Community for Workers of Member States and their Families ([1968] OJ (Special Edition) (II) 485) sets out more fully than Article 39 the right of entry and residence, and amplifies several procedural aspects of the right of free movement.

It, along with a great deal of other relevant documentation may be consulted *via* the Commission's website, at http://europa.eu.int/comm/justice_home/index_en.htm. Commission attempts to secure the adoption of a revised text that would extend the scope of protection beyond Directive 68/360 have not yet fallen on fertile political soil; see most recently the proposal for an amending Directive on the abolition of restrictions on movement and residence within the Community for workers of Member States and their families, COM (98) 394 [1998] OJ C344.

Some confusion has arisen as a result of the reference to a residence permit in Article 4 of Directive 68/360. The Court has been obliged to explain that documents may be required of migrant workers; but that they are evidence of rights, not their source. Any penalties for failure to acquire a permit must accordingly respect the principle of proportionality.

ARTICLE 4 OF DIRECTIVE 68/360

1. Member States shall grant the right of residence in their territory to the persons referred to in Article 1 [nationals of the Member States and of members of their families to whom Regulation (EEC) No 1612/68 applies] who are able to produce the documents listed in paragraph 3.

2. As proof of the right of residence, a document entitled 'Residence Permit for a National of a Member State of the EEC' shall be issued. This document must include a statement that it has been issued pursuant to Regulation (EEC) No 1612/68 and to the measures taken by the Member

States for the implementation of the present Directive. The text of such statement is given in the Annex to this Directive.

3. For the issue of a Residence Permit for a National of a Member State of the EEC, Member States may require only the production of the following documents;

— by the worker:
   (a) the document with which he entered their territory;
   (b) a confirmation of engagement from the employer or a certificate of employment;
— by the members of the worker's family:
   (c) the document with which they entered the territory;
   (d) a document issued by the competent authority of the State of origin or the State whence they came, proving their relationship;
   (e) in the cases referred to in Article 10(1) and (2) of Regulation (EEC) No 1612/68, a document issued by the competent authority of the State of origin or the State whence they came, testifying that they are dependent on the worker or that they live under his roof in such country.

4. A member of the family who is not a national of a Member State shall be issued with a residence document which shall have the same validity as that issued to the worker on whom he is dependent.

R v *Pieck* (Case 157/79)
[1980] ECR 2171, [1980] 3 CMLR 220, Court of Justice of the European Communities

Pieck, a Dutch national working in Wales, was charged with overstaying his six-month limited leave to remain in the UK. He held no residence permit. The Pontypridd magistrates' court made a preliminary reference in respect of the implications of EC law. The Court dealt with the grant of limited leave by reference to existing case law.

[13] The Court has already stated in its judgment of 14 July 1977 in Case 8/77 *Sagulo, Brenca and Bakhouche* [1977] ECR 1495 that the issue of a special residence document provided for in Article 4 above-mentioned has only a declaratory effect and that, for aliens to whom Article 48 of the Treaty or parallel provisions give rights, it cannot be assimilated to a residence permit such as is prescribed for aliens in general, in connexion with the issue of which the national authorities have a discretion. The Court went on to say that a Member State may not therefore require from a person enjoying the protection of Community law that he should possess a general residence permit instead of the document provided for in Article 4 of Directive No 68/360.

On penalties for non-conformity with formalities:

[18] Among the penalties attaching to a failure to comply with the formalities required as proof of the right of residence of a worker enjoying the protection of Community law, deportation is certainly incompatible with the provisions of the Treaty since, as the Court has already confirmed in other cases, such a measure negates the very right conferred and guaranteed by the Treaty.

[19] As regards other penalties such as fines and imprisonment, whilst the national authorities are entitled to impose penalties in respect of failure to comply with the terms of provisions relating to residence permits which are comparable to those attaching to minor offences by nationals, they are not justified in imposing a penalty so disproportionate to the gravity of the infringement that it becomes an obstacle to the free movement of persons. This would be especially so if that penalty included imprisonment.

[20] It follows that the failure on the part of a national of a Member State of the Community, to whom the rules on freedom of movement for workers apply, to obtain the special residence permit prescribed in Article 4 of Directive No 68/360 may not be punished by a recommendation for deportation or by measures which go as far as imprisonment.

NOTE

See also *Messner* (Case C-265/88) [1989] ECR 4209, [1991] 2 CMLR 545; *Commission v Netherlands* (Case C-68/89) [1991] ECR I-2637; and Case C-378/97 *Florius Ariel Wijsenbeck* [1999] ECR I-6207 (in which the effect of what is now Article 18 EC was considered).

Regulation 1612/68 ensures that the migrant worker, once settled in the host State, shall enjoy non-discriminatory treatment in relation to access to employment and provision of employment-related benefits. Family members are also covered. These provisions are wide-ranging on their face, but have been taken still further by the Court.

COUNCIL REGULATION 1612/68 ON FREEDOM OF MOVEMENT FOR WORKERS WITHIN THE COMMUNITY, ARTICLES 1–12
[1968] OJ (Special Edition) (II) 475

TITLE I ELIGIBILITY FOR EMPLOYMENT

Article 1

1. Any national of a Member State, shall, irrespective of his place of residence, have the right to take up an activity as an employed person, and to pursue such activity, within the territory of another Member State in accordance with the provisions laid down by law, regulation or administrative action governing the employment of nationals of that State.

2. He shall, in particular, have the right to take up available employment in the territory of another Member State with the same priority as nationals of the State.

Article 2

Any national of a Member State and any employer pursuing an activity in the territory of a Member State may exchange their applications for and offers of employment, and may conclude and perform contracts of employment in accordance with the provisions in force laid down by law, regulation or administrative action, without any discrimination resulting therefrom.

Article 3

1. Under this Regulation, provisions laid down by law, regulation or administrative action or administrative practices of a Member State shall not apply.

— where they limit application for and offers of employment, or the right of foreign nationals to take up and pursue employment or subject these to conditions not applicable in respect of their own nationals; or
— where, though applicable irrespective of nationality, their exclusive or principal aim or effect is to keep nationals of other Member States away from the employment offered.

This provision shall not apply to conditions relating to linguistic knowledge required by reason of the nature of the post to be filled.

2. There shall be included in particular among the provisions or practices of a Member State referred to in the first subparagraph of paragraph 1 those which:

(a) prescribe a special recruitment procedure for foreign nationals;
(b) limit or restrict the advertising of vacancies in the press or through any other medium or subject it to conditions other than those applicable in respect of employers pursuing their activities in the territory of that Member State;
(c) subject eligibility for employment to conditions of registration with employment offices or impede recruitment of individual workers, where persons who do not reside in the territory of that State are concerned.

Article 4

1. Provisions laid down by law, regulation or administrative action of the Member States which restrict by number or percentage the employment of foreign nationals in any undertaking,

branch of activity or region, or at a national level, shall not apply to nationals of the other Member States.

2. When in a Member State the granting of any benefit to undertakings is subject to a minimum percentage of national workers being employed, nationals of the other Member States shall be counted as national workers, subject to the provisions of the Council Directive of 15 October 1963.

Article 5

A national of a Member State who seeks employment in the territory of another Member State shall receive the same assistance there as that afforded by the employment offices in that State to their own nationals seeking employment.

Article 6

1. The engagement and recruitment of a national of one Member State for a post in another Member State shall not depend on medical, vocational or other criteria which are discriminatory on grounds of nationality by comparison with those applied to nationals of the other Member State who wish to pursue the same activity.

2. Nevertheless, a national who holds an offer in his name from an employer in a Member State other than that of which he is a national may have to undergo a vocational test, if the employer expressly requests this when making his offer of employment.

TITLE II EMPLOYMENT AND EQUALITY OF TREATMENT

Article 7

1. A worker who is a national of a Member State may not, in the territory of another Member State, be treated differently from national workers by reason of his nationality in respect of any conditions of employment and work, in particular as regards remuneration, dismissal, and should he become unemployed, reinstatement or re-employment;

2. He shall enjoy the same social and tax advantages as national workers.

3. He shall also, by virtue of the same right and under the same conditions as national workers, have access to training in vocational schools and retraining centres.

4. Any clause of a collective or individual agreement or of any other collective regulation concerning eligibility for employment, employment, remuneration and other conditions of work or dismissal shall be null and void in so far as it lays down or authorises discriminatory conditions in respect of workers who are nationals of the other Member States.

Article 8

1. A worker who is a national of a Member State and who is employed in the territory of another Member State shall enjoy equality of treatment as regards membership of trade unions and the exercise of rights attaching thereto, including the right to vote and to be eligible for the administration or management posts of a trade union; he may be excluded from taking part in the management of bodies governed by public law and from holding an office governed by public law. Furthermore, he shall have the right of eligibility for workers' representative bodies in the undertaking. The provisions of this Article shall not affect laws or regulations in certain Member States which grant more extensive rights to workers coming from the other Member States.

2. This Article shall be reviewed by the Council on the basis of a proposal from the Commission which shall be submitted within not more than two years.

Article 9

1. A worker who is a national of a Member State and who is employed in the territory of another Member State shall enjoy all the rights and benefits accorded to national workers in matters of housing, including ownership of the housing he needs.

2. Such worker may, with the same right as nationals, put his name down on the housing lists in the region in which he is employed, where such lists exist; he shall enjoy the resultant benefits and priorities.

If his family has remained in the country whence he came, they shall be considered for this purpose as residing in the said region, where national workers benefit from a similar presumption.

TITLE III WORKERS' FAMILIES

Article 10

1. The following shall, irrespective of their nationality, have the right to install themselves with a worker who is a national of one Member State and who is employed in the territory of another Member State:

    (a) his spouse and their descendants who are under the age of 21 years or are dependants;
    (b) dependent relatives in the ascending line of the worker and his spouse.

    2. Member States shall facilitate the admission of any member of the family not coming within the provisions of paragraph 1 if dependent on the worker referred to above or living under his roof in the country whence he comes.

    3. For the purposes of paragraphs 1 and 2, the worker must have available for his family housing considered as normal for national workers in the region where he is employed; this provision, however must not give rise to discrimination between national workers and workers from the other Member States.

Article 11

Where a national of a Member State is pursuing an activity as an employed or self-employed person in the territory of another Member State, his spouse and those of the children who are under the age of 21 years or dependent on him shall have the right to take up any activity as an employed person throughout the territory of that same State, even if they are not nationals of any Member State.

Article 12

The children of a national of a Member State who is or has been employed in the territory of another Member State shall be admitted to that State's general educational, apprenticeship and vocational training courses under the same conditions as the nationals of that State, if such children are residing in its territory.

    Member States shall encourage all efforts to enable such children to attend these courses under the best possible conditions.

NOTE
Article 7(2) of the Regulation provides a striking example of a provision which has been developed by the Court in a perhaps unexpectedly broad manner.

Cristini v *SNCF* (Case 32/75)

[1975] ECR 1085, [1975] 1 CMLR 573, Court of Justice of the European Communities

SNCF, the French railway company, offered a fare reduction for large families. Cristini, an Italian national resident in France and the widow of an Italian national who had worked in France, was refused the reduction card on the basis of nationality. SNCF argued that Article 7(2) of Regulation 1612/68 covered only advantages connected with the contract of employment. The Court did not agree.

[12] . . . [T]he reference to 'social advantages' in Article 7(2) cannot be interpreted restrictively.

[13] It therefore follows that, in view of the equality of treatment which the provision seeks to achieve, the substantive area of application must be delineated so as to include all social and tax advantages, whether or not attached to the contract of employment, such as reductions in fares for large families.

[14] It then becomes necessary to examine whether such an advantage must be granted to the widow and children after the death of the migrant worker when the national law provides that, at the request of the head of the family, each member of the family shall be issued with an identity card entitling him or her to the reduction.

[15] If the widow and infant children of a national of the Member State in question are entitled to such cards provided that the request had been made by the father before his death, the same must apply where the deceased father was a migrant worker and a national of another Member State.

[16] It would be contrary to the purpose and the spirit of the Community rules on freedom of movement for workers to deprive the survivors of such a benefit following the death of the worker whilst granting the same benefit to the survivors of a national.

[17] In this respect it is important to note the provisions of Regulation (EEC) No 1251/70 of the Commission on the right of workers to remain in the territory of a Member State after having been employed in that State.

[18] Article 3(1) of that regulation provides that if a worker has acquired the right to remain in the territory of a Member State, the members of his family who are residing with him shall be entitled to remain there after his death, whilst Article 7 provides that: 'The right to equality of treatment, established by Council Regulation (EEC) No 1612/68, shall apply also to persons coming under the provisions of this regulation'.

[19] Accordingly the answer to the question should be that Article 7(2) of Regulation (EEC) No 1612/68 of the Council must be interpreted as meaning that the social advantages referred to by that provision include fares reduction cards issued by a national railway authority to large families and that this applies, even if the said advantage is only sought after the worker's death, to the benefit of his family remaining in the same Member State.

NOTE
Regulation 1251/70 ([1970] OJ (Special Edition) (II) 402), referred to in the judgment, confers rights on the worker to remain in the host State after retirement.

There is a dual focus to the Court's broad interpretation of Article 7(2) of Regulation 1612/68. On one level, the Court's actions may be seen as intruding on a State's social welfare system, by guaranteeing the individual 'social and tax advantages' which operate beyond the employment relationship and which affect on the wider sphere of life as a citizen. Yet at another level the conferral of such benefits may be presented as an instrument of market integration. Without the lure of extended equal treatment, labour mobility would in practice prove an illusion. This is a controversial debate both in its substance – *should* the Community touch on welfare laws? – and in its institutional aspects – is this the job of the Court or the legislature? This theme is readdressed more generally in Chapters 19 and 20.

Article 7(2) of Regulation 1612/68 ensures non-discrimination. It does not confer an absolute right to a rail concession; it confers a right to such provision on terms which do not discriminate according to nationality. So in principle the migrant worker cannot enjoy rights above the ceiling of national provision. If further rights are to be made available, Community legislation must be passed. This re-opens the controversial debate about the proper scope of Community social legislation.

The Commission has sought to achieve the recasting of secondary legislation in this area in order to reflect and advance the process of removal of internal frontiers and the creation of Citizenship. This was first aired in COM (93) 545. Subsequently, the High Level Group on the Free Movement of Persons, chaired by Simone Veil, which reported to the Commission in March 1997, concluded that the essential legislation was in place but advocated *inter alia* better cooperation between Member States in securing the effective application of the rules and improved dissemination of information about individual rights. Consolidation of relevant legislation was supported as a means of realizing these objectives. The impetus to secure formal recasting of the rules appears subsequently to have stalled.

The Community also has legislation on social security provision. These measures are based on perceptions similar to those underlying Regulation 1612/68. They are, however, measures of extraordinary complexity, and are best left for discussion in specialist works.

SECTION 3: **EXCEPTIONS**

Article 39(3) and (4) (p.427 above) contain derogations from the basic principle of free movement. In common with all provisions which are hostile to free movement, these clauses are to be interpreted narrowly. This approach is confirmed by Directive 64/221 which elaborates the substance and procedure of derogation under the third paragraph.

COUNCIL DIRECTIVE 64/221/EEC ON THE COORDINATION OF SPECIAL MEASURES CONCERNING THE MOVEMENT AND RESIDENCE OF FOREIGN NATIONALS WHICH ARE JUSTIFIED ON GROUNDS OF PUBLIC POLICY, PUBLIC SECURITY OR PUBLIC HEALTH, ARTICLES 1–10
[1963–64] OJ (Special Edition) 117

Article 1
1. The provisions of this Directive shall apply to any national of a Member State who resides in or travels to another Member State of the Community, either in order to pursue an activity as an employed or self-employed person, or as a recipient of services.

2. These provisions shall apply also to the spouse and to members of the family who come within the provisions of the regulations and directives adopted in this field in pursuance of the Treaty.

Article 2
1. This Directive relates to all measures concerning entry into their territory, issue or renewal of residence permits, or expulsion from their territory, taken by Member States on grounds of public policy, public security or public health.

2. Such grounds shall not be invoked to service economic ends.

Article 3
1. Measures taken on grounds of public policy or of public security shall be based exclusively on the personal conduct of the individual concerned.

2. Previous criminal convictions shall not in themselves constitute grounds for the taking of such measures.

3. Expiry of the identity card or passport used by the person concerned to enter the host country and to obtain a residence permit shall not justify expulsion from the territory.

4. The State which issued the identity card or passport shall allow the holder of such document

to re-enter its territory without any formality even if the document is no longer valid or the nationality of the holder is in dispute.

Article 4

1. The only diseases or disabilities justifying refusal of entry into a territory or refusal to issue a first residence permit shall be those listed in the Annex to this Directive.

2. Diseases or disabilities occurring after a first residence permit has been issued shall not justify refusal to renew the residence permit or expulsion from the territory.

3. Member States shall not introduce new provisions or practices which are more restrictive than those in force at the date of notification of this Directive.

Article 5

1. A decision to grant or to refuse a first residence permit shall be taken as soon as possible and in any event not later than six months from the date of application for the permit.

The person concerned shall be allowed to remain temporarily in the territory pending a decision either to grant or to refuse a residence permit.

2. The host country may, in cases where this is considered essential, request the Member State of origin of the applicant, and if need be other Member States, to provide information concerning any previous police record. Such enquiries shall not be made as a matter of routine. The Member State consulted shall give its reply within two months.

Article 6

The person concerned shall be informed of the grounds of public policy, public security, or public health upon which the decision taken in his case is based, unless this is contrary to the interests of the security of the State involved.

Article 7

The person concerned shall be officially notified of any decision to refuse the issue or renewal of a residence permit or to expel him from the territory. The period allowed for leaving the territory shall be stated in this notification. Save in cases of urgency, this period shall be not less than fifteen days if the person concerned has not yet been granted a residence permit and not less than one month in all other cases.

Article 8

The person concerned shall have the same legal remedies in respect of any decision concerning entry, or refusing the issue or renewal of a residence permit, or ordering expulsion from the territory, as are available to nationals of the State concerned in respect of acts of the administration.

Article 9

1. Where there is no right of appeal to a court of law, or where such appeal may be only in respect the legal validity of the decision, or where the appeal cannot have suspensory effect, a decision refusing renewal of a residence permit or ordering the expulsion of the holder of a residence permit from the territory shall not be taken by the administrative authority, save in cases of urgency, until an opinion has been obtained from a competent authority of the host country before which the person concerned enjoys such rights of defence and of assistance or representation as the domestic law of that country provides for.

This authority shall not be the same as that empowered to take the decision refusing renewal of the residence permit or ordering expulsion.

2. Any decision refusing the issue of a first residence permit or ordering expulsion of the person concerned before the issue of the permit shall, where that person so requests, be referred for consideration to the authority whose prior opinion is required under paragraph I. The person concerned shall then be entitled to submit his defence in person, except where this would be contrary to the interests of national security.

Article 10

1. Member States shall within six months of notification of this Directive put into force the measures necessary to comply with its provisions and shall forthwith inform the Commission thereof.

2. Member States shall ensure that the texts of the main provisions of national law which they adopt in the field governed by this Directive are communicated to the Commission.

NOTE

The following case was one of the earliest involving the UK to reach the Court after accession.

Van Duyn v *Home Office* (Case 41/74)

[1974] ECR 1337, [1975] 1 CMLR 1, Court of Justice of the European Communities

Ms Van Duyn, a Dutch national, was refused leave to enter the UK to work for the Church of Scientology because the UK Government considered the Church's activities to be socially harmful. Ms Van Duyn's reliance on Community law led to a preliminary reference by the High Court. The European Court first held Article 48 of the EC Treaty (now, after amendment, Article 39 EC) and Article 3(1) of Directive 64/221 (above) directly effective and accordingly enforceable before national courts by private individuals. The Court then turned to the substance of the case.

[17] It is necessary, first, to consider whether association with a body or an organization can in itself constitute personal conduct within the meaning of Article 3 of Directive No 64/221. Although a person's past association cannot in general, justify a decision refusing him the right to move freely within the Community, it is nevertheless the case that present association, which reflects participation in the activities of the body or of the organization as well as identification with its aims and its designs, may be considered a voluntary act of the person concerned and, consequently, as part of his personal conduct within the meaning of the provision cited.

[18] This third question further raises the problem of what importance must be attributed to the fact that the activities of the organization in question, which are considered by the Member State as contrary to the public good are not however prohibited by national law. It should be emphasized that the concept of public policy in the context of the Community and where, in particular, it is used as a justification for derogating from the fundamental principle of freedom of movement for workers, must be interpreted strictly, so that its scope cannot be determined unilaterally by each Member State without being subject to control by the institutions of the Community. Nevertheless the particular circumstances justifying recourse to the concept of public policy may vary from one country to another and from one period to another, and it is therefore necessary in this matter to allow the competent national authorities an area of discretion within the limits imposed by the Treaty.

[19] It follows from the above that where the competent authorities of a Member State have clearly defined their standpoint as regards the activities of a particular organization and where, considering it to be socially harmful, they have taken administrative measures to counteract these activities, the Member State cannot be required, before it can rely on the concept of public policy, to make such activities unlawful, if recourse to such a measure is not thought appropriate in the circumstances.

[20] The question raises finally the problem of whether a Member State is entitled, on grounds of public policy, to prevent a national of another Member State from taking gainful employment within its territory with a body or organization, it being the case that no similar restriction is placed upon its own nationals.

[21] In this connexion, the Treaty, while enshrining the principle of freedom of movement for workers without any discrimination on grounds of nationality, admits, in Article 48 (3), limitations justified on grounds of public policy, public security or public health to the rights deriving from this principle. Under the terms of the provision cited above, the right to accept offers of employment actually made, the right to move freely within the territory of Member States for this purpose, and the right

to stay in a Member State for the purpose of employment are, among others, all subject to such limitations. Consequently, the effect of such limitations, when they apply, is that leave to enter the territory of a Member State and the right to reside there may be refused to a national of another Member State.

[22] Furthermore, it is a principle of international law, which the EEC Treaty cannot be assumed to disregard in the relations between Member States, that a State is precluded from refusing its own nationals the right of entry or residence.

[23] It follows that a Member State, for reasons of public policy, can, where it deems necessary, refuse a national of another Member State the benefit of the principle of freedom of movement for workers in a case where such a national proposes to take up a particular offer of employment even though the Member State does not place a similar restriction upon its own nationals.

[24] Accordingly, the reply to the third question must be that Article 48 of the EEC Treaty and Article 3(1) of Directive No 64/221 are to be interpreted as meaning that a Member State, in imposing restrictions justified on grounds of public policy, is entitled to take into account, as a matter of personal conduct of the individual concerned, the fact that the individual is associated with some body or organization the activities of which the Member State considers socially harmful but which are not unlawful in that State, despite the fact that no restriction is placed upon nationals of the said Member State who wish to take similar employment with these same bodies or organizations.

NOTE
In both the following decisions, the Court adopted a narrow interpretation of the legitimate scope of Member State action against individual workers.

R v *Bouchereau* (Case 30/77)
[1977] ECR 1999, [1977] 2 CMLR 800, Court of Justice of the European Communities

Bouchereau, a French national working in England, was convicted of unlawful possession of drugs. He fought proposed deportation using Community law. Could the UK authorities show that his case fell within the exception then located in Article 48(3), now Article 39(3)? The matter reached the Court by way of a preliminary reference. The Court examined the relevance of previous criminal convictions.

[27] The terms of Article 3(2) of the directive, which states that 'previous criminal convictions shall not in themselves constitute grounds for the taking of such measures' must be understood as requiring the national authorities to carry out a specific appraisal from the point of view of the interests inherent in protecting the requirements of public policy, which does not necessarily coincide with the appraisals which formed the basis of the criminal conviction.

[28] The existence of a previous criminal conviction can, therefore, only be taken into account in so far as the circumstances which gave rise to that conviction are evidence of personal conduct constituting a present threat to the requirements of public policy.

[29] Although, in general, a finding that such a threat exists implies the existence in the individual concerned of a propensity to act in the same way in the future, it is possible that past conduct alone may constitute such a threat to the requirements of public policy.

The Court then proceeded to consider the notion of 'public policy' mentioned in Article 48(3) of the EC Treaty (now, after amendment, Article 39(3) EC).

[33] In its judgment of 4 December 1974 (Case 41/74, *Van Duyn v Home Office*, [1974] ECR 1337, at p.1350) the Court emphasized that the concept of public policy in the context of the Community and where, in particular, it is used as a justification for derogating from the fundamental principle of freedom of movement for workers, must be interpreted strictly, so that its scope cannot be

determined unilaterally by each Member State without being subject to control by the institutions of the Community.

[34] Nevertheless, it is stated in the same judgment that the particular circumstances justifying recourse to the concept of public policy may vary from one country to another and from one period to another and it is therefore necessary in this matter to allow the competent national authorities an area of discretion within the limits imposed by the Treaty and the provisions adopted for its implementation.

[35] In so far as it may justify certain restrictions on the free movement of persons subject to Community law, recourse by a national authority to the concept of public policy presupposes, in any event, the existence, in addition to the perturbation of the social order which any infringement of the law involves, of a genuine and sufficiently serious threat to the requirements of public policy affecting one of the fundamental interests of society.

Adoui and Cornuaille v *Belgian State* (Cases 115 & 116/81)
[1982] ECR 1665, [1982] 3 CMLR 631, Court of Justice of the European Communities

The applicants were French nationals refused permission to reside in Belgium on public policy grounds. The Court delicately described them as waitresses in a Liège bar which was considered 'suspect from the point of view of morals'. It was more direct in the body of the judgment.

[6] Those questions are motivated by the fact that prostitution as such is not prohibited by Belgian legislation, although the Law does prohibit certain incidental activities, which are particularly harmful from the social point of view, such as the exploitation of prostitution by third parties and various forms of incitement to debauchery.

[7] The reservations contained in Articles 48 and 56 of the EEC Treaty permit Member States to adopt, with respect to the nationals of other Member States and on the grounds specified in those provisions, in particular grounds justified by the requirements of public policy, measures which they cannot apply to their own nationals, inasmuch as they have no authority to expel the latter from the national territory or to deny them access thereto. Although that difference of treatment, which bears upon the nature of the measures available, must therefore be allowed, it must nevertheless be stressed that, in a Member State, the authority empowered to adopt such measures must not base the exercise of its powers on assessments of certain conduct which would have the effect of applying an arbitrary distinction to the detriment of nationals of other Member States.

[8] It should be noted in that regard that reliance by a national authority upon the concept of public policy presupposes, as the Court held in its judgment of 27 October 1977 in Case 30/77 *Bouchereau* [1977] ECR 1999, the existence of 'a genuine and sufficiently serious threat affecting one of the fundamental interests of society'. Although Community law does not impose upon the Member States a uniform scale of values as regards the assessment of conduct which may be considered as contrary to public policy, it should nevertheless be stated that conduct may not be considered as being of a sufficiently serious nature to justify restrictions on the admission to or residence within the territory of a Member State of a national of another Member State in a case where the former Member State does not adopt, with respect to the same conduct on the part of its own nationals repressive measures or other genuine and effective measures intended to combat such conduct

[9] The answer to Questions 1 to 9, 11 and 12 should therefore be that a Member State may not, by virtue of the reservation relating to public policy contained in Articles 48 and 56 of the Treaty, expel a national of another Member State from its territory or refuse him access to its territory by reason of conduct which, when attributable to the former State's own nationals, does not give rise to repressive measures or other genuine and effective measures intended to combat such conduct.

[10] In the tenth question, the national court asks whether the action taken by a Member State which, 'anxious to remove from its territory prostitutes from a given country because they could promote criminal activities, does so systematically, declaring that their business of prostitution

endangers the requirements of public policy and not taking the trouble to consider whether the persons concerned may or may not be suspected of contact with the "underworld"', constitutes a measure of a general preventive nature within the meaning of Article 3 of Directive No 64/221.

[11] It should be noted that Article 3(1) of the directive provides that measures taken on grounds of public policy or of public security are to be based exclusively on the personal conduct of the individual concerned. In that regard it is sufficient to refer to the judgment of 26 February 1975 in Case 67/74 *Bonsignore* [1975] ECR 297, in which the Court held that 'measures adopted on grounds of public policy and for the maintenance of public security against the nationals of Member States of the Community cannot be justified on grounds extraneous to the individual case, as is shown in particular by the requirements set out in paragraph (1) that "only" the "personal conduct" of those affected by the measures is to be regarded as determinative'.

■ QUESTION

There are two aspects of *Van Duyn* (Case 41/74) (p.439 above) which are of particular interest in the present context: (i) its discussion of the nature of 'personal conduct', mentioned in Article 3(1) of Directive 64/221; (ii) its approach to the competence of Member States to control that conduct, taking account of how nationals behaving in a similar fashion would be treated. Explain how the Court has developed a more rigorous stance since *Van Duyn*.

Donatella Calfa (Case C-348/96)
[1999] ECR I-11, Court of Justice of the European Communities

Ms Calfa, an Italian tourist in Greece, was found guilty of a drugs-related offence. She was sentenced to three months' imprisonment and expelled for life from Greek territory. The case concerned the receipt of services, rather than a worker, and therefore Articles 49–55 EC were relevant (p.445 below), but the principles of derogation apply *mutatis mutandis* and the Court cited familiar case law concerning workers.

[20] Article 56 [now 46] permits Member States to adopt, with respect to nationals of other Member States, and in particular on the grounds of public policy, measures which they cannot apply to their own nationals, inasmuch as they have no authority to expel the latter from the territory or to deny them access thereto (see Case 41/74 *Van Duyn* v *Home Office* [1974] ECR 1337, paragraphs 22 and 23, Joined Cases 115/81 and 116/81 *Adoui and Cornuaille* v *Belgium* [1982] ECR 1665, paragraph 7, and Joined Cases C-65/95 and C-111/95 *Shingara and Radiom* [1997] ECR I-3343, paragraph 28).

[21] Under the Court's case law, the concept of public policy may be relied upon in the event of a genuine and sufficiently serious threat to the requirements of public policy affecting one of the fundamental interests of society (see Case 30/77 *Bouchereau* [1977] ECR 1999, paragraph 35).

[22] In this respect, it must be accepted that a Member State may consider that the use of drugs constitutes a danger for society such as to justify special measures against foreign nationals who contravene its laws on drugs, in order to maintain public order.

[23] However, as the Court has repeatedly stated, the public policy exception, like all derogations from a fundamental principle of the Treaty, must be interpreted restrictively.

[24] In that regard, Directive 64/221, Article 1(1) of which provides that the directive is to apply to *inter alia* any national of a Member State who travels to another Member State as a recipient of services, sets certain limits on the right of Member States to expel foreign nationals on the grounds of public policy. Article 3 of that directive states that measures taken on grounds of public policy or of public security that have the effect of restricting the residence of a national of another Member State must be based exclusively on the personal conduct of the individual concerned. In addition, previous criminal convictions cannot in themselves constitute grounds for the taking of such meas-

ures. It follows that the existence of a previous criminal conviction can, therefore, only be taken into account in so far as the circumstances which gave rise to that conviction are evidence of personal conduct constituting a present threat to the requirements of public policy (*Bouchereau*, paragraph 28).

[25] It follows that an expulsion order could be made against a Community national such as Ms Calfa only if, besides her having committed an offence under drugs laws, her personal conduct created a genuine and sufficiently serious threat affecting one of the fundamental interests of society.

[26] In the present case, the legislation at issue in the main proceedings requires nationals of other Member States found guilty, on the national territory in which that legislation applies, of an offence under the drugs laws, to be expelled for life from that territory, unless compelling reasons, in particular family reasons, justify their continued residence in the country. The penalty can be revoked only by a decision taken at the discretion of the Minister for Justice after a period of three years.

[27] Therefore, expulsion for life automatically follows a criminal conviction, without any account being taken of the personal conduct of the offender or of the danger which that person represents for the requirements of public policy.

[28] It follows that the conditions for the application of the public policy exception provided for in Directive 64/221, as interpreted by the Court of Justice, are not fulfilled and that the public policy exception cannot be successfully relied upon to justify a restriction on the freedom to provide services, such as that imposed by the legislation at issue in the main proceedings.

NOTES

1. These rights are frequently invoked at relatively low levels within national legal systems. Several decisions of the Immigration Appeal Tribunal in the UK demonstrate a healthy appreciation of the implications of Community law. In *Monteil* v *Secretary of State* [1984] 1 CMLR 264, the Tribunal ruled against the deportation of a French national who had been convicted of criminal offences and had spent time in gaol. It was shown that he had been cured of the illness which had led to his crimes, and that accordingly he posed no sufficient present threat to society.

2. It remains to be seen how the Article 39(3) derogations can be applied in practice in the light of the Article 14 commitment to an area without internal frontiers. The intimate relationship between the EC rules on free movement and action in common under the EU's 'third pillar' (p.9 above) in *inter alia* asylum policy, immigration policy, and police cooperation was acknowledged at Maastricht by the 'transfer' procedure between what were then Article K.9 TEU and Article 100c EC. This remained unused. Partly in consequence of dissatisfaction with the progress made under structures fashioned at Maastricht, the Member States agreed at Amsterdam to adjust the legal framework in favour of increased 'communitiarization' of the material relevant to securing the free movement of persons. The EC Treaty post-Amsterdam contains a Title on 'Visas, asylum, immigration and other policies related to free movement of persons' which is dedicated to the progressive establishment of 'an area of freedom, security and justice'. This is Title IV and comprises Articles 61–69 EC. It is set out and discussed in Chapter 15, p.479 below. This arrangement casts further doubt on the role in practice of Article 39(3) EC.

■ QUESTION

Ken, a British national, travels to Belgium with his aged grandmother. He takes up part-time work in a café, where he earns below the national minimum wage. He takes part in an anti-racist march organized by a group which, while not illegal in Belgium, is nonetheless one on which the authorities have determined to keep a close watch.

The Belgian authorities serve a deportation order on Ken, stating that his wage is too low for him to obtain any rights under Community law. The Belgian authorities contend that in any event Ken's presence in the country is contrary to the public good on the grounds that:

(a) he is linked to an organization of which the State disapproves;

(b) he may be forced to turn to crime to support his relative; and

(c) it is contrary to public policy to permit undermining of standard wage rates.

Discuss the relevant principles of Community law.

NOTE

Article 39(4), the 'public service' exception, has been subjected by the Court to a parallel narrow interpretation.

Commission v *Belgium* (Case 149/79)

[1980] ECR 3881, [1981] 2 CMLR 413, Court of Justice of the European Communities

The case involved the restriction to Belgians alone of several posts on Belgian railways, including trainee drivers, shunters, and signallers, and also posts with the City of Brussels for, *inter alia*, hospital nurses, plumbers, and electricians. The Court's statements of principle included the following, directed at Article 48(4) of the EC Treaty (now, after amendment, Article 39(4) EC):

[10] That provision removes from the ambit of Article 48(1) to (3) a series of posts which involve direct or indirect participation in the exercise of powers conferred by public law and duties designed to safeguard the general interests of the State or of other public authorities. Such posts in fact presume on the part of those occupying them the existence of a special relationship of allegiance to the State and reciprocity of rights and duties which form the foundation of the bond of nationality.

[11] The scope of the derogation made by Article 48(4) to the principles of freedom of movement and equality of treatment laid down in the first three paragraphs of the article should therefore be determined on the basis of the aim pursued by that article. However, determining the sphere of application of Article 48(4) raises special difficulties since in the various Member States authorities acting under powers conferred by public law have assumed responsibilities of an economic and social nature or are involved in activities which are not identifiable with the functions which are typical of the public service yet which by their nature still come under the sphere of application of the Treaty. In these circumstances the effect of extending the exception contained in Article 48(4) to posts which, whilst coming under the State or other organizations governed by public law, still do not involve any association with tasks belonging to the public service properly so called, would be to remove a considerable number of posts from the ambit of the principles set out in the Treaty and to create inequalities between Member States according to the different ways in which the State and certain sectors of economic life are organized.

[12] Consequently it is appropriate to examine whether the posts covered by the action may be associated with the concept of public service within the meaning of Article 48(4), which requires uniform interpretation and application throughout the Community. It must be acknowledged that the application of the distinguishing criteria indicated above gives rise to problems of appraisal and demarcation in specific cases. It follows from the foregoing that such a classification depends on whether or not the posts in question are typical of the specific activities of the public service in so far as the exercise of powers conferred by public law and responsibility for safeguarding the general interests of the State are vested in it.

NOTE

The Court felt it had insufficient information to rule in the case itself; the follow-up judgment appears at [1982] ECR 1845.

For additional material and resources see the Companion Website at: www.oup.co.uk/best.textbooks/law/weatherill6e

14

Freedom of Establishment and the Free Movement of Services: Articles 43 and 49

SECTION 1: **THE RIGHTS**

Articles 43 and 49 extend the rights of free movement beyond 'workers' to include free movement of individuals who are self-employed and wish to establish themselves in another Member State, or to provide services there. These rights are granted not just to the natural person who wishes to migrate, but also to the legal person – i.e., the company.

ARTICLES 43 AND 49 EC

Article 43

Within the framework of the provisions set out below, restrictions on the freedom of establishment of nationals of a Member State in the territory of another Member State shall be prohibited. Such prohibition shall also apply to restrictions on the setting up of agencies, branches or subsidiaries by nationals of any Member State established in the territory of any Member State.

Freedom of establishment shall include the right to take up and pursue activities as self-employed persons and to set up and manage undertakings, in particular companies or firms within the meaning of the second paragraph of Article 48, under the conditions laid down for its own nationals by the law of the country where such establishment is effected, subject to the provisions of the Chapter relating to capital.

Article 49

Within the framework of the provisions set out below, restrictions on freedom to provide services within the Community shall be prohibited in respect of nationals of Member States who are established in a State of the Community other than that of the person for whom the services are intended.

The Council may, acting by a qualified majority on a proposal from the Commission, extend the provisions of the Chapter to nationals of a third country who provide services and who are established within the Community.

NOTES
1. The Treaty of Amsterdam effected merely cosmetic changes to these provisions by removing references to the transitional period. On re-numbering (p.12 above), what are now Articles 43 and 49 replaced what were previously Articles 52 and 59. These numerical games must be borne in mind in reading the pre-Amsterdam material in this Chapter.

    The distinction between Article 43, the right of establishment, and Article 49, the right to provide services, is rather artificial. The former envisages a more permanent presence in the host Member State than the latter, but at the margin it may be difficult to select the correct classification. Broadly, however, the problem is unlikely to arise in an acute form, because the

Court has wisely recognised the common purpose of the provisions and has shown itself prepared to interpret them in parallel fashion. Article 39 too joins in this shared purpose; see, e.g., *Procureur du Roi* v *Royer* (Case 48/75) [1976] ECR 497; *Walrave* v *Association Union Cycliste Internationale* (Case 36/74) [1974] ECR 1405; *Roux* v *Belgian State* (Case C-363/89) [1991] ECR I-273.

The rights of the migrating individual to non-discriminatory treatment according to nationality are amplified by Directive 73/148 on the Abolition of Restrictions on Movement and Residence within the Community for Nationals of Member States with regard to Establishment and the Provision of Services, Articles 1–8 [1973] OJ L172/14. This measure is analogous to Directive 68/360 applicable to workers (p.431 above).

2. Directive 75/34 [1975] OJ L14/10 confers rights to remain in the host State. It is analogous to Regulation 1251/70, mentioned at p.436 above. These two Directives are available *via* http://europa.eu.int/comm/justice_home/index_en.htm.

Derogation from the rights is possible in a fashion comparable to Article 39 (p.427 above); see Articles 45, 46, and 55. This complementarity was encountered in *Donatella Calfa* (Case C-348/96), p.442 above.

SECTION 2: **NON-DISCRIMINATION**

The following case illustrates the application of the principle of non-discrimination.

Thieffry v Conseil de l'Ordre des Avocats à la Cour de Paris (Case 71/76)
[1977] ECR 765, [1977] 2 CMLR 373, Court of Justice of the European Communities

Thieffry, a Belgian advocate, held a Belgian diploma of Doctor of Laws, recognized by a French university as equivalent to the French licenciate's degree in law. Despite this recognition of equivalence, he was refused entry to the Paris Bar because he held no French diploma of the required level. Thieffry's challenge reached the Court via the preliminary reference procedure (Chapter 7). The Court cited the General Programme for the abolition of restrictions on freedom of establishment, adopted in 1961, and continued:

[15]. . . [F]reedom of establishment, subject to observance of professional rules justified by the general good, is one of the objectives of the Treaty.

[16] In so far as Community law makes no special provision, these objectives may be attained by measures enacted by the Member States, which under Article 5 of the Treaty are bound to take 'all appropriate measures, whether general or particular, to ensure fulfilment of the obligations arising out of this Treaty or resulting from action taken by the institutions of the Community', and to abstain 'from any measure which could jeopardize the attainment of the objectives of this Treaty'.

[17] Consequently, if the freedom of establishment provided for by Article 52 can be ensured in a Member State either under the provisions of the laws and regulations in force, or by virtue of the practices of the public service or of professional bodies, a person subject to Community law cannot be denied the practical benefit of that freedom solely by virtue of the fact that, for a particular profession, the directives provided for by Article 57 of the Treaty have not yet been adopted.

[18] Since the practical enjoyment of freedom of establishment can thus in certain circumstances depend upon national practice or legislation, it is incumbent upon the competent public authorities –

including legally recognised professional bodies – to ensure that such practice or legislation is applied in accordance with the objective defined by the provisions of the Treaty relating to freedom of establishment.

[19] In particular, there is an unjustified restriction on that freedom where, in a Member State, admission to a particular profession is refused to a person covered by the Treaty who holds a diploma which has been recognised as an equivalent qualification by the competent authority of the country of establishment and who furthermore has fulfilled the specific conditions regarding professional training in force in that country, solely by reason of the fact that the person concerned does not possess the national diploma corresponding to the diploma which he holds and which has been recognised as an equivalent qualification.

The Court was accordingly able to conclude, in terms obviously favourable to Thieffry:

[27] In these circumstances, the answer to the question referred to the Court should be that when a national of one Member State desirous of exercising a professional activity such as the profession of advocate in another Member State has obtained a diploma in his country of origin which has been recognized as an equivalent qualification by the competent authority under the legislation of the country of establishment and which has thus enabled him to sit and pass the special qualifying examination for the profession in question, the act of demanding the national diploma prescribed by the legislation of the country of establishment constitutes, even in the absence of the directives provided for in Article 57, a restriction incompatible with the freedom of establishment guaranteed by Article 52 of the Treaty.

NOTES
1. A similar approach had been taken in *Reyners v Belgian State* (Case 2/74) [1974] ECR 631, [1974] 2 CMLR 305, where the Court insisted that the principle of non-discrimination had direct effect even in the absence of implementing Directives.
2. The Court has extended the scope of these Treaty Articles in order to accommodate tourists. Tourists are neither self-employed nor providers of services, but they are recipients of services and thus fall within the scope of Article 49.

Cowan v *Le Trésor Public* (Case 186/87)
[1986] ECR 195, Court of Justice of the European Communities

Mr Cowan, a British national, was attacked and robbed while visiting Paris as a tourist. He was refused criminal injuries compensation by the French authorities because of his nationality. He challenged this refusal using Community law. The matter reached the Court as a preliminary reference. The Court placed great emphasis on the principle of non-discrimination on grounds of nationality under (what was then) Article 7 EEC. It should be noted that this became Article 6 EC after the entry into force of the Maastricht Treaty on European Union and post-Amsterdam it is Article 12 EC.

[14] Under Article 7 of the Treaty the prohibition of discrimination applies 'within the scope of application of this Treaty' and 'without prejudice to any special provisions contained therein'. This latter expression refers particularly to other provisions of the Treaty in which the application of the general principle set out in that article is given concrete form in respect of specific situations. Examples of that are the provisions concerning free movement of workers, the right of establishment and the freedom to provide services.

[15] On that last point, in its judgment of 31 January 1984 in Joined Cases 286/82 and 26/83 *Luisi and Carbone v Ministero del Tesoro* [1984] ECR 377, the Court held that the freedom to provide services includes the freedom for the recipients of services to go to another Member State in order to receive a service there, without being obstructed by restrictions, and that tourists, among others, must be regarded as recipients of services.

[16] At the hearing the French Government submitted that as Community law now stands a recipient of services may not rely on the prohibition of discrimination to the extent that the national law at issue does not create any barrier to freedom of movement. A provision such as that at issue in the main proceedings, it says, imposes no restrictions in that respect. Furthermore, it concerns a right which is a manifestation of the principle of national solidarity. Such a right presupposes a closer bond with the State than that of a recipient of services, and for that reason it may be restricted to persons who are either nationals of that State or foreign nationals resident on the territory of that State.

[17] That reasoning cannot be accepted. When Community law guarantees a natural person the freedom to go to another Member State the protection of that person from harm in the Member State in question, on the same basis as that of nationals and persons residing there, is a corollary of that freedom of movement. It follows that the prohibition of discrimination is applicable to recipients of services within the meaning of the Treaty as regards protection against the risk of assault and the right to obtain financial compensation provided for by national law when that risk materializes. The fact that the compensation at issue is financed by the Public Treasury cannot alter the rules regarding the protection of the rights guaranteed by the Treaty.

[18] The French Government also submitted that compensation such as that at issue in the main proceedings is not subject to the prohibition of discrimination because it falls within the law of criminal procedure, which is not included within the scope of the Treaty.

[19] Although in principle criminal legislation and the rules of criminal procedure, among which the national provision in issue is to be found, are matters for which the Member States are responsible, the Court has consistently held (see *inter alia* the judgment of 11 November 1981 in Case 203/80 *Casati* [1981] ECR 2595) that Community law sets certain limits to their power. Such legislative provisions may not discriminate against persons to whom Community law gives the right to equal treatment or restrict the fundamental freedoms guaranteed by Community law.

[20] In the light of all the foregoing the answer to the question submitted must be that the prohibition of discrimination laid down in particular in Article 7 of the EEC Treaty must be interpreted as meaning that in respect of persons whose freedom to travel to a Member State, in particular as recipients of services, is guaranteed by Community law that State may not make the award of State compensation for harm caused in that State to the victim of an assault resulting in physical injury subject to the condition that he hold a residence permit or be a national of a country which has entered into a reciprocal agreement with that Member State.

NOTE
Greeting *Cowan* (Case 186/87), F. Mancini has congratulated the Court on 'one of its shrewdest judgments' ((1989) 26 CML Rev 595); see also S. Weatherill (1989) 26 CML Rev 563 and (pre-*Cowan*) M. van der Woude and P. Mead (1988) 25 CML Rev 117. *Donatella Calfa* (Case C-348/96) (p.442 above) was similarly a case concerning a tourist who fell within the scope of application of the Treaty provisions on services.

The scope of the principle of non-discrimination, which as *Cowan* (Case 186/87) indicates derives fundamentally from Article 12 EC post-Amsterdam, remains unclear. One might suppose that there is no right to equality in all matters, and that the tourist would not be able to use Article 12 EC in so extensive a manner as the worker is able to rely on Article 7(2) of Regulation 1612/68 (see cases at p.435 above). However, this reading now seems to be challenged by the Court's case law concerning Citizenship. This is addressed at p.488 below.

It is also worth noting that each time an enhanced competence is conferred on the Community, as has occurred on periodic Treaty revision at Maastricht, Amsterdam, and (less significantly) at Nice, so the scope of application of *inter alia* Article 12 is correspondingly widened. The field of education provides a good example of such increasing occupation by requirements drawn from Community law; see J. Shaw, 'From the Margins to the Centre: Education and Training Law and Policy' in P. Craig and G. De Búrca, *The Evolution of EU Law* (1999).

■ QUESTIONS

1. In its case law, the Court is trying to strike a balance between, on the one hand, applying and extending the principle of non-discrimination already set out in both the Treaty and secondary legislation, and, on the other, acknowledging that some areas are dependent on legislative action to extend the law. Has it gone beyond the scope of due judicial restraint?

2. What is the legal basis of the Commission's action publicized in this Press Release of 14 July 1989:

> The Commission scored a success following a complaint by an Irish citizen, resident in Ireland, who was refused admission to pilot training courses organized by British Aerospace because he was not a British citizen. After an approach to British Airways by the Commission, an assurance was received that the company would not discriminate on grounds of nationality or residence against Community citizens wishing to enrol on vocational training courses such as those mentioned or to become British Airways pilots. (Commission Press Release IP (89) 575.)

How might the would be pilot have sought to protect himself had the Commission refused to assist him? On the horizontal direct effect of these Treaty provisions see *URBSFA* v *Bosman* (Case C-415/93) [1995] ECR I-4921, and the most important recent decision, *Roman Angonese* (Case C-281/98) [2000] ECR I-4139. Read S. Van den Bogaert, 'Horizontality', Ch. 5 in C. Barnard and J. Scott (eds), *The Law of the Single European Market* (Oxford: Hart Publishing, 2002).

NOTE

In 1990 three Directives were adopted which were designed to extend the protection of Community law. These Directives provide a General Right of Residence (Directive 90/364 [1990] OJ L180/26); a Right of Residence for employees and self-employed persons who have ceased their occupational activity (Directive 90/365 [1990] OJ L180/28) and a Right of Residence for Students (Directive 90/366 [1990] OJ L180/30; this Directive was annulled by the Court for choice of incorrect legal base in *Parliament* v *Council* (Case C-295/90) [1992] ECR I-4193, although the Court ordered that its provisions should remain in force pending the making of a new measure on the correct base which occurred in Directive 93/96 [1993] OJ L317/59). The advances made by these Directives were severely limited by the requirement in each that, according to the Preambles, the 'beneficiaries of the right of residence must not become an unreasonable burden on the public finances of the host Member State'. This considerable limitation is reflected in the specific provisions of each measure. The Commission has issued a report on the implementation of these Directives: COM (99) 127.

SECTION 3: **BEYOND DISCRIMINATION**

The limits of the non-discrimination approach to market integration are significant. Consider *Thieffry* (Case 71/76) (p.446 above). The key to the application of the principle of non-discrimination was the recognition of Thieffry's Belgian degree as sufficient for French purposes. Without recognition, he could have been excluded from the French lawyer's market. There would have been no nationality discrimination; no one could act as *avocat* without a French degree, irrespective of nationality. (See, e.g., *Procureur de la République* v *Bouchoucha* (Case C-61/89) [1990] ECR I-3551.)

This problem is serious for the professional person, who is faced by the need to meet the professional qualification requirements of the host State; in the absence of cross-recognition as in *Thieffry* (Case 71/76), home State qualifications are unlikely to suffice. Similarly, a company may face serious problems in offering services across borders, because it may find that certain regulations are imposed on all firms supplying services in the host State, but with which it, a non-national firm, does not comply. Articles 43(2) and 50(3) declare that the host State may continue to apply its rules equally to all those active on its market.

....

A: **Challenging and justifying obstructive national measures**

It should be immediately apparent that there are potentially close connections with the '*Cassis de Dijon*' case law under Article 28 (Chapter 12). The problem here too arises in relation to national measures which are not discriminatory, but which hinder the exercise of free movement rights. The principles according to which the permissibility of such national measures shall be judged appear to be the same under both Article 28 and Article 49, in so far as both enshrine fundamental Treaty freedoms (*cf* Case C-55/94 *Gebhard*, p.321 above). However, the Court's scrutiny of regulatory diversity between the Member States in the context of Article 49 has until recently been couched in similar but not identical language to that which occurs under Article 28.

Commission v *Germany* (Case 205/84)
[1986] ECR 3755, [1987] 2 CMLR 69, Court of Justice of the European Communities

The case involved German law regulating the provision of insurance services on German territory. *All* insurers had to have a permanent establishment in Germany. *All* insurers had to be authorised by the German State. Plainly, insurers from other States wishing to offer services in Germany were impeded by these requirements. The Commission argued that the rules violated Articles 59 and 60 of the EC Treaty (now, after amendment, Articles 49 and 50 EC). The matter reached the Court under Article 169 of the EC Treaty (now Article 226 EC: see Chapter 4)). The first extract sets out the Court's approach.

[25] According to the well-established case-law of the Court, Articles 59 and 60 of the EEC Treaty became directly applicable on the expiry of the transitional period, and their applicability was not conditional on the harmonisation or the coordination of the laws of the Member States. Those articles require the removal not only of all discrimination against a provider of a service on the grounds of his nationality but also all restrictions on his freedom to provide services imposed by reason of the fact that he is established in a Member State other than that in which the service is to be provided.

[26] Since the German Government and certain other of the governments intervening in its support have referred to the third paragraph of Article 60 as a basis for their contention that the State of the person insured can also apply its supervisory legislation to insurers established in another Member State, it should be added, as the Court made clear in particular in its judgment of 17 December 1981 (Case 279/80 *Webb* [1981] ECR 3305), that the principal aim of that paragraph is to enable the provider of the service to pursue his activities in the Member State where the service is

given without suffering discrimination in favour of the nationals of the State. However, it does not follow from that paragraph that all national legislation applicable to nationals of that State and usually applied to the permanent activities of undertakings established therein may be similarly applied in its entirety to the temporary activities of undertakings which are established in other Member States.

[27] The Court has nevertheless accepted, in particular in its judgments of 18 January 1979 (Joined Cases 110 and 111/78 *Ministère public and Another* v *van Wesemael and Others* [1979] ECR 35) and 17 December 1981 (Case 279/80 *Webb*, cited above), that regard being had to the particular nature of certain services, specific requirements imposed on the provider of the services cannot be considered to be incompatible with the Treaty where they have as their purpose the application of rules governing such activities. However, the freedom to provide services, as one of the fundamental principles of the Treaty, may be restricted only by provisions which are justified by the general good and which are applied to all persons or undertakings operating within the territory of the State in which the service is provided in so far as that interest is not safeguarded by the provisions to which the provider of a service is subject in the Member State of his establishment. In addition, such requirements must be objectively justified by the need to ensure that professional rules of conduct are complied with and that the interests which such rules are designed to safeguard are protected.

[28] It must be stated that the requirements in question in these proceedings, namely that an insurer who is established in another Member State, authorised by the supervisory authority of that State and subject to the supervision of that authority, must have a permanent establishment within the territory of the State in which the service is provided and that he must obtain a separate authorisation from the supervisory authority of that State, constitute restrictions on the freedom to provide services inasmuch as they increase the cost of such services in the State in which they are provided, in particular where the insurer conducts business in that State only occasionally.

[29] It follows that those requirements may be regarded as compatible with Articles 59 and 60 of the EEC Treaty only if it is established that in the field of activity concerned there are imperative reasons relating to the public interest which justify restrictions on the freedom to provide services, that the public interest is not already protected by the rules of the State of establishment and that the same result cannot be obtained by less restrictive rules.

The Court then proceeded to accept the existence of a protectable interest in this area:

[30] As the German Government and the parties intervening in its support have maintained, without being contradicted by the Commission or the United Kingdom and Netherlands Governments, the insurance sector is a particularly sensitive area from the point of view of the protection of the consumer both as a policy-holder and as an insured person. This is so in particular because of the specific nature of the service provided by the insurer, which is linked to future events, the occurrence of which, or at least the timing of which, is uncertain at the time when the contract is concluded. An insured person who does not obtain payment under a policy following an event giving rise to a claim may find himself in a very precarious position. Similarly, it is as a rule very difficult for a person seeking insurance to judge whether the likely future development of the insurer's financial position and the terms of the contract, usually imposed by the insurer, offer him sufficient guarantees that he will receive payment under the policy if a claimable event occurs.

[31] It must also be borne in mind, as the German Government has pointed out, that in certain fields insurance has become a mass phenomenon. Contracts are concluded by such enormous numbers of policy-holders that the protection of the interests of insured persons and injured third parties affects virtually the whole population.

[32] Those special characteristics, which are peculiar to the insurance sector, have led all the Member States to introduce legislation making insurance undertakings subject to mandatory rules both as regards their financial position and the conditions of insurance which they apply, and to permanent supervision to ensure that those rules are complied with.

[33] It therefore appears that in the field in question there are imperative reasons relating to the public interest which may justify restrictions on the freedom to provide services, provided, however, that the rules of the State of establishment are not adequate in order to achieve the necessary level of protection and that the requirements of the State in which the service is provided do not exceed what is necessary in that respect.

NOTE

After due examination, the Court concluded that the public interest was *not* adequately protected by the rules of the State of establishment. In the abstract, then, Germany could lawfully restrict trade in order to serve the public interest. It then fell to be determined whether the actual rules enacted could satisfy Community law. The Court refused to accept that a blanket requirement of establishment in Germany was compatible with Community law. However, it took a rather different view of the necessity to undergo an authorisation procedure.

Commission v Germany (Case 205/84)

[1986] ECR 3755, [1987] 2 CMLR 69, Court of Justice of the European Communities

[42] The Commission does not dispute that the State in which the service is provided is entitled to exercise a certain control over insurance undertakings which provide services within its territory. At the hearing it even accepted that it was permissible to provide for certain measures of supervision of the undertaking concerned to be applied prior to its conducting any business in the context of the provision of services. It nevertheless maintained that such supervision should take a form less restrictive than that of authorization. It did not however explain how such a system might work.

[43] The German Government and the governments intervening in its support maintain that the necessary supervision can be carried out only by means of an authorization procedure which makes it possible to investigate the undertaking before it commences its activities, to monitor those activities continuously and to withdraw the authorization in the event of serious and repeated infringements.

[44] In that respect it should be noted that in all the Member States the supervision of insurance undertakings is organized in the form of an authorization procedure and that the necessity of such a procedure is recognized in the two first coordination directives as regards the activities to which they refer. In each of those directives Article 6 thereof provides that each Member State must make the taking-up of the business of insurance in its territory subject to an official authorization. An undertaking which sets up branches and agencies in Member States other than that in which its head office is situated must therefore obtain an authorization from the supervisory authority of each of those States.

[45] It must also be observed that the proposal for a second directive provides for the retention of that system. The undertaking must obtain an official authorization from each Member State in which it wishes to conduct business in the context of the provision of services. Although, according to that proposal, the authorization must be obtained from the supervisory authority of the State of establishment, that authority must first consult the authority of the State in which the service is to be provided and send it all the relevant papers. The proposal also envisages permanent cooperation between the two supervisory authorities, thus making it possible, in particular, for the authority of the State of establishment to take all appropriate measures, which may extend to withdrawal of the authorization, to put an end to the infringements which have been notified to it by the supervisory authority of the State in which the service is provided.

[46] In those circumstances the German Government's argument to the effect that only the requirement of an authorization can provide an effective means of ensuring the supervision which, having regard to the foregoing considerations, is justified on grounds relating to the protection of the consumer both as a policy-holder and as an insured person, must be accepted. Since a system such as that proposed in the draft for a second directive, which entrusts the operation of the authorization procedure to the Member State in which the undertaking is established, working in close cooperation with the State in which the service is provided, can be set up only by legislation, it

must also be acknowledged that, in the present state of Community law, it is for the State in which the service is provided to grant and withdraw that authorization.

[47] It should however be emphasized that the authorization must be granted on request to any undertaking established in another Member State which meets the conditions laid down by the legislation of the State in which the service is provided, that those conditions may not duplicate equivalent statutory conditions which have already been satisfied in the State in which the under-taking is established and that the supervisory authority of the State in which the service is provided must take into account supervision and verifications which have already been carried out in the Member State of establishment. According to the German Government, which has not been contradicted on that point by the Commission, the German authorization procedure conforms fully to those requirements.

[48] It is still necessary to consider whether the requirement of authorization which, under the Insurance Supervision Law, applies to any insurance business other than transport insurance, is justified in all its applications. In that respect it has been pointed out, in particular by the United Kingdom Government, that the free movement of services is of importance principally for com-mercial insurance and that with regard to that particular type of insurance the grounds relating to the protection of policy-holders relied on by the German Government and the governments interven-ing in its support do not apply

[49] It follows from the foregoing that the requirement of authorization may be maintained only in so far as it is justified on the grounds relating to the protection of policy-holders and insured persons relied upon by the German Government. It must also be recognized that those grounds are not equally important in every sector of insurance and that there may be cases where, because of the nature of the risk insured and of the party seeking insurance, there is no need to protect the latter by the application of the mandatory rules of his national law.

[50] However, although it is true that the proposal for a second directive takes account of those considerations by excluding *inter alia* commercial insurance, which is defined in detail, from the scope of the mandatory rules of the State in which the service is provided, it must also be observed that, in the light of the legal and factual arguments which have been presented before it, the Court is not in a position to make such a general distinction and to lay down the limits of that distinction with sufficient precision to determine the individual cases in which the needs of protection, which are characteristic of insurance business in general, do not justify the requirement of an authorization.

[51] It follows from the foregoing that the Commission's first head of claim must be rejected in so far as it is directed against the requirement of authorization.

NOTES
1. See comment by D. Edward (1987) 12 EL Rev 231; R. Hodgin (1987) 24 CML Rev 273; J. Steenbergen (1987) CDE 526; D. Lasok (1988) 51 MLR 706.
2. Insurance regulation is increasingly subject to Community legislation (see generally J. Usher, *The Law of Money and Financial Services in the EC* (Oxford: OUP, 2000); and the Commission has a dedicated website containing relevant documentation, http://europa.eu.int/comm/ internal_market/insurance/index_en.htm). The Commission has published an interpretative communication relevant to the sector at [2000] OJ C43/5 (*cf* pp.364 and 410 above on the role of such communications). However, the principle that non-discriminatory national rules which have the effect of protecting domestic industry can be challenged under Article 49 applies across the services sector. Increasingly the market for services has been liberalized through the application of the primary Treaty provisions without the need to resort to har-monization. As suggested above at p.450, there are clear parallels with the Court's approach in *Cassis de Dijon* (Case 120/78, p.381 above); see, e.g., the language of para 29 of the above judgment in Case 205/84. The issue is similar. One State demands compliance with its rules. *All* firms must adhere, but importers/migrants suffer because they too are subjected to con-trols in their home State. The next case provides an example. The Commission considered France was in violation of Article 59 of the EC Treaty (now, after amendment, Article 49 EC) by making the provision of services by tourist guides accompanying groups of tourists from

another Member State subject to the possession of a licence, itself dependent on possession of a particular qualification. The Court agreed with the Commission.

Commission v France (Case C-154/89)
[1991] ECR I-659, Court of Justice of the European Communities

[12] It should further be pointed out that Articles 59 and 60 of the Treaty require not only the abolition of any discrimination against a person providing services on account of his nationality but also the abolition of any restriction on the freedom to provide services imposed on the ground that the person providing a service is established in a Member State other than the one in which the service is provided. In particular, the Member State cannot make the performance of the services in its territory subject to observance of all the conditions required for establishment; were it to do so the provisions securing freedom to provide services would be deprived of all practical effect.

[13] The requirement imposed by the abovementioned provisions of French legislation amount to such a restriction. By making the provision of services by tourist guides accompanying a group of tourists from another Member State subject to possession of a specific qualification, that legislation prevents both tour companies from providing that service with their own staff and self-employed tourist guides from offering their services to those companies for organized tours. It also prevents tourists taking part in such organized tours from availing themselves at will of the services in question.

[14] However, in view of the specific requirements in relation to certain services, the fact that a Member State makes the provision thereof subject to conditions as to the qualifications of the person providing them, pursuant to rules governing such activities within its jurisdiction, cannot be considered incompatible with Articles 59 and 60 of the Treaty. Nevertheless, as one of the fundamental principles of the Treaty the freedom to provide services may be restricted only by rules which are justified in the general interest and are applied to all persons and undertakings operating in the territory of the State where the service is provided, in so far as that interest is not safeguarded by the rules to which the provider of such a service is subject in the Member State where he is established. In addition, such requirements must be objectively justified by the need to ensure that professional rules of conduct are complied with and that the interests which such rules are designed to safeguard are protected (see *inter alia* the judgment in Case 205/84 *Commission* v *Germany* [1986] ECR 3755, at paragraph 27).

[15] Accordingly, those requirements can be regarded as compatible with Articles 59 and 60 of the Treaty only if it is established that with regard to the activity in question there are overriding reasons relating to the public interest which justify restrictions on the freedom to provide services, that the public interest is not already protected by the rules of the State of establishment and that the same result cannot be obtained by less restrictive rules.

[16] The French Government contends that the French legislation in question seeks to ensure the protection of general interests relating to the proper appreciation of places and things of historical interest and the widest possible dissemination of knowledge of the artistic and cultural heritage of the country. According to the French Government, those interests are not adequately safeguarded by the rules to which the provider of the services, in this case the tour company, is subject in the Member State in which it is established. Several States require no occupational qualifications for tourist guides or demand no special knowledge of the historical and cultural heritage of other countries. In the absence of harmonization on that point the French legislation is not, therefore, incompatible with Article 59 of the EEC Treaty.

[17] The general interest in the proper appreciation of places and things of historical interest and the widest possible dissemination of knowledge of the artistic and cultural heritage of a country can constitute an overriding reason justifying a restriction on the freedom to provide services. However, the requirement in question contained in the French legislation goes beyond what is necessary to ensure the safeguarding of that interest inasmuch as it makes the activities of a tourist guide accompanying groups of tourists from another Member State subject to possession of a licence.

[18] The service of accompanying tourists is performed under quite specific conditions. The independent or employed tourist guide travels with the tourists and accompanies them in a closed group; in that group they move temporarily from the Member State of establishment to the Member State to be visited.

[19] In those circumstances a licence requirement imposed by the Member State of destination has the effect of reducing the number of tourist guides qualified to accompany tourists in a closed group, which may lead a tour operator to have recourse instead to local guides employed or established in the Member State in which the service is to be performed. However, that consequence may have the drawback that tourists who are the recipients of the services in question do not have a guide who is familiar with their language, their interests and their specific expectations.

[20] Moreover, the profitable operation of such group tours depends on the commercial reputation of the operator, who faces competitive pressure from other tour companies; the need to maintain that reputation and the competitive pressure themselves compel companies to be selective in employing tourist guides and exercise some control over the quality of their services. Depending on the specific expectations of the groups of tourists in question, that factor is likely to contribute to the proper appreciation of places and things of historical interest and to the widest possible dissemination of knowledge relating to the artistic and cultural heritage, in the case of conducted tours of places other than museums or historical monuments which may be visited only with a professional guide.

[21] It follows that in view of the scale of the restrictions it imposes, the legislation in issue is disproportionate in relation to the objective pursued, namely to ensure the proper appreciation of places and things of historical interest and the widest dissemination of knowledge of the artistic and cultural heritage of the Member State in which the tour is conducted.

NOTE

In this way a host State's reliance on qualification requirements as a condition of access to its market is put to the test of EC trade law. The preference in para 20 for market rather than regulatory solutions is striking. The Court has subsequently made clear that a State is required actively to assess whether a migrant's qualification is adequate, though different from local requirements. Vlassopoulou was a Greek national and a member of the Athens Bar. She wished to work as a lawyer in Germany. The case was decided in the context of Article 52, which has become Article 43 post-Amsterdam and which sets out the right of establishment, but appears to enshrine a general principle of Community trade law.

Vlassopoulou v *Ministerium für Justiz, Bundes- und Europaangelegenheiten Baden-Württemberg* (Case C-340/89)

[1991] ECR I-2357, Court of Justice of the European Communities

[14] [I]t is also clear from the judgment in Case 71/76 *Thieffry* v *Conseil de l'Ordre des Avocats à la Cour de Paris* [1977] ECR 765, at paragraph 16, that, in so far as Community law makes no special provision, the objectives of the Treaty, and in particular freedom of establishment, may be achieved by measures enacted by the Member States, which, under Article 5 of the Treaty, must take 'all appropriate measures, whether general or particular, to ensure fulfilment of the obligations arising out of this Treaty or resulting from action taken by the institutions of the Community' and abstain from 'any measure which could jeopardize the attainment of the objectives of this Treaty'.

[15] It must be stated in this regard that, even if applied without any discrimination on the basis of nationality, national requirements concerning qualifications may have the effect of hindering nationals of other Member States in the exercise of their right of establishment guaranteed to them by Article 52 of the EEC Treaty. That could be the case if the national rules in question took no account of the knowledge and qualifications already acquired by the person concerned in another Member State.

[16] Consequently, a Member State which receives a request to admit a person to a profession to which access, under national law, depends upon the possession of a diploma or a professional

qualification must take into consideration the diplomas, certificates and other evidence of qualifications which the person concerned has acquired in order to exercise the same profession in another Member State by making a comparison between the specialized knowledge and abilities certified by those diplomas and the knowledge and qualifications required by the national rules.

[17] That examination procedure must enable the authorities of the host Member State to assure themselves, on an objective basis, that the foreign diploma certifies that its holder has knowledge and qualifications which are, if not identical, at least equivalent to those certified by the national diploma. That assessment of the equivalence of the foreign diploma must be carried out exclusively in the light of the level of knowledge and qualifications which its holder can be assumed to possess in the light of that diploma, having regard to the nature and duration of the studies and practical training to which the diploma relates (see the judgment in Case 222/86 *Unectef* v *Heylens* [1987] ECR 4097, paragraph 13).

[18] In the course of that examination, a Member State may, however, take into consideration objective differences relating to both the legal framework of the profession in question in the Member State of origin and to its field of activity. In the case of the profession of lawyer, a Member State may therefore carry out a comparative examination of diplomas, taking account of the differences identified between the national legal systems concerned.

The Court concluded:

[23] Consequently, the answer to the question submitted by the Bundesgerichtshof must be that Article 52 of the EEC Treaty must be interpreted as requiring the national authorities of a Member State to which an application for admission to the profession of lawyer is made by a Community subject who is already admitted to practise as a lawyer in his country of origin and who practises as a legal adviser in the first-mentioned Member State to examine to what extent the knowledge and qualifications attested by the diploma obtained by the person concerned in his country of origin correspond to those required by the rules of the host State; if those diplomas correspond only partially, the national authorities in question are entitled to require the person concerned to prove that he has acquired the knowledge and qualifications which are lacking.

NOTE

This approach was confirmed by the Court in *Gebhard* (Case C-55/94, p.321 above) where explicit reference was made to paras 15 and 16 of the ruling in *Vlassopoulou*. *Vlassopoulou* is also cited in para 21 of *Commission* v *Spain* (Case C-232/99 judgment of 16 May 2002). In its Twelfth Annual Report on monitoring the application of Community law, the Commission notes that the Dutch *Raad van State* has applied the principle illustrated by the ruling in *Vlassopoulou*, although the Court's conclusion was that the relevant Dutch minister had acted properly in withholding recognition of an East German qualification after making comparisons between that qualification and Dutch requirements ([1995] OJ C254/166–7).

Several of the cases in this Chapter display the determination of commercial operators to exploit the freedoms found in Articles 43 and 49 of the EC Treaty to establish themselves or to provide services in another State. Typically such parties are anxious to rely on EC law to preclude the host State insisting on conformity with part or all of its regulatory requirements as a pre-condition of market access. Reducing costs by relying on EC law to evade those burdens is commercially attractive and should intensify consumer-friendly competition. As seen above, the Court has developed a formula, inspired by *Cassis de Dijon*, designed to weigh the balance between trade integration and local regulatory concerns. Consider also *Stichting Collectieve Antennevoorziening Gouda* v *Commissariaat voor de Media* (Case C-288/89) [1991] ECR I-4007 (which examines the extent to which cultural policy may constitute a requirement in the general interest justifying a restriction on the freedom to provide services); *Säger* v *Dennemeyer & Co. Ltd* (Case C-76/90) [1991]

ECR I-4221; *Customs and Excise Commissioners* v *Schindler and Schindler* (Case C-275/92) [1994] ECR I-1039 (in which UK controls over lotteries were ruled capable of justification based on social and cultural considerations – prior to the National Lottery Act 1993!); *Markku Juhani Läärä, Cotswold Microsystems Ltd, Oy Transatlantic Software Ltd* (Case C-124/97) [1999] ECR I-6067 (which concerns Finnish rules reserving to a public body the right to run the operation of slot machines). For an overview see S. O'Leary, 'The Free Movement of Persons and Services', in P. Craig and G. de Búrca, *The Evolution of EU Law* (1999); V. Hatzopoulous, 'Recent developments of the case law of the ECJ in the field of services' (2000) 37 CML Rev 43. The Commission itself published an interpretative communication on this area of law at [1993] OJ C334/3 (*cf* pp.364, 410 and 453 above on the role of such communications).

Although there is a strong, deregulatory impulse in this case law, the Court insists that 'the fact that one Member State imposes less strict rules than another Member State does not mean that the latter's rules are disproportionate and hence incompatible with Community law' (e.g., Case C-3/95 *Reiseburo Broede* v *Gerd Sanker* [1996] ECR I-6511; Case C-124/97, mentioned in the previous paragraph). This conforms to the pattern under Articles 28–30 (p.409). Respect for national regulatory choices is also visible in the next case, in which the Court found itself asked to deal with the question of the permissibility of national measures of market regulation which impede cross-border provision of services in a rather different context.

Alpine Investments BV v *Minister van Financiën* (Case C-384/93)
[1995] ECR I 1141, Court of Justice of the European Communities

Alpine Investments, a provider of financial services, was prevented by Dutch rules from contacting potential customers by telephone without their prior written consent. This ban on 'cold calling' extended to offers made to individuals both inside and outside The Netherlands. The Court ruled that the matter fell within Article 59 of the EC Treaty (now, after amendment, Article 49 EC) by observing that the restriction impeded offers made by a provider in one Member State to a potential recipient established outside that State. But the restriction applied to all Dutch providers, irrespective of the location of their target clients. The UK and Dutch Governments argued by analogy with *Keck* (Cases C-267 and 268/91, p.397 above) that the rule should be regarded as falling outside the scope of the Treaty rules governing free movement. The Court commented that the ban 'deprives the operators concerned of a rapid and direct technique for marketing and for contacting potential clients in other Member States'. It then stated of the challenged Dutch rules that:

[36] Such a prohibition is not analogous to the legislation concerning selling arrangements held in *Keck and Mithouard* to fall outside the scope of Article 30 of the Treaty.

[37] According to that judgment, the application to products from other Member States of national provisions restricting or prohibiting, within the Member State of importation, certain selling arrangements is not such as to hinder trade between Member States so long as, first, those provisions apply to all relevant traders operating within the national territory and, secondly, they affect in the same manner, in law and in fact, the marketing of domestic products and of those from other Member States. The reason is that the application of such provisions is not such as to prevent

access by the latter to the market of the Member State of importation or to impede such access more than it impedes access by domestic products.

[38] A prohibition such as that at issue is imposed by the Member State in which the provider of services is established and affects not only offers made by him to addressees who are established in that State or move there in order to receive services but also offers made to potential recipients in another Member State. It therefore directly affects access to the market in services in the other Member States and is thus capable of hindering intra-Community trade in services.

NOTE

The reader should consider whether this finding sheds any light on the unclear limits to the scope of EC trade law discussed in connection with *Keck* at p.399 above. Is this approach peculiar to cases involving 'export'? (For a recent survey of the case law and literature see C. Barnard, 'Fitting the remaining pieces into the goods and persons jigsaw' (2001) 26 EL Rev 35.) The Court's treatment of Swedish restrictions on advertising in *Konsumentombudsmannen* v *De Agostini and TV Shop* (Joined Cases C-34/95, C-35/95, and C-36/95) was considered in the light of Article 28 at p.404 above. For the purposes of Article 49, the Court observed that a restriction on freedom to provide services was imposed where an undertaking established in the broadcasting State was impeded in broadcasting advertisements directed at the public in the receiving State on behalf of advertisers established in that State. It was for the national court to determine whether such trade restrictions were justified (against standards plainly inspired by *Cassis de Dijon*). Articles 28 and 49 appear to have been handled differently by the Court in this decision, although it is notable that the Court focused on the position of the advertiser in its discussion of Article 28, but on that of the broadcaster in approaching Article 49 (for comment see J. Stuyck (1997) 34 CML Rev 1445).

The finding that the measure in *Alpine Investments* hindered intra-Community trade such as to trigger the application of Article 59 of the EC Treaty (now, after amendment, Article 49 EC) then required the Court to examine the justifications advanced in support of the Dutch intervention in the market. The Court was invited to assess various methods of available regulatory techniques in determining whether the Dutch choice was permissible under Community law.

Alpine Investments BV v *Minister van Financiën* (Case C-384/93)
[1995] ECR I-1141, Court of Justice of the European Communities

[40] The national court's third question asks whether imperative reasons of public interest justify the prohibition of cold calling and whether that prohibition must be considered to be objectively necessary and proportionate to the objective pursued.

[41] The Netherlands Government argues that the prohibition of cold calling in off-market commodities futures trading seeks both to safeguard the reputation of the Netherlands financial markets and to protect the investing public.

[42] Financial markets play an important role in the financing of economic operators and, given the speculative nature and the complexity of commodities futures contracts, the smooth operation of financial markets is largely contingent on the confidence they inspire in investors. That confidence depends in particular on the existence of professional regulations serving to ensure the competence and trustworthiness of the financial intermediaries on whom investors are particularly reliant.

[43] Although the protection of consumers in the other Member States is not, as such, a matter for the Netherlands authorities, the nature and extent of that protection does none the less have a direct effect on the good reputation of Netherlands financial services.

[44] Maintaining the good reputation of the national financial sector may therefore constitute an imperative reason of public interest capable of justifying restrictions on the freedom to provide financial services.

[45] As for the proportionality of the restriction at issue, it is settled case-law that requirements imposed on the providers of services must be appropriate to ensure achievement of the intended

aim and must not go beyond that which is necessary in order to achieve that objective (see Case C-288/89 *Collectieve Antennevoorziening Gouda and Others* v *Commissariaat voor de Media* [1991] ECR I-4007, paragraph 15).

[46] As the Netherlands Government has justifiably submitted, in the case of cold calling the individual, generally caught unawares, is in a position neither to ascertain the risks inherent in the type of transactions offered to him nor to compare the quality and price of the caller's services with competitors' offers. Since the commodities futures market is highly speculative and barely comprehensible for non-expert investors, it was necessary to protect them from the most aggressive selling techniques.

[47] Alpine Investments argues however that the Netherlands Government's prohibition of cold calling is not necessary because the Member State of the provider of services should rely on the controls imposed by the Member State of the recipient.

[48] That argument must be rejected. The Member State from which the telephone call is made is best placed to regulate cold calling. Even if the receiving State wishes to prohibit cold calling or to make it subject to certain conditions, it is not in a position to prevent or control telephone calls from another Member State without the cooperation of the competent authorities of that State.

[49] Consequently, the prohibition of cold calling by the Member State from which the telephone call is made, with a view to protecting investor confidence in the financial markets of that State, cannot be considered to be inappropriate to achieve the objective of securing the integrity of those markets.

[50] Alpine Investments also argues that a general prohibition of telephone canvassing of potential clients is not necessary for the achievement of the objectives pursued by the Netherlands authorities. Requiring broking firms to tape-record unsolicited telephone calls made by them would suffice to protect consumers effectively. Such rules have moreover been adopted in the United Kingdom by the Securities and Futures Authority.

[51] That point of view cannot be accepted. As the Advocate-General correctly states in point 88 of his Opinion, the fact that one Member State imposes less strict rules than another Member State does not mean that the latter's rules are disproportionate and hence incompatible with Community law.

[52] Alpine Investments argues finally that, since it is of a general nature, the prohibition of cold calling does not take into account the conduct of individual undertakings and accordingly imposes an unnecessary burden on undertakings which have never been the subject of complaints by consumers.

[53] That argument must also be rejected. Limiting the prohibition of cold calling to certain undertakings because of their past conduct might not be sufficient to achieve the objective of restoring and maintaining investor confidence in the national securities markets in general.

[54] In any event, the rules at issue are limited in scope. First, they prohibit only the contacting of potential clients by telephone or in person without their prior agreement in writing, while other techniques for making contact are still permitted. Next, the measure affects relations with potential clients but not with existing clients who may still give their written agreement to further calls. Finally, the prohibition of unsolicited telephone calls is limited to the sector in which abuses have been found, namely the commodities futures market.

[55] In the light of the above, the prohibition of cold calling does not appear disproportionate to the objective which it pursues.

[56] The answer to the third question is therefore that Article 59 does not preclude national rules which, in order to protect investor confidence in national financial markets, prohibit the practice of making unsolicited telephone calls to potential clients resident in other Member States to offer them services linked to investment in commodities futures.

NOTE

Telephone selling reflects and advances market integration; it is a medium which renders physical borders irrelevant. At paras 47–49 in its ruling in *Alpine Investments*, the Court shows a shrewd awareness of the limits placed on 'destination State control' in such circumstances. Compare the discussion of problems of enforcing laws that differ from those of other Member States which emerge in an integrating market at p.371 above.

■ QUESTIONS

1. Is there an irreconcilability between the Court's acceptance at para 48 that home State control of technologically advanced marketing practices is more effective than destination State control and its comment at para 43 that protection of consumers in other States is not as such a matter for the Dutch authorities? Do you agree that The Netherlands should not be able to export its high standards of consumer protection other than indirectly, as part of a method for securing the high reputation of its own financial services sector (paras 43, 44)?

2. How can the Dutch consumer 'cold-called' from outside The Netherlands be protected? Does this case suggest a need for Community-wide harmonization, or does it display an acceptable level of regulatory diversity within the common market?

....

B: **Cases dealing with company law**

These Treaty provisions have been eagerly exploited by commercial operators seeking advantages in cross-border mobility. This theme is prominent in the next case. It involves a company formed in accordance with the law of one Member State wishing to open a branch in another Member State. This is covered by the right granted by Article 43 EC. But the company was not commercially active in the State in which it was formed. It planned to be active in the State in which its branch was to be located.

Centros Ltd v *Erhervs- og Selskabhysstyrelsen* (Case C-212/97)
[1999] ECR I-1459, Court of Justice of the European Communities

Centros Ltd was a private limited company registered in the UK in accordance with English law. Its shares were held by Mr and Mrs Bryde, who were Danish nationals. Centros did not trade in the UK. It planned to trade in Denmark. Its application to register a branch in Denmark was refused by the other party to the proceedings, the Danish Trade and Companies Board, on the ground that Centros was in fact attempting to establish not a branch but a principal establishment in Denmark, which would have involved subjection to Danish regulatory requirements, including the paying-up of minimum share capital, which were far more onerous than those demanded under English law. Centros was, in short, a consumer of competition between (State) regulators (p.322 above); but could it rely on EC law to entitle it to act in this way? A preliminary reference seeking an interpretation of Articles 52, 56, and 58 of the EC Treaty (now, after amendment, Articles 43, 46, and 48 EC) was made by a Danish court before which Centros's challenge had been pursued. The European Court treated the refusal to register the branch as an obstacle to the exercise of the freedom of establishment.

[23] According to the Danish authorities, however, Mr and Mrs Bryde cannot rely on those provisions, since the sole purpose of the company formation which they have in mind is to circumvent the application of the national law governing formation of private limited companies and therefore constitutes abuse of the freedom of establishment. In their submission, the Kingdom of Denmark is therefore entitled to take steps to prevent such abuse by refusing to register the branch.

[24] It is true that according to the case-law of the Court a Member State is entitled to take measures designed to prevent certain of its nationals from attempting, under cover of the rights created by the Treaty, improperly to circumvent their national legislation or to prevent individuals from improperly or fraudulently taking advantage of provisions of Community law (see, in particular, regarding freedom to supply services, Case 33/74 *Van Binsbergen* v *Bedrijfsvereniging Metaalnijverheid* [1974] ECR 1299, paragraph 13, Case C-148/91 *Veronica Omroep Organisatie* v *Commissariaat voor de Media* [1993] ECR I-487, paragraph 12, and Case C-23/93 *TV 10* v *Commissariaat voor de Media* [1994] ECR I-4795, paragraph 21; regarding freedom of establishment, Case 115/78 *Knoors* [1979] ECR 399, paragraph 25, and Case C-61/89 *Bouchoucha* [1990] ECR I-3551, paragraph 14; regarding the free movement of goods, Case 229/83 *Leclerc and Others* v *'Au Blé Vert' and Others* [1985] ECR 1, paragraph 27; regarding social security, Case C-206/94 *Brennet* v *Paletta* [1996] ECR I-2357, *'Paletta II'*, paragraph 24; regarding freedom of movement for workers, Case 39/86 *Lair* v *Universität Hannover* [1988] ECR 3161, paragraph 43; regarding the common agricultural policy, Case C-8/92 *General Milk Products* v *Hauptzollamt Hamburg-Jonas* [1993] ECR I-779, paragraph 21, and regarding company law, Case C-367/96 *Kefalas and Others* v *Greece* [1998] ECR I-2843, paragraph 20).

[25] However, although, in such circumstances, the national courts may, case by case, take account – on the basis of objective evidence – of abuse or fraudulent conduct on the part of the persons concerned in order, where appropriate, to deny them the benefit of the provisions of Community law on which they seek to rely, they must nevertheless assess such conduct in the light of the objectives pursued by those provisions (*Paletta II*, paragraph 25).

[26] In the present case, the provisions of national law, application of which the parties concerned have sought to avoid, are rules governing the formation of companies and not rules concerning the carrying on of certain trades, professions or businesses. The provisions of the Treaty on freedom of establishment are intended specifically to enable companies formed in accordance with the law of a Member State and having their registered office, central administration or principal place of business within the Community to pursue activities in other Member States through an agency, branch or subsidiary.

[27] That being so, the fact that a national of a Member State who wishes to set up a company chooses to form it in the Member State whose rules of company law seem to him the least restrictive and to set up branches in other Member States cannot, in itself, constitute an abuse of the right of establishment. The right to form a company in accordance with the law of a Member State and to set up branches in other Member States is inherent in the exercise, in a single market, of the freedom of establishment guaranteed by the Treaty.

[28] In this connection, the fact that company law is not completely harmonised in the Community is of little consequence. Moreover, it is always open to the Council, on the basis of the powers conferred upon it by Article 54(3)(g) of the EC Treaty, to achieve complete harmonisation.

[29] In addition, it is clear from paragraph 16 of *Segers* [Case 79/85 [1986] ECR 2375] that the fact that a company does not conduct any business in the Member State in which it has its registered office and pursues its activities only in the Member State where its branch is established is not sufficient to prove the existence of abuse or fraudulent conduct which would entitle the latter Member State to deny that company the benefit of the provisions of Community law relating to the right of establishment.

[30] Accordingly, the refusal of a Member State to register a branch of a company formed in accordance with the law of another Member State in which it has its registered office on the grounds that the branch is intended to enable the company to carry on all its economic activity in the host

State, with the result that the secondary establishment escapes national rules on the provision for and the paying-up of a minimum capital, is incompatible with Articles 52 and 58 of the Treaty, in so far as it prevents any exercise of the right freely to set up a secondary establishment which Articles 52 and 58 are specifically intended to guarantee.

[31] The final question to be considered is whether the national practice in question might not be justified for the reasons put forward by the Danish authorities.

[32] Referring both to Article 56 of the Treaty and to the case-law of the Court on imperative requirements in the general interest, the Board argues that the requirement that private limited companies provide for and pay up a minimum share capital pursues a dual objective: first, to reinforce the financial soundness of those companies in order to protect public creditors against the risk of seeing the public debts owing to them become irrecoverable since, unlike private creditors, they cannot secure those debts by means of guarantees and, second, and more generally, to protect all creditors, whether public or private, by anticipating the risk of fraudulent bankruptcy due to the insolvency of companies whose initial capitalisation was inadequate.

[33] The Board adds that there is no less restrictive means of attaining this dual objective. The other way of protecting creditors, namely by introducing rules making it possible for shareholders to incur personal liability, under certain conditions, would be more restrictive than the requirement to provide for and pay up a minimum share capital.

[34] It should be observed, first, that the reasons put forward do not fall within the ambit of Article 56 of the Treaty. Next, it should be borne in mind that, according to the Court's case-law, national measures liable to hinder or make less attractive the exercise of fundamental freedoms guaranteed by the Treaty must fulfil four conditions: they must be applied in a non-discriminatory manner; they must be justified by imperative requirements in the general interest; they must be suitable for securing the attainment of the objective which they pursue; and they must not go beyond what is necessary in order to attain it (see Case C-19/92 *Kraus* v *Land Baden-Württemberg* [1993] ECR I-1663, paragraph 32, and Case C-55/94 *Gebhard* v *Consiglio dell'Ordine degli Avvocati e Procuratori di Milano* [1995] ECR I-4165, paragraph 37).

[35] Those conditions are not fulfilled in the case in the main proceedings. First, the practice in question is not such as to attain the objective of protecting creditors which it purports to pursue since, if the company concerned had conducted business in the United Kingdom, its branch would have been registered in Denmark, even though Danish creditors might have been equally exposed to risk.

[36] Since the company concerned in the main proceedings holds itself out as a company governed by the law of England and Wales and not as a company governed by Danish law, its creditors are on notice that it is covered by laws different from those which govern the formation of private limited companies in Denmark and they can refer to certain rules of Community law which protect them, such as the Fourth Council Directive 78/660/EEC of 25 July 1978 based on Article 54(3)(g) of the Treaty on the annual accounts of certain types of companies (OJ 1978 L 222, p.11), and the Eleventh Council Directive 89/666/EEC of 21 December 1989 concerning disclosure requirements in respect of branches opened in a Member State by certain types of company governed by the law of another State (OJ 1989 L 395, p.36).

[37] Second, contrary to the arguments of the Danish authorities, it is possible to adopt measures which are less restrictive, or which interfere less with fundamental freedoms, by, for example, making it possible in law for public creditors to obtain the necessary guarantees.

[38] Lastly, the fact that a Member State may not refuse to register a branch of a company formed in accordance with the law of another Member State in which it has its registered office does not preclude that first State from adopting any appropriate measure for preventing or penalising fraud, either in relation to the company itself, if need be in cooperation with the Member State in which it was formed, or in relation to its members, where it has been established that they are in fact attempting, by means of the formation of the company, to evade their obligations towards private or public creditors established on the territory of a Member State concerned. In any event, combating

fraud cannot justify a practice of refusing to register a branch of a company which has its registered office in another Member State.

[39] The answer to the question referred must therefore be that it is contrary to Articles 52 and 58 of the Treaty for a Member State to refuse to register a branch of a company formed in accordance with the law of another Member State in which it has its registered office but in which it conducts no business where the branch is intended to enable the company in question to carry on its entire business in the State in which that branch is to be created, while avoiding the need to form a company there, thus evading application of the rules governing the formation of companies which, in that State, are more restrictive as regards the paying up of a minimum share capital. That interpretation does not, however, prevent the authorities of the Member State concerned from adopting any appropriate measure for preventing or penalising fraud, either in relation to the company itself, if need be in cooperation with the Member State in which it was formed, or in relation to its members, where it has been established that they are in fact attempting, by means of the formation of a company, to evade their obligations towards private or public creditors established in the territory of the Member State concerned.

NOTE

This ruling does not set aside the ability of Member States to exercise supervision over companies active on their territory in pursuit of economic freedoms guaranteed by the EC Treaty. Paragraph 34 is familiar territory to the student of EC trade law (cf p. 321 above). However, the ruling confines the scope of permissible public control in cases of strategic choices about company formation. Moreover, it offers possibilities for future exploitation of patterns of interstate regulatory competition by firms seeking what the judgment refers to as the 'least restrictive' regime (para 27). More litigation in these realms may be expected (see prognosis by W.-H. Roth (2000) 37 CML Rev 147; P. Calral and P. Cunha (2000) 25 EL Rev 157; C. Loostijn-Clearie (2000) 49 ICLQ 621). The next case is not on precisely the same point as *Centros*, but it adds to the stock of EC case law to which national company law must adjust.

Überseering BV v *Nordic Construction Company Baumanagement GmbH (NCC)* (C-208/00)

Judgment of 5 November 2002, Court of Justice of the European Communities

For the purposes of the preliminary reference, German company law was treated as providing that a company's legal capacity is determined by reference to the law applicable in the place where its actual centre of administration is established ('Sitztheorie' or company seat principle), as opposed to the 'Gründungstheorie' or incorporation principle, by virtue of which legal capacity is determined in accordance with the law of the State in which the company is incorporated. Überseering was a company incorporated under Dutch law that had transferred its actual centre of administration to Germany once its shares had been acquired by two German nationals. So before German courts Überseering, as a Dutch company administered in Germany, was treated as lacking legal capacity. The question was whether this violated Article 43 EC. The German rules had the effect of requiring Überseering to reincorporate in Germany in order to sue. This was 'tantamount to outright negation of freedom of establishment' (para 81). Nor could the rules be justified:

[91] The Netherlands and United Kingdom Governments, the Commission and the EFTA Surveillance Authority submit that the restriction in question is not justified. They point out in particular that the aim of protecting creditors was also invoked by the Danish authorities in *Centros* to justify the refusal to register in Denmark a branch of a company which had been validly incorporated in the United Kingdom and all of whose business was to be carried on in Denmark but which did not meet the requirements of Danish law regarding the provision and paying-up of a minimum amount of share

capital. They add that it is not certain that requirements associated with a minimum amount of share capital are an effective way of protecting creditors.

[92] It is not inconceivable that overriding requirements relating to the general interest, such as the protection of the interests of creditors, minority shareholders, employees and even the taxation authorities, may, in certain circumstances and subject to certain conditions, justify restrictions on freedom of establishment.

[93] Such objectives cannot, however, justify denying the legal capacity and, consequently, the capacity to be a party to legal proceedings of a company properly incorporated in another Member State in which it has its registered office. Such a measure is tantamount to an outright negation of the freedom of establishment conferred on companies by Articles 43 EC and 48 EC.

[94] Accordingly, the answer to the first question must be that, where a company formed in accordance with the law of a Member State ('A') in which it has its registered office is deemed, under the law of another Member State ('B'), to have moved its actual centre of administration to Member State B, Articles 43 EC and 48 EC preclude Member State B from denying the company legal capacity and, consequently, the capacity to bring legal proceedings before its national courts for the purpose of enforcing rights under a contract with a company established in Member State B.

NOTE

For analysis see W.-H. Roth, 'From *Centros* to *Uberseering*: Free Movement of Companies, Private International Law, and Community Law' (2003) 52 ICLQ 177.

C: **Cases dealing with particularly sensitive State choices**

The cases considered above brought the law of market integration into collision with technical national rules of market regulation. Much broader and, arguably, more important national interests may clash with the integrative process. The next case considers the extent to which the provision of health care services may be subjected to market competition. The potential impact on national welfare provision as an element in securing social cohesion makes this litigation unavoidably sensitive. The Court is not deterred. It sanctions a form of inter-State competition in the provision of medical care, and it also takes the opportunity to demonstrate its awareness that the effective application of the Community rules is heavily dependent on ensuring that national decisions are taken on a transparent basis.

B.S.M. Geraets-Smits v *Stichting Ziekenfonds VGZ, H.T.M. Peerbooms* v *Stichting CZ Groep Zorgverzekeringen* (Case C-157/99)
[2001] ECR I-5473, Court of Justice of the European Communities

Mrs Geraets-Smits, a Dutch national, suffered from Parkinson's disease. She had been treated in Germany and sought reimbursement of the costs of care from the Dutch sickness insurance scheme. Mr Peerbooms had fallen into a coma following a road accident. He was taken to hospital in The Netherlands and then transferred in a vegetative state to a Clinic in Innsbruck in Austria. His neurologist sought payment of the costs of treatment from the Dutch scheme (ZFW). Both applications were rejected, for reasons explained in the Court's summary of the questions referred to it by a Dutch court under Article 234 EC (Chapter 7).

[43] By its two questions, which fall to be dealt with together, the national court is asking essentially whether Articles 59 and 60 of the Treaty are to be interpreted as precluding legislation of a Member State, such as the legislation at issue in the main proceedings, which makes the assumption of the costs of care provided in a hospital establishment in another Member State conditional upon prior authorisation by the sickness insurance fund with which the insured person is registered, that authorisation being granted only in so far as the following two conditions are satisfied. First, the proposed treatment must be among the benefits for which the sickness insurance scheme of the first Member State assumes responsibility, which means that the treatment must be regarded as 'normal in the professional circles concerned'. Second, the treatment abroad must be necessary in terms of the medical condition of the person concerned, which supposes that adequate care cannot be provided without undue delay by a care provider which has entered into an agreement with a sickness insurance fund in the first Member State.

The Court first addressed the question of the competence of the EC to intrude on national social security systems. It offered a classic statement of the 'spillover' effect of trade law.

[44] . . . it should be remembered at the outset that, according to settled case-law, Community law does not detract from the power of the Member States to organise their social security systems (Case 238/82 *Duphar and Others* [1984] ECR 523, paragraph 16, Case C-70/95 *Sodemare and Others* [1997] ECR I-3395, paragraph 27, and Case C-158/96 *Kohll* [1998] ECR I-1931, paragraph 17).

[45] In the absence of harmonisation at Community level, it is therefore for the legislation of each Member State to determine, first, the conditions concerning the right or duty to be insured with a social security scheme (. . .*Kohll*, paragraph 18) and, second, the conditions for entitlement to benefits (. . .*Kohll*, paragraph 18).

[46] Nevertheless, the Member States must comply with Community law when exercising that power.

So the absence of a general Community legislative competence in the field of social security (Chapter 2) did not preclude *national* social security rules falling within the scope of application of the law of free movement. The next objection faced by the Court was that Article 50 (ex 60) EC provides that services are subject to the Treaty rules 'where they are normally provided for remuneration'. Does this cover hospital services where the patient receives care without having to pay for it where all or part of the cost is reimbursed?

[55] With regard more particularly to the argument that hospital services provided in the context of a sickness insurance scheme providing benefits in kind, such as that governed by the ZFW, should not be classified as services within the meaning of Article 60 of the Treaty, it should be noted that, far from falling under such a scheme, the medical treatment at issue in the main proceedings, which was provided in Member States other than those in which the persons concerned were insured, did lead to the establishments providing the treatment being paid directly by the patients. It must be accepted that a medical service provided in one Member State and paid for by the patient should not cease to fall within the scope of the freedom to provide services guaranteed by the Treaty merely because reimbursement of the costs of the treatment involved is applied for under another Member State's sickness insurance legislation which is essentially of the type which provides for benefits in kind.

[56] Furthermore, the fact that hospital medical treatment is financed directly by the sickness insurance funds on the basis of agreements and pre-set scales of fees is not in any event such as to remove such treatment from the sphere of services within the meaning of Article 60 of the Treaty.

[57] First, it should be borne in mind that Article 60 of the Treaty does not require that the service be paid for by those for whom it is performed (Case 352/85 *Bond van Adverteerders and Others*

[1988] ECR 2085, paragraph 16, and Joined Cases C-51/96 and C-191/97 *Deliège* [2000] ECR I-2549, paragraph 56).

[58] Second, Article 60 of the Treaty states that it applies to services normally provided for remuneration and it has been held that, for the purposes of that provision, the essential characteristic of remuneration lies in the fact that it constitutes consideration for the service in question (*Humbel*, paragraph 17). In the present cases, the payments made by the sickness insurance funds under the contractual arrangements provided for by the ZFW, albeit set at a flat rate, are indeed the consideration for the hospital services and unquestionably represent remuneration for the hospital which receives them and which is engaged in an activity of an economic character.

The Court turned to consider whether there was a restriction on freedom to provide services where the costs of treatment provided in a hospital in another Member State was reimbursed by the local sickness insurance scheme provided that the insured person complied with rules laid down by the Dutch scheme.

[61] According to settled case-law, Article 59 of the Treaty precludes the application of any national rules which have the effect of making the provision of services between Member States more difficult than the provision of services purely within one Member State (Case C-381/93 *Commission* v *France* [1994] ECR I-5145, paragraph 17, and *Kohll*, paragraph 33).

[62] In the present case, while the ZFW does not deprive insured persons of the possibility of using a provider of services established in another Member State, it does nevertheless make reimbursement of the costs incurred in another Member State subject to prior authorisation and provides for such reimbursement to be refused where the two requirements referred to in paragraph 60 above are not satisfied.

[63] As regards the first of those requirements, namely that the proposed treatment must be treatment covered by the ZFW, in other words treatment which can be regarded as 'normal in the professional circles concerned', it is sufficient to point out that by its very essence such a condition is liable to lead to refusals of authorisation. It is only the precise frequency with which authorisation is refused, not refusal itself, that will be determined by the interpretation of 'normal' treatment and 'the professional circles concerned'.

[64] As regards the second requirement, namely that provision of hospital treatment in another Member State must be a medical necessity, which will be the case only if adequate treatment cannot be obtained without undue delay in contracted hospitals in the Member State in which the person seeking treatment is insured, this requirement by its very nature will severely limit the circumstances in which such authorisation can be obtained.

Were the rules justified? This drew the Court into assessment of the nature and purpose of a State's social security system.

[71] In that regard, it is first necessary to determine whether there are overriding reasons which can be accepted as justifying barriers to freedom to provide medical services supplied in the context of a hospital infrastructure, then to determine whether the prior authorisation principle is justifiable in the light of such overriding needs and last to consider whether the conditions governing the grant of prior authorisation can themselves be justified.

Overriding considerations which may be relied on to justify barriers to the exercise of freedom to provide services in the sphere of hospital treatment

[72] As all the governments which have submitted observations to the Court have pointed out, the Court has held that it cannot be excluded that the possible risk of seriously undermining a social security system's financial balance may constitute an overriding reason in the general interest capable of justifying a barrier to the principle of freedom to provide services (*Kohll*, paragraph 41).

[73] The Court has likewise recognised that, as regards the objective of maintaining a balanced medical and hospital service open to all, that objective, even if intrinsically linked to the method of

financing the social security system, may also fall within the derogations on grounds of public health under Article 56 of the EC Treaty (now, after amendment, Article 46 EC), in so far as it contributes to the attainment of a high level of health protection (*Kohll*, paragraph 50).

[74] The Court has further held that Article 56 of the Treaty permits Member States to restrict the freedom to provide medical and hospital services in so far as the maintenance of treatment capacity or medical competence on national territory is essential for the public health, and even the survival of, the population (*Kohll*, paragraph 51).

[75] It is therefore necessary to determine whether the national rules at issue in the main proceedings can actually be justified in the light of such overriding reasons and, in such a case, in accordance with settled case-law, to make sure that they do not exceed what is objectively necessary for that purpose and that the same result cannot be achieved by less restrictive rules (Case 205/84 *Commission* v *Germany* [1986] ECR 3755, paragraphs 27 and 29; Case C-180/89 *Commission* v *Italy* [1991] ECR I-709, paragraphs 17 and 18; and Case C-106/91 *Ramrath* [1992] ECR I-3351, paragraphs 30 and 31).

The prior authorisation requirement

[76] As regards the prior authorisation requirement to which the ZFW subjects the assumption of the costs of treatment provided in another Member State by a non-contracted care provider, the Court accepts, as all the governments which have submitted observations have argued, that, by comparison with medical services provided by practitioners in their surgeries or at the patient's home, medical services provided in a hospital take place within an infrastructure with, undoubtedly, certain very distinct characteristics. It is thus well known that the number of hospitals, their geographical distribution, the mode of their organisation and the equipment with which they are provided, and even the nature of the medical services which they are able to offer, are all matters for which planning must be possible.

[77] As may be seen, in particular, from the contracting system involved in the main proceedings, this kind of planning therefore broadly meets a variety of concerns.

[78] For one thing, it seeks to achieve the aim of ensuring that there is sufficient and permanent access to a balanced range of high-quality hospital treatment in the State concerned.

[79] For another thing, it assists in meeting a desire to control costs and to prevent, as far as possible, any wastage of financial, technical and human resources. Such wastage is all the more damaging because it is generally recognised that the hospital care sector generates considerable costs and must satisfy increasing needs, while the financial resources which may be made available for health care are not unlimited, whatever the mode of funding applied.

[80] From both those perspectives, a requirement that the assumption of costs, under a national social security system, of hospital treatment provided in another Member State must be subject to prior authorisation appears to be a measure which is both necessary and reasonable.

[81] Looking at the system set up by the ZFW, it is clear that, if insured persons were at liberty, regardless of the circumstances, to use the services of hospitals with which their sickness insurance fund had no contractual arrangements, whether they were situated in the Netherlands or in another Member State, all the planning which goes into the contractual system in an effort to guarantee a rationalised, stable, balanced and accessible supply of hospital services would be jeopardised at a stroke.

[82] Although, for the considerations set out above, Community law does not in principle preclude a system of prior authorisation, the conditions attached to the grant of such authorisation must none the less be justified with regard to the overriding considerations examined and must satisfy the requirement of proportionality referred to in paragraph 75 above.

A prior authorization system may be justified. But was this one? The Court had already conceded that it is for the legislation of each Member State to organize its national social security system, which includes a competence to fix limits on entitlement to benefits and access to medical treatment paid for by the social security scheme (paras 44–46 above). Equally Community trade law cannot be disregarded.

[90] It likewise follows from settled case-law that a scheme of prior authorisation cannot legitimise discretionary decisions taken by the national authorities which are liable to negate the effectiveness of provisions of Community law, in particular those relating to a fundamental freedom such as that at issue in the main proceedings (see, to that effect, Joined Cases C-358/93 and C-416/93 *Bordessa and Others* [1995] ECR I-361, paragraph 25; Joined Cases C-163/94, C-165/94 and C-250/94 *Sanz de Lera and Others* [1995] ECR I-4821, paragraphs 23 to 28, and Case C-205/99 *Analir and Others* [2001] ECR I-1271, paragraph 37). Therefore, in order for a prior administrative authorisation scheme to be justified even though it derogates from such a fundamental freedom, it must, in any event, be based on objective, non-discriminatory criteria which are known in advance, in such a way as to circumscribe the exercise of the national authorities' discretion, so that it is not used arbitrarily (*Analir and Others*, paragraph 38). Such a prior administrative authorisation scheme must likewise be based on a procedural system which is easily accessible and capable of ensuring that a request for authorisation will be dealt with objectively and impartially within a reasonable time and refusals to grant authorisation must also be capable of being challenged in judicial or quasi-judicial proceedings.

After examining the Dutch scheme the Court observed that:

[95] It follows from the those requirements that the institution of a system such as that at issue in the main proceedings, under which the authorisation decision needed to undergo hospital treatment in another Member State is entrusted to the sickness insurance funds, means that the criteria which those funds must apply in reaching that decision must be objective and independent where the providers of treatment are established.

[96] To allow only treatment habitually carried out on national territory and scientific views prevailing in national medical circles to determine what is or is not normal will not offer those guarantees and will make it likely that Netherlands providers of treatment will always be preferred in practice.

[97] If, on the other hand, the condition that treatment must be regarded as 'normal' is extended in such a way that, where treatment is sufficiently tried and tested by international medical science, the authorisation sought under the ZFW cannot be refused on that ground, such a condition, which is objective and applies without distinction to treatment provided in the Netherlands and to treatment provided abroad, is justifiable in view of the need to maintain an adequate, balanced and permanent supply of hospital care on national territory and to ensure the financial stability of the sickness insurance system, so that the restriction of the freedom to provide services of hospitals situated in other Member States which might result from the application of that condition does not infringe Article 59 of the Treaty.

[98] Further, where, as in the present case, a Member State decides that medical or hospital treatment must be sufficiently tried and tested before its cost will be assumed under its social security system, the national authorities called on to decide, for authorisation purposes, whether hospital treatment provided in another Member States satisfies that criterion must take into consideration all the relevant available information, including, in particular, existing scientific literature and studies, the authorised opinions of specialists and the fact that the proposed treatment is covered or not covered by the sickness insurance system of the Member State in which the treatment is provided.

. . .

The condition concerning the necessity of the proposed treatment

[103] In view of what is stated in paragraph 90 above, it can be concluded that the condition concerning the necessity of the treatment, laid down by the rules at issue in the main proceedings,

can be justified under Article 59 of the Treaty, provided that the condition is construed to the effect that authorisation to receive treatment in another Member State may be refused on that ground only if the same or equally effective treatment can be obtained without undue delay from an establishment with which the insured person's sickness insurance fund has contractual arrangements.

[104] Furthermore, in order to determine whether equally effective treatment can be obtained without undue delay from an establishment having contractual arrangements with the insured person's fund, the national authorities are required to have regard to all the circumstances of each specific case and to take due account not only of the patient's medical condition at the time when authorisation is sought but also of his past record.

[105] Such a condition can allow an adequate, balanced and permanent supply of high-quality hospital treatment to be maintained on the national territory and the financial stability of the sickness insurance system to be assured.

The Court concluded:

[108] In view of all the foregoing considerations, the answer to be given to the national court must be that Articles 59 and 60 of the Treaty do not preclude legislation of a Member State, such as that at issue in the main proceedings, which makes the assumption of the costs of treatment provided in a hospital located in another Member State subject to prior authorisation from the insured person's sickness insurance fund and the grant of such authorisation subject to the condition that (i) the treatment must be regarded as 'normal in the professional circles concerned', a criterion also applied in determining whether hospital treatment provided on national territory is covered, and (ii) the insured person's medical treatment must require that treatment. However, that applies only in so far as

— the requirement that the treatment must be regarded as 'normal' is construed to the effect that authorisation cannot be refused on that ground where it appears that the treatment concerned is sufficiently tried and tested by international medical science, and

— authorisation can be refused on the ground of lack of medical necessity only if the same or equally effective treatment can be obtained without undue delay at an establishment having a contractual arrangement with the insured person's sickness insurance fund.

NOTE

The Court has not thrown the provision of medical care on to the mercy of the market at the expense of State involvement, but it has adjusted the 'balance of power' between the insured person's freedom to receive services and the State's competence to define the terms of the provisions of health care. The Court's case law nudges our assumptions about the discharge of a State's responsibility to its citizens in an era of transnational economic growth.

FURTHER READING

Davies, G., 'Welfare as a Service' [2002-1] LIEI 27.

Fuchs, M., 'Free Movement of Services and Social Security – Quo Vadis?' (2002) 8 ELJ 536.

Hervey, T., 'Social Solidarity: a Buttress against Internal Market Law?' in J. Shaw (ed), *Social Law and Policy in an Evolving EU* (Oxford: Hart Publishing, 2001).

Szyszczak, E., 'Free Trade as a Fundamental Value of the EU' in K. Economides (ed), *Fundamental Values* (Oxford: Hart Publishing, 2000).

Society for the Protection of Unborn Children Ireland Ltd (SPUC) v *Grogan*
(Case C-159/90)
[1991] ECR I-4685, [1991] 3 CMLR 849, Court of Justice of the European Communities

The litigation arose against the background of the right to life of the unborn under the Irish Constitution. Thousands of Irish women travel annually to London to receive abortion services because they are unable to receive such services in Ireland. A Students' Union in Dublin provided information about services lawfully available in London. This practice was challenged before the Irish courts by SPUC. The Students' Union claimed that as a matter of Community law it was entitled to distribute such information, relying on Articles 59–66 of the EC Treaty (now, after amendment, Articles 49–55 EC).

The European Court accepted that abortion was a commercial service within the meaning of then Article 60 of the EC Treaty (now, after amendment, Article 50 EC). It then observed that the Students' Union did not in any way cooperate with the clinics whose addresses were published. It declared that:

[26] The information to which the national court's questions refer is not distributed on behalf of an economic operator established in another Member State. On the contrary, the information constitutes a manifestation of freedom of expression and of the freedom to impart and receive information which is independent of the economic activity carried on by clinics established in another Member State.

[27] It follows that, in any event, a prohibition of the distribution of information in circumstances such as those which are the subject of the main proceedings cannot be regarded as a restriction within the meaning of Article 59 of the Treaty.

This perception that there was no economic motivation in the case allowed the Court to conclude that:

It is not contrary to Community law for a Member State in which medical termination of pregnancy is forbidden to prohibit students associations from distributing information about the identity and location of clinics in another Member State where voluntary termination of pregnancy is lawfully carried out and the means of communicating with those clinics, where the clinics in question have no involvement in the distribution of the said information.

NOTE
The Court thus sidestepped the need to make an assessment which Advocate-General van Gerven had characterized in his Opinion as a balancing exercise.

The question remains whether it is consonant with the general principles of Community law with regard to fundamental rights and freedoms for a Member State to prohibit the provision and receipt of information by way of assistance about abortions lawfully carried out in other Member States, thereby infringing individuals' freedom of expression. It is a question here of *balancing* two fundamental rights, on the one hand the right to life as defined and declared to be applicable to unborn life by a Member State, and on the other the freedom of expression, which is one of the general principles of Community law on the basis of the constitutional traditions of the Member States and the European and international treaties and declarations on fundamental rights, in particular Article 10 of the European Convention on Human Rights.

The Advocate-General, in contrast to the Court, explored these difficult issues. He concluded his Opinion by proposing that the following answer should be given to the referring court:

The Treaty provisions with regard to the freedom to provide services do not prevent a Member State where the protection of unborn life is recognised in the Constitution and in its legislation as a fundamental principle from imposing a general prohibition, applying to everyone regardless of their nationality or place of establishment, on the provision of assistance to pregnant women, regardless of their nationality, with a view to the termination of their pregnancy, more specifically through the distribution of information as to the identity and location of and method of communication with clinics located in another Member State where abortions are carried out, even though the services of medical termination of pregnancy and the information relating thereto are provided in accordance with the law in force in that second Member State.

The final clause of the Court's ruling clearly indicated the potential for future litigation where the required commercial link is shown to exist. A Protocol annexed to the Maastricht Treaty on European Union declares that nothing therein 'shall affect the application in Ireland' of the relevant provision of the Irish Constitution. The protection which that Protocol afforded Ireland against further EC-derived litigation was soon seen to be a mixed blessing as a combination of domestic and European pressures led to reconsideration of the nature of the Constitutional guarantees (see R. Pearce, 'Abortion and the Right to Life under the Irish Constitution' [1993] JSWFL 396).

Looking beyond the specific problem of abortion and Irish law, the litigation strikingly illustrates the potential depth of the intrusion of Community law into national life and the potential of the European Court to assume a controversial adjudicative role far beyond the economic sphere as narrowly understood. The following articles draw broader conclusions about the development of Community law from the process of the litigation in *SPUC* v *Grogan* (Case C-159/90):

de Búrca, G., 'Fundamental Human Rights and the Reach of EC Law' (1993) 13 OJLS 283.

Hervey, T., 'Buy Baby: The European Union and Regulation of Human Reproduction' (1998) 18 OJLS 207.

O'Leary, S., 'The Court of Justice as a Reluctant Constitutional Adjudicator' (1992) 71 EL Rev 138.

Spalin, E., 'Abortion, Speech and the European Community' (1992) *Journal of Social Welfare and Family Law* 17.

■ QUESTION

'[R]ights to travel or freedom of information are rights with which men [rather than women] can more easily identify. By focussing on matters which are peripheral to the abortion issue itself, the media, in common with politicians, have sought refuge in the discourse of liberal legalism which more easily accommodates rights to travel or information than rights to abortion' (M. Fox and T. Murphy, 'Irish Abortion: Seeking Refuge in a Jurisprudence of Doubt and Delegation' (1992) 19 *Journal of Law and Society* 454, 457). Might this criticism be extended to apply to the structure of European Community law?

SECTION 4: **HARMONIZATION**

The Court, in its judgments discussed in the previous section, recognises, as it did in *'Cassis de Dijon'* (p.381 above), that where a genuine interest is the subject of protection, national restrictive rules may remain compatible with the Treaty. So professional qualifications, designed to maintain standards and integrity, obstruct free movement but may be lawful. So, too, rules protecting the consumer or the investor, or the reputation of financial markets. Here lie the limits of the Court's role. This suggests a role for legislative harmonization.

Harmonization requires all professionals to meet common standards, wherever qualified. There is then no obstruction to free movement (see, e.g., *Auer* v *Ministère Public* (Case 271/82) [1983] ECR 2727). Yet achieving such harmonization has proved extremely difficult. Profession by profession, progress has been painfully slow, doubtless because vested interests, many of them perfectly legitimate, are at stake. A 'New Approach' has been initiated. This sets broad common standards which must be met, but avoids the detailed, laborious approach of old. Again, an analogy with the free movement of goods is appropriate, for in that field, too, it has been recognized that the inclusion of excessive detail in Community measures is counter-productive (see p.619).

The first measure which adopted the 'New Approach' to harmonization in this field was Directive 89/48 on a General System for the Recognition of Higher Education Diplomas [1989] OJ L19/16. Directive 89/48 is now supplemented by Directive 92/51 [1992] OJ L209/25, which extends beyond training in higher education of at least three years' duration, and further supplemented by Directive 99/42 [1999] OJ L201/77. Both Directives 89/48 and 92/51 were amended by Directive 2001/19 [2001] OJ L206/1.

For lawyers, then, as for other professions, cross-border competition should become a reality. The barriers created by long-standing professional requirements should fall. The migrant lawyer must demonstrate a basic ability, but is not to be subjected to the full period of professional training normal in the host State. (Primary law already plays a role; note that the dispute in Case C-340/89 *Vlassopoulou* (p.455 above) pre-dated the entry into force of Directive 89/48. See also Case C-55/94 *Gebhard* (p.321 above), annotated from the perspective of its impact on the mobility of lawyers by J. Lonbay (1996) 33 CML Rev 1073.) UK lawyers can expect to face developing competition from outside the UK; but the process is two-way, and UK lawyers can also look to expand their own activities beyond traditional frontiers. Strictly, the Directive is not of purely internal effect. It is concerned with migration. Yet the Directive is likely to supplement the many factors currently operative as catalysts in the reform of the English legal profession. It would be a strange result indeed if lawyers who are nationals of other Member States enjoy access to all English courts, leaving only English solicitors beyond the pale. The market for legal services has undergone further adjustment as a result of Directive 98/5 [1998] OJ L77/36, the deadline for implementation of which was 14 March 2000. Lawyers are to be entitled to pursue specified activities on a permanent basis in another Member State while using their home-State professional title. Moreover, a lawyer so practising who has 'effectively and regularly' pursued an activity in the host State in that State's law or Community law for at least three years is exempted from the conditions of Article 4(1)(b) of Directive 89/48 with regard to gaining admission to the profession of lawyer in the host State.

Similar initiatives aim to remove trade barriers resulting from divergent company law and other regulatory regimes, which hinder the free movement of services provided by companies. The Second Banking Directive (Directive 89/646 [1989]

OJ L386/1) illustrates the use of the New Approach in this area. Consider also the relevance of the initiative to tackle 'Harmful Tax Competition' (p.339 above). These issues are considered further in Chapter 19, which discusses some of the policy implications of the new style of harmonization.

NOTE

For additional material and resources see the Companion Website at: www.oup.co.uk/best.textbooks/law/weatherill6e

15

European Citizenship Within an Area of
Freedom, Security, and Justice

SECTION 1: **INTRODUCTION**

The case law and legislation examined in the previous two Chapters is straining to break the bounds of economics. The law governing the free movement of persons and services is rooted in Treaty Articles which are squeezed in between provisions dealing with the free movement of goods, agriculture, and the free movement of capital. This is trade law. Persons and services are treated as factors of production, and their enhanced mobility is a means to improve competition and economic performance in Europe. And all this remains true. But this is only part of the story. The mobility of people implicates more than simply economic indicators. It concerns the individual human being.

This has always been true. But more recently the growth of the scope of activities of the European Union has generated new momentum in the quest to devise a coherent law of persons for the EU that is not confined to economic performance. Part of this new dimension is directed at ensuring that the economic law provisions are interpreted with due respect for the dignity of the person. Part of it is more ambitious, and is directed at shaping a case for the treatment of people in the European Union that is distinct from market economics.

This is law and policy in flux. There is a profound lack of agreement about what should be the scope of the EU's relationship with the peoples of Europe. The EU Charter of Fundamental Rights, set out in Chapter 1 (p.16 above), promises to be of major significance, but even so it remains non-binding. Policy-making is at times awkward and tentative, at others vigorous and demanding. The next case represents a powerful assertion by the Court that once a matter is shown to fall within the scope of application of the Community rules on the free movement of persons, the range of legal sources that become relevant in influencing the legal protection afforded by what is nominally EC 'trade law' is broad indeed. But it is a ruling which in some respects is hard to fathom, and its full implications are unlikely to be apparent for some time to come. That is why it is chosen. It captures the dynamic nature of this area of law.

Mary Carpenter v *Secretary of State for the Home Department* (Case C-60/00)
Judgment of 11 July 2002, Court of Justice of the European Communities

Mrs Carpenter, a national of the Philippines, had entered the UK on a six months' visa, stayed after its expiry without receiving any extension, and then married Peter Carpenter, a UK national. She was subsequently served with a deportation order, against which she appealed. Points of Community law were referred to Luxembourg by the Immigration Appeal Tribunal.

As a third country national, Mrs Carpenter's rights under EC law, if any, were not free-standing but rather derived from her husband. But he was a national of the UK living in the UK. In *Morson* v *State of the Netherlands* (Cases 35 and 36/82) [1982] ECR 3723, [1983] 2 CMLR 720, the Court held that Dutch nationals working in the Netherlands had no rights under Article 48 of the EC Treaty (now, after amendment, Article 39 EC) and therefore could not rely on the Community secondary legislation discussed below to protect their Surinamese mothers who wished to join them. By contrast, in *R* v *IAT and Singh, ex parte Secretary of State* (Case C-370/90) [1992] ECR I-4265, [1992] 3 CMLR 358, a British national was able to rely on Community law to protect an Indian spouse when returning to the UK after working in Germany.

Mr Carpenter ran a business selling advertising space in medical and scientific journals and offering various administrative and publishing services to the editors of those journals. The business was established in the UK, but a significant proportion of the business was conducted with advertisers established in other Member States of the European Community. Mr Carpenter travelled to other Member States for the purpose of his business. It was argued that his wife's deportation would require him to go to live with her in the Philippines or separate the members of the family unit if he remained in the United Kingdom. In both cases his business would be affected.

Mr Carpenter seemed to be more mobile than Morson but less mobile than Singh.

[28] It is to be noted, at the outset, that the provisions of the Treaty relating to the freedom to provide services, and the rules adopted for their implementation, are not applicable to situations which do not present any link to any of the situations envisaged by Community law (see, to that effect, among others, Case C-97/98 *Jägerskiöld* [1999] ECR I-7319, paragraphs 42 to 45).

[29] As is apparent from paragraph 14 of this judgment, a significant proportion of Mr Carpenter's business consists of providing services, for remuneration, to advertisers established in other Member States. Such services come within the meaning of 'services' in Article 49 EC both in so far as the provider travels for that purpose to the Member State of the recipient and in so far as he provides cross-border services without leaving the Member State in which he is established (see, in respect of 'cold-calling', Case C-384/93 *Alpine Investments* [1995] ECR I-1141, paragraphs 15 and 20 to 22).

[30] Mr Carpenter is therefore availing himself of the right freely to provide services guaranteed by Article 49 EC. Moreover, as the Court has frequently held, that right may be relied on by a provider as against the State in which he is established if the services are provided for persons established in another Member State (see, among others, *Alpine Investments*, cited above, paragraph 30).

The Court was remarkably quick to find the case fell within the scope of the Treaty. Would someone moving to *receive* services also be protected? If so, is it rational to leave out of the scope of protection the few people who doggedly never move across a border? Is that a task for the Court or for the legislature? For a survey and analysis see N. NicShuibhne, 'Free Movement of Persons and the Wholly Internal Rule: Time to Move On?' (2002) 39 CML Rev 731.

Directive 73/148 on the abolition of restrictions on movement and residence within the Community for nationals of Member States with regard to establishment and the provision of services (p.446 above) was of no assistance to the Carpenters. It applies to cases where nationals of Member States leave their Member State of origin and move to another Member State, not to cases concerning the right of residence of members of the family in the home State of the right-holder. So the matter fell for resolution in the light of general principles.

[38] In that context it should be remembered that the Community legislature has recognised the importance of ensuring the protection of the family life of nationals of the Member States in order to eliminate obstacles to the exercise of the fundamental freedoms guaranteed by the Treaty, as is particularly apparent from the provisions of the Council regulations and directives on the freedom of movement of employed and self-employed workers within the Community (see, for example, Article 10 of Council Regulation (EEC) No 1612/68 of 15 October 1968 on freedom of movement for workers within the Community (OJ, English Special Edition 1968 (II), p.475); Articles 1 and 4 of Council Directive 68/360/EEC of 15 October 1968 on the abolition of restrictions on movement and residence within the Community for workers of Member States and their families (OJ, English Special Edition 1968 (II), p.485), and Articles 1(1)(c) and 4 of the Directive).

[39] It is clear that the separation of Mr and Mrs Carpenter would be detrimental to their family life and, therefore, to the conditions under which Mr Carpenter exercises a fundamental freedom. That freedom could not be fully effective if Mr Carpenter were to be deterred from exercising it by obstacles raised in his country of origin to the entry and residence of his spouse (see, to that effect, *Singh*, cited above, paragraph 23).

[40] A Member State may invoke reasons of public interest to justify a national measure which is likely to obstruct the exercise of the freedom to provide services only if that measure is compatible with the fundamental rights whose observance the Court ensures (see, to that effect, Case C-260/89 *ERT* [1991] ECR I-2925, paragraph 43, and Case C-368/95 *Familiapress* [1997] ECR I-3689, paragraph 24).

[41] The decision to deport Mrs Carpenter constitutes an interference with the exercise by Mr Carpenter of his right to respect for his family life within the meaning of Article 8 of the Convention for the Protection of Human Rights and Fundamental Freedoms, signed at Rome on 4 November 1950 (hereinafter 'the Convention'), which is among the fundamental rights which, according to the Court's settled case-law, restated by the Preamble to the Single European Act and by Article 6(2) EU, are protected in Community law.

[42] Even though no right of an alien to enter or to reside in a particular country is as such guaranteed by the Convention, the removal of a person from a country where close members of his family are living may amount to an infringement of the right to respect for family life as guaranteed by Article 8(1) of the Convention. Such an interference will infringe the Convention if it does not meet the requirements of paragraph 2 of that article, that is unless it is 'in accordance with the law', motivated by one or more of the legitimate aims under that paragraph and 'necessary in a democratic society', that is to say justified by a pressing social need and, in particular, proportionate to the legitimate aim pursued (see, in particular, *Boultif* v *Switzerland*, no 54273/00, §§ 39, 41 and 46, ECHR 2001-IX).

[43] A decision to deport Mrs Carpenter taken in circumstances such as those in the main proceedings, does not strike a fair balance between the competing interests, that is, on the one hand, the right of Mr Carpenter to respect for his family life, and, on the other hand, the maintenance of public order and public safety.

[44] Although, in the main proceedings, Mr Carpenter's spouse has infringed the immigration laws of the United Kingdom by not leaving the country prior to the expiry of her leave to remain as a visitor, her conduct, since her arrival in the United Kingdom in September 1994, has not been the subject of any other complaint that could give cause to fear that she might in the future constitute a danger to public order or public safety. Moreover, it is clear that Mr and Mrs Carpenter's marriage, which was celebrated in the United Kingdom in 1996, is genuine and that Mrs Carpenter continues

to lead a true family life there, in particular by looking after her husband's children from a previous marriage.

[45] In those circumstances, the decision to deport Mrs Carpenter constitutes an infringement which is not proportionate to the objective pursued.

[46] In view of all the foregoing, the answer to the question referred to the Court is that Article 49 EC, read in the light of the fundamental right to respect for family life, is to be interpreted as precluding, in circumstances such as those in the main proceedings, a refusal, by the Member State of origin of a provider of services established in that Member State who provides services to recipients established in other Member States, of the right to reside in its territory to that provider's spouse, who is a national of a third country.

NOTE

It is striking how little effort the Court makes to establish a connection between the threatened deportation and the perceived impediment to trade. If EC trade law can achieve a result as remarkable as this, what is the need for any extra level of fundamental rights protection? And what need is there for a status of Citizenship? (This book's Companion Website will supply references to academic comment on this striking decision.)

SECTION 2: FREE MOVEMENT OF PERSONS WITHIN AN AREA OF FREEDOM, SECURITY, AND JUSTICE

Article 14 EC's insistence on the removal of internal frontiers within the Community at the end of 1992 was discussed in Chapter 9 at p.299 above. It suggested that date as a 'Big Bang' in the historical evolution of the Community. For consumers, there was certainly a very specific advantage to be enjoyed at the turn of the year 1992. It became possible to buy goods for private consumption in another Member State and to return home with those goods without the need to pay any duties to the home State. However, frontier controls did not vanish at the end of 1992; '1992' – Article 14 EC – is not legally unambiguous.

In December 1992, the European Council meeting in Edinburgh concluded that:

The European Council has had to take note of the fact that free movement of persons within the Community, in accordance with Article 8a of the Treaty of Rome [converted with amendment at Amsterdam into Article 14 EC], cannot be completely assured on 1 January 1993. The work necessary to achieve this result without creating dangers for public security and compromising the fight against illegal immigration, although having progressed, is still under way. Further progress is needed in particular to complete the ratification process of the Dublin Asylum Convention, to conclude the External Frontiers Convention and to complete negotiations on a Convention on the European Information System.

The view of the European Council is constitutionally not the final word within the EC system. The authoritative source of interpretation of EC law is the European Court. In 1999, the European Court finally had the opportunity to rule on the point. In Case C-378/97 *Florius Ariel Wijsenbeek* [1999] ECR I-6207, decided in the light of the law of the post-Maastricht, pre-Amsterdam period, the Court accepted that a Member State was entitled to require a person crossing an internal EU frontier to establish his or her nationality. The expiry of the 1992 deadline had not altered this. Article 14 EC has no automatic effect. The Court referred to the need for, and absence of, common rules governing, in particular, the crossing of the external frontiers of the EU as a precondition to elimination of internal frontiers. The Treaty provisions on European Citizenship (Article 18 EC, p.483 below) were also considered insufficient to deprive the Member States of the legal right to perform border checks.

The 'flanking measures', the adoption of which the European Council in 1992 regarded as necessary preconditions for securing the free movement of persons in accordance with what is now Article 14, were not envisaged as creatures of the EC legal order. They were primarily the province of cooperation between the Member States in Justice in Home Affairs, the 'third pillar' of the EU created at Maastricht (p.9 above). However, negligible progress was made in agreeing flanking measures outwith the EC structure. The Treaty of Amsterdam altered the structure by substantially re-working the provisions governing the free movement of persons, in particular by modifying relevant material from the 'third pillar' created at Maastricht (Justice and Home Affairs, p.11 above) and transferring it to the first, EC, pillar. The EC Treaty post-Amsterdam contains a Title on 'Visas, asylum, immigration and other policies related to free movement of persons' which is dedicated to the progressive establishment of 'an area of freedom, security and justice'. This is Title IV, and comprises Articles 61–69 EC. As already suggested at p.11 above, this 'communitiarization' suggests that Amsterdam saw a triumph of EC institutional and constitutional method over the species of intergovern-mentalism found in the non-EC EU, although the validity of that observation must be judged after an inspection of the relevant provisions, which display some characteristics which are, at least, unorthodox in EC practice. The following is the text of the Title, which deserves careful reading.

TITLE IV

VISAS, ASYLUM, IMMIGRATION AND OTHER POLICIES RELATED TO FREE MOVEMENT OF PERSONS

Article 61

In order to establish progressively an area of freedom, security and justice, the Council shall adopt:

(a) within a period of five years after the entry into force of the Treaty of Amsterdam, measures aimed at ensuring the free movement of persons in accordance with Article 14, in conjunction with directly related flanking measures with respect to external border controls, asylum and immigration, in accordance with the provisions of Article 62(2) and (3) and Article 63(1)(a) and (2)(a), and measures to prevent and combat crime in accordance with the provisions of Article 31(e) of the Treaty on European Union;

(b) other measures in the fields of asylum, immigration and safeguarding the rights of nationals of third countries, in accordance with the provisions of Article 63;

(c) measures in the field of judicial cooperation in civil matters as provided for in Article 65;

(d) appropriate measures to encourage and strengthen administrative cooperation, as provided for in Article 66;

(e) measures in the field of police and judicial cooperation in criminal matters aimed at a high level of security by preventing and combating crime within the Union in accordance with the provisions of the Treaty on European Union.

Article 62

The Council, acting in accordance with the procedure referred to in Article 67, shall, within a period of five years after the entry into force of the Treaty of Amsterdam, adopt:

1. measures with a view to ensuring, in compliance with Article 14, the absence of any controls

on persons, be they citizens of the Union or nationals of third countries, when crossing internal borders;

2. measures on the crossing of the external borders of the Member States which shall establish:

   (a) standards and procedures to be followed by Member States in carrying out checks on persons at such borders;

   (b) rules on visas for intended stays of no more than three months, including:

      (i) the list of third countries whose nationals must be in possession of visas when crossing the external borders and those whose nationals are exempt from that requirement;

      (ii) the procedures and conditions for issuing visas by Member States;

      (iii) a uniform format for visas;

      (iv) rules on a uniform visa;

3. measures setting out the conditions under which nationals of third countries shall have the freedom to travel within the territory of the Member States during a period of no more than three months.

Article 63

The Council, acting in accordance with the procedure referred to in Article 67, shall, within a period of five years after the entry into force of the Treaty of Amsterdam, adopt:

1. Measures on asylum, in accordance with the Geneva Convention of 28 July 1951 and the Protocol of 31 January 1967 relating to the status of refugees and other relevant treaties, within the following areas:

   (a) criteria and mechanisms for determining which Member State is responsible for considering an application for asylum submitted by a national of a third country in one of the Member States,

   (b) minimum standards on the reception of asylum seekers in Member States,

   (c) minimum standards with respect to the qualification of nationals of third countries as refugees,

   (d) minimum standards on procedures in Member States for granting or withdrawing refugee status;

2. Measures on refugees and displaced persons within the following areas:

   (a) minimum standards for giving temporary protection to displaced persons from third countries who cannot return to their country of origin and for persons who otherwise need international protection,

   (b) promoting a balance of effort between Member States in receiving and bearing the consequences of receiving refugees and displaced persons;

3. Measures on immigration policy within the following areas:

   (a) conditions of entry and residence, and standards on procedures for the issue by Member States of long-term visas and residence permits, including those for the purpose of family reunion,

   (b) illegal immigration and illegal residence, including repatriation of illegal residents;

4. Measures defining the rights and conditions under which nationals of third countries who are legally resident in a Member State may reside in other Member States.

Measures adopted by the Council pursuant to points 3 and 4 shall not prevent any Member State from maintaining or introducing in the areas concerned national provisions which are compatible with this Treaty and with international agreements.

Measures to be adopted pursuant to points 2(b), 3(a) and 4 shall not be subject to the five-year period referred to above.

Article 64

1. This title shall not affect the exercise of the responsibilities incumbent upon Member States with regard to the maintenance of law and order and the safeguarding of internal security.

2. In the event of one or more Member States being confronted with an emergency situation characterised by a sudden inflow of nationals of third countries and without prejudice to paragraph 1, the Council may, acting by qualified majority on a proposal from the Commission, adopt provisional measures of a duration not exceeding six months for the benefit of the Member States concerned.

Article 65

Measures in the field of judicial cooperation in civil matters having cross-border implications, to be taken in accordance with Article 67 and in so far as necessary for the proper functioning of the internal market, shall include:

- (a) improving and simplifying:
  - — the system for cross-border service of judicial and extrajudicial documents,
  - — cooperation in the taking of evidence,
  - — the recognition and enforcement of decisions in civil and commercial cases, including decisions in extrajudicial cases;
- (b) promoting the compatibility of the rules applicable in the Member States concerning the conflict of laws and of jurisdiction;
- (c) eliminating obstacles to the good functioning of civil proceedings, if necessary by promoting the compatibility of the rules on civil procedure applicable in the Member States.

Article 66

The Council, acting in accordance with the procedure referred to in Article 67, shall take measures to ensure cooperation between the relevant departments of the administrations of the Member States in the areas covered by this title, as well as between those departments and the Commission.

Article 67

1. During a transitional period of five years following the entry into force of the Treaty of Amsterdam, the Council shall act unanimously on a proposal from the Commission or on the initiative of a Member State and after consulting the European Parliament.
    2. After this period of five years:

- — the Council shall act on proposals from the Commission; the Commission shall examine any request made by a Member State that it submit a proposal to the Council,
- — the Council, acting unanimously after consulting the European Parliament, shall take a decision with a view to providing for all or parts of the areas covered by this title to be governed by the procedure referred to in Article 251 and adapting the provisions relating to the powers of the Court of Justice.

3. By derogation from paragraphs 1 and 2, measures referred to in Article 62(2)(b) (i) and (iii) shall, from the entry into force of the Treaty of Amsterdam, be adopted by the Council acting by a qualified majority on a proposal from the Commission and after consulting the European Parliament.

4. By derogation from paragraph 2, measures referred to in Article 62(2)(b) (ii) and (iv) shall, after a period of five years following the entry into force of the Treaty of Amsterdam, be adopted by the Council acting in accordance with the procedure referred to in Article 251.

5. By derogation from paragraph 1, the Council shall adopt, in accordance with the procedure referred to in Article 251:

- — the measures provided for in Article 63(1) and (2)(a) provided that the Council has previously adopted, in accordance with paragraph 1 of this article, Community legislation defining the common rules and basic principles governing these issues,
- — the measures provided for in Article 65 with the exception of aspects relating to family law.

Article 68

1. Article 234 shall apply to this title under the following circumstances and conditions: where a question on the interpretation of this title or on the validity or interpretation of acts of the institutions of the Community based on this title is raised in a case pending before a court or a tribunal of a Member State against whose decisions there is no judicial remedy under national law, that court or tribunal shall, if it considers that a decision on the question is necessary to enable it to give judgment, request the Court of Justice to give a ruling thereon.

2. In any event, the Court of Justice shall not have jurisdiction to rule on any measure or decision taken pursuant to Article 62(1) relating to the maintenance of law and order and the safeguarding of internal security.

3. The Council, the Commission or a Member State may request the Court of Justice to give a ruling on a question of interpretation of this title or of acts of the institutions of the Community based on this title. The ruling given by the Court of Justice in response to such a request shall not apply to judgments of courts or tribunals of the Member States which have become res judicata.

Article 69

The application of this title shall be subject to the provisions of the Protocol on the position of the United Kingdom and Ireland and to the Protocol on the position of Denmark and without prejudice to the Protocol on the application of certain aspects of Article 14 of the Treaty establishing the European Community to the United Kingdom and to Ireland.

■ QUESTION

Assess the competing weight of the *advantages* of these provisions in moving beyond the Maastricht Treaty by establishing a fuller and time-limited framework within the EC 'pillar' for achieving the free movement of persons within an area of freedom, security, and justice, and their *disadvantages* in the shape of what may be regarded as regression from standard EC method in, e.g., Articles 67(1) and 68. Are these prices worth paying for (imperfect) communitiarization?

Article 68 EC deserves your close attention, in particular its second paragraph. If the Court of Justice is denied jurisdiction over such Council acts, how *is* supervision to be achieved? Is Article 68(2) EC consistent with the rule of law?

Note also the nature of the Protocols mentioned in Article 69 EC, which, in different ways, exclude the UK, Ireland, and Denmark from the full impact of this new Title. Here is a form of 'flexible' integration (see further p.665); here is a further price to be paid for the progress towards open borders achieved at Amsterdam via communtiarization of 'third pillar' and Schengen material. The UK has subsequently chosen to join parts of the cooperation from which the Protocol to the Amsterdam Treaty allows it to stand aside. For discussion of the implications, see the Report of the House of Lords Select Committee on the European Union, HL 34, 1999–2000.

NOTE

The Tampere European Council of October 1999 was significant in accelerating the momentum towards adding legislative meat to the area of freedom, security, and justice. A substantial body of legislation has now been adopted pursuant to these provisions, ranging from matters in the criminal field to border control issues. The perceived threat of illegal immigration has been a factor in promoting recourse to these procedures. The distinct issue of asylum has also been a major feature. The events of 11 September 2001 have plainly hastened the speed at which the programme has been agreed (for good or ill). The record can be consulted *via* http://europa.eu.int/comm/justice_home/index_en.htm

FURTHER READING

Den Boer, M., and Monar, J., '11 September and the Challenge of Global Terrorism to the EU as a Security Actor' (2002) 40 JCMS Annual Review 11.

Peers, S., 'Who's Judging the Watchmen? The Judicial System of the Area of Freedom, Security and Justice' (1998) 18 YEL 337.

Peers, S., 'EU Responses to Terrorism' (2003) 52 ICLQ 227.

Thym, D.,'The Schengen Law: A Challenge for Legal Accountability in the European Union' (2002) 8 ELJ 218.

Wagner, E., 'The Integration of Schengen into the Framework of the EU' [1998/2] LIEI 1.

Walker, N., 'Freedom, Security and Justice' in B. De Witte (ed), *Ten Reflections on the Constitutional Treaty for Europe* (Florence: Robert Schuman Centre, 2003), available *via* http://www.iue.it/RSCAS/Research/Institutions/EuropeanTreaties.shtml

See also essays by O'Keeffe, D., Hedemann-Robinson, M., den Boer, M., Hervey, T., and Twomey, P., in O'Keeffe, D. and Twomey, P., *Legal Issues of the Amsterdam Treaty* (Oxford: Hart Publishing, 1999).

SECTION 3: **EUROPEAN CITIZENSHIP**

Shiny labels abound. Fundamental rights . . . the area of 'freedom, security and justice' . . . and Citizenship of the Union.

The Maastricht Treaty introduced into the EC Treaty a new Part Two, 'Citizenship of the Union'. This comprised Articles 8–8e EC. These were adjusted by the Treaty of Amsterdam, albeit in rather minor ways. Articles 8–8e EC became Articles 17–22 EC on re-numbering. The Treaty of Nice adjusted Article 18 alone among these provisions and the post-Nice Articles read as follows.

PART TWO

CITIZENSHIP OF THE UNION

Article 17

1. Citizenship of the Union is hereby established. Every person holding the nationality of a Member State shall be a citizen of the Union. Citizenship of the Union shall complement and not replace national citizenship.

2. Citizens of the Union shall enjoy the rights conferred by this Treaty and shall be subject to the duties imposed thereby.

Article 18

1. Every citizen of the Union shall have the right to move and reside freely within the territory of the Member States, subject to the limitations and conditions laid down in this Treaty and by the measures adopted to give it effect.

2. If action by the Community should prove necessary to attain this objective and this Treaty has not provided the necessary powers, the Council may adopt provisions with a view to facilitating the exercise of the rights referred to in paragraph 1. The Council shall act in accordance with the procedure referred to in Article 251.

3. Paragraph 2 shall not apply to provisions on passports, identity cards, residence permits or any other such document or to provisions on social security or social protection.

Article 19

1. Every citizen of the Union residing in a Member State of which he is not a national shall have the right to vote and to stand as a candidate at municipal elections in the Member State in which he resides, under the same conditions as nationals of that State. This right shall be exercised subject to detailed arrangements adopted by the Council, acting unanimously on a proposal from the Commission and after consulting the European Parliament; these arrangements may provide for derogations where warranted by problems specific to a Member State.

2. Without prejudice to Article 190(4) and to the provisions adopted for its implementation, every citizen of the Union residing in a Member State of which he is not a national shall have the right to vote and to stand as a candidate in elections to the European Parliament in the Member State in which he resides, under the same conditions as nationals of that State. This right shall be exercised subject to detailed arrangements adopted by the Council, acting unanimously on a proposal from the Commission and after consulting the European Parliament; these arrangements may provide for derogations where warranted by problems specific to a Member State.

Article 20

Every citizen of the Union shall, in the territory of a third country in which the Member State of which he is a national is not represented, be entitled to protection by the diplomatic or consular authorities of any Member State, on the same conditions as the nationals of that State. Member States shall establish the necessary rules among themselves and start the international negotiations required to secure this protection.

Article 21

Every citizen of the Union shall have the right to petition the European Parliament in accordance with Article 194.

Every citizen of the Union may apply to the Ombudsman established in accordance with Article 195.

Every citizen of the Union may write to any of the institutions or bodies referred to in this Article or in Article 7 in one of the languages mentioned in Article 314 and have an answer in the same language.

Article 22

The Commission shall report to the European Parliament, to the Council and to the Economic and Social Committee every three years on the application of the provisions of this Part. This report shall take account of the development of the Union.

On this basis, and without prejudice to the other provisions of this Treaty, the Council, acting unanimously on a proposal from the Commission and after consulting the European Parliament, may adopt provisions to strengthen or to add to the rights laid down in this Part, which it shall recommend to the Member States for adoption in accordance with their respective constitutional requirements.

NOTE
Remember also the EU Charter of Fundamental Rights, p.16 above.

Article 45 Charter: Freedom of movement and of residence

1. Every citizen of the Union has the right to move and reside freely within the territory of the Member States.

2. Freedom of movement and residence may be granted, in accordance with the Treaty establishing the European Community, to nationals of third countries legally resident in the territory of a Member State.

The precise nature of Citizenship of the Union required elaboration when it was introduced at Maastricht and it still requires elaboration today. For the German Federal Constitutional Court in its *Maastricht* decision, Union citizenship represents 'a lasting legal tie . . . knotted between the nationals of the individual Member States' (p.686 below). Nevertheless, it remains unclear how far in practical terms citizenship of the Union transcends the pre-existing law, which already conferred on migrants a bundle of rights which *de facto* created a form of Community citizenship (e.g., A. Evans, 'European Citizenship' (1982) 45 MLR 497). As a label, Union citizenship hints at a step beyond the largely economic focus of the history of EC law applied to persons. But closer inspection of the text is less encouraging to the proponent of a more overtly political connection between the Union and nationals of the Member States. To this extent one cannot be confident that the Citizen of the Union is much, if at all, different from the migrant economic actor: see M. Everson, 'The Legacy of the Market Citizen' in J. Shaw and G. More (eds), *New Legal Dynamics of the European Union* (Oxford: OUP, 1995).

Plainly European Citizenship does not at all imply a transfer of status from State to European level. Indeed Article 17(1) EC provides that 'Citizenship of the Union shall complement and not replace national citizenship.' But the very language of *Citizenship* suggests an attempt to convey something of the shifting sands of allegiance and legitimacy that flow from the deepening role of the European Union, and to add a (supplementary) European level of democratic legitimacy. It has not done very well on this score. But it could. In so far as it involves the construction of a sense of European identity which is, first, in supplement to and not in replacement for national loyalties and, second, built around social values not ethnicity or nationhood, then European Citizenship has some potential for developing an appealingly inclusive notion of political belonging. One may therefore argue for a distinct form of European identity-formation built around shared constitutional values. (Consider in this vein J. Habermas, *The Inclusion of the Other: Studies in Political Theory* (London: Polity Press, 1999); N. MacCormick, 'Democracy, Subsidiarity and Citizenship in the European Commonwealth' (1997) 16 *Law and Philosophy* 331.) This would not be a static notion but would be susceptible to development and, in particular, to widening. This could begin to help to underpin multiple sites of political authority with a degree of social legitimacy and begin to challenge approaches that too readily assume that membership of a single political community is descriptively and normatively orthodox. So one cannot sensibly attempt to get to grips with the nature of citizenship without considering what it is in the EU that people are classified as citizens *of*. Chapter 21 will present a more general discussion of what the Union is and might become.

For the time being, the status of Citizenship of the Union offers more promise than fulfilment.

C. Closa, 'The Concept of Citizenship in the Treaty on European Union' (1992) 29 CML Rev 1137, 1162

. . . the character of the union citizenship is determined by the progressive acquisition of rights stemming from the dynamic development of the Union. That is, the gradual acquisition by the European citizen of specific rights in new policy-areas transferred to the Union. This evolutive character, which is in itself the most characteristic feature of the citizenship of the Union, was developed by the contributions to the conference as a channel for incorporating controversial socio-economic rights.

. . . The Commission also endorsed this dynamic character (i.e. Citizenship would be progressively developed) in its opinion. Indeed, the Commission included as one element of Union citizenship the establishment of targets for the civic, economic and social rights of the individuals to be properly defined in a later stage. When it presented its contribution to the IGC, the Commission explained that the dynamic character was one of the principles on which Union citizenship was based: it *reflects the aims of the Union, involving as it does an indivisible body of rights and obligations stemming from the gradual and coherent development of the Union's political, economic and social dimension.* The Commission wanted to avoid the concept of citizenship being restricted to economic rights in the framework of the Rome Treaties and, at the same time, it sought to provide the basis for its future updating as the union developed. Therefore, the provisions proposed laid down objectives for the granting of rights in the future and for defining obligations, specially in the social field, with the possibility of eventually *enlarging* (and only enlarging, not reducing) the catalogue of citizens' rights by a unanimous Council vote on a Commission proposal.

4. Conclusions

The concept of union citizenship embodied by the Treaty on European Union has formalized or constitutionalized certain already existing rights within the Community ambit; it has introduced certain new rights and, above all, it has provided a solid basis for further enlargement of the catalogue of rights attached to citizenship. From this point of view, it represents an advance on the situation under the Rome Treaty and the SEA. The institutional role for the development of the dynamic character of citizenship will be the determinant factor to produce a qualitative leap forward.

However, citizenship of the Union has not superseded nationality of the Member States, in much the same way as the European Union has not abolished the sovereign existence of the Member States. This is particularly evident regarding certain political rights not included in the Treaty: national elections – the mechanism to actualize sovereignty and the source of a state policy on the Union itself – are the exclusive domain of *nationals*. The same applies to referendum: without being a procedure common to all twelve Member States, referendums have had a decisive role in Community developments, as the latest Danish and French referendums prove. The important point is that the decisive entitlement for individuals' decisions on the Union is not citizenship but nationality. It remains to be seen whether the basis of citizenship of the Union provided by the Treaty could evolve in the future to develop a political subject for the Union.

H.U. Jessurun D'Oliveira, 'Union Citizenship: Pie in the Sky?'
in A. Rosas and E. Antola (eds), A Citizen's Europe
(London: Sage Publications, 1995), pp.82–84

(Footnotes omitted.)

Up till now, as far as citizenship is concerned, the European market is a 'futures' market. Citizenship is, in other words, nearly exclusively a symbolic plaything without substantive content, and in the Maastricht Treaty very little is added to the existing status of nationals of Member States. It is worth noting that, whereas in the Member States the notion of citizenship historically accrued around the *political* rights of the individual, it is around the freedom of movement that the notion of Union citizenship is crystallising.

It is unclear which rights and duties together are connected with Union citizenship because there is no cohesive notion of this new citizenship, and because the political dimension of citizenship here is underdeveloped. The instruments for participation in the public life of the Union are lacking as this public life itself, as distinguished from public life in the Member States, is virtually non-existent: a weak Parliament, next to no direct access to the European Courts, and so on.

Furthermore, the rights and obligations of the European citizen as granted by the Maastricht Treaty do differentiate only very partially between citizens and non-citizens. Several rights, such as the freedom of movement, are granted to large categories of non-nationals, such as nationals of the EFTA countries, or even to 'everyone', or normally to those legally resident in the territory of one of the Member States. Thus, European citizenship is not only severely underdeveloped, but also insufficiently distinctive between those who 'belong' and those who do not. In this situation, and also for policy reasons, it is better to forge a Union citizenship not only for nationals of Member States, but for resident aliens as part of the population of the Member States of the Union as well. This would increase rationality and cohesiveness of such a larger concept, and would reinforce democratic access to participation in the cultural, political and economic life of the Union and Community of the resident population of the Member States.

One must not forget, after all, that the creation, albeit in an as yet very rudimentary form, of a concept of citizenship which is related to a community of states, marks a significant departure from the traditional link between nationality and citizenship in the nation-state. It represents a loosening of the metaphysical ties between persons and a state, and forms a symptom of cosmopolitisation of citizenship. The rising concept of European citizenship is not the concept of national citizenship writ large: its quality has changed in that it does not presuppose any more a large set of common or shared values. It is a clear indication of a phenomenon which is also to be observed in the component parts of the European Community: that the Member States have to a large extent become multicultural and multi-ethnic societies which may be bound together not in the first place by a set of common values, but by a developing competence of persons to deal with differences in their dealing with others who do not necessarily share the same values and with redefined institutions. It is this competence to deal with differences which may be the nucleus of modern active citizenship, and European citizenship may be useful as a laboratory for this procedural concept of proto-cosmopolitan citizenship.

As it stands, Union citizenship is misleading in that it suggests that the Union is a state-like entity. This connotation is less adequate than ever as the Union moves more and more away from federal and supranational aspirations. It is furthermore misleading as the elements added to the European Community, and especially the third pillar of the Union, are inaccessible to the political influence of the so-called citizens. Nobody in his or her right mind would use the word citizen to describe the relationship between people and international organisations like GATT or the Hague Conference for private international law. To indicate the position of people under the Maastricht Treaty as citizenship is nearly as gross a misnomer. The populations of the Member States have not asked for citizenship; it has graciously been bestowed upon them as a cover-up for the still existing democratic deficit. As an alibi it may please Brussels; whether it changes anything in the sceptical attitude and weak position of the populations of the Member States is, in my view, rather improbable.

NOTE

In its periodic reports, the Commission has claimed that the insertion of the Citizenship provisions into the Treaty has elevated the status of the people to a new constitutional plane in the Community legal order. See, for example, COM (93) 702, COM (97) 230. For up-to-date information on developments see: http://europa.eu.int/comm/dg15/en/people/index.htm. In its Third Report the Commission takes care to place Citizenship in a wider context that confirms the trends 'beyond economics'.

THE COMMISSION'S THIRD REPORT ON CITIZENSHIP OF THE UNION, COM (2001) 506, pp.1, 6

This report focuses on the rights provided for in the second part of the EC Treaty. However, it includes advances in areas closely related to citizenship in the wider sense, such as the protection of fundamental rights, including measures to combat all forms of illegal discrimination. Two texts deserve special mention here: the proposal for a Directive on the right of citizens of the Union and their family members to move and reside freely within the territory of the Member States and the Charter of Fundamental Rights of the European Union . . .

. . . The rights that feature in Part Two of the Treaty, under the heading Citizenship of the Union, thus form the core of the rights conferred by citizenship, but are not an exhaustive list. The EC Treaty confers on citizens of the Union other rights which appear elsewhere in the Treaties, such as protection from all forms of discrimination on grounds of nationality (Article 12). It is therefore legitimate for this Third Report on Citizenship of the Union to go beyond the specific rights featuring in the second part of the EC Treaty and to examine subjects that have an obvious connection with citizenship of the Union, such as the fight against all forms of discrimination and, more generally, the protection of fundamental rights in the Union.

On the wider sweep of discrimination law, see D. Schiek, 'A New Framework on Equal Treatment of Persons in EC Law?' (2002) 8 ELJ 290.

Pending elaboration of the content of European Citizenship through legislation and/or Treaty revision, it has been an intriguing, and familiar, question in EC law and policy whether the Court will employ the admittedly guarded wording of the relevant Treaty provisions as a basis for dynamic interpretation of the law in order to enhance the status of the individual. In Cases C-64/96 and C-65/96 *Land Nordrhein Westfalen* v *Uecker, Jacquet* [1997] ECR I-3171 the Court ruled that the insertion of these provisions is not intended to extend the material scope of the Treaty to internal situations with no link to Community law. It preferred to adhere to the perceived existing limitations on the scope of the Treaty.

In Case C-91/92 *Paola Faccini Dori* (p.148 above) it declined the invitation of its Advocate-General, Mr Lenz, to secure the equality of the European Citizen before the law by embracing the horizontal direct effect of Directives. This would pre-clude the variation in the impact of Directives State-by-State which is caused by uneven local fidelity to the obligation of timely transposition. But the Court stuck doggedly to its rejection of the phenomenon of horizontal direct effect in the case of Directives. However, a glimpse of a more dynamic role for European citizenship emerges from the Court's ruling in *Maria Martinez Sala* v *Freistaat Bayern* (Case C-85/96) [1998] ECR I-2691. It ruled that a national of a Member State lawfully residing in the territory of another Member State falls within the personal scope of the Treaty provisions on European Citizenship. This triggered a right to, *inter alia*, protection from discrimination on grounds of nationality within the material scope of application of the Treaty. In *Martinez Sala* this allowed the applicant access to benefits which, one might previously have supposed, would have been available to her only had she held a more active economic status than mere lawful residence in the host State. *Martinez Sala* may prove to be the key ruling that breaks the ground between the orthodoxy of economic rights for economic migrants and new horizons lit up by comprehensive rights to equal treatment for Union citizens. See S. Fries and J. Shaw, 'Citizenship of the Union: First Steps in the Court of Justice' (1998) 4 *European Public Law* 533; O'Leary, 'Putting Flesh on the Bones of European Union Citizenship' (1999) 24 EL Rev 68. But what if the applicant had *not* been lawfully resident in Germany? Would the Treaty provisions on citizenship secure that right, even for individuals falling outwith the scope of the familiar economically-focused Treaty provisions and the package of secondary legislation adopted in 1990 (p.449)? *Martinez Sala* does not answer this question. Closa's prediction at p.485 above of the 'progressive acquisition of rights [by the Union citizen] stemming from the dynamic develop-ment of the Union' invites us, a decade later, to reflect on nothing more than incremental progress in this area.

And yet although it is not yet summer, *Martinez Sala* is not the only swallow.

Rudy Grzelczyk v *Centre public d'aide sociale d'Ottignies-Louvain-la-Neuve* (Case C-184/99)

[2001] ECR I-6193, Court of Justice of the European Communities

The applicant, a French national studying in Belgium, had been denied the 'minimex', a minimum subsistence allowance paid in Belgium. Previous case law established that the minimex was a social advantage within the meaning of Regula-tion 1612/68, p.433 above. But Regulation 1612/68 concerns workers. Grzelczyk was not a worker. He was a student.

[29] It is clear from the documents before the Court that a student of Belgian nationality, though not a worker within the meaning of Regulation No 1612/68, who found himself in exactly the same circumstances as Mr Grzelczyk would satisfy the conditions for obtaining the minimex. The fact that Mr Grzelczyk is not of Belgian nationality is the only bar to its being granted to him. It is not therefore in dispute that the case is one of discrimination solely on the ground of nationality.

[30] Within the sphere of application of the Treaty, such discrimination is, in principle, prohibited by Article 6 [now 12]. In the present case, Article 6 [now 12] must be read in conjunction with the provisions of the Treaty concerning citizenship of the Union in order to determine its sphere of application.

[31] Union citizenship is destined to be the fundamental status of nationals of the Member States, enabling those who find themselves in the same situation to enjoy the same treatment in law irrespective of their nationality, subject to such exceptions as are expressly provided for.

[32] As the Court held in paragraph 63 of its judgment in *Martínez Sala*, cited above, a citizen of the European Union, lawfully resident in the territory of a host Member State, can rely on Article 6 of the Treaty in all situations which fall within the scope *ratione materiae* of Community law.

[33] Those situations include those involving the exercise of the fundamental freedoms guaranteed by the Treaty and those involving the exercise of the right to move and reside freely in another Member State, as conferred by Article 8a of the Treaty (see Case C-274/96 *Bickel and Franz* [1998] ECR I 7637, paragraphs 15 and 16).

[34] It is true that, in paragraph 18 of its judgment in Case 197/86 *Brown* [1988] ECR 3205, the Court held that, at that stage in the development of Community law, assistance given to students for maintenance and training fell in principle outside the scope of the EEC Treaty for the purposes of Article 7 thereof (later Article 6 of the EC Treaty [and now Article 12]).

[35] However, since *Brown*, the Treaty on European Union has introduced citizenship of the European Union into the EC Treaty and added to Title VIII of Part Three a new chapter 3 devoted to education and vocational training. There is nothing in the amended text of the Treaty to suggest that students who are citizens of the Union, when they move to another Member State to study there, lose the rights which the Treaty confers on citizens of the Union. Furthermore, since *Brown*, the Council has also adopted Directive 93/96, which provides that the Member States must grant right of residence to student nationals of a Member State who satisfy certain requirements.

[36] The fact that a Union citizen pursues university studies in a Member State other than the State of which he is a national cannot, of itself, deprive him of the possibility of relying on the prohibition of all discrimination on grounds of nationality laid down in Article 6 of the Treaty.

[37] As pointed out in paragraph 30 above, in the present case that prohibition must be read in conjunction with Article 8a(1) of the Treaty, which proclaims 'the right to move and reside freely within the territory of the Member States, subject to the limitations and conditions laid down in this Treaty and by the measures adopted to give it effect'.

NOTE

The Court agreed that Directive 93/96, mentioned in para 35 and introduced at p.449 above, envisages that a host State may require migrant students to have means to support themselves without falling back on the host State's system of social assistance as a precondition for enjoying rights of residence under the Directive. A student may lose the right of residence under the Directive if incapable of self-support. But this was no basis for excusing the discrimination practised by Belgium.

It was commented at p.448 above that the scope of Article 12 (ex 6) EC is enhanced each time that Treaty revision extends the scope of Community competence. But something different is at stake here. Once the individual's case is shown to have a connection with Community law there then arises an entitlement to equal treatment with a home State national by virtue of Article 12 (ex 6) read with the Citizenship provisions. The Court's vivid insistence that 'Union citizenship is destined to be the fundamental status of nationals of the Member States' pleads for a single basis for entitlements. Once the applicant had squeezed inside the personal scope of Community competence – as a lawful resident of Belgium – the pull of Citizenship plus Article 12 (ex 6) took over, and secured him the same treatment as a Belgian student. This gives a strong appearance of case law moving away from the grant of particular rights to particular groups of (economic) actors and instead embracing a powerful mission of protection of individual rights. The gap in legal protection between the migrant economic actor and the Citizen of the Union gets ever smaller. You might consider whether *Mary Carpenter* (Case C-60/00) discloses any functional similarities to these cases which confer rights on Citizens of the Union.

See also, in the same vein as *Grzelczyk*, *Marie-Nathalie D'Hoop v Office national de l'emploi* (Case C-224/98 judgment of 11 July 2002); *Baumbast* (Case C-413/99 judgment of 17 September 2002).

■ QUESTIONS

1. Wilkinson asserts that 'this mythical European citizen might, to paraphrase Mark Twain, complain that rumours of his or her *birth* have been greatly exaggerated' ((1995) 1 *European Public Law* 417). Do you agree? What suggestions for nurture would you make?

2. 'Citizenship is part of the political development of the EU. As such, it is likely to evolve in the classic Union fashion: gradually and eliptically, with gaps and inconsistencies, as opportunities, agents and sponsors can be found. In that fascinating struggle, "European" citizenship will move beyond its formally frozen condition, but in a direction and to an extent that it would be foolhardy to predict' (A. Warleigh, 'Purposeful Opportunists? EU Institutions and the Struggle over European Citizenship' in R. Bellamy and A. Warleigh, *Citizenship and Governance in the EU* (London: Continuum, 2001), pp.34–35). Discuss.

FURTHER READING

Barnard, C., 'Article 13: Through the Looking Glass of Union Citizenship' in D. O'Keeffe and P. Twomey, *Legal Issues of the Amsterdam Treaty* (Oxford: Hart Publishing, 1999).

De Búrca, G., 'The Quest for Legitimacy in the European Union' (1996) 59 MLR 349.

Douglas Scott, S., 'In Search of Union Citizenship' (1998) 18 YEL 29.

Faist, T., 'Social Citizenship in the European Union' (2001) 39 JCMS 37.

Jacqueson, C., 'Union Citizenship and the Court of Justice' (2002) 27 EL Rev 260.

Jessurun d'Oliveira, H., 'Nationality and the European Union after Amsterdam' in D. O'Keeffe and P. Twomey, *Legal Issues of the Amsterdam Treaty* (Oxford: Hart Publishing, 1999).

Lardy, H., 'The Political Rights of Union Citizenship' (1996) 2 *European Public Law* 611.

Lyons, C., 'A Voyage around Article 8: an Historical and Comparative Evaluation of the Fate of European Union Citizenship' (1997) 17 YEL 135.

Reich, N., 'Union Citizenship – Metaphor or Source of Rights' (2001) 7 ELJ 4.

Shaw, J., 'The Many Pasts and Futures of Citizenship in the European Union' (1997) 22 EL Rev 554.

NOTE

 For additional material and resources see the Companion Website at: www.oup.co.uk/best.textbooks/law/weatherill6e

Epilogue to Part Two

It is worth taking a moment to reflect on the remarkable change in emphasis in Community policy-making. In the late 1980s and early 1990s the completion of the internal market was the dominant feature of the political landscape, and the relevant legal provisions were similarly high-profile. Yet in recent years the internal market has taken a lower profile. It is not yesterday's news; it is not even complete, as the Commission itself has conceded (p.310). But political priorities move on. Citizenship of the Union, the protection of Fundamental Rights and the creation of an area of 'freedom, security, and justice' all jostle for attention as the means to earn the EU fresh legitimacy. It seems that economic growth is of itself no longer sufficient for these purposes. Is this progress? The matter will be re-addressed at a general level in Chapter 21, but for the time being it is valuable to reflect on which of the issues tackled in Part Two of this book were significant agenda items at the Convention on the 'Future of Europe' and which were relegated to the sidelines.

As was explained at pp.30–32 above, the June 2003 draft constitutional text agreed at the Convention on the Future of Europe is based on four Parts. Part One received the lion's share of the attention. That is intended to supply the constitutional core of the system. It is no surprise to find that Citizenship of the Union is dealt with in Part One. And draft Article I-4 refers in its first paragraph to the economic freedoms: 'Free movement of persons, goods, services and capital, and freedom of establishment shall be guaranteed within and by the Union, in accordance with the provisions of this Constitution'. But it is the third Part of the draft text which contains detailed treatment of substantive competences, policies, and the functioning of the Union. It is here that the bulk of the matters of law and policy examined in Part Two of this book is located. The Convention was not even able to find time to propose textual refinement of the relevant provisions. This may occur before or during the intergovernmental conference scheduled to begin in the Autumn of 2003. Moreover, one of the principal attractions of separating the detailed rules of trade law from the more glamorous constitutional fundamentals located in Part One was to allow inclusion of an abridged amendment procedure for the former. This idea now appears to have fallen out of favour, so, under the June 2003 proposals, alteration of Part Three would, like alteration of Part One, demand Treaty revision backed by unanimity. It remains to be seen whether the intergovernmental conference will look again at the procedures for amendment. But, whatever may be the fate of Part Three of the draft constitutional text, it is plain that the law governing free movement will continue to occupy a central role in the system, and that the lively interplay between the Court and the political institutions in the evolution of the law will continue to supply an enduringly rich source of intellectual fascination.

PART THREE

Competition Law

16

Article 81: Cartels

SECTION 1: **INTRODUCTION TO COMPETITION LAW**

The author holds the conviction that no student of EU law can afford to be unfamiliar with the mainstream of competition law. Equally, however, there is a great deal of complex and fast-moving material in the field that can be safely left aside by the student looking at the big picture. The purpose of this Chapter and the two that follow are to chart the general structure of the law without delving too deeply into sector-specific issues or obscure economists' wrangles.

The competition law provisions of the EC Treaty are probably the most important of all from the perspective of the commercial lawyer or business person. Nothing could illustrate this more vividly than the fines, occasionally well in excess of €10 million, which have been imposed on firms by the Commission, which is responsible for the administration of these rules, subject to supervision by the Court (initially, the Court of First Instance). Moreover the Court itself is not shy in emphasizing the central role of the Treaty competition rules.

Eco Swiss China Time Ltd v *Benetton International NV* (Case C-126/97)
[1999] ECR I 3055, Court of Justice of the European Communities

[36] . . . according to Article 3(g) of the EC Treaty (now, after amendment, Article 3(1)(g) EC), Article 81 EC (ex Article 85) constitutes a fundamental provision which is essential for the accomplishment of the tasks entrusted to the Community and, in particular, for the functioning of the internal market. The importance of such a provision led the framers of the Treaty to provide expressly, in Article 81(2) EC (ex Article 85(2)), that any agreements or decisions prohibited pursuant to that article are to be automatically void.

The function of the competition rules was summarized by the Court in the following dictum:

Metro-SB-Grossmärkte GmbH & Co. KG v *Commission* (Case 26/76)
[1977] ECR 1875, [1978] 2 CMLR 1, Court of Justice of the European Communities

The requirement contained in Articles 3 and 85 of the EEC Treaty [now Articles 3 and 81 of the EC Treaty] that competition shall not be distorted implies the existence on the market of workable competition, that is to say the degree of competition necessary to ensure the observance of the basic requirements and attainment of the objectives of the Treaty, in particular the creation of a single market achieving conditions similar to those of a domestic market.

NOTE

Two ringing phrases may be extracted from that dictum: *workable competition* and *a single market*.

The first, the notion that the Treaty competition rules are concerned to promote *workable competition*, reflects a kind of economic pragmatism. 'Perfect' competition, where producers respond instantly and inevitably to consumer demand and where the efficient allocation of resources is ensured, is in practice an illusion. 'Workable' competition is concerned to achieve the most efficient resource allocation available, given the constraints of a modern economy where consumer choice cannot be perfectly expressed. So EC competition law controls cartels under Article 81, because such arrangements tend to suppress improvements normally stimulated by competition and to reduce consumer choice. Yet some cartels yield benefits, for example, through the ability of firms to specialize; this is reflected in Article 81(3), which allows exemption from prohibition for economically desirable cartels. Community law accepts that monopolies – 'dominant positions' in Community terminology – exist and may yield inefficient results. So it uses Article 82 to prohibit abuse of that position of economic strength.

The second idea, that of the *single market*, is a familiar one. Here we see the special role of competition law in a common market. Articles 81 and 82 are concerned with market integration as well as with suppressing anti-competitive conduct. In fact, Articles 81 and 82 have much in common with Articles 25, 28, 39, etc., which aim to eliminate State barriers to trade and to convert a fragmented market into a common market. Articles 81 and 82 perform a similar role but they operate in the private sector. It will be seen that firms which agree to carve up the common market along national lines are targets for severe penalties under Community competition law.

Much of the theory and practice of competition law is tied up with economic lore. This contributes to the intellectual challenge of this area of the law. At this stage, no further analysis will be provided in the abstract. However, where specific issues are dealt with, references to the relevant general literature which questions the impact of competition law will be provided. It is a matter of personal choice how deeply a student wishes to inquire into the implications of the choice of particular legal rules. However, it is suggested that basic economic theory is not as forbidding as it may first appear, and that study in this area will greatly assist understanding of the application of the legal rules.

SECTION 2: **ARTICLE 81**

ARTICLE 81 EC

1. The following shall be prohibited as incompatible with the common market: all agreements between undertakings, decisions by associations of undertakings and concerted practices which may affect trade between Member States and which have as their object or effect the prevention, restriction or distortion of competition within the common market, and in particular those which:

(a) directly or indirectly fix purchase or selling prices or any other trading conditions;
(b) limit or control production, markets, technical development, or investment;
(c) share markets or sources of supply;
(d) apply dissimilar conditions to equivalent transactions with other trading parties, thereby placing them at a competitive disadvantage;
(e) make the conclusion of contracts subject to acceptance by the other parties of supplementary obligations which, by their nature or according to commercial usage, have no connection with the subject of such contracts.

2. Any agreements or decisions prohibited pursuant to this Article shall be automatically void.
3. The provisions of paragraph 1 may, however, be declared inapplicable in the case of:

— any agreement or category of agreements between undertakings;
— any decision or category of decisions by associations of undertakings;
— any concerted practice or category of concerted practices;

which contributes to improving the production or distribution of goods or to promoting technical or economic progress, while allowing consumers a fair share of the resulting benefit, and which does not:

(a) impose on the undertakings concerned restrictions which are not indispensable to the attainment of these objectives;

(b) afford such undertakings the possibility of eliminating competition in respect of a substantial part of the products in question.

NOTE

The text of this provision was untouched by both the Amsterdam and the Nice Treaty. However, Article 81's pre-Amsterdam number was 85. This must be borne in mind in reading the material contained in this Chapter.

No case better illustrates the nature and purpose of Article 81 than the following:

Établissements Consten SA and *Grundig GmbH* v *Commission* (Cases 56 and 58/64)

[1966] ECR 299, [1966] CMLR 418, Court of Justice of the European Communities

Consten, a French firm, agreed to handle only German-made Grundig electrical products in France. Grundig agreed to supply only Consten in France and to ensure that its customers outside France were restrained from delivering the goods into France. This was an 'exclusive distribution' deal which conferred 'absolute territorial protection' in France on Consten. The Commission found the agreement unlawful and the parties applied to the Court for annulment of that decision. The Court's ruling deserves close attention. Remember that Article 85 is now, post-Amsterdam, Article 81.

The applicants submit that the prohibition in Article 85(1) applies only to so-called horizontal agreements. The Italian Government submits furthermore that sole distributorship contracts do not constitute 'agreements between undertakings' within the meaning of that provision, since the parties are not on a footing of equality. With regard to these contracts, freedom of competition may only be protected by virtue of Article 86 of the Treaty.

Neither the wording of Article 85 nor that of Article 86 gives any ground for holding that distinct areas of application are to be assigned to each of the two Articles according to the level in the economy at which the contracting parties operate. Article 85 refers in a general way to all agreements which distort competition within the Common Market and does not lay down any distinction between those agreements based on whether they are made between competitors operating at the same level in the economic process or between non-competing persons operating at different levels. In principle, no distinction can be made where the Treaty does not make any distinction.

Furthermore, the possible application of Article 85 to a sole distributorship contract cannot be excluded merely because the grantor and the concessionnaire are not competitors *inter se* and not on a footing of equality. Competition may be distorted within the meaning of Article 85(1) not only by agreements which limit it as between the parties, but also by agreements which prevent or restrict the competition which might take place between one of them and third parties. For this purpose, it is irrelevant whether the parties to the agreement are or are not on a footing of equality as regards their position and function in the economy. This applies all the more, since, by such an agreement, the parties might seek, by preventing or limiting the competition of third parties in respect of the products, to create or guarantee for their benefit an unjustified advantage at the expense of the consumer or user, contrary to the general aims of Article 85.

It is thus possible that, without involving an abuse of a dominant position, an agreement between economic operators at different levels may affect trade between Member States and at the same time have as its object or effect the prevention, restriction or distortion of competition, thus falling under the prohibition of Article 85(1).

In addition, it is pointless to compare on the one hand the situation, to which Article 85 applies, of a producer bound by a sole distributorship agreement to the distributor of his products with on the other hand that of a producer who includes within his undertaking the distribution of his own products by some means, for example, by commercial representatives, to which Article 85 does not apply. These situations are distinct in law and, moreover, need to be assessed differently, since two marketing organizations, one of which is integrated into the manufacturer's undertaking whilst the other is not, may not necessarily have the same efficiency. The wording of Article 85 causes the prohibition to apply, provided that the other conditions are met, to an agreement between several undertakings. Thus it does not apply where a sole undertaking integrates its own distribution network into its business organization. It does not thereby follow, however, that the contractual situation based on an agreement between a manufacturing and a distributing undertaking is rendered legally acceptable by a simple process of economic analogy – which is in any case incomplete and in contradiction with the said Article. Furthermore, although in the first case the Treaty intended in Article 85 to leave untouched the internal organization of an undertaking and to render it liable to be called in question, by means of Article 86, only in cases where it reaches such a degree of seriousness as to amount to an abuse of a dominant position, the same reservation could not apply when the impediments to competition result from agreement between two different undertakings which then as a general rule simply require to be prohibited.

Finally, an agreement between producer and distributor which might tend to restore the national divisions in trade between Member States might be such as to frustrate the most fundamental object of the Community. The Treaty, whose preamble and content aim at abolishing the barriers between States, and which in several provisions gives evidence of a stern attitude with regard to their reappearance, could not allow undertakings to reconstruct such barriers. Article 85(1) is designed to pursue this aim, even in the case of agreements between undertakings placed at different levels in the economic process.

The submissions set out above are consequently unfounded . . .

The complaints relating to the concept of 'agreements . . . which may affect trade between Member States'

The applicants and the German Government maintain that the Commission has relied on a mistaken interpretation of the concept of an agreement which may affect trade between Member States and has not shown that such trade would have been greater without the agreement in dispute.

The defendant replies that this requirement in Article 85(1) is fulfilled once trade between Member States develops, as a result of the agreement, differently from the way in which it would have done without the restriction resulting from the agreement, and once the influence of the agreement on market conditions reaches a certain degree. Such is the case here, according to the defendant, particularly in view of the impediments resulting within the Common Market from the disputed agreement as regards the exporting and importing of Grundig products to and from France.

The concept of an agreement 'which may affect trade between Member States' is intended to define, in the law governing cartels, the boundary between the areas respectively covered by Community law and national law. It is only to the extent to which the agreement may affect trade between Member States that the deterioration in competition caused by the agreement falls under the prohibition of Community law contained in Article 85; otherwise it escapes the prohibition.

In this connexion, what is particularly important is whether the agreement is capable of constituting a threat, either direct or indirect, actual or potential, to freedom of trade between Member States in a manner which might harm the attainment of the objectives of a single market between States. Thus the fact that an agreement encourages an increase, even a large one, in the volume of trade between States is not sufficient to exclude the possibility that the agreement may 'affect' such trade in the abovementioned manner. In the present case, the contract between Grundig and Consten, on the one hand by preventing undertakings other than Consten from importing Grundig products into France, and on the other hand by prohibiting Consten from re-exporting those products to other countries of the Common Market, indisputably affects trade between Member States. These limitations on the freedom of trade, as well as those which might ensue for third parties from the registration in France by Consten of the GINT trade mark, which Grundig places on all its products, are enough to satisfy the requirement in question.

Consequently, the complaints raised in this respect must be dismissed.

The complaints concerning the criterion of restriction on competition

The applicants and the German Government maintain that since the Commission restricted its examination solely to Grundig products the decision was based upon a false concept of competition and of the rules on prohibition contained in Article 85(1), since this concept applies particularly to competition between similar products of different makes; the Commission, before declaring Article 85(1) to be applicable, should, by basing itself upon the 'rule of reason', have considered the economic effects of the disputed contract upon competition between the different makes. There is a presumption that vertical sole distributorship agreements are not harmful to competition and in the present case there is nothing to invalidate that presumption. On the contrary, the contract in question has increased the competition between similar products of different makes.

The principle of freedom of competition concerns the various stages and manifestations of competition. Although competition between producers is generally more noticeable than that between distributors of products of the same make, it does not thereby follow that an agreement tending to restrict the latter kind of competition should escape the prohibition of Article 85(1) merely because it might increase the former.

Besides, for the purpose of applying Article 85(1), there is no need to take account of the concrete effects of an agreement once it appears that it has as its object the prevention, restriction or distortion of competition.

Therefore the absence in the contested decision of any analysis of the effects of the agreement on competition between similar products of different makes does not, of itself, constitute a defect in the decision.

It thus remains to consider whether the contested decision was right in founding the prohibition of the disputed agreement under Article 85(1) on the restriction on competition created by the agreement in the sphere of the distribution of Grundig products alone. The infringement which was found to exist by the contested decision results from the absolute territorial protection created by the said contract in favour of Consten on the basis of French law. The applicants thus wished to eliminate any possibility of competition at the wholesale level in Grundig products in the territory specified in the contract essentially by two methods.

First, Grundig undertook not to deliver even indirectly to third parties products intended for the area covered by the contract. The restrictive nature of that undertaking is obvious if it is considered in the light of the prohibition on exporting which was imposed not only on Consten but also on all the other sole concessionnaires of Grundig, as well as the German wholesalers. Secondly, the registration in France by Consten of the GINT trade mark, which Grundig affixes to all its products, is intended to increase the protection inherent in the disputed agreement, against the risk of parallel imports into France of Grundig products, by adding the protection deriving from the law on industrial property rights. Thus no third party could import Grundig products from other Member States of the Community for resale in France without running serious risks.

The defendant properly took into account the whole distribution system thus set up by Grundig. In order to arrive at a true representation of the contractual position the contract must be placed in the economic and legal context in the light of which it was concluded by the parties. Such a procedure is not to be regarded as an unwarrantable interference in legal transactions or circumstances which were not the subject of the proceedings before the Commission.

The situation as ascertained above results in the isolation of the French market and makes it possible to charge for the products in question prices which are sheltered from all effective competition. In addition, the more producers succeed in their efforts to render their own makes of product individually distinct in the eyes of the consumer, the more the effectiveness of competition between producers tends to diminish. Because of the considerable impact of distribution costs on the aggregate cost price, it seems important that competition between dealers should also be stimulated. The efforts of the dealer are stimulated by competition between distributors of products of the same make. Since the agreement thus aims at isolating the French market for Grundig products and maintaining artificially, for products of a very well-known brand, separate national markets within the Community, it is therefore such as to distort competition in the Common Market.

It was therefore proper for the contested decision to hold that the agreement constitutes an infringement of Article 85(1). No further considerations, whether of economic data (price differences between France and Germany, representative character of the type of appliance considered, level of overheads borne by Consten) or of the corrections of the criteria upon which the Commission relied in its comparisons between the situations of the French and German markets, and no possible favourable effects of the agreement in other respects, can in any way lead, in the face of abovementioned restrictions, to a different solution under Article 85(1).

NOTE

Was this an *anti-competitive* deal? In one sense it was, because Grundig goods were available in France from just one source, Consten. But did it really matter? After all, if Consten had sold Grundig goods at unreasonably high prices, consumers would simply have bought the electrical products of other manufacturers. Competition between different brands of the goods would restrain Consten.

So, adopting this perspective, the US Supreme Court declared in *Continental TV* v *Sylvania* 433 US 36 (1977) that:

Interbrand competition . . . is the primary concern of antitrust law . . . When interbrand competition exists . . . it provides a significant check on the exploitation of intrabrand market power because of the ability of consumers to substitute a different brand of the same product.

■ QUESTION

Explain how and why this perception went largely ignored in *Consten* (Cases 56 and 58/64). Notice the Court's concern to preserve 'parallel trade'; cross-border intrabrand competition must be secured, whatever the interbrand competitive situation may be.

NOTE

So EC competition law has special objectives. It aims to further *market integration*. It is different from US law, and, for that matter, from UK or German law. *Consten* (Cases 56 and 58/64), then, has caused us to ask some important questions about the *purpose* of competition law. It seems that EC law may have suspicions about 'vertical' deals which improve product distribution which would not be entertained by other competition law systems which are not designed to help market integration.

But *should* it? Is interventionism of this type, even in markets shown to be characterised by interbrand competition, truly justified or is market integration but a shibboleth? Even if such an approach *was* so justified, can it remain so in the post-1992 climate of an internal market? These questions about the shape of EC competition policy were among those that prompted the Commission to publish a Green Paper on *Vertical Restraints in EC Competition Policy* in January 1997 (COM (96) 721), which initiated a wide-ranging review of the application of Article 81 to vertical restraints (those between traders at different points in the supply chain), including distribution agreements of the *Consten and Grundig* type. This review culminated in the adoption of Regulation 2790/1999 on vertical restraints in December 1999, which is examined below at p.535, after the structure of Article 81 has been placed in its full context.

SECTION 3: **JURISDICTION**

Community competition law applies only to deals which 'affect trade between Member States'. Most deals which involve parties in more than one State will raise no great difficulty under this head. Obviously, the Consten/Grundig arrangement affected trade between Member States; so too the Dyestuffs concerted practice (*ICI* v *Commission* (Case 48/69)) discussed at p.505 below. However, the ambit of

EC competition law is broad. Two situations may seem prima facie to fall out-with Article 81; first, where the parties to the deal are all located within one Member State; secondly, where the parties to the deal are all located outside the Community. Both may nevertheless fall within Article 81.

The first issue, a deal apparently internal to one Member State, is discussed in the next case.

Cooperatieve Stremsel- en Kleurselfabriek v *Commission* (Case 61/80)

[1981] ECR 851, Court of Justice of the European Communities

A cooperative of producers in the dairy sector required all its members to buy exclusively from each other. All the members were Dutch. The Commission held that an effect on inter-State trade had been established. The Court agreed, for the following reasons:

[12] ... [I]t should be recalled that for the agreement at issue to be caught by the prohibition contained in Article 85(1) it must have 'as its object or effect the prevention, restriction or distortion of competition within the common market'. The Cooperative's rules, which require its members to purchase from the Cooperative all the rennet and colouring agents for cheese which they need, and which reinforce that obligation by stipulating the payment of a not inconsiderable sum in the event of resignation or expulsion, have clearly as their object to prevent members from obtaining supplies from other suppliers of rennet or colouring agents or from making them themselves should those alternatives offer advantages from the point of view of quality or price. Since, according to information which has not been challenged, the members now account for more than 90% of Netherlands cheese output, those provisions in addition contribute to maintaining the present situation, in which the Cooperative is virtually the only supplier of rennet on the Netherlands market.

[13] Those provisions are thus of such a nature as to prevent competition, at the level of the supply of rennet and colouring agents for cheese, between producers holding a large part of the Community market in cheese, and also tend to rule out the possibility of creating a competitive situation on the whole of the Netherlands market in these ancillary substances which are indispensable in the making of cheese. In the circumstances, there is no need to examine the question whether other factors help to maintain the Cooperative's dominant position on the relevant market and whether such factors are sufficient to consolidate that position, even in the absence of the aforesaid provisions.

[14] In order to determine whether the agreement is contrary to Article 85(1) it is also necessary to consider whether it is liable to affect trade between Member States, that is to say whether, according to the consistent case-law of the Court, it is possible to foresee with a sufficient degree of probability that it may have an influence, direct or indirect, actual or potential, on the pattern of trade between Member States, thus rendering more difficult the interpenetration of trade which the Treaty is intended to create.

[15] It emerges from information supplied by the Commission that there is already trade in animal rennet and colouring agents between Member States and no mention has been made of technical or economic difficulties standing in the way of the expansion of such trade. On the other hand, bearing in mind the economic context to which they belong, the obligations contained in the rules of the Cooperative are precisely of such a nature as to reinforce the partitioning of markets on a national basis, thereby holding up the economic interpenetration which the Treaty is designed to bring about.

NOTE
Notice how the stress on preventing the isolation of national markets has much in common with the rationale of the *'Cassis de Dijon'* (Case 120/78) line of authority under Article 28. It can also be identified in *Keck* (Cases C-267 and 268/91) (p.397 above). This is the law of market integration rather than a set of individual Treaty provisions.

The second issue, the deal external to the Community's borders, was examined by the Court in the 'Woodpulp' cartel case.

Ahlström Osakyhtio v Commission (Cases 89, 104, 114, 116, 117, and 125–129/85)

[1988] ECR 5193, [1988] 4 CMLR 901, Court of Justice of the European Communities

[12] It should be noted that the main sources of supply of wood pulp are outside the Community, in Canada, the United States, Sweden and Finland and that the market therefore has global dimensions. Where wood pulp producers established in those countries sell directly to purchasers established in the Community and engage in price competition in order to win orders from those customers, that constitutes competition within the common market.

[13] It follows that where those producers concert on the prices to be charged to their customers in the Community and put that concertation into effect by selling at prices which are actually coordinated, they are taking part in concertation which has the object and effect of restricting competition within the common market within the meaning of Article 85 of the Treaty.

[14] Accordingly, it must be concluded that by applying the competition rules in the Treaty in the circumstances of this case to undertakings whose registered offices are situated outside the Community, the Commission has not made an incorrect assessment of the territorial scope of Article 85.

[15] The applicants have submitted that the decision is incompatible with public international law on the grounds that the application of the competition rules in this case was founded exclusively on the economic repercussions within the common market of conduct restricting competition which was adopted outside the Community.

[16] It should be observed that an infringement of Article 85, such as the conclusion of an agreement which has had the effect of restricting competition within the common market, consists of conduct made up of two elements, the formation of the agreement, decision or concerted practice and the implementation thereof. If the applicability of prohibitions laid down under competition law were made to depend on the place where the agreement, decision or concerted practice was formed, the result would obviously be to give undertakings an easy means of evading those prohibitions. The decisive factor is therefore the place where it is implemented.

[17] The producers in this case implemented their pricing agreement within the common market. It is immaterial in that respect whether or not they had recourse to subsidiaries, agents, sub-agents, or branches within the Community in order to make their contacts with purchasers within the Community.

[18] Accordingly the Community's jurisdiction to apply its competition rules to such conduct is covered by the territoriality principle as universally recognized in public international law.

[19] As regards the argument based on the infringement of the principle of non-interference, it should be pointed out that the applicants who are members of KEA have referred to a rule according to which where two States have jurisdiction to lay down and enforce rules and the effect of those rules is that a person finds himself subject to contradictory orders as to the conduct he must adopt, each State is obliged to exercise its jurisdiction with moderation. The applicants have concluded that by disregarding that rule in applying its competition rules the Community has infringed the principle of non-interference.

[20] There is no need to enquire into the existence in international law of such a rule since it suffices to observe that the conditions for its application are in any event not satisfied. There is not, in this case, any contradiction between the conduct required by the United States and that required by the Community since the Webb Pomerene Act merely exempts the conclusion of export cartels from the application of United States anti-trust laws but does not require such cartels to be concluded.

[21] It should further be pointed out that the United States authorities raised no objections regarding any conflict of jurisdiction when consulted by the Commission pursuant to the OECD Council

Recommendation of 25 October 1979 concerning cooperation between member countries on restrictive business practices affecting international trade (*Acts of the organization*, Vol. 19, p.376).

[22] As regards the argument relating to disregard of international comity, it suffices to observe that it amounts to calling in question the Community's jurisdiction to apply its competition rules to conduct such as that found to exist in this case and that, as such, that argument has already been rejected.

[23] Accordingly it must be concluded that the Commission's decision is not contrary to Article 85 of the Treaty or to the rules of public international law relied on by the applicants.

NOTE

The Court, by concentrating on 'implementation' (para 16), is obviously skirting around an explicit adoption of the 'effects doctrine' of jurisdiction under international law. Advocate-General Darmon, after examining relevant authorities, had concluded ([1988] ECR, at p.5227) that:

. . . there is no rule of international law which is capable of being relied upon against the criterion of the direct, substantial and foreseeable effect. Nor does the concept of international comity, in view of its uncertain scope, militate against that criterion either.

In the absence of any such prohibitive rule and in the light of widespread State practice, I would therefore propose that in view of its appropriateness to the field of competition, it be adopted as a criterion for the jurisdiction of the Community.

■ QUESTION

Has the Court adopted a test which is distinct in practice from the 'effects doctrine'? For comment, read, e.g., J. B. Lange and D. Sandage (1989) 26 CML Rev 137; F. Mann (1989) 38 ICLQ 375; A. V. Lowe (1989) 48 CLJ 9.

SECTION 4: **AN AGREEMENT**

The 'agreement' which may be caught by Article 81 goes beyond the formal contract. Article 81 is aimed at the parties' intent, not the form in which that may be expressed. It covers informal agreements, claimed to be non-binding, secret cartels, and even imposed agreements. The next case involves the uncovering of the multi-faceted 'Quinine Cartel'.

ACF Chemiefarma v *Commission* (Cases 41, 44, and 45/69)

[1970] ECR 661, Court of Justice of the European Communities

[106] The applicant complains that the Commission considered that the export agreement relating to trade with third countries and the gentlemen's agreement governing the conduct of its members in the Common Market constituted an indivisible entity as far as Article 85 was concerned.

[107] The applicant states that the gentlemen's agreement, unlike the export agreement, did not constitute an agreement within the meaning of Article 85(1) and in any event it definitively ceased to exist from the end of October 1962.

[108] The conduct of the parties to the export agreement does not in the applicant's view indicate that they continued the restrictions on competition which were originally provided for in the gentlemen's agreement.

[109] The opposite conclusions reached by the contested decision are therefore alleged to be vitiated because they are based on incorrect findings.

[110] The gentlemen's agreement, which the applicant admits existed until the end of October 1962, had as its object the restriction of competition within the Common Market.

[111] The parties to the export agreement mutually declared themselves willing to abide by the gentlemen's agreement and concede that they did so until the end of October 1962.

[112] This document thus amounted to the faithful expression of the joint intention of the parties to the agreement with regard to their conduct in the Common Market.

[113] Furthermore it contained a provision to the effect that infringement of the gentlemen's agreement would *ipso facto* constitute an infringement of the export agreement.

[114] In those circumstances account must be taken of this connexion in assessing the effects of the gentlemen's agreement with regard to the categories of acts prohibited by Article 85(1).

[115] The defendant bases its view that the gentlemen's agreement was continued until February 1965 on documents and declarations emanating from the parties to the agreement the tenor of which is indistinct and indeed contradictory so that it is impossible to conclude whether those undertakings intended to terminate the gentlemen's agreement at their meeting on 29 October 1962.

[116] The conduct of the undertakings in the Common Market after 29 October 1962 must therefore be considered in relation to the following four points: sharing out of domestic markets, fixing of common prices, determination of sales quotas and prohibition against manufacturing synthetic quinidine.

[117] The gentlemen's agreement guaranteed protection of each domestic market for the producers in the various Member States.

[118] After October 1962 when significant supplies were delivered on one of those markets by producers who were not nationals, as for example in the case of sales of quinine and quinidine in France, there was a substantial alignment of prices conforming to French domestic prices which were higher than the export prices to third countries.

[119] It does not appear that there were alterations in the insignificant volume of trade between the other Member States referred to by the clause relating to domestic protection in spite of considerable differences in the prices prevailing in each of those States.

[120] The divergences between the domestic legislation of those States cannot by itself explain those differences in price or the substantial absence of trade.

[121] Obstacles which might arise in the trade in quinine and quinidine from differences between national legislation governing pharmaceutical products under trade-mark cannot relevantly be invoked to explain those facts.

[122] The correspondence exchanged in October and November 1963 between the parties to the export agreement with regard to the protection of domestic markets merely confirmed the intention of those undertakings to allow this state of affairs to remain unchanged.

[123] This intention was subsequently confirmed by Nedchem during the meeting of the undertakings concerned in Brussels on 14 March 1964.

[124] From those circumstances it is clear that with regard to the restriction on competition arising from the protection of the producers' domestic markets the producers continued after the meeting on 29 October 1962 to abide by the gentlemen's agreement of 1960 and confirmed their common intention to do so.

NOTE

Read also *BMW v Belgium* (Case 32/78) [1979] ECR 2435, [1980] 1 CMLR 370 and for a recent indication that covert cartels involving market-sharing and price-fixing are far from things of the past see Decision 2003/2 *Vitamins* [2003] OJ L6/1.

SECTION 5: **THE CONCERTED PRACTICE**

Even arrangements which are less formal than an agreement are caught by Article 81 if they constitute a 'concerted practice'. In fact, because both the agreement and the concerted practice fall within Article 81, there may be little point distinguishing between them. However, it remains crucial to differentiate collusion, whether agreement or concerted practice, from mere parallel behaviour, for the latter remains perfectly lawful. The next case illustrates the notion of the concerted practice and raises complex questions about the reach of Article 81. It is concerned with the dyestuffs industry and is commonly referred to as the 'Dyestuffs' case. Remember: Article 81 was Article 85 prior to the re-numbering effected by the Amsterdam Treaty (p.12 above).

ICI v _Commission_ (Case 48/69)
[1972] ECR 619, Court of Justice of the European Communities

The Court first examined the concept of a concerted practice.

[64] Article 85 draws a distinction between the concept of 'concerted practices' and that of 'agreements between undertakings' or of 'decisions by associations of undertakings'; the object is to bring within the prohibition of that article a form of coordination between undertakings which, without having reached the stage where an agreement properly so-called has been concluded, knowingly substitutes practical cooperation between them for the risks of competition.

[65] By its very nature, then, a concerted practice does not have all the elements of a contract but may _inter alia_ arise out of coordination which becomes apparent from the behaviour of the participants.

[66] Although parallel behaviour may not by itself be identified with a concerted practice, it may however amount to strong evidence of such a practice if it leads to conditions of competition which do not correspond to the normal conditions of the market, having regard to the nature of the products, the size and number of the undertakings, and the volume of the said market.

[67] This is especially the case if the parallel conduct is such as to enable those concerned to attempt to stabilize prices at a level different from that to which competition would have led, and to consolidate established positions to the detriment of effective freedom of movement of the products in the Common Market and of the freedom of consumers to choose their suppliers.

[68] Therefore the question whether there was a concerted action in this case can only be correctly determined if the evidence upon which the contested decision is based is considered, not in isolation, but as a whole, account being taken of the specific features of the market in the products in question.

The Court then proceeded to explore the nature of the dyestuffs market.

[69] The market in dyestuffs is characterised by the fact that 80% of the market is supplied by about ten producers, very large ones in the main, which often manufacture these products together with other chemical products or pharmaceutical specialities.

[70] The production patterns and therefore the cost structures of these manufacturers are very different, and this makes it difficult to ascertain competing manufacturers' costs.

[71] The total number of dyestuffs is very high, each undertaking producing more than a thousand.

[72] The average extent to which these products can be replaced by others is considered relatively good for standard dyes, but it can be very low or even non-existent for speciality dyes.

[73] As regards speciality products, the market tends in certain cases towards an oligopolistic situation.

[74] Since the price of dyestuffs forms a relatively small part of the price of the final product of the user undertaking, there is little elasticity of demand for dyestuffs on the market as a whole and this encourages price increases in the short term.

[75] Another factor is that the total demand for dyestuffs is constantly increasing, and this tends to induce producers to adopt a policy enabling them to take advantage of this increase.

[76] In the territory of the Community, the market in dyestuffs in fact consists of five separate national markets with different price levels which cannot be explained by differences in costs and charges affecting producers in those countries.

[77] Thus the establishment of the Common Market would not appear to have had any effect on this situation, since the differences between national price levels have scarcely decreased.

[78] On the contrary, it is clear that each of the national markets has the characteristics of an oligopoly and that in most of them price levels are established under the influence of a 'priceleader', who in some cases is the largest producer in the country concerned, and in other cases is a producer in another Member State or a third State, acting through a subsidiary.

[79] According to the experts this dividing-up of the market is due to the need to supply local technical assistance to users and to ensure immediate delivery, generally in small quantities, since, apart from exceptional cases, producers supply their subsidiaries established in the different Member States and maintain a network of agents and depots to ensure that user undertakings receive specific assistance and supplies.

[80] It appears from the data produced during the course of the proceedings that even in cases where a producer establishes direct contact with an important user in another Member State, prices are usually fixed in relation to the place where the user is established and tend to follow the level of prices on the national market.

[81] Although the foremost reason why producers have acted in this way is in order to adapt themselves to the special features of the market in dyestuffs and to the needs of their customers, the fact remains that the dividing-up of the market which results tends, by fragmenting the effects of competition, to isolate users in their national market, and to prevent a general confrontation between producers throughout the Common Market.

[82] It is in this context, which is peculiar to the way in which the dyestuffs market works, that the facts of the case should be considered.

The increases of 1964, 1965 and 1967

[83] The increases of 1964, 1965 and 1967 covered by the contested decision are interconnected.

[84] The increase of 15% in the prices of most aniline dyes in Germany on 1 January 1965 was in reality nothing more than the extension to another national market of the increase applied in January 1964 in Italy, the Netherlands, Belgium and Luxembourg.

[85] The increase in the prices of certain dyes and pigments introduced on 1 January 1965 in all the Member States, except France, applied to all the products which had been excluded from the first increase.

[86] The reason why the price increase of 8% introduced in the autumn of 1967 was raised to 12% for France was that there was a wish to make up for the increases of 1964 and 1965 in which that market had not taken part because of the price control system.

[87] Therefore the three increases cannot be isolated from one another, even though they did not take place under identical conditions.

[88] In 1964 all the undertakings in question announced their increases and immediately put them

into effect, the initiative coming from Ciba-Italy which, on 7 January 1964, following instructions from Ciba-Switzerland, announced and immediately introduced an increase of 15%. This initiative was followed by the other producers on the Italian market within two or three days.

[89] On 9 January ICI Holland took the initiative in introducing the same increase in the Netherlands, whilst on the same day Bayer took the same initiative on the Belgo-Luxembourg market.

[90] With minor differences, particularly between the price increases by the German undertakings on the one hand and the Swiss and United Kingdom undertakings on the other, these increases concerned the same range of products for the various producers and markets, namely, most aniline dyes other than pigments, food colourings and cosmetics.

[91] As regards the increase of 1965 certain undertakings announced in advance price increases amounting, for the German market, to an increase of 15% for products whose prices had already been similarly increased on the other markets, and to 10% for products whose prices had not yet been increased. These announcements were spread over the period between 14 October and 28 December 1964.

[92] The first announcement was made by BASF, on 14 October 1964, followed by an announcement by Bayer on 30 October and by Casella on 5 November.

[93] These increases were simultaneously applied on 1 January 1965 on all the markets except for the French market because of the price freeze in that State, and the Italian market where, as a result of the refusal by the principal Italian producer, ACNA, to increase its prices on the said market, the other producers also decided not to increase theirs.

[94] ACNA also refrained from putting its prices up by 10% on the German market.

[95] Otherwise the increase was general, was simultaneously introduced by all the producers mentioned in the contested decision, and was applied without any differences concerning the range of products.

[96] As regards the increase of 1967, during a meeting held at Basel on 19 August 1967, which was attended by all the producers mentioned in the contested decision except ACNA, the Geigy undertaking announced its intention to increase its selling prices by 8% with effect from 16 October 1967.

[97] On that same occasion the representatives of Bayer and Francolor stated that their undertakings were also considering an increase.

[98] From mid-September all the undertakings mentioned in the contested decision announced a price increase of 8%, raised to 12% for France, to take effect on 16 October in all the countries except Italy, where ACNA again refused to increase its prices, although it was willing to follow the movement in prices on two other markets, albeit on dates other than 16 October.

[99] Viewed as a whole, the three consecutive increases reveal progressive cooperation between the undertakings concerned.

[100] In fact, after the experience of 1964, when the announcement of the increases and their application coincided, although with minor differences as regards the range of products affected, the increases of 1965 and 1967 indicate a different mode of operation. Here, the undertakings taking the initiative, BASF and Geigy respectively, announced their intentions of making an increase some time in advance, which allowed the undertakings to observe each other's reactions on the different markets, and to adapt themselves accordingly.

[101] By means of these advance announcements the various undertakings eliminated all uncertainty between them as to their future conduct and, in doing so, also eliminated a large part of the risk usually inherent in any independent change of conduct on one or several markets.

[102] This was all the more the case since these announcements, which led to the fixing of general and equal increases in prices for the markets in dyestuffs, rendered the market transparent as regard the percentage rates of increase.

[103] Therefore, by the way in which they acted, the undertakings in question temporarily eliminated with respect to prices some of the preconditions for competition on the market which stood in the way of the achievement of parallel uniformity of conduct.

[104] The fact that this conduct was not spontaneous is corroborated by an examination of other aspects of the market.

[105] In fact, from the number of producers concerned it is not possible to say that the European market in dyestuffs is, in the strict sense, an oligopoly in which price competition could no longer play a substantial role.

[106] These producers are sufficiently powerful and numerous to create a considerable risk that in times of rising prices some of them might not follow the general movement but might instead try to increase their share of the market by behaving in an individual way.

[107] Furthermore, the dividing-up of the Common Market into five national markets with different price levels and structures makes it improbable that a spontaneous and equal price increase would occur on all the national markets.

[108] Although a general, spontaneous increase on each of the national markets is just conceivable, these increases might be expected to differ according to the particular characteristics of the different national markets.

[109] Therefore, although parallel conduct in respect of prices may well have been an attractive and risk-free objective for the undertakings concerned, it is hardly conceivable that the same action could be taken spontaneously at the same time, on the same national markets and for the same range of products.

[110] Nor is it any more plausible that the increases of January 1964, introduced on the Italian market and copied on the Netherlands and Belgo-Luxembourg markets, which have little in common with each other either as regards the level of prices or the pattern of competition, could have been brought into effect within a period of two to three days without prior concertation.

[111] As regards the increases of 1965 and 1967 concertation took place openly, since all the announcements of the intention to increase prices with effect from a certain date and for a certain range of products made it possible for producers to decide on their conduct regarding the special cases of France and Italy.

[112] In proceeding in this way, the undertakings mutually eliminated in advance any uncertainties concerning their reciprocal behaviour on the different markets and thereby also eliminated a large part of the risk inherent in any independent change of conduct on those markets.

[113] The general and uniform increase on those different markets can only be explained by a common intention on the part of those undertakings, first, to adjust the level of prices and the situation resulting from competition in the form of discounts, and secondly, to avoid the risk, which is inherent in any price increase, of changing the conditions of competition.

NOTE

The key point about the 'Dyestuffs' case is that the Court decided that there was *no* oligopoly. There must, the Court deduced, have been a concerted practice which explained the absence of effective competition. Proof of concertation is problematic. You should carefully examine the 'Dyestuffs' judgment *and the Commission's decision* ([1969] CMLR D23) in order to determine which pieces of evidence you may take into account in locating a concerted practice.

The development of the law has been distorted because procedural irregularities have led to the annulment of some Commission Decisions which have found the existence of concerted practices. The 'Woodpulp Cartel' was considered above in connection with jurisdictional aspects (p.502). The substance was dealt with by the Court in 1993, when it largely annulled the Decision. However, the Court provided important comment on proof of concertation. It said that parallel conduct is not proof of concertation unless concertation represents the only plausible explanation for such conduct. It then applied this principle to the producers' quarterly price announcements which the Commission had used as evidence of concertation:

Ahlström O Sakyhtio v *Commission* (Cases C-89, 104, 114, 116–7, 125–129/85)
[1993] ECR I-1307, [1993] 4 CMLR 407

[126] . . . [I]t must be stated that, in this case, concertation is not the only plausible explanation for the parallel conduct. To begin with, the system of price announcements may be regarded as constituting a rational response to the fact that the pulp market constituted a long-term market and to the need felt by both buyers and sellers to limit commercial risks. Further, the similarity in the dates of price announcements may be regarded as a direct result of the high degree of market transparency, which does not have to be described as artificial. Finally, the parallelism of prices and the price trends may be satisfactorily explained by the oligopolistic tendencies of the market and by the specific circumstances prevailing in certain periods. Accordingly, the parallel conduct established by the Commission does not constitute evidence of concertation.

[127] In the absence of a firm, precise and consistent body of evidence, it must be held that concertation regarding announced prices has not been established by the Commission. Article 1(1) of the contested decision must therefore be annulled.

NOTE
See comment by A. Jones (1993) 14 ECLR 273; G. Cumming [1994] JBL 165; C. Osti [1994] ECLR 176.

Consider also *John Deere* v *Commission* (Case T-35/92) [1994] ECR II-957, for a case in which information exchange was found to violate Article 81, in part because of the confidential nature of the data exchanged. Residual market competition was inhibited by the reduced uncertainty about strategies planned by rival firms. In such litigation the Court of First Instance is today responsible for carrying out the function of checking the compatibility of the Commission's conduct of an investigation with Community law (see, e.g., on concertation, Case T-334/94 *Sarrio* v *Commission* [1998] ECR II-1439). The unsuccessful appeal in *John Deere* v *Commission* (Case C-7/95P) [1998] ECR I-3111 provides an example of the European Court's treatment of appeals against such CFI decisions; see also *Commission* v *Anic* (Case C-49/92P [1999] ECR I-4125).

Where a true oligopoly exists (which in the view of both Court and Commission was *not* the case in 'Dyestuffs'), firms may make parallel decisions without colluding. Yet the observable result on the market would be more or less the same as if they had colluded. The inadequacies of the collusion-based Article 81 as a method for controlling true oligopolies have tempted the Commission to move in the direction of treating firms in an oligopoly as collectively dominant and subject to control under Article 82. But the Commission has suffered economic and legal setbacks in developing this notion, which is one of profound complexity and escapes exploration in this Chapter. See R. Whish, *Competition Law* (4th ed, London: Butterworths, 2001), Ch.14.

■ QUESTION

You are asked to advise Alpha, a producer in a market which contains only three other producers. Would the following be caught by Article 81?

    (a) Alpha's announcement of a 10% price rise, communicated 14 days in advance through a statement in the trade's leading journal;

    (b) Alpha's Christmas card, sent to the other three producers, which adds to seasonal greetings the comment: 'Life would be so much easier if we simply followed each other's prices! But of course we'd never get away with it'. Alpha's 5% price rise on 1 January is followed by the other three producers on 10 January;

    (c) the establishment of a trade association of which all four producers are members.

SECTION 6: **RESTRICTION OF COMPETITION**

The deal, having satisfied the preceding requirements, must have as its 'object or effect the prevention, restriction or distortion of competition within the common market'. Each word in this phrase has some independent relevance, but the classic broad statement of the requirements of this test was supplied in *Société Technique Minière* v *Maschinenbau Ulm* (Case 56/65) [1966] ECR 235:

It must be possible to foresee with a sufficient degree of probability on the basis of a set of objective factors of law or fact that the agreement in question may have an influence, direct or indirect, actual or potential, on the pattern of trade between Member States.

Often this is not a difficult test to satisfy. In *Consten* (Cases 56 and 58/64), the contract clearly distorted normal competitive conditions. In *Cooperatieve Stremsel-* (Case 61/80), the Court explained how the arrangement distorted patterns of trade between The Netherlands and the rest of the common market. But we have already seen the problems associated with an over-extensive interpretation of EC trade law in connection with Article 28 EC (Chapter 11) and some comparable sensitivities are at stake in determining the scope of Article 81(1) EC.

· ·

A: **Preventing or distorting competition**

A balance needs to be struck in the legal control of agreements which may contain terms seemingly restrictive of competition, yet which also may serve to promote market integration and product distribution. The next case examines whether the required element of market distortion may be found in an agreement which contributes to furthering competition and distribution in circumstances where both were previously lacking.

Nungesser v *Commission* (Case 258/78)
[1982] ECR 2015, [1983] 1 CMLR 278, Court of Justice of the European Communities

There is considerable technical expertise involved in the development of new types of seeds. The case involves techniques of cultivating new types of maize varieties. These skills are passed between plant breeders and are valuable. An agreement which may be subject to Article 81 is concluded where technical knowledge is transferred between traders in different Member States. The transfer in this case conferred exclusive rights for Germany on Nungesser. The Court was asked to annul the Commission's decision relating to the lawfulness of the agreement.

[44] . . . [T]he applicants criticize the Commission for wrongly taking the view that an exclusive licence of breeders' rights must by its very nature be treated as an agreement prohibited by Article 85(1) of the Treaty. They submit that the Commission's opinion in that respect is unfounded in so far as the exclusive licence constitutes the sole means, as regards seeds which have been recently developed in a Member State and which have not yet penetrated the market of another Member State, of promoting competition between the new product and comparable products in that other Member State; indeed, no grower or trader would take the risk of launching the new product on a new market if he were not protected against direct competition from the holder of the breeders' rights and from his other licensees.

The Court went on to examine the nature of the licences at issue; there were two distinct types.

[53] . . . The first case concerns a so-called open exclusive licence or assignment and the exclusivity of the licence relates solely to the contractual relationship between the owner of the right and the licensee, whereby the owner merely undertakes not to grant other licences in respect of the same territory and not to compete himself with the licensee on that territory. On the other hand, the second case involves an exclusive licence or assignment with absolute territorial protection, under which the parties to the contract propose, as regards the products and the territory in question, to eliminate all competition from third parties, such as parallel importers or licensees for other territories.

[54] That point having been clarified, it is necessary to examine whether, in the present case, the exclusive nature of the licence, in so far as it is an open licence, has the effect of preventing or distorting competition within the meaning of Article 85(1) of the Treaty.

[55] In that respect the Government of the Federal Republic of Germany emphasized that the protection of agricultural innovations by means of breeders' rights constitutes a means of encouraging such innovations and the grant of exclusive rights for a limited period, is capable of providing a further incentive to innovative efforts.

From that it infers that a total prohibition of every exclusive licence, even an open one, would cause the interest of undertakings in licences to fall away, which would be prejudicial to the dissemination of knowledge and techniques in the Community.

[56] The exclusive licence which forms the subject-matter of the contested decision concerns the cultivation and marketing of hybrid maize seeds which were developed by INRA after years of research and experimentation and were unknown to German farmers at the time when the cooperation between INRA and the applicants was taking shape. For that reason the concern shown by the interveners as regards the protection of new technology is justified.

[57] In fact, in the case of a licence of breeders' rights over hybrid maize seeds newly developed in one Member State, an undertaking established in another Member State which was not certain that it would not encounter competition from other licensees for the territory granted to it, or from the owner of the right himself, might be deterred from accepting the risk of cultivating and marketing that product; such a result would be damaging to the dissemination of a new technology and would prejudice competition in the Community between the new product and similar existing products.

[58] Having regard to the specific nature of the products in question, the Court concludes that, in a case such as the present, the grant of an open exclusive licence, that is to say a licence which does not affect the position of third parties such as parallel importers and licensees for other territories, is not in itself incompatible with Article 85(1) of the Treaty.

[59] Part B of the third submission is thus justified to the extent to which it concerns that aspect of the exclusive nature of the licence.

[60] As regard to the position of third parties, the Commission in essence criticizes the parties to the contract for having extended the definition of exclusivity to importers who are not bound to the contract, in particular parallel importers. Parallel importers or exporters, such as Louis David KG in Germany and Robert Bomberault in France who offered INRA seed for sale to German buyers, had found themselves subjected to pressure and legal proceedings by INRA, Frasema and the applicants, the purpose of which was to maintain the exclusive position of the applicants on the German market.

[61] The Court has consistently held (cf. Joined Cases 56 and 58/64 *Consten and Grundig* v *Commission* [1966] ECR 299) that absolute territorial protection granted to a licensee in order to enable parallel imports to be controlled and prevented results in the artificial maintenance of separate national markets, contrary to the Treaty.

NOTE

The Court is prepared to accept that some apparent restrictions on trade are immune from control under Article 81(1), provided that they are necessary as part of a package for securing the conclusion of desirable deals. Yet a balance must be struck: only reasonable restraints are permitted to escape Article 81. Unduly tight or lengthy restrictions will not escape the prohibition in this way. So in *Nungesser* (Case 258/78) the Court would not countenance a licence which suppressed parallel trade (paras 53, 61). And in *Consten* (Cases 56 and 58/64) itself (p.497 above), a deal which enhanced product distribution was held incompatible with the Treaty because of the extra clause which forbade parallel trade.

> **J. Peeters**, 'The Rule of Reason Revisited: Prohibition on Restraints of
> Competition in the Sherman Act and the EEC Treaty'
> (1989) 37 American Journal of Comparative Law 521, 550–57, 568–70

(Footnotes omitted.)

Under the traditional analysis, such an open exclusive license is restrictive of competition within the meaning of Article 85(1) since the licensor undertakes to license no one else for the licensed territory, a restriction on the freedom of action of the parties to the agreement having a perceptible effect on third parties. The Court's holding [in *Nungesser*] that such a license is not in itself incompatible with Article 85(1) is, however, in no way based on a balancing of the restrictions imposed on intra-brand competition with the enhancement of inter-brand competition. Rather, the Court refers to the need to protect the licensee against competition from licensees for the same territory or the licensor himself to induce him to make the necessary investments in a new technology being licensed. Only 'in a case such as the present' will an open exclusive license not be incompatible with Article 85(1), implying that the Court has probably applied the doctrine of market opening. This doctrine starts from the premise that introducing a new product in the territory granted to the licensee, implies that the product itself was not yet available in that area, meaning no intrabrand competition could be restricted but inter brand competition will be created. Although one can argue that under such type of analysis the Court should not have objected to absolute territorial protection, including protection against parallel importers, such an argument tends to forget the goal of market integration and should therefore be rejected.

NOTE

In the following case the Court considered the application of Article 85 of the EC Treaty (now Article 81 EC) to franchising agreements. Once again, it accepted that some apparent restraints on competition are simply part of a wider, desirable deal and therefore unaffected by Article 85 of the EC Treaty (now Article 81 EC).

Pronuptia de Paris GmbH v *Pronuptia de Paris Irmgaard Schillgalis* (Case 161/84)

[1986] ECR 353, [1986] 1 CMLR 414, Court of Justice of the European Communities

The first question referred under the preliminary reference procedure (Chapter 7) by the German court asked: Is Article 85(1) of the Treaty [now Article 81(1)] applicable to franchise agreements such as the contracts between the parties, which have as their object the establishment of a special distribution system whereby the franchisor provides to the franchisee, in addition to goods, certain trade names, trademarks, merchandising material, and services?

[27] . . . the answer to the first question must be that:

(1) The compatibility of franchise agreements for the distribution of goods with Article 85(1) depends on the provisions contained therein and on their economic context.

(2) Provisions which are strictly necessary in order to ensure that the know-how and assistance provided by the franchisor do not benefit competitors do not constitute restrictions of competition for the purposes of Article 85(1).

(3) Provisions which establish the control strictly necessary for maintaining the identity and reputation of the network identified by the common name or symbol do not constitute restrictions of competition for the purposes of Article 85(1).

(4) Provisions which share markets between the franchisor and the franchisee or between franchisees constitute restrictions of competition for the purposes of Article 85(1).

(5) The fact that the franchisor makes price recommendations to the franchisee does not constitute a restriction of competition, so long as there is no concerted practice between the franchisor and the franchisees or between the franchisees themselves for the actual application of such prices.

(6) Franchise agreements for the distribution of goods which contain provisions sharing markets between the franchisor and the franchisees or between franchisees are capable of affecting trade between Member States.

NOTE

For a casenote see J. Venit (1986) 11 EL Rev 213. In relation to several types of agreement, including distribution and franchising agreements, it has long ago been decided that the uncertainty which surrounds the application of Article 81 can best be allayed by the introduction of Block Exemption Regulations. These constitute, more or less, lists of permissible and impermissible clauses, and are of immense practical importance to the commercial lawyer Regulation 2790/99 now governs vertical restraints (see below p.533).

The use of this so-called 'rule of reason' approach as a means to cut down the scope of application of the basic prohibition against restrictions on competition is well-established in US antitrust law. There are, however, reasons for doubting whether the US analogy can usefully be transplanted into EC law. Under the Sherman Act in the US the case for a cautiously narrow interpretation of the prohibition is strengthened by the absence of any statutory exemption for practices judged restrictive of competition yet beneficial. By contrast in Europe, the prohibition in Article 81(1) is accompanied by the exemption provision of Article 81(3) (p.496 above). So, one may argue, a wide interpretation of the basic prohibition, and a rejection of its curtailment by a 'rule of reason', is a proper consequence of the choice made under the EC system to assess costs and benefits pursuant to Article 81(3) which is unavailable in the US. Whether this structural difference is sufficient to *justify* a refusal to transplant a 'rule of reason' from the US to the EC as a softening of Article 81(1) remains controversial. But it is, undoubtedly, a difference. For discussion of the nature of the rule of reason in this context, contrast R. Whish and B. Sufrin, 'Article 85 and the Rule of Reason' (1987) 7 YEL 1 with the approach of B. Hawk, 'System Failure: Vertical Restraints and EC Competition Law' (1995) 32 CML Rev 973. In policy terms, restricting the reach of Article 81(1) would doubtless permit greater commercial freedom, while also curtailing the heavy emphasis on the role of exemption under Article 81(3). The reader should be aware that an extra motivation for this shift has long been the Commission's monopoly over the grant of exemption pursuant to Article 81(3). The Commission's inability to deal efficiently with the workload imposed by this monopoly has led many frustrated commentators to urge a narrower reading of Article 81(1) as a means to liberate firms from dependence on the Commission. From 1 May 2004 the Commission's exclusive grip on Article 81(3) is lifted by Regulation 1/2003, examined in Chapter 18. The force of the case against a European 'rule of reason' that is driven by administrative concerns is therefore likely to be diminished. The EC's new regime applicable to *vertical restraints,* discussed at p.533 below, should be assessed with awareness of this debate.

In the next case the Court of First Instance directly addresses the status of a 'rule of reason' in EC competition law. Notice that the rulings in both *Nungesser* (Case 258/78) and *Pronuptia* (Case 161/84) are cited.

Métropole télévision (M6), Suez-Lyonnaise des eaux, France Télécom v *Télévision française 1 SA (TF1)* (Case T-112/99)

[2001] ECR II-2159, Court of First Instance of the European Communities

[72] According to the applicants, as a consequence of the existence of a rule of reason in Community competition law, when Article 85(1) of the Treaty is applied it is necessary to weigh the pro and anti-competitive effects of an agreement in order to determine whether it is caught by the prohibition laid down in that article. It should, however, be observed, first of all, that contrary to the applicants' assertions the existence of such a rule has not, as such, been confirmed by the Community courts. Quite to the contrary, in various judgments the Court of Justice and the Court of First Instance have been at pains to indicate that the existence of a rule of reason in Community competition law is doubtful (see Case C-235/92 *P. Montecatini* v *Commission*]1999] ECR I-4539, paragraph 133 ('. . . even if the rule of reason did have a place in the context of Article 85(1) of the Treaty), and Case T-14/89 *Montedipe* v *Commission* [1992] ECR II-1155, paragraph 265, and in Case T-148/89 *Tréfilunion* v *Commission* [1995] ECR II-1063, paragraph 109).

[73] Next, it must be observed that an interpretation of Article 85(1) of the Treaty, in the form suggested by the applicants, is difficult to reconcile with the rules prescribed by that provision.

[74] Article 85 of the Treaty expressly provides, in its third paragraph, for the possibility of exempting agreements that restrict competition where they satisfy a number of conditions, in particular where they are indispensable to the attainment of certain objectives and do not afford undertakings the possibility of eliminating competition in respect of a substantial part of the products in question. It is only in the precise framework of that provision that the pro and anti-competitive aspects of a restriction may be weighed (see, to that effect, Case 161/84 *Pronuptia* [1986] ECR 353, paragraph 24, and Case T-17/93 *Matra Hachette* v *Commission* [1994] ECR II-595, paragraph 48, and *European Night Services and Others* v *Commission*, cited in paragraph 34 above, [Cases T-374/94 *et al*] paragraph 136). Article 85(3) of the Treaty would lose much of its effectiveness if such an examination had to be carried out already under Article 85(1) of the Treaty.

[75] It is true that in a number of judgments the Court of Justice and the Court of First Instance have favoured a more flexible interpretation of the prohibition laid down in Article 85(1) of the Treaty (see, in particular, *Société technique minière* and *Oude Luttikhuis and Others* [Case C-399/93], cited in paragraph 70 above, *Nungesser and Eisele* v *Commission* and *Coditel* v *Ciné-Vog Films* [Case 262/81], cited in paragraph 68 above, *Pronuptia*, cited in paragraph 74 above, and *European Night Services and Others* v *Commission*, cited in paragraph 34 above, as well as the judgment in Case C-250/92 *DLG* [1994] ECR I-5641, paragraphs 31 to 35).

[76] Those judgments cannot, however, be interpreted as establishing the existence of a rule of reason in Community competition law. They are, rather, part of a broader trend in the case-law according to which it is not necessary to hold, wholly abstractly and without drawing any distinction, that any agreement restricting the freedom of action of one or more of the parties is necessarily caught by the prohibition laid down in Article 85(1) of the Treaty. In assessing the applicability of Article 85(1) to an agreement, account should be taken of the actual conditions in which it functions, in particular the economic context in which the undertakings operate, the products or services covered by the agreement and the actual structure of the market concerned (see, in particular, *European Night Services and Others* v *Commission*, cited in paragraph 34 above, paragraph 136, *Oude Luttikhuis*, cited in paragraph 70 above, paragraph 10, and *VGB and Others* v *Commission*, cited in paragraph 70 above, [Case T-77/94] paragraph 140, as well as the judgment in Case C-234/89 *Delimitis* [1991] ECR I-935, paragraph 31).

[77] That interpretation, while observing the substantive scheme of Article 85 of the Treaty and, in particular, preserving the effectiveness of Article 85(3), makes it possible to prevent the prohibition in Article 85(1) from extending wholly abstractly and without distinction to all agreements whose effect is to restrict the freedom of action of one or more of the parties. It must, however, be emphasised that such an approach does not mean that it is necessary to weigh the pro and anti-competitive effects of an agreement when determining whether the prohibition laid down in Article 85(1) of the Treaty applies.

NOTE

For comment see P. Manzini, 'The European Rule of Reason – Crossing the Sea of Doubt' [2002] ECLR 392.

B: **Agreements of minor importance**

Some agreements have an insignificant economic impact. In such circumstances the market distortion test is not met and Article 81 is inapplicable. The Court accepted the validity of this analysis in *Volk* v *Verwaecke* (Case 5/69) [1969] ECR 295, and the Commission has sought to bring clarity to its scope by issuing an explanatory Notice on agreements of minor importance ('de minimis'). Such a Notice is not legislation, but its terms are influential, particularly in respect of Commission enforcement practice.

COMMISSION NOTICE ON AGREEMENTS OF MINOR IMPORTANCE WHICH DO NOT APPRECIABLY RESTRICT COMPETITION UNDER ARTICLE 81(1) OF THE TREATY ESTABLISHING THE EUROPEAN COMMUNITY (DE MINIMIS)[1]
[2001] OJ C368/13

I

1. Article 81(1) prohibits agreements between undertakings which may affect trade between Member States and which have as their object or effect the prevention, restriction or distortion of competition within the common market. The Court of Justice of the European Communities has clarified that this provision is not applicable where the impact of the agreement on intra-Community trade or on competition is not appreciable.

2. In this notice the Commission quantifies, with the help of market share thresholds, what is not an appreciable restriction of competition under Article 81 of the EC Treaty. This negative definition of appreciability does not imply that agreements between undertakings which exceed the thresholds set out in this notice appreciably restrict competition. Such agreements may still have only a negligible effect on competition and may therefore not be prohibited by Article 81(1).[2]

3. Agreements may in addition not fall under Article 81(1) because they are not capable of appreciably affecting trade between Member States. This notice does not deal with this issue. It does not quantify what does not constitute an appreciable effect on trade. It is however acknowledged that agreements between small and medium-sized undertakings, as defined in the Annex

---

1 This notice replaces the notice on agreements of minor importance published in OJ C 372, 9.12.1997.

2 See, for instance, the judgment of the Court of Justice in Joined Cases C-215/96 and C-216/96 *Bagnasco (Carlos)* v *Banca Popolare di Novara and Casa di Risparmio di Genova e Imperia* (1999) ECR I-135, points 34–35. This notice is also without prejudice to the principles for assessment under Article 81(1) as expressed in the Commission notice 'Guidelines on the applicability of Article 81 of the EC Treaty to horizontal cooperation agreements', OJ C 3, 6.1.2001, in particular points 17–31 inclusive, and in the Commission notice 'Guidelines on vertical restraints', OJ C 291, 13.10.2000, in particular points 5–20 inclusive.

to Commission Recommendation 96/280/EC[3], are rarely capable of appreciably affecting trade between Member States. Small and medium-sized undertakings are currently defined in that recommendation as undertakings which have fewer than 250 employees and have either an annual turnover not exceeding EUR 40 million or an annual balance-sheet total not exceeding EUR 27 million.

4. In cases covered by this notice the Commission will not institute proceedings either upon application or on its own initiative. Where undertakings assume in good faith that an agreement is covered by this notice, the Commission will not impose fines. Although not binding on them, this notice also intends to give guidance to the courts and authorities of the Member States in their application of Article 81.

5. This notice also applies to decisions by associations of undertakings and to concerted practices.

6. This notice is without prejudice to any interpretation of Article 81 which may be given by the Court of Justice or the Court of First Instance of the European Communities.

II

7. The Commission holds the view that agreements between undertakings which affect trade between Member States do not appreciably restrict competition within the meaning of Article 81(1):

- (a) if the aggregate market share held by the parties to the agreement does not exceed 10% on any of the relevant markets affected by the agreement, where the agreement is made between undertakings which are actual or potential competitors on any of these markets (agreements between competitors)[4]; or
- (b) if the market share held by each of the parties to the agreement does not exceed 15% on any of the relevant markets affected by the agreement, where the agreement is made between undertakings which are not actual or potential competitors on any of these markets (agreements between non-competitors). In cases where it is difficult to classify the agreement as either an agreement between competitors or an agreement between non-competitors the 10% threshold is applicable.

8. Where in a relevant market competition is restricted by the cumulative effect of agreements for the sale of goods or services entered into by different suppliers or distributors (cumulative foreclosure effect of parallel networks of agreements having similar effects on the market), the market share thresholds under point 7 are reduced to 5%, both for agreements between competitors and for agreements between non-competitors. Individual suppliers or distributors with a market share not exceeding 5% are in general not considered to contribute significantly to a cumulative foreclosure effect.[5] A cumulative foreclosure effect is unlikely to exist if less than 30% of the relevant market is covered by parallel (networks of) agreements having similar effects.

---

3 OJ L 107, 30.4.1996, p.4. This recommendation will be revised. It is envisaged to increase the annual turnover threshold from EUR 40 million to EUR 50 million and the annual balance-sheet total threshold from EUR 27 million to EUR 43 million.

4 On what are actual or potential competitors, see the Commission notice 'Guidelines on the applicability of Article 81 of the EC Treaty to horizontal cooperation agreements', OJ C 3, 6.1.2001, paragraph 9. A firm is treated as an actual competitor if it is either active on the same relevant market or if, in the absence of the agreement, it is able to switch production to the relevant products and market them in the short term without incurring significant additional costs or risks in response to a small and permanent increase in relative prices (immediate supply-side substitutability). A firm is treated as a potential competitor if there is evidence that, absent the agreement, this firm could and would be likely to undertake the necessary additional investments or other necessary switching costs so that it could enter the relevant market in response to a small and permanent increase in relative prices.

5 See also the Commission notice 'Guidelines on vertical restraints', OJ C 291, 13.10.2000, in particular paragraphs 73, 142, 143 and 189. While in the guidelines on vertical restraints in relation to certain restrictions reference is made not only to the total but also to the tied market share of a particular supplier or buyer, in this notice all market share thresholds refer to total market shares.

9. The Commission also holds the view that agreements are not restrictive of competition if the market shares do not exceed the thresholds of respectively 10%, 15% and 5% set out in points 7 and 8 during two successive calendar years by more than 2 percentage points.

10. In order to calculate the market share, it is necessary to determine the relevant market. This consists of the relevant product market and the relevant geographic market. When defining the relevant market, reference should be had to the notice on the definition of the relevant market for the purposes of Community competition law.[6] The market shares are to be calculated on the basis of sales value data or, where appropriate, purchase value data. If value data are not available, estimates based on other reliable market information, including volume data, may be used.

11. Points 7, 8 and 9 do not apply to agreements containing any of the following hardcore restrictions:

(1) as regards agreements between competitors as defined in point 7, restrictions which, directly or indirectly, in isolation or in combination with other factors under the control of the parties, have as their object:[7]

(a) the fixing of prices when selling the products to third parties;

(b) the limitation of output or sales;

(c) the allocation of markets or customers;

(2) as regards agreements between non-competitors as defined in point 7, restrictions which, directly or indirectly, in isolation or in combination with other factors under the control of the parties, have as their object:

(a) the restriction of the buyer's ability to determine its sale price, without prejudice to the possibility of the supplier imposing a maximum sale price or recommending a sale price, provided that they do not amount to a fixed or minimum sale price as a result of pressure from, or incentives offered by, any of the parties;

(b) the restriction of the territory into which, or of the customers to whom, the buyer may sell the contract goods or services, except the following restrictions which are not hardcore:

— the restriction of active sales into the exclusive territory or to an exclusive customer group reserved to the supplier or allocated by the supplier to another buyer, where such a restriction does not limit sales by the customers of the buyer,

— the restriction of sales to end users by a buyer operating at the wholesale level of trade,

— the restriction of sales to unauthorised distributors by the members of a selective distribution system, and

— the restriction of the buyer's ability to sell components, supplied for the purposes of incorporation, to customers who would use them to manufacture the same type of goods as those produced by the supplier;

(c) the restriction of active or passive sales to end users by members of a selective distribution system operating at the retail level of trade, without prejudice to the possibility of prohibiting a member of the system from operating out of an unauthorised place of establishment;

(d) the restriction of cross-supplies between distributors within a selective distribution system, including between distributors operating at different levels of trade;

(e) the restriction agreed between a supplier of components and a buyer who incorporates those components, which limits the supplier's ability to sell the components as spare parts to end users or to repairers or other service providers not entrusted by the buyer with the repair or servicing of its goods;

---

6 OJ C 372, 9.12.1997, p.5.

7 Without prejudice to situations of joint production with or without joint distribution as defined in Article 5, paragraph 2, of Commission Regulation (EC) No 2658/2000 and Article 5, paragraph 2, of Commission Regulation (EC) No 2659/2000, OJ L 304, 5.12.2000, pp.3 and 7 respectively.

(3) as regards agreements between competitors as defined in point 7, where the competitors operate, for the purposes of the agreement, at a different level of the production or distribution chain, any of the hardcore restrictions listed in paragraph (1) and (2) above.

12. (1) For the purposes of this notice, the terms 'undertaking', 'party to the agreement', 'distributor', 'supplier' and 'buyer' shall include their respective connected undertakings.
    (2) 'Connected undertakings' are:
        (a) undertakings in which a party to the agreement, directly or indirectly:
            — has the power to exercise more than half the voting rights, or
            — has the power to appoint more than half the members of the supervisory board, board of management or bodies legally representing the undertaking, or
            — has the right to manage the undertaking's affairs;
        (b) undertakings which directly or indirectly have, over a party to the agreement, the rights or powers listed in (a);
        (c) undertakings in which an undertaking referred to in (b) has, directly or indirectly, the rights or powers listed in (a);
        (d) undertakings in which a party to the agreement together with one or more of the undertakings referred to in (a), (b) or (c), or in which two or more of the latter undertakings, jointly have the rights or powers listed in (a);
        (e) undertakings in which the rights or the powers listed in (a) are jointly held by:
            — parties to the agreement or their respective connected undertakings referred to in (a) to (d), or
            — one or more of the parties to the agreement or one or more of their connected undertakings referred to in (a) to (d) and one or more third parties.
    (3) For the purposes of paragraph 2(e), the market share held by these jointly held undertakings shall be apportioned equally to each undertaking having the rights or the powers listed in paragraph 2(a).

NOTE

In assessing the economic impact of an agreement, its wider context must be appraised. An apparently minor agreement may fall foul of Article 81 if in reality it forms part of a network of similar agreements (*cf* para 8 of the Notice).

Brasserie de Haecht SA v *Wilkin* (Case 23/67)
[1967] ECR 407, [1968] CMLR 26, Court of Justice of the European Communities

The agreement was between a brewery and a café owner in Belgium. However, a number of similar agreements between the brewery and other café owners also existed.

. . . Article 85(1) mentions agreements, decisions and practices. By referring in the same sentence to agreements between undertakings, decisions by associations of undertakings and concerted practices, which may involve many parties, Article 85(1) implies that the constituent elements of those agreements, decisions and practices may be considered together as a whole.

Furthermore, by basing its application to agreements, decisions or practices not only on their subject-matter but also on their effects in relation to competition, Article 85(1) implies that regard must be had to such effects in the context in which they occur, that is to say, in the economic and legal context of such agreements, decisions or practices and where they might combine with others to have a cumulative effect on competition. In fact, it would be pointless to consider an agreement, decision or practice by reason of its effects if those effects were to be taken distinct from the market in which they are seen to operate and could only be examined apart from the body of effects, whether convergent or not, surrounding their implementation. Thus in order to examine whether it is caught by Article 85(1) an agreement cannot be examined in isolation from the above context, that is, from the factual or legal circumstances causing it to prevent, restrict or distort competition. The existence of similar contracts may be taken into consideration for this objective to the extent to which the general body of contracts of this type is capable of restricting the freedom of trade.

Lastly, it is only to the extent to which agreements, decisions or practices are capable of affecting trade between Member States that the alteration of competition comes under Community prohibitions. In order to satisfy this condition, it must be possible for the agreement, decision or practice, when viewed in the light of a combination of the objective, factual or legal circumstances, to appear to be capable of having some influence, direct or indirect, on trade between Member States, of being conducive to a partitioning of the market and of hampering the economic inter-penetration sought by the Treaty. When this point is considered the agreement, decision or practice cannot therefore be isolated from all the others of which it is one.

The existence of similar contracts is a circumstance which, together with others, is capable of being a factor in the economic and legal context within which the contract must be judged. Accordingly, whilst such a situation must be taken into account it should not be considered as decisive by itself, but merely as one among others in judging whether trade between Member States is capable of being affected through any alteration in competition.

NOTE

The link with defining the jurisdictional reach of Article 81 is plain. In similar fashion, an agreement which seems of purely local impact may have cross-border implications if viewed in its true context. See also *Windsurfing v Commission* (Case 193/83) [1986] ECR 611.

The Court pronounced further on this issue in *Stergios Delimitis* v *Henninger Brau* (Case C-234/89). As in the previous case, the litigation involved beer supply agreements.

Stergios Delimitis v *Henninger Brau* (Case C-234/89)
[1991] ECR I-935, Court of Justice of the European Communities

[14] In its judgment in Case 23/67 *Brasserie De Haecht* v *Wilkin* [1967] ECR 407, the Court held that the effects of such an agreement had to be assessed in the context in which they occur and where they might combine with others to have a cumulative effect on competition. It also follows from that judgment that the cumulative effect of several similar agreements constitutes one factor amongst others in ascertaining whether, by way of a possible alteration of competition, trade between Member States is capable of being affected.

[15] Consequently, in the present case it is necessary to analyse the effects of a beer supply agreement, taken together with other contracts of the same type, on the opportunities of national competitors or those from other Member States, to gain access to the market for beer consumption or to increase their market share and, accordingly, the effects on the range of products offered to consumers.

[16] In making that analysis, the relevant market must first be determined. The relevant market is primarily defined on the basis of the nature of the economic activity in question, in this case the sale of beer. Beer is sold through both retail channels and premises for the sale and consumption of drinks. From the consumer's point of view, the latter sector, comprising in particular public houses and restaurants, may be distinguished from the retail sector on the grounds that the sale of beer in public houses does not solely consist of the purchase of a product but is also linked with the provision of services, and that beer consumption in public houses is not essentially dependent on economic considerations. The specific nature of the public house trade is borne out by the fact that the breweries organize specific distribution systems for this sector which require special installations, and that the prices charged in that sector are generally higher than retail prices.

[17] It follows that in the present case the reference market is that for the distribution of beer in premises for the sale and consumption of drinks. That finding is not affected by the fact that there is a certain overlap between the two distribution networks, namely inasmuch as retail sales allow new competitors to make their brands known and to use their reputation in order to gain access to the market constituted by premises for the sale and consumption of drinks.

[18] Secondly, the relevant market is delimited from a geographical point of view. It should be noted that most beer supply agreements are still entered into at a national level. It follows that, in applying the Community competition rules, account is to be taken of the national market for beer distribution in premises for the sale and consumption of drinks.

[19] In order to assess whether the existence of several beer supply agreements impedes access to the market as so defined, it is further necessary to examine the nature and extent of those agreements in their totality, comprising all similar contracts tying a large number of points of sale to several national producers (judgment in Case 43/69 *Bilger* v *Jehle* [1970] ECR 127). The effect of those networks of contracts on access to the market depends specifically on the number of outlets thus tied to national producers in relation to the number of public houses which are not so tied, the duration of the commitments entered into, the quantities of beer to which those commitments relate, and on the proportion between those quantities and the quantities sold by free distributors.

[20] The existence of a bundle of similar contracts, even if it has a considerable effect on the opportunities for gaining access to the market, is not, however, sufficient in itself to support a finding that the relevant market is inaccessible, inasmuch as it is only one factor, amongst others, pertaining to the economic and legal context in which an agreement must be appraised (Case 23/67 *Brasserie De Haecht*, cited above). The other factors to be taken into account are, in the first instance, those also relating to opportunities for access.

[21] In that connection it is necessary to examine whether there are real concrete possibilities for a new competitor to penetrate the bundle of contracts by acquiring a brewery already established on the market together with its network of sales outlets, or to circumvent the bundle of contracts by opening new public houses. For that purpose it is necessary to have regard to the legal rules and agreements on the acquisition of companies and the establishment of outlets, and to the minimum number of outlets necessary for the economic operation of a distribution system. The presence of beer wholesalers not tied to producers who are active on the market is also a factor capable of facilitating a new producer's access to that market since he can make use of those wholesalers' sales networks to distribute his own beer.

[22] Secondly, account must be taken of the conditions under which competitive forces operate on the relevant market. In that connection it is necessary to know not only the number and the size of producers present on the market, but also the degree of saturation of that market and customer fidelity to existing brands, for it is generally more difficult to penetrate a saturated market in which customers are loyal to a small number of large producers than a market in full expansion in which a large number of small producers are operating without any strong brand names. The trend in beer sales in the retail trade provides useful information on the development of demand and thus an indication of the degree of saturation of the beer market as a whole. The analysis of that trend is, moreover, of interest in evaluating brand loyalty. A steady increase in sales of beer under new brand names may confer on the owners of those brand names a reputation which they may turn to account in gaining access to the public-house market.

[23] If an examination of all similar contracts entered into on the relevant market and the other factors relevant to the economic and legal context in which the contract must be examined shows that those agreements do not have the cumulative effect of denying access to that market to new national and foreign competitors, the individual agreements comprising the bundle of agreements cannot be held to restrict competition within the meaning of Article 85(1) of the Treaty. They do not, therefore, fall under the prohibition laid down in that provision.

[24] If, on the other hand, such examination reveals that it is difficult to gain access to the relevant market, it is necessary to assess the extent to which the agreements entered into by the brewery in question contribute to the cumulative effect produced in that respect by the totality of the similar contracts found on that market. Under the Community rules on competition, responsibility for such an effect of closing off the market must be attributed to the breweries which make an appreciable contribution thereto. Beer supply agreements entered into by breweries whose contribution to the cumulative effect is insignificant do not therefore fall under the prohibition under Article 85(1).

[25] In order to assess the extent of the contribution of the beer supply agreements entered into by a brewery to the cumulative sealing-off effect mentioned above, the market position of the contracting parties must be taken into consideration. That position is not determined solely by the market share held by the brewery and any group to which it may belong, but also by the number of outlets tied to it or to its group, in relation to the total number of premises for the sale and consumption of drinks found in the relevant market.

[26] The contribution of the individual contracts entered into by a brewery to the sealing-off of that market also depends on their duration. If the duration is manifestly excessive in relation to the average duration of beer supply agreements generally entered into on the relevant market, the individual contract falls under the prohibition under Article 85(1). A brewery with a relatively small market share which ties its sales outlets for many years may make as significant a contribution to a sealing-off of the market as a brewery in a relatively strong market position which regularly releases sales outlets at shorter intervals.

[27] The reply to be given to the first three questions is therefore that a beer supply agreement is prohibited by Article 85(1) of the EEC Treaty, if two cumulative conditions are met. The first is that, having regard to the economic and legal context of the agreement at issue, it is difficult for competitors who could enter the market or increase their market share to gain access to the national market for the distribution of beer in premises for the sale and consumption of drinks. The fact that, in that market, the agreement in issue is one of a number of similar agreements having a cumulative effect on competition constitutes only one factor amongst others in assessing whether access to that market is indeed difficult. The second condition is that the agreement in question must make a significant contribution to the sealing-off effect brought about by the totality of those agreements in their economic and legal context. The extent of the contribution made by the individual agreement depends on the position of the contracting parties in the relevant market and on the duration of the agreement.

■ QUESTION

Do you perceive any shift in emphasis in this ruling?

NOTE

The Commission's view of the implications of the *Delimitis* ruling for beer supply agreements was set out in a Notice published at [1992] OJ C121/2. This a further example of the Commission's work in developing policy from the accidents of litigation, *cf* pp.364, 410, and 453 above. More generally see now Regulation 2790/1999 on the application of Article 81(3) of the Treaty to categories of vertical agreements and concerted practice, p.535 below.

Municipality of Almelo and Others v *Energiebedrijf IJsselmij NV* (Case C-393/92)
[1994] ECR I-1477, Court of Justice of the European Communities

The Court was asked to consider the application of Article 85 of the EC Treaty (now Article 81 EC) to distribution patterns for electricity in The Netherlands. These included a requirement imposed on local distributors to purchase exclusively from a Dutch supplier, which precluded importation of electricity.

[34] Article 85 of the Treaty applies, in its own terms, to agreements between undertakings which restrict competition and affect trade between Member States.

[35] As regards the existence of an agreement between undertakings, it is to be observed, as the Commission found in the 1991 Decision, that the electricity distribution system in the Netherlands is based on a network of contractual legal relationships between generators, between generators and regional distributors, between regional distributors and local distributors and, finally between local distributors and end-users. The exclusive purchasing clause in issue before the national court is contained in the general conditions for the supply of electric power by a regional distributor to local distributors and therefore constitutes a clause contained in an agreement as referred to in Article 85 of the Treaty.

[36] An agreement containing such a clause has a restrictive effect on competition, inasmuch as the clause prohibits the local distributors from obtaining electricity supplies from other suppliers.

[37] In order to determine whether such an agreement has an appreciable effect on trade between Member States, it is necessary, as the Court observed in its judgments in Case 23/67 *Brasserie de Haecht* [1967] ECR 525 and Case C-234/89 *Delimitis* [1991] ECR I-935, to assess it in its economic and legal context and to take account of any cumulative effect resulting from the existence of other exclusivity agreements.

[38] In that regard, it appears from the documents before the Court that the general conditions governing the relations between the parties to the main proceedings, which contain the exclusivity clause, follow the model General Terms and Conditions for the supply of electricity drawn up by the Association of Operators of Electricity Undertakings in the Netherlands.

[39] Those contractual relationships have the cumulative effect of compartmentalising the national market, inasmuch as they have the effect of prohibiting local distributors established in the Netherlands from obtaining supplies of electricity from distributors or producers in other Member States.

NOTE

For another example of the Court's insistence on appraising the pattern of contractual relationships in their true economic and legal context, see Case C-306/96 *Javico et al* v *Yves St Laurent Parfums* [1998] ECR I-1983; and C-214/99 *Neste Markkinointi Oy* [2000] ECR I-11121 (in which the length of notice periods in the relevant contracts was regarded as relevant to assessment of the degree of foreclosure caused by the network of agreements).

....

C: **Assessing a 'restriction of competition' in its full context**

Account must be taken of the legal and economic context in which practices occur. *Nungesser* and *Pronuptia* should be read as revealing the Court's concern to examine apparent restrictions on competition in their full economic and legal context for the purposes of application of Article 81(1). *Delimitis*, which is mentioned in para 76 of *M6* (Case T-112/99 p.514 above), demonstrates a comparable concern. One may disagree with the Court's conclusions on the particular facts of the cases, but the point of principle is that a mechanical assumption that any contractual or other restriction on freedom inevitably falls within the scope of Article 81(1) is false. Article 81(1) is not so broad. But what matters are contextually relevant for the purposes of this inquiry?

Wouters, J.W. Savelbergh, Price Waterhouse Belastingadviseurs BV v *Algemene Raad van de Nederlandse Orde van Advocaten* (Case C-309/99)
[2002] ECR I-1577, Court of Justice of the European Communities

The Court was asked to rule on the application of Article 81 in the context of Dutch rules prohibiting multi-disciplinary partnerships between members of the Bar and accountants.

[86] It appears to the Court that the national legislation in issue in the main proceedings has an adverse effect on competition and may affect trade between Member States.

[87] As regards the adverse effect on competition, the areas of expertise of members of the Bar and of accountants may be complementary. Since legal services, especially in business law, more and more frequently require recourse to an accountant, a multi-disciplinary partnership of members of the Bar and accountants would make it possible to offer a wider range of services, and indeed to

propose new ones. Clients would thus be able to turn to a single structure for a large part of the services necessary for the organisation, management and operation of their business (the 'one-stop shop' advantage).

[88] Furthermore, a multi-disciplinary partnership of members of the Bar and accountants would be capable of satisfying the needs created by the increasing interpenetration of national markets and the consequent necessity for continuous adaptation to national and international legislation.

[89] Nor, finally, is it inconceivable that the economies of scale resulting from such multi-disciplinary partnerships might have positive effects on the cost of services.

[90] A prohibition of multi-disciplinary partnerships of members of the Bar and accountants, such as that laid down in the 1993 Regulation, is therefore liable to limit production and technical development within the meaning of Article 85(1)(b) of the Treaty. . . .

[95] . . . As regards the question whether intra-Community trade is affected, it is sufficient to observe that an agreement, decision or concerted practice extending over the whole of the territory of a Member State has, by its very nature, the effect of reinforcing the partitioning of markets on a national basis, thereby holding up the economic interpenetration which the Treaty is designed to bring about (Case 8/72 *Vereeniging van Cementhandelaren* v *Commission* [1972] ECR 977, paragraph 29; Case 42/84 *Remia and Others* v *Commission* [1985] ECR 2545, paragraph 22; and *CNSD*, paragraph 48).

[96] That effect is all the more appreciable in the present case because the 1993 Regulation applies equally to visiting lawyers who are registered members of the Bar of another Member State, because economic and commercial law more and more frequently regulates transnational transactions and, lastly, because the firms of accountants looking for lawyers as partners are generally international groups present in several Member States.

[97] However, not every agreement between undertakings or every decision of an association of undertakings which restricts the freedom of action of the parties or of one of them necessarily falls within the prohibition laid down in Article 85(1) of the Treaty. For the purposes of application of that provision to a particular case, account must first of all be taken of the overall context in which the decision of the association of undertakings was taken or produces its effects. More particularly, account must be taken of its objectives, which are here connected with the need to make rules relating to organisation, qualifications, professional ethics, supervision and liability, in order to ensure that the ultimate consumers of legal services and the sound administration of justice are provided with the necessary guarantees in relation to integrity and experience (see, to that effect, Case C-3/95 *Reisebüro Broede* [1996] ECR I-6511, paragraph 38). It has then to be considered whether the consequential effects restrictive of competition are inherent in the pursuit of those objectives.

[98] Account must be taken of the legal framework applicable in the Netherlands, on the one hand, to members of the Bar and to the Bar of the Netherlands, which comprises all the registered members of the Bar in that Member State, and on the other hand, to accountants.

[99] As regards members of the Bar, it has consistently been held that, in the absence of specific Community rules in the field, each Member State is in principle free to regulate the exercise of the legal profession in its territory (Case 107/83 *Klopp* [1984] ECR 2971, paragraph 17, and *Reisebüro*, paragraph 37). For that reason, the rules applicable to that profession may differ greatly from one Member State to another.

[100] The current approach of the Netherlands, where Article 28 of the Advocatenwet entrusts the Bar of the Netherlands with responsibility for adopting regulations designed to ensure the proper practice of the profession, is that the essential rules adopted for that purpose are, in particular, the duty to act for clients in complete independence and in their sole interest, the duty, mentioned above, to avoid all risk of conflict of interest and the duty to observe strict professional secrecy.

[101] Those obligations of professional conduct have not inconsiderable implications for the

structure of the market in legal services, and more particularly for the possibilities for the practice of law jointly with other liberal professions which are active on that market.

[102] Thus, they require of members of the Bar that they should be in a situation of independence *vis-à-vis* the public authorities, other operators and third parties, by whom they must never be influenced. They must furnish, in that respect, guarantees that all steps taken in a case are taken in the sole interest of the client.

[103] By contrast, the profession of accountant is not subject, in general, and more particularly, in the Netherlands, to comparable requirements of professional conduct.

[104] As the Advocate-General has rightly pointed out in paragraphs 185 and 186 of his Opinion, there may be a degree of incompatibility between the 'advisory' activities carried out by a member of the Bar and the 'supervisory' activities carried out by an accountant. The written observations submitted by the respondent in the main proceedings show that accountants in the Netherlands perform a task of certification of accounts. They undertake an objective examination and audit of their clients' accounts, so as to be able to impart to interested third parties their personal opinion concerning the reliability of those accounts. It follows that in the Member State concerned accountants are not bound by a rule of professional secrecy comparable to that of members of the Bar, unlike the position under German law, for example.

[105] The aim of the 1993 Regulation is therefore to ensure that, in the Member State concerned, the rules of professional conduct for members of the Bar are complied with, having regard to the prevailing perceptions of the profession in that State. The Bar of the Netherlands was entitled to consider that members of the Bar might no longer be in a position to advise and represent their clients independently and in the observance of strict professional secrecy if they belonged to an organisation which is also responsible for producing an account of the financial results of the transactions in respect of which their services were called upon and for certifying those accounts.

[106] Moreover, the concurrent pursuit of the activities of statutory auditor and of adviser, in particular legal adviser, also raises questions within the accountancy profession itself, as may be seen from the Commission Green Paper 96/C/321/01 'The role, the position and the liability of the statutory auditor within the European Union' (OJ 1996 C 321, p.1; see, in particular, paragraphs 4.12 to 4.14).

[107] A regulation such as the 1993 Regulation could therefore reasonably be considered to be necessary in order to ensure the proper practice of the legal profession, as it is organised in the Member State concerned.

[108] Furthermore, the fact that different rules may be applicable in another Member State does not mean that the rules in force in the former State are incompatible with Community law (see, to that effect, Case C-108/96 *Mac Quen and Others* [2001] ECR I-837, paragraph 33). Even if multi-disciplinary partnerships of lawyers and accountants are allowed in some Member States, the Bar of the Netherlands is entitled to consider that the objectives pursued by the 1993 Regulation cannot, having regard in particular to the legal regimes by which members of the Bar and accountants are respectively governed in the Netherlands, be attained by less restrictive means (see, to that effect, with regard to a law reserving judicial debt-recovery activity to lawyers, *Reisebüro*, paragraph 41).

[109] In light of those considerations, it does not appear that the effects restrictive of competition such as those resulting for members of the Bar practising in the Netherlands from a regulation such as the 1993 Regulation go beyond what is necessary in order to ensure the proper practice of the legal profession (see, to that effect, Case C-250/92 *DLG* [1994] ECR I-5641, paragraph 35).

[110] Having regard to all the foregoing considerations, the answer to be given to the second question must be that a national regulation such as the 1993 Regulation adopted by a body such as the Bar of the Netherlands does not infringe Article 85(1) of the Treaty, since that body could reasonably have considered that that regulation, despite the effects restrictive of competition that

are inherent in it, is necessary for the proper practice of the legal profession, as organised in the Member State concerned.

NOTE

The Court does not deny that the Dutch rules constitute a restriction of competition, viewed in the abstract. But it takes account of the contribution of the rules to the sound administration of justice. This is part of the relevant context within which to assess the reach of Article 81(1). The next case is further demonstration of the Court's broad understanding of the context within which to locate legal interpretation of the Article 81(1) prohibition.

Albany International v *Stichting Bedrijfspensioenfonds Textielindustrie* (Case C-67/96)

[1999] ECR I-5751, Court of Justice of the European Communities

As foreseen under Dutch legislation, management and labour had jointly requested the public authorities to make affiliation to a sectoral pension fund compulsory. But did this collective agreement struck between both sides of industry constitute an agreement within the meaning of Article 81(1) (ex 85(1)) EC? After all, it envisaged the exclusion from the market of pension providers outside the system that was to be made compulsory. It was argued that this would damage competition and, ultimately, consumer choice.

[52] It is necessary to consider first whether a decision taken by the organisations representing employers and workers in a given sector, in the context of a collective agreement, to set up in that sector a single pension fund responsible for managing a supplementary pension scheme and to request the public authorities to make affiliation to that fund compulsory for all workers in that sector is contrary to Article 85 of the Treaty.

[53] It must be noted, first, that Article 85(1) of the Treaty prohibits all agreements between undertakings, decisions by associations of undertakings and concerted practices which may affect trade between Member States and which have as their object or effect the prevention, restriction or distortion of competition within the common market. The importance of that rule prompted the authors of the Treaty to provide expressly in Article 85(2) of the Treaty that any agreements or decisions prohibited pursuant to that article are to be automatically void.

[54] Next, it is important to bear in mind that, under Article 3(g) and (i) of the EC Treaty (now, after amendment, Article 3(1)(g) and (j) EC), the activities of the Community are to include not only a 'system ensuring that competition in the internal market is not distorted' but also 'a policy in the social sphere'. Article 2 of the EC Treaty (now, after amendment, Article 2 EC) provides that a particular task of the Community is 'to promote throughout the Community a harmonious and balanced development of economic activities' and 'a high level of employment and of social protection'.

[55] In that connection, Article 118 of the EC Treaty (Articles 117 to 120 of the EC Treaty have been replaced by Articles 136 EC to 143 EC) provides that the Commission is to promote close cooperation between Member States in the social field, particularly in matters relating to the right of association and collective bargaining between employers and workers.

[56] Article 118b of the EC Treaty (Articles 117 to 120 of the EC Treaty having been replaced by Articles 136 EC to 143 EC) adds that the Commission is to endeavour to develop the dialogue between management and labour at European level which could, if the two sides consider it desirable, lead to relations based on agreement.

[57] Moreover, Article 1 of the Agreement on social policy (OJ 1992 C 191, p.91) states that the objectives to be pursued by the Community and the Member States include improved living and working conditions, proper social protection, dialogue between management and labour, the development of human resources with a view to lasting high employment and the combatting of exclusion.

[58] Under Article 4(1) and (2) of the Agreement, the dialogue between management and labour at Community level may lead, if they so desire, to contractual relations, including agreements, which will be implemented either in accordance with the procedures and practices specific to management and labour and the Member States, or, at the joint request of the signatory parties, by a Council decision on a proposal from the Commission.

[59] It is beyond question that certain restrictions of competition are inherent in collective agreements between organisations representing employers and workers. However, the social policy objectives pursued by such agreements would be seriously undermined if management and labour were subject to Article 85(1) of the Treaty when seeking jointly to adopt measures to improve conditions of work and employment.

[60] It therefore follows from an interpretation of the provisions of the Treaty as a whole which is both effective and consistent that agreements concluded in the context of collective negotiations between management and labour in pursuit of such objectives must, by virtue of their nature and purpose, be regarded as falling outside the scope of Article 85(1) of the Treaty.

NOTE

In the light of this statement the Court proceeded to examine the particular arrangements at issue in the case. The vital point, however, is that, as in *Wouters* (Case C-309/99 above), the Court in *Albany International* did not deny that the rules restricted competition. But it placed its investigation into the scope of Article 81(1) in a wider context. The Treaty competition rules are porous: the very scope of Article 81(1) is influenced by policy objectives located elsewhere in the framework of EC law and policy. It is worth recalling that both Articles 28 and 49 EC on the free movement of goods and services respectively offer similar insight into the way in which the Court interprets EC trade law in a manner that seeks to avoid trampling other regulatory objectives underfoot. In fact an apparent convergence between the assumptions of EC law of free movement and EC competition law emerges form the ruling in *Wouters*. The Dutch rules prohibiting multi-disciplinary partnerships between members of the Bar and accountants were not only attacked as violations of Article 81 but also as violations of Articles 49 (ex 59) EC concerning the free movement of services (Chapter 13). The Court was curt.

Wouters, J.W. Savelbergh, Price Waterhouse Belastingadviseurs BV v *Algemene Raad van de Nederlandse Orde van Advocaten* (Case C-309/99)
[2002] ECR I-1577, Court of Justice of the European Communities

[120] It should be observed at the outset that compliance with Articles 52 and 59 of the Treaty is also required in the case of rules which are not public in nature but which are designed to regulate, collectively, self-employment and the provision of services. The abolition, as between Member States, of obstacles to freedom of movement for persons would be compromised if the abolition of State barriers could be neutralised by obstacles resulting from the exercise of their legal autonomy by associations or organisations not governed by public law (Case 36/74 *Walrave and Koch* [1974] ECR 1405, paragraphs 17, 23 and 24; Case 13/76 *Donà* [1976] ECR 1333, paragraphs 17 and 18; Case C-415/93 *Bosman* [1995] ECR I-4921, paragraphs 83 and 84, and Case C-281/98 *Angonese* [2000] ECR I-4139, paragraph 32).

[121] In those circumstances, the Court may be called upon to determine whether the Treaty provisions concerning the right of establishment and freedom to provide services are applicable to a regulation such as the 1993 Regulation.

[122] On the assumption that the provisions concerning the right of establishment and/or freedom to provide services are applicable to a prohibition of any multi-disciplinary partnerships between members of the Bar and accountants such as that laid down in the 1993 Regulation and that that regulation constitutes a restriction on one or both of those freedoms, that restriction would in any event appear to be justified for the reasons set out in paragraphs 97 to 109 above.

■ QUESTION

The key to this case law seems to be a refusal explicitly to accommodate a 'rule of reason' within EC competition law but a readiness to use the interpretative rule that restrictions on competition be seen in their full legal and economic context as a basis for permitting Article 81(1)'s scope to be affected by a range of (loosely stated) public interest considerations. Is this approach sufficiently reliable and predictable as a basis for the regulation of commerce under a regime which includes the possibility of the imposition of heavy fines? If not, what improvements would you advocate for this regime?

FURTHER READING

Deards, E., 'Closed Shop Versus One Stop Shop: the Battle Goes On' (2002) 27 EL Rev 618.

Giubboni, S., 'Social Insurance Monopolies in Community Competition Law and the Italian Constitution: Practical Convergences and Theoretical Conflicts' (2001) 7 ELJ 69.

Monti, G., 'Article 81 EC and Public Policy' (2002) 39 CML Rev 1057.

Mortelmans, K., 'Towards Convergence in the Application of the Rules on Free Movement and on Competition?' (2001) 38 CML Rev 613.

Van den Bergh, R. and Camesasca, P., 'Irreconcilable Principles? The Court of Justice Exempts Collective Labour Agreements from the Wrath of Antitrust' (2000) 25 EL Rev 492.

Vossestein, A.J., 'Annotation of *Wouters*' (Case C-309/99), (2002) 39 CML Rev 841.

··

D: **State involvement**

What if the State is involved in the practice which causes market distortion? The approach of Community law depends on the precise nature of State participation. If the State is simply pursuing a commercial activity in, perhaps, the guise of a nationalized industry, then Article 81 will apply to any agreements struck (e.g., *Aluminium Products* [1985] OJ L92/1). If the body is a public undertaking or an undertaking to which the State grants special or exclusive rights, Article 86 applies. Article 86 requires conformity with the requirements of Article 81, but offers exception in its second paragraph where this is necessary to enable the entity to perform its assigned tasks. This is a narrow exception. Where the State obstructs cross-border trade by legislative or administrative action, Article 28 applies (Chapter 10). So the price-fixing cases such as *Tasca* (Case 65/75) (discussed above, at p.365) involve obligations imposed on private firms to set prices within certain bands, but the measure caught by Community law is the State compulsion which falls within the definition of Article 28's prohibition on MEQRs. The State which subsidizes domestic industry is liable to distort the market. Article 87 controls State aids.

Where the State legislates to permit or encourage a breach of the competition rules, then not only do the parties to the agreement act in breach of the Treaty, but also the State has violated its duty to cooperate in the pursuit of the objectives of the Community. It may be in breach of Article 10 (which was Article 5 pre-Amsterdam) read with the competition provisions. In the next case, the issue arose in relation to State approval of airline fare structures.

Ahmed Saeed Flugreisen v Zentrale zur Bekämpfung unlauteren Wettbewerbs (Case 66/86)

[1989] ECR 803, [1990] 4 CMLR 102, Court of Justice of the European Communities

[48] . . . [I]t should be borne in mind in the first place that, as the Court has consistently held, while it is true that the competition rules set out in Articles 85 and 86 concern the conduct of undertakings and not measures of the authorities in the Member States, Article 5 of the Treaty nevertheless imposes a duty on those authorities not to adopt or maintain in force any measure which could deprive those competition rules of their effectiveness. That would be the case, in particular, if a Member State were to require or favour the adoption of agreements, decisions or concerted practices contrary to Article 85 or reinforce their effects (see, most recently, the judgment of 1 October 1987 in Case 311/85 *Vereniging van Vlaamse Reisbureaus* v *Sociaale Dienst van de plaatselijke en gewestelijke Overheidsdiensten* [1987] ECR 3801).

[49] It must be concluded as a result that the approval by the aeronautical authorities of tariff agreements contrary to Article 85(1) is not compatible with Community law and in particular with Article 5 of the Treaty. It also follows that the aeronautical authorities must refrain from taking any measure which might be construed as encouraging airlines to conclude tariff agreements contrary to the Treaty.

[50] In the specific case of tariffs for scheduled flights that interpretation of the Treaty is borne out by Article 90(1) of the Treaty, which provides that in the case of undertakings to which Member States grant special or exclusive rights – such as rights to operate on an air route alone or with one or two other undertakings – Member States must not enact or maintain in force any measure contrary to the competition rules laid down in Articles 85 and 86. Moreover, it is stated in the preambles to Council Regulations Nos 3975 and 3976/87 that those regulations do not prejudge the application of Article 90 of the Treaty.

[51] Admittedly, in the preamble to Regulation No 3976/87 the Council expressed a desire to increase competition in air transport services between Member States gradually so as to provide time for the sector concerned to adapt to a system different from the present system of establishing a network of agreements between Member States and air carriers. However, that concern can be respected only within the limits laid down by the provisions of the Treaty.

[52] Whilst, as a result, the new rules laid down by the Council and the Commission leave the Community institutions and the authorities in the Member States free to encourage the airlines to organize mutual consultations on the tariffs to be applied on certain routes served by scheduled flights, such as the consultations provided for in Directive 87/601/EEC, the Treaty nevertheless strictly prohibits them from giving encouragement, in any form whatsoever, to the adoption of agreements or concerted practices with regard to tariffs contrary to Article 85(1) or Article 86, as the case may be.

[53] The national court also refers to Article 90(3), but that provision appears to be of no relevance for the purpose of resolving the problems raised by this case. That provision places the Commission under a duty to ensure the application of the provisions of Article 90 and to address, where necessary, appropriate directives or decisions to Member States; it does not, however, preclude the application of paragraphs (1) and (2) of that article where the Commission fails to act.

[54] In contrast, Article 90(2) might entail consequences for decisions by the aeronautical authorities with regard to the approval of tariffs. That provision provides *inter alia* that undertakings entrusted with the operation of services of general economic interest are to be subject to the competition rules contained in the Treaty, in so far however as the application of such rules does not obstruct the performance of the particular tasks assigned to them.

[55] That provision may be applied to carriers who may be obliged, by the public authorities, to operate on routes which are not commercially viable but which it is necessary to operate for reasons of the general interest. It is necessary in each case for the competent national administrative or judicial authorities to establish whether the airline in question has actually been entrusted with the task of operating on such routes by an act of the public authority (judgment of 27 March 1974 in Case 127/73 *Belgische Radio en Televisie* v *Sabam ('BRT-II')* [1974] ECR 313).

[56] However, for it to be possible for the effect of the competition rules to be restricted pursuant to Article 90(2) by needs arising from performance of a task of general interest, the national authorities responsible for the approval of tariffs and the courts to which disputes relating thereto are submitted must be able to determine the exact nature of the needs in question and their impact on the structure of the tariffs applied by the airlines in question.

[57] Indeed, where there is no effective transparency of the tariff structure it is difficult, if not impossible, to assess the influence of the task of general interest on the application of the competition rules in the field of tariffs. It is for the national court to make the necessary findings of fact in that connection.

[58] It follows from the foregoing considerations that it should be stated in reply to the third question submitted by the national court that Articles 5 and 90 of the EEC Treaty must be interpreted as:

(i) prohibiting the national authorities from encouraging the conclusion of agreements on tariffs contrary to Article 85(1) or Article 86 of the Treaty, as the case may be;

(ii) precluding the approval by those authorities of tariffs resulting from such agreements;

(iii) not precluding a limitation of the effects of the competition rules in so far as it is indispensable for the performance of a task of general interest which air carriers are required to carry out, provided that the nature of that task and its impact on the tariff structure are clearly established.

NOTE

German legislation which restricted the growth of a market in employment procurement services was at issue in the next case. The Court made it clear that a State which nurtures an uncompetitive market may violate the Treaty rules. The result of the application of the Community rules is market liberalization.

Höfner v *Macrotron* (Case C-41/90)

[1991] ECR I-1979, Court of Justice of the European Communities

[34]   [A] public employment agency engaged in employment procurement activities is subject to the prohibition contained in Article 86 of the Treaty [now Article 82], so long as the application of that provision does not obstruct the performance of the particular task assigned to it. A Member State which has conferred an exclusive right to carry on that activity upon the public employment agency is in breach of Article 90(1) of the Treaty [now Article 86(1)] where it creates a situation in which that agency cannot avoid infringing Article 86 of the Treaty [now Article 82]. That is the case, in particular, where the following conditions are satisfied:

— the exclusive right extends to executive recruitment activities;

— the public employment agency is manifestly incapable of satisfying demand prevailing on the market for such activities;

— the actual pursuit of those activities by private recruitment consultants is rendered impossible by the maintenance in force of a statutory provision under which such activities are prohibited and non-observance of that prohibition renders the contracts concerned void;

— the activities in question may extend to the nationals or to the territory of other Member States.

NOTE

The profile of EC law's supervision of anticompetitive State laws has increased markedly since the late-1980s. This has given rise to challenges to long-standing national monopolies in areas such as energy supply and telecommunications. It is beyond the scope of this book to provide extended coverage. Its purpose is simply to alert the reader to the shape of the law. The following articles offer scope for further reading:

Edward, D. and Hoskins, M., 'Article 90: Deregulation and EC Law. Reflections arising from the XVI FIDE Conference' (1995) 32 CML Rev 157.

Ehlermann, C.-D., 'Managing Monopolies: the Role of the State in Controlling Market Dominance in the European Community' (1993) 14 ECLR 61.

Ross, M., 'Article 16 EC and Services of General Interest: from Derogation to Obligation' (2000) 25 EL Rev 22.

Szyszczak, E., 'Public Service Provision in Competitive Markets' (2001) 20 YEL 35.

NOTE
Nevertheless, the Court does not assert a general power to supervise all State intervention in the market. It is necessary to establish the application of one or more specific Treaty provisions. In the next case the Court picks its way carefully through the Treaty provisions to which reference is made by the national court and concludes that none prevents the application of the Italian rules in question.

DIP SpA v *Comune di Bassano del Grappa* (Case C-140/94), *LIDL Italia SrL* v *Comune di Chioggia* (Case C-141/94), *Lingral SrL* v *Comune di Chioggia* (Case C-142/94)
[1995] ECR I-3257, Court of Justice of the European Communities

The three applicants had been refused licences to open retail premises. Under the relevant Italian legislation, opening a new shop is subject to the issue of a licence by the local mayor on the opinion of a municipal committee, taking into account the criteria laid down in a commercial development plan drawn up by each municipality after consulting the committee. The committee membership is determined by law and its precise composition differs depending whether the municipality has more or fewer than 50,000 inhabitants. However, in either instance, members include public officials, an urban planning expert and traffic expert appointed by the town council, experts on distribution problems appointed with the involvement of trade and consumer representative organizations, and, finally, workers' representatives. The Court first considered whether the State could be held in violation of Article 5 read with Articles 85 and 86 of the EC Treaty (now Articles 10, 81, and 82 EC) by introducing or maintaining in force measures which may render ineffective the competition rules applicable to undertakings. It stated that:

[15] The Court has held that Articles 5 and 85 are infringed where a Member State requires or favours the adoption of agreements, decisions or concerted practices contrary to Article 85 or reinforces their effects, or where it deprives its own rules of the character of legislation by delegating to private economic operators responsibility for taking decisions affecting the economic sphere.

The Court continued:

[17] As regards rules such as those contained in the Italian Law, it should first be pointed out that members appointed or nominated by traders' organisations are in a minority on the municipal committees, side by side with workers' representatives, representatives of public authorities and experts appointed by the latter.

[18] Moreover, as expressly indicated in that law, the members appointed or nominated by traders' organisations are present as experts on distribution problems and not in order to represent their own business interests, and in drawing up its opinions the municipal committee is to observe the public interest.

[19] It follows from the foregoing considerations that in a trading licence system such as that established by the Italian Law, the opinions adopted by the municipal committee cannot be regarded as agreements between traders which the public authorities have required or favoured or the effects of which they have reinforced.

[20] It must next be considered . . . whether the public authorities have delegated their powers in the matter of trading licences to private economic operators.

[21] The Italian Law provides that licences are to be issued by the mayor of the municipality concerned, taking into account the criteria laid down in the municipal commercial development plan. The purpose of that plan is to provide the best possible service for consumers and the best possible balance between permanent trading establishments and foreseeable demand from the population.

[22] Furthermore, the municipal committee is called on to give the mayor merely an opinion on individual licenses. It is only where the municipality does not yet have an approved commercial development plan that licences may not be issued unless the committee's opinion is favourable.

[23] It follows from the foregoing considerations that, in a system such as that established by the Italian Law, the public authorities have not delegated their powers to private economic operators.

[24] Articles 3(g), 5 and 86 of the Treaty could apply to rules such as those contained in the Italian Law only if it were proved that that law creates a position of economic strength for an undertaking which enables it to prevent effective competition being maintained on the relevant market by affording it the power to behave to an appreciable extent independently of its competitors, its customers and, ultimately, the consumers (judgment in Case 85/76 *Hoffmann-La Roche v Commission* [1979] ECR 461, paragraph 38).

[25] The Court has held that Article 86 of the Treaty prohibits abusive practices resulting from the exploitation, by one or more undertakings, of a dominant position on the common market or in a substantial part of it, in so far as those practices may affect trade between Member States (judgment in Case C-393/92 *Almelo and Others v Energiebedriff IJsselmij* [1994] ECR I-1477, paragraph 40).

[26] In order to find that a collective dominant position exists, the undertakings in question must be linked in such a way that they adopt the same conduct on the market (judgment in *Almelo*, paragraph 42).

[27] National rules which require a licence to be obtained before a new shop can be opened and limit the number of shops in the municipality in order to achieve a balance between supply and demand cannot be considered to put individual traders in dominant positions or all the traders established in a municipality in a collective dominant position, a salient feature of which would be that traders did not compete against one another.

[28] It follows that Articles 85 and 86, in conjunction with Articles 3(g) and 5, of the Treaty do not preclude rules such as those contained in the Italian Law.

The Court then completed its exploration of EC trade law by adding reference to Article 30 of the EC Treaty (now, after amendment, Article 28: Chapters 7 and 8):

[29] On this point, it is sufficient to observe that rules such as those contained in the Italian Law make no distinction according to the origin of the goods distributed by the business concerned, that their purpose is not to regulate trade in goods with other Member States and that the restrictive effects which they might have on the free movement of goods are too uncertain and indirect for the obligation which they impose to be regarded as being capable of hindering trade between Member States (judgment in Case C-379/92 *Peralta* [1994] ECR I-3453, paragraph 24, and the decisions cited above).

[30] Article 30 does not therefore preclude legislation such as the Italian Law.

■ QUESTIONS

1. The referring national court did not ask about the potential application of Articles 52 or 59 of the EC Treaty (now, after amendment, Articles 43 and 49 respectively), which govern establishment and provision of services respectively. What would be the relevance of those Treaty provisions in such circumstances?

2. Laws such as that in issue in this decision place barriers to entry on to the market by potential new suppliers. Where a licence is refused, this may forestall a widening of consumer choice and may allow existing operators to cushion themselves from (potentially price-cutting) competitors. So is the European Court well advised to decline to take a stand on the permissibility of such a rule?

NOTE

See also Case C-38/97 *Autotrasporti Librandi Snc di Librandi F & C* [1998] ECR I-5955. The market regulation in question is treated by the Court as a matter of national competence untouched by EC trade law. The decision should be read in conjunction with discussion elsewhere of the outer limits to EC trade law (pp.392, 458). In adopting a relatively narrow focus, the Court has declined the temptation to create a general economic constitutional law for the Community (see N. Bernard, 'Discrimination and Free Movement in EC Law' (1996) 45 ICLQ 82; P. Davies, 'Market Integration and Social Policy' (1995) 25 ILJ 49; D. Gerber, 'Constitutionalising the Economy: German Neo-Liberalism, Competition Law and the "New" Europe' (1994) 42 AJCL 25; T. Hervey, 'Social Solidarity: a Buttress Against Internal Market' in J. Shaw (ed), *Social Law and Policy in an Evolving European Union* (Oxford: Hart Publishing, 2000); H. Schepel, 'Delegation of Regulatory Powers to Private Parties under EC Competition Law: Towards a Procedural Public Interest Test' (2002) 39 CML Rev 31).

SECTION 7: **EXEMPTION**

Article 81(3) permits exemption of agreements falling within Article 81(1). It is set out at p.496 above. It implies a cost-benefit assessment, whereby the advantages of collaboration are balanced against the disadvantages of impeded competition. However, the terms of Article 81(3) are rather more specific than general economic cost-benefit. The provision contains four elements; two positive conditions and two negative conditions. All must be satisfied. The two positive conditions demand a yield of economic progress, a fair share of which must percolate to the consumer; the two negative conditions forbid unnecessary extra restraints and the elimination of competition.

Typically, a Commission Decision relating to Article 81(3) will appraise the general economic context of an agreement and then proceed to apply these four elements. Despite this step-by-step approach, all four elements are inter-linked. The following Decision illustrates the types of argument relevant under Article 81(3) and the application of the conditions, two positive, two negative.

Prym-Werke
[1973] CMLR D250; [1973] OJ L296/24, Commission Decision 73/323

Prym agreed to give up making needles. It agreed to buy its needle needs from Beka. Beka agreed to supply Prym. Beka could then specialize in needle production. The Commission decided to exempt the agreement after the following analysis.

. . . [T]he concentration of manufacturing agreed on by Prym and Beka has, from the point of view of the improvement of production, favourable effects analogous to those of specialisation; it causes an increase of at least 50 per cent in the quantity of needles to be manufactured in the Eupen factory, which makes it possible to make more intensive use of the existing plant and to introduce production-line manufacture.

This rationalisation of production has in particular made it possible to reduce the very large proportion of labour costs in the producer's cost price. The producer's cost price of 'Standard' quality needles, which fell by some 20 per cent in 1970 after the concentration of production at Eupen, was still lower at the end of 1972 than in 1969 in spite of the increases in wages and in the cost of raw materials which had occurred during those four years. The introduction of mechanised production-line manufacture with increased productive capacity also makes it possible to manufacture articles of a more even quality.

The agreement allows consumers a fair share of the benefit resulting from it, as it must be supposed that because of the pressure of competition existing on the needle market the advantages resulting from rationalisation will be passed on to consumers.

The agreement does not contain restrictions which are not indispensable to the attainment of the said advantages. The favourable effects of the agreement are due essentially to the improvement in productivity resulting from a more intensive utilisation of productive capacity, and that more intensive utilisation is only possible if the quantities of needles to be manufactured are, and are to remain, considerably larger than before. That being so, it is essential that Prym should enter into a commitment for a long period, not only to cease manufacture, but also to purchase all its requirements of needles for domestic sewing machines from Beka, so as to provide a guarantee for an increased output by the latter.

The long-term commitments by Prym to obtain its supplies exclusively from Beka thus represents an indispensable restriction if the favourable effects of the agreement are to be achieved and, moreover, maintained. That commitment, moreover, does not go beyond what is strictly necessary, since it allows Prym the possibility, in the event of Beka being unable to meet its commitments, of buying from other sources and since, in any case, Prym gets the benefit of preferential prices.

The agreement does not afford the parties the possibility of eliminating competition in respect of a substantial part of the products in question. In the amended version in force since 10 October 1972 the agreement no longer prevents Beka and Prym from competing with each other on any EEC market, whether geographic or sectoral. Both undertakings rest exposed to the keen competition from other, sometimes larger, producers who appear as sellers within the EEC.

All the conditions necessary for the application of Article 85(3) of the Treaty [now Article 81(3)] are thus fulfilled.

■ QUESTION

Why was exemption unavailable to the Consten/Grundig deal (p.497 above)? After all, it improved product distribution; German goods were available in France. Consider each of the four elements of Article 81(3).

NOTE

It is relatively uncommon for an agreement to be denied exemption due to failure to satisfy one element only. See, e.g., *WANO Schwarzpulver* [1978] OJ L322/26, [1979] 1 CMLR 403, for an example of a Commission Decision which finds several reasons for refusal and illustrates how the four elements of Article 81(3) are connected.

SECTION 8: **BLOCK EXEMPTION**

The four elements of Article 81(3) find practical expression in Block Exemption Regulations. These measures apply the criteria for exemption to particular types of collaboration. As charters for lawful agreements, they assist in the practical administration of the competition rules by the Commission; and in commercial planning by firms. At the beginning of 2000 there were several Block Exemption Regulations in force. They covered several types of agreement. Some regulations dealt with agreements of a vertical type (those between traders at different points in the supply chain). Others covered agreements more typically struck on a horizontal basis (between traders at the same point on the supply chain). But the Commission's approach to block exemptions has been radically overhauled. It launched an extensive review of its treatment of vertical restraints in its Green Paper on *Vertical Restraints in EC Competition Policy,* published in January 1997 (COM (96) 721). As already mentioned at pp.500 and 513 above, this review was initiated against a background of increasing pressure from commercial interests and from some academics in favour of relaxing the grip of Article 81 on private contractual autonomy. Concerns rooted in both policy and administration underpin the review. 'Background and reasons for the Green Paper' form the opening section of its Executive Summary:

GREEN PAPER ON VERTICAL RESTRAINTS IN EC COMPETITION POLICY, EXECUTIVE SUMMARY

(Footnotes omitted.)

Background and reasons for Green Paper

1. The creation of a single market is one of the main objectives of the European Union's competition policy. Whilst great progress has been made further efforts are still necessary if the full economic advantages of integration are to be realised.

2. The single market represents an opportunity for EU firms to enter new markets that may have been previously closed to them because of government barriers. This penetration of new markets takes time and investment and is risky. The process is often facilitated by agreements between producers who want to break into a new market and local distributors. Efficient distribution with appropriate pre- and after-sales support is part of the competitive process that brings benefits to consumers.

However, arrangements between producers and distributors can also be used to continue the partitioning of the market and exclude new entrants who would intensify competition and lead to downward pressure on prices. Agreements between producers and distributors (vertical restraints) can therefore be used pro-competitively to promote market integration and efficient distribution or anti-competitively to block integration and competition. The price differences between Member States that are still found provide the incentive for companies to enter new markets as well as to erect barriers against new competition.

3. Because of their strong links to market integration that can be either positive or negative, vertical restraints have been of particular importance to the Union's competition policy. Whilst this policy has been successful in over 30 years of application a review is now necessary because

    — the single market legislation for the free movement of products is now largely in place
    — the Regulations governing vertical restraints expire, and
    — there have been major changes in methods of distribution that may have implications for policy.

4. In addition, as the world's largest trading block, the Union is committed to the development of open and fair international trade. Just as vertical restraints can either promote or hinder the creation of a real single market, they can be either beneficial or detrimental to international trade. The Union's policy in this area is therefore of wider international importance. Our experience may be useful for analysing market access impediments in third countries.

5. The review of policy takes the form of a Green Paper, which sets out the relevant issues as understood by the Commission. Several policy options (point VIII below) are set out which will form the basis for a wide reaching public consultation involving Parliament, Member States, the Economic and Social Committee and Committee of Regions as well as all interested parties

(producers, distributors, workers' representatives and consumers). This consultation will allow the Commission to decide on the direction and form of future policy in the full light of all the facts. This review and consultation also constitute the Commission's response to the exciting challenge of taking forward this key area of competition policy into the next millennium.

The Green Paper generated the lively debate that one would expect of a document which represented an invitation to consider the 'modernization' of EC competition law after almost 40 years of experience (see, e.g., C. Bright, 'EU Competition Policy: Rules, Objectives and Deregulation' (1996) 16 OxJLS 535; R. Wesseling, 'Subsidiarity in Community Antitrust Law: Setting the Right Agenda' (1997) 22 EL Rev 35). After an intense period of consultation, the main lines of planned reform were set out in the Commission *Communication on the application of EC competition rules to vertical restraints*, COM (98) 544. Council Regulation 1215/99 then amended Regulation 19/65 to empower the Commission to adopt a block exemption for vertical restraints. It duly adopted Regulation 2790/1999 on the application of Article 81(3) of the Treaty to categories of vertical agreements and concerted practices, which is set out below. This altered the law by adjusting the conditions for exempting vertical deals (as defined) from the prohibition in Article 81. The Regulation entered into force on 1 January 2000, but its key provisions applied from 1 June 2000 (Article 13). It replaces the pre-existing block exemptions governing exclusive distribution, exclusive purchasing, and franchising.

COMMISSION REGULATION (EC) 2790/1999 OF 22 DECEMBER 1999 ON THE APPLICATION OF ARTICLE 81(3) OF THE TREATY TO CATEGORIES OF VERTICAL AGREEMENTS AND CONCERTED PRACTICES
[1999] OJ L336/21

THE COMMISSION OF THE EUROPEAN COMMUNITIES,

Having regard to the Treaty establishing the European Community, Having regard to Council Regulation No 19/65/EEC of 2 March 1965 on the application of Article 85(3) of the Treaty to certain categories of agreements and concerted practices [OJ 36, 6.3.1965, p.533/65], as last amended by Regulation (EC) No 1215/1999 [1999] OJ L148/1, and in particular Article 1 thereof,

Having published a draft of this Regulation [1999] OJ C270/7,

Having consulted the Advisory Committee on Restrictive Practices and Dominant Positions,

Whereas:

(1) Regulation No 19/65/EEC empowers the Commission to apply Article 81(3) of the Treaty (formerly Article 85(3)) by regulation to certain categories of vertical agreements and corresponding concerted practices falling within Article 81(1).

(2) Experience acquired to date makes it possible to define a category of vertical agreements which can be regarded as normally satisfying the conditions laid down in Article 81(3).

(3) This category includes vertical agreements for the purchase or sale of goods or services where these agreements are concluded between non-competing undertakings, between certain competitors or by certain associations of retailers of goods; it also includes vertical agreements containing ancillary provisions on the assignment or use of intellectual property rights; for the purposes of this Regulation, the term 'vertical agreements' includes the corresponding concerted practices.

(4) For the application of Article 81(3) by regulation, it is not necessary to define those vertical agreements which are capable of falling within Article 81(1); in the individual assessment of agreements under Article 81(1), account has to be taken of several factors, and in particular the market structure on the supply and purchase side.

(5) The benefit of the block exemption should be limited to vertical agreements for which it can be assumed with sufficient certainty that they satisfy the conditions of Article 81(3).

(6) Vertical agreements of the category defined in this Regulation can improve economic efficiency within a chain of production or distribution by facilitating better coordination between the participating undertakings; in particular, they can lead to a reduction in the transaction and distribution costs of the parties and to an optimisation of their sales and investment levels.

(7) The likelihood that such efficiency-enhancing effects will outweigh any anti-competitive effects due to restrictions contained in vertical agreements depends on the degree of market power of the undertakings concerned and, therefore, on the extent to which those undertakings face competition from other suppliers of goods or services regarded by the buyer as interchangeable or substitutable for one another, by reason of the products' characteristics, their prices and their intended use.

(8) It can be presumed that, where the share of the relevant market accounted for by the supplier does not exceed 30%, vertical agreements which do not contain certain types of severely anti-competitive restraints generally lead to an improvement in production or distribution and allow consumers a fair share of the resulting benefits; in the case of vertical agreements containing exclusive supply obligations, it is the market share of the buyer which is relevant in determining the overall effects of such vertical agreements on the market.

(9) Above the market share threshold of 30%, there can be no presumption that vertical agreements falling within the scope of Article 81(1) will usually give rise to objective advantages of such a character and size as to compensate for the disadvantages which they create for competition.

(10) This Regulation should not exempt vertical agreements containing restrictions which are not indispensable to the attainment of the positive effects mentioned above; in particular, vertical agreements containing certain types of severely anti-competitive restraints such as minimum and fixed resale-prices, as well as certain types of territorial protection, should be excluded from the benefit of the block exemption established by this Regulation irrespective of the market share of the undertakings concerned.

(11) In order to ensure access to or to prevent collusion on the relevant market, certain conditions are to be attached to the block exemption; to this end, the exemption of non-compete obligations should be limited to obligations which do not exceed a definite duration; for the same reasons, any direct or indirect obligation causing the members of a selective distribution system not to sell the brands of particular competing suppliers should be excluded from the benefit of this Regulation.

(12) The market-share limitation, the non-exemption of certain vertical agreements and the conditions provided for in this Regulation normally ensure that the agreements to which the block exemption applies do not enable the participating undertakings to eliminate competition in respect of a substantial part of the products in question.

(13) In particular cases in which the agreements falling under this Regulation nevertheless have effects incompatible with Article 81(3), the Commission may withdraw the benefit of the block exemption; this may occur in particular where the buyer has significant market power in the relevant market in which it resells the goods or provides the services or where parallel networks of vertical agreements have similar effects which significantly restrict access to a relevant market or competition therein; such cumulative effects may, for example, arise in the case of selective distribution or non-compete obligations.

(14) Regulation No 19/65/EEC empowers the competent authorities of Member States to withdraw the benefit of the block exemption in respect of vertical agreements having effects incompatible with the conditions laid down in Article 81(3), where such effects are felt in their respective territory, or in a part thereof; and where such territory has the characteristics of a distinct geographic market; Member States should ensure that the exercise of this power of withdrawal does not prejudice the uniform application throughout the common market of the Community competition rules or the full effect of the measures adopted in implementation of those rules.

(15) In order to strengthen supervision of parallel networks of vertical agreements which have

similar restrictive effects and which cover more than 50% of a given market, the Commission may declare this Regulation inapplicable to vertical agreements containing specific restraints relating to the market concerned, thereby restoring the full application of Article 81 to such agreements.

(16) This Regulation is without prejudice to the application of Article 82.

(17) In accordance with the principle of the primacy of Community law, no measure taken pursuant to national laws on competition should prejudice the uniform application throughout the common market of the Community competition rules or the full effect of any measures adopted in implementation of those rules, including this Regulation,

HAS ADOPTED THIS REGULATION:

Article 1

For the purposes of this Regulation:

(a) 'competing undertakings' means actual or potential suppliers in the same product market; the, product market includes goods or services which are regarded by the buyer as interchangeable with or substitutable for the contract goods or services, by reason of the products' characteristics, their prices and their intended use;

(b) 'non-compete obligation' means any direct or indirect obligation causing the buyer not to manufacture, purchase, sell or resell goods or services which compete with the contract goods or services, or any direct or indirect obligation on the buyer to purchase from the supplier or from another undertaking designated by the supplier more than 80% of the buyer's total purchases of the contract goods or services and their substitutes on the relevant market, calculated on the basis of the value of its purchases in the preceding calendar year;

(c) 'exclusive supply obligation' means any direct or indirect obligation causing the supplier to sell the goods or services specified in the agreement only to one buyer inside the Community for the purposes of a specific use or for resale;

(d) 'Selective distribution system' means a distribution system where the supplier undertakes to sell the contract goods or services, either directly or indirectly, only to distributors selected on the basis of specified criteria and where these distributors undertake not to sell such goods or services to unauthorised distributors;

(e) 'intellectual property rights' includes industrial property rights, copyright and neighbouring rights;

(f) 'know-how' means a package of non-patented practical information, resulting from experience and testing by the supplier, which is secret, substantial and identified: in this context, 'secret' means that the know-how, as a body or in the precise configuration and assembly of its components, is not generally known or easily accessible; 'substantial' means that the know-how includes information which is indispensable to the buyer for the use, sale or resale of the contract goods or services; 'identified' means that the know-how must be described in a sufficiently comprehensive manner so as to make it possible to verify that it fulfils the criteria of secrecy and substantiality;

(g) 'buyer' includes an undertaking which, under an agreement falling within Article 81(1) of the Treaty, sells goods or services on behalf of another undertaking.

Article 2

1. Pursuant to Article 81(3) of the Treaty and subject to the provisions of this Regulation, it is hereby declared that Article 81(1) shall not apply to agreements or concerted practices entered into between two or more undertakings each of which operates, for the purposes of the agreement, at a different level of the production or distribution chain, and relating to the conditions under which the parties may purchase, sell or resell certain goods or services ('vertical agreements').

This exemption shall apply to the extent that such agreements contain restrictions of competition falling within the scope of Article 81(1) ('vertical restraints').

2. The exemption provided for in paragraph 1 shall apply to vertical agreements entered into between an association of undertakings and its members, or between such an association and its suppliers, only if all its members are retailers of goods and if no individual member of the association, together with its connected undertakings, has a total annual turnover exceeding EUR 50 million; vertical agreements entered into by such associations shall be covered by this Regulation without prejudice to the application of Article 81 to horizontal agreements concluded between the members of the association or decisions adopted by the association.

3. The exemption provided for in paragraph 1 shall apply to vertical agreements containing provisions which relate to the assignment to the buyer or use by the buyer of intellectual property rights, provided that those provisions do not constitute the primary object of such agreements and are directly related to the use, sale or resale of goods or services by the buyer or its customers. The exemption applies on condition that, in relation to the contract goods or services, those provisions do not contain restrictions of competition having the same object or effect as vertical restraints which are not exempted under this Regulation.

4. The exemption provided for in paragraph 1 shall not apply to vertical agreements entered into between competing undertakings; however, it shall apply where competing undertakings enter into a non-reciprocal vertical agreement and:

(a) the buyer has a total annual turnover not exceeding EUR 100 million, or
(b) the supplier is a manufacturer and a distributor of goods, while the buyer is a distributor not manufacturing goods competing with the contract goods, or
(c) the supplier is a provider of services at several levels of trade, while the buyer does not provide competing services at the level of trade where it purchases the contract services.

5. This Regulation shall not apply to vertical agreements the subject matter of which falls within the scope of any other block exemption regulation.

Article 3

1. Subject to paragraph 2 of this Article, the exemption provided for in Article 2 shall apply on condition that the market share held by the supplier does not exceed 30% of the relevant market on which it sells the contract goods or services.

2. In the case of vertical agreements containing exclusive supply obligations, the exemption provided for in Article 2 shall apply on condition that the market share held by the buyer does not exceed 30% of the relevant market on which it purchases the contract goods or services.

Article 4

The exemption provided for in Article 2 shall not apply to vertical agreements which, directly or indirectly, in isolation or in combination with other factors under the control of the parties, have as their object:

(a) the restriction of the buyer's ability to determine its sale price, without prejudice to the possibility of the supplier's imposing a maximum sale price or recommending a sale price, provided that they do not amount to a fixed or minimum sale price as a result of pressure from, or incentives offered by, any of the parties;
(b) the restriction of the territory into which, or of the customers to whom, the buyer may sell the contract goods or services, except:
— the restriction of active sales into the exclusive territory or to an exclusive customer group reserved to the supplier or allocated by the supplier to another buyer, where such a restriction does not limit sales by the customers of the buyer,
— the restriction of sales to end users by a buyer operating at the wholesale level of trade,
— the restriction of sales to unauthorised distributors by the members of a selective distribution system, and
— the restriction of the buyer's ability to sell components, supplied for the purposes of incorporation, to customers who would use them to manufacture the same type of goods as those produced by the supplier;

(c) the restriction of active or passive sales to end users by members of a selective distribution system operating at the retail level of trade, without prejudice to the possibility of prohibiting a member of the system from operating out of an unauthorised place of establishment;

(d) the restriction of cross-supplies between distributors within a selective distribution system, including between distributors operating at different level of trade;

(e) the restriction agreed between a supplier of components and a buyer who incorporates those components, which limits the supplier to selling the components as spare parts to end-users or to repairers or other service providers not entrusted by the buyer with the repair or servicing of its goods.

Article 5

The exemption provided for in Article 2 shall not apply to any of the following obligations contained in vertical agreements:

(a) any direct or indirect non-compete obligation, the duration of which is indefinite or exceeds five years. A non-compete obligation which is tacitly renewable beyond a period of five years is to be deemed to have been concluded for an indefinite duration. However, the time limitation of five years shall not apply where the contract goods or services are sold by the buyer from premises and land owned by the supplier or leased by the supplier from third parties not connected with the buyer, provided that the duration of the non-compete obligation does not exceed the period of occupancy of the premises and land by the buyer;

(b) any direct or indirect obligation causing the buyer, after termination of the agreement, not to manufacture, purchase, sell or resell goods or services, unless such obligation:
— relates to goods or services which compete with the contract goods or services, and
— is limited to the premises and land from which the buyer has operated during the contract period, and
— is indispensable to protect know-how transferred by the supplier to the buyer, and provided that the duration of such non-compete obligation is limited to a period of one year after termination of the agreement; this obligation is without prejudice to the possibility of imposing a restriction which is unlimited in time on the use and disclosure of know-how which has not entered the public domain;

(c) any direct or indirect obligation causing the members of a selective distribution system not to sell the brands of particular competing suppliers.

Article 6

The Commission may withdraw the benefit of this Regulation, pursuant to Article 7(1) of Regulation No 19/65/EEC, where it finds in any particular case that vertical agreements to which this Regulation applies nevertheless have effects which are incompatible with the conditions laid down in Article 81(3) of the Treaty, and in particular where access to the relevant market or competition therein is significantly restricted by the cumulative effect of parallel networks of similar vertical restraints implemented by competing suppliers or buyers.

Article 7

Where in any particular case vertical agreements to which the exemption provided for in Article 2 applies have effects incompatible with the conditions laid down in Article 81(3) of the Treaty in the territory of a Member State, or in a part thereof, which has all the characteristics of a distinct geographic market, the competent authority of that Member State may withdraw the benefit of application of this Regulation in respect of that territory, under the same conditions as provided in Article 6.

Article 8

1. Pursuant to Article 1 a of Regulation No 19/65/EEC, the Commission may by regulation declare that, where parallel networks of similar vertical restraints cover more than 50% of a relevant

market, this Regulation shall not apply to vertical agreements containing specific restraints relating to that market.

2. A regulation pursuant to paragraph 1 shall not become applicable earlier than six months following its adoption.

Article 9

1. The market share of 30% provided for in Article 3(1) shall be calculated on the basis of the market sales value of the contract goods or services and other goods or services sold by the supplier, which are regarded as interchangeable or substitutable by the buyer, by reason of the products' characteristics, their prices and their intended use; if market sales value data are not available, estimates based on other reliable market information, including market sales volumes, may be used to establish the market share of the undertaking concerned. For the purposes of Article 3(2), it is either the market purchase value or estimates thereof which shall be used to calculate the market share.

   2. For the purposes of applying the market share threshold provided for in Article 3 the following rules shall apply:

   (a) the market share shall be calculated on the basis of data relating to the preceding calendar year;
   (b) the market share shall include any goods or services supplied to integrated distributors for the purposes of sale;
   (c) if the market share is initially not more than 30% but subsequently rises above that level without exceeding 35%, the exemption provided for in Article 2 shall continue to apply for a period of two consecutive calendar years following the year in which the 30% market share threshold was first exceeded;
   (d) if the market share is initially not more than 30% but subsequently rises above 35%, the exemption provided for in Article 2 shall continue to apply for one calendar year following the year in which the level of 35% was first exceeded;
   (e) the benefit of points (c) and (d) may not be combined so as to exceed a period of two calendar years.

Article 10

1. For the purpose of calculating total annual turnover within the meaning of Article 2(2) and (4), the turnover achieved during the previous financial year by the relevant party to the vertical agreement and the turnover achieved by its connected undertakings in respect of all goods and services, excluding all taxes and other duties, shall be added together. For this purpose, no account shall be taken of dealings between the party to the vertical agreement and its connected undertakings or between its connected undertakings.

   2. The exemption provided for in Article 2 shall remain applicable where, for any period of two consecutive financial years, the total annual turnover threshold is exceeded by no more than 10%.

Article 11

1. For the purposes of this Regulation, the terms 'undertaking', 'supplier' and 'buyer' shall include their respective connected undertakings.

   2. 'Connected undertakings' are:

   (a) undertakings in which a party to the agreement, directly or indirectly:
       — has the power to exercise more than half the voting rights, or
       — has the power to appoint more than half the members of the supervisory board, board of management or bodies legally representing the undertaking, or
       — has the right to manage the undertaking's affairs;
   (b) undertakings which directly or indirectly have, over a party to the agreement, the rights or powers listed in (a);
   (c) undertakings in which an undertaking referred to in (b) has, directly or indirectly, the rights or powers listed in (a);
   (d) undertakings in which a party to the agreement together with one or more of

the undertakings referred to in (a), (b) or (c), or in which two or more of the latter undertakings, jointly have the rights or powers listed in (a);

(e) undertakings in which the rights or the powers listed in (a) are jointly held by:
— parties to the agreement or their respective connected undertakings referred to in (a) to (d), or
— one or more of the parties to the agreement or one or more of their connected undertakings referred to in (a) to (d) and one or more third parties.

3. For the purposes of Article 3, the market share held by the undertakings referred to in paragraph 2(e) of this Article shall be apportioned equally to each undertaking having the rights or the powers listed in paragraph 2(a).

Article 12

1. The exemptions provided for in Commission Regulations (EEC) No 1983/83 [OJ L 173, 30.6.1983, p.1], (EEC) No 1984/83 [OJ L 173, 30.6.1983, p.5] and (EEC) No 4087/88 [OJ L 359, 28.12.1988, p.46] shall continue to apply until 31 May 2000.

2. The prohibition laid down in Article 81(1) of the EC Treaty shall not apply during the period from 1 June 2000 to 31 December 2001 in respect of agreements already in force on 31 May 2000 which do not satisfy the conditions for exemption provided for in this Regulation but which satisfy the conditions for exemption provided for in Regulations (EEC) No 1983/83, (EEC) No 1984/83 or (EEC) No 4087/88.

Article 13

This Regulation shall enter into force on 1 January 2000.
It shall apply from 1 June 2000, except for Article 12(1) which shall apply from 1 January 2000.
This Regulation shall expire on 31 May 2010.

This Regulation shall be binding in its entirety and directly applicable in all Member States.
Done at Brussels, 22 December 1999.

■ QUESTIONS

1. Explain, with reference to particular clauses, how the requirements of Article 81(3) are reflected in this Block Exemption Regulation.

2. A major element in the Commission's modernization programme is the drive to ensure the efficient allocation of its scarce enforcement resources while also reducing burdens on business. The use of market share threshold criteria (Articles 3, 8, 9 of Regulation 2790/1999; and *cf* the Notice on Agreements of Minor Importance, p.515 above) forms part of this strategy. It is hoped to set aside the task of scrutinizing deals with an insignificant impact on market competition in favour of a focus on agreements with seriously prejudicial potential. Do 'safe havens' defined by market share criteria serve this purpose? What are their limitations? (Consider also the Commission *Notice on the Definition of the Relevant Market*, extracted at p.550 below.)

3. Could the Commission have achieved its objects in the area of control of vertical restraints simply by adopting a narrower interpretation of the scope of Article 81(1)? To what extent is the rule of reason approach, discussed at p.513 above, relevant in assessing the contribution of this Regulation to the modernization of EC competition law and policy?

4. How is the golden thread of market integration in EC law reflected in Regulation 2790/1999?

FURTHER READING

Nazerali, J. and Cowan, D., 'Unlocking EU Distribution Rules – Has the European Commission Found the Right Keys?' [2000] ECLR 50.

Neubauer, S. and Lever, J., 'Vertical Restraints, their Motivation and Justification' [2000] ECLR 7.

Whish, R., 'Regulation 2790/99: the Commission's New Style Block Exemption for Vertical Agreements' (2000) 37 CML Rev 887.

NOTE

The Commission spent time in 1999 and 2000 pursuing consultation on its treatment of horizontal restraints. Here too modernization has won the day. New Block Exemption Regulations on the application of Article 81(3) to categories of specialization agreements (Regulation 2658/2000 [2000] OJ L304/3) and research and development agreements (Regulation 2659/2000 [2000] OJ L304/7) were adopted, supplemented by new Guidelines on the applicability of Article 81 to horizontal co-operation agreements ([2001] OJ C3/2). Here too the Commission wishes to free both itself and commercial actors of burdens associated with supervision of deals that are insignificant in competition terms in order to target resources more efficiently on more serious cases. A more flexible regime is the result.

■ QUESTION

Pursuit of market integration has served as a canon of interpretation in EC competition law in the past; in the light of the accession of Central and Eastern European countries lacking developed economic links with Western Europe, ought market integration to retain its leading role also in the future?

NOTE

For additional material and resources see the Companion Website at: www.oup.co.uk/best.textbooks/law/weatherill6e

17

Article 82: Dominant Positions

ARTICLE 82 EC

Any abuse by one or more undertakings of a dominant position within the common market or in a substantial part of it shall be prohibited as incompatible with the common market in so far as it may affect trade between Member States.

Such abuse may, in particular, consist in:

(a) directly or indirectly imposing unfair purchase or selling prices or other unfair trading conditions;

(b) limiting production, markets or technical development to the prejudice of consumers;

(c) applying dissimilar conditions to equivalent transactions with other trading parties, thereby placing them at a competitive disadvantage;

(d) making the conclusion of contracts subject to acceptance by the other parties of supplementary obligations which, by their nature or according to commercial usage, have no connection with the subject of such contracts.

The text of Article 82 was untouched by the Amsterdam and Nice Treaties, but it must be borne in mind in reading the material in this Chapter that what is now Article 82 was numbered Article 86 until the entry into force of the Amsterdam Treaty on 1 May 1999 (p.12 above).

Article 82 stands alongside Article 81 as the second of the twin pillars of the Community's competition law system. Like Article 81, it controls undertakings, depends on an effect on trade between Member States, and has as its objective the control of market distortion. However, unlike Article 81, it controls the conduct of a single firm, rather than two or more firms. Articles 81 and 82 complement each other and should be read together as a competition law regime, not as two independent provisions.

The rationale for controlling the conduct of a single firm is found in the damage which it can wreak on the market. The firm may charge high prices, or it may refuse to supply customers. None of this matters in a competitive market. Our firm will simply lose business. But where our firm is economically powerful, it may be able to distort the market without fear of effective competition. The result may be inefficiency as a result of mismatch between the influence of supply and demand. The law, then, has reason to control the conduct of a single firm, but only where the firm has passed a threshold of economic power. English law has called that threshold the monopoly; Article 82 refers to it as the dominant position.

But it is not the dominant position that is condemned. It is the *abuse* of a dominant position, not its existence, which is unlawful. Article 82, set out above, supplies an illustrative list of the type of practice which may be held abusive.

Logically, there are two elements to an analysis under Article 82. First, is the firm *in a dominant position*? If so, secondly, has it *abused* that dominant position? The discussion uses as its framework the Court's decision in *United Brands* v *Commission* (Case 27/76), a famous case which touches on many of the issues of law and policy in this area.

SECTION 1: **THE DOMINANT POSITION: DEFINING THE MARKET**

The question, 'Is this firm in a dominant position?,' is simply answered: 'It depends!' And it depends on exactly what it is that the firm is alleged to be dominating. The producer of 80% of a nation's ox liver dominates the ox liver market. But there is no lack of competition if the consumer will freely switch preference to lamb's liver in the event of the ox liver producer raising prices. The breadth of the market, then, has to be defined accurately before one can logically accuse a firm of dominance on that market, and before one can claim a rationale for intervention to control dominance.

United Brands v *Commission* (Case 27/76)
[1978] ECR 207, [1978] 1 CMLR 429, Court of Justice of the European Communities

The United Brands Company (UBC) was found by the Commission to have abused a dominant position in the banana market. The firm sought annulment of that Decision before the Court. The following extract involves assessment of the market, defined according to product.

[12] As far as the product market is concerned it is first of all necessary to ascertain whether, as the applicant maintains, bananas are an integral part of the fresh fruit market, because they are reasonably interchangeable by consumers with other kinds of fresh fruit such as apples, oranges, grapes, peaches, strawberries, etc. or whether the relevant market consists solely of the banana market which includes both branded bananas and unlabelled bananas and is a market sufficiently homogeneous and distinct from the market of other fresh fruit.

[13] The applicant submits in support of its argument that bananas compete with other fresh fruit in the same shops, on the same shelves, at prices which can be compared, satisfying the same needs: consumption as a dessert or between meals.

[14] The statistics produced show that consumer expenditure on the purchase of bananas is at its lowest between June and December when there is a plentiful supply of domestic fresh fruit on the market.

[15] Studies carried out by the Food and Agriculture Organization (FAO) (especially in 1975) confirm that banana prices are relatively weak during the summer months and that the price of apples for example has a statistically appreciable impact on the consumption of bananas in the Federal Republic of Germany.

[16] Again according to these studies some easing of prices is noticeable at the end of the year during the 'orange season'.

[17] The seasonal peak periods when there is a plentiful supply of other fresh fruit exert an influence not only on the prices but also on the volume of sales of bananas and consequently on the volume of imports thereof.

[18] The applicant concludes from these findings that bananas and other fresh fruit form only one

market and that UBC's operations should have been examined in this context for the purpose of any application of Article 86 of the Treaty.

[19] The Commission maintains that there is a demand for bananas which is distinct from the demand for other fresh fruit especially as the banana is a very important part of the diet of certain sections of the community.

[20] The specific qualities of the banana influence customer preference and induce him not to readily accept other fruits as a substitute.

[21] The Commission draws the conclusion from the studies quoted by the applicant that the influence of the prices and availabilities of other types of fruit on the prices and availabilities of bananas on the relevant market is very ineffective and that these effects are too brief and too spasmodic for such other fruit to be regarded as forming part of the same market as bananas or as a substitute therefor.

[22] For the banana to be regarded as forming a market which is sufficiently differentiated from other fruit markets it must be possible for it to be singled out by such special features distinguishing it from other fruits that it is only to a limited extent interchangeable with them and is only exposed to their competition in a way that is hardly perceptible.

[23] The ripening of bananas takes place the whole year round without any season having to be taken into account.

[24] Throughout the year production exceeds demand and can satisfy it at any time.

[25] Owing to this particular feature the banana is a privileged fruit and its production and marketing can be adapted to the seasonal fluctuations of other fresh fruit which are known and can be computed.

[26] There is no unavoidable seasonal substitution since the consumer can obtain this fruit all the year round.

[27] Since the banana is a fruit which is always available in sufficient quantities the question whether it can be replaced by other fruits must be determined over the whole of the year for the purpose of ascertaining the degree of competition between it and other fresh fruit.

[28] The studies of the banana market on the Court's file show that on the latter market there is no significant long term cross elasticity any more than – as has been mentioned – there is any seasonal substitutability in general between the banana and all the seasonal fruits, as this only exists between the banana and two fruits (peaches and table grapes) in one of the countries (West Germany) of the relevant geographic market.

[29] As far as concerns the two fruits available throughout the year (oranges and apples) the first are not interchangeable and in the case of the second there is only a relative degree of substitutability.

[30] This small degree of substitutability is accounted for by the specific features of the banana and all the factors which influence consumer choice.

[31] The banana has certain characteristics, appearance, taste, softness, seedlessness, easy handling, a constant level of production which enable it to satisfy the constant needs of an important section of the population consisting of the very young, the old and the sick.

[32] As far as prices are concerned two FAO studies show that the banana is only affected by the prices – falling prices – of other fruits (and only of peaches and table grapes) during the summer months and mainly in July and then by an amount not exceeding 20%.

[33] Although it cannot be denied that during these months and some weeks at the end of the year this product is exposed to competition from other fruits, the flexible way in which the volume of imports and their marketing on the relevant geographic market is adjusted means that the conditions of competition are extremely limited and that its price adapts without any serious difficulties to this situation where supplies of fruit are plentiful.

[34] It follows from all these considerations that a very large number of consumers having a constant need for bananas are not noticeably or even appreciably enticed away from the consumption of this product by the arrival of other fresh fruit on the market and that even the personal peak periods only affect it for a limited period of time and to a very limited extent from the point of view of substitutability.

[35] Consequently the banana market is a market which is sufficiently distinct from the other fresh fruit markets.

NOTE

The Commission had adopted a narrower market definition than that advocated by United Brands. The narrower the definition, the more likely that dominance will be established. Disagreement between Commission and undertaking in this fashion is a common feature of Article 82 cases.

Markets may also be defined by reference to their territorial scope. Even if consumers will not switch from ox liver to other types of liver, the single national ox liver producer is not dominant if producers of ox liver in other States can import their produce as competition.

United Brands v *Commission* (Case 27/76)
[1978] ECR 207, [1978] 1 CMLR 429, Court of Justice of the European Communities

The Commission had analysed UBC's conduct in a market comprising Germany, Ireland, Denmark, Belgium, The Netherlands, and Luxembourg, but excluding the other three Member States at that time, the UK, France, and Italy. UBC argued that the geographic market 'should only comprise areas where the conditions of competition are homogeneous' and that this test was not satisfied by the Commission's chosen market. The Court, however, agreed with the Commission:

[44] The conditions for the application of Article 86 to an undertaking in a dominant position presuppose the clear delimitation of the substantial part of the Common Market in which it may be able to engage in abuses which hinder effective competition and this is an area where the objective conditions of competition applying to the product in question must be the same for all traders.

[45] The Community has not established a common organization of the agricultural market in bananas.

[46] Consequently import arrangements vary considerably from one Member State to another and reflect a specific commercial policy peculiar to the States concerned.

[47] This explains why for example the French market owing to its national organization is restricted upstream by a particular import arrangement and obstructed downstream by a retail price monitored by the Administration.

[48] This market, in addition to adopting certain measures relating to a 'target price' ('prix objectif') fixed each year and to packaging and grading standards and the minimum qualities required, reserves about two thirds of the market for the production of the overseas departments and one third to that of certain countries enjoying preferential relations with France (Ivory Coast, Madagascar, Cameroon) the bananas whereof are imported duty-free, and it includes a system the running of which is entrusted to the 'Comité interprofessionnel bananier' ('CIB').

[49] The United Kingdom market enjoys 'Commonwealth preferences', a system of which the main feature is the maintenance of a level of production favouring the developing countries of the Commonwealth and of a price paid to the associations of producers directly linked to the selling price of the green banana charged in the United Kingdom.

[50] On the Italian market, since the abolition in 1965 of the State Monopoly responsible for marketing bananas, a national system of quota restrictions has been introduced, the Ministry for Shipping and the Exchange Control Office supervising the imports and the charterparties relating to the foreign ships which carry the bananas.

[51] The effect of the national organization of these three markets is that the applicant's bananas do not compete on equal terms with the other bananas sold in these States which benefit from a preferential system and the Commission was right to exclude these three national markets from the geographic market under consideration.

[52] On the other hand the six other States are markets which are completely free, although the applicable tariff provisions and transport costs are of necessity different but not discriminatory, and in which the conditions of competition are the same for all.

[53] From the standpoint of being able to engage in free competition these six States form an area which is sufficiently homogeneous to be considered in its entirety.

[54] UBC has arranged for its subsidiary in Rotterdam – UBCBV – to market its products. UBCBV is for this purpose a single centre for the whole of this part of the Community.

[55] Transport costs do not in fact stand in the way of the distribution policy chosen by UBC which consists in selling f.o.r. Rotterdam and Bremerhaven, the two ports where the bananas are unloaded.

[56] These are factors which go to make relevant market a single market.

[57] It follows from all these considerations that the geographic market as determined by the Commission which constitutes a substantial part of the common market must be regarded as the relevant market for the purpose of determining whether the applicant may be in a dominant position.

The defined market, then, was internally more or less homogeneous and distinct in material respects from the wider market, defined by product and by territory. The next question was whether United Brands dominated that market. The Court established its test:

[65] The dominant position referred to in this article relates to a position of economic strength enjoyed by an undertaking which enables it to prevent effective competition being maintained on the relevant market by giving it the power to behave to an appreciable extent independently of its competitors, customers and ultimately of its consumers.

[66] In general a dominant position derives from a combination of several factors which, taken separately, are not necessarily determinative.

The first set of factors then analysed relate to the structure of UBC.

[69] It is advisable to examine in turn UBC's resources for and methods of producing, packaging, transporting, selling and displaying its product.

[70] UBC is an undertaking vertically integrated to a high degree.

[71] This integration is evident at each of the stages from the plantation to the loading on wagons or lorries in the ports of delivery and after those stages, as far as ripening and sale prices are concerned, UBC even extends its control to ripener/distributors and wholesalers by setting up a complete network of agents.

[72] At the production stage UBC owns large plantations in Central and South America.

[73] In so far as UBC's own production does not meet its requirements it can obtain supplies without any difficulty from independent planters since it is an established fact that unless circumstances are exceptional there is a production surplus.

[74] Furthermore several independent producers have links with UBC through contracts for the growing of bananas which have caused them to grow the varieties of bananas which UBC has advised them to adopt

[75] The effects of natural disasters which could jeopardize supplies are greatly reduced by the fact

that the plantations are spread over a wide geographic area and by the selection of varieties not very susceptible to diseases.

[76] This situation was born out by the way in which UBC was able to react to the consequences of hurricane 'Fifi' in 1974.

[77] At the production stage UBC therefore knows that it can comply with all the requests which it receives.

[78] At the stage of packaging and presentation on its premises UBC has at its disposal factories, manpower, plant and material which enable it to handle the goods independently.

[79] The bananas are carried from the place of production to the port of shipment by its own means of transport including railways.

[80] At the carriage by sea stage it has been acknowledged that UBC is the only undertaking of its kind which is capable of carrying two thirds of its exports by means of its own banana fleet.

[81] Thus UBC knows that it is able to transport regularly, without running the risk of its own ships not being used and whatever the market situation may be, two thirds of its average volume of sales and is alone able to ensure that three regular consignments reach Europe each week, and all this guarantees it commercial stability and well being.

[82] In the field of technical knowledge and as a result of continual research UBC keeps on improving the productivity and yield of its plantations by improving the draining system, making good soil deficiencies and combating effectively plant disease.

[83] It has perfected new ripening methods in which its technicians instruct the distributor/ripeners of the Chiquita banana.

[84] That is another factor to be borne in mind when considering UBC's position since competing firms cannot develop research at a comparable level and are in this respect at a disadvantage compared with the applicant.

[85] It is acknowledged that at the stage where the goods are given the final finish and undergo quality control UBC not only controls the distributor/ripeners which are direct customers but also those who work for the account of its important customers such as the Scipio group.

[86] Even if the object of the clause prohibiting the sale of green bananas was only strict quality control, it in fact gives UBC absolute control of all trade in its goods so long as they are marketable wholesale, that is to say before the ripening process begins which makes an immediate sale unavoidable.

[87] This general quality control of a homogeneous product makes the advertising of the brand name effective.

[88] Since 1967 UBC has based its general policy in the relevant market on the quality of its Chiquita brand banana.

[89] There is no doubt that this policy gives UBC control over the transformation of the product into bananas for consumption even though most of this product no longer belongs to it.

[90] This policy has been based on a thorough reorganization of the arrangements for production, packaging, carriage, ripening (new plant with ventilation and a cooling system) and sale (a network of agents).

[91] UBC has made this product distinctive by large-scale repeated advertising and promotion campaigns which have induced the consumer to show a preference for it in spite of the difference between the price of labelled and unlabelled bananas (in the region of 30 to 40%) and also of Chiquita bananas and those which have been labelled with another brand name (in the region of 7 to 10%).

[92] It was the first to take full advantage of the opportunities presented by labelling in the tropics for

the purpose of large-scale advertising and this, to use UBC's own words, has 'revolutionized the commercial exploitation of the banana' (Annex II (a) to the application, p.10).

[93] It has thus attained a privileged position by making Chiquita the premier banana brand name on the relevant market with the result that the distributor cannot afford not to offer it to the consumer.

[94] At the selling stage this distinguishing factor – justified by the unchanging quality of the banana bearing this label – ensures that it has regular customers and consolidates its economic strength.

[95] The effect of its sales networks only covering a limited number of customers, large groups or distributor/ripeners, is a simplification of its supply policy and economies of scale.

[96] Since UBC's supply policy consists – in spite of the production surplus – in only meeting the requests for Chiquita bananas parsimoniously and sometimes incompletely UBC is in a position of strength at the selling stage.

The Court went on to examine the competitive situation on the market. UBC was by no means the only active trader. The Court declared that 'an undertaking does not have to have eliminated all opportunity for competition in order to be in a dominant position'; and it observed that UBC's market share, fixed by the Court at 40–45%, was several times greater than its nearest rival. Limited price wars had not altered market shares. The Court came to the conclusion that:

[121] UBC's economic strength has thus enabled it to adopt a flexible overall strategy directed against new competitors establishing themselves on the whole of the relevant market.

[122] The particular barriers to competitors entering the market are the exceptionally large capital investments required for the creation and running of banana plantations, the need to increase sources of supply in order to avoid the effects of fruit diseases and bad weather (hurricanes, floods), the introduction of an essential system of logistics which the distribution of a very perishable product makes necessary, economies of scale from which newcomers to the market cannot derive any immediate benefit and the actual cost of entry made up *inter alia* of all the general expenses incurred in penetrating the market such as the setting up of an adequate commercial network, the mounting of very large-scale advertising campaigns, all those financial risks, the costs of which are irrecoverable if the attempt fails.

[123] Thus, although, as UBC has pointed out, it is true that competitors are able to use the same methods of production and distribution as the applicant, they come up against almost insuperable practical and financial obstacles.

[124] That is another factor peculiar to a dominant position.

[125] However UBC takes into account the losses which its banana division made from 1971 to 1976 – whereas during this period its competitors made profits – for the purpose of inferring that, since dominance is in essence the power to fix prices, making losses is inconsistent with the existence of a dominant position.

[126] An undertaking's economic strength is not measured by its profitability; a reduced profit margin or even losses for a time are not incompatible with a dominant position, just as large profits may be compatible with a situation where there is effective competition.

[127] The fact that UBC's profitability is for a time moderate or non-existent must be considered in the light of the whole of its operations.

[128] The finding that, whatever losses UBC may make, the customers continue to buy more goods from UBC which is the dearest vendor, is more significant and this fact is a particular feature of the dominant position and its verification is determinative in this case.

[129] The cumulative effect of all the advantages enjoyed by UBC thus ensures that it has a dominant position on the relevant market.

NOTE

Of course, the bigger the market share, the more likely that dominance is established. But *United Brands* (Case 27/76) emphasizes that each market requires special attention and must be judged according to its own peculiarities.

In 1997, the Commission sought to make its approach to market definition more transparent. In reading this text, remember it is a pre-Amsterdam document. Articles 81 and 82 are the post-Amsterdam numbers of Articles 85 and 86 respectively.

COMMISSION NOTICE ON THE DEFINITION OF THE RELEVANT MARKET FOR THE PURPOSES OF COMMUNITY COMPETITION LAW
[1997] OJ C372/5

I. INTRODUCTION

1. The purpose of this notice is to provide guidance as to how the Commission applies the concept of relevant product and geographic market in its ongoing enforcement of Community competition law, in particular the application of Council Regulation No 17 and (EEC) No 4064/89, their equivalents in other sectoral applications such as transport, coal and steel, and agriculture, and the relevant provisions of the EEA Agreement.[1] Throughout this notice, references to Articles 85 and 86 of the Treaty and to merger control are to be understood as referring to the equivalent provisions in the EEA Agreement and the ECSC Treaty.

2. Market definition is a tool to identify and define the boundaries of competition between firms. It serves to establish the framework within which competition policy is applied by the Commission. The main purpose of market definition is to identify in a systematic way the competitive constraints that the undertakings involved[2] face. The objective of defining a market in both its product and geographic dimension is to identify those actual competitors of the undertakings involved that are capable of constraining those undertakings' behaviour and of preventing them from behaving independently of effective competitive pressure. It is from this perspective that the market definition makes it possible *inter alia* to calculate market shares that would convey meaningful information regarding market power for the purposes of assessing dominance or for the purposes of applying Article 85.

3. It follows from point 2 that the concept of 'relevant market' is different from other definitions of market often used in other contexts. For instance, companies often use the term 'market' to refer to the area where it sells its products or to refer broadly to the industry or sector where it belongs.

4. The definition of the relevant market in both its product and its geographic dimensions often has a decisive influence on the assessment of a competition case. By rendering public the procedures which the Commission follows when considering market definition and by indicating the criteria and evidence on which it relies to reach a decision, the Commission expects to increase the transparency of its policy and decision-making in the area of competition policy.

5. Increased transparency will also result in companies and their advisers being able to better anticipate the possibility that the Commission may raise competition concerns in an individual case. Companies could, therefore, take such a possibility into account in their own internal decision-making when contemplating, for instance, acquisitions, the creation of joint ventures, or the establishment of certain agreements. It is also intended that companies should be in a

---

1 The focus of assessment in State aid cases is the aid recipient and the industry/sector concerned rather than identification of competitive constraints faced by the aid recipient. When consideration of market power and therefore of the relevant market are raised in any particular case, elements of the approach outlined here might serve as a basis for the assessment of State aid cases.

2 For the purposes of this notice, the undertakings involved will be, in the case of a concentration, the parties to the concentration; in investigations within the meaning of Article 86 of the Treaty, the undertaking being investigated or the complainants; for investigations within the meaning of Article 85, the parties to the Agreement.

better position to understand what sort of information the Commission considers relevant for the purposes of market definition.

6. The Commission's interpretation of 'relevant market' is without prejudice to the interpretation which may be given by the Court of Justice or the Court of First Instance of the European Communities.

II. DEFINITION OF RELEVANT MARKET

Definition of relevant product market and relevant geographic market

7. The Regulations based on Articles 85 and 86 of the Treaty, in particular in section 6 of Form A/B with respect to Regulation No 17, as well as in section 6 of Form CO with respect to Regulation (EEC) No 4064/89 on the control of concentrations having a Community dimension have laid down the following definitions. 'Relevant product markets' are defined as follows:

> 'A relevant product market comprises all those products and/or services which are regarded as interchangeable or substitutable by the consumer, by reason of the products' characteristics, their prices and their intended use'.

8. 'Relevant geographic markets' are defined as follows:

> 'The relevant geographic market comprises the area in which the undertakings concerned are involved in the supply and demand of products or services, in which the conditions of competition are sufficiently homogeneous and which can be distinguished from neighbouring areas because the conditions of competition are appreciably different in those areas'.

9. The relevant market within which to assess a given competition issue is therefore established by the combination of the product and geographic markets. The Commission interprets the definitions in paragraphs 7 and 8 (which reflect the case-law of the Court of Justice and the Court of First Instance as well as its own decision-making practice) according to the orientations defined in this notice.

Concept of relevant market and objectives of Community competition policy

10. The concept of relevant market is closely related to the objectives pursued under Community competition policy. For example, under the Community's merger control, the objective in controlling structural changes in the supply of a product/service is to prevent the creation or reinforcement of a dominant position as a result of which effective competition would be significantly impeded in a substantial part of the common market. Under the Community's competition rules, a dominant position is such that a firm or group of firms would be in a position to behave to an appreciable extent independently of its competitors, customers and ultimately of its consumers.[3] Such a position would usually arise when a firm or group of firms accounted for a large share of the supply in any given market, provided that other factors analysed in the assessment (such as entry barriers, customers' capacity to react, etc.) point in the same direction.

11. The same approach is followed by the Commission in its application of Article 86 of the Treaty to firms that enjoy a single or collective dominant position. Within the meaning of Regulation No 17, the Commission has the power to investigate and bring to an end abuses of such a dominant position, which must also be defined by reference to the relevant market. Markets may also need to be defined in the application of Article 85 of the Treaty, in particular, in determining whether an appreciable restriction of competition exists or in establishing if the condition pursuant to Article 85(3)(b) for an exemption from the application of Article 85(1) is met.

12. The criteria for defining the relevant market are applied generally for the analysis of certain types of behaviour in the market and for the analysis of structural changes in the supply of products. This methodology, though, might lead to different results depending on the nature

---

3 Definition given by the Court of Justice in its judgment of 13 February 1979 in Case 85/76, *Hoffmann-La Roche* [1979] ECR 461, and confirmed in subsequent judgments.

of the competition issue being examined. For instance, the scope of the geographic market might be different when analysing a concentration, where the analysis is essentially prospective, from an analysis of past behaviour. The different time horizon considered in each case might lead to the result that different geographic markets are defined for the same products depending on whether the Commission is examining a change in the structure of supply, such as a concentration or a cooperative joint venture, or examining issues relating to certain past behaviour.

Basic principles for market definition

Competitive constraints

13. Firms are subject to three main sources or competitive constraints: demand substitutability, supply substitutability and potential competition. From an economic point of view, for the definition of the relevant market, demand substitution constitutes the most immediate and effective disciplinary force on the suppliers of a given product, in particular in relation to their pricing decisions. A firm or a group of firms cannot have a significant impact on the prevailing conditions of sale, such as prices, if its customers are in a position to switch easily to available substitute products or to suppliers located elsewhere. Basically, the exercise of market definition consists in identifying the effective alternative sources of supply for the customers of the undertakings involved, in terms both of products/services and of geographic location of suppliers.

14. The competitive constraints arising from supply side substitutability other than those described in paragraphs 20 to 23 and from potential competition are in general less immediate and in any case require an analysis of additional factors. As a result such constraints are taken into account at the assessment stage of competition analysis.

Demand substitution

15. The assessment of demand substitution entails a determination of the range of products which are viewed as substitutes by the consumer. One way of making this determination can be viewed as a speculative experiment, postulating a hypothetical small, lasting change in relative prices and evaluating the likely reactions of customers to that increase. The exercise of market definition focuses on prices for operational and practical purposes, and more precisely on demand substitution arising from small, permanent changes in relative prices. This concept can provide clear indications as to the evidence that is relevant in defining markets.

16. Conceptually, this approach means that, starting from the type of products that the undertakings involved sell and the area in which they sell them, additional products and areas will be included in, or excluded from, the market definition depending on whether competition from these other products and areas affect or restrain sufficiently the pricing of the parties' products in the short term.

17. The question to be answered is whether the parties' customers would switch to readily available substitutes or to suppliers located elsewhere in response to a hypothetical small (in the range 5% to 10%) but permanent relative price increase in the products and areas being considered. If substitution were enough to make the price increase unprofitable because of the resulting loss of sales, additional substitutes and areas are included in the relevant market. This would be done until the set of products and geographical areas is such that small, permanent increases in relative prices would be profitable. The equivalent analysis is applicable in cases concerning the concentration of buying power, where the starting point would then be the supplier and the price test serves to identify the alternative distribution channels or outlets for the supplier's products. In the application of these principles, careful account should be taken of certain particular situations as described within paragraphs 56 and 58.

18. A practical example of this test can be provided by its application to a merger of, for instance, soft-drink bottlers. An issue to examine in such a case would be to decide whether different flavours of soft drinks belong to the same market. In practice, the question to address would be whether consumers of flavour A would switch to other flavours when confronted with a permanent price increase of 5% to 10% for flavour A. If a sufficient number of consumers would switch to, say, flavour B, to such an extent that the price increase for flavour A would not be profitable owing to the resulting loss of sales, then the market would comprise at least flavours A and B. The process would have to be extended in addition to other available

flavours until a set of products is identified for which a price rise would not induce a sufficient substitution in demand.

19. Generally, and in particular for the analysis of merger cases, the price to take into account will be the prevailing market price. This may not be the case where the prevailing price has been determined in the absence of sufficient competition. In particular for the investigation of abuses of dominant positions, the fact that the prevailing price might already have been substantially increased will be taken into account.

Supply substitution

20. Supply-side substitutability may also be taken into account when defining markets in those situations in which its effects are equivalent to those of demand substitution in terms of effectiveness and immediacy. This means that suppliers are able to switch production to the relevant products and market them in the short term[4] without incurring significant additional costs or risks in response to small and permanent changes in relative prices. When these conditions are met, the additional production that is put on the market will have a disciplinary effect on the competitive behaviour of the companies involved. Such an impact in terms of effectiveness and immediacy is equivalent to the demand substitution effect.

21. These situations typically arise when companies market a wide range of qualities or grades of one product; even if, for a given final customer or group of consumers, the different qualities are not substitutable, the different qualities will be grouped into one product market, provided that most of the suppliers are able to offer and sell the various qualities immediately and without the significant increases in costs described above. In such cases, the relevant product market will encompass all products that are substitutable in demand and supply, and the current sales of those products will be aggregated so as to give the total value or volume of the market. The same reasoning may lead to group different geographic areas.

22. A practical example of the approach to supply-side substitutability when defining product markets is to be found in the case of paper. Paper is usually supplied in a range of different qualities, from standard writing paper to high quality papers to be used, for instance, to publish art books. From a demand point of view, different qualities of paper cannot be used for any given use, i.e., an art book or a high quality publication cannot be based on lower quality papers. However, paper plants are prepared to manufacture the different qualities, and production can be adjusted with negligible costs and in a short time-frame. In the absence of particular difficulties in distribution, paper manufacturers are able therefore, to compete for orders of the various qualities, in particular if orders are placed with sufficient lead time to allow for modification of production plans. Under such circumstances, the Commission would not define a separate market for each quality of paper and its respective use. The various qualities of paper are included in the relevant market, and their sales added up to estimate total market value and volume.

23. When supply-side substitutability would entail the need to adjust significantly existing tangible and intangible assets, additional investments, strategic decisions or time delays, it will not be considered at the stage of market definition. Examples where supply-side substitution did not induce the Commission to enlarge the market are offered in the area of consumer products, in particular for branded beverages. Although bottling plants may in principle bottle different beverages, there are costs and lead times involved (in terms of advertising, product testing and distribution) before the products can actually be sold. In these cases, the effects of supply-side substitutability and other forms of potential competition would then be examined at a later stage.

Potential competition

24. The third source of competitive constraint, potential competition, is not taken into account when defining markets, since the conditions under which potential competition will actually represent an effective competitive constraint depend on the analysis of specific factors and circumstances related to the conditions of entry. If required, this analysis is only carried out at a subsequent stage, in general once the position of the companies involved in the relevant market

---

4 That is such a period that does not entail a significant adjustment of existing tangible and intangible assets (see paragraph 23).

has already been ascertained, and when such position gives rise to concerns from a competition point of view.

III. EVIDENCE RELIED ON TO DEFINE RELEVANT MARKETS

The process of defining the relevant market in practice

Product dimension

25. There is a range of evidence permitting an assessment of the extent to which substitution would take place. In individual cases, certain types of evidence will be determinant, depending very much on the characteristics and specificity of the industry and products or services that are being examined. The same type of evidence may be of no importance in other cases. In most cases, a decision will have to be based on the consideration of a number of criteria and different items of evidence. The Commission follows an open approach to empirical evidence, aimed at making an effective use of all available information which may be relevant in individual cases. The Commission does not follow a rigid hierarchy of different sources of information or types of evidence.

26. The process of defining relevant markets may be summarized as follows: on the basis of the preliminary information available or information submitted by the undertakings involved, the Commission will usually be in a position to broadly establish the possible relevant markets within which, for instance, a concentration or a restriction of competition has to be assessed. In general, and for all practical purposes when handling individual cases, the question will usually be to decide on a few alternative possible relevant markets. For instance, with respect to the product market, the issue will often be to establish whether product A and product B belong or do not belong to the same product market. It is often the case that the inclusion of product B would be enough to remove any competition concerns.

27. In such situations it is not necessary to consider whether the market includes additional products, or to reach a definitive conclusion on the precise product market. If under the conceivable alternative market definitions the operation in question does not raise competition concerns, the question of market definition will be left open, reducing thereby the burden on companies to supply information.

Geographic dimension

28. The Commission's approach to geographic market definition might be summarized as follows: it will take a preliminary view of the scope of the geographic market on the basis of broad indications as to the distribution of market shares between the parties and their competitors, as well as a preliminary analysis of pricing and price differences at national and Community or EEA level. This initial view is used basically as a working hypothesis to focus the Commission's enquiries for the purposes of arriving at a precise geographic market definition.

29. The reasons behind any particular configuration of prices and market shares need to be explored. Companies might enjoy high market shares in their domestic markets just because of the weight of the past, and conversely, a homogeneous presence of companies throughout the EEA might be consistent with national or regional geographic markets. The initial working hypothesis will therefore be checked against an analysis of demand characteristics (importance of national or local preferences, current patterns of purchases of customers, product differentiation/ brands, other) in order to establish whether companies in different areas do indeed constitute a real alternative source of supply for consumers. The theoretical experiment is again based on substitution arising from changes in relative prices, and the question to answer is again whether the customers of the parties would switch their orders to companies located elsewhere in the short term and at a negligible cost.

30. If necessary, a further check on supply factors will be carried out to ensure that those companies located in differing areas do not face impediments in developing their sales on competitive terms throughout the whole geographic market. This analysis will include an examination of requirements for a local presence in order to sell in that area the conditions of access to distribution channels, costs associated with setting up a distribution network, and the presence or

absence of regulatory barriers arising from public procurement, price regulations, quotas and tariffs limiting trade or production, technical standards, monopolies, freedom of establishment, requirements for administrative authorizations, packaging regulations, etc. In short, the Commission will identify possible obstacles and barriers isolating companies located in a given area from the competitive pressure of companies located outside that area, so as to determine the precise degree of market interpenetration at national, European or global level.

31. The actual pattern and evolution of trade flows offers useful supplementary indications as to the economic importance of each demand or supply factor mentioned above, and the extent to which they may or may not constitute actual barriers creating different geographic markets. The analysis of trade flows will generally address the question of transport costs and the extent to which these may hinder trade between different areas, having regard to plant location, costs of production and relative price levels.

Market integration in the Community

32. Finally, the Commission also takes into account the continuing process of market integration, in particular in the Community, when defining geographic markets, especially in the area of concentrations and structural joint ventures. The measures adopted and implemented in the internal market programme to remove barriers to trade and further integrate the Community markets cannot be ignored when assessing the effects on competition of a concentration or a structural joint venture. A situation where national markets have been artifically isolated from each other because of the existence of legislative barriers that have now been removed will generally lead to a cautious assessment of past evidence regarding prices, market shares or trade patterns. A process of market integration that would, in the short term, lead to wider geographic markets may therefore be taken into consideration when defining the geographic market for the purposes of assessing concentrations and joint ventures.

The process of gathering evidence

33. When a precise market definition is deemed necessary, the Commission will often contact the main customers and the main companies in the industry to enquire into their views about the boundaries of product and geographic markets and to obtain the necessary factual evidence to reach a conclusion. The Commission might also contact the relevant professional associations, and companies active in upstream markets, so as to be able to define, in so far as necessary, separate product and geographic markets, for different levels of production or distribution of the products/services in question. It might also request additional information to the undertakings involved.

34. Where appropriate, the Commission will address written requests for information to the market players mentioned above. These requests will usually include questions relating to the perceptions of companies about reactions to hypothetical price increases and their views of the boundaries of the relevant market. They will also ask for provision of the factual information the Commission deems necessary to reach a conclusion on the extent of the relevant market. The Commission might also discuss with marketing directors or other officers of those companies to gain a better understanding on how negotiations between suppliers and customers take place and better understand issues relating to the definition of the relevant market. Where appropriate, they might also carry out visits or inspections to the premises of the parties, their customers and/or their competitors, in order to better understand how products are manufactured and sold.

35. The type of evidence relevant to reach a conclusion as to the product market can be categorized as follows:

Evidence to define markets – product dimension

36. An analysis of the product characteristics and its intended use allows the Commission, as a first step, to limit the field of investigation of possible substitutes. However, product characteristics and intended use are insufficient to show whether two products are demand substitutes. Functional interchangeability or similarity in characteristics may not, in themselves, provide sufficient criteria, because the responsiveness of customers to relative price changes may be determined by other considerations as well. For example, there may be different competitive

constraints in the original equipment market for car components and in spare parts, thereby leading to a separate delineation of two relevant markets. Conversely, differences in product characteristics are not in themselves sufficient to exclude demand substitutability, since this will depend to a large extent on how customers value different characteristics.

37. The type of evidence the Commission considers relevant to assess whether two products are demand substitutes can be categorized as follows:

38. *Evidence of substitution in the recent past.* In certain cases, it is possible to analyse evidence relating to recent past events or shocks in the market that offer actual examples of substitution between two products. When available, this sort of information will normally be fundamental for market definition. If there have been changes in relative prices in the past (all else being equal), the reactions in terms of quantities demanded will be determinant in establishing substitutability. Launches of new products in the past can also offer useful information, when it is possible to precisely analyse which products have lost sales to the new product.

39. There are a number of *quantitative tests* that have specifically been designed for the purpose of delineating markets. These tests consist of various econometric and statistical approaches, estimates of elasticities and cross-price elasticities[5] for the demand of a product, tests based on similarity of price movements over time, the analysis of causality between price series and similarity of price levels and/or their convergence. The Commission takes into account the available quantitative evidence capable of withstanding rigorous scrutiny for the purposes of establishing patterns of substitution in the past.

40. *Views of customers and competitors.* The Commission often contacts the main customers and competitors of the companies involved in its enquiries, to gather their views on the boundaries of the product market as well as most of the factual information it requires to reach a conclusion on the scope of the market. Reasoned answers of customers and competitors as to what would happen if relative prices for the candidate products were to increase in the candidate geographic area by a small amount (for instance of 5% to 10%) are taken into account when they are sufficiently backed by factual evidence.

41. *Consumer preferences.* In the case of consumer goods, it may be difficult for the Commission to gather the direct views of end consumers about substitute products. *Marketing studies* that companies have commissioned in the past and that are used by companies in their own decision-making as to pricing of their products and/or marketing actions may provide useful information for the Commission's delineation of the relevant market. Consumer surveys on usage patterns and attitudes, data from consumer's purchasing patterns, the views expressed by retailers and more generally, market research studies submitted by the parties and their competitors are taken into account to establish whether an economically significant proportion of consumers consider two products as substitutable, also taking into account the importance of brands for the products in question. The methodology followed in consumer surveys carried out *ad hoc* by the undertakings involved or their competitors for the purposes of a merger procedure or a procedure pursuant to Regulation No.17 will usually be scrutinized with utmost care. Unlike pre-existing studies, they have not been prepared in the normal course of business for the adoption of business decisions.

42. *Barriers and costs associated with switching demand to potential substitutes.* There are a number of barriers and costs that might prevent the Commission from considering two *prima facie* demand substitutes as belonging to one single product market. It is not possible to provide an exhaustive list of all the possible barriers to substitution and of switching costs. These barriers or obstacles might have a wide range of origins, and in its decisions, the Commission has been confronted with regulatory barriers or other forms of State intervention, constraints arising in downstream markets, need to incur specific capital investment or loss in current output in order to switch to alternative inputs, the location of customers, specific investment in production process, learning and human capital investment, retooling costs or other investments, uncertainty about quality and reputation of unknown suppliers, and others.

---

5 Own-price elasticity of demand for product X is a measure of the responsiveness of demand for X to percentage change in its own price. Cross-price elasticity between products X and Y is the responsiveness of demand for product X to percentage change in the price of product Y.

43. *Different categories of customers and price discrimination*. The extent of the product market might be narrowed in the presence of distinct groups of customers. A distinct group of customers for the relevant product may constitute a narrower, distinct market when such a group could be subject to price discrimination. This will usually be the case when two conditions are met: (a) it is possible to identify clearly which group an individual customer belongs to at the moment of selling the relevant products to him, and (b) trade among customers or arbitrage by third parties should not be feasible.

Evidence for defining markets – geographic dimension

44. The type of evidence the Commission considers relevant to reach a conclusion as to the geographic market can be categorized as follows:

45. *Past evidence of diversion of orders to other areas*. In certain cases, evidence on changes in prices between different areas and consequent reactions by customers might be available. Generally, the same quantitative tests used for product market definition might as well be used in geographic market definition, bearing in mind that international comparisons of prices might be more complex due to a number of factors such as exchange rate movements, taxation and product differentiation.

46. *Basic demand characteristics*. The nature of demand for the relevant product may in itself determine the scope of the geographical market. Factors such as national preferences or preferences for national brands, language, culture and life style, and the need for a local presence have a strong potential to limit the geographic scope of competition.

47. *Views of customers and competitors*. Where appropriate, the Commission will contact the main customers and competitors of the parties in its enquiries, to gather their views on the boundaries of the geographic market as well as most of the factual information it requires to reach a conclusion on the scope of the market when they are sufficiently backed by factual evidence.

48. *Current geographic pattern of purchases*. An examination of the customers' current geographic pattern of purchases provides useful evidence as to the possible scope of the geographic market. When customers purchase from companies located anywhere in the Community or the EEA on similar terms, or they procure their supplies through effective tendering procedures in which companies from anywhere in the Community or the EEA submit bids, usually the geographic market will be considered to be Community wide.

49. *Trade flows/pattern of shipments*. When the number of customers is so large that it is not possible to obtain through them a clear picture of geographic purchasing patterns, information on trade flows might be used alternatively, provided that the trade statistics are available with a sufficient degree of detail for the relevant products. Trade flows, and above all, the rationale behind trade flows provide useful insights and information for the purpose of establishing the scope of the geographic market but are not in themselves conclusive.

50. *Barriers and switching costs associated to divert orders to companies located in other areas*. The absence of trans-border purchases or trade flows, for instance, does not necessarily mean that the market is at most national in scope. Still, barriers isolating the national market have to identified before it is concluded that the relevant geographic market in such a case is national. Perhaps the clearest obstacle for a customer to divert its orders to other areas is the impact of transport costs and transport restrictions arising from legislation or from the nature of the relevant products. The impact of transport costs will usually limit the scope of the geographic market for bulky, low-value products, bearing in mind that a transport disadvantage might also be compensated by a comparative advantage in other costs (labour costs or raw materials). Access to distribution in a given area, regulatory barriers still existing in certain sectors, quotas and custom tariffs might also constitute barriers isolating a geographic area from the competitive pressure of companies located outside that area. Significant switching costs in procuring supplies from companies located in other countries constitute additional sources of such barriers.

51. On the basis of the evidence gathered, the Commission will then define a geographic market that could range from a local dimension to a global one, and there are examples of both local and global markets in past decisions of the Commission.

52. The paragraphs above describe the different factors which might be relevant to define markets. This does not imply that in each individual case it will be necessary to obtain evidence

and assess each of these factors. Often in practice the evidence provided by a subset of these factors will be sufficient to reach a conclusion, as shown in the past decisional practice of the Commission.

IV. CALCULATION OF MARKET SHARE

53. The definition of the relevant market in both its product and geographic dimensions allows the identification of the suppliers and the customers/consumers active on that market. On that basis, a total market size and market shares for each supplier can be calculated on the basis of their sales of the relevant products in the relevant area. In practice, the total market size and market shares are often available from market sources, i.e., companies' estimates, studies commissioned from industry consultants and/or trade associations. When this is not the case, or when available estimates are not reliable, the Commission will usually ask each supplier in the relevant market to provide its own sales in order to calculate total market size and market shares.

54. If sales are usually the reference to calculate market shares, there are nevertheless other indications that, depending on the specific products or industry in question, can offer useful information such as, in particular, capacity, the number of players in bidding markets, units of fleet as in aerospace, or the reserves held in the case of sectors such as mining.

55. As a rule of thumb, both volume sales and value sales provide useful information. In cases of differentiated products, sales in value and their associated market share will usually be considered to better reflect the relative position and strength of each supplier.

V. ADDITIONAL CONSIDERATIONS

56. There are certain areas where the application of the principles above has to be undertaken with care. This is the case when considering primary and secondary markets, in particular, when the behaviour of undertakings at a point in time has to be analysed pursuant to Article 86. The method of defining markets in these cases is the same, i.e., assessing the responses of customers based on their purchasing decisions to relative price changes, but taking into account as well, constraints on substitution imposed by conditions in the connected markets. A narrow definition of market for secondary products, for instance, spare parts, may result when compatibility with the primary product is important. Problems of finding compatible secondary products together with the existence of high prices and a long lifetime of the primary products may render relative price increases of secondary products profitable. A different market definition may result if significant substitution between secondary products is possible or if the characteristics of the primary products make quick and direct consumer responses to relative price increases of the secondary products feasible.

57. In certain cases, the existence of chains of substitution might lead to the definition of a relevant market where products or areas at the extreme of the market are not directly substitutable. An example might be provided by the geographic dimension of a product with significant transport costs. In such cases, deliveries from a given plant are limited to a certain area around each plant by the impact of transport costs. In principle, such an area could constitute the relevant geographic market. However, if the distribution of plants is such that there are considerable overlaps between the areas around different plants, it is possible that the pricing of those products will be constrained by a chain substitution effect, and lead to the definition of a broader geographic market. The same reasoning may apply if product B is a demand substitute for products A and C. Even if products A and C are not direct demand substitutes, they might be found to be in the same relevant product market since their respective pricing might be constrained by substitution to B.

58. From a practical perspective, the concept of chains of substitution has to be corroborated by actual evidence, for instance related to price interdependence at the extremes of the chains of substitution, in order to lead to an extension of the relevant market in an individual case. Price levels at the extremes of the chains would have to be of the same magnitude as well.

NOTE

It is constitutionally plain that the Court, not the Commission, serves as the authoritative source of interpretation of Community law. This is made explicit in para 6 of the Notice. However, the

Commission's direct, though not exclusive, control over the practical administration of competition policy (examined in the next Chapter) ensures that this Notice will have considerable influence in the treatment of cases. A test for determining substitutability based on customer reaction to a 'small [5–10%], non-transitory change in relative prices' (paras 15, 17) is not to be found in such terms in judgments delivered by the European Court, but is instead drawn directly from North American practice. An illustration of the application of this test by the Commission is provided by Commission Decision 2000/12 *1998 Football World Cup* [2000] OJ L5/55. The market for match tickets for the tournament stood alone from the perspective of the consumer.

It should be obvious from the approach taken in *United Brands* (Case 27/76), that defining a market involves a calculation of the barriers which surround that market (see para 122). At one extreme, even 100% occupation of a market is not a cause for concern where any other firm is able freely to enter that market. Potential competition controls the liberty of the firm in occupation. (See the annulment of an economically inadequate Commission Decision in *Continental Can* v *Commission* (Case 6/72) [1973] ECR 215.) However, the Commission's Notice prefers to treat this not as a matter of market definition, but rather as a (logically subsequent) matter of market power (para 24). The stage at which the role of potential competition is taken into account in the analysis should not be of any practical significance to the outcome.

Should you wish to explore economic theory in this area, the classic work is J.S. Bain, *Barriers to New Competition* (Cambridge, Mass.: Harvard University Press, 1956). Try also W. Baumol, J. Panzar, and R. Willig, *Contestable Markets and the Theory of Industrial Structure* (New York: Harcourt Brace Jovanovitch, 1982). P. A. Geroski and A. Jacquemin, 'Industrial change, barriers to mobility and European industrial policy' (1985) 1 *Economic Policy* 170 provide a useful synthesis.

Over-estimation of entry barriers leads to unduly narrow market definition, which leads to unnecessary intervention in markets which would correct themselves. The next case has been criticized from this perspective.

Hugin Kassaregister AB v *Commission* (Case 22/78)

[1979] ECR 1869, [1979] 3 CMLR 345, Court of Justice of the European Communities

The Commission held Hugin in breach of Article 86 of the EC Treaty (now Article 82 EC) for refusal to supply spare parts for Hugin cash registers to Liptons. It defined the market as comprising spare parts for Hugin machines needed by independent repairers. Hugin argued the proper market definition covered the fiercely competitive cash register market in general. The Court dealt with the dispute as follows.

[5] To resolve the dispute it is necessary, first, to determine the relevant market. In this respect account must be taken of the fact that the conduct alleged against Hugin consists in the refusal to supply spare parts to Liptons and, generally, to any independent undertaking outside its distribution network. The question is, therefore, whether the supply of spare parts constitutes a specific market or whether it forms part of a wider market. To answer that question it is necessary to determine the category of clients who require such parts.

[6] In this respect it is established, on the one hand, that cash registers are of such a technical nature that the user cannot fit the spare parts into the machine but requires the services of a specialized technician and, on the other, that the value of the spare parts is of little significance in relation to the cost of maintenance and repairs. That being the case, users of cash registers do not operate on the market as purchasers of spare parts, however they have their machines maintained and repaired. Whether they avail themselves of Hugin's after-sales service or whether they rely on independent undertakings engaged in maintenance and repair work, their spare part requirements are not manifested directly and independently on the market. While there certainly exists amongst users a market for maintenance and repairs which is distinct from the

market in new cash registers, it is essentially a market for the provision of services and not for the sale of a product such as spare parts, the refusal to supply which forms the subject-matter of the Commission's decision.

[7] On the other hand, there exists a separate market for Hugin spare parts at another level, namely that of independent undertakings which specialize in the maintenance and repair of cash registers, in the reconditioning of used machines and in the sale of used machines and the renting out of machines. The rôle of those undertakings on the market is that of businesses which require spare parts for their various activities. They need such parts in order to provide services for cash register users in the form of maintenance and repairs and for the reconditioning of used machines intended for re-sale or renting out. Finally, they require spare parts for the maintenance and repair of new or used machines belonging to them which are rented out to their clients. It is, moreover, established that there is a specific demand for Hugin spare parts, since those parts are not interchangeable with spare parts for cash registers of other makes.

[8] Consequently the market thus constituted by Hugin spare parts required by independent undertakings must be regarded as the relevant market for the purposes of the application of Article 86 of the facts of the case. It is in fact the market on which the alleged abuse was committed.

[9] It is necessary to examine next whether Hugin occupies a dominant position on that market. In this respect Hugin admits that it has a monopoly in new spare parts. For commercial reasons any competing production of spare parts which could be used in Hugin cash registers is not conceivable in practice. Hugin argues nevertheless that another source of supply does exist, namely the purchase and dismantling of used machines. The value of that source of supply is disputed by the parties. Although the file appears to show that the practice of dismantling used machines is current in the cash register sector it cannot be regarded as constituting a sufficient alternative source of supply. Indeed the figures relating to Liptons' turnover during the years when Hugin refused to sell spare parts to it show that Liptons' business in the selling, renting out and repairing of Hugin machines diminished considerably, not only when expressed in absolute terms but even more so in real terms, taking inflation into account.

NOTE
So Hugin dominated the market for its own spare parts. However, the Court went on to annul the Decision because it was not satisfied that any impact on trade between Member States had been shown.

The finding of dominance in *Hugin* (Case 22/78) is challenged in the next extract.

E. Fox, 'Monopolization and Dominance in the US and the EC:
Efficiency, Opportunity and Fairness'
(1986) 61 Notre Dame Law Rev 981, at pp.1003, 1004
[© 1983 by Matthew Bender & Co. Inc., and reproduced by permission of
1983 Fordham Corporate Law Institute]

Having analysed *United Brands* (Case 27/76) and uncovered discrepancies between US and EC law, Fox continues:

In *Hugin-Liptons*, we find an even greater gap between US and Common Market law. First, in the United States, a company's own brand of product is almost never a market.[89] Under Community law, customer dependence may qualify a brand as a market. In *Hugin-Liptons*, the Court of Justice defined the market as spare parts for Hugin machines in view of the demand by independent servicers and renting agents. In doing so it ignored facts that US courts would deem material; namely, that the independents could get spare parts for the other cash registers from their

89 See *Calculators Hawaii, Inc.* v *Brandt, Inc.*, 724 F 2d 1332, 1337 (9th Cir 1983); *Telex Corp* v *IBM Corp* 510 F 2d 894,914–19 (10th Cir 1975), *cert. dismissed*, 423 US 802 (1975); *Rea* v *Ford Motor Co.*, 497 F 2d 577, 590 n 28 (3d Cir 1974), *cert. denied*, 419 US 868 (1974).

producers and that Liptons could be expected to shift its business to the servicing and renting of more cash registers produced by other firms. A healthy market of independents who serviced and rented cash registers (made by other producers) would have remained.

When one asks whether Hugin's termination of Liptons was an effort to monopolize, the misfit of the monopoly framework becomes plain. Hugin was not a dominant cash register firm. It surely could not get a monopoly by charging a supracompetitive price for spare parts, and it would undercut its competitive attractiveness as a supplier of new machines if it developed a reputation for overcharging for repairs. Only two hypotheses seem plausible. Either Hugin was charging a low price for service and was providing rapid reliable service itself or through its authorized distributors, so as to wage more effective competition against its highly aggressive competitors, or Hugin wanted to keep the servicing business for itself and its authorized distributors and they were providing at least as good a price/service package as Liptons. Both for lack of dominance and lack of anticompetitive conduct, American courts would dismiss the case against Hugin. . . .

One suspects that the Court of Justice concludes too quickly that refusals to deal harm consumers. To base a result on harm to consumers where neither evidence nor theory indicates that such harm exists undermines the legitimacy of Court of Justice judgments, although those judgments might have been justified by an interest in protecting entrepreneurs.

NOTE

The economic analysis remains instructive in the search to grasp the nature and purpose of these legal rules, even though practice in this area in both jurisdictions has moved on; see, in the US, the Supreme Court's ruling in *Eastman Kodak Co.* v *Image Technical Services, Inc* 112 S. Ct. 2072 (1992) and, in the EC, the Commission's decision in *Pelikan* (XXVth Report on Competition on Policy, para 87, 1995), both of which are noted by D. Maldoom [1996] 8 ECLR 473. See also on markets for spare parts, para 56 of the Notice, p.558 above. Refusal to deal is discussed further at p.565.

Other cases which deserve attention for their approach to market definition include: *Hoffmann la Roche* v *Commission* (Case 85/76) [1979] ECR 461; *Michelin* v *Commission* (Case 322/81) [1983] ECR 3461; *Continental Can* v *Commission* (Case 6/72), above.

Comparable issues arise in EC merger control which, since 21 September 1990, has been dealt with under the 'Merger Regulation', Regulation 4064/89 ([1989] OJ L395/1, corrected version published [1990] OJ L257/14), amended with effect from 1 March 1998 by Regulation 1310/97 [1997] OJ L180/1, corrig. *ibid.* L199/69. (For treatment of the Regulation, see F. Navarro Varona, *Merger Control in the EU: Law, Economics and Practice* (Oxford: OUP, 2002).) Like Article 82, merger control is motivated by the need to keep a check on market power and the specialized merger regime has many features in common with Article 82. This is evident from the cross-references in the Commission's Notice on Definition of the Relevant Market, p.550 above. Article 2(3) of the Regulation provides that:

> A concentration which creates or strengthens a dominant position as a result of which effective competition would be significantly impeded in the common market or in a substantial part of it shall be declared incompatible with the common market.

The Commission Decision in M053 *Aerospatiale Alenia/De Havilland* [1991] OJ L334/42, [1992] 4 CMLR M2, provides a good example of the process of market definition under the Regulation, covering matters such as substitutability and the impact of governmental regulation of airlines. Once the market was defined to cover specific types of short haul commuter aircraft the merger was blocked as incompatible with the Regulation. The Commission has lately published a proposal for a revised Merger Regulation [OJ 2003 C20/4]. The text and background information is available at http://europa.eu.int/comm/competition/mergers/review/.

■ QUESTION

Are the Community institutions consistent in these cases in their approach to the role of potential competition brought about by adaptation of existing techniques? Are they too ready to permit intervention in the market?

SECTION 2: **ABUSE**

Dominance is not unlawful. Once the firm has been held dominant, it is necessary to decide whether it has abused that dominance. Again, *United Brands* (Case 27/76) provides an example of the types of conduct subject to control.

United Brands v *Commission* (Case 27/76)
[1978] ECR 207, [1978] 1 CMLR 429, Court of Justice of the European Communities

First, UBC forbade its distributors from reselling bananas when still green. The Commission considered this an abusive tactic, because it effectively prohibited cross-border trade in green bananas. UBC also routinely undersupplied in response to orders so as to force distributors to sell locally rather than seek to penetrate new markets. UBC was controlling the structure of the market.

Secondly, UBC cut off supply of Chiquita bananas to Olesen, a Danish distributor, in response to Olesen's participation in a promotion of Dole bananas, a rival brand.

The third practice condemned by the Commission related to UBC's selling prices, which differed dependent on the customer's Member State. These price differences were imposed at the banana's port of entry into the Community, before any supplement based on transport costs within the Community might have caused such discrepancy.

Finally, the Commission accused UBC of charging unfair prices; prices 'excessive in relation to the economic value of the product supplied'.

[157] [In response to the first practice.] To impose on the ripener the obligation not to resell bananas so long as he has not had them ripened and to cut down the operations of such a ripener to contacts only with retailers is a restriction of competition.

[158] Although it is commendable and lawful to pursue a policy of quality, especially by choosing sellers according to objective criteria relating to the qualifications of the seller, his staff and his facilities, such a practice can only be justified if it does not raise obstacles, the effect of which goes beyond the objective to be attained.

[159] In this case, although these conditions for selection have been laid down in a way which is objective and not discriminatory, the prohibition on resale imposed upon duly appointed Chiquita ripeners and the prohibition of the resale of unbranded bananas – even if the perishable nature of the banana in practice restricted the opportunities of reselling to the duration of a specific period of time – when without any doubt an abuse of the dominant position since they limit markets to the prejudice of consumers and affects trade between Member States, in particular by partitioning national markets.

[160] Thus UBC's organization of the market confined the ripeners to the role of suppliers of the local market and prevented them from developing their capacity to trade *vis-à-vis* UBC, which moreover tightened its economic hold on them by supplying less goods than they ordered.

[161] It follows from all these considerations that the clause at issue forbidding the sale of green bananas infringes Article 86 of the Treaty.

. . .

[182] [In response to the second practice.] . . . [I]t is advisable to assert positively from the outset that an undertaking in a dominant position for the purpose of marketing a product – which cashes in on the reputation of a brand name known to and valued by the consumers – cannot stop supplying a long standing customer who abides by regular commercial practice, if the orders placed by that customer are in no way out of the ordinary.

[183] Such conduct is inconsistent with the objectives laid down in Article 3(f) of the Treaty, which are set out in detail in Article 86, especially in paragraphs (b) and (c), since the refusal to sell would limit markets to the prejudice of consumers and would amount to discrimination which might in the end eliminate a trading party from the relevant market.

[184] It is therefore necessary to ascertain whether the discontinuance of supplies by UBC in October 1973 was justified.

[185] The reason given is in the applicant's letter of 11 October 1973 in which it upbraided Olesen in no uncertain manner for having participated in an advertising campaign for one of its competitors.

[186] Later on UBC added to this reason a number of complaints, for example, that Olesen was the exclusive representative of its main competitor on the Danish market.

[187] This was not a new situation since it goes back to 1969 and was not in any case inconsistent with fair trade practices.

[188] Finally UBC has not put forward any relevant argument to justify the refusal of supplies.

[189] Although it is true, as the applicant points out, that the fact that an undertaking is in a dominant position cannot disentitle it from protecting its own commercial interests if they are attacked, and that such an undertaking must be conceded the right to take such reasonable steps as it deems appropriate to protect its said interests, such behaviour cannot be countenanced if its actual purpose is to strengthen this dominant position and abuse it.

[190] Even if the possibility of a counter-attack is acceptable that attack must still be proportionate to the threat taking into account the economic strength of the undertakings confronting each other.

[191] The sanction consisting of a refusal to supply by an undertaking in a dominant position was in excess of what might, if such a situation were to arise, reasonably be contemplated as a sanction for conduct similar to that for which UBC blamed Olesen.

[192] In fact UBC could not be unaware of that fact that by acting in this way it would discourage its other ripener/distributors from supporting the advertising of other brand names and that the deterrent effect of the sanction imposed upon one of them would make its position of strength on the relevant market that much more effective.

[193] Such a course of conduct amounts therefore to a serious interference with the independence of small and medium sized firms in their commercial relations with the undertaking in a dominant position and this independence implies the right to give preference to competitors' goods.

[194] In this case the adoption of such a course of conduct is designed to have a serious adverse effect on competition on the relevant banana market by only allowing firms dependant upon the dominant undertaking to stay in business.

. . .

[227] [In response to the third practice.] Although the responsibility for establishing the single banana market does not lie with the applicant, it can only endeavour to take 'what the market can bear' provided that it complies with the rules for the regulation and coordination of the market laid down by the Treaty.

[228] Once it can be grasped that differences in transport costs, taxation, customs duties, the wages of the labour force, the conditions of marketing, the differences in the parity of currencies, the density of competition may eventually culminate in different retail selling price levels according to the Member States, then it follows those differences are factors which UBC only has to take into account to a limited extent since it sells a product which is always the same and at the same place to ripener/distributors who – alone – bear the risks of the consumers' market.

[229] The interplay of supply and demand should, owing to its nature, only be applied to each stage where it is really manifest.

[230] The mechanisms of the market are adversely affected if the price is calculated by leaving out

one stage of the market and taking into account the law of supply and demand as between the vendor and the ultimate consumer and not as between the vendor (UBC) and the purchaser (the ripener/distributors).

[231] Thus, by reason of its dominant position UBC, fed with information by its local representatives, was in fact able to impose its selling price on the intermediate purchaser. This price and also the 'weekly quota allocated' is only fixed and notified to the customer four days before the vessel carrying the bananas berths.

[232] These discriminatory prices, which varied according to the circumstances of the Member States, were just so many obstacles to the free movement of goods and their effect was intensified by the clause forbidding the resale of bananas while still green and by reducing the deliveries of the quantities ordered.

[233] A rigid partitioning of national markets was thus created at price levels, which were artificially different, placing certain distributor/ripeners at a competitive disadvantage, since compared with what it should have been competition had thereby been distorted.

[234] Consequently the policy of differing prices enabling UBC to apply dissimilar conditions to equivalent transactions with other trading parties, thereby placing them at a competitive disadvantage, was an abuse of a dominant position.

. . .

[248] [In response to the last practice.] The imposition by an undertaking in a dominant position directly or indirectly of unfair purchase or selling prices is an abuse to which exception can be taken under Article 86 of the Treaty.

[249] It is advisable therefore to ascertain whether the dominant undertaking has made use of the opportunities arising out of its dominant position in such a way as to reap trading benefits which it would not have reaped if there had been normal and sufficiently effective competition.

[250] In this case charging a price which is excessive because it has no reasonable relation to the economic value of the product supplied would be such an abuse.

[251] This excess could, *inter alia*, be determined objectively if it were possible for it to be calculated by making a comparison between the selling price of the product in question and its cost of production, which would disclose the amount of the profit margin; however the Commission has not done this since it has not analysed UBC's costs structure.

[252] The questions therefore to be determined are whether the difference between the costs actually incurred and the price actually charged is excessive, and, if the answer to this question is in the affirmative, whether a price has been imposed which is either unfair in itself or when compared to competing products.

The Court decided that the Commission had not proved this last allegation and annulled this part of the Decision.

NOTE

Unfairness in pricing is obviously hard to pin down. For discussion see R. Whish, *Competition Law* (London: Butterworths, 2001), Ch. 18.

■ QUESTION

Consider which aspects of United Brands' policy were likely to exploit consumers directly; and which were more indirect in that they served to reduce or suppress competition. Article 82 is broad enough to cover both types of practice.

NOTE

One of the several matters considered in *United Brands* (Case 27/76) was the conduct of a dominant firm towards the supply of its customers. The Court accepts that the dominant firm is precluded from arbitrary conduct (paras 182–89). The precise nature of the control exercised in this area depends on the nature of the market in issue. The next case is an important decision on abusive refusal to supply.

Istituto Chemicoterapico Italiano SpA and Commercial Solvents Corporation v Commission (Cases 6 and 7/73)

[1974] ECR 223, [1974] 1 CMLR 309, Court of Justice of the European Communities

Commercial Solvents (CSC) stopped supplying Zoja with aminobutanol, a raw material used in the production of ethambutol. The Commission held CSC dominant in the market for aminobutanol. The firm challenged the subsequent finding that it had abused that dominance by refusing to continue supplies to Zoja.

[23] The applicants state that they ought not to be held responsible for stopping supplies of aminobutanol to Zoja for this was due to the fact that in the spring of 1970 Zoja itself informed Istituto that it was cancelling the purchase of large quantities of aminobutanol which had been provided for in a contract then in force between Istituto and Zoja. When at the end of 1970 Zoja again contacted Istituto to obtain this product, the latter was obliged to reply, after consulting CSC, that in the meantime CSC had changed its commercial policy and that the product was no longer available. The change of policy by CSC was, they claim, inspired by a legitimate consideration of the advantage that would accrue to it of expanding its production to include the manufacture of finished products and not limiting itself to that of raw material or intermediate products. In pursuance of this policy it decided to improve its product and no longer to supply aminobutanol save in respect of commitments already entered into by its distributors.

[24] It appears from the documents and from the hearing that the suppliers of raw material are limited, as regards the EEC, to Istituto, which, as stated in the claim by CSC, started in 1968 to develop its own specialities based on ethambutol, and in November 1969 obtained the approval of the Italian government necessary for the manufacture and in 1970 started manufacturing its own specialities. When Zoja sought to obtain further supplies of aminobutanol, it received a negative reply. CSC had decided to limit, if not completely to cease, the supply of nitropropane and aminobutanol to certain parties in order to facilitate its own access to the market for the derivatives.

[25] However, an undertaking being in a dominant position as regards the production of raw material and therefore able to control the supply to manufacturers of derivatives, cannot, just because it decides to start manufacturing these derivatives (in competition with its former customers) act in such a way as to eliminate their competition which in the case in question, would amount to eliminating one of the principal manufacturers of ethambutol in the Common Market. Since such conduct is contrary to the objectives expressed in Article 3(f) of the Treaty and set out in greater detail in Articles 85 and 86, it follows that an undertaking which has a dominant position in the market in raw materials and which, with the object of reserving such raw material for manufacturing its own derivatives, refuses to supply a customer, which is itself a manufacturer of these derivatives, and therefore risks eliminating all competition on the part of this customer, is abusing its dominant position within the meaning of Article 86. In this context it does not matter that the undertaking ceased to supply in the spring of 1970 because of the cancellation of the purchases by Zoja, because it appears from the applicants' own statement that, when the supplies provided for in the contract had been completed, the sale of aminobutanol would have stopped in any case.

[26] It is also unnecessary to examine, as the applicants have asked, whether Zoja had an urgent need for aminobutanol in 1970 and 1971 or whether this company still had large quantities of this product which would enable it to reorganize its production in good time, since that question is not relevant to the consideration of the conduct of the applicants.

The Court upheld the finding of abuse.

NOTE
A different market yielded a different result in the next case.

BP v *Commission* (Case 77/77)

[1978] ECR 1511, Court of Justice of the European Communities

The Commission found abusive BP's reduction in supply of oil to ABG, a Dutch customer, during the oil crisis of the early-1970s. The Court disagreed.

[28] It emerges from the contested decision that the fact that BP in November 1972 terminated its commercial relations with ABG was connected with the regrouping of BP's operational activities which was made necessary by the nationalization of a large part of that company's interests in the production sector and by the participation of the producer countries in its extracting activities and is thus explained by considerations which have nothing to do with its relations with ABG.

[29] It therefore follows that at the time of the crisis and even from November 1972, ABG's position in relation to BP was no longer, as regards the supply of motor spirit, that of a contractual customer but that of an occasional customer.

[30] The principle laid down by the contested decision that reductions in supplies ought to have been carried out on the basis of a reference period fixed in the year before the crisis, although it may be explicable in cases in which a continued supply relationship has been maintained, during that period, between seller and purchaser, cannot be applied when the supplier ceased during the course of that same period to carry on such relations with its customer, regard being had in particular to the fact that the plans of any undertaking are normally based on reasonable forecasts.

[31] Moreover, the advances in petrol against crude oil agreed to by BP in pursuance of the processing agreement, as they occur within the context of an agreement whose purpose was solely the refining of crude oil supplied by ABG and not the supplying of ABG with motor spirit, cannot serve as a valid argument to compare ABG's position in this case in relation to BP with that of a traditional customer of BP during the above-mentioned reference period.

[32] For all these reasons, since ABG's position in relation to BP had been, for several months before the crisis occurred, that of an occasional customer, BP cannot be accused of having applied to it during the crisis less favourable treatment than that which it reserved for its traditional customers.

■ QUESTION

Explain the major features which distinguish these two cases. You might also look at the decision of the Court of First Instance in *BPB Industries and British Gypsum Ltd* v *Commission* (Case T-65/89) [1993] ECR II-389, [1993] 5 CMLR 32 (the subject of an unsuccessful appeal dealing only with procedural matters in *BPB Industries and British Gypsum Ltd* v *Commission* (Case C-310/93P) [1995] ECR I-865) and that of the Court of Justice in Case C-333/94P *Tetra Pak* v *Commission* [1996] ECR I-5951.

NOTE

Broadly, this type of intervention can be justified as an attempt to preserve vestiges of competition and to curb potential inefficiencies flowing from the dominator's tactics. The cases have, not surprisingly, aroused some concern about the nature of the policy pursued. Read, for example, A. Pathak, 'Vertical Restraints in EEC Competition Law' [1988/2] LIEI 15, who questions whom the Commission is trying to protect in this area; consumer, small trader . . . or the broader competitive process?

In the next case the Court upheld the Commission's extension of control to cover a refusal to supply a first-time customer.

Radio Téléfis Eireann and Independent Television Publications v *Commission* (Cases C-241/91P, C-242/91P)

[1995] ECR I-801, [1995] 4 CMLR 718, Court of Justice of the European Communities

Three British and Irish television companies, RTE, BBC, and ITP, held copyright over programme listings. Each produced a guide to its own programmes, but they did not produce a single guide available to Irish consumers containing the combined listings. Third party publishers were unable to produce a comprehensive guide, because the companies refused to license use of the copyright-protected material. The Court of First Instance rejected an application for the annulment of the Commission Decision that the companies were abusing their dominant position (Case T-69/89 [1991] ECR II-485). The companies' appeal to the European Court was also unsuccessful. In reading this extract from the judgment remember that Article 86 should be read with post-Amsterdam eyes as Article 82.

[52] Among the circumstances taken into account by the Court of First Instance in concluding that such conduct was abusive was, first, the fact that there was, according to the findings of the Court of First Instance, no actual or potential substitute for a weekly television guide offering information on the programmes for the week ahead. On this point, the Court of First Instance confirmed the Commission's finding that the complete lists of programmes for a 24-hour period – and for a 48-hour period at weekends and before public holidays – published in certain daily and Sunday newspapers, and the television sections of certain magazines covering, in addition, 'highlights' of the week's programmes, were only to a limited extent substitutable for advance information to viewers on all the week's programmes. Only weekly television guides containing comprehensive listings for the week ahead would enable users to decide in advance which programmes they wished to follow and arrange their leisure activities for the week accordingly. The Court of First Instance also established that there was a specific, constant and regular potential demand on the part of consumers (see the *RTE* judgment, paragraph 62, and the *ITP* judgment, paragraph 48).

[53] Thus the appellants – who were, by force of circumstances, the only sources of the basic information on programme scheduling which is the indispensable raw material for compiling a weekly television guide – gave viewers wishing to obtain information on the choice of programmes for the week ahead no choice but to buy the weekly guides for each station and draw from each of them the information they needed to make comparisons.

[54] The appellants' refusal to provide basic information by relying on national copyright provisions thus prevented the appearance of a new product, a comprehensive weekly guide to television programmes, which the appellants did not offer and for which there was a potential consumer demand. Such refusal constitutes an abuse under heading (b) of the second paragraph of Article 86 of the Treaty.

[55] Second, there was no justification for such refusal either in the activity of television broadcasting or in that of publishing television magazines (*RTE* judgment, paragraph 73, and *ITP* judgment, paragraph 58).

[56] Third, and finally, as the Court of First Instance also held, the appellants, by their conduct, reserved to themselves the secondary market of weekly television guides by excluding all competition on that market (see the judgment in Joined Cases 6/73 and 7/73 *Commercial Solvents* v *Commission* [1974] ECR 223, paragraph 25) since they denied access to the basic information which is the raw material indispensable for the compilation of such a guide.

[57] In the light of all those circumstances, the Court of First Instance did not err in law in holding that the appellants' conduct was an abuse of a dominant position within the meaning of Article 86 of the Treaty.

NOTE
The decision is remarkable for its assertion of control of the firms' exercise of exclusive rights under national copyright law. P. Crowther comments that '[t]aken literally, the court's pronouncement on the fact that the copyright was used to restrict competition on a derivative market leaves the owner of an intellectual property right in a very precarious position . . . the upshot . . . is that owners of intellectual property rights, controlling "indispensable

raw materials", might think twice about launching expensive R[esearch] & D[evelopment] programmes' ((1995) 20 EL Rev 521, 528).

■ QUESTION

Has the Court established a satisfactory balance between the consumer interest in a market that is currently competitive and the consumer interest in a market which encourages innovators by rewarding them through shelter from competition?

NOTE

The Court of First Instance subsequently ruled that a refusal to supply may be condemned under Article 82 only where supply is essential to the activity in question or where the refusal prevents the introduction of a new product subject to consumer demand (Case T-504/93 *Tiercé Ladbroke* v *Commission* [1997] ECR II-923). And in the next case the European Court offered a further hint that the treatment of the market for television listings which led it to impose an obligation to contract on the dominant firm is likely to be regarded as exceptional.

Oscar Bronner GmbH & Co. KG v Mediaprint (Case C-7/97)
[1998] ECR I-7791, Court of Justice of the European Communities

This was a preliminary reference made by an Austrian court. Mediaprint, a publisher, had established a nationwide home-delivery scheme for newspapers. No competing facility existed in Austria. Oscar Bronner claimed that Mediaprint was acting in breach of Article 86 of the EC Treaty (now Article 82 EC) by refusing to include Bronner's newspaper, *Der Standard*, in the delivery service (for which Bronner was prepared to pay). Mediaprint pointed to the considerable investment it had made in developing the service and submitted that even though it held considerable market power in the Austrian daily newspaper market, it was not obliged to assist competing companies by allowing access to its facility. The Court agreed with Mediaprint.

[32] In examining whether an undertaking holds a dominant position within the meaning of Article 86 of the Treaty, it is of fundamental importance, as the Court has emphasised many times, to define the market in question and to define the substantial part of the common market in which the undertaking may be able to engage in abuses which hinder effective competition (Case C-242/95 *GT-Link* v *DSB* [1997] ECR I-4449, paragraph 36).

[33] It is settled case-law that, for the purposes of applying Article 86 of the Treaty, the market for the product or service in question comprises all the products or services which in view of their characteristics are particularly suited to satisfy constant needs and are only to a limited extent interchangeable with other products or services (Case 31/80 *L'Oréal* v *De Nieuwe AMCK* [1980] ECR 3775, paragraph 25; Case C-62/86 *AKZO* v *Commission* [1991] ECR I-3359, paragraph 51).

[34] As regards the definition of the market at issue in the main proceedings, it is therefore for the national court to determine, *inter alia*, whether home-delivery schemes constitute a separate market, or whether other methods of distributing daily newspapers, such as sale in shops or at kiosks or delivery by post, are sufficiently interchangeable with them to have to be taken into account also. In deciding whether there is a dominant position the court must also take account, as the Commission has emphasised, of the possible existence of regional home-delivery schemes.

[35] If that examination leads the national court to conclude that a separate market in home-delivery schemes does exist, and that there is an insufficient degree of interchangeability between Mediaprint's nationwide scheme and other, regional, schemes, it must hold that Mediaprint, which according to the information in the order for reference operates the only nationwide home-delivery service in Austria, is *de facto* in a monopoly situation in the market thus defined, and thus holds a dominant position in it.

[36] In that event, the national court would also have to find that Mediaprint holds a dominant position in a substantial part of the common market, since the case-law indicates that the territory of a Member State over which a dominant position extends is capable of constituting a substantial part of the common market (see, to that effect, Case 322/81 *Michelin* v *Commission* [1983] FCR 3461, paragraph 28; Case C-323/93 *Centre d'Insémination de la Crespelle* [1994] ECR I-5077, paragraph 17).

[37] Finally, it would need to be determined whether the refusal by the owner of the only nationwide home-delivery scheme in the territory of a Member State, which uses that scheme to distribute its own daily newspapers, to allow the publisher of a rival daily newspaper access to it constitutes an abuse of a dominant position within the meaning of Article 86 of the Treaty, on the ground that such refusal deprives that competitor of a means of distribution judged essential for the sale of its newspaper.

[38] Although in *Commercial Solvents* v *Commission* [Cases 6 & 7/73 p.488 above] and CBEM [v *CLT and IPB* Case 311/84 [1985] ECR 3261] cited above, the Court of Justice held the refusal by an undertaking holding a dominant position in a given market to supply an undertaking with which it was in competition in a neighbouring market with raw materials (*Commercial Solvents* v *Commission*, paragraph 25) and services (*CBEM*, paragraph 26) respectively, which were indispensable to carrying on the rival's business, to constitute an abuse, it should be noted, first, that the Court did so to the extent that the conduct in question was likely to eliminate all competition on the part of that undertaking.

[39] Secondly, in *Magill* [Cases C-241/91P, C-242/91P *RTE and ITP* v *Commission*, above], at paragraphs 49 and 50, the Court held that refusal by the owner of an intellectual property right to grant a licence, even if it is the act of an undertaking holding a dominant position, cannot in itself constitute abuse of a dominant position, but that the exercise of an exclusive right by the proprietor may, in exceptional circumstances, involve an abuse.

[40] In *Magill*, the Court found such exceptional circumstances in the fact that the refusal in question concerned a product (information on the weekly schedules of certain television channels) the supply of which was indispensable for carrying on the business in question (the publishing of a general television guide), in that, without that information, the person wishing to produce such a guide would find it impossible to publish it and offer it for sale (paragraph 53), the fact that such refusal prevented the appearance of a new product for which there was a potential consumer demand (paragraph 54), the fact that it was not justified by objective considerations (paragraph 55), and that it was likely to exclude all competition in the secondary market of television guides (paragraph 56).

[41] Therefore, even if that case-law on the exercise of an intellectual property right were applicable to the exercise of any property right whatever, it would still be necessary, for the *Magill* judgment to be effectively relied upon in order to plead the existence of an abuse within the meaning of Article 86 of the Treaty in a situation such as that which forms the subject-matter of the first question, not only that the refusal of the service comprised in home delivery be likely to eliminate all competition in the daily newspaper market on the part of the person requesting the service and that such refusal be incapable of being objectively justified, but also that the service in itself be indispensable to carrying on that person's business, inasmuch as there is no actual or potential substitute in existence for that home-delivery scheme.

[42] That is certainly not the case even if, as in the case which is the subject of the main proceedings, there is only one nationwide home-delivery scheme in the territory of a Member State and, moreover, the owner of that scheme holds a dominant position in the market for services constituted by that scheme or of which it forms part.

[43] In the first place, it is undisputed that other methods of distributing daily newspapers, such as by post and through sale in shops and at kiosks, even though they may be less advantageous for the distribution of certain newspapers, exist and are used by the publishers of those daily newspapers.

[44] Moreover, it does not appear that there are any technical, legal or even economic obstacles capable of making it impossible, or even unreasonably difficult, for any other publisher of daily

newspapers to establish, alone or in cooperation with other publishers, its own nationwide home-delivery scheme and use it to distribute its own daily newspapers.

[45] It should be emphasised in that respect that, in order to demonstrate that the creation of such a system is not a realistic potential alternative and that access to the existing system is therefore indispensable, it is not enough to argue that it is not economically viable by reason of the small circulation of the daily newspaper or newspapers to be distributed.

[46] For such access to be capable of being regarded as indispensable, it would be necessary at the very least to establish, as the Advocate General has pointed out at point 68 of his Opinion, that it is not economically viable to create a second home-delivery scheme for the distribution of daily newspapers with a circulation comparable to that of the daily newspapers distributed by the existing scheme.

[47] In the light of the foregoing considerations, the answer to the first question must be that the refusal by a press undertaking which holds a very large share of the daily newspaper market in a Member State and operates the only nationwide newspaper home-delivery scheme in that Member State to allow the publisher of a rival newspaper, which by reason of its small circulation is unable either alone or in cooperation with other publishers to set up and operate its own home-delivery scheme in economically reasonable conditions, to have access to that scheme for appropriate remuneration does not constitute abuse of a dominant position within the meaning of Article 86 of the Treaty.

■ QUESTION

Alpha plc is the sole UK manufacturer of Brillyarn, and its output of Brillyarn constitutes 50% of production of the fibre in the EC. There are only two other EC producers: Heinz, a German firm responsible for 30% of the EC output; and Ventoux, a French firm responsible for the remaining 20% of EC production.

Brillyarn cannot be manufactured without the constituent material, 'Coralfoam'. The only supplier of 'Coralfoam' presently active in the EC is an Italian firm, Donadoni, although several American companies also produce 'Coralfoam', but have not attempted to enter the European market due to the costs of transporting 'Coralfoam' across the Atlantic.

Donadoni has supplied Alpha with 'Coralfoam' for six years, since the discovery of the process for manufacturing Brillyarn. However, when Alpha orders an increase in supplies of 'Coralfoam' as part of an expansion programme, Donadoni rejects the order and informs Alpha that it no longer intends to do business with it. Donadoni explains that it has concluded an exclusive dealing contract with Heinz, designed to permit Heinz to purchase all Donadoni's supplies of 'Coralfoam' with a view to rapid expansion.

Alpha seeks your advice as to whether any infringements of the EC Treaty have been committed.

Advise Alpha.

How, if at all, would your answer differ if Donadoni had agreed to continue supplying Alpha but had insisted on an immediate 50% price increase?

NOTE

For additional material and resources see the Companion Website at: www.oup.co.uk/best.textbooks/law/weatherill6e

18

The Enforcement of the Competition Rules

Article 83 (ex 87) EC empowers the Council to adopt measures to give effect to the principles contained in Articles 81 and 82 (ex 85 and 86). This has duly occurred. But the relevant legal rules governing the enforcement of the Treaty competition rules have been radically altered by Regulation 1/2003. With effect from 1 May 2004, the long-standing system of enforcement, first established by Regulation 17/62 and subsequently elaborated in case law, has been replaced by the new regime contained in Regulation 1/2003. So the forward-thinking reader must focus attention on the future – Council Regulation 1/2003, based on Article 83 EC.

The new regime is not a clean slate, for some of the pre-existing practice and case law will remain influential in so far as aspects of the long-standing scheme of Regulation 17/62 have been retained, albeit in the new form provided by Regulation 1/2003. For example, the structure of the Commission's powers of investigation into suspected infringements of the competition rules has been largely retained. Accordingly the case law that has developed governing procedural protection for firms subject to Commission inquiry has an enduring significance. However, other aspects of previous practice are consigned to history. A dominant feature of the regime established by Regulation 17/62 was the conferral on the Commission of exclusive competence to grant exemption pursuant to Article 81(3) EC. Firms were expected to notify agreements subject to Article 81(1) and await Commission approval. This helped to secure uniformity in the interpretation and application of Article 81(3). It also made a bottleneck of the Commission. Its workload was immense, and its inability to supply the required output of formal decisions meant that a great deal of practice was of an informal nature. This in turn risked leaving national courts and competition authorities in a state of uncertainty when asked to apply the EC rules to commercial practices. Articles 81(1), 81(2), and 82 are directly effective, but Article 81(3) was not because of the exclusive reservation of decision-making competence to the Commission. The beginning of the Regulation's Preamble is helpful in setting out the principal motivations for 'modernization' of the regime.

COUNCIL REGULATION (EC) NO 1/2003 OF 16 DECEMBER 2002 ON THE IMPLEMENTATION OF THE RULES ON COMPETITION LAID DOWN IN ARTICLES 81 AND 82 OF THE TREATY (TEXT WITH EEA RELEVANCE)

[2003] OJ L/1/1, Preamble

(1) In order to establish a system which ensures that competition in the common market is not distorted, Articles 81 and 82 of the Treaty must be applied effectively and uniformly in the Community. Council Regulation No 17 of 6 February 1962, First Regulation implementing Articles 81 and 82(4) of the Treaty, has allowed a Community competition policy to develop that has helped to disseminate a competition culture within the Community. In the light of experience, however, that Regulation should now be replaced by legislation designed to meet the challenges of an integrated market and a future enlargement of the Community.

(2) In particular, there is a need to rethink the arrangements for applying the exception from the prohibition on agreements, which restrict competition, laid down in Article 81(3) of the Treaty. Under Article 83(2)(b) of the Treaty, account must be taken in this regard of the need to ensure effective supervision, on the one hand, and to simplify administration to the greatest possible extent, on the other.

(3) The centralised scheme set up by Regulation No 17 no longer secures a balance between those two objectives. It hampers application of the Community competition rules by the courts and competition authorities of the Member States, and the system of notification it involves prevents the Commission from concentrating its resources on curbing the most serious infringements. It also imposes considerable costs on undertakings.

(4) The present system should therefore be replaced by a directly applicable exception system in which the competition authorities and courts of the Member States have the power to apply not only Article 81(1) and Article 82 of the Treaty, which have direct applicability by virtue of the case-law of the Court of Justice of the European Communities, but also Article 81(3) of the Treaty.

NOTE

The abandonment of the system of notification and the lifting of the Commission's exclusive grip over the grant of exemption pursuant to Article 81(3) represents a profound adjustment in the orthodox assumptions and the very structure of competition law enforcement.

■ QUESTION

Is it surprising that this decentralization has occurred shortly before imminent enlargement into Central and Eastern Europe? Is the 'competition culture' mentioned above in the first recital sufficiently well-entrenched to guard against the risk that divergent decisions among the newly empowered courts and competition authorities of the Member States will imperil the uniform application of EC competition law across the territory of the Union?

COUNCIL REGULATION (EC) NO 1/2003 OF 16 DECEMBER 2002 ON THE IMPLEMENTATION OF THE RULES ON COMPETITION LAID DOWN IN ARTICLES 81 AND 82 OF THE TREATY (TEXT WITH EEA RELEVANCE)

[2003] OJ L/1/1

CHAPTER I: PRINCIPLES

Article 1: Application of Articles 81 and 82 of the Treaty

1. Agreements, decisions and concerted practices caught by Article 81(1) of the Treaty which do not satisfy the conditions of Article 81(3) of the Treaty shall be prohibited, no prior decision to that effect being required.

2. Agreements, decisions and concerted practices caught by Article 81(1) of the Treaty which satisfy the conditions of Article 81(3) of the Treaty shall not be prohibited, no prior decision to that effect being required.

3. The abuse of a dominant position referred to in Article 82 of the Treaty shall be prohibited, no prior decision to that effect being required.

Article 2: Burden of proof

In any national or Community proceedings for the application of Articles 81 and 82 of the Treaty, the burden of proving an infringement of Article 81(1) or of Article 82 of the Treaty shall rest on the party or the authority alleging the infringement. The undertaking or association of undertakings claiming the benefit of Article 81(3) of the Treaty shall bear the burden of proving that the conditions of that paragraph are fulfilled.

Article 3: Relationship between Articles 81 and 82 of the Treaty and national competition laws

1. Where the competition authorities of the Member States or national courts apply national competition law to agreements, decisions by associations of undertakings or concerted practices within the meaning of Article 81(1) of the Treaty which may affect trade between Member States within the meaning of that provision, they shall also apply Article 81 of the Treaty to such agreements, decisions or concerted practices. Where the competition authorities of the Member States or national courts apply national competition law to any abuse prohibited by Article 82 of the Treaty, they shall also apply Article 82 of the Treaty.

2. The application of national competition law may not lead to the prohibition of agreements, decisions by associations of undertakings or concerted practices which may affect trade between Member States but which do not restrict competition within the meaning of Article 81(1) of the Treaty, or which fulfil the conditions of Article 81(3) of the Treaty or which are covered by a Regulation for the application of Article 81(3) of the Treaty. Member States shall not under this Regulation be precluded from adopting and applying on their territory stricter national laws which prohibit or sanction unilateral conduct engaged in by undertakings.

3. Without prejudice to general principles and other provisions of Community law, paragraphs 1 and 2 do not apply when the competition authorities and the courts of the Member States apply national merger control laws nor do they preclude the application of provisions of national law that predominantly pursue an objective different from that pursued by Articles 81 and 82 of the Treaty.

CHAPTER II: POWERS

Article 4: Powers of the Commission

For the purpose of applying Articles 81 and 82 of the Treaty, the Commission shall have the powers provided for by this Regulation.

Article 5: Powers of the competition authorities of the Member States

The competition authorities of the Member States shall have the power to apply Articles 81 and 82 of the Treaty in individual cases. For this purpose, acting on their own initiative or on a complaint, they may take the following decisions:

— requiring that an infringement be brought to an end,
— ordering interim measures,
— accepting commitments,
— imposing fines, periodic penalty payments or any other penalty provided for in their national law.

Where on the basis of the information in their possession the conditions for prohibition are not met they may likewise decide that there are no grounds for action on their part.

Article 6: Powers of the national courts

National courts shall have the power to apply Articles 81 and 82 of the Treaty.

CHAPTER III: COMMISSION DECISIONS

Article 7: Finding and termination of infringement

1. Where the Commission, acting on a complaint or on its own initiative, finds that there is an infringement of Article 81 or of Article 82 of the Treaty, it may by decision require the undertakings and associations of undertakings concerned to bring such infringement to an end. For this purpose, it may impose on them any behavioural or structural remedies which are proportionate to the infringement committed and necessary to bring the infringement effectively to an end. Structural remedies can only be imposed either where there is no equally effective behavioural remedy or where any equally effective behavioural remedy would be more burdensome for the undertaking concerned than the structural remedy. If the Commission has a legitimate interest in doing so, it may also find that an infringement has been committed in the past.

2. Those entitled to lodge a complaint for the purposes of paragraph 1 are natural or legal persons who can show a legitimate interest and Member States.

Article 8: Interim measures

1. In cases of urgency due to the risk of serious and irreparable damage to competition, the Commission, acting on its own initiative may by decision, on the basis of a prima facie finding of infringement, order interim measures.

2. A decision under paragraph 1 shall apply for a specified period of time and may be renewed in so far this is necessary and appropriate.

Article 9: Commitments

1. Where the Commission intends to adopt a decision requiring that an infringement be brought to an end and the undertakings concerned offer commitments to meet the concerns expressed to them by the Commission in its preliminary assessment, the Commission may by decision make those commitments binding on the undertakings. Such a decision may be adopted for a specified period and shall conclude that there are no longer grounds for action by the Commission.

2. The Commission may, upon request or on its own initiative, reopen the proceedings:

> (a) where there has been a material change in any of the facts on which the decision was based;
> (b) where the undertakings concerned act contrary to their commitments; or
> (c) where the decision was based on incomplete, incorrect or misleading information provided by the parties.

Article 10: Finding of inapplicability

Where the Community public interest relating to the application of Articles 81 and 82 of the Treaty so requires, the Commission, acting on its own initiative, may by decision find that Article 81 of the Treaty is not applicable to an agreement, a decision by an association of undertakings or a concerted practice, either because the conditions of Article 81(1) of the Treaty are not fulfilled, or because the conditions of Article 81(3) of the Treaty are satisfied.

The Commission may likewise make such a finding with reference to Article 82 of the Treaty.

CHAPTER IV: COOPERATION

Article 11: Cooperation between the Commission and the competition authorities of the Member States

1. The Commission and the competition authorities of the Member States shall apply the Community competition rules in close cooperation.

2. The Commission shall transmit to the competition authorities of the Member States copies of the most important documents it has collected with a view to applying Articles 7, 8, 9, 10 and Article 29(1). At the request of the competition authority of a Member State, the Commission shall provide it with a copy of other existing documents necessary for the assessment of the case.

3. The competition authorities of the Member States shall, when acting under Article 81 or Article 82 of the Treaty, inform the Commission in writing before or without delay after

commencing the first formal investigative measure. This information may also be made available to the competition authorities of the other Member States.

4. No later than 30 days before the adoption of a decision requiring that an infringement be brought to an end, accepting commitments or withdrawing the benefit of a block exemption Regulation, the competition authorities of the Member States shall inform the Commission. To that effect, they shall provide the Commission with a summary of the case, the envisaged decision or, in the absence thereof, any other document indicating the proposed course of action. This information may also be made available to the competition authorities of the other Member States. At the request of the Commission, the acting competition authority shall make available to the Commission other documents it holds which are necessary for the assessment of the case. The information supplied to the Commission may be made available to the competition authorities of the other Member States. National competition authorities may also exchange between themselves information necessary for the assessment of a case that they are dealing with under Article 81 or Article 82 of the Treaty.

5. The competition authorities of the Member States may consult the Commission on any case involving the application of Community law.

6. The initiation by the Commission of proceedings for the adoption of a decision under Chapter III shall relieve the competition authorities of the Member States of their competence to apply Articles 81 and 82 of the Treaty. If a competition authority of a Member State is already acting on a case, the Commission shall only initiate proceedings after consulting with that national competition authority.

Article 12: Exchange of information

1. For the purpose of applying Articles 81 and 82 of the Treaty the Commission and the competition authorities of the Member States shall have the power to provide one another with and use in evidence any matter of fact or of law, including confidential information.

2. Information exchanged shall only be used in evidence for the purpose of applying Article 81 or Article 82 of the Treaty and in respect of the subject-matter for which it was collected by the transmitting authority. However, where national competition law is applied in the same case and in parallel to Community competition law and does not lead to a different outcome, information exchanged under this Article may also be used for the application of national competition law.

3. Information exchanged pursuant to paragraph 1 can only be used in evidence to impose sanctions on natural persons where:

— the law of the transmitting authority foresees sanctions of a similar kind in relation to an infringement of Article 81 or Article 82 of the Treaty or, in the absence thereof,
— the information has been collected in a way which respects the same level of protection of the rights of defence of natural persons as provided for under the national rules of the receiving authority. However, in this case, the information exchanged cannot be used by the receiving authority to impose custodial sanctions.

Article 13: Suspension or termination of proceedings

1. Where competition authorities of two or more Member States have received a complaint or are acting on their own initiative under Article 81 or Article 82 of the Treaty against the same agreement, decision of an association or practice, the fact that one authority is dealing with the case shall be sufficient grounds for the others to suspend the proceedings before them or to reject the complaint. The Commission may likewise reject a complaint on the ground that a competition authority of a Member State is dealing with the case.

2. Where a competition authority of a Member State or the Commission has received a complaint against an agreement, decision of an association or practice which has already been dealt with by another competition authority, it may reject it.

Article 14: Advisory Committee

1. The Commission shall consult an Advisory Committee on Restrictive Practices and Dominant Positions prior to the taking of any decision under Articles 7, 8, 9, 10, 23, Article 24(2) and Article 29(1).

2. For the discussion of individual cases, the Advisory Committee shall be composed of representatives of the competition authorities of the Member States. For meetings in which issues other than individual cases are being discussed, an additional Member State representative competent in competition matters may be appointed. Representatives may, if unable to attend, be replaced by other representatives.

3. The consultation may take place at a meeting convened and chaired by the Commission, held not earlier than 14 days after dispatch of the notice convening it, together with a summary of the case, an indication of the most important documents and a preliminary draft decision. In respect of decisions pursuant to Article 8, the meeting may be held seven days after the dispatch of the operative part of a draft decision. Where the Commission dispatches a notice convening the meeting which gives a shorter period of notice than those specified above, the meeting may take place on the proposed date in the absence of an objection by any Member State. The Advisory Committee shall deliver a written opinion on the Commission's preliminary draft decision. It may deliver an opinion even if some members are absent and are not represented. At the request of one or several members, the positions stated in the opinion shall be reasoned.

4. Consultation may also take place by written procedure. However, if any Member State so requests, the Commission shall convene a meeting. In case of written procedure, the Commission shall determine a time-limit of not less than 14 days within which the Member States are to put forward their observations for circulation to all other Member States. In case of decisions to be taken pursuant to Article 8, the time-limit of 14 days is replaced by seven days. Where the Commission determines a time-limit for the written procedure which is shorter than those specified above, the proposed time-limit shall be applicable in the absence of an objection by any Member State.

5. The Commission shall take the utmost account of the opinion delivered by the Advisory Committee. It shall inform the Committee of the manner in which its opinion has been taken into account.

6. Where the Advisory Committee delivers a written opinion, this opinion shall be appended to the draft decision. If the Advisory Committee recommends publication of the opinion, the Commission shall carry out such publication taking into account the legitimate interest of undertakings in the protection of their business secrets.

7. At the request of a competition authority of a Member State, the Commission shall include on the agenda of the Advisory Committee cases that are being dealt with by a competition authority of a Member State under Article 81 or Article 82 of the Treaty. The Commission may also do so on its own initiative. In either case, the Commission shall inform the competition authority concerned.

A request may in particular be made by a competition authority of a Member State in respect of a case where the Commission intends to initiate proceedings with the effect of Article 11(6).

The Advisory Committee shall not issue opinions on cases dealt with by competition authorities of the Member States. The Advisory Committee may also discuss general issues of Community competition law.

Article 15: Cooperation with national courts

1. In proceedings for the application of Article 81 or Article 82 of the Treaty, courts of the Member States may ask the Commission to transmit to them information in its possession or its opinion on questions concerning the application of the Community competition rules.

2 Member States shall forward to the Commission a copy of any written judgment of national courts deciding on the application of Article 81 or Article 82 of the Treaty. Such copy shall be forwarded without delay after the full written judgment is notified to the parties.

3. Competition authorities of the Member States, acting on their own initiative, may submit written observations to the national courts of their Member State on issues relating to the application of Article 81 or Article 82 of the Treaty. With the permission of the court in question, they may also submit oral observations to the national courts of their Member State. Where the coherent application of Article 81 or Article 82 of the Treaty so requires, the Commission, acting on its own initiative, may submit written observations to courts of the Member States. With the permission of

the court in question, it may also make oral observations. For the purpose of the preparation of their observations only, the competition authorities of the Member States and the Commission may request the relevant court of the Member State to transmit or ensure the transmission to them of any documents necessary for the assessment of the case.

4. This Article is without prejudice to wider powers to make observations before courts conferred on competition authorities of the Member States under the law of their Member State.

Article 16: Uniform application of Community competition law

1. When national courts rule on agreements, decisions or practices under Article 81 or Article 82 of the Treaty which are already the subject of a Commission decision, they cannot take decisions running counter to the decision adopted by the Commission. They must also avoid giving decisions which would conflict with a decision contemplated by the Commission in proceedings it has initiated. To that effect, the national court may assess whether it is necessary to stay its proceedings. This obligation is without prejudice to the rights and obligations under Article 234 of the Treaty.

2. When competition authorities of the Member States rule on agreements, decisions or practices under Article 81 or Article 82 of the Treaty which are already the subject of a Commission decision, they cannot take decisions which would run counter to the decision adopted by the Commission.

CHAPTER V: POWERS OF INVESTIGATION

Article 17: Investigations into sectors of the economy and into types of agreements

1. Where the trend of trade between Member States, the rigidity of prices or other circumstances suggest that competition may be restricted or distorted within the common market, the Commission may conduct its inquiry into a particular sector of the economy or into a particular type of agreements across various sectors. In the course of that inquiry, the Commission may request the undertakings or associations of undertakings concerned to supply the information necessary for giving effect to Articles 81 and 82 of the Treaty and may carry out any inspections necessary for that purpose.

The Commission may in particular request the undertakings or associations of undertakings concerned to communicate to it all agreements, decisions and concerted practices.

The Commission may publish a report on the results of its inquiry into particular sectors of the economy or particular types of agreements across various sectors and invite comments from interested parties.

2. Articles 14, 18, 19, 20, 22, 23 and 24 shall apply mutatis mutandis.

Article 18: Requests for information

1. In order to carry out the duties assigned to it by this Regulation, the Commission may, by simple request or by decision, require undertakings and associations of undertakings to provide all necessary information.

2. When sending a simple request for information to an undertaking or association of undertakings, the Commission shall state the legal basis and the purpose of the request, specify what information is required and fix the time-limit within which the information is to be provided, and the penalties provided for in Article 23 for supplying incorrect or misleading information.

3. Where the Commission requires undertakings and associations of undertakings to supply information by decision, it shall state the legal basis and the purpose of the request, specify what information is required and fix the time-limit within which it is to be provided. It shall also indicate the penalties provided for in Article 23 and indicate or impose the penalties provided for in Article 24. It shall further indicate the right to have the decision reviewed by the Court of Justice.

4. The owners of the undertakings or their representatives and, in the case of legal persons, companies or firms, or associations having no legal personality, the persons authorised to represent them by law or by their constitution shall supply the information requested on behalf of the undertaking or the association of undertakings concerned. Lawyers duly authorised to act may

supply the information on behalf of their clients. The latter shall remain fully responsible if the information supplied is incomplete, incorrect or misleading.

5. The Commission shall without delay forward a copy of the simple request or of the decision to the competition authority of the Member State in whose territory the seat of the undertaking or association of undertakings is situated and the competition authority of the Member State whose territory is affected.

6. At the request of the Commission the governments and competition authorities of the Member States shall provide the Commission with all necessary information to carry out the duties assigned to it by this Regulation.

Article 19: Power to take statements

1. In order to carry out the duties assigned to it by this Regulation, the Commission may inter-view any natural or legal person who consents to be interviewed for the purpose of collecting information relating to the subject-matter of an investigation.

2. Where an interview pursuant to paragraph 1 is conducted in the premises of an undertaking, the Commission shall inform the competition authority of the Member State in whose territory the interview takes place. If so requested by the competition authority of that Member State, its officials may assist the officials and other accompanying persons authorised by the Commission to conduct the interview.

Article 20: The Commission's powers of inspection

1. In order to carry out the duties assigned to it by this Regulation, the Commission may conduct all necessary inspections of undertakings and associations of undertakings.

2. The officials and other accompanying persons authorised by the Commission to conduct an inspection are empowered:

> (a) to enter any premises, land and means of transport of undertakings and associations of undertakings;
> (b) to examine the books and other records related to the business, irrespective of the medium on which they are stored;
> (c) to take or obtain in any form copies of or extracts from such books or records;
> (d) to seal any business premises and books or records for the period and to the extent necessary for the inspection;
> (e) to ask any representative or member of staff of the undertaking or association of undertakings for explanations on facts or documents relating to the subject-matter and purpose of the inspection and to record the answers.

3. The officials and other accompanying persons authorised by the Commission to conduct an inspection shall exercise their powers upon production of a written authorisation specifying the subject matter and purpose of the inspection and the penalties provided for in Article 23 in case the production of the required books or other records related to the business is incomplete or where the answers to questions asked under paragraph 2 of the present Article are incorrect or misleading. In good time before the inspection, the Commission shall give notice of the inspection to the competition authority of the Member State in whose territory it is to be conducted.

4. Undertakings and associations of undertakings are required to submit to inspections ordered by decision of the Commission. The decision shall specify the subject matter and purpose of the inspection, appoint the date on which it is to begin and indicate the penalties provided for in Articles 23 and 24 and the right to have the decision reviewed by the Court of Justice. The Commission shall take such decisions after consulting the competition authority of the Member State in whose territory the inspection is to be conducted.

5. Officials of as well as those authorised or appointed by the competition authority of the Member State in whose territory the inspection is to be conducted shall, at the request of that authority or of the Commission, actively assist the officials and other accompanying persons authorised by the Commission. To this end, they shall enjoy the powers specified in paragraph 2.

6. Where the officials and other accompanying persons authorised by the Commission find that an undertaking opposes an inspection ordered pursuant to this Article, the Member State concerned shall afford them the necessary assistance, requesting where appropriate the assistance of the police or of an equivalent enforcement authority, so as to enable them to conduct their inspection.

7. If the assistance provided for in paragraph 6 requires authorisation from a judicial authority according to national rules, such authorisation shall be applied for. Such authorisation may also be applied for as a precautionary measure.

8. Where authorisation as referred to in paragraph 7 is applied for, the national judicial authority shall control that the Commission decision is authentic and that the coercive measures envisaged are neither arbitrary nor excessive having regard to the subject matter of the inspection. In its control of the proportionality of the coercive measures, the national judicial authority may ask the Commission, directly or through the Member State competition authority, for detailed explanations in particular on the grounds the Commission has for suspecting infringement of Articles 81 and 82 of the Treaty, as well as on the seriousness of the suspected infringement and on the nature of the involvement of the undertaking concerned. However, the national judicial authority may not call into question the necessity for the inspection nor demand that it be provided with the information in the Commission's file. The lawfulness of the Commission decision shall be subject to review only by the Court of Justice.

Article 21: Inspection of other premises

1. If a reasonable suspicion exists that books or other records related to the business and to the subject-matter of the inspection, which may be relevant to prove a serious violation of Article 81 or Article 82 of the Treaty, are being kept in any other premises, land and means of transport, including the homes of directors, managers and other members of staff of the undertakings and associations of undertakings concerned, the Commission can by decision order an inspection to be conducted in such other premises, land and means of transport.

2. The decision shall specify the subject matter and purpose of the inspection, appoint the date on which it is to begin and indicate the right to have the decision reviewed by the Court of Justice. It shall in particular state the reasons that have led the Commission to conclude that a suspicion in the sense of paragraph 1 exists. The Commission shall take such decisions after consulting the competition authority of the Member State in whose territory the inspection is to be conducted.

3. A decision adopted pursuant to paragraph 1 cannot be executed without prior authorisation from the national judicial authority of the Member State concerned. The national judicial authority shall control that the Commission decision is authentic and that the coercive measures envisaged are neither arbitrary nor excessive having regard in particular to the seriousness of the suspected infringement, to the importance of the evidence sought, to the involvement of the undertaking concerned and to the reasonable likelihood that business books and records relating to the subject matter of the inspection are kept in the premises for which the authorisation is requested. The national judicial authority may ask the Commission, directly or through the Member State competition authority, for detailed explanations on those elements which are necessary to allow its control of the proportionality of the coercive measures envisaged.

However, the national judicial authority may not call into question the necessity for the inspection nor demand that it be provided with information in the Commission's file. The lawfulness of the Commission decision shall be subject to review only by the Court of Justice.

4. The officials and other accompanying persons authorised by the Commission to conduct an inspection ordered in accordance with paragraph 1 of this Article shall have the powers set out in Article 20(2)(a), (b) and (c). Article 20(5) and (6) shall apply mutatis mutandis.

Article 22: Investigations by competition authorities of Member States

1. The competition authority of a Member State may in its own territory carry out any inspection or other fact-finding measure under its national law on behalf and for the account of the competition authority of another Member State in order to establish whether there has been an infringement of Article 81 or Article 82 of the Treaty. Any exchange and use of the information collected shall be carried out in accordance with Article 12.

2. At the request of the Commission, the competition authorities of the Member States shall undertake the inspections which the Commission considers to be necessary under Article 20(1) or which it has ordered by decision pursuant to Article 20(4). The officials of the competition authorities of the Member States who are responsible for conducting these inspections as well as those authorised or appointed by them shall exercise their powers in accordance with their national law. If so requested by the Commission or by the competition authority of the Member State in whose territory the inspection is to be conducted, officials and other accompanying persons authorised by the Commission may assist the officials of the authority concerned.

CHAPTER VI: PENALTIES

Article 23: Fines

1. The Commission may by decision impose on undertakings and associations of undertakings fines not exceeding 1% of the total turnover in the preceding business year where, intentionally or negligently:

    (a) they supply incorrect or misleading information in response to a request made pursuant to Article 17 or Article 18(2);

    (b) in response to a request made by decision adopted pursuant to Article 17 or Article 18(3), they supply incorrect, incomplete or misleading information or do not supply information within the required time-limit;

    (c) they produce the required books or other records related to the business in incomplete form during inspections under Article 20 or refuse to submit to inspections ordered by a decision adopted pursuant to Article 20(4);

    (d) in response to a question asked in accordance with Article 20(2)(e),

        — they give an incorrect or misleading answer,

        — they fail to rectify within a time-limit set by the Commission an incorrect, incomplete or misleading answer given by a member of staff, or

        — they fail or refuse to provide a complete answer on facts relating to the subject-matter and purpose of an inspection ordered by a decision adopted pursuant to Article 20(4);

    (e) seals affixed in accordance with Article 20(2)(d) by officials or other accompanying persons authorised by the Commission have been broken.

2. The Commission may by decision impose fines on undertakings and associations of undertakings where, either intentionally or negligently:

    (a) they infringe Article 81 or Article 82 of the Treaty; or

    (b) they contravene a decision ordering interim measures under Article 8; or

    (c) they fail to comply with a commitment made binding by a decision pursuant to Article 9.

For each undertaking and association of undertakings participating in the infringement, the fine shall not exceed 10% of its total turnover in the preceding business year.

Where the infringement of an association relates to the activities of its members, the fine shall not exceed 10% of the sum of the total turnover of each member active on the market affected by the infringement of the association.

3. In fixing the amount of the fine, regard shall be had both to the gravity and to the duration of the infringement.

4. When a fine is imposed on an association of undertakings taking account of the turnover of its members and the association is not solvent, the association is obliged to call for contributions from its members to cover the amount of the fine. Where such contributions have not been made to the association within a time-limit fixed by the Commission, the Commission may require payment of the fine directly by any of the undertakings whose representatives were members of the decision-making bodies concerned of the association.

After the Commission has required payment under the second subparagraph, where necessary to ensure full payment of the fine, the Commission may require payment of the balance by any of the members of the association which were active on the market on which the infringement occurred.

However, the Commission shall not require payment under the second or the third subparagraph from undertakings which show that they have not implemented the infringing decision of the association and either were not aware of its existence or have actively distanced themselves from it before the Commission started investigating the case. The financial liability of each undertaking in respect of the payment of the fine shall not exceed 10% of its total turnover in the preceding business year.

5. Decisions taken pursuant to paragraphs 1 and 2 shall not be of a criminal law nature.

Article 24: Periodic penalty payments

1. The Commission may, by decision, impose on undertakings or associations of undertakings periodic penalty payments not exceeding 5% of the average daily turnover in the preceding business year per day and calculated from the date appointed by the decision, in order to compel them:

> (a) to put an end to an infringement of Article 81 or Article 82 of the Treaty, in accordance with a decision taken pursuant to Article 7;
> (b) to comply with a decision ordering interim measures taken pursuant to Article 8;
> (c) to comply with a commitment made binding by a decision pursuant to Article 9;
> (d) to supply complete and correct information which it has requested by decision taken pursuant to Article 17 or Article 18(3);
> (e) to submit to an inspection which it has ordered by decision taken pursuant to Article 20(4).

2. Where the undertakings or associations of undertakings have satisfied the obligation which the periodic penalty payment was intended to enforce, the Commission may fix the definitive amount of the periodic penalty payment at a figure lower than that which would arise under the original decision. Article 23(4) shall apply correspondingly.

CHAPTER VII: LIMITATION PERIODS

Article 25: Limitation periods for the imposition of penalties

1.The powers conferred on the Commission by Articles 23 and 24 shall be subject to the following limitation periods:

> (a) three years in the case of infringements of provisions concerning requests for information or the conduct of inspections;
> (b) five years in the case of all other infringements.

2. Time shall begin to run on the day on which the infringement is committed. However, in the case of continuing or repeated infringements, time shall begin to run on the day on which the infringement ceases.

3. Any action taken by the Commission or by the competition authority of a Member State for the purpose of the investigation or proceedings in respect of an infringement shall interrupt the limitation period for the imposition of fines or periodic penalty payments. The limitation period shall be interrupted with effect from the date on which the action is notified to at least one undertaking or association of undertakings which has participated in the infringement. Actions which interrupt the running of the period shall include in particular the following:

> (a) written requests for information by the Commission or by the competition authority of a Member State;
> (b) written authorisations to conduct inspections issued to its officials by the Commission or by the competition authority of a Member State;
> (c) the initiation of proceedings by the Commission or by the competition authority of a Member State;

(d) notification of the statement of objections of the Commission or of the competition authority of a Member State.

4. The interruption of the limitation period shall apply for all the undertakings or associations of undertakings which have participated in the infringement.

5. Each interruption shall start time running afresh. However, the limitation period shall expire at the latest on the day on which a period equal to twice the limitation period has elapsed without the Commission having imposed a fine or a periodic penalty payment. That period shall be extended by the time during which limitation is suspended pursuant to paragraph 6.

6. The limitation period for the imposition of fines or periodic penalty payments shall be suspended for as long as the decision of the Commission is the subject of proceedings pending before the Court of Justice.

Article 26: Limitation period for the enforcement of penalties

1. The power of the Commission to enforce decisions taken pursuant to Articles 23 and 24 shall be subject to a limitation period of five years.

2. Time shall begin to run on the day on which the decision becomes final.

3. The limitation period for the enforcement of penalties shall be interrupted:

(a) by notification of a decision varying the original amount of the fine or periodic penalty payment or refusing an application for variation;

(b) by any action of the Commission or of a Member State, acting at the request of the Commission, designed to enforce payment of the fine or periodic penalty payment.

4. Each interruption shall start time running afresh.

5. The limitation period for the enforcement of penalties shall be suspended for so long as:

(a) time to pay is allowed;

(b) enforcement of payment is suspended pursuant to a decision of the Court of Justice.

CHAPTER VIII: HEARINGS AND PROFESSIONAL SECRECY

Article 27: Hearing of the parties, complainants and others

1. Before taking decisions as provided for in Articles 7, 8, 23 and Article 24(2), the Commission shall give the undertakings or associations of undertakings which are the subject of the proceedings conducted by the Commission the opportunity of being heard on the matters to which the Commission has taken objection. The Commission shall base its decisions only on objections on which the parties concerned have been able to comment. Complainants shall be associated closely with the proceedings.

2. The rights of defence of the parties concerned shall be fully respected in the proceedings. They shall be entitled to have access to the Commission's file, subject to the legitimate interest of undertakings in the protection of their business secrets. The right of access to the file shall not extend to confidential information and internal documents of the Commission or the competition authorities of the Member States. In particular, the right of access shall not extend to correspondence between the Commission and the competition authorities of the Member States, or between the latter, including documents drawn up pursuant to Articles 11 and 14. Nothing in this paragraph shall prevent the Commission from disclosing and using information necessary to prove an infringement.

3. If the Commission considers it necessary, it may also hear other natural or legal persons. Applications to be heard on the part of such persons shall, where they show a sufficient interest, be granted. The competition authorities of the Member States may also ask the Commission to hear other natural or legal persons.

4. Where the Commission intends to adopt a decision pursuant to Article 9 or Article 10, it shall publish a concise summary of the case and the main content of the commitments or of the proposed course of action. Interested third parties may submit their observations within a time limit which is fixed by the Commission in its publication and which may not be less than one

month. Publication shall have regard to the legitimate interest of undertakings in the protection of their business secrets.

Article 28: Professional secrecy

1. Without prejudice to Articles 12 and 15, information collected pursuant to Articles 17 to 22 shall be used only for the purpose for which it was acquired.

2. Without prejudice to the exchange and to the use of information foreseen in Articles 11, 12, 14, 15 and 27, the Commission and the competition authorities of the Member States, their officials, servants and other persons working under the supervision of these authorities as well as officials and civil servants of other authorities of the Member States shall not disclose information acquired or exchanged by them pursuant to this Regulation and of the kind covered by the obligation of professional secrecy. This obligation also applies to all representatives and experts of Member States attending meetings of the Advisory Committee pursuant to Article 14.

CHAPTER IX: EXEMPTION REGULATIONS

Article 29: Withdrawal in individual cases

1. Where the Commission, empowered by a Council Regulation, such as Regulations 19/65/EEC, (EEC) No 2821/71, (EEC) No 3976/87, (EEC) No 1534/91 or (EEC) No 479/92, to apply Article 81(3) of the Treaty by regulation, has declared Article 81(1) of the Treaty inapplicable to certain categories of agreements, decisions by associations of undertakings or concerted practices, it may, acting on its own initiative or on a complaint, withdraw the benefit of such an exemption Regulation when it finds that in any particular case an agreement, decision or concerted practice to which the exemption Regulation applies has certain effects which are incompatible with Article 81(3) of the Treaty.

2. Where, in any particular case, agreements, decisions by associations of undertakings or concerted practices to which a Commission Regulation referred to in paragraph 1 applies have effects which are incompatible with Article 81(3) of the Treaty in the territory of a Member State, or in a part thereof, which has all the characteristics of a distinct geographic market, the competition authority of that Member State may withdraw the benefit of the Regulation in question in respect of that territory.

CHAPTER X: GENERAL PROVISIONS

Article 30: Publication of decisions

1. The Commission shall publish the decisions, which it takes pursuant to Articles 7 to 10, 23 and 24.

2. The publication shall state the names of the parties and the main content of the decision, including any penalties imposed. It shall have regard to the legitimate interest of undertakings in the protection of their business secrets.

Article 31: Review by the Court of Justice

The Court of Justice shall have unlimited jurisdiction to review decisions whereby the Commission has fixed a fine or periodic penalty payment. It may cancel, reduce or increase the fine or periodic penalty payment imposed.

Article 32: Exclusions

This Regulation shall not apply to:

(a) international tramp vessel services as defined in Article 1(3)(a) of Regulation (EEC) No 4056/86;

(b) a maritime transport service that takes place exclusively between ports in one and the same Member State as foreseen in Article (2) of Regulation (EEC) No 4056/86;

(c) air transport between Community airports and third countries.

Article 33: Implementing provisions

1. The Commission shall be authorised to take such measures as may be appropriate in order to apply this Regulation. The measures may concern, *inter alia*: (a) the form, content and other details of complaints lodged pursuant to Article 7 and the procedure for rejecting complaints; (b) the practical arrangements for the exchange of information and consultations provided for in Article 11; (c) the practical arrangements for the hearings provided for in Article 27.

2. Before the adoption of any measures pursuant to paragraph 1, the Commission shall publish a draft thereof and invite all interested parties to submit their comments within the time-limit it lays down, which may not be less than one month. Before publishing a draft measure and before adopting it, the Commission shall consult the Advisory Committee on Restrictive Practices and Dominant Positions.

CHAPTER XI: TRANSITIONAL, AMENDING AND FINAL PROVISIONS

Article 34: Transitional provisions

1. Applications made to the Commission under Article 2 of Regulation No 17, notifications made under Articles 4 and 5 of that Regulation and the corresponding applications and notifications made under Regulations (EEC) No 1017/68, (EEC) No 4056/86 and (EEC) No 3975/87 shall lapse as from the date of application of this Regulation.

2. Procedural steps taken under Regulation No 17 and Regulations (EEC) No 1017/68, (EEC) No 4056/86 and (EEC) No 3975/87 shall continue to have effect for the purposes of applying this Regulation.

Article 35: Designation of competition authorities of Member States

1. The Member States shall designate the competition authority or authorities responsible for the application of Articles 81 and 82 of the Treaty in such a way that the provisions of this regulation are effectively complied with. The measures necessary to empower those authorities to apply those Articles shall be taken before 1 May 2004. The authorities designated may include courts.

2. When enforcement of Community competition law is entrusted to national administrative and judicial authorities, the Member States may allocate different powers and functions to those different national authorities, whether administrative or judicial.

3. The effects of Article 11(6) apply to the authorities designated by the Member States including courts that exercise functions regarding the preparation and the adoption of the types of decisions foreseen in Article 5. The effects of Article 11(6) do not extend to courts insofar as they act as review courts in respect of the types of decisions foreseen in Article 5.

4. Notwithstanding paragraph 3, in the Member States where, for the adoption of certain types of decisions foreseen in Article 5, an authority brings an action before a judicial authority that is separate and different from the prosecuting authority and provided that the terms of this paragraph are complied with, the effects of Article 11(6) shall be limited to the authority prosecuting the case which shall withdraw its claim before the judicial authority when the Commission opens proceedings and this withdrawal shall bring the national proceedings effectively to an end.

Articles 36–42 deal with the amendment of Regulations 1017/68, 2988/74, 4056/86, 3975/87, 19/65, 2821/71 and 1534/91, 3976/87, and 479/92.

Article 43: Repeal of Regulations No 17 and No 141

1. Regulation No 17 is repealed with the exception of Article 8(3) which continues to apply to decisions adopted pursuant to Article 81(3) of the Treaty prior to the date of application of this Regulation until the date of expiration of those decisions.

2. Regulation No 141 is repealed.

3. References to the repealed Regulations shall be construed as references to this Regulation.

Article 44: Report on the application of the present Regulation

Five years from the date of application of this Regulation, the Commission shall report to the European Parliament and the Council on the functioning of this Regulation, in particular on the application of Article 11(6) and Article 17.

On the basis of this report, the Commission shall assess whether it is appropriate to propose to the Council a revision of this Regulation.

Article 45: Entry into force

This Regulation shall enter into force on the 20th day following that of its publication in the Official Journal of the European Communities.

It shall apply from 1 May 2004.

This Regulation shall be binding in its entirety and directly applicable in all Member States.

NOTE

Regulation 1/2003 promises deeper and more effective enforcement of EC competition law. Both Community level – the Commission – and national level – the competition authorities and the courts – are involved: Chapter II, Articles 4–6 of Regulation 1/2003 above. Article 1(2) of Regulation 1/2003 eliminates the Commission's exclusive grip over Article 81(3). This permits all these bodies to play a full part in supervising the application of the rules untainted by the pre-existing reliance on the Commission alone as the source of exemption. Deals will be valid from the date of conclusion provided they satisfy the Article 81(3) criteria without the need for notification to the Commission. There is no longer any requirement of an administrative decision confirming exemption. And the Commission in turn is able to re-allocate resources from the notification process to more intense investigation of covert anti-competitive practices which in the past would certainly not have been notified by the participants. The risk is plainly that these benefits will come at cost, largely paid in the currency of diverse approaches to the availability of (in particular) Article 81(3) exemption taken by national authorities and courts. Commercial distortion may result from a decentralization of enforcement that in practice spills over into fragmented and disunified enforcement. In response to this peril, Chapter IV of the Regulation in particular is directed at the establishment of an effective system of co-operation between the several bodies charged with the responsibility of applying the Treaty provisions. The aim is to minimize the risk of the law being applied in different ways in different States. Future research will be needed to reveal the extent to which this process of modernization, built on decentralization, can be prevented from generating damaging unevenness in the application of the Treaty rules governing competition law across the territory of the Union. To place the problem in context, it is worth recalling that the system created by Regulation 1/2003 is comparable to the system of enforcement according to the pattern of 'dual vigilance' that applies to Community law generally. As Chapter 4 demonstrates, the enforcement of Community law generally is placed in the hands of both Community and national-level bodies, with a corresponding risk of diversity in practice. After all, both Article 30 EC and the Court's 'mandatory requirements', which offer the possibility of justifying national measures that restrict inter-State trade, are capable of application by national courts. There is no reservation of competence to the Commission. To this extent one may choose to regard the old system of Commission exclusivity over Article 81(3) as abnormal, and Regulation 1/2003 as a transfer of the practice of competition law enforcement back to the *communautaire* mainstream.

FURTHER READING

(i) On the 1999 White Paper on modernization that made the case for (what became) Regulation 1/2003

'Reforming EC Competition Law Procedures', report of the House of Lords Select Committee, HL 33 1999–2000.

Ehlermann, C.-D. and Atanasiu, I. (eds), *European Competition Law Annual 2000: The Modernisation of EC Antitrust Policy* (Oxford: Hart Publishing, 2001).

Klimisch, A. and Krueger, B., 'Decentralised Application of EC Competition Law: Current Practice and Future Prospects' (1999) 24 EL Rev 463.

Rodger, B., 'The Commission White Paper on Modernisation of the Rules Implementing Articles 81 and 82 of the EC Treaty' (1999) 24 EL Rev 653.

Wesseling, R., 'The Commission White Paper on Modernisation of EC Antitrust Law' [1999] ECLR 420.

(ii) On Regulation 1/2003 itself

See also the Companion Website to this book for references to the latest literature.

■ QUESTION

The substantive alignment of national competition law with the EC model has been a feature of recent years (see, e.g., I. Maher, 'Alignment of Competition Laws in the European Community' (1996) 16 YEL 223). To what extent will this serve to diminish the risk of misunderstanding of EC practice by the national courts and administrators newly empowered by Regulation 1/2003?

NOTE

Achieving a balance between the needs of effective enforcement of the competition rules and the protection of firms subject to the rules is a difficult but vital issue. Chapter V of Regulation 1/2003 contains *Powers of Investigation*. Article 20, the Commission's powers of investigation, and Article 21, Inspection of other premises, are especially significant. These govern the so-called 'dawn raids' of premises, which, since the Commission prefers to find buildings open, tend not to happen at dawn. The procedure assumes a Commission Decision with which a firm must comply but, in the event of non-compliance, recourse to national procedures to secure compliance is envisaged. Equipping the Commission with tough powers of this type is plainly important in creating an effective regime that will be capable of uncovering secret cartels, which are likely to be the most pernicious of all. Equally firms subject to such intrusion have a proper concern for protection from undue or unfair administrative interference.

Article 14 of Regulation 17/62 contained a procedure that is recognisably the precursor of the set of powers now found in Chapter V of Regulation 1/2003. However, the provisions of Regulation 1/2003 represent a significant adjustment of the pre-existing regime. Article 21 of Regulation 1/2003 constitutes a significant widening of the scope of the power to search. And the provisions of Regulation 1/2003 absorb the important decisions handed down in this area by the Court. The exercise of these powers of the Commission has been the subject of regular challenges which have permitted the Court to elaborate its own view of the appropriate scope of procedural protection for natural or legal persons subject to investigation. Regulation 1/2003 will doubtless generate its own case law, but it is worth briefly setting out the key components of decisions of the Court dealing with Regulation 17/62, both in order to expose the source of some of the wording found in the Articles contained in Chapter V of Regulation 1/2003 and also to identify the source of inspiration of the Court in developing these legal principles. The latter point is of more general importance. The Court's cases in this area are important in competition law, but they also reflect the development of Community notions of fundamental rights (p.78 above). Its major decisions include *National Panasonic v Commission* (Case 136/79) [1980] ECR 2033; *Musique Diffusion Française v Commission* (Cases 100–103/80) [1983] ECR 1825; *Transocean Marine Paint v Commission* (Case 17/74) [1974] ECR 1063, discussed at p.88 above for its value as an example of Community legal technique; and *AKZO v Commission* (Case 5/85) [1986] ECR 2585.

The Court of First Instance has now assumed jurisdiction in this area and it too has begun to establish important ground rules. However, the following decision of the Court of Justice remains highly significant.

Hoechst v *Commission* (Case 46/87)

[1989] ECR 2859, Court of Justice of the European Communities

The Commission suspected Hoechst was implicated in a cartel. Seeking information, it arrived unannounced at Hoechst's premises, as it was entitled to do under Article 14 of Regulation 17/62 (the precursor of Article 20 of Regulation 1/2003, albeit that the latter is a much more elaborate provision). Hoechst refused to admit the Commission officials and argued that it was entitled to exclude them until a search warrant had been obtained through national procedures. The Commission eventually obtained access using this route, but imposed financial penalties on Hoechst for refusal to comply with the original decision under Article 14. Hoechst sought the annulment of that decision before the Court.

[12] It should be noted, before the nature and scope of the Commission's powers of investigation under Article 14 of Regulation No 17 are examined, that that article cannot be interpreted in such a way as to give rise to results which are incompatible with the general principles of Community law and in particular with fundamental rights.

[13] The Court has consistently held that fundamental rights are an integral part of the general principles of law the observance of which the Court ensures, in accordance with constitutional traditions common to the Member States, and the international treaties on which the Member States have collaborated or of which they are signatories (see, in particular, the judgment of 14 May 1974 in Case 4/73 *Nold* v *Commission* [1974] ECR 491). The European Convention for the Protection of Human Rights and Fundamental Freedoms of 4 November 1950 (hereinafter referred to as 'the European Convention on Human Rights') is of particular significance in that regard (see, in particular, the judgment of 15 May 1986 in Case 222/84 *Johnston* v *Chief Constable of the Royal Ulster Constabulary* [1986] ECR 1651).

[14] In interpreting Article 14 of Regulation No 17, regard must be had in particular to the rights of the defence, a principle whose fundamental nature has been stressed on numerous occasions in the Court's decisions (see, in particular, the judgment of 9 November 1983 in Case 322/81 *Michelin* v *Commission* [1983] ECR 3461, paragraph 7).

[15] In that judgment, the Court pointed out that the rights of the defence must be observed in administrative procedures which may lead to the imposition of penalties. But it is also necessary to prevent those rights from being irremediably impaired during preliminary inquiry procedures including, in particular, investigations which may be decisive in providing evidence of the unlawful nature of conduct engaged in by undertakings for which they may be liable.

[16] Consequently, although certain rights of the defence relate only to the contentious proceedings which follow the delivery of the statement of objections, other rights, such as the right to legal representation and the privileged nature of correspondence between lawyer and client (recognised by the Court in the judgment of 18 May 1982 in Case 155/79 *AM & S* v *Commission* [1982] ECR 1575) must be respected as from the preliminary-inquiry stage.

[17] Since the applicant has also relied on the requirements stemming from the fundamental right to the inviolability of the home, it should be observed that, although the existence of such a right must be recognised in the Community legal order as a principle common to the laws of the Member States in regard to the private dwellings of natural persons, the same is not true in regard to undertakings, because there are not inconsiderable divergences between the legal systems of the Member States in regard to the nature and degree of protection afforded to business premises against intervention by the public authorities.

[18] No other inference is to be drawn from Article 8(1) of the European Convention on Human Rights which provides that: 'Everyone has the right to respect for his private and family life, his home and his correspondence'. The protective scope of that article is concerned with the development of man's personal freedom and may not therefore be extended to business premises.

Furthermore, it should be noted that there is no case law of the European Court of Human Rights on that subject.

[19] None the less, in all the legal systems of the Member States, any intervention by the public authorities in the sphere of private activities of any person, whether natural or legal, must have a legal basis and be justified on the grounds laid down by law, and, consequently, those systems provide, albeit in different forms, protection against arbitrary or disproportionate intervention. The need for such protection must be recognised as a general principle of Community law. In that regard, it should be pointed out that the Court has held that it has the power to determine whether measures of investigation taken by the Commission under the ECSC Treaty are excessive (judgment of 14 December 1962 in Joined Cases 5 to 11 and 13 to 15/62 *San Michele and Others* v *Commission* [1962] ECR 449).

These statements of principle echo the discussion of fundamental rights within EU law in Chapter 2 (p.78 above). The Court then turned to consider the nature and scope of Article 14 of Regulation 17/62 in detail. The entry into force of Regulation 1/2003 on 1 May 2004 removes the practical value of pursuing a close examination of this aspect of the judgment, but the observations regarding an inspection conducted without the co-operation of the firm under investigation merit setting out:

[32] . . . the Commission's officials may, on the basis of Article 14(6) and without the cooperation of the undertakings, search for any information necessary for the investigation with the assistance of the national authorities, which are required to afford them the assistance necessary for the performance of their duties. Although such assistance is required only if the undertaking expresses its opposition, it may also be requested as a precautionary measure, in order to overcome any opposition on the part of the undertaking.

[33] It follows from Article 14(6) that it is for each Member State to determine the conditions under which the national authorities will afford assistance to the Commission's officials. In that regard, the Member States are required to ensure that the Commission's action is effective, while respecting the general principles set out above. It follows that, within those limits, the appropriate procedural rules designed to ensure respect for undertakings' rights are those laid down by national law.

[34] Consequently, if the Commission intends, with the assistance of the national authorities, to carry out an investigation other than with the cooperation of the undertakings concerned, it is required to respect the relevant procedural guarantees laid down by national law.

[35] The Commission must make sure that the competent body under national law has all that it needs to exercise its own supervisory powers. It should be pointed out that that body, whether judicial or otherwise, cannot in this respect substitute its own assessment of the need for the investigations ordered for that of the Commission, the lawfulness of whose assessments of fact and law is subject only to review by the Court of Justice. On the other hand, it is within the powers of the national body, after satisfying itself that the decision ordering the investigation is authentic, to consider whether the measures of constraint envisaged are arbitrary or excessive having regard to the subject-matter of the investigation and to ensure that the rules of national law are complied with in the application of those measures.

The Court concluded that in the case itself there was no violation by the Commission of these requirements. Its Decision was sufficiently well-reasoned.

[41] As has been stated above, the Commission's obligation to specify the subject-matter and purpose of the investigation constitutes a fundamental guarantee of the rights of the defence of the undertakings concerned. It follows that the scope of the obligation to state the reasons on which decisions ordering investigations are based cannot be restricted on the basis of considerations concerning the effectiveness of the investigation. Although the Commission is not required to communicate to the addressee of a decision ordering an investigation all the information

at its disposal concerning the presumed infringements, or to make a precise legal analysis of those infringements, it must none the less clearly indicate the presumed facts which it intends to investigate.

[42] Although the statement of the reasons on which the contested decision is based is drawn up in very general terms which might well have been made more precise, and is therefore open to criticism in that respect, it none the less contains the essential indications prescribed by Article 14(3) of Regulation No 17. The decision at issue refers in particular to information suggesting the existence and application of agreements or concerted practices between certain producers and suppliers of PVC and polyethylene (including, but not limited to, LdPE) in the EEC, concerning prices, quantities or sales targets for those products. It states that those agreements and practices may constitute a serious infringement of Article 85(1) of the Treaty. According to Article 1 of the decision in question, the applicant 'is required to submit to an investigation concerning its possible participation' in those agreements or concerted practices and, consequently, to give the Commission's officials access to its premises and to produce or allow copies to be made for the purpose of inspection of business documents 'related to the subject-matter of the Investigation'.

[43] In those circumstances, the submission alleging that the statement of reasons is insufficient must be rejected.

Roquette Frères SA v Directeur général de la concurrence, de la consommation et de la répression des frauds (Case C-94/00)
Judgment of 22 October 2002, Court of Justice of the European Communities

The Commission adopted a decision pursuant to Article 14 of Regulation 17/62 requiring Roquette Frères to submit to an investigation. The Commission requested the French Government to take the necessary steps to ensure that, in the event of opposition by Roquette Frères, the national authorities would provide assistance of the type envisaged by Article 14 of Regulation 17/62. The competent French administrative authorities duly sought a court order providing authorization to enter the premises of Roquette Frères and seize documents. The application before the French court consisted in essence of a copy of the Commission decision and the text of the judgment in *Hoechst*. The order was granted and Roquette Frères co-operated, but then appealed against the authorization order. The company asserted that it was not open to the French judge to order entry onto private premises without first determining that there were indeed reasonable grounds for suspecting the existence of anti-competitive practices such as to justify the grant of coercive powers. This determination had not been made, nor did the Commission decision disclose any relevant information explaining its briefly stated view that the company was engaging in practices contrary to the EC Treaty. The matter was referred to the European Court under the Article 234 procedure (Chapter 7), and the Court was invited to consider the development of the law since *Hoechst*.

THE EFFECT OF GENERAL PRINCIPLES OF COMMUNITY LAW

[22] As is apparent from the Judgment making the reference, the Cour de cassation is uncertain as to the possible effect on the principles established by the Court in *Hoechst*, and hence on the answers to be given to its questions, of certain developments which have taken place in the field of the protection of human rights since delivery of the judgment in *Hoechst*.

[23] According to settled case-law, fundamental rights form an integral part of the general principles of law observance of which the Court ensures. For that purpose, the Court draws inspiration from the constitutional traditions common to the Member States and from the guidelines supplied by international treaties for the protection of human rights on which the Member States have collaborated or to which they are signatories. The ECHR has special significance in that respect (see,

in particular, *Hoechst*, paragraph 13, and Case C-274/99 P *Connolly* v *Commission* [2001] ECR I-1611, paragraph 37).

[24] As the Court has also stated, the principles established by that case-law have been reaffirmed in the preamble to the Single European Act and in Article F.2 of the Treaty on European Union (Case C-415/93 *Bosman* [1995] ECR I-4921, paragraph 79). They are now set out in Article 6(2) EU (*Connolly* v *Commission*, cited above, paragraph 38).

[25] In a different connection, the Court has likewise consistently held that, where national rules fall within the scope of Community law and reference is made to it for a preliminary ruling, it must provide all the criteria of interpretation needed by the national court to determine whether those rules are compatible with the fundamental rights the observance of which the Court ensures and which derive in particular from the ECHR (see, in particular, Case C-260/89 *ERT* [1991] ECR I-2925, paragraph 42, and Case C-159/90 *Society for the Protection of Unborn Children Ireland* [1991] ECR I-4685, paragraph 31).

[26] Since the questions referred relate in essence to the scope of the review which may be carried out by a court of a Member State where that court is called upon to act on a request by the Commission for assistance pursuant to Article 14(6) of Regulation No 17, the Court of Justice is clearly competent to provide the referring court with all the criteria of interpretation needed by that court to determine whether the applicable national rules are compatible, for the purposes of such review, with Community law, including, as the case may be, the rights established by the ECHR as general principles of law observance of which is to be ensured by the Court of Justice.

[27] It should be recalled in that regard that, in paragraph 19 of the judgment in *Hoechst*, the Court recognised that the need for protection against arbitrary or disproportionate intervention by public authorities in the sphere of the private activities of any person, whether natural or legal, constitutes a general principle of Community law.

[28] The Court has likewise stated that the competent authorities of the Member States are required to respect that general principle when they are called upon to act in response to a request for assistance made by the Commission pursuant to Article 14(6) of Regulation No 17 (see *Hoechst*, paragraphs 19 and 33).

[29] For the purposes of determining the scope of that principle in relation to the protection of business premises, regard must be had to the case-law of the European Court of Human Rights subsequent to the judgment in *Hoechst*. According to that case-law, first, the protection of the home provided for in Article 8 of the ECHR may in certain circumstances be extended to cover such premises (see, in particular, the judgment of 16 April 2002 in *Colas Est and Others v. France*, not yet published in the *Reports of Judgments and Decisions*, § 41) and, second, the right of interference established by Article 8(2) of the ECHR 'might well be more far-reaching where professional or business activities or premises were involved than would otherwise be the case' (Niemietz v. Germany, cited above, § 31).

As in *Hoechst,* so in *Roquette Frères* – the material in Chapter 2 dealing with the infusion of EU law by rules protecting fundamental rights should be recalled (p.78 above). The Court proceeded to consider the more detailed questions concerning the position of a national court called on to issue an order in support of a Commission Decision authorising an inspection of premises.

[35] According to the Court's case-law . . . the Member States, when exercising that power, are subject to a twofold obligation imposed on them by Community law. They are required to ensure that the Commission's action is effective, while respecting various general principles of Community law (*Hoechst*, paragraph 33).

[36] Precisely with a view to ensuring observance of the general principle referred to in paragraph 27 of this judgment, the Court has ruled that it is for the competent national body to consider whether the coercive measures envisaged are arbitrary or excessive having regard to the subject-matter of the investigation (*Hoechst*, paragraph 35).

[37] The Court has likewise held that the Commission is for its part obliged to make sure that the national body in question has all that it needs to perform that supervisory task and to ensure that, in the implementation of the coercive measures, the national rules are respected (*Hoechst*, paragraphs 34 and 35).

[38] The questions referred in the present case concern the scope of the review which may need to be undertaken by a national court having jurisdiction under domestic law to authorise entry onto the premises of undertakings suspected of having infringed the competition rules where that court is seised of an application pursuant to a request by the Commission for assistance made under Article 14(6) of Regulation No 17, and the nature of the information which the Commission must provide to that court to enable it to carry out such review.

The purpose of the review to be carried out by the competent national court

[39] It should be noted, as a preliminary point, that, according to the case-law of the Court, the competent national court, when considering the matter, may not substitute its own assessment of the need for the investigations ordered for that of the Commission, the lawfulness of whose assessments of fact and law is subject only to review by the Community judicature (*Hoechst*, paragraph 35).

[40] The review carried out by the competent national court, which must concern itself only with the coercive measures applied for, may not go beyond an examination, as required by Community law, to establish that the coercive measures in question are not arbitrary and that they are proportionate to the subject-matter of the investigation. Such an examination exhausts the jurisdiction of that court as regards the review of the justification of the coercive measures applied for in pursuance of a request by the Commission for assistance under Article 14(6) of Regulation No 17.

The scope of the review to be carried out by the competent national court

[41] To determine the scope of the review thus required by Community law to be carried out by the competent national court, it is necessary at the outset to recall the context surrounding the coercive measures to which that review relates.

[42] First, it should be borne in mind that the powers conferred on the Commission by Article 14(1) of Regulation No 17 are designed to enable it to perform its task of ensuring that the competition rules are applied in the common market, the function of those rules being to prevent competition from being distorted to the detriment of the public interest, individual undertakings and consumers (*Hoechst*, paragraph 25), thereby ensuring economic well-being in the Community.

[43] Second, it should be noted that Community law provides a range of guarantees.

[44] First of all, the coercive measures for which application may be made to national authorities in the implementation of Article 14(6) of Regulation No 17 are intended solely to enable Commission officials to exercise the investigatory powers vested in that institution. Those powers, which are listed in Article 14(1) of that regulation, are themselves clearly circumscribed.

[45] Thus, the scope of the Commission's investigatory powers does not extend to cover, in particular, documents of a non-business nature, that is to say, documents not relating to the market activities of the undertaking (Case 155/79 *AM & S Europe* v *Commission* [1982] ECR 1575, paragraph 16).

[46] Next, without prejudice to the guarantees under domestic law governing the implementation of coercive measures, undertakings under investigation are protected by various Community guarantees, including, in particular, the right to legal representation and the privileged nature of correspondence between lawyer and client (*AM & S Europe* v *Commission*, cited above, paragraphs 18 to 27; *Hoechst*, paragraph 16; Case 85/87 *Dow Benelux* v *Commission* [1989] ECR 3137, paragraph 27).

[47] Lastly, Article 14(3) of Regulation No 17 requires the Commission to state reasons for the decision ordering an investigation by specifying its subject-matter and purpose. As the Court has

held, this is a fundamental requirement, designed not merely to show that the proposed entry onto the premises of the undertakings concerned is justified but also to enable those undertakings to assess the scope of their duty to cooperate whilst at the same time safeguarding their rights of defence (*Hoechst*, paragraph 29).

[48] The Commission is likewise obliged to state in that decision, as precisely as possible, what it is looking for and the matters to which the investigation must relate (Case 136/79 *National Panasonic* v *Commission* [1980] ECR 2033, paragraphs 26 and 27). As the Court has held, that requirement is intended to protect the rights of defence of the undertakings concerned, which would be seriously compromised if the Commission could rely on evidence against undertakings which was obtained during an investigation but was not related to the subject-matter or purpose thereof (*Dow Benelux* v *Commission*, cited above, paragraph 18).

[49] Third, an undertaking against which the Commission has ordered an investigation may bring an action against that decision before the Community judicature under the fourth paragraph of Article 173 of the EC Treaty (now, after amendment, the fourth paragraph of Article 230 EC). If the decision in question were annulled by the Community judicature, the Commission would in that event be prevented from using, for the purposes of proceeding in respect of an infringement of the Community competition rules, any documents or evidence which it might have obtained in the course of that investigation, as otherwise the decision on the infringement might, in so far as it was based on such evidence, be annulled by the Community judicature (see the orders of 26 March 1987 in Case 46/87R *Hoechst* v *Commission* [1987] ECR 1549, paragraph 34, and of 28 October 1987 in Case 85/87R *Dow Chemical Nederland* v *Commission* [1987] ECR 4367, paragraph 17).

[50] Clearly, the existence of the power of judicial review so conferred on the Community judicature and the detailed rules, particularly those referred to in paragraphs 43 to 48 above, governing the exercise by the Commission of its investigatory powers, help to protect undertakings against arbitrary measures and to keep such measures within the limits of what is necessary in order to pursue the legitimate interests specified in paragraph 42 of this judgment.

[51] Fourth, as emerges from paragraphs 35 and 39 of this judgment, the competent national court is required to ensure that the Commission's action is effective and to refrain from substituting its own assessment of the need for the investigations ordered for that of the Commission, the lawfulness of whose assessments of fact and law may be reviewed only by the Community judicature.

[52] Although the national court with jurisdiction to authorise coercive measures must take into account the particular context in which its jurisdiction has been invoked, as well as the considerations set out in paragraphs 42 to 51 above, those requirements cannot prevent or absolve it from performing its obligation to ensure, in the specific circumstances of each individual case, that the coercive measure envisaged is not arbitrary or disproportionate to the subject-matter of the investigation ordered (see, by analogy, Eur. Court HR, Funke v. France judgment of 25 February 1993, Series A No 256-A, § 55, Camenzind v. Switzerland judgment of 16 December 1997, *Reports of Judgments and Decisions* 1997-VIII, § 45, and in *Colas Est and Others v. France*, cited above, § 47).

[53] In the light of the foregoing considerations, it is necessary to determine more precisely what is involved in carrying out such a review and the nature of the information which the national court in question must have at its disposal. A distinction must be drawn in that regard between review to ensure that the coercive measures envisaged are not arbitrary and review of their proportionality to the subject-matter of the investigation.

Review to ensure that the coercive measures are not arbitrary and the information which the Commission may be required to provide to that end

[54] First, when conducting its review to ensure that there is nothing arbitrary about a coercive measure designed to permit implementation of an investigation ordered by the Commission, the competent national court is required, in essence, to satisfy itself that there exist reasonable grounds for suspecting an infringement of the competition rules by the undertaking concerned.

[55] It is true that there is no fundamental difference between that review and the review which the

Community judicature may be called upon to carry out for the purposes of ensuring that the investigation decision itself is in no way arbitrary, that is to say, that it has not been adopted in the absence of facts capable of justifying the investigation (Joined Cases 97/87 to 99/87 *Dow Chemical Ibérica and Others* v *Commission* [1989] ECR 3165, paragraph 52). It must be borne in mind in that regard that the investigations carried out by the Commission are intended to enable it to gather the necessary documentary evidence to check the actual existence and scope of a given factual and legal situation concerning which the Commission already possesses certain information (*National Panasonic* v *Commission*, cited above, paragraphs 13 and 21).

[56] However, that similarity in the nature of the review carried out by the Community judicature and that undertaken by the competent national body must not obscure the distinction between the objectives which those two types of review respectively seek to attain.

[57] The investigatory powers conferred on the Commission by Article 14(1) of Regulation No 17 are limited to authorising its officials to enter such premises as they choose and to have shown to them the documents they request and the contents of any piece of furniture which they indicate (*Hoechst*, paragraph 31).

[58] For their part, the coercive measures falling within the competence of the national authorities entail the power to gain access to premises or furniture by force or to oblige the staff of the undertaking to give them such access, and to carry out searches without the permission of the management of the undertaking (*Hoechst*, paragraph 31).

[59] Having regard to the invasion of privacy which they entail, recourse to such coercive measures necessitates the ability of the competent national body autonomously to satisfy itself that they are not arbitrary.

[60] In particular, such an examination of possible arbitrariness cannot be precluded on the ground that, in satisfying itself as to the existence of reasonable grounds for suspecting an infringement of the competition rules, the competent national body might, in accordance with paragraph 35 of the judgment in *Hoechst*, substitute its own assessment of the need for the investigations ordered for that of the Commission and call in question the latter's assessments of fact and law.

[61] It follows that, for the purposes of enabling the competent national court to satisfy itself that the coercive measures sought are not arbitrary, the Commission is required to provide that court with explanations showing, in a properly substantiated manner, that the Commission is in possession of information and evidence providing reasonable grounds for suspecting infringement of the competition rules by the undertaking concerned.

[62] On the other hand, the competent national court may not demand that it be provided with the information and evidence in the Commission's file on which the latter's suspicions are based.

[63] In that regard, it is necessary to take into consideration the obligation of the Member States, pointed out in paragraph 35 of this judgment, to ensure that the Commission's action is effective.

[64] First, as the Commission and the German and United Kingdom Governments have rightly observed, the Commission's ability to guarantee the anonymity of certain of its sources of information is of crucial importance with a view to ensuring the effective prevention of prohibited anti-competitive practices.

[65] Clearly, if the Commission were obliged to send to the various national competition authorities factual information and evidence revealing the identity of its sources of information, or enabling that identity to be deduced, that might well increase the risks to informants of disclosure of their identity to third parties, in view, particularly, of the procedural requirements of national law.

[66] Second, it must also be borne in mind that the physical transmission to the competent national authorities of the various items of factual information and evidence held in the Commission's file could give rise to other risks as regards the effectiveness of the action taken by the Community,

especially in cases involving parallel investigations to be carried out simultaneously in more than one Member State. Account must be taken of the uncertainties and delays that may affect such transmission and the different procedural rules with which they may have to comply under the legal systems of the Member States concerned, as well as the time which the authorities in question may need to consider potentially complex and voluminous documents.

[67] In the context of the allocation of competences in terms of Article 234 EC, it is in principle for the competent national court to assess whether, in a given case, the explanations referred to in paragraph 61 of this judgment have been properly provided and to carry out, on that basis, the review which it is required to undertake under Community law. In addition, where the national court is called upon to rule on a request for assistance submitted by the Commission pursuant to Article 14(6) of Regulation No 17, it must pay even greater heed to that allocation of competences, inasmuch as a reference for a preliminary ruling – unless made, as in the present case, after the investigations have been carried out – is apt to delay the decision of that court and may bring the request for assistance into the public domain, thereby creating a risk that the Commission's action may be paralysed and that any subsequent investigation may serve no useful purpose.

[68] In the light of those considerations, the Court of Justice, when called upon to give a preliminary ruling, can provide the referring court with all the criteria of interpretation within the scope of Community law which may enable that court to determine the case before it.

[69] As regards the main proceedings in the present case, it is clear from the reasons contained in the investigation decision of 10 September 1998, as reiterated in paragraph 11 of this judgment, that the Commission gave a very precise account of the suspicions harboured by it with regard to Roquette Frères and the other participants in the suspected cartel, providing detailed information as to the holding of regular secret meetings and as to what was discussed and agreed at those meetings.

[70] Although the Commission has not indicated the nature of the evidence on which its suspicions are based, such as a complaint, testimony or documents exchanged between the participants in the suspected cartel, the mere fact that no such indication is given cannot suffice to cast doubt on the existence of reasonable grounds for those suspicions where, as in the main proceedings, the detailed account of the information held by the Commission concerning the specific subject-matter of the suspected cartel is such as to enable the competent national court to establish a firm basis for its conclusion that the Commission does indeed possess such evidence.

Review of the proportionality of the coercive measures to the subject-matter of the investigation and the information which the Commission may be required to provide to that end

[71] Second, as regards the need to verify that the coercive measures are proportionate to the subject-matter of the investigation ordered by the Commission, it should be noted that this involves establishing that such measures are appropriate to ensure that the investigation can be carried out.

[72] In that regard, it must be borne in mind, in particular, that Article 14(3) of Regulation No 17 requires the undertakings concerned to submit to investigations ordered by decision of the Commission and that Article 14(6) provides for Member States to afford assistance to the officials authorised by the Commission only in the event that an undertaking opposes such an investigation.

[73] It is true that the Court has acknowledged that the assistance may be requested as a precautionary measure, in order to overcome any opposition on the part of the undertaking (*Hoechst*, paragraph 32).

[74] However, coercive measures may be so requested on a precautionary basis only in so far as there are grounds for apprehending opposition to the investigation and/or attempts at concealing or disposing of evidence in the event that an investigation ordered pursuant to Article 14(3) of Regulation No 17 is notified to the undertaking concerned.

[75] Consequently, it is for the Commission to provide the competent national court with the explanations needed by that court to satisfy itself that, if the Commission were unable to obtain, as

a precautionary measure, the requisite assistance in order to overcome any opposition on the part of the undertaking, it would be impossible, or very difficult, to establish the facts amounting to the infringement.

[76] In addition, review of the proportionality of the coercive measures envisaged to the subject-matter of the investigation involves establishing that such measures do not constitute, in relation to the aim pursued by the investigation in question, a disproportionate and intolerable interference (Case C-331/88 *Fedesa and Others* [1990] ECR I-4023, paragraph 13; Joined Cases C-143/88 and C-92/89 *Zuckerfabrik Süderdithmarschen and Zuckerfabrik Soest* [1991] ECR I-415, paragraph 73; Case C-233/94 *Germany* v *Parliament and Council* [1997] ECR I-2405, paragraph 57; and Case C-200/96 *Metronome Musik* [1998] ECR I-1953, paragraphs 21 and 26).

[77] In that regard, it should certainly be kept in view that, in relation to the proportionality of the investigation measure itself, the Court has held that the Commission's choice between an investigation by straightforward authorisation and an investigation ordered by a decision does not depend on matters such as the particular seriousness of the situation, extreme urgency or the need for absolute discretion, but rather on the need for an appropriate inquiry, having regard to the special features of the case. The Court has concluded in that regard that, where an investigation decision is solely intended to enable the Commission to gather the information needed to assess whether the Treaty has been infringed, such a decision is not contrary to the principle of proportionality (*National Panasonic* v *Commission*, cited above, paragraphs 28 to 30).

[78] Similarly, it is in principle for the Commission to decide whether a particular item of information is necessary to enable it to bring to light an infringement of the competition rules (*AM & S Europe* v *Commission*, paragraph 17; Case 374/87 *Orkem* v *Commission* [1989] ECR 3283, paragraph 15). Even if it already has evidence, or indeed proof, of the existence of an infringement, the Commission may legitimately take the view that it is necessary to order further investigations enabling it to better define the scope of the infringement, to determine its duration or to identify the circle of undertakings involved (see to that effect, in relation to requests for additional information, *Orkem* v *Commission*, cited above, paragraph 15).

[79] However, if the scope of the review to be carried out by the competent national court is to be meaningful, and if proper account is to be taken of the invasion of privacy that recourse to law-enforcement authorities entails, it must be acknowledged, with regard to such a measure, that the national authority cannot carry out its review of proportionality without regard to factors such as the seriousness of the suspected infringement, the nature of the involvement of the undertaking concerned or the importance of the evidence sought.

[80] Consequently, it must be open to the competent national court to refuse to grant the coercive measures applied for where the suspected impairment of competition is so minimal, the extent of the likely involvement of the undertaking concerned so limited, or the evidence sought so peripheral, that the intervention in the sphere of the private activities of a legal person which a search using law-enforcement authorities entails necessarily appears manifestly disproportionate and intolerable in the light of the objectives pursued by the investigation.

[81] It follows that, in order for the competent national court to be able to carry out the review of proportionality which it is required to undertake, the Commission must in principle inform that court of the essential features of the suspected infringement, so as to enable it to assess their seriousness, by indicating the market thought to be affected, the nature of the suspected restrictions of competition and the supposed degree of involvement of the undertaking concerned.

[82] On the other hand, as the Court has previously held in relation to the statement of reasons for investigation decisions themselves, it is not indispensable that the information communicated should precisely define the relevant market, set out the exact legal nature of the presumed infringements or indicate the period during which those infringements were committed (*Dow Benelux* v *Commission*, cited above, paragraph 10).

[83] The Commission is also obliged to indicate as precisely as possible the evidence sought and the

matters to which the investigation must relate (*National Panasonic* v *Commission*, cited above, paragraphs 26 and 27), as well as the powers conferred on the Community investigators.

[84] However, the Commission cannot be required to limit its investigation to requesting the production of documents or files which it is able to identify precisely in advance. That would, in effect, render nugatory its right of access to such documents or files. On the contrary, as the Court has held, such a right implies the power to search for various items of information which are not already known or fully identified (*Hoechst*, paragraph 27).

[85] As stated in paragraph 67 above, it is in principle for the competent national court to assess whether, in a given case, the information referred to in paragraphs 75, 81 and 83 above has been properly provided by the Commission and to carry out, on that basis, the review which it is required to undertake under Community law.

[86] However, as is pointed out in paragraph 68 above, the Court of Justice is competent to provide all such criteria of interpretation within the scope of Community law as may enable the referring court to determine the case before it.

[87] As regards the main proceedings in the present case, it is clear from the grounds of the investigation decision of 10 September 1998, as reiterated in paragraph 11 above, that the Commission gave a sufficient account of the features of the suspected cartel, indicated its seriousness and stated that Roquette Frères had participated in the meetings described.

[88] Likewise, the Commission stated, first, that Roquette Frères might hold information which the Commission needed in order to pursue its inquiries. Second, it stated that the very nature of the suspected agreements suggested that they were being implemented by secret means, so that an investigation was the most appropriate way of gathering evidence of their existence, and that it was necessary to compel the undertaking, by a decision, to submit to an investigation pursuant to Article 14(3) of Regulation No 17. Those statements are, it would seem, such as to enable the competent national court to assess the need to grant, as a precautionary measure, the authorisation sought.

[89] As to the subject-matter of the investigations to be carried out, it is apparent from the operative part and the grounds of the investigation decision of 10 September 1998, as reiterated in paragraphs 10 and 11 above respectively, that the Commission was concerned to discover all the facts concerning the suspected agreements and/or concerted practices and to establish whether Roquette Frères had participated therein. To that end, the decision orders that undertaking to give the officials authorised by the Commission access to its premises, to produce the books and other business records required by those officials, to allow them to inspect and copy those books and records and to provide the officials in question with any oral explanations they may request in connection with the subject-matter of the investigation. Those statements adequately indicate what the Commission was looking for and the powers to which recourse could be had for that purpose.

The approach to be adopted by the competent national court and by the Commission in the event that the information communicated by the latter proves to be insufficient

[90] Where a national court having jurisdiction under domestic law to authorise entry onto premises considers that the information communicated by the Commission does not fulfil the requirements set out in paragraphs 75, 81 and 83 above, it cannot simply dismiss the application brought before it.

[91] In such circumstances, the court in question and the Commission are required, in compliance with the obligation to cooperate in good faith referred to in paragraphs 30 to 32 above, to collaborate with each other with a view to overcoming the problems arising and to cooperate in the implementation of the investigation decision ordered by the Commission (see, by analogy, Case 52/84 *Commission* v *Belgium* [1986] ECR 89, paragraph 16, and Case C-217/88 *Commission* v *Germany* [1990] ECR I-2879, paragraph 33).

[92] In order to comply fully with that obligation and to assist, as it must, in ensuring that the

Commission's action is effective, the competent national court is therefore required as rapidly as possible to inform the Commission, or the national authority which has brought the latter's request before it, of the difficulties encountered, where necessary by asking for the additional information needed to enable it to carry out the review which it is to undertake. In such circumstances, that court must pay particular heed to the need for coordination, expedition and discretion needing to be fulfilled in order to ensure the effectiveness of parallel investigations as referred to in paragraph 66 of this judgment.

[93] Similarly, the Commission's duty to cooperate in good faith is of particular importance *vis-à-vis* the judicial authorities of a Member State who are responsible for ensuring that Community law is applied and respected in the national legal system (order in *Zwartfeld*, cited above, paragraph 18). The Commission must therefore provide, with the minimum of delay, any additional information thus requested by the competent national court which is such as to satisfy the requirements set out in paragraph 90 of this judgment.

[94] Not until it is provided with such clarifications, if any, or the Commission fails to take any practical steps in response to its request, may the competent national court refuse to grant the assistance sought where it cannot be concluded, in the light of the information available to that court, that the coercive measures envisaged are not arbitrary or disproportionate to the subject-matter of those measures.

The manner in which information can be brought to the knowledge of the competent national court

[95] As to the manner in which the requisite information can be brought to the knowledge of the competent national court, it should be observed that the main reason for which the referring court has asked the Court of Justice to give a ruling in relation to the adequacy of the statement of reasons for the investigation decision of 10 September 1998 is that, in the main proceedings, the only material submitted for assessment to the competent national court is the text of that decision.

[96] However, as far as a national court is concerned, the relevance of the statement of reasons contained in such an investigation decision is to enable that court to satisfy itself that the coercive measure sought is neither arbitrary nor disproportionate to the subject-matter of the investigation. Review of the adequacy of the reasons given for any Commission decision ordering an investigation, as defined in Article 14(3) of Regulation No 17, falls within the exclusive competence of the Community judicature.

[97] Whilst the matters which must feature in the investigation decision itself, particularly under Article 14(3) of Regulation No 17, correspond in part to the information which must be communicated to the competent national court so as to enable that court to carry out its review, that information may also emanate from other sources.

[98] In that regard, Community law does not require information communicated to the competent national court to be in any particular form. Since the purpose is to enable that court to carry out the review which it is required to undertake, such information may be contained either in the investigation decision itself or in the request made to the national authorities under Article 14(6) of Regulation No 17, or indeed in an answer – even given orally – to a question put by that court.

[99] Having regard to all the foregoing considerations, the answers to be given to the questions referred must be as follows:

— In accordance with the general principle of Community law affording protection against arbitrary or disproportionate intervention by public authorities in the sphere of the private activities of any person, whether natural or legal, a national court having jurisdiction under domestic law to authorise entry upon and seizures at the premises of undertakings suspected of having infringed the competition rules is required to verify that the coercive measures sought in pursuance of a request by the Commission for assistance under Article 14(6) of

Regulation No 17 are not arbitrary or disproportionate to the subject-matter of the investigation ordered. Without prejudice to any rules of domestic law governing the implementation of coercive measures, Community law precludes review by the national court of the justification of those measures beyond what is required by the foregoing general principle.

— Community law requires the Commission to ensure that the national court in question has at its disposal all the information which it needs in order to carry out the review which it is required to undertake. In that regard, the information supplied by the Commission must in principle include:

— a description of the essential features of the suspected infringement, that is to say, at the very least, an indication of the market thought to be affected and of the nature of the suspected restrictions of competition;

— explanations concerning the manner in which the undertaking at which the coercive measures are aimed is thought to be involved in the infringement in question;

— detailed explanations showing that the Commission possesses solid factual information and evidence providing grounds for suspecting such infringement on the part of the undertaking concerned;

— as precise as possible an indication of the evidence sought, of the matters to which the investigation must relate and of the powers conferred on the Community investigators; and

— in the event that the assistance of the national authorities is requested by the Commission as a precautionary measure, in order to overcome any opposition on the part of the undertaking concerned, explanations enabling the national court to satisfy itself that, if authorisation for the coercive measures were not granted on precautionary grounds, it would be impossible, or very difficult, to establish the facts amounting to the infringement.

— On the other hand, the national court may not demand that it be provided with the evidence in the Commission's file on which the latter's suspicions are based.

— Where the national court considers that the information communicated by the Commission does not fulfil the requirements set out above, it cannot, without violating Article 14(6) of Regulation No 17 and Article 5 of the Treaty, simply dismiss the application brought before it. In such circumstances, it is required as rapidly as possible to inform the Commission, or the national authority which has brought the latter's request before it, of the difficulties encountered, where necessary by asking for any clarification which it may need in order to carry out the review which it is to undertake. Not until any such clarification is forthcoming, or the Commission fails to take any practical steps in response to its request, may the national court refuse to grant the assistance sought on the ground that, in the light of the information available to it, it is unable to hold that the coercive measures envisaged are not arbitrary or disproportionate to the subject-matter of those measures.

— The information to be provided by the Commission to the national court may be contained either in the investigation decision itself or in the request made to the national authorities under Article 14(6) of Regulation No 17, or indeed in an answer – even given orally – to a question put by that court.

NOTE

In formal terms this judgment is not relevant to the interpretation of Articles 20 and 21 of Regulation 1/2003. It pre-dates it. But the textual connections are impossible to miss. The judgment should therefore be taken to provide a helpful insight into the way in which Articles 20 and 21 of Regulation 1/2003 are likely to be interpreted and applied.

■ **QUESTION**

How successful is the Court's balance between the interests of the Commission and of the firm under investigation?

NOTE

Important secondary legislation amplifies the procedural protection to which firms under scrutiny are entitled. In particular Regulation 2842/98 governing hearings deserves attention.

COMMISSION REGULATION (EC) NO 2842/98 OF 22 DECEMBER 1998 ON THE HEARING OF PARTIES IN CERTAIN PROCEEDINGS UNDER ARTICLES 85 AND 86 [NOW 81 AND 82] OF THE EC TREATY

[1998] OJ L354/18

CHAPTER 1: SCOPE

Article 1

This Regulation shall apply to the hearing of parties under Article 19(1) and (2) of Regulation No 17, Article 26(1) and (2) of Regulation (EEC) No 1017/68, Article 23(1) and (2) of Regulation (EEC) No 4056/86 and Article 16(1) and (2) of Regulation (EEC) No 3975/87.

CHAPTER II: HEARING OF PARTIES TO WHICH THE COMMISSION HAS ADDRESSED OBJECTIONS

Article 2

1. The Commission shall hear the parties to which it has addressed objections before consulting the appropriate Advisory Committee under Article 10(3) of Regulation No 17, Article 16(3) of Regulation (EEC) No 1017/68, Article 15(3) of Regulation (EEC) No 4056/86 or Article 8(3) of Regulation (EEC) No 3975/87.

2. The Commission shall in its decisions deal only with objections in respect of which the parties have been afforded the opportunity of making their views known.

Article 3

1. The Commission shall inform the parties in writing of the objections raised against them. The objections shall be notified to each of them or to a duly appointed agent.

2. The Commission may inform the parties by giving notice in the Official Journal of the European Communities, if from the circumstances of the case this appears appropriate, in particular where notice is to be given to a number of undertakings but no joint agent has been appointed. The notice shall have regard to the legitimate interests of the undertakings in the protection of their business secrets and other confidential information.

3. A fine or a periodic penalty payment may be imposed on a party only if the objections have been notified in the manner provided for in paragraph 1.

4. The Commission shall, when giving notice of objections, set a date by which the parties may inform it in writing of their views.

5. The Commission shall set a date by which the parties may indicate any parts of the objections which in their view contain business secrets or other confidential material. If they do not do so by that date, the Commission may assume that the objections do not contain such information.

Article 4

1. Parties which wish to make known their views on the objections raised against them shall do so in writing and by the date referred to in Article 3(4). The Commission shall not be obliged to take into account written comments received after that date.

2. The parties may in their written comments set out all matters relevant to their defence. They may attach any relevant documents as proof of the facts set out and may also propose that the Commission hear persons who may corroborate those facts.

Article 5

The Commission shall afford to parties against which objections have been raised the opportunity to develop their arguments at an oral hearing, if they so request in their written comments.

CHAPTER III: HEARING OF APPLICANTS AND COMPLAINANTS

Article 6

Where the Commission, having received an application made under Article 3(2) of Regulation No 17 or a complaint made under Article 10 of Regulation (EEC) No 1017/68, Article 10 of Regulation

(EEC) No 4056/86 or Article 3(1) of Regulation (EEC) No 3975/87, considers that on the basis of the information in its possession there are insufficient grounds for granting the application or acting on the complaint, it shall inform the applicant or complainant of its reasons and set a date by which the applicant or complainant may make known its views in writing.

Article 7

Where the Commission raises objections relating to an issue in respect of which it has received an application on a complaint as referred to in Article 6, it shall provide an applicant or complainant with a copy of the non-confidential version of the objections and set a date by which the applicant or complainant may make known its views in writing.

Article 8

The Commission may, where appropriate, afford to applicants and complainants the opportunity of orally expressing their views, if they so request in their written comments.

CHAPTER IV: HEARING OF OTHER THIRD PARTIES

Article 9

1. If parties other than those referred to in Chapters II and III apply to be heard and show a sufficient interest, the Commission shall inform them in writing of the nature and subject matter of the procedure and shall set a date by which they may make known their views in writing.

2. The Commission may, where appropriate, invite parties referred to in paragraph 1 to develop their arguments at the oral hearing of the parties against which objections have been raised, if they so request in their written comments.

3. The Commission may afford to any other third parties the opportunity of orally expressing their views.

CHAPTER V: GENERAL PROVISIONS

Article 10

Hearings shall be conducted by the Hearing Officer.

Article 11

1. The Commission shall invite the persons to be heard to attend the oral hearing on such date as it shall appoint.

2. The Commission shall invite the competent authorities of the Member States to take part in the oral hearing.

Article 12

1. Persons invited to attend shall either appear in person or be represented by legal representatives or by representatives authorised by their constitution as appropriate. Undertakings and associations of undertakings may be represented by a duly authorised agent appointed from among their permanent staff.

2. Persons heard by the Commission may be assisted by their legal advisers or other qualified persons admitted by the Hearing Officer.

3. Oral hearings shall not be public. Each person shall be heard separately or in the presence of other persons invited to attend. In the latter case, regard shall be had to the legitimate interest of the undertakings in the protection of their business secrets and other confidential information.

4. The statements made by each person heard shall be recorded on tape. The recording shall be made available to such persons on request, by means of a copy from which business secrets and other confidential information shall be deleted.

Article 13

1. Information, including documents, shall not be communicated or made accessible in so far as it contains business secrets of any party, including the parties to which the Commission has

addressed objections, applicants and complainants and other third parties, or other confidential information or where internal documents of the authorities are concerned. The Commission shall make appropriate arrangements for allowing access to the file, taking due account of the need to protect business secrets, internal Commission documents and other confidential information.

2. Any party which makes known its views under the provisions of this Regulation shall clearly identify any material which it considers to be confidential, giving reasons, and provide a separate non-confidential version by the date set by the Commission. If it does not do so by the set date, the Commission may assume that the submission does not contain such material.

Article 14

In setting the dates provided for in Articles 3(4), 6, 7 and 9(1), the Commission shall have regard both to the time required for preparation of the submission and to the urgency of the case. The time allowed in each case shall be at least two weeks; it may be extended.

CHAPTER VI: FINAL PROVISIONS

Article 15

1. Regulations No 99/63/EEC and (EEC) No 1630/69 are repealed.
    2. Sections II of Regulations (EEC) No 4260/88 and (EEC) No 4261/88 are deleted.

Article 16

This Regulation shall enter into force on 1 February 1999.

This Regulation shall be binding in its entirety and directly applicable in all Member States.

NOTE
Chapter V of Regulation 2842/98 refers to the Hearing Officer. That officer's role is amplified by Commission Decision 2001/462 on the terms of reference of hearing officers in certain competition proceedings ([2001] OJ L162/21).

Having obtained the necessary information, and respected the requirements of Regulation 2842/98, the Commission is in a position to conclude the matter. In Regulation 1/2003 Chapter III, *Commission Decisions* (p.574 above), and Chapter VI, *Penalties* (p.580 above), are of particular relevance.

Article 23 of Regulation 1/2003 confers the power to fine on the Commission. As a deterrent, this power is a key element in an effective system. Hunting secret cartels is a difficult job, and the Commission uses the lure of partial or even total immunity from fines to encourage participants to own up. The latest version of the Commission's notice on immunity from fines and reduction of fines in cartel cases was published in 2002 ([2002] OJ C45/3). The use of explanatory Notices conforms with practice visible elsewhere in the competition field, e.g., in relation to market definition (p.551).

The structure explained above is based on a striking concentration of function in the hands of the Commission in Brussels. The next case is a decision of the European Commission on Human Rights – *it is outside the formal sphere of Community law*. However, not only does it provide an academically interesting analogy, it is also likely to come to exert practical influence on the Community system.

Société Stenuit v *France*
Judgment of 27 February 1992, Series A No 232-A, European Commission on Human Rights

A firm party to an alleged cartel was fined 50,000 FF by the Minister of Economic and Financial Affairs under French competition law. The fine was characterized under French law as administrative rather than criminal. A complaint was made to the European Commission on Human Rights of violation of Article 6(1) of the European Convention. The relevant section reads:

In the determination of his civil rights and obligations or of any criminal charge against him, everyone is entitled to a fair and public hearing within a reasonable time by an independent and impartial tribunal established by law.

The Human Rights Commission decided the fine was of a criminal nature and considered that there was a violation of Article 6(1) in the absence of a separate tribunal which determined the criminal charge (the Conseil d'Etat's review function was in this respect considered inadequate). The reasoning which led to the conclusion that this was a criminal matter was as follows:

62. The Commission observes in this connection that the aim pursued by the impugned provisions of the Order of 30 June 1945 was to maintain free competition within the French market. The Order thus affected the general interests of society normally protected by criminal law (application no 7341/76, case of *Eggs* v *Switzerland*, Commission's report of 4 March 1978, Decisions and Reports (DR) no 15, 35, § 79). The penalties imposed by the Minister were measures directed against firms or corporate bodies which had committed acts constituting '*infractions*'. The Commission further points out that the Minister could refer the case to the prosecuting authorities with a view to their instituting criminal proceedings against the '*contrevenant*'. Furthermore, after transmitting the file to the prosecuting authorities, the Minister could no longer impose a fine. A fine was therefore a substitute for the penalty the criminal courts might have imposed if the case had been referred to the prosecuting authorities.

63. With regard to the nature and severity of the penalty to which those responsible for infringements made themselves liable, the Commission observes first of all that 'according to the ordinary meaning of the terms, there generally come within the ambit of the criminal law offences that make their perpetrator liable to penalties intended [. . .] to be deterrent and usually consisting of fines and of measures depriving the person of his liberty' (Eur. Court H. R., above-mentioned *Oztürk* judgment, p.20, § 53 *Oztürk* v *Germany*, judgment of 21 February 1984, Series A no 73). However, that does not imply that every penalty involving deprivation of liberty or every fine necessarily belongs to the criminal law (Eur. Court H. R., above-mentioned *Engel* judgment, p.36, § 85 *Engel and others* v *The Netherlands*, judgment of 8 June 1976, Series A no 22).

64. In the present case the penalty imposed by the Minister was a fine of 50,000 FRF, a sum which, in itself, is not negligible. But it is above all the fact that the maximum fine, i.e., the penalty to which those responsible for infringements made themselves liable, was 5% of the annual turnover for a firm and 5,000,000 FRF for other '*contrevenants*' (see paragraph 32 of the report) which shows quite clearly that the penalty in question was intended to be deterrent.

65. In the Commission's view the criminal aspect of the case for the purposes of the Convention is revealed unambiguously by the combination of concordant factors noted above. The Commission points out that in certain circumstances a charge could, for the purposes of Article 6 § 1 of the Convention, be defined as the official notification given to an individual by the competent authority, of an allegation that he has committed a criminal offence (see paragraph 55 of the Commission's opinion). This had already taken place in the present case when the Minister consulted the Competition Commission and when the latter recommended that the applicant be fined 100,000 FRF. In any case, the Minister's decision to impose a fine constituted, for the purposes of the Convention, determination of a criminal charge, and the fine had all the aspects of a criminal penalty.

66. However, the Government seem to raise an objection, albeit indirectly, by maintaining that corporate bodies cannot be liable under criminal law. The Commission observes in the first place that the Convention contains no provision to that effect. It further observes that the question of the criminal liability of corporate bodies is dealt with in different ways in the various legal systems of the member countries of the Council of Europe. It points out that French law establishes exceptions to the principle that corporate bodies may not be held criminally liable. The Court of Cassation

has recognised the existence of such exceptions where they are prescribed by law (see paragraph 47 of the report). Lastly, the Commission notes that there is no doubt that the penalty imposed in this case was imposed on a corporate body. The Commission therefore takes the view that in a situation such as the one under consideration in this case, it is possible under French law for a corporate body to face a criminal charge. Consequently, the question which arises under the Convention is whether the guarantees it confers on natural persons may or may not be afforded to corporate bodies which suffer a violation of its provisions. In this connection the Commission points out that the institutions of the Convention have already recognised in the past that corporate bodies can exercise a number of rights usually enjoyed by natural persons, such as the right to freedom of expression (Eur. Court H. R., *Sunday Times* v *the United Kingdom* judgment of 26 April 1979, Series A no 30; application no 13166/86, *Times Newspapers Ltd and Andrew Neil* v *the United Kingdom*. Commission's report of 12 July 1990) or the rights set forth in Article 9 of the Convention (application no 8118/77, decision of 19 March 1981, DR 25, pp.105–117). Lastly, the Commission points out that the institutions of the Convention have consistently emphasised the importance of Article 6 of the Convention, which reflects 'the fundamental principle of the rule of law' (Eur. Court H. R., above-mentioned *Sunday Times* judgment, p.34. n 55) and that a restrictive interpretation of that article 'would not be consonant with the object and purpose of the provision' (Eur. Court H. R., *De Cubber* v *Belgium* judgment of 26 October 1984, Series A no 86, p.16, n 30). In the light of the above considerations, the Commission considers that a corporate body can claim the protection of Article 6 of the Convention when a 'criminal charge' has been made against it.

67. In conclusion, Article 6 was applicable in this case.

NOTE

A friendly settlement was reached before the European Court of Human Rights came to rule on the matter. The case was accordingly struck from the list.

■ **QUESTION**

In Community law, Article 23(5) of Regulation 1/2003 denies the criminal nature of fining decisions taken by the Commission in Brussels. But could the Community's competition law procedures be classified as criminal on the reasoning offered in *Société Stenuit* by the Human Rights Commission? If the answer is 'Yes', would the Community's structure conform to Article 6(1) of the Convention? If the answer to that second question is 'No', how might a challenge to the Community system's compatibility with the Convention be brought (*cf* pp.78–88 above)?

So much for enforcement by the Commission. Enforcement at two levels is a familiar feature of the Community legal order. Action may be taken both by the Commission at Community level and by private individuals relying on the direct effect of Community law before national courts. The competition rules are in this respect no different from provisions such as Articles 25, 28, and 90 considered elsewhere in this book. And, on the entry into force of Regulation 1/2003 on 1 May 2004, the alignment is still closer. The pre-existing exclusive competence to grant exemption under Article 81(3) vested in the Commission is lifted, and national competition authorities and courts are empowered to apply Article 81(3) as well as Articles 81(1), 81(2), and 82. In the wake of this 'decentralization' of enforcement practice much of the material in Part 1 of this book dealing with patterns of enforcement is largely applicable also to the competition rules. Domestic enforcement serves as a hugely important supplement to the power of the Commission to select the cases to which it will devote its own scarce enforcement resources.

In this vein, the rules of State liability discussed in Chapter 6 deserve consideration in the context of competition law. A victim of anti-competitive conduct may be interested not merely in putting an end to the practice but in claiming compensation for loss suffered. Article 6 of Regulation 1/2003 provides simply that 'National courts shall have the power to apply Articles 81 and 82 of the Treaty'. The question of remedies is not addressed. But the case law is already more ambitious. In the preliminary reference in *H. Banks & Co. Ltd* v *British Coal Corporation* (Case C-128/92) [1994] ECR I-1209 Advocate-General Van Gerven had analysed *Francovich* liability as part of the general system of Community law and, in pursuit of effective protection of Community law rights against both public and private sector defendants, he favoured its application to violations by private parties. However, the Court, in a cautious ruling carefully confined to the Coal and Steel Treaty, held that an action for damages before a national court could not be pursued in the absence of a Commission finding of violation. But the next case revealed the Court's approach to the availability of compensation for breach of the competition rules.

Courage Ltd v *Bernard Crehan* (Case C-453/99)
[2001] ECR I-6297, Court of Justice of the European Communities

Crehan was not a third-party victim of an anti-competitive practice. He was party to an agreement that was susceptible to challenge as a violation of Article 81. He was a tenant of a public house who had been sued for money due under a contract obliging him to buy his beer from Courage, the brewer. His defence to the claim was that the 'beer tie' violated Article 81, that he was therefore not liable to pay and he also counter-claimed for damages for loss suffered as a result of the illegality. The English courts were minded to treat him as a participant in an anti-competitive practice, not a victim of one, and to deny in principle his claim for compensation. A preliminary reference was made to Luxembourg, asking for guidance on the impact of EC law.

[19] It should be borne in mind, first of all, that the Treaty has created its own legal order, which is integrated into the legal systems of the Member States and which their courts are bound to apply. The subjects of that legal order are not only the Member States but also their nationals. Just as it imposes burdens on individuals, Community law is also intended to give rise to rights which become part of their legal assets. Those rights arise not only where they are expressly granted by the Treaty but also by virtue of obligations which the Treaty imposes in a clearly defined manner both on individuals and on the Member States and the Community institutions (see the judgments in Case 26/62 *Van Gend en Loos* [1963] ECR 1, Case 6/64 *Costa* [1964] ECR 585 and Joined Cases C-6/90 and C-9/90 *Francovich and Others* [1991] ECR I-5357, paragraph 31).

[20] Secondly, according to Article 3(g) of the EC Treaty (now, after amendment, Article 3(1)(g) EC), Article 85 of the Treaty constitutes a fundamental provision which is essential for the accomplishment of the tasks entrusted to the Community and, in particular, for the functioning of the internal market (judgment in Case C-126/97 *Eco Swiss* [1999] ECR I-3055, paragraph 36 [p.495 above]).

[21] Indeed, the importance of such a provision led the framers of the Treaty to provide expressly, in Article 85(2) of the Treaty, that any agreements or decisions prohibited pursuant to that article are to be automatically void (judgment in *Eco Swiss*, cited above, paragraph 36).

[22] That principle of automatic nullity can be relied on by anyone, and the courts are bound by it once the conditions for the application of Article 85(1) are met and so long as the agreement concerned does not justify the grant of an exemption under Article 85(3) of the Treaty (on the latter point, see *inter alia* Case 10/69 *Portelange* [1969] ECR 309, paragraph 10). Since the nullity referred to in Article 85(2) is absolute, an agreement which is null and void by virtue of this provision has no effect as between the contracting parties and cannot be set up against third parties (see the judgment in Case 22/71 *Béguelin* [1971] ECR 949, paragraph 29). Moreover, it is capable of having a

bearing on all the effects, either past or future, of the agreement or decision concerned (see the judgment in Case 48/72 *Brasserie de Haecht II* [1973] ECR 77, paragraph 26).

[23] Thirdly, it should be borne in mind that the Court has held that Article 85(1) of the Treaty and Article 86 of the EC Treaty (now Article 82 EC) produce direct effects in relations between individuals and create rights for the individuals concerned which the national courts must safeguard (judgments in Case 127/73 *BRT and SABAM* [1974] ECR 51, paragraph 16, ('*BRT I*) and Case C-282/95P *Guérin Automobiles* v *Commission* [1997] ECR I-1503, paragraph 39).

[24] It follows from the foregoing considerations that any individual can rely on a breach of Article 85(1) of the Treaty before a national court even where he is a party to a contract that is liable to restrict or distort competition within the meaning of that provision.

[25] As regards the possibility of seeking compensation for loss caused by a contract or by conduct liable to restrict or distort competition, it should be remembered from the outset that, in accordance with settled case-law, the national courts whose task it is to apply the provisions of Community law in areas within their jurisdiction must ensure that those rules take full effect and must protect the rights which they confer on individuals (see *inter alia* the judgments in Case 106/77 *Simmenthal* [1978] ECR 629, paragraph 16, and in Case C-213/89 *Factortame* [1990] ECR I-2433, paragraph 19).

[26] The full effectiveness of Article 85 of the Treaty and, in particular, the practical effect of the prohibition laid down in Article 85(1) would be put at risk if it were not open to any individual to claim damages for loss caused to him by a contract or by conduct liable to restrict or distort competition.

[27] Indeed, the existence of such a right strengthens the working of the Community competition rules and discourages agreements or practices, which are frequently covert, which are liable to restrict or distort competition. From that point of view, actions for damages before the national courts can make a significant contribution to the maintenance of effective competition in the Community.

[28] There should not therefore be any absolute bar to such an action being brought by a party to a contract which would be held to violate the competition rules.

[29] However, in the absence of Community rules governing the matter, it is for the domestic legal system of each Member State to designate the courts and tribunals having jurisdiction and to lay down the detailed procedural rules governing actions for safeguarding rights which individuals derive directly from Community law, provided that such rules are not less favourable than those governing similar domestic actions (principle of equivalence) and that they do not render practically impossible or excessively difficult the exercise of rights conferred by Community law (principle of effectiveness) (see Case C-261/95 *Palmisani* [1997] ECR I-4025, paragraph 27).

[30] In that regard, the Court has held that Community law does not prevent national courts from taking steps to ensure that the protection of the rights guaranteed by Community law does not entail the unjust enrichment of those who enjoy them (see, in particular, Case 238/78 *Ireks-Arkady* v *Council and Commission* [1979] ECR 2955, paragraph 14, Case 68/79 *Just* [1980] ECR 501, paragraph 26, and Joined Cases C-441/98 and C-442/98 *Michaïlidis* [2000] ECR I-7145, paragraph 31).

[31] Similarly, provided that the principles of equivalence and effectiveness are respected (see *Palmisani*, cited above, paragraph 27), Community law does not preclude national law from denying a party who is found to bear significant responsibility for the distortion of competition the right to obtain damages from the other contracting party. Under a principle which is recognised in most of the legal systems of the Member States and which the Court has applied in the past (see Case 39/72 *Commission* v *Italy* [1973] ECR 101, paragraph 10), a litigant should not profit from his own unlawful conduct, where this is proven.

[32] In that regard, the matters to be taken into account by the competent national court include the economic and legal context in which the parties find themselves and, as the United Kingdom Government rightly points out, the respective bargaining power and conduct of the two parties to the contract.

[33] In particular, it is for the national court to ascertain whether the party who claims to have suffered loss through concluding a contract that is liable to restrict or distort competition found himself in a markedly weaker position than the other party, such as seriously to compromise or even eliminate his freedom to negotiate the terms of the contract and his capacity to avoid the loss or reduce its extent, in particular by availing himself in good time of all the legal remedies available to him.

[34] Referring to the judgments in Case 23/67 *Brasserie de Haecht* [1967] ECR 127 and Case C-234/89 *Delimitis* [1991] ECR I-935, paragraphs 14 to 26, the Commission and the United Kingdom Government also rightly point out that a contract might prove to be contrary to Article 85(1) of the Treaty for the sole reason that it is part of a network of similar contracts which have a cumulative effect on competition. In such a case, the party contracting with the person controlling the network cannot bear significant responsibility for the breach of Article 85, particularly where in practice the terms of the contract were imposed on him by the party controlling the network.

[35] Contrary to the submission of Courage, making a distinction as to the extent of the parties' liability does not conflict with the case-law of the Court to the effect that it does not matter, for the purposes of the application of Article 85 of the Treaty, whether the parties to an agreement are on an equal footing as regards their economic position and function (see *inter alia* Joined Cases 56/64 and 58/64 *Consten and Grundig* v *Commission* [1966] ECR 382). That case-law concerns the conditions for application of Article 85 of the Treaty while the questions put before the Court in the present case concern certain consequences in civil law of a breach of that provision.

[36] Having regard to all the foregoing considerations, the questions referred are to be answered as follows:

— a party to a contract liable to restrict or distort competition within the meaning of Article 85 of the Treaty can rely on the breach of that article to obtain relief from the other contracting party;

— Article 85 of the Treaty precludes a rule of national law under which a party to a contract liable to restrict or distort competition within the meaning of that provision is barred from claiming damages for loss caused by performance of that contract on the sole ground that the claimant is a party to that contract;

— Community law does not preclude a rule of national law barring a party to a contract liable to restrict or distort competition from relying on his own unlawful actions to obtain damages where it is established that that party bears significant responsibility for the distortion of competition.

NOTE

The anxiety to promote the *effectiveness* of private enforcement is prominent in this ruling (paras 26 and 27). This tool of legal reasoning has been encountered elsewhere in comparable circumstances in which the Court delivers a ruling that, in so far as it improves methods for policing the rules of Community law, is likely to be welcomed by the Commission (*cf*, e.g., p.315).

FURTHER READING ON PATTERNS OF PRIVATE ENFORCEMENT

(i) Pre-Courage v Crehan

Jones, C., *Private Enforcement of Antitrust Law in the EU, UK and USA* (Oxford: OUP, 1999).

Shaw, J., 'Decentralised Law Enforcement in EC Competition Law' (1995) 15 *Legal Studies* 128.

Waller, A., 'Decentralization of the Enforcement Process of EC Competition Law – The Greater Role of National Courts' [1996/2] LIEI 1.

Yeung, K., 'Privatising Competition Regulation' (1998) 18 OxJLS 581.

(ii) Post-Courage v Crehan

Komninos, A., 'New Prospects for Private Enforcement of EC Competition Law' (2002) 39
 CML Rev 457.

Monti, G., 'Anticompetitive Agreements: the Innocent Party's Right to Damages' (2002) 27
 EL Rev 282.

NOTE

For additional material and resources see the Companion Website at: www.oup.co.uk/
best.textbooks/law/weatherill6e

Competition Law – Epilogue to Part Three

A. Albors-Llorens, 'Competition Policy and the Shaping of the Single Market',
Ch. 12 in C. Barnard and J. Scott, *The Law of the Single European Market:
Unpacking the Premises* (Oxford: Hart Publishing, 2002), pp.330–1.

(Footnotes omitted.)

Has the time come for the single market objective to play a less prominent role in the context of competition policy? After all, it could be argued that the 31 December 1992 deadline has long expired and that competition policy should move into a more economically based terrain. This idea infused the debate on vertical restraints and culminated in the adoption of the new block exemption regulations on vertical and horizontal agreements [p.535 above]. In the context of that debate some authors and the Commission itself have already argued that it might be too early to relax the importance of that goal given the price differentials still subsisting between the Member States, the minimum impact of cross-border purchasing groups, and the prospective further enlargement of the Union. Furthermore, two additional factors may have a decisive influence on the way the single market objective is deployed in the interpretation of Articles 81 and 82 EC. First, the fully decentralised system for the enforcement of these provisions envisaged by the Commission in its 1999 *White Paper* is likely to have an impact on this area [see now Reg 1/2003 p.572 above]. While it is true that the Commission will continue to play a pivotal role in directing competition policy in the new system, it remains to be seen whether national competition authorities and national courts will be as motivated as the Commission is by the goal of market integration. Second, the growing trend towards economic globalisation, which is progressively leading to the international integration of markets, may also have a diluting effect on the single market aim.

■ QUESTION

In the light of these trends and pressures, which direction do you expect EC competition law to take? Which direction should it take?

PART FOUR

Policy-Making, Governance, and the Constitutional Debate

19

Harmonization and Common Policy-Making

SECTION 1: **INTRODUCTION**

Much – perhaps too much – of this book has concentrated on the *negative* aspects of the Community's substantive law. Articles 25, 28, 39, and 90, for example, all forbid the maintenance of national rules which restrict free movement. The suppression by law of trade barriers assists in market integration. Yet the development of the Community is also dependent on a *positive* contribution by the law. A common market can only be fully realised by common policy-making; by creating positive Community rules. Both Articles 2 and 3 of the EC Treaty, set out at pp.290 and 293 above, insist on the importance of both negative and positive action. The positive elements of Community policy-making may assume many forms and may be adopted under a wide range of Treaty provisions. This Chapter is by no means an exhaustive survey of Community policy-making. Instead, it selects particular areas as illustrations and endeavours to extract and illuminate key themes and endemic problems in the shaping of Community policies.

The first extract presents a useful overview of the issues. It reintroduces some aspects already touched on in Chapter 9. It is also a decade and-a-half old. Deliberately so. These are not simply today's issues. These are yesterday's issues and they are tomorrow's issues too.

> **J. Lodge**, The European Community and the Challenge of the Future
> (London: Pinter Publishers, 1989), pp.83–85

(Footnote omitted.)

The 1990s are clearly going to be preoccupied with issues arising out of the attempt to realize the Single European Market (SEM). An artificial distinction can be made between what might loosely be defined as 'internal' and 'external' policies. However, it must be remembered that internal policies have external effects and the idea of an impenetrable barrier separating the two is misleading. By 'internal' policies, we mean that group of policies whose goals are directly related to the accomplishment of targets within the EC: they are inner-directed; they seek to modify in some way policy activities within the domestic settings of the EC and its member states. 'External policies' are outer-directed and aim at producing a degree of agreement and/or consensual policies among the Twelve towards non-EC, often known as 'third', states . . .

However, 'domestic' policies like the C[ommon] A[gricultural] P[olicy], attempts to manage difficult sectoral areas (like steel and textiles) and to advance EC monetary integration, fiscal harmonization and capital and labour mobility as well as new efforts in the environmental and information technology (IT) trade spheres spill-out into the external arena. As a result, the EC's own arrangements for initiating, managing and executing policies in those sectors become stressed by the absence of appropriate mechanisms to manage effectively external effects of domestic policies that are often highly sensitive. Moreover, the goal of achieving a common market (as in the 1950s) and now a SEM inadvertently encourages policymakers at all levels from the EC itself through national government down to local government to focus on internal problems and on the difficulties associated with member states having to adjust to new policy environments and conditions. Since the effects of policies are largely unknown at the outset, and since subsequent wrangling is likely to result from unpalatable effects within certain sectors or member states, it is to be expected that policymakers will not necessarily anticipate possibly deleterious external effects. Moreover, in dealing with them (as in the case of Mediterranean enlargement), they have to adopt some means of prioritizing the claims of those who feel that their interests (usually trade interests) have been harmed as a result. The criteria they choose will almost always be contested.

It is obvious that neither a common market nor the SEM can be established without often unwelcome consequences for third states. The mere establishment of a Common External Tariff demands adjustments both by members of the bloc applying that tariff and by those who export to the bloc. Various forms of protectionism and market support also have trade diversifying effects. The year 1992 has become shorthand for the completion of the SEM. While its consolidation will extend beyond the 1990s, many third states and commercial interests within them are operating as if the SEM will assume concrete shape by 1992. This is especially true of the EC's major trading partners, including the rump EFTA . . . Third states are forced to adapt to the EC's policies and its anticipated effects. EC rim states seem to be following parallel actions, at a minimum, to minimize anticipated difficulties from the SEM's establishment.

While such effects are largely an unknown quantity, they are recognized. Predicting and managing them is, however, difficult. Equally, the internal consequences of a limited range of inner-directed policies are often overlooked, or insufficient resources are set aside to encourage appropriate supranantional-led action. Economic and political considerations explain this. Certainly this has been the EC's experience. The accent on the removal of obstacles to trade within the EC led, for example, to the EC being castigated as a 'rich man's club'. The SEM has been similarly construed as a commercial ploy whose uncertain benefits would gravitate towards already rich centres – the Golden Triangle – wealthy elites and powerful companies already in a position to benefit from the hypothesized economies of scale consequent upon the SEM. . . . Whereas the Rome Treaty establishing the EEC made some provisions to assist poorer sectors, it did not 'flag' them in the way in which Commission President Delors did.

The qualitative difference to European integration in the 1990s inheres not simply in the modifications to the Rome Treaty introduced through the Single European Act, but in the way in which they have been interpreted in the public domaine. The politico-economic context in which the SEA unfurled partly accounts for this. The era of Green parties on mainland Europe and generalized high unemployment with its attendant social problems meant that something more than mere lip-service had to be paid to sectors that clearly were high on the Member States' domestic political agenda. Equally important, however, was M. Delors's intention to define the EC's *raison d'être*. Since its inception, this issue had been side-stepped. . . . The Monnet-Schuman visions and methods stressed the establishment of concrete achievements to create real solidarity and to realise the common good. However, the goal of European Union had been obfuscated by the process. Gradualism reigned supreme: indeed, had to assume centre stage at a time when national sovereignty was not only sorely tried but was still being slowly granted to the new West German state by its Western allies.

The phrase 'an ever closer union' disguised or hid the likely extensive implications of the creation of a common market for thirty years. National governments occasionally protested loudly at steps likely to augment the authority and competence of the EC's institutions. Such protestations seemed to reflect anxiety over an inability to make others in the EC follow a line prescribed by one state's national interest. A well thought-out understanding of what the various sectoral policy measures to advance integration implied in the longer term for both the Member States' and the EC's capacity to deliver the goods proved elusive. No matter how serious and protracted disagreements among the Member States, it was clear that the EC was not only an acceptable forum for the pursuit of goals but one which soon attracted more members. The effect on the EC of many states using it instrumentally to advance national interests was, paradoxically and contrary to the assumptions implicit in many integration theories, to reinforce and consolidate rather than weaken it. Many appreciated that the political implications of the processes of economic integration could not be forever ignored. Few appreciated that greater political integration would have consequences for macro and microeconomic sectoral integration.

It was comparatively easy in the early stages of European integration to deride and dismiss the future visions as 'federalist rantings'. By the 1980s, as Mrs Thatcher was to learn, this ceased to be the case. Many still abhor 'federalism' (often without understanding what it implies). But it is also clear that the EC's *raison d'être* needs some clarification. Public and elite expectations of what it can deliver exceed its capacity. The notion that the EC is a political animal is accepted. M. Delors tried to set out some parameters and to project a vision of a future EC. The precise details of the vision are less important than the fact that the vision makes clear that domestic and external policy sectors are irrevocably intertwined; that any benefits from economic integration must be shared in the name of social justice and its disadvantages offset. While the 'Social Europe' package was disappointing, the highlighting of different tranches of the SEM has imprinted a socialist element firmly on the EC.

A faint socialist watermark is clear in the Rome Treaty. Conscience calls for measures to deal with the negative effects of integration. Some incentives exist for labour mobility. By and large, however, the 'social' aspects of integration have played a secondary role. Attention has focused on removing barriers to trade and other forms of economic discrimination that might adversely affect intra-EC trade. The creation of the SEM and an industrial base for the EC remains frustrated by weaknesses in the EC's policy processes, the absence of consensus over macroeconomic goals and the continuing wrangling among the Twelve over the locus of authority.

Problems also inhere in the piecemeal approach to policymaking, the identification and implementation of sectoral policy goals that require a horizontal rather than a vertical approach to ensure rational and optimal outcomes. Moreover, the domestic organization and funding of agencies and departments charged with implementing and enforcing EC policy varies so greatly as to further frustrate rational and approximately common outcomes. Moreover, the EC lacks an overall economic plan (the SEM only partly disguises this). Instead of coherent over-arching economic policy, the EC has a series of economic instruments, often designed to prevent national actions that will distort competition (such as non-tariff and technical barriers to trade, state aids, export premiums, preferential energy and freight rates for exports, for example) or that unfairly give or allow companies to abuse a dominant position . . .

NOTE

To repeat Professor Lodge's words – 'Many appreciated that the political implications of the processes of economic integration could not be forever ignored' . . . 'it is also clear that the EC's *raison d'être* needs some clarification'. And how! Although Professor Lodge's book was published in a 2nd edition in 1993, the above extract from the 1st edition has been retained as an introduction to this Chapter in order to emphasise the enduring nature of the problems that confront the EC. The reader who has reached this stage of the book will have no difficulty in identifying how these comments may be extended beyond the SEM project to *inter alia* the prospects for Economic and Monetary Union, the role of the Charter on Fundamental Rights, the imminent Enlargement, and the path *via* the Convention on the 'Future of Europe' towards an intergovernmental conference in 2004.

SECTION 2: **HARMONIZATION POLICY**

Even at the simple level of the quest for market access, it is obvious that not just *negative* but also *positive* rule making is required. Articles 28 and 39, for example, do not forbid all national rules which partition the market. There are derogations in Article 30 and Article 39(3) which envisage the maintenance of lawful trade barriers. Moreover the *Cassis de Dijon* principle introduced a principle of mutual recognition that was qualified by the admission that a regulating State is entitled to show a justification in the public interest for its rules even if they impeded inter-State trade (see Chapter 12 dealing with Article 28 EC, Chapter 14 dealing with Article 49). Article 90 forbids discriminatory internal taxation, but the tax systems of the Member States remain different, and consequently trade barriers may remain justified in order to allow the collection of taxes. A *positive* set of rules is needed to remove such lawful trade barriers. This explains the need for the Community's harmonization programme. (*Cf* p.376 above.)

THE COMMISSION'S SECOND BIENNIAL REPORT ON THE APPLICATION OF THE PRINCIPLE OF MUTUAL RECOGNITION IN THE SINGLE MARKET, COM (2002) 419, PARA 3

Mutual recognition is not always a miracle solution for ensuring the free movement of goods in the single market. Harmonisation or further harmonisation remains without doubt one of the most effective instruments, both for economic operators and for the national administrations.

Harmonization sets common Community standards of, for example, health protection, which deprive States of the ability to take unilateral action in defence of such interests which would inhibit free trade.

....

A: Harmonization as an introduction to the wider debate

The old Article 100a served as the legal base for a wide variety of harmonization Directives connected with the process of building the internal market, stretching from, for example, procedures for the award of public works contracts (Dir. 93/37 [1993] OJ L199/54) to unfair terms in consumer contracts (Dir. 93/13 [1993] OJ L95/29). On the entry into force of the Amsterdam Treaty (p.11 above), Article 100a was amended and re-numbered Article 95 EC. It has been encountered before in this book (p.59) but its text deserves repetition.

ARTICLE 95 EC

Article 95

1. By way of derogation from Article 94 and save where otherwise provided in this Treaty, the following provisions shall apply for the achievement of the objectives set out in Article 14. The Council shall, acting in accordance with the procedure referred to in Article 251 and after consulting the Economic and Social Committee, adopt the measures for the approximation of the provisions laid down by law, regulation or administrative action in Member States which have as their object the establishment and functioning of the internal market.

    2. Paragraph 1 shall not apply to fiscal provisions, to those relating to the free movement of persons nor to those relating to the rights and interests of employed persons.

    3. The Commission, in its proposals envisaged in paragraph 1 concerning health, safety, environmental protection and consumer protection, will take as a base a high level of protection, taking account in particular of any new development based on scientific facts. Within their respective powers, the European Parliament and the Council will also seek to achieve this objective.

4. If, after the adoption by the Council or by the Commission of a harmonisation measure, a Member State deems it necessary to maintain national provisions on grounds of major needs referred to in Article 30, or relating to the protection of the environment or the working environment, it shall notify the Commission of these provisions as well as the grounds for maintaining them.

5. Moreover, without prejudice to paragraph 4, if, after the adoption by the Council or by the Commission of a harmonisation measure, a Member State deems it necessary to introduce national provisions based on new scientific evidence relating to the protection of the environment or the working environment on grounds of a problem specific to that Member State arising after the adoption of the harmonisation measure, it shall notify the Commission of the envisaged provisions as well as the grounds for introducing them.

6. The Commission shall, within six months of the notifications as referred to in paragraphs 4 and 5, approve or reject the national provisions involved after having verified whether or not they are a means of arbitrary discrimination or a disguised restriction on trade between Member States and whether or not they shall constitute an obstacle to the functioning of the internal market.

In the absence of a decision by the Commission within this period the national provisions referred to in paragraphs 4 and 5 shall be deemed to have been approved.

When justified by the complexity of the matter and in the absence of danger for human health, the Commission may notify the Member State concerned that the period referred to in this paragraph may be extended for a further period of up to six months.

7. When, pursuant to paragraph 6, a Member State is authorised to maintain or introduce national provisions derogating from a harmonisation measure, the Commission shall immediately examine whether to propose an adaptation to that measure.

8. When a Member State raises a specific problem on public health in a field which has been the subject of prior harmonisation measures, it shall bring it to the attention of the Commission which shall immediately examine whether to propose appropriate measures to the Council.

9. By way of derogation from the procedure laid down in Articles 226 and 227, the Commission and any Member State may bring the matter directly before the Court of Justice if it considers that another Member State is making improper use of the powers provided for in this Article.

10. The harmonisation measures referred to above shall, in appropriate cases, include a safeguard clause authorising the Member States to take, for one or more of the non-economic reasons referred to in Article 30, provisional measures subject to a Community control procedure.

NOTE

It was established in Chapter 2 that Article 95 does not confer an open-ended competence on the Community to approximate or to harmonize laws. The 'Tobacco Advertising' case (Case C-376/98 *Germany* v *European Parliament and Council of the European Union* [2000] ECR I-8419), examined at p.60 above, insists on the demonstration of an adequate link between the measure of harmonization and the process of market-making in Europe. This, at bottom, reflects the constitutionally vital principle of attributed competence found in Article 5(1) EC.

ARTICLE 5(1) EC

The Community shall act within the limits of the powers conferred upon it by this Treaty and of the objectives assigned to it therein.

NOTE

Article 5(1) EC and the scrupulously careful reading of the scope of Article 95 evident in the Court's ruling in 'Tobacco Advertising' represent the formal constitutional dimension of a much deeper set of policy questions. These may be grouped around the general inquiry – *how much Europe*? Or more precisely, *how much European Union*? 'Tobacco Advertising' emphasizes the Court's readiness to police the limits of the powers granted to the EC by the Treaty, but there are broader normative questions about what *should be* the nature of the relationship between the Union and its Member States. It is undisputed that in some areas action in common is required in order to achieve the objectives of the European Union. Member States have agreed that they will surrender aspects of local autonomy in favour of a centralized decision-making competence. But how much action in common? Across how many fields? Professor Lodge's sketch (p.613 above) reveals some of the tensions associated with the expansion of Union activity, and this is a process that has evolved according to ever more complex patterns as the experiment has continued. The fact that each successive round of Treaty revision has tended to add new competences to the Union's list, combined with the steady enlargement of the Union, once six States, now 15 and soon many more (p.14), has deepened the scope of action in common. Moreover, many EC competences – and, in much more limited respects, some non-EC EU competences – are capable of exercise by Qualified Majority Vote in Council according to Article 251 EC. This is true of Article 95, above. The release of State veto power in Council accentuates the impression of a Union which possesses a degree of self-momentum – or at least a Union in which majoritarian practices hold sway. And so the hubbub of debate has grown louder – has the European Union been tipped too far in favour of centralized decision-making authority to the detriment of local autonomy?

This Chapter explores the contours of the debate: *how much Europe, how much European Union?* Harmonization pursuant to Article 95 EC offers a helpfully illuminating introduction to the investigation. There are important policy issues which emerge from the harmonization programme. Harmonization is designed to protect interests such as public health in the framework of an integrating Community in which the advantages of free trade will be secured. Harmonization, then, has a dual aim: protection of the citizen and facilitation of free trade. The difficulty of achieving both objectives was discussed in the context of the free movement of goods in the several extracts presented at pp.415–425 above. The problems of fiscal harmonization were discussed at p.336 above. Harmonization, as a process of replacing diverse national rules with common Community rules for a common market, is a perfect example of the triumph of centralized rule-making over local autonomy. Market integration seems to demand such a transfer of regulatory authority, but the functional and geographical expansion of the Union increasingly reveals that harmonization cannot be treated merely as a technical process. It is capable of affecting important national interests. In Article 95 itself, the tensions involved in attempting to satisfy all interests affected by harmonization emerge in the procedure found in paras (4) *et seq*. This demonstrates that 'levelling the playing field' is not of itself a strong enough rationale to persuade States to surrender all regulatory leeway in a harmonized field. And Article 95(3) suggests anxiety about the *quality* of the regime to be introduced as the harmonized basis for regulating the market.

At least two arguments may be advanced to question the feasibility and desirability of harmonization:

(a) Harmonization of this nature tends to be *conservative*. The standard is fixed until such time as the legislator is able to alter it – a laborious process, especially at Community level. The inflexible, rigid standard hinders innovation (e.g., in respect of cheaper or safer devices), and is consequently inefficient.

(b) Harmonization of this nature suppresses national tradition. Why should one single Community rule replace national preference? Is free trade a goal which overrides the capacity of individual States to retain higher standards of, say, environmental and consumer protection?

B: **The New Approach to harmonization policy**

The difficulties in achieving the harmonization of technical rules relating to products led in the 1980s to a new impetus in Community harmonization policy. The problems of old style harmonization are well explained in the following extract.

J. Pelkmans, 'The New Approach to Technical Harmonization and Standardization' (1986–87) 25 JCMS 249, 251–53

(Footnote omitted.)

THE 'TRADITIONAL' APPROACH OF THE POLICY REGIME

For more than one and a half decades the European Commission has tried to pursue an ambitious harmonization programme. Following a few ad hoc cases, and a prudent first step towards the harmonization of the national regulations concerning pharmaceutical products, in March 1968, the Commission proposed a General Programme. From that time until the so called Mutual Information Directive 83/189/EEC [now replaced by Directive 98/34: pp.153, 315 above], an incredible amount of energy on the part of civil servants and experts had been devoted to the production of an extremely limited number of Council Directives. Many of these directives focus on specific technical *aspects* of products and they therefore fail to solve all the problems of access in product markets. During these fifteen years the EC has adopted on average only a little over ten technical directives a year.

It is doubtful, to say the least, whether such a slow speed can actually bring about a net reduction in the technical barriers to trade in the Community in view of the simultaneous accretion of regulations in Member States. To put it more strongly, given the increase in bureaucratic regulatory capacity in recent decades in all Member States and the greater societal preference for environmental and consumer protection, it can safely be presumed that the tempo of national regulation has, for many years, exceeded by far that of the annual output of 'aspect-directives' at EC level with respect to a rather limited group of products. Apart from being *inefficient* – due to extensive and drawn out consultations on technical specifications – the method was *ineffective* as well: a general improvement of mutual market access was not achieved, at best there was only a slowing down of the rate of increase of technical barriers.

Nor did the wider European standardization processes proceed smoothly. The history of CEN (European Standardization Committee) shows clearly that, without some connection with the EC's own harmonization policy, progress at the wider European level tends to be exceedingly difficult. A serious drawback of the functioning of CEN is that no long-term programmes are being developed to remove the trade-impeding effects of different national standards (notwithstanding their private and voluntary character) . . .

DRAWBACKS OF THE 'TRADITIONAL' APPROACH

In earlier work I have analysed extensively the considerable disadvantages and shortcomings of the traditional strategy of technical harmonization (and standardization) of the Community. Briefly these consist of:

1. time-consuming and cumbersome procedures
2. excessive uniformity
3. unanimity (ex Art. 100, EEC) [now 94 EC]
4. the failure, except rarely, to develop a linkage between the harmonization of technical regulations and European standardization, leading to wasteful duplication, useless inconsistencies and time lost
5. the slowness of European harmonization and standardization relative to national regulation and standardization
6. a neglect of the problems of certification and testing

7. the incapacity to solve the third country problem
8. implementation problems in Member States
9. a lack of political interest by the Ministers.

It is not surprising that by the early 1980s the question of the removal of technical barriers to trade in the EC had led to profound feelings of frustration and disappointment.

The policy climate in which the elimination of technical barriers to trade in the EC had to be realized was such that the individual protectionist was thriving whereas the dynamic exporter, attempting to encroach upon other markets, was hampered. Of course, the opposite climate should characterize European market integration for the benefit of the Community's economy at large.

NOTE

Consequently, the Council adopted in 1985 a Resolution approving a *New Approach* to technical harmonization.

COUNCIL RESOLUTION OF 7 MAY 1985 ON A NEW APPROACH TO TECHNICAL HARMONIZATION AND STANDARDS [1985] OJ C136/1; ANNEX, 'GUIDELINES FOR A NEW APPROACH TO TECHNICAL HARMONIZATION AND STANDARDS'

The following are the four fundamental principals [sic] on which the new approach is based:

(i) legislative harmonization is limited to the adoption, by means of Directives based on Article 100 of the EEC Treaty, of the essential safety requirements (or other requirements in the general interest) with which products put on the market must conform, and which should therefore enjoy free movement throughout the Community.

(ii) the task of drawing up the technical specifications needed for the production and placing on the market of products conforming to the essential requirements established by the Directives, while taking into account the current stage of technology, is entrusted to organizations competent in the standardization area,

(iii) these technical specifications are not mandatory and maintain their status of voluntary standards,

(iv) but at the same time national authorities are obliged to recognise that products manufactured in conformity with harmonized standards (or, provisionally, with national standards) are presumed to conform to the 'essential requirements' established by the Directive. (This signifies that the producer has the choice of not manufacturing in conformity with the standards but that in this event he has an obligation to prove that his products conform to the essential requirements of the Directive).

In order that this system may operate it is necessary:

(i) on the one hand that the standards offer a guarantee of quality with regard to the 'essential requirements' established by the Directives.

(ii) on the other hand that the public authorities keep intact their responsibility for the protection of safety (or other requirements envisaged) on their territory.

The quality of harmonized standards must be ensured by standardization mandates, conferred by the Commission, the execution of which must conform to the general guidelines which have been the subject of agreement between the Commission and the European standardization organizations. In so far as national standards are concerned their quality must be verified by a procedure at Community level managed by the Commission, assisted by a standing committee composed of officials from national administrations.

At the same time safeguard procedures must be provided for, under the management of the Commission assisted by the same committee, in order to allow the competent public authorities the possibility of contesting the conformity of a product, the validity of a certificate or the quality of a standard.

In following this system of legislative harmonization in each area in which it is feasible, the Commission intends to be able to halt the proliferation of excessively technical separate Directives for each product. The scope of Directives according to the 'general reference to standards' formula should encompass wide product categories and types of risk.

The Community could on the one hand, therefore, complete the extremely complex undertaking of harmonizing technical legislation and on the other hand promote the development and application of European standards. These are essential conditions for the improvement of the competitiveness of its industry.

NOTE

Accordingly, Directives conforming to the New Approach need not include detailed specifications. They instead set broad performance standards. Products meeting those standards are entitled to access to the markets of all the Member States. See, for example, Directive 2001/95, the Directive on General Product Safety [2002] OJ L11/4 (replacing Directive 92/59 with effect from 15 January 2004).

The advantages of the New Approach are manifold.

J. Pelkmans, 'The New Approach to Technical Harmonization and Standardization' (1986–87) 25 ICMS 249, 257–61

(Footnotes omitted.)

ADVANTAGES OF THE 'NEW APPROACH'

The most important potential advantages of the 'new approach' are (i) greater coherence between the policy regime and the legal regime to eliminate technical barriers, and (ii) the better conveyance between European harmonization of technical regulations and European standardization. As stated earlier, the Council will have to assume the task of reaching a 'European doctrine' in the fields of safety, health, etc., so that the technical barriers to intra-EC free movement can disappear. The new approach is a serious attempt to achieve this coherence by combining *total harmonization* of the objectives at issue (safety, etc.) with a *flexible approach* of the means (standardization). It also improves the scope for a timely interchange of information so that national draft-standards and technical draft-regulations can be altered or converted into European ones before formally taking effect.

These advantages are commendable and may explain the willingness in Member States and in various circles to view the new approach with a 'prejugé favourable'. They are however *potential* advantages because a great deal depends on the actual results, both in the Council, with respect to the total harmonization of objectives of health, safety, etc., and also from the standardization processes in the CEN/CENELEC framework.

The advantages can be formulated in a less abstract way by examining which *dis*advantages of the traditional approach, as mentioned before, will be reduced or eliminated by the new approach. The effects on these nine disadvantages and deficiencies are summed up below. The reader is warned that for the time being a speculative evaluation concerning the 'quality policy' is needed in some cases. The author considers the model directive to be a sufficient basis to develop an adequate quality policy from the coordinated work of the Commission, the Standing Committee 'Reference to Standards' and CEN/CENELEC. Given this presumption, the effects on the 'old' approach disadvantages are summarized as follows:

1. Time-consuming and laborious procedures

Both the Commission and the Council (and the Coreper bodies) could save a considerable amount of time, not only because technical specifications do not need to be approved twice, but also because technical aspects – within the quality policy – are in fact delegated. Whether this time-saving can be transformed into acceleration depends on the speed of standardization. Standardization speed can be increased by pressure originating from the procedures under the Mutual Information Directive and by apportioning Commission payments for the implementation of mandates to CEN and CENELEC. It is not precluded (indeed, it is implicit in the new approach) that, should the safety objectives, etc., be agreed, legislation can also lead to greater pressure being exerted to speed up standardization.

2. Uniformity

The advantage here has already been reported: the combination of uniform safety objectives (etc.) with the desired variability in the means for industry or for the consumers. Moreover, the fact that no mandatory reference takes place leaves room for original solutions in existing products and for product innovation.

3. Unanimity

The central question remains whether unanimity with respect to the objectives, including the demands on the quality policy, will always be achieved so easily. This question is even more pressing because the new approach is applied to relatively comprehensive product groups. The way out in the Council that is apparently used with the first 'new approach' proposals of the Commission is to negotiate 'mixed forms' of the old and the new approach, with some technical specification in the directive itself but not as detailed as before. The 'traditional' approach will not completely disappear: the White Paper contains some 90 industrial and 60 agricultural proposals of the traditional type. Recent experience with lead-free petrol and with the reduction of exhaust gases of motor vehicles has shown that even unanimity *can* lead to decisions if the pressure of time arising from the Mutual Information Directive together with economic (export) interests increase the willingness to reach compromises.

The newly agreed Art. 100-A [now Art. 95 EC], included in the Single European Act and providing for qualified majority voting, could constitute a significant boost in overcoming the resistance of a single country. It is expected to enhance the room for manoeuvre of the Commission, which was almost non-existent under unanimity. Nevertheless, the usage of products for workers and the possibility of safeguards (subject to Court review) may continue to cause occasional problems in case of majority voting (given paragraphs 3, 4 and 5 of this new Article).

4. Harmonization not related to standardization

For every case in which the 'new approach' is applied, this problem is by definition solved.

5. EC standardization slower than national standardization

Because standards are included in the Mutual Information Directive, and because 'reference to standards' will be used in directives, an increase in the tempo and in the volume of European standardization can reasonably be expected.

With regard to the short-term, it is doubtful whether this acceleration and volume increase is sufficient to bring about a net reduction in the barriers; in the long run this is certainly possible. It should be ensured that the volume increase does not merely consist of CEN approval of all sorts of sectoral standards which in certain sectors have already been agreed at European level for a long time. Indeed, to the extent that this is a 'cosmetic' operation, little value can be attached to it. To the extent that the standards were not actually followed, it does have significance. Moreover, where government contracts are at stake, the European Commission can possibly extend the significance further. Ultimately a strong tempo and volume increase by CEN and CENELEC depends on capacity limitations and the rapidity with which these can be overcome.

6. Limited attention to tests and certification

Except for a vague promise nothing can be found on this in the new approach. This serious weakness of the new approach must be dealt with soon . . .

7. The third country problem

Here also the effect of the new approach is still not clear.

8. Application and implementation

It seems reasonable to accept that the combination of total harmonization of health/safety objectives, European standards linked to an adequate quality policy of the Council and the already existing legislation, will have a favourable effect on the actual application of the directives in the

Member States. Of course, it is the details of application that will be decisive for the economic agents in the market. Proper implementation is, however, a slow process and substantial improvement is not to be expected before the 1990s [for recent practice, see p.309 above]. It can be speeded up by the greater potential which careful total harmonization of objectives offers for the national judicial process. However the real problems are sometimes deep seated, for instance, reference to national standards in insurance contracts, in the conditions for connection imposed by public utilities or in local delivery conditions.

9. Lack of political interest

Total harmonization of the objectives as well as the comprehensiveness of the product groups form the arguments which give rise to the presumption that *more political interest* in the Internal Market Council and in the Commission will be mustered.

Taking everything together, improvements can be perceived with respect to seven of the nine disadvantages of the 'traditional' approach. The extent of these advantages, however, is at the moment far from obvious and the length of time before they will be felt by industry and consumers could be considerable. Nevertheless this does not detract from the fact that the 'new approach' looks as though it will be *qualitatively an enormous improvement* over the traditional approach.

Finally, two advantages must be pointed out which are directly connected with the nine points just mentioned, but are of such potential importance that they deserve to be mentioned separately and emphatically.

In the first place the new approach is linked to the issue of *improvement in the competitiveness of European industry*. Harmonization and standardization are still viewed in many branches of industry or in individual companies as a potential threat to the market position or a cause of unwanted adaptation costs. Except for extremely specific conditions in a large market, however, protectionism leads in due course to a worsening international competitiveness.

If, on the other hand, *standard quality* is such that penetration into many foreign markets is possible, then standardization can be seen in quite another light. Because specialization is becoming ever more refined, and scale effects in many cases form an important determinant of the export position, the quality approach offers a much better perspective, not only for industry and the consumer but also for the economy as a whole. Seen in this way, emphasis will come to lie on quality and international acceptance of the standard, two matters which – except in the case of far-fetched protectionism – are closely connected. The new approach stimulates this because it aims at making market penetration easier and at the same time at pursuing a quality policy. This is further stimulated by Art. 100-A, sub 3 of the Single European Act. Considering the weaknesses widely observed in the competitiveness of European industry, this advantage can be described as carrying some weight.

In some branches of industry the positive impact of European standardization on competitiveness will weigh even more heavily. Standards can have a market-creating effect or, in other words, the lack of a standard between adjoining countries can make the Euromarket (i.e., trade between Member States) impossible, as is for instance the case with car telephones. Standards can also have an anticipatory effect. For instance, sufficient investment in product development, process technology and further innovations takes place in some products only when compatibility is secured first. Interesting examples of this are the recently proposed Council directives concerning standardization in the field of information technologies and telecom and concerning the mutual recognition of type approval of terminal equipment for telecommunication, the latter now having been adopted. Given the very close relationship between telecom and information technologies, the key to promoting European product development and greater intra-EC trade is a system of European standards which provides specifications in much more detail than the CCITT world standards. When (different) computers or word processors communicate at a distance, compatibility standards require precise conventions (on the basis of which information exchange takes place) while safeguarding the inter-operability of the systems for processing and communicating the information. European industry lacks these standards and, thereby, a necessary condition for maintaining and improving its world competitive position.

Secondly, it can be expected that the workload on some Commission services will be considerably reduced by the new approach and that the excessively detailed regulations will gradually become of lesser importance. The Commission has already withdrawn various draft directives which were laid before the Council in the context of the traditional approach. *The reduction in the Commission's workload* is welcome because attention can then be given to more urgent problems in the field of technical trade barriers which have a more direct and greater effect on the free intra-EC movement of goods. A couple of urgent problems ask for that attention: the whole set of problems concerning testing, inspections and certification marks; and the consultation procedures in the framework of the Mutual Information Directive which are labour intensive but prevent many potential bottlenecks in the national draft regulations at an early stage.

Reduction in the Commission's workload can also lead to more attention being given to implementation and enforcement questions in the Member States. For many years responses have only been made to complaints and the question is whether even these have been pursued adequately.

NOTE

Many of the perceived economic advantages of the New Approach should be familiar from the material found in Chapter 9. See also G. Bermann, 'The Single European Act: A New Constitution for the Community?' (1989) 27 *Columbia Journal of Transnational Law* 529; D. Waelbroeck, 'L'harmonisation des règles et normes téchniques dans la CEE' (1988) CDE 243.

....

C: **Questioning the New Approach**

Nonetheless, fears have been expressed on several levels about the desirability of the New Approach. First, it has been alleged that the New Approach is liable to reduce effective protection of the citizen by diminishing the explicit detailed commitment to social protection. A connection should here be made with the discussion at p.420 above of the arguably related shift in balance in favour of free trade achieved by the '*Cassis de Dijon*' (Case 120/78) judgment and its subsequent interpretation. The following extract discusses the matter in connection with the free movement of foodstuffs.

> **O. Brouwer**, 'Free Movement of Foodstuffs and Quality Requirements;
> Has the Commission got it Wrong?'
> (1988) 25 CML Rev 237, 248–52

(Some footnotes omitted.)

4. Critical remarks

The Commission's rejection of detailed recipes in Community legislation can be qualified as a minimalist approach; the Commission leaves quality policy with regard to foodstuffs to the Member States and leaves the enforcement and further realisation of the free movement of foodstuffs in this respect to the judiciary. A minimalist approach is not necessarily a bad one; however, in the present case, the foundations for the adoption of this approach are shaky, for the reasons discussed below.

4.1 The borderline between quality requirements and public health requirements

It must first of all be noted that, in general, the composition or manufacturing characteristics of a foodstuff cannot be isolated from matters which are covered by public health requirements. The use of certain ingredients may have as a corollary the use of certain pesticides or additives (the German beer case provides a striking example in this respect [p.387 above]), or the prescription of a certain manufacturing process or treatment which is regulated by law to protect public health (e.g., a biotechnological process). In consequence, the mutual recognition of quality requirements is often only one aspect when the question arises whether a foodstuff, which is lawfully manufactured and marketed in one Member State, may be marketed in another Member State. In any event, it seems inevitable that the free movement of foodstuffs within the Community will remain dependent on the harmonisation of public health requirements (and methods of inspection, analysis and sampling) and the further development and coordination of a public health policy with regard to foodstuffs at Community level.

However, the point at issue is that difficulties may arise as to the borderline between quality requirements and issues of public health even with regard to recipe laws as such. The Commission rightly admits in its Communication that it may be necessary, in the interest of public health, to define in law the nature and composition of a foodstuff, even if the purchaser is adequately informed, by a label, of these elements. The fear then arises that the new legislative approach of the Commission, as set out in its Communication, may partly be jeopardised; after all, who is going to establish whether a given composition of a foodstuff, despite the fact that it may have been lawfully produced and marketed in the exporting Member State, may be undesirable from the point of view of public health in the Member State of import? It must be borne clearly in mind that the Court has in this respect consistently held that the eating habits in the Member State of import comprise one of the elements which may be taken into account when considering potential dangers for public health.

The Commission's viewpoint seems to indicate that it is the task of national courts and the Court of Justice to assess this matter. In fact, the judiciary has been able in a number of cases to dismiss the plea of public health when manifestly ill-founded or when the national legislation in question was clearly disproportionate.[29] However, apart from these situations, the general problem arises to what extent the judiciary is equipped to assess whether products are or may be positively harmful to health. Often scientists, who have been called as expert witnesses in legal proceedings, do not agree, or, findings of scientific research show that uncertainties remain. If one adds to this difficulty the fact that the Court has consistently held that, insofar as scientific uncertainties remain, it is in principle for the Member States, in the absence of harmonisation, to decide what degree of protection of public health they intend to assure,[31] it seems justified to conclude that the judiciary may often not be in a position to overrule the view of the national legislator.

4.2 Is the Commission's approach desirable?

Apart from the preceding observations, it is submitted that the rigorousness of the Commission's new approach is not desirable. The absolute priority accorded to the principle of free movement of goods, and the abandonment, as a matter of principle, of further harmonisation, is undesirable for several reasons.

4.2.1 The protection of the consumer

4.2.1.1 Foodstuffs which lack essential characteristics
It is not my intention to rehearse once again the frequent criticism that the *Cassis de Dijon* ruling will automatically lead to a general reduction in quality, since the most liberal national rule will become general practice. This question has already been discussed *in extenso* on many occasions and the Commission is probably right to reject this criticism in general. The Commission is equally right to reject the similar criticism that a lack of Community compositional rules will automatically lead to a general reduction in quality.

However, the question which seems more appropriate in the context of its Communication and which the Commission does not discuss, is whether the Commission should, as a matter of principle, abandon the introduction of any Community legislation in this field. It may turn out in the end to be highly undesirable with regard to the protection of the consumer to abandon such legislation. In particular, if foodstuffs are brought on the market which lack essential characteristics and are nutritionally inferior, the argument that the choice should be left to the consumer comes across as a bromide. Such situations do not necessarily stem from the disparity in national recipe laws, but may

---

29 The German beer case is a clear example in this respect [Case 178/84, p.387 above].

31 See in particular Case 174/82, *Sandoz*, [1983] ECR 2445 [p.373].

stem from the fact that a foodstuff is not subject to any regulation in the exporting Member State or has been exempted therefrom.

The food laws of the Member States provide numerous exemptions for the manufacturing of foodstuffs which are intended for export. An illustration of this can be found again in the Italian pasta cases: the mandatory use of durum wheat meal is not prescribed for pasta intended for export. Moreover, it may be noted that a number of Member States have exempted products which are intended for export from the official inspections which are prescribed by national legislation with regard to foodstuffs, to ensure protection against public health risks and fraud. But apparently, even if there is no such exemption, the competent authorities of Member States do often, in practice, not carry out any inspections with regard to foodstuffs intended for export.

NOTE

Also worth reading in this vein are H.-C. Von Heydebrand u.d. Lasa, 'Free Movement of Food-stuffs, Consumer Protection and Food Standards in the European Community: has the Court of Justice got it wrong?' (1991) 16 EL Rev 391; C. MacMaolain, 'Free movement of foodstuffs, quality requirements and consumer protection: have the Court and Commission both got it wrong?' (2001) 26 EL Rev 413.

Concern has also been expressed about what has been seen as the privatization of the stand-ards making process under the New Approach. The next extract addresses some questions about the democratic accountability of aspects of the legislative process which emerges from the New Approach's shift in emphasis.

R. Dehousse, '1992 and Beyond: the Institutional Dimension of the
Internal Market Programme'
[1989/1] LIEI 109, 125–27

(Footnotes omitted.)

A. DELEGATION OF POWERS: EFFICIENCY v DEMOCRACY?

We have seen that the internal market programme was framed under the assumption that no major alteration to the key principle of decision-making by consensus was likely to take place in the near future. In spite of the long-term effects they might possibly have, the modifications contained in the Single Act did not fundamentally change the nature of the problem. If a leap forward is to be realised, it is therefore necessary to think of alternative ways of avoiding the protracted bargaining to which decision-making by consensus amounts most of the time.

One such way is of course to reduce the legislative agenda, which is as we saw one of the main advantages of the principle of mutual recognition. Another way is to limit the Council's work-load by delegating more decision-making powers to other bodies. This latter way has been more actively explored at Community level in recent years, be it in the field of standardisation or through an increase in the Commission's powers as regards the implementation of Community legislation. Although these two techniques involve different kinds of problems, they raise similar political issues.

The new strategy defined by the Commission in the wake of *Cassis de Dijon* not only limits the extent to which harmonisation is necessary, but also involves a new approach to ways of harmonisa-tion. The basic feature of this new line is the distinction drawn between essential safety require-ments, which must be adopted at Community level, and technical specifications, the defining of which can be entrusted to private standardisation bodies. This new approach was defined by the Council even before the White Paper on the internal market was finalised. Later on, the 'Model directive' on technical harmonisation made it clear that although standards defined by European bodies like CEN or CENELEC – or, in their absence, by national bodies – were to retain their non-mandatory character, products manufactured according to these technical specifications were to be regarded as conforming to the essential requirements laid down by the directives.

One of the reasons used to justify this mechanism is that since harmonisation is of direct interest to the industry and industrialists have a more direct knowledge of the technical problems involved, it would be unwise to give this task to an already overburdened Community legislator. It is clear that the reference to standards can also ease the updating of technical regulations, which is often a delicate matter. But this search for greater efficiency cannot ignore the basic requirements of the Commission legal system. It has been stressed that since compliance with standards entitles a product to free movement, the reference to standards in directives amounts to a delegation of competence from the Council to private bodies. It can therefore only be made in accordance with the general principles laid down by the Court of Justice: delegated powers must be of a clearly defined executive nature and subject to the same conditions as those imposed on the delegating institution, such as the duty to state reasons and the necessary [sic] of judicial control [*Meroni* (Case 9/56)]. These requirements are in a way the transportation in legal terms of more general concerns. If reference to standards is to become a permanent feature of Community regulatory policy, the transparency of this process must be ensured so as to guarantee that the interests of all parties concerned (the industry, of course, but consumers as well, for instance) are duly taken into account. In other words, a balance must be struck between public and private concerns.

How could the requirements laid down by the Court be satisfied? It has been suggested that standards could be published as an annex to which harmonisation directives will refer, in order to make judicial control possible. To some extent, the difficulty was also anticipated by the Model Directive. The need to assign clear limits to the delegated powers surfaces in the description which is given of the essential requirements to be covered by harmonisation directives:

'The essential safety requirements . . . shall be worded precisely enough in order to create, on transposition into national law, legally binding obligations which can be enforced. They should be so formulated as to enable the certifications straight away to certify products as being in conformity, having regard to those requirements in the absence of standards.'

While this line of conduct is probably able to reconcile the somewhat contradictory requirements of legitimacy and efficiency, the practical difficulties should not be underestimated: whereas too much discretion given to private bodies could be regarded as incompatible with the guidelines given by the Court, a too detailed directive would amount to no less than a return to the 'old approach'. The implementation of the new approach will therefore be no easy task.

■ QUESTION

P. Birkenshaw, I. Harden, and N. Lewis, in *Government by Moonlight* (London: Unwin, 1990), conclude a survey of the implications for democratic accountability of privatization in the UK context as follows:

It would be a fine irony if British citizens were to get a bill of rights only to find that the 'public' authorities against which the rights might be impleaded had largely been replaced by 'private' bodies, which can be rendered accountable only through private law mechanisms.

To what extent do you think that the privatizating trend of the New Approach yields a parallel (and perhaps greater) democratic deficit at Community level?

NOTES
1. See R. Dehousse in R. Bieber *et al* (eds), at p.423 above; S. Weatherill and A. McGee (1990) 53 MLR 578, 582–87; N. Burrows, *ibid.* at p.597. But contrast L. Gormley [1989/1] LIEI 9, 13, n.18; J. Stoodley, quoted in N. Burrows, at pp.601–02. The general issue is how to assess the efficiency and legitimacy of the harmonization programme as a basis for managing the market created pursuant to the rules of the EC Treaty. As the extracts above demonstrate, this is not a narrow technical matter. And it is an enduring area of interest. For more recent debate in related areas, see G. Spindler, 'Market Processes, Standardisation, and Tort Law' (1998) 4 ELJ 316; E. Vos, *Institutional Frameworks of Community Health and Safety Regulation: Committees, Agencies and Private Bodies* (Oxford: Hart Publishing, 1999).

In conclusion, it should be pointed out that the New Approach, although now firmly embedded within Community regulatory strategy, is not seen as appropriate for *all* future harmonization. The realisation of economies of scale within the wider market will sometimes be dependent on effective Community-wide harmonisation. In the absence of uniformity, as H. von Sydow has observed (in R. Bieber *et al*, at p.97), 'it will be possible to buy an electrical appliance in any part of the Community and to take it across the border without restriction, but, once at home, it may still prove impossible to plug it into the wall socket'.

2. The second important component in the shift of emphasis in the Commission's harmonization programme was the change in voting rules introduced by the Single European Act. In Article 100a, an important move towards qualified majority voting in place of unanimity was made. This is now found in Article 95 post-Amsterdam. Yet States still retain some protection against the risk that their standards would be lowered by the harmonized rule. This is the purpose of Articles 95(3) and (4) *et seq*. See p.616 above for the text: as already suggested, these provisions show the sensitivity of trying to introduce a common rule into a system characterized by the diversity that is a feature (and strength) of Europe. This is the thematic issue that holds together the material traversed in this Chapter.

SECTION 3: **METHODS OF HARMONIZATION**

A: **Harmonization and the allocation of competence between the EC and the Member States**

When the Community adopts secondary legislation, what is the impact on the competence of Member States in the area covered by the EC measure? Some provisions of the Treaty that authorize the adoption of secondary legislation explicitly address this question. Others do not.

Article 153 deals with consumer protection. The Community is authorized to legislate in order to promote the interests of consumers and to ensure a high level of consumer protection. It shall do so by adopting measures pursuant to Article 95 in the context of the completion of the internal market (Article 153(3)(a)) and also by adopting measures which support, supplement, and monitor the policy pursued by the Member States (Article 153(2)(b)). In the latter case it explicitly provided that such measures 'shall not prevent any Member State from maintaining or introducing more stringent protective measures. Such measures must be compatible with this Treaty. The Commission shall be notified of them'. This is Article 153(5) EC.

A similar formula governs the impact of EC action on national competence to legislate in the field of environmental protection. Article 175 EC provides a base for the adoption of measures to protect the environment. Article 176 then declares that 'The protective measures adopted pursuant to Article 175 shall not prevent any Member State from maintaining or introducing more stringent protective measures. Such measures must be compatible with this Treaty. They shall be notified to the Commission'.

Accordingly Community legislation governing consumer protection adopted under Article 153 and environmental protection adopted under Article 175 does not displace national competence to act. The Member States must comply with the Community rules but, if they so choose, they can also go further to protect the consumer and the environment. The Community rules operate as a *minimum* standard.

In December 1992, the Edinburgh European Council concluded that:

> ... where it is necessary to set standards at Community level, consideration should be given to setting minimum standards, with freedom for Member States to set higher standards, not only in the areas where the Treaty so requires ... but also in other areas where this would not conflict with the objectives of the proposed measure or with the Treaty.

What of harmonization? In contrast to Articles 153 and 176 the Treaty provisions governing harmonization do not make clear what shall be the effect of EC legislation on national competence. Article 94 (ex 100) is completely silent on the issue. Article 95 (ex 100a) contains within it only the strictly limited derogation foreseen by Articles 95(4) *et seq*. Article 95 is set out in full above (p.616) but the relevant paragraphs deserve repetition.

ARTICLE 95(4)–(5)

4. If, after the adoption by the Council or by the Commission of a harmonisation measure, a Member State deems it necessary to maintain national provisions on grounds of major needs referred to in Article 30, or relating to the protection of the environment or the working environment, it shall notify the Commission of these provisions as well as the grounds for maintaining them.

5. Moreover, without prejudice to paragraph 4, if, after the adoption by the Council or by the Commission of a harmonisation measure, a Member State deems it necessary to introduce national provisions based on new scientific evidence relating to the protection of the environment or the working environment on grounds of a problem specific to that Member State arising after the adoption of the harmonisation measure, it shall notify the Commission of the envisaged provisions as well as the grounds for introducing them.

The paragraphs that follow within Article 95 map out the manner in which the Commission shall manage this procedure (p.616 above).

The first question asks how this procedure is handled. The second question is a more general one – if the procedure set out in Article 95(4) *et seq* is not invoked, what competence (if any) do Member States retain to legislate in areas covered by a measure of harmonization? Can *minimum harmonization* play a role in the area of harmonization of laws?

....

B: **The management of Article 95(4)** *et seq*

On the first question: in the next case the Court decided that a narrow interpretation should be placed on these provisions, for they challenge the attainment of a fundamental Treaty objective, the integration of the market for goods.

France v *Commission* (Case C-41/93)
[1994] ECR I-1829, Court of Justice of the European Communities

[19] One of the objectives of the Community set out in Articles 2 and 3 of the EEC Treaty is the creation of a common market. The Court has consistently held that the establishment of the common market is intended to remove barriers to intra-Community trade with a view to merging

national markets into a single market achieving conditions as close as possible to those of a genuine domestic market.

[20] Article 8a of the EEC Treaty (Article 7a of the EC Treaty [now Article 14 EC]) provides that the internal market is to be progressively established by measures adopted by the Community in accordance with the provisions of the article and of the other provisions mentioned therein, including Article 100a.

[21] By way of derogation from Article 100 and save where otherwise provided in the Treaty, the provisions of Article 100a apply for the achievement of the objectives set out in Article 8a.

[22] According to Article 100a(1), those objectives are to be implemented by measures, including directives to be adopted by the Council in accordance with the procedure laid down therein and which have as their object the abolition of barriers to trade arising from differences between the provisions laid down by law, regulation or administrative action in Member States.

[23] Under that system, however, if the conditions which Article 100a(4) lays down are fulfilled, that provision allows a Member State to apply rules derogating from a harmonisation measure adopted in accordance with the procedure laid down in Paragraph 1.

[24] As this possibility constitutes a derogation from a common measure aimed at attaining one of the fundamental objectives of the Treaty, namely the abolition of obstacles to the free movement of goods between Member States, Article 100a(4) makes it subject to review by the Commission and the Court of Justice.

[25] It is in the light of those considerations that it is necessary to examine the procedure according to which the Commission must review and, where appropriate, confirm the national provisions of which it is notified by a Member State.

[26] In the first place, where, after the expiry of the time allowed for transposing, or after the entry into force of, a harmonisation measure mentioned in Article 100a(1), a Member State intends, as in this case, to continue to apply national provisions derogating from the measure, it is required to notify the Commission of those provisions.

[27] The Commission must then satisfy itself that all the conditions for a Member State to be able to rely on the exception provided for by Article 100a(4) are fulfilled. In particular, it must establish whether the provisions in question are justified on grounds of the major needs mentioned in the first subparagraph of Article 100a(4) and are not a means of arbitrary discrimination or a disguised restriction on trade between Member States.

[28] The procedure laid down by that provision is intended to ensure that no Member State may apply national rules derogating from the harmonised rules without obtaining confirmation from the Commission.

[29] Measures for the approximation of the provisions laid down by law, regulation or administrative action in Member States which are such as to hinder intra-Community trade would be rendered ineffective if the Member States retained the right to apply unilaterally national rules derogating from those measures.

[30] A Member State is not, therefore, authorised to apply the national provisions notified by it until after it has obtained a decision from the Commission confirming them.

NOTE

The Court adopted the same narrow approach to the interpretation of this device in Case C-319/97 *Antoine Kortas* [1999] ECR I-3143. (It should be noted *en passant* that the details of the procedure were significantly amended and made more sophisticated by the Amsterdam Treaty and the fact pattern of *Kortas* could not recur.)

But the procedure offers at least the possibility of a departure from harmonized orthodoxy – provided Commission authorisation is forthcoming.

Denmark v Commission (Case C-3/00)
Judgment of 20 March 2003, Court of Justice of the European Communities

Denmark had notified the Commission of more restrictive rules governing food additives than were laid down in the relevant Community harmonization Directive. The Commission found the measures excessive and refused to authorize them. In a Danish challenge to the Commission Decision, the Court insisted on the (admittedly limited) degree of respect for diversity which is the hallmark of the procedure in Article 95(4) *et seq.*

[63] The applicant Member State may, in order to justify maintaining such derogating national provisions, put forward the fact that its assessment of the risk to public health is different from that made by the Community legislature in the harmonisation measure. In the light of the uncertainty inherent in assessing the public health risks posed by, *inter alia*, the use of food additives, divergent assessments of those risks can legitimately be made, without necessarily being based on new or different scientific evidence.

[64] A Member State may base an application to maintain its already existing national provisions on an assessment of the risk to public health different from that accepted by the Community legislature when it adopted the harmonisation measure from which the national provisions derogate. To that end, it falls to the applicant Member State to prove that those national provisions ensure a level of health protection which is higher than the Community harmonisation measure and that they do not go beyond what is necessary to attain that objective.

The Court found the Commission's assessment of the relevant evidence to be flawed and it annulled the Decision. A report of the Community's Scientific Committee for Food had made a 'highly critical evaluation' of the maximum amounts for additives set by the Directive (para 110), but the Court considered the Commission had failed to take sufficient account of this opinion in rejecting the Danish application. However, it is plain that derogation of this type will not be lightly permitted.

Commission practice follows suit. It is not readily persuaded of the need to depart from the agreed Community standard for fear of damage to the process of market integration. Information on the treatment of applications for derogations from harmonization measures pursuant to Article 95 is routinely provided in the Annual Reports on Monitoring the Application of Community Law, currently available via http://europa.eu.int/comm/secretariat_general/sgb/droit_com/index_en.htm. The next case is simply an illustration.

Decision 2001/571/EC Commission Decision of 18 July 2001 on the national provisions notified by Germany in the field of pharmacovigilance
[2001] OJ L202/46

The aim of Directive 2000/38/EC was to remodel pharmacovigilance systems, previously primarily paper-based and organized at national level, into a Community-wide electronic data system. The obligation imposed on a trader to report adverse reactions to a medicinal product under German law (the 'AMG') differed from the obligation under the Directive in two respects. First, German law required notification of an adverse reaction irrespective of whether the suspected case occurred inside or outside Germany, whereas the Directive required only notification to the competent authority of the Member State in which the adverse reaction took place. Second, adverse reactions occurring outside the Community had to be notified pursuant to the Directive only if unexpected, whereas German

law contained no such restriction. Germany applied under Article 95(4) for authorization to maintain its pre-existing regime.

[17] The Commission can only approve a notification pursuant to Article 95(4) of the EC Treaty if all of
the conditions listed in Article 95 of the EC Treaty are met. In particular, maintaining the national
provisions must be justified on grounds of major needs referred to in Article 30 of the EC Treaty,
or relating to protection of the environment or the working environment (Article 95(4) of the EC
Treaty). In addition the national provisions may neither be a means of arbitrary discrimination or a
disguised restriction on trade between Member States; neither can they constitute an obstacle to
the functioning of the internal market (Article 95(6) of the EC Treaty).

[18] When examining whether the national measures notified under Article 95(4) are justified by
major needs, the Commission has to take as a basis 'the grounds' put forward by the Member State
to justify the maintenance of its national provisions. This means that, according to the provisions of
the Treaty, the responsibility for proving that these measures are justified lies with the requesting
Member State. Given the procedural framework established by Article 95 of the EC Treaty, in
principle the Commission has to limit itself to examining the relevance of the elements which are
submitted by the requesting Member State, without itself having to seek possible grounds of
justification.

[19] Germany invokes major needs to protect the health and life of humans and consequently one of
the circumstances referred to in Article 30 of the EC Treaty. Maintaining the obligations to report as
provided for in the current provisions of sentences 2 to 8 of Section 95(1) AMG would attain the
highest possible level of health protection for the population in their use of medicinal products. This
high national level of protection was endangered by Directive 2000/38/EC since, firstly, adverse
reactions will in future only be reported to the Member state in which they take place and, secondly,
adverse reactions which take place in a non-member country are only covered by the obligation to
report when they are 'unexpected'.

The Commission examined the detail of the matter, and was not convinced by
Germany's submission. On the first point, it ruled that the system of information
sharing foreseen by Directive 2000/38 would adequately protect health.

[24] . . . no major needs within the meaning of Article 30 of the EC Treaty can be recognised which
could justify maintaining the obligation to report adverse reactions from other Member States.
Rather the restriction contained in the new version of Article 29d(2) [of the Directive] represents a
logical conclusion to the establishment of the new data network. This will make the same information available to the Member States as previously, but presentation will be improved. Maintaining
the previous obligations to report would place an unnecessary and unjustifiable burden on the
respective marketing authorisation holders.

Neither did the Commission accept Germany's second point, which was directed
against the Directive's limitation to notification of *unexpected* reactions in the case
of events occurring outside the Community.

[27] . . . any expected adverse reactions have to be taken into account during the testing and
authorisation of a product, while obviously this is not possible when these are unexpected, During
the subsequent monitoring of a medicinal product in the framework of pharmacovigilance, special
significance is thus attached to unexpected as opposed to expected adverse reactions. For this
reason, the general reporting and evaluation of adverse reactions, even when they occur outside the
Community, appears necessary only when these are unexpected.

[28] This conclusion is based on scientific evidence acquired in recent years relating to the medicinal
products approved as part of the centralized Community procedure pursuant to Regulation (EEC)
2309/93. This procedure is obligatory for certain products of the biotechnology and high technology
industries, which are regarded as particularly complex and sensitive. None the less the second
subparagraph of Article 22(1) of Regulation (EEC) 2309/93 restricts the obligation to report the

adverse reactions of such medicinal products which occur in non-member countries to those which are unexpected. Analyses and evaluations of the information on adverse reactions generated from centrally authorised medicinal products have confirmed that it is also not necessary to report and evaluate information on expected adverse reactions from non-member countries.

[29] This assessment is further supported by the fact that the Federal Republic of Germany is the only Member State which does not restrict the obligation to report adverse reactions occurring in non-member countries to those which are unexpected, but extends this obligation to adverse reactions which are expected. This highlights the fact that none of the other Member States considers it necessary, in order to protect the health and life of humans, to include reports of suspected serious expected adverse reactions from non-member countries in the pharmacovigilance systems.

[30] Consequently, in maintaining an obligation to report suspected serious expected adverse reactions from non-member countries, Germany is not able to invoke major needs within the meaning of Article 30 of the EC Treaty. The provision of the new version of Article 29d(4) applies new scientific evidence without prejudicing the high level of health protection in the Community.

The Commission rejected the application. Notice the concern for burdens imposed on traders (para 24) and the relevance of choices made by other Member States (para 29). A connection should be made with the broader discussion of the scope allowed to States to justify trade barriers under Article 28 (pp.366, 408) and Article 49 (p.456).

....

C: **Harmonization, competence, and the scope for minimum rules**

The second question posed above (p.629) is a more general one – if the procedure set out in Article 95(4) *et seq* is not invoked, what competence (if any) do Member States retain to legislate in areas covered by a measure of harmonization?

The legal aspects of this issue under Articles 28–30 EC were discussed in *Rewe* (Case 4/75) and *Moormann* (Case 190/87), at p.376 above. It was there demonstrated that action taken to harmonize national laws by the Community legislature may have the effect of depriving Member States of the competence to resort to Article 30 justify obstructive trading rules in the field covered by the Directive. The relevant jargon holds that the Community has 'occupied the field'; it has 'pre-empted' national competence. Free trade proceeds on the basis of a rule which is identical throughout the Community and States are deprived of the ability to set standards which diverge from the Community norm. In the next case the Court's interpretation of Directive 76/756 in 'Dim Dip' follows this resolutely pro-integrative line. The UK is held to have acted in breach of the Treaty by imposing a requirement not included in the exhaustive list of requirements permissible under the relevant Directive. It prohibited the use of motor vehicles not equipped with dim dip lighting.

Commission v *UK* (Case 60/86)
[1988] ECR 3921, Court of Justice of the European Communities

[10] It is clear from the documents before the Court that the reason for which dim-dip devices were not included in the provisions, even as optional devices, is that the technical committee of national experts did not consider them acceptable given the state of technical progress at the time. In addition, it was not considered appropriate to adapt Directive 76/756/EEC, after its entry into force, so as to take account of technical progress in accordance with the procedure laid down in Article 13

of Directive 70/156/EEC and Article 5 of Directive 76/756/EEC, by bringing dim-dip devices within the scope of the latter directive.

[11] Such an interpretation of the exhaustive nature of the list of lighting and light-signalling devices set out in Annex I to the directive is consistent with the purpose of Directive 70/156/EEC which is to reduce, and even eliminate, hindrances to trade within the Community resulting from the fact that mandatory technical requirements differ from one Member State to another (see the first and second recitals in the preamble to Directive 70/156/EEC). In the context of Directive 76/756/EEC that objective is reflected in the obligation imposed on the Member States to adopt the same requirements 'either in addition to or in place of their existing rules' (second recital).

[12] It follows that the Member States cannot unilaterally require manufacturers who have complied with the harmonized technical requirements set out in Directive 76/756/EEC to comply with a requirement which is not imposed by that directive, since motor vehicles complying with the technical requirements laid down therein must be able to move freely within the common market.

[13] It must therefore be declared that, by prohibiting, in breach of Council Directive 76/756/EEC of 27 July 1976, the use of motor vehicles manufactured after 1 October 1986 and put into service after 1 April 1987 which are not equipped with a dim-dip device, the United Kingdom has failed to fulfil its obligations under Community law.

NOTE

The approach taken in *Commission* v *UK* (Case 60/86) is obviously potentially of relevance beyond its facts. The same approach might be taken, for example, to the effect of rules relating to the quality of goods or the qualifications which a migrant professional must possess.

But the Court's interpretative approach in this case is based on the purpose of the Directive. It is not rooted in the Treaty provision on which the Directive was based. As mentioned above, neither Article 94 or 95 (ex 100 and 100a) EC make explicit what should be the impact of EC legislation on residual national competence. Articles 153 and 176, by contrast, stipulate that Community legislation adopted under those provisions governing consumer and environmental protection respectively establish *minimum* rules only. One may assume that the minimum formula is appropriate in the fields of environmental and consumer protection because the dominant purpose of the relevant Treaty provisions is to pursue the objectives of those policies and not explicitly to integrate markets, whereas, by contrast, one might choose to argue that Articles 94 and 95, as foundation stones of market building, should always pre-empt national competence to act in the occupied field. Were it otherwise, there would loom the possibility of an uneven 'playing field' for traders in so far as States choose to set rules above the Community minimum.

But the Court's case law is not quite so neat. In the next case the Court rejected a submission that a Directive should be interpreted as setting both floor and ceiling (total harmonization) and finding instead that it fixed a floor only (minimum harmonization). Stricter State rules were therefore not pre-empted by the Directive.

Hans Hönig v *Stadt Stockach* (Case C-128/94)

[1995] ECR I-3389, Court of Justice of the European Communities

Directive 88/166 established standards for the protection of laying hens kept in battery cages. German rules required larger cages than were provided for under the Directive. Hönig, a German farmer, submitted that to allow a State to set a stricter rule would frustrate the Directive's capacity to achieve uniform conditions of competition in the EC. The Directive's legal base was Article 43 (now, in amended form,

37) EC, governing the common organization of agricultural markets. (Where EC legislation concerns the production and marketing of agricultural products and contributes to the achievement of one or more of the aims of the objectives of the common agricultural policy, this Treaty provision applies; the Treaty provisions governing harmonization cannot be relied upon as a ground for restricting its scope, see recently, e.g., Case C-269/97 *Commission v Council* [2000] ECR I-2257.) *Via* the preliminary reference procedure, a German court sought the European Court's interpretation of the leeway permitted to Member States under the Directive. The Court based its ruling on both the text and the purpose of the Directive.

[9] As the Court has emphasised in its decisions, it is necessary in interpreting a provision of Community law to consider not only its wording but also the context in which it occurs and the objects of the rules of which it is part (judgment in Case 292/82 *Merck v Hauptzollamt Hamburg-Jonas* [1983] ECR 3781, paragraph 12, and in Case 337/82 *St Nikolaus Brennerei v Hauptzollamt Krefeld* [1984] ECR 1051, paragraph 10).

[10] As regards in the first place the wording of the directive, Article 3(1)(a) of the Annex provides as follows:

> Member States shall ensure that from 1 January 1988:
>
> — all newly built cages for use within the Community,
> — all cages brought into use for the first time,
>
> at least comply with the following requirements:
>
> (a) at least 450cm2 of cage area . . . shall be provided for each laying hen. . . .

[11] On the wording of the provision, therefore, the Member States may not lay down a minimum surface area of less than 450cm2 per cage, but may lay down a minimum cage area per hen greater than that provided for; that is shown, moreover, by the title of the directive and Article 1 thereof, which provides that 'this directive lays down the minimum standards for the protection of laying hens kept in battery cages'.

[12] The minimum standards contained in the directive were laid down as a consequence of the Council Resolution of 22 July 1980 on the protection of laying hens in cages (OJ 1980 C 196, p.1) and in Council Decision 78/923/EEC of 19 June 1978 approving the European Convention for the Protection of Animals kept for Farming Purposes (OJ 1978 L 323, p.12).

[13] Next, the purpose of the directive must be considered.

[14] As the Advocate General pointed out in paragraph 13 of his Opinion, the directive seeks first to provide protection for animals kept for farming purposes and secondly to reduce the disparities in conditions of competition as between Member States on the market in eggs and poultry.

[15] The Community legislature therefore sought to reconcile the interests of the proper functioning of the organisation of the market in eggs and poultry with those of animal protection by laying down, according to the third recital in the preamble to the directive, common minimum requirements applicable to all intensive housing systems, including those for laying hens kept in battery cages.

[16] Lastly, the use of the words 'as a first step' in the third recital, and the content of the fourth recital in the preamble to the directive, indicate that the latter seeks only a certain degree of harmonisation in the protection of hens by means of provisions laying down minimum standards.

[17] Admittedly, that interpretation of the directive's provisions may lead, as the plaintiff in the main action has pointed out, to battery hen farmers in one Member State receiving less favourable treatment than those in other Member States, thus allowing some inequalities in competition to persist. However, those are the consequences of the level of harmonisation sought by those provisions, which lay down minimum standards.

NOTE

Inspection of the Directive's purpose led the Court to its conclusion. These were minimum rules only, so a degree of local regulatory autonomy remained, unsuppressed by centralized rule-making. There are individual Directives formally adopted as measures of harmonization designed to advance the building of an integrated market which contain a minimum clause. This is common in the batch of measures harmonizing the legal protection of the economic interests of consumers. Directive 85/577 governing 'Doorstep Selling' provides an example. (It was, you may remember, the Directive at stake in *Dori* (Case C-91/92), in which the Court rejected the horizontal direct effect of Directives: Chapter 5, p.148 above.)

DIRECTIVE 85/577 ON THE PROTECTION OF THE CONSUMER IN RESPECT OF CONTRACTS NEGOTIATED AWAY FROM BUSINESS PREMISES
[1985] OJ L372/31

Article 8

This Directive shall not prevent Member States from adopting or maintaining more favourable provisions to protect consumers in the field which it covers.

NOTE

Ministère Public v *Buet* (Case 382/87 [1989] ECR 1235) was encountered in Chapter 11 (p.400). A French decision to ban doorstep selling of certain materials was not treated as pre-empted by the existence of Directive 85/577, which governs exactly that marketing practice and which requires only that the consumer be given a seven-day cooling off period after concluding such a contract. The Court took the view that because the Directive, though adopted under Article 100 (now 94), provides explicitly for Member States to apply measures more favourable to the consumer, stricter rules were allowed even where they obstructed imported goods, provided only that they were justified (which the Court thought they could be, given their function of protecting vulnerable consumers, as explained at p.401 above).

However, our understanding of this notion of 'minimum harmonization' appears now to be changed by the Court's ruling in the *Tobacco Advertising* case, more properly *Germany v Parliament and Council*, examined at length in Chapter 2 (p.60 above). This reveals that the presence in a Directive of a clause which permits a Member State to introduce stricter rules that impede imports complying with the requirements of the harmonization Directive may be relevant in determining whether use of Article 95 is valid.

Germany v *European Parliament and Council of the European Union*
(Case C-376/98)
[2000] ECR I-8419, Court of Justice of the European Communities

The Court annulled Directive 98/43, which imposed severe restrictions on the advertising of tobacco products. It was based on Article 100a, now, after amendment, Article 95 (and also Articles 57(2) and 66, now Articles 47(2) and 55, governing the services sector). But it did not sufficiently contribute to market-making. Among the Court's objections to the Directive was that:

[101] Moreover, the Directive does not ensure free movement of products which are in conformity with its provisions.

[102] Contrary to the contentions of the Parliament and Council, Article 3(2) of the Directive, relating to diversification products, cannot be construed as meaning that, where the conditions laid down in

the Directive are fulfilled, products of that kind in which trade is allowed in one Member State may move freely in the other Member States, including those where such products are prohibited.

[103] Under Article 5 of the Directive, Member States retain the right to lay down, in accordance with the Treaty, such stricter requirements concerning the advertising or sponsorship of tobacco products as they deem necessary to guarantee the health protection of individuals.

[104] Furthermore, the Directive contains no provision ensuring the free movement of products which conform to its provisions, in contrast to other directives allowing Member States to adopt stricter measures for the protection of a general interest (see, in particular, Article 7(1) of Council Directive 90/239/EEC of 17 May 1990 on the approximation of the laws, regulations and administrative provisions of the Member States concerning the maximum tar yield of cigarettes (OJ 1990 L 137, p.36) and Article 8(1) of Council Directive 89/622/EEC of 13 November 1989 on the approximation of the laws, regulations and administrative provisions of the Member States concerning the labelling of tobacco products (OJ 1989 L 359, p.1)).

[105] In those circumstances, it must be held that the Community legislature cannot rely on the need to eliminate obstacles to the free movement of advertising media and the freedom to provide services in order to adopt the Directive on the basis of Articles 100a, 57(2) and 66 of Treaty.

NOTE

Chapter 2 also considered the unsuccessful legal challenge to the validity of Directive 2001/37 on tobacco labelling (p.66 above). It was based on Article 95 EC and, in view of its impact on external trade, Article 133 EC. It contained a clause requiring Member States to accept on to their market goods complying with the terms of the Directive; put another way, it prohibited the application of stricter rules. This was an element in the Court's finding that the Directive was valid.

R v *Secretary of State for Health, ex parte British American Tobacco (Investments) Ltd and Imperial Tobacco Ltd* (Case C-491/01)
Judgment of 10 December 2002, Court of Justice of the European Communities

[74] It must be added that, unlike the directive at issue in the case giving rise to the tobacco advertising judgment, the Directive contains a provision, Article 13(1), which guarantees the free movement of products which comply with its requirements. By forbidding the Member States to prevent, on grounds relating to the matters harmonised by the Directive, the import, sale or consumption of tobacco products which do comply, that provision gives the Directive its full effect in relation to its object of improving the conditions for the functioning of the internal market.

[75] It follows that the Directive genuinely has as its object the improvement of the conditions for the functioning of the internal market and that it was, therefore, possible for it to be adopted on the basis of Article 95 EC, and it is no bar that the protection of public health was a decisive factor in the choices involved in the harmonising measures which it defines.

NOTE

Minimum harmonization therefore seems to be treated as a contradiction in terms. A measure of harmonization adopted on the basis of Article 94 or 95 takes as one of its constitutional rationales the suppression of local regulatory competence to maintain or introduce stricter rules that impede the access to the local market of goods or services from other Member States that comply with the harmonized standard. A State wishing to demand higher standards of imports has available to it only the procedure set out in Article 95(4) *et seq.* The Court's willingness in *Buet* to entertain justification for rules stricter than those laid down in Directive 85/577 now seems incompatible with the rulings in the 'tobacco' cases of 2000 and 2002. And Directive 85/577's concession that 'This Directive shall not prevent Member States from adopting or maintaining more favourable provisions to protect consumers in the field which it covers' (p.636 above) now seems *either* fatal to the Directive's validity as a measure of harmonization *or else*, less savagely, properly interpreted to allow the application of more favourable rules only to domestic goods, and not to imports.

SECTION 4: **THE EXAMPLE OF CONSUMER LAW**

The field of consumer law deserves attention as a case study in choice of patterns of harmonization. The key to understanding the apparent paradox of a measure of harmonization, designed to build an integrated market, which includes a 'minimum clause' permitting States to introduce (doubtless varying) stricter rules lies in the enduringly important issue of choosing a legal base in the Treaty that authorises the adoption of secondary legislation. Directive 85/577 in fact had little to do with market-building, even though it was adopted on the basis of Article 100. The Directive reflected unanimous political preference for the development of a legislative programme of consumer protection at a time when the Treaty conferred no relevant competence in that field. (What is now) Article 153 governing consumer protection was inserted into the Treaty only with effect from 1993, when the Maastricht Treaty entered into force. In fact, a number of Directives dealing with the harmonization of laws protecting the economic interests of consumers include the minimum formula. Examples include Directive 93/13 on unfair terms in consumer contracts and Directive 94/46 on timeshare [1993] OJ L95/29 and [1994] OJ L280/83 respectively; see further S. Weatherill, *EC Consumer Law and Policy* (Harlow: Longman, 1997).

A: **Minimum harmonization**

The next extract, from an article published in 1988, is written against the background of this history. It sets out the appeal of minimum harmonization, but plainly now requires reading in the light of the Court's more recent case law dealing with the consequences for national competence of harmonization undertaken by the Community legislature.

K. Mortelmans, 'Minimum Harmonization and Consumer Law'
[1988] ECLJ 2, 5–7

(Footnotes omitted.)

The double objective of harmonization, i.e., the establishment of a Common Market and the protection of the interests of the consumer, may be related to the technique of minimum harmonization. Free movement is facilitated as the harmonization of legislation removes distortions in competition; but, since consumer legislation in a number of Member States provides more stringent safeguards, such Member States regard harmonization as a minimum and, on the basis of a provision in the directive, they are authorized to introduce more stringent national measures . . .

The provisions for minimum harmonization arise primarily in directives aimed specifically at the protection of the consumer, the environment or other justified interests and where the abolition of obstacles to free movement of goods comes in second place. In such cases the public interest, in this context in terms of consumer protection, acquires relative precedence over the free movement of goods. More stringent national measures most often arise when scholarly or legal doubts obtain in respect of the protection required for certain specific situations, persons or geographical areas. This then leads to national legislation with different levels of protection.

The technique of minimum harmonization is consequently [a more] than honourable means of reconciling the common market with consumer interests . . .

NOTE

At a descriptive level, the concluding comment now comfortably fits Article 153 EC, but, post-'*Tobacco Advertising*' (Case C-376/98), not Article 95.

■ **QUESTION**

Does the Court's approach in Case C-376/98 (p.636) and Case C-491/01 (p.637) to the place of 'minimum clauses' in measures of legislative harmonization represent an undue emphasis on market integration promoted by centralized rule-making at the expense of local regulatory preferences?

NOTE

The next section concerns a Directive concerned with the harmonization of civil liability rules. Once again, the policy issue relates to the accommodation of diverse aspirations within a regime devoted to free trade.

....

B: **The Product Liability Directive**

Directive 85/374 [1985] OJ L210/29 as amended by Directive 99/34 [1999] L141/20 harmonizes the rules on liability for injury caused by defective consumer products. It was adopted on the basis of Article 100 (now 94) of the Treaty. Article 1 provides that, 'The producer shall be liable for damage caused by a defect in his product'. The Directive is a classic 'dual aim' harmonization measure.

R. Merkin, A Guide to the Consumer Protection Act 1987

(London: Financial Training Publications, 1987), pp.4–5

. . . Reasons for the Directive

The introduction of a uniform code of product liability within the European Community is perceived by the Community authorities as being necessary to bring about two broad sets of objectives: consumer protection objectives and market unity objectives.

The importance of consumer protection is recognised by the second recital of the product liability Directive, which states that:

> . . . liability without fault on the part of the producer is the sole means of adequately solving the problem, peculiar to our age of increasing technicality, of a fair apportionment of the risks inherent in modern technological production.

This broad statement encompasses a number of distinct arguments in favour of strict liability:

(a) The general desire to spread loss throughout society rather than to allow it to fall on individual consumers.

(b) The belief that producers can insure against third-party risks at a lower cost than individual consumers could insure against first-party risks, so that strict liability is the cheapest form of risk-spreading.

(c) The possibility that strict liability will provide manufacturers with the incentive to increase safety and standards generally, an incentive which is not diminished by the probable existence of liability insurance, given the dangers of premium-rating and of adverse publicity.

(d) The illogicality and expense of maintaining a fault-based system.

The market unity arguments for strict liability are rather more subtle. The first recital of the Directive asserts that:

> . . . the existing divergences [between the laws of Member States] may distort competition and affect the movement of goods within the common market and entail a differing degree of protection of the consumer.

Two distinct issues are at stake here:

(a) The principle that goods must be allowed to move freely between Member States, enshrined in articles 30 to 36 [now 28–30] of the Treaty of Rome, is overridden by mandatory consumer protection laws which prevent the sale of dangerous goods, imported or otherwise. By imposing strict liability, standards will improve and goods will be permitted to circulate more freely as between Member States.

(b) If the laws of one Member State are less generous to manufacturers than the laws of other Member States, by the imposition of strict liability, those manufacturers subject to strict liability will be at a competitive disadvantage when exporting to Member States offering a lesser degree of consumer protection. This is so because their products will be more expensive, either as a result of the costs of higher safety standards or as a result of the price of the goods containing an element representing domestic liability insurance premiums. Failure to implement strict liability is thus seen as a form of indirect protectionism.

■ QUESTION

That the Directive promotes consumer protection is plain. But it is a harmonization measure based on Article 100 (now 94). Are the 'market unity' arguments strong enough to secure the Directive against allegations that it is inadequately closely tied to the process of market-making to constitute a valid measure of harmonization? See Chapter 2, p.60 above, for discussion in this vein of Case C-376/98 'Tobacco Advertising'.

NOTE

Two distinct issues associated with the effect of the Directive on national competence arise. The first concerns the scope for local choice expressly allowed within the scope of application of the Directive. The second concerns 'pre-emption' – does the Directive leave any scope for national rules governing product liability that are more generous to the consumer than those mandated by the Directive?

On the first issue, one might suppose that a measure of harmonization should exclude a menu of options from which Member States could select. Yet it was not possible to achieve unanimity in drafting a final version of the Directive which would apply without derogation to all Member States.

R. Merkin, A Guide to the Consumer Protection Act 1987
(London: Financial Training Publications, 1987), pp.6–7

One interesting feature of the Directive is that it permits three 'derogations', i.e., matters in respect of which each Member State is free to determine whether or not it wishes to follow the terms of the Directive. The derogations are as follows:

(a) Agricultural products and game. Article 1 of the Directive provides that there is to be no strict liability upon the producers of these products, although Article 15.1(a) permits Member States to impose such liability if they so wish. . . .

(b) A 'development risks' defence. The Directive contains, in Article 7(e), a defence open to a manufacturer to the effect that the state of scientific and technical knowledge was not such as to enable the defect to be discovered when the product was put into circulation. However, Article 15.1(b) allows Member States to extend strict liability to cover development risks of this nature. It would appear that the majority of Member States intend to avail themselves of the derogation, but the UK has again opted to follow the Directive and to retain the defence . . . [In fact, it emerged that most Member States permit the defence; COM (00) 893, Commission's second report on the Directive, relates that only Finland and Luxembourg exclude it in full, while Spain, France and Germany exclude it in some sectors].

(c) Maximum liability. Article 16 allows the imposition of a maximum liability in respect of individual claims or in respect of aggregate claims arising out of a particular defect in a product, of some £40 million. The UK did not think it necessary to limit liability in this way . . .

The operation of these three derogations is to be assessed in July 1995 to determine whether they should be abandoned or made mandatory . . . [In both COM (95) 617 and COM (00) 893, the Commission's two reports on the Directive, no modification to the Directive was proposed. However, agricultural products and game (point (a)) *are* now subject to the liability régime as a result of amending Directive 99/34, introduced 'in the aftermath of the mad cow crisis', COM (00) 893, p.6.]

NOTE

A major stumbling block was the argument over whether or not to include the 'development risks' defence; derogation (b) in the preceding extract. Its absence would, it was alleged, lead, *inter alia*, to undesirable inhibition of technical innovation.

R. Merkin, A Guide to the Consumer Protection Act 1987
(London: Financial Training Publications, 1987), pp.35–36

. . . The most important justification of the development risks defence is that it encourages research into new products. The argument runs that a producer facing absolute liability for unforeseeable defects will simply not risk marketing new products, to the ultimate detriment of all consumers, because of the cost of potential liability from doing so and because of the danger of damage to reputation resulting from widely publicised successful proceedings.

The validity of the cost approach rests upon two assumptions. First, it presupposes that insurance will not be available for development risk liability. The preliminary view of the Association of British Insurers is, as already noted, that premiums will not be increased significantly by the imposition of strict liability as long as the development risks defence is available, but that there will be a substantial rise if absolute liability is imposed. Given, however, that insurance is available – albeit at a price – the question becomes whether it is proper to allow loss by development risks to fall upon individuals, or whether it is more desirable to require all consumers to contribute to the costs of insurance when making their purchases.

The underlying assumption of product liability is that the latter option is the most desirable. It might also be questioned whether premiums would in fact have to rise as steeply as has been predicted by the Association of British Insurers: most of the calculations were done by assessing the American experience, although the high levels of damages there awarded and the contingency fee system may both render any comparison with the UK misleading.

The second assumption is that producers will not face development risk liability if a development risks defence is included. This, however, is not the case. First, an exporter to other Member States of the EEC may, depending upon the conflict of laws rules prevailing in those States, face absolute liability. Secondly, the original producer may face liability in the UK under the Sale of Goods Act 1979, where a chain action is commenced. Finally, there is always the possibility that, following expensive litigation, the defence cannot be made out. Consequently, it would appear that UK suppliers would be unwise not to carry development risk cover irrespective of the position under the Consumer Protection Act 1987.

The reputation argument would not appear to be significant. In the absence of a development risks defence there would appear not to be a need for litigation, and all manufacturers would in any event face the same liability, so that there ought not be a fear of competitive disadvantage. In addition, reputation may be lost as much in successfully defending litigation as in accepting liability quietly.

NOTE

The existence of the development risk defence has been criticized as a severe curtailment of the ability of the measure to provide effective consumer protection. For example, a modern parallel to the thalidomide tragedy would probably still go uncompensated in the UK because of the producer's ability to rely on the defence. See Cmnd. 7054 (1978), para 1259, *Report of the Pearson Commission on Civil Liability and Compensation for Personal Injury*. See also C. Newdick, 'The

Future of Negligence in Product Liability' (1987) 103 LQR 288; M. Shapo, 'Comparing Products Liability: Concepts in European and American Law' (1993) 26 Cornell Intl LJ 279; G. Howells and T. Wilhelmsson, 'EC and US Approaches to Consumer Protection – Should the Gap be Bridged?' (1997) 17 YEL 207; and, more broadly J. Stapleton, *Product Liability* (Oxford: OUP, 1994).

Furthermore, the nature of the defence and its implementation in the UK has provoked controversy; Article 7(e) of Directive 85/374 provides that 'the producer shall not be liable as result of this Directive if he proves that the state of scientific and technical knowledge at the time when he put the product into circulation was not such as to enable the existence of the defect to be discovered'. The UK's implementing Consumer Protection Act 1987, s. 4(1)(e), provides that it is a defence to show 'that the state of scientific and technical knowledge at the relevant time was not such that a producer of products of the same description as the product in question might be expected to have discovered the defect if it had existed in his products while they were under his control'. For a challenging argument that the UK's implementation is in fact correct, notwithstanding the textual discrepancy, see C. Newdick, 'The Development Risk Defence of the Consumer Protection Act 1987' (1988) 47 CLJ 455 and 'Risk, Uncertainty and "Knowledge" in the Development Risk Defence' [1991] Anglo-Amer LR 127. The Court was provided with the opportunity to clarify the position by Commission infringement proceedings brought against the United Kingdom under Article 169 (now 226) EC, but the Court's ruling did not entirely resolve the matters of substance.

Commission v *United Kingdom* (Case C-300/95)
[1997] ECR I-2649, Court of Justice of the European Communities

The core of the Commission's complaint is summarized as follows:

[16] In its application, the Commission argues that the United Kingdom legislature has broadened the defence under Article 7(e) of the Directive to a considerable degree and converted the strict liability imposed by Article 1 of the Directive into mere liability for negligence.

[17] The Commission submits that the test in Article 7(e) of the Directive is objective in that it refers to a state of knowledge, and not to the capacity of the producer of the product in question, or to that of another producer of a product of the same description, to discover the defect. However, by its use of the words 'a producer of products of the same description as the product in question [who] might be expected to have discovered the defect', section 4(1)(e) of the Act presupposes a subjective assessment based on the behaviour of a reasonable producer. It is easier for the producer of a defective product to demonstrate, under section 4(1)(e), that neither he nor a producer of similar products could have identified the defect at the material time, provided that the standard precautions in the particular industry were taken and there was no negligence, than to show, under Article 7(e), that the state of scientific and technical knowledge was such that no-one would have been able to discover the defect.

The Court proceeded to reject the Commission's application:

[23] In order to determine whether the national implementing provision at issue is clearly contrary to Article 7(e) as the Commission argues, the scope of the Community provision which it purports to implement must first be considered.

[24] In order for a producer to incur liability for defective products under Article 4 of the Directive, the victim must prove the damage, the defect and the causal relationship between defect and damage, but not that the producer was at fault. However, in accordance with the principle of fair apportionment of risk between the injured person and the producer set forth in the seventh recital in the preamble to the Directive, Article 7 provides that the producer has a defence if he can prove certain facts exonerating him from liability, including 'that the state of scientific and technical knowledge at the time when he put the product into circulation was not such as to enable the existence of the defect to be discovered' (Article 7(e)).

[25] Certain general observations can be made as to the wording of Article 7(e) of the Directive.

[26] First, as the Advocate General rightly observes in paragraph 20 of his Opinion, since that provision refers to 'scientific and technical knowledge at the time when [the producer] put the product into circulation', Article 7(e) is not specifically directed at the practices and safety standards in use in the industrial sector in which the producer is operating, but, unreservedly, at the state of scientific and technical knowledge, including the most advanced level of such knowledge, at the time when the product in question was put into circulation.

[27] Second, the clause providing for the defence in question does not contemplate the state of knowledge of which the producer in question actually or subjectively was or could have been apprised, but the objective state of scientific and technical knowledge of which the producer is presumed to have been informed.

[28] However, it is implicit in the wording of Article 7(e) that the relevant scientific and technical knowledge must have been accessible at the time when the product in question was put into circulation.

[29] It follows that, in order to have a defence under Article 7(e) of the Directive, the producer of a defective product must prove that the objective state of scientific and technical knowledge, including the most advanced level of such knowledge, at the time when the product in question was put into circulation was not such as to enable the existence of the defect to be discovered. Further, in order for the relevant scientific and technical knowledge to be successfully pleaded against the producer, that knowledge must have been accessible at the time when the product in question was put into circulation. On this last point, contrary to what the Commission seems to consider, Article 7(e) of the Directive raises difficulties of interpretation which, in the event of litigation, the national courts will have to resolve having recourse, if necessary, to Article 177 of the EC Treaty.

[30] For the present, it is the heads of claim raised by the Commission in support of its application that have to be considered.

[31] In proceedings brought under Article 169 of the Treaty the Commission is required to prove the alleged infringement. The Commission must provide the Court with the material necessary for it to determine whether the infringement is made out and may not rely on any presumption (see, in particular, Case C-62/89 *Commission v France* [1990] ECR I-925, paragraph 37).

[32] The Commission takes the view that inasmuch as section 4(1)(e) of the Act refers to what may be expected of a producer of products of the same description as the product in question, its wording clearly conflicts with Article 7(e) of the Directive in that it permits account to be taken of the subjective knowledge of a producer taking reasonable care, having regard to the standard precautions taken in the industrial sector in question.

[33] That argument must be rejected in so far as it selectively stresses particular terms used in section 4(1)(e) without demonstrating that the general legal context of the provision at issue fails effectively to secure full application of the Directive. Taking that context into account, the Commission has failed to make out its claim that the result intended by Article 7(e) of the Directive would clearly not be achieved in the domestic legal order.

[34] First, section 4(1)(e) of the Act places the burden of proof on the producer wishing to rely on the defence, as Article 7 of the Directive requires.

[35] Second, section 4(1)(e) places no restriction on the state and degree of scientific and technical knowledge at the material time which is to be taken into account.

[36] Third, its wording as such does not suggest, as the Commission alleges that the availability of the defence depends on the subjective knowledge of a producer taking reasonable care in the light of the standard precautions taken in the industrial sector in question.

[37] Fourth, the Court has consistently held that the scope of national laws, regulations or administrative provisions must be assessed in the light of the interpretation given to them by national courts

(see, in particular, Case C-382/92 *Commission* v *United Kingdom* [1994] ECR I-2435, paragraph 36). Yet in this case the Commission has not referred in support of its application to any national judicial decision which, in its view, interprets the domestic provision at issue inconsistently with the Directive.

[38] Lastly, there is nothing in the material produced to the Court to suggest that the courts in the United Kingdom, if called upon to interpret section 4(1)(e), would not do so in the light of the wording and the purpose of the Directive so as to achieve the result which it has in view and thereby comply with the third paragraph of Article 189 of the Treaty (see, in particular, Case C-91/92 *Faccini Dori* v *Recreb* [1994] ECR I-3325, paragraph 26). Moreover, section 1(1) of the Act expressly imposes such an obligation on the national courts.

[39] It follows that the Commission has failed to make out its allegation that, having regard to its general legal context and especially section 1(1) of the Act, section 4(1)(e) clearly conflicts with Article 7(e) of the Directive. As a result, the application must be dismissed.

■ QUESTION

How does one determine when knowledge is 'accessible'? Is such an issue apt for preliminary reference to the European Court, as suggested in para 29 of the ruling above?

....

C: **Uniform application of Community consumer law**

For our purposes the central question must be whether the existence of the options in the Directive tracked in the previous sub-section represents a satisfactory compromise between the demands of free trade and consumer protection. But there is another question inextricably associated with this inquiry, and it is introduced in the next extract.

G. Howells, 'Implications of the Implementation and Non-Implementation
of the EC Products Liability Directive'
(1990) 41 NILQ 22, 25–27

(Footnotes omitted.)

THE THREAT TO HARMONISATION

. . . The options resulted, of course, from compromises which had to be reached in order for the Directive to be acceptable to all the Member States in the first place. Article 15(2) does provide a partial safeguard, in that it provides that a Member State wishing to derogate from Article 7(e) (the development risks defence) must communicate the proposed text to the Commission, who must then inform the other Member States. In general, however, the problem of not knowing how other Member States will decide on the optional provisions has been a disincentive to Member States to provide more than a minimalist level of consumer protection . . . with so many rumours abounding about the form which implementing legislation would take across the Community, it is easy to understand the confusion . . .

There also seems to be a more subtle threat to harmonisation implicit in the Directive's definition of 'defect' as including a product which does not provide 'the safety which a person is entitled to expect'. Although the same test will be applied in each Member State, will the answer vary between them? One might wonder, for example, whether a Greek consumer has the same expectations as a West German?

NOTE

The final paragraph of this extract raises a connected point of great significance. Beyond the existence of options, one can legitimately question whether the terms of the Directive are sufficiently clear and precise to lead to effective harmonization. (*Cf* Brouwer's discussion of food law, at p.624 above.) Of course Article 234 is the channel of communication between national courts and European Court established by the Treaty for the purposes of securing uniform interpretation of EC law (see Chapter 7). But how 'uniform' can one realistically expect the application of such broad notions to be? The field of private law remains illuminating – from tort/delict above, to contract law below.

COMMUNICATION FROM THE COMMISSION TO THE COUNCIL AND THE EUROPEAN PARLIAMENT ON EUROPEAN CONTRACT LAW
[2001] OJ C255/1, COM (2001) 398

The Commission's Communication was designed to prompt debate about the role of the EC in the development of Contract Law. Thus far its role is mainly concerned with the adoption of harmonization measures affecting contract law – Directive 85/577 on Doorstep Selling and Directive 93/13 on unfair terms in consumer contracts have both been encountered above. Four options are floated for the future:

(i) No EC action – based on the perception that markets have a capacity to achieve self-correction that should not be underestimated;
(ii) The promotion of the development of common contract law principles leading to greater convergence of national laws – there should be Commission support for research into comparative law and deeper co-operation between academic and practising lawyers;
(iii) Improving the quality of legislation already in place. This builds on the existing SLIM initiative – 'simpler legislation for the internal market';
(iv) The adoption of new comprehensive legislation at EC level – an idea that is floated conspicuously cautiously.

One question is whether the EC is even legally competent to pursue these ambitions. In paras 23–33 of the Communication on Contract Law the Commission calls explicitly for information on whether diversity between national contract laws 'directly or indirectly obstructs the functioning of the internal market, and if so to what extent', with a view to considering appropriate action by the EC's institutions. To what extent do you think this is inspired by awareness of the limits of Article 95 revealed by the Court's judgment in 'Tobacco Advertising' (Case C-376/98), p.60 above?

The Commission also addresses the issue of uniformity. This extract offers a salutary reminder that 'harmonization' is a long-term process, rather than an one-off act.

3.3. Uniform application of Community law

[34] The European Community legislator must ensure consistency in the drafting of Community legislation as well as in its implementation and application in the Member States. The measures adopted by the European Community must be consistent with each other, interpreted in the same manner and produce the same effects in all Member States. The Court of Justice of the European Communities (the ECJ) has stated that 'the need for uniform application of Community law and

the principle of equality require that the terms of a provision of Community law which makes no express reference to the law of the Member States for the purpose of determining its meaning and scope must normally be given an autonomous and uniform interpretation throughout the Community.[16]

[35] In the area of contract law the European legislator has taken a 'piecemeal' approach to harmonisation. This approach combined with unforeseen market developments, could lead to inconsistencies in the application of Community law. For example, under certain circumstances[17] it is possible to apply both the doorstep selling Directive and the timeshare Directive. Both Directives give the consumer a right of withdrawal; however the time period during which the consumer can exercise this right is different. Although such cases of conflicts between rules are exceptional, the Commission would welcome information on problems resulting from possible inconsistencies between Community rules.

[36] Using abstract terms in Community law can also cause problems for implementing and applying Community law and national measures in a non-uniform way. Abstract terms may represent a legal concept for which there are different rules in each national body of law.[18]

[37] In general, differences between provisions in directives can be explained by differences in the problems which those directives seek to solve. One cannot, therefore, require that a term used to solve one problem is interpreted and applied in precisely the same manner in a different context. However, differences in terms and concepts that cannot be explained by differences in the problems being addressed should be eliminated.

[38] In addition, domestic legislation adopted by Member States to implement Community directives refers to domestic concepts of these abstract terms. These concepts vary significantly from one Member State to another.[19] The absence of a uniform understanding in Community law of general terms and concepts (at least in specific or linked areas) may lead to different results in commercial and legal practice in different Member States.[20]

---

16 Case C-357/98 *The Queen v Secretary of State for the Home Department ex parte Nana Yaa Konadu Yiadom* [2000] ECR-9265, at paragraph 26. See also Case C-287/98 *Luxemburg v Linster* [2000] ECR-6917, at paragraph 43; Case C-387/97 *Commission v Greece* [2000] ECR-5047; Case C-327/82 *Ekro v Produktschap voor Vee en Vlees* [1984] ECR I-107, at paragraph 11. The principle of uniform application also applies in the area of private law see Case C-373/97 *Dionisios Diamantis v Elliniko Dimosio (Greek State), Organismos Ikonomikis Anasinkrotisis Epikhiriseon AE (OAE)* [2000] ECR I-1705, at paragraph 34; Case C-441/93 *Pafitis and Others v TKE and Others* [1996] ECR I-1347, at paragraphs 68 to 70.

17 See Case C-423/97, *Travel-Vac S.L. and Manuel José Antelm Sanchís* [1999] ECR I-2195.

18 These matters have recently been examined by a European Parliament study, drafted by a team of high ranking independent legal experts. It states with regard to the example of the term 'damage' that 'The European laws governing liability do not yet have even a reasonably uniform idea of what damage is or how it can be defined, which naturally threatens to frustrate any efforts to develop European directives in this field'; European Parliament, DG for Research: 'Study of the systems of private law in the EU with regard to discrimination and the creation of a European civil code' (PE 168.511, p.56). Some Directives (Article 9 of Directive 85/374/EEC, Article 17 of Directive 86/653/EEC) contain differing definitions of the term 'damage'. Each definition, however, is intended solely for the purpose of each respective Directive. Other Directives (Article 5 of Directive 90/314/EEC) use the term without defining it.

19 This problem is highlighted by a case pending with the Court of Justice (C-168/00, *Simone Leitner/TUI Deutschland GmbH & Co. KG*). On the basis of a package travel contract concluded under Austrian law with a German tour operator, the complainant seeks compensation for 'moral damages' (unrecoverable holiday spent in hospital). Austrian law does not grant compensation for this kind of damage, but the laws of Germany and some other Member States do. The complainant points to Article 5 of the package travel Directive, saying that this Article establishes a specific concept of 'damage' that includes 'moral damage'.

20 The Commission has emphasised for example in its report on the application of the commercial agents Directive (COM(1996) 364 final of 23 July 1996) that the application of the system of compensation for damage foreseen in the Directive concerning the same factual situation produces completely different practical results in France and the UK due to different methods of calculation for the quantum of compensation.

[39] This kind of problem does not only apply to horizontal questions concerning general terms of contract law as mentioned above. It is also relevant to specific economic sectors.[21]

[40] The Commission is reflecting whether, in order to avoid the kind of problems described above, the necessary consistency could be ensured through the continuation of the existing approach or should be improved through other means. The Commission is therefore interested in receiving information on practical problems relating to contract law resulting from the way that Community rules are applied and implemented in the Member States.

NOTE

A follow-up to the 2001 Communication was published in February 2003: the Action Plan on a more coherent European Contract Law, COM (2003) 68.

■ QUESTION

The development risk defence under the Product Liability Directive is an example of optional differentiated integration within a Community measure. It also allows appreciation of the problems in securing a uniform interpretation and application of notionally 'harmonized' terms. Might one see failure to implement Directives in the national legal order as a further means of choosing differentiated integration? How effective are the Community rules on the direct and indirect effect of Directives (see Chapter 5) as controls over inadequate national implementation of Directives? What might be the impact of the ruling in *Francovich* (Cases C-6, C-9/90), p.168 above?

....

D: **The Product Liability Directive and pre-emption**

The inquiry above concentrates on derogations and options expressly foreseen by the Product Liability Directive, and on its uniform interpretation. What of the *pre-emptive effect* of Directive 85/374? Are different national liability systems to be tolerated? Article 13 provides that 'This Directive shall not affect any rights which an injured person may have according to the rules of the law of contractual or non-contractual liability or a special liability system existing at the moment when this Directive is notified'. The meaning of this provision was elucidated in the next case.

María Victoria González Sánchez v Medicina Asturiana SA (Case C-183/00)
Judgment of 25 April 2002, Court of Justice of the European Communities

Ms González Sánchez sued Medicina Asturiana for compensation for injury allegedly caused on their premises belonging to Medicina Asturiana in the course of a blood transfusion. She claimed to have been infected by the Hepatitis C virus. The Spanish court concluded that the rights afforded to consumers under pre-existing Spanish law were more extensive than those available under the rules introduced to transpose Directive 85/374 into domestic law. The European Court was asked for a preliminary ruling on the question whether Article 13 of the Directive should be

---

21 *The problem referred to here also exists outside the contract law area. Thus in its report on the regulation of European securities markets, the Committee of Wise Men led by Alexandre Lamfalussy pointed to problems resulting from the use in certain Directives in the financial area of ambiguous notions, which allowed Member States to apply these Directives in a disparate manner. Final report, Brussels, 15 February 2001, Annex 5 (initial report of 9 November 2000).*

interpreted as precluding the restriction or limitation, as a result of transposition of the Directive, of rights granted to consumers under the legislation of the Member State.

[22] By its question the referring court is essentially seeking to ascertain whether Article 13 of the Directive must be interpreted as meaning that the rights conferred under the legislation of a Member State on victims of damage caused by a defective product may be limited or restricted as a result of the Directive's transposition into the domestic law of that State.

[23] It should be noted that the Directive was adopted by the Council by unanimity under Article 100 of the EEC Treaty (amended to Article 100 of the EC Treaty, now Article 94 EC) concerning the approximation of such laws, regulations or administrative provisions of the Member States as directly affect the establishment or functioning of the common market. Unlike Article 100a of the EC Treaty (now, after amendment, Article 95 EC), which was inserted into the Treaty after the adoption of the Directive and allows for certain derogations, [see Art 95(4) *et seq* p.629 above] that legal basis provides no possibility for the Member States to maintain or establish provisions departing from Community harmonising measures.

[24] Nor can Article 153 EC, likewise inserted into the Treaty after the adoption of the Directive, be relied on in order to justify interpreting the directive as seeking a minimum harmonisation of the laws of the Member States which could not preclude one of them from retaining or adopting protective measures stricter than the Community measures. In fact, the competence conferred in that respect on the Member States by Article 153(5) EC concerns only the measures mentioned at paragraph 3(b) of that article, that is to say measures supporting, supplementing and monitoring the policy pursued by the Member States. That competence does not extend to the measures referred to in paragraph 3(a) of Article 153 EC, that is to say the measures adopted pursuant to Article 95 EC in the context of attainment of the internal market with which in that respect the measures adopted under Article 94 EC must be equated. Furthermore, as the Advocate General noted at point 43 of his Opinion, Article 153 EC is worded in the form of an instruction addressed to the Community concerning its future policy and cannot permit the Member States, owing to the direct risk that would pose for the *acquis communautaire*, autonomously to adopt measures contrary to the Community law contained in the directives already adopted at the time of entry into force of that law.

[25] Accordingly, the margin of discretion available to the Member States in order to make provision for product liability is entirely determined by the Directive itself and must be inferred from its wording, purpose and structure.

[26] In that connection it should be pointed out first that, as is clear from the first recital thereto, the purpose of the Directive in establishing a harmonised system of civil liability on the part of producers in respect of damage caused by defective products is to ensure undistorted competition between traders, to facilitate the free movement of goods and to avoid differences in levels of consumer protection.

[27] Secondly, it is important to note that unlike, for example, Council Directive 93/13/EEC of 5 April 1993 on unfair terms in consumer contracts (OJ 1993 L 95, p.29), the Directive contains no provision expressly authorising the Member States to adopt or to maintain more stringent provisions in matters in respect of which it makes provision, in order to secure a higher level of consumer protection.

[28] Thirdly, the fact that the Directive provides for certain derogations or refers in certain cases to national law does not mean that in regard to the matters which it regulates harmonisation is not complete.

[29] Although Articles 15(1)(a) and (b) and 16 of the Directive permit the Member States to depart from the rules laid down therein, the possibility of derogation applies only in regard to the matters exhaustively specified and it is narrowly defined. Moreover, it is subject *inter alia* to conditions as to assessment with a view to further harmonisation, to which the penultimate recital in the preamble expressly refers. An illustration of progressive harmonisation of that kind is afforded by Directive

1999/34/EC of the European Parliament and of the Council of 10 May 1999 amending Council Directive 85/374/EEC (OJ 1999 L 141, p.20), which by bringing agricultural products within the scope of the Directive removes the option afforded by Article 15(1)(a) thereof.

[30] In those circumstances Article 13 of the Directive cannot be interpreted as giving the Member States the possibility of maintaining a general system of product liability different from that provided for in the Directive.

[31] The reference in Article 13 of the Directive to the rights which an injured person may rely on under the rules of the law of contractual or non-contractual liability must be interpreted as meaning that the system of rules put in place by the Directive, which in Article 4 enables the victim to seek compensation where he proves damage, the defect in the product and the causal link between that defect and the damage, does not preclude the application of other systems of contractual or non-contractual liability based on other grounds, such as fault or a warranty in respect of latent defects.

[32] Likewise the reference in Article 13 to the rights which an injured person may rely on under a special liability system existing at the time when the Directive was notified must be construed, as is clear from the third clause of the 13th recital thereto, as referring to a specific scheme limited to a given sector of production (see judgments of today in Case C-52/00 *Commission v France* [2002] ECR I-3827, paragraphs 13 to 23, and Case C-154/00 *Commission v Greece* [2002] ECR I-3879, paragraphs 9 to 19).

[33] Conversely, a system of producer liability founded on the same basis as that put in place by the Directive and not limited to a given sector of production does not come within any of the systems of liability referred to in Article 13 of the Directive. That provision cannot therefore be relied on in such a case in order to justify the maintenance in force of national provisions affording greater protection than those of the Directive.

[34] The reply to the question raised must therefore be that Article 13 of the Directive must be interpreted as meaning that the rights conferred under the legislation of a Member State on the victims of damage caused by a defective product under a general system of liability having the same basis as that put in place by the Directive may be limited or restricted as a result of the Directive's transposition into the domestic law of that State.

NOTE
The same identification of a 'complete' system of harmonisation (para 28 above) emerges from the Court's two other rulings of the same day dealing with Directive 85/374: Case C-52/00 *Commission v France*, Case C-154/00 *Commission v Greece* mentioned in para 32 above. This ruling fits into the pattern of *inter alia* that in 'Tobacco Advertising' (Case C-376/98) in its thematic insistence on legislative harmonisation as an instrument for building an internal market.

■ QUESTION

Para 27 of this judgment refers briefly to the inclusion in Directive 93/13 on unfair terms in consumer contracts of a provision expressly authorizing the Member States to adopt or to maintain more stringent provisions in order to secure a higher level of consumer protection. This was also referred to at p 638 above. But Directive 93/13 was adopted under Article 100a (now, after amendment, 95): what is the status today of such a 'minimum clause' in a measure of harmonization?

NOTE
The Court's interpretation of Article 13 of the Directive is vulnerable to the criticism that it locates competence in this field exclusively in the hands of the Community legislature and that it accordingly precludes the expression of local diversity and regulatory innovation. The troubling implications of this prompted the Council to adopt the following Resolution.

COUNCIL RESOLUTION OF 19 DECEMBER 2002 ON AMENDMENT
OF THE LIABILITY FOR DEFECTIVE PRODUCTS DIRECTIVE
[2003] OJ C26/02

THE COUNCIL OF THE EUROPEAN UNION, RECALLING THAT:

[1] Council Directive 85/374/EEC of 25 July 1985 on the approximation of the laws, regulations and administrative provisions of the Member States concerning liability for defective products (OJ 1985 L210), as amended by European Parliament and Council Directive 1999/34/EC of 10 May 1999 (OJ 1999 L141), seeks to achieve an approximation of the laws of the Member States concerning the liability of the producer for damage caused by the defectiveness of his products because the existing divergences may distort competition and affect the movement of goods within the common market and entail a differing degree of protection of the consumer against damage caused by a defective product to his health or property. To provide an adequate solution to the problem, peculiar to our age of increasing technicality, of a fair apportionment of the risks inherent in modern technological production, the Directive imposes liability on the producer without fault on his part for damage caused by the defectiveness of his products.

[2] The producer is considered to be the manufacturer of a finished product, the producer of any raw material or the manufacturer of a component part and any person who, by putting his name, trade mark or other distinguishing feature on the product, presents himself as the producer, cf. Article 3(1) of the Directive. Without prejudice to the liability of the producer, any person who imports into the Community a product for sale, hire, leasing or any form of distribution in the course of his business shall be deemed to be a producer and shall be responsible as a producer, cf. Article 3(2) of the Directive.

[3] Where the producer or the importer of the product cannot be identified, each supplier of the product shall be treated as its producer unless he informs the injured person, within a reasonable time, of the identity of the producer or the importer or of the person who supplied him with the product, cf. Article 3(3) of the Directive. Apart from this specific Article the Directive contains no provisions concerning the liability of the supplier.

[4] At the time of the adoption of the Directive (Session 1025 of the Council, 25 July 1985), the following joint statement of the Council and the Commission concerning the scope of the Directive was inserted in the Council minutes: 'With regard to the interpretation of Articles 3 and 12, the Council and the Commission are in agreement that there is nothing to prevent individual Member States from laying down in their national legislation rules regarding liability for intermediaries, since intermediary liability is not covered by the Directive. There is further agreement that under the Directive the Member States may determine rules on the final mutual apportionment of liability among several liable producers (see Article 3) and intermediaries.' At the same time the following statement was inserted in the Council minutes concerning the understanding of Article 3(3): 'The Council notes that the word "supplier" within the meaning of Article 3(3) means the person who operates in the chain of distribution.'

[5] In a judgment of 25 April 2002 (Case C-52/00) the Court of Justice of the European Communities established that the Directive seeks to achieve, in the matters regulated by it, complete harmonisation of the laws, regulations and administrative provisions of the Member States (see also judgments of the same date in cases C-154/00 and C-183/00). Furthermore, the Court of Justice also established in case C-52/00 that a national legislation providing that the supplier of a defective product is to be liable in all cases and on the same basis as the producer constitutes a violation of the Directive.

[6] Thus, it seems that Member States may no longer lay down rules on liability of suppliers, i.e., persons who operate in the chain of distribution, based on the same ground as the liability system in the Directive concerning liability of producers. Except for cases provided for in Article 3(3) a system of liability of suppliers based on strict liability therefore seems to be precluded.

[7] This legal situation gives rise to concern, since as pointed out in paragraph 3 the Directive does not, apart from Article 3(3), contain provisions concerning the liability of the supplier.

[8] The possibility to lay down rules on liability of suppliers, including rules on strict liability, could involve benefits to the consumers, regardless of whether these rules are laid down at national or Community level. In relevant cases the consumer would then be able to raise his claim against the producer, subsequent suppliers, including the seller of the product, or them all. This could improve consumer's possibility of actually obtaining compensation. The Council also recalls that one of the general objectives of the Community is to promote consumer interests and ensure a high level of consumer protection, cf. Articles 95 and 153 of the Treaty.

[9] THE COUNCIL CONSIDERS that against this background there is a need to assess whether Directive 85/374/EEC, as amended by Directive 1999/34/EC, should be modified in such a way as to allow for national rules on liability of suppliers based on the same ground as the liability system in the Directive concerning liability of producers.

■ QUESTION

What does this tell you about the perils of 'complete harmonization'? What does this tell you about the perils of adding statements to Council minutes that are not carried through in the formal text of adopted legislation?

NOTE

For additional material and resources see the Companion Website at: www.oup.co.uk/best.textbooks/law/weatherill6e

20

Subsidiarity, Flexibility, and New Forms of Governance

Chapter 19 explored the extent to which EC rule-making need not result in an all-or-nothing transfer of competence from Member States to Community. Minimum harmonization in the fields of consumer and environmental protection provides a good example of the rise of a system of 'multi-level governance', within which both State and Community authorities may be active as regulators. Sub-national and regional actors within the States may be involved too – so might international bodies. There are layers of legal authority in today's interdependent world. However, the process of harmonization as a basis for constructing an internal market carries a different emphasis. Derogations within the scope of a Directive are possible, as the case of the Product Liability Directive illustrates (p.639). But the recent case law is strongly motivated by the perceived need to establish the agreed Community rule as the basis for cross-border trade and market integration, and to exclude the possibility of Member States treating the harmonized rule as a minimum.

But there is much more to consider in appreciating the sweep of the Community's regulatory strategy and, in particular, the extent to which the pressure for centralized decision-making is softened by respect for local autonomy and diversity.

The next issue asks: even if the Community is, as a general observation, competent to act, should it exercise that competence in a particular case, or should it instead leave the matter in the hands of the Member States? This is Subsidiarity, and it is treated in Section 1.

Then, to what extent is it desirable to establish systems for decision-making in common which do not implicate all the Member States? This is not a derogation of the detailed type of which the Product Liability Directive offers an illustration, nor even an individual opt-out. It is more fundamental. It suggests a European Union of varying intensities of integration, within which States may choose the depth of their commitment to available common projects. Section 2 covers this.

A further question of governance relates to the instruments to be used. Can the relationship between central and local legal and political authority be better managed by using 'softer' instruments of law- and policy-making that are more conducive to local preferences and regulatory reform than binding instruments such as Regulations and Directives envisaged by Article 249 EC? This is the terrain covered in Section 3.

SECTION 1: **SUBSIDIARITY**

Neither the Treaty of Rome nor the Single European Act contained explicit reference to the principle of subsidiarity. Its essence appears, however, in (what was) Article 130r(4), a provision inserted by the Single European Act.

4. The Community shall take action relating to the environment to the extent to which the objectives referred to in paragraph 1 *can be attained better at Community level than at the level of the individual Member States.* (emphasis added)

NOTE
The Maastricht Treaty introduced a broader formulation of the principle of subsidiarity. It was Article 3b EC and is now, in unamended form, found in the second paragraph of Article 5 post-Amsterdam. It is unaffected by the Nice Treaty.

ARTICLE 5 EC

The Community shall act within the limits of the powers conferred upon it by this Treaty and of the objectives assigned to it therein.

In areas which do not fall within its exclusive competence, the Community shall take action, in accordance with the principle of subsidiarity, only if and in so far as the objectives of the proposed action cannot be sufficiently achieved by the Member States and can therefore, by reason of the scale or effects of the proposed action, be better achieved by the Community.

Any action by the Community shall not go beyond what is necessary to achieve the objectives of this Treaty.

NOTES
1. Article 5(1) contains the principle of attributed competence (p.59 above); Article 5(2) states the subsidiarity pinciple; Article 5(3) reflects the proportionality principle (p.72).
2. The principle of subsidiarity has been cited in connection with the withdrawal of a number of legislative proposals in recent years. The Product Liability Directive (85/374) was examined in the preceding Chapter. The Commission proposed that this liability system for the supply of defective goods should by complemented by a Directive governing liability for supply of defective services (COM (90) 482). In the Commission's report submitted to the Edinburgh European Council in December 1992, which reviewed existing and proposed legislation in the light of the subsidiarity principle, the Commission included the draft Directive in its list of excessively detailed instruments which required revision. It became plain that there was an absence of political will behind the proposed Directive. Eventually, in a Communication on new directions on the liability of suppliers of services (COM (94) 260), the Commission concluded that its 'proposal stands no chance of being adopted without sweeping changes which would risk voiding it of much of its substance'. It therefore withdrew it.
3. 'Subsidiarity' has been employed as a slogan for challenging the expansion of Community activity. Yet the wording of Article 5 is directed at identification of the appropriate level at which action should be taken. It is not based on any entrenched preconception in favour of State action at the expense of the Community. The nature and purpose of the principle of subsidiarity in the context of allocating competences between States and Community has been subjected to increasing scrutiny as the Community continues to develop. The next extract was written at an early stage of the EU's 'subsidiarity mood', and it sets the scene.

M. Wilke and H. Wallace, 'Subsidiarity: Approaches to Power-Sharing
in the European Community'
RIIA Discussion Paper No 27 (1990) pp.21, 30–31

(Some footnotes omitted.)

The current British political debate links the principle of subsidiarity exclusively to the debate about the European Community. Policy-makers and academics are attempting to develop new definitions of the concept, recognizing that Roman Catholic sources have supplied the basic foundations. It is not surprising, however, given that British experience is different from Dutch or German, that a considerable confusion persists when it comes to 'pinning down' the principle of subsidiarity.

In February 1990, the Legal Adviser of the Select Committee on European Legislation of the House of Commons was asked to produce a note on subsidiarity.[23] Mentioning the Madrid European Council and the different interventions on the subject made by Jacques Delors, the note states that, in absence of a 'precise identity', it is time 'to start with . . . a clean sheet of paper' as 'the concept of subsidiarity is assigned a major constitutional role'. This last assumption necessitates a clarification of the subsidiarity concept, which is 'clearly established as a manufactured term; and accordingly there is ample scope for argument about the meaning to be ascribed to it today'.

The note attempts to clarify the political function of the principle of subsidiarity. The concept might facilitate more efficient and productive policy-making and implementation, thus following the exhortation given by the House of Lords Select Committee on the EC, in its *Report on the Community Social Charter*, which stated that 'the Community should act only where objectives can be attained better at Community level than at the level of the individual Member States'?[26] If so, 'the Commission is likely to take a more generous view of the benefits of Community action and of its own capability than Member States may be disposed to do'. Does the principle of subsidiarity serve the common interest, as mentioned the Commission's Programme for 1989? Is the principle to add to democratic accountability, as Leon Brittan suggested in his speech of 13 July 1989? If so, stated the note, 'little would be appropriate for Community action because ordinarily Member States will be much closer to the people affected'. Or is it Francis Maude's definition of subsidiarity that should stand, namely 'that things should not be done at Community level unless they cannot be done at national level'? This definition, the note concludes, 'would raise substantially the barrier which the Community must cross'. Its author believed, however, that the definition given by House of Lords Select Committee on the EC, using the wording 'attained better', would 'command the greatest measure of support'.

The issue which justifies these speculations, and which 'is in the air' remains: whether to incorporate the principle of subsidiarity into the EC Treaties. 'Any such suggestion', states the note 'would be received with alarm by lawyers brought up in the common law tradition. For if written in as a pure statement of principle, it would serve no purpose. And if written in as something more, it could do great harm'.

. . .

Subsidiarity has thus been introduced into the debate about EC institutions and policies. Its wide-ranging character has not, however, been derived from a concrete formulation of the principle. The Commission has over the last two years attempted to clarify, define and explore how it might help to identify the appropriate level of policy competence. But so far each case for its application has rested on a separate analysis, in relation to criteria of efficiency, proportionality and judicial soundness.

Jacques Delors has become the leading exponent of the principle of subsidiarity. His political, philosophical and social background suggests some familiarity with the concept. Through his readings of Emmanuel Mounier, Jacques Delors acquired a specific perception of the individual in society. Mounier, born in Grenoble in 1905 and founder of the prestigious review *Esprit*, became a

23 See the House of Commons Foreign Affairs Committee, *The Operation of the Single European Act: Minutes of Evidence*, 17 January 1990, Select Committee on European Legislation, House of Commons, Session 1989–1990, pp.68–72.

26 House of Lords Select Committee of the European Communities, *Report on a Community Social Charter*, House of Lords Paper 6 (1989–90), 5 December 1989, p.26.

major spokesman for the so-called *personalisme* movement, which sought to reconcile Christianity and socialism.

Jacques Delors was inspired by the idea that a global approach rather than particular solutions was needed to define the proper place of the individual in society. As a member of a community, the individual was enabled to participate in the creation of a growing socio-economical world. Finding and implementing the 'difficile équilibre entre la nécessaire affirmation de la volonté collective par l'Etat et le libre jeu de tous les centres de décisions' became a leading objective of Jacques Delors' political career. Any member of society is to be allocated a considerable autonomy in his activities, an idea cherished by Jacques Delors since his earliest participation in the semi-religious movement *Vie Nouvelle*. These thoughts were further elaborated during his first encounters with socialism, which focused on the development of the so-called 'communautés de base', as an alternative to the omnipresent state . . .

. . . Leon Brittan, in his Granada lecture of November 1989, stated that it was 'impossible to set down in advance clear guidelines as to when the subsidiarity principle should apply'. Nevertheless

> if the EC is to prove a liberating influence and not a centralizing and corporatist one, we must further develop and apply the principle that decisions should be taken at the lowest appropriate level: as close as possible, that is, to the people who are affected by them.

There is a challenge involved here, Brittan believed, as

> we should ask ourselves, particularly in the social domain, is this really a decision that needs to be taken at Community level? If it is not, the Community would be wise to set out the general objective, but leave it to the individual Member State to achieve that as they wish, according to their own traditions and their own laws.

Leon Brittan, a lawyer himself, argued that subsidiarity 'should not be seen as something for the theologians of Community law, but as something *intensely practical*: where to draw the dividing line between what is best done by the Community and what is best done by national governments'. Subsidiarity 'needs to be developed and applied with much more vigour in practice'.

NOTE

The frequently-observed British tendency to view European federalism as a centralizing process may be corrected by a fuller understanding of the implications of the principle of subsidiarity. Indeed, far from leading inevitably to centralization, Community development may have quite the reverse effect.

M. Wilke and H. Wallace, 'Subsidiarity: Approaches to Power-Sharing
in the European Community'
RIIA Discussion Paper No 27 (1990), p.8

In addition it should be borne in mind that the concern of the German Länder is not about the balance of powers between the Community and the Member States, but about the impact on the regional level of government for a country with a federal constitution. The logic of their complaint is that the EC should not be empowered to make EC legislation in areas of Länder competence, unless the Länder themselves have endorsed the measure. One can envisage similar arguments being made in Belgium, Italy or Spain. To follow this logic would be enormously to complicate the EC process and would also set a model which could become an issue in other Member States with rather different internal arrangements. Thus within the UK one could envisage the supporters of Scottish devolution, who in any event can also plead differences between Scottish and English law, rushing to exploit the precedent. There is an important question here about whether this regional dimension should be recognized in any way at the EC level or left to the constitutional rules and political practice of individual Member States.

■ QUESTION

'. . . the chief advantage of [subsidiarity] seems to be its capacity to mean all things to all interested parties – simultaneously' (Mary Robinson [when President of

Ireland], 'Constitutional Shifts in Europe and the US: Learning from each other' (1996) 32 Stanford Jnl Int L 1, 10). Is this a good thing or a bad thing? Is this law or politics?

NOTE

The general issue of competence allocation and identification of the appropriate respective contributions of the Community and the Member States to the evolution of the Community/ Union is quite fundamental to any perspective on the future of Europe. Subsidiarity has acted as a catchphrase for that debate (and not always helpfully, as the quote from Mary Robinson above suggests). Its high profile is accordingly hardly surprising. The quest to imbue the subsidiarity principle with a degree of operational value in determining whether or not the Community should act prompted the attachment of a Protocol on the application of the principles of subsidiarity and proportionality to the EC Treaty by the Treaty of Amsterdam. Does this Protocol help you to grasp the intended impact of subsidiarity on the EC's institutional culture?

PROTOCOL ON THE APPLICATION OF THE PRINCIPLES OF SUBSIDIARITY AND PROPORTIONALITY

THE HIGH CONTRACTING PARTIES,

DETERMINED to establish the conditions for the application of the principles of subsidiarity and proportionality enshrined in Article 3b [now 5] of the Treaty establishing the European Community with a view to defining more precisely the criteria for applying them and to ensure their strict observance and consistent implementation by all institutions;

WISHING to ensure that decisions are taken as closely as possible to the citizens of the Union;

TAKING ACCOUNT of the Interinstitutional Agreement of 25 October 1993 between the European Parliament, the Council and the Commission on procedures for implementing the principle of subsidiarity;

HAVE CONFIRMED that the conclusions of the Birmingham European Council on 16 October 1992 and the overall approach to the application of the subsidiarity principle agreed by the European Council meeting in Edinburgh on 11–12 December 1992 will continue to guide the action of the Union's institutions as well as the development of the application of the principle of subsidiarity, and, for this purpose,

HAVE AGREED UPON the following provisions which shall be annexed to the Treaty establishing the European Community:

(1) In exercising the powers conferred on it, each institution shall ensure that the principle of subsidiarity is complied with. It shall also ensure compliance with the principle of proportionality, according to which any action by the Community shall not go beyond what is necessary to achieve the objectives of the Treaty.

(2) The application of the principles of subsidiarity and proportionality shall respect the general provisions and the objectives of the Treaty, particularly as regards the maintaining in full of the acquis communautaire and the institutional balance; it shall not affect the principles developed by the Court of Justice regarding the relationship between national and Community law, and it should take into account Article F(4) [now 6(4)] of the Treaty on European Union, according to which 'the Union shall provide itself with the means necessary to attain its objectives and carry through its policies'.

(3) The principle of subsidiarity does not call into question the powers conferred on the European Community by the Treaty, as interpreted by the Court of Justice. The criteria referred to in the second paragraph of Article 3b [now 5] of the Treaty shall relate to areas for which the Community does not have exclusive competence. The principle of subsidiarity provides a guide as to how those powers are to be exercised at the Community level. Subsidiarity is a dynamic concept and

should be applied in the light of the objectives set out in the Treaty. It allows Community action within the limits of its powers to be expanded where circumstances so require, and conversely, to be restricted or discontinued where it is no longer justified.

(4) For any proposed Community legislation, the reasons on which it is based shall be stated with a view to justifying its compliance with the principles of subsidiarity and proportionality; the reasons for concluding that a Community objective can be better achieved by the Community must be substantiated by qualitative or, wherever possible, quantitative indicators.

(5) For Community action to be justified, both aspects of the subsidiarity principle shall be met: the objectives of the proposed action cannot be sufficiently achieved by Member States' action in the framework of their national constitutional system and can therefore be better achieved by action on the part of the Community.

The following guidelines should be used in examining whether the abovementioned condition is fulfilled:

— the issue under consideration has transnational aspects which cannot be satisfactorily regulated by action by Member States;
— actions by Member States alone or lack of Community action would conflict with the requirements of the Treaty (such as the need to correct distortion of competition or avoid disguised restrictions on trade or strengthen economic and social cohesion) or would otherwise significantly damage Member States' interests;
— action at Community level would produce clear benefits by reason of its scale or effects compared with action at the level of the Member States.

(6) The form of Community action shall be as simple as possible, consistent with satisfactory achievement of the objective of the measure and the need for effective enforcement. The Community shall legislate only to the extent necessary. Other things being equal, directives should be preferred to regulations and framework directives to detailed measures. Directives as provided for in Article 189 [now 249] of the Treaty, while binding upon each Member State to which they are addressed as to the result to be achieved, shall leave to the national authorities the choice of form and methods.

(7) Regarding the nature and the extent of Community action, Community measures should leave as much scope for national decision as possible, consistent with securing the aim of the measure and observing the requirements of the Treaty. While respecting Community law, care should be taken to respect well established national arrangements and the organisation and working of Member States' legal systems. Where appropriate and subject to the need for proper enforcement; Community measures should provide Member States with alternative ways to achieve the objectives of the measures.

(8) Where the application of the principle of subsidiarity leads to no action being taken by the Community, Member States are required in their action to comply with the general rules laid down in Article 5 [now 10] of the Treaty, by taking all appropriate measures to ensure fulfilment of their obligations under the Treaty and by abstaining from any measure which could jeopardise the attainment of the objectives of the Treaty.

(9) Without prejudice to its right of initiative, the Commission should:

— except in cases of particular urgency or confidentiality, consult widely before proposing legislation and, wherever appropriate, publish consultation documents;
— justify the relevance of its proposals with regard to the principle of subsidiarity: whenever necessary, the explanatory memorandum accompanying a proposal will give details in this respect. The financing of Community action in whole or in part from the Community budget shall require an explanation;
— take duly into account the need for any burden, whether financial or administrative, falling upon the Community, national governments, local authorities, economic operators and citizens, to be minimised and proportionate to the objective to be achieved;
— submit an annual report to the European Council, the European Parliament and the

Council on the application of Article 3b [now 5] of the Treaty. This annual report shall also be sent to the Committee of the Regions and to the Economic and Social Committee.

(10) The European Council shall take account of the Commission report referred to in the fourth indent of point 9 within the report on the progress achieved by the Union which it is required to submit to the European Parliament in accordance with Article D [now 4] of the Treaty on European Union.

(11) While fully observing the procedures applicable, the European Parliament and the Council shall, as an integral part of the overall examination of Commission proposals, consider their consistency with Article 3b [now 5] of the Treaty. This concerns the original Commission proposal as well as amendments which the European Parliament and the Council envisage making to the proposal.

(12) In the course of the procedures referred to in Articles 189b [now 251] and 189c [now 252] of the Treaty, the European Parliament shall be informed of the Council's position on the application of Article 3b [now 5] of the Treaty, by way of a statement of the reasons which led the Council to adopt its common position. The Council shall inform the European Parliament of the reasons on the basis of which all or part of a Commission proposal is deemed to be inconsistent with Article 3b [now 5] of the Treaty.

(13) Compliance with the principle of subsidiarity shall be reviewed in accordance with the rules laid down by the Treaty.

■ QUESTION

The idea of subsidiarity, if not the word, has been familiar for decades in the Community. Consider, for example, how you might use subsidiarity to analyse:

(a) The division of function between national and Community courts under the Article 234 preliminary reference procedure (Chapter 7).

(b) The distinction between the Regulation and the Directive under Article 249; p.42 above).

(c) The scope of Article 28, as illuminated by the rulings of the European Court In *Torfaen* v B & Q *plc* (Case 145/88); *Stoke-on-Trent and Norwich City Councils* v B & Q (Case C-169/91); and *Keck and Mithouard* (Joined Cases C-267 and C-268/91) (Chapter 11).

(d) The enforcement of competition law envisaged by Regulation 1/2003 (p.572 above).

To what extent is it possible for the European Court to use subsidiarity under Article 5 as an enforceable legal rule in adjudication in these or other areas? Do you agree with the Commission's view that 'subsidiarity cannot be reduced to a set of procedural rules; it is primarily a state of mind' (COM (93) 545)? What, then, of the Amsterdam Protocol? You might also consider the Commission's tart comment in its first annual report on the subsidiarity principle that 'one cannot help observing that principle and practice are often far apart with Member States meeting within the Council often adopting positions on individual cases at variance with their respect in principle for Article 3b' (COM (94) 533; see subsequently COM (98) 715, COM (99) 562).

NOTE

The Court's approach to the subsidiarity principle as a specifically *legal* rule has taken some time to become clear. The next far-sighted extract explains how the changing patterns of governance in the EC made it inevitable that the Court would eventually find itself invited to explore the nature of subsidiarity in the context of a legal challenge to adopted legislation.

W. Robinson, 'The Court of Justice after Maastricht'
in D. O'Keeffe and P. Twomey (eds), Legal Issues of the Maastricht Treaty
(Chichester: Chancery Law Publishing, 1994), 187–9

The principle of subsidiarity has been described as a 'national precedence',[43] a 'best level' test,[44] 'an anti-competitive arrangement among executive branches',[45] 'an elementary principle of good government'[46] and 'a principle of social organisation developed to be used in combination with other principles of collective and individual action'.[47] Any definition of 'subsidiarity' will therefore include an ideological underpinning. It serves for the purposes of this article merely to cite the second paragraph of Article 3b as a working definition of the inherently imprecise principle:

> In areas which do not fall within its exclusive competence, the Community shall take action, in accordance with the principle of subsidiarity, only if and in so far as the objectives of the proposed action cannot be sufficiently achieved by the Member States and can therefore, by reason of the scale or effects of the proposed action, be better achieved by the Community.

Whilst it is clear therefore that all parties accept the binding nature of Article 3b EC, their purposes for such acceptance are markedly different. The political motivations range the *Länder*'s fear of the extension of Community responsibility into areas within their exclusive competence under the *Grundgesetz*, through the UK's desire to preserve 'sovereignty' at a national level to the introduction of subsidiarity as an acceptance of federalism. Article 3b has enabled national politicians to claim that the Treaty of European Union, and Community law, will serve their requirements. Clearly, the uniformity of interpretation which will arise from the Court of Justice's jurisprudence on the principle will not enable the expectations of all the Member States to be met. Professor Curtin's statement that 'subsidiarity is presented in terms capable of papering over any number of cracks and crevices in the structure of the Maastricht Treaty'[48] reflects the difference between the political and legal implications of the principle.

The Treaty on European Union has increased the use of qualified majority voting in the Council. This follows the precedent set by the Single European Act. The combination of varying political perceptions of the principle of subsidiarity and the increase in qualified majority voting is likely to result in litigation. Member States who argued, unsuccessfully, within the Council that the Community should not act on a particular matter may challenge the adopted legislation before the Court on the principle of subsidiarity. The Court of Justice will, seemingly inevitably, be drawn into political dispute resolution which has arisen within one institution, rather than between institutions. This may be regarded as the first significant difference from the Court's existing constitutional jurisprudence.

Secondly, the Court of Justice has determined the majority of its constitutional cases on the interpretation of the aim and content of the particular legislative act, as seen above, the text and spirit of the Treaties and the general principles of law. Challenges by Member States to enacted legislation on the principle of subsidiarity will not, however, seek to annul legislation on the determination of the aim and content of the measure itself, but upon the question whether those aims should be pursued at a Community level at all. Put another way, should those aims exist at all at the Community level within Community legislation?

The way a particular act is phrased will suggest that the Community is indeed both competent in that area and should enact legislation. The adopted act must state the reasons for its adoption.

---

43 Major, speech to the Conservative Group for Europe, 22 April 1993.

44 Brittan, 'Institutional Developments of the European Community' (1992) *Public Law*, 567–579 at 574.

45 Allott, 'Europe after Maastricht: Interim Report', First Report from the foreign Affairs Committee, HC 205, 1992–93, Ev at 51.

46 MacKenzie-Stuart, 'Assessment of the view expressed and introduction to a panel discussion' in *Subsidiarity: the Challenge of Change* (1991), European Institute of Public Administration at 38.

47 Wilke and Wallace, *Subsidiarity: Approaches to Power-Sharing in the European Community* (1990) at 11.

48 Curtin, *The Irish Times*, 16 October 1992 at 16.

These will have been drafted in order to give effect to the wishes of the majority. The reasons for Community action will therefore be stated on the face of the act. The arguments of the dissenting voices will not appear. The content and aim of the act is therefore unlikely to assist the Court. The Court would consider the Treaty provisions upon which basis the act was adopted. Unless the act is *ultra vires*, the provision will provide jurisdiction for the Community to act, albeit concurrently with Member States. This is unlikely to provide guidance for the level of action. Similarly, the spirit of the Treaty has been interpreted, to date, as integrating action at a Community level in the pursuit of an 'ever closer union among the peoples of Europe'. The existing *acquis communautaire* and the drafting of the disputed act are unlikely to assist the Court. The applicants would, however, argue that the Community should not have acted at all. The general principle of subsidiarity will require the Court to 'step back' from the particular act and the existing *acquis communautaire* to consider the level at which the measure should have been adopted. This is an almost unprecedented task, which requires the Court to place constraints upon its methods of interpretation and to consider arguments based on a general principle against an adopted act and the spirit of the Treaty itself.

NOTE

William Robinson accurately predicts the emergence of *subsidiarity* in challenges to the validity of adopted legislation before the Court. The lack of clarity in the early litigation was instructive. In Case C-84/94 *UK* v *Council* [1996] ECR I-5755, the almost entirely unsuccessful challenge to the 'Working Time' Directive extracted at p.54 above, the Court felt able to reject the argument based on subsidiarity 'at the outset'. Advocate-General Leger was more blunt: the UK 'created some confusion by regularly invoking the principle of subsidiarity in the course of the proceedings – without, however, relying on it as a ground of annulment – and seemingly equating it with the principle of proportionality'. The applicant was also unsuccessful in Case C-223/94 *Germany* v *Parliament and Council* [1997] ECR I-2304.

But – by no means for the first time in this book! – the search for insight takes us to the Court's rulings in Case C-376/98 *Germany* v *European Parliament and Council of the European Union* [2000] ECR I-8419 ('Tobacco Advertising', p.60 above) and in Case C-491/01 *R v Secretary of State, ex parte BAT and Imperial Tobacco* judgment of 10 December 2002, p.66 above.

Subsidiarity was not mentioned by the Court in its judgment in the 'Tobacco Advertising' case, other than simply to acknowledge that Germany had invoked its violation as one of the bases for its application for annulment. There is a perfectly logical explanation for the Court's silence. Once the Directive had been shown to lie beyond the Community's competence, it fell to be annulled and its conformity with the subsidiarity principle was irrelevant. In this sense, the first hurdle that a disputed Community act must cross is that presented by Article 5(1) EC, p.654 above, the principle of attributed competence. Only if that hurdle is crossed does Article 5(2), the subsidiarity principle, come into play as a basis for judicial review.

The 'Tobacco Advertising' judgment is therefore hugely significant for its reminder that the relationship between Member State and Community competences is in the first place fixed by Article 5(1) EC. Subsidiarity is then relevant – and sensitive – in determining whether a competence once established should be exercised in a particular sector.

The Commission's 2001 Communication on Contract Law was introduced above (p.645). It deserves critical scrutiny from this perspective.

COMMUNICATION FROM THE COMMISSION TO THE COUNCIL
AND THE EUROPEAN PARLIAMENT ON EUROPEAN CONTRACT LAW
[2001] OJ C255/1, COM (2001) 398

(Footnotes omitted.)

4. OPTIONS FOR FUTURE COMMUNITY INITIATIVES IN CONTRACT LAW

[41] Responses to this document may show that there are impediments to the functioning of the internal market for cross-border transactions. If these problems cannot be solved satisfactorily through a case-by-case approach, a horizontal measure providing for comprehensive harmonisation of contract law rules could be envisaged at Community level. However, there are of course limits to the power of the Commission and the other Community institutions to intervene in this area.

[42] Any measure must be in accordance with the principles of subsidiarity and proportionality, as described in Article 5 of the EC Treaty and the Protocol on subsidiarity and proportionality. As the European Parliament pointed out in its resolutions on the better lawmaking reports, the subsidiarity principle is a binding legal standard that does not rule out the legitimate exercise of the Community's competencies. The need to achieve balanced application of this principle has been highlighted by a number of Member States and the European institutions.

[43] The principle of subsidiarity serves as a guide as to how the Community powers are to be exercised at Community level. Subsidiarity is a dynamic concept and should be applied in the light of the objectives set out in the Treaty. It allows Community action within the limits of its powers to be expanded where circumstances so require, and conversely, to be restricted or discontinued where it is no longer justified. There should be clear benefits to taking action at Community level instead of national level. Where the intention is to have an impact throughout the Community, Community-level action is undoubtedly the best way of ensuring homogeneous treatment within national systems and stimulating effective cooperation between the Member States.

[44] Moreover, legislation should be effective and should not impose any excessive constraints on national, regional or local authorities or on the private sector, including civil society. The principle of proportionality, which is one of the general principles of Community law, requires that measures adopted by Community institutions do not exceed the limits of what is appropriate and necessary in order to attain the objectives legitimately pursued by the legislation in question; when there is a choice between several appropriate measures recourse must be had to the least onerous, and the disadvantages caused must not be disproportionate to the aims pursued. Clearly, the Commission is duty-bound to propose whatever measures are necessary to supplement Member States' efforts to achieve the Treaty's objectives. The Commission follows two criteria designed to guarantee that fixed objectives are complied with in both political and legal terms: the ability of national and regional authorities, and of civil society, to act to achieve the objectives laid down in a Community provision, and the compatibility or conformity of these objectives with national or sectoral practices.

■ QUESTION

To what extent are these matters truly associated with Article 5(1) EC rather than Articles 5(2) and (3) EC? What are the practical differences between the application of the principle of 'attributed competence' or 'conferred powers' under Article 5(1) EC and the application of the principle of subsidiarity in Article 5(2)?

NOTE

After the annulment of Directive 98/43 in 'Tobacco Advertising' (Case C-376/98) on the ground that it fell outside the Community's competence, an outstanding question was how the subsidiarity principle would be used to check the validity of a measure of harmonization that did fall within the scope of EC competence. This in turn demanded an answer to the question whether Article 95 falls within an area of exclusive competence enjoyed by the Community – if so, then according to the explicit terms of Article 5(2) (p.654 above), subsidiarity has no role to play. In 'Tobacco Advertising' Advocate-General Fennelly expressed the opinion that Article 95 is a matter of exclusive competence and that accordingly review of an adopted act against the requirements of the subsidiarity principle was excluded. The Court did not address the issue in that case, but in the next case it did: and it took the opposite view from Mr Fennelly.

R v *Secretary of State, ex parte BAT and Imperial Tobacco* (Case C-491/01)
Judgment of 10 December 2002, Court of Justice of the European Communities

[177] The principle of subsidiarity is set out in the second paragraph of Article 5 EC, according to which, in areas which do not fall within its exclusive competence, the Community is to take action only if and in so far as the objectives of the proposed action cannot be sufficiently achieved by the Member States and can therefore, by reason of the scale or effects of the proposed action, be better achieved at Community level.

[178] Article 3 of the protocol on the application of the principles of subsidiarity and proportionality, annexed to the Treaty establishing the European Community, states that the principle of subsidiarity does not call into question the powers conferred on the Community by the Treaty as interpreted by the Court.

[179] It is to be noted, as a preliminary, that the principle of subsidiarity applies where the Community legislature makes use of Article 95 EC, inasmuch as that provision does not give it exclusive competence to regulate economic activity on the internal market, but only a certain competence for the purpose of improving the conditions for its establishment and functioning, by eliminating barriers to the free movement of goods and the freedom to provide services or by removing distortions of competition (see, to that effect, the tobacco advertising judgment, paragraphs 83 and 95).

[180] As regards the question whether the Directive was adopted in keeping with the principle of subsidiarity, it must first be considered whether the objective of the proposed action could be better achieved at Community level.

[181] As the Court has stated in paragraph 124 above, the Directive's objective is to eliminate the barriers raised by the differences which still exist between the Member States' laws, regulations and administrative provisions on the manufacture, presentation and sale of tobacco products, while ensuring a high level of health protection, in accordance with Article 95(3) EC.

[182] Such an objective cannot be sufficiently achieved by the Member States individually and calls for action at Community level, as demonstrated by the multifarious development of national laws in this case (see paragraph 61 above).

[183] It follows that, in the case of the Directive, the objective of the proposed action could be better achieved at Community level.

[184] Second, the intensity of the action undertaken by the Community in this instance was also in keeping with the requirements of the principle of subsidiarity in that, as paragraphs 122 to 141 above make clear, it did not go beyond what was necessary to achieve the objective pursued.

[185] It follows from the foregoing conclusions concerning Question 1(f) that the Directive is not invalid by reason of infringement of the principle of subsidiarity.

■ QUESTION

Can you envisage a measure of harmonization that would be validly adopted pursuant to Article 95 EC yet ruled invalid for violation of the subsidiarity principle in Article 5(2) EC?

FURTHER READING ON THE PRINCIPLE OF SUBSIDIARITY

Bermann, G., 'Proportionality and Subsidiarity' in Barnard C., and Scott J. (eds), *The Law of the Single European Market: Unpacking the Premises* (Oxford: Hart Publishing, 2002).

Bernard, N., 'The Future of European Economic Law in the Light of the Principle of Subsidiarity' (1996) 33 CML Rev 633.

Breyer, S., Does Federalism make a difference? [1999] Public Law 651.

Cass, D., 'The Word that Saves Maastricht? The Principle of Subsidiarity and the Division of Powers within the European Community' (1992) 29 CML Rev 1107.

De Búrca, G., 'Reappraising Subsidiarity's Significance after Amsterdam' Harvard Law School Jean Monnet Working Papers 7/99 (via http://www.jeanmonnetprogram.org/).

Edwards, D., 'Fearing Federalism's Failure: Subsidiarity in the EU' (1996) 44 AJCL 537.

Timmermans, C., 'Subsidiarity and Transparency' (1999) 22 Fordham Intl Law Jnl 5106.

Wyatt, D., 'Is subsidiarity justiciable?' in O'Keeffe, D. (ed), *Liber Amicorum Gordon Slynn* (The Hague: Kluwer, 2000).

The general issue of competence allocation and identification of the appropriate respective contributions of the Community and the Member States to the evolution of the Community/Union is quite fundamental to any perspective on the future of Europe. So too the need to provide reliable institutional arrangements for deciding controversies. Defining and policing the limits of EC competence is part of this inquiry (Article 5(1)); so is subsidiarity (Article 5(2)).

De Búrca, G. and De Witte, B., 'The Delimitation of Powers between the EU and its Member States', Ch. 12 in A. Arnull and D. Wincott, *Accountability and Legitimacy in the European Union* (Oxford: OUP, 2002).

Verges Bausili, A., 'Rethinking the methods of dividing and exercising powers in the EU: reforming subsidiarity and national Parliaments' available via http://eiop.or.at/cgi-bin/erpa-search.pl?site=JeanMonnet&cmd=search or http://www.jeanmonnetprogram.org.

Von Bogdandy, A. and Bast, J., 'The European Union's vertical order of competences: the current law and proposals for its reform' (2002) 39 CMLRev 227.

The Convention on the 'Future of Europe' has, of course, looked closely at these issues and its approach deserves inspection via the Convention website (p.30 above). Consult also this book's Companion Website.

■ QUESTION

'The federalist structure of the United States Constitution was designed in part to gain the States' acceptance of a stronger central government by assuring meaningful residual state sovereignty', S. Day O'Connor, 'Altered States: Federalism and Devolution at the Real Turn of the Millennium' (2001) 60 CLJ 493, 507. To what extent is a comparable bargain being struck today in the European Union? How reliable are the instruments for weighing the claims of centralization against local autonomy? (Comparisons between the USA and Europe must pay heed to the different historical and political context, but, if treated with due caution, such investigation is potentially fascinating; see K. Nicolaidis and R. Howse, *The Federal Vision: Legitimacy and Levels of Governance in the United States and the European Union* (Oxford: OUP, 2001).)

SECTION 2: **VARIABLE INTEGRATION AND FLEXIBILITY**

The discussion so far in this Chapter has taken account of the pressures caused by an expansion in Community competence. The extent to which legislative action by the Community pre-empts national competence has been considered. The criteria that govern the exercise of a Community competence have been discussed, under the catchphrase 'subsidiarity'. This represents an inquiry into the tension between centralized rule-making and preservation of local diversity. A further element in this volatile debate relates to the question of whether a majority decision among the Member States in favour of pursuit of a particular common policy should bind all participants, or whether dissentient States can be permitted to 'opt-out' (and thereby to 'compete' against the standards chosen by the majority). This raises the prospect of the 'two (or more)-speed Europe', or patterns of 'variable' or 'differentiated' integration. As already mentioned in Chapter 9, pressures in this direction have increased as the Community enlarges. The next extract was written in 1992 at a time when the issue first came to prominence.

J. Harrop, The Political Economy of Integration in the EC
(2nd ed, Aldershot: Edward Elgar Publishing, 1992), 262–67

B Differentiated and flexible integration

Enlargement is likely to accelerate the more pragmatic and flexible approach to integration. However, a range of basic common policies have formed the building blocks of the Community. Countries have to conform to the Treaties and to the ongoing legislation from Community institutions. The basic foundations of the EC, such as the principle of non-discrimination against its members, have to be respected and countries cannot reimpose trading barriers against other members of the Community. Unless these principles are applied, the EC cannot operate effectively and will be undermined. Nevertheless, a pursuit of excessive common standardisation and an attempt to impose uniformity for its own sake is undesirable and certainly less practicable for a Community of twelve different countries. The Community has acknowledged this, using various instruments such as gradual and phased directives, plus some derogations, and some national discretion in how measures are to be applied . . .

The Community is likely to be confined to core policies, though there is no consensus over what they should be; for example, R. Dahrendorf's list in a Europe *à la carte* included foreign policy, trade, monetary policy and overseas development. France approved a variable-geometry Community in the 1970's, particularly in industrial and technological policy. The *'acquis communautaire'* applies to core policies, but in other areas countries may choose whether to participate or not. Even some non-members of the EC have participated in the EUREKA project and projects of nuclear fusion, such as the Joint European Torus (JET).

The new Community of twelve cannot be optimal for all activities. It has striven hard to obtain basic agreement in key areas and indeed it is surprising in some respects that the Community has been able to make as much progress as it has, given the differences and at times the unco-operativeness of new members. A much looser pattern of integration seems inevitable in the future and the UK may look back wistfully on why it could not attain flexibility to a greater extent in the first place in sectors such as agriculture. A more variegated pattern of integration enables the more dynamic countries to press on ahead, acting as catalysts to new policy areas and providing a way of breaking the soul-destroying deadlock and paralysis of the EC . . . Perhaps the SEA, with more use of majority voting, will help to overcome a damaging split of the Community into two groups.

NOTES

1. This extract floats the idea that there are core areas where a rule of action in common cannot be abandoned but also areas in which looser patterns of involvement may be tolerated, even encouraged. This is a fine line to tread. 'Flexibility', to which Harrop refers, is an appealing, even irresistible, word, yet what can it really mean in a *common* market and a European *Union*? The question whether the emerging structure of a two (or more)-speed Europe represents a fragmentation or an evolution in the entity's endeavours already deserves the reader's attention. 'Flexibility' as a catchphrase encompasses not only constructive but also perilous trends for the Union.

2. Social policy has provided one battleground. There are fundamentally important questions about the extent to which the EC should develop common policies designed to regulate the market in the wake of the process of integration. Some States, most notably the UK, have expressed fears about perceived 'over-regulation' of the European market. The administrations of Margaret Thatcher (1979–1990) and John Major (1990–1997) were marked by stubborn resistance to new legislative measures in the social policy field. Only in the limited areas where the Council could act by qualified majority vote was advancing the social policy agenda possible: this is the background to the legal wrangle over the 'legal base' of the 'Working Time' Directive in Case C-84/94 *UK* v *Council*, considered in Chapter 2 (p.54 above). At Maastricht the other Member States were determined to amend the Treaty to extend the possibilities for social policy-making. The UK was implacably opposed. A novel deal was struck.

Edward Moxon-Browne, 'Social Europe' in J. Lodge (ed.),
The European Community and the Challenge of the Future
(2nd ed, London: Pinter Publishers, 1993) p.156

In the Maastricht Treaty, social policy was given more publicity than might have been the case because it became the issue on which Britain again parted company with the other member states; and this disagreement led to a unique solution: the other eleven member states agreed a protocol on social policy between them whereby they would make progress 'borrowing' the EC's institutions to do so. The isolation of the UK on the social chapter of the Maastricht Treaty was simply the reflection of very different traditions and policies in the field of labour law. Britain is unusual in the EC in the degree of which hours of work, overtime, holidays and employment contracts are left to employers or collective bargaining (Towers, 'Two Speed ahead: social Europe and the UK after Maastricht' (1992) *Industrial Relations Journal*, 23(2), 83–91). Among other member states, however, there was the suspicion that the UK, by opting out of the Maastricht section on social policy, was in fact seeking an unfair advantage over its partners: 'A UK outside the Social Chapter but within the EC tariff wall could become very attractive to inward investors capable of raising productivity to European levels without paying the full labour cost price' (Towers, 1992: 83) . . .

   Although Maastricht undoubtedly reinforces the position of social policy within the framework of the EC's development, it also complicates it. The Prime Minister, John Major, was under strong political pressure from within his own party to bring back visible evidence of having secured a treaty favourable to Britain. What *The Economist* (14 December 1991) referred to as the 'unprecedented institutional fix' relating to the Social Chapter of the treaty, coupled with the loophole for Britain on EMU, provided this evidence. The resulting formula may have long-term consequences for the EC inasmuch as other member states in the future may adopt an *à la carte* attitude towards extensions of the EC's competence . . .

NOTE

The device was widely described as the UK's 'opt-out' from deeper EC social policy-making, although a strict reading might have labelled it as an 'opt-in' by the other 11 (now 14) Member States. Whichever formulation is preferred, the structure envisaged the uneven development of social policy among the 12 (now 15) Member States of the Community. The Maastricht Protocol was more symbol than reality. Little legislation was in fact adopted under its provisions (see C. McGlynn, 'An Exercise in Futility: the practical effects of the social policy opt-out' (1998)

49 NILQ 60). And after the Labour Government took power in May 1997, the political climate changed so that agreement at Amsterdam led to that Treaty eliminating even the possibility of a separate stream of social policy legislation applying to all Member States save the UK. Accordingly, the modestly ambitious social policy arrangements found in the Protocol were amalgamated with the existing, and in part modified, long-standing provisions on social policy found in the Treaty 'proper'. They have become Chapter 1, 'Social Provisions', of Title XI, 'Social Policy, Education, Vocational Training and Youth', comprising Articles 136–145 of the renumbered Treaty. In this sphere, 'variable integration' is at an end.

But the symbol was vivid. The critical questions for the future were the extent to which willingness in the social policy sphere to allow a dissenting minority to opt out of common policy-making would and should become a model for resolving disagreements about the path the Union should follow. In times of geographic and functional expansion, there is a probability that consensus will be increasingly elusive. The temptation for a majority to push ahead, without waiting to persuade a reluctant minority, will be powerful. Yet, for some, such variable integration undermines the traditional notions of the European common market.

At stake is the identification of the proper and achievable scope of Community intervention into the market. There is a fierce debate about the extent to which the Community should combine a commitment to market liberalization with a readiness to establish a common basis for the regulation of the market. As mentioned in Chapter 9 (p.322 above), this is reducible (with a risk of oversimplification) to the battle between a 'competition between regulators' (which favours a basic rule of mutual market access against a background of regulatory diversity which breeds competition and releases comparative advantage) and the 'level playing field' (which prefers a greater degree of rule making in common in order to equalize competitive conditions and deepen interdependence between the Member States).

This debate is being conducted in many sectors. For example, in the social policy field, anxiety is frequently expressed that inadequate common rules will release a market for regulation in which firms will re-locate to jurisdictions offering them the cheapest regime, thereby driving down social standards in Europe. From another perspective, this is precisely the sort of competition that will equip European firms with the efficiency required to succeed in global markets, thereby enhancing job creation. For discussion, see C. Barnard, 'Social dumping and race to the bottom: some lessons for the EU from Delaware?' (2000) 25 EL Rev 57. In another sector: to what extent should the liberalization of the market for financial services be accompanied by the fixing of standards that must be met before a provider may claim access to the integrated market? And should any Community standards that are set be minimum standards only? See Chapter 14; and for a comprehensive investigation, see N. Moloney, *EC Securities Regulation* (Oxford: OUP, 2002).

■ QUESTION

'. . . competition processes among jurisdictions . . . up until now . . . are not seen as being an integral part of the process of European integration . . . It seems rather that advocates of European integration have a hostile attitude toward the idea of competition among jurisdictions . . . The core of the problem is that simultaneous realization of mobility and decentralization logically implies the existence of competition among jurisdictions', '. . . if we want simultaneous mobility and decentralisation, then we must accept interjurisdictional competition and we must think about ways to make competition processes workable', W. Kerber, 'Inter-jurisdictional Competition within the European Union' (2000) 23 Fordham Intl Law Jnl S217, S221, S249. Discuss. Do we want decentralization? How much decentralization?

The significance of developments in the social policy sphere is that the Member States at Maastricht were prepared to abandon the search for an agreed common path through this policy maze. One State, the UK, was allowed to opt out; one State, the UK, was allowed to maintain regulatory diversity and compete with its partners by offering firms a lighter regulatory regime. Elsewhere, in relation to the third stage of Economic and Monetary Union, two States, Denmark and the UK, have been allowed to choose whether or not to proceed, whereas all other Member States are committed according to the Treaty.

Such variable integration – or 'flexibility' – raises questions of the highest significance in judging the future institutional and constitutional shaping of the Union. Is it possible to permit a degree of 'flexibility' but to subject it to pre-conditions that would ensure that such arrangements were permitted only pro-vided they did not imperil the achievement of the Union's mission? A pragmatic concern is that any attempt to maintain the 'purity' of an all-or-nothing approach to participation in activities conducted under the Union umbrella is not likely to persuade groupings of States wishing to develop co-operation mechanisms in fields unattractive to some of their partners to abandon their plans if unable to secure unanimous support. Rather it would likely provoke those States to deepen co-operation outwith the EU's relatively well-developed institutional and constitutional apparatus. In the negotiations leading up to agreement at Amsterdam, the anxiety to craft a workable system for variable integration, which had become regarded as a necessary element of the EU system, was driven by a desire to fashion a model that would be objectively justifiable and comprehensible as a new feature of the Union's *constitutionalized* structure. The Maastricht social policy arrangements, underpinned by nothing other than political intransigence, were treated as an *ad hoc* aberration.

The two brief extracts that follow draw attention to the key point that 'flexibility' is likely to be tolerable within the EU only provided it does not infect core areas of action in common. They should be read with regard both to 'agenda-setting' for the 1996 Intergovernmental Conference which generated the Treaty of Amsterdam in 1997 and, looking further ahead, to the structures needed for the potential growth of the Union to embrace most of Europe early in the new millennium. The section then concludes with the provisions found in the Treaty of Amsterdam designed to provide a general framework for integration at different speeds – so-called 'closer cooperation', p.672 below.

D. Curtin, 'The Shaping of a European Constitution and the 1996 IGC'
(1995) 50 Aussenwirtschaft 237, 244–49

4. Towards a systematisation of 'flexibility'

In many respects the EC has always been a multi-speed phenomenon and multiple speed integration in this almost classic sense can be defined as integration whereby the policy objective is the same for all the Member States and has been agreed to by all of them: it is only the speed at which it is achieved which varies.[23] Generally such differentiation must be capable of objective justification and be temporary in nature. The reason for the introduction of this type of divergence which is mainly to be found in the application of secondary Community law is to account for internal (social or economic) difficulties of one or several Member States which are expected to be overcome during the period of exception.[24] Nevertheless the underlying legislative act (often a harmonising directive) is based on the principle of unanimous will of all the Member States including the declared intention of the excluded Member State(s) to introduce the harmonised standard at the agreed and fixed date. The ultimate aim is clearly a *uniform rule* for a fully integrated market.[25]

The transition to the third stage of EMU as regulated in the TEU is another example of multiple speed integration more or less in the classic sense, albeit regulated via a Treaty amendment: it does not undermine the Community legal order as such nor arguably impair the cohesion of the internal market. Rather it enables a leading group of Member States to proceed with further cooperation and integration on the basis of objectively defined criteria with the intention that the other Member States will in principle, in the ripeness of time, join this leading group in the path ahead which has been forged. The controversial point is the inevitable creation of two classes of membership without adequate provision for common action to enable weaker economies to catch up and earn their membership of the common currency regime.

In the EMU system, the possibility of a leading group is explicitly accepted by *all* the EU Member States in the TEU, including the UK and Denmark, although they have secured an opt-out for themselves. It can be argued however that the emergence of an EMU leading group is not only compatible with the internal market but enables additional profit to be obtained from it.[26] The quibble one can have with the opt-out's which Denmark and the UK obtained in Maastricht and Edinburgh regarding the move to the final stage of the EMU is that they provide the possibility of *permanently* 'opting out' of the provisions laid down in the Treaty on the third stage of the EMU (in the sense of an indefinite period as opposed to a merely undefined period) and that they were obtained for purely political reasons (as opposed to social and economic factors which were the only objective justification in the classic approach[27]). To this extent one can indeed claim that the opt-outs do in fact contribute to the undermining of the Community legal order.

The bottom line in a multiple (or two) speed approach such as that encapsulated in the EMU is that it probably is possible to a considerable extent to maintain the principle of the single institutional framework as enshrined in article C of the Treaty [now Art. 3 EU] on the assumption that, although temporary derogations or special arrangements might be granted, 'all those who are party to the single institutional framework share the same framework and are ready in time to conform to the same system'.[28]

However another different form of graduated integration may also be distinguished and this is one which gives rise to more serious problems. *Variable geometry* is quite different from variable speeds in the sense that the group of Member States deciding to proceed with closer integration actually agree *among themselves* their policy objectives as well as the tempo for their realisation.[29] In this

---

23 See the House of Commons Foreign Affairs Committee, *The Operation of the Single European Act: Minutes of Evidence*, 17 January 1990, Select Committee on European Legislation, House of Commons, Session 1989–1990, pp.68–72.

24 See further, Feenstra and Mortelmans, 33–34. See too, Article 35 of the European Parliaments Draft Treaty on European Union, 1984 which accepted the idea of the differentiated application of Community rules provided that such differentiation was limited in time, being 'designed to facilitate the subsequent application of all the provisions of the law to all of its addressees'. See further, Louis, 'Europese Unie en gedifferentieerde integratie', SEW 6 (1985) 410.

25 Feenstra and Mortelmans, *op. cit*. 33.

26 House of Lords Select Committee of the European Communities, *Report on a Community Social Charter*, House of Lords Paper 6 (1989–90), 5 December 1989, p.26.

27 See, in general Ehlermann, 'How flexible is Community law? An unusual approach to the concept of "two speeds" ' in (1984) Michigan Law Review. 136, 151.

28 Ludlow, Beyond Maastricht, Brussels, 1993, p.70.

29 See, in general, Maillet and Velo, (eds.), *L'Europe a geometrie variable. Transition vers l'integration* (Paris, 1994).

construction those left 'behind' are not at all involved and simply 'opt out' of any agreement as to the policy objectives. So it is not only the speed but also the specific policy objectives and the means of achieving these which varies for different groups of countries.

It is submitted that this (disintegrative) formula should *not* be applied to the so-called 'hard core' of Community law and in particular not to those policy areas which might impair the cohesion of the internal market. The same is arguably also true with regard to the organisation of the Union's external economic relations as well as solidarity within the Union.[30]

The substantive *hard core* of the Union can be tentatively defined for present purposes as the rules and obligations entailed in the establishment of the internal market including the necessary harmonisation of legislation, the five freedoms and the common competition, agriculture, transport and trade policies as well as certain aspects of the EMU which constitute a necessary addition to the internal market.[31] This definition does not necessarily exclude the right for small groups of countries to take more *far-reaching measures* in certain areas of 'supplementary policy' which essentially seek to establish *minimum* norms (for example, environmental policy, social policy, research and technological policy, etc).[32]

For the internal market and the foundations of the Community system (the substantive 'hard core' and the institutional core *acquis*), it is mandatory, at least from the perspective of the *acquis communautaire,* that the Community decision making procedure as such is followed and that *all* Member States *participate* (albeit with the possibility of different speeds, see *supra*) with regard to Community policy. Moreover, when action is envisaged in the so-called 'hard core' of the Community then the principle of institutional unity and balance as envisaged in the Treaty itself must be respected. Finally, the fundamental rule is that of the equality of the Member States, thereby prohibiting the exclusion of one or more Member States from a particular policy area. These are the three fundamental rules mandated by the *acquis communautaire* with regard to the substantive 'hard core' of the Community.[33]

R. Harmsen, 'A European Union of Variable Geometry: Problems and Perspectives'
(1994) 45 NILQ 109, 129–33

IV. THE LIMITS OF VARIABILITY

If 'variable geometry' corresponds to deep-seated political trends, it nonetheless also poses significant problems with respect to both the maintenance of system legitimacy and the practical functioning of institutions. As regards the legitimacy of the politico-legal system, extensive recourse to variable institutional structures risks undermining the minimal sense of 'community' necessary for the creation or maintenance of a cohesive political unit. At a more practical level, problems are presented by the coexistence of parallel legal orders as well as by the need to redesign common political institutions in a way which corresponds to jurisdictional variations. Straddling the line between abstract considerations of legitimacy and more practical problems of institutional design, the overall level of systemic complexity further gives cause for concern.

. . . considerations of legitimacy and practicality overlap. In part, as suggested by the preceding discussion of institutional mechanics, the limits of variability are set by the practical capacity of a legal or political system to cope with complexity. However, beyond the internal manageability of the system, attention must be paid to its external intelligibility. Simply put, institutional variability, though it may correspond to very real political necessity, also renders the politico-legal system as a whole exceptionally opaque. For the European Union, already sharply criticised for a relatively low

---

30 See, Maillet and Velo, *op. cit.,* 125.

31 See further, the interesting discussion by Verloren van Themaat. 'Epiloog, De horizon 2000', in: Kapteyn, Verloren van Themaat *et al, Jnleiding tot het Recht van de Europese Gemeenschappen,* 5th ed, 1995, forthcoming.

32 See, Dutch government policy document on enlargement, *op. cit* where it suggests the test in each case whether the differentiation of norms and policy in this way will gradually undermine the level playing field of the internal market.

33 See further, Feenstra and Mortelmans, *op. cit.*

degree of intelligibility, there is a very real danger that further moves down the path of 'variable geometry' will render still more difficult its legitimation in the eyes of often sceptical national publics.

CONCLUSION

It has clearly emerged in the preceding sections that multiple forms of both 'structural' and 'jurisdictional' variability have been accepted within the European Union and that these variable institutional structures correspond to deeply embedded political imperatives. It is equally clear, however, that such differentiated institutional structures pose significant problems, potentially even calling into question basic precepts of the entire integration project. More than most problems of institutional design, there is no readily apparent way of resolving this tension between strong demands for diversity and an equally compelling logic of uniformity. Nevertheless, a promising path forward has been sketched out by the Court of Justice, with its tentative acceptance of a notion of 'supraconstitutionality' at the supranational level.

Although essentially unknown in the common-law world, the idea of 'supraconstitutionality' has been a staple of post-war public-law theory in much of continental Western Europe.[71] As the term implies, 'supraconstitutionality' refers to the existence of principles or positive law norms which are logically prior to and therefore in some sense 'above' the written constitution. It follows that these principles or norms must be respected by every governmental and legislative act, including constitutional amendment. Most simply, one notes the prohibition on the abolition of the Republican form of government contained in both the French and the Italian Constitutions; 'Republicanism' is defined as a prior value which even the constitutional legislator must respect.[72] In a more elaborate fashion, Article 79(3) of the German Basic Law enumerates a number of 'unrevisable' provisions, placing certain basic individual rights and the federal character of the State beyond the realm of constitutional amendment. In each case, while one may question the practical effectiveness of such provisions, they unquestionably make explicit the core or constitutive values of the regime.

In the Community context, the Court of Justice broached the idea of supraconstitutionality in its first decision concerning the EEA Agreement, handed down on 14 December 1991.[73] Specifically, the Commission asked the Court to rule on whether any incompatibilities found to exist between the judicial mechanism provided for in the EEA Agreement and the EC founding treaties might be resolved by way of amendment to the Treaty of Rome. The Commission envisaged a simple amendment to Article 238, permitting the establishment of the court system agreed. The Court of Justice, in response, ruled that even Treaty amendment would 'not cure the incompatibility', as the proposed system of courts (functionally integrating the CJEC and the Court of First Instance into EEA courts for EEA purposes) conflicted 'with the very foundations of the Community.'[74]In other words, the autonomy and integrity of the Community legal system has been held by the Court of Justice to constitute a 'prior' or 'supraconstitutional' value of the Community order, which even Treaty amendment should not be allowed to violate.

Relative to the present concern with 'variable geometry', the CJEC's decision crucially underlines the need for variable or asymmetrical structures to be conceived with reference to a Community 'core'.[75] Simply put, increased institutional variability must inevitably call forward a stronger and

---

71 The doctrinal background is discussed in Stéphane Rials. 'Supraconstitutionnalité et systématicité du droit' [1986] 31 *Archives de Philosophie du Droit* 57. A somewhat more empirical survey may be found in Arne. 'Existe-t-il des normes supra-constitutionnelles? Contribution à l'étude des fondamentaux et de la constitutionnalité' (1993) 205 *Revue du Droit public* 459.

72 Art 89 of the Constitution of the French Fifth Republic: Art 139 of the present Italian Constitution.

73 *Re The Draft Treaty on a European Economic Area*. Opinion 1/91. [1992] 1 CMLR 245. Commentaries and follow-up are cited *supra*, n45. The 'supraconstitutional' dimension of the decision is discussed in Dutheil de la Rochère, *supra*, n52, at 607.

74 Opinion 1/91 at 275.

75 It may be argued that the European Convention on Human Rights already has such a core, in so far as contracting States may not derogate, even in time of emergency, from specified central Articles (*viz* 2, 3, 4/1 and 7). See Arné, *op cit*, p.466.

more explicit conception of which principles, values, and policies integrally define the Community. Although the exact parameters of such a core can emerge only gradually, its constituent elements must reasonably include the basic precepts of the common market, the underlying principles of the legal order, and some sense of a common political destiny (parallelling, at the supranational level, Renan's classic definition of a nation in terms of a *vouloir vivre ensemble*).

At the same time, the limits of a Community-level reliance on the notion of supraconstitutionality must also be underlined. First, concerning the substantive definition of a Community core, it is essential that the *noyau communautaire* not be confused with the *acquis communautaire*. The core, by definition, must include only those principles which are constitutive of the Community order, not the sum total of all policies and practices which might have developed under the Community rubric. Second, at a procedural level, the part played by the Court of Justice in defining this supra-constitutional core must be carefully limited relative to the role of political actors. In this regard, it should be borne in mind that a Community supraconstitutionality lacks the inherent legitimacy of its national counterparts, as it refers only to fairly abstract concepts of 'order', rather than to basic human rights or founding principles of liberal democracy.

In sum, a logic of supraconstitutionality would appear to offer a conceptual framework within which an increasing variability of institutional structures might be reconciled with the need to pre-serve the basic tenets of the Union as an economic, legal, and political order. Nevertheless, whether through the adoption of such a framework or through another means, it is clear that an increasing structural and jurisdictional variability must be accompanied by a more explicit definition of the Union's invariable core. Therein lies a task, whatever their initial differences, which would seem singularly well suited to a co-operative effort on the part of lawyers and political scientists.

■ QUESTION

Do you find attractive the attempt in these two extracts to identify a 'hard core' of Community obligations? What machinery could be used to define the content and to secure the inviolability of such a hard core?

NOTE

One of the more innovative amendments made by the Treaty of Amsterdam was the intro-duction of new provisions designed to permit 'enhanced' or 'closer' cooperation, through which some, but not all, Member States may choose to deepen their mutual interdependence. These provisions are by no means exhaustive of the models of 'flexibility' available to the Member States, but they represent an illuminating attempt to chart a course in the Treaty for forms of action that may be thought to carry a disturbing momentum towards fragmentation of the unity of the legal order. Rigorous criteria must be satisfied before 'enhanced cooperation' is permitted. The 'master' provisions governing 'closer cooperation' are Articles 43–45 of the Treaty on European Union, and they were amended by the Treaty of Nice. This is the post-Nice version:

TREATY ON EUROPEAN UNION

TITLE VII PROVISIONS ON ENHANCED COOPERATION

Article 43

Member States which intend to establish enhanced cooperation between themselves may make use of the institutions, procedures and mechanisms laid down by this Treaty and by the Treaty establishing the European Community provided that the proposed cooperation:

(a) is aimed at furthering the objectives of the Union and of the Community, at protecting and serving their interests and at reinforcing their process of integration;

(b) respects the said Treaties and the single institutional framework of the Union;

(c) respects the acquis communautaire and the measures adopted under the other provisions of the said Treaties;

(d) remains within the limits of the powers of the Union or of the Community and does not concern the areas which fall within the exclusive competence of the Community;

(e) does not undermine the internal market as defined in Article 14(2) of the Treaty establishing the European Community, or the economic and social cohesion established in accordance with Title XVII of that Treaty;

(f) does not constitute a barrier to or discrimination in trade between the Member States and does not distort competition between them;

(g) involves a minimum of eight Member States;

(h) respects the competences, rights and obligations of those Member States which do not participate therein;

(i) does not affect the provisions of the Protocol integrating the Schengen acquis into the framework of the European Union;

(j) is open to all the Member States, in accordance with Article 43b.

Article 43a

Enhanced cooperation may be undertaken only as a last resort, when it has been established within the Council that the objectives of such cooperation cannot be attained within a reasonable period by applying the relevant provisions of the Treaties.

Article 43b

When enhanced cooperation is being established, it shall be open to all Member States. It shall also be open to them at any time, in accordance with Articles 27e and 40b of this Treaty and with Article 11a of the Treaty establishing the European Community, subject to compliance with the basic decision and with the decisions taken within that framework. The Commission and the Member States participating in enhanced cooperation shall ensure that as many Member States as possible are encouraged to take part.

Article 44

1. For the purposes of the adoption of the acts and decisions necessary for the implementation of enhanced cooperation referred to in Article 43, the relevant institutional provisions of this Treaty and of the Treaty establishing the European Community shall apply. However, while all members of the Council shall be able to take part in the deliberations, only those representing Member States participating in enhanced cooperation shall take part in the adoption of decisions. The qualified majority shall be defined as the same proportion of the weighted votes and the same proportion of the number of the Council members concerned as laid down in Article 205(2) of the Treaty establishing the European Community, and in the second and third subparagraphs of Article 23(2) of this Treaty as regards enhanced cooperation established on the basis of Article 27c. Unanimity shall be constituted by only those Council members concerned.

Such acts and decisions shall not form part of the Union acquis.

2. Member States shall apply, as far as they are concerned, the acts and decisions adopted for the implementation of the enhanced cooperation in which they participate. Such acts and decisions shall be binding only on those Member States which participate in such cooperation and, as appropriate, shall be directly applicable only in those States. Member States which do not participate in such cooperation shall not impede the implementation thereof by the participating Member States.

Article 44a

Expenditure resulting from implementation of enhanced cooperation, other than administrative costs entailed for the institutions, shall be borne by the participating Member States, unless all members of the Council, acting unanimously after consulting the European Parliament, decide otherwise.

Article 45

The Council and the Commission shall ensure the consistency of activities undertaken on the basis of this title and the consistency of such activities with the policies of the Union and the Community, and shall cooperate to that end.

NOTE

Provisions in both the EU Treaty and the EC Treaty build on this base. In the former instance, Articles 27a–27e EU permit closer or enhanced co-operation between some, but not all, Member States in the field of foreign and security policy, while Articles 40–40b EU permits closer co-operation between some, but not all, Member States in pursuit of accelerated development towards an area of freedom, security, and justice. These provisions' cousins in the EC Treaty as amended by the Treaties of Amsterdam and Nice are Articles 11–11a EC.

Article 11

1. Member States which intend to establish enhanced cooperation between themselves in one of the areas referred to in this Treaty shall address a request to the Commission, which may submit a proposal to the Council to that effect. In the event of the Commission not submitting a proposal, it shall inform the Member States concerned of the reasons for not doing so.

2. Authorisation to establish enhanced cooperation as referred to in paragraph 1 shall be granted, in compliance with Articles 43 to 45 of the Treaty on European Union, by the Council, acting by a qualified majority on a proposal from the Commission and after consulting the European Parliament. When enhanced cooperation relates to an area covered by the procedure referred to in Article 251 of this Treaty, the assent of the European Parliament shall be required.

A member of the Council may request that the matter be referred to the European Council. After that matter has been raised before the European Council, the Council may act in accordance with the first subparagraph of this paragraph.

3. The acts and decisions necessary for the implementation of enhanced cooperation activities shall be subject to all the relevant provisions of this Treaty, save as otherwise provided in this Article and in Articles 43 to 45 of the Treaty on European Union.

Article 11a

Any Member State which wishes to participate in enhanced cooperation established in accordance with Article 11 shall notify its intention to the Council and to the Commission, which shall give an opinion to the Council within three months of the date of receipt of that notification. Within four months of the date of receipt of that notification, the Commission shall take a decision on it, and on such specific arrangements as it may deem necessary.

NOTE

The adjustments made by the Nice Treaty to the wording of these provisions was in some respects purely cosmetic but in others more significant. In the latter category, the requirement that closer co-operation involves a minimum of eight Member States (Article 43(g) EU) replaces the Amsterdam requirement of a majority of States. This is designed to facilitate resort to this device after enlargement. Moreover, a brake envisaged by the Amsterdam Treaty has been deleted from Article 11(2) EC (and *mutatis mutandis* from Article 40 EU). This had provided that a member of the Council could declare that, for important and stated reasons of national policy, it intended to oppose the granting of an authorization by qualified majority, whereupon a vote would not be taken and the Council was able, acting by a qualified majority, to request that the matter be referred to the Council, meeting in the composition of the Heads of State or Government, for decision by unanimity. The elimination of this control is designed to improve the likelihood of reliance on the provisions on closer co-operation. *As yet there has been no use made of this procedure to promote forms of enhanced or closer co-operation.*

■ QUESTIONS

1. Try to construct a form of closer co-operation which would satisfy all the criteria imposed by Articles 43–45 EU and Articles 11–11a EC.

2. Would a two-speed model of social policy of the type invented at Maastricht (and abandoned at Amsterdam, p.667 above) comply with the Treaty provisions controlling the establishment of a framework for closer co-operation

between some, but not all, Member States? Would the pattern for securing an Area of Freedom, Security, and Justice, which, as explained in Chapter 14, includes opt-outs comply?

3. Review the post-Nice provisions on closer co-operation in the light of the two extracts above, pp.668–672. Are the anxieties and suggestions expounded by Curtin and Harmsen reflected in these provisions?

NOTE

The Convention on the 'Future of Europe' has entertained a lively debate about the nature and purpose of these provisions. This has embraced both their detail and, more generally, the question of where they should be located in any new Treaty. A central question of intellectual preference asks whether the device of enhanced co-operation, and the notion of flexibility more generally, constitute methods for achieving the EU's objectives, or whether in a deeper sense they represent a guiding principle of respect for diversity. The Convention's progress was tracked at pp.30–32 above and the reader should also consult this book's Companion Website.

FURTHER READING

(i) On the general phenomenon of 'flexibility'

Bieber, R., 'On the Mutual Completion of Overlapping Legal Systems: the Case of the European Communities and the National Legal Orders' (1988) 13 EL Rev 147.

De Búrca, G. and Scott, J. (eds), *Constitutional Change in the EU: from uniformity to flexibility?* (Oxford: Hart Publishing, 2000).

Ehlermann, C-D., 'How Flexible is Community Law? An Unusual Approach to the Concept of "Two Speeds" ' (1984) 82 Michigan Law Rev 1274.

Scharpf, F., 'The problem-solving capacity of multi-level governance' (1997) 4 *Journal of European Public Policy* 520.

Stubb, A., 'The 1996 Intergovernmental Conference and the management of flexible integration' (1997) 4 *Journal of European Public Policy* 37.

Usher, J., 'Variable Geometry or Concentric Circles: Patterns for the EU' (1997) 46 ICLQ 243.

(ii) On closer co-operation under the Amsterdam Treaty

Constantinesco, V., 'Les clauses de coopération renforcée' (1997) 33 RTDE 751.

Ehlermann, C.-D., 'Differentiation, Flexibility, Closer Co-operation: The New Provisions of the Amsterdam Treaty' (1998) 4 ELJ 246.

Gaja, G., 'How flexible is flexibility under the Amsterdam Treaty?' (1998) 35 CML Rev 855.

Shaw, J., 'The Treaty of Amsterdam: Challenges of Flexibility and Legitimacy' (1998) 4 ELJ 63.

Tuytschaever, F., *Differentiation in European Union Law* (Oxford: Hart Publishing, 1999).

Usher, J., 'Flexibility and Enhanced Cooperation', in T. Heukels, N. Blokker, and M. Brus (eds), *The European Union after Amsterdam* (The Hague: Kluwer Law International, 1998), Ch. 14.

Walker, N., 'Sovereignty and Differentiated Integration in the European Union' (1998) 4 ELJ 355.

Weatherill, S., ' "If I'd wanted you to understand I would have explained it better": what is the purpose of the provisions on closer co-operation introduced by the Treaty of Amsterdam?' in D. O'Keeffe and P. Twomey (eds), *Legal Issues of the Amsterdam Treaty* (Oxford: Hart Publishing, 1999).

(iii) On the impact on closer co-operation of the Nice Treaty

Usher, J., 'Enhanced Co-Operation or Flexibility in the Post-Nice Era', Ch. 6 in A. Arnull and D. Wincott, *Accountability and Legitimacy in the European Union* (Oxford: OUP, 2002).

(iv) On the 'post-Nice' debate about future patterns of flexibility

Philippart, E., 'A new mechanism of enhanced co-operation for the enlarged European Union' *Notre Europe*, Studies and Research Paper No 22 (2003), available *via* http://www.notre-europe.asso.fr/fichiers/Etud22-en.pdf.

Shaw, J., 'Flexibility in a Reorganized and Simplified Treaty' in B. De Witte (ed), *Ten Reflections on the Constitutional Treaty for Europe* (Florence, 2003), available *via* http://www.iue.it/RSCAS/Research/Institutions/EuropeanTreaties.shtml.

SECTION 3: **INSTRUMENTS OF GOVERNANCE**

How should the Union go about achieving its tasks? Can the relationship between central and local legal and political authority be better managed by using 'softer' instruments of law and policy-making that are more conducive to respect for local preferences and pursuit of effective regulatory reform than binding instruments such as Regulations and Directives envisaged by Article 249 EC?

In March 2000 the European Council held a special meeting in Lisbon at which a new Strategic Goal For the Next Decade was agreed.

Presidency Conclusions, Lisbon European Council, March 23 and 24 2000

A STRATEGIC GOAL FOR THE NEXT DECADE

The new challenge

1. The European Union is confronted with a quantum shift resulting from globalisation and the challenges of a new knowledge-driven economy. These changes are affecting every aspect of people's lives and require a radical transformation of the European economy. The Union must shape these changes in a manner consistent with its values and concepts of society and also with a view to the forthcoming enlargement.

2. The rapid and accelerating pace of change means it is urgent for the Union to act now to harness the full benefits of the opportunities presented. Hence the need for the Union to set a clear strategic goal and agree a challenging programme for building knowledge infrastructures, enhancing innovation and economic reform, and modernising social welfare and education systems.

The Union's strengths and weaknesses

3. The Union is experiencing its best macro-economic outlook for a generation. As a result of stability-oriented monetary policy supported by sound fiscal policies in a context of wage moderation, inflation and interest rates are low, public sector deficits have been reduced remarkably and the EU's balance of payments is healthy. The euro has been successfully introduced and is delivering the expected benefits for the European economy. The internal market is largely complete and is yielding tangible benefits for consumers and businesses alike. The forthcoming enlargement will create new opportunities for growth and employment. The Union possesses a generally well-educated workforce as well as social protection systems able to provide, beyond their intrinsic value, the stable framework required for managing the structural changes involved in moving towards a knowledge-based society. Growth and job creation have resumed.

4. These strengths should not distract our attention from a number of weaknesses. More than 15 million Europeans are still out of work. The employment rate is too low and is characterised by insufficient participation in the labour market by women and older workers. Long-term structural

unemployment and marked regional unemployment imbalances remain endemic in parts of the Union. The services sector is underdeveloped, particularly in the areas of telecommunications and the Internet. There is a widening skills gap, especially in information technology where increasing numbers of jobs remain unfilled. With the current improved economic situation, the time is right to undertake both economic and social reforms as part of a positive strategy which combines competitiveness and social cohesion.

The way forward

5. The Union has today set itself a **new strategic goal** for the next decade: *to become the most competitive and dynamic knowledge-based economy in the world, capable of sustainable economic growth with more and better jobs and greater social cohesion.* Achieving this goal requires an **overall strategy** aimed at:

— preparing the transition to a knowledge-based economy and society by better policies for the information society and R&D, as well as by stepping up the process of structural reform for competitiveness and innovation and by completing the internal market;

— modernising the European social model, investing in people and combating social exclusion;

— sustaining the healthy economic outlook and favourable growth prospects by applying an appropriate macro-economic policy mix.

6. This strategy is designed to enable the Union to regain the conditions for full employment, and to strengthen regional cohesion in the European Union. The European Council needs to set a goal for full employment in Europe in an emerging new society which is more adapted to the personal choices of women and men. If the measures set out below are implemented against a sound macro-economic background, an average economic growth rate of around 3% should be a realistic prospect for the coming years.

7. Implementing this strategy will be achieved by improving the existing processes, introducing a **new open method of coordination** at all levels, coupled with a stronger guiding and coordinating role for the European Council to ensure more coherent strategic direction and effective monitoring of progress. A meeting of the European Council to be held every Spring will define the relevant mandates and ensure that they are followed up.

NOTE

Some of these aspirations are intimately related with long-standing Union objectives. Others are new. Others again are woolly. But it is immediately apparent that the quest to advance economic integration, even if taken to include a generous spillover into choices about social policy, is treated as but part of a much broader readiness to identify social matters as an arena for co-operation under the European Union umbrella.

Improving social cohesion and combatting social exclusion are daunting tasks. It is particularly significant that the means envisaged for the realization of these objectives are broader than the normal array of Union instruments. The broad sweep of ambition plain in this statement is matched by a desire to develop new techniques of governance. In particular, the binding legal acts put at the Union's disposal by its Treaty – Articles 249 EC and Articles 12 and 34(2) EU (pp.42–45 above) – are here not even mentioned. Paragraph 7 of the Lisbon Conclusions refers to a *new open method of coordination* at all levels. The intent is amplified later in the Conclusions.

PUTTING DECISIONS INTO PRACTICE: A MORE COHERENT AND SYSTEMATIC APPROACH

Improving the existing processes

35. No new process is needed. The existing Broad Economic Policy Guidelines and the Luxembourg, Cardiff and Cologne processes offer the necessary instruments, provided they are simplified and better coordinated, in particular through other Council formations contributing to the preparation

by the ECOFIN Council of the Broad Economic Policy Guidelines. Moreover, the Broad Economic Policy Guidelines should focus increasingly on the medium- and long-term implications of structural policies and on reforms aimed at promoting economic growth potential, employment and social cohesion, as well as on the transition towards a knowledge-based economy. The Cardiff and Luxembourg processes will make it possible to deal with their respective subject matters in greater detail.

36. These improvements will be underpinned by the European Council taking on a pre-eminent guiding and coordinating role to ensure overall coherence and the effective monitoring of progress towards the new strategic goal. The European Council will accordingly hold a meeting every Spring devoted to economic and social questions. Work should consequently be organised both upstream and downstream from that meeting. The European Council invites the Commission to draw up an annual synthesis report on progress on the basis of structural indicators to be agreed relating to employment, innovation, economic reform and social cohesion.

Implementing a new open method of coordination

37. Implementation of the strategic goal will be facilitated by applying a new open method of coordination as the means of spreading best practice and achieving greater convergence towards the main EU goals. This method, which is designed to help Member States to progressively develop their own policies, involves:

— fixing guidelines for the Union combined with specific timetables for achieving the goals which they set in the short, medium and long terms;
— establishing, where appropriate, quantitative and qualitative indicators and benchmarks against the best in the world and tailored to the needs of different Member States and sectors as a means of comparing best practice;
— translating these European guidelines into national and regional policies by setting specific targets and adopting measures, taking into account national and regional differences;
— periodic monitoring, evaluation and peer review organised as mutual learning processes.

38. A fully decentralised approach will be applied in line with the principle of subsidiarity in which the Union, the Member States, the regional and local levels, as well as the social partners and civil society, will be actively involved, using variable forms of partnership. A method of benchmarking best practices on managing change will be devised by the European Commission networking with different providers and users, namely the social partners, companies and NGOs.

39. The European Council makes a special appeal to companies' corporate sense of social responsibility regarding best practices on lifelong learning, work organisation, equal opportunities, social inclusion and sustainable development.

40. A High Level Forum, bringing together the Union institutions and bodies and the social partners, will be held in June to take stock of the Luxembourg, Cardiff and Cologne processes and of the contributions of the various actors to enhancing the content of the European Employment Pact.

Mobilising the necessary means

41. Achieving the new strategic goal will rely primarily on the private sector, as well as on public-private partnerships. It will depend on mobilising the resources available on the markets, as well as on efforts by Member States. The Union's role is to act as a catalyst in this process, by establishing an effective framework for mobilising all available resources for the transition to the knowledge-based economy and by adding its own contribution to this effort under existing Community policies while respecting Agenda 2000. Furthermore, the European Council welcomes the contribution that the EIB stands ready to make in the areas of human capital formation, SMEs and entrepreneurship, R&D, networks in the information technology and telecom sectors, and innovation. With the 'Innovation 2000 Initiative', the EIB should go ahead with its plans to make another billion euro available for venture capital operations for SMEs and its dedicated lending programme of 12 to 15 billion euro over the next 3 years for the priority areas.

D. Hodson and I. Maher, 'The Open Method as a New Mode of Governance:
the Case of Soft Economic Policy Co-Ordination'
(2001) 39 JCMS 719, 721–22

There are three reasons why the open method may be seen as a new mode of governance. First, taking developments in economic policy as our case study, the open method emerged to deal with the specific issue of factor (capital and labour) and product market flexibility under EMU. Within the current paradigm of sound money and sound finance, national responses in the framework of commonly agreed parameters to this issue are deemed superior to either unco-ordinated national action or action via the traditional and more legally structured Community method. Second, as EU policy-making moves into politically sensitive areas such as immigration, defence and taxation, the centralisation of policy formation encapsulated in the Monnet method is more problematic due to difficulties in achieving policy convergence and popular dissatisfaction with the Union. This has prompted the development of new methods of governance that facilitate further Europeaniza-tion outside existing institutional forms. Third, the open method provides a pragmatic rather than principled answer to the Achilles' heel of the EU – legitimacy. Legitimation is presumed for policy formed at the national level and, even if contested, arguments are framed in national rather than EU terms and hence are unlikely to call into question fundamentally the role of the EU in facilitating co-ordination. It is, however, debatable whether the open method transcends the usual criticisms of governance in the EU, notably elitism and opacity.

  Whether the open method is merely a transitional method governance is answered in part by Dyson's view that it is intended to bring about a convergence in policy-makers' attitudes towards specific issues. '*Benchmarking* can be a factor in reframing domestic discourse and shifting the distribution of power over ideas and agenda setting' [K. Dyson, *The Politics of the Eurozone: Stability or Breakdown* (OUP, 2000), p.5]. This suggests that the sound money, sound finance paradigm is currently seen as a necessary truth, although such truths can become contingent in the presence of a changing conceptual paradigm. For example, the view that the heterogenous nature of national economies made monetary union impossible was prevalent in many states in the years before EMU. Once member governments accepted the sound money, sound finance paradigm for monetary policy, other pre-existing barriers, such as diversity in national economies, were surmounted. Arguably, as common values begin to grow (through the open method), the possibility of a transfer in competence to the EU level could increase. If this happens, the open method would be transitional and its novelty as a mode of governance would diminish.

Hodson and Maher proceed to reflect on the Open Method in the light of other trends and techniques explored in this Chapter.

  First, subsidiarity (p.728):

[Subsidiarity] now forms an important part of the cultural frame within which policy formation takes place and is a tool in deciding whether or not particular action should be taken by the EU . . . The open method seems entirely consistent with the principle, with its emphasis on policy learning among different levels of government. The Lisbon Conclusions themselves note that a fully decentralized approach will be applied in line with the principle (. . . para 38 [see above]). Arguably, the open method goes further and radicalises subsidiarity; this is a static principle with its focus on what level of government at a particular time of rule formation in the policy process and with a continuing emphasis on hierarchy of structures. The open method, being focused on horizontal learning processes and peer pressure where individual action runs counter to broadly accepted principles, is dynamic in nature, heterarchical, decentered as a *modus operandi* and without any particular rule or single policy objective as an objective . . .

And then 'flexibility' (pp.730–31):

The open method can also be seen as a form of 'soft' flexibility in contrast to that found under Art. 11 EC and Art. 40–43 EU. These provisions allow for closer co-operation between states aspiring to greater integration than is currently envisaged under the treaties, by setting down specific steps that have to be taken in order to protect the interests of non-participants and the *acquis* . . . The provisions have yet to be invoked, although the amendments introduced in Nice may change that . . . Even with reform, the provisions form a legal straitjacket determining how much further co-operation can take place and reflect an anxiety about the ability of the EU to control outcomes. This can be contrasted with the open method that occurs in a space devoid of formal legal norms apart from the Treaty provisions themselves and the decisions establishing the relevant committees. There is no formal attempt to control outcomes (outside of fiscal policy of course), and process is determined by a system of benchmarking and lesson-drawing, emphasising state competence and the voluntary alignment of policies. Thus the open method provides real flexibility and marks a further maturation of the integration process. The desire of the EC to control outcomes, as manifest in the directive as the rule of choice in the single market, with its emphasis on common outcomes if not methods, is overcome by recognition of the importance of diversity at the national level in relation to policy formation, legal frameworks, ideational references and popular perceptions and reactions to either the European project generally or the specific policy being co-ordinated.

NOTE

The desire to craft a European Union that is enriched by a constructive relationship with its Member States, and not simply seen as an elite-driven, 'top-down' project is plain here, and it binds together much of the material collected in this Chapter. Rigid hierarchies may make the European Union seem aloof. And yet Hodson and Maher, discussing the Open Method, identify a real problem already remarked upon by Harmsen in examining 'variable geometry' (p.670). The more complex the system becomes, the more intransparent and alienating it becomes. Hierarchical structures are at least intelligible. The Union is grappling with some dauntingly difficult dilemmas here.

This is rich fare for the Convention on the 'Future of Europe', and the next round of Treaty revision. The Open Method is firmly on the agenda.

Paper 6/2003 Constitutionalising the Open Method of Coordination
By *Gráinne de Búrca* (European University Institute/Columbia Law School) *and*
Jonathan Zeitlin (European Union Center, University of Wisconsin-Madison)

Thinking Outside the Box Editorial Series, Paper 6/2003: JURIST EU,
available via http://www.fd.unl.pt/je/edit_pap.htm

Within the Convention process, the final reports of no less than four separate working groups – those on Simplification, Complementary Competences, Economic Governance and Social Europe respectively – have come out in favour of including the 'Open Method of Coordination' (OMC) within the Constitutional Treaty. The reasons for this relatively broad agreement, as expressed in the various reports, stem from an apparently widespread recognition of the usefulness, efficiency, and flexibility of this new form of national policy coordination for dealing jointly with issues of common interest to the Member States. Several of the reports point out that in addition to the two Treaty-based coordination mechanisms in employment and economic policy launched during the 1990s, the Lisbon European Council authorised the extension of this method to a broad range of other policy domains, such as information society, enterprise policy, research and development, education and training, combating social exclusion and modernising social protection. Since then, significant OMC processes have been developed in a number of these fields, especially social protection (inclusion, pensions, health care), while new ones have begun to emerge in other areas like immigration and asylum, as well as industrial policy, youth policy and disability policy . . .

We argue that the value of the OMC lies not simply in its general usefulness, efficiency, and flexibility as an instrument of EU policymaking. Rather, because the OMC encourages convergence of national objectives, performance and policy approaches rather than specific institutions, rules and programs, this mechanism is particularly well suited to identifying and advancing the common concerns and interests of the Member States while simultaneously respecting their autonomy and diversity. It is neither strictly a supranational nor an intergovernmental method of governance, but one which is genuinely joint and multilevel in its operation. By committing the Member States to share information, compare themselves to one another, and reassess current policies against their relative performance, the OMC is also proving to be a valuable tool for promoting deliberative problem-solving and crossnational learning across the EU. It is for precisely these reasons that the OMC has so rapidly become a virtual template for Community policymaking in complex, domestically sensitive areas where diversity among the Member States precludes harmonisation but inaction is politically unacceptable, and where widespread strategic uncertainty recommends mutual learning at the national as well as the European level.

The authors recommend that the Open Method be admitted to the Constitutional Treaty. It should be applicable to the existing coordination processes in employment and economic policy, added to the social policy field and, moreover, 'a flexible generic enabling OMC provision should be introduced for areas other than these three'. The OMC should not be used in a way which would undermine or weaken the existing EU acquis, nor as a permanent substitute for Union legislative action permissible under the Constitutional Treaty. All OMC processes should be conducted as openly as possible in accordance with the principle of transparency. The reader is invited to consult the website of the Convention on the 'Future of Europe' (p.30 above) and this book's Companion Website in order to acquire up-dated information about the progress of this and related debates.

In fact, a great deal of vigorous re-thinking is accompanying the debate about methods of governance for a functionally and geographically enlarged Union. The *Community method* is increasingly regarded as inapt to provide an effective basis for advancing the rich variety of policy objectives that have been embedded within the system. At the same time there is a genuine anxiety that departures from the *Community method* may heedlessly abandon the very core of the 'constitutionalized' legal order that has contributed so much to stabilizing the successes of the integration experiment achieved so far. Can there be adaptation without fragmentation? It is a debate that first emerged in a vigorous fashion at the time of the creation of the European Union by the Treaty of Maastricht, when the deliberate crafting of the two non-EC pillars of the EU under arrangements that were institutionally and constitutionally distinct from – and less sophisticated than – those reigning in the EC attracted criticism for its perceived undermining of *Community method*. Since then other features of the EU's evolution have presented themselves as further candidates for the sceptic, anxious lest cherished features of the EC's style of governance be diluted.

In July 2001 the Commission published a White Paper on Governance. It defines *governance* to mean 'rules, processes and behaviour that affect the way in which powers are exercised at European level, particularly as regards openness, participation, accountability, effectiveness and coherence' (p.8).

EUROPEAN GOVERNANCE: A WHITE PAPER, COM (2001) 428, pp.7–9

I. WHY REFORM EUROPEAN GOVERNANCE?

European integration has delivered fifty years of stability, peace and economic prosperity. It has helped to raise standards of living, built an internal market and strengthened the Union's voice in the world. It has achieved results which would not have been possible by individual Member States acting on their own. It has attracted a succession of applications for membership and in a few years time it will expand on a continental scale. It has also served as a model for regional integration across the world.

These results have been achieved by democratic means. The Union is built on the rule of law; it can draw on the Charter of fundamental rights, and it has a double democratic mandate through a Parliament representing EU citizens and a Council representing the elected governments of the Member States. Yet despite its achievements, many Europeans feel alienated from the Union's work. This feeling is not confined to the European Institutions. It affects politics and political institutions around the globe. But for the Union, it reflects particular tensions and uncertainty about what the Union is and what it aspires to become, about its geographical boundaries, its political objectives and the way these powers are shared with the Member States. The decreasing turnout in the European Parliament elections and the Irish 'No' vote also serve to show the widening gulf between the European Union and the people it serves:

- There is a perceived inability of the Union to act effectively where a clear case exists, for instance, unemployment, food safety scares, crime, the conflicts on the EU's borders and its role in the world.
- Where the Union does act effectively, it rarely gets proper credit for its actions. People do not see that improvements in their rights and quality of life actually come from European rather than national decisions. But at the same time, they expect the Union to act as effectively and visibly as their national governments.
- By the same token, Member States do not communicate well about what the Union is doing and what they are doing in the Union. 'Brussels' is too easily blamed by Member States for difficult decisions that they themselves have agreed or even requested.
- Finally, many people do not know the difference between the Institutions. They do not understand who takes the decisions that affect them and do not feel the Institutions act as an effective channel for their views and concerns. People do not necessarily feel less European. They still expect Europe-wide action in many domains, but they no longer trust the complex system to deliver what they want. In other words, people have disappointed expectations, but expectations nevertheless.

The debate on the future of Europe and the scope of the White Paper

This disenchantment and with it the fundamental questions concerning the future of Europe will be the subject of intense debate in the run up to the Inter-Governmental Conference. However, in preparing for further institutional change, the Union must start the process of reform now. There is much that can be done to change the way the Union works under the existing Treaties. This is why the Commission decided to launch in early 2000 the reform of European governance as a strategic objective – well in advance of the Nice European Council. Reforming governance addresses the question of how the EU uses the powers given by its citizens. It is about how things could and should be done. The goal is to open up policy-making to make it more inclusive and accountable. A better use of powers should connect the EU more closely to its citizens and lead to more effective policies.

In order to achieve this, the Union must better combine different policy tools such as legislation, social dialogue, structural funding, and action programmes. This would contribute to strengthening the Community method. Reforming European governance implies that the Commission must refocus on its core mission. The proposals in this paper will improve the quality of the way it initiates policy. They will ensure more clarity and effectiveness in policy execution, and maximise the impact of the Commission's actions as guardian of the Treaty.

What is the Community method?

The Community method guarantees both the diversity and effectiveness of the Union. It ensures the fair treatment of all Member States from the largest to the smallest. It provides a means to arbitrate between different interests by passing them through two successive filters: the general interest at the level of the Commission; and democratic representation, European and national, at the level of the Council and European Parliament, together the Union's legislature.

— The **European Commission** alone makes legislative and policy proposals. Its independence strengthens its ability to execute policy, act as the guardian of the Treaty and represent the Community in international negotiations.

— Legislative and budgetary acts are adopted by the **Council of Ministers** (representing Member States) and the **European Parliament** (representing citizens). The use of qualified majority voting in the Council is an essential element in ensuring the effectiveness of this method. Execution of policy is entrusted to the Commission and national authorities.

— The **European Court of Justice** guarantees respect for the rule of law.

NOTE

The White Paper on Governance has stimulated a lively debate, and is plainly part of the general process of introspection that dominates the European Union as it considers the 'Future of Europe' (p.30 above). This extract champions the 'Community method'. Some commentators have identified a tone of conservatism and even defensiveness in the White Paper's commitment to the virtues of the Community method: see for example C. Scott, 'The Governance of the European Union: the Potential for Multi-Level Control' (2002) 8 ELJ 59; D. Wincott, 'The Governance White Paper, the Commission and the Search for Legitimacy', Ch. 22 in A. Arnull and D. Wincott, *Accountability and Legitimacy in the European Union* (Oxford: OUP, 2002).

The next extract pursues the debate on a more specifically legal plane. The authors define new governance as any major departure from 'Classic Community method' ('CCM'), covering departures within CCM and alternatives to it. They then identify the following dimensions as characteristic of new forms of governance:

J. Scott and D. Trubek, 'Mind the Gap: Law and New Approaches
to Governance in the European Union'
(2002) 8 ELJ 1, 5–6

A Participation and Power-Sharing

Many of the new governance approaches involve novel ways to expand participation by elements of civil society in policy making. And some entail a greater degree of power sharing than traditional legislation or regulation. This in some cases, policy making may be seen not as something to be done by autonomous regulators but rather as a process of mutual problem-solving among stakeholders from government and the private sector, and from different levels of government.

B Multi-level integration

New governance tends to accept the necessity for coordination of action and actors at many levels of government, as well as between government and private actors. This means that new governance mechanisms may include machinery that brings actors from various levels of government (localities, sub-national regions, national, European) together in ways that facilitate dialogue and coordination.

C Diversity and Decentralisation

New governance, unlike much EU legislation and regulation, accepts the possibility of coordinated diversity and the advantages of leaving final policy making to the lowest possible level when this is feasible. To that end, several new governance mechanisms are designed more to support and coordinate Member State policies than to create uniformity across the Union.

D Deliberation

Many of the new governance mechanisms are designed to foster extended deliberation among stakeholders over the nature of problems, the best way to solve them, and the challenge of carrying out solutions within the widely differing contexts of the fifteen Member States. Deliberation serves both to improve problem-solving capabilities and possibly provide some degree of democratic legitimation.

E Flexibility and Revisability

Many of the approaches emerging in the area of 'new governance', including some that are carried through the Community method, rely less on formal rules and 'hard law' than on open-ended standards, flexible and revisable guidelines, and other forms of 'soft law'. In this way, these mechanisms can adopt to diversity, tolerate alternative approaches to problem solving, and make it easier to revise strategies and standards in light of evolving knowledge.

F Experimentaion and Knowledge Creation

Some new governance mechanisms facilitate experimentation and the creation of new knowledge. New knowledge may come from deliberative processes, from combining local experimentation with multilateral surveillance, and from formal and informal ways of exchanging results, benchmaking performance, and sharing best practices.

FURTHER READING ON ASPECTS OF 'NEW GOVERNANCE'

De La Porte, C., 'Is the Open Method of Coordination Appropriate for Organising Activities at European Level in Sensitive Policy Areas?' (2002) 8 ELJ 38.

Mosher, J.S. and Trubek, D., 'Alternative Approaches to Governance in the EU: EU Social Policy and the European Employment Strategy' (2003) 41 JCMS 63.

Syrpis, P., 'Legitimising European Governance: Taking Subsidiarity Seriously Within the Open Method of Coordination', Working Paper of the European University Institute, Law 2002/10 (http://www.iue.it/PUB/law02–10.pdf).

■ QUESTION

Norbert Reich has commented that 'the more competences the Community is acquiring, the less exclusive will be its jurisdiction' ((1992) 29 CML Rev 861, 895). What are the manifestations of this development? Is it desirable?

NOTE

 For additional material and resources see the Companion Website at: www.oup.co.uk/ best.textbooks/law/weatherill6e

What Sort of 'Europe'?

Chapters 19 and, in particular, 20 were by no means designed to show that the core assumptions of the nature and purpose of Community policy-making are now outmoded, but it was designed to show the widening variety of methods of governance that now contribute to the workings of the Union. The remarkable tale of the 'constitutionalization' of the Treaties provided the binding thread for the material in Part One of this book. That story was built on a legal order for the EC that is supreme: a 'new legal order' according to the Court. This Chapter is designed to survey some of the challenges to the European Court's portrayal of the nature of EC law. This discussion connects to the Laeken Declaration and the current Constitutional Convention on the 'Future of Europe', the quest for Constitutional 'Finality', Enlargement and the 2004 IGC. As with Chapters 19 and 20, so with Chapter 21: the intent is not at all to suggest received wisdom about the nature and purpose of the European Union is flawed, but rather to suggest that the geographical and functional growth of the system has generated a much wider debate about the ramifications of what is and should be done in the name of European integration.

One of the notions lurking in the previous Chapter was that of *legitimacy*. It also surfaced in Chapter 1 (pp.15, 23 above). This is a notion that carries heavy weight.

With hindsight one of the most remarkable features of the early years of the Union's development was the small amount of attention paid to the fundamental constitutional questions of what really was being created. A new legal order, that was supreme over the laws of the Member States. Was this State-building? State-*replacing*?

SECTION 1: **THE CHALLENGE OF NATIONAL CONSTITUTIONAL COURTS**

Denmark ratified the Maastricht Treaty in 1993 after a popular referendum voted in favour of ratification. But this was the second bite of the cherry. In 1992 the Danes had voted 'No'. Discontent had been reduced from majority to minority sentiment in the period between the first and second referendum, but the jolt to assumptions about the popular appeal of the European integration process was profound. Nor was Denmark alone in ratifying the Maastricht Treaty only after considerable internal difficulty. It was mentioned in Chapter 1 (at p.9) that Germany was the last State to ratify the Maastricht Treaty and that it did so only after its Constitutional Court (*Bundesverfassungsgericht*) approved ratification. The German Court rejected an individual's constitutional complaint, but the ruling is remarkable for observations about the Treaty-defined limits of Community competence and the inapplicability of acts of the Community's institutions which trespass on areas of exclusive national competence.

The ruling is by no means the inevitable starting point in any debate about the true nature of the European Union and its relationship with its Member States. But it is nevertheless worthy of attention. After decades of assumptions that European integration was a project handled by élites, the rocky road to ratification of the Maastricht Treaty changed perceptions.

The Danish 'No' must be taken as an expression of popular disquiet. But it is hard to draw clear lessons from the result of a single-issue, single-answer referendum, not least because of the tiny majorities involved in both votes. By contrast the intervention of the German *Bundesverfassungsgericht* provides us with more tangible bases for understanding what is at stake.

In the following extract the German Federal Constitutional Court considers its perception of the nature of the European Union, both generally and in the light of Germany's 'Basic Law':

Ruling of the Federal Constitutional Court, Second Division, 12 October 1993, 2 BvR 2134/92, 2 BvR 2159/92 (*Brunner* v *European Union Treaty*)

. . . b 1) The European Union is, in accordance with its understanding of itself as a union of the peoples of Europe (Art. A para 2 Union Treaty), a confederation of allied democratic states whose objectives include dynamic development (see, e.g., Arts. B para 1 last indent and C para 1, Union Treaty). If the Union carries out its sovereign duties and thereby exercises sovereign powers, it is in the first place the nationals of the Member States through their national parliaments who have to legitimise this democratically.

At the same time, with the development of the functions and powers of the Community it becomes increasingly necessary to allow the democratic legitimation and influence provided by way of national parliaments to be accompanied by a representation of the nationals of a Member State through a European Parliament as the source of a supplementary democratic support for the policies of the European Union. With the establishment of union citizenship by the Maastricht Treaty, a lasting legal tie is knotted between the nationals of the individual Member States which, though not as strong as the common nationality of a single state, provides a legally binding expression of the degree of *de facto* community already in existence (see especially Art. 8b paras. 1 and 2, EC Treaty). The influence extending from the citizens of the Union can eventually become a part of the democratic legitimation of the European institutions, to the extent that the peoples of the European Union fulfill the necessary preconditions for such.

Democracy, if it is not to remain as merely a formal principle of accountability, is dependent on the existence of certain pre-legal conditions, such as a continuous free debate between opposing social forces, interests, and ideas, in which political goals become clarified and change course (see 5 BVerfGE 85 at 135, 198 and 205; 69 BVerfGE 315 at 344 *et seq*) and out of which a public opinion emerges which starts to shape a political will. This also means that the decision-making processes of the organs exercising sovereign powers and the various political objectives pursued can be generally perceived and understood, and therefore that citizens entitled to vote can communicate, in their own language, with the sovereign authority to which they are subject.

Such factual conditions, to the extent that they do not yet exist, can develop in the course of time within the institutional framework of the European Union. Such development to no small extent is dependent on a process for imparting the objectives of the Community institutions and the effects of their decisions to the member nations. Parties, associations, the press and the broadcasting services are as much a medium as a factor of this process, out of which a European public opinion may come into being (see Art. 138a, EC Treaty). The European Council is also eager for more openness and transparency in the European decision-making process (see Birmingham Declaration: A Community close to its citizens nos, 2, 3, BullBReg. No 115 of 23 Oct. 1992, p.1058; Final Conclusions of the European Council Presidency in Edinburgh, 11/12 Dec. 1992, part A, sect. 7, and annex 3 BullBReg. No 140 of 28 Dec. 1992, pp.1278, 1284 *et seq.*

b 2) In the confederation of allied states formed by the European Union, therefore, democratic legitimation necessarily comes about through the feed-back of the actions of the European institutions into the parliaments of the Member States; within the institutional structure of the Union there is the additional factor (which increases as European nations grow closer together) of the provision of democratic legitimation by means of the European Parliament which is elected by the citizens of the Member States. Already at the present stage of development the legitimation of the European Parliament has a supporting function, which could become stronger were it to be elected by uniform voting rules in all the Member States in accordance with Art. 138 para 3 of the EC Treaty and if its influence on the policies and legislation of the European Community were to increase. What is decisive is that the democratic bases of the European Union are built up in step with integration, and that as integration proceeds a thriving democracy is also maintained in the Member States. Excessive functions and powers within the sphere of responsibility of the European confederation of states would effectively weaken democracy at the national level, so that the parliaments of the Member States could no longer adequately provide the legitimation for the sovereign power exercised by the Union.

If, as at present, the peoples of the individual states provide democratic legitimation through their national parliaments, limits to the extension of the European Communities' functions and powers are then set by virtue of the democratic principle. Each of the peoples of the individual states is the starting point for the public authority relating to that people. The states need sufficiently important spheres of activity of their own in which the peoples of each can develop and articulate in a process of political will – formation which it legitimates and controls, in order to give legal expression to what – relatively homogeneously – binds the people spiritually, socially, and politically together (see H. Heller, *Politische Demokratie and soziale Homogenität, Gesammelte Schriften*, Vol. 2 (1971), p.421 at 427 *et seq*).

From all that it follows that functions and powers of substantial importance must remain for the German *Bundestag*.

c) The exercise of sovereign power through a confederation of allied states such as the European Union is based on authorisations from states which remain sovereign and which in international matters generally act through their governments and thereby control the integration process. It is therefore primarily governmentally determined. If such a community power is to rest on the political will-formation which is supplied by the people of each individual state, and is to that extent democratic, it presupposes that the power is exercised by an entity made up of representatives sent by Member States' governments, which in turn are subject to democratic control. The issue of European legal regulations may – without prejudice to the need for democratic control of the government – as well lie with an institution composed of representatives of Member States' governments, i.e., an executive organ, to a greater extent than would be constitutionally acceptable at national level.

3. As the German voter essentially exercises his right to participate in the democratic legitimation of the institutions and agencies entrusted with sovereign powers by means of the elections for the German *Bundestag*, the *Bundestag* must also decide on German membership in the European Union and on its continuation and development.

Article 38 of the Basic Law is accordingly breached if a law that opens up the German legal system to the direct validity and application of the law of the – supranational – European Communities does not establish with adequate certainty what powers are transferred and the intended program of integration (see 58 BVerfGE 1 at 37). When it is unclear to what extent and degree the German legislature has assented to the transfer of the exercise of sovereign powers, then the European Communities may possibly claim functions and powers that were not specified. That would be equivalent to a general authorisation, and therefore would be a relinquishment of powers, against which Art. 38 of the Basic Law provides protection.

In view of the fact that the text of an international treaty must be negotiated by the treaty parties, the certainty and tightness of the treaty provisions cannot be set in the same way as for a law under parliamentary jurisdiction (see 77 BVerfGE 170 at 231 *et seq*). What is decisive is that Germany's membership and the pendant rights and duties – especially the immediately binding legal effect of the Communities' actions within the national sphere – have been defined in the Treaty so as to be predictable for the legislature and are enacted by it in the Law on Accession with sufficient certainty (see 58 BVerfGE 1 at 37; 68 BVerfGE 1 at 98 *et seq*). At the same time that means that subsequent important changes to the integration program set up in the Union Treaty and to the Union's powers of action are no longer covered by the Law on Accession to the present Treaty (see *ibid*; Mosler in *Handbuch des Staatsrechts*, Vol. VII, 1992, sec. 175, n. 60). Thus, if European institutions or agencies were to treat or develop the Union Treaty in a way that was no longer covered by the Treaty in the form that is the basis for the Law on Accession, the resulting legislative instruments would not be legally binding within the sphere of German sovereignty. The German state organs would be prevented, for constitutional reasons, from applying them in Germany. Accordingly, the Federal Constitutional Court reviews legal instruments of European institutions and organs to see whether they remain within the limits of the sovereign rights conferred on them or whether they transgress those limits (see 58 BVerfGE 1 at 30 *et seq*; 75 BVerfGE 223 at 235, 242) . . .

The German court concluded that the Union Treaty measured up to these standards, thereby clearing the way for German ratification. However, in the later stages of the ruling it reaffirmed its sensitivity to the location of the outer limits of Community competence:

. . . Inasmuch as the Treaties establishing the European Communities on the one hand in limited circumstances confer sovereign rights, and on the other hand regulate Treaty amendments – through a normal and also in a simplified procedure – does this distinction take on meaning for the future treatment of the individual powers. Whereas a dynamic extension of the existing Treaties has been supported so far on the basis of a broad treatment of Art. 235 of the EEC Treaty [now Art. 308 EC] in the sense of a 'lacuna-filling competence' (*Vertragsabrundungskompetenz*) and on the basis of considerations relating to the implied powers of the Communities and of Treaty interpretation as allowing maximum exploitation of Community powers of 'effect utile' (see Zuleeg in: von der Groeben/Thiesing/Ehlermann, *EWG-Vertrag*, 4th ed. 1991, Art. 2, note 3), in future the interpretation of enabling provisions by institutions and agencies of the Community will have to consider that the Union Treaty basically distinguishes between the exercise of a conferred limited sovereign power and the amendment of the Treaty, thus the interpretation will not result in an extension of the Treaty: such an interpretation of enabling provisions would not have a binding effect for Germany . . .

The *Bundesverfassungsgericht's* parting shot was:

The Maastricht Treaty – especially by the extension of EC competences and the inclusion of monetary policy – confers further essential functions and powers on European organs – which at Treaty level are not yet supported by a corresponding strengthening and extension of the democratic bases. It sets up a new stage of European unification, which according to the stated intentions of the Contracting Parties is to enhance further the democratic and efficient functioning of the institutions (fifth considérant of the Preamble). Democracy and efficiency are here not to be separated; it is also expected that the strengthening of the democratic principle will improve work at the Community level in all its organs. At the same time, in accordance with Art. F para 1 of the Union Treaty [now Art. 6 TEU], the Union will respect the national identities of its Member States, the governmental systems of which are based on democratic principles. To that extent the Union preserves the democratic bases already existing in the Member States and builds on them.

Any further development of the European Union cannot evade the conceptual framework set out above. The constitution-amending legislature had in connection with this Treaty taken that into account when they inserted Art. 23 into the Basic Law, as there the development of the European Union is expressly mentioned, subject to the principles of democracy and the rule of law, social and federal principles, and the subsidiarity principle. It is decisive, therefore, from the point of view of both the Treaties and of constitutional law, that the democratic bases of the Union will be built in step with integration, and also as integration progresses a living democracy will be maintained in the Member States.

It is hard to read these observations other than as warnings for the future. Note that they are addressed to *all* the Community/Union institutions. H. Hauser and A. Muller summarize the Court's view in the following terms ((1995) 50 *Aussenwirtschaft* 17, 30):

> EU institutions provide no primary source for democratic legitimisation. The democratic systems of the Member States are the primary source for democratic legitimisation of EU legislation. Because citizen participation is only guaranteed on the national and not on the European level, democratic legitimisation needs clearly defined restrictions on the transfer of sovereignty. National constitutional courts should have the ultimate interpretation whether EU legislation corresponds to the principle of specific delegation of power.

It is important to realize that the German court is, in effect, threatening to deprive the European Court of exclusive competence to determine the limits of EC competence, but that it is doing so out of a declared perception based on the need to secure effective democratic control of political decision-making. Nevertheless, there is much to be said for the view that the *Bundesverfassungsgericht's* concerns are not prompted by the pattern of the Maastricht Treaty itself, but rather by a belated recognition of expansionist trends in the evolution of Community law and policy through legislative and judicial activism over an extended period (the subject matter of this book!). J. Weiler suggests that for the *Bundesverfassungsgericht* 'the only way out was to legitimate the past by . . . weak notions of Member State democratic mediation, and put the polity on notice that German constitutionalism will not be caught napping again.' ('Does Europe need a Constitution? Reflections on Demos, Telos, and the German Maastricht Decision') (1995) 1 *European Law Journal* 219, 237). It has been suggested at several points in this book that a new post-Maastricht sensitivity affects the Community institutions when they are invited to act at the outer limits of Community competence; and that this is in part attributable to an awareness that the Community system, built on willing and active cooperation between Community and national bodies, can survive only if negative reactions at national level are absorbed and answered at Community level. Examples might include *Dori* (Case C-91/92, p.148) and *Tobacco Advertising* (Case C-376/98, p.60). It is, of course, in the interest of the European Court to maintain the loyal support of national courts, for the evolution of the EC legal system and its practical enforcement depend heavily on the inter-penetration of Community law and national law. Coercive measures are not available to the European Court, so it must seek to persuade.

In fact, this is a two-way process of dialogue. The harsh tone of the *Maastricht* judgment should be contrasted with the more emollient expressions of a more recent ruling of the *Bundesverfassungsgericht*.

BANANAS, ORDER OF THE SECOND SENATE OF 7 JUNE 2000 – 2 BvL 1/97

I

Submissions of cases to the Federal Constitutional Court for constitutional review under Article 100(1) GG which refer to rules that are part of secondary European Community law are only admissible if their grounds show in detail that the present evolution of law concerning the protection of fundamental rights in European Community law, especially in case law of the Court of Justice of the European Communities, does not generally ensure the protection of fundamental rights required unconditionally in the respective case. Certainly the submitting court has, in a way which meets the requirements under Article 80 (2), sentence 1 of the BVerfGG [*Bundesverfassungsgerichtsgesetz – Federal Constitutional Court Act*] set forth its conviction that, and for what reasons, it regards the application of the submitted legal rules as unconstitutional (cf. BVerfGE [*Bundesverfassungsgerichtsentscheidungen – Decisions of the Federal Constitutional Court*] 37, 328 <333 *et seq*>; 66, 265 <269 *et seq*>; 84, 160 <165>; 86, 52 <57>). Its opinion that the decision it must take depends on the decision on the issue submitted is clearly stated in the decision for submission (cf. BVerfGE 97, 49 <60>, 98, 169 <199>). However, the submitting court's position that the rules of Articles 17–19 and Article 21 (2) of Regulation (EEC) No 404/93 as well as other secondary rules of Community law to which it objects may be submitted to the Federal Constitutional Court for constitutional review under Article 100(1) GG cannot be supported.

II

1. In its decision of 29 May 1974 – 2 BvL 52/71 (BVerfGE 37, 271 – 'As long as . . . Decision' [*Solange I*]), the competent Senate of the Federal Constitutional Court had, with reference to actual jurisdiction, come to the result that the integration process of the Community had not progressed so far that Community law also contained a codified catalogue of fundamental rights decided on by a Parliament and of settled validity, which was adequate in comparison with the catalogue of fundamental rights contained in the Basic Law. For this reason, the Senate regarded the reference by a court of the Federal Republic of Germany to the Federal Constitutional Court in constitutional review proceedings, following the obtaining of a ruling of the Court of Justice of the European Communities under Article 177 of the EEC Treaty, which was required at that time, as admissible and necessary if the German court regards the rule of Community law that is relevant to its decision as inapplicable in the interpretation given by the Court of Justice of the European Communities because and in so far as it conflicts with one of the fundamental rights of the Basic Law (BVerfGE 37, 271 <285>).

2 a) In its decision of 22 October 1986 – 2 BvR 197/83 (BVerfGE 73, 339 – [*Solange II*]), the Senate holds that a measure of protection of fundamental rights has been established in the meantime within the sovereign jurisdiction of the European Community which in its conception, substance and manner of implementation is essentially comparable with the standards of fundamental rights provided in the Basic Law, and that there are no decisive factors to lead one to conclude that the standard of fundamental rights which has been achieved under Community law is not adequately consolidated and only of a transitory nature (BVerfGE 73, 339 <378>).

On the basis of individual decisions of the Court of Justice of the European Communities, the Senate made statements concerning the standard of fundamental rights, and holds that this standard, particularly through the decisions of the Court of Justice of the European Communities, has been formulated in content, consolidated and adequately guaranteed (BVerfGE 73, 339 <378–381>). In this context, the Senate commented on the decisions of the Court of Justice of the European Communities concerning the fundamental rights and freedoms relating to economic activities, such as the right to property and the freedom to pursue economic activities (above, p.380), but also on the freedom of association, on the general principle of equal treatment and the prohibition of arbitrary acts, religious freedom and the protection of the family, as well as on the principles, which follow from the rule of law, of the prohibition of excessive action and of proportionality as general legal principles in achieving a balance between the common interest objectives of the Community legal system, and on the safeguarding of the essential content of fundamental rights (above, p.380).

In summary, the Senate made the following statement: As long as the European Communities, in particular European case law, generally ensure effective protection of fundamental rights as against the sovereign powers of the Communities which is to be regarded as substantially similar to the protection of fundamental rights required unconditionally by the Basic Law, and in so far as they generally safeguard the essential content of fundamental rights, the Federal Constitutional Court will no longer exercise its jurisdiction to decide on the applicability of secondary Community legislation cited as the legal basis for any acts of German courts or authorities within the sovereign jurisdiction of the Federal Republic of Germany, and it will no longer review such legislation by the standard of fundamental rights contained in the Basic Law. References (of rules of secondary Community law to the Federal Constitutional Court) under Article 100(1) GG are therefore inadmissible (BVerfGE 73, 339 <387>).

b) In its Maastricht Decision (BVerfGE 89, 155), the Senate maintained this view. In this decision, the Senate stressed that the Federal Constitutional Court, through its jurisdiction, guarantees, in co-operation with the Court of Justice of the European Communities, that effective protection of fundamental rights for the residents of Germany will also be secured against the sovereign powers of the Communities and is generally to be regarded as substantially similar to the protection of fundamental rights required unconditionally by the Basic Law, and that in particular the Court provides a general safeguard of the essential contents of the fundamental rights. The Federal Constitutional Court thus guarantees this essential content against the sovereign powers of the Community as well (BVerfGE 89, 155 <174–175>, with reference to BVerfGE 37, 271 <280 et seq> and 73, 339 <376–377, 386>). Under the preconditions the Senate has formulated in BVerfGE 73, 339 – 'Solange II' –, the Court of Justice of the European Communities is also competent for the protection of the fundamental rights of the citizens of the Federal Republic of Germany against acts done by the national (German) public authority on account of secondary Community law. The Federal Constitutional Court will only become active again in the framework of its jurisdiction should the Court of Justice of the European Communities depart from the standard of fundamental rights stated by the Senate in BVerfGE 73, 339 (378–381).

c) Article 23 (1), sentence 1 GG (inserted pursuant to the Law amending the Basic Law of 21 December 1992 – BGBI I, p.2086 –) confirms this ruling. Pursuant to this law, the Federal Republic of Germany shall participate, with a view to establishing a united Europe, in the development of the European Union that is committed to democratic, social, and federal principles, to the rule of law, and to the principle of subsidiarity, and that guarantees a level of protection of fundamental rights essentially comparable to that afforded by the Basic Law. An identical protection in the different areas of fundamental rights afforded by European Community law and by the rulings of the Court of Justice of the European Communities, which are based on Community law, is not called for. The constitutional requirements are satisfied in accordance with the preconditions mentioned in BVerfGE 73, 339 (340, 387) if the rulings of the Court of Justice of the European Communities generally ensure effective protection of fundamental rights as against the sovereign powers of the Communities which is to be regarded as substantially similar to the protection of fundamental rights required unconditionally by the Basic Law, and in so far as they generally safeguard the essential content of fundamental rights.

d) Thus, constitutional complaints and submissions by courts are, also pursuant to the Senate decision in BVerfG 89, 155, inadmissible from the outset if their grounds do not state that the evolution of European law, including the rulings of the Court of Justice of the European Communities, has resulted in a decline below the required standard of fundamental rights after the 'Solange II' decision (BVerfGE 73, 339 <378–381>). Therefore, the grounds for a submission by a national court of justice or of a constitutional complaint which puts forward an infringement by secondary European Community Law of the fundamental rights guaranteed in the Basic Law must state in detail that the protection of fundamental rights required unconditionally by the Basic Law is not generally assured in the respective case. This requires a comparison of the protection of fundamental rights on the national and on the Community level similar to the one made by the Federal Constitutional Court in BVerfGE 73, 339 (378–381).

III

Such a statement is lacking in this case.

1. The grounds of this submission fail from the outset to satisfy the special requirement for admissibility, as they are based on a misunderstanding of the Maastricht decision. The submitting court is of the opinion that the Federal Constitutional Court, pursuant to the Maastricht decision, contrary to the Solange II decision, explicitly exercises its review authority again, albeit in co-operation with the Court of Justice of the European Communities.

This conclusion cannot be drawn from the Maastricht decision. In the passage to which the Administrative Court refers, the Senate of the Federal Constitutional Court explicitly quotes the statements of its 'Solange II' decision that shows that it exercises its jurisdiction to a limited extent. The fact that the Senate in its Maastricht decision has neither in this passage nor elsewhere given up its opinion laid down in BVerfGE 73, 339, on the delimitation of the authority for jurisdiction of the Court of Justice of the European Communities vis-à-vis the Federal Constitutional Court and vice versa is also evident from the previous considerations (BVerfGE 89, 155, 174–175). Finally, the Senate discusses these questions in the passage on the admissibility of relief being sought with reference to the Constitution, not in the passage that deals with the question whether the submission is well-founded (BVerfGE 89, 155 <174>, beginning of 2.). Also under this aspect, the assumption of a contradiction between the Solange II and the Maastricht decisions lacks a sound basis.

2. In the present case there was, beyond these requirements, a special cause for detailed statements concerning a negative evolution of the standard of fundamental rights in the jurisdiction of the Court of Justice of the European Communities, as the Court of Justice of the European Communities had, in its decision of 26 November 1996 (Case C-68/95 – *T. Port GmbH & Co. KG* v *Bundesanstalt für Landwirtschaft und Ernährung*, European Court Reports 1996, p.I-6065), which had been taken after the decision for submission had been issued, required the Commission pursuant to Article 30 of Regulation No 404/93 to take any transitional measures it judges necessary. Such transitional measures must serve, according to this judgement, to overcome the difficulties which occurred after the common organisation of the market came into but originated in the state of the national markets before the enactment of the Regulation. This decision and its possible consequences for the admissibility of the decision for submission had been specifically pointed out to the submitting court.

At this point in time, the submitting court should have recognised the insufficiency of its submission and should have remedied it (cf. BVerfGE 51, 161 <163 *et seq*>; 85, 191 <203>). For doing so, the reply, which was made by the presiding judge of the chamber alone, was already insufficient for formal reasons because the presiding judge, as a member of a court composed of several judges, is not allowed to take the decision to submit the case on his own (in this context, cf. BVerfGE 1, 80 <81–82>; 21, 148 <149> already), it is quite out of the question for him alone to be in charge of and observe the admissibility of the submitted decision until the decision of the Federal Constitutional Court is taken. As to their contents, the statements made by the presiding judge also head into the wrong direction. There is a contradiction between them and the grounds of the decision for submission, which especially criticises the lack of transitional measures and derives the unconstitutionality of Regulation 404/93 from this fact. It would, however, not have been possible for the Administrative Court to infer a general decline of the standard of fundamental rights in the jurisdiction of the Court of Justice of the European Communities against the background of this decision of the Court of Justice of the European Communities.

Moreover, the Administrative Court should have seen that the decision of the Court of Justice of the European Communities had been preceded by the decision of the First Chamber of the Second Senate of the Federal Constitutional Court of 25 November 1995 – 2 BvR 2689/94 and 2 BvR 52/95 – (EuZW [Europäische Zeitschrift für Wirtschaftsrecht] 1995, p.126). The Court of Justice of the European Communities judged the necessity of a provisional hardship arrangement that follows from the guarantee of property in a similar manner as the Federal Court of Justice did. Thus, both decisions illustrate that the judicial protection of fundamental rights by national courts of justice and Community courts of justice interlock on the European level.

NOTE

Bananas concerns review of acts for compliance with fundamental rights; *Maastricht* concerned alleged trespass beyond the outer limits of Treaty-conferred competence. But the pivotal issue was the same – what competence did a national court enjoy when faced with a plea that an EC act was invalid according to domestic constitutional standards? The pure logic of supremacy insists that the EC act must prevail; and the European Court's view is that that act can be set aside only by the European Court itself applying the rules of the EC legal order (Case 314/85 *Foto-Frost*, p.245 above). But this is not what the *Bundesverfassungsgericht* decides. The *Bundesverfassungsgericht* does not concede to the European Court an exclusive jurisdiction to decide on the validity of Community law The ruling in *Bananas* is stated to be consistent with that in the *Maastricht* case, and indeed it is. It maintains an ultimate review competence vested in the German court in the event that review of EC acts against the standards of fundamental rights by the European Court is shown to be deficient judged by German constitutional standards. But it places a heavy burden on the applicant seeking to demonstrate such deficiency. This ruling is strikingly more concerned than *Maastricht* to assert the extreme improbability that the German court would rule in favour of the disapplication of a Community act on German territory. In form this is not compatible with the European Court's insistence that it and it alone is competent to rule on the validity of Community legislative acts. But in practice the disagreement matters little, at least while the German courts remain content with the steering role played by the European Court.

Several questions emerge. What kind of unstable legal order is this? How can we truly bask in the successful remaking of the EC legal order as an independent source of law which is, moreover, supreme over conflicting national laws when such audacious claims are so readily challenged by a national court? Has the European Court been exposed as the Walter Mitty of European legal hierarchies?

And yet the quest to hammer out an answer to the question 'who is boss?' should not be lightly undertaken by Europeans. History reveals what happens when one group seeks to impose its views on others. Is acquiescence in 'constitutional plurality' feasible in Europe?

Miguel Poiares Maduro, 'Europe and the Constitution: *What if this is As Good As It Gets*?'
Constitutionalism Web-Papers (University of Manchester)
http://les1.man.ac.uk/conweb/ ConWEB No 5/2000

Who Decides Who Decides?

Constitutional law has usually been considered as the higher degree and ultimate source of legitimacy of the legal system and its rules. Independently of ones conception of constitutional law as a 'grundnorm', a set of rules of recognition, positivized natural law, an higher command of a sovereign supported by an habit of obedience, or other, constitutional law has always been conceived as the higher law of the legal system, criterion of legitimacy and validity of other sources of the law. European integration 'attacks' this hierarchical understanding of the law. In reality, both national and European constitutional law assume in the internal logic of their respective legal systems the role of higher law. According to the internal conception of the EU legal order developed by the European Court of Justice, Community primary law will be the 'higher law' of the Union, the criterion of validity of secondary rules and decisions as well as that of all national legal rules and decisions within its scope. Moreover, the Court of Justice is the higher court of this legal system. However, a different perspective is taken by national legal orders and national constitutions. Here, Community Law owes its supremacy to its reception by a higher national law (normally constitutions). The higher law remains, in the national legal orders, the national constitution and the ultimate power of legal adjudication belongs to national constitutional courts. In this way, the question of who decides who decides has different answers in the European and the national legal orders[42] and when viewed from a perspective outside both national and Community legal orders requires a conception of the law which is no longer dependent upon an hierarchical construction. Such form of legal pluralism has already been convincingly argued by Neil MacCormick.[43] However, the Maastricht Decision of the German Constitutional Court and the possibility of this Court striking down a Community legal act on its decision on the Bananas regulation,[44] have again raised fears of actual conflicts between national courts and the ECJ disrupting the European Union legal order and ultimately the process of European integration. In my view, the question of 'who decides who decides' has long been present within constitutionalism. It is a normal consequence of the divided powers system inherent in constitutionalism. In fact, it can be considered as an expected result of the Madisonian view of separation of powers as creating a mechanism of checks and balances. The conflicts surrounding the exercise of judicial review, for example, are linked to this question: when a Court strikes down a piece of legislation according to its interpretation of a constitutional norm which could be object of different interpretations two opposing positions can be argued: one, arguing that the Court has done nothing else but apply the higher law; another, arguing that the Court has overstepped its role since the indeterminacy of the constitutional norm meant that it was for the legislator to choose one among several possible interpretations of that norm. Of course, in the operation of national constitutions and where constitutional judicial review exists it is expected for the legislator to accept the Court's decision and therefore it is stated that it is the later that has the 'right to decide who decides'. But that is a more a result of the historical development of separation of powers than a logical conclusion to be derived from the foundations of constitutionalism. Moreover, the reality is that the political system can still impact upon the judiciary (for example by changing the members of the constitutional court)[45] and, in this way, still has an important share of the power 'to decide who decides'. I am not going to address the complex questions involved in judicial review and separation of powers. What I want to stress is that the paradox of 'who decides who decides' is inherent to the values of constitutionalism as one of its guarantees of limited power. If the question of 'who decides who decides' was constitutionally allocated to a single institution all the mechanisms of countervailing powers and checks and balances would be easily undermined. Therefore, in a multi-level or federal system it is the vertical or federal conception of constitutionalism (as a form of limited government at the State and federal level) that requires for the decision on 'who decides who decides' to be left unresolved. The open question should be left open. What then, are conflicts unavoidable? Should the conflicts between EU law and national constitutional law be subject to a *primus inter pares* (for example, international law[46] or a new Constitutional Court composed of EU and National constitutional judges[47])? Can't different legal orders coexist in the same sphere of

---

42 Rossa Phelan has made a detailed analysis of the different viewpoints on the relationship between national and the European legal order depending on whether it is observed from the perspective of EC law, national constitutional law or even public international law. See D. Rossa Phelan, *Revolt or Revolution: The Constitutional Boundaries of the European Community*, Dublin: Sweet & Maxwell, 1997.

43 N. MacCormick, 'Beyond the Sovereign State', (1993) 56 Modern Law Review 1.

44 See, for example, M. Kumm, 'Who Is the Final Arbiter of Constitutionality in Europe?', Harvard Jean Monnet Chair Working Papers 10/98. Among other relevant issues (mainly, the direct effect of the GATT rules in the German legal order), the argument is made by some German Companies which traditionally imported Bananas from Latin-American countries that the EC Regulation discriminates against those importers in favor of intra-EC Bananas producers (mainly from Canarias and Madeira) and importers from ACP countries.

45 An exemplary case, is Roosevelt's 're-packaging' of the American Supreme Court to change the classical economic due process interpretation of the American Constitution.

46 N. MacCormick, 'Risking Constitutional Collision in Europe?', (1998) 18 *Oxford Journal of Legal Studies* 517. Although, MacCormick suggests subjecting such conflicts to the arbitration of international law as a possible direction he does not really take that path and prefers to remain faithful to a totally legal pluralistic solution where the question of conflict is left open.

47 J. Weiler, 'The European Union Belongs to Its Citizens: Three Immodest Proposals', (1997) 22 *European Law Review* 150.

application under different claims of legitimacy?[48] And if they can, how can conflicts be avoided or dealt with?

The general tendency may be for national courts to comply with the 'European Constitution' but there is still on the part of several national high courts a challenge to the absolute supremacy of EU law. This is visible either in the description that national constitutionalism makes of itself or in the dependence of EU law effectiveness upon national law and national courts. National law still holds a veto power over national law[49] and that is important even when not used. It is well known that many developments in EU law can be explained by the European Court of Justice perception of the possible reactions by national courts. A hierarchical alternative imposing a monist authority of European law and its judicial institutions over national law would be difficult to impose in practical terms and could undermine the legitimacy basis on which European law has developed.[50] Though the grammar used by EU lawyers in describing the process of constitutionalisation may assume a top-down approach, the reality is that the legitimacy of European constitutionalism as developed in close co-operation with national courts and national legal communities which have an increasing bottom-up effect on the nature of the European legal order.[51]

We have to start reasoning in the realm of what could be called counterpunctual law. Counterpoint is the musical method of harmonising different melodies that are not in a hierarchical relationship among them. The discovery that different melodies could be heard at the same time in an harmonic manner was one of the greatest developments in musical history and greatly enhanced the pleasure and art of music. In law we too have to learn how to manage the non-hierarchical relationship between different legal orders and institutions and to discover how to gain from the diversity and choices that offer us without generating conflicts that ultimately will destroy those legal orders and the values they sustain. There is much to be gained from a pluralist conception of the EU legal order. In a world where problems and interests have no boundaries, it is a mistake to concentrate the ultimate authority and normative monopoly in a single source. Legal pluralism constitutes a form of checks and balances in the organisation of power in the European and national polities and, in this sense, it is an expression of constitutionalism and its paradoxes. But, to take full advantage of this legal pluralism we need to conceive forms of reducing or managing the potential conflicts between legal orders while promoting exchanges between them and requiring courts to conceive their decisions and the conflicts of interests at hand in the light of a broader European context. This will also highlight the trans-national character of much of these conflicts which is often ignored by national constitutional law. Catherine Richmond has proposed an attractive framework for the 'legal indeterminacy' entailed in the non-hierarchical relationship between national and European legal orders. She argues that each legal order has its own viewpoint over the same set of norms[52] and that each is to take into account the changes in that set of norms arising from the other legal orders: 'each time a norm is created or amended in one particular legal order, the cognitive arrangement of norms must, from our one particular viewpoint, be shuffled around in order to accommodate the change'.[53] However, no legal order should be forced to abandon its own viewpoint (or, if you prefer, its own cognitive framework). In her own words: 'A state of legal indeterminacy is only

---

48 Rossa Phelan, above n.42, for example, argues that 'revolt or revolution' is unavoidable unless Community law partly redraws its claim of supremacy over national law. For a critical review of Rossa Phelan's position see MacCormick, above n.46 and Poiares Maduro, 'The Heteronyms of European Law', (1999) 5 *European Law Journal, Annual Review of Books*, Weiler and Poiares Maduro (eds.), at 160.

49 See D. Chalmers, 'Judicial Preferences and the Community Legal Order', (1997) 60 Modern Law Review 164 at 180.

50 In the words of Chalmers, 'the regime is able to develop provided it does not significantly disrupt the egalitarian relations enjoyed between national courts and the Court of Justice', ibidem.

51 Kamiel Mortelmans, 'Community Law: More than a Functional Area of Law, Less than a Legal System', *Legal Issues of European Integration*, 1996/1, 23, at 42–43.

52 In the suggestive expression of Jo Shaw: 'each national constitution creates a different "gateway" for the EU legal order'. Postnational Constitutionalism, n.2.

53 Catherine Richmond, 'Preserving the Identity Crisis: Autonomy, System and Sovereignty in European Law', (1997) 16 *Law and Philosophy* 377 at 417.

stable, however, as long as no *normative* challenge is made to it which challenges the *political* basis of the cognitive model adopted (. . .). Therefore it is in all parties' interest to preserve the indeterminacy in the Community, enabling each to latch on to the model of legal authority that is politically most comfortable'.[54] Identity is lost if it is not self-determined. On the other hand, such self-determination should not dispute the self-determined identity of the other legal orders. In my view, one of the consequences ought to be that each time a legal order changes the set of norms shared with the broader European legal community it ought to do it in a manner that can be accommodated by the other legal orders (a good example being the introduction of fundamental rights protection in the Community legal order). The EU legal order should be conceived as integrating both the claims of validity of national and EU constitutional law. Any judicial body (national or European) would be obliged to reason and justify its decisions in the context of a coherent and integrated EU legal order. In this way, I do not share the view that the best form of safeguarding legal pluralism is to recognise, pragmatically and normatively, the possibility for national constitutional authorities to derogate from EU law so long as that would not itself be recognised by EU law and will be valid under national constitutional law but not EU law. For Kumm, who has powerfully argued in favour of such a view,[55] the fact that the deviations will take place under national law and not EU law will mean that the integrity and uniformity of EU law would be safeguarded. But this will be so from a purely formal perspective. Further, the fact that the deviations would be legitimised on purely national grounds and 'not affect' EU law may promote the use and abuse of that national constitutional exceptions without any form of EU control. Ultimately, it could lead to a 'race to the bottom' between national courts in the uniform application of EU law. I argue that national deviations can still be possible but they need to be argued in 'universal' terms, safeguarding the coherence and integrity of the EU legal order. The idea is to promote the universalisability of national decisions on EU law and integrate them into a coherent system of interpretation of EU law by national courts. In other words, national decisions on EU law should not be seen as separated national interpretations and applications of EU law but as decisions to be integrated in a system of law requiring compatibility and coherence. This may raise fears of corrosion of EU law since it appears to promote and multiply national deviations from the European rule of law. However, this assumption must be confronted with the dynamics of law and legal reasoning. If a national constitutional court is aware that the decision that it will take becomes part of European law as interpreted by the 'community' of national courts, it will internalise in its decisions the consequences in future cases and the system as a whole. This will prevent national courts from using the autonomy of their legal system as a form of evasion and free-riding and will engage the different national courts and the ECJ in a true discourse and coherent construction of the EU pluralist legal order. At the same time, we should improve European legal pluralism by raising in each legal order the awareness of the constitutional boundaries of the other legal orders. And, in here, an important role is to be played by the changes in constitutional thinking which I have been arguing for, particularly the abandoning of single constitutionalism which has dominated the conceptions of national constitutionalism. The conception of European legal pluralism or contrapunctual law argued for in here safeguards the constitutional value of the paradox of who decides who decides by preserving the identity of each legal order while at the same time promoting its inclusiveness through what, following Luhmann's and Teubner's autopoeisis, could be described as a process of reflexivity. It is not only identity but also communication that needs to be fostered between national and European legal orders. In this case, 'the fact that we define our identity by exclusion from the other does not ultimately exclude because there is no way of knowing where the next redefinition will go'.[56] This discourse between different legal orders and different institutions resulting from the emerging European polity is a further promotion of constitutionalism, broadening its deliberative elements beyond the exclusive deliberative communities involved in each national institution.

---

54 Ibid.

55 Kumm, above n.44.

56 Z. Bankowski and E. Christodoulidis, 'The European Union as an Essentially Contested Project', (1998) 4 *European Law Journal* 341 at 351–352.

FURTHER READING ON THE IMPLICATIONS OF THE JUDICIAL DIALOGUE ABOUT THE NATURE OF THE EUROPEAN LEGAL ORDER

Aziz, M., 'Sovereignty Lost, Sovereignty Regained? Some Reflections on the Bundesverfassungsgericht's Bananas Judgment' Constitutionalism Web-Papers (University of Manchester), http://les1.man.ac.uk/conweb/ ConWEB No 3/2003

Boom, S. J., 'The European Union after the Maastricht Decision: Will Germany be the "Virginia of Europe"?' (1995) XLIII Amer J Comp Law 177.

Petersmann, E.-U., 'Proposals for a New Constitution for the European Union: Building Blocks for a Constitutional Theory and Constitutional Law of the EU' (1995) 32 CML Rev 1123.

Rasmussen, H., 'Confrontation or Peaceful Co-Existence?' Ch 24 in D O'Keeffe (ed), *Judicial Review in European Union Law: Liber Amicorum Gordon Slynn* (Kluwer, 2000) – *discussing Danish developments*.

Schmid, C., 'All Bark and no Bite: Notes on the Federal Constitutional Court's Banana Decision' (2001) 7 ELJ 95.

Slaughter, A.-M., Stone Sweet, A., and Weiler, J.H.H. (eds), *The European Courts and National Courts: Doctrine and Jurisprudence* (Oxford: Hart Publishing, 1997)

Zuleeg, M., 'The European Constitution under Constitutional Constraints: The German Scenario' (1997) 22 EL Rev 19.

You might also read P. Kirchhof, 'The Balance of Powers between National and European Institutions' (1999) 5 ELJ 225; the author was a member of the *Bundesverfassungsgericht* and widely supposed to have exerted significant influence over the drafting of its 'Maastricht' judgment. It is of interest that his discussion includes explicit reference to judicial anxieties expressed in other Member States (pp.240–41).

SECTION 2: **STATES AND BEYOND: MULTI-LEVEL GOVERNANCE AND CONSTITUTIONALISM**

This complex layering of multi-level legal authority, which seems to resist reduction to a simple hierarchy, finds an echo in the even wider phenomemon of the political character of the Union itself. Is it a State or is not a State? And whose benchmark do we employ to measure what it really is? In fact, these kinds of 'simple questions' are exactly the numbingly pedestrian questions that preclude necessary leaps of imagination. The European Union need not be a State – on some accounts, *should* not be a State – and yet may fulfil its role. At the core of the debate is the question of where lies the legitimate source of authority? And, as with the search to locate the 'constitutional right answer' on whose law should prevail, there is much to be said for an approach which respects the different and differently motivated voices of claimants instead of demanding that one win, and others lose.

 The following two extracts build beyond the 'Maastricht ruling' of the *Bundesverfassungsgericht* to discuss the present and future shaping of the Union.

H. Hauser and A. Müller, 'Legitimacy: The Missing Link for
Explaining EU-Institution Building'
(1995) 50 Aussenwirtschaft 17, 18–22

(Footnotes omitted, small linguistic alterations made with the copyright holder's permission.)

1.1. FROM INTERGOVERNMENTAL TO SUPRANATIONAL

The EU is an institution 'sui generis' with no historical precedent. Accordingly, it is difficult to describe the institution in traditional terms. . . . The institutional structure goes far beyond an international agreement between sovereign states, even beyond a confederation between sovereign states with unlimited veto power. On the other hand, the EU clearly lacks main features of a federal state. Until now the European Union was qualified as a supranational co-operation, but this organisation never achieved the quality of a state. The Preamble speaks about the growing union of the peoples of Europe. It is difficult to qualify the nature of the European Union, e.g., the German Constitutional Court in the judgment of Maastricht talks about a 'parent organisation' . . . and other new qualifications. Similarly, when the German Constitutional Court talks about the future of Europe, it explains itself very carefully, 'state-connection' . . . and 'growing union of the peoples of Europe' . . . are expressions which reveal its fear of becoming more concrete. The Court describes the European Union not as no state, not even a 'federal' one . . ., but as a process of integration of its own nature as an 'interstate establishment'. . . . The complex structure of supranational and inter-governmental elements in institutions and decision making processes must be at the core of a theoretical discussion of EU institutional development.

The Treaty incorporates two intergovernmental pillars, whereas the EC pillar contains inter-governmental as well as supranational elements. A mix of intergovernmental and supranational can also be observed in procedural questions. The most striking examples for this complex set of supranational and intergovernmental elements are the following:

(a) The EC as economic pillar of the EU has strong supranational elements whereas CFSP and WEU as well as the cooperation in the field of justice and Home Affairs have intergovernmental structures. Besides the competences of the Union which are exercised on a supranational level, the intergovern-mental competences also have to be regarded. The CFSP is an example of unfinished integration, it is still an intergovernmental co-operation. The Member States remain responsible in this area even if the competences have been brought nearer to the European Union. But even if operations are organised in common (Art. J.3 and Art. K. 3 2 EU), the decisions can only be made unanimously.

(b) Revisions of the supranational EU treaty are prepared by intergovernmental conferences and not by a constitutional assembly. The intergovernmental orientation of constitutional amendments is also exemplified by the fact that they need unanimous approval by all member states. Article N EU Treaty says: '*The amendments shall enter into force after being ratified by all Member States in accordance with their respective constitutional requirements.*'

(c) In the exercise of competences, the mix between intergovernmental and supranational aspects is also obvious. Competences of the EU must be based on specific delegation of power by the Treaty. The union can only legislate in areas which are directly mentioned in the Treaty of Maastricht. As a general rule, 'exclusive competences' . . . of the European Union have to be the exception and are only accepted under restrictive conditions. If the European Union is not explicitly entitled to act, competences remain with the Member States. Nevertheless, this principle does not have the intended limiting effect, because the European Court of Justice developed the theory of implied powers, which justifies further regulations if it is in the logic of the goals of integration. Even if a regulation has no basis in the Treaty, it can be enacted by the Union due to this principle. The teleological interpretation of EU competences by the European Court of Justice and the former frequent use of Art. 235 of the EC Treaty have opened the door for expanding EU competences and have reduced the binding effect of the principle of specific delegation.

(d) The legislative power of the EU is further strengthened by the priority of European law over national law and by the judgments of the European Court of Justice, which have 'prejudicial effects' on judgments of the national courts. The recent Karlsruhe decision of the German Constitutional Court [on the Maastricht Treaty, above] highlights a fundamental ambiguity: Should the European Court of Justice or should national constitutional courts of member countries decide in the event of disagreement on the separation of power between the EU and its Member States? Presently, we have no case in question, but the potential for future conflicts exists. Jurisprudence of the Court of Justice clearly states that a decision about the distribution of competences is only decided by the European Court of Justice, whereas the ruling of Karlsruhe places the final decision about the distribution of competences in the hands of national self-determination.

(e) It is difficult to decide whether decision making in the EU is supranational or intergovernmental. The important role of the Commission, co-decision rights of the Parliament and majority voting in the Council are clearly supranational elements. The fact that legislative power is vested primarily with the Council, which is composed of delegate ministers of member states, the fact that important decisions, particularly in fiscal issues, still require unanimity, and the decision procedures for defining fiscal guidelines are closer to intergovernmental structures. Intergovernmental is also the distribution of voting rights, which give smaller Member States a more than proportional representation in decision-making. By the Treaty of Maastricht, the Parliament acquires co-decision, but this does not give Parliament the final say in the legislative procedure. All legislation must still be approved by the Council, so the democratic deficit problem remains. Nevertheless, a veto by the Parliament ends the legislative process. The co-decision procedure has only led to a modest increase in the Parliament's participation.

(f) The evolution toward a supranational organisation is also reflected in the ambition to create a 'European Law' having primacy over the national legislatures. EU primary law, within the limitations of direct applicability as defined by the European Court of Justice, and regulations as part of secondary law is clearly supranational law. Directives must be translated into national law by the national legislature, but the increasing specificity of directives and the ruling of the European Court of Justice that directives can develop direct applicability under certain conditions bring them also very close to supranational law. EU institutions can create directly applicable supranational law within a broad range of competences with unclear boundaries. At least in the field of economic regulation, there seem to be no effective constitutional restrictions for EU institutions to take over responsibility. According to the European Court of Justice, the European Treaty is seen as a Constitution and has priority over national constitutions. Since the Treaty of Maastricht, the ruling of the Court has even more importance under the new Article 171 [now Art. 228 EC]: '*If the Member State concerned fails to take the necessary measures to comply with the Court's judgment within the time-limit laid down by the Commission, the latter may bring the case before the Court of Justice. In so doing it shall specify the amount of the lump sum or penalty payment to be paid by the Member State concerned which it considered appropriate in the circumstances. If the Court of Justice finds that the Member State concerned has not complied with its judgment it may impose a lump sum or penalty payment on it.*' This possibility of the European Court of Justice to force Member States to transform EU ruling into national legislation points out the strong supranational power of the EU.

To summarise: Institutional tensions in the EU can best be explained by the weak correspondence between the distribution of power to regulate and the institutional structure of decision making. With regard to the separation of power in the field of economic regulation, the EU comes very close to a federation: within the broad competences of the Maastricht Treaty, EU institutions decide on the separation of power (with the restriction of unanimity vote in some areas), the European Court of Justice has the right for authoritative interpretation, in areas of majority voting Member States have lost control over future regulation. Institutional structures do not follow these developments. The separation of power within the EU does not correspond to requirements of a democratic state: EU legislation is in the hands of members of the executive of Member States, the executive function in the EU is a shared responsibility of the Commission and the Council, the exclusive right to initiatives gives the Commission an important role in the legislative process, members of the Commission and of the European Court of Justice are delegated by national governments and not appointed by the legislator.

The tension between the regulative power of a federation and the weak institutional structure which does not meet basic requirements of a democratic state is at the heart of most critical voices in the academic and political debate. . . . Complaints about democratic deficits, weak accountability of EU institutions, inefficient decision procedures, or over-centralisation are the symptoms. Reforms to either better restrict EU competences or to develop democratic EU institutions are proposals to ease the underlying tensions . . .

NOTE

The reader would profit at this point from re-visiting some of the material contained in Chapter 1 of this book. In particular, consider the extent to which the *Laeken Declaration* (p.25) fits the authors' descriptive and prescriptive summary in the concluding two paragraphs of this extract. Which of the two routes suggested in the final sentence has been preferred by the Convention on the 'Future of Europe'? (p.30).

J. Habermas, 'Remarks on Dieter Grimm's "Does Europe Need a Constitution?" '
(1995) 1 European Law Journal 303–07

The Diagnosis

From a constitutional perspective, one may discern a contradiction in the European Union's present situation. On the one hand, the EU is a supranational organisation established by international treaties and without a constitution of its own. In this respect it is not a state (in the modern sense of a constitutional state characterised by a monopoly on violence and a domestically and internationally recognised sovereignty). On the other hand, Community institutions create European law that binds the Member States – thus the EU exercises a supreme authority previously claimed only by individual states. From this results the oft-bemoaned democratic deficit. Commission and Council pronouncements, as well as decisions by the European Court, are intervening ever more profoundly into the Member States' internal affairs. Within the framework of the rights conferred upon the Union, the European Executive may enforce its pronouncements over and against the opposition of the national governments. At the same time, as long as the European Parliament is equipped with only weak competences, these pronouncements and enactments lack direct democratic legitimation. The executive institutions of the community derive their legitimacy from that of the member governments. They are not institutions of a state that is itself constituted by the act of will on the part of the united citizens of Europe. The European passport is not as yet associated with rights constitutive for democratic citizenship.

Political Conclusion

In contrast with the Federalists, who recommend a democratic pattern for the EU, Grimm warns [in an article to be found in the same issue of the *European Law Journal*] against any further European-law-induced eroding of national competences. The democratic deficit would not be effectively filled by a 'statist shortcut' to the problem, but rather deepened. New political institutions such as a European Parliament with the usual powers, a government formed out of the Commission, a Second Chamber replacing the Council, and a European Court of Justice with expanded competences, as such offer no solutions. If they are not filled with life, they will instead accelerate tendencies already apparent within the national frameworks, tendencies towards autonomisation of bureaucratised politics. The real prerequisites for a European-wide integration of citizen will-formation have been absent up to now. Constitutional Euroscepticism thus amounts to the empirically-based argument that runs as such: as long as there is not a European people which is sufficiently 'homogenous' to form a democratic will, there should be no constitution.

The Discussion

My reflections are directed against (a) the insufficient account of alternative courses and (b) the not entirely unambiguous normative underpinnings of the functional requirements for democratic will-formation.

(a) Grimm sets before us the undesired consequences that would result from the transition of the European Community to a democratically-constituted, federal state should the new institutions not take root. So long as a European-networked civil society, a European-wide political public sphere and a common political culture are lacking, the supranational decision processes would become increasingly independent of the still nationally organised opinion- and will-formation processes. This dangerous prognosis is plausible as far as I am concerned. However what is the alternative? Grimm's option seems to suggest that the constitutional status quo can at least freeze the extant democratic deficit. Completely independent of constitutional innovations however this deficit expands day by day because the economic and social dynamics even within the existing institutional framework perpetuate the erosion of national powers through European law. As Grimm himself acknowledges: 'The democratic principle is valid for the Member States whose own decision capabilities are however diminishing: decisional capability is accruing to the European Community where the democracy principle is developing only weakly.' But if the gap is steadily widening between the European authorities' expanding scope and the inadequate legitimation of the proliferating European regulations, then decisively adhering to an exclusively nation-state mode of legitimation does not necessarily mean opting for the lesser evil. The Federalists at least face the foreseeable – and perhaps avoidable – risk of the autonomisation of supranational organisations as a challenge. The Eurosceptics have, from the start, acquiesced in the supposedly irresistible erosion of democratic substance so that they do not have to leave what appears as the reliable shelter of the nation-state.

In fact the shelter is becoming increasingly less comfortable. The debates on national economic competitiveness and the international division of labour in which we are engaged make us aware of quite another gap – a gap between the nation state's increasingly limited maneuverability, and the imperatives of modes of production interwoven worldwide. Modern revenue-states profit from their respective economies only so long as there are 'national economies' that can still be influenced by political means. With the denationalisation of the economy, especially of the financial markets and of industrial production itself, national governments today are increasingly compelled to accept permanently high unemployment and the marginalisation of a growing minority for the sake of international competitiveness. If there is to be at least some substantive maintaining of the welfare state and some avoiding the further segmentation of an underclass, then institutions capable of acting supranationally must be formed. Only regionally comprehensive regimes like the European Community can still affect the global system in line with a coordinated world domestic policy.

In Grimm's account, the EU appears as an institution to be *put up with*, and with whose abstractions we must live. The reasons why we should *want* it politically are not presented. I would submit that the greater danger is posed by the autonomisation of globalised networks and markets which simultaneously contribute to the fragmentation of public consciousness. If these systemic pressures are not met by politically capable institutions then the crippling fatalism of the Old Empires will grow again in the midst of a highly mobile economic modernity. The decisive elements of this future scenario would be the postindustrial misery of the 'surplus' population produced by the surplus society – the Third world within the First – and an accompanying moral erosion of community. *This* future-present would in retrospect view itself as the future of a past illusion – the democratic illusion according to which societies could still determine their own destinies through political will and consciousness.

(b) *Apropos* the second problem. Naturally any assessment of the chances for a European-wide democracy depends in the first place upon empirically grounded arguments. But we first have to determine the functional requirements; and for that the normative perspective in which the former are supposed to fit is crucial.

Grimm rejects a European constitution 'because there is as yet no European people'. This would on first glance seem founded upon the same premise that informed the tenor of the German Constitutional Court's Maastricht judgment: namely, the view that the basis of the state's democratic legitimation requires a certain homogeneity of the state-constituting people. However Grimm immediately distances himself from a Schmittian kind of definition of *völkischen* homogeneity: 'The presuppositions for democracy are developed here not of the people, but from the society that wants to constitute itself as a political unit. But this presumes a collective identity, if it wants to settle its conflicts without violence, accept majority rule and practice solidarity.' This formulation leaves open the question of how the called-for collective identity is to be understood. I see the nub of republicanism in the fact that the forms and procedures of the constitutional state together with the democratic mode of legitimation simultaneously forge a new level of social integration. Democratic citizenship establishes an abstract, legally mediated solidarity among strangers. This form of social integration which first emerges with the nation-state is realised in the form of a politically socialising *communicative context*. Indeed this is dependent upon the satisfaction of certain important functional requirements that cannot be fulfilled by administrative means. To these belong conditions in which an ethical political self-understanding of citizens can communicatively develop and likewise be reproduced – but in no way a collective identity that is *independent of the democratic process itself* and as such existing prior to that process. What unites a nation of citizens as opposed to a *Volksnation* is not some primordial substrate but rather an intersubjectively shared context of possible understanding.

It is therefore crucial in this context whether one uses the term 'people', in the juristically neutral sense of 'state-constituting people', or whether one associates the term with notions of identity of some other kind. In Grimm's view the identity of a nation of citizens 'need not' be 'rooted in ethnic origin, but may also have other bases'. I think on the contrary that it *must* have another basis if the democratic process is to finally guarantee the social integration of a differentiated – and today increasingly differentiating – society. This burden must not be shifted from the levels of political will-formation to pre-political, pre-supposed substrates because the constitutional state guarantees that it will foster necessary social integration in the legally abstract form of political participation and that it will actually secure the status of citizenship in democratic ways. The examples of culturally and ideologically pluralistic societies only serve to emphasise this normative point. The multicultural self-understanding of the nations of citizens formed in classical countries of immigration like the USA is more instructive in this respect than that derived from the assimilationist French model. If in the same democratic political community various cultural, religious and ethnic forms of life are to exist among and with each other then the majority culture must be sufficiently detached from its traditional fusion with the *political* culture shared by all citizens.

To be sure, a politically constituted context of solidarity among citizens who despite remaining strangers to one another are supposed to stand up for each other is a communicative context *rich in prerequisites*. In this point there is no dissent. The core is formed by a political public sphere which enables citizens to take positions at the same time on the same topics of the same relevance. This public sphere must be deformed neither through external nor internal coercion. It must be embedded in the context of a freedom-valuing political culture and be supported by a liberal associational structure of a civil society. Socially relevant experience from still-intact private spheres must flow into such a civil society so that they may be processed there for public treatment. The political parties – not state-dependent – must remain rooted in this complex so as to mediate between the spheres of informal public communication, on the one hand, and the institutionalised deliberation and decision processes, on the other. Accordingly, from a normative perspective, there can be no European Federal state worthy of the name of a democratic Europe unless a European-wide, integrated public sphere develops in the ambit of a common political culture: a civil society with interest associations; non-governmental organisations; citizens' movements etc.; and naturally a party system appropriate to a European arena. In short, this entails public communication that transcends the boundaries of the until now limited national public spheres.

Certainly, the ambitious functional requirements of democratic will-formation can scarcely be fulfilled in the nation-state framework; this is all the more true for Europe. What concerns me, however, is the perspective from which these functional prerequisites are normatively justified; for this, as it were, prejudices the empirical evaluation of the present difficulties. These must, for the time being, seem insuperable if a pre-political collective identity is regarded as necessary, that is an independent cultural substrate which is *articulated only* in the fulfilment of the said functional requirements. But a communications-theoretical understanding of democracy, one that Grimm also seems to favour, can no longer rest upon such a concretistic understanding of 'the people'. This notion falsely pretends homogeneity, where in fact something still quite heterogeneous is met.

The ethical-political self-understanding of citizens in a democratic community must not be taken as an historical-cultural *a priori* that makes democratic will-formation possible, but rather as the flowing contents of a circulatory process that is generated through the legal institutionalisation of citizens' communication. This is precisely how national identities were formed in modern Europe.

Therefore it is to be expected that the political institutions to be created by a European constitution would have an inducing effect. Europe has been integrating economically, socially and administratively for some time and in addition can base itself on a common cultural background and the shared historical experience of having happily overcome nationalism. Given the political will, there is no *a priori* reason why it cannot subsequently create the politically necessary communicative context as soon as it is constitutionally *prepared* to do so. Even the requirement of a common language – English as a second first language – ought not be an insurmountable obstacle with the existing level of formal schooling. European identity can in any case mean nothing other than unity in national diversity. And perhaps German Federalism, as it developed after Prussia was shattered and the confessional division overcome, might not be the worst model.

■ QUESTION

How can democratic participation best be secured within the EU? Insofar as the EU is a response to the inadequacies of a system based on the nation-State, is it helpful to look to the national level as a model for the future institutional and constitutional development of the EU?

NOTE

The diminished capacity of the nation-State to provide a 'reliable shelter', to which Habermas refers at p.701 above, continues to attract differing views on what could and should be put in its place, or at least what could and should supplement it. This is central to imagining what we want 'Europe' to deliver more than half a century after the end of the Second World War. But Europe today is built on a multi-level system of governance. In this vein Pernice treats the European Union as a divided power system, and sees 'a progressive constitution of legitimate institutions and powers at the European level, which are complementary to the national constitutions and designed to meet the challenges of an evolving global society' (I. Pernice, 'Multi-level constitutionalism and the Treaty of Amsterdam: European Constitution-Making Revisited' (1999) 36 CML Rev 703).

This an unsettlingly ambiguous environment. It envisages arenas for problem-solving (which might involve problem-avoiding) within an overall system which emphasizes the necessary interconnection of national and European constitutional legal orders. In so far as it is an attempt to provide an arena within which national and transnational law and politics can co-exist it is inevitably characterized in Europe by a certain imprecision for, after all, what is at stake is nothing less than a challenge to the hegemony of national constitutional law and the development of a legal order that involves a re-distribution of power. In fact, as already investigated in the context of the intervention of the *Bundesverfassungsgericht* (p.686 above), the system works (for the time being) precisely because each participant can rest its consent to involvement on different bases which may be constitutionally irreconcilable in a purely formal sense but which do not cause any practical need to choose. It would be problematic only if there was some attempt to find the 'correct' answer – that is, to adjudicate who is the winner and who the loser – the either/or question. So 'Multi-level governance' acts as a rather neat shorthand for describing the way in which Europe (and not only Europe) is the subject of many layers of intersecting legal and political authority, some territorially defined, others sectorally defined, not necessarily capable of subjection to a single, internally consistent rule of authority, yet working more or less successfully because of adaptation along the way and the vested interest of participants in avoiding conflict.

SECTION 3: **LEGITIMACY AND DEMOCRACY**

Multi-level constitutionalism possesses the singular attraction that it frees us from the trap that treats the increase in private economic power in supra-State domains as a basis for shifting extra public power to that same level, which would in turn draw demands for greater institutional accountability to be transplanted to that level, a process which is then seen to impoverish the domestic political sphere. This is a self-defeating prognosis (*cf* Epilogue to Part One, p.275 above). Instead a multi-level approach argues for the importance of different levels of governance in dealing with the growth of transnational economic activity.

What does this mean from the perspective of *legitimacy*?

> **A. Menon and S. Weatherill**, 'Legitimacy, Accountability and Delegation in the European Union', Ch. 7 in A. Arnull and D Wincott, *Accountability and Legitimacy in the European Union* (Oxford: OUP, 2002), pp.115–16, 129–31

LEGITIMACY AND THE EUROPEAN UNION

Fritz Scharpf has drawn a distinction between input and output legitimacy in assessing the European Union. Democratic self-determination, he insists, requires that choices made by the given political system be driven by the authentic preferences of citizens. This suggests a chain of accountability linking those governing to those governed. It is input legitimation, or government by the people. But democratic self-determination also demands that those exercising political power are able to achieve a high degree of effectiveness in meeting the expectations of the governed. The democratic process is, for Scharpf, an 'empty ritual' without such delivery – output legitimacy, or government for the people. Scharpf argues vigorously and persuasively that although the Union is regularly and (to some extent) justifiably criticised for deficiencies in input legitimacy, too little attention is paid to the inadequacies of States when judged from the standpoint of output legitimacy. This tends to breed an inflated assumption of the claim of States to legitimacy. Scharpf's key point is that in at least some policy areas it may be possible to conceive of the EU as capable of legitimation by reference to its output, even if input legitimation is lacking.

In a similar vein, Giandomenico Majone famously describes the EU as a 'regulatory State', drawing attention to the remarkable gulf between the Union (and especially the Community's) extensive rule-making capacity and its negligible administrative infrastructure.[1] Policy-implementation is heavily reliant on the Member States' own legal and administrative agencies. Majone draws normative conclusions. He finds a ready legitimation of the EU through its outputs provided that its activities are confined to securing efficient outcomes. This suggests a temptingly clean-cut model according to which to define the proper limits of regulatory activity 'above' the State. It makes the important claim that legitimation may require assessment in different ways in different policy sectors.

The insights of Scharpf and Majone carry great weight in guiding our understanding of the problems associated with the growth of regulatory activity 'above' the State. They are especially valuable in emphasising the value that is properly attached to output legitimacy. This is especially important in the light of the effect that membership of the EU exerts in confining policy options available to Member States while not recreating equal opportunities for rule-making at transnational level. Under such arrangements, orthodox assumptions about securing input legitimacy for decisions by public bodies are undermined. A response based on reversion to unilateral, bilateral or ad hoc multilateral State action will be confronted by limitations in achieving effective problem-solving. A response based on re-creating State structures at transnational level, in order to re-locate sites of input legitimacy, raises all manner of awkward problems associated with the disinclination of citizens simply to shift their sense of allegiance. As Fritz Scharpf puts it:

---

1 *Regulating Europe* (London, Routledge, 1996).

Given the historical, linguistic, cultural, ethnic and institutional diversity of its member states, there is no question that the Union is very far from having achieved the 'thick' collective identity that we have come to take for granted in national democracies – and in its absence, institutional reforms will not greatly increase the input-oriented legitimacy of decisions taken by majority rule.[2]

Consequently, input legitimacy must be seen as one important element in assessing the legitimacy of the European Union, but it should be assessed in combination with an unavoidable appreciation of the virtues of output legitimacy. It is in the very nature of the Union that it invites such nuanced examination. And it is therefore quite proper to identify a road to legitimacy paved by the ability of the Union to deliver responses to problems that would be insoluble or even simply less effectively solved by individual States. . . .

CONCLUSION

. . . The 'problem with States' is not merely that they may be incapable of effective problem-solving. The rise of transnational economies also tends to accentuate the extent to which State decisions may be driven by the orthodox pressures of national-level representative democracy and yet impose costs on actors who are intimately affected by those decisions yet who are not represented or only inadequately represented in the State's political processes. The juxtaposition of State political decision-making and burgeoning transnational economic activity allows or even induces States to externalise costs and a method is required for reducing, if not eliminating, the ability of the State to take decisions which are neglectful of costs imposed on parties who are not able to gain (adequate) access to the (domestic) market for votes. A supranational legal order is capable of achieving this, and exploration of its legitimacy should encompass respect for this capacity.

Assessing problems of legitimacy by extending emphasis on European-level governance can *always* be criticised for its illegitimacy by those who assume the pre-eminence of national-level political structures. It is the specious but primitively compelling 'loss of sovereignty' argument, but such debates cannot sensibly be conducted pending liberation from (frequently unwitting) preconceptions about sites of legitimacy. So solutions must be pragmatic, incremental and cautious. They must identify the different strands of legitimacy and be aware that tweaking one tweaks all. A starting point might have been that output legitimacy is a Union strength while input legitimacy is a State strength but in fact the interconnections are decidedly more sophisticated than such a model will allow. The least ambitious case made by this paper is that it is wrong to make assumptions about which element to privilege. The more ambitious, and as yet relatively tentative, claim is that we can have it all – provided that all elements are cherished and treated as mutually reinforcing aspects of a broad and multi-level conception of European constitutionalism.[3] That is, a legitimacy test insisting on both input and output legitimacy may be failed both by States and the EU, though in respect of different criteria and/or by different degrees, but taken together, the combination passes. In so far as this represents the essence of transnational governance, it should be seen as a necessarily dynamic and creative process.

There is not the space here to draw out fully the implications of this analysis. One important, though by no means the only such issue concerns the appropriate scope of EU action. Both Majone and Scharpf argue that the EU should remain somewhat restricted in scope because of the necessary 'strong' (input) legitimation that must underpin many areas of public policy and which the EC lacks.[4] Such preferences should be expressed, if at all, only by Member States. Yet at a time when the EU is embarking on its experiment with a single currency, such arguments seem curiously anachronistic. It may well be that the Union is confronted with the stark choice between on the one hand risking its potential to deliver effective outputs by controlling monetary policy in the euro zone without an effective fiscal policy to redress regional disparities and, on the other, venturing into

2 F. Scharpf *Governing in Europe: Effective and Democratic?* (Oxford, OUP 1998), p.9.

3 Similarly Maduro [extract above, p.693].

4 Scharpf talks of the need for EU policies to satisfy the conditions of low visibility and being conflict minimising, whilst Majone insists on the need for the Union to steer clear of redistributive policies. Fritz Scharpf, *Governing in Europe*, pp. 21–25; G. Majone, *Regulating Europe* (London, Routledge, 1996).

larger scale redistributive policies that surpass its capacity to muster input legitimacy. There are no easy solutions to such dilemmas. The most that we can hope to have achieved here is to suggest that by looking at the structure of the multi-level European constitutional system as a whole, rather than performing misleading 'legitimacy tests' based on standards developed for nation states upon the EU alone, we may have suggested a more appropriate and effective way of beginning the task of thinking about the legitimacy of the Union.

NOTE

The reader is invited to add these arguments to reflection on the suggestion advanced above by Hauser and Müller that 'Reforms to either better restrict EU competences or to develop democratic EU institutions are proposals to ease the underlying tensions' (p.700), and to re-visit both the vista presented by the *Laeken Declaration* (p.25) and the conclusions of the Convention on the 'Future of Europe'? (p.30). Is *legitimacy* achievable in Europe? And what of democracy?

T. Kostakopoulou, 'Democracy-talk in the European Union: the Need for a Reflexive Approach' (version to be published in the Columbia Journal of European Law, 2003)

(Some footnotes omitted.)

III. The Centrality of Antinomic Co-operation in European Governance

The European Union is a complex and unique edifice. Good theorising about democracy in the European Union needs to address its distinctive features. For example, the Community's founding Treaties (ECSC, Euratom and EEC) do not represent the crystallisation of a unified and homogeneous constituent political will. Although the Community has its origins in international law, the founding of a 'Community', that is, the inauguration of a framework of co-operation among states and peoples, did not represent a way of 'doing that it comes naturally'. Its architects took 'a leap in the dark'[32] and proposed a framework for integration that transcended the traditional framework of interdependence.

Anchored in the memory of war, the urgent need for post-war economic reconstruction, and against a background of popular movements championing federalist ideas, the European Community, in its early days, represented the organisation of industrial sector communities setting up integration in limited, but vital, economic fields (i.e., coal and steel). The avowed objectives of the founders of the European Coal and Steel Community[33] included the prospect of a 'European federation'. The political dimensions of the integrationist framework featured in the Schuman Plan (1950): closer co-operation between France and Germany would furnish a 'broader and deeper community among peoples long divided by bloody conflicts'.[34] Ensuring peace and prosperity in Europe through a supranationalist experiment with no historical precedent has been a 'master ideal' of the Community,[36] alongside ensuring undistorted competition in a barrier-free market, raising the standard of living, promoting social cohesion and so on.

Although European integration is oriented to the realisation of these ideals,[37] the Community lacks a set of generalised shared beliefs concerning how to go about realising these ideals, a clear conception of its development and the scope of its competences, a settled constitutional structure and so on. The Treaties make no reference to a shared political end, the ultimate telos of European

---

32 J. Monnet, *Memoirs* (Collins 1978), 305.

33 ECSC [18 April 1951] 25 July 1952.

34 See the preamble to the Treaty of Paris, 18 April 1951.

36 The term is borrowed from Philip Selznick, 'Sociology and Natural Law', (1961) *Natural Law Forum* pp.84–108. For a critical discussion of the ideals of the Community, see J. Weiler, 'Fin de Siecle Europe', in R. Dehousse (ed.), *Europe After Maastricht: An Ever Closer Union* (Beck 1994), pp.203–216.

37 One could see the 'master ideals' of the Community as signposts or road maps. On this, see Z. Bankowski and E. Christodoulidis, 'The European Union as an Essentially Contested Project', (1998) 4(4) *European Law Journal* pp.341–354 at p.342. On the member states' divergent preferences over the institutional structure of the Coal and Steel Community, see B. Rittberger, 'Which Institutions for Europe? Explaining the Birth of a Unique Institutional Structure', Paper presented at the *ECSA 7th Biennial International Conference*, May 31–June 2, Madison, USA. Weiler argues that the European Union suffers from a 'crisis of ideals'; Weiler, *The Constitution of Europe, op. cit.*, 238–245, 259–262.

integration. Questions about the nature and the end of European integration and the role and future of the state are thus the primary source of disagreement. Europe is a contested polity.[38]

In this contested polity of crosscutting levels of decision-making, Community law does not reflect the consensus of competing constituencies. Instead, it delineates an evolving and ambiguous system of relationships. Both the incremental development of the human rights policy and the evolving constitutional framework in relation to the vertical division of powers attest to this. This rules out the application of a Rawlsian approach to the EU whereby we would have to assume that the European legislative process does not involve fundamental disagreements about matters of principle, for these have been settled at an earlier stage.[39] Nor can it be argued that an agreement about the norms of deliberation is what binds the Community together. Moments of crisis in the European integration process, such as the failure of the European Defence Community or the Empty Chair Crisis in 1965 highlight the fact that the norms of deliberation themselves can be the subject of much contention thereby leading to a renegotiation of the rules of the game.

If I am correct on this, then the European Community cannot be analysed as a community like any other. Its operation disproves Hayek's argument that democracy can only work in the long run if the great majority has in common at least a general conception of the type of society desired.[40] The master ideals of the Community form a 'fuzzy' presuppositional framework within which the actors declare their willingness to engage in a process of devising the rules and terms of their interaction without presupposing commonalities, common interests, shared beliefs about the common good and shared dispositions. The European Community is not a complete, homogeneous and unified body governed by a set of closed, coherent and definite rules. Although Monnet was correct to state that the union of Europe cannot be based on goodwill alone and that nothing lasts without institutions,[41] it is interesting that both the scope and nature of these rules continue to be the subject of debate. For example, national constitutional courts have not unconditionally accepted the principle of the supremacy of the Community law.[42] The debates concerning the meaning and justiciability of the principle of subsidiarity in post-Maastricht Europe and on the meaning and implications of flexibility in post-Amsterdam Europe also confirm this.[43] The grammar of the Community legal order thus remains incomplete, contested and unsettled.

The European Court of Justice has made a vital contribution to furnishing the basic tenets of this grammar. In *Van Gend Loos* it pronounced that the Community constitutes a new legal order of international law, and subsequently it held that the Treaty constitutes the constitutional charter of a Community based on the rule of law.[44] The ECJ has also adjudicated the numerous inter-institutional conflicts and helped delineate the powers and prerogatives of the institutions on the basis of the principle of institutional balance. In the *Isoglucose* cases, the Court established the European Parliament's participation in the legislative process through consultation,[45] and in the *Chernobyl*

---

38 Z. Bankowski and E. Christodoulidis, 'The European Union as an Essentially Contested Project'; T. Banchoff and M. P. Smith (eds.), *Legitimacy and the European Union: the contested polity* (Routledge 1999).

39 For a critique, see J. Waldron, *The Dignity of Legislation* (Cambridge University Press 1999), 71.

40 F. Hayek, *The Constitution of Liberty* (Routledge and Kegan Paul 1960).

41 Jean Monnet, *Memoirs, op. cit.*

42 See Case 11/70, *Internationale Handelsgesellshaft mbH v Einfuhr* [1970] ECR 1125, [1972] CMLR 255; *Internationale Handelsgesellshaft mbH v Einfuhr* [1972] CMLR 177; *Raul Georges Nicolo* [1990] 1 CMLR 173; *Brunner v The European Union Treaty* [1994] 1 CMLR 57; *Frontini v Ministero delle Finanze* [1974] 2 CMLR 372.

43 On subsidiarity, see A. G. Toth, 'A Legal Analysis of Subsidiarity', in D. O'Keeffe and P. Twomey (eds), *Legal Issues of the Maastricht Treaty* (Wiley 1994); J. Steiner, 'Subsidiarity under the Maastricht Treaty', in *Legal Issues of the Maastricht Treaty*; N. Emiliou, 'Subsidiarity: An Effective Barrier Against the "Enterprises of Ambition"?', in *Legal Issues of the Maastricht Treaty*. On flexibility, see C. D. Ehlermann, *Differentiation, Flexibility, Closer Co-operation: The New Provisions of the Amsterdam Treaty* (European University Institute 1998); J. Shaw, 'The Treaty of Amsterdam: Challenges of Flexibility and Legitimacy, (1998) 4(1) *European Law Journal* pp.63–86; N. Walker, 'Theoretical Reflections on Flexibility and Europe's Future', in G. de Burca and J. Scott (eds), *Constitutional Change in the EU: From Uniformity to Flexibility?* (Hart Publishing 2000).

44 Case 26/62 *Van Gend Loos* [1963] ECR 1, [1963] CMLR 105; Case 294/83 *Parti Ecologiste 'Les Verts' v European Parliament* [1986] ECR 1339, [1987] 2 CMLR 343; Opinion 1/91 [1991] (Draft Treaty on a European Economic Area) ECR I-6079, [1992] 1 CMLR 245.

45 Case 138/79 *Roquette Freres v Council* [1980] ECR 3333; Case 139/79 *Maizena v Council* [1980] ECR 3393.

case[46] it gave the EP standing to challenge the acts of the other institutions under Article 230 EC in order to protect its prerogatives, thereby reversing its earlier position.[47] All this disproves the argument that democratic politics can be deeply satisfactory only to the extent that fairly clear normative standards are accepted by the participants at the outset, just as overarching rules are required to enjoy playing games.[48]

Additionally, unlike modern liberal communities, the Community is neither a community of shared ends nor a community of destiny.[49] European integration is a process and an adventure. It is akin to a conversation that evolves endlessly as the parties engage in a collective quest for community. And although the conversation does not mean the same thing for everyone at the same time, since domestic constraints inform state preferences and shape the various interpretations of the European output, it is, nevertheless, shared. As Preuss has put it, 'the dynamic character and the openness of the European Union require a constitutional framework which does not fix boundaries to the evolution and self-transformation of the Union – boundaries of objectives and of competences – but provides appropriate institutional schemes with the help of which the deliberations about the next step of the political transformation can be performed and the changes, if considered necessary and desirable, can be accomplished'.[50] The ongoing and open-ended European conversation,[51] however, has to be conducted within the context of a culturally heterogeneous political community that is open to disagreements, to critique, to new ideas and cultural collisions.

It is true that strong disagreements and dissent often put pressure on the delicate institutional balances of the Community, and conflicts on the policies of the EU often take the form of conflicts on the EU itself in national arenas. Intergovernmental reflexes have also exercised a strong hold on the trend towards supranationalism in the 1990s. In addition, the forthcoming enlargement is bound to accentuate pressures for differentiated and asymmetrical solutions. But at the same time, however, the constituent units demonstrate a deep commitment to continued co-operation and to the joint creation of common, albeit contested, institutional realities. The absence of either some kind of consensus over the final shape of the Union, or an agreement over a common set of determinate values[52] is counterbalanced by a strong commitment on behalf of the constituent units to co-operation, in the sense that 'we are all in this together and we will collectively shape this process by designing appropriate institutions and common rules'.[53] The European political community is a community of concern and engagement.[54] It is perhaps the member states' awareness of the indispensability of their involvement in the European collective adventure – and not their conviction that 'Europe' will produce answers or solutions on which all will agree,[55] that leads them to comply with even those European norms that conflict with conventional understandings and settled traditions in domestic arenas.

---

46 C-70/88 *European Parliament v Council (Chernobyl)* [1990] ECR I-2041.

47 Case 302/87 *European Parliament v Council* [1988] ECR 5616.

48 See J. Elster, 1986.

49 P. Howe, 'A Community of Europeans: The Requisite Underpinnings', (1995) 33(1) *Journal of Common Market Studies* pp.27–46; 'Insiders and Outsiders in a Community of Europeans: A Reply to Kostakopoulou', (1997) 35(2) *Journal of Common Market Studies* pp.309–14.

50 U. Preuss, 'The Constitution of a European Democracy and the Role of the Nation-State', (1999) 12(4) *Ratio Juris* pp.417–28, at p.427.

51 J. Shaw, 'Postnational Constitutionalism in the European Union', (1999) 6(4) *Journal of European Public Policy* pp.579–97.

52 P. Lehning, 'European Citizenship: A Mirage?', in P. Lehning and A. Weale (eds), *Citizenship, Democracy and Justice in the New Europe* (Routledge 1997), 175–99. But compare Siedentop's argument for the need of a 'moral consensus' or a common 'culture of consent' in the European Union.

53 T. Kostakopoulou, 'Towards a Theory of Constructive Citizenship in Europe', (1996) 4(4) *Journal of Political Philosophy* pp.337–358.

54 T. Kostakopoulou, *Citizenship, Identity and Immigration in the European Union: Between Past and Future* (Manchester University Press 2001).

55 Walker has argued that the present pattern of differentiated integration has evolved as a result of a series of strategic compromises and gambits, of policy-driven sectoral initiatives, and of accommodations of new geo-political forces; N. Walker, 'Sovereignty and Differentiated Integration in the European Union, (1998) 4(4) *European Law Journal* pp.355–388, at p.374.

The delicate balance between co-operation and antinomy (antinomic co-operation) can be seen in the following table, which outlines the prospects for democratic governance.

Cooperation⇒Antinomy ⇓	Intensive	Relaxed
Weak	Low	Low
Strong	Low	High

The opportunities for democratic governance are higher when co-operation is relaxed and antinomy is strong. Too much emphasis on co-operation will lead to the obliteration of antinomy and will thus undermine the maintenance of a democratic community. On the other hand, enhanced voice must be accompanied with the awareness that the parties have embarked upon a common journey or a common quest for understanding and the design of institutions that accommodate conflicting interests and meet common as well as distinct needs – rather than for a 'common weal' or a common good'. It is precisely this awareness that binds the units together and makes outside options unappealing. In sum, the art of European association requires antinomic co-operation.

A prominent and rather permanent feature of the incipient political culture of the EU is the politics of 'becoming'. Unlike its constituent units, the member states, the European Community is a community of multifarious minorities whose perspectives, interests and opinions are equally legitimate. The process of collective collaboration of diverse political communities cannot but induce fundamental changes and facilitate an awareness of both the contestability and relativity of their own positions, assumptions and beliefs. For the same reason, European institutions are characterised by conditionality and reflexivity; they recognise their cognitive and coercive limits, seek to accommodate multiple and often contending visions even within a single provision or a legislative instrument and, more importantly, their output is open to review and renegotiation. Contestation is thus as much as a discursive process as an institutional fact. Disagreements and conflicts do not have a fleeting quality; they do not evaporate when Treaty amendments are agreed or secondary legislation is published in the Official Journal. Rather, they continue as much as after deliberation as during and before it. And European Community law serves as a surface for the inscription of disagreement and strife as well as a medium for the (co-ordinated) management and maintenance of dissent and antinomy. But this does not make the European Community democratically unstable or disorderly. On the contrary, it makes it precisely what it is; namely, a community of antinomic co-operation and a site for reflexive governance.

V. Conclusion

If we are to take the task of democratising the European Union seriously, be it in the sense of strengthening recent institutional reforms, or perfecting and deepening democracy in certain areas, or making the transition to democracy in other areas, then we need to reflect on the models of democracy we use in order to theorise and measure democracy at the European level. Quite often lens-shaped problems either create an 'apparent democratic deficit effect' or magnify or even conceal crucial deficiencies of democracy in institutional design and practice. The main rationale of this paper has been to show that the European democracy question cannot be addressed adequately without first addressing the suitability of existing models of national democracy for the European polity in formation, and perhaps without radically transforming these models. Premised on the ideals of consensus and stability such models are ill equipped to capture the process of the formation of a community at the European level in which there are strong disagreements about the type of community desired and its scope, divergent interpretations of civic values, an incomplete legal grammar and contested rules. The European political community has been created and is being sustained through practices of antinomic co-operation. Such practices of antinomic co-operation presuppose neither the presence of a constituent European people, nor the existence of a relatively stable background of settled cultural-cum-political norms. Although it has long been assumed that the latter are necessary conditions of democracy, the process of European integration has shown that democratic processes and institutional design do not need consensus, be it over a set of meanings, or a set of principles or the rules of the game, in order to advance.

But they do need a more serious effort on the part of European institutional actors to engage critically with the national-statist frames of reference they use, to reflect seriously on the models of democracy they employ at the European setting and their tensions, competing demands and incoherences, and to direct their focus towards the search for avenues for democratisation in the EU, rather than insisting on a particular notion of democracy or blending several notions of it.

Essential as they are, solving the 'paradox of democracy' and shifting the focus from the inherited models of democracy to democratisation are not the only relevant criteria for devising a complex model of democracy beyond the nation-state. Ensuring fairness in representation, rethinking the model of representative democracy itself, introducing mechanisms to improve the responsiveness of the system, searching for institutional devices that improve the citizens' inclusion in the policy process, including their ability to initiate legislation and Europe-wide referenda, are equally important. Nothing I have said in this paper should be taken to imply that the search for a postnational model of democracy that is suited to the evolving European experimental community is an easy task.[76] However, it seems to me that two ingredients are necessary for any significant advance. First, we need to identify problems, to understand the bias of our frames, to search for solutions beyond the confines of existing models of national democracy and to be more imaginative in the design of mechanisms to control political power and to enhance citizen participation. Secondly, it would be wise to abandon the logic of the 'eclipsing binaries' of the EU and the state, and to embrace the democratisation of institutions and sociopolitical life both vertically, that is, at all levels of governance, and horizontally.

FURTHER READING ON THE DEBATE ABOUT LEGITIMACY, DEMOCRACY, AND CONSTITUTIONS

Special Issue on Sovereignty, Citizenship and the European Constitution, (1995) 1/3 *European Law Journal*.

Special Issue on Legal Theory in the European Union, (1998) 4/4 *European Law Journal*.

Special Issue on Constructing Legal Systems: ' "European Union" in Legal Theory', (1997) 163/4 *Law and Philosophy*.

Craig, P., 'Democracy and Rule-Making within the EC: an Empirical and Normative Assessment' (1997) 3 ELJ 105.

Hooghe, L., and Marks, G., *Multi-Level Governance and European Integration* (Rowman and Littlefield, 2001).

Horeth, M., 'No Way Out for the Beast? The Unsolved Legitimacy Problem of European Governance' (1999) 6 JEPP 249.

Pernice, I., 'Multi-level Constitutionalism in the European Union' (2002) 27 ELRev 511.

Shaw, J., 'Postnational Constitutionalism in the European Union' (1999) 6 JEPP 579.

Stone Sweet, A. and Sandholtz, W., 'European Integration and Supranational Governance' (1997) 4 JEPP 297.

Walker, N., 'The Idea of Constitutional Pluralism' (2002) 65 MLR 317.

Weatherill, S., 'Is Constitutional Finality Feasible or Desirable? On the Cases for European Constitutionalism and a European Constitution', Constitutionalism Web-Papers (University of Manchester), http://les1.man.ac.uk/conweb/ ConWEB No 7/2002

Wouters, J., 'Institutional and Constitutional Challenges for the European Union – Some Reflections in the Light of the Treaty of Nice' (2001) 26 ELRev 342.

---

76 See E. Grande, 'Postnational Democracy in Europe', in M. T. Greven and L. W. Pauly (eds), *Democracy Beyond the Nation-State* (Rowman and Littlefield 2000).

Epilogue to Part Four – Europe's True Soul

And where is 'Europe's true soul'? The next and final extract finds it in the principle of 'constitutional tolerance'.

J. Weiler, 'The Function and Future of European Law' in V. Heiskanen and K. Kulovesi (eds), Function and Future of European Law (Helsinki,1999), pp.12–16

There are, it seems to me, two basic human strategies of dealing with the alien and these two strategies have played a decisive role in Western civilisation. One strategy is to remove the boundaries. It is the spirit of 'come, be one of us'. It is noble since it involves, of course, elimination of prejudice, of the notion that there are boundaries that cannot be eradicated. But the 'be one of us,' however well intentioned, is often an invitation to the alien to be one of us, by being us. Vis-à-vis the alien, it risks robbing him of his identity. Vis-à-vis one's self, it may be a subtle manifestation of intolerance. If I cannot tolerate the alien, one way of resolving the dilemma is to make him like me, no longer an alien. This is, of course, infinitely, better than the physical annihilation. But it is still a form of dangerous internal and external intolerance.

The alternative strategy is to acknowledge the validity of certain forms of bounded identity but simultaneously to reach across boundaries. We acknowledge and respect difference (and what is special and unique about ourselves as individuals and groups) and yet we reach across differences in recognition of our essential humanity. I never tire of referring to Hermann Cohen (1842–1918), the great neo-Kantian philosopher of religion, in an exquisite modern interpretation of the Mosaic law on this subject which captures its deep meaning in a way which retains its vitality even in today's ever closer union. It can be summarised as follows: The law of shielding the alien from all wrong is of vital significance. The alien was to be protected, not because he was a member of one's family, clan, religious community or people; but because he was a human being. In the alien, therefore, man discovered the idea of humanity. What is significant in this are the two elements I have mentioned. On the one hand, the identity of the alien, as such, is maintained. One is not invited to go out and, for example, 'save him' by inviting him to be one of you. One is not invited to recast the boundary. On the other hand, despite the boundaries which are maintained, and constitute the I and the Alien, one is commanded to reach over the boundary and love him, in his alienship, as oneself. The alien is accorded human dignity. The soul of the I is tended to not by eliminating the temptation to oppress but by maintaining it and overcoming it.

Europe represents this alternative, civilising strategy of dealing with the 'other'. This is, more than peace and prosperity, Europe's true soul. The constitutional expression of this strategy is the principle of Constitutional Tolerance and it is encapsulated in that most basic articulation of its meta-political objective in the Preamble of the EC Treaty:

> Determined to lay the foundations of an ever closer union among the peoples of Europe.

No matter how close the Union, it is to remain among distinct peoples. An ever closer union could be achieved by an amalgam of distinct peoples into one nation – which is both the ideal and/or the de facto experience of most federal and non federal states. The rejection by Europe of that one nation ideal, or destiny, is usually understood as intended to preserve the rich diversity – cultural and other – of the distinct European peoples as well as to respect their political self-determination. But 'the European choice' has an even deeper spiritual meaning.

An ever closer union is altogether more easy if differences among the components are eliminated, if they come to resemble each other, if they aspire to become one. The more identical the 'Other's' identity is to my own, the easier it is for me to identify with him and accept him. It demands less of me to accept another if he is very much like me. It is altogether more difficult to attain an ever closer Union if the components of that Union preserve their distinct identities, if they retain their 'otherness' vis-à-vis each other, if they do not become 'one flesh,' politically speaking.

Herein resides the principle of Constitutional Tolerance. Inevitably I define my distinct identity by a boundary which differentiates me from those who are unlike me. My continued existence as a distinct identity depends, ontologically, on that boundary and, psychologically and sociologically, on preserving that sentiment of otherness. The call to bond with those very others in an ever closer union demands an internalisation (individual and societal) of a very high degree of toleration. The Leviticus imperative to love thy neighbour as oneself is so difficult and hence civilising because that neighbour is not like myself. Living the Kantian categorical imperative is most meaningful when it is extended to those who are unlike me.

It is in legal terms that the principle of Constitutional Tolerance finds its deepest and most remarkable expression. The European *Courts* of Justice – in Luxembourg and the various Member States – have enjoined us to accept European law as the supreme law of the land. This, despite the fact that at face value this law defies the normal premise of democracy. Normally in democracy, we demand democratic discipline, i.e., accepting the authority of the majority over the minority only within a polity which understands itself as being constituted of one people, however defined. A majority demanding obedience from a minority which does not regard itself as belonging to the same people is usually regarded as subjugation. And yet, in the Community, through the doctrines of direct effect and supremacy we subject the European peoples to the discipline of democracy even though the European polity is composed of distinct peoples. It is a remarkable instance of Constitutional Tolerance to accept to be bound by a decision not by 'my people' but by a majority among peoples which are precisely not mine – a people, if you wish, of 'others'. I compromise my self-determination in this fashion as an expression of this kind of internal (towards myself) and external (towards others) Constitutional Tolerance.

However – and there is a big 'however' at this point. This, the Union's most fundamental principle, that of Constitutional Tolerance, becomes a travesty if the norms I follow, if the democratic discipline I obey is not adopted by others, my fellow European citizens, with whom I do not share the bonds of peoplehood but instead the bonds of a community of values and a new civic and political culture of transnational tolerance, but by a technocratic bureaucracy over which I have little control – presided over in the unreachable supranational Olympus of the European Council (and even European Parliament) and within the infranational netherworld of comitology. A non-democratic Europe extinguishes the principle of Constitutional Tolerance just as a statal or a one nation Europe would.

And that exactly is the weakness of the European Court of Justice ('ECJ') and some of its national counterparts. Their scant regard for, and weak sensibility to, the democratic processes by which the norms of which they demand supreme loyalty are enacted. It was evident in the Court's historic decisions such as *Van Gend en Loos* [see Chapter 3] where the Court said:

> The objective of the EEC Treaty, which is to establish a Common Market, the functioning of which is of direct concern to interested parties in the Community, implies that this Treaty is more than an agreement which merely creates mutual obligations between the contracting states. This view is confirmed by the preamble to the Treaty which refers not only to governments but to peoples. It is also confirmed more specifically by the establishment of institutions endowed with sovereign rights, the exercise of which affects Member States and also their citizens. *Furthermore, it must be noted that the nationals of the states brought together in the Community are called upon to cooperate in the functioning of this Community through the intermediary of the European Parliament and the Economic and Social Committee.'* (Recital 10, emphasis added)

There is something deeply unsettling to present the European Parliament and the Economic and Social Committee as a chamber that can be said to express a meaningful democratic notion of citizen cooperation in governance and justify rendering laws coming out of the Community process an obligatory nature binding upon States and individuals:

Independently of the legislation of Member States. (Recital 12)

This original sin of the Court and its acceptance by national jurisdictions may have been justified at the time when the international legal nature of the Community was strong and ratification of the EC Treaty in national parliaments could have been considered as an effective means for democratic legitimacy. But in today's incredibly complex and wide ranging Community when national ratification after each Inter-Governmental Conference ('IGC') is an impossible take-it-or-leave-it pact, reminiscent of the worst plebiscites in authoritarian regimes and nothing more than a formal act rather than a civic exercise of democracy, the continued indifference of the Court to the weak democratic basis of many of the norms which it upholds – notably in those coming out of the comitology process is more than unsettling – it is an act of Constitutional abdication.[4]

The late Judge Mancini was right: The Court assumes that – respectable democracy – which is not there.[5]

NOTE

And where next? And how? Will the Convention on the 'Future of Europe' and its aftermath (p.30 above) dispel Weiler's gloomy concluding anxieties?

This is plainly an enormous debate. It is of the most profound importance. It deserves to be pursued with rigour and energy in examining the proposals that emerge out of the current and evolving debate on the 'Future of Europe', but it deserves to be taken on to a broader plane. If this Chapter in particular, and this book in general, has left you with the impression that if only someone can put their hands on the 'right answer' then the mysteries of European integration can be resolved in a simple Treaty text, then the author has failed miserably in his endeavours and offers humble apologies. European integration is an evolving process with no defined end in view.

■ QUESTIONS

1. '. . . [S]tates in the European Union are being melded gently into a multilevel polity by their leaders and by the actions of numerous subnational and supra-national actors. State-centric theorists are right when they argue that states are extremely powerful institutions that are capable of crushing direct threats to their existence. The organizational form of the state emerged because it proved a particularly effective means of systematically wielding violence, and it is difficult to imagine any generalized challenge along these lines. But this is not the only, nor even the most important, issue facing the institution of the state. One does not have to argue that states are on the verge of political extinction to believe that their control of those living in their territories has significantly weakened'. (L. Hooghe and G. Marks, 'Contending Models of Governance in the European Union', in A. Cafruny and C. Lankowski, *Europe's Ambiguous Unity: Conflict and Consensus in the Post-Maastricht Era* (Boulder 1997), Ch. 1, p.38.)

Assess the contribution of the European Union (i) to the weakening of State power and (ii) to offering a secure basis for subjecting power dispersed from States to transnational actors and markets to effective and democratically legitimate supervision.

---

4 For the debate about Comitology, democracy and the courts see, e.g., the various essays in C. Joerges and E. Voss, *EU Committees: Social Regulation, Law and Politics* (Hart Publishing, Oxford 1999).

5 See Mancini v Weiler, *Europe – The Case for Statehood . . . and the Case Against: An Exchange*. Harvard Jean Monnet Working Paper No 6/98, available at http://law.harvard.edu/programs/Jean/Monnet (also Vol. 4 ELJ (1998)). [This is a particularly vivid and vigorous exchange – SW].

2. '. . . it could be argued that an ideal democracy, as conceived by accepted standards, is neither a purely popular democracy nor a purely constitutionalist one
   [that is, one in which majoritarianism is confined by e.g., a Bill of Rights, judicial
   control, territorial or functional devolution], but rather a system able to realize
   a satisfactory equilibrium between the two . . . to conform to the principles at
   the basis of its constitution, any ideal democracy should seek to balance one
   element with the other, taking great care that none of the components offsets
   the other. If this analysis is correct, it can be argued that the growing dissatisfaction with democracy, particularly in Europe, is the result of the continuing
   expansion of the constitutional pillar to the detriment of the popular one.
   Democratic citizens have the feeling that their votes matter less and less . . .'
   (Y. Mény, *'De la démocratie en Europe*: Old Concepts and New Challenges' (2002)
   41 JCMS 1. Is this accurate? If so, what can be done?

NOTE

For additional material and resources see the Companion Website at www.oup.co.uk/
best.textbooks/law/weatherill6e

Final Questions

1. 'EC law represents, more evidently perhaps than most other academic subjects, an intricate web of politics, economics and law. It virtually calls out to be understood by means of a political economy of law or from an interdisciplinary, contextual or critical approach. Nevertheless, it has often been regarded . . . simply as a highly technical set of rules, a dense doctrinal thicket where only the ignorant or the foolish would jump in and scratch out their eyes . . .' (F. Snyder, *New Directions in European Community Law*, p.9.) Discuss.

2. '. . . [T]here are two vital differences between the formal structure of traditional international law and that of European Community law. These differences represent a particularly strong limitation upon State sovereignty and justify the common description of the Community as "supranational" rather than an international entity. First, even viewed from the limited perspective of the traditional subjects of international law – the sovereign Member States – the formal structure of European Community law displays those features that characterize a well-developed legal system as opposed to a simple set of primary rules. Second, Community law and the Community legal system penetrate deeply and pervasively into the Member States. This penetration is manifested in particular by the direct and indirect modification of the legal position of individuals – the traditional subjects of municipal law.' (M. Jones, 'The Legal Nature of the European Community: A Jurisprudential Analysis using H.L.A. Hart's Model of Law and a Legal System', (1984) 17 *Cornell International Law Journal* 1, 15–16.) Discuss.

3. 'There is no motivation for European unification that is surpassed by the desire for peace'. Discuss.

Selected Bibliography

This bibliography is by no means exhaustive. However, in it the student should find enough sources to assist in deeper exploration of EU law.

Concentrating on substantive law

Barnard, C. and Scott, J., *The Law of the Single European Market: Unpacking the Premises* (Oxford: Hart Publishing, 2002).

Chalmers, D. and Szyszczak, E., *European Union Law Two: Towards a European Policy?* (Aldershot: Ashgate, 1998).

Oliver, P., *Free Movement of Goods in the EC*, 4th ed (London: Sweet & Maxwell, 2003).

Snell, J., *Goods and Services in EC Law* (Oxford: OUP, 2002).

Concentrating on institutional and constitutional law and practice

Andenas, M. Hadjiemanuill, C., Gormley, L., and Harden, I. (eds), *European Economic and Monetary Union: The Institutional Framework* (Dordrecht: Kluwer, 1997).

Chalmers, D. and Szyszczak, E., *European Union Law One: Law and EU Government* (Aldershot: Ashgate, 1998).

Hartley, T., *The Foundations of EC Law*, 4th ed (Oxford: OUP, 1998).

Hix, S., *The Political System of the European Union* (Basingstoke: Macmillan, 1999).

Lenaerts, K. and Arts, D., *Procedural Law of the European Union* (ed Bray) (London: Sweet & Maxwell, 1999).

Lenaerts, K. and Van Nuffel, P., *Constitutional Law of the European Union* (ed Bray) (London: Sweet & Maxwell, 1999).

Neville Brown, L. and Kennedy, T., *The Court of Justice of the European Communities*, 5th ed (London: Sweet & Maxwell, 2000).

Weiler, J.H.H., *The Constitution of Europe: Do the New Clothes Have an Emperor?* (Cambridge: CUP, 1999).

Concentrating on competition law

Bellamy, C. and Child, G., *EC Market Law of Competition*, 5th ed (London: Sweet & Maxwell, 2001).

Furse, M., *Competition Law of the UK and EC* (Oxford: OUP, 2003).

Kerse, C.S., *EC Antitrust Procedure*, 4th ed (London: Sweet & Maxwell, 1998).

Korah, V., *An Introductory Guide to EC Competition Law and Practice*, 7th ed (Oxford: Hart Publishing, 2000).

Whish, R., *Competition Law*, 4th ed (London: Butterworths, 2001).

Covering all or most aspects of the Community legal order

Arnull, A., *The European Union and its Court of Justice* (Oxford: OUP, 1999).

Craig, P. and De Búrca, G., *The Evolution of EU Law* (Oxford: OUP, 1999).

Craig, P. and De Búrca, G., *EU Law*, 3rd ed (Oxford: OUP, 2002).

Kapteyn, P. and Verloren van Themaat, P., *Introduction to the Law of the European Communities*, 3rd ed (ed Gormley) (London: Kluwer, Deventer/ Graham and Trotman, 1998).

Mathijsen, P., *A Guide to European Union Law*, 7th ed (London: Sweet & Maxwell, 1999).

Shaw, J., *European Community Law*, 3rd ed (Basingstoke: Macmillan, 2000).

Steiner, J. and Woods, L., *Textbook on EC Law*, 8th ed (Oxford: OUP, 2003).

Weatherill, S. and Beaumont, P., *EU Law*, 3rd ed (London: Penguin, 1999).

Wyatt, D. and Dashwood, A., *European Union Law*, 4th ed (London: Sweet & Maxwell, 2000).

Covering development of aspects of the Community legal order

Alter, K., *Establishing the Supremacy of European Law* (Oxford: OUP, 2001).

Dehousse, R., *The European Court of Justice* (Basingstoke: Macmillan, 1998).

Heukels, T., Blokker, N., and Brus, M., *The European Union after Amsterdam: A Legal Analysis* (The Hague: Kluwer, 1998).

Krämer, L., Micklitz, H.-W., and Tonner, K., *Law and Diffuse Interests in the European Legal Order* (Baden-Baden: Nomos, 1997).

Nielsen, R., and Szyszczak, E., *The Social Dimension of the European Union*, 3rd ed (Copenhagen: Handelsøskolens Forlag, 1997).

O'Keeffe D., and Twomey P., *Legal Issues of the Amsterdam Treaty* (Oxford: Hart Publishing, 1999).

O'Keeffe, D. and Twomey, P. (eds), *Legal Issues of the Maastricht Treaty* (Chichester: Chancery, 1994).

Rasmussen, H., *On Law and Policy in the European Court of Justice* (Dordrecht: Martinus Nijhoff, 1986).

Rasmussen, H., *European Court of Justice* (Copenhagen: Gadjura, 1998).

Shaw, J. and More, G., *New Legal Dynamics of European Union* (Oxford: OUP, 1995).

Snyder, F., *New Directions in European Community Law* (London: Weidenfeld and Nicolson, 1990).

Tridimas, T., *The General Principles of EC Law* (Oxford: OUP, 1999).

Weatherill, S., *Law and Integration in the European Union* (Oxford: OUP, Clarendon Law Series, 1995).

INDEX

accountability 7, 52, 308, 627–628
acte clair 203–206
advertising
  free movement 195–196, 361–364, 401–408,
    458
  see also Tobacco Advertising
Amsterdam Treaty 11 13, 34, 54, 443, 479, 617
  effect on choice of legal base 53, 58, 294, 668
annulment of Community acts 216–234
  acts subject to review 217–218, 219–220
  anti-dumping cases 219, 226–231, 262–263
  direct concern 224–225, 266
  effects of annulment 217, 261
  grounds 231–233, 259
  individual concern 220–224, 266, 267, 269,
    273
  interim relief 117, 233–234
  liberalisation of rules affecting private parties
    230–231, 262–274
  preliminary references, role of 207–209, 248–
    261, 268, 271, 273
  standing of Parliament 218
  standing of private parties 219–231, 262–274
anti-dumping cases 219, 226–231, 262–263
area of freedom security and justice 11, 45, 443,
  478–483, 675
assent (legislative) procedure 41
attributed competence 45–46, 53, 59–68, 465,
  618, 655, 662, 665, 696
  exclusive review by ECJ 207, 254, 268, 688–
    696
  non-discrimination on grounds of nationality
    448, 489

Block Exemption 513, 534–542
Bundesverfassungsgericht 9, 86–87, 149, 209,
  259, 484, 688–696, 700

cartels see restrictive practices
Cecchini Report 299, 316, 317
Churchill, Winston 5, 6
citizenship 10, 16, 427, 436, 448, 478, 479,
  483–490, 491
closer co-operation see enhanced co-operation
Coal and Steel Community 5, 6, 7, 34, 74, 604
Cockfield, Lord 299, 344

collective agreement 525–527
Commission 38–40
  management of Art 95(4) 629–634
  right of initiative 38, 46
  three pillars 10, 33, 38, 46
  see also Competition law
Committee of the Regions 46
Common Foreign and Security Policy 9, 33,
  44–45, 46, 79, 675
common market 7, 289, 290–294, 345
competition law
  Commission power of investigation 572–604
  convergence with free movement law 501, 526
  damages 604–607
  fines 495, 578, 602, 604
  fundamental rights 587–589, 602–604
  market share, as threshold 541–542
  modernisation 535, 572, 586
  national level enforcement 586, 604 607
  overall objectives 495–496, 500, 543
  State involvement 527–532
  see also restrictive practices
Constitution, as next step 29, 30–32, 96, 284
constitutionalisation 96, 129, 216, 262, 275–285,
  688, 697–700, 700–706, 713
consultation (legislative) procedure 40 41
consumer protection
  harmonisation 616, 617, 637, 638–651, 655
  legal base 629, 635, 638
  subsidiarity 658
  trade law 371, 401, 407–408, 409–410, 413,
    415–425, 626, 638
contract law
  harmonisation 616, 636, 638, 647–649, 650,
    662–663
  notification directive 156–159
Convention
Charter 23–24, 87
  Future of Europe 25, 30–32, 68, 87, 284, 491,
    616, 664, 675, 681–682, 689, 703
co-decision (legislative) procedure 40, 46, 53, 93
co-operation (legislative) procedure 41, 48–49,
  52
co-operation in Justice and Home Affairs 9, 11,
  479
Council 36–38

Council – *contd*
three pillars 10, 33, 37, 46
voting rules 14, 37, 46, 48–49, 54, 60, 65, 294, 619, 629
Council of Europe 80
see also Fundamental Rights
Court
jurisdiction in third pillar 10, 11–12, 33, 46, 80, 198
First Instance, demarcation of roles 215, 219, 264, 509
fundamental rights, scope of jurisdiction 80, 470–471
inter-pillar disputes 53–54, 215
interpretative technique 33, 71, 88–97, 100, 128, 171–174, 276, 345–346
interpretation in the light of directives 159–165
relationship with legislature and treaty revision 92–97, 270, 273, 447
subsidiarity 660–664
temporal effects of rulings 127–128, 200, 261
see also preliminary reference, national courts
culture, legal base 50–51
free movement 410, 456–457
customs duty 109–110, 189, 326–330, 335–336
customs formalities 349
customs union 290–292, 325

dawn raids 587
De Gaulle 5, 7
Decision 42
judicial review 43; and see annulment
Denmark, Maastricht referendum 9, 14, 15, 689
development co-operation 79
direct applicability 103
distinguished from direct effect 141
direct effect 123–131, 188, 275, 294, 345, 447
competition law 607–611
criteria 123–128
distinguished from direct applicability 141
non-EC EU pillars 128
source 109–110, 128–131
see also Directives
Directive 42
conform-interpretation 159–165
direct effect accepted 141–144
direct effect curtailed 144–149
enforcement against the State 146–147, 149–152, 159–160
enforcement against private parties 147–149, 152, 159–160, 488
implementation 141, 143, 164, 309–310, 651
incidental direct effect 152–159, 315
indirect effect 159–165
discrimination
scope of law against gender discrimination 93–96
nationality 102, 117, 136, 447–448, 488
sex directives 144, 159–160

tax 330–336
see also free movement
distribution agreements 497–500, 510–515, 518–522, 534–542
dominant position
abuse 562–570
market analysis 544–561
duty-free shopping 338, 478

EEA 10
EEC, creation 7, 34; renamed EC 9, 34
Economic and Social Committee 46
education 448
see also students
EMU 10, 34, 317–323, 339, 615, 668
enhanced co-operation 12, 323, 669, 673–676
enlargement 13, 14, 24, 31, 198, 572, *613, 619,* 665, 689
environmental protection
fines 120
trade law 413–414
legal base 48–50, 51–52, 53, 629, 634
standing to challenge EC acts 266–268
subsidiarity 658
equality 93–94, 96, 487
equal pay 123, 125–127, 133
establishment 445–446
beyond discrimination 449–471
company law 460–464, 472–473
non-discrimination 446–449
Euratom, creation 7, 34
exemption see restrictive practices

Factortame 117–119, 136–140, 177–184, 255, 260
failure to act 114, 234–236
fair hearing 88–92, 599–602
flexibility see variable integration
franchising 512–513, 535
free movement
Community legislation challenged 410
convergence of freedoms 322, 450, 453, 458
convergence with competition law 501, 529
discrimination , role of 332–333, 344, 353, 373, 381, 409, 413–414, 446–449, 449–450
effect as key 326, 344, 357, 386, 501
export restrictions 457–458
justification for obstacles 332–334, 341, 345, 366–367, 408–414, 456–457, 458–460, 470–471, 526–527, 586, 615–616, 635
company law 463
consumer protection 371, 401, 407–408, 409–410, 413, 415–425, 460, 628, 638
culture 410, 456–457
discrimination, relevance of 413–414
environmental protection 413–414
media plurality 411–412
public health 371–378, 389, 406, 464–469
public morality 367–371
public policy 371, 440, 441, 442

public service 444
persons 437–444, 446, 478–479
lowest common denominator 409, 457
trade barrier defined 344, 392–408, 457–458,
    532
freedom of expression 65, 411–412
fundamental Rights 78–88, 101, 357, 696
    Charter 16–24, 80, 87, 96, 270, 273, 357, 410,
        414, 475, 484, 615
    competition law 587–589, 601–604
    ECHR 23, 80, 83, 87, 92, 601–604
    trade law 357, 410–413, 470–471, 478
Future of Europe see Convention

Giscard d'Estaing, Valery 29, 30, 31
governance defined 683
    distinguished from classic community method
        683–686
    new forms 676–684
    see also White Paper on Governance

harmonization
    company law 472–473
    consumer protection, see separate entry
    dual aim 376, 619, 639
    effect of Cassis ruling 417, 453
    effect on national competence 107, 338–339,
        348, 376–379, 414, 619–620, 628–637,
        640–641, 647–651
    fiscal 336–339, 618
    function 322, 336, 341, 349, 376–379, 424,
        471–473, 613, 616–617,
    legal base 48–50, 51–52, 53, 59–68, 618–618,
        637, 645
    minimum 338–339, 628–629, 634–636,
        639–640, 649, 653, 667
    new approach 172, 619–628
    professional qualifications 472
    subsidiarity 662–664
    voting rules 619, 629
health, see public health
Hearing Officer 601
horizontal clauses in the Treaty 52–53
horizontal application
of Treaty provisions 122–123, 125–127, 364–365,
    449
    of Directives 147–149, 152, 159, 488
horizontal restraints 542, 609

incidental direct effect 152–159, 315
industry, legal base 50–51,
infringement procedure 39, 109, 111–122
    fines 120–121
    individual complaint 114, 121–122
    interim orders 116–119
    private parties, unavailable against 123
institutional balance 13, 36–42
insurance 450–453
intergovernmentalism 7, 11, 15, 33, 276, 479
interim proceedings

against EC institution before national court
    208–209, 255–260
against EC institution before Community
    judicature 233–234
against State before Community judicature
    116–119
against State before national courts 136–140
preliminary references 191
internal market
    "1992" 7, 8, 34, 289, 294–299, 316, 321, 379,
        478
    contribution of competition law 495–496
    economic benefits 299–303, 345, 409, 418,
        421, 456
    management 309–317, 357, 364, 421
    measurement of effects 303–307, 316
    scoreboard 309
    White Paper 8, 295, 336–337, 418–419
    see also Free Movement; Harmonisation
Ireland
    abortion 470–471
    ratification of Nice Treaty 14, 15

Laeken Declaration 25–30, 31, 68, 284, 685, 700,
    709
lawyers
    free movement 321–322, 446–447, 455–456,
        472
    partnerships and competition law 522–525,
        525–526
legislative process
    acts 42–45, 653, 676–684
    attributed competence 45–46, 59–68
    choice of legal base 46–58, 294, 449, 638, 667
    institutional overview 36–42
    majority voting, implications 8, 46, 54, 60, 65,
        619, 629, 666
    reasons 68–71
    see also accountability, Open Method of Co-
        Ordination, White Paper on governance
legitimacy 15–16, 23, 275, 485, 687,
    697–700, 703–709, 710–716
liability for breach of EC law
    EC institutions185, 239–248
    private parties 607–611
    State 121, 122, 167–186, 241–244
limitation periods before national courts
    132–133, 135–136, 171

Maastricht treaty 9–10, 34, 294, 483
    power to fine States 120
    Protocol, Ireland 471
    fundamental Rights 80
    three pillars 9, 10, 34, 53, 443, 479, 681
    subsidiarity introduced 654
    see also opt out
Major, John 9, 323, 666
merger control 562
Monnet, Jean 5–6
Monti, Mario 311

multi-level governance 653, 698–703, 705
mutual recognition 421, 616–617

national courts
  competition law 586, 603–607
  dialogue with ECJ 86–87, 101, 129–130,
    686–697
  procedure and remedies 131–140, 170–174
  review of Validity of EC acts 65, 87, 199,
    207–209, 248–261, 692, 696
see also Liability; direct effect; preliminary
    reference
Nice Treaty 13–14, 34, 294
  Declaration on the Future of the Union 24–25
  preliminary rulings 198, 213
  standing of Parliament in judicial review 218
numbering of Treaty changed at Amsterdam 12

oligopoly 508–509
ombudsman 42, 121
open method of co-ordination 679–681
opt out
  at Maastricht 10, 318, 323, 666–668
  at Amsterdam 11, 482
origin marking 352–354

Parliament 40–42
  Maastricht 10
  Nice 14
  standing in judicial review 218
  three pillars 46
persons
  free movement, horizontal application 123,
    449
  law in flux 427, 475, 485, 489–490
  third country national 476
  see also free movement
plea of illegality 237–238
Police and Judicial co-operation 11, 33, 45, 46
pre-emption 104–7, 338, 637, 634, 641,
    647–651
preliminary reference
  acte clair 203–206
  Art 68 version 168, 482
  bodies competent to refer 200–202
  Court of First Instance 198, 213
  effect of a ruling 199–200, 260–261
  obligation to refer 203–206
  power to refer 207–209
  purpose 187–188
  reform 211–213
  rejection of references 191–198, 273
  separation of functions 188–198, 396
  third pillar 198
  validity of EC acts in issue 207–209, 248–261,
    268, 271, 273, 695
  volume of references 198
principle of effectiveness 133, 135–140, 158,
    170–171, 177, 188, 604
principle of equivalence 133–135, 158

proportionality 58, 65, 71–78, 233, 250, 367,
    373, 414, 431, 654
public health
  legal base 61, 65, 66, 67
  free movement 371–378, 464–469,
    631–633
public procurement 133, 151–152, 184, 309,
    417–418, 616
public service 529

quantitative restriction 341–343

reasons
  legislation 68–71
  trade barriers 455–456, 467–468
refusal to supply 565–570
Regulation 42
  direct applicability 103
  judicial review 43; and see annulment
research and development 543
residence permit 431–433
restrictive practices
  agreements 503–504
  block Exemption 533–542
  concerted practice 505–509
  contextual examination 521–527
  exemption criteria 513, 532–533
  exemption, Commission monopoly 513,
    572–573, 585, 603
  jurisdiction 500–503
  minor agreements 515–522
  networks 518–522
  notification 572–573, 585
  preventing competition 510–515
  see also rule of reason
Rome Treaties 7, 34, 35
rule of reason 345, 414, 512–515, 527, 541

Schuman Plan 4–5, 6
SEA 7–9, 34, 295, 628
September 11th 482
services
  abortion 470–471
  beyond discrimination 449–471
  company law 460–464, 472–473
  exports 457–458
  health care 464–469
  liability 658
  non-discrimination 446–449
  recipients 442, 447–448, 476
  rights 445–446
see also free movement
single market see internal market
social policy
  competition law 525–527
  discrimination law, scope of 93–96
  legal base disputes 54–58, 75
  Lisbon Conclusions 677–678
  UK opt out 10, 58, 323, 666–668
social security 437, 465

soft law 339, 657, 676–684
  judicial review 44, 364
  role of guidelines 364, 410, 453, 457, 520
SOLVIT 312
Spinelli Aldo 5,7
state aid 339, 362, 527
students 449, 488–490
subsidiarity 16, 24, 57–58, 65, 67, 72, 251, 421,
      424, 654–664, 681
  exclusive competence 663
  Protocol 657–659
substitutability 333–336, 559, 560
Sunday trading 393–397
supremacy 99–107, 130–131, 188, 275, 294, 345,
      695
  dialogue with national courts 86–87, 101, 695
  non-EC EU pillars 99

tax competition 339, 473
tax discrimination 112, 330–336
Thatcher, Margaret 5, 322, 665
Tobacco Advertising 60–68, 617, 636–637, 640,
      643, 649, 661
tort law, harmonisation 639–644, 647–651, 654
tourists 442, 447–448

UK
  attitude to federalism 656
  free movement of persons 482
  Maastricht ratification 9
  social policy 10, 58, 666–668
  sovereignty and supremacy 136, 140
  use of referenda 15
Union, EU vs EC law 11, 33, 99, 128, 215, 443,
      479
  compare USA 664
  State like 15, 284–285
  legitimacy 15–16, 23, 275, 485, 688, 695–697,
      700–706, 706–710

variable geometry 323, 653, 665–676, 680
vertical restraints 497–500, 513–514, 518–522,
      533–542, 609

White Paper on Governance 116, 314, 681–683
worker defined 428–431
  advantages 431–437, 448, 488
  exceptions 437–444
  see also free movement
Working Time 54–58, 75, 233, 661, 666
WTO 105, 259